A Companio

Blackwell Companions to Philosophy

This outstanding student reference series offers a comprehensive and authoritative survey of philosophy as a whole. Written by today's leading philosophers, each volume provides lucid and engaging coverage of the key figures, terms, topics, and problems of the field. Taken together, the volumes provide the ideal basis for course use, representing an unparalleled work of reference for students and specialists alike.

Already published in the series:

A Companion
to Aristotle

Edited by

Georgios Anagnostopoulos

A John Wiley & Sons, Ltd., Publication

Blackwell Publishing was acquired by John Wiley & Sons in February 2007. Blackwell's publishing program has been merged with Wiley's global Scientific, Technical, and Medical business to form Wiley-Blackwell.

Registered Office
John Wiley & Sons Ltd, The Atrium, Southern Gate, Chichester, West Sussex, PO19 8SQ, UK

Editorial Offices
350 Main Street, Malden, MA 02148-5020, USA
9600 Garsington Road, Oxford, OX4 2DQ, UK
The Atrium, Southern Gate, Chichester, West Sussex, PO19 8SQ, UK

For details of our global editorial offices, for customer services, and for information about how to apply for permission to reuse the copyright material in this book please see our website at www.wiley.com/wiley-blackwell.

The right of Georgios Anagnostopoulos to be identified as the author of the editorial material in this work has been asserted in accordance with the UK Copyright, Designs and Patents Act 1988.

Library of Congress Cataloging-in-Publication Data

A companion to Aristotle / edited by Georgios Anagnostopoulos.
p. cm. – (Blackwell companions to philosophy)
Includes bibliographical references and index.
ISBN 978-1-4051-2223-8 (hardcover : alk. paper); ISBN 978-1-118-59243-4 (pbk. : alk. paper)
1. Aristotle.   I. Anagnostopoulos, Georgios.
B485.C59 2009
185–dc22   2008036223

A catalogue record for this book is available from the British Library.

Cover image: Roman bust of Aristotle. Naples, National Museum. Photo © 1990 Scala, courtesy of the Ministero Beni e Att. Culturali.
Cover design by Workhaus.

Set in 10 on 12.5 pt Photina by Toppan Best-set Premedia Limited
Printed in Malaysia by Ho Printing (M) Sdn Bhd

1   2013

Μνήμη μητρὸς Δήμητρας
(1904–2006)

Contents

B. Art

Notes on Contributors

Georgios Anagnostopoulos is a Professor of Philosophy at the University of California, San Diego. His research interests primarily focus on ancient Greek philosophy, ethics, and metaphysics. He has authored *Aristotle on the Goals and Exactness of Ethics* (1994), edited *Law and Rights in the Ancient Greek Tradition* (a supplementary volume of *Philosophical Inquiry*, 2006), and has published a number of articles on ancient Greek philosophy and medicine.

Elizabeth Belfiore is Professor of Classics at the University of Minnesota, Twin Cities. Her two main areas of research are ancient philosophy and Greek tragedy. She is the author of *Tragic Pleasures: Aristotle on Plot and Emotion* (1992), *Murder Among Friends: Violation of Philia in Greek Tragedy* (2000), and numerous articles in these fields.

Sarah Broadie taught at the University of Edinburgh, the University of Texas at Austin, Yale, Rutgers, and Princeton, before taking up her present position at the University of St. Andrews. She has wide interests in philosophy and her collection *Aristotle and Beyond: Essays in Metaphysics and Ethics* was published in 2007.

Victor Caston is Professor of Philosophy and Classical Studies at the University of Michigan. His research concentrates on issues in the philosophy of mind throughout antiquity, and he has published extensively on Aristotle, including papers on perception, phantasia, and intellect, with a focus on mind–body issues, mental causation, intentionality, and consciousness. He is currently at work on a book on the problem of intentionality in ancient philosophy.

S. Marc Cohen is Professor of Philosophy at the University of Washington, where he teaches courses in the history of ancient Greek philosophy, logic, and the philosophy of language. He has also taught at Minnesota, Rutgers, Berkeley, and Indiana. His publications have mainly concerned the metaphysics and epistemology of Plato and Aristotle. He is co-editor of *Readings in Ancient Greek Philosophy* (2005) and co-author of *Ammonius: On Aristotle's Categories* (1991).

Ursula Coope is Fellow of Corpus Christi College and University Lecturer at Oxford University. She is the author of *Time for Aristotle: "Physics" IV.10–14* (2005).

Paolo Crivelli teaches philosophy at New College, Oxford. His areas of research are Ancient Philosophy, mainly Plato, Aristotle, and the Stoics. He has published a book *Aristotle on Truth* (2004) and several articles in various journals (*Archiv fuer Geschichte der Philosophie*, *Phronesis*, *Oxford Studies in Ancient Philosophy*, among others), along with collections of essays.

Norman O. Dahl is Professor of Philosophy, Emeritus, University of Minnesota. His main areas of research interest are ethics and ancient Greek philosophy. Publications in the latter area include: *Practical Reason, Aristotle, and Weakness of the Will*, (1984); "Plato's Defense of Justice," *Philosophy and Phenomenological Research* (1991); "Substance, Sameness, and Essence in *Metaphysics* VII 6," *Ancient Philosophy* (2007); and *Nicomachean Ethics* Books III–IV, "Theses and Arguments" and "Alternative Interpretations," Project Archelogos.

Michael Ferejohn is an Associate Professor of Philosophy at Duke University, and specializes in Platonic and Aristotelian metaphysics and epistemology and Socratic ethics. He is the author of *The Origins of Aristotelian Science* (1991) as well as numerous articles on Plato and Aristotle in scholarly journals.

R. J. Hankinson was educated at Oxford and Cambridge, and is Professor of Philosophy and Classics at the University of Texas at Austin. He has also taught at McGill University, and was a Research Fellow of King's Cambridge. He has published numerous articles on various aspects of Greek philosophy and science, and is the author of several books, including *The Sceptics* (1995) and *Cause and Explanation in Ancient Greek Thought* (1998). He is currently working on a history of the concept of demonstration.

Robert Heinaman of University College London specializes in ancient philosophy. His recent publications include: "Why Justice Does Not Pay in Plato's *Republic*," *Classical Quarterly* (2004); "Actuality, Potentiality and *De Anima* II.5," *Phronesis* (2007); and "Aristotle on the Activity *Eudaimonia*," *Oxford Studies in Ancient Philosophy* (2007).

Devin M. Henry of the University of Western Ontario, researches in ancient philosophy and science, and philosophy of biology. Selected publications include: "Organismal Natures," *Apeiron* (2008); "How Sexist is Aristotle's Developmental Biology?" *Phronesis* (2007); "Aristotle on the Mechanisms of Inheritance," *Journal of the History of Biology* (2006); "Embryological Models in Ancient Philosophy," *Phronesis* (2005), and "Themistius and Spontaneous Generation in Aristotle's *Metaphysics*," *Oxford Studies in Ancient Philosophy* (2003).

David Keyt is a professor of philosophy at the University of Washington. His current research is on Plato and Aristotle. He is the author of *Aristotle: Politics V and VI* (1999) and co-editor with Fred D. Miller, Jr. of *A Companion to Aristotle's Politics* (1991), and *Freedom, Reason, and the Polis: Essays in Ancient Greek Political Philosophy* (2007).

Gavin Lawrence is Professor at the Department of Philosophy, UCLA. He works mainly in ancient philosophy, practical philosophy, and later Wittgenstein.

Gabriel Richardson Lear is Associate Professor of Philosophy at the University of Chicago. She is currently writing about topics in Plato's and Aristotle's ethics and aesthetics. Her publications include: *Happy Lives and the Highest Good: An Essay on*

Aristotle's "Nicomachean Ethics" (2004) and "Aristotle on Moral Virtue and the Fine" in *The Blackwell Guide to Aristotle's "Nicomachean Ethics"* (2005).

Stephen Leighton is Professor of Philosophy at Queen's University, Canada. His research interests include Plato, Aristotle (particularly their philosophical psychologies and understandings of value), theories of the emotions, and value theory.

James G. Lennox is Professor of History and Philosophy of Science at the University of Pittsburgh. His research focuses on the history and philosophy of biology and especially on Aristotle and the Aristotelian tradition and Charles Darwin and Darwinism. His publications include a translation with commentary of *Aristotle: On the "Parts of Animals" I–IV* (2001) and a collection of essays entitled *Aristotle's Philosophy of Biology: Studies in the Origins of Life Science* (2001).

Frank A. Lewis is Professor of Philosophy at the University of Southern California. He is the author of *Substance and Predication in Aristotle* (1991), and co-editor (with Robert Bolton) of *Form, Matter, and Mixture in Aristotle* (1996). Recent publications deal mostly with topics in Aristotle's metaphysics and natural philosophy.

Michael J. Loux is Shuster Professor of Philosophy at the University of Notre Dame. His areas of research include metaphysics and Aristotle. Among his publications are: *Substance and Attribute*, *Primary Ousia*, *Metaphysics: A Contemporary Introduction* (3rd edn.), and *Nature, Norm, and Psyche*.

Mohan Matthen is Canada Research Chair in Philosophy, Perception, and Communication at the University of Toronto. Previously he taught at the University of British Columbia and the University of Alberta. He has worked on ancient science and metaphysics, and on connections between the two. Currently, his main area of research is the philosophy of perception: *Seeing, Doing, and Knowing: A Philosophical Theory of Sense-perception* (2005).

Gareth B. Matthews is Emeritus Professor of Philosophy at the University of Massachusetts, Amherst. He taught previously at the University of Virginia and the University of Minnesota. He is the author of a number of books and articles on ancient and medieval philosophy, including *Socratic Perplexity and the Nature of Philosophy* (1999) and *Augustine* (2005).

Robert Mayhew is Professor of Philosophy at Seton Hall University. His research interests include the moral and political thought of Plato and Aristotle, and the twentieth-century novelist-philosopher Ayn Rand. His recent books are *The Female in Aristotle's Biology: Reason or Rationalization* (2004) and *Plato: "Laws" 10* (2008). He has recently finished a book on Prodicus of Ceos and is currently working on a revised edition of the Aristotelian *Problemata*.

Fred D. Miller, Jr. is Professor of Philosophy and Executive Director of the Social Philosophy and Policy Center at Bowling Green State University. He is the author of *Nature, Justice, and Rights in Aristotle's Politics* (1995) and co-editor of numerous collections, including *A Companion to Aristotle's Politics* (1991), of *Freedom, Reason, and the Polis: Essays in Ancient Greek Political Philosophy* (2007), and *A History of the Philosophy* *of Law from the Ancient Greeks to the Scholastics*, volume 6 of *A Treatise of Legal Philosophy and General Jurisprudence* (2007).

Deborah Karen Ward Modrak is a Professor of Philosophy at the University of Rochester. She has published articles on a wide range of topics in ancient Greek philosophy. She is the author of *Aristotle: The Power of Perception* (1987) and *Aristotle's Theory of Language and Meaning* (2001).

Michael Pakaluk is Professor of Philosophy and Director of Integrative Research at the Institute for the Psychological Sciences in Arlington, VA. His work currently focuses on Aristotelian psychology, moral psychology, and philosophy of action. His books include the Clarendon Aristotle volume on *Nicomachean Ethics*, Books VIII and IX, *Aristotle's Nicomachean Ethics: An Introduction* (2005), and *Aristotelian Moral Psychology and Philosophy of Action* (with Giles Pearson, forthcoming).

Christof Rapp is Professor of Philosophy at the Humboldt-University at Berlin. His areas of research include ancient philosophy, ontology, ethics, philosophy of rhetoric. Among his publications are: *Vorsokratiker* (1997, 2007), *Aristoteles zur Einführung* (2001, 2008), *Aristoteles, Werke in deutscher Übersetzung, Bd. 4: "Rhetorik"* (2002).

C. D. C. Reeve is Delta Kappa Epsilon Distinguished Professor of Philosophy at the University of North Carolina at Chapel Hill. He works in ancient Greek philosophy, ethics, metaphysics, and the philosophy of film. He is the author of *Love's Confusions* (2005), *Women in the Academy* (2001), *Substantial Knowledge* (2000), *Practices of Reason* (1992), *Socrates in the Apology* (1989), and *Philosopher-Kings* (1988, 2006). He has translated Plato's *Cratylus* (1997), *Euthyphro, Apology, Crito* (2002), *Republic* (2004), *Meno* (2006), and Aristotle's *Politics* (1998).

Jean Roberts is an Associate Professor of Philosophy at the University of Washington, Seattle. She has written mainly on Plato's and Aristotle's moral and political theory and is working on a book on Aristotle's *Politics*.

George Rudebusch is Professor of Philosophy at Northern Arizona University. He is the author of *Socrates, Pleasure, and Value* (1999) and *Socrates* (forthcoming).

Theodore Scaltsas, University of Edinburgh, works on ancient philosophy and contemporary metaphysics. His books include: *Substances and Universals in Aristotle's Metaphysics, Unity, Identity and Explanation in Aristotle's "Metaphysics,"* the *Philosophy of Zeno*, the *Philosophy of Epictetus*. His recent articles are on the topics of plural subjects and relations in Plato, ontological composition, and being determinate in Aristotle. He is the founder and director of Project Archelogos.

Christopher Shields is Fellow of Lady Margaret Hall and Professor of Classical Philosophy in the University of Oxford. He is the author of *Aristotle, Order in Multiplicity: Homonymy in the Philosophy of Aristotle, Aristotle, "De Anima": Translation and Commentary, Classical Philosophy: A Contemporary Introduction*, and (with Robert Pasnau) *The Philosophy of Thomas Aquinas*. He is also editor of *The Blackwell Guide to Ancient Philosophy* and *The Oxford Handbook on Aristotle*.

Robin Smith is Professor of Philosophy at Texas A&M University. His areas of research include ancient Greek philosophy, especially Aristotle and ancient logic. Among his publications are *Aristotle, "Prior Analytics,"* (1989) and *Aristotle, Topics I, VIII and Selections* (1997).

Richard Stalley is Professor of Ancient Philosophy at the University of Glasgow. He has worked mainly on the moral and political philosophy of Plato and Aristotle and on Scottish Philosophy. His publications include *An Introduction to Plato's Laws* (1983) and *Aristotle's "Politics"* (1995).

Michael V. Wedin is Professor of Philosophy at the University of California, Davis. Apart from a brace of articles on Wittgenstein's *Tractatus*, and an occasional foray into Plato, his essays focus chiefly on Aristotle's logic and semantics, philosophy of mind, and metaphysics. Lengthier efforts include *Mind and Imagination in Aristotle* (1988) and *Aristotle's Theory of Substance*: *The "Categories" and "Metaphyiscs" Zeta* (2000). He has also completed a book on the logical structure of Parmenides' "Way of Truth."

Michael J. White is Professor of Philosophy at Arizona State University and Professor of Law at the Sandra Day O'Connor College of Law, Arizona State University. His principal areas of research are history of philosophy, of natural science, and of mathematics, political philosophy, jurisprudence, and mathematical logic. His publications include: "Plato and Mathematics," in *A Companion to Plato* (2006); "On Doubling the Cube: Mechanics and Conics, *Apeiron*, 2006; "Stoic Natural Philosophy (Physics and Cosmology)," in *The Cambridge Companion to the Stoics* (2003), and "The Problem of Aristotle's *Nous Poiêtikos*" (*Review of Metaphysics* (2004)).

Paul Woodruff is Darrell K. Royal Preofessor of Ethics and American Society at the University of Texas where he serves in the departments of philosophy and classics. With Peter Meineck, he has published a complete translation of Sophocles' plays. One of his recent books is *The Necessity of Theater: The Art of Watching and Being Watched*.

Charles M. Young is Professor of Philosophy at Claremont Graduate University. He is currently completing a monograph on Aristotle's accounts of virtue and the virtues and the module on *Nicomachean Ethics* V for Project Archelogos, after which he plans work on Aristotelian grace (the impulse to return good for good received) and on Aristotle's *Rhetoric* and Shakespeare's *Julius Caesar*.

Preface

The present volume does not provide a survey of all of Aristotle's thought, and it was not intended to do so. Its aim is to treat some central topics of his philosophy in as much depth as is possible within the space of a short chapter. Ancient and later biographers and historians of philosophy attribute to Aristotle a large number of works, two-thirds of which have not survived. Even what has survived is an astounding achievement, both in its size and scope. Aristotle's extant works add up to more than two thousand printed pages and range over an astonishingly large number of topics – from the highly abstract problems of being, substance, essence, form, and matter to those relating solely to the natural world, and especially to living things (e.g., nutrition and the other faculties of the soul, generation, sleep, memory, dreaming, movement, and so on), the human good and excellences, the political association and types of constitutions, rhetoric, tragedy, and so on.

Clearly, not all the topics Aristotle examines in his works could be discussed in a single volume, and choices had to be made as to which ones to include. The choices were guided by an intuitive consideration – e.g., the centrality a topic has in the totality of the Aristotelian corpus (e.g., substance, essence, cause, teleology) or in a single, major work (e.g., the categories, the soul, and the generation of animals are the central topics in three different Aristotelian treatises). These considerations produced a first list. Still, the list was too long for a single volume, and had to be shortened. The topics that made the final list seemed to the editor to be the ones that any volume with the objectives of this one has to include. Others might have come up with different lists, but they would not be radically different from this. The overwhelming majority of the topics discussed below would be on every list that was aiming to achieve the objectives of this volume. Individually, each one of these topics receives an extensive treatment in Aristotle's works, and the views he articulates on them, when put together, give a good sense of the kinds of problems that exercised Aristotle's mind and the immense and lasting contributions he made in his investigations of them.

The contents of the volume are divided into five parts, with part I covering Aristotle's life and certain issues about the number, edition, and chronology of his works. The division of the remaining chapters is based on the way Aristotle frequently characterizes groups of inquiries in terms of their goals. Thus, part II consists of a number of chapters discussing topics from the treatises that have been traditionally called *Organon*, i.e., those studying the instruments or tools for reasoning, demonstrating and, in general, attaining knowledge and truth. Aristotle does not label these works (*Categories, On Interpretation, Prior Analytics, Posterior Analytics, Topics, On Sophistical Refutations*) *Organon*, but in several passages in his extant works he indicates that he views them as the instruments of inquiry and knowledge. The division of the remaining chapters into three parts – Theoretical, Practical, and Productive Knowledge – is, of course, based on the way Aristotle himself frequently divides the various inquiries on the basis of their ultimate goals – knowledge, action, and production. The chapters included in each one of these parts are further subdivided into groups on the basis of the subfield of Aristotelian philosophy to which a topic or the work(s) treating it belong – Metaphysics (seven chapters), Physics (three), Psychology (three), Biology (three) in part III (theoretical knowledge); Ethics (eight) and Politics (five) in part IV (practical knowledge); and Rhetoric (two) and Art (two) in part V (productive knowledge). Of course, several topics (e.g., cause, teleology, substance) are discussed in many different Aristotelian treatises, with some of them falling into different groups with respect to their ultimate goals – e.g., substance is explored in both the *Categories* (*Organon*) and the *Metaphysics* (theoretical knowledge).

The contributors to the volume are many, and no attempt was made to impose a uniform style with respect to writing, presentation, or argumentation. Each contributor was left free to use her/his favored approach, except in the way references to Aristotle's works or citations of specific passages in them are made – a uniform system has been adopted. Although in some instances the whole title of a work (e.g., *Politics*) is given, most frequently an abbreviation is used (e.g., *Pol*: see list of abbreviations). Citations of passages in the Aristotelian corpus are made by giving: (1) the title of the specific work, (e.g., *Pol* or *An* for *de Anima*); (2) the Book for those Aristotelian treatises that are divided into Books in Roman numerals (e.g., I, II) – except for *Met* where Books are identified by uppercase Greek letters (e.g., Γ, Θ) and lowercase alpha (α) for the second Book; (3) the chapter within the Book or treatise in Arabic numerals; (4) and the Bekker page and line number – e.g., *An* II.1 412a3, or *Met* Γ.4 1008b15. Each chapter includes a short bibliography listing the sources cited in it and in some cases additional works on the topic discussed that might be of interest to the reader. Space limitations did not permit the inclusion of a comprehensive bibliography on Aristotle.

Working on the volume gave me the opportunity to reconnect with colleagues I have known over the years and to come in contact with others with whom I had no previous exchanges. Collaborating with them has been rewarding in more than one way, and I want to thank all of them for accepting the invitation to be a part of the project and for their contributions. I also wish to thank several people at Blackwell who made the publication of the volume a reality and, most of all, for their patience: Nick Bellorini for inviting me to edit the volume, Liz Cremona, and Graeme Leonard.

Abbreviations of Aristotle's Works

Categories (Categoriae)	Cat
Eudemian Ethics (Ethica Eudemia)	EE
Generation of Animals (de Generatione Animalium)	GA
History of Animals (Historia Animalium)	HA
Interpretations (de Interpretatione)	Int
Magna Moralia	MM
Metaphysics (Metaphysica)	Met
Meteorology (Meteorologica)	Meteor
Movement of Animals (de Motu Animalium)	MA
Nicomachean Ethics (Ethica Nicomachea)	NE
On Dreams (de Insomniis)	Insomn
On Generation and Corruption (de Generatione et Corruptione)	GC
On the Heavens (de Caelo)	Cael
On Memory (de Memoria et Reminiscentia)	Mem
On the Soul (de Anima)	An
On the Universe (de Mundo)	Mund
On Virtues and Vices (de Vertutibus et Vitiis)	VV
Parts of Animals (de Partibus Animalium)	PA
Physics (Physica)	Phys
Poetics (Poetica)	Poet
Politics (Politica)	Pol
Posterior Analytics (Analytica Posteriora)	An. Post
Prior Analytics (Analytica Priora)	An. Pr
Problems (Problemata)	Prob
Progression of Animals (de Incessu Animalium)	IA
Rhetoric (Rhetorica)	Rhet
Sense and Sensibilia (de Sensu et Sensibilibus)	Sens
Sophistical Refutations (Sophistici Elenchi)	SE
Topics (Topica)	Top

Part I

Aristotle's Life and Works

1

Aristotle's Life

GEORGIOS ANAGNOSTOPOULOS

To many, Aristotle is the last great figure in the distinguished philosophical tradition of Greece that is thought to begin with Thales (ca. 600 BCE). Of course, Greek philosophy did not end with Aristotle; it continued for several centuries in the various schools – those of the Epicureans, Skeptics, and Stoics as well as Plato's Academy and Aristotle's own Peripatetic School – that flourished in Athens and elsewhere up to the early centuries of the Byzantine Empire. Yet there is considerable truth in the opinion of the many, if viewed as a claim about great *individual* figures in the Greek philosophical tradition. For Aristotle was the last great individual philosopher of ancient times, one of the three thinkers – the others being Socrates (470–399 BCE) and Plato (427–347 BCE) – that comprise what many consider to be the greatest philosophical trio of all time. Their philosophical careers span more than a hundred years, and all three were major figures in the lively philosophical scene of fifth- and fourth-century Athens. It was a unique moment in the history of philosophy, one that saw Socrates engaging in discussions with Plato – by far the most distinguished of his followers – and Plato instructing and debating with Aristotle – by far the most eminent student to graduate from and do research in his own school, the Academy.

While Socrates and Plato were born and spent their entire lives in Athens – indeed, Socrates took pride in the fact he left Athens only for military service (Plato, *Crito* 52b–c) – Aristotle was not born in Athens, never became a citizen of it and, according to some, never felt at home in it, despite his extended stays there. He spent most of his life and died away from his birthplace. Aristotle's life may conveniently be divided into the following five periods, which correspond to his residency in certain parts of the Greek world and, according to some, to the main stages of his intellectual growth.

Early Years in Stageira

Aristotle spent the first seventeen years of his life in the ancient Greek city-state of Stageira, where he was born in 384 BCE. Stageira, colonized by Andros (an Aegean island) and Chalcis of Euboia, is located in the eastern-most finger of the Chalcidici Peninsula, a region of the ancient Greek world located about 500 km north of Athens. His father's family had its origins in Messenia at the south-western tip of the

Peloponnesos; the family of his mother, Phaistis, came from Chalcis of Euboia, an island on the Aegean Sea, a few kilometers west of Athens. While there is no evidence that Aristotle retained any contact with Messenia, he stayed connected to his mother's family and estate in Chalcis; he spent the last year of his life and died there. Aristotle's father, Nicomachos, belonged to the Asclepiadae medical guild and served as a court physician to the Macedonian King Amyntas II. Aristotle probably spent some of his childhood in the Macedonian palace in Pella, thus establishing connections with the Macedonian monarchy that were to last throughout his whole life. Both of Aristotle's parents died when he was still a boy, and his upbringing was entrusted to a family relative named Proxenos, whose own son, Nicanor, was later adopted by Aristotle.

The paucity of information on Aristotle's childhood has made it difficult to answer questions about influences on him during the early, formative years of his life, and it has provided ample ground for speculation. Some have wondered how one of the world's greatest and most influential minds could have come from a rather remote part of the Greek world and far away from Athens. Such wondering seems unfounded. As G. E. R. Lloyd (1968: 3) observes, in the ancient Greek world, many great thinkers were born or flourished in places far away from Athens. Democritus, whose atomistic conception of matter has shaped the scientific account of the natural world for centuries, came from a place (Abdera) that is farther away from Athens than is Aristotle's birthplace. It is perhaps more interesting to ask about the influence his early surroundings may have had on Aristotle's attitudes or ideas. For example, one might puzzle about the personal basis of Aristotle's views on the ideal size of a polis (city-state). At the time he was articulating these views, Alexander the Great was creating a political entity that extended eastward from the Greek mainland to India, something Aristotle would not identify as a polis on account of its size. Many of the Greek city-states that were most familiar to Aristotle, including those of Athens and Sparta, far exceeded in size his ideal polis which, according to him: (a) should be self sufficient (*Pol* VII.5 1326b26 and throughout this work); (b) should have a population "that is the largest number sufficient for the purposes of life and can be taken at a single view" (VII.4 1326b25); and (c) its territory must be able to be taken in at one view (VII.5 1327a3). Of course, Aristotle gives arguments in support of his views, and any assessment of the plausibility of the latter would solely depend on the soundness and validity of these arguments. Yet it is striking how well Aristotle's birthplace met the requirements he sets for his ideal city. Its timber,[1] mining, and fishing industries probably provided enough for the sustenance of its citizens, and from the highest point of the site that is now identified with ancient Stageira one can see in one view what most likely was the whole city-state. Also, its proximity to the sea satisfied Aristotle's defense and commercial requirements (VII.5, 6). Its relatively small number of citizens would also have made it possible for its residents to know each other and develop the kind of friendship among themselves that Aristotle considers desirable in a polis. It is not unreasonable to suppose that his childhood experiences of living in Stageira left lasting impressions in Aristotle's mind and colored his attitudes toward and beliefs about aspects of the polis.

Scholarly opinion is almost unanimous in supposing Aristotle's interest in biology and on the empirical approach to inquiry, both evident throughout his works, were due to his father's influence during his childhood years. He and his associates compiled a vast body of facts and developed some far-reaching theories about nearly every biological phenomenon with which they were familiar. Indeed, Aristotle seems to be startled by the phenomena of living things, even ordinary ones (e.g., that trees have roots), and his desire to find explanations for them and, in turn, fit these into a comprehensive explanatory scheme is boundless. Members of the Asclepiadae guild were well-known in antiquity for carrying on empirical research that included dissections and, according to Galen (*On Anatomical Procedures* II.1), they also trained their sons in such research, suggesting that Aristotle's strong interest in the study of living things, his strong reliance on observation in such studies, and the doing of dissections were learned from his father and instilled in him from his early childhood. In his biological works, he makes references to dissections and even to works titled *Dissections*, which appear on the ancient lists of his writings but have not survived. These same lists include lost works on medicine.[2] It is apparent from the frequent references to medicine throughout his extant corpus that he had well-defined views about medicine as a scientific inquiry and healing art (*Sens* 436a17, and throughout his ethical works and *Met*). In addition, the surroundings of Aristotle's childhood were an ideal environment for the interest that was kindled by the family to flourish. The densely wooded area of his birthplace was teeming with animals as was the Aegean Sea with marine life, providing a large variety of specimens for observation and study, further exciting Aristotle's inquisitive mind.

First Athenian Period

In 367 and at the age of seventeen/eighteen, Aristotle entered Plato's Academy, where he stayed for the next nineteen years, until Plato's death. The specific reasons that led Aristotle to join Plato's school are not known and, once more, scholarly speculation tries to fill the void. Thus W. D. Ross (1995: 1) surmises that "We need not suppose that it was any attraction to the life of philosophy that drew him to the Academy; he was simply getting the best education that Greece could offer." Given that in Plato's/ Aristotle's time philosophy encompassed all disciplines – including mathematics, physics, astronomy, biology, politics, ethics, etc. – it is difficult to make sense of the distinction between education and philosophy Ross wishes to draw. More importantly, given the fact that Aristotle lived the life of philosophy and in his ethics defends the view that the ideal life for a human is the contemplative life, it is quite likely that what attracted him to Plato's Academy was precisely the life of philosophy.

Whatever Aristotle's reasons for entering the Academy, his long stay makes it abundantly clear that he found the aims, intellectual approaches, and research endeavors of the school to his liking. It seems that Aristotle did not have personal contact with or come under the direct influence of Plato in the first two years in the Academy, since the latter was absent in Sicily. But there is no doubt that those responsible for his instruction while he was a student were following the instructional guidelines of the Academy, which reflected Plato's own approach to education and the main tenets of his philosophical thinking. Aristotle, as was probably the case with the other prominent members of the Academy, shared some of the main tenets of Platonism, first as a student and then as an associate in the school, when he participated in teaching and engaged in research. According to Diogenes Laertius (third century CE) – one of our important sources of information on Aristotle's life – he was "the most genuine student of Plato"

(V.1). Years after his sojourn in Plato's school, he continues to speak with affection toward those sharing the Platonist outlook, some of whom had been his associates in the Academy, considers them friends, and appears to include himself among the followers of Plato (*NE* I.6 1096a11).

What survives from his early writings during his stay in the Academy clearly reflects his general, but not necessarily complete, adherence to Platonism with respect to the topics he discussed, the views he articulated, and even the genre of writing he chose for expressing these views. Like the master of the Academy, he chose the dialogue as the vehicle of philosophical inquiry, writing a number of dialogues, some having titles identical to dialogues of his teacher. While only fragments of these early writings survive, it appears that he was quite successful in the use of Socrates' and Plato's favorite way of philosophizing. The praise he received in antiquity from Cicero and Quintilian for his graceful style is probably for his dialogues. But the issues examined in his early writings are also within that set of questions that were Plato's main concern during his middle years – education, immortality of the soul, the nature of philosophy – and his own positions on them do not stray far from those of his teacher. But even in these early writings one can see that Aristotle does not hesitate to pursue lines that deviate from those of Plato. And if the works included in the Aristotelian *Organon* belong, as is commonly thought, to Aristotle's period in the Academy, Plato's student did not hesitate at all to challenge the teacher – indeed, to question some of the pillars of the edifice of Platonism. The relation of Aristotle's thought to that of his teacher is a rather complicated matter, and it will be touched on in the next chapter. What I wish to stress here is that, while we may all agree that Platonism left an indelible mark on Aristotle's thinking, it would be simplistic to suppose that we can identify a stage in his life, or that his stay in the Academy was precisely that stage, during which he was a blind follower of his teacher. Conversely, while Aristotle struck out in many new directions that are different from those taken by Plato and advanced competing theories that challenge fundamental Platonic tenets, it would also be equally simplistic to suppose that we can identify a stage in Aristotle's life when he cleanly and irrevocably broke away from Platonism, thereafter writing works that bear no connection to any of the views or approaches of his teacher.

Scholarly controversies also abound about Aristotle's departure from the Academy, both about the time it happened and his reasons. While Diogenes Laertius reports that Aristotle left the Academy while Plato was still alive, most scholars today believe that he departed soon after Plato died in 347. But what led Aristotle to leave the most prestigious and intellectually stimulating institution of learning of his time? Various reasons have been proposed. I. Düring (1957: 459), for example, has suggested that Aristotle's departure was in response to the rising anti-Macedonian sentiment in Athens after the sacking of Olynthus by Philip in 348. Most likely, this was a factor in Aristotle's decision. But many scholars believe that Aristotle's reasons primarily had to do with the choice of Plato's successor as head of the Academy, the changes that occurred in Plato's school following his death, and Aristotle's deteriorating relationship with him. There might be some truth to the last claim, which is echoed in Plato's alleged remark that "Aristotle spurns me, as colts kick the mother who bore them" (Diogenes Laertius V.1.2). But the most important reason, supposedly, was that he, like Xenocrates (another prominent member of the Academy), was not chosen to succeed Plato as director of the Academy on account of "doctrinal unorthodoxy" (G. E. R. Lloyd 1968: 4–5), with the position going instead to Plato's nephew, Speusippus.

We hardly have any direct evidence as to why Aristotle was bypassed for the directorship of the Academy. But it is unlikely that the decision in favor of Speusippus and against both Aristotle and Xenocrates had much to do with doctrinal orthodoxy/ unorthodoxy. Speusippus was no more doctrinally orthodox than the other two, having been openly critical of the canonical theory of Forms.[3] W. Jaeger, one of the twentieth century's most eminent Aristotelian scholars, took the opposite line: He recognized Speusippus' supposed unorthodoxy (Jaeger 1962: 111) and argued in support of Aristotle's and Xenocrates' faithfulness to Platonism, seeing the break of the latter two from the Academy as their response to the choice of a successor to Plato who did not represent Platonism. According to him, "Aristotle's departure from Athens was the expression of a crisis in his inner life" and "The departure of Aristotle and Xenocrates from the Academy was a secession: They went to Asia Minor in the conviction that Speusippus inherited merely the office and not the spirit [of the Academy]" (pp. 110–11). Jaeger may be right in stressing Speusippus' deviation from aspects of Platonism, but his assumptions that Aristotle faithfully adhered to Platonism at this stage of his life – a central element in Jaeger's account of Aristotle's philosophical development (see ch. 2) – that a doctrinal chasm existed between him and Plato's successor, and that the latter was the sole reason for Aristotle's not being chosen to succeed Plato are questionable. As Lloyd (1968: 5) points out, Xenocrates, who eventually succeeded Speusippus, was the one who remained faithful to Platonism and, if that were the basis of choosing Plato's successor, he, and not Speusippus, should have been the clear choice.

More recently, scholars have posited pragmatic reasons for bypassing Aristotle (and Xenocrates) for head of the Academy that had nothing to do with doctrinal differences among the eligible candidates. Aristotle and Xenocrates were not citizens of Athens and, as a consequence, they faced legal barriers with respect to owning property in the city. Speusippus, on the other hand, was an Athenian citizen and, most importantly, Plato's relative. This last fact might have been a major factor in his being appointed head of the Academy; it guaranteed that Plato's property remained in the family. At the same time, Aristotle's decision to leave Plato's school and Athens may have had as much, and possibly more, to do with an exceptional opportunity that arose around the time of Plato's death – namely, to carry out research, with his close associates at an almost ideal setting – than with his being bypassed as Plato's successor or with alleged doctrinal disagreements among the most prominent members of the Academy. In any case, his leaving Athens does not necessarily mean that he moved away from the circle of the Academy.

Period of Travels

Around the time of Plato's death, Aristotle was invited by Hermeias, a former fellow-student in Plato's Academy who had risen from slavery to become the ruler of Atarneus and Assos in the north-western coast of Asia Minor and who maintained close connections with the Macedonian palace, to join a small group of other Academics gathered around him that included Erastus and Coriscus. The Sixth letter attributed to Plato indicates that he viewed Hermeias' Academic circle as an extension of the Academy. Aristotle moved to Hermeias' court with Xenocrates, to be joined later by Theophrastus of Lesbos – a life-long associate of Aristotle who eventually succeeded him as director of his school upon his death – and Aristotle's nephew Callisthenes. Thus Aristotle's departure from Athens need not imply a complete break from the Academic circle. In the view of Jaeger "nothing more than a colony of the Athenian Academy was taking shape in Assos at this time, and there was laid the foundation of the school of Aristotle." (p. 115) In speaking of "the foundation of the school of Aristotle," Jaeger is thinking of areas of study and approaches to inquiry that are associated with Aristotle and his school – i.e., the study of living things, and nature in general, and the empiricist approach. The evidence bears this out. While at the court of Hermeias, Aristotle and his associates embarked on an extensive research program in biology, especially a study of the marine life of the area, which was essentially empirical in its character. It continued when he and his team moved to the nearby island of Lesbos. Place-names in his biological treatises, especially *HA*, indicate that the north-western coast of Asia Minor, the Hellespont, and the Propontis were frequented by Aristotle while carrying out his biological investigations (see Lee 1948; Thompson 1913).

Aristotle's relationship to Hermeias was a close one. He married his niece and adopted daughter, Pythias, with whom he had a daughter by the same name. After Pythias' death, Aristotle lived till his death with a native of Stageira named Herpyllis who, according to Diogenes Laertius (V.1), bore him a son,[4] Nicomachos, for whom his *Nicomachean Ethics* is named. The closeness of the relationship between Aristotle and Hermeias is evident in a hymn and epitaph (see Diogenes Laertius V.6, 7–8) the philosopher composed for his friend; both are highly laudatory of his friend and for that reason they were used against Aristotle in his final days in Athens (see below).

In 342, King Philip of Macedon invited Aristotle to his palace and entrusted him with the education of his son Alexander, who was at the time thirteen years old. Aristotle accepted the invitation, and spent two years in Pella and at the royal estate in Mieza, where there was a complete school. Again, we possess very little concrete information about what Aristotle taught the young Alexander, the future general and empire-builder, and about the kind of relationship the two had, thus leaving much room for speculation. Most scholars believe that while Aristotle's teaching relied heavily on Homer and the tragic poets, he also introduced the young Alexander to political studies and possibly wrote for him two works: on *Monarchy* and on *Colonies*, which are included in lists of Aristotle's works in antiquity but have not survived. Most likely, it was at this time that Aristotle also embarked on his major project of studying many of the existing constitutions (158 of them) in the Greek world.

The relationship between Aristotle and Alexander probably lasted until the latter died. Although tradition has it that Alexander contributed a major sum of money toward Aristotle's school in Athens, it is unlikely that the two were close.[5] Whatever the nature of the relationship was, it was not based on an affinity of their respective views on the end of human life or the best political association for humans. For Aristotle, the contemplative life is the best, happiest, and most pleasant one a human can attain, and he lived such a life. Alexander, on the other hand, chose the life of action and of empire-building. Aristotle argues that war cannot be the final end of human life (*NE* X.7), and while it is most likely that the ultimate objectives of Alexander and his father

8

aimed beyond warfare and conquest – possibly the Hellenizing of the world of the East – Aristotle seems to have had deep doubts and profound reservations about such a project. He had advised Phillip against trying to build a mixed empire of Hellenic and non-Hellenic subjects, and his steadfast defense of the city-state as the ideal political community reveals his strong opposition to Alexander's objectives. He thought that a state like the one his former pupil was aiming to build was neither conducive to nor necessary for the kind of human flourishing the polis, according to Aristotle, aims to achieve. His remark at *NE* X.8 1179a10 that "it is possible to perform noble acts without being ruler of land and sea," makes clear what he thought of Alexander's kind of undertaking: conquering the world, building an empire, and engaging in endless warfare are not necessary for attaining the highest goals a human being can aim at. Again, his remarks on states and rulers bent on or giving primacy to war, warrior virtues, and despotic rule over non-free subjects (*Pol* VII.13) are at odds with his former pupil's ambitions.

In 340 Aristotle returned to Stageira, where he stayed until the death of Philip and the latter's succession by Alexander in 336, settling shortly after in Athens once more.

Second Period in Athens

Aristotle's second stay in Athens, 335–323, is considered the most productive period of his life, the time when he composed or completed most of his major philosophical treatises. This is also the time when he established, with financial support from Alexander, his own school, the Lyceum, named after the area of Athens located just outside the city between the Hill of Lycabettus and the Illisos River, often frequented by Socrates. In the mid-1990s, archaeologists excavated ruins of several structures located in what was the Lyceum area of ancient Athens, which they believe to have been a part of Aristotle's school. Aristotle, not being a citizen of Athens, could not own the property constituting his school; he rented it. The wooded grove of the Lyceum provided an ideal setting for what tradition reports as his favorite way of teaching – taking a walk (*peripatos*) "up and down philosophizing together with his students . . . hence the name 'Peripatetic'" (Diogenes Laertius V.2). The school is reputed to have had a major library, which contained hundreds of manuscripts, maps, and other objects essential to the teaching of natural science, and became the model of the great libraries of antiquity in Alexandria and Pergamon.[6]

Aristotle spent half his life in Athens, longer than he resided anywhere else. Yet evidence suggests that the city might have never felt like home to him and it, in turn, might not have been very warm to him. As a foreigner non-citizen (metic), he did not enjoy all the rights or privileges of Athenians. In a letter to his close friend, Antipater, he complains that "In Athens the same things are not proper for a foreigner as they are for a citizen; it is difficult to stay in Athens" (see *Vita Marciana* in Düring 1957: 105, and the latter's comments, p. 459). Undoubtedly he was self-conscious of his own status as a foreigner in Athens, and when in *Pol* VII.2 1324a14 he asks "which life is more choice-worthy, the one that involves taking part in politics with other people and participating in a city-state or the life of an alien cut off from the political community?"

he is probably articulating something of personal and profound significance to himself.[7] His critical attitude towards Athenian participatory democracy might have rubbed the wrong way ardent supporters of it, especially his exact contemporary Demosthenes,[8] and raised suspicions about him. His stay in Athens came to an abrupt end when Alexander died in 323. Diogenes Laertius (V.1.6) reports that he "was indicted for impiety by Eurymedon" or "according to Favorinus, by Demophilus, the ground of the charge being the hymn he [Aristotle] composed to . . . Hermeias as well as the . . . inscription for his [Hermeias'] statue at Delphi."

The impiety charge by Eurymedon may not be altogether baseless, given Aristotle's views on the gods. In the *Met* (983a6, 1072b13, 1074b33) Aristotle sees god as engaging only in self-contemplation; in *NE* he speaks of the gap separating gods from humans (VIII.7) and of the senselessness of thinking about the gods as acting like humans (X.7), claims that sharply contrast with popular religious beliefs of his time. At *Met* Λ.8 1074b Aristotle questions and rejects even more openly the anthropomorphism of popular religion and sides with the view of earlier thinkers that the natural world or the first substance are gods.[9] Eurymedon's charge of impiety brings to mind the similar charge against Socrates. The latter argues in Plato's *Apology* that the real reasons behind his indictment had nothing to do with his religious beliefs. There is good reason to believe that the same is true in Aristotle's case. The timing of the indictment suggests that the reasons were political.

The charge by Demophilus seems to be even less believable, if it was based on the contents of Aristotle's hymn to and epitaph for Hermeias. There seems to be nothing offensive in them. But again, the real reasons behind the charge might have been different – once more, political. Aristotle's profuse praises for Hermeias, a person with a life-long connection to the Macedonian palace, most likely, irritated Athenian democrats at a time when anti-Macedonian sentiment was sweeping the city upon Alexander's death. Aristotle's connection to Alexander and an even closer one to Antipater – named by Aristotle the executor of his will, a member of the inner circle, and perhaps the closest advisor of Alexander, who appointed him regent of Macedonia and the rest of Greece during his eastern expeditions – made him an obvious target. Aristotle was forced to leave Athens, reportedly in order to "save it from sinning against philosophy twice," (for the testimonies, see Düring 1957: 341–2) and leave Theophrastus as head of the Lyceum.

Last Year in Chalcis, Euboia

After leaving Athens, Aristotle settled at his mother's estate in Chalcis, where he died a year later (322). In the biographical tradition, many report that he died on account of his deep sorrow for being unable to explain the natural phenomenon of the powerful tide currents of Euripus, the narrow straight separating Euboia from the Greek mainland.[10] Given Aristotle's character and life-long pursuit of explanations of natural phenomena, this seems improbable. Most scholars believe that Aristotle died from a chronic intestinal condition.

The appearance, manners, character, personality, and abilities of Aristotle attracted the attention of ancient and later biographers, and some of their comments have survived (see Düring 1957: 349–51). Diogenes Laertius, for instance, reports that Aristotle "spoke with a lisp . . . his calves were slender, his eyes small, and he was conspicuous by his attire, his rings, and the cut of his hair" (V.1.1); and that Plato, comparing Xenocrates' quickness of mind to Aristotle's, said "the one needed a spur [Xenocrates], the other a bridle [Aristotle]" and "see what an ass [Xenocrates] I am training and what a horse [Aristotle] he has to run against" (IV.2.1). But it is difficult to know whether any of these are true. Fortunately, concerning Aristotle's intellectual abilities, his writings provide ample testimony. Concerning his character, we have his will, which gives us a glimpse into his feelings and attitudes. In it, he leaves instructions for his daughter's marriage and his son's supervision, and makes provisions for both of them as well as for Herpyllis, about whom he speaks with affection and gratitude. He asks that his first wife's bones be buried wherever he is buried, honoring her request. He also makes arrangements for his household slaves, stipulating that none should be sold and that they should be freed when they are of age and if they deserve it. The latter might seem puzzling, given his defense of slavery in his *Pol* (especially I.3–6); but, in fact, it is in agreement with what he promises to discuss in a later Book of the same work (*Pol* VII.10 1330a33) but never does. Finally, he leaves instructions for the placements of statues of intimate associates and of his mother that he has already commissioned as well for the commissioning and placement of life-size statues of Zeus and Athena in Stageira. These concerns of his and the whole tenor of his will show Aristotle to have been a person with strong attachments to associates and members of his household, including slaves with whom he might have enjoyed the kind of friendship he deems possible between master and slave (*Pol* I.6 1255b12 and *NE* VIII.11 1161b1). Commenting on the will, Jaeger remarks "There is something affecting in the spectacle of the exile putting his affairs in order. He is constantly calling to mind his home in Stageira and the lonely house of his parents far away . . . Between the lines of the sober dispositions . . . we read a strange language . . . It is the warm tone of true humanity, and at the same time of an almost terrifying gulf between him and the persons by whom he was surrounded. These words were written by a lonely man." (pp. 320–1)[11] While there might be a bit of hyperbole and speculation on Jaeger's part here, he is correct in seeing true humanity in Aristotle's will – a humanity that permeates his practical philosophy, even when he emphasizes the theoretic life. As Jaeger goes on to say, Aristotle's "full life was not exhausted, as a superficial eye might suppose, by all its science and research. His 'theoretic life' was rooted in a second life, hidden and profoundly personal, from which that ideal derived its force. The picture of Aristotle as nothing but a scientist is the reverse of the truth" (p. 361). In Aristotle's thought, the pull of the theoretic life is strong; yet the life of action guided by practical wisdom and the excellences of character has its rightful place. There is no doubt that Aristotle shared in the first kind of life; his will shows the great extent to which he shared in the second as well.[12]

Notes

[1] Timber is one of the two commodities Aristotle mentions in his discussion of the territory of the ideal polis (*Pol* VII.5 1327a8).

[2] Works by Aristotle on dissections appear in all three detailed lists of his works from antiquity and later. Following Düring's (1957) numbering system, they are as follows: in Diogenes Laertius nos. 103 and 104; in Hesychius nos. 93 and 94; in Ptolemy al-Garib no. 48. Works on medicine are: in Diogenes Laertius no. 110; Hesychius nos. 98 and 167; Ptolemy al-Garib no. 99. Works on medicine are also mentioned in *Vita Marciana* and *Vita Lascaris*.

[3] Ross (1995: 3) cites views of Speusippus on Plato's theories with which Aristotle disagreed; W. Jaeger (1962: 111) goes further, claiming that "Speusippus had himself declared the theory of Ideas untenable during Plato's own lifetime, and had also abandoned the Ideal numbers suggested by Plato in his last period; he differed from him in other fundamental particulars as well." Aristotle criticizes Speusippus' views on the Forms, identifying him by name (*Met* Z.2 1028b21, Λ.7 1072b30) or his positions (A.9 992a32, M.6 1080b15, 8 1083a20, 9 1085a33).

[4] That Aristotle's son was with Herpyllis is also asserted in *Vita Hesychii* and in Suda, among others, and accepted by Ross (1995: 3) and Lloyd (1968: 8); but there are doubts. Düring, (1957: 262–7), citing a sentence in an Arabic version of Aristotle's will that is missing from the Greek text and other testimony, says that, if we accept this sentence "we must conclude that N[ichomachus] was Aristotle's legitimate son in his marriage with Pythias" (p. 261). J. Barnes (1995: 3) takes the same position.

[5] Comments on the relation between Aristotle and Alexander (and Philip) can be found in the biographical tradition of late antiquity (see Düring 1957: 284–8), but most scholars consider them an unreliable source.

[6] There is diversity of scholarly opinion about many matters relating to Aristotle's school. Despite ancient testimony (see Düring 1957: 404–11) that Aristotle established a school, Düring (pp. 460–1) argues that Aristotle did not found a school like Plato's Academy, and that the peripatetic school was established after his death. Barnes (1982: 5) also doubts that Aristotle established a formal school in the Lyceum; Ackrill (1981: 4) claims that he did. On *peripatos* and the name of Aristotle's school, Diogenes Laertius gives two different accounts, and there are additional ones in the biographical tradition (see Düring, 1957: 405–11). Allan (1978: 5) also rejects the idea that the name of Aristotle's school had anything to do with Aristotle lecturing while walking. As to Aristotle's library, while ancient testimony (see Düring, 1957: 337–8) supports the existence of it in Aristotle's school, Düring himself (p. 338) concludes that, while Aristotle owned many books, he kept them at his house. For a more detailed discussion on Aristotle's school, see J. Lynch (1972).

[7] According to Düring (1957: 459), "at the age of seventeen he [Aristotle] came as a stranger to Athens. He was looked upon as a stranger throughout his life."

[8] For a discussion of the parallel lives of Aristotle and Demosthenes and their respective views on rights and democracy, see Fred D. Miller, Jr., in G. Anagnostopoulos (ed.), *Law and Rights in the Ancient Greek Tradition*, Supplementary Volume of *Philosophical Inquiry* (Athens, 2006), pp. 27–60.

[9] "Our forefathers in the most remote ages have handed down to their posterity a tradition, in the form of myth, that these bodies are gods and that the divine encloses the whole of nature. The rest of the tradition has been added later in mythical form with a view of the persuasion of the multitude and to its utilitarian expediency; they say these gods are in the form of men . . . But if one were to separate the first point from these additions and take it alone – that they thought the first substance to be gods, one must regard this as an inspired utterance."

[10] See the accounts of Justin Martyr, Gregorius Nazianzenus, Procopius, and Eustathius about the connection between Aristotle's death and his inability to explain the tides of Euripus in Düring (1957: 347).

[11] Düring (p. 462) reaches conclusions similar to Jaeger's: "Aristotle left Athens in the middle of a political turmoil and died the same year, a lonely man. He had few real friends and numerous enemies."

[12] I would like to thank Gerasimos Santas and Andreas Anagnostopoulos for helpful comments and suggestions.

Bibliography

Ackrill, J. L. (1981). *Aristotle the Philosopher* (Oxford: Oxford University Press).

Allan, D. J. (1978). *The Philosophy of Aristotle* (Oxford: Oxford University Press).

Anagnostopoulos, G. (ed.) (2006). *Law and Rights in the Ancient Greek Tradition*, supple. vol. of *Philosophical Inquiry*.

Barnes, J. (1982). *Aristotle* (Oxford: Oxford University Press).

Barnes, J. (ed.) (1995). *The Cambridge Companion to Aristotle* (Cambridge: Cambridge University Press).

Diogenes Laertius (1972). *Lives of Eminent Philosophers*, vol. 1 (Cambridge, MA: Harvard University Press).

Düring, I. (1957). *Aristotle in the Ancient Biological Tradition* (Göteborg: Institute of Classical Studies of the University of Göteborg).

Grayeff, F. (1974). *Aristotle and His School* (London: Duckworth).

Jackson, H. (1920). "Aristotle's Lecture-room and Lectures," *Journal of Philology*, 35, pp. 191–200.

Jaeger, W. (1962). *Aristotle: Fundamentals of the History of his Development* (Oxford: Oxford University Press).

Lee, H. D. P. (1948). "Place-names and the Date of Aristotle's Biological Works," *Classical Quarterly*, pp. 61–7.

Lloyd, G. E. R. (1968). *Aristotle: The Growth and Structure of his Thought* (Cambridge: Cambridge University Press).

Lynch, J. (1972). *Aristotle's School* (Berkeley, CA: University of California Press).

Miller, F. D., Jr. (2006). "Legal and Political Rights in Demosthenes and Aristotle," in G. Anagnostopoulos (ed.), *Law and Rights in the Ancient Greek Tradition*, supple. vol. of *Philosophical Inquiry*, pp. 27–60.

Ross, W. D. [1923] (1995). *Aristotle* (London/New York: Routledge).

Thompson, W. D. (1913). *On Aristotle as a Biologist* (Oxford: Clarendon Press).

2

Aristotle's Works and the Development of His Thought

GEORGIOS ANAGNOSTOPOULOS

Catalogues and Editions of Aristotle's Works

From the biographical tradition of late antiquity we have inherited three itemized lists of works attributed to Aristotle.[1] Diogenes Laertius (third century CE) credits Aristotle with 143 works; Hesychius (sixth century CE) attributes to him 187; and the Ptolemy al-Garib (fourth century CE?) catalogue includes 99 works. (The totals given here are based on the numbering system used by Düring, 1957.) The obvious differences in the numbers of works included in these lists are due primarily to the different ways a work may appear on a list. For example, the *Eudemian Ethics* appears as a single work in one list while in another the various Books of that same work are listed as separate items. When one takes into account that Aristotle's works are parsed in different ways by those cataloguing them, then, it will become apparent that the three lists overlap considerably although not completely.

However one counts the items in these lists, what is included in them constitutes a most impressive achievement in terms of quantity, scope of topics covered, and quality – facts that did not escape Diogenes. He introduces his list by remarking that "His [Aristotle's] writings are very numerous and, considering the man's all-round excellence, I deemed it incumbent on me to catalogue them" (V.21) and concludes by estimating that the items in his catalogue add up to "in all 445, 270 lines" (V.27).[2] Aristotle's contributions across almost all philosophical areas are major; in the words of J. Barnes (1982: 1), "He bestrode antiquity like an intellectual colossus. No man before him had contributed so much to learning. No man after him could hope to rival his achievements." But in some fields he was not a mere contributor. He was a pioneer and his theories defined these fields of inquiry for centuries, especially logic and biology. With respect to the former, he seems self-conscious of his achievement in articulating the syllogistic system of deductive inference. At the conclusion of *SE* (34 184b1) he remarks that "on the subject of deduction we had absolutely nothing else of an earlier age to mention" and views the results of his own systematic inquiries on deduction as satisfactory. With respect to his contributions in biology, the opinion of the late M. Delbrück, Nobel laureate in biology (1969), will give a sense of his achievement. Delbrück suggested that Aristotle should be awarded posthumously the Nobel Prize on account of his theory of biological form as the carrier, from one generation to the other, of the kind of genetic information identified in DNA theories (Delbrück 1971).

But how accurate are these lists? Do they include everything Aristotle wrote? Do they include more than he wrote? Undoubtedly, the latter is true. Already in antiquity, biographers and scholars were aware that certain works attributed to Aristotle were not his. Hesychius concludes his list by appending ten works (items 188–97) he labels as spurious (*pseudoepigrapha*). Moreover, there are reasons to believe that such works were known to Andronicus, the first editor of Aristotle's works (see below), several centuries earlier (Düring 1957: 91). Indeed, almost all of the last twenty-nine items listed as non-spurious in Hesychius' catalogue do not correspond to any items in the lists of Diogenes Laertius or Ptolemy al-Garib and their authenticity is questionable, with some scholars surmising that they are titles of books that were in the libraries of Rhodes or Pergamon (see Düring 1957: 91). Even items that appear in all three lists may not be Aristotle's works, although some of them have survived and are included in modern editions of the Aristotelian corpus.[3] Surprisingly, Diogenes' catalogue omits several major works by Aristotle – including *On the Soul* (*de Anima*), *Parts of Animals* and *Generation of Animals* – whose authenticity has never been in doubt.

The above lists were based on a biography of Aristotle by Hermippus (third century CE), which has been lost, and possibly on the work of the peripatetic scholar Andronicus of Rhodes, who is credited with the systematic cataloguing and editing of Aristotle's works around the middle of first century BCE. While the details of Andronicus' plan for cataloguing and editing Aristotle's works are unclear and the subject of many scholarly controversies, those regarding the fate of Aristotle's writings after his death and the way they landed into his first editor's hands are the subject of a legend. As the legend goes, when Aristotle died, his successor at the Lyceum, Theophrastus, inherited his library and it then was passed on to the latter's nephew Neleus, who took it to the city of Scepsis in Asia Minor and left it with his relatives who, in turn, hid it underground. The contents of Aristotle's library, the legend continues, remained hidden for almost two centuries and suffered considerable damage, till they were moved first to Athens and then to Rome where Andronicus prepared his edition (see Düring 1957: 412–25). The legend has given rise to a tale about the availability and influence of Aristotle's writings over the years during which they were supposedly hidden underground: They were not available to anyone, even to those in Aristotle's own school and, as a consequence, his works were hardly read by or had any influence on anyone; however, Andronicus' edition changed all that and revived interest in Aristotelianism.[4] While Andronicus' editorial achievements, which have shaped the Aristotelian corpus as we have it today, are not in doubt, most everything in both the legend and the tale is contested.

First of all, it is unlikely that Aristotelian manuscripts had disappeared from all locations, including Aristotle's own school, from Theophrastus' death until the time Andronicus edited them. Most probably, the Lyceum had copies of some, if not of all, of Aristotle's works as did libraries and some individuals. Most scholars believe that there was considerable interest in and philosophical discussion of the views of Aristotle during these same years in the many philosophical centers, including those of Athens, Rome, Asia Minor, and additional cities along the shores of the eastern Mediterranean.[5]

15

Furthermore, the parts of the legend concerning the transference of Aristotle's works to and from their underground storage in Asia Minor as well as the extent of the damage they suffered have been questioned. Concerning the latter, in particular, some see behind it a bias against Aristotle and the peripatetic school among biographers and commentators.[6]

There is, however, considerable testimony about Andronicus' cataloguing and editing of the Aristotelian corpus that seems reliable, and it appears that he was well-prepared for what must have been a major editorial undertaking. He was a peripatetic and an accomplished scholar himself, who is reputed to have lectured on Aristotle and his school and to have authored some philosophical works of his own, including a work that was an introduction to his edition of Aristotle's texts which may have been titled *On Aristotle's Writings* (Düring 1957: 442).[7] But what exactly were the materials that Andronicus catalogued and edited and what did his editing amount to? Surviving testimony as to the materials inherited by Neleus, stored underground in Scepsis, moved to Rome and, eventually, catalogued and edited by Andronicus is at best ambiguous and conflicting. In some cases the materials are described as Aristotle's own writings (*autographa*); in others, as Aristotle's library; and in yet others, as Aristotle's and Theophrastus' libraries. Tradition has it that Aristotle, in addition to his own works, bought books by others and had a library; Theophrastus, who inherited Aristotle's library and is credited by Diogenes Laertius with having authored "a large number of writings" (227, to be exact), also had a library that probably included books written by others, bequeathing all of these to Neleus (see Theophrastus' will in Diogenes Laertius, V. 52). Thus the collection of works that ended up in Andronicus' hands, after its incredible journey (Athens–Scepsis–Athens–Rome) may have included works by Theophrastus and other peripatetics. Hence, claims in late antiquity that some works attributed to Aristotle were not by him but, instead, were written by other peripatetics, might not be completely baseless. But at least one source (Ammonius in his commentary on Aristotle's *Int* 5.24) reports that Andronicus was judicious in his work, that he used rigorous criteria for ascertaining whether or not a treatise was a genuine Aristotelian text – e.g., diction, methods of exposition, and relationship with other genuine works by Aristotle (see also Gottschalk 1990, p. 58ff). While these criteria seem reasonable, they do not remove all doubts; the works of other peripatetics could easily pass Andronicus' test. Indeed, some of the works making up the Aristotelian corpus today but whose authenticity is questioned are thought to have been authored by members of the peripatos (e.g., *Problems*).

As to the nature of Andronicus' editing of the Aristotelian corpus, the consensus among scholars is that it has shaped Aristotle's works as we know them and, thus, it has had a major influence in the way his works have been read and understood during the past two millennia. What is meant by this is not necessarily that Andronicus altered Aristotle's texts, but that he organized what were probably separate, short texts into the treatises we have today and, in addition, divided the treatises into groups on the basis of their subject-matter (e.g., ethical, physical, psychological, or logical), or their intended audience and possibly philosophical rigor or significance, or their use in inquiry (e.g., the ones that are or investigate the instruments of inquiry – the logical treatises constituting the *Organon* – vs. those that investigate a certain domain). Scholars find evidence for this in Porphyry's account (*Vita Plotini* ca. 24) of Andronicus' method of editing Aristotle's works, which he claims to have used himself as a model in editing the works of Plotinus. Porphyry speaks of such organization of writings according to their subject into a single treatise and possibly of grouping together of treatises. Thus, Barnes (1995: 11) sees the *Top* as such a collection of essays on related themes, appearing as different items in Diogenes Laertius' list but made into a single work by Andronicus, who has thus influenced once and for all the way we read these separate pieces – i.e., as parts of a unified work. Of course, the same can be said about many of Aristotle's works, including his physical treatises, his ethical ones, and what has come to be called *Metaphysics*, perhaps the most daring attempt by Andronicus (and possibly others – see below) at creating a single treatise out of what seem to be separate and disparate essays – an attempt that, according to many, has not succeeded in producing a work possessing unity or coherence.

But how did Andronicus arrive at the editorial principles that have organized Aristotle's writings in the way we know them today and which are perhaps responsible for all or most of the systematicity we find in them? Düring argues that Andronicus had worked out a comprehensive view of Aristotle as a systematic thinker and of the contents of his many treatises as the articulation of a single system. He thinks that such views were the centerpieces of Andronicus' lost book referred to earlier (*On Aristotle's writings*), which functioned as an introduction to his edition of Aristotle's works, and that those same views guided his cataloguing and editing of the Aristotelian corpus. In Düring's opinion, Andronicus proceeded to (a) organize the treatises according to subject-matter, disregarding their chronology; (b) artificially create a department of knowledge called "metaphysics," corresponding to Aristotle's "first philosophy;" (c) accept the distinction between "exoteric" (i.e., works for a wider audience) and "acroamatic" or "acroatic" (or "esoteric," i.e., those intended for a select and trained audience), restricting the former to Aristotle's early dialogues and other popular writings and minimizing their importance, on the one hand, while equating the acroamatic or esoteric with the treatises and viewing them as the only important works and "the only true expression of Aristotle's thought," on the other; and (d) capitalize on an idea "mentioned only in passing by Aristotle, namely that logic and dialectics are the instruments of philosophy" and proceed to arrange "all the logical writings in a corpus to which he gave the name *Organon*" (Düring 1957: 422–3).

Düring's opinion about Andronicus' editorial principles can be easily gleaned from what is asserted (a)–(d), but he emphatically states that, "In his work on Aristotle's writings Andronicus was inspired by some typically Hellenistic but very un-Aristotelian ideas. He believed that Aristotle had written his scholarly treatises as part of a philosophic system; he tried to arrange the writings according to this idea" (pp. 422–3). According to this view, Andronicus was guided by editorial principles that were not applicable to Aristotle, in the end *creating* a philosophical system where presumably there was none. Given that the canonical, modern edition of Aristotle's works by Immanuel Bekker (Berlin 1831) – on which the numbering system for referring to any passage in any Aristotelian text is based – derives directly from Andronicus' edition, it should not come as a surprise that the unity/disunity of or the order of the Books within several treatises are hotly contested. Once the view articulated above about the inappropriateness of Andronicus' editorial principles is accepted – as it is by many – disputes seem inevitable. Thus, scholars disagree about the placement of the middle Books of the *Pol*, the common Books of the *EE* and *NE*, the appropriateness of including Book I of *Phys* in that treatise, and, of course, about the *Met*. Regarding the last treatise, its unity is not the only issue. As (b) shows, according to Düring, Aristotle had no conception of metaphysics as a subfield of philosophy; it was fabricated by the editor of his texts. Many point out that Aristotle did not name any of his works *Metaphysics* and he never uses the term "metaphysics" or its cognates. The term is believed to have originated with Andronicus who grouped a number of Aristotle's writings into a single volume and placed it after (*meta*) the physical treatises (*physika*). Thus the term *metaphysica*, which became the name of Aristotle's work, did not mean what it subsequently came to mean – a subfield of philosophy. These facts about the origin and meaning of the term "metaphysics" have been used by some recent opponents of metaphysics, not only to support the claim that Aristotle had no conception of metaphysics and was not a metaphysician, but also as evidence for their contention that such a subfield does not exist or is impossible. It is clear that the reasoning behind these last claims is a *non sequitur*. From the fact that Aristotle did not name one of his treatises *Metaphysics* – did he name all or most of his other works? – or had no single term corresponding to "metaphysics," does not follow that he had no conception of metaphysics as a subfield of inquiry or that he did not write on metaphysical issues. Plato did not have a term for metaphysics either, but hardly anyone denies that he was a metaphysician. Needless to say, nothing also follows from such linguistic facts about the existence/non-existence or possibility/impossibility of metaphysics.

Now, while it is wise to exercise caution about Andronicus' editorial decisions, there is also the danger of going overboard, especially when our primary access to Aristotle's texts is through Andronicus' edition. Those seeing a heavy-handed approach in Andronicus' editing assume that Aristotle had no system whatsoever and that Andronicus imposed a comprehensive one on his work. Both of these assumptions should be questioned. It is doubtful that Aristotle's works, as edited by Andronicus, constitute a comprehensive system of thought into which everything he says fits neatly. But there is systematic thinking in them about many things – the nature of the sciences, the faculties of the soul, the types and correctness of political constitutions, the nature of causes, the nature of physical bodies and that of heavenly ones and the relation between the two, to mention a few. These fragments of systematic thinking have not been created by Andronicus; they are to be found in Aristotle's texts. Why then suppose that Aristotle had no philosophical system, or even that he did not treat systematically any topic, and that it was his editor who invented either a single comprehensive one or many mini-systems for him out of nowhere?

And should we dismiss any and all attempts to group various texts by Aristotle into single works, along the lines Andronicus attempted to do? Admittedly, the criteria for determining whether the different parts making up the *NE*, *Pol*, or *Phys* constitute a unity in each case are less well-defined and more likely to be contested than diction or method. But even with unity there are some limits, which Andronicus seems to have observed. He does not group the essays making up the *Top* with those of *Rhet* or *An. Pr*, or those of the *NE* with those of *Pol*, although there are connections between the works in the first group, and the treatises in the second exhibit not only strong connections but an obvious continuity – the *NE* leads directly into the *Pol*. And, in many instances, for every argument questioning Andronicus' judgment in grouping some texts together and forming a single treatise or placing the Books of an Aristotelian treatise in a certain order within it, one can come up with an argument supporting his judgment. Thus, one can see that the general discussion of the inquiry into nature fits nicely as an introductory chapter (Book I) of the *Phys*. And it seems that Andronicus' grouping the logical treatises into the *Organon* need not be inconsistent with Aristotle's views. He repeatedly indicates that such treatises are the tools of all inquiry (*NE* I.3 1094b19, *Met* Γ.3 1005b2, Γ.4 1006a5).

The case of *Met* is, of course, much more complicated, and for that reason even greater caution is required before reaching sweeping conclusions about its unity or what it tells us about its author's metaphysical quest. While one can admit that it consists of individual texts probably composed during different periods in Aristotle's life (something not unique to this treatise) and that there is considerable variation in the topics discussed, one can reasonably resist the conclusions that Andronicus fabricated a subfield Aristotle had no idea of and there is no unity or coherence to this work whatsoever. It is clear from the discussion in Books A, α, and B that the knowledge Aristotle aims to achieve in his inquiries in what is now called *Metaphysics* is of a special kind, similar in some respects to, but also different from, that aimed at in the canonical sciences. It is the most universal and abstract and aims to understand the first principles and highest causes. He does not call it "metaphysical knowledge" but the features he attributes to it bring to mind the kind of knowledge traditional metaphysics hopes to attain. Again, Aristotle's discussion in Book Γ of truths about things on account of the fact that they simply are – in contrast to truths on account of the fact that they are of some kind or other – and his contention that there are both a science and axioms of Being shows that he was aware the knowledge he was seeking was of a special kind. The well-known passage in Z.1 claiming that "the question which, both now and of old, has always been raised, and always been the subject of doubt, viz. what being is, is just the question, what is substance?"; the discussion on substance, form, matter, and essence in the same Book; and the examination of change and of the divine in the later Books of the treatise are on topics that are the staple of traditional metaphysics. Even a cursory reading of Aristotle's treatise that now bears the label *Metaphysics* will convince anyone that its author was dealing with many of the topics we associate with traditional metaphysics and that he was fully aware he was aiming at a special kind of knowledge. Andronicus, of course, might have reached the very same conclusion and for similar reasons.

The question of the unity of the *Met* is, of course, a separate issue. But it is not clear how much weight one should attach to this. Some works of Aristotle exhibit greater unity than others. The *An*, for example, focusing on the soul and its faculties, exhibits greater unity than either the *NE* or *Pol*, which range over a much larger number of topics that are not as tightly connected with each other as those dealt with within the *An*. When speaking of lack of unity in connection with the *Met*, scholars often focus on two things: (1) the apparent independent and different views on what seems to be the same issue; and (2) the supposed fact that the various Books of the treatise have been collected into a single work by many, different editors. Thus C. Kirwan (1971: 75) accepts the many-editors-view of the *Met*, as do many others,[8] and argues that there is no connection between the kind of knowledge of first principles that Books A, α, and B outline and that of the type of science of Being presented in Book Γ. But S. Menn (1995:

19

202–8) has raised serious doubts about both claims, especially about the claim that there is clear evidence for the many-editors-view of the *Met*.[9]

Chronology of Aristotle's Works

As they have done in the case of the Platonic corpus, scholars have been hard at work attempting to understand the chronological sequence of Aristotle's works. Achieving such understanding is of importance for speaking meaningfully about Aristotle's intellectual development – assuming that there was one. While the scholarly disagreements about the chronology of Plato's works have not ended, there is a broad consensus about the place of most of his dialogues in the three chronological classes into which his writings are grouped – Socratic or Early, Middle, and Late Dialogues. The situation is far less clear and much more difficult in the case of Aristotle's writings. First of all, Aristotle did not date his works and no one else close to him, who might have known when specific works were written, did it for him. Most agree that the dialogues attributed to him, of which only fragments survive, belong in Aristotle's early life – the time of his first stay in Athens, when he was in Plato's Academy – but beyond that it has been difficult to attach either an absolute or even a relative date to his works. Scholars have relied on the following in their efforts to understand the chronological order of the works comprising the Aristotelian corpus.

Cross-references within Aristotle's works

This criterion was touted by Ross as a reliable means for determining relative chronology among works (Ross 1960: 16; Kenny 1978: ch. 2). If a work (e.g., the *An. Post*) is referred to in another (e.g., the *NE* VI.3), it must have been written before the latter. Leaving aside the reliability of the criterion itself, since the two works could have been written at the same time, Barnes has raised serious doubts as to whether cross-references in Aristotle's works are really Aristotle's own. According to him, they probably have been added by editors or commentators, and they should not be used as evidence of the relative chronology of Aristotle's works (Barnes 1995: 19). Barnes may be correct in urging caution, but not all cross-references should be dismissed as evidence for dating a work. In some cases, including the one just cited from *NE*, the cross-reference is an integral part of Aristotle's argument and if Aristotle kept revising his treatises over many years, as many believe, some of the cross-references might have been added later by him.

References to historical events in Aristotle's works

In some of his works Aristotle refers to historical events that occurred in his lifetime, which may tell us something about the date of the writing of that work or, at least, a part of it. Thus, the latest event Aristotle refers to in his *Pol* (V.10 1311b2) is the assassination of King Philip of Macedonia in 336, which tells us that Aristotle could not have written *Pol* V (or a part of it) before this date. Given that each of the lengthy treatises of Aristotle was probably written over several years, other Books of the *Pol* could have been written before this date; and, given the uncertainty about the order of the Books of the *Pol* alluded to earlier, it will not be easy to identify which these are. In addition, dating a work by references to historical events that might occur in it does not necessarily produce any precise results. In the case of the *Pol*, even if we had reason to believe that the whole of the treatise was written after Philip's assassination, we would only be able to infer that it was written sometime within the fourteen years following that event – between 336 and Aristotle's death in 322.[10]

Philosophical views, presuppositions, or advances

As Barnes points out, scholars have relied heavily on this test for determining chronology – namely, by trying to determine whether or not the philosophical view elaborated in one work (the earlier one) is used or presupposed in another (the later one); or by trying to determine whether or not one work (the later) develops or advances the argument of another (the earlier). Thus, it has been recognized that an account of the syllogism, articulated in *An. Pr*, is presupposed by the theory of demonstrative knowledge presented in *An. Post*, leading most to conclude that the former work precedes the latter. The accounts of the good and the virtues elaborated in the *EE* seem to be further developed and refined in the *NE*, easily leading many to the conclusion that the latter was written after the former. But perhaps the most convincing application of this kind of test seems to have been the relative dating of the *HA*. In Book I of that treatise (I.6 491a9), Aristotle puts forward his methodological principle that supposedly guides his researches into animals: "Our object being to determine first of all the differences that exist and the actual facts in the case of all of them. Having done this, we must attempt to discover the causes. And, after all, this is the natural method of procedure . . ." In the several volumes of the *HA* he collects an astonishingly large number of facts, while *PA* and *GA* carry out the second component of his methodological directive by developing the comprehensive theories that presumably give the causes of the facts. Naturally, it has been taken for granted by scholars that *HA* preceded *PA* and *GA*.

Yet in none of these cases has the application of the test settled the disputes about the relative chronology of the treatises just mentioned. Recently, scholars have adduced plausible reasons in favor of the view that the *An. Post* was written first and that Aristotle developed the syllogistic theory of the *An. Pr* afterwards (Barnes 1993 and 1995: 21–2; Smith 1982: 327–35; Düring 1957: 369). Over the years, there have been as many arguments in favor of the *NE* being later than the *EE* as there have been in favor of the reverse. Surprisingly, the relative dating of the *HA* has also been questioned. D. Balme, after a thorough examination of common phrases occurring in the factual biological work (*HA*) and the theoretical ones (*PA*, *GA*), reached the conclusion that the latter two were written before the former, raising deep doubts as to whether Aristotle's methodological directive can provide any evidence about the relative chronology of his biological treatises (see Balme 1986; but cf. Lennox 1996). Indeed, Barnes has raised deep doubts about the reliability of this criterion for the relative dating of Aristotle's works, especially when it relies on comparing how developed or mature a view or an argument is. He thinks that such parameters are subjective and it is unlikely that agreement can be reached about which one of two, and possibly more, articulations of a view or argument occurring in different works is the more developed or mature.

Stylometry

This approach eschews concern with content or judgments about features of it that may raise the issue of subjectivity, and instead focuses on linguistic features of the text. By comparing statistical data on such linguistic features from different works one might be able to locate the chronological position of one of Aristotle's works relative to the position of others (see, for example, Kenny 1978: chs. 4–6). The use of computers in recent years has made it possible for scholars to easily compile the necessary data for such stylometric studies. But doubts remain about its effectiveness when applied to Aristotle. What we know about the nature of his works seems to raise problems for this, and possibly any, approach to dating his texts (see below).

Is it likely that the search for an absolute or relative dating of Aristotle's works will ever end successfully? The nature of Aristotle's writings, especially of the treatises, makes it very difficult, if not impossible. But some scholars go even further, claiming that, given this nature, "it makes no sense to attempt to provide a chronology of Aristotle's writings" (Barnes 1995: 21). Aristotle's works are believed to be his lecture notes, some more polished than others, which he kept revising over many years, possibly decades; and most likely he continued reworking sets of notes that now constitute different treatises at the same time. If this is the nature of what survives as Aristotle's treatises, what exactly can we expect to determine when seeking the date of a certain work? Even relative dating will be a problem in many cases. Consider the NE and Pol. The former contains many programmatic statements about politics and the latter presupposes or incorporates many of Aristotle's views developed in the former, and these facts have led to the view that NE preceded the Pol. Yet nothing in these facts excludes the possibility that Aristotle was working on the different sets of lecture notes constituting these two treatises at the same time, over many years, incorporating into his notes on political topics the relevant views from his notes on ethical matters. If these two treatises co-developed over many years, what sense is there to the question of which one preceded the other? It should not come as surprise, then, that not much progress has been made in fixing with any degree of certainty the chronology of Aristotle's works. While most agree that Aristotle's dialogues were written early in his life and that the logical treatises may also belong to the same period, the chronological ordering of most of his other writings remains quite tentative, and little has been added to Jaeger's (1923, 1934) proposals and to the revisions of them made by Ross (1995, 1960).

The Development of Aristotle's Thought

While Plato's works were looked at as reflecting a system of thought that had gone through considerable development during the long life of its author, for centuries the opposite was true with his student's works. Aristotle's writings were thought to articulate a comprehensive, consistent, and static system that did not develop at all during his life. Indeed, some contend that the conviction about the static character of Aristotle's thought led those copying his manuscripts through the centuries to excise or edit lines in his texts that they took to be inconsistent with the presumed static system. They never considered the possibility that Aristotle might have changed his mind about anything. This view of Aristotle's thought was challenged in the twentieth century and has been abandoned. According to Ross (1960: 2), the first to question the static conception was Thomas Case (Case 1910). But the scholar who most forcefully challenged the prevailing view and articulated a systematic alternative to it was Werner Jaeger in his first publication on the topic of development (Jaeger 1912) and his seminal work *Aristoteles, Grundlegung einer Geschichte seiner Entwicklung* (Berlin 1923; appearing in English as *Aristotle: Fundamentals of the History of his Development*, 1934). As the title of Jaeger's work indicates, he was convinced that there was development in Aristotle's thought, and the bulk of his book outlines and documents the supposed precise course of this development, which Jaeger saw as roughly corresponding to the three major periods in Aristotle's life: the first period in Athens, a period of travels, and the second period in Athens (see ch. 1). In very brief outline, the gist of Jaeger's view is that during his twenty years in Plato's Academy Aristotle remained a faithful Platonist, and his early dialogues (*Eudemus* and *Protrepticus*) clearly confirm such faithfulness. Indeed, Jaeger argues that Aristotle's departure from the Academy at Plato's death is a sign of his profound disappointment with Plato's successor who, according to Jaeger, Aristotle thought had "inherited merely the office and not the spirit" of Platonism. The period of travels, according to Jaeger, saw the beginning of Aristotle's movement away from Platonism, especially in his metaphysical and epistemological views, leading towards empiricism; the development continued during Aristotle's second period in Athens, when Aristotle headed his own school and, according to Jaeger, abandoned Platonism completely and became a full-fledged empiricist.

Jaeger's systematic arguments for his position are impressive, and his correlation of Aristotle's alleged intellectual development to the main periods of his life makes for a neat account of the growth of one of the most prolific philosophers. Jaeger's view has had a major influence (see Chroust 1973), but in the eyes of some the account is in fact too neat. Most scholars, while they accept the general claim that there is development in Aristotle's thought, question Jaeger's specific trajectory of it from early faithfulness to Platonism to empiricism. They doubt that Aristotle ever was the kind of faithful Platonist Jaeger makes him out to be and believe that what survives from Aristotle's early dialogues does not reflect a blind faithfulness to Plato's doctrines (see Ackrill 1981: 4; Allan 1968: 5; Barnes 1995: 17; Lloyd 1968: 19–41). Most likely, Aristotle began to articulate criticisms of and alternatives to certain views of Plato while he was still in the latter's Academy, even in his earliest writings, the dialogues (see Lloyd 1968: 28–41). Two such salient criticisms and alternatives are presented in the *Cat* (the criticism of the priority of kinds and the formulation of his account of substance) and *An. Post* (the criticism of Plato's theory of recollection or innate ideas and the formulation of his own account of the grasping of first principles), both of which are considered relatively early works. As to the onset of Aristotle's empiricism, it has been well-established that during his period of travels Aristotle embarked on a major research project in the shores of Asia Minor that was empirical in character (see ch. 1). It is unlikely that such a project could have been started by someone who was as committed a Platonist as Jaeger makes Aristotle to be. As argued in the previous chapter,

Aristotle had considerable training in empirical research and medicine, and it was probably his life-long interest in and affinity for the empirical study of nature that made his transition from a member of the Academy in Athens to a student of the marine life of the Aegean Sea such a natural one. Indeed, his early metaphysical and logical views – his account of primary substance as individual and the relation between it and secondary substance (species and genera) as well as his views on definition in the works comprising the *Organon* – provide the necessary ontological and logical foundation for the kind of scientific inquiry he embarked on upon leaving Athens.[11]

Leaving aside the question about when Aristotle drifted into empiricism, did he ever abandon Platonism altogether and become a complete empiricist? Most doubt that this ever happened. Aristotle's relation to Platonism, whatever is meant by the latter, is a rather complicated matter. As Owen shows in his discussion of Aristotle's views on dialectic, logic and metaphysics, Plato's student was a very astute but also a very selective critic and follower of his teacher (Owen 1986b: 200–20). Many scholars believe that no clear path from Platonism to empiricism (or non-Platonism) can be identified in Aristotle's works. Platonism concerned Aristotle all his life, as is evident in many of his works, especially the *Met.* It is true that he argues against tenets of Platonism in these works, but that is different from the claim that he abandoned every bit of Plato's thought. Indeed, Owen comes to a conclusion that is very different from Jaeger's: "It seems possible now to trace that progress [in logic and metaphysics] from sharp and rather schematic criticism of Plato to an avowed sympathy with Plato's general metaphysical program. But the sympathy is one thing, the concrete problems and procedures which give content to Aristotle's project are another. They are his own, worked out and improved in the course of his own thinking about science and dialectic. There seems no evidence of a stage in that thinking in which he confused admiration with acquiescence" (p. 220). Still others reach conclusions that are even more starkly opposed to those of Jaeger. Düring (2005), for instance, argues that Aristotle's development was exactly the opposite of what Jaeger claims – from empiricism to Platonism.

Searching for the path of Aristotle's development exclusively or primarily from the perspective of the relation of his thought to that of Plato has produced conclusions that are conflicting and perhaps not very informative. This may not be an accident. If there is a developmental story to be told about Aristotle's thought, the trajectory of the relation of his thinking throughout his philosophical career to Platonism could be only a part, not the whole, of that story. The relation of the thought of the two thinkers need not always be the overriding concern when it comes to questions about Aristotle's intellectual development, and making it such may not produce the most illuminating results. Perhaps the engine driving whatever development there is in Aristotle's thought has more to do with the puzzles, both philosophical and scientific, he was encountering than with his changing attitudes toward Platonism. As Owen observes, it is the concrete problems Aristotle faced and the procedures he relied on in dealing with them, both worked on and revised over many years, which give content to his project. It might be wise then, when asking the developmental question, to set to one side the perennial puzzle about the relation of Aristotle's thought to that of Plato and, instead, make as our focus the problems Aristotle grappled with, the methods he used, and the answers he considered and often repeatedly reconsidered over the years. Concentrating, for instance, on the growth of his biological views as they unfold in his treatises on animals, or the increasing complexity of his views about substance, essence, form, and matter as they take shape in the relevant works of his, might lead to a deeper understanding of Aristotle's development than has been achieved by making his relation to Platonism the central and overarching concern. Some recent studies[12] have begun to move in this direction.

Notes

[1] Of course, there are others, e.g., *Vita Marciana*, *Vita Vulgata*, *Vita Lascaris*, and *Vita Latina*, which mention only a few works or list the classes into which the works are grouped. In addition to Düring (1957), detailed discussion on the lists of Aristotle's books can be found in Moraux (1951).

[2] Barnes (1995: 9) calculates that the modern equivalent of Diogenes' estimate is six thousand pages, of which less than two thousand have survived.

[3] Barnes (1984: vol. 1, x) lists fifteen items in his edition of the complete works of Aristotle whose "authenticity has been seriously questioned" or "spuriousness has never been doubted."

[4] Barnes (1995: 10) considers this a "modern story," but the claims about the unavailability of the Aristotelian texts go back to late antiquity (see the relevant sources in and comments Düring (1957: 382–93, 312–425); also Tarán (2001: 490–3) as well as Barnes' own exhaustive discussion of the travails and edition of Aristotle's texts in Barnes (1997: 1–69).

[5] While in some testimony it is claimed that Aristotle's works were unknown to all, Plutarch (*Vita Sullae* 26) claims that "they were not accurately known to the many." On the availability of Aristotle's works, including in libraries, and the influence of his texts prior to Andronicus' edition see, Gomperz (1969: 33), Moraux (1973: ch. 1), Tarán (2001: 484), Barnes (1997), and Gottschalk (1990: 55–82).

[6] On the anti-peripatos bias, see e.g., Düring (1957: 462–3) and Tarán (2001: 489–90); Gomperz (1969: 33), on the other hand, claims that "no doubt is permissible as to the actual occurrence of these events [recounted in the legend and tale]" but "the case is different when we come to inquire into the range of their significance."

[7] While there is some testimony (Ammonius, Elias) that Andronicus was even the head of the Peripatetic School in Athens, most think it is not true (see Düring 1957: 420), but Moraux (1973: 52ff) concurs with it. As to the date of Andronicus' editing of Aristotle's works, Düring (1957: 421) proposes 40–20 BCE, but Gottschalk (1990: 62) argues that it cannot be later than 60 BCE.

[8] See Ackrill (1981: 116); Barnes (1995: 67–8); Ross (1924), but in his 1923 book (1923, 1995: 12), he claims that most Books of the *Met* "were worked up into a fairly well-knit whole, linked together by frequent cross-references which may well go back to Aristotle."

[9] Search for unity in the *Met* has followed different lines. P. Merlan (1968) argues that it is to be found in Aristotle's concern with the divine, which he equates with Aristotle's being-*qua*-being. For another approach to the unity of certain parts of the *Met* see Frede (1987), as well as Wedin, ch. 8 of this volume. A systematic defense of the unity of certain Books of the *Met* (A-Γ and Z-Θ) on the basis of being the knowledge Aristotle designates as first philosophy and science of being *qua* being is developed by Irwin (1988).

[10] Ross (1995: 15) points to Aristotle's reference (*Pol* V.10 1312b10) to the expulsion of Dionysius by Dion from Syracuse in 357–6 as an event that has happened *nun* (now), and concludes that Aristotle started work on the *Pol* during his first period in Athens. Ross's view, which implies that Aristotle was working on the *Pol* for at least twenty years, is rejected by all recent translators of the work.

[11] Cf. Owen (1986a), who argues that Aristotle's concerns with science and dialectic during his stay in the Academy led him to positions that differ from Plato's but doubts that Aristotle had at this time any training or interest in empirical research.

[12] Lloyd (1968) approaches the study of Aristotle's growth from such a perspective, as do many of the contributors to the volume by Wians (1996).

Bibliography

Ackrill, J. L. (1981). *Aristotle the Philosopher* (Oxford: Oxford University Press).

Allan, D. J. (1968). *The Philosophy of Aristotle* (Oxford: Oxford University Press).

Balme, D. (1986). "The Place of Biology in Aristotle's Philosophy," in A. Gotthelf and J. Lennox (eds.), *Philosophical Issues in Aristotle's Biology* (Cambridge: Cambridge University Press), pp. 9–20.

Barnes, J. (1982). *Aristotle* (Oxford: Oxford University Press).

Barnes, J. (1993). *Aristotle: "Posterior Analytics"* (Oxford: Clarendon Press).

Barnes, J. (1995). *The Cambridge Companion to Aristotle* (Cambridge: Cambridge University Press).

Barnes, J. (1997). "Roman Aristotle," in J. Barnes and M. Griffin (eds.), *Philosophia Togata II* (Oxford: Clarendon Press).

Barnes, J. (ed.) (1984). *The Collected Works of Aristotle* (Princeton, NJ: Princeton University Press).

Case, T. (1910). "Aristotle," *Encyclopaedia Britannica*, 2, pp. 501–22.

Chroust, A.-H. (1973). "The First Thirty Years of Modern Aristotelian Scholarship," *Classica et Mediaevalia*, 24, pp. 27–57.

Delbrück, M. (1971). "Aristotle-totle-totle," in J. Monod and E. Borek (eds.), *Of Microbes and Life* (New York: Columbia University Press), pp. 50–4.

Düring, I. (1957). *Aristotle in the Ancient Biographical Tradition* (Göteborg: Institute of Classical Studies of the University of Göteborg).

Düring, I. (2005). *Aristoteles: Darstellung und Interpretation seines Denkens* (Heidelberg: Carl Winter-Universitäts Verlag).

Frede, M. (1987). "The Unity of General and Special Metaphysics: Aristotle's Conception of Metaphysics," in M. Frede, *Essays in Ancient Philosophy* (Oxford: Clarendon Press), pp. 81–95.

Gomperz, T. (1969). *The Greek Thinkers*, vol. 4 (London: John Murray).

Gottschalk, H. B. (1990). "The Earliest Aristotelian Commentators," in R. Sorabji (ed.), *Aristotle Transformed: The Ancient Commentators and Their Influence* (London: Duckworth), pp. 55–82.

Irwin, T. (1988). *Aristotle's First Principles* (Oxford: Clarendon Press).

Jaeger, W. (1912). *Studien zur Entstehungsgeschichte der Metaphysik des Aristoteles* (Berlin: Weidmann).

Jaeger, W. (1934). *Aristotle: Fundamentals of the History of his Development* (Oxford: Oxford University Press).

Kenny, A. (1978). *The Aristotelian Ethics* (Oxford: Clarendon Press).

Lennox, J. (1996). "Aristotle's Biological Development: The Balme Hypothesis," in W. Wians (ed.), *Aristotle's Philosophical Development* (London: Rowman and Littlefield), pp. 229–48.

Lloyd, G. E. L. (1968). *Aristotle: The Growth and Structure of His Thought* (Cambridge: Cambridge University Press).

Merlan, P. (1968). "On the Terms 'Metaphysics' and Being-*qua*-Being," *Monist*, 52 (2), pp. 174–94.

Menn, S. (1995). "The Editors of the *Metaphysics*," *Phronesis*, 40 (2), pp. 202–8.

Moraux, P. (1951). *Les listes anciennes des ouvrages d'Aristote* (Louvain: Éditions uiniversitares de Louvain).

Moraux, P. (1973). *Der Aristotelismus bei den Griechen von Andronikos bis Alexander von Aphrodisias*, Band I (Berlin/New York: De Gruyter).

Owen, G. E. L. (1986a). "Aristotle: Method, Physics and Cosmology," in Owen, *Logic, Science and Dialectic* (Ithaca, NY: Cornell University Press), pp. 152–64.

Owen, G. E. L. (1986b). "The Platonism of Aristotle," in Owen, *Logic, Science and Dialectic* (Ithaca, NY: Cornell University Press), pp. 200–20.

Ross, W. D. (1924). *Aristotle's "Metaphysics"* (Oxford: Oxford University Press).

Ross, W. D. (1960). "The Development of Aristotle's Thought," in I. Düring and G. E. L. Owen (eds.), *Aristotle and Plato in the Mid-fourth Century* (Göteborg: Institute of Classical Studies of the University of Göteborg), pp. 1–17.

Ross, W. D. [1923] (1995). *Aristotle* (London: Routledge).

Smith, R. (1982). "The Relationship between Aristotle's Two *Analytics*," *Classical Quarterly*, 32, pp. 327–35.

Tarán, L. (2001). "Aristotelianism in the First Century B.C.," in Tarán, *Collected Papers (1962–1999)* (Leiden: Brill), pp. 479–524.

Wians, W. (ed.) (1996). *Aristotle's Philosophical Development* (London: Rowman and Littlefield).

Part II

The Tools of Inquiry

3

Deductive Logic

DAVID KEYT

Introduction

The first sentence of the *Prior Analytics*, Aristotle's great work on deductive logic, declares that the work is about demonstration and demonstrative knowledge, and lists the syllogism only as a subordinate topic (I.1 24a10–15; all references in this chapter, unless otherwise indicated, are to this treatise). Since demonstration and demonstrative knowledge are the subject of the *Posterior Analytics*, Aristotle, in his very first sentence, unites the treatises that came later to be distinguished as "prior" and "posterior." In his other works he refers to the two simply as *The Analytics* (*Top* VIII.11 162a11; *Met* Z.12 1037b8; *NE* VI.3 1139b27, and elsewhere); and when, in the "posterior" treatise, he wishes to refer to the "prior" one, he speaks of "the discussions concerning the syllogism" (*An. Post* I.3 73a14, 11 77a35).

To understand the relation of the *Prior* to the *Posterior Analytics*, it is helpful to distinguish a deductive theory from the logic that undergirds it. In modern logic a deductive theory is a set of sentences in a given language closed under deducibility in a given logical system (Mates 1972: 183–204). Formal number theory consists, for example, of all the sentences in the language of arithmetic that can be deduced from Peano's postulates in first-order logic. The only science in Aristotle's day that approached an axiomatized theory was plane geometry, but Aristotle grasped the importance of the axiomatic method and attempted in the *Prior* and *Posterior Analytics* to give an account of it. In the *Prior Analytics* he lays out the underlying logic, the instrument for producing theorems in a deductive theory; in the *Posterior Analytics* he attempts to characterize the axioms, or first principles, from which the theorems in such a theory are derived.

One puzzle about the *Analytics* and Aristotle's other works on logic is where they fit in his classification of the sciences. Logic does not seem to be either a theoretical, a practical, or a productive science (for the division see *Top* VI.6 145a15–16; *Met* E.1 1025b25, K.7 1064a16–19; *NE* VI.2 1139a26–8). If logic were any of the three, it would have to be a theoretical science; but the only species of theoretical science that Aristotle recognizes are first philosophy (ontology and theology), natural philosophy (physics, biology, astronomy, and psychology), and mathematics (*Met* E.1 1026a18–19, K.7 1064b1–3; together with *Phys* II.1 192b8–12; *Cael* III.1 298a27–32; *An* I.1 403a27–b2); and logic belongs to none of these. Faced with this problem, the great Aristotelian scholar Alexander of Aphrodisias claimed that logic was an instrument, or *organon*, of science – of theoretical science in particular – rather than a science in its own right (*in An. Pr* I.9, II.3). Though Aristotle never refers to logic as an *organon* himself, he does think of it as prior to, rather than a part of, the special sciences – something one studies before one comes to a special science (*Met* Γ.3 1005b2–5, 4 1006a5–11; *NE* I.3 1094b19–27). It is a mark of the uneducated, he says, to introduce questions of logic into an investigation in one of the special sciences. Alexander's notion that logic is not a science, but an instrument in the service of science, is consonant with this idea.

To attempt to understand Aristotle's syllogistic strictly in its own terms, without making use of the resources of either modern or traditional logic, would be pointless. By modern logic I mean the mathematical logic of the twentieth century that sprang from the great works of Gottlob Frege; by traditional logic I mean the logic, called "Aristotelian" in contemporary logic texts, that developed from the *Prior Analytics* through the accretion of many small refinements over the course of the more than two millennia that separate Aristotle and Frege. Helpful as traditional logic is at many points, the deepest insights into Aristotle's project in the *Prior Analytics* come from modern logic.

A large part of the *Prior Analytics* is devoted to modal logic, the logic of necessity and possibility. In recent years this part of the treatise has generated more discussion than Aristotle's better understood account of assertoric logic, the logic of mere fact. Due to space limitations we shall not, however, have the opportunity to enter the interesting controversies swirling around this topic (for which, see van Rijen 1989; Patterson 1995).

Statements

The language of Aristotle's syllogistic is a natural language, ancient Greek, not, as in modern logic, a simple artificial language. But not every natural language sentence comes within the purview of his logic; prayers, for example, do not. Aristotle's logic is restricted to assertions, or statements, that is to say, to sentences that are true or false (*Int* 4 17a2–7). Nor does it apply even to every statement. It deals only with subject-predicate, or categorical statements, not with disjunctive or conditional statements. The predicate of a categorical statement in Aristotle's view refers to a universal, whereas its subject may refer to either a particular or a universal. The things explicitly counted as universals in the *Prior Analytics* cover a wide range: man, horse, swan, raven, animal, substance, wild, black, white, good, snow, stone, cloak, unit, line, number, wisdom, knowledge, ignorance, inanimate.

In the *De Interpretatione* singular statements such as *Callias is wise*, in which the subject refers to a particular, are considered along with those in which both predicate and subject refer to universals (*Int* 7 17b1–3, 26–9). But singular statements go unmentioned when Aristotle surveys the various types of categorical statement at the beginning of the *Prior Analytics* (I.1 24a16–22), and examples of such statements in the treatise are rare (I.33 47b21–37; II.27 70a16–18, 26–8). Why singular statements are ignored for the most part in the *Prior Analytics* is a matter of conjecture. Perhaps they are ignored because, as Aristotle says, "discussions and inquiries are mostly about species" (I.27 43a42–3; Ross: 289), or perhaps he wishes to deal only with terms that can occupy both subject and predicate position (Łukasiewicz 1957: 5–7). We shall return to singular statements at the end of the chapter, but focus on nonsingular until then.

The natural way of connecting the subject and predicate of a categorical statement is by the copula – *S is P* – and this is the mode of expression favored in the *De Interpretatione* (*Int* 7). In the *Prior Analytics* Aristotle eschews the natural mode in favor of three artificial idioms: (i) *P belongs (huparchei) to S*, (ii) *P is predicated (katêgoreitai) of S*, and (iii) *P is said (legetai) of S*. (The natural mode of expression is not nonexistent in the *Prior Analytics*, though it is rare (I.2 25a6–12, II.27 70a26–7).) Aristotle never explains why he introduces this technical idiom. His reason may have been that it facilitates the use of letters for concrete terms by avoiding the syntactical ambiguity that can result in Greek when such letters are used with the copula (Kneale and Kneale 1962: 62–3), or he may have thought that it reveals the logical structure of categorical sentences more clearly than the natural idiom (Patzig 1968: 9–12, developing an idea in Alexander, *in An. Pr* 54.21–9).

Categorical statements are distinguished by their quantity, quality, and modality. In modality such a statement is assertoric, necessary, or possible; in quality it is affirmative or negative; and in quantity it is universal (*all*), particular (*in part*), singular, or indeterminate (I.2 25a1–5). Excluding singular statements and setting indeterminate statements aside for the moment, one is left with four types of assertoric categorical statement: (i) universal affirmative (*P belongs to every S*), (ii) universal negative (*P belongs to no S*), (iii) particular affirmative (*P belongs to some S*), and (iv) particular negative (*P does not belong to some S*). Using the customary four vowels *a*, *e*, *i*, and *o* for the four combinations of quality and quantity, we can symbolize the four types of statement respectively as *PaS*, *PeS*, *PiS*, and *PoS*.

Statements of indeterminate quantity play little role in Aristotle's syllogistic. Some scholars, such as John Ackrill, lament the fact that they are mentioned at all (Ackrill 1963: 129). But Aristotle's treatment of them may be of interest, for it raises an important issue in the philosophy of logic. Aristotle's prime example of an indeterminate statement is *Pleasure is good*. Lacking a quantifier, it can mean either (i) that *all* pleasure is good or (ii) that *some* pleaure is good (*Top* III.6 120a6–20). How should logic deal with such a statement and with ambiguity in general? A modern logician would regard the disambiguation of an indeterminate statement as a preliminary step that should be taken before logic is applied, whereas Aristotle seems tempted to apply logic to ambiguous statements. A similar issue arises in post-Aristotelian logic over vague, or borderline, statements such as *Fifty grains of wheat make a heap*. A logician honed on mathematics and wedded to precise concepts and standard two-valued logic will want to sharpen a vague statement before applying logic to it, whereas a philosophical logician interested in natural languages might experiment with a logic – a many-valued logic perhaps – that can be applied to vague statements as they stand (see, for example, Beall and Van Fraassen 2003: 131–45). The debate between the mathematical and the philosophical logician concerns the degree to which logic should be Procrustean: Are the vague and ambiguous statements of natural languages to be made unambiguous and precise to fit logic or logic expanded to fit them? Aristotle's treatment of indeterminate statements suggests sympathy for a non-Procrustean logic. (As we saw in the

33

previous paragraph, this does not mean there is no regimentation of natural language in Aristotle's logic.)

The Square of Opposition

Aristotle discusses the relations of the four categorical statements in the *De Interpretatione*:

> I call an affirmation and a negation *contradictory* opposites when what one signifies universally the other signifies not universally, e.g. *every man is white* and *not every man is white*, *no man is white* and *some man is white*. But I call the universal affirmation and the universal negation *contrary* opposites, e.g. *every man is just* and *no man is just*. So these cannot be true together, but their opposites may both be true with respect to the same thing, e.g. *not every man is white* and *some man is white*. (*Int* 7 17b16–26, Ackrill's translation with typographical alterations)

By Aristotle's definition of "contradictory opposite" *a* and *o* statements have opposite truth values, and so do *e* and *i*; that is to say, an *a* is the contradictory of the corresponding *o*, and an *e* is the contradictory of the corresponding *i*. Aristotle also says that corresponding *a* and *e* statements are contrary opposites: they cannot be true together, though their contradictories can be. That is to say, corresponding *a* and *e* statements cannot both be true, though they can both be false. Given that corresponding *a* and *e* statements are contraries, it follows that an *a* statement entails the corresponding *i* and an *e* entails the corresponding *o*. For the truth of an *a* statement entails the falsity of the corresponding *e*, which in turn entails the truth of its contradictory, the corresponding *i*; and the truth of an *e* statement entails the falsity of the corresponding *a*, which in turn entails the truth of its contradictory, the corresponding *o*. Moreover, if corresponding *a* and *e* statements are contraries, corresponding *i* and *o* statements must be subcontraries – that is to say, they cannot both be false, though they can both be true. For the falsity of an *i* statement entails the truth of the corresponding *e*, which in turn entails the truth of the corresponding *o*; and the falsity of an *o* statement entails the true of the corresponding *a*, which in turn entails the truth of the corresponding *i*. Thus, the three logical facts, that an *a* statement is the contradictory of the corresponding *o*, that an *e* statement is the contradictory of the corresponding *i*, and that corresponding *a* and *e* statements are contraries, yield the following Square of Opposition with contraries along the top, subcontraries along the bottom, entailments down, but not up, the verticals, and contradictories across the diagonals as shown in the figure.

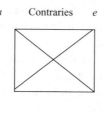

a Contraries e

i Subcontraries o

Only one of these relations, the relation across the diagonals, is preserved under the standard, or most natural, rendition of the four categorical statements in modern monadic logic. The symbolization usually found in modern logic textbooks is the following (where $\forall$ and $\exists$ are the universal and existential quantifiers respectively, $\neg$ the sign of negation, $\rightarrow$ the sign of material implication, and "Fx" and "Gx" symbolize "x is F" and "x is G"):

$$a \quad \forall x \, (Fx \rightarrow Gx)$$
(For all x, if x is F, then x is G)
$$i \quad \exists x \, (Fx \,\&\, Gx)$$
(There is an x such that x is F and x is G)
$$e \quad \forall x \, (Fx \rightarrow \neg Gx)$$
(For all x, if x is F, then x is not G)
$$o \quad \exists x \, (Fx \,\&\, \neg Gx)$$
(There is an x such that x is F and x is not G)

Under this symbolization an *a* statement is the contradictory of the corresponding *o*, and an *e* of the corresponding *i*. But none of the other relations holds. In particular, if there are no *F*s, corresponding *a* and *e* statements are both true. That is because on the standard symbolization *a* and *e* statements do not have "existential import." Suppose we try to make a repair by adding $\exists x Fx$ (*There is an x such that x is F*) as a conjunct to the above rendition of *a* and *e* statements. In this case, corresponding *a* and *e* statements become contraries; an *a* statement superentails (i.e., entails, but is not in turn entailed by) a corresponding *i*; and an *e* superentails a corresponding *o*. But now none of the other relations of the Aristotelian Square holds: corresponding *a* and *o* statements are contraries, not contradictories; and the same is true of corresponding *e* and *i* statements. Furthermore, corresponding *i* and *o* statements are now logically independent. The reason these symbolizations fail is that the Aristotelian Square *presupposes* (but does not *assert*) that the universal denoted by the subject of an *a* or an *e* statement is instantiated. (The Aristotelian Square leaves it open whether this must also be true of the predicate.) The difference between a presupposition of a logic and an assertion within it is that the assertion can be denied within the logic but the presupposition cannot. That *a* and *e* statements have existential import within Aristotle's logic is sometimes thought to be a defect, or at least a limitation, of his logic. But there is a Modern Square (see figure) that demonstrates a similar presupposition of modern logic (where the formulas at the four corners can be read as *Everything is G, Nothing is G, Something is G,* and *Something is not G*).

$$\forall x Gx \qquad \forall x \neg Gx$$

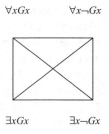

$$\exists x Gx \qquad \exists x \neg Gx$$

In this Modern Square, as in the Aristotelian Square, the sentences across the diagonals are contradictories; the sentences along the top of the square are contraries; those along the bottom are subcontraries; and the upper sentences superentail the sentences directly below them. These relations all hold because the Modern Square presupposes the existence of at least one individual. Standard modern logic does not apply to null universes. When this assumption of modern logic is dropped, as in free logic, the relations in the Modern Square crumble just as they do in the Aristotelian Square when a, e, i, and o statements are standardly symbolized. Moreover, when a repair is attempted by conjoining an assertion of existence with $\forall x\ Gx$ and $\forall x\ \neg Gx$, the repair fails to restore the relations in the Modern Square for the same reason that the analogous repair of the standard symbolization of a and e statements fails.

Figure and Mood

Aristotle defines a *syllogism* as "an argument (*logos*) in which, (i) certain things having been supposed, (ii) something different from the things supposed (iii) results of necessity (iv) because these things are so" (I.1 24b18–20; all quotations from the *Prior Analytics* are modified versions of Robin Smith's careful rendering). Each of the numbered phrases requires comment. The first refers to the premises of a syllogism. Being in the plural ("certain things"), it indicates that a syllogism has more than one premise. Immediate inferences such as "No man is a swan; therefore, no swan is a man" are not syllogisms. The second phrase refers to the conclusion of a syllogism, and rules out inferences that, in some contexts at least, would be regarded as fallacious, such as arguing "that a given thing is so if [i.e. on the ground that] it is so" (II.16 65a7–9; see also *An. Post* I.3 73a4–6). To argue in this way – to include among the premises of an argument the very point at issue – is to "beg the question" or commit the fallacy of *petitio principii*. This is not a *logical* fallacy, of course, since the conclusion of such an argument certainly follows from the premises. The third phrase of Aristotle's definition says that the conclusion of a syllogism follows "of necessity" from its premises: only *valid* arguments are syllogisms. Aristotle explains that by the fourth phrase he means "needing no further term [i.e. premise] from outside in order for the necessity to come about" (I.1 24b20–2). The point here is that the conclusion of a syllogism must follow from explicit, rather than tacit or suppressed, premises (see I.32 47a22–8). (For Aristotle's definition of "syllogism" see especially Frede 1987: 110–16.)

The Greek work *syllogismos* is often rendered "deduction" rather than "syllogism." But this seems wrong. "Deduction" is a syntactic, or proof theoretic, concept, whereas the reference to necessity in Aristotle's definition would seem to indicate that he is defining a semantic, or model theoretic, concept.

The extension of "syllogism," as Aristotle defines the term, is almost as broad as the extension of "valid argument." But one sort of syllogism, that consisting of three categorical statements sharing three terms, each term occurring in two different statements, is the prime focus of Aristotle's logic. Aristotle begins by thoroughly investigating this sort of syllogism (I. 4–7), and regards it as basic and fundamental throughout his logic (I.25 41b36–7, 42a30–2; *An. Post* I.19 81b10). It will be convenient to reserve the adjective "syllogistic" for that which pertains to *arguments* consisting of three such categorical statements and to refer to a *valid* syllogistic argument as a "basic syllogism." (To reiterate, only valid arguments are syllogisms.)

In order to conduct his investigation of syllogistic arguments, Aristotle needs a way of cataloging their forms. He does this with "figure" and "mood." The *figure* is the arrangement of the three terms in a syllogistic argument; the *mood* is the quality and quantity of each of its three categorical statements.

Each of the three terms of a syllogistic argument must have its own name if their different arrangements are to be described. Aristotle calls the term shared by the premises of a syllogistic argument the "middle" term (*An. Pr* I.32 47a39–40) and calls the two others the "extremes" (*An. Pr* I.4 25b36–7, 6 28a13). The extremes are then distinguished as "major" and "minor." Aristotle defines "major" and "minor" for each figure separately (I.4 26a21–3, 5 26b37–8, 6 28a13–14) though a single definition will suffice if the *order* of the two premises is taken into account. Since Aristotle does pay attention to order in I.4–6, he could have defined the major term (as we shall do here) as the extreme occurring in the first (or major) premise, and the minor term as the extreme occurring in the second (or minor) premise. These definitions can be used to define the figure of a syllogistic argument once we specify which extreme is the subject of the conclusion and which the predicate. Aristotle's practice in I.4–6 is to take the major term as predicate and the minor as subject.

If A, B, and C are the major, minor, and middle terms respectively of a syllogistic argument, the argument is said to be in the *first figure* if A is predicated of C and C of B; in the *second figure* if C is predicated of both A and B; and in the *third figure* if both A and B are predicated of C (I.23 41a13–16 together with I.5 26b34–9 and I.6 28a10–15).

In traditional logic the ordered triplet of vowels (for example, *eae*) indicating the quality and quantity of the premises and conclusion of a syllogistic argument is called the *mood* of the argument. Aristotle uses the concept of mood in the *Prior Analytics* without ever giving it a name; that is to say, within each figure he distinguishes the form of one syllogistic argument from that of another by specifying the quality and quantity of the statements composing the arguments.

There are 192 forms of syllogistic argument that come within Aristotle's purview in I.4–6: 64 moods ($4 \times 4 \times 4$) in each of the three figures. Aristotle cleverly reduces the number of cases that he needs to examine by focusing just on premise-sets. Let us call an ordered pair of categorical statements that share exactly one term a *linked pair*. A linked pair has a figure and mood just like a syllogistic argument. Its figure is the figure of the syllogistic argument of which it is a premise-set, and its mood is the ordered pair of letters indicating the quality and quantity of its two elements. There are only 48 forms of linked pair: 16 combinations of a, e, i, and o statements (4×4) in each of the three figures. Borrowing the graphic terminology of Lear (1980: 54), let us say that the mood xy of a linked pair in a given figure is *fertile* if there is a z such that xyz is a valid syllogistic mood in the given figure; otherwise it is *sterile*. (The variables x, y, and z range over the constants a, e, i, and o.) Aristotle's task in I.4–6 is reduced to determining the fertility or sterility of each of the sixteen linked-pair moods in each of the three figures.

Aristotle's project in the *Prior Analytics* is difficult to describe without invoking the notion of logical form. Since Aristotle's own distinction between form and matter provides the conceptual resources for an account of logical form, it is surprising to discover that he never uses that conjugal pair anywhere in the *Prior Analytics*. The word for matter, *hulê*, does not occur in the treatise. The concept of matter is applied to the syllogism at only one place in the Aristotelian corpus. At *Physics* II.3 195a18–19 Aristotle says that "the hypotheses [are matter] of the conclusion." (By "hypotheses" he presumably means "premises.") This idea, however, has nothing to do with logical form. The concept in the *Prior Analytics* that comes closest to that of form is figure (*schêma*). But the figure of a syllogistic argument only partially characterizes the argument's form. It is a genus within which the specific form of the argument is differentiated by the mood. By this line of thought the matter of a syllogistic argument is the three concrete terms that fill the specific form to produce an actual argument. This, at any rate, is the path taken by Alexander in commenting on the *Prior Analytics* (see Alexander, *in An. Pr* 6.16–22, 52.19–25). Figure and mood, it should be noted, have the attractive feature of capturing the form of a syllogistic argument without the use of variables. (For more on this topic see Barnes 1990.)

Deduction

"I call a syllogism *perfect* (*teleion*)," Aristotle writes, "if it stands in need of nothing else besides the things taken in order for the necessity to be evident (*phanênai*); I call it *imperfect* (*atelê*) if it still needs either one or several additional things which are necessary because of the terms assumed, but yet were not taken by means of premises" (I.1 24b22–6). A perfect syllogism differs from an imperfect one, not in being valid – all syllogisms are valid arguments – but in being transparently valid. Imperfect syllogisms need to be "unveiled" for their validity to become evident (Alexander, *in An. Pr* 24.10). Aristotle refers to them as "potential syllogisms" (I.5 27a2, 6 28a16, 24 41b33), meaning apparently that their validity is potentially but not actually evident. An imperfect syllogism is *perfected* (*teleiountai*) by "leading it back" or "reducing it" to a perfect syllogism (I.7 29b1, 16 23.40b17–19, 32 46b40, 45 51b1–2), though it does not thereby become itself a perfect syllogism.

Aristotle distinguishes the process of perfecting from the syllogism to which it is applied. An imperfect syllogism consists simply of a premise-set and a conclusion. Such a syllogism is perfected, its validity made evident, by deducing its conclusion from its premises by means of a series of transparently valid steps: it is perfected when its premises and conclusion become the first and last steps respectively of a deduction. Perfect syllogisms stand to imperfect syllogisms as axioms stand to theorems in a deductive theory; and the proof of a theorem in such a theory is the analogue of the leading back, or reduction, of an imperfect syllogism to a perfect one (Corcoran 1974: 91–2).

The only perfect syllogisms in Aristotle's syllogistic are the four syllogisms in the first figure: Barbara, Celarent, Darii, and Ferio, to give them their medieval names. (The three vowels in each name encode the mood of the syllogism.) The syllogisms are perfect, Aristotle claims, because "they are all brought to perfection through the premises initially taken" (I.4 26b29–30). The deduction in each case consists, in other words, simply of the syllogism itself.

An imperfect syllogism is led back, or reduced to, one of the four perfect syllogisms in either of two ways: conversion or indirect proof. The rules of conversion allow the terms of an *e* or an *i* statement to be interchanged (conversion in full) and allow an *i* statement with terms interchanged to be inferred from a corresponding *a* (conversion in part) (I.2 25a5–13). The rule of indirect proof operates in conjunction with the relations of contradiction and contrariety across the diagonals and along the top of the Square of Opposition.

Once the conversion rules are in place it can be seen that Aristotle's syllogistic presupposes the nonemptiness of the predicate, as well as the subject, of every categorical statement. A presupposition of a statement, to reiterate, is a condition that holds whether the statement be true or false. Given that an *e* statement converts in full and that its subject cannot be empty, its predicate cannot be empty either if the statement is true; and if it is false, the corresponding *i* statement must be true and again the predicate cannot be empty. Since an *a* statement converts in part, its predicate cannot be empty if it is true. Suppose, on the other hand, that it is false and its predicate empty. If its predicate is empty, the corresponding *i* statement must of course be false and the corresponding *e* statement, by the Square of Opposition, true. But the predicate of a true *e* statement, as we have just seen, cannot be empty. The supposition, therefore, that the predicate of the given *a* statement is empty entails that the predicate is not empty. So it is not empty. Thus, the predicate of an *a* statement cannot be empty if the *a* statement is false. Therefore, both *a* and *e* statements presuppose the nonemptiness of both their subjects and their predicates. Since *a* and *e* statements are the contradictories of *o* and *i* statements respectively, *o* and *i* statements must have the same presuppositions.

Aristotle's reduction of Ferison in the third figure to Ferio is an example of a direct proof: "If the negative term [i.e. premise] is universal, then when the major is negative and the minor positive there will be a syllogism. For if *P* belongs to no *S* and *R* belongs to some *S*, then *P* will not belong to some *R* (for it will again be the first figure when premise *RS* has been converted)" (I.6 28b31–5). This deduction can be displayed as follows:

(1) *PeS* Premise.
(2) *RiS* Premise.

To show: PoR.

(3) *SiR* Conversion of (2).
(4) *PoR* From (1) and (3) by Ferio.

One point to notice is that the thesis Aristotle seeks to establish is not a syllogism itself but an assertion *about* a type of syllogism: "If the negative term is universal, then when the major is negative and the minor positive *there will be a syllogism*." In modern logic this would be termed a "metatheorem." Another point is that the letter-formulas, for which Aristotle is famous, enter into the proof but not the statement of the thesis. The letters seem to be, not variables, but uninterpreted, or dummy, constants like the *F* in $\forall x F x$ of first-order logic or the schematic letters *a*, *b*, and *c* (as distinct from the variable *x*) in the algebraic equation $ax^2 + bx + c = 0$. Using letters Aristotle establishes the validity of one instance of Ferison and then generalizes to his metatheorem (Frede 1987: 113).

Aristotle's reduction of Darapti in the third figure to Celarent is an example of indirect proof: "if both *A* and *B* belong to every *C*, then *A* will belong to some *B*: for if it belongs to none and *B* to every *C*, then *A* will belong to no *C*: but it belonged to every *C*" (I.7 29a37–9). This deduction can be displayed as follows:

(1) *AaC* Premise.
(2) *BaC* Premise.

To show: *AiB*.

(3) *AeB* Provisional assumption of the contradictory of *AiB*.
(4) *AeC* The contrary of (1) from (3) and (2) by Celarent.

This example of indirect proof brings to the fore two notable features of Aristotle's syllogistic. The first is that it contains no sign of negation. That is why it needs the Square of Opposition. The second is that Aristotle's rule of indirect proof is weaker than the rule of *reductio ad absurdum* usually found in modern systems of natural deduction. The modern rule allows multiple nested uses within a single deduction, whereas Aristotle's rule of indirect proof, to judge from his use of it, allows only one (Corcoran 1972: 699).

In a fashion typical of the *Prior Analytics* the thesis Aristotle announces in the passage above is expressed as a conditional. One might infer from this that an Aristotelian syllogism is a conditional statement rather than (as we have been assuming) an argument and that Aristotle is concerned with the truth or falsity of certain forms of statement rather than with the validity or invalidity of certain forms of argument (Łukasiewicz 1957: 20–3). That this would be a mistake is indicated by Aristotle's use of Celarent in the argument we have just laid out. He must deduce either *AoC* or *AeC* to reach an inconsistency ("but [*A*] belonged to every *C*"). If the perfect syllogism to which appeal is made were the conditional *If AeB and BaC, then AeC*, he would not be able to separate the consequent from the antecedent without a rule of detachment. But he does not appeal to such rule in the passage above nor does he develop a logic in which such a rule would have a place. (For Aristotle's syllogistic as an axiomatized theory formulated in the pure predicate calculus see Mates 1972: 188–91.)

We are now in a position to define "deduction" and "deducibility" in a way that reflects Aristotle's practice and his account of "arguments through impossibility." A *deduction* of a categorical statement φ from a set of categorical statements Δ is either (i) a sequence of categorical statements terminating in φ, each element of which is either (a) a member of Δ, (b) the conversion of an earlier statement, or (c) the conclusion (from statements earlier in the sequence) of a perfect syllogism or (ii) a sequence of categorical statements terminating in the contrary or the contradictory of a member of Δ each element of which is either (a) a member of the union of Δ and the set whose sole member is the contradictory of φ, (b) the conversion of an earlier element, or (c) the conclusion (from statements earlier in the sequence) of a perfect syllogism (for (ii) see I.23 41a22–b1 and Smith 1989: 141–2). (i) is a direct proof; (ii) an indirect. φ is *deducible from* Δ if, and only if, there is a deduction of φ from Δ.

Counterexamples

In I.4–6 Aristotle identifies fourteen fertile forms of linked pairs. To be thorough he needs to show that the remaining thirty-four forms are sterile. To establish sterility he uses the method of counterexample. A counterexample is an argument of a given form with true premises and a false conclusion. Since such an argument must be invalid and since every instance of a valid form of argument is valid, a counterexample establishes the invalidity of the form of which it is an instance.

Four counterexamples are needed to establish the sterility of a single mood of a linked pair in a given figure, one for each targeted conclusion (where a targeted conclusion is a categorical statement whose predicate and subject are the major and minor terms respectively of the linked pair). Thus, to establish the sterility of the 34 moods in the 3 figures for which proofs of fertility are lacking requires 136 counterexamples. But Aristotle always gets at least 4 counterexamples from just 2 triplets of concrete terms. Here is how he disposes of the mood *ae* in the third figure: "if *R* belongs to no *S* and *P* to every *S*, then there will not be a syllogism (terms for belonging are *animal, horse, man*; for not belonging, *animal, inanimate, man*)" (I.6 28a30–3). *P, R,* and *S* stand for the major, minor, and middle term respectively; and major-minor-middle is the order in which the concrete terms are listed. Taking *animal, horse,* and *man* to be the major, minor, and middle terms of a linked pair of the mood *ae* in the third figure, we can form the three statements: (i) *Animal belongs to every man*, (ii) *Horse belongs to no man*, and (iii) *Animal belongs to every horse.* All three statements are true, so we do not yet have a counterexample. But (iii) is an *a* statement, and by the Square of Opposition an *a* statement can be true only if the corresponding *e* and *o* statements – (iv) *Animal belongs to no horse* and (v) *Animal does not belong to some horse* – are false. The triplet of concrete terms thus generates two syllogistic arguments that combine true premises with a false conclusion and are, consequently, invalid: "(i); (ii); therefore, (iv)" and "(i); (ii); therefore, (v)." The first is in the mood *aee* in the third figure, the second in the mood *aeo.* Since every instance of a valid form of argument is valid, these moods are invalid. The triplet *animal-inanimate-man* provides counterexamples for *aea* and *aei* in the third figure, completing the proof of the sterility of the linked pair mood *ae* in the third figure. This is not the limit of Aristotle's cleverness with counterexamples; through the adroit selection of triplets of concrete terms he is often able to establish the sterility of more than one mood of a form of linked pair with a single pair of triplets.

Independence

One important question about any system of inference rules is whether the rules are independent of each other. Are some of the rules redundant in that their work can be done by others? Aristotle is alive to this issue, and addresses the question of the independence of his four perfect syllogisms in I.7 and of his conversion rules at I.2 25a14–26.

Aristotle offers an elaborate argument to show that the only perfect syllogisms needed in his system are the universal ones (Barbara and Celarent): (a) all imperfect

41

syllogisms, that is to say, all syllogisms not in the first-figure, are reducible to first-figure syllogisms (I.7 29a30–1); (b) the particular syllogisms of the first figure are reducible to second-figure syllogisms (I.7 29b17–18); (c) all second-figure syllogisms are reducible to the universal syllogisms in the first figure (I.7 29b15–17); (d) reducibility is transitive; (e) the universal syllogisms in the first figure are trivially reducible to themselves; therefore, (f) every syllogism is reducible to a universal syllogism of the first figure (I.7 29b1–2). This is an impressive metaproof of an important metatheorem.

Aristotle implies that the only premise of this argument that has not already been established is the one he proceeds to argue for – premise (b). But this is not quite true. Aristotle did not establish in I.4–6 that every imperfect syllogism is reducible to a first-figure syllogism. As we shall see, there are several imperfect syllogisms that escape his net. Furthermore, Aristotle did not reduce all second-figure syllogisms to the universal syllogisms in the first figure. As the initial letter of its Latin name indicates, he reduced the second-figure syllogism Festino, not to Barbara or Celarent, but to Ferio (I.5 27a32–6). Festino can be reduced to Celarent through an indirect proof, but Aristotle does not give the reduction.

Aristotle reduces Darii to the second-figure syllogism Cesare (I.7 29b6–11), having previously reduced Cesare to Celarent (I.5 27a9–14, following Smith's deviation from Ross's text at 27a10). We can combine the two reductions into a single one as follows:

(1) *PaM* Premise
(2) *MiS* Premise

To show: PiS

(3) *PeS* Provisional assumption
(4) *SeP* Conversion of (3)
(5) *SeM* By Celarent from (4) and (1)
(6) *MeS* Conversion of (5), the contradictory of (2)

The corresponding reduction of Ferio to Celarent, which combines the reduction of Ferio to Camestres (*An. Pr* I.7 29b11–15) and the reduction of Camestres to Celarent (I.5 27a5–9), is even shorter:

(1) *PeM* Premise
(2) *MiS* Premise

To show: PoS

(3) *PaS* Provisional assumption
(4) *MeP* Conversion of (1)
(5) *MeS* By Celarent from (4) and (3), the contradictory of (2).

Aristotle also shows how to reduce the rules for converting *i* and *a* statements to the rule for converting an *e* (I.2 25a14–26):

42

(1) *SiP* Premise

To show: PiS

(2) *PeS* Provisional assumption
(3) *SeP* e-conversion of (2), the contradictory of (1)

---

(1) *SaP* Premise

To show: PiS

(2) *PeS* Provisional assumption
(3) *SeP* e-conversion of (2), the contrary of (1)

Aristotle's syllogistic thus rests upon six basic, or primitive, rules:

(1) Barbara
(2) Celarent
(3) *e*-conversion
(4) Contrariety of corresponding *a* and *e* statements
(5) Contradictoriness of corresponding *a* and *o* statements
(6) Contradictoriness of corresponding *e* and *i* statements

It is easily proved that this set of rules is independent. No further reduction is possible.

Soundness

The whole point of deductive logic is the transmission of truth from premises to conclusion. Any system of deductive logic that allows a false conclusion to be deduced from true premises is unsound. The most important question about Aristotle's syllogistic, then, is whether its rules preserve truth. Is it possible to deduce a false conclusion from true premises by means of Aristotle's rules? Phrased another way, do Aristotle's methods of reduction and counterexample cohere or conflict?

One might answer this question by giving a semantic analysis of each of his rules. Such an analysis of Celarent might run as follows. Suppose that *P*, *M*, and *S* are the major, middle, and minor terms of a syllogistic argument in Celarent and that its conclusion, *PeS*, is false. We need to show that at least one of its premises must be false. Well, if *PeS* is false, there must be some particular, call it "*j*," that is both *S* and *P*. *j* is either *M* or not. If *j* is *M*, then *j* is both *M* and *P* and the major premise, *PeM*, must be false; if *j* is not *M*, then *j* is *S* but not *M* and the minor premise, *MaS*, must be false. Thus, at least one premise of the argument is false.

Aristotle offers an argument similar to this for the soundness of e-conversion: "Now, if *A* belongs to none of the *B*s, then neither will *B* belong to any of the *A*s. For if it [i.e. *B*] does belong to some (for instance to *C*), it will not be true that *A* belongs to none of the *Bs*, since *C* is one of the *Bs*" (I.2 25a15–17). Alexander suggests that we take "*C*" to refer to a particular, say, Theo (*in An. Pr* 33.2–12), an idea also suggested by Aristotle's reference to *C* as "one (*ti*) of the *Bs*." The argument would then be this. Suppose that *BeA* is false. Then there must be a particular, call it "Theo," that is both *B* and *A*. But in that case (since conjunction is commutative) *AeB* must be false. Thus, it is not possible for the premise to be true and the conclusion false.

Aristotle does not try to establish the soundness of his other rules by such an argument. It is easy to see why. Unless arguments *about* a logistic system are sharply distinguished from arguments *within* such a system it will seem that we are involved in either a circle or an infinite regress (see *An. Post* I.3). The argument in the last paragraph assumes the commutativity of conjunction, and the argument of the paragraph before last has the form of a constructive dilemma. Where did these logical principles come from? Are they sound? If we seek to answer these questions by arguments within the logistic system we are developing, we will have taken the first step in a circle or a regress.

What, then, is the basis of Aristotle's confidence that his rules of inference, the perfect syllogisms Barbara and Celarent in particular, are sound? All he says on this score is that a perfect syllogism stands in need of nothing extraneous "for its necessity to be evident" (*pros to phanênai to anagkaion*) (*An. Pr* I.1 24b22–4), which seems to mean that the validity of a perfect syllogism is transparent.

This transparency must be due to some distinctive feature of first-figure syllogisms. The most striking difference between syllogisms in the first figure and those in the other figures is the position of the middle term. When the premise-pair of a first-figure syllogism is written as Aristotle writes it – *PxM, MxS* – the middle term is exactly where its name indicates it should be, in the middle. Furthermore, the major and minor terms are in the same positions, far left and far right, that they occupy in the conclusion. The conjecture, then, is that Aristotle thought the validity of first-figure syllogisms more transparent than the validity of syllogisms in the other figures because he thought that the similarity of syntax between premise-pairs and conclusion found only in the first translated into a shorter and psychically easier step from premises to conclusion. The reader can judge the plausibility of this conjecture for himself by comparing the transparency of the validity of Celarent ("If A is predicated of no B and B of every C, it is necessary that A will belong to no C" (*An. Pr* I.4 25b40–26a2)) and Camestres in the second figure ("If M belongs to every N but to no X, then neither will N belong to any X" (*An. Pr* I.5 27a9–10)). (On this topic see especially Patzig 1968: 43–87.)

Completeness: Syllogistic Arguments

Completeness is the complement of soundness. A system of inference rules is sound if it stays within its proper bounds, if it does not allow the deduction of a false conclusion from true premises. A system of inference rules is complete if it can reach its proper bounds, if the deductive power of its rules is such that the valid conclusion of any argument the system is designed to analyze is deducible from the premises of the argument. The combination of the method of reduction and the method of counterexamples in I.4–6 shows that Aristotle was alive to the issue of completeness, though these three chapters do not by any means exhaust Aristotle's interest in the subject.

To determine whether a logical system is complete, one must first determine the sort of arguments the system is designed to analyze. Aristotle proceeds in stages, gradually expanding the types of argument he wishes to bring within the scope of his system. In the first stage he considers only syllogistic arguments, arguments composed of three categorical statements sharing three terms, each term occurring in two different statements. Aristotle's syllogistic is complete within this narrow range if every valid syllogistic argument – every basic syllogism – is reducible to Barbara or Celarent. Since there are only finitely many forms of syllogistic argument, one way to establish that every basic syllogism is so reducible is to examine each form of syllogistic argument in turn and provide either a counterexample or a reduction. As we have seen, Aristotle does something different; in each of his three figures he focuses on the forms of premise-pairs rather than of entire arguments. The question is whether this will do the trick. There are two problems with Aristotle's proof.

The first problem is that the fertile forms of premise-pairs are not thoroughly investigated. Aristotle points out that every conclusion deducible from a fertile pair except for an o statement leads to a further deducible conclusion (II.1 53a3–14). If an a statement is deducible, so is a corresponding i (and its converse); and if an e is deducible, so is its converse as well as a corresponding o (and its converse). (SxP is the converse of PxS.) Moreover, if an a (or an e) statement is deducible from a linked pair of the mood xy, the soundness of the rules and the Square of Opposition guarantee the existence of counterexamples showing that the moods xye and xyo (xya and xyi) in the figure of the linked pair are invalid. On the other hand, if an i (or an o) statement is deducible from a linked pair of the mood xy, nothing follows about the deducibility of a corresponding a or o (e or i) statement or the invalidity of the moods xya and xyo (xye and xyi) in the figure of the linked pair. Thus, in the cases where Aristotle establishes the fertility of a linked-pair mood xy in a given figure by showing how to deduce an i (or an o) statement from a linked pair in that mood and figure – which he does only if an a (or an e) is *not* deducible – he needs to provide counterexamples to show that xya and xyo (xye and xyi) are invalid moods in the figure of the linked pair; otherwise there may be syllogistic arguments that are neither invalid nor reducible to Barbara or Celarent. This gap in the completeness proof has a bearing on Aristotle's claim that at least one of the premises of a basic syllogism must be of the same quality as its conclusion (I.24 41b27–31). Since he offers no reason for this assertion, it is evidently supposed to rest on a survey of all cases. But it has not been shown to hold in all cases. Aristotle has not shown, for example, that *aio* in the third figure is invalid.

The second problem is that Aristotle's initial understanding of what we have called "fertility" and "sterility" is too narrow. After determining the fertility or sterility of every linked-pair mood in each of his three figures in I.4–6 Aristotle notes in the very next chapter that some sterile linked-pair moods are in fact fertile (I.7 28a19–29)! The moods he identifies are *ae* and *ie* in the first figure, whose sterility was presumably established by counterexamples at I.4 26a2–9, 36–9. Aristotle now shows how to deduce an o statement from a linked pair in both of these moods (I.7 29a23–6). If his syllogistic is sound, how can the same linked pair be both fertile and sterile? The answer is that sterility is relative to a targeted set of conclusions, and the target has changed. In the chapters on the three figures (I.4–6) the targeted conclusion is a categorical statement whose predicate and subject are the major and minor terms respectively of the linked-pair. If the target is changed by switching predicate and subject, some linked pair moods that are sterile relative to the old target are fertile relative to the new, *ae* and *ie* in the first figure being two such moods. (Traditional logic deals with this problem by holding to the original target and introducing a fourth figure in which the middle term is predicate of the major premise and subject of the minor.)

Let us say that a linked-pair mood in a given figure is *fertile in the broad sense* if it is fertile relative to either target; otherwise it is *sterile in the broad sense*. A thorough investigation must consider both targets.

We need to ask whether Aristotle has uncovered all the linked-pair moods in the first figure that are fertile in the broad sense. Are *ae* and *ie* together with *aa*, *ea*, *ai*, and *ei* all there are? The answer is affirmative. There are just these six fertile moods in the first figure. Aristotle has not, however, established this fact. His proof of the sterility of the other ten moods is incomplete. To establish the sterility in the broad sense of a linked-pair mood in the first figure Aristotle needs to provide eight counterexamples, one for each PxS and SxP where x ranges over a, e, i, and o, and P and S are the major and minor terms respectively of the pair. He provides only four.

The second and third figures do not present a similar problem. In these, unlike the first, a mood xy is fertile in the broad sense if either xy or yx is fertile in the original, or narrow, sense. However, when a linked pair targets SxP, as well as PxS, six linked-pair moods in each of these two figures become redundant. That leaves thirty-six linked-pair moods in all three figures together. Excluding the redundant moods, there are three linked-pair moods in the second figure that are fertile in the broad sense (*ae*, *ao*, and *ei*) and five in the third (*aa*, *ae*, *ai*, *ao*, and *ei*), giving a total of fourteen in all three figures together. Subtracting the fertile moods from the total moods leaves twenty-two that are sterile in the broad sense.

Counterexamples are easily provided to fill the gaps in Aristotle's proof. His syllogistic is complete within the narrow range of syllogistic arguments: every basic syllogism is reducible to Barbara or Celarent.

Completeness: Categorical Arguments

In I.23, which is separated from I.7 by a lengthy excursion into modal logic, Aristotle extends the scope of his logical system. He writes: "That the syllogisms in these [three] figures are both perfected through the universal syllogisms in the first figure and led back into them is clear from what has been said. But that this holds for every syllogism without qualification will now be evident, when every one has been proved to come about through some one of these figures" (I.23 40b17–22). What does Aristotle mean by a "syllogism without qualification" (*sullogismos haplôs*)? This is a matter of controversy, but an argument can be made that a syllogism "in these [three] figures" is what we have been calling a "basic" syllogism and that a syllogism without qualification is a valid argument with *two or more* categorical premises and a categorical conclusion (Smiley 1994: 25). On this interpretation, syllogism without qualification is a genus of which basic syllogism is one species. That this more general sort of argument is under discussion in I.25 is beyond dispute; the issue is whether such arguments are introduced for the first time in I.25 or whether they are precisely the syllogisms without qualification mentioned at the beginning of I.23. I shall follow Timothy Smiley in supposing that they are the latter and that Aristotle in I.23 is extending the completeness proof he began in I.4–7 (Smiley 1994).

It will be convenient to call an argument consisting entirely of categorical statements a *categorical argument*. A *syllogism without qualification* will thus be a *valid* categorical argument. When Aristotle's logic is extended to include categorical arguments, the question of completeness becomes the question whether the conclusion of every valid categorical argument is deducible from its premises by means of Aristotle's inference rules.

Aristotle's proof of completeness, as Smiley interprets it, proceeds in two stages. To understand the first stage, we need the notion of a chain argument, an argument in which the various premises are linked together as in a chain by a series of middle terms. Let *XY* be either *XxY* or *YxX*. Then a *chain argument* is an argument of the form "*AC, CD, DE, EF,* . . . *GH, HB*; therefore, *AB.*" In the first stage (I.23 40b30–41a13) Aristotle attempts (unsuccessfully) to establish that every valid categorical argument is a chain argument. In the second stage (I.23 41a13–20) he attempts to prove that the conclusion of every valid chain argument is deducible from its premises through a series of basic syllogisms, called "prosyllogisms" in traditional logic. The completeness of the extended system would then follow.

Smiley provides a detailed reconstruction of the second stage of Aristotle's metaproof (Smiley 1994: 33–4), which I here reproduce with one correction. Suppose that "*AC, CD, DE,* . . . *GH, HB*; therefore, *AB*" is a valid chain argument. (*A, B, C,* . . . *G, H* are uninterpreted constants.) We want to show that *AB* is deducible from *AC, CD, DE,* . . . *GH, HB* through a series of prosyllogisms. We begin by showing that the argument must be invalid if *AC, CD* is a sterile pair. Suppose, then, that *AC, CD* is a sterile pair. Let *A* be *man*, and let *B* also be *man* if *AB* is negative; otherwise let *B* be *swan*. (Thus, if *AB* is *BaA*, *AB* is *Swan is predicated of every man.*) *AB* is false. Let each term in the sequence *B, H, G,* . . . *D* after the first be the same as the term preceding it in the sequence (*man* or *swan*) if the premise containing it and its predecessor is affirmative; otherwise let it be the other concrete term. Under this interpretation of the letters *B, H, G,* . . . *D, DE,* . . . *GH, HB* are all true. We need to find a term to assign to *C* by which *AC* and *CD* are also true. *AC, CD* is an instance of one among the 22 sterile forms of linked pair. Examining each of these forms in turn, we discover that if we have terms for a proper subset of *man* (say, *Greek*) and of *swan* (say *cob* (*male swan*)), for a set of which *man* and *swan* are proper subsets (say, *biped*), and for a set that excludes both *man* and *swan* (say, *stone*), then in each of the 22 cases we can always find a *C* such that *AC* and *CD* are both true. Thus, on the supposition that *AC, CD* is a sterile pair, the original argument, having true premises and a false conclusion, is invalid. So *AC, CD* must be a fertile pair.

Now, let *AD* be the strongest statement containing *A* and *D* deducible from *AC, CD* if there is a strongest. (One statement is *stronger* than another if the one superentails the other.) If there is a tie among the strongest, let *AD* be either. We need to show now that the original argument must be invalid if *AD, DE* is a sterile pair. Suppose, then, that *AD, DE* is sterile. Following the strategy outlined in the previous paragraph, we can make all of *AD, DE,* . . . *GH, HB* true and *AB* false. But we also need to make *AC* and *CD* true. *AC, CD* is an instance of one among the fourteen fertile forms. Examining

47

each of these cases in turn, we discover that terms can be found for *C* if in addition to the concrete terms used so far we have terms for *S* minus *P* whenever *AD* is *PoS* (if *S* is *swan* and *P* is *cob*, *C* will be *female swan*, or *pen*). Thus, on the supposition that *AD*, *DE* is a sterile pair, the original argument must be invalid. So *AD*, *DE* is fertile. As before let *AE* be a statement deducible from *AD*, *DE* of which no statement containing *A* and *E* is stronger.

Continuing in this way we can generate *AD*, *AE*, . . . *AG*, *AH*. *AH* is deducible from *AG*, *GH*; . . . *AE* from *AD*, *DE*; and *AD* from *AC*, *CD*. *AB* is also deducible from *AH* and *HB*. For if not, the fact established in the last section, that every valid syllogistic conclusion is deducible from its two premises, guarantees the existence of a term *H* by which *AH* and *HB* are true and *AB* false; and by the process outlined in the preceding paragraph we can find terms by which all of *AC*, *CD*, *DE*, . . . *GH*, *HB* are true and *AB* false, contradicting validity. It follows that *AB* is deducible from *AC*, *CD*, *DE*, . . . *GH*, *HB* through a series of prosyllogisms.

We have, then, that the conclusion of every valid chain argument is deducible from its premises by means of Aristotle's inference rules. If every valid categorical argument is a chain argument, the conclusion of every such argument is deducible from its premises by means of Aristotle's inference rules. Since Aristotle is unable to establish the antecedent of the preceding conditional, the question arises whether it can be dropped. Can it be proven that the conclusion of every valid categorical argument is deducible from its premises by means of Aristotle's inference rules without first proving that every such argument is a chain argument? The answer is that it can be. Using the sophisticated methods of modern metatheory John Corcoran has done it (Corcoran 1972). But, unlike Smiley's, Corcoran's proof is nonconstructive: it provides no recipe, no step-by-step procedure, for actually deducing the conclusion of a valid categorical argument from its premises.

Completeness: Arguments in General

At the beginning of I.32 Aristotle says that his next project is to consider "how we may lead syllogisms back into the aforementioned figures" (I.32 46b40–47a1), and at the end of I.45 announces the completion of this project (I.45 51b3–5). His project is generally taken to be that of showing how to recast, or formalize, valid arguments as valid categorical arguments (Ross 1949: 2, 400; Lear 1980: 11; Smith 1989: 161). Did Aristotle maintain that *every* valid argument can be recast as a categorical argument? The answer to this question is not crystal clear. But in I.32–45 Aristotle does discuss each of the three items that, from a modern perspective, stand in the way of such an ambitious claim: singular terms, polyadic predicates, and complex statements.

Statements containing singular terms are rare in the *Prior Analytics*, occurring only at I.33 and II.27. As we noted earlier, Aristotle may have good reason for excluding singular terms from his syllogistic proper. This makes his comment about the following argument all the more interesting: *The ambitious are generous; Pittakos is ambitious; therefore, Pittakos is generous* (II.27 70a26–7). Aristotle takes this argument to be a universal first-figure syllogism (II.27 70a29–30), that is to say, a syllogism in Barbara. This means that he, like traditional logic later, assimilates singular statements to *a* statements. Such an assimilation implicitly turns proper names (in certain contexts at least) into predicates – "Pittakos" into, say, "is identical with Pittakos." When "Pittakos" is so understood, the foregoing argument slips neatly into the proper form: *The ambitious are generous; all who are identical with Pittakos are ambitious; therefore, all who are identical with Pittakos are generous.* Statements containing singular terms can easily be brought within the scope of Aristotle's syllogistic.

Polyadic predicates such as "*x* loves *y*" and "*x* is between *y* and *z*" are a different story. But Aristotle seems prepared to broaden his understanding of categorical statements to bring at least some *dyadic* relations within the scope of his syllogistic. He seems to take the following argument (translated literally to preserve its form) to be an instance of Barbara: "If wisdom is knowledge, and of the good is wisdom, the conclusion is that of the good is knowledge; accordingly, the good is not knowledge; but wisdom is knowledge" (I.36 48b10–14). As Aristotle points out in the second half of his sentence, the conclusion expresses some relation other than the relation of predication between the good and knowledge. The preposition in the phrase "of the good" renders an objective genitive in the Greek (*tou agathou*). Following Ross one might interpret the argument as follows: *Wisdom is knowledge; the good is an object of wisdom; therefore, the good is an object of knowledge* (Ross 1949: 405). So interpreted, it seems to be a valid argument involving a dyadic relation. The question is whether it is a valid *syllogistic* argument. It is difficult to see how it can be. Aristotle takes the major, middle, and minor terms to be "knowledge," "wisdom," and "the good" respectively. The connecting verb in the major premise is "is," and the connecting phrase in the minor premise and conclusion is "is of" (or "is an object of"). But, as Aristotle points outs, "is" and "is of" denote different relations. The former denotes the inclusion of one set or kind or form in another, whereas the latter denotes the dyadic relation *being an object of.* And if the major term bears a different relation to the middle than the middle bears to the minor, it cannot be an argument in Barbara where the relation is the same in both premises. Aristotle's attempt to bring dyadic relations into his syllogistic must be judged a failure.

We come finally to complex statements, and Aristotle's discussion of arguments involving conditionals. At I.44 50a19–28 Aristotle discusses an extended argument involving both *modus ponens* and *modus tollens*. (For the following reconstruction see Ross 1949: 416; square brackets signify implicit premises.)

(1)　If there were a single potentiality for both health and sickness, the same thing would be at the same time well and ill.

(2)　[The same thing cannot be at the same time well and ill.]

(3)　Therefore, there is not a single potentiality for both health and sickness.

(4)　[Health and sickness are a pair of contraries.]

(5)　Therefore, there is not a single potentiality for every pair of contraries.

(6)　If there is not a single potentiality for every pair of contraries, then there is not a single science of them.

(7)　Therefore, there is not a single science for every pair of contraries.

This extended argument consists of three two-premise subarguments, the conclusions of the first and second being premises of the second and third respectively. Aristotle makes no comment on the first, says that the second is "presumably" a syllogism (presumably in Felapton in the third figure), and denies that the third is a syllogism (I.44 50a16–18, 27–8). Since Aristotle in this very chapter explicitly calls such arguments as the third "syllogisms" (I.44 50a16, 50b3), he must, when commenting on the above argument, be using the word as an ellipsis for "syllogism in the figures." But in that case he is denying that every valid argument can be recast as a valid categorical argument.

Aristotle bequeaths the logic of complex statements to the Stoics. (For the debate between the Stoics and the Peripatetics see Barnes 1983.)

Note

I am grateful to S. Marc Cohen and my son, Aaron Keyt, for helpful comments on an earlier draft.

Bibliography

Ackrill, J. L. (1963). *Aristotle's "Categories" and "De Interpretatione"* (Oxford: Clarendon Press).

Barnes, Jonathan (1983). "Terms and Sentences: Theophrastus on Hypothetical Syllogisms," *Proceedings of the British Academy*, 69, pp. 279–326.

Barnes, Jonathan (1990). "Logical Form and Logical Matter," in Antonina Alberti (ed.), *Logica, Mente e Persona* (Florence: Olschki).

Barnes, Jonathan, Bobzien, Susanne, Flannery, Kevin, and Ierodiakonou, Katerina (1991). *Alexander of Aphrodisias: On Aristotle "Prior Analytics" 1.1–7* (London: Duckworth).

Beall, J. C. and Van Fraassen, Bas C. (2003). *Possibilities and Paradox* (Oxford: Oxford University Press).

Corcoran, John (1972). "Completeness of an Ancient Logic," *Journal of Symbolic Logic*, 37, pp. 696–702.

Corcoran, John (1974). "Aristotle's Natural Deduction System," in John Corcoran (ed.), *Ancient Logic and its Interpretations* (Dordrecht: Reidel).

Frede, Michael (1987). "Stoic vs. Aristotelian Syllogistic," in M. Frede, *Essays in Ancient Philosophy* (Minneapolis, MN: University of Minnesota Press).

Kneale, William and Kneale, Martha (1962). *The Development of Logic* (Oxford: Clarendon Press).

Lear, Jonathan (1980). *Aristotle and Logical Theory* (Cambridge: Cambridge University Press).

Łukasiewicz, Jan (1957). *Aristotle's Syllogistic from the Standpoint of Modern Formal Logic*, 2nd edn. (Oxford: Clarendon Press).

Mates, Benson (1972). *Elementary Logic*, 2nd edn. (Oxford: Oxford University Press).

Patterson, Richard (1995). *Aristotle's Modal Logic* (Cambridge: Cambridge University Press).

Patzig, Günther (1968). *Aristotle's Theory of the Syllogism*, trans. from the German by Jonathan Barnes (Dordrecht: Reidel).

Ross, W. D. (1949). *Aristotle's "Prior" and "Posterior Analytics"* (Oxford: Clarendon Press). (Repr. New York: Garland 1980.)

Smiley, Timothy (1994). "Aristotle's Completeness Proof," *Ancient Philosophy*, 14, special issue, pp. 25–38.

Smith, Robin (1989). *Aristotle, "Prior Analytics"* (Indianapolis: Hackett).

van Rijen, Jeroen (1989). *Aspects of Aristotle's Logic of Modalities* (Dordrecht: Kluwer).

4

Aristotle's Theory of Demonstration

ROBIN SMITH

Posterior Analytics I is about a kind of knowledge. Aristotle calls it *epistêmê*, one of several Greek words for knowledge. He is fairly careful about using *epistêmê* in this sense and distinguishing this kind of knowledge from others (for which he uses other words fairly indifferently); it is best to translate it with a special term. I will follow the old-fashioned way of translating it as as "science," though the modern experimental connotations of that word should not be assumed. Aristotle defines science as knowledge of the causes why things must be as they are (*An. Post* I.2 71b9–12). Only that which cannot be otherwise than it is, therefore, can be an object of science. Anglophone philosophers brought up on a diet of epistemological debate about the definition of knowledge need to keep this point constantly in mind.

For Aristotle, science depends on *demonstrations* (*apodeixis*). In simplest terms, a demonstration is a "scientific syllogism," i.e. "a syllogism such that we have science in virtue of possessing it" (71b18–19). I shall have more to say shortly about what a syllogism is, but for the moment we can say it is an argument consisting of some premises and a conclusion which follows from them (in modern terms, a valid argument: but see below). What must an argument be like if it is to be scientific in this sense, and what is it to "possess" a demonstration? The main business of *Posterior Analytics* I is to answer these questions, especially the first. In addition, Aristotle addresses a further question: are demonstrations in fact possible? To understand why this last question is important, we need to examine the background of issues and problems against which Aristotle developed his own position. If we can recover the problems he is dealing with, we can better understand the point behind many aspects of his views. This is critically important with some of the more technical details of his views on demonstration. A modern interpreter often sees a similarity between a passage in Aristotle and a result of contemporary logical theory and on that basis interprets Aristotle as having approached that result. Sometimes this is useful, but sometimes it leads us to miss the even more interesting issue Aristotle is actually concerned with.

A case in point is the relationship of Aristotle's theory to contemporary epistemology. The defining issue for epistemology has long been the problem of skepticism, and responses to skepticism typically take the form of definitions of knowledge. If we suppose that Aristotle must be addressing these same questions, we will, I think, find his position disappointing and at times mystifying, but that is because he is addressing a different set of problems. Similarly, it has sometimes been supposed that demonstration is a method of inquiry, which then leads to a double problem: first, it would have to be strongly aprioristic, which does not sit well with Aristotle's own frequent insistence on the indispensability of making observations in science; second, it is surprising that Aristotle does not appear to follow anything like that method in his own scientific treatises. In what follows, I shall try to show that Aristotle's concerns arise out of the context of the early Academy, and in particular that they rest on criticisms of Plato's view of science (like Aristotle, he prefers the word *epistêmê* for the philosopher's knowledge). Demonstration, for Aristotle, is not a method for acquiring knowledge but, rather, something inseparable from science itself: if something has a demonstration, then to have science of it just is to possess that demonstration. Thus, Aristotle says in *NE* VI that science is a "demonstrative capacity" or "demonstrative condition" (*hexis apodeiktikê*, 3 1139b31–2).

In what follows, I shall rely heavily not just on the *Posterior Analytics* but also on its companion, the *Prior Analytics*, a work which declares in its first sentence that it too is about "demonstration and demonstrative science." In fact, Aristotle almost certainly means this to apply to the *Analytics* as a single treatise consisting of our *Prior* or *Posterior Analytics*. Many contemporary interpreters do not see these two works as so closely connected, so I should confess my own viewpoint up front. As discussed in chapter 3 of this volume, Aristotle's theory of the syllogism is his account of deductive logic. Its presentation in the *Prior Analytics* is technically sophisticated and masterful. By contrast, what we find of this same theory in the *Posterior Analytics* is often much less well developed and at times even commits errors it is hard to imagine the author of the *Prior Analytics* committing. Some interpreters have accordingly argued that the integration between these two works is limited at best and that the *Prior Analytics* is a later and substantially independent work. I believe instead that the development of the theory of the syllogism in the *Prior Analytics*, and in fact almost all the contents of that work, grew out of Aristotle's efforts to resolve the problems he addresses in the *Posterior Analytics*. For that very reason, he could only have written the *Prior Analytics* after the general outlines of the theory in the *Posterior* were already reasonably fixed in his thought. This explains the greater theoretical sophistication of the *Prior* that is evident if we compare the many treatments of similar issues in the two works.

Let us begin, then with what "syllogism" means. Aristotle defines this in several places (*Top* I.2, 100a25–7; *SE* 1 164b27–165a2; *An. Pr* I.1 24b18–20) in essentially the same way: an argument in which something follows of necessity from some other suppositions. This is a reasonably general definition of "valid argument" in modern terms. The English word "syllogism," however, has come to have the much narrower meaning of a two-premise argument composed of sentences of certain limited forms ("categorical sentences"). Making things worse, validity is *not* essential to a syllogism in the modern sense, so that "valid syllogism" is not redundant and "invalid syllogism" not self-contradictory, as they would be for Aristotle. Now, as a matter of fact, Aristotle does grant special importance to the forms of argument *we* call (valid) syllogisms, though his term for them is "arguments in the figures": he thinks all valid arguments whatsoever can be reduced to these, and indeed he believes he has proved this in *Prior Analytics* I. This is far from a trivial claim (and I would agree with virtually all modern logicians that it is clearly false). He believes that the theory of "syllogisms" (in the narrow modern sense) is in fact the entire theory of deductive logic. Having said this, I will nevertheless use "syllogism" as a translation of Aristotle's word *sullogismos*. I will also follow tradition and call the theory of such arguments developed in *Prior Analytics* I.1–22 the *syllogistic*. As long as we remember that for Aristotle, this is not just *a* logical theory but *the only possible* logical theory, I do not think this will lead to any confusion.

What properties, then, must a syllogism have in order to be a demonstration? According to *An. Post* I.2, that is a matter of the nature of its premises. They must be:

1 True
2 "First" or "primary"
3 "Immediate" or "unmiddled"
4 "More familiar" or "more intelligible" than the conclusion
5 "Prior" to the conclusion
6 The cause of the conclusion.

Each of these requires further explanation, but first we should take note of what is not on this list. Aristotle does not say that the premises must be necessary, and he does not say that they must be known (he does speak of their being "more familiar" than the conclusion, but of that more below). For that matter, his definition makes no explicit reference to an epistemic subject (a knower). Returning to what Aristotle *does* say, the first (truth) seems an obvious requirement (since we cannot know what is false), so I will start with "immediate." A modern reader may take this for an epistemic term ("known directly" or "known without the intervention of anything else,") but for Aristotle its content is logical. Since he believes that the syllogistic is the only correct theory of inference, he also believes that the premises of a demonstration must have the forms recognized by that theory. That is, he supposes that any premise must be either the affirmation or the denial of one term of another: "A is true of B," "A is not true of B." with an added distinction between universal and particular affirmations and denials. Now, in the syllogistic, every syllogism deduces its conclusion from two premises, each of which has a predicate and a subject term, where these premises have one term in common. This term is called the *middle* term. Consider now a proposition with predicate A and subject B, and suppose that it is a true proposition. If in addition there are two true premises from which it can be deduced, then those premises will have to share a third term, C. If there is no such middle term – that is, if there is no pair of such true premises – then the proposition in question is *amesos*, "unmiddled." This is what "immediate" means for Aristotle.

Here is perhaps the most critical place where the syllogistic shapes Aristotle's account of science. The term "immediate" is only meaningful against a background of the syllogistic as the theory of deduction. Now, as it happens, Aristotle's logical theory has properties that make this notion of immediacy of far greater interest. Consider the proposition "A is true of every B" (I will write AaB). Suppose that it is true and that it has a middle term C, so that there are true premises AaC, CaB from which AaB follows. What further consequences might we derive from this situation? In the syllogistic, we can deduce a collection of particular affirmative propositions: "A belongs to some B" (I write AiB), BiA, AiC, CiA, BiC, CiB. However, that is as far as it goes: the set $\{AaB, BaC,$

53

AaC, AiB, BiA, AiC, CiA, BiC, CiB} is deductively closed. Moreover, within this set, the propositions *AaB* and *BaC* are not deducible from any other propositions in the set, even including the entire set minus themselves: *AaB* cannot be derived from the set {*BaC, AaC, BiA, AiC, CiA, BiC, CiB*}. This is a crucial fact distinguishing the syllogistic as a deductive system from modern propositional logic: in the latter, no such sets are possible. If we start with just a single proposition *p*, its logical consequences include not only all the infinitely many tautologies but also all the infinitely many propositions equivalent to it: *p&p, p&(q∨~q), p∨p*, etc. If we take the deductive closure of {*p*} and subtract *p* from it, we can deduce *p* from the remainder. The significance of this is that in Aristotle's system, there can be true propositions that cannot be deduced from any other true propositions, even including all other true propositions. These are the immediate propositions. If there are immediate propositions, then there cannot be any demonstration of them, since they cannot even be deduced from other true propositions. Immediate propositions are thus indemonstrable on purely logical grounds, and if there is any knowledge of them it cannot consist of possessing a demonstration.

Next on Aristotle's list is the requirement that the premises be "first" or "primary." Aristotle's use of this term elsewhere shows that it is actually a virtual synonym for "immediate": A is predicated of B "first" if there is no other term C *prior* to B of which A is predicated, i.e. if there is no term C such that *AaC* and *CaB*, i.e. if *AaB* is immediate. (In *An. Post* I.15 and elsewhere, he adds a third term, "atomic," with roughly the same sense: *AaB* is atomic if it is immediate.)

Turning now to requirements 4–6, we do find a property that appears to have something to do with epistemic status: the premises must be "more familiar" or "better known" or "more intelligible" than the conclusion (these are all proposed translations of the same word *gnôrimôteron*). We might suppose this means that a demonstration must be from premises better known *by the person for whom it is a demonstration* than the conclusion. The opening sentence of the *Posterior Analytics*, which declares that "all teaching and all rational learning arises from previously existing knowledge" (71a1–2), could be taken to reinforce this. However, Aristotle thinks of "familiarity" in absolute terms. He distinguishes between what is more familiar *to us* and what is more familiar *by nature*: what is more familiar to us is what is closer to perception, whereas what is more familiar by nature is what is furthest from perception, that is, universals. It is only the latter that matters for demonstrations. However, in order for me to *possess* a demonstration, it must become the case that those same premises are also more familiar *for me* than the conclusion. Aristotle puts this point most forcibly in *Metaphysics* Z 3:

> just as in conduct our work is to start from what is good for each and make what is good in itself good for each, so it is our work to start from what is more intelligible [familiar] to oneself and make what is intelligible [familiar] by nature also intelligible to oneself. Now what is intelligible and first for particular sets of people is often intelligible only to a very small extent and has little or nothing of reality. (1029b3–10)

Thus, far from supposing us to have an innate ability to recognize indemonstrable premises, Aristotle holds instead that familiarity or intelligibility *to us* is changeable through habituation. To the possessor of science, different things are familiar and obvious than what is familiar and obvious to us in our uneducated state. We can see here an indication of what it is to "possess" a demonstration: it is to be disposed to find its premises more familiar or intelligible than its conclusion. This is analogous, as Aristotle says, to the ethical case, where our dispositions to feel pleasure and pain at our actions indicate, not whether the actions themselves are right or wrong, but whether *we* are virtuous.

As a result, "more familiar" or "more intelligible" turns out again to be closely connected to "immediate," since immediate propositions are by nature prior deductively to all others. This same sense of priority explains what "prior" means (and in any event Aristotle equates "prior" and "more familiar" at 71b33–72a4).

The last of the six requirements is that the premises of a demonstration give the *cause* or *reason* (*aition, aitia*) of its conclusion. Without entering into a full discussion of Aristotle's views on causes, I think we can see a connection between this and the notion of immediacy. Aristotle's account of demonstration, as we have considered it so far, is this: science is knowledge of the cause why something must be as it is; we possess science when we possess a demonstration. A demonstration is a syllogism the premises of which are true and immediate. Possessing a demonstration requires bringing it about that its immediate premises also are more familiar or more intelligible to us than the conclusion. Now, this account raises two questions: (1) If we cannot have demonstrative science of the premises of a demonstration, then what kind of knowledge *do* we have of them? (2) What reason is there for thinking that there are immediate propositions at all? Aristotle addresses (1) by considering two rival views about demonstration that he rejects. As it happens, his response leads him to give a detailed answer to (2).

According to Aristotle, some people argued that demonstrative science is impossible because of the problem of knowledge of the indemonstrable premises. Scholars differ about who these people may have been; I shall just call them the "anti-demonstrators." Their position rests on two claims:

1   The premises of a demonstration must be known scientifically
2   Only what is demonstrated is known scientifically

They then observe that this gives rise to a regress of premises. If the premises of a demonstration are known, then they must be demonstrated from yet other premises, and these from yet others, and so on. Now, either this regress comes to a stop at some point or it goes on without end. In the latter case, say the anti-demonstrators, there is no demonstration because "we cannot know posterior things from prior things of which there are none that are first" (72b9–10). Turning to the other horn of the dilemma, suppose that the regress comes to a stop. It would come to a stop whenever we reached some premise to which nothing was prior, that is (as we can say against the background of Aristotle's logic), an immediate premise. The anti-demonstrators then invoke (2) to conclude that an immediate premise cannot be known, and thus by (1) they conclude that there is no demonstration in this case either.

Aristotle answers each horn of the dilemma separately. First, he agrees with the anti-demonstrators that demonstration is impossible where there is an infinite regress of premises, but he argues that such regresses never actually occur. This argument occupies a major part of *Posterior Analytics* I. He must then reject (2) and instead hold that the knowledge of the immediate premises is something other than demonstration. (Aristotle's usage is not quite consistent: in I.2, he speaks of "non-demonstrative" science, but elsewhere he identifies science with demonstrative science and uses a different term for the knowledge that goes with immediate premises.) We should notice how strongly this response depends on the syllogistic. It is only in the syllogistic that the notion of a regress of premises "coming to a stop" makes sense. Moreover, if a premise regress does terminate in immediate premises, then by reversing the regress we will have a deduction of the premise we started with from immediates. Consequently, if every regress terminates in immediates, then every proposition is either itself immediate (and thus not demonstrable at all) or deducible from immediates (and thus we will have its demonstration). This would be a powerful result to establish: added to an account of what knowledge of the immediate propositions consists in, it would show how demonstration, and therefore science, is possible.

In addition to the anti-demonstrators, Aristotle rejects the position of another group, the circular demonstrators. He says that these thinkers accept the claim that only demonstration produces science but think that every scientific proposition can be demonstrated through "circular demonstration" of premises from each other. Aristotle gives three arguments against this view. First, if the premises of a demonstration must be prior to its conclusion, then (no matter how we understand prior, so long as it is an asymmetrical relation) the same premises will have to appear now as premises and now as conclusions, and so they will be both prior and posterior to themselves, which is absurd. Second, circular demonstration is logically equivalent to deducing something from itself, but if that counts as a demonstration then any proposition whatever can be demonstrated.

These two objections do not depend on any particular characteristics of Aristotle's logical theory. However, he adds a third that is irreducibly syllogistic, appealing to a result established in *Prior Analytics* II.5–7 concerning "circular and reciprocal proof," (defined in syllogistic terms). Aristotle proves there that this kind of circular proof is only possible when two of the terms are "convertible," that is, are universally true of one another. So, he says in *Posterior Analytics* I.3, since "such things are rare in demonstrations, clearly it is both pointless and impossible to say that the demonstration is reciprocal and through this that there can be demonstration of everything" (73a18–20). The connection between these two sections of these two treatises illustrates what I see as the main relationship between the two works: the *Posterior Analytics* raises questions which set the agenda for more detailed discussions of technical points taken up in the *Prior*.

To return to my subject, the argument against the possibility of an infinite premise regress is perhaps the most important of all such connections between the *Prior* and *Posterior Analytics*. In *An. Post.* I.19–23, Aristotle develops a lengthy argument for this resting on the syllogistic (at least in a simplified version). His strategy is as follows. Consider first a regress of true premises beginning with a universal affirmative conclusion *AaB*. There is only one way of deducing an *a* conclusion: premises for *AaB* must be of the form *AaC*, *CaB*. Using language Aristotle employs in this connection, let us say that when *AaB* is true, B is *below* A. We can then represent this graphically as in figure 4.1.

If the regress continues further with premises for *AaC* and *CaB*, then there will be middle terms D, E falling in the intervals AC and CB as shown in figure 4.2.

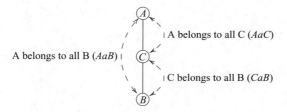

Figure 4.1   A chain of terms

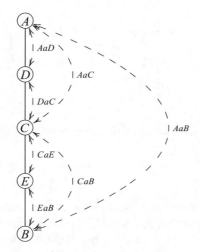

Figure 4.2   Filling in a proof for a universal affirmative proposition, *AaB*

Each further step in this regress must introduce a new term into the "chain" (as Aristotle calls it) between A and B. If the regress were to continue forever, then there would be infinitely many terms in this chain. Thus, we have a simple condition for the termination of all regresses. Suppose that no "chain" is infinite either upwards or downwards. Then, since the series of terms between A and B is both an upwards and a downwards chain, and since an infinite regress would insert terms into it without end, every regress for a universal affirmative would have to terminate.

Aristotle next shows that the finiteness of all upwards or downwards chains would entail that every premise regress for a universal negative (*e*) conclusion terminates. His proof can be summarized graphically as follows. A regress for *AeB* must have premises of one of three forms: *AeC* and *CaB* (celarent), *CeA* and *CaB* (cesare), or *CaA* and *CeB* (camestres). In each case, the middle term will be above one of the terms A, B and in an *e* premise with the other as shown in figure 4.3.

Continuing the regress for the *a* premise falls under the case already covered. A continued regress for the *e* premise will again have one of the three forms mentioned, and its middle term will again be added atop a chain rising either from A or from B. So, if every chain is finite, then these regresses are finite.

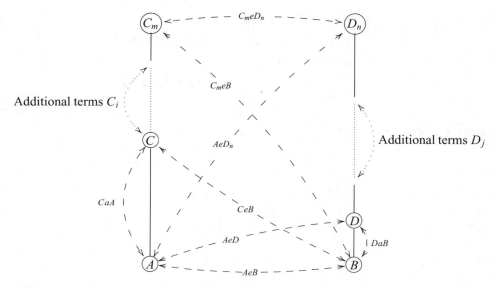

Figure 4.3 Filling in a proof for a universal negative proposition, AeB

Before we turn to the final step in Aristotle's argument, showing that every chain is finite, let us take note of what this remarkable argument shows about the role of the syllogistic in the theory of demonstration. Since Aristotle thinks of the syllogistic as embracing all valid arguments, he is drawing conclusions about what can be proved by considering all the possible structures of a proof. It does not seem to me unreasonable to compare this, at least broadly, with proof theory in the modern sense. It also seems possible to me that the goal of establishing this and related results motivated the development of the syllogistic as we find it in the *Prior Analytics*: Aristotle first develops an austere formal theory (I.1–7) and then argues that all arguments can be "analyzed" into its limited forms (see *An. Pr* I.32 for the statement of his program). This is not what we would expect of a teacher of critical thinking, but it is exactly what we would expect of a logical theorist.

Aristotle argues for the termination of all chains in *An. Post* I.22 on the basis of his theory of predication and his concept of essence. A thorough treatment of these issues would take us outside the purview of this chapter; in summary, his argument is that we do know some essences; that we could not know them if they were infinite; and that they would be infinite if there were infinite chains of predication.

The core of Aristotle's theory of demonstration, then, can be summarized as follows:

1 Science, or demonstrative science (he often equates the two) is knowledge that consists in possessing a demonstration.
2 A demonstration is a syllogism with immediate (and therefore indemonstrable) premises.

3   Possessing a demonstration requires finding its premises to be more intelligible than its conclusion.
4   Every truth either is itself an immediate proposition or is deducible from immediate propositions.

Aristotle still owes us an explanation of one further claim essential to his theory:

5   Knowledge of immediate propositions is possible through some means other than demonstration.

I will return briefly to (5) below, though a full treatment of this issue falls to another chapter in this volume. First, however, let me consider several issues that have been important in the scholarly discussions of Aristotle's account of demonstration against the background of my interpretation. (Aristotle uses the term *archê*, "beginning" or "origin", for a premise of a demonstration. This is traditionally translated "principle", and for convenience I will use this term in what follows.)

Necessity and Predication "Through Itself"

Aristotle says that a demonstration must show the cause why something is necessarily as it is. As I noted above, he does not include necessity among the properties that the premises of a demonstration must have when he enumerates those in *An. Post* I.2. Where does this necessity enter into a demonstration? Aristotle turns his attention to necessity at the beginning of *An. Post.* I.4 and says that he will give an account of the sorts of premises demonstrations can be from. However, instead of discussing necessity at once, he examines what he calls predication "through itself" or "in virtue of itself" (*kath' hauto*, often rendered with the Latin translation *per se*). When A is predicated of B, it is predicated of B "through itself" if either (1) A is part of the definition of B or (2) B is part of the definition of A (as Aristotle's use makes clear, the phrase "through itself" attaches to B, the subject of the predication). To take an example of the first case, humans are essentially a species of animal, and so animal is predicated of human through itself. Elsewhere, Aristotle also calls this "essential predication" or "predication in the what it is" (see for instance *Top* I.7). The second case is illustrated by predicates which by their nature can only belong to subjects from a certain genus, as for example "straight" and "curved" can only belong to lines or "odd" and "even" can only belong to numbers. So, a straight line is straight through itself, and an odd number is odd through itself. Predication that is not "through itself" is "incidental" or "accidental" (*kata sumbebêkos*).

   If A is true of B through B itself, then B could not fail to be A without failing to be itself, and thus through-itself predications of the first kind are necessary. It is less obvious how to make the case for necessity in the case of the second kind of through-itself predication, and in fact Aristotle's usage on this point is unsettled. "Odd" is a through-itself predicate of numbers, though not of all numbers. Is the number three odd through itself? It is plausible to say that three could not fail to be odd without failing to be three, though this example is complicated by the fact that numbers could be argued to have only necessary properties. "Male" and "female" are predicates of "animal" through itself, since each includes "animal" in its definition. Are male animals then necessarily male animals, and female animals necessarily female animals? As far as Aristotle's biology is concerned, it is at least conceivable that this is the case, i.e., that a given animal could not change from male to female, or conversely, without ceasing to be the animal that it is, but this is at best speculative.

Suppose that AaB and that there is a middle term C for it, so that AaC and CaB. Can we then say that C is the *cause* of A belonging to B? According to Aristotle, we need to know more. In particular, if there is another middle term between A and C (which will therefore be a wider universal than C), then C cannot be the cause: only that middle is the cause which is the most universal term to which A belongs that also belongs to B. Aristotle's example will help clarify this. Let A be "has internal angles equal to two right angles" (I will abbreviate this as "has 2R") and let B be an isosceles triangle. Why does A belong to B? The answer "Because it is an isosceles triangle" does not give the true cause, for Aristotle, since there is a wider term, "triangle," to which A belongs. He reasons that if being an isosceles triangle were the cause of *this* figure's having 2R, then it would also have to be the cause of having 2R for *every* figure that has it. Instead, we have found the cause of being A when we have found the "first universal" of which A is universally true. Aristotle's thought here is influenced by the mathematics of his time. Mathematics frequently advances by discovering more general proofs that embrace results proved by several less general ones. In such a case, Aristotle regards the more general proof as giving the real cause of the subsidiary cases. For example, it can be proved that every isosceles triangle has 2R as follows: bisect the triangle's base and connect this to its opposite vertex, producing two congruent triangles. Invert one of these halves and join it to the other, producing a rectangle. It is then evident that the angles of the two triangles add up to four right angles, so the angles of each add up to two. From Aristotle's perspective, this is not really a demonstration since it cannot explain why *all* triangles have 2R, even though all triangles do have 2R.

We may make a case, then, that for Aristotle necessity is a consequence of through-itself predication, so that if principles must involve only such predication they will be necessary. However, Aristotle himself seems to be of two minds about whether this is the right way to proceed. In *An. Post* I.6, he proposes an alternative account on which a demonstration would just be by definition a syllogism with necessary premises: "It is possible to syllogize from true premises without demonstrating, but it is not possible to syllogize from necessary premises without demonstrating, since that is already what belongs to demonstration" (74b15–18). I will not attempt here to resolve this issue, but it is noteworthy that despite the implied promise at the beginning of *An. Post* I.4 of a discussion of syllogisms from necessary premises, what we actually find in the *Posterior Analytics* on that score is very sketchy: hardly more than the assertion that if the premises are necessary, then the conclusion must be necessary (see 75a1–11). We might speculate that the detailed study of syllogisms with necessary premises in *Prior Analytics* I.8–10 is inspired by just this issue.

Demonstrations, Universals, and the Objects of Scientific Knowledge

Aristotle says that scientific knowledge concerns "universals" (*ta katholou*). We could take this to mean that the propositions known by sciences are all universal generalizations. Aristotle would no doubt agree that this is true of sciences, but his own way of conceiving of the objects of science is different. He takes science to be a knowledge of universals *themselves*: arithmetic is knowledge of number, not (or not merely) knowledge of propositions about number. This implies that science is possible only if such things as universals exist. What exactly are these universals? This was a central issue of debate in the early Academy. Aristotle rejected Plato's view that universals are objects of a kind totally different from perceptible individuals (Platonic forms, as we usually call them), and he spends a great deal of time in the *Metaphysics* working out his alternative. This is a subject well beyond the purview of this chapter. However, a few brief remarks about how this affects his views on science may not be amiss here.

First, it is worth noting some peculiarities of the various Greek idioms that are usually translated with the verb "know." English makes the verb "know" serve both for *knowing that* something is the case ("I know that Socrates is bald") and for *being acquainted* with something or someone ("I know Socrates"). In this respect, English is quite different from other modern European languages, which use different verbs for these two senses (*wissen/kennen, savoir/connaître, saber/conocer*) and have no single verb with the full breadth of "know." In ancient Greek, matters are different again, and somewhat more complicated. Among the common verbs that are often translated "know," some (e.g. *gignôskein*) can be used, like English "know," both for propositional knowledge and for acquaintance, while others (e.g. *eidenai, sunienai, epistasthai*) are mostly confined to propositional knowledge. Moreover, there is a Greek idiom, common in both Plato and Aristotle, that is hard to capture in English. Instead of saying "I know that Socrates is bald," I can also say, "I know Socrates that he is bald." Modern philosophers may be tempted to construe this as a sort of *de re* idiom, equivalent to "I know, of Socrates, that he is bald," but Aristotle does not seem to regard it as different in meaning from "I know that Socrates is bald." This idiom may have made it natural for Aristotle to treat knowing a proposition about Socrates (i.e. knowing that it is true) as a matter of knowing Socrates (that is, being acquainted with Socrates). This would make it easy for him to treat knowledge that A belongs to B as a matter of *knowing B*.

Next, I believe it is best to see Aristotle's view of science, like so much else in his thought, as a revision of a Platonic position. Plato held that the objects of science (*epistêmê*, the term he prefers for the knowledge that philosophers seek) are necessarily as they are, that these objects are not the same as perceptible objects, and that they explain why things are as they are. Aristotle actually agrees with each of these views. He differs from Plato, first, in rejecting "separation" (the thesis that universals exist separately from perceptible objects), and second in denying Plato's view that we have innate knowledge of them. Now, Plato made use of an argument in the *Phaedo* which he thought established both the separate existence of universals and that we have innate knowledge of them. He observes that we do, as a matter of fact, have knowledge of such things as equality itself, or mathematical objects, or other universals, since we are able to make judgments involving them. However, we never perceive such objects with our senses. Therefore, Plato concludes, we must have been born with this knowledge and, since it is not the knowledge of any perceptible object, its objects must exist in separation from the perceptible world. Aristotle believes that science is possible but

61

denies both separation and innate knowledge. Instead, he holds that universals do indeed exist, but in perceptible things rather than apart from them. He also holds that these same universals can exist in our intellects. Universals do have causal powers, and through those powers they are able to cause themselves to exist in other individuals: it is the form of human in the parent that causes the form in the child. There is also a causality that operates on our intellects and our senses. When we perceive, the universals in the object perceived cause those same universals to exist in our minds, so that we perceive something by taking on its form without its matter. In an analogous way, when we come to know what a human being is, what happens is that our intellect takes on the form of a human. (There are many problems in understanding just how this process is supposed to take place, and I will not try to address them here; it is clear, however, that Aristotle does think it takes place: see *An. Post* I.18, 81b2; *An. Post* II.19, 100a10–11; *EN* VI.3). Now, if we suppose that knowing a universal is a matter of knowing its definition or essence and also that knowing the essence of something entails knowing its through-itself predicates, then this picture can be fitted plausibly together with Aristotle's picture of demonstrations as resting on immediate premises. The immediates at which a premise regress "comes to a stop" would then be the same immediates known as a direct result of the perceptual process through which universals come to be in the intellect.

The Route to the Principles

In *Prior Analytics* I.27–8, Aristotle gives us an account of "the road through which we can get the principles of anything" (43a21–2). Suppose that we want to find true premises from which to deduce a proposition having A as its predicate and E as its subject. Begin by collecting all the truths involving A or E and then assemble the following six sets of terms:

B: whatever is true of all A (i.e. BaA)   F: whatever is true of all E (i.e. FaE)
C: whatever A is true of all of (AaC)   G: whatever E is true of all of (EaG)
D: whatever cannot belong to A (DeA)   H: whatever cannot belong to E (HeE)

Aristotle then shows, for each of the premises we can construct using A as predicate and B as subject, how premises can be found for it by looking for a common term in some one of the first three sets (B, C, D) and some one of the second three (F, G, H). For instance, if we need premises for AaE, we will need a term X such that AaX and XaE. What we need in this case is a term that is in both C and F: if X is in C, then AaX, and if X is in F, then XaE. Aristotle works through all the combinations possible, thus showing for each possible conclusion all the ways we might find premises for this. This is not merely a heuristic procedure: if, as Aristotle believed, the syllogistic is the one true logic, then this method will discover a middle term for a premise if and only if one exists. Therefore, if this method does not find a middle, then there is not one to be found, and that premise is immediate. Aristotle's method, then, is a systematic way of carrying out a premise regress until it "comes to a stop" at immediates.

How are these sets of terms to be collected? Evidently, by collecting all the true propositions about some subject matter. This, at any rate, is what Aristotle says in *An. Pr* I.30: if we take care to leave none of the relevant truths out of our "history" (*historia*: 46a24–5), then we will be in a position to "reveal the demonstration" of whatever can be demonstrated as well as to make it evident when we have found something that has no demonstration.

Axioms, Common Principles, and Self-evidence

Aristotle is sometimes taken to say that principles must be self-evident, though it is hard to find a clear statement of such a view in his works. Perhaps the closest is in *Top* I.1, where he says that scientific premises should "get their conviction (*pistis*) through themselves" or "be convincing (*pistên*) themselves through themselves" (100b8–22). However, there are certain specific propositions for which he does claim something like self-evidence. In *Met* Γ.3, he argues that the principle of non-contradiction is "the most secure of all principles" because no one can possibly disbelieve it. This same argument is alluded to in *An. Post* I.10, 76b22–4, which speaks of "what through itself both necessarily is and necessarily is believed." Finally, in *An. Post* I.2, in a passage evidently classifying the different types of "immediate syllogistic principles," Aristotle says "I call that a *thesis* which cannot be proved and which it is not necessary for someone who is going to learn something to possess; that which it is necessary for someone who is going to learn any given thing to possess I call an *axiom*" (72a16–17). To many interpreters, "what necessarily is believed" and "what it is necessary for anyone to learn any given thing to possess" sound rather close, so that "axioms" would be those principles that everyone must believe, or at any rate everyone who is going to learn anything. Are "axioms" self-evident, then? And just what are they?

Aristotle has more to say about "axioms" in *An. Post* I.7 and I.10. He tells us that there are "three things" in every demonstrative science:

> There are three things in demonstrations: one is what is demonstrated, that is, the conclusion (this is what belongs to some genus through itself); one is the axioms (the axioms are that from which); and the third is the subject genus, of which the demonstration reveals the attributes and the through-itself accidents. (I.7 75a39–b2)

> Every demonstrative science concerns three things: what it assumes to be (this is the genus, of which it studies the through-itself attributes); and the commonly called axioms (from which first things it demonstrates); and third the attributes, of which it supposes what each signifies. (I.10 76b11–16)

In each case, Aristotle only says that the "axioms" are "that from which," an expression that usually means "premises" for him. Since there is no mention of any other premises, we might think that "axiom" here just means "premise", as it does in many other places. However, matters are complicated by the phrase "the commonly called axioms" in the second passage. This points to an issue that both these passages are concerned with. Aristotle holds that there is no single science that covers all of knowledge and that both reality and our knowledge of it are irreducibly divided into "categories." In the *Posterior Analytics*, he says that each science has its own proper subject matter and its own proper principles and that it is not in general possible to prove anything about the subject matter of one science from the principles of another (the only exception is if one science is subordinate to the other, as for Aristotle optics is to geometry or music to arithmetic). Nevertheless, Aristotle says, there are certain "common things" (he usually just says *ta koina*, "common," without an associated noun) that are not proper to any science and can be made use of by all sciences (e.g. 77a26–35). He says almost as little about just what these "common things" are as he does about axioms, but he gives a few examples: "when equals are subtracted from equals, the remainders are equal" (76a41, 76b20–1, 77a30–1), the law of excluded middle (77a30). Both non-contradiction and excluded middle appear in *An. Post* I.11, a difficult section to interpret (see Barnes's commentary). Outside the *Analytics*, Aristotle does mention "common principles" or "common locations" in the *Topics* and the *Rhetoric*, and the possibility of a general art of dialectical argument rests on them. However, he also insists that dialectic is not a science or the method of a science, and he says in *SE* 11 that it is not the universal science of being.

Are these "common things" what Aristotle means by "axioms"? The evidence is far from conclusive, and I am inclined to think not. There is only one passage in which he actually restricts the word "axiom" to a special class of proposition, and the surrounding context of that passage has other difficulties (see Barnes 1993 and Ross 1949 on 72a11–14 in particular). I think it more likely that "axiom" just means "proposition" and that what he means in *An. Post* I.7–10 is that *among* the premises used in demonstrations, some are common. See, however, Hintikka (1972).

Demonstration and Analysis

Aristotle consistently refers to the *Analytics* with that title. Why? The most likely reason, I think, is that he has in mind the notion of analysis that was already established in Greek mathematics. In rough terms, analysis was the process of assuming that a problem had been solved, or a proof found, and then working backwards deductively to previously established results; then, a proof or solution could be obtained by reversing the steps. Aristotle is certainly familiar with this usage, as a passage in the *Nicomachean Ethics* shows (III.3 1112b20–4). He also refers in several places to the "road up" (to the principles) and the "road down" (from the principles to what is proved from them), and these can be taken to refer to analysis and synthesis in a very broad sense. Connecting this specifically with the purpose of the *Analytics* is more speculative, but I would offer this suggestion. I have argued that premise regresses are both a major issue in the *Posterior Analytics* and a major point of connection between the *Posterior* and the *Prior*. A premise regress is, in fact, what an analysis would be: a process that looks for premises from which a given conclusion follows. By its very construction, a regress can always be reversed to yield a deduction of the proposition with which it started from the premises with which it ends. One of the few places in which Aristotle speaks of "analyzing" is in just such a connection, at the beginning of *Prior Analytics*

I.32, in a passage which summarizes what he believes he has accomplished in his exposition of the syllogistic:

> So, then, what demonstrations arise from, and how, and what we should look to in the case of each problem, is evident from what has been said. But how we may reduce syllogisms into the previously mentioned figures would be the next thing to explain after this, since that is what remains of our inquiry. For if we have both studied the origins of syllogisms and have the ability to discover them, and moreover if we can analyze existing syllogisms into the figures mentioned, our original project would reach its goal. It will at the same time follow that the things said previously are reinforced and that it is more obvious that they are so, because of what we are about to say. For whatever is true must be in agreement with itself in all ways. (46b38–47a9).

Bibliography

Barnes, Jonathan (1981). "Proof and the Syllogism," in Berti (ed.) (1985), pp. 17–59.

Barnes, Jonathan (1993). *Aristotle, "Posterior Analytics,"* 2nd edn. (Oxford: Oxford University Press, Clarendon Aristotle Series).

Berti, Enrico (ed.) (1985). *Aristotle on Science: The "Posterior Analytics" (Proceedings of the Eighth Symposium Aristotelicum* (Padua: Antenore).

Burnyeat, Myles (1985). "Aristotle on Understanding Knowledge," in Berti (ed.) (1985), pp. 97–139.

Ferejohn, Michael (1991). *The Origins of Aristotelian Science* (New Haven, CT: Yale University Press).

Hintikka, Jaakko (1972). "On the Ingredients of an Aristotelian Science," *Nous*, 6, pp. 55–69.

McKirahan, Richard (1992). *Principles and Proofs: Aristotle's Theory of Demonstrative Science.* (Princeton, NJ: Princeton University Press).

Mignucci, Mario (1975). *L'argomentazione dimostrative in Aristotele* (Padua: Antenore).

Mignucci, Mario (2007). *Aristotele, Analitici Secondi: Organon III*, trans. and comm. by M. Mignucci., intro. by J. Barnes (Rome: Editori Laterza).

Pellegrin, Pierre (2005). *Aristote: Seconds Analytiques*, intro., trans., notes, bib., and index by Pierre Pellegrin (Paris: Editions Flammarion).

Ross, W. D. (1949). *Aristotle's "Prior" and "Posterior Analytics": A Revised Text with Introduction and Commentary* (Oxford: Clarendon Press).

Solmsen, Friedrich [1929] (2001). *Die Entwicklung der aristotelischen Logik und Rhetoric* (Berlin: Weidmannsche Buchhandlung). (Repr. Hildesheim: Georg Olms Verlag.)

5

Empiricism and the First Principles of Aristotelian Science

MICHAEL FEREJOHN

> All teaching and all learning of the discursive sort arises out of pre-existent knowledge.
>
> *Posterior Analytics*, I.1 71a1–2

With this, the very first sentence of his treatise on scientific explanation, Aristotle announces a striking epistemic principle in a manner quite possibly intended to bring to mind the Platonic doctrine of recollection in the *Meno*.

(P1)   Every piece of knowledge arises out of some pre-existent knowledge.

At first sight, this principle seems quite anti-foundationalist in spirit. It is, therefore, somewhat surprising that two chapters later it is pressed into service by Aristotle to support a foundationalist theory of epistemic justification. The main topic of the treatise is a very special type of knowledge, indeed what Aristotle regards as the very highest form of knowledge, or what he calls "knowledge *simpliciter*." His settled view throughout the *Analytics* is that one doesn't really know a given truth in the fullest sense unless one knows not merely *that* it is true but also *why* it is true. And since, within the theory of deductive inference developed in the *Prior Analytics* and presupposed throughout the *Posterior Analytics*, to know why something is true is to have constructed an adequate syllogistic demonstration that establishes the proposition in question, he understandably equates knowledge *simpliciter* with demonstrated knowledge.

In *Posterior Analytics* I.3, Aristotle considers the implications of (P1) for his theory of demonstrative knowledge. He reasons that if *all* knowledge were demonstrative, then according to (P1) either all demonstrations are infinite (which, for Aristotle, would mean there could be no knowledge whatsoever), or circular proof is possible. But since Aristotle takes it as an incontestable fact that there *is* knowledge, when he goes on to argue at 72b25–73a20 that circular demonstration is in fact impossible, he concludes, contrary to the initial supposition, (1) that not all knowledge is demonstrated knowledge, and further, (2) that every piece of demonstrated knowledge rests upon premises which are known but not demonstrated.

However, Aristotle evidently also recognizes that to argue that knowledge of these ultimate demonstrative premises doesn't come about through demonstration does not exempt them from (P1) altogether. For even though the arguments of I.3 effectively remove questions about the origin of this sort of knowledge from the relatively narrow scope of his investigation into the nature and generation of knowledge *simpliciter* (i.e., demonstrative knowledge), from a more general epistemological point of view Aristotle understandably feels obliged to say something at some point or other about how knowledge of such ultimate premises of demonstration is acquired in the first place.

Nearly every commentator agrees that this is the central issue of *Posterior Analytics* II.19, the treatise's final chapter (though, as we shall see, it is a matter of some dispute whether this is the only place in the treatise where the issue is addressed). Unfortunately, this chapter is also generally regarded as one of the most perplexing in the *Analytics*, in large part because it seems on its face to present two *mutually inconsistent* theories of knowledge. The chapter is plainly divided into two sections, the first and longer of which (from the beginning of the chapter to 100b5) has often been interpreted as putting forward an "empiricist" account of the acquisition of non-inferential knowledge. This is then followed by a short closing section, which appears to be an enunciation of a "rationalistic" account of the foundations of epistemic justification.

My chief objective here will be to challenge a number of "empiricist" interpretations of the first section of the chapter. Many such interpretations are encouraged by the presence of a line of reasoning at the very beginning of the chapter (99b20–34) from which Aristotle draws the moral – not to say a logical consequence – that perception (*aisthesis*) plays a central role in the apprehension of ultimate demonstrative principles. Let us begin, then, by taking a close look at this reasoning.

I

Aristotle prefaces this argument by recalling his earlier conclusion in *Post. An* I.3 that the possibility of demonstrative knowledge requires that prior to the demonstration, one had already possessed knowledge of first principles (*archai*) that serve as ultimate premises of the demonstration. With respect to this prior apprehension of these first principles, then, he asks whether the same issue that arose in the case of demonstrative knowledge also arises here, which issue I take to be the applicability of (P1). He does this by asking whether the correct account of the pre-existent apprehension of ultimate demonstrative principles will (a) involve postulating the emergence of entirely new cognitive states (*hexeis*) in the soul of the knowing subject, or will instead (b) require the postulation of some further pre-existent *hexeis* in the soul of which the subject is unaware. In Aristotle's own words,

> [We must inquire] whether cognitive states not [already] present in the subject come into being, or whether they had [simply] not been noticed to be within the subject. (99b21–6)

At this point Aristotle proceeds to argue that the apparent dilemma formed by the disjunction of (a) and (b) is only apparent because one can reject both (a) and (b) in favor of some third alternative. He moves directly against (a) at 99b28–30 by recalling his pronouncement in I.1 that it is not possible for knowledge or learning to arise out

67

of a complete lack of cognition on the subject's part. His rejection of (b), on the other hand, is qualified: he claims at 99b26–7 that it would be absurd (*atopon*) to think that one could possess a cognitive *hexis* that is "more accurate" (*akribesteras*) than demonstrative knowledge while remaining ignorant that one possessed it. The qualification here turns out to be significant, for Aristotle's subsequent proposal for avoiding the dilemma is to deny (a) by holding that there is a certain pre-existent *hexis* from which the apprehension of first principles ultimately arises, while at the same time avoiding (b) by denying that the *hexis* in question is an *occurrent* cognitive state (which would presumably have to be "more accurate" than demonstrative knowledge, and could therefore not be possessed inadvertently). Rather, he maintains, the *hexis* in question is a certain kind of cognitive capacity (*dunamis*) for *acquiring* such occurrent states, but which is not more "accurate" than those occurrent states themselves:

> However, it is apparent both that one cannot possess such states without knowing so, and also that they could not come to be if one didn't possess any [prior] state at all; therefore, it is necessary for one to have a certain sort of capacity (*dunamis*) but one which will not be "more worthy with respect to accuracy" (*timiotera kat' akribeian*) than those others. (99b30–4).

As I have just interpreted him, Aristotle's rejection of alternative (a) is based on the germinal idea of (P1), namely that it is impossible for a piece of knowledge to arise out of a total absence of cognition. In his commentary on this passage, Jonathan Barnes agrees with this interpretation.[1] But he then goes on to criticize Aristotle on this account by arguing first that as (P1) is announced in I.1, it should be interpreted narrowly to require only that every occurrent state of knowledge must arise out of another pre-existent *occurrent* cognitive state. On this basis, Barnes then argues that (P1) therefore has no legitimate application to II.19, where Aristotle is trying to establish that certain cognitive achievements – namely the apprehension of the first principles of demonstration – arise not out of earlier occurrent cognitive states, but instead out of a cognitive *capacity*.

Notice, however, that as (P1) is actually expressed in I.1, it explicitly conveys only the more modest point that all knowledge must arise out of *some sort* of pre-existent cognition (*gnôsis*) but it does not specify further, as Barnes understands it, that this prior cognition must be a piece of occurrent knowledge, even though it is true that the principle is *applied* later in Book I to establish that a certain type of occurrent cognitive state (namely, demonstrative knowledge, or knowledge *simpliciter*) arises out of another type of occurrent cognitive state (knowledge of first principles). Hence, given the strong indication that the same principle is also in play in the argument of II.19, I believe we should understand it as expressing a more general, if less determinate, idea that could be thought of as *Epistemological Eleaticism*. What I have in mind is this. The details of his particular arguments against change aside, one can understand Parmenides as pressing the compelling metaphysical insight that various types of change (say, generation or alteration) would be impossible if upon analysis they turned out to require that certain entities (be they things, qualities, or states of affairs) can come to be out of nothing at all. I propose that we should understand (P1) as expressing an analogous point in an epistemological setting, namely that the acquisition of knowledge would be impossible if it required that any cognitive states could come into being entirely *ex nihilo*, that is, out of a complete and utter lack of any cognition whatsoever. Understood in this way, the principle would leave room for the possibility argued for in II.19, that the occurrent knowledge of principles could arise out of a cognitive capacity.

Whatever the source of its ultimate premises, the most Aristotle's argument at 99b20–34 establishes is that undemonstrated knowledge of first principles arises out of *some cognitive capacity or other*. It tells us nothing at all about what specific capacity that might be. However, in the very next sentence Aristotle goes on to identify this *dunamis* as "the 'discerning' capacity, present in all animals, which is called 'perception'" (99b35–6). But this abrupt statement is potentially misleading because it can give the impression that Aristotle believes that perception is the *only* cognitive capacity involved in coming to know demonstrative first principles. This is clearly not the case, for in the immediate sequel he describes in some detail an epistemic process, which he calls *epagoge*, in which believes such knowledge is acquired, and this description mentions at least three other cognitive capacities *besides* perception.

A useful way to think about the roles of these other capacities in *epagôgê* is by means of a series of thought-experiments. To begin with, if we start from the idea that Aristotle regards perception as necessary for coming to know first principles, we might consider first the case of a hypothetical sentient animal that lacked even minimal (i.e., shortest-term) memory. While such an animal could be affected momentarily by things (or events) in its environment, no trace of these interactions would survive their initial occurrence. For such an animal, every taste, sight, sound and smell would be absolutely novel. To invoke the old and familiar wax-tablet metaphor introduced in Plato's *Theaetetus*, it would be as if the wax of the tablet was so soft and fluid that it could not hold the imprint of the signet even for an instant. Such an animal, on Aristotle's view, would be no more capable of coming to know first principles than it would be if it were completely insentient.

Next, we might imagine yet another hypothetical animal that could both perceive and retain memory traces of those perceptions, yet for which each such retained experience was entirely *sui generis*. That is to say, it would be able to remember having perceived one object of a given type (say, white), and another object of that type, but would have no way of understanding that it had perceived two objects of the *same* type. Such an animal, on Aristotle's view would lack the faculty of *empeiria* (usually translated as "experience"), which we might think of roughly as the ability to classify retained percepts into general kinds. Aristotle's view, which again seems quite reasonable, is that such an animal would be no more able to know first principles than would its perfectly insentient and perfectly forgetful counterparts.

Aristotle's insistence on the indispensability in coming to know first principles of yet a fourth cognitive capacity (besides perception, memory, and experience) will not seem so uncontroversial. He believes an animal that could do nothing more than (1) perceive, (2) retain memories of those perceptions, and (3) group those memories into appropriate (natural) categories would *still* not be able to know first principles. This is because the objects of thought for such an animal would all be particulars (particular memory traces, or perhaps memories of particular perceived objects), whereas Aristotle believes as a separate matter that all scientific knowledge (and therefore, the knowledge of principles on which it rests) must be about universals. Consequently, he posits a

69

fourth capacity, which he calls *nous*, and which might be thought of the distinctly human ability to move from general, "nominalistic" beliefs about (natural) classes of particulars gained through *empeiria* to necessary, "realist" knowledge concerning (relations among) the universals instantiated by those particulars.

But even though Aristotle's full account on this matter has perception as just one of four different cognitive capacities involved in *epagôgê*, his decision to mention only perception at 99b35–6 as *the* capacity from which knowledge of first principles arises does seem to indicate that he gives it some special status vis-à-vis the others. In the following section, I shall offer an explanation of this special status that turns upon recognizing a crucial difference between the Aristotelian and more modern conceptions of the operation of perception. For now, however, it will suffice to notice that the apparent prominence of perception in Aristotle's account of the acquisition of first principles (together, perhaps, with the fact that the term *epagôgê* is commonly translated as "induction") quite understandably invites comparisons (and perhaps confusions) with later empiricist epistemologies, and that this may be what lies behind the tendency among some scholars to interpret Aristotle's position in the chapter as "empiricist." In what follows, I shall argue that some of these interpretations are resistant to meaningful assessment because they are intolerably imprecise about what the term "empiricism" might mean in this ancient epistemological setting, while others fail because they mistake the import of certain key passages both inside and outside *An. Post* II.19.

II

In his final comments on II.19, Barnes remarks in passing that the position Aristotle defends on the question of how first principles are acquired is "whole-heartedly empiricist" (270), presumably referring back to his detailed comments on 99b35–6 and its context. However, it is very difficult to discern in those comments an argument for this conclusion. More importantly, nowhere in his commentary does Barnes offer a formulation of empiricism against which to measure Aristotle's position. He instead seems just to assume that any account on which perceptual experience is made the starting point for the acquisition of knowledge *ipso facto* is an instance of empiricism. But this is not at all obvious. Suppose, as a first approximation, we characterize empiricism by the following familiar thesis.

(P2)   All knowledge (or perhaps all knowledge of a certain type) must arise ultimately out of perceptual experience.

Pretty clearly, as it stands this is too vague to distinguish empiricist from non-empiricist epistemologies. Many different sorts (or grades) of necessity might reasonably be expressed by the modal idiom "must," and many rationalists could comfortably endorse (P2) by construing it as involving suitably weak, yet perfectly natural, conceptions of necessity. In Plato's *Republic*, for example, certain facts about the human condition (most importantly, that the semi-divine proper instrument for knowing the Forms finds itself encased in an imperfect mortal vessel) entail the impossibility of a prospective ruler coming to know the Forms without first considering the difference and relationship between concrete mundane objects on the one hand, and representations of such objects on the other. But I take it that no one would want to classify the epistemology of the *Republic* as "empiricist" on that account.

To capture what is distinctive about empiricism, then, we might want to specify that the necessity involved in (P2) is sufficiently strong to rule out acceptance by clear-cut rationalists such as Plato. If we take our lead from the empiricists of the seventeenth and eighteenth century, we might then plausibly disambiguate (P2) by specifying what might be thought of as a sort of "informational necessity"

(P3)　The *content* of all knowledge (or all knowledge of a certain type) must be given by perceptual experience.

Clearly, a rationalist such as Plato could not embrace this principle if he holds that the content of the knowledge the ruler eventually obtains is originally given in some pre-natal existence, and that sense experience acts merely as a triggering device to reawaken consciousness of what she had already apprehended prior to having any perceptions at all.

But even though it is possible to exclude obvious rationalists like Plato by means of (P3), we risk anachronism if we try to use it to make Aristotle into an empiricist. This is because the modern empiricists plainly understood (P3) in a very special way colored by their concurrent commitment to the following principle,

(P4)　Because the *object* of perception is always a particular, the *content* provided by perception is always particular.

Because of this dual commitment they were understandably troubled by the problem of how it could be possible to "abstract" knowledge of universals out of perceptual experience of particulars. Of course, this is a genuine problem if one has an "ultra-empiricist" theory of perception and knowledge according to which both the object and the *content* of a perceptual experience must be "perfectly particular." But this is precisely the kind of theory that Aristotle does *not* have. To be sure, he reacts vigorously against the Platonist's *separation* of universals from the visible world, but he is every bit as much a realist – *albeit* an immanent realist – as the target of those attacks. Consequently, his metaphysics allows him to analyze perception, as Plato cannot, as acquaintance not just with an individual mundane object, but also with whatever immanent universals are instantiated by that object. This is possible because these universals are for him (as they are not for Plato) actually present at the site of perception. Hence, Aristotle is not the least bit troubled by the so-called "problem of abstraction" which so exercised the modern empiricists because he explicitly rejects (P4). This occurs in a striking passage at 100a18–b2, where he declares

> Even though it is the particular (*to kath' hekaston*) that is perceived (*aisthanetai*), the perception (*hê aisthesis*) is of the universal (*tou katholou*).

My point is that in light of his distinctive theory of perception and the metaphysics on which it rests, it is inappropriate to classify Aristotle according to the later distinction

71

between rationalist and empiricist epistemologies. The most we can say is that Aristotle differs from paradigmatic rationalists like Plato with respect to (P3), but that, because of his denial of (P4), his understanding of (P3) is so much different from that of modern empiricists that grouping him together with them would be grossly misleading.

III

To this point I have been arguing in effect that it is not possible, as Barnes wants to do, to simply read a commitment to empiricism off Aristotle's discussion *within* II.19 of perception and its role in *epagôgê*. I want now to consider a pair of more subtle attempts to classify Aristotle as an empiricist by invoking passages elsewhere in the *Analytics*. The first of these is contained in an extremely influential 1973 article by James Lesher.[2] Lesher begins by arguing, quite plausibly I think, that the appearance that *Posterior Analytics* II.19 advances a "schizoid" epistemology can be dispelled by an appreciation of the fact that the two sections of the chapter are in fact addressed to two very different questions. According to Lesher, the long first section describes the "inductive" *process* by which one apprehends demonstrative first principles, whereas the short closing section is concerned with identifying the *cognitive faculty*, which is in operation during this process. Lesher puts the point as follows.

> The relation between *nous* and *epagôgê* turns out to be a typically Aristotelian one: there is one activity, grasping the universal principle, but it admits of various descriptions; to speak of it as an act of *noesis* is to give an epistemological characterization, while to char-acterize it as *epagôgê* is to speak of methodology. (p. 58)

Again, I do find this a plausible way of reconciling the apparent strain between the two sections of II.19, but it is also important to notice that there is nothing in this that contradicts my conclusion in the preceding section that it would be wrong to classify the activity in question as empiricist. I am, however, now concerned with Lesher's concurrent attempt to make Aristotle into an empiricist by assimilating the "noetic" apprehension of the first principles of demonstration in *epagôgê* with another "noetic" activity which Lesher claims to find evidenced by remarks scattered throughout the whole of the *Posterior Analytics*. According to Lesher, this activity occurs in the context of scientific inquiry, when one constructs a demonstrative syllogism by hitting upon the "universal cause" of some fact to be explained after perceptual exposure to a suffi-cient number of instances in which that fact is present.

Now even though Lesher himself admits that the evidence for assigning this activity to *nous* is skimpy, scattered, and exceedingly indirect, I have no serious objection to entertaining it in the spirit it is offered, as an interesting speculative hypothesis about Aristotle's views concerning the construction of syllogisms in earlier chapters of the *Posterior Analytics*. On the other hand, I do have misgivings when Lesher subsequently turns to the interpretation of II.19 and claims to find the very same sort of syllogism construction activity in evidence in that chapter. In response to the long-standing ques-tion, instigated by an ambiguity in the term *horos*, of whether Aristotle is concerned in this chapter with the apprehension of universal (definitional) *principles* or with the understanding of universal *terms* (or concepts), Lesher argues that *horos* is in fact never used in the *Posterior Analytics* to mean "term" and that Aristotle must therefore be concerned in the chapter with items that are propositional in nature. I am not so much interested here with the correctness of his reasoning as I am with the surprising manner in which he expresses this conclusion.

> Thus "to grasp the universal" . . . in the *Posterior Analytics* is to grasp a universal principle (e.g., to see that all Xes are Yes, *or that X is a Phi because X is a Psi, and all Psis are Phis*). If this is concept formation, it is exemplified not by a man who is learning the meaning of the word "man," but by the scientist who is developing a scientific demonstration of the nature of man by demonstrating certain attributes to inhere essentially, necessarily, and universally in men. (p. 61, emphasis added)

Now I certainly agree that what Aristotle is concerned with here is not merely a person learning the meaning of a word (or understanding a concept), and also that "grasping a universal" throughout the *Posterior Analytics* should generally be understood as apprehending a universal principle (that is, some proposition of the form "All Xs are Ys"). What I cannot understand is why Lesher includes in his parenthetical schematic specification of the grasped items the following *syllogistic* form.

"X is a Phi because X is a Psi, and all Psis are Phi."

Aristotle nowhere refers to full syllogisms as *horoi*, or for that matter, as either *archai* or *amesous*, yet these are the terms he uses to pick out his subject matter in II.19. So far as I can tell, Lesher's grounds for this parenthetical inclusion is nothing more than his own earlier speculation about a certain sort of "noetic" activity described *outside* of II.19, even though he conceded that there was no evidence for identifying that activity with anything discussed in B 19.

I also have doubts about the implication of Lesher's account that the "inductive" process described in the first section of II.19 is something typically practiced by a scientist engaged in the construction of syllogistic demonstrations. If this were so, it would be extremely puzzling that Aristotle never once mentions the construction of syllogisms in the entire chapter. Further, it would be hard to explain why he seems so clearly in earlier passages (e.g., at 88a9–10) to be *postponing* a discussion of the acquisition the first principles if, as Lesher holds, he had been discussing that subject intermittently all along. Finally, Aristotle's description at 99b35–100a9 of a sequence of different sorts of animals with progressively more sophisticated cognitive capacities strongly suggests that the terminus of the series is simply the biological kind *human*, and not some narrower, socially defined subclass of humans who had mastered the theory of the syllogism and could employ it to generate scientific explanations. For this reason, I prefer to interpret *Posterior Analytics* II.19 as locating the *hexis* which apprehends the immediate first principles of demonstration in the cluster of capacities that belong universally and especially to humans *qua* rational beings. Hence, on my view, the chapter is extremely well placed, and should indeed be thought of as something like an appendix to the main treatise. It is not concerned with demonstration proper, but rather with the source of the "pre-existent" cognitive material required to get that justificatory program off the ground. On this understanding, the "inductive" process the chapter describes is one that could be performed (and in fact is performed) not just by the Aristotelian scientist, but by virtually *any* well-developed mature human specimen solely by virtue of having a rational soul, and quite independently of whether it had any inclination or ability for the scientific enterprise. In other words, as *Posterior Analytics* II.19 characterizes the manner in which the definitional first principles of demonstration are initially apprehended, it is simply the process of general concept formation which is available to all humans, and which must already have been accomplished before there can be any question of doing Aristotelian science.

IV

Another somewhat different attempt to find Aristotle broaching the subject of how demonstrative first principles are acquired in the *Posterior Analytics* outside II.19 was first suggested by L. A. Kosman in an article[3] that appeared in the same year as Lesher's (1973), and to some extent is adopted, modified, and supported in a recent book by Richard McKirahan.[4] The final note to Kosman's paper suggests that his account in turn develops and extends some suggestions in a group of enormously influential papers published or informally circulated by Myles Burnyeat in the early 1970s. In these papers Burnyeat offered an interpretation of the final section of the *Theaetetus* according to which Plato is there exploring (if not quite endorsing) the idea that possession of the highest possible form of knowledge of some object or proposition requires that one not only have an isolated linear justification of that item, but that one also sees the item in question as but one element among many in a wide and systematically organized field of study. To take a well-known example employed by Plato in the *Meno* (85c–d), the idea is that possessing a single proof of a single geometrical theorem is not sufficient to ground the claim that one knows that theorem. For that one would also need to have mastered the wider field of geometry and appreciate the place of that theorem in that systematically interrelated field of axioms, postulates, definitions and other theorems. This view is often referred to as the "interrelatedness" model of epistemic justification.

Then, in a paper published in 1981[5] (but circulated much earlier) Burnyeat turned his attention to Aristotle and made a persuasive case for the presence of the "interrelatedness" model in the *Posterior Analytics*. On this interpretation, Aristotle is not willing to characterize a proposition as an object of *epistêmê haplôs* (a term Burnyeat plausibly translates as "understanding") simply because one possesses an isolated syllogistic demonstration of it. Rather, on this view, each demonstrative science is properly concerned with a certain genus (for example, arithmetic with numbers, geometry with figures, etc.), and to *understand* a given demonstrated proposition requires a grasp of all or most of the principles pertinent to that science as well as an appreciation of how those principles combine to provide demonstrations of a sufficiently wide range of other propositions within the subject-genus.

This work of Burnyeat's has had enormous influence on subsequent interpretations of both Plato and Aristotle. What is novel and distinctive, and ultimately questionable, in Kosman's approach, however, is that he attempts to extend Burnyeat's point that a *theorem* of demonstration can be epistemically "upgraded" by recognition of its inter-relatedness to other elements within its proper scientific field by arguing that the same point applies to the demonstrative *principles* themselves. Italicizing the word "under-standing" to mark his affinity with Burnyeat, Kosman represents the position this way.

> *Understanding* [first principles], the noetic grasp we have of them as principles, concerns our ability to use them in explaining and making intelligible the world of phenomena. *Nous* therefore is a feature of our understanding of all explanatory principles or premises . . . just insofar as we understand them *qua* principles and not *qua explicanda.* (p. 389)

Evidently the idea here is that the epistemic warrant for a demonstrative principle is partly derived from the recognition that it functions successfully *as a principle* within some systematic demonstrative scientific field (or genus). This is an idea found in con-temporary discussions within the philosophy of science, for Kosman's language puts one in mind of familiar "explanatory scope" or "explanatory power" adequacy condi-tions on scientific theories and hypotheses. And since, on Kosman's account, this sort of understanding is developed in the more or less "empirical" activity of attempting to use the principle in question (in conjunction with others) to construct demonstrations of various observed facts, it is possible to think of the procedure as in keeping with the general spirit of empiricism. Hence, by suggesting that evidence for this procedure is to be found in II.19, Kosman is in effect claiming to find in that chapter a more subtle and sophisticated form of empiricism than those examined earlier. But is there any textual basis for locating this more subtle form of empiricism in II.19 or anywhere else in the *Analytics?*

I shall eventually want to look closely at the textual arguments Kosman employs to support this interpretation. But first I want to examine the view he ascribes to Aristotle from a purely philosophical perspective. Putting historical questions aside for a moment, those familiar with recent trends in contemporary epistemology will recognize in Kosman's interpretation an intriguing (if not, in the end, fully intelligible) thesis associ-ated with so-called coherence theories of epistemic justification. On Kosman's account, Aristotle seemingly would allow the possibility of *unending* justificatory sequences, wherein some principle is justified because it entails certain facts, which in turn are justified because they are entailed by certain principles, which are in turn justified because they explain certain facts, and so on. In the event that the elements in the justificatory system are finite in number, the interminability of such a sequence entails that some elements appear more than once, which is the familiar hallmark of coherence theories.

But for precisely this reason it is extremely unlikely that Aristotle could endorse such a view. For he takes pains in *Posterior Analytics* I.3 to argue *against* the possibility of unending justificatory sequences by first ruling out the possibility of such sequences involving an infinite number of elements, and then attacking the finite case by arguing in effect that small circular justifications are not legitimate, and that simply adding more elements to them cannot rectify the situation. For this reason, I believe Aristotle would have deep philosophical reasons, stemming from his general epistemology, for rejecting the position Kosman attributes to him.

Let us now look more carefully at the arguments Kosman employs to support this questionable attribution. Again, one undeniable fact about II.19 is that it contains no *explicit* discussion of the use of principles in syllogistic demonstration. So, rather than providing direct evidence from II.19 itself for his interpretation, Kosman, like Lesher, is compelled to rely instead on other passages elsewhere in the *Analytics*. He points to a number of passages (e.g., *Prior Analytics* II.22 67a13–21, *Posterior Analytics* I.1 71a21–9, 2 71b9–12) where Aristotle seems in one way or another to express the view that the possession of a genuine demonstration of a given explicandum requires that the subject know not merely that the appropriate explanatory principles are true, but also that they entail the explicandum in question. Here we have yet another idea echoed in contemporary philosophical literature, this time in the form of the epistemological principle that having a justification for a given belief requires that one not merely have other beliefs which in fact imply it, but also know that these implications obtain.

I believe that Kosman correctly understands the immediate point of the passages on which he relies, but that he distorts their import when he attempts to press them into the service of his own interpretation. We may concede that these passages express something like the following.

(P5) To conduct a successful demonstration of F from $P_1 \ldots P_n$, one must know that F is derivable from $P_1 \ldots P_n$.

Notice however, that Kosman paraphrases Aristotle's remarks in these passages as meaning that successful demonstration requires not merely that the subject know that the pertinent principles are true, but also that they "in fact *are* principles" (p. 387), which is to say that he takes (P5) as equivalent to

(P6) To conduct a successful demonstration of F from $P_1 \ldots P_n$, one must know that $P_1 \ldots P_n$ are principles (of F, etc.).

Moreover, on Kosman's way of understanding this, it is in turn equivalent to saying that to have a demonstration, it is not enough for one merely to know the principles; one must "come to know (or understand) them *qua* principles" (p. 387),[6] or in other words knowing that they are the principles of some specific set of explicanda:

(P7) To conduct a successful demonstration of F from $P_1 \ldots P_n$, one must know (or understand) $P_1 \ldots P_n$ *qua* principles (of F, etc.).

But now, since the phrase "coming to know a principle *qua* principle" is very naturally construed as describing a distinctive sort of cognitive apprehension of the principle in question, and the general topic of II.19 is unquestionably some sort of apprehension of demonstrative principles, Kosman believes himself justified in conjecturing that the topic of II.19 is nothing other than the "empirical" process, described in (P5), of discovering that the principles in question do actually explain some body of facts.

Even before we examine the details of this allegedly seamless progression from (P5)–(P7), we should have some textual grounds for wondering about it. For many of the contexts from which Kosman extracts the passages expressing (P5) plainly concern conditions Aristotle places upon knowledge *simpliciter*, yet Aristotle is quite clear throughout the treatise that the only items that can be known in this manner are the theorems, or *products*, of demonstration (see, for example, 73a20–9). Hence, it is somewhat suspicious, to say the least, that Kosman should cite passages from these contexts to support an interpretation of Aristotle's views about how one comes to gain knowledge of the *principles* of demonstration.

Indeed, a closer look at Kosman's language in (P5)–(P7) reinforces this suspicion. For expressions such as

"S knows that P is a principle."

and

"S knows P *qua* principle."

are in a very obvious way ambiguous, and I believe Kosman's attempt to link the passages expressing (P5) to II.19 via (P6) and (P7) trades on this ambiguity. Evidently, Kosman himself wants always to understand these expressions in a way that makes the parentheses in (P6) and (P7) indispensable, so that what is said to be known in both formulations is that the principles in question bear a certain appropriate *relationship* (presumably syllogistic implication) to a certain set of explicanda. This "relational" interpretation of (P6) and (P7) comes across more or less clearly when Kosman represents Aristotle as holding

> Understanding . . . principles as *principles* is just . . . seeing them in their capacity *to explain*. (388, emphasis his)

and it is even more explicit in the following parallel passage in McKirahan.

> Finally comes the stage where we know principles (100a8). [We should] keep in mind that "principle" is a relative term: a principle is a principle of *something*. To grasp something as a principle is to understand how the things of which it is a principle depend on it. (pp. 243–4, emphasis his.)

Moreover, Kosman must think this is the *only* possible Aristotelian manner of construing what it is to know of principles *qua* principles when he assumes without argument that the function of *nous* in Aristotle's theory must either be

(i)   to grasp that the principles *are true* (or "exist"). (p. 383, emphasis his.)

or

(ii) to grasp that the principles *are principles*, that is, [to] know them *as* the principles for a given body of phenomena and/or *how* they are the principles, that is, how it is that the phenomena are explained by them. (p. 383, emphasis his.)

77

and then proceeds to argue from the obvious untenability of (i) to the correctness of (ii) as if these were the only two possibilities.

If (i) and (ii) were in fact the only way to understand the relevant expressions in (P6) and (P7), I suppose the connections between those principles and (P5) would be unobjectionable, and it might then seem plausible to carry this "relational" construal of knowledge of principles right through into II.19, as Kosman wants to do. However, in my view, his strategy founders because not only is there is another, "non-relational" way of understanding these expressions, but it is one that seems much more in keeping with Aristotle's usual way of thinking about this issue.

Aristotle would certainly agree with McKirahan's remark that "principle" is a relative term in the *minimal* sense that to call something a principle is to imply that there are things of which it is a principle. However, he certainly would *not* agree that it is a relative term in the *stronger* sense there are no objective and context-independent features that make some things acceptable as principles and other things not. For Aristotle's theory of demonstration is first and last a theory of *objective* explanation. One of its central features is that the order of demonstration must always be from facts or things which are further removed from perception but more intelligible "in themselves" (or "by nature") to those that are closer to perception (and so more familiar) but less intelligible "in themselves." (71b34–72a6). Thus, it is an indispensable part of his theory that the *ultimate* principles of demonstration must be those items that are the *most* intelligible in themselves. Moreover, Aristotle evidently believes that this "absolute" intelligibility is grounded on certain non-relational features of the principles themselves that are not dependent in any way on how (or even whether) they are actually deployed in scientific demonstrations. But if this is so, it seems to open for Aristotle the possibility that one could come to "know that the principles are principles," or come to "know them *qua* principles" simply by grasping their "absolute intelligibility" without ever having actually used them to explain anything at all. If, however, this "non-relational" way of understanding these expressions is indeed Aristotelian, then Kosman's argument that his preferred "relational" understanding must apply by default to the apprehension of principles discussed in II.19 misses its mark.

But, it may be asked, is there any textual basis for such a "non-relational" understanding of what it is to be a principle? I believe that a number of "non-relational" features of demonstrative principles on which their "intelligibility by nature" depends are introduced at 71b20–22 in *Posterior Analytics* I.2.

> Now if knowing is as we posited, demonstrative knowledge must come from premises which are (1) true (*alethon*), (2) primary (*proton*), (3) immediate (*ameson*), (4) better known than (*gnorimoteron*), (5) prior to (*proteron*), and (6) causative of (*aition*) the conclusion.

Oddly enough, McKirahan, who is apparently impressed by Aristotle's use of comparatives to formulate conditions (4) and (5), paraphrases this very same passage in a way that seems to reinforces Kosman's "relational" understanding of what it means to know a principle:

> to grasp something as a principle is to grasp it *as* true, immediate, primary, and prior to, grounds of, and more naturally intelligible than the connections for which it is a principle. (p. 243, emphasis his.)

I believe that McKirahan mistakes both the general topic and the specific import of this passage. To begin with, Aristotle is not here talking about what is involved in *grasping* principles, as McKirahan's paraphrase makes it seem, but simply about what conditions a proposition must satisfy in order to *be* a principle. Furthermore, it seems to me that each of these conditions is ultimately non-relational. With respect to the first three listed conditions, which are not even expressed by comparatives, it should be immediately obvious that one could detect their presence in a given principle without having an inkling of how the principle might subsequently be deployed in demonstrations. I can, for example, surely know that the proposition that all squares are rectangles is both true and immediate, and therefore primary, without a thought about what use, demonstrative or otherwise, I might want to put it to later on. And even though the fourth and fifth conditions listed at 71b20–2 are given by comparatives, and the sixth condition (that the principle must be "causative of" (*aition*) the conclusion) might plausibly be regarded as comparative in spirit, I believe that Aristotle is here really just describing a *single* condition – which I take to be absolute "intelligibility in nature," and that he uses comparatives here simply to match his usual, comparative way of making the distinction in terms of "intelligibility to us" and "intelligibility in nature." If I'm right about this, Aristotle does have a notion of "absolute intelligibility in nature," and sees no difficulty about the possibility of someone discerning this feature in a principle prior to, and independent of, any employment of that principle in demonstrations. My principal contention is that such discernment of "absolute intelligibility" is the subject of II.19. But even if I'm not right about whether this is the subject of II.19, my point against McKirahan, that the grasp of ultimate principles is *not* the subject of I.2, would still stand.

I would now like to close with a pair of disclaimers. To begin with, I should acknowledge that most or all of the accounts I have been criticizing are motivated largely by the desire to counteract an earlier tendency to interpret II.19 as congenial to rationalist epistemology, where that is understood as the tendency to postulate an intellectual faculty of "intuition" or "mental vision," which somehow generates flashes of "insight" concurrently with, but independently of, the operations of the perceptual faculties. My arguments here should not be taken as an endorsement of that misguided view. In resisting various recent attempts to characterize Aristotle as an empiricist, I certainly don't mean to make him out as a rationalist – or at least a rationalist of *that* sort. Rather, I have in effect been arguing that Aristotle's position in II.19 resists classification according to the crude dichotomy between rationalism and empiricism.

Finally, it may be objected that in rejecting Lesher's and Kosman's interpretations of II.19, I have offered no positive account in their place of how *nous* functions in the acquisition of principles. For whatever else may be said about these "empiricist" interpretations, it can't be denied that they tell an elegant and readily understandable (and even currently respectable) story of how someone might reasonably think about knowledge of ultimate explanatory principles. Hence, the complaint will go, the exclusively critical arguments given here, if successful, accomplish little more than to return this perplexing Aristotelian doctrine to its previous mysterious status.

Here I am afraid I can do no more than sympathize with the complaint, and raise the possibility that this situation may not be due to a failure of philosophical imagination on my part. Rather, it may be because Aristotle simply had no positive account of the operations of *nous* at hand when the *Posterior Analytics* was composed. In other words, it is quite possible that at that point in his thinking, he was convinced – perhaps by his own argument in II.19 – that humans, *qua* rational, must possess a very special cognitive faculty which allows for the grasp of the ultimate explanatory principles, but had not the slightest idea of what exactly this faculty is, or how it could perform this function.

Notes

[1] J. Barnes (1994).
[2] J. Lesher (1973).
[3] L. A. Kosman (1973).
[4] R. McKirahan (1992).
[5] M. Burnyeat (1981).
[6] Cf. McKirahan (1992).

Bibliography

Barnes, J. (1994). *Aristotle: "Posterior Analytics,"* 2nd edn. (Oxford: Clarendon Press).

Burnyeat, M. (1981). "Aristotle on Understanding Knowledge," in E. Berti (ed.), *Aristotle on Science: The "Posterior Analytics,"* Proceedings of the Eighth Symposium Aristotelicum (Padua and New York: Editrice Antenore), pp. 97–139.

Kosman, L. A. (1973). "Understanding, Explanation, and Insight in Aristotle's *Posterior Analytics,"* in E. Lee, A. Mourelatos, and R. Rorty (eds.), *Exegesis and Argument* (Assen: Van Gorcum), pp. 374–92.

Lesher, J. (1973). "The Meaning of NOUS in the *Posterior Analytics,"* Phronesis, 18, pp. 44–68.

McKirahan, R. (1992). *Principles and Proofs: Aristotle's Theory of Demonstrative Science* (Princeton, NJ: Princeton University Press).

6

Aristotle on Signification and Truth

PAOLO CRIVELLI

Aristotle discusses signification and truth in passages from several works, mainly the *Categories*, *de Interpretatione*, *Sophistici Elenchi*, *de Anima*, the *Metaphysics*, and the *Poetics*. Signification and truth are not the main topic of these works: their discussions of these subjects are asides. This study reconstructs some views on signification and truth to which Aristotle can be plausibly taken to be committed by his scattered remarks.

Signification

Universals To expound Aristotle's ideas on signification and truth, I must present some of his views on universals. Luckily, it is not necessary to embark on the daunting task of a complete exposition of Aristotle's views on universals.

Aristotle is to this extent a realist about universals: in his view, universals are objects whose nature is neither mental nor linguistic (they are neither concepts nor linguistic expressions). He believes that every universal exists just when it is instantiated by some individual or other that at some time or other exists.

Let me now make three remarks about terminology. First, I often refer to a universal by writing "the universal" followed by an inscription which is an italicized version of those which in other contexts normally introduce that universal: for example, I sometimes refer to a certain universal by writing "the universal *man*." Second, I use "just when" in a temporal sense, i.e. as equivalent to "at all and only the times at which." Third, one might wonder why the words "at some time or other" occur in the last paragraph's last sentence. For Aristotle, some universals are sometimes instantiated by individuals that do not exist then, but exist at other times. For example, Aristotle seems to think that at any time the universal *poet* is instantiated by all and only those individuals (including those which at that time do not exist) which by that time have authored some poem. In particular, Aristotle would probably grant that although Homer does not exist now, he instantiates now the universal *poet*. It is because of universals of this sort that the words "at some time or other" are used.

Some claims about signification Near the beginning of *de Interpretatione* 1 16a3–8 Aristotle makes seven claims:

1   Uttered nouns, verbs, phrases, and sentences are tokens of affections of the soul.
2   Written nouns, verbs, phrases, and sentences are tokens of uttered nouns, verbs, phrases, and sentences.
3   Inscriptions are not the same for all people.
4   Utterances are not the same for all people.
5   Affections of the soul which are likenesses of objects are the first items of which utterances are signs.
6   Affections of the soul are the same for all people.
7   Objects are the same for all people.

Claim (5) probably commits Aristotle to a further claim:

8   Objects of which affections of the soul are likenesses are the second items of which utterances are signs.

These claims introduce three relations (being-a-token-of, being-a-likeness-of, and being-a-sign-of) obtaining between items of six kinds (uttered nouns, verbs, phrases, and sentences, affections of the soul, written nouns, verbs, phrases, and sentences, inscriptions, utterances, and objects). The next subsection discusses the items involved, while the relations obtaining between them are examined in later subsections.

The items in Aristotle's analysis   The uttered nouns, verbs, phrases, and sentences mentioned in (1) and (2) are individual events of speech occurring over short portions of time. They are identical with the utterances mentioned in (4), (5), and (8) ("utterances" is a stylistic variant of "uttered nouns, verbs, phrases, and sentences"). Uttered nouns include, at least, uttered proper names (for example, certain utterances of "Socrates"), uttered substantive nouns (for example, certain utterances of "horse"), uttered adjectives (for example, certain utterances of "white"), and uttered participles (for example, certain utterances of "running"). I say "certain utterences of . . ." because utterances produced by parrots are not uttered nouns.

The affections of the soul mentioned in (1), (5), (6), and (8) are thoughts, i.e. individual events of thinking. Numerically distinct thinkers have numerically distinct thoughts: for example, every thought of Jim's is numerically distinct from every thought of Tim's.

The written nouns, verbs, phrases, and sentences mentioned in (2) are individual marks on some medium (for example, wax or paper). They are identical with the inscriptions mentioned in (3) ("inscriptions" is a stylistic variant of "written nouns, verbs, phrases, and sentences").

The objects mentioned in (5), (7), and (8) can be anything: individuals, universals, or states of affairs. (For states of affairs, read on.)

Being-a-token-of   In *Sophistici Elenchi* 1, Aristotle says: "It is not possible to converse by bringing in the objects themselves, but instead of the objects we use words as tokens" (165a6–8). Thus, for Aristotle, in certain cases, if certain items (for example, objects) cannot be used in a certain way (for example, brought in) to achieve a certain effect (for example, conversing), and if other items (for example, words) can be used in a certain way so as to achieve that effect, then the second items are tokens of the first ones. I assume that when in *de Interpretatione* 1 he speaks of tokens, Aristotle has in mind, among other things, such a use of them.

Suppose that inside my pocket there is a triangular button, and I want to inform you that inside my pocket there is a button of that sort. One way for me to achieve my aim is to get you to look at that button. Now suppose that I had a thought of a certain sort (for example, I judged that Socrates is seated), and I want to inform you that I had a thought of that sort. Since I could not get you to look at that thought (because thoughts cannot be looked at), I must proceed differently. If we are within hearing range, I can produce an appropriate utterance (for example, one of "Socrates is seated") and cause you to hear it. In most cases, your hearing my utterance will bring about my aim, i.e. informing you that I had a thought of the given sort.

Situations of this kind are part of what Aristotle has in mind when he says that uttered nouns, verbs, phrases, and sentences are tokens of affections of the soul. If an uttered linguistic expression *u* is a token of a thought *t*, then *t* was a thought of the speaker and the speaker produced *u* with the purpose of getting an audience to hear *u* and thereby bringing about the same effect that he or she would have brought about by getting the audience to look at *t* (the effect the speaker desires is to inform the audience that he or she had a thought of the sort which is in fact that of *t*).

If we are beyond hearing range, I cannot achieve my aim of informing you that I had a thought of a certain sort by causing you to hear my utterances. However, if I find a messenger, I can resort to different means: I can produce a suitable inscription and cause you to read it. In most cases, your reading my inscription will bring about my aim, i.e. informing you that I had a thought of a certain sort.

Situations of this kind are part of what Aristotle has in mind when he says that written nouns, verbs, phrases, and sentences are tokens of uttered nouns, verbs, phrases, and sentences. If a written linguistic expression *w* is a token of an uttered linguistic expression *u*, then *u* was produced by the writer and the writer produced *w* with the purpose of getting someone to read *w* and thereby bringing about the same effect that he or she would have brought about by getting the reader to hear *u* (the effect the writer desires is to inform the reader that he or she had a thought of a certain sort).

Tokens depend on convention   The relation of being-a-token-of depends on convention. In the case of uttered linguistic expressions which are tokens of thoughts, this dependence on convention is revealed by utterances of different languages. Suppose that Bernard had a thought of a certain sort (for example, one of the universal *man*), and wants to inform Peter and Pierre that he had a thought of this sort. Since he could not get them to look at his thought, he achieves his aim by producing an appropriate uttered expression in English (for example, an utterance of "man") and causing Peter to hear it, and by producing an appropriate uttered expression in French (for example, an utterance of "homme") and causing Pierre to hear it. The uttered linguistic expressions produced by Bernard for Peter and Pierre are of different kinds, but are tokens of the same thought. Hence it is not the case that uttered linguistic expressions which are tokens of the same thought are of the same kind for all people.

Similarly, in the case of written linguistic expressions which are tokens of uttered linguistic expressions, the fact that the relation of being-a-token-of depends on convention is revealed by inscriptions of different systems of writing. Suppose that Bernard produced a certain uttered linguistic expression (for example, an utterance of "man"). Bernard wants to inform Peter and Frank that he had a thought of a certain sort. Since he could not get them to hear his utterance, he achieves his aim by producing an appropriate Roman alphabet inscription and causing Peter to read it, and by producing an appropriate Morse code inscription and causing Frank to read it. The written linguistic expressions produced by Bernard for Peter and Frank are of different kinds, but are tokens of the same uttered linguistic expression. Hence it is not the case that written linguistic expressions which are tokens of the same uttered linguistic expression are of the same kind for all people.

Being-a-likeness-of   What is Aristotle committing himself to when he claims that thoughts are likenesses of objects? Since immediately after making this claim he says that "these matters are discussed in the treatises on the soul" (16a8–9), we should look there. In *de Anima* II.5 (418a4–5) Aristotle says that when the faculty of perception is not similar to an object, it is affected by it, and once it has been affected by the object it has been likened to it. In *de Anima* II.4 (429a10–11, 429a13–16, and 429a23) he says that thinking is like perceiving, that thinking is something like being affected by what is being thought of, and that the intellect, which is the part of the soul whereby the soul thinks, is able to receive the form of what is being thought of and is potentially like it. I cannot discuss here Aristotle's views on the relationship of thought to its objects, and, in particular, I cannot address the vexed question of how the intellect receives the form of an object which is being thought of. I merely draw three plausible consequences of Aristotle's views. The first is that thoughts can be described as "affections of the soul" and "likenesses of objects." The second is that a thought is of an object just if it is a likeness of it. The third consequence is that to be a likeness of an object is to be the result of a process of likening of which that object is a cause (note that for Aristotle any item that can be appropriately mentioned in explaining why a process began is a cause of that process, and such an item can be a universal). Hence all thoughts which are likenesses of the same object or objects are results of processes of likening caused by the same object or objects, and therefore are of the same kind (because for Aristotle membership of a kind is fixed by causal history). Hence thoughts which are likenesses of the same object or objects are of the same kind for all people. In Aristotle's view this fact shows that the relation of a thought to the object or objects it is a likeness of is (not conventional, but) natural.

Being-a-sign-of   There are two main differences between the relations of being-a-token-of and being-a-sign-of. First, the two relations embody different perspectives on the same items, i.e. uttered nouns, verbs, phrases, and sentences: the relation of being-a-token-of embodies the speaker's perspective (for the speaker views the utterances as tokens of thoughts he or she could not get the audience to look at), whereas the relation of being-a-sign-of embodies the audience's perspective (for the audience view the utterances as signs of something). Second, while the relation of being-a-token-of relies by its very nature on convention, that of being-a-sign-of does not: some signs are conventional signs, others are natural signs (for example, some screams produced by beasts are not conventional, but natural signs of their pain).

Before Aristotle a debate raged between some thinkers who held that human language is significant by nature and others who maintained that it is significant by convention, a debate staged in Plato's *Cratylus*. Aristotle sides with the conventionalists: At *de Interpretatione* 2 16a19–20 and 4 17a1–2 he claims that uttered nouns, verbs, phrases, and sentences are significant by convention.

Utterances are conventional signs both of thoughts and of objects   Aristotle claims that affections of the soul which are likenesses of objects are the first items of which utterances are signs, and he thereby probably commits himself to the further claim that objects of which affections of the soul are likenesses are the second items of which utterances are signs. Aristotle therefore probably commits himself to distinguishing two ways in which uttered nouns, verbs, phrases, and sentences are conventional signs: uttered nouns, verbs, phrases, and sentences are both conventional signs of thoughts and conventional signs of objects.

Conventional signs of thoughts   Aristotle never defines what it is for uttered linguistic expressions to be conventional signs of thoughts. He would probably grant the following characterization: an uttered linguistic expression is a conventional sign of a thought just if it is a token of it.

Here are some examples: an utterance of "Socrates" is a conventional sign of a thought of Socrates just if it is a token of it, an utterance of "man" is a conventional sign of a thought of the universal *man* just if it is a token of that thought, and an utterance of "Socrates is seated" is a conventional sign of a judgment that Socrates is seated just if it is a token of it.

A question about conventional signs of thoughts   If an uttered linguistic expression is a conventional sign of a thought, what use do the audience make of that uttered linguistic expression when they interpret it as a conventional sign of thoughts? Since Aristotle never addresses this question, I offer the answer that seems most plausible within the context of his views.

Thoughts are individual mental events. Let us then look at how we use signs of individual non-mental events. If a geological phenomenon g is a sign of a particular earthquake e (which, let us suppose, occurred before humankind existed), and if geologists accurately interpret g as a sign of earthquakes, then they infer that some earthquake of a certain sort occurred in a certain place at a certain time, and e really was of this sort. Analogously, if an uttered linguistic expression u is a conventional sign of a thought t, and if the audience accurately interpret u as a conventional sign of thoughts, then they infer that some thought of a certain sort occurred in the speaker shortly before u was produced, and t really was of this sort.

Conventional signs of objects   Aristotle never defines what it is for uttered linguistic expressions to be conventional signs of objects. However, he is probably committed to two claims: that thoughts which are likenesses of objects are the first items of which uttered nouns, verbs, phrases, and sentences are conventional signs, and that the objects of which thoughts are likenesses are the second items of which uttered nouns, verbs, phrases, and sentences are conventional signs. Why does Aristotle hold that in

85

a situation where a certain thought is a likeness of a certain object, the thought and the object are, respectively, the first and the second item of which an uttered noun, verb, phrase, or sentence is a conventional sign? I guess that it is because he endorses the following account of what it is for uttered linguistic expressions to be conventional signs of objects: an uttered linguistic expression is a conventional sign of an object just if it is a token of some thought which was a likeness of that object. The position I am attributing to Aristotle resembles some which several commentators from Antiquity onwards (for example, Boethius and Ammonius) have attributed to him. Let it however be emphasized that this attribution is a guess that goes beyond the available evidence: Aristotle's words are compatible with other, quite different accounts of what it is for uttered linguistic expressions to be conventional signs of objects (indeed, they are compatible even with the absence of any such account).

Here are some examples: an utterance of "Socrates" is a conventional sign of Socrates just if it is a token of some thought which was a likeness of Socrates; an utterance of "man" is a conventional sign of the universal *man* just if it is a token of some thought which was a likeness of the universal *man*; an utterance of "Socrates is seated" is a conventional sign of the state of affairs that Socrates is seated just if it is a token of some thought which was a likeness of this state of affairs; an utterance of "Socrates and Coriscus" is a conventional sign of Socrates and Coriscus just if it is a token of some thought which was a likeness of Socrates and Coriscus (because every uttered linguistic expression is a token of at most one thought); and an utterance of "walking white man" is a conventional sign of the universal *man*, the universal *walking*, and the universal *white* just if it is a token of some thought which was a likeness of these three universals.

Our results so far enable us to offer the following sketchy summary of Aristotle's conception of conventional signification of objects: an uttered linguistic expression is a conventional sign of the object or objects which the speaker had in mind in producing it. Therefore conventional signification of objects, as Aristotle conceives of it, is close to what modern philosophers call "speaker's meaning."

A question about conventional signs of objects   If an uttered linguistic expression is a conventional sign of an object, what use do the audience make of that uttered linguistic expression when they interpret it as a conventional sign of objects? Aristotle never addresses this question. However, in *de Interpretatione* 3 he says of an uttered linguistic expression of a certain sort that it "signifies something, for the speaker arrests his thought and the hearer pauses" (16b19–21). He probably means that the thought of the speaker, of which the uttered linguistic expression is a token, and the thought of the hearer, which is prompted by the hearer's interpreting the uttered linguistic expression as a conventional sign, both "come to a stop" by focusing on the same object or objects. Therefore, Aristotle's view is probably that, if the audience hear an uttered linguistic expression and interpret it as a conventional sign of objects, then they are likely to come to think of any object which the speaker's thought, of which that uttered linguistic expression is a token, was of. I now offer a plausible answer to the above question that incorporates this position.

Suppose that an uttered linguistic expression u is a conventional sign of an object o. Then u is a token of some thought t which was a likeness of o. Therefore u is a conventional sign of *t* and *t* is of *o*. Suppose also that the audience accurately interpret *u* as a conventional sign of thoughts: then they infer that some thought of a certain sort occurred in the speaker shortly before *u* was produced, and *t* really was of this sort (cf. the penultimate subsection). At this stage, if the audience believe about any object (or objects) that every thought of the sort in question is of it and only of it (or of all of them and only of them), then they are likely to come to think of that object (or of all those objects). Finally, suppose that the audience correctly believe about some object (or objects) that every thought of the sort in question is of it and only of it (or of all of them and only of them). Then the audience are likely to come to think of that object (or of all those objects), and every thought of the sort in question is of that object and only of it (or of all of those objects and only of them). Since *t* is a thought of the sort in question, and since *t* is of *o*, it follows that *o* is that object (or one of those objects). Therefore the audience are likely to come to think of *o*.

A question about conventional signs of thoughts and objects   Why should one assume that some uttered linguistic expressions are conventional signs not only of objects, but also of thoughts? As before, I offer the answer that seems most plausible within the context of the position I am attributing to Aristotle.

The most straightforward explanation of the difference between uttered linguistic expressions that constitute speech acts of different sorts appeals to the use the audience make of uttered linguistic expressions when they interpret them as conventional signs of thoughts. For example, consider utterances of "Socrates is seated" and "Is Socrates seated?" The first utterance is a token, and therefore a conventional sign, of a judgment of its speaker to the effect that Socrates is seated (this judgment is an individual mental event). If they are accurate when they interpret the utterance as a conventional sign of thoughts, the audience infer that some judgment of this sort occurred in the speaker. The second utterance is a token, and therefore a conventional sign, of a desire of its speaker to know whether Socrates is seated (this desire is an individual mental event). If they are accurate when they interpret the utterance as a conventional sign of thoughts, the audience infer that some desire of this sort occurred in the speaker.

One might however insist that at least with regard to those uttered linguistic expressions that constitute the most basic conventional signs, i.e. uttered proper names, Aristotle is wrong: "In baptisms we name individuals, not thoughts of individuals! Therefore, uttered proper names are conventional signs of individuals directly, not by being tokens of thoughts of individuals; and when we interpret uttered proper names as conventional signs of objects, we come to think of individuals directly, without passing through thoughts of which they are tokens."

Is the objector right? It is true that in baptisms we name individuals, not thoughts of individuals. But the conclusions the objector infers with regard to what uttered proper names are conventional signs of and how we interpret them do not follow. In fact, these conclusions are false. Consider an utterance of "Zeno was brave" produced by Jim and an utterance of "Zeno was brave" produced by Tim. The utterance of "Zeno" within Jim's utterance is a conventional sign of Zeno of Citium because it is a token of a particular thought of Jim's which was of Zeno of Citium. Moreover, when I interpreted this utterance of "Zeno," I came to think of Zeno of Citium because I inferred that Jim had a thought which was of him (Jim and I had just been speaking about the moral traits of Stoic philosophers). On the other hand, the utterance of "Zeno" within Tim's utterance is a conventional sign of Zeno of Elea because it is a token of a particular thought of Tim's which was of Zeno of Elea. Moreover, when I interpreted this utterance of "Zeno," I came to think of Zeno of Elea because I inferred that Tim had a thought which was of him (Tim and I had just been speaking about the Eleatics).

Uttered nouns, verbs, and phrases   Aristotle maintains that all conventionally significant utterances are articulate, i.e. composed of elementary utterances of certain sorts. He is however committed to denying the converse, i.e. to claiming that some articulate significant utterances (for example, some produced by certain birds) are significant not by convention, but by nature. He observes that while some conventionally significant articulate utterances have parts which also are conventionally significant on their own, others have no such parts. For example, in certain circumstances an utterance of "Socrates is seated" is conventionally significant and has among its parts an utterance of "Socrates," which is conventionally significant on its own but has no part that is conventionally significant on its own (even the part of it that is an utterance of "rat" is not conventionally significant on its own). Every uttered phrase or sentence is a conventionally significant articulate utterance some part of which is conventionally significant on its own; every uttered noun or verb is a conventionally significant articulate utterance no part of which is conventionally significant on its own.

Every uttered compound noun (like some utterances of "blueberry" and "goatstag") is an uttered noun, and therefore has no part that is conventionally significant on its own. Some part of an uttered compound noun does conventionally signify something, but not on its own: for example, the utterances of "blue" and "berry" which are parts of a certain utterance of "blueberry" do conventionally signify something, but not on their own, and the utterances of "goat" and "stag" which are parts of a certain utterance of "goatstag" conventionally signify something, but not on their own. An analogy may help: if Jim and Tim are dragging a boat on the beach in a joint effort, then Jim and Tim are dragging the boat, but neither of them is doing it on his own. The situation of certain parts of uttered compound nouns with respect to conventional signification resembles the situation of Jim and Tim with respect to dragging the boat. The fact that Jim and Tim contribute to dragging the boat enables each of them to be described as dragging the boat, but not on his own; so the fact that the utterances of "blue" and "berry" which are parts of a certain utterance of "blueberry" contribute to its overall conventional signification enables each of them to be described as conventionally signifying the universal *blueberry*, but not on its own; and the fact that the utterances of "goat" and "stag" which are parts of a certain utterance of "goatstag" contribute to its overall conventional signification enables each of them to be described as conventionally signifying both the universal *goat* and the universal *stag*, but not on its own. On the other hand, the utterance of "blueb" which is a part of a certain utterance of "blueberry" does not conventionally signify anything, neither on its own nor not on its own. Its status is similar to that of the mereological sum of Jim and the left arm of Tim: although Jim and Tim contribute to dragging the boat, the mereological sum of Jim and the left arm of Tim does not.

Is an utterance consisting of an utterance of "is" followed by an uttered noun or noun-like phrase (like some utterances of "is seated" or "is a white horse") an uttered verb? Aristotle does not say. Perhaps he thinks that every such utterance is not an uttered verb, but an uttered verb-like phrase some part of which is conventionally significant on its own (for example, in certain circumstances an utterance of "is seated" is a conventionally significant verb-like phrase and has among its parts an utterance of "seated" which is conventionally significant on its own).

Some abbreviations   Henceforth, whenever conventional signs of objects are in question, I use expressions from the family of "to signify" and "signification" (without adding "conventionally" or "conventional"), whereas whenever conventional signs of thoughts are in question, I resort to expressions constructed around the word "token." Moreover I omit writing "uttered": I write "noun" for "uttered noun," "verb" for "uttered verb," and similarly with "phrase," "sentence," "preposition," "conjunction," and "quantifying expression" (Aristotle himself often omits "uttered" in his own formulations).

Uttered linguistic expressions signifying one or more objects   Aristotle thinks that certain nouns, verbs, and noun-like or verb-like phrases signify exactly one object, which is a universal: for example, he would grant that some utterances of "man" signify the universal *man* but no other object (he would of course recognize that utterances of "man" produced by a parrot lack such a signification). He also thinks that certain nouns signify exactly one object, which is an individual: for example, he would grant that some utterances of "Socrates" signify Socrates but no other object (again, he would recognize that the utterances produced by a parrot are out of the question). In *Categories* 4 1b25–2a4 Aristotle commits himself to the view that if a noun, a verb, or a phrase signifies exactly one object, this object falls under one of ten headings – the categories. The categories are very important in Aristotle's philosophy, but I cannot discuss them here: I restrict myself to hinting at their connection with signification.

Aristotle thinks that certain nouns, verbs, and phrases signify more than one universal: for example, he would concede that some utterance of "walking white man" signifies three universals (the universal *man*, the universal *walking*, and the universal *white*, which do not coalesce in a single universal) because it is a token of some thought which was a likeness of these universals. "Empty" nouns are of this sort. For example, no utterance of "goatstag" signifies a universal *goatstag* because there is no such universal. However, some utterances of "goatstag" signify the universal *goat* and the universal *stag*. Any sentence containing an utterance of "goatstag" is semantically complex and is equivalent to a sentence consisting of two or more sentences which are linked by conjunctions and concern the universal *goat* and the universal *stag*.

Uttered linguistic expressions signifying no objects   No preposition, conjunction, or quantifying expression, and no utterance of a form of "to be," is a token of any thought which was a likeness of any object. For what could such an object be? Aristotle therefore seems committed to conceding that such utterances signify no objects. In fact, in *Poetics* 20 1456b38–1457a10 and *de Interpretatione* 3 16b19–25 and 10 20a12–14 he concedes this while insisting that such utterances make a contribution to what is signified by phrases or sentences containing them: phrases and sentences containing them are tokens of thoughts of certain sorts which were likenesses of objects of certain sorts.

89

Homonymy   Two objects are homonyms relatively to a certain expression-type just if the definition of the first object that corresponds to that expression-type is different from the definition of the second object that corresponds to that expression-type (for example, that bird over there and that machine in the shipyard are homonyms relatively to "crane" because the definition of that bird that corresponds to "crane" is different from the definition of that machine that corresponds to this same word-type). Two objects are synonyms relatively to a certain expression-type just if the definition of the first object that corresponds to that expression-type is identical with the definition of the second object that corresponds to that expression-type.

Aristotle scrutinizes homonymy. He has several reasons for doing so. One is that homonymy can induce invalid moves both in dialectical debates and in philosophical research (Aristotle himself often begins an inquiry by explaining "in how many ways things are thus called," i.e. by mapping out a homonymy). Another reason is epistemological. For Aristotle, expression-types do not reliably indicate what sciences there are: no science studies both the birds and the machines to which "crane" applies. Notwithstanding, Aristotle insists that sometimes there is a science corresponding to an expression-type that gives rise to homonymy: this is when the different definitions of objects that correspond to that expression-type are reciprocally associated. For example, although "being" gives rise to homonymy, Aristotle (at least in his mature thought) maintains that there is a single science corresponding to "being" because the different definitions of objects that correspond to "being" are reciprocally associated. Specifically, the different definitions of objects that correspond to "being" are associated by converging on a core, namely substance (commentators describe situations of this sort as cases of *focal meaning*).

Truth

What can be true or false?   For Aristotle, items that are true or false are of three main kinds: sentences, thoughts, and certain objects whose nature is neither mental nor linguistic. They are true or false at times: some of them are always true, others always false, yet others true at one time and false at another. The view that the bearers of truth or falsehood are true or false at times was widespread in Antiquity – in fact, it remained unchallenged.

Since for Aristotle sentences are utterances, i.e. individual events of speech occurring over short portions of time, Aristotle is committed to the view that some utterances are true or false at times, and that some of them are even true at one time and false at another. The time when an utterance is produced must not be confused with the time or times when it is true or false: an utterance is true or false even at times very distant from that when it is produced.

What are the objects that are true or false?   Aristotle holds that among items that are true or false there are objects (I sometimes use "object" to mean "object whose nature is neither mental nor linguistic": I trust that the context will clarify whether a given occurrence of "object" is to be understood in this narrow sense). These objects that are true or false play a central role within Aristotle's views on truth. What are they?

In *Metaphysics* Θ.10 1051a34–1052a4 Aristotle distinguishes two kinds of objects that are true or false: composite objects and simple objects. I address composite objects first. Some composite objects that are true or false are states of affairs. "State of affairs" is used in several senses: I use it to denote objects of a "propositional" nature of which it is sensible to say both that they obtain and that they do not obtain at a time. Aristotle's most overt discussion of states of affairs occurs at *Metaphysics* Δ.29 1024b17–21. Every state of affairs is an object and is composed of two further objects: one of these is a universal, the other is either a universal or an individual. A state of affairs is true just when the objects it is composed of are combined in a certain way; it is false just when the objects it is composed of are divided in a certain way. For example, the state of affairs that Socrates is seated is composed of the universal *seated* and Socrates; it is true just when the universal *seated* is combined in a certain way with Socrates, i.e. just when Socrates is seated; it is false just when the universal *seated* is divided in a certain way from Socrates, i.e. just when Socrates is not seated. Again, the state of affairs that every diagonal is commensurable is composed of the universal *commensurable* and the universal *diagonal*; it is true just when the universal *commensurable* is combined in a certain way with the universal *diagonal*, i.e. just when every diagonal is commensurable; it is false just when the universal *commensurable* is divided in a certain way from the universal *diagonal*, i.e. just when some diagonal is not commensurable. Since no diagonal ever is commensurable, the state of affairs that every diagonal is commensurable is never true, but always false. For Aristotle, at least in the *Metaphysics*, there are only "affirmative" states of affairs: there are the state of affairs that Socrates is seated and the state of affairs that every diagonal is commensurable, but there is no state of affairs that Socrates is not seated nor one that not every diagonal is commensurable. In principle, a state of affairs can exist at a time when it is false, i.e. when the objects of which it is composed are divided in the relevant way. For example, at certain times the state of affairs that Socrates is seated exists and is false, and the state of affairs that every diagonal is commensurable always exists and is always false. The combination that makes a state of affairs true must not be confused with the composition whereby the state of affairs is composed of further objects, and the division that makes a state of affairs false does not dissolve the composition whereby the state of affairs is composed of further objects (otherwise the state of affairs could not, even in principle, exist when it is false). For example, the state of affairs that Socrates is seated remains composed of the universal *seated* and Socrates even when the universal *seated* is divided from Socrates in such a way as to make the state of affairs in question false. It remains unclear whether for Aristotle all states of affairs are everlasting: does Aristotle believe that the state of affairs that Socrates is seated exists before and after Socrates exists? A state of affairs, as Aristotle conceives of it, is best understood as an object corresponding to a present-tense affirmative predicative assertion, and as being composed of the objects signified by the assertion's predicate and subject. For example, the state of affairs that Socrates is seated corresponds to some utterance of "Socrates is seated," and is composed of the universal *seated*, which is signified by the assertion's predicate (an utterance of "is seated"), and Socrates, who is signified by the subject (an utterance of "Socrates").

As I said, some composite objects that are true or false are states of affairs. For Aristotle, material substances (for example, Socrates and the horse Bucephalus) are composite objects in that they consist of form and matter. Material substances are not states of affairs, but resemble them in interesting respects: as for a state of affairs to be true is to be combined, so for a material substance to exist is to be combined, i.e. it is for its form to be combined with its matter; as for a state of affairs to be false is to be divided, so for a material substance not to exist is to be divided, i.e. it is for its form to be divided from its matter. Aristotle perhaps thinks that material substances rank among the composite objects that are true or false, that for a material substance to be true is to exist, and that for a material substance to be false is not to exist. Note that while some states of affairs exist at times when they are false, no material substances exist when they are false (because for a material substance to be false is not to exist).

Aristotle's views on simple objects are presented in *Metaphysics* Θ.10 1051b17–1052a4 and E.4 1027b18–1028a4 and in *de Anima* III.6 430a26–430b6 and 430b26–31. Since a simple object has no components between which combination or division could obtain, for a simple object to be true cannot be to be combined, nor can for it to be false be to be divided. Rather, for a simple object to be true is simply to exist, and for it to be false is simply not to exist. Aristotle distinguishes two kinds of simple objects: essences and incorporeal substances. Essences are natural kinds, for example, the kind horse. (Aristotle's remarks on essence are obscure and variously interpreted: the view I am attributing to Aristotle here, that essences are natural kinds, is "minimal" in that it is compatible with, and perhaps implied by, several of these interpretations.) The remaining simple objects, incorporeal substances, are God and (perhaps) the intellects that move the heavenly spheres. Both essences and incorporeal substances are everlasting, i.e. exist always. Hence, all simple objects exist always.

The sense of "true" and "false" whereby they apply to objects is probably Aristotle's own creation: it is an extension of the ordinary sense of these expressions which enables Aristotle to construct a more elegant account of truth.

Objects that are true or false play three roles   First, they contribute to explaining what it is to be true or false for items of other kinds, i.e. for thoughts and sentences; second, they are bearers of modal attributes; third, they are targets of propositional attitudes. In what follows I concentrate on their first role, i.e. their contribution to explaining what it is to be true or false for thoughts and sentences. This role recalls a strategy often adopted by modern philosophers, from Frege onwards: explaining the truth and false-hood of certain mental or linguistic items by appealing to the truth and falsehood of propositions (abstract entities whose nature is neither mental nor linguistic). Although there are important differences between Aristotle's conception and the modern strat-egy, here I wish to underscore their resemblance. Let me now say something about thoughts and sentences that are true or false.

Truth-evaluable sentences   Every sentence is a significant utterance, and signifies one or more objects by being a token of some thought which was a likeness of that object or those objects. Aristotle's views on truth-evaluable sentences are presented at *de Interpretatione* 4 16b33–17a4. Sentences of certain kinds (for example, prayers) are always neither true nor false. Every sentence that at any time is either true or false is an assertoric sentence, or (as Aristotle often calls it) an assertion. The converse fails:

some assertions are sometimes neither true nor false. Assertions coincide with truth-evaluable sentences, i.e. the sentences about which the question "Is it now true or false?" can be reasonably asked. Note that this question cannot be reasonably asked about certain sentences (for example, prayers). With regard to some sentences about which the question "Is it now true or false?" can be reasonably asked, the correct answer is "Neither." An analogy clarifies. Physical objects coincide with color-evaluable objects, i.e. the objects about which the question "What color is it?" can be reasonably asked. Note that this question cannot be reasonably asked about certain objects (for example, numbers). With regard to some objects about which the question "What color is it?" can be reasonably asked, the correct answer is "None" (for example, transparent objects like lenses).

Truth-evaluable thoughts   Aristotle never isolates a class of truth-evaluable thoughts that constitute the mental counterparts of assertions. However, since he regards the spheres of thought and speech as almost isomorphic, he probably believes that there is such a class of truth-evaluable thoughts. Some of Aristotle's remarks indicate that he would agree that every judgment is a truth-evaluable thought, i.e. a thought with regard to which the question "Is it now true or false?" can be reasonably asked.

Simple and composite assertions   At *de Interpretatione* 5 and 6 (17a8–26) Aristotle distinguishes two kinds of assertions: simple assertions and composite assertions. An assertion is simple just if it signifies exactly one object; it is composite just if it signifies more objects. Every simple assertion is either affirmative or negative. Composite assertions are equivalent to assertions constructed from several simple assertions linked by conjunctions.

Aristotle concentrates on simple assertions. He says little about composite assertions: he acknowledges them, but they remain beyond the horizon of his gaze. He never states that some sentences that are true or false lack assertoric force (like the utterances of "Socrates is seated" within one of "If Socrates is seated, Socrates is seated").

Simple judgments   Aristotle does not explicitly isolate a class of simple judgments that are the mental counterparts of simple assertions. However, since (as I said) he regards the spheres of thought and speech as almost isomorphic, he probably takes such a class for granted. Perhaps he thinks that a judgment is simple just if it is a likeness of exactly one object, and that every simple judgment is either affirmative or negative.

Truth and falsehood defined   Having outlined Aristotle's conception of thoughts and sentences that are true or false, I can now address his views on how objects that are true or false contribute to explaining what it is to be true or false for thoughts and sentences. Objects play this role, in particular, with regard to simple judgments and simple assertions.

Aristotle's views on the truth and falsehood of simple judgments and assertions are governed by a general definition of truth and falsehood (henceforth "*DTF*"):

DTF   Every simple judgment, or assertion, is a likeness of, or signifies, exactly one object, and is either affirmative or negative. Every affirmative simple judgment, or assertion, posits that its object is true. Accordingly, it is true (or false) just when its object is true (or false). Every negative simple judgment, or assertion, posits that its object is false. Accordingly, it is true (or false) just when its object is false (or true).

Aristotle never states *DTF*. But in a famous passage from *Metaphysics* Γ.7 he offers a definition of truth and falsehood which seems to commit him to the part of *DTF* concerning assertions: "To say that what is is not, or that what is not is, is false; to say that what is is, and that what is not is not, is true" (1011b26–7).

DTF covers at one blow all simple judgments and assertions, both those that are likenesses of, or signify, composite objects and those that are likenesses of, or signify, simple ones. It is worthwhile working out the details for each case. In particular, let us study the forms taken on by *DTF* for simple judgments, or assertions, which are likenesses of, or signify, (1) those composite objects that are states of affairs, (2) those composite objects that are material substances, and (3) simple objects.

Predicative assertions and judgments   The simple assertions that signify those composite objects that are states of affairs are predicative assertions; similarly, the simple judgments that are likenesses of those composite objects that are states of affairs are predicative judgments. Let me first outline Aristotle's views on predicative assertions and predicative judgments.

Every predicative assertion has exactly one part that constitutes its predicate (it is a verb or a verb-like phrase) and exactly one that constitutes its subject (it is a noun or a noun-like phrase). Every predicative assertion is a sentence, and therefore a significant utterance. Specifically, in every predicative assertion the predicate signifies exactly one object, which is a universal, and the subject also signifies exactly one object, which is either a universal or an individual. For example, in any predicative assertion that is an utterance of "Socrates is seated" the subject is the part that is an utterance of "Socrates" and signifies Socrates (and no other object), and the predicate is the part that is an utterance of "is seated" and signifies the universal *seated* (and no other object).

Every predicative assertion is either affirmative (for example, some utterances of "Socrates is seated") or negative (for example, some utterances of "Socrates is not seated"). (Not all utterances of "Socrates is seated" or "Socrates is not seated" are predicative assertions: for example, those produced by parrots are not.) Many predicative assertions have one further part over and above their predicate and their subject: they contain either an utterance of "not" or a quantifying expression (an utterance of "every," "no," "some," or "not every").

Every predicative judgment has exactly one part that constitutes its predicate and exactly one that constitutes its subject. In every predicative judgment the predicate is a likeness of exactly one object, which is a universal, and the subject also is a likeness of exactly one object, which is either a universal or an individual. For example, in Peter's judgment that Socrates is seated, the predicate is the part that is a likeness of the universal *seated*, and the subject is the part that is a likeness of Socrates. Every predicative judgment is either affirmative or negative. In some cases a predicative assertion is a token of a predicative judgment (for example, Peter's utterance of "Socrates is seated" is a token of his judgment that Socrates is seated): of course, not every predicative judgment comes to be outwardly expressed in a predicative assertion.

Predications classified In *de Interpretatione* 7 17a38–17b22, Aristotle presents a classification of predicative assertions. On the assumption that for Aristotle predicative judgments correspond to predicative assertions, I now present a classification of predicative judgments and assertions which can be plausibly attributed to Aristotle. Predicative judgments and assertions divide into two main groups: *singular* and *general* predicative judgments and assertions. A predicative judgment, or assertion, is singular just if its subject is a likeness of, or signifies, an individual; it is general just if its subject is a likeness of, or signifies, a universal. For example, some utterances of "Socrates is seated" and "Socrates is not seated" are singular predicative assertions (again, utterances produced by parrots are not predicative assertions). General predicative judgments and assertions divide into two subgroups: *indeterminate* and *quantified* predicative judgments and assertions. For example, some utterances of "A horse is white" and "A horse is not white" are indeterminate predicative assertions. Quantified predicative judgments and assertions divide into two subgroups: *particular* and *universal* predicative judgments and assertions. For example, some utterances of "Some horse is white" and "Not every horse is white" are particular predicative assertions, whereas some utterances of "Every horse is white" and "No horse is white" are universal predicative assertions.

The distinction between affirmative and negative predicative judgments and assertions cuts across the above classification: every group within this classification is divided into an affirmative and a negative subgroup. That is, universal predicative judgments and assertions divide into *universal affirmative* and *universal negative* predicative judgments and assertions; particular predicative judgments and assertions divide into *particular affirmative* and *particular negative* predicative judgments and assertions; similarly with indeterminate and singular predicative judgments and assertions. Since Aristotle says little about indeterminate predicative judgments and assertions, I shall also gloss over them.

Predications and states of affairs I can now report Aristotle's views on how predicative judgments and assertions are related to states of affairs. Every predicative judgment, or assertion, is a likeness of, or signifies, exactly one state of affairs whose two components are, first, the universal which the predicate of the judgment, or the assertion, is a likeness of, or signifies, and, second, the object (a universal or an individual) which the subject of the judgment, or the assertion, is a likeness of, or signifies.

For example, Peter's predicative judgment that Socrates is seated is a likeness of the state of affairs that Socrates is seated, which is composed of the universal *seated* (which the judgment's predicate is a likeness of) and Socrates (whom the judgment's subject is a likeness of). Frank's predicative judgment that Socrates is not seated is a likeness of the same state of affairs: the state of affairs that Socrates is seated. Peter's utterance of "Socrates is seated," a token of his judgment, signifies the same state of affairs.

DTF and predications With regard to predicative judgments, *DTF* is specified as follows. An affirmative predicative judgment is true (or false) just when the state of affairs it is a likeness of is true (or false), i.e. just when the components of this state of affairs are appropriately combined (or divided), i.e. just when the universal which the predicate

95

is a likeness of is appropriately combined with (or divided from) the object (a universal or an individual) which the subject is a likeness of. A negative predicative judgment is true (or false) just when the state of affairs it is a likeness of is false (or true), i.e. just when the components of this state of affairs are appropriately divided (or combined), i.e. just when the universal which the predicate is a likeness of is appropriately divided from (or combined with) the object which the subject is a likeness of. This account concerns *judgments*. To obtain the corresponding account concerning *assertions*, replace "judgment" with "assertion" and "is a likeness of" with "signifies."

Truth-conditions for predications that differ in "quantity"   Aristotle probably thinks that different relations of combination and division are associated with predicative judgments and assertions that differ in "quantity" (i.e. by being universal, particular, or singular). I offer first an abstract exposition, then an example. Although Aristotle never explicitly formulates the conception I am now presenting, there are plausible grounds for attributing it to him (cf. *Prior Analytics* I.1 24b26–30).

(a)   Every universal affirmative predicative judgment posits that the universal which its predicate is a likeness of is combined with the universal which its subject is a likeness of in such a way as universally to hold of it. Accordingly, a universal affirmative predicative judgment is true (or false) just when the universal which its predicate is a likeness of is combined with (or divided from) the universal which its subject is a likeness of in such a way as universally to hold of it (or not universally to hold of it).

(b)   Every universal negative predicative judgment posits that the universal which its predicate is a likeness of is divided from the universal which its subject is a likeness of in such a way as universally to fail to hold of it. Accordingly, a universal negative predicative judgment is true (or false) just when the universal which its predicate is a likeness of is divided from (or combined with) the universal which its subject is a likeness of in such a way as universally to fail to hold of it (or not universally to fail to hold of it).

(c)   Every particular affirmative predicative judgment posits that the universal which its predicate is a likeness of is combined with the universal which its subject is a likeness of in such a way as not universally to fail to hold of it. Accordingly, a particular affirmative predicative judgment is true (or false) just when the universal which its predicate is a likeness of is combined with (or divided from) the universal which its subject is a likeness of in such a way as not universally to fail to hold of it (or universally to fail to hold of it).

(d)   Every particular negative predicative judgment posits that the universal which its predicate is a likeness of is divided from the universal which its subject is a likeness of in such a way as not universally to hold of it. Accordingly, a particular negative predicative judgment is true (or false) just when the universal which its predicate is a likeness of is divided from (or combined with) the universal which its subject is a likeness of in such a way as not universally to hold of it (or universally to hold of it).

(e)   Every singular affirmative predicative judgment posits that the universal which its predicate is a likeness of is combined with the individual which its subject is a likeness of in such a way as to hold of it. Accordingly, a singular affirmative predicative judgment is true (or false) just when the universal which its predicate is a likeness of is combined with (or divided from) the individual which its subject is a likeness of in such a way as to hold of it (or hold outside it).

(f)   Every singular negative predicative judgment posits that the universal which its predicate is a likeness of is divided from the individual which its subject is a likeness of in such a way as to hold outside it. Accordingly, a singular negative predicative judgment is true (or false) just when the universal which its predicate is a likeness of is divided from (or combined with) the individual which its subject is a likeness of in such a way as to hold outside it (or hold of it).

To pin down the above, a definition of the relevant relations of combination and division is called for. A universal *u* is combined with a universal *v* in such a way as universally to hold of it just when every individual that instantiates *v* instantiates *u*. A universal *u* is divided from a universal *v* in such a way as universally to fail to hold of it just when every individual that instantiates *v* is other than every individual that instantiates *u*. A universal *u* is combined with a universal *v* in such a way as not universally to fail to hold of it just when at least one individual that instantiates *v* instantiates *u*. A universal *u* is divided from a universal *v* in such a way as not universally to hold of it just when at least one individual that instantiates *v* is other than every individual that instantiates *u*. A universal *u* is combined with an individual *i* in such a way as to hold of it just when *i* instantiates *u*. A universal *u* is divided from an individual *i* in such a way as to hold outside it just when *i* is other than every individual that instantiates *u*.

Propositions (a)–(f) concern *judgments*. To obtain the corresponding truth-conditions concerning *assertions*, replace "judgment" with "assertion" and "is a likeness of" with "signifies."

Example   An example will clarify this abstract exposition. Peter's universal affirmative predicative judgment that every horse is white posits that the universal *white*, of which the judgment's predicate is a likeness, is combined with the universal *horse*, of which the judgment's subject is a likeness, in such a way as universally to hold of it. Accordingly, this judgment is true just when the universal *white* is combined with the universal *horse* in such a way as universally to hold of it, i.e. just when every individual that instantiates the universal *horse* instantiates the universal *white*. Since it is not the case that every individual that now instantiates the universal *horse* instantiates now the universal *white*, this judgment is not true now.

DTF and material substances   With regard to those composite objects that are material substances, *DTF* is specified as follows: An affirmative simple judgment which is a likeness of a material substance is true (or false) just when this material substance is true (or false), i.e. just when it exists (or does not exist), i.e. just when its form is combined with (or divided from) its matter. A negative simple judgment which is a likeness of a material substance is true (or false) just when this material substance is false (or true), i.e. just when it does not exist (or exists), i.e. just when its form is divided from (or combined with) its matter. The truth-conditions just offered concern *judgments*. To obtain the corresponding truth-conditions concerning *assertions*, replace "judgment" with "assertion" and "is a likeness of" with "signifies."

The above truth-conditions indicate that simple judgments and assertions that are likenesses of, or signify, material substances are singular existential judgments and assertions (for example, Peter's judgment that Socrates exists and some utterances of "Socrates exists"). These truth-conditions recall those for predicative judgments and assertions: for example, as some utterance of "Socrates does not exist" is true just when Socrates' form is divided from his matter, so some utterance of "Socrates is not seated" is true just when the universal *seated* is divided from Socrates in such a way as to hold outside him.

When a material substance no longer exists, i.e. when its form is divided from its matter, a singular affirmative existential judgment, or assertion, which is a likeness of, or signifies, it is false, and a singular negative existential judgment, or assertion, which is a likeness of, or signifies, it is true. Existential judgments and assertions of this sort require that the material substances they are likenesses of, or signify, exist at some time or other. Singular existential judgments or assertions about what never exists as a material substance (for example, my present judgment that Pegasus does not exist) remain unexplained.

DTF and simple objects   With regard to simple objects, *DTF* is specified as follows: An affirmative simple judgment which is a likeness of a simple object is true (or false) just when this simple object is true (or false), i.e. exists (or does not exist). A negative simple judgment which is a likeness of a simple object is true (or false) just when this simple object is false (or true), i.e. does not exist (or exists). As usual, the corresponding truth conditions for assertions are obtained by replacing "judgment" with "assertion" and "is a likeness of" with "signifies." Thus, simple judgments and assertions of this kind also are existential judgments and assertions. For example, some utterance of "Man exists," which is an affirmative simple existential assertion signifying the universal *man* (an essence, hence a simple object), is true just when man exists.

Since all simple objects exist always, every affirmative existential judgment, or assertion, which is a likeness of, or signifies, a simple object is always true: for example, some utterance of "Man exists" is always true because the simple object it signifies, the universal *man*, exists always. In *Metaphysics* Θ.10 (1051b25–8 and b30–2) Aristotle describes thoughts about simple objects as unerring: he means that all affirmative existential judgments about simple objects are always true (he forgoes mentioning that all negative existential judgments about simple objects are always false). Note that no corresponding result holds for material substances: since some material substances are not everlasting, some singular affirmative existential judgments about material substances are sometimes false.

My interpretation of Aristotle's views on truth concerning simple items differs from the traditional interpretation (for example, de Rijk and Wilpert). According to the traditional interpretation, thoughts about simple items are (not existential judgments, but) concepts which are true whenever they grasp their simple objects, and linguistic expressions about simple items are (not existential assertions, but) noun-like expressions which are true whenever they signify their simple objects. Thoughts and linguistic expressions about simple items are therefore always true (because they always grasp or signify their simple objects), and their truth is of a non-propositional character. This traditional interpretation is unsatisfactory because it saddles Aristotle with a conception of truth which is broken-backed in that it involves two different and unrelated concepts of truth.

Truth as correspondence?   Most commentators claim that Aristotle propounds a correspondence theory of truth. Are they right? There are various conceptions of what a correspondence theory of truth amounts to. According to *DTF*, the definition of truth and falsehood for simple judgments and assertions, an affirmative simple judgment, or assertion, posits that the object it is a likeness of, or signifies, is true, and is true just when this object is true; a negative simple judgment, or assertion, posits that the object it is a likeness of, or signifies, is false, and is true just when this object is false. Since every simple judgment, or assertion, is either affirmative or negative, *DTF* entails that every simple judgment, or assertion, is true just when it "posits its object to be as it is." Such a claim has been traditionally regarded as characteristic of correspondence theories of truth.

Some hold that a correspondence theory of truth must claim that being true is corresponding to some fact. If *this* is how a correspondence theory of truth is understood, then Aristotle does not have a correspondence theory of truth because he does not mention facts. Note that no Greek count-noun can be used like the English "fact" in a Greek construction which corresponds word for word to the English "the fact that . . . ."

Future-tense assertions   In *de Interpretatione* 9 Aristotle claims that some future-tense assertions are sometimes neither true nor false. His reason for making this claim is his conception of the history of the universe as an accumulation of events: as time unfolds, new events are added to the stock of earlier ones to constitute the universe "to date." At any time, while all of its past and present are given in their full determinateness, not all of its future is given yet: that time's future is a multiplicity of equally possible developments of the events accumulated until then, and the only part of this future that is already given is what is common to all these alternative developments (this represents what at the given time is already necessary). All that at any given time has already happened is necessary then in the sense that it cannot be changed ("if the milk has been spilled, nothing can be done about it now"). By contrast, at least part of a time's future is not necessary then: something can be done then to modify it. Suppose every future-tense assertion were always either true or false. Hence at any given time it would be either true or false. Its truth or falsehood at that time would be something which has already happened then, and would therefore be necessary then. This necessity would transfer from the truth or falsehood of the future-tense assertion to what it predicts, so that the future of the given time would be necessary then as much as its past and present. In order to avoid this consequence, Aristotle concedes that not every future-tense assertion is always either true or false. It is worth mentioning that the interpretation of *de Interpretatione* 9 is highly controversial: commentators have offered radically different exegeses (see for example, Fine, Frede, Hintikka, and Weidemann).

Note

I would like to thank Francesco Ademollo and David Charles for their comments on earlier drafts of this paper, and Benjamin Morison and Annamaria Schiaparelli for discussions on some of the issues it addresses. The responsibility for the remaining deficiencies is only mine.

Further Reading

Ammonius (1897). *In Aristotelis de Interpretatione Commentarius*, ed. A. Busse (Berlin: Reimer).

Boethius (1877/80). *Commentarii in Librum Aristotelis ΠΕΡΙ ΕΡΜΗΝΕΙΑΣ*, ed. C. Meiser (Leipzig: Teubner).

Charles, D. (2000). *Aristotle on Meaning and Essence* (Oxford: Oxford University Press).

Crivelli, P. (2004). *Aristotle on Truth* (Cambridge: Cambridge University Press).

De Rijk, L.M. (1952). *The Place of the Categories of Being in Aristotle's Philosophy* (Assen: Van Gorcum).

Fine, G. (1984). "Truth and Necessity in *De Interpretatione 9*," *History of Philosophy Quarterly*, 1, pp. 23–47.

Frede, D. (1985). "The Sea-battle Reconsidered: A Defence of the Traditional Interpretation," *Oxford Studies in Ancient Philosophy*, 3, pp. 31–87.

Hintikka, J. (1973). *Time & Necessity: Studies in Aristotle's Theory of Modality* (Oxford: Clarendon Press).

Künne, W. (2003). *Conceptions of Truth* (Oxford: Oxford University Press).

Modrak, D.K. (2001). *Aristotle's Theory of Language and Meaning* (Cambridge: Cambridge University Press).

Weidemann, H. (trans. and comm.) (2002). *Aristoteles, Peri hermeneias*, 2nd edn. (Berlin: Akademie Verlag).

Wilpert, P. (1940). "Zum aristotelischen Wahrheitsbegriff," *Philosophisches Jahrbuch der Görres-Gesellschaft*, 53, pp. 3–16.

7

Aristotle's Methods

GEORGIOS ANAGNOSTOPOULOS

Introduction

Questions about Aristotle's methods may be asking a variety of things, e.g.: (1) What method(s), if any, does he identify as appropriate for attaining knowledge? (2) What method(s) does he use in his own treatises? In turn, these questions can be understood in different ways, e.g., as questions about (3) methods of discovery; (4) methods of confirmation, proof, or systematic presentation. Each of these questions poses different challenges, and none is easy to answer. Focusing on (2), for instance, one quickly realizes the challenges it poses when bringing to mind the number of treatises constituting the extant Aristotelian corpus and the variety of areas they investigate – from art to zoology and almost everything in between. Naturally, one may wonder at the outset whether Aristotle could have relied on a single method in his inquiries across so many different fields – from his logical investigations in the *Organon* to his study in the practical (ethics and politics) and productive (rhetoric and poetics) areas, the theoretical inquiries into nature and the first principles of Being (mathematics, treatises on nature, metaphysics), and so on. "Method" can mean different things to different people, and I will understand it here as broadly as possible. As might be expected, Aristotle relies on a number of methods in his own inquiries – e.g., analysis, analogy, collection of observational data, demonstration, developmental stages, dialectic, division, induction, and so on. And in most of his works he constantly switches from one method to another. Thus in the opening chapter of the *Pol* he announces that in his investigation of the state he will proceed with "the method that has hitherto guided us," i.e., analyzing "a compound into the simplest elements or least parts of the whole" (I.1 1252a20; see also his treatment of slavery by analysis at I.8 1256a). In the next chapter, he claims that the clearest view of the nature of the state will be attained by investigating its growth and origin from the union of male and female, the household, and the village (I.2 1252a25). While it is possible in some cases for constitutive elements or parts and originating elements to be identical (e.g., the household in the case of the state), it is not necessary that they are; wealth is counted as a part but it is not one of the originating elements of the state. And the inquiry into the parts of animals in *PA*, on which Aristotle's methodological approach to the identification of the parts of a state or constitution is based in the *Pol* (IV.4 1290b21) is modeled, is not necessarily equivalent to a developmental study of an animal from its origins. (The origin of a plant, a seed, is not a part of the plant.) Yet additional methods are employed in the *Pol*, including dialectic, analogy, fact gathering. In some instances, scholars disagree as to what method Aristotle is relying on for reaching a certain position, and it is possible that he employs more than one. The opening statement of the treatise, identifying the nature and goal of the state, has been seen as a dialectical inference, an inductive inference based on Aristotle's research on 158 constitutions of the ancient world, a deductive inference from other well-established truths, and as a principle whose truth is not inferred from that of others but is grasped immediately. Thus, not only might it be difficult to identify a method as Aristotle's method throughout his works, it might be equally problematic to do so for a single work of his.

The present study then cannot investigate all the methods Aristotle uses throughout his corpus; indeed, it cannot even examine all the methods he avails himself to in a single work, for these could be equally many. It will focus on the most prominent ones, those that he identifies as central to his account of scientific knowledge or uses in his own treatises.

Aristotle's Presuppositions and Demonstration

Methods may rest on substantive presuppositions and, in turn, have important implications as to the kinds of result they produce. In thinking about the methods Aristotle uses or advocates, it is important to consider his presuppositions with respect to the character of the domains to which they are applied, the objectives inquiry aims to attain, and the implications both of these have for the nature of the methods of inquiry. Doing so is necessary for determining whether or not the methods he uses or advocates are appropriate for the kinds of domain that are subject to investigation and, more importantly, for assessing whether or not they are adequate for the type of results he thinks inquiry should attain.

At *NE* VI.2 1139a30 and 1139b12, Aristotle claims that the aim of the intellect – whether its investigations are theoretical, practical, or productive – is truth. This is of some importance since it shows that he takes the aim of all inquiry to be the same, at least at a general level. But since Aristotle often claims that practical inquiry is pursued for the sake of action and productive inquiry for the sake of production, the aim of such inquiries has been taken to be something other than attaining or knowing the truth. But there is no inconsistency in Aristotle's statements: The *ultimate* goal of some types of inquiry or science, e.g., practical and productive ones, may be something other than truth, but their *immediate* end is knowledge of truth. And this leaves the possibility open that, other things being equal, the methods in all or most types of inquiry could be completely or, to a significant extent, the same.

What is Aristotle's conception of truth? His well-known account is given at *Met* Γ.7 1011b25: "To say of what is that it is not, or of what is not that it is, is false, while to say of what is that it is, and of what is not that it is not, is true." Most scholars take Aristotle's statement to imply a correspondence theory of truth. Certainly, there is no mention of coherence as the criterion of truth in Aristotle's statement. In addition, there is no hint that truth is relative to linguistic, conceptual, or other frameworks or to speakers. The last option is explicitly rejected in Aristotle's argument against the relativism of Protagoras and the conception of truth it implies (*Met* Γ.5). His own conception of truth seems to be absolutist in character, taking a statement or an account to be true if it captures the way things are. The philosophical tradition that advocates such a non-coherentist and non-relativist conception of truth is often also committed to a robust metaphysical realism concerning the nature of the world – namely, that the world possesses a determinate and fixed structure that is independent of any and every linguistic, conceptual, or belief system. Aristotle is one of the most prominent figures in that tradition. In addition, while arguing against relativism and what it implies about the nature of things, Aristotle claims that Protagoras' doctrine does away with the essences and necessary properties of things, thus making clear his own commitment to metaphysical essentialism (*Met* Γ.4 1007a20, 5 1010b26). The latter, of course, runs through all of Aristotle's works.

Aristotle's robust metaphysical essentialism is presupposed in his account of scientific knowledge or understanding and the demonstrative method that produces it. If we were to ask "What do we seek when we inquire after the truth about x?" the answer, according to Aristotle, would be that we seek to know the causes of x. This is true of inquiries in the canonical sciences, which seek the causes or principles within a specific domain (e.g., arithmetic or zoology), as well as in metaphysics, which seeks to identify the first principles or causes of all that is (*Phys* I.1 184a; *Met* A.3 983a25).

The account of demonstration he develops in the *An. Post* aims to explain how scientific knowledge or understanding (*epistêmê*) of something can be attained through a deductive inference from those things that are its causes or that explain it[1]: "We think we know [or understand (*epistasthai*)] a thing *simpliciter* when we think we are aware of the explanation [or cause (*aitia*)] because of which the object holds that it is its explanation [cause], and also that it is not possible for it to be otherwise . . . Whether there is also another type of understanding we shall say later: here we assert that we do know things through demonstration [*apodeixis*]. By demonstration I mean a scientific deduction [*epistêmonikos syllogismos*]; and by scientific I mean one in virtue of which, by having it, we understand [or know (*epistametha*)] something" (*An. Post* I.2 71b9). The goals of inquiry – strict knowledge of the causes or explanations of things – are attained by scientific deduction or the demonstrative syllogism, and Aristotle proceeds to spell out the requirements a stretch of deductive reasoning must meet in order to be such a syllogism and produce scientific knowledge or understanding. According to him, in order for a deduction to be a demonstrative syllogism its premises must be:

(a) true
(b) primitive
(c) immediate
(d) more familiar (or better known) than the conclusion
(e) prior to the conclusion
(f) explanatory of the conclusion. (*An. Post* I.2 71b20).

To these Aristotle adds what seems to be implied by his definition of scientific knowledge or understanding, i.e., that both the premises and the conclusion of a demonstrative syllogism must be

(g) necessary. (I.4 73a22).

These conditions are necessary elements in Aristotle's conception of the demonstrative syllogism and the kind of knowledge or understanding resulting from it: "there can be deduction even if these conditions [(a)–(g)] are not met, but there cannot be demonstration; for it [the deductive reasoning that does not meet (a)–(g)] will not bring about understanding [*epistêmê*]" (I.2 71b24). The above conditions are strictly the conditions that must be met by the most basic elements of a science, its starting points or axioms, which Aristotle most often calls "principles" (*archai*), and from which the other truths of the science (its theorems) are deductively derived.[2]

When identifying and explaining these conditions Aristotle moves without any hesitation at all from thinking of them as features of the propositions or statements in a demonstrative syllogism to thinking of the things in the world these propositions/statements are about. Indeed, for Aristotle it is the fact that certain things in the world have the features specified in (a)–(g) that is primary and explains why the propositions about these things also have the same features. It is because some x in the world is primitive, immediate, a cause, or more knowable that the propositions about x have these same features. And all these features are understood in absolute terms. Thus, what is more or most knowable is not that which is so in relation to us, but absolutely (I.2 72a). The point in geometry is a primitive in terms of which line must be defined and, although we could define the point in terms of the line for some purposes, the definition would not be capturing the way things really are but would be defining what is more intelligible and prior in nature by what is less intelligible and posterior (*Top* VI.4 141b15). Again, Aristotle argues that a demonstration must capture the causal structure in the world.

The metaphysical presuppositions of a strict Aristotelian science are considerable. As many have pointed out (see Barnes 1994; Scholz 1930; Irwin 1988), they include a commitment to absolutely basic or foundational elements of a domain that is a subject of a demonstrative discipline, invariant essences, necessary connections among properties and an objective causal structure.[3] In turn, a canonical Aristotelian demonstrative science of a certain domain consists of primitive and indemonstrable principles, which are known non-inferentially and are proper to and absolutely foundational for that domain, and of the theorems derived from them. The features Aristotle attributes to the principles show that he conceives of the scientific account of a domain as mirroring the independent structure, causal order of, and necessary connections among, the objects and properties of that domain.

It is clear that much rides on the principles of an Aristotelian demonstrative science. For instance, the truth of whatever is derived from them (of theorems) depends upon the truth of the principles, and for this reason, Aristotle argues, "you must not only already know the primitives (either all or some of them), you must actually know them better [than what is demonstrated from them] . . . Hence if we know and are convinced of something because of the primitives, then we know and are convinced of them better, since it is because of them that we know and are convinced of the posterior items" (I.2 72a27ff). How strong must be our conviction of the principles? Aristotle goes on to say that it must be unshakable: "Anyone who is going to possess understanding through demonstration must not only get to know the principles better and be more convinced of them than he is of what is being proved: in addition, there must be no other item more convincing to him or more familiar among the opposites of the principles from which the deduction of the contrary error may proceed – given that anyone who understands anything *simpliciter* must be incapable of being persuaded to change his mind" (I.2 72a39).

The description of knowledge of principles appears to set an unreachable standard. In fact, it is unclear how the principles of an Aristotelian science can be known, even if such knowledge need not be absolutely unshakable. The primitiveness and immediacy of the principles seem to imply that they are indemonstrable (see Barnes 1994: 94–5, and below), and even that they can be known only through themselves and non-inferentially (Irwin 1988: 130–1). So Aristotle claims that "the principles are known through themselves" (*An. Pr* II.16 64b36) and that "Things are true and primitive which are convincing on the strength not of anything else but of themselves; for in regard to the first principles of science it is improper to ask any further for the why and wherefore of them; each of the first principles should command belief in and by itself" (*Top* I.1100a30).[4]

Induction (*epagôgê*) and Comprehension or Intuition (*nous*)

How do we arrive at the first principles? Aristotle poses the question whether there is a kind of knowledge or understanding that is different from that which comes about by demonstration as soon as he offers his definition of scientific knowledge, and promises to deal with the question later (*An. Post* I.2 71b16). Although he does not identify what the objects of this different kind of understanding are, it is quite clear that he is thinking of the principles. Aristotle offers a preliminary response to this question in the next chapter, where he tries to meet the skeptical challenges he thinks arise if one equates knowledge with what is produced by demonstration. The skeptic argues that, if one does so, one is led to an infinite regress because one needs to demonstrate the principles; and if one were to end the regress by stopping giving demonstrations somewhere, the starting points will be unknown and the only kind of knowledge one could have of the things inferred from such principles will be hypothetical and not strict. He also rejects circular proof as a way of demonstrating the principles and meeting the skeptical challenge: "We assert that not all understanding [knowledge, *epistêmê*] is demonstrative: rather, in the case of immediate items understanding is indemonstrable. And it is clear that this must be so; for if you must understand [have knowledge of, *epistasthai*] the items which are prior and from which the demonstration proceeds, and if things come to a stop at some point, then these immediates must be indemonstrable. We agree in this way; and we also assert that there is not only understanding but also some principle of understanding by which we get to know [*gnôrizomen*] the definitions" (I.3 72b19; see also I.9 76a16). Thus Aristotle agrees with the skeptic that, if there is to be demonstrative knowledge or understanding, there must be some kind of cognition of the first principles and, therefore, some way different from demonstration by which such cognition comes about. Obviously, he thinks there is demonstrative knowledge or understanding, and therefore asserts that there is knowledge of the principles. While at the beginning of the passage just quoted Aristotle uses the terms "*epistêmê*" and "*epistasthai*" to refer to both the cognitive state that results from demonstration and we have in relation to that which is inferred (demonstrated) from the principles (the theorems of a discipline) as well as to the one we have in relation to the principles, it is clear that he is committed to the view that there cannot be demonstration of the principles and that the cognition we have of them cannot be identical with (demonstrative) understanding. His use in the last line of the passage of the more general and non-technical term (*gnôrizomen*) for the knowledge one can have in relation to principles (axioms) indicates that he has already concluded it cannot be the same as that one has of the theorems and which results from demonstration. But he does not explain at this stage what this cognition is and from what it comes about.

Aristotle offers explanations of both the means (process or method) of getting to the principles and the cognitive state resulting from it in the last chapter of *An. Post* (II.19), fifty-one chapters after he makes the statements quoted above. This chapter is one of the most compressed and dense in this work, and seems to stand alone and without clear connections to the chapters preceding it. Not surprisingly, some have concluded it was written separately from the rest of the work and later appended to it (see Barnes 1994: 271). Be that as it may, once he returns to the questions about the means to and nature of the cognition of principles he proceeds methodically to answer two questions:

> As for the principles – [1] how they become familiar [*pôs te gignontai gnôrimoi*] and [2] what is the state which gets to know them [*tis ê gnôrizousa hexis*] – this will be plain from what follows, when we have first set out the puzzles. (99b17)

In answering [1], Aristotle rejects the Platonic view that knowledge of the principles is innate (II.19 99b27, 100a10; also *Met* A.9 993b), and articulates his view of the cognitive processes and stages by which we get the principles. He claims that the process begins with the activities of the lowest cognitive faculty, sensation, in which all animals share. But some animals possess also memory, from which experience arises which, in turn, makes it possible for a universal to be established in the soul. He concludes his answer to [1] by saying

> Let us say again what we have just said but not said clearly. When one of the undifferentiated items makes a stand there is a primitive universal in the soul; for although you perceive particulars, perception is of the universals, – e.g., of man, not of Callias the man. Next, a stand is made among these items, until something partless and universal makes a stand. E.g., such-and-such an animal makes a stand, until animal does; and with animal a stand is made in the same way. Thus it is plain that we must get to know [*gnôrizomen*] the primitives by induction [*epagôgê*]; for this is the way perception instills universals. (II.19 100a15)

The problems with Aristotle's account are many, and differences of opinion with regard to precisely what it says abound in the scholarly tradition.[5] At first glance, the passage appears to be restating Aristotle's view of how we get to know universals from particulars, which is repeated on several occasions in the *An. Post* and elsewhere (see e.g., 71a8, 81b2, 88a4). But on these occasions Aristotle does not go on to identify a particular cognitive state that results from induction. However once Aristotle concludes that "we must get to know the primitives by induction," he goes on to identify the intellectual states by which different things – e.g., principles (axioms) and theorems – are grasped:

106

Of the intellectual states [*hexeis*] by which we grasp truth, some are always true and some admit falsehood (e.g., opinion and calculation do – whereas understanding [*epistêmê*] and comprehension [*nous*] are always true); and no kind apart from comprehension is more exact than understanding. Again the principles of demonstrations are more familiar [or known – *gnôrimôterai*], and all understanding involves an account. Hence there will not be understanding of the principles; and since nothing apart from comprehension (*nous*) can be truer than understanding, there will be comprehension (*nous*) of the principles. (II.19 100b10)

Everything in this passage has given rise to scholarly controversies, especially the translation of "*nous*" and, consequently, the nature of whatever this term stands for. One thing, however, is beyond controversy. The way Aristotle sets up the problem (see 99b17 above) to be addressed and his twofold answer in terms of *epagôgê* and *nous* show, as Barnes points out, that Aristotle thought two very different questions about first principles need to be answered: the way we get to them and the state we are in when we have them. Recognizing this is, according to Barnes, of great importance in guarding against misinterpretations of *nous*. Thus we may schematically present Aristotle's answers to how we get to theorems and axioms and in what state we are in relation to each one of them:

Type of thing cognized	Method	State of cognition
Principles (axioms)	Induction (*epagôgê*)	Comprehension (*nous*)
Theorems	Demonstration	Understanding (*epistêmê*)

Traditionally, *nous* has been understood as rational intuition, an act resembling some-what mental vision grasping non-inferentially that some propositions are true or as kind of faculty, perhaps a part of or the faculty of reason itself (Zeller 1890: 184; Mure 1964: 213; Allan 1978: 111, 118). Such an interpretation has been based on the belief that the epistemic features Aristotle attributes to the cognitive state designated as *nous* (infallibility, certainty) cannot be true of any cognition that involves, or ultimately derives from sensation and rests on induction. The rationalist interpretation is consis-tent with Aristotle's rejection of Plato's innate ideas; rational intuition could be viewed as the last step in a process that begins with sensation and does not require innate knowledge.[6] And it also easily meets Aristotle's requirement that the cognition of prin-ciples, unlike that of theorems, is not the result of an account or inference; intuition presumably just grasps that certain things are principles, that they meet all the condi-tions Aristotle imposes on principles. For that is precisely how intuition is understood to work – grasping, without the need of any justification, necessary truths. The ratio-nalist interpretation of *nous* has been given its strongest defense by Irwin (1988), who develops compelling arguments to show that Aristotle's kind of foundationalism and the epistemic conditions it imposes on principles require that *nous* is intuition. Indeed, Irwin argues that the nature of Aristotle's metaphysical/epistemological framework requires an intuition with a role that is similar to Descartes' conception of intuition and its activity (see especially ch. 7).

Scholars have focused, for support of this interpretation, on a remark at *NE* VI.2 1143a35:

> And comprehension [*nous*] is concerned with the ultimates in both directions; for both the primary definitions and the ultimates are objects of comprehension [*nous*] and not of argument, and in demonstrations comprehension grasps the unchangeable and primary definitions, while in practical reasoning it grasps the last and contingent fact . . . For these are the starting-points of that for the sake of which; since the universals are reached from the particulars; of these therefore we must have perception, and this is comprehension [*nous*].

As Barnes (1994: 268) points out, Aristotle here connects a *nous* that deals with individuals and is like perception with the *nous* of the *An. Post* that knows the principles. Some have taken this evidence in support of intuition, but Barnes doubts that this passage provides any support for the rationalist reading of *nous* (but cf. Reeve 1992; Kosman 1973; Lesher 1973). Evidence in support of the rationalist reading of *nous* has also been sought in Aristotle's account of the faculty of reason or intellect (*nous*) in *An* III.4. In explaining the functioning of this faculty, Aristotle argues that it is causally affected by and receives the intelligible form without the matter, i.e., what some kind of thing is, in very much the same way that sensation is causally affected by and receives the perceptible form without the matter. Yet it is unclear whether the cognitive state described here has the features Aristotle ascribes to that whose object are the principles.

   Some have raised doubts in the past as to whether the rationalist interpretation of *nous* is supported by the text of II.19 (Grote 1880: ch. 8; Gomperz 1912 and 1969: 75). Others have found the coupling of induction and intuition in the rationalist position, which leaves Aristotle with two theories about the cognition of principles, puzzling. More recently, the criticism of the supporters of the rationalist interpretation (Barnes' orthodoxy) and those puzzled by Aristotle's apparent failure to choose between the two theories (Barnes' unorthodoxy) are most serious (see also Bolton 1991). As Barnes (1994: 268) puts it, "There is a powerful objection to the orthodox view which tells equally against this rejection to it: both orthodoxy and its enemies assume that *nous* and induction are elements in the answer to a single question. But the assumption is false: Aristotle carefully distinguishes his first question from his second; and he clearly indicates that induction figures in the answer to the first, *nous* in the answer to the second. If the questions are genuinely distinct, their answers cannot conflict in the way the unorthodoxy fear, nor need they be reconciled after the fashion of the orthodoxy." According to Barnes, Aristotle unequivocally says that the method by which we gain knowledge of the principles is inductive. Aristotle's *nous* is not meant to pick out some faculty or method, but the cognitive state or disposition that stands to induction in the way *epistêmê* stands to demonstration. What is the state designated by "*nous?*" Barnes claims that this is not an important question, and Aristotle could have used an invented term to designate the state associated with the principles; what matters is that they "are not susceptible to demonstrative *epistêmê*."

   The text of the *An. Post* seems to support Barnes' contention. Throughout this work and elsewhere Aristotle claims that we come to know universals inductively, and *nous* does not appear as another way of doing it. The process is always described as having its basis in sensation, without which there can be no knowledge of any kind (*An* III.8 454a7 and *An. Post* I.18 81b5). Also in the account Aristotle gives in *Met* A.1 of how the higher cognitive states come about from sensation, which parallels the account of *An. Post* II.19, we find no reference to *nous*. Yet there are problems, perhaps due to the analogy between demonstration/understanding (*epistêmê*) and induction/comprehension (*nous*) that Barnes wishes to stress. The epistemic features of understanding are justified by the nature of demonstration. But what justifies the much stronger epistemic features Aristotle attributes to comprehension, even though the epistemic strength of induction does not match that of demonstration? Aristotle seems to offer a genetic/causal account of induction and comprehension, and thus the problem of how one can justify that induction can give rise to a state that has the epistemic features of *nous* (infallibility, highest exactness, etc.) remains unanswered. The rationalist's puzzle does not go away easily. Perhaps the aspect of necessity of the principles can be accommodated within perception and induction, even if it is understood to be different from universality.[7] While in the modern tradition necessity has been primarily viewed as an epistemic feature that is known a priori, Kripke's work (1980) has questioned this view and defended an alternative – that it is a metaphysical feature and that necessary connections can be known a posteriori. The essential definition of animal, for example, as "living thing with sensation," might state a necessary connection that can be known a posteriori. If so there will be no need to bring in reason or rational intuition to deal with the necessity Aristotle requires of principles and the connections in the world they denote. But it is difficult to see how the remaining features (especially the kind of conviction he attributes to the cognition of principles, which is higher than that he associates with *epistêmê*) can be the result of induction that begins with sensation, even if we take into account some of Aristotle's claims about sensation that speak in favor of its veridicality and, possibly, the reliability of some of the cognitive states built on it.

First, there is his causal account of sensation, according to which the sense organ becomes like the object it perceives and receives the perceptible form without the matter in the way a piece of wax receives the shape of a signet-ring without its matter (*An* II.11 424a, II.12 424a20). The veridicality of sensation implied by this model is restricted to our cognition of the proper objects of sensation, but Aristotle admits the possibility of error when judgments based on sensation are made. Second, he defends the role sensation plays in the survival of an animal, which argues in favor of the reliability of sensation (*An* III.13 434a30, *Sens* 1 436b10). But, again, it is hard to see how a case for the survival value of the cognition Aristotle designates as *nous* could be made. And given his views about the reasons inquiry is pursued – they have nothing to do with survival – Aristotle would not put much weight on such an argument (*Met* A.2). It is unlikely that those who are skeptically inclined would be convinced that the cognitive state Aristotle derives from the operations of sensation and the rest of the states that build on it can have the epistemic features he attributes to it. And perhaps, marshaling these supposed facts about sensation in support of the truth of some principles amounts to offering a kind of inferential justification of it.

Perhaps if we could find in Aristotle's treatises particular principles, with an indication as to how they were arrived at, this might shed some light on the dispute about the cognition of principles. Unfortunately, we hardly find anything along these lines, except perhaps in the discussion of the axioms of the science of Being in *Met* Γ. There he identifies the Principle of Non-Contradiction (PNC) as the highest principle that is firmest and immune to doubt. Aristotle argues that the PNC cannot be demonstrated and he claims that asking for a demonstrative proof of it is a sign of lack of training. He then proceeds to offer a number of arguments aiming to show that the PNC cannot be meaningfully denied (see Wedin, ch. 8, in this volume). But neither induction nor intuition obviously figures in these arguments, although some scholars claim that the PNC is known by induction (Ross, 1923 and 1995: 54;) or *nous* (Mure 1964: 218).

The fact we do not find explicitly identified first principles in Aristotle's treatises is, according to many scholars, not an accident. While all agree that Aristotle's articulation of the demonstrative method is a major achievement that succeeded in systematizing the intuitions of philosophers and mathematicians alike about the structure of scientific knowledge, many insist that the system of demonstration is meant only as an ideal, or as something to be used for the systematization, presentation or teaching of knowledge that we already possess and not for the discovery of truths, the latter being what Aristotle is doing in his treatises. Hence, it should not be surprising that we find no clearly identifiable principles or many demonstrations in his works. Thus, Barnes (1995: 26; 1982: 38–9) points out that Aristotle's works contain few formal deductions and rarely are principles of the kind he speaks of in his logical works identified in his treatises; Reeve (1992: 32) argues that the reason Aristotle's works do not have the syllogistic structure is that they are nascent sciences, arguing to first principles and not from them. Some of these claims are correct, but others seem to go too far. That Aristotle articulates an ideal of finished knowledge is most likely correct, as is the claim that none of his extant works realizes the ideal. Of course, many of his works have not survived, and we do not know whether or not some of the lost ones were reasonable approximations of the demonstrative ideal. But leaving speculations about lost works aside, one may accept that Aristotle was articulating an ideal and his works do not realize it but not accept any conclusion that sees his works as bearing no resemblance to the ideal.

One form basic principles take is that of definitions articulating the essential structure of the genus studied by a discipline, e.g., the essential definition of the genus *animal* in the case of zoology. While Aristotle does not identify it as the, or a, principle of zoology, there is no doubt that it plays such a role in many explanatory inferences he makes in the zoological treatises. For example, when at *GA* I.23 731a24 he defends the view that reproduction is not the only function of animals, the definition of the genus is the pivotal premise in his argument. The definition of the human good in terms of function is used as kind of principle in the *NE* in terms of which the most general account of virtue is explicated. The argument in support of the functional account of the human good *NE* and several arguments in *Pol* in support of what Keyt (1991) has called "theorems" in that treatise can be reconstructed as rigorous proofs (Keyt 1983: 366–8; Santas 2001: 236–7). And in *Poet*, the work that would seem the farthest removed from concerns with demonstrative principles and syllogisms, Aristotle offers a definition of tragedy in terms of its essence, which includes its genus (representation of action), and proceeds to deductively derive from it the parts of tragedy (I.5 49b35ff). Indeed, he offers a proof that one part, plot, is the most important one. This proof uses as a foundational premise the portion of the definition of tragedy identifying its genus (I.6 50a15). Are all of these clear principles or fully articulated demonstrations that meet the standards of *An. Post*? Perhaps not, but some may do so more than others. In his treatises we find many instances in which his reasoning has something of the structure Aristotle wants in a proof.

Collecting Facts and Finding Causes

Aristotle's aim in his logical treatise (*An. Post*) might be the articulation, in terms of the demonstrative syllogism, of the strict apodeictic structure into which the results of a completed inquiry into some domain must be organized, if there is to be knowledge or understanding of it. Induction and *nous* answer an important question about the formation/cognition of the principles that are the foundations of the apodeictic structure. The highly compressed and rather abstruse account of how induction and *nous* lead to principles gives the impression that, although the process of getting to principles is more complex than having sensations or forming memories, it is nonetheless analogous to it – somehow universals get established in the soul from perceptions of individuals. Yet this account cannot, and is not meant to, be a description of what an inquirer must do to get to causes or principles. These latter things are far more complicated than simply perceiving individuals of a kind and grasping the nature of the kind, which can be articulated by a definition stating the genus and differentia of the kind. In some of his own inquiries as presented in the extant treatises, especially those on nature, Aristotle makes methodological remarks that might more accurately reflect his own practices as a researcher, and perhaps one should look at these kinds of remarks as constituting his more concrete methodological recommendations as far as *actual inquiry* is concerned. On such occasions, he stresses the role observation and familiarity with the facts of a certain domain of inquiry play in the search for causal explanations in nature. Looking at these remarks, one cannot help being struck by the apparent difference between the simplicity of the *An. Post* II.19 account of how principles come to be in and cognized by the soul, on the one hand, and the complexity, and even messiness, of the path to causes and explanatory principles he outlines and follows in some of his research treatises, on the other.

At *GC* I.2 316a5, for example, Aristotle makes a very general claim about the importance of experience in getting hold of the facts and its usefulness to formulating the appropriate principles that explain them:

> Lack of experience diminishes our power of taking a comprehensive view of the admitted facts. Hence those who dwell in intimate association with nature and its phenomena grow more and more able to formulate, as the foundations of their theories, principles such as to admit of a wide and coherent development: while those whom devotion to abstract discussion has rendered unobservant of the facts are too ready to dogmatize on the basis of a few observations. The rival treatments of the subject now before us will serve to illustrate how great is the difference between "scientific" and "dialectical" method of inquiry. For whereas the Platonists argue that there must be atomic magnitudes 'because otherwise "The Triangle" will be more than one', Democritus would appear to have been convinced by arguments appropriate to the subject, i.e., drawn from the science of nature.

Aristotle appears to follow the more "scientific" method of Democritus in the above quotation in his discussion of the steps to be taken in the study of animals. He empha-

111

sizes the need to begin with a familiarity, based largely on observation, with certain facts about, and differentiating features among, animals in order eventually to arrive at causes and principles appropriate to zoology:

> our object being to determine first of all the differences that exist [in the case of animals] and the actual facts in the case of all of them. Having done this, we must attempt to discover the causes. And, after all, this is the natural method of procedure – to do this only after we have before us the ascertained facts about each item, for this will give us a clear indication of the subjects with which our exposition is to be concerned and the principles upon which it must be based. (HA I.6 491a10)

The same approach to inquiry is advocated at PA I.1 639b8:

> Should the student of nature follow the same sort of procedure as the mathematicians follow in their astronomical expositions – that is to say, should he consider first of all the phenomena which occur in animals, and the parts of each of them, and having done that go on to state the why [reasons, to dia ti] and the causes [aitias]; or should he follow some other way?

Aristotle opts for the first option. Now, when Aristotle speaks of facts or phenomena, he often has in mind something broader than what we typically designate as observational facts or phenomena. At times he includes conceptual distinctions, opinions, or reports by third persons among the facts, and there numerous references to the latter in the HA (e.g., reports by fishermen or just hearsay) and the other biological treatises. But there is little doubt in the above statements, he has in mind primarily facts and phenomena that we come to have by observations and empirical research.[8] Doubts have been raised as to whether Aristotle's own biological treatises follow the methodological directive enunciated in the above passage from HA; Balme (1986) suggests that he composed the more theoretical biological treatises, those that articulate the basic explanatory principles of the genus animal (PA and GA), prior to writing the one (HA) that presents the vast body of facts he and his associates had collected. But this does not affect the substantive issue here, for Aristotle's concern is with how one proceeds in inquiring after causes or principles and not when one writes down the results of one's inquiry. The above statements make clear (1) the recognition on Aristotle's part that the process of getting to principles is far more complex than the account given in the An. Post in terms of the cognitive state of nous that comes about by inductively getting hold of a universal from the experience of some particulars – if such a cognitive state comes about, it comes after thorough empirical inquiry (see Burnyeat 1981; Kosman 1973) – and (2) the importance he places on the collection of facts or observational data for his own and all inquiries.

Focusing on (1), the above quotations imply that getting to any principle (basic or intermediate) or cause (ultimate or non-ultimate) is a far more arduous and labor intensive task and requires a far greater familiarity with a domain than Aristotle's account of how a number of perceptions of individuals of a certain kind leads us inductively to knowledge of the kind, which can be articulated as a definition in terms of its genus and differentia. Induction may be the way to principles, but the inductive base may need to be considerable and the resulting definition might be far more complex than what a logician supposes. Thus, according to Aristotle, the process of inquiring about animals involves the collection of observational data about every aspect of animals – their parts, ways of feeding, reproducing, stages of growth, movement, habitat, dispositions, behavior, and so on, as well as the differences in each one of these aspects from one species to another – and in some cases the facts will become apparent only by doing dissections, to which Aristotle makes numerous references in his works in zoology. It is this kind of inquiry that will lead one to the identification of patterns in the vast array of zoological phenomena, which in turn will be the basis of formulating causal explanations for them. To be sure, such an observationally guided approach to seeking causes is already present in the *An. Post.* Aristotle may deny that seeing an eclipse or leaf-shedding by trees constitutes scientific knowledge or understanding of these types of phenomena, but he shows how from such observations we can reason to causes and definitions of the respective features of nature (see e.g., II.8–13 and Bolton 1987 and Lennox, ch. 21, in this volume). The observation-guided process of inquiring after causes touched on in *An. Post* is put to work in the comprehensive research project of the *Researches into Animals* (*Tôn peri ta zô(i)a historiôn, Historia Animalium*) and some of the other biological treatises. The facts amassed in this work give us a better sense of what an inductive base for finding causes and principles about animals must look like. And there may be additional, significant rewards to the labor intensive empirical inquiry; they may include the opening of a window for the investigator to the kind of complexity, richness and, possibly, intractability of nature that cannot be captured or exhausted by the kind of definition the logician insists on – i.e., specifying a genus and a differentia. Systematic observation, for instance, may reveal that what gives us a better insight into the nature of a kind is a cluster – possibly with a very large number of components – of features and not the single differentia the logician's definition dictates.[9] It also may lead the inquirer to realize that the possibility of identifying a genus in certain cases is not to be taken for granted or that the one-genus requirement in the logician's definition may not be satisfied everywhere in nature. So in his researches on animals, Aristotle encounters species whose genus is problematic since they straddle the genera *animal* and *plant*, the type he designates "dualizers" (*HA* VIII.1 588b5).

The need to gather the facts or data in order to move on to causes is not a peculiarity of zoology, or even natural science, for Aristotle. This brings us to (2). It is to be found in his work on politics, ethics, psychology, and so on. Focusing on the *Pol*,[10] his remark at II.5 1264a5 that "the matter [unity in the state] would become particularly evident, however, if one could see such a constitution actually been instituted" makes clear the value he placed on observation and empirical evidence. In the *Pol* he continuously makes use of observed facts, including ones about non-human animals, and often seems to work in some important respects like a political scientist of the empiricist tradition. Thus in trying to elucidate the differences between household management and wealth acquisition (*Pol* I.8), he presents observational facts about the different ways of life and food acquisition of non-human animals and points to the corresponding facts on these matters in the case of humans. As he makes clear at *Pol* IV.4, the approach to be used for the classification of constitutions is modeled on the one proposed for the classification of animals in *PA*: "If we wanted to grasp the kinds of animals, we would first determine what it is necessary for every animal to have: for example, certain of the sense organs, something to work on and absorb food . . . and also parts

113

by which it moves . . . It is the same way with constitutions we have mentioned. For city-states are constituted not out of one but many parts, as we have often said" (*Pol* IV.4 1290b25–38).[11] Much of the empirical investigation on the parts of animals and how they differ from one species to the other is carried on in *HA*, where he defines his aim as follows: "So first of all we must consider the parts of animals – the parts of which they are composed; for it is in respect of its parts first and foremost that any animal differs from another" (*HA* I.6 491a15). Aristotle's emphasis on the parts of the state and the empirical approach by which they are identified can be seen at the very beginning of the *Pol*, when he claims that "if we also examine the parts that make up a city-state, we shall see better both how these differ from each other, and whether or not it is possible to gain some expertise in connection with each of the things we have mentioned" (*Pol* I.1 1252a20). This emphasis runs through the whole treatise. He identifies a number of things as parts of the state, including: the associations from which the state comes to be – family, household, village; classes in terms of possession of property – the wealthy and the poor; occupational classes – farmers, craftsmen, traders, hired laborers, defensive warriors.

The empirical data about the parts of the state Aristotle uses in his political investigation have important consequences for some of the views he develops in the *Pol*. Perhaps his discussions of democracy and oligarchy provide the best example of this. While he often views democracy as the rule of the many and oligarchy as that of the few, the empirically established factual connections between the many and being poor and the few and being wealthy play a decisive role in his thinking about democracy and oligarchy. For instance, when he explains why both oligarchy and democracy are deviant forms of constitution or government, the reasons he gives are not that the former is a rule aiming at the benefit of the few and the latter at the benefit of the many, but that "oligarchy is for the benefit of the rich, and democracy for the benefit of the poor" (*Pol* III.7 1279b6). And this is not surprising, given what his empirical researches have revealed about the important features of these types of government:

> What this argument seems to make clear is that it is a coincidence that the few have authority in oligarchies and the many in democracies, a result of the fact that everywhere the rich are few and the poor many . . . What does distinguish democracy and oligarchy from one another is poverty and wealth: whenever some, whether a minority or a majority, rule because of their wealth, the constitution is necessarily an oligarchy, and whenever the poor rule, it is necessarily a democracy. But it turns out, as we said, that the former are in fact few and the latter many. (*Pol* III.9 1279b34)

The emphasis he places on these factual connections between democracy and poverty, on the one hand, and oligarchy and wealth, on the other, creates challenges for him when he tries to define these two forms of government more fully; and the accounts he finally gives of them are much more complex than the intuitive view supposes when it equates democracy with the rule of the many and oligarchy with that of the few. The accounts are far richer, too, reflecting the empirical connections that hold between parts of the state and revealing that both of these forms of government can only be understood in terms of a cluster of features. Thus, Aristotle criticizes Plato, who in his *Statesman* (291d) equates democracy with the rule of the many, and instead argues that

One should not assert . . . that democracy is simply where the multitude is in authority . . . Nor should an oligarchy be regarded as being where the few are in authority over the constitution. For if there were a total of thirteen hundred people, out of which a thousand were rich people who give no share in office to three hundred poor ones, no one would say that the latter were democratically governed even if they were free and otherwise similar to the rich. Similarly, if the poor were few, but stronger than the rich, who were a majority, no one would call such a constitution an oligarchy if the others, though rich, did not participate in office. Thus it is better to say that a democracy exists when the free are in authority and an oligarchy exists when the rich are, but it happens that the former are many and the latter few, since many are free and few are rich. (*Pol* IV.4 1290a30)

But the above does not satisfy Aristotle; it does not fully capture the complex nature of these types of government, and he goes on to elaborate further:

Yet these are not sufficient to distinguish these constitutions. Rather, since both democracy and oligarchy have a number of parts, we must further grasp that it is not a democracy if a few free people rule over a majority who are not free . . . Nor is it an oligarchy if the rich rule because they are a multitude . . . Rather, it is a democracy when the free and the poor who are a majority have the authority to rule, and an oligarchy when the rich and well born, who are few, do. (*Pol* IV.4 1290b7)

Aristotle's methodological directive, which emphasizes empirical research and the collection of observational data, is not thought of as being applicable only to the study of animals or the polis. It has a much wider application. In his ethics, for example, he appeals often to what he considers to be the facts about the soul. Yet it is not clear that even this more complex and intensive empirical inquiry into the facts prior to and as the basis to seeking causes or principles fares any better as a way of getting to the principles or first causes of the kind Aristotle demands than the simpler and more limited one discussed at the end of *An. Post*. The problems with getting to Aristotelian principles stem primarily from his metaphysical commitments, his foundationalism, the epistemic conditions he places on principles, and the kind of scientific knowledge or understanding he wants to attain. As long as all these requirements remain in place, the problem of how to arrive at the kind of knowledge of principles Aristotle insists on will likely persist. Yet the rewards of the intensive empirical inquiry alluded to earlier are not insignificant.

Dialectic and its Uses

Simple perception or intensive empirical inquiry, together with induction and *nous*, however, are not the only ways to principles. While Aristotle takes a dim view of the kind of dialectic used by Platonists in the investigation of generation and corruption (see passage from *GC* quoted earlier) or nature generally (see *An* I.1), the kind involving abstract reasoning about abstract objects, he thinks that the kind dealt with in his own works devoted to the study of dialectic (*Top*, *SE*) can have several uses, one of them in connection to reaching the first principles of the sciences. At *Top* I.2 101a35, he claims that:

> They [uses] are three – [a] intellectual training, [b] casual encounters, and [c] the philosophical sciences . . . For the study of the philosophical sciences it [dialectic] is useful, because [c_1] the ability to puzzle on both sides of a subject will make us detect more easily the truth and error about the several points that arise. [c_2] It has a further use in relation to the principles used in the several sciences. For it is impossible to discuss them at all from the principles proper to the particular science in hand, seeing that the principles are primitive in relation to everything else: it is through reputable opinions (*endoxa*) about them that these have to be discussed, and this task belongs properly, or most appropriately, to dialectic; for dialectic is a process of criticism wherein lies the path to the principles of all inquiries.

Use [c_1] appears to be consistent with the character of dialectical deductions and of their premises, as Aristotle understands them, and we find many instances in his works where he "puzzles on both sides of a subject." But use [c_2] seems controversial precisely on account of the way Aristotle understands the nature of dialectical reasoning, on the one hand, and the nature of first principles and their epistemic status, on the other. At *Top* I.1 100a25, he contrasts demonstrative deductions with dialectical ones, leaving no doubt about the distance separating the two. He claims that a deduction

> is a demonstration, when the premises from which the deduction starts are true and primitive, or are such that our knowledge of them has originally come through premises which are primitive and true; and it is a dialectical deduction, if it reasons from reputable opinions (*endoxa*). Things are true and primitive which are convincing not on the strength of anything else but of themselves; for in regard to the first principles of science it is improper to ask any further for the why and wherefore of them; each of the first principles should command belief in and of itself. On the other hand, those opinions are reputable (*endoxa*) which are accepted by everyone or by the majority or by the wise – i.e., by all, or by the majority, or by the most notable and reputable of them. (see also I.10 104a10)

If the difference between the starting points of demonstration and dialectical reasoning is what Aristotle says it is, then how could reasoning from dialectical propositions lead one to the kind of cognition Aristotle associates with principles? Dialectical reasoning from reputable opinions will, at best, reach an opinion or establish the plausibility of something, not the kind of necessity or certainty associated with scientific knowledge or understanding (*An. Post* I.19 81b18).

Socrates and Plato rejected any appeal to or reasoning from opinions in the quest for knowledge, and it is reasonable to suppose that Aristotle had some reasons for placing the weight he does place on opinions – at least on the reputable ones. On several occasions throughout his writings, he insists on the importance the views of earlier thinkers have for any inquiry since "the same opinions appear in cycles among men not once nor twice nor occasionally, but infinitely often" (*Meteor* I.3 339b28; see also *Cael* I.3 270b19: "the same ideas . . . recur in men's minds not once or twice but again and again"), and that "while probably each art and science has often been developed as far as possible and has again perished, these opinions [of the early natural philosophers about the divine] have been preserved like relics until the present" (*Met* Λ.8 1074b10). For this reason, Aristotle argues that "we should not disregard the experiences of ages" (*Pol* II.5 1264a) but instead "we should make the best use of what has been already discovered, and try to correct deficiencies" (*Pol* VII.10 1329b34). Actually, he goes a step further by claiming that not only the few wise thinkers but everyone "says something true about the nature of things," that both those with whose views we agree and those with whose views we disagree "contributed something," and that, thus, inquiring after the truth is a collective effort that can succeed:

> The investigation of the truth is in one way hard, in another easy. An indication of this is found in the fact that no one is able to attain the truth adequately, while on the other hand, we do not collectively fail, but every one says something true about the nature of things, and while individually we contribute little or nothing to the truth, by the union of all a considerable amount is amassed . . . It is just that we should be grateful, not only to those with whose views we may agree, but also to those who have expressed more superficial views; for these also contributed something, by developing before us the powers of thought. It is true that if there had been no Timotheus we should have been without much of our lyric poetry; but if there had been no Phrynis there would have been no Timotheus. The same holds good of those who have expressed views about the truth; for from some thinkers we have inherited certain opinions, while the others have been responsible for the appearance of the former. (*Met* α.1 993a30–b18)

The generous view expressed here, which credits *everyone* with making a contribution to knowledge of the truth is likely based on his views about the nature and veridicality of sensation and its role in survival, mentioned earlier. As he claims at *Rhet* I.1 1355a15, humans have "a natural capacity for the truth and indeed in most cases attain to it." Opinions are not experiences, but they may have their origins in experiences.

Elsewhere, we find limits to Aristotle's generosity: he thinks that some opinions are worthless. At *EE* I.3 1214b28 he dismisses the views about happiness of most: "To examine then all the views held about happiness is superfluous, for children, sick people, and the insane all have views, but no sane person would dispute over them . . . Similarly we have not to consider the views of the multitudes (for they talk without consideration about almost everything, and most about happiness); for it is absurd to apply argument to those who need not argument but experience." But Aristotle's doubts about the worthiness of opinions extend beyond those of the children, the sick, the insane, and of the multitude. At times he questions the worthiness of the views of people reputed for their wisdom. Thus, while he considers it possible that Thales made some contribution to the early accounts of nature, "Hippo no one would think fit to include among these thinkers, because of the paltriness of his thought" (*Met* A.3 984a2). According to Aristotle, Empedocles "contradicts his own statements as well as the observed facts [about change and alteration]" (*GC* I.1 315a4). Aristotle, in fact, takes a dim view of all of his predecessors, except Democritus, with respect to their accounts of coming-to-be and passing-away: "Not one of them penetrated below the surface or made a thorough examination of a single one of the problems . . . none of the other [than Democritus] philosophers made any definite statement about growth, except such as any amateur might have made" (*GC* I.1 315a35). In his review of the contributions of his predecessors on causes at *Met* A, he complains than nothing was articulated clearly by them (986b2), although they might have had some inkling but spoke vaguely (988a18), and that they seek the causes vaguely and "although in a sense they [causes] have been described before in a sense they have not been described at all. For the earliest philosophy is on all subjects, like one who lisps" (993a13). These remarks seem to raise questions about the usefulness of Aristotle's distinction between reputable and non-reputable opinions, the former being those held by the most notable and reputable people. As he admits, "not every opinion that seems reputable actually is reputable. For none of the opinions which we call reputable show their character entirely on the surface" (*Top* I.1 100b26).[12]

For certain uses of dialectic, the status of opinions from which they reason may be of no concern. Uses [a] and [b] (intellectual training and casual encounters) perhaps fall in the first class. For some others, the dialectician may not need to make at the outset any significant assumptions about the nature of the opinions; his own reasoning may sort out which ones are of value. This seems to be the case in the first philosophical use of dialectic, that of setting the puzzles. In the well-known passage from *Met* B.1 995a23, where Aristotle explains why it is important in inquiry to start with the opinions of others and set out the puzzles, he does not stipulate that only some opinions are to be used and not others. Similarly, when at *NE* VII.1 he proposes to review the opinions of others about incontinence, he does not indicate that only some opinions make the grade for this purpose. Presumably, for such purposes it is the task of dialectic to shift through all the opinions and arrive at the genuine puzzles about the problem at hand. In addition to setting forth the puzzles dialectic also aims, in philosophical contexts, to establish or prove (*deikninai*) the *endoxa* or use *endoxa* to support one's conclusions arrived at by a different route. At *NE* VII, the task is to explore the nature of continence and incontinence, and Aristotle relies on the same strategy of setting out the phenomena, going through the puzzles, and establishing the truth of "all the *endoxa* . . . or failing that, of the majority of them and most authoritative" (1145b2). Aristotle lists seven different opinions about continence and incontinence that seem to be common beliefs of the same status, and sets out the difficulties. But it is clear that, as Aristotle's argument unfolds, the opinion about incontinence that becomes the focus of the discussion and that he is most concerned to establish is that of Socrates and, as Reeve (1992: 36–7) points out, the opinion has considerable authority on account of being the view of a person, Socrates, who is reputed to be wise. At *NE* I.8 1098b10, however, when Aristotle seeks corroboration of his conclusion from the function argument, he characterizes the opinion that the goods of the soul are goods in the fullest sense as an opinion "of long standing, and generally accepted by philosophers." This is a different criterion, for Socrates' opinion on incontinence is neither "of long standing" nor "generally accepted." A few lines later (1098b25), while considering whether the characteristics that are believed to be true of happiness – e.g., virtue, a kind of wisdom or practical wisdom, pleasure, prosperity – belong to the human good as he defines it, he claims that "Some of these views have been held by many people and from ancient times, others by a few distinguished men, and neither class is likely to be altogether mistaken; the probability is that their beliefs are at least partly, or indeed mainly, correct."

The criteria he gives for which opinions ought to be established, and which beliefs ought to be used for corroboration of his own views are not precise and it is not clear what relative weight he places on each one of them. Perhaps the criteria he lists in the passages just quoted may suffice for the less ambitious purposes just discussed. A more difficult challenge is to provide a criterion that singles a subclass of endoxa that can lead, through the use of dialectic alone, to first principles. This is made difficult both by Aristotle's foundationalist framework and by the conditions – objectivity, necessity, epistemic priority, non-inferential cognition – he places on principles in the *An. Post*. No opinion is a principle, and one cannot try to justify its being one by appealing to the above kind of criteria, or to the reasons mentioned earlier in support of the veracity of perception, or the natural capacity of humans to hit the truth. Even if such justification were possible, it would be based on inference, and so undermine the status of the desired principles as *first* principles. Dialectical reasoning can at most establish coherence among opinions; it cannot prove that certain propositions are Aristotelian principles, even if we were to assume that such a proof was permitted within Aristotle's foundationalist framework. It seems then that dialectic of the kind we have been discussing, the kind Irwin calls "pure," can take us only up to a certain point, very much as, according to the rationalist interpretation of *nous*, induction does in the account of the cognition of principles in *An. Post*. How does dialectic gets us to the principles?

Some scholars conclude that intuition takes over where dialectic ends. Reeve (1992: 62–3), for instance, argues that this is Aristotle's position (see also Mure 1964: 218). In such an interpretation, the role of dialectic and its reliance on opinions is the counterpart to that of induction and its reliance on the data of the senses, with the final stage in both methods being the contribution of intuition in the grasping of the principles. Thus criteria for singling out a set of *endoxa* that may lead to an intuitive grasp of principles at the end of the dialectical process may be of importance. With respect to the intuitive grasp of principles, starting from or focusing on the most authoritative *endoxa* may be as important in dialectic as beginning with the appropriate experiential data is in induction.

Not all think that the above is Aristotle's view – that dialectic's way to the principles is, once more, via intuition. Irwin argues that Aristotle's foundationalist framework in *An. Post* and its implication that the cognition of first principles is non-inferential rule out the possibility that the reasoning of pure dialectic from common beliefs can lead to first principles. Intuition is necessary for that, if foundationalism remains in place and there is only pure dialectic (Irwin 1988: ch. 7). But he does not think that Aristotle takes that route. Instead, Irwin argues, he moves away from the foundationalism of the *An. Post*, and thus opens the door for some type of justification of first principles. The justification is not demonstrative, but dialectical. But the dialectic appropriate for this cannot be pure dialectic, the kind that solely relies on common beliefs and cannot reach objective truths. Irwin argues that the justification Aristotle offers in the *Met* for the highest principles of the science of being, e.g., of the PNC, uses what he terms "strong dialectic." Strong dialectic does not rely on any and all common beliefs, but on an appropriate, restricted subset of them, and for this reason has a claim to objective truth. In the dialectical defense of the PNC Aristotle reasons from beliefs about there being objects suitable for scientific inquiry, and the science of being he articulates, according to Irwin, identifies those universal features (substance with an essence) that are necessary for being an object of scientific inquiry. Irwin argues that the dialectical justification of the principles of the science of being makes it possible for Aristotle to move beyond the puzzles pure dialectic sets forth in works like *An*, *NE*, and *Pol*, and develop his psychological, ethical, and political views. These works depend on what has been established in the *Met* about substance and essence, and the method they employ is strong dialectic. Because of the latter, they and parts of the *Met* are viewed as being the philosophical works and as standing apart from other treatises of Aristotle.

Irwin's comprehensive study of Aristotle's works and overarching argument about first principles offers a powerful alternative to the intuitionist account of first principles and illuminates many parts of Aristotle's thought. Clearly, much rides on the distinction he makes between pure and strong dialectic. Yet there is no clear evidence that Aristotle makes such a distinction. But while the absence of such distinction in Aristotle's texts raises doubts as to whether the alternative to principles Irwin offers is Aristotle's as well, it does not affect the point Irwin often wishes to make – namely, that Aristotle needs strong dialectic in order to get the kind of principles he wants.

As I said at the outset, Aristotle relies on more methods than the ones discussed here. Of particular importance is that of division on which he relies heavily in his biological works on the classification of animals. Several recent studies explore aspects of this method.[13]

Notes

[1] For passages from the *An. Post* I use the translation of that work by Barnes (1994). In this translation Barnes renders several key terms in Aristotle's account of scientific knowledge in ways that deviate from earlier translations (*epistêmê* is rendered as "understanding," *aitia* as "explanation," and *nous* as "comprehension"). Where possible, I indicate the more traditional ways of rendering these terms.

[2] Aristotle identifies three kinds of things as principles: axioms (propositions true of everything, e.g., the Principle of Non-Contradiction and the Excluded Middle, or propositions common to several sciences, e.g., if equals are taken from equals, equals remain), definitions (an account of what something is), and hypotheses (existence claims, e.g., so-and-so is or is not). The concern here is primarily with the first two kinds of principles. For discussion of the conditions Aristotle requires of premises, see Barnes (1994), Irwin (1988), McKirahan (1992), and R. Smith, ch. 4, in this volume.

[3] Aristotle claims that some domains do not exhibit these features to the same extent as those of the most rigorous disciplines and, therefore, the sciences studying them lack the exactness of the rigorous ones. Aristotle's views on these matters are discussed in Anagnostopoulos (1994) and Reeve (1992).

[4] There is disagreement as to whether principles are self-explanatory (Barnes 1994; Burnyeat 1981; Reeve 1994) or self-evident (Irwin 1988).

[5] Aristotle's account is in terms of something like percepts, but the principles are general propositions. Also, although he seems to be thinking of a process of abstraction that takes one from different particulars to a universal, he does not mention abstraction. His claim that, although we perceive particulars, perception is of universals is also highly problematic in view of the fact that he takes the proper objects of perception to be colors, sounds, smells, etc.

[6] There is considerable disagreement among scholars as to whether *nous* reaches into induction or is simply the cognitive state resulting from it; on this, see Lesher (1973), Kosman (1973), Kahn (1981), Irwin (1988).

[7] Often Aristotle speaks of necessity in terms of universality (e.g., *An. Post* I.4 73b27), but at others he thinks of the necessary as that which cannot be otherwise.

[8] See Owen (1961) on the different things Aristotle means by "phainomena." Irwin (1988: 31–2) argues that Aristotle has in mind observations or observed facts when he speaks of the role of experience in inquiry.

[9] Furth (1988: 105) says "a good definition of man might be a million pages long."

[10] His empirical study of 158 constitutions of ancient Greek city-states is to the study of the polis what his researches on animals are to zoology. And Aristotle concludes the *NE* (X.9 1181b 18) by saying "in the light of the constitutions we have collected let us study what sorts of influence preserve and destroy states, and what sorts preserve and destroy the particular kinds of constitution, and to what causes it is due that some are well and others ill administered." This suggests that the empirical survey of the constitutions was completed before the *Pol* was written and that the survey provided the empirical data used in the Pol. But such inferences are not certain. The authenticity of the passage just quoted has been questioned; in addition, the dates (absolute or relative) of *NE*, *Pol*, and the survey are uncertain. Although facts about constitutions are to be found throughout the *Pol*, especially in Book II.9–12, in speaking of the reliance on empirical observations and facts I mean facts of all kinds, some of which are about existing constitutions and may be based on his survey of them.

[11] Robinson (1962: 81) claims that Aristotle "seems here to suggest that he might have arrived at his species without any observation"; for different views that stress observation see Lloyd (1961) and Balme (1972).

[12] Views differ on what are *endoxa*. Some scholars take them to be common beliefs; others claim that they are beliefs or opinions of some weight – see Irwin (1988: 37–9) and Reeve (1992: 36–7).

[13] I would like to thank Andreas Anagnostopoulos and Thalia Anagnostopoulos for some very helpful comments.

Bibliography

Anagnostopoulos, G. (1994). *Aristotle on the Goals and Exactness of Ethics* (Berkeley, CA: University of California Press).

Allan, D. J. (1978). *The Philosophy of Aristotle* (Oxford: Oxford University Press).

Balme, D. (1972). *Aristotle's "De Partibus Animalium" and "De Generatione Animalium"* (Oxford: Oxford Univerity Press).

Balme, D. (1986). "The Place of Biology in Aristotle's Philosophy," in A. Gotthelf and J. Lennox (eds.), *Philosophical Issues in Aristotle's Biology* (Cambridge: Cambridge University Press), pp. 9–20.

Barnes, J. (1982). *Aristotle* (Oxford: Oxford University Press).

Barnes, J. (1994). *Aristotle: "Posterior Analytics"* (Oxford: Clarendon Press).

Barnes, J. (1995). *The Cambridge Companion to Aristotle* (Cambridge: Cambridge University Press).

Bolton, R. (1987). "Definition and Scientific Method in Aristotle's *Posterior Analytics* and *Generation of Animals*," in A. Gotthelf and J. Lennox (eds.), *Philosophical Issues in Aristotle's Biology* (Cambridge: Cambridge University Press), pp. 120–66.

Bolton, R. (1991), "Aristotle's Method in Natural Science: *Physics* I," in L. Judson (ed.), *Aristotle's "Physics"* (Oxford: Oxford University Press), pp. 1–29.

Burnyeat, M. (1981). "Aristotle on Understanding Knowledge," in E. Berti (ed.), *Aristotle on Science: The "Posterior Analytics"* (Padua: Editrice Antinore), pp. 97–139.

Furth, M. (1988). *Substance, Form and Psyche: An Aristotelian Metaphysics* (Cambridge: Cambridge University Press).

Gomperz, T. [1912] (1969). *Greek Thinkers*, vol. 4 (London: John Murray).

Grote, G. (1880). *Aristotle* (London: John Murray).

Irwin, T. (1988). *Aristotle's Principles* (Oxford: Clarendon Press).

Kahn, C. (1981). "The Role of *Nous* in the Cognition of First Principles in *Posterior Analytics*," in E. Berti (ed.), *Aristotle on Science: The "Posterior Analytics"* (Padua: Editrice Antinore), pp. 385–414.

Keyt, D. (1983). "Intellectualism in Aristotle," in J. P. Anton and A. Preus (eds.), *Essays in Ancient Greek Philosophy*, vol. 2 (Albany, NY: State University of New York), pp. 364–87.

Keyt, D. (1991). "Three Basic Theorems in Aristotle's *Politics*," in D. Keyt and F. D. Miller (eds.), *A Companion to Aristotle's "Politics"* (Oxford: Blackwell), pp. 118–41.

Kosman, A. (1973). "Understanding, Explanation, and Insight in the *Posterior Analytics*," in E. N. Lee, A. D. Mourelatos, and R. M. Rorty (eds.), *Exegesis and Argument* (Assen: Van Gorcum), pp. 374–92.

Kripke, S. (1980). *Naming and Necessity* (Cambridge, MA: Harvard University Press).

Lesher, J. (1973). "The Meaning of *Nous* in the *Posterior Analytics*," *Phronesis*, 18, pp. 44–68.

Lloyd, G. E. R. (1961). "The Development of Aristotle's Theory of the Classification of Animals," *Phronesis*, 6, pp. 59–81.

McKirahan, R. (1992). *Principles and Proofs* (Princeton, NJ: Princeton University Press)

Mure, G. R. G. (1964). *Aristotle* (New York: Oxford University Press).

Owen, G. E. L. [1961] (1986). *Tithenai ta Phainomena*. Repr. in Owen, *Logic, Science and Dialectic* (Ithaca, NJ: Cornell University Press, 1986), pp. 239–51.

Reeve, C. D. C. (1992). *Practices of Reason* (Oxford: Oxford University Press).

Robinson, R. (1962), *Aristotle's "Politics," Books III and IV* (Oxford: Oxford University Press).

Ross, W. D. [1923] (1995). *Aristotle* (London: Routledge).

Santas, G. (2001). *Goodness and Justice* (Oxford: Blackwell)

Scholz, H. [1930] (1975). "The Ancient Axiomatic Theory." Repr. in J. Barnes, M. Schofield and R. Sorabji (eds.), *Articles on Aristotle*, vol. 1, pp. 50–64.

Zeller, E. (1890). *Greek Philosophy* (New York: Henry Holt).

Part III

Theoretical Knowledge

A. Metaphysics

8

The Science and Axioms of Being

MICHAEL V. WEDIN

Aristotle's first editor, Andronicus of Rhodes, placed the fourteen books now known as the *Metaphysics* after the *Physics*, whence comes the word "metaphysics," which literally means "after the physics." Some have used this fact to buttress the claim that the work as a whole has no focused subject, but rather is a collection of loosely linked essays. There is some warrant for this skeptical assessment. The first chapter of the first Book, Book A,[1] announces that "we" are seeking a certain kind of theoretical knowledge, something Aristotle calls "wisdom" (*sophia*). Because wisdom is knowledge of first causes and principles, the task is to investigate what sorts of causes and principles are suited to play this role. The reader might expect Aristotle to then proceed on just such a course of inquiry. After A, however, the term "wisdom" effectively disappears from the treatise.[2] In B's set of puzzles we get instead the "science of substance," in Γ we are introduced to the "science of being *qua* being," and in Book E preference appears to be given to "first philosophy" and "theology." Are these the same or different enterprises and, if different, are they independent or related, and, if related, how? These questions can be addressed by seeing how Aristotle's treatment of wisdom follows a coherent, if complicated, path through much of the *Metaphysics*, beginning with the science of being *qua* being.

Aristotle's Declaration of a General Science of Being *qua* Being

Book Γ of the *Metaphysics* opens with the declaration that there is a science of being *qua* being and distinguishes this from special sciences, such as physics or geometry, which carve out part of being for study:

> There is a science which studies (A) that which is *qua* that which is and (B) what things hold of this in its own right. This is not the same as any of the so-called special sciences, for none of them investigates universally that which is *qua* thing that is, but all select some part of it. (1003a21–4)

125

I shall refer to this as the Declaration Statement and to (A) and (B) as Provisions. The phrase commonly translated "being *qua* being" is rendered by Kirwan "that which is *qua* that which is" (unless otherwise noted, I use, or follow, the translation of Kirwan 1971). Provision (A) uses this expression to fix the domain of the science. Provision (B), which I turn to in the next section, covers what the science will say *about* the items in the domain.

Every science studies that which is but not in the same way, and none of the special sciences will study that which is in the same way as the general science of being. Still the cases are importantly parallel. For example, Aristotle can say that physics studies that which is *qua* having an internal principle of motion and rest. Here the occurrence of "that which is" before the *qua* operator can be replaced by a variable and what follows the *qua* specifies the property that will be studied by the science (which property, implicitly, restricts the range of values for the variable). So, switching to a more transparent idiom, we can say that physics studies *x insofar as x* has an internal principle of motion and rest. Similarly, biology studies *x* insofar as *x* has the capacity for living, and geometry studies *x* insofar as *x* is the limit of a solid. The second sentence of the Declaration Statement suggests that special sciences may investigate universally, but what they investigate universally is only a part of that which is. So the special sciences satisfy universally quantified formulae – physics studies *any x* insofar as *x* has an internal principle of rest and motion, biology studies *any x* insofar as *x* has the capacity for living, and so on.

The general science of being does not, then, differ formally from the special sciences, at least as so far characterized. It also studies that which is, and, like them, it does so under a specification that fixes its domain. But the specification in question is rather different. The expression translated above as "that which is *qua* that which is" is typically rendered as "being *qua* being." This tends to obscure the expression's function, something better captured by the more transparent idiom, "that which is *insofar as* it is." Thus, the general science of being studies things simply insofar as they *are*, that is, it studies any *x* insofar as *x is*. This idiom also shows what is misleading about the expression "being *qua* being" – it is too easily taken to function as a semantic unit that picks out an object, *being-qua-being*. But this mistakenly takes "*qua* being" to modify the noun "being"; rather the phrase has adverbial force and goes with "study," indicating *how* the given science will investigate things. There is no fancy object to serve as the referent of the expression "being *qua* being." On the contrary, for the most part, there are only the ordinary objects studied in the various sciences. In the general science of being, however, these ordinary objects will be studied in a quite extraordinary way. In particular, to study them *insofar as* they *are* entails that the general science of being will study *everything* that is.

The fact that Γ characterizes the general science of being in terms that apply to the special sciences suggests that Aristotle conceives of this science on the model of the demonstrative sciences outlined in the *Posterior Analytics*. This impression gains force from the fact that particular sciences demonstrate of a subject those attributes that hold of the subject in its own right. This is just what Provision (B) of the Declaration Statement says about the science of *being*. Just as geometry investigates what holds in its own right of things insofar as they are the limits of solids, so the general science of being will investigate what holds in its own right of things insofar as they are. So it will investigate notions that apply to everything, notions such as being, difference and similarity. Most especially, as we shall see shortly, it also will study axioms – the paradigms of principles that hold of everything. Before pursuing this further, however, we must address a worry that threatens the very possibility of a general science of being.

A Problem for the Science of Being

The worry stems from the requirement, laid down in *An. Post* I.28, that every demonstrative science has a subject genus, which the science is *about*. This is precisely what is specified by the phrases following "insofar as *x* has . . ." three paragraphs back in our characterizations of physics, biology, and geometry. The Subject Condition, as I shall call this, is invoked in Γ.1, where the so-called special sciences are said to select some part of being and study its properties. Thus, physics is specified by the subject genus, *having an internal principle of motion and rest*. In the *Posterior Analytics*, however, the Subject Condition is entertained as a requirement on sciences in general. So in considering the science that investigates "universally that which is insofar as it is," it is natural to ask for the subject genus of this science, the general science of being. The obvious choice would seem to be *being* itself. Unfortunately, the obvious choice is not available, for Aristotle routinely insists (e.g., at *Metaphysics* H.6 1045a33–b7) and twice argues (at *Metaphysics* B.3 998b22–7 and K.1 1059b24–34) that *being* is not a genus.

We, thus, appear to be faced with a dilemma. Given the Subject Condition,

    1a.   Every science has a genus,

and the prohibition against being as a genus,

    1b.   Being is not a genus,

we seem forced to conclude,

    1c.   There is no general science of being.

So two of Aristotle's favored doctrines appear to exclude the enterprise he so easily affirms at the outset of Γ. One might complain that (1a) holds only for demonstrative sciences and, thus, that (1c) ought to read that there is no *demonstrative* general science of being. But for Aristotle there is no other notion of a science available here, and so (1c) appears to stand.

How, then, can Book Γ assert, without qualm or qualification, that there is a general science of being? There are, I think, two strategies for explaining this. According to the first, developmental, strategy the Subject Condition dates from an early period when Aristotle eschewed a science of being. By the time of Γ's composition, however, he had discovered a new way to unify the domain of a science, by relaxing the Subject Condition from the *Posterior Analytics*. Proponents of this strategy might find Aristotle doing just this in Γ.2, at 1003b12–14 (and, in a slightly different formulation, at 1004a24–5), where he signals that there are two ways for a group of things to qualify for investigation by a single science:

it falls to one science to study not only (i) things that are called what they are by virtue of one thing but also (ii) things that are called what they are by reference to one nature.

For a number of things to be called something *by virtue of one thing* is for them to fall uneventfully under a single genus. For example, a number of things will be called "animal" by falling under the genus *animal*. This explains why they are animals and provides a natural principle of unity for the domain under investigation (namely, animals). Thus, alternative (i) states the early *Posterior Analytics* condition on the subject matter of a science: one genus for every science. Alternative (ii), however, announces a new way to unify a domain for scientific investigation. For a number of things to be called something *by reference to one nature* the things need not belong to the same genus. Quite disparate things are healthy without falling into a single genus – witness exercise and food. Yet there is, we are told, a science of health, or, in Γ.1's idiom, a science of things insofar as they are healthy. Aristotle's two alternatives may be captured by the following formulation:

2.   There is a science, S, & S studies $x \ldots$ & $\ldots y \leftrightarrow$ (i) $x \ldots$ & $\ldots y$ are called what they are in virtue of one thing (i.e., they fall under a single genus) $\lor$ (ii) $x \ldots$ & $\ldots y$ are called what they are by reference to one thing.

The next step in the developmental strategy is to give a plausible account of (ii), the new way of unifying a domain, in particular its use of what Owen (1960) famously called "focal meaning." Aristotle illustrates the notion with ordinary cases and then extends it to the science of being. Taking the case already introduced, things may be called healthy for quite different reasons but they are so-called by reference to one thing, namely health. Some produce health, some preserve it, some are a sign of it, and so on. Thus, things as diverse as nutrition, exercise, complexion, and climate are counted healthy because of standing in some such relation to health. And because of this "reference to health" they are included in a single science of health. Further, while there may be various senses of "healthy" distributed among the diverse things that are healthy, all have a common focus, namely, health. Hence, the term has focal meaning, and its domain has what might be called focal unity. Things that *are* also enjoy focal unity. Thus, that which is is said in many ways but with reference to one thing or principle. The idiom, "being is said in many ways," typically refers to the senses of being demarcated by the ten categories. Thus, to be is to be a substance, a quality, a quantity, a place, etc. Because items other than substances *are* thanks to their dependence on substances, they are said to *be* by reference to another thing that *is*, namely, substance.

Owen made much of focal meaning in his influential developmentalist account. In particular, he seized on a passage from *Eudemian Ethics* I.8 as conclusive proof of Aristotle's change of mind about a science of being. In 1217b25–35, after remarking that being is said in as many ways as the categories, Aristotle concludes

> So, just as being is not a single thing embracing the things mentioned [namely, the categories], the good is not either; nor is there a single science of being or the good (following Woods 1982).

The *Eudemian Ethics* is an early work and, according to Owen, it fails to allow that "being" enjoys focal meaning. Thus, Aristotle had little choice but to disallow a single science of being. By the same token, Γ's later extension of focal meaning to "being" enables the general science of being. Owen takes Aristotle, now fully armed with focal meaning, to hold that being (that which *is*) is so-called by reference to one thing, *rather than* in virtue of one thing. In terms of (2) above, this means that he takes (i) and (ii) to be exclusive alternatives. Since (i) corresponds to the Subject Condition, Aristotle is held to drop the condition as a requirement on a science. And so he rejects premise (1a) of the argument that generated the dilemma at the beginning of this section.

More than a little puzzling for this account is the fact that *EE* VII.2 1236a7–33, embraces focal meaning, awarding it to "friendship" on the model of "medical." Owen is aware of this, and, therefore, contends that in the *Eudemian Ethics* Aristotle simply is unable to *apply* focal meaning to "being." Although there is more to the notion (see two paragraphs below), the core idea is that substance individuals are the primary instances of being and that all other "beings" depend on them for their being. Because Aristotle knows this from the *Categories*, another early work, Owen's contention is implausible. Moreover, the contention is called for only on the assumption that the *EE* I.8 passage, 1217b25–35, denies focal meaning to being. Precisely this is brought into question by the second strategy for dealing with Aristotle's apparent change of mind on the possibility of a science of being.

Due to Code (1996), the strategy proceeds, in effect, by rejecting the assumption that (2)'s alternatives, (i) and (ii), are incompatible. Crucially, it neutralizes Owen's use of the *Eudemian Ethics* passage by cautioning that the passage is part of an anti-Platonist salvo against the possibility of a science of being and the good *of the sort envisioned by Plato*. These sciences *would* have the Platonic objects, *Being* and *the Good*, as their subjects. Aristotle is, thus, objecting to Plato's science of being. He is not rejecting focal meaning for "being," and so he is not rejecting his own version of a science of being. Moreover, (i) and (ii) are compatible even for Aristotle's special sciences. Drawing on the point that the *Posterior Analytics* does not require the *propria* of a demonstrative science to belong to the subject genus of the science, Code shows how a special science can satisfy the Subject Condition and still investigate items that fall outside its single subject genus. Generally, the claim that a science is *officially about* Gs is distinct from the claim that it *investigates* Gs. To consider the categories, nothing prevents a science whose subject genus falls in one category, say a science of time, from investigating, as needed, items from another category. Likewise, nothing prevents a science of substance from investigating items, perhaps all items, falling outside the subject genus, namely, substance. This is precisely the situation for the science of being.

Given the parallel with health, we might expect Aristotle to say that each of the things that are *is* by reference to one thing, namely *being*. But, of course, this option is not available because, unlike health, in the case of *being* there is no such one thing or nature – Platonic or other. Faced with this, Aristotle adopts a two-part strategy. First, he borrows an entrenched thesis from the *Categories*, namely, the thesis that things other than substances depend for their existence on substances, and strengthens the thesis by insisting that a non-substantial item is *called* a thing that *is* because it is an affection of a substance, or because it is a quality of a substance, and so on. For the primacy of substance is now linked with *explaining*, for everything else that is, *what it*

129

is to be a thing that is. Indeed, the second formulation of focal unity, at 1004a24–5, takes us beyond the mere ontological dependence of the *Categories* to a stronger tie by insisting that the *formulae* of the disparate items are such as to refer to the primary item, in this case, substance. With this, the thesis gains semantical force not evident in the *Categories*: for something to be a quality, for example, just means for it to be a quality of a substance, and so on. Second, in Γ.2 Aristotle claims that each science is funda-mentally concerned with what might be called the primary item in its domain, namely, that on which the others depend and because of which they are called what they are. Further, because this primary item provides the science with its subject genus, the science satisfies the Subject Condition. But even this is not quite enough for a general science of being, for while things other than substance depend on *substance*, nonethe-less these things are said to *be*. So in Γ.2 Aristotle also insists on the point that sub-stances are the primary things that *are* and, further, that dependence on the primary kind of *being* explains why the dependent items are called things that *are* and how substances can be the one thing that unifies everything in the domain of that which *is*. (Note that the parallel with health would be exact were Aristotle to accept that the primary instance of health is a certain ratio of physiological elements in the body. That would be the primary thing that is healthy and so other things would merit the term "healthy" by producing, or sustaining this ratio, and so on.)

Thus, the general science of being has a legitimate subject genus, substance, and so can claim to universally investigate things that *are* without countenancing being as a genus. In terms of the argument that generated the dilemma at the beginning of this section, (1a) and (1b) are true, but entail (1c) only on the assumption that if there is a general science of being, then its subject genus must be being. Since there is no reason to hold Aristotle to this assumption, the dilemma disappears, and there is no cause to adopt Owen's developmental account.

An additional plus for non-developmentalism is its ability to explain a puzzling passage in Γ.2. At 1003b14–15, after indicating that things-that-are are called what they are by reference to one thing, Aristotle adds, "indeed in a certain sense they are called what they are in virtue of one thing." To say that they are called what they are in virtue of one thing means that they are so-called thanks to the existence of a proper subject genus, namely substance; but at the same time they are not all proper members of the genus; nonetheless, as we have seen, all are called what they are by reference to the subject genus. This agrees with Code's judgment that (2)'s alternatives, (i) and (ii), are compatible. On the other hand, it is hard to see how Owen's developmental account squares with 1003b14–15's acknowledgment of agreement between (i) and (ii).

Quite independently of the issue of developmentalism, we need to call attention to the troublesome fact that (2) is formulated as a biconditional. The formulation is forth-coming from 1003b12–14, where alternatives (i) and (ii) are given as necessary condi-tions for the subject matter of a science, and 1004a24–5, where their negations are necessary conditions for failure of a single science: "it will fall to another science [to study disparate things] not if they are called what they are in several ways [what is the case with *being*] but only if the formulae are connected neither by virtue of one thing [i.e., neither (i)] nor by reference to one thing [i.e., nor (ii)]." This is just equivalent to: if either (i) or (ii) hold, there is a single science. So (i) and (ii) are sufficient as well as necessary conditions for the singleness of a science. Now were (i) and (ii) only necessary conditions, Aristotle would be committed to holding that something satisfying them *might* be a science. More might be called for, including provisions from the *Posterior Analytics*. By making (i) and (ii) sufficient conditions, however, (2) requires that what satisfies them *is* a science. And herein lies the trouble, for why should there not be a science of the political or even the comical, since both terms seem to be enjoy focal meaning every bit as much as "medical"? Granted, Aristotle sometimes speaks of politics as a *practical* science. But there is no room for this in the *Metaphysics*, where sciences one and all are theoretical disciplines. So the argument that focal meaning is the basis for a science of *being* may prove too much.

The Content of the General Science of Being

So far we have discussed only Provision (A), the provision of the Declaration Statement that fixes the domain of the science of being. But Provision (B) commits the science of being to studying what holds "in its own right" of that which is insofar as it is. What does Aristotle have in mind by this? First, he is not denying that *unity* or *sameness*, to take two such things, apply, for example, to animals. They do. But they apply to things that are animals not insofar as they are animals but rather insofar as they are things that *are*. The same holds for rocks, plants, and everything else. Second, Aristotle explains Provision (B) by, again, referring to special sciences. There are, for example, properties distinctive of number *qua* number – properties such as oddness, evenness, and commensurability – and these, Aristotle says, "hold good of numbers both in their own right and [i.e., "or"] with reference to one another" (1004b12–13). Similarly, there are properties or features distinctive of being *qua* being, that is, properties or features holding of anything at all simply insofar as it is a thing that is. Such a property, feature, or thing will hold of everything that is. So one might think of Provision (B) as proposing to examine the absolutely most general concepts or notions that apply to things in general.

One way to carry out this proposal is to investigate concepts that are coextensive with *being*. Now this could be done *ad seriatim*, taking one coextensive concept after another. And this may be the style of treatment recommended at the end of Γ.2 for *priority*, *posteriority*, *genus*, *form*, *part* and *whole*. (Although I hasten to add that, taken singly, it is implausible to suppose that all these are coextensive with *being*. Prospects are, however, better for disjoined pairs. Thus, it is considerably more plausible to suppose that everything is *prior* or *posterior*, that everything is *part* or *whole*, and so on. Still, it is unlikely that every concept studied by the science of being *qua* being is coextensive with *being* even as one term of a disjoined pair.) In any event, Aristotle prefers that the concepts in question be related to *being* in some stronger fashion – recall his remark at 1004b12–13, in the above paragraph, that the properties distinctive of number hold good "with reference to one another." Certainly, this inter-connectedness holds for *unity*. He begins in Γ.2 with an argument for the coextensivity of *being* and *unity*: because everything that *is* is *one* thing and every thing that is *one* is a thing that *is*, *unity* applies to everything *being* applies to and conversely. "Each follows from the other . . . not as being indicated by one formula," but "it helps" if they are (1003b24–6). He then adds that reduplicating the "is" in "*S* is one man" yields "*S* is one man that *is*," without, however, generating a sentence that indicates anything different. The

131

reduplication shows, Aristotle seems to think, that *being* and *unity* are of the same nature. Whatever this means, it goes beyond coextensivity.

A number of inter-connected "metaphysical facts" flow from the proposition that the general science of being studies *unity*. Because, generally, a science that studies a given property will also study its opposite, the general science of being studies *plurality* in addition to *unity* or the *one*. As such, it will also study the various (general) kinds of plurality and the kinds of these kinds (perhaps, echoing 1003b19–22's charge that one science studies the forms of that which is *qua* that which is and the forms of these forms). Thus, *otherness* is a kind of *plurality*, *difference* a kind of *otherness*, and *contrariety* a kind of *difference*. So, as a matter of conceptual analysis, *contrariety* is a kind of *plurality*. And, thus, as a matter of conceptual analysis, the science of being *qua* being studies *contrariety*. In particular, it studies contrariety under Provision (B) as something that holds "in its own right" of that which is *qua* thing that is.

Including Axioms in the General Science of Being

In *Met* Γ.2 Aristotle legitimizes the general science of being by reducing it to the science of substance. Indeed, in *Met* Z.1 he is able to report that the question, "What is being?" just is the question, "What is substance?" So when Γ.3 asserts "it is obvious" that the science of substance deals with axioms, it is affirming that the general science of being deals with the axioms. Less obvious, however, are the grounds for including axioms, the star example of which is the principle of non-contradiction (PNC). One might think that any science that studies contrariety *ipso facto* studies contradiction. Of course, Aristotle clearly distinguishes between contrary and contradictory propositions. But there is a way contraries *imply* contradictories: where a subject, *a*, has the contrary of a property, *F*, *a* does not have *F*; and so were *a* to have *F* and its contrary, it would have *F* and not have *F*. This fact might be used to include PNC in the general science of being. Something like this may be proposed by Code (1987: 138), who argues that contradiction is the primary form of opposition and that the proper study of other modes of opposition, such as contrariety, calls for studying the primary mode. So PNC is included by virtue of its conceptual links to *opposition* and, hence, to *plurality* and *being*.

Unfortunately, it is by no means certain that Aristotle followed this course. In Γ.3 he indicates that axioms are included in the study of substance because "they hold good of *everything* that is." So also in the second aporia from B's set of puzzles, which asks whether the science of substance also deals with the starting points of demonstrations. Aristotle offers as examples the principle of non-contradiction and law of excluded middle (LEM), and says they are called *axioms* and, as such, are the "most universal and the principles of all things." In both places PNC is included in the science of substance because it is an axiom that holds universally of everything that is. Thus, coextensivity with *being* appears to be the basis for including PNC in the science of substance.

In any case, inclusion of PNC in the science of substance is not without complication. First, since any demonstration or deductive reasoning presupposes it, PNC itself cannot be demonstrated or proven to be true. So any argument in support of it must proceed by other means. Therefore, when Aristotle turns to a defense of the principle in Γ.4, he admits that it can be shown only elenctically or "in the manner of a refutation." Second, one need not prove the truth of a principle in order to prove various things about it. Aristotle does just this in Γ.3 in proving that PNC has the property of firmness, indeed, that it is the firmest of all principles.

The Notion of the Firmest Principle

Midway through *Met* Γ.3 Aristotle reiterates that it falls to the philosopher to investigate things that are *qua* things that are and adds that, as such, he should be able to state the firmest principles of everything. He then offers an account of what it is to be a firmest principle (1005b11–18), and immediately identifies the principle of non-contradiction as the firmest principle of all (1005b18–22). The balance of the chapter (1005b22–32) contains a proof for this identification, which I shall call the Indubitability Proof, and a closing flourish promoting PNC as the ultimate principle.

Aristotle's account of firmness is captured by the following claim:

3.   If (a) error is impossible regarding a principle, *P*, then (b) *P* is firmest.

According to (3) firmness is a property of a principle and is connected to the principle's immunity to error.

Although Aristotle supports (3) with an extended argument (see Wedin 2004a), here I shall call attention only to his claims that a principle immune to error (i.e., one that satisfies [3a]) is *most intelligible* and *non-hypothetical*. The notion of a most intelligible principle has Aristotelian warrant. He insists after all that the premises of a demonstration are better known than the conclusion. By extension, for *P* to be the most intelligible principle is for it to be more intelligible than any other principle and for there to be no principle as intelligible as it. The second claim, that a principle immune to error is non-hypothetical, carries no presumption of knowledge, but simply constrains the non-hypothetical to what is not provable (see Kirwan 1971; Wedin 2004a).

So a principle is firmest if there can be no principle more intelligible than it and it is more intelligible than all other principles, and if it is not provable, i.e., if there is no principle from which it may be proved. These two proximate sufficient conditions for firmness are inherited by any principle that is immune to error. For this reason, Aristotle is free to restrict himself to immunity to error as the qualifying condition for a firmest principle. He does just this in the Indubitability Proof, where he argues that is impossible for someone to believe the negation of PNC.

Proving Something about an Axiom: the Indubitability Proof of PNC

The firmest principle of all is the principle of non-contradiction:

> For the same thing to hold and not to hold of the same thing at the same time and in the same respect is impossible, given any further specifications added to guard against dialectical objections. (1005b19–22)

133

This provides an ontological version of PNC insofar as it ranges over things and their properties. Because it holds of anything that is simply insofar as it is, PNC functions as a principle of that which is *qua* thing that is. So in the terms of the Declaration Statement, PNC falls under Provision (B)'s charge to study "what things hold in its own right" of that which is *qua* thing that is. The Indubitability Proof, which does not aspire to demonstrate PNC itself but rather to prove something *about* it, does just this.

The proof relies on the general thesis that, if it is possible to err about something, *p*, then it must be possible to believe the negation of *p*. Thus, Reggie can be mistaken about the fact that there are ten polar bears in the Brookfield Zoo, only if he can have a belief to the effect that there are not ten such animals in the zoo. So, if *x* can be in error about PNC, then it must be possible for *x* to believe "not-PNC." But, Aristotle argues, this sort of belief is impossible and so PNC is immune to error and, thus, is declared the firmest of all principles.

When Aristotle says that PNC is the firmest *principle*, we may assume that he takes immunity to error to be a property of the principle itself. However, the Indubitability Proof might establish this in one of two ways: either by showing that it is impossible to believe an instance of the negation of PNC or by showing that it is impossible to believe the negation of PNC, the principle, itself. More formally, on the first option the Indubitability Proof targets

4. $\neg\Diamond(\exists x)(\exists z)(x\ bel\ (Fz \wedge \neg Fz))$

as its conclusion. On this option, there cannot be a person and a thing such that the person believes the thing is *F* and not-*F*. On the second option the targeted conclusion is

5. $\neg\Diamond(\exists x)(x\ bel\ \Diamond(\exists z)(Fz \wedge \neg Fz))$.

This option declares that there cannot be a person who believes that it is possible that there is a something that is *F* and not-*F*. These are importantly different. According to (4), any proposition of the form *Fz*, say *Ga*, is such that it is impossible to believe the proposition and its negation. So (4) declares that it is impossible to believe the negation of *instances* of PNC, whereas what (5) declares impossible is believing the negation of the *principle itself*. Thus, (4) proscribes belief in particular propositions of the sort allegedly asserted by Heraclitus, for example, that water is good and not good. But this does not establish (5). For someone might agree that every proposition he happens to believe is such that he cannot believe it and its negation (the situation [4] describes) but none the less insist that there might be *some* proposition such that it and its negation can be believed (what (5) denies). But if one can hold (4) and deny (5), (4) cannot entail (5).

Most commentators agree that the Indubitability Proof establishes at most (4), by barring joint belief in a particular proposition and its negation. The proof utilizes two general theses about beliefs. First, if someone, *x*, believes something, say *Fa*, then *x* has a "doxastic" *property* corresponding to *the belief that Fa*. Second, if *x* believes *p and q*, then *x* believes *p* and *x* believes *q* (conservatively, as a discrete inference, and not, controversially, as an instance of the thesis that belief is closed under entailment). Third, *the belief that Fa* is the contrary of *the belief that not-Fa*. Thus, if *x* believes *Fa and not-Fa*, then x has the property (corresponding to) *the belief that Fa* and the property (corresponding to) *the belief that not-Fa*. So x has a certain doxastic property and has the contrary of that property. But to have the contrary of a property is not to have the property. Therefore, x has the doxastic property in question and does not have it. But PNC itself declares this to be impossible. So no instances of the negation of PNC can be believed; and, thus, Aristotle can report at the beginning of *Met* Γ.4 that by assuming PNC he has shown that it is the firmest of all principles.

PNC as the Ultimate Principle

Aristotle closes Γ.3 with a flourish. PNC is not only the firmest principle, but also the principle "all who demonstrate go back to in the end" and "the principle of all the other axioms" (1005b32–4). Commentators have objected to these claims. Lukasiewicz (1910) urged rejection of the view that PNC is the highest principle of all demonstrations and held that many logical principles are independent of PNC. Kirwan (1971: 90) complained that immunity to disbelief does not establish that every argument relies on PNC but only that no argument questions it.

However, Aristotle's ultimacy claim is not so easily dismissed. Let us take him at his word when he says that in the end all demonstrating goes back to PNC, and let us suppose, further, that the reasoning is deductive. Then he is claiming that all deductive reasoning somehow goes back to PNC. Arguably, this calls for a connection between patterns of deductive reasoning and PNC. To take a familiar case, many instances of demonstration use the rule of *modus ponens*. As such, they depend on the validity of

6. $((p \rightarrow q) \wedge p) \rightarrow q.$

The outer parenthesized schema may be said to *imply q*. Thus, the conjunction of the antecedent with the negation of the consequent should lead to an inconsistency (with Quine 1966, 100: "One schema implies another if and only if the one in conjunction with the other's negation is inconsistent"). In the case of (6), we would have on the left: $\neg(p \wedge \neg q) \wedge p$; and on the right: $\neg q$. But the left side is equivalent to $(\neg p \vee q) \wedge p$ and this yields q. So, we are left with q and $\neg q$. We, thus, confirm that (6) is valid. More to the point, however, we do so by appeal to the principle of non-contradiction. Hence, one can conclude that the validity of (6) depends on the principle of non-contradiction, even if no application of (6) or instances of (6) *uses* the principle. The same result is yielded by any pattern of reasoning that is deductively valid.

So, arguably, there is a sense in which PNC is the doctrine that everyone who demonstrates goes back to in the end – not as the principle *from which* all deductions start, in which case it would be used in all deductions, but rather as a presupposition of the *validity* of the principles that are used in such deductions, namely, the principles of deductive reasoning. In this way PNC's claim to ultimacy holds despite the fact that it is not *used* in all cases of deductive reasoning.

There remains a worry. If PNC is such a presupposition, then does it not parade as a principle that is somehow "deeper" than other logical principles? This, of course, will be challenged on the grounds that the validity of principles such as $p \wedge q \rightarrow p$ or $p \rightarrow p$

is hardly less transparent than that of $\neg(p \wedge \neg p)$. Nonetheless, there is a reason Aristotle gives pride of place to PNC. Recall his claim that it is *because* PNC is the firmest of principles that it is the principle every demonstration goes back to. From this point of view, we may take the principle not as *establishing* the validity of principles of deduction but rather as *displaying* their deductive firmness. Someone might suppose it possible to grant their deductive utility, even validity, but still insist that they are not immune to error, that is, that someone might be mistaken about them. This, however, requires that it is possible to believe the negation of a principle of demonstration, and, assuming that belief is closed under logical entailment (controversially, but see Wedin 2004a, Sect. 7, for some conciliatory remarks), this belief in turn requires that it is possible to believe that PNC fails to hold. But, by Γ.3's Indubitability Proof, such a belief is impossible. Hence, the firmness attaching to PNC is inherited by all principles whose denials involve flouting the principle of non-contradiction. Because these principles inherit their firmness *from* PNC and because PNC establishes its *own* firmness, he declares that it is the principle of all other principles. Thanks to its role in *explaining* the firmness of other principles, PNC can be declared *the* firmest principle of all. Thus, the ultimacy claim completes the argument in favor of the singular status of the principle of non-contradiction. So far from being merely *one* of the firmest principles, it assures that PNC is *the* firmest principle – just as Aristotle promised.

Defending an Axiom: the Elenctic Proof of PNC

It is one thing to prove something *about* an ultimate principle such as PNC, but quite another thing to prove the principle itself. Aristotle unambiguously rejects the latter project precisely because PNC is presupposed by all demonstrative reasoning. Asking for such a proof only reveals "lack of training." At the same time, a number of Aristotle's predecessors affirm, or are committed to affirming, contradictory propositions – some for the sake of argument and some, including "many writers on nature," because of honest theoretical perplexity. Against these "opponents" of PNC Aristotle mounts a two-part defense. First, he claims to refute them by an elenctic demonstration, that is, by demonstrating "in the manner of a refutation." This he does in the first part of Γ.4. Second, in the balance of Γ.4 and, indeed, in the remainder of the Book, Aristotle retails a number of absurd, unacceptable, or embarrassing consequences facing those who would deny PNC. Here I shall deal only with the elenctic proof.

Aristotle's chief reservation in Γ.4 about a rational defense of PNC is not the admitted absence of premises from which it could be properly demonstrated. (As Code 1986 points out, the fact that PNC cannot be properly demonstrated means that the elenctic proof, whatever its weight, could not and does not aspire to *explain* the conclusion of the proof. For this is just what proper demonstrations do.) Rather he raises the specter of begging the question. Aristotle's low opinion of their training notwithstanding, the opponents presumably demand some sort of proof of PNC. This means they are open to deductive reasoning, in particular, we may suppose, any reasoning not *using* PNC. If such a course of reasoning proceeds from premises set down by Aristotle, then the entire argument is open to the charge of begging the question – at least according to Aristotle. Because of this he needs the opponent to enter something into discourse so that reasoning may begin at his expense. From this Aristotle will derive PNC. Although he denies PNC, this denial need not be what the opponent utters. Contrary to certain commentators, Aristotle does not require this but only that the opponent utters something, and this something, it appears, may be a single word. The opponent then is bound to agree that what he has said is significant (otherwise he counts as no better that a plant). This allows Aristotle to introduce semantical conditions on the significance of a word and to argue that these conditions entail that use of the word must accord with PNC. Since this holds for any significant word, the proof may be generalized. Thus, anyone who utters anything significant is committed to holding PNC.

Suppose, then, that the opponent utters "man." According to Aristotle "man" signifies one thing, namely, *two-footedness* or "what it is to be a man." Because this is what a man is *essentially*, it follows that necessarily anything that is a man is two-footed. But this is equivalent to the claim that it is impossible that anything be a man and not be two-footed. This, in turn, entails that it is impossible that anything be a man and not be a man. So if "man" signifies *two-footedness*, then there cannot be an x that is man and not man. By, thus, applying essentialist semantics to terms like "man," Aristotle's elenctic proof shows that it is impossible for anything to satisfy a frame like "x is a man and is not a man." (For two different ways of reconstructing the proof, see Kirwan 1971 and Wedin 2000b.)

Some commentators are concerned that the elenctic proof deploys a strongly essentialist notion of significance. Why should an opponent accept the semantics of Aristotelian essences? Well, an Aristotelian might reply that the opponent is obliged to accept *some* semantics, and, arguably, even a modestly robust notion of meaning will yield a similar result. A second concern is that the proof works at most for essential predications, and, thus, that it fails to establish a fully general version of PNC. Here, defenders of the proof can make use of recent accounts that extend the range of the proof (e.g., Wedin 2000b). Finally, there remains the worry that what is proved are simply *instances* of PNC relative to given significant utterances, not a general version of PNC. We could, however, provide the requisite generality by endowing the proof with counter-factual force, that is, by providing a formulation that captures the idiom, "*were* σ to be uttered, σ *would* signify Σ," where σ is a variable for words and Σ for essences. This would be true to the spirit, if not to the letter, of Aristotle's proof.

Theology and the General Science of Being

Recall that in the first chapter of the *Metaphysics*, Aristotle sets his sights on first principles and causes, and labels the science that investigates these "wisdom." Book B lists several puzzles confronting this science but without referring to it as "wisdom." It speaks, rather, of the "science of substance." And we have just examined how Aristotle reduces the general science of being to the science of substance, and includes the axioms in it, without mentioning wisdom as such. Now, finally, we come to Book E, where "first philosophy" and "theology" enjoy prominence, but, again, there is no allusion to "wisdom." Do all of these "metaphysical" enterprises fit together or is the *Metaphysics* after all a fractured treatise?

One suggestion is to take these enterprises as executing parts of the strategy for the science of wisdom. Because they are parts of wisdom, no one of the metaphysical enterprises is singled out as wisdom. There are signs of this in A.2, where Aristotle lists several general marks of the sort of knowledge that counts as wisdom. Such knowledge, to take three such marks, should be universal (the wise man should know everything); its object should be what is most knowable; and it should be authoritative. B's set of puzzles makes it clear that the science of substance is to count as wisdom or, at least, a chief part of wisdom. But how can such a science be universal – after all there is more to the world than substances? Aristotle's answer, we have seen, is to articulate a general science of being, the science of being *qua* being, and to reduce it to the science of substance. Further A.2 goes on to say that one knows all things by knowing the most universal notions. These are just the sorts of general notions that comprise the content of the science of being *qua* being – unity, sameness, and the like. Thus, the first two marks of wisdom are satisfied. Finally, A.2 reports that having the most authoritative knowledge amounts to knowing the supreme end or good in the whole of nature. This mark of wisdom will be satisfied by knowledge that focuses on divine objects and, perhaps, even the unmoved mover of Book Λ. But an investigation that focuses on such special objects is in danger of conflicting with an investigation focusing on being *qua* being because the latter is a topic-neutral investigation of *everything*.

It is clear that there is a problem with wisdom's encompassing both kinds of investigation. Because the science of substance that embraces the science of being *qua* being is fully general, nothing bars it from considering special changeless substances such as the unmoved mover. However, in Book E the primary discipline, or as Aristotle says "first philosophy," deals with the primary or best kinds of objects. Here the science of substance is the science of separate and changeless substances, and, as such, it appears to exclude most of what would be studied by the science of being *qua* being. So how could anything, wisdom included, be *the* science of substance?

The problem is at the center of E.1. After elevating theoretical over practical disciplines, Aristotle distinguishes three theoretical disciplines in terms of the objects they range over. Every object is, on the one hand, either separate or not separate, and, on the other hand, changeless or not changeless. Separate objects are those that *exist* separately, or "on their own," as do Callias, Socrates, and the other primary substances of the *Categories*. The science of physics studies objects that are separate and not changeless. Mathematics studies objects that are changeless and not separate. In studying triangularity, for example, mathematics studies a property of material objects. Although such a property does not exist independently of objects, mathematicians treat the property *as if* it existed separately and *were not* subject to change. Finally, objects that are separate and changeless are reserved for theology, appropriately, in light of their divinity. No discipline studies objects that are not separate and not changeless because these are accidents, and, as E.2 insists, there is no science of what happens coincidentally.

The three theoretical disciplines are not of equal value because their objects are not of equal value. Separate objects are prior to objects that are not separate. Thus, the separate objects of physics, being changeable substances, are prior to the objects of mathematics, which are, for example, the limits of such substances. For this reason physics is prior to mathematics. Indeed, Aristotle says that were there only natural (i.e., changeable) substances, then physics would the primary discipline. However, changeless substances are prior to changeable substances and, so, the primary discipline would have these as its objects. Hence, theology would be first philosophy. Therefore, if wisdom is first philosophy, wisdom is theology. But theology is a special science, and so wisdom cannot be identified with the general science of being. Moreover, this threatens one of the chief marks of wisdom, namely, that it provides a certain kind of knowledge of *everything*.

Commentators have anguished over the fact that Aristotle appears to endorse, in M. Frede's apt phrase, "two radically different conceptions of the enterprise of the *Metaphysics*" (Frede 1987: 83). Aristotle himself is aware of this tension. The beginning of E.1 reprises the familiar theme that "we" are seeking the principles and causes of that which is *qua* thing that is, and at the chapter's end Aristotle feels compelled to explain how this is possible if theology is the highest discipline. Here is what he says:

> One might be perplexed as to whether the primary philosophy really is universal, or deals with a particular genus and one particular nature . . . If there is no other substance apart from those constituted naturally, the discipline concerned with nature would be primary. But if there is some changeless substance, this is prior and is primary philosophy, and universal in this way, because it is primary; and it would fall to it to study that which is *qua* thing that is, both what it is and what holds of it *qua* thing-that-is. (1026a23–32).

So theology is the primary philosophy. Nonetheless, (*i*) theology is "universal in this way, because it is primary" and, therefore, (*ii*) theology studies being *qua* being. Merlan (1968) attempted to explain this by proposing that "being *qua* being" all along refers to divine being rather than being in general. However, the mere fact that (*i*) is presented as explaining (*ii*), and thereby as solving a *problem*, excludes Merlan's heroic proposal. More promising might be to focus on the fact that not-separate objects (those of mathematics) are causally dependent on separate and not-changeless objects (those of physics) and that separate and not-changeless objects are causally dependent on separate and changeless objects (those of theology). So in some sense everything else is causally dependent on divine objects. Nevertheless, there are two worries about simple causal dependence, as I shall call this solution. First, in adverting to Λ's unmoved mover, it relies on a text that many discount as a late add-on to the *Metaphysics*. Second, and more troubling, simple causal dependence connects items in a purely external way. But without a stronger, internal connection, nothing ensures that such items will be *explained* by the same principles. In short, the domain of causally dependent items may not be sufficiently unified for a single science. More is needed.

The most important proposal is due to Patzig in his classic 1960 article. According to this, Aristotle recognizes two levels of focal meaning. (Although he employed "paronymy" in the original 1960 article, in a footnote to the 1979 translation Patzig welcomes Owen's idiom of focal meaning.) Horizontally, everything other than substance is focally dependent on substances. This focally unifies the domain of everything that is and so makes possible the general science of being *qua* being. This much is familiar. But Patzig also applies focal meaning vertically within the category of substance. Substances other than the changeless and separate substance that is the unmoved mover are focally dependent on the unmoved mover for their being. Thus, the unmoved mover has the sort of primacy capable of unifying the domain of substance. So theology, the science of the unmoved mover(s), is also the science of (all) substance, and, presumably, because the science of (all) substance studies everything that is *qua* thing that is, theology also studies everything that is (that is, it is universal) and so studies being *qua* being.

Some will worry about Patzig's extension of focal meaning to the "vertical" relation between the unmoved moving substance and the other substances. Although simple causal dependence holds here, Owen plausibly insisted that ontological dependence on substances was not enough to make items in non-substantial categories focally dependent on substances. Certainly, Aristotle argues in Book Λ that the motions of sublunary bodies depend on the existence of an unmoved mover, but it is not clear that the causal dependence established by the argument offers more than ontological dependence. Patzig is aware of the problem for he emphasizes (1960: 42) that "the concept of an *ousia* [substance] other than the *ousia* [substance] of the first mover logically presupposes the concept of the 'first mover'." It is correct that the unified domain required for a science calls for something like logical dependence between items in the domain. Unfortunately, it is not obvious how to move from causal dependence to logical dependence.

Frede (1987) aims to validate the essential correctness of Patzig's proposal by identifying a set of logical presuppositions that would logically unify the vertically structured domain of substances. He maintains that objects of theology have a particular *way of being* that is different from the way of being enjoyed by objects of physics. Although hedgehogs and foxes are different *kinds* of beings, they, along with all natural substances, have the same *way* of being. They are matter-form compounds. The divine objects of theology, on the other hand, have no matter and so are "pure actualities, and thus forms, and thus substances, and thus beings in a paradigmatic way in that they are perfectly real" (Frede 1987: 90). Thus, they have a different way of being.

According to Frede, this distinction validates Patzig's account because the way of being of divine objects provides one term of explanation for all other ways of being. It is the "focal way of being" because it must be understood in order to understand other ways of being, and in this way the vertical domain of substances is internally connected. The notion of form now becomes central. The substantiality of natural substances is explained in terms of their substantial forms (substantial forms$_1$), whereas divine substances just are substantial forms (substantial forms$_2$). Substantial forms$_1$ have a different way of being from substantial forms$_2$. Moreover, substantial forms$_2$ straightforwardly satisfy three requirements for substancehood set down in Z.3: separateness, individuality, and subjecthood. Substantial forms$_1$ do so only in a qualified way – they are separate in account only, they could have been universals rather than particulars, and their associated compounds are better candidates for subjects of predication. Nonetheless, to properly understand what it is to be a substantial form$_1$ we must understand how they satisfy these three conditions.

The critical point is that understanding what it is to be a form and, thus, to be a substance entails understanding how separate forms are substances, i.e., how they satisfy the three Z.3 conditions, and then weakening the conditions for material forms. We may put the point as follows:

7.   *x* understands a substantial form$_1$ to be a substance $\rightarrow$ *x* understands how some substantial form$_2$ is a substance.

So understanding what it is for a natural, enmattered form to be a substance *requires* understanding how an immaterial form is a substance. This would provide a logical link between the two kinds of substances, just as Patzig proposed. Unfortunately, there are difficulties. First, (7) structures the domain of substances by establishing dependence relations between their *forms*. Some will worry that this changes the subject or, worse, that it illicitly identifies the form of a form-matter compound with the compound itself. And, in any event, why should the form of a form-matter compound have a different way of being from a pure form just because the form-matter *compound* does? Some will even worry that (7) requires Aristotle's unmoved moving substance itself to be a form, something that is not explicitly stated and does not follow from the fact that it is a pure actuality. Second, if substantial forms$_1$ are universals, it is not clear how this can be understood by weakening an *individuality* condition no matter how it is satisfied by a divine *particular* substance. So (7) obligates us to accept the controversial proposal that the substantial forms of natural substances are themselves particulars. Third, there does not appear to be an Aristotelian relation that captures the dependence between the kinds of understanding marked by the arrow in (7). It cannot be the dependence between what is better known to us and what is better known by nature since this would have to mean that forms$_2$ are better know *than* forms$_1$. This works, in the standard case, for a genus and its species, but no such relation holds between enmattered forms and pure forms; and it is doubtful that there is an appropriate relation that does work. Fourth, (7) implies that we cannot *understand* the forms of natural substances unless we understand pure forms. There are two worries about this. Taken as an independent claim, (7) seems to get things reversed – surely it is more plausible to suppose that understanding forms of natural things might help us get a grasp on the less accessible pure forms. The other worry concerns Aristotle's remark in E.1, cited above, that were there only natural substances, then physics would be first philosophy. There is no hint here that in such circumstances our understanding of natural objects would be in any way deficient. On the contrary, physics would rate as the primary kind of knowledge. So how could understanding objects of physics *require*, as (7) insists, understanding pure forms?

For Aristotle the science of wisdom was to encompass the general science of being (the science of being *qua* being), the science of substance, and first philosophy or theology. The crux of this project is harmonizing the general science of being with theology, the science of the highest kind of being. Unfortunately, his proposal for accomplishing this consists of the single remark that theology "is universal because it is first." Although it has proven suggestive, the idiom continues to resist settled interpretation. But even if this part of Aristotle's project fails, the scope and force of the general science of being remain intact.[3]

Notes

[1] It is customary to indicate Books of the *Metaphysics* by uppercase Greek letters, with the exception of the diminutive second Book, which is denoted by lower case Alpha (α).

[2] The term occurs in B.2 but only by way of referring back to A.2's marks of wisdom. It also reappears in K. But K is just a precis of Books B, Γ, and E (with, in its second half, material from the *Physics*); plus, some doubt that K was even written by Aristotle.

141

[3] Once again, I am indebted to my Davis colleague, John Malcolm, for careful comments on an early draft of this article. David Freelove spotted a nontrivial oversight in my account of Owen on focal meaning, and Frank Lewis provided extensive written remarks that left the final product substantially improved and free of at least one serious error. I am grateful to all three, especially Lewis, who has agreed to shoulder blame for any remaining blunders. Finally, I wish to tip my hat to Georgios Anagnostopoulos, for spearheading this project and, more importantly, for his friendship over the years.

Bibliography

Barnes, J. (1969). "The Law of Contradiction," *Philosophical Quarterly*, 10, pp. 302–9.

Code, A. (1986). "Aristotle's Investigation of a Basic Logical Principle: Which Science Investigates the Principle of Non-contradiction?," *Canadian Journal of Philosophy*, 16, pp. 341–58.

Code, A. (1987). "Metaphysics and Logic," in M. Matthen (ed.), *Aristotle Today: Essays on Aristotle's Ideal of Science* (Edmonton: Academic Printing and Publishing), pp. 127–49.

Code, A. (1996). "Owen on the Development of Aristotle's Metaphysics," in W. Wians (ed.), *Aristotle's Philosophical Development* (Lanham, MD: Rowman and Littlefield), pp. 303–25.

Cohen, S. M. (1986). "Aristotle on the Principle of Non-contradiction," *Canadian Journal of Philosophy*, 16, pp. 359–70.

Frede, M. (1987). "The Unity of General and Special Metaphysics: Aristotle's Conception of Metaphysics," in M. Frede, *Essays in Ancient Philosophy* (Oxford: Clarendon Press), pp. 81–95.

Kirwan, C. (1971). *Aristotle's "Metaphysics": Books ΓΔΕ*, trans. with notes (Oxford: Clarendon Press).

Lukasiewicz, J. (1910). "Über den satz des widerspruchs des Aristotles," *Bull. Intern. de l'Academie des Sciences de Cracovie*, authorized trans. M. V. Wedin (as Vernon E. Wedin), "Aristotle on the Principle of Contradiction," *Review of Metaphysics*, 24, pp. 485–509.

Merlan, P. (1968). "On the Terms 'Metaphysics' and 'Being-*Qua*-Being'," *Monist*, 52, pp. 174–94.

Owen, G. E. L. (1960). "Logic and Metaphysics in Some Early Works of Aristotle," in I. Düring and G. E. L. Owen (eds.), *Aristotle and Plato in the Mid-fourth Century* (Göteborg: Almqvist and Wiksell), pp. 163–90. (Repr. in J. Barnes, M. Schofield, and R. Sorabji (eds.), *Articles on Aristotle* (London: Duckworth), vol. 3, pp. 13–32.)

Patzig, G. (1960). "Theologie und ontology in der 'Metaphysik' des Aristoteles," *Kant-Studien*, 52, pp. 185–205; trans. J. and J. Barnes, "Theology and Ontology in Aristotle's Metaphysics," in J. Barnes, M. Schofield, and R. Sorabji (eds.), *Articles on Aristotle* (London: Duckworth), vol. 3, pp. 33–49.

Quine, W. V. O. (1966). *Methods of Logic* (New York: Holt, Reinhart and Winston).

Ross, W. D. [1924] (1953). *Aristotle's "Metaphysics,"* revd. with intro. and comm., (Oxford: Clarendon Press); corrected edn. 1953, 2 vols.

Wedin, M. V. (2000a). *Aristotle's Theory of Substance: The "Categories" and "Metaphysics" Zeta* (Oxford: Oxford University Press).

Wedin, M. V. (2000b). "Some Logical Problems in *Metaphysics* Gamma," *Oxford Studies in Ancient Philosophy*, 19, pp. 113–62.

Wedin, M. V. (2004a). "Aristotle on the Firmness of the Principle of Non-contradiction," *Phronesis*, 44, 225–65.

Wedin, M. V. (2004b). "On the Use and Abuse of Non-contradiction: Aristotle's Critique of Protagoras and Heraclitus in *Metaphysics* Gamma 5," *Oxford Studies in Ancient Philosophy*, 26, pp. 213–39.

Woods, M. (1982). *Aristotle's "Eudemian Ethics,"* Books I, II, III, trans. with comm. (Oxford: Clarendon Press).

9

Aristotelian Categories

GARETH B. MATTHEWS

That which is there to be spoken of and thought of, must be.

Parmenides, Fragment 6 (McKirahan trans.)

The short treatise entitled *Categories* enjoys pride of place in Aristotle's writings. It is the very first work in the standard edition of Aristotle's texts. Each line of the thirty columns that make up this treatise has been pored over by commentators, from the first century BCE down to the present. Moreover, its gnomic sentences still retain their fascination for both philosophers and scholars, even today.

In the tradition of Aristotelian commentary, the first works of Aristotle are said to make up the *Organon*, which begins with the logic of terms (the *Categories*), then moves on to the logic of propositions (the *De Interpretatione*) and then to the logic of syllogistic argumentation (the *Prior Analytics*). But to say that the *Categories* presents the logic of terms may leave the misleading impression that it is about words rather than about things. That is not the case. This little treatise is certainly about words. But it is no less about things. It is about terms and the ways in which they can be combined; but this "logic" of terms is also meant to be a guide to what there is, that is, to ontology, and more generally, to metaphysics.

The *Categories* text was not given its title by Aristotle himself. Indeed, there has long been a controversy over whether the work was even written by Aristotle. Michael Frede's discussion of this issue in "The Title, Unity, and Authenticity of Aristotle's *Categories*" (Frede 1987: 11–28) is as close to being definitive on this issue as is possible. Frede concludes that the *Categories* can only be the work of Aristotle himself or one of his students.

The question of authenticity is often connected with the issue of whether the last part of the *Categories*, chapters 10–15, traditionally called the "*Postpraedicamenta*," and the earlier chapters really belong to the same work. We shall have very little to say about the *Postpraedicamenta* here.

The Fourfold Classification

We learn in chapter 4 of the *Categories* that there are ten categories of entities: substance, quantity, quality, relative, place, time, being-in-a-position, having, action, and passion. But before we get this Tenfold Classification, we come, in chapter 2, to a Fourfold Classification. It is laid out in the following way:

T1. Among things that are, (a) some are *said of* a subject but are *not in* any subject. For example man is said of a subject, the individual man, but is not in any subject; (b) Some are *in* a subject but are *not said of* any subject . . . For example, the individual knowledge-of-grammar is in a subject, the soul, but is not said of any subject; and the individual white is in a subject, the body (for all color is in a body), but is not said of any subject. (c) Some are *both said of* a subject and *in* a subject. For example, knowledge is in a subject, the soul, and is also said of a subject, knowledge-of-grammar. (d) Some are *neither in* a subject *nor said of* a subject, for example, the individual man or individual horse – for nothing of this sort is either in a subject or said of a subject. Things that are individual and numerically one are, without exception, not said of any subject, but there is nothing to prevent some of them from being in a subject – the individual knowledge-of-grammar is one of the things in a subject (1a20–21b9).[1]

The fourfold classification Aristotle gives us in T1 yields the table shown.

	Not in a subject	In a subject
Said of a subject	man horse	knowledge
Not said of a subject	the individual man the individual horse	the individual knowledge of grammar the individual white

We can see right away that Aristotle recognizes two sorts of things that are individual and numerically one – some that are not in a subject, and some that are in a subject. An individual thing that is not in a subject is a basic, or independent, thing. The examples Aristotle gives here are the individual man, say, Socrates, and the individual horse, say, the famous horse of Alexander the Great, Bucephalus.

What Aristotle understands to be an individual thing in a subject is highly controversial. I shall take up the controversy later on. Aristotle's first example of such a thing is the individual knowledge of grammar. His second example is the individual white. He must also suppose that there is such a thing as the individual wisdom, the individual bravery, and so on. The subject that the individual knowledge of grammar is in, Aristotle says, is the soul. This knowledge might be in, for example, the soul of Socrates. We cannot tell here whether Aristotle thinks of the soul of Socrates as something distinct from Socrates. What seems clear is that, if the individual knowledge of grammar is in the soul of Socrates, then Socrates himself has a certain knowledge of grammar.

What does Aristotle mean by "things said of a subject"? For Aristotle in this work, but not necessarily in his later writings, the phrase "said of something as a subject" [*kath' hupokeimenou tinos legetai*] is best thought of as expressing a basic classification relation. *Man* (that is, human being, *anthrôpos*) is said of the individual man, say, Socrates. And what that means is that Socrates is classified basically and fundamentally as *a man*. Put the other way around, *man* is said of Socrates means that *man* classifies Socrates in a fundamental way. Analogously, *knowledge* is said of the individual

145

knowledge of grammar. That is to say, *knowledge* classifies the individual knowledge of grammar. The individual knowledge of grammar is an example of knowledge.

Not being in a subject makes something a substance (*ousia*). Not being in a subject conjoined with not even being said of a subject makes something a *primary* substance. As we shall see in a moment, primary substances, according to Aristotle, are subjects for everything else. That includes, first of all, things that, while they are not in primary substances, are said of primary substances. Man and horse are examples of that group. Thus, although man is not in Socrates, man is said of Socrates. Similarly, horse is not in Bucephalus, but horse is said of Bucephalus. Because man and horse are not in any subject, they, too, count as substances, along with Socrates and Bucephalus. But because man and horse are said of subjects, that is, classify them, they are only secondary substances.

Here one might wonder why we shouldn't say that *Socrates* is said of Socrates, and *Bucephalus* is said of Bucephalus. The reason seems to be that *Socrates* does not classify Socrates; it names him, just as *Bucephalus* names Bucephalus. And being said of, we need to remember, is a classifying relation.

So things on the left side of the box are substances, either primary (on the bottom) or secondary (on top). What now about things in the right-hand column, things that are in a subject? What are they? I shall call them "properties." I use "property" here in the modern sense in which each quality or feature or characteristic of a thing counts as a property of that thing.[2] A philosopher today might most naturally think of properties as being the properties *of* substances. But Aristotle thinks of them as being *in* substances. Following him in this use of "in," we can think of substances as being, metaphorically, jewel boxes. We can say that the jewels in a given jewel box are that particular box's properties. An individual jewel box will be a primary substance. And a basic kind of jewel box will be a secondary substance.

The Greek word we transliterate as "categories," namely, *katêgoriai*, comes from a verb Aristotle uses to mean "to predicate." What the editor or commentator who first named this treatise *Categories* had in mind with the title he gave it is presumably that Aristotle, in this work, makes distinctions among statements or predications that, as we might want to put the matter today, reveal the "deep structure" of very simple and basic predications. Revealing this deep structure in turn illuminates the metaphysical status of what gets predicated and what it gets predicated of.

Consider now the simplest subject-predicate predications of the schematic form, "S is F." There are, according to T1, two ways in which it will be correct to state of S that it is F. We might correctly state of S that it is F if

(1)   S is [fundamentally classified as an] F.

Alternatively, we might correctly state of S that it is F if

(2)   There is something, x, such that x is in S and x is [fundamentally classified as an] F.

Now compare these examples:

(a)   Bucephalus is a horse.
(b)   Bucephalus is brown.

If (a) is true, it will be true, according to Aristotle, because, in line with (1) above,

(a*)   Bucephalus is fundamentally classified as a horse.

That is, *horse* is said of Bucephalus. By contrast, if (b) is true, it will be so because, in line with (2) above,

(b*)   There is something, x, such that x is in Bucephalus and x is [fundamentally classified as a] brown.

The distinction between primary and secondary substances – substances said of a subject and those not said of a subject – is relatively straightforward. It is a distinction between concrete individuals – paradigmatically, for Aristotle, living organisms – and their species and genera. We could also adopt the "primary"–"secondary" terminology to distinguish ground-level properties from their species and genera, although Aristotle himself does not do this. The "primary properties" would then be the things in a subject that are not said of a subject; that is, they would be properties that are not themselves the species or genera of properties. "Secondary properties" would be properties that are the species and genera of primary properties.

Now we need to ask what exactly it is that counts as being a "primary," that is, individual property. What exactly are, to use Aristotle's own examples, this individual knowledge-of-grammar and this individual white?

Tropes

How to answer that question has been much debated among commentators. For the time being I am going to make use of my own interpretation of what primary properties are. Later on I shall consider an alternative account.

On my interpretation, a "primary" or individual property is what is called by metaphysicians today a "trope." A trope in this modern usage[3] is not, as one might have thought, a figure of speech; rather, it is an abstract particular. It is a non-repeatable instance of some property – what Bertrand Russell called a "unit quality." Thus, if two roses have exactly the same shade of pink, it will still be true that the pink in this rose is distinct from the pink in that rose. Each rose will have its own individual color property, its own individual pink, even if the two properties are of the very same shade and hue. One individual pink will be in a subject (say, an individual rose), and in no other subject. Its being individual means that it is not said of anything else; in particular, it is not said of, that is, does not classify, any other instance of color, even one of the same shade and hue.

If we accept this understanding of what it is to be an individual quality, something "in a subject, but not said of a subject," we have the materials for a very interesting solution to "the problem of the one and the many," a problem that Aristotle inherited from Plato. Thus Plato has his character, Socrates, wonder in the dialogue, *Philebus*, whether one ought to suppose there is some one thing, man (that is human being), some one thing, ox, some one thing, the beautiful, and so on. He asks, "how we are to

147

conceive that each of them, being always one and the same and subject neither to generation nor destruction, nevertheless is, to begin with, most assuredly this single unity and yet subsequently comes to be in the infinite number of things that come into being – an identical unity being thus found simultaneously in unity and in plurality. (*Philebus* 15b, Hackforth trans.)

According to the solution to the one-over-many problem I am drawing from Aristotle's *Categories*, there can be no property, and hence no individual property either, that is not a property of some kind or other. To be an individual color, for example, is to be a color of some shade and hue. But it is also to be in some individual subject, say this rose, and in no other. If this rose is destroyed, so is the individual pink that was in it. Of course, there might be another rose of exactly the same shade and hue as the rose that was destroyed. But the individual color in the other rose, though qualitatively identical with the old one, would be distinct from it. Pink gets to be in distinct things, say, this rose and that, by there being in each thing some trope that is classified as a pink.

Somewhat surprisingly, Plato also seems to have conceived the idea of tropes. In his dialogue, *Phaedo*, Plato has his character, Phaedo, speak, not just of Tallness and Shortness, but also of the individual tallness, or shortness, in Simmias. (102b–103a) Daniel Devereux notes the parallel. He comments that "in the *Phaedo* we see, if not the origin of, at least a close parallel to Aristotle's conception of individuals in non-substance categories" (Devereux 1992: 117).

The difference between the Aristotle of the *Cagtegories* and the Plato of the *Phaedo* on the tallness in Simmias is that Tallness itself is, according to Plato, a thing apart from the tallness in x and y and z, whereas according to the Aristotle, it is not. We shall have more to say about this very shortly.

Although there is admittedly no passage in the *Categories* that requires us to understand individual qualities as tropes, the last part of T1 seems clearly to invite this understanding, where the individual property under discussion is the individual knowledge of grammar, rather than the individual pink:

> T1a. Things that are individual and numerically one are, without exception, not said of any subject, but there is nothing to prevent some of them from being in a subject – the individual knowledge-of-grammar is one of the things in a subject. (1b6–9)

Thus both Socrates and his individual wisdom are numerically one and therefore not said of any subject; but whereas Socrates is not in any subject either, his individual wisdom is; in fact it is in him and him alone.

Aristotle's Principle

Everything that exists, according to Aristotle, has a basic classification. We can put this point by saying that everything that exists is *a* something or other. Aristotle couldn't express himself that way, since Greek has no indefinite article. But that was his idea. J. L. Austin is reported to have made the point dramatically in his lectures at Oxford by saying that, when God called out to Moses from the burning bush, "I am," Moses should have shot back, "You are *a* what?" Let's call this "Aristotle's principle," or "AP."

AP: Everything that exists is *a* something or other.

According to AP, there are no bare particulars. There is no Socrates apart from there being a certain man, who is, at the same time, a certain animal and a certain living thing. According to *Categories*, the relationship between Socrates and man (that is, "human-ness") is not correctly thought of as a relationship between two quite separate things; rather, Socrates, in being the individual he is, is (already) an individual man. And, in general:

AP*: Every existing individual is an individual something or other.

AP* applies, not only to substances, but also to properties. For there to be an individual property, say, the wisdom of Socrates, is for there to be an individual of a certain kind – in this case, of the kind or species, wisdom. Thus every individual – whether individual substance or individual property – is an individual something or other. There is for Aristotle no deep problem about how there can be the one and the many because to be many is to be many somethings – many Fs, or many Gs.

So far, then, we have this fourfold classification of "the things that there are":

1   *Individual substances*, such as this man (say, Socrates) and this tree: these are *not in a subject* and *not said of a subject*, and they are called by Aristotle "primary substances."
2   *Species and genera of substances*, such as man, horse, animal, oak, and tree: these are *not in a subject* but *said of a subject* (man is said of Socrates and animal is both said of Socrates and also said of man). Items in this grouping are called by Aristotle "secondary substances."
3   *Individual properties*, such as the very paleness of Socrates and his particular wisdom, and other *non-substance individuals*. These are *in a subject* but *not said of a subject*.
4   *Species and genera* of *properties*, such as wisdom and virtue. These are *in a subject* and also *said of a subject*.

In a Subject

The interpretation I have been suggesting, according to which individual, or primary, properties are tropes, faces challenges on more than one front. But the most obvious challenge arises from a sentence I left out of T1. In J.L. Ackrill's translation it reads this way:

T2. By "in a subject" I mean what is in something, not as a part, and cannot exist separately from that which it is in. (1a24–5)

149

In 1965 G.E.L. Owen published an influential paper, "Inherence," in which he rejected John Ackrill's reading (in Ackrill 1963: 74–5) of T2. Ackrill had understood the last clause of T2 to mean this:

(A) . . . cannot exist apart from whatever it is in.

But according to T2, on Ackrill's reading of it, we could infer from the statement

1   Color is in this ball

together with

2   What is in a subject cannot exist apart from whatever it is in

that

3   Color cannot exist apart from this ball.

which is absurd. Surprisingly, Ackrill simply agrees that (3) would follow from (1) and (2) and, rather than have Aristotle reject (2), has him reject (1). On his reading of Aristotle, the only thing color can be in is body, not this particular body or that.

Something, however, has gone terribly wrong here. Surely, on the picture Aristotle gives us in the *Categories*, color can be, not just in body in general, but in this body, say, in this ball. Indeed, Aristotle gives us explicit reasoning for the conclusion that color is in individual bodies:

T3. Again, color is in body and *therefore* also in an individual body. (2b1–2)

Ackrill has to write off T3 as "compressed and careless" (Ackrill 1963: 83). But that is implausible. If, as Ackrill supposes, the inseparability requirement, i.e., (A) above, requires a "monogamous" (this is my term, not Ackrill's) relationship between a given quality and what it can be truly said to be in, then surely Aristotle would not say, "Color is in body and therefore (!) in an individual body." But that is, in fact, what he does say.

Owen's Reading

Rejecting (A) as an interpretation of the last clause of T2, Owen proposed instead that that clause be read this way:

(O) . . . cannot exist apart from being in something or other

What the Greek says is more literally this:

(R) . . . cannot exist apart from that which it is in [*adunaton chôris einai tou en hô estin*].

It is natural to read (R) in Ackrill's way, that is, as claiming that that each thing that is in a subject is such that it cannot exist apart from *whatever* it is in. By contrast, reading (R) Owen's way is a stretch. Owen has to motivate his reading by pointing out the unwelcome consequences of Ackrill's reading, especially the one I have just mentioned.

By contrast, Owen's reading has the welcome consequence that color can be in both body and this body, as Aristotle explicitly claims to be the case. For Owen the inseparability requirement amounts only to the insistence that color, and indeed anything whatsoever that is in a subject, must have some host or other. Thus there is no color unless something is colored. Indeed, there is no color red, or color crimson, unless there is something it is in. Such a consequence would, of course, be rejected by any Platonist. For the Platonist the existence of color is logically and metaphysically prior to there being any instances of color whatsoever. But it certainly seems to be at least part of the point of the *Categories* to find an alternative to Platonist metaphysics.

What is an individual quality, according to Owen? It is, for example, a particular shade of pink, which Owen suggests calling "vink." What makes vink individual and, as Aristotle adds, "one in number" is only, according to Owen, that it is not said of any more determinate shade. That is, there are no two even slightly different shades of pink that both count as being vink.

We should note that, on Owen's reading of T2, Aristotle's idea of individual properties does not address the issue of the one and the many, as I have been supposing it does. Even though vink is a maximally determinate shade of pink, it is still a *shade* of pink, and not a trope. Many balloons can have the very same color, vink. And so there is no analogy, as I have been suggesting there is, between a primary substance, such as Socrates, who is at the same time an individual and, by AP*, an individual something or other, and a particular, non-repeatable quality – there being no such thing as a non-repeatable quality on Owen's reading.

Frede's Reading

Ackrill's and Owen's suggestions do not exhaust the alternatives for reading the last clause of T2. Michael Frede (in Frede 1987: 49–71) has suggested that we read the last clause of (T2) this way:

(F) . . . there is something it cannot exist apart from.

Frede's idea is that, according to Aristotle, there is, for each item in a subject, something that we might call its "primary host." Perhaps for color the primary host is body. Then color cannot exist apart from body. If all bodies were destroyed, there would be no color. Still, color can be in this body, say, this particular ball, even though it can exist after the total extinction of this particular ball.

Whereas Ackrill's reading of T2 is, in my judgment, the most natural reading of the sentence, (R), and Owen's reading of (R) is a real stretch, Frede's reading is only a very small stretch. Here is a paraphrase that may suggest how Frede gets his reading:

151

(T2*) By "[thing] in a subject" I mean what is in something, x, not as a part, and cannot exist separately from x (although, for all we have said, it may also be in something else, y, and be able to exist apart from y).

Unlike the other interpretations, which take Aristotle to be defining a two-place predicate, "x is in y," Frede takes him to be defining a one place predicate, "x is in a subject." Put another way, Frede takes Aristotle to be defining "x is an accident" rather than "x inheres in y."

So here we have three interpretations of the final clause of T2. I call the Ackrill reading the "Monogamous Parasite" interpretation, Owen's reading, the "Promiscuous Parasite" reading, and Frede's the "Primary Host" interpretation. Owen thought, quite correctly, that Ackrill's reading, which restricts each thing in a subject to one and only one subject, leads to the conclusion that there are unit qualities, or tropes. Owen himself thought the doctrine of tropes to be an incoherent doctrine. He wanted to save Aristotle from incoherence. (See Wedin 1993 for good responses to Owen's claim of incoherence.) He also wanted to take Aristotle's claim in T3 seriously. So he proposed that we can fend off incoherence by reading the last phrase of T2 to mean (O).

One might, however, reject Ackrill's reading of T2 and still suppose, on quite other grounds, that Aristotle has tropes in mind when he speaks of properties that are in a subject but not said of any subject . Thus one might understand Aristotle to be proposing, as I have been suggesting, a general solution to the one-over-many problem by insisting that there are particular, non-repeatable qualities, in analogy to primary substances, and that each of them is a particular of some kind. (See Matthews and Cohen 1968.)

Differentiae

Frede sets his reading of T2 in a more general discussion of what it is to be an individual in Aristotle's *Categories*. That discussion supports several other enlightening suggestions, one of which I single out now for special mention.

From 3a7 to 3a21 Aristotle argues that no substance is in a subject. We are not surprised to learn that neither this man nor this horse is in a subject. However, we might think that humanity and animality are in a subject, in fact, in Socrates. A first thing to note is that such things as humanity and animality are not explicitly under discussion in the *Categories*. It is man (or human being, *anthrôpos*) and animal that Aristotle talks about. But what about rationality? Shouldn't Aristotle agree that rationality is in Socrates?

In the very first chapter of the *Categories* Aristotle introduces us to the idea of "paronymy," which he illustrates as the relation between, for example, the terms, "brave" and "bravery" (1a14–15). His idea is that, when a person is brave, it is bravery that is in that person. So if Socrates is a rational animal and therefore rational, why shouldn't we say that rationality is in Socrates? At 3a21 Aristotle says that, not only is no substance in a subject, no differentia is in a subject either. Why should that be the case?

Frede's answer is that Aristotle understands "part" in T2 differently from what we might well have expected. He writes:

from the third chapter [of the *Categories*], we can see that Aristotle maintains that a differentia can occur only in a single genus and not in two independent genera. If "rational" were the *differentia specifica* that constitutes the species man, "rational" could not also, at least not in the sense relevant to the species man, appear in another genus; but this implies that we can specify a subject for the differentia without which it could not exist, viz., the species it constitutes. For the differentia is said of this species and, hence, has it as its subject.

Now it seems as if Aristotle wishes to rule out precisely this case by requiring, in 1a24–25, not only that there must be a subject, without which the thing in question could not exist, but also that this thing must not be a part of its subject. The *differentia specifica* however, is a part of the species, since it constitutes it. This interpretation presupposes that Aristotle is thinking of "conceptual" parts, when he is speaking of parts in 1a24–25. As we can see from Bonitz's *Index* (455b32ff.), Aristotle uses "part" in this sense quite frequently. (Frede 1987: 61)

If we follow Frede in the way he takes "part" in T2, then all things that are in a subject will be accidents, what we would today call "accidental properties" of some substance. The differentia of a given species, say rationality, which is perhaps the differentia of man, will not be in a subject and so not either in man in general or in Socrates in particular, because it is a conceptual part of the species, man.

Options for "In a Subject"

So where do we stand on the vexed the issue of how to understand Aristotle's expression, "in a subject"? I have discussed three options: (i) Ackrill's, (ii) Owen's, and (iii) Frede's. I have said that Ackrill's reading of T2 is the most natural, whereas Owen's is the least natural. But Ackrill's reading clashes immediately with Aristotle's claim,

T3. Color is in body and therefore also in an individual body; for where it not in some individual body it would not be in body at all. (2b1–3)

Moreover, and this is a highly significant point, Aristotle goes on immediately to add:

T4. Thus all the other things are either said of the primary substances as subjects or in them as subjects. (2b3–5; previously stated at 2a34–5)

I'm going to call this the "Reduction Thesis" and emphasize its importance for the metaphysics of the *Categories*. The Reduction Thesis is, of course, false if we read T2 in Ackrill's way. It is false because color is one of the things there are and, on Ackrill's reading of "in a subject," color, though it is something that is in a subject, is not in any primary substance; indeed it could not be in any primary substance unless color ceased to exist upon the demise of that primary substance, which is absurd. On Ackrill's reading of "in a subject," color can only be in body, without being in any particular body.

If we eliminate Ackrill's reading of "in a subject," we have two possibilities left, Owen's reading and Frede's reading. I myself don't really see how to get Owen's reading out of the Greek. By contrast, Frede's reading, though it requires some stage setting, seems to me to rest on a defensible translation of the text. So I opt for Frede's reading.

Ironically, Frede himself supposes that the things in a subject but not said of a subject are, as Owen maintains, fully determinate properties, such as a shade of color, but not tropes, that is, not non-repeatable unit qualities. His main reason for agreeing with Owen that individual qualities are not tropes is that, if we read T2 in the way he suggests, we are *not forced* to draw the conclusion that they are tropes. "The assumption, then, that there are individual properties that are individuated by their bearers," Frede writes, "is by no means as obvious or natural as its proponents would have us believe" (Frede 1987: 63). Perhaps that is right. But I have argued that there are still good and interesting reasons for supposing that individual properties in the *Categories* are tropes.

In any case, I suggest we accept Frede's reading of T2, including his suggestion about what "part" means here. But I suggest we also take seriously the idea that Aristotle may have a general response in the *Categories* to the infamous problem of the one and the many.

The Tenfold Classification

One of the main puzzles that Aristotle's *Categories* presents is the puzzle about why Aristotle wants a Tenfold Classification of the things there are, as well as the Fourfold Classification we have been discussing. We assume, I think, that living organisms will be Aristotle's main examples of substances – "things not in a subject," whether primary substances or their species and genera, that is, secondary substances. Yet, even though there are many, many living organisms in the world, as well as many, many basic classifications of these organisms (tree, oak, animal, dog, and so on) the vast majority of "things that there are" will not be substances at all, but rather qualities, amounts, relations, places, times, and so on. The only place for these hoards of non-substances in the Fourfold Classification scheme will be as "things in a subject." If we take "in a subject" to mean "accidental feature of some substance," and if we suppose, as I think Aristotle does in the *Categories*, that everything else besides substances is an accidental feature of some substance, then we can call everything else "in a subject." But, given the important differences between, say, qualities and quantities, or between places and times, it will also be important to recognize those differences through the Tenfold Classification scheme.

So that is my explanation of why Aristotle wants both a Fourfold Classification scheme and a Tenfold Classification scheme. He wants the former as part of his "reduction project," that is, he attempt to show how everything there is, is either a primary substance, or the basic classification (or conceptual part of the classification) of a primary substance, or something in a primary substance, or the classification of something in a primary substance.

With his Reduction Thesis Aristotle turns Plato upside down. Instead of the eternal and unchanging Forms being the primary substances, it is, he says in the *Categories*, concrete individual things, especially living organisms, that are the primary substances.

Still, despite the central importance of the Fourfold Classification scheme to the metaphysics of Aristotle's *Categories*, Aristotle also thinks it important to outline the categorical differences between the ways in which non-substances can be features of primary substances. Being six feet tall is a very different sort of property from being blue-eyed, or being the teacher of someone, or being sitting rather than standing. The Tenfold Classification scheme brings out these categorical differences.

So how does Aristotle arrive at his list of just ten categories? In fact, he does not always list ten, sometimes he gives just seven (for example, in *Metaphysics* K.12 1068a8) and sometimes even fewer. Here is his list, with examples, from the *Categories*:

> Of things said without any combination, each signifies either substance or quantity or qualification or a relative or where or when or being-in-a-position or having or doing or being-affected. To give a rough idea, examples of substance are man, horse; of quality: four-foot, five-foot; of qualification: white, grammatical; of a relative: double, half, larger; of where: in the Lyceum, in the market-place; of when: yesterday, last-year; of being-in-a-position: is-lying, is-sitting; of having: has-shoes-on, has-armour-on; of doing: cutting, burning; of being-affected: being-cut, being-burned. (1b25–2a4)

It is significant that Aristotle often uses an interrogative pronoun to name a category. Not here, but elsewhere, he refers to secondary substance as "the what." Quantity is "the how much." Quality is "the how qualified." Place is "the where," and so on. No doubt one reason Aristotle uses interrogative pronouns to name the categories is that, in most cases, he doesn't have abstract terms readily available in the Greek of his time. But a more interesting reasoning fits his Reduction Thesis. Consider place. What kind of thing is a place? To answer that it is a "where" doesn't help much, until we realize that, on Aristotle's reductionist view, any given place is going to have to be an accident of one or more primary substances.

The container metaphor for accidents (that is, there being said to be "in a subject") is especially counterintuitive for place. Thus suppose that Coriscus is in the Lyceum. Following the Fourfold Classification we shall have to say that in-the-Lyceum is in Coriscus. Here the interrogative pronoun is helpful. In-the-Lyceum is "a where" by being where Coriscus or Callias, or whoever, is or was or will be.

Substance

Aristotle devotes chapter 5 of the *Categories* to substance. His idea of what it is to be a substance is important for all later philosophy.

One characteristic of substance he considers here, and takes up later in the *Metaphysics* (see ch. 12, "Substances") is being a certain "this." He writes:

> T5. As regards the primary substances, it is indisputably true that each of them signifies a certain "this"; for the thing revealed is individual and numerically one. But as regards the secondary substances, though it appears from the form of the name – when one speaks of man or animal – that a secondary substance likewise signifies a certain "this," this is not really true; rather, it signifies a certain qualification, for the subject is not, as the primary substance is, one, but man and animal are said of many things. (3b10–18)

Aristotle considers whether it is peculiar to substance to have nothing contrary to it. He rejects that criterion, on the ground that there is nothing contrary to a definite quantity either, such as four-foot, or ten (3b29–30).

A peculiarity of substance he does accept is that substance is not called more or less:

> T6. For one man is not more of a man than another, as one pale thing is more pale than another and one beautiful thing more beautiful than another . . . Thus substance does not admit of a more and a less. (3b37–4a9)

Finally he hits on his most important criterion:

> T7. It seems most distinctive of substance that what is numerically one and the same is able to receive contraries. In no other case could one bring forward anything, numerically one, which is able to receive contraries. For example, a color which is numerically one and the same will not be black and white, nor will numerically one and the same action be bad and good; and similarly with everything else that is not a substance. A substance, however, numerically one and the same is able to receive contraries. For example, an individual man – one and the same – becomes pale at one time and dark at another, and hot and cold, and bad and good. Nothing like this is to be seen in any other case. (4a10–22)

This criterion of substance is not preserved in Aristotle's later metaphysics. (See ch. 12, "Substances.")

Relatives

It is important to realize that there is, for Aristotle, no category of relations. Instead there is a category of *relatives*, such as double, half, mother, child, master, and slave. In fact, it was not really until the logic of relations was developed in the nineteenth century that philosophers and logicians developed a clear conception of relations. Aristotle did, however, seek to establish some principles about relatives. He says things like "when there is a double there is a half, and when there is a slave there a master." But there cannot be a full-fledged logic of relatives in the way that there is a logic of relations. And so Aristotle has none.

Although Aristotle in the *Categories* does not use the notion of an "accidental unity," what I have elsewhere called a "kooky object" (Matthews 1982) or the idea of (merely) accidental sameness, it is clear that the relatives of the *Categories* are what Aristotle will later in his career call accidental unities. Thus, he will also want to say that if Corsicus is a father, the father that is Coriscus will not be identical with Coriscus, but only accidentally the same as Corsicus.

While relatives are themselves accidental unities, items in other categories, when combined with primary substances, also constitute accidental unities. Thus musical Coriscus is made up of the primary substance, Coriscus, plus the quality of musicality, and seated Socrates is the primary substance, Socrates, plus being in the position, namely, the position of being seated.

The Place of the Categories in Aristotle's Thought

Central to Aristotle's mature metaphysics is the idea of hylomorphism, that is, the idea that concrete substances are composed of form and matter. One might want to say that the idea of form is present as species in the *Categories*, since species is there recognized as secondary substance. But that would be wrong, or at the very least, misleading. The characteristically Aristotelian idea of form is not present until it is coupled with the idea of matter. And the idea of matter does not make an appearance in Aristotle's writings until we get to Book I of the *Physics*.

What leads Aristotle to introduce the idea of matter is the idea of substantial change, that is, the idea of a concrete substance coming to be or passing away. Each concrete substance comes to be out of matter and passes away into matter. Moreover, during the time that a concrete substance exists, its matter underlies its form.

Is the world of the *Categories* simply a static world? No, not at all. Aristotle does allow in this work for alteration, that is, for a primary substance to take on and lose properties. In fact, as we have seen, he tells us that what is most characteristic of substance is that it admits of opposites, now light and now dark, or now short and now tall. The kind of change that that the *Categories* has nothing to say about is substantial change, a primary substance either coming into being or passing out of being.

We have no good way of knowing whether Aristotle developed his concept of matter after he wrote, or perhaps dictated, the *Categories*, or whether Aristotle simply ignored matter in the *Categories* so as to be able to focus more clearly on other issues. In any case, we can say that the concept of matter Aristotle develops in the *Physics* does not force Aristotle to take back anything he says in the *Categories*. At most it requires him to reject the implicit suggestion that the Fourfold Classification and the Tenfold Classification are each exhaustive of what there is.

Things are rather different with respect to the question of what substance should count as primary. As we have seen, concrete individuals, especially living organisms, count as primary substances in the *Categories*. By contrast, what seems to count primarily as substance in *Metaphysics*, Book Z, is form. Here we seem to have a change in metaphysical doctrine. Michael Frede sums up the development this way:

> The idea of the *Categories* that substances are that which underlies everything else is retained [in Aristotle's *Metaphysics*], as we see in Z.1 and Z.3. However, the answer to the question what is it that underlies everything else has changed: now it is the substantial form [rather than concrete individuals]. Aristotle also adds two new conditions for substancehood quite generally, conditions which, in the *Categories*, applied only to primary substances. They must be tode ti [a certain this], and they must exist independently, i.e., not depend for their existence on any other entities. (Frede 1987: 26)

Being Said in Many Ways

A hallmark of Aristotelian philosophy is the claim concerning many of the most contentious terms in philosophy that they are "said in many ways." Thus, for example, Aristotle tries to show us that we can make significant progress in philosophy when we recognize that his word for "cause" or "explanation" (*aitia*) is said in at least four ways, that is, for the material cause, the formal cause, the final cause and the efficient cause.

Especially important for later Aristotle is the claim that "to be" is said in many ways (Owen 1960). Sometimes when Aristotle makes that claim he unpacks it by saying that "to be" is said in as many ways as there are categories. When Aristotle makes that claim about "to be," he goes on to say that it is substance that is, or exists, in the primary sense of "is." We can easily combine that claim with the Reduction Thesis of the *Categories* in the following way. For Socrates to exist is for him to be a substance. However, for wisdom to exist is for it to be a "how qualified" (*poion*), in particular, to be how some substance is qualified. For three cubits to exist for it to be a "how much" (*poson*), in particular, to be how much or how tall some substance is, and so on.

In fact, the idea of a term being said in many ways – being, that is, a *pollachôs legomenon* – does not appear in the first nine chapters of the *Categories*. However, chapter 10, the beginning of the last part, the *Postpraedicamenta*, itself begins with the claim that "is the opposite of " is said in four ways. This fact, among others, suggests that the last six chapters were probably written later than the first nine and then added to the earlier part. On the other hand, the distinction between the ten different categories in chapter 4 and Aristotle's idea throughout the early chapters of the *Categories* that non-substances are dependent entities, indeed, dependent in the ways that the categorical distinctions bring out, prepares the ground for the later assertions that "to be" is said in as many ways as there are categories.

Two Systems?

In 1987 Daniel Graham published a book, *Aristotle's Two Systems*, in which he argued for these two theses:

(1)   There are two incompatible philosophic systems in Aristotle, namely those expressed in the *Organon* and the physical-metaphysical treatises, respectively.

(2)   These systems stand in a genetic relationship to one another: the latter is posterior in time and results from a transformation of the former. (Graham 1987: 15)

Graham characterizes the ontology of the first system, that of the *Categories*, this way:

According to this ontology, the realities of which the world is composed are atomic objects which are to be identified with biological individuals; these are organized under universals which are to be identified with natural kinds. In general, natural kinds are analyzable into differentiae and genera which uniquely define them and constitute their essence. In the first place the atomic objects and in the second place the kinds they fall under are called substances. Attributes are instantiated primarily in individual substances and secondarily in universal substances. These attributes, called accidents, characterize substances without belonging to them necessarily. (Graham 1987: 54)

Graham characterizes the second system – that of the *Physics* but especially of *Metaphysics* Zeta – this way:

The ontologically simple entities of S_1 [i.e., the system of the *Categories*] that Aristotle calls primary substances in S_1 have no counterpart in S_2 [i.e., the system of, say, *Metaphysics* Z]. The sensible substances, which serve as paradigm cases of primary substances in S_1, are found to be ontological complexes in S_2. Decomposed into form and matter, the compound substance holds no intrinsic interest in S_2, but rather forfeits its ontological primacy to its components. Aristotle considers both form and matter for the role of primary substance and settles on form, although the argument is not clear. Other theses of S_2 seem similar to S_1, *mutatis mutandis*. However, a new dimension in Aristotelian metaphysics is created by the addition of a theory of actuality which correlates degree of completeness of an object with its degree of actuality. (Graham 1987: 81)

Michael Wedin, in his book, *Aristotle's Theory of Substance: The* Categories *and Metaphysics Zeta*, has tried to argue for a single metaphysical system in Aristotle. He tries to do this by distinguishing between the one-place predicate, "is a substance," and the two-place predicate, "is the substance of." His idea is that what counts as a substance in the *Categories* still counts as a substance in *Metaphysics* Z, but, according to the later work, form is the substance of, say, this man or this horse.

Wedin concedes that the honorific qualifier, "primary," shifts in Aristotle from the concrete individual substance to its form. He seeks to domesticate that shift in the following way:

Compatibilists still need to explain why Aristotle should appear to withdraw *primacy* from c-substances [i.e., the primary substances of the *Categories*] and attach it to their forms . . . Resolution is achieved by seeing that the primacy of *Categories* primary substances . . . is a kind of ontological primacy, whereas the primacy of form is a kind of structural or explanatory primacy. (Wedin 2000: 452–3)

An ingenious and illuminating way of understanding the relationship between the metaphysics of the *Categories* and that of *Metaphysics* Zeta can be found in this volume, ch. 12, "Substances."

The Afterlife of the Doctrine of Categories

The idea that entities belong to different categories and especially the question of how many categories there are were much discussed and debated in late antiquity, in medieval philosophy, and in early modern philosophy. Among the many difficulties discussed is the question of whether Socrates will have to count as an accident of place, since he cannot exist apart from being in a place. Ammonius, a Neoplatonic commentator of the late fifth and early sixth centuries CE, responds this way:

We reply then that Socrates can exist apart from what he is in. For if we suppose him to have left behind the place where he was earlier and gone to another place, he is no less Socrates, whereas the accident separated from its subject has been destroyed. (Sorabji 2004: 110)

Among other problems the ancient commentators posed for Aristotle's *Categories* is one about how to understand the fact that the fragrance of an apple be can both in the apple and also in the air surrounding the apple. For a discussion of what they had to say about this problem see Ellis 1990. And for other interesting problems with the *Categories* that these commentators identified see Sorabji 2004.

Kant, in his *Critique of Pure Reason*, develops a "Table of Categories" (A80/B105), which he says has the same purpose as Aristotle's account of the categories. In fact, Kant's theory is so different from Aristotle's that one must work hard to find the points of similarity between the two theories.

Closer in spirit to Aristotle is the use Gilbert Ryle makes of the idea of categories with his conception of a "category mistake." Notoriously, Ryle ridicules Descartes' mind–body dualism as the theory of "the Ghost in the Machine" and analyzes the mistake it embodies as a category mistake – the mistake of thinking that minds and bodies belong to the same category, namely, the category of substance. In Ryle's view minds are not "things," i.e., substances, additional to the bodies that have them. Rather they are, to put the matter rather crudely, complex and at least partially learned dispositions of certain bodies to behave in purposive ways that count as being intelligent.

Ryle couples his diagnosis of mind-body dualism as a category mistake with the idea from later Aristotle that "is," or "exists," has as many different senses as there are categories:

> It is perfectly proper to say, in one logical tone of voice, that there exist minds and to say, in another logical tone of voice, that there exist bodies. But these expressions do not indicate two different species of existence, for "existence" is not a generic word like "coloured" or "sexed." They indicate two different senses of "exist," somewhat as "rising" has different senses in "the tide is rising," "hope are rising," and "the average age of death is rising." A man would be thought to be making a poor joke who said that three things are now rising, namely the tide, hopes and the average age of death. (Ryle 1949: 23)

Other philosophers have taken over Ryle's idea of a category mistake without accepting Ryle's critique of Cartesian dualism, let alone accepting the specific details of Aristotle's original doctrine of the categories. Thus the Aristotelian idea of categories, at least in a generalized form, lives on in philosophy today, even though there is no agreement about exactly what a category is, how many categories there are, or what makes it the case that two given candidates for being categories are, or are not, distinct categories.[4]

Notes

[1] All translations from the *Categories* will be taken from Ackrill 1963, with occasional modifications.

[2] In an older and more traditional sense of "property," a property is a *proprium* (Latin) or an *idion* (Greek), that is, a feature of a thing that necessarily belongs to it, even though it does not belong to the essence of the thing. The idea of there being such a thing as a property in this traditional sense requires that one understand "essence" in rather different ways from what is often called "Aristotelian essentialism" today. See Matthews 1990.

[3] We owe this modern use of "trope" to my old teacher, Donald Carey Williams, in Williams 1953.

[4] I owe thanks to Marc Cohen for suggesting several improvements over an earlier version of this chapter.

Bibliography

Ackrill, J. L. (1963). *Aristotle's "Categories" and "De Interpretatione"* (Oxford: Clarendon Press).

Devereux, D. T. (1992). "Inherence and Primary Substance in Aristotle's *Categories*," *Ancient Philosophy*, 12, pp. 113–31.

Ellis, J. (1990). "The Trouble with Fragrance," *Phronesis*, 35, pp. 290–302.

Frede, M. (1987). *Essays in Ancient Philosophy* (Minneapolis, MN: University of Minnesota Press).

Graham, D. W. (1987). *Aristotle's Two Systems* (Oxford: Clarendon Press).

Matthews, G. B. (1982). "Accidental unities," in M. Schofiled and M. Nussbaum (eds.), *Language and Logos* (Cambridge: Cambridge University Press), pp. 223–40.

Matthews, G. B. (1990). "Aristotelian Essentialism," *Philosophy and Phenomenological Research*, 50, supple., pp. 251–62.

Matthews. G. B. (1991). "Container Metaphysics according to Aristotle's Greek Commentators," *Canadian Journal of Philosophy*, 17, supple., pp. 7–23.

Matthews, G. B. and Cohen, S. M. (1968). "The One and the Many," *Review of Metaphysics*, 21, pp. 630–55.

Owen, G. E. L. [1960] (1986). "Logic and Metaphysics in Some Earlier Works of Aristotle," in I. Düring and G. E. L. Owen (eds.), *Aristotle and Plato in the Mid-fourth Century* (Göteborg: Elanders Boktryckeri Aktiebolag), pp. 163–90. (Repr. in Owen, 1986, pp. 180–99.)

Owen, G. E. L. [1965] (1986). "Inherence," *Phronesis*, 10, pp. 97–105. (Repr. in Owen, (1986), pp. 252–8.)

Owen, G. E. L. (1986). *Logic, Science and Dialectic*, ed. M. Nussbaum (Ithaca, NY: Cornell University Press).

Ryle, G. [1938] (1971). "Categories," *Proceedings of the Aristotelian Society*, 38, pp. 189–206. (Repr. in *Collected Papers*, vol. 2, *Collected Essays 1929–1968* (London: Hutchinson, 1971), pp. 170–84.)

Ryle, G. (1949). *The Concept of Mind* (London: Hutchinson's University Library).

Sorabji, R. (2004). *The Philosophy of the Commentators, 200–600 AD* (London: Duckworth).

Wedin, M. V. (1993). "Nonsubstantial Individuals," *Phronesis*, 38, pp. 137–63.

Wedin, M. V. (2000). *Aristotle's Theory of Substance: The "Categories" and "Metaphysics" Zeta* (Oxford: Oxford University Press).

Williams, D. C. (1953). "On the Elements of Being," *Review of Metaphysics*, 7, pp. 3–18, 171–92.

10

Form and Matter

FRANK A. LEWIS

The topic of Aristotle's theory of form and matter is a large one, and even the limited survey here will take us through substantial portions of his metaphysics and natural philosophy.

Some Metaphysical Preliminaries

We begin at a place where the theory is conspicuously absent. In the *Cat*, Aristotle appears to present a general metaphysical theory, dividing "things that are" into four classes, but with no mention of form or matter. Instead, we get an ontology of individual substances (this man, this horse) and their kinds (man, animal), along with their accidents, lowest-level or otherwise – but nothing more. In the theory that Aristotle constructs out of these materials, individual substances are members of kinds (lowest-level kinds, like man, and the higher-level kinds above them) and also subjects to accidents (pallor, generosity, and the like).

Form and matter, however, are nowhere in evidence – perhaps (the "developmental" view) because Aristotle has not thought of them yet. Or he may already have thought of them, but holds them irrelevant in one way or another to the current project. For example (the "pedagogical" view), the *Cat* is a "primer," and stops short of such complications. Alternatively, the theory of form and matter is at a different level of analysis from what we read in the *Cat*. At this deeper level of explanation, what it is for Archimedes (say) to be a member of a kind, and the very notion of a kind itself, are explained in terms of – even reduced to – the mechanism of form and matter.

As we shall see below, the new theory also promises to repair two problems left unresolved in the *Cat*. In the *Cat*, first, individual substances count as primary, because items from the three remaining classes – substance kinds, lowest-level accidents and accident kinds – all owe their existence to the fact that they are (metaphysically) predicated of individual substances as their subjects. (Think of *metaphysical* predication as the relation between entities that makes the corresponding *linguistic* predication true, as the fact that pallor is metaphysically predicated of Socrates (say) makes true the linguistic predication, "Socrates is pale.") Puzzlingly, the existential dependence by everything else on individual substances is matched by an essential dependence in the opposite

162

direction by individual members of the different categories on their kinds. Archimedes cannot exist without being a man; the purple of his cloak cannot exist unless it is a color or, more broadly, a quality; and so on. This second, reverse dependence undoubtedly disturbs what Aristotle sees as the primacy of individual substances.

A second unresolved issue involves change. The *Cat* contains only the barest reference to change of any sort: the remark that "it seems distinctive above all of substance that what is the same and one in number is receptive of contraries" (5 4a10ff, cf. 6 5b39–6a4) must presuppose a reference to time – an individual substance, Archimedes, can be now pale, now dark; worthy or unworthy. But this minimal account breaks down for coming to be and destruction: for something to come to be cannot be for it to lose one contrary and acquire another, for it would have to exist as the subject of the first contrary before coming into existence by acquiring the second; and for similar reasons, its ceasing to exist cannot be explained in terms of its gaining and losing contraries.

The Introduction of Matter and Form

In *Phys* I, the bare suggestion from the *Cat* that change is between contraries becomes part of a general account of change: not just the cases of change in accidents envisioned in the *Cat*, but also the coming to be and perishing of an individual substance, where entities other than individual substances will be the subjects of contraries.

Aristotle's chief aim in *Phys* I is to establish the first principles on which the science of natural philosophy rests. These principles, he thinks, must be reached from outside natural philosophy itself; for this reason, he mentions the notions of form and matter, which are central to his natural philosophy, only glancingly in the last chapters of the Book, where they are his counterparts within natural philosophy of the apparatus uncovered in the earlier, preliminary inquiry. In the body of I, accordingly, Aristotle turns for help to dialectic or some allied technique, for example, "induction" or the review of cases. Dialectic treads where the special sciences are not meant to go. It is concerned to uncover general principles that apply across the sciences; or that are preliminary to, and hence lie outside, the business of a given science (*Top* I.2, 101a36–b4).

Contraries and the underlying subject

Typical also of dialectic is the appeal to other philosophers, or to what is commonly thought, as a source for views on the subject-matter at hand. Thus, in both the early going and at the end of *Phys* I.5, Aristotle turns to his predecessors for the view that all change is between contraries. (By "contraries," it appears, he means *polar* contraries, which exhibit maximum or complete difference (*Cat* 6 6a17–18; *Met* I.4 1055a4, 16; see Bogen (1992)), accompanied typically but not always by intermediates: black and white, for example, and the various intermediate colors.) His view is also backed up by argument (if this is the right translation of *epi tou logou*, 188b31): a review of cases indicates that the pale man turns dark, or the stingy man generous; while if the pale man turns generous, this is because it is an accident of the stingy man that he is also pale.

163

The exact character of Aristotle's argument in I.5 is the subject of controversy. It is agreed that his argument takes place outside the bounds of natural philosophy. Beyond this, however, is he arguing for a logical, even conceptual doctrine? Or is his argument, instead, empirically based? On the usual story, Aristotle is appealing to the supposedly a priori truth that all change takes place along "incompatibility ranges." But he has also been taken to be arguing by "induction" – by a review of cases – for the claim that only the accidental (which for him is by definition irregular) disturbs the regular pattern of change between contraries.

Having made the case that change is between contraries, Aristotle argues in I.6 that in addition to a given pair of contraries, we must also make room for what underlies them – the *subject* they qualify – that *persists* through the exchange of contraries. There cannot be just one principle (since contraries come in pairs); but not an unlimited number either. But however small a number of principles we end up with, there could not be just two of them: various puzzles show that we must posit some additional nature to underlie the contraries. By this point, Aristotle's discussion of principles has quietly shifted from a count of *stuffs* and *contraries*, to counting the different *functional work* that the various stuffs and contraries will do. Commentators also remark on the "tentative," even cursory nature of the puzzles of I.6, which rely freely on views from the *Cat*, with little attention to how well those views are suited to their new context.

How we talk about change

In earlier chapters of *Phys* I, Aristotle makes extensive use of the views of others (or of his own other self in the *Cat*). In I.7, by contrast, he seeks to put his own stamp on the account of change. Aristotle agrees with his predecessors that some third entity under-lies the contraries. On this score, there are three principles – but no more. Or rather, it is a puzzle whether they are three in number, or just two. In the end, however, we may put down as one of the central tenets of natural philosophy, the existence of a persisting substratum of change, with its attendant contraries, both in genuine coming to be and destruction, but also in cases of accidental change.

On the way to these conclusions, Aristotle begins with coming-to-be generally, and only later separates out "simply coming to be" – the coming to be (and perishing) of a thing – from accidental change (its "coming to be something"). In some cases, we say that

1   The man becomes musical;

but not that

*2   From the man, he comes to be musical.

In other cases, however, both ways of speaking are available:

3   The unmusical becomes musical;
4   From the unmusical, he comes to be musical.

In the use of "from" Aristotle has in mind in (4), if a thing comes to be "from X," then X disappears (this is not the "from" of constitution, where if a thing is "from X," then X is a constituent of the thing). Because (3) can be rewritten as (4), while (1) has no such counterpart, Aristotle concludes that what comes to be "<something>," as in (1) and (3) – what underlies the change – divides into two cases:

> The man remains when he becomes musical, and is a man; but the not musical, i.e., the unmusical, does not remain. (190a10–13)

And these, he says, the man and the unmusical, are one in number but two in form or account, for "the being of man is not the same as the being of unmusical" (190a17).

That there is something underlying that does the coming to be is plain in cases of accidental change, where a substance underlies its various qualities and the rest. (This is "what underlies" in the sense of what also persists through the change.) But on a closer look, in the case of substances too, there is something that underlies (and also persists) when a substance comes to be – the statue by change of shape (here, the marble is what underlies), a house by "composition" (the bricks and mortar underlie), and so on.

Change and constitution

The analysis of change and its antecedents immediately becomes a premiss in the account of the metaphysical constitution of the product of change, so that "everything comes to be out of the underlying thing and the form" (190b20). The "out of" or "from" here is the "from" of constitution: Aristotle is listing the constituents of things that have come to be. The underlying thing, meanwhile, "though one in number, is two in form": on the one hand, the man, the gold, and in general the "countable matter" (*hulê arithmêtê*) (the variety of "underlying thing" that also persists); but on the other hand, the "privation" (the unmusical man, say, or perhaps just his lack of musicality). Finally, we have the form: the arrangement, or the knowledge of music.

For the present, Aristotle is concerned above all with the number of principles: what underlies and the form (two principles); or what underlies and persists (selecting for one of the two notions of "what underlies" presumably rolled together in the count that gives the answer, two), the privation, and the form (three principles). Or we have the two contraries, form and privation (two principles); or the two contraries and what underlies and persists (three principles). He makes only passing use of the terms "form" and "matter," which remain unexplained. But he does append an account "by analogy" of his notion of the underlying nature that persists:

> As bronze to a statue, or wood to a bed, or the matter and the formless before it acquires a form to anything else which has a definite form, so this [= the underlying nature] stands to a reality, to a this, to what is.

This is not analogy in our sense, in which one thing is compared to a second. Rather, what is compared is a relationship between one pair of items, set against fresh instances of the same relationship among further pairs of items. In each case, Aristotle suggests, one member of each pair stands as the underlying thing to the other as the reality, or finished product.

Aristotle flags one item that awaits resolution in *Phys* II: it is "not yet clear" whether the form or the underlying thing is substance. (In II, as we shall see, he is clear that the preference lies with form.)

Aristotle ends I.7 by declaring settled the inquiry into the number of principles. One point, however, deserves further notice. Aristotle's stated uncertainty over how many principles to recognize hangs on a point about sameness. In one way, the man and the unmusical, for example, are the same; but in another, they are different. Aristotle explains: "the underlying thing is one in number, but two in form or account, for being for <the> man and for <the> unmusical are not the same" (190a15–17, cf. b23–7). Equally, "the being of <the> man is different from the being of <the> unmusical, and the being of <the> shapeless is different from the being of the bronze" (190b35–191a3). It may well be that the distinction in kinds of sameness is where he thinks the distinctive contribution of the chapter lies. At any rate, as we shall see, the distinction is also behind his criticism of Plato in the last chapter of I: by failing to draw this distinction, Aristotle thinks, Plato was led to miss the further distinction between the matter of a thing and the privation.

In distinguishing the man and the unmusical, Aristotle's point is not merely that, in the course of change, one and the same thing can be assigned different descriptions: Archimedes under the description "man," in contrast to Archimedes under the description "unmusical" (say). Nor is the difference that between Archimedes and the accident unmusicality – these are straightforwardly two. Rather (although the point is controversial), the distinction is best seen as between Archimedes and unmusical Archimedes, a.k.a. Archimedes + unmusical – between Archimedes and (in one ready jargon) the *accidental compound* of Archimedes with the accident, unmusicality, where these are accidentally the same, but not identical. Similarly, we distinguish the matter – the bronze that at one time is relatively shapeless, at another has the shape of a statue – from the compound of the matter with the privation. We will say more about compounds below.

Parmenides and Plato

In the last two chapters of *Phys* I, Aristotle compares the views developed in previous chapters with those of two notable predecessors: in I.8, Parmenides, and in I.9, Plato. His difference with Plato revolves around their different conceptions of "what underlies." As Aristotle sees it, Plato holds that things come to be from what is one not only in number, but also in possibility, which for Aristotle is a different thing altogether. According to Plato, the underlying thing is joint cause with the form of the things that come to be. But the remaining contrary, the privation, is left out of Plato's story. For his part, Aristotle insists on the contrast between the matter and the privation. The privation is contrary to the form; and matter strives after the form. If, then, as Plato supposes, the matter and the privation are the same, the matter is contrary to the form and strives after its own contrary, which is absurd.

Aristotle ends the Book by stepping out of dialectical mode, and lining up his own concept of matter with what underlies:

By matter, I mean that primary underlying thing in each case, out of which as a constituent (*enuparchontos*) and not by virtue of an accident something comes to be. (192a31–2)

To the idea of a preexisting matter, Aristotle adds the requirement that the matter persist (*enuparchontos*) in the product of change. The persistence requirement calls for separate discussion below. As for "the principle in the sense of form," discussion of whether there are one or many of these, and their nature, can be left to first philosophy; but "natural and perishable forms" – the forms of natural, perishable objects? – are his next topic.

Explanation and natural philosophy

In *Phys* I, Aristotle works towards the notions of matter and form that are parts of his own theory by a painstaking process that employs methods and concepts that lie outside the domain of natural philosophy proper. *Phys* II begins with a fresh start, but his approach to matter and form is similarly circuitous. In this case, however, he arrives at the target notions more quickly, midway through the first chapter. First, (i), to help fix ideas, he lists things typically thought to have natures. There follows, (ii), a definition of the nature of a thing, as an internal principle of its behavior. Finally, (iii), Aristotle explains which items in his official ontology answer to the specification given: in their different ways, and to different degrees, both the matter and the form of a thing qualify as its nature.

It is worth attending to how Aristotle secures the "fit" between his definition at stage (ii), and the notions of form and matter from his own theory, which belong at stage (iii). Warrant for thinking that the matter of a thing satisfies the definition of its nature or substance is found in Antiphon's bed experiment (193a12–17, b8–12); and found also among Aristotle's materialist reductionist predecessors, for whom what stands at the very bottom of the chain of material constituents in a thing will count as its substance, everything else being the "affections, states, or dispositions" of these basic ingredients. Aristotle himself, on the other hand, argues that the better claim for being a thing's nature or substance belongs to its shape or form, which (in contrast to Plato's forms) is separable only in account. In this way, a thing's behavior can be explained in certain ways by reference to its matter, in other ways by reference to its form; but the preferred modes of explanation will rely on the form.

With the topic of explanation, the third of three major projects falls into place. Aristotle's inquiry in I.7 had two main targets: the analysis of change already under way in earlier chapters, and the accompanying analysis of the metaphysical composition of concrete particulars out of an underlying subject and some favored contrary. In *Phys* II, a third aim becomes apparent: to augment the account of change in Book I with a wholly general account of explanation in natural philosophy. Such a theory of explanation – Aristotle's notion of the so-called four causes – is possible, thanks to the view that emerges in II.1, that we are to think of natural objects as consisting of the form and the matter together – as *compounds* of form and matter (*to ek toutôn*, 193b5). His scheme of causes is built around the twin notions of matter and form; the scheme is genuinely explanatory, presumably, because it is tailor-made for a domain of objects with this very constitution – with matter and form as their constituents.

Aristotle's talk of form-matter compounds requires comment. In general, Aristotle will analyze individual substances, a and the rest, as compounds of form and matter, so that for some matter, m, and form, ψ, $a = m + \psi$. (The "+" notation expresses the notion of compounding, which is primitive in his theory; associations the notation may have in other contexts should be disregarded.) Talk of individual substances as compounds follows Aristotle's own idioms: they are a "this-in-this," or "what is out of these," or a "composite," or a "composite substance." Form-matter compounds can be compared to accidental compounds, discussed above. We return briefly to compounding below.

Form, matter, and the Categories once more

The theory outlined in the *Phys* helps answer questions left unresolved in the *Cat*. First, as we saw, the *Cat* only hints at an account of accidental change, and says nothing about the coming to be and passing away of individual substances, which cannot involve the exchange of contraries by an individual substance. But an account of coming to be and passing away is available, without absurdity, if we "drop a level" in comparison with the account of accidental change gestured at in the *Cat*, so that the structure present in accidental change applies one level down, to a thing's matter, and to the privation and the form that in turn qualify the matter.

Aristotle's theory in the *Cat* is also subject to strain from the fact that we have reason to think both that the individual substance is primary, and also that it is, in a different way, dependent on the kinds under which it falls and in this respect not primary after all. With the advent of matter and form, on most accounts of Aristotle, the individual loses its primacy. In *Phys* I, Aristotle is inclined to wonder whether the form or the matter of a thing ranks first; in *Phys* II, however, and in the *Met*, he plumps unequivocally for the primacy of form. It is the form of a thing that above all determines its nature, or that is "the cause of being" and "the cause of being one" for the thing (*Met* Z.17, H.2). And if its form is the cause of being for the thing, Aristotle can now explain what it is for an individual to belong to a kind. The kinds or secondary substances of the *Cat* are no longer substances at all, but "compounds of this form and this matter, taken universally"; and for a thing to belong to a given kind is for its matter to be informed by the form that typifies the kind.

Some problems of persistence

The *Phys* account of change, featuring a pair of contraries and a persisting subject of the change, is hardly free of controversy. When the shapeless lump is worked up into a statue, for example, surely the shapeless lump no longer exists, once the statue is made, contrary to Aristotle's persistence requirement. Against this, we need to distinguish the underlying subject – a quantity of bronze (say), which does persist – from the compound of the subject with the privative contrary – the (relatively) shapeless lump, which does not persist.

But if the *Phys* itself is clear about contraries and a persisting subject, the persistence requirement comes under pressure from other Aristotelian views, as the theory of form and matter is applied to the complexities of the natural world. How, for example, is persistence to be understood in the result of *mixing* (below), where Aristotle supposes that the product is uniform through and through, and what counts as matter exists only potentially in the product? Again, what, if anything, persists through the exchange of elemental contraries in the mutual transformation of the elements? (This is the question of *prime matter*, below.)

Aristotle's persistence requirement also intersects in a troubling way with his notion of *homonymy*, as it appears to apply to the matter of a living thing. The stuffs and structures that serve as matter for a living animal, for example, cannot exist in the absence of the form that characterizes the whole. For example, only the living eye can be part of the matter of an animal – and to be living, it must be endowed with the form or soul of the whole creature. How, then, can it be independent of the form, in the way that Aristotle's notion of the persistence of matter apparently requires? We will return to this difficulty below.

The Hierarchy of Form and Matter

Phys I and II provide a blueprint for work in natural philosophy: an account of the metaphysical constitution of natural objects, and how such things can be subject to generation and destruction; and an account of what in general counts as explanation for the behavior of objects of this sort. But the detailed application to the natural world (and perhaps, in the case of the Unmoved Mover, beyond the natural world as well) is left to other works.

Aristotle outlines the scope of natural philosophy at the beginning of the *Meteor*, through successively more complex domains of nature, culminating in the most important branch of natural philosophy, namely, psychology. At every point, various stuffs or structures serve as matter, and are acted on or constrained in one way or another by form. (Aristotle will say that a given stuff or structure is the *matter of* a form-matter compound – some higher-level matter, perhaps, or a finished substance – and that the first is as *proximate matter* to the second, if no intermediate matter lies between the two.)

The different levels in the constitution of a thing are an acknowledged part of Presocratic natural philosophy (*Phys* II.1 193a9–28). Aristotle has his own view of the different levels of form and matter in the constitution of living things. In the biological works, he describes how the so-called elements, earth, air, fire, and water, are the matter for the *uniform* parts; these in turn are the matter for the *nonuniform* parts (there are also "ambiguous" parts that are in one way uniform, in another nonuniform); the nonuniform parts, finally, are the matter for the completed animal.

In this sequence, the clearly uniform parts include blood, flesh, and bone. These are uniform (following the Greek, *homoiomerous*, "like-parted"), because (on Aristotle's view, but not ours) they are what they are, flesh (say), "through and through": every part is like every other, and each is like the whole. Aristotle's notion of uniform parts, and the process of mixing by which these are produced, are directed against Empedocles and the atomists, for whom things are put together in the way that a wall is made out of bricks and stones, which (if one's eyes were only sharp enough) are still to be seen in the product.

The clearly nonuniform parts, next, include the familiar organs of the living animal – the head, for example, ears, eyes, and horns. An eye, for example is nonuniform, because the whole has a structure in such a way that its parts are not all like the whole (and not all like each other). Meanwhile, the ambiguous parts include such items as the viscera (for Aristotle, the system of internal organs connected by the blood vessels), which are composed of a single uniform substance, and so are in one way uniform, in another, nonuniform.

At the bottom of the sequence, meanwhile, the simplest perceptible constituents of the sublunary world are the so-called elements: unhappily named, for Aristotle, because they are neither eternal nor simple. Not eternal: in his work "On the Elements" (*GC* II.1–8), Aristotle argues against Empedocles for the mutual *transformation* of the elements, which he thinks is a datum of experience. Not simple: their mutual transformation requires that they each consist of the appropriate two from the four elemental contraries, hot, cold, wet, dry, together with, on the traditional view, prime matter. (Thus, earth is dry and cold; water, moist and cold; air, moist and hot; and fire, dry and hot.) As *Phys* I maintains, generation is to contraries and from contraries; given the presence of contraries in their constitution, then, it follows that, by nature, the different elements can transform reciprocally into each other.

The transformation of one element into another – where the one is generated and the other destroyed – can take place when one constituent contrary in a given element is overwhelmed by the presence of its contrary: when the contrary, moist, for example, that helps constitute a portion of air, is overwhelmed by the presence of its contrary, dry, so that the air is transformed into fire. (Here, Aristotle says, the contraries "are not equal"). But it can also happen, as the elements come in contact, that the various contraries are present in more or less equal amounts. In this case the contraries act on each other in such a way as to achieve a mean or an intermediate – each "destroys the other's excesses" – and the result is a *mixture*, in Aristotle's technical sense, Fine ([1995] 1996), (1998), in which the elements that have been mixed are not destroyed, but are present potentially.

Aristotle's view of the different stuffs and structures found in the composition of natural objects offers a sequence of matters from which successive layers are composed. But he is emphatic that the different stages in the composition of a thing are described best of all teleologically, via their definition and final cause, which are present at every level, from the elements up. The role of form in the definition of a given part is matched by its role in how that part comes to be. At *GA* II.1 734b28–31, 33–735a5, he uses an analogy with human craftsmanship to make the point; similar (but less sweeping) claims appear in *Meteor* IV.12 390b3ff.

Aristotle argues for his teleological view in *PA* II.1. As often (compare *PA* I.1), "being is before becoming," even if the process of coming-to-be is temporally prior. An animal "makes its coming-to-be" from one principle to another – from a first mover, *with its own definite nature*, to a form or some such end: even here, where the underlying matter and the process of coming-to-be come first in time, "it takes a human being to beget a human being." Again, the essence and the form of the product are first in definition, as the definition of the coming-to-be shows: the definition of building contains that of the house, but not vice versa. So the product or end is definitionally prior, and the matter comprising the elements, which comes temporally first, exists for the sake of the uniform stuffs, which come later; and similarly for the uniform and the nonuniform parts.

But could the ordering of the stages in the constitution of a thing have been otherwise – the uniform parts, for example, composed of the nonuniform? An animal exhibits its distinctive behavior – its many actions and movements – by the use of its nonuniform parts – its eyes, nose, hands, and so on. But the different, even conflicting, powers are distributed singly among the uniform parts – how else could they be uniform? The full array of powers that give a single nonuniform part, a hand (say), its distinctive behavior, can be present there, only if that single nonuniform part is assembled out of many uniform parts, each with its own distinctive power. So the very complexity of a hand, reflected in the variety of the powers that are "useful" to it, requires that it have the (simple) uniform parts as its constituents, rather than vice versa. In this way, even the ordering of the sequence of stuffs and structures in the constitution of natural objects is teleologically determined. We will return to Aristotelian teleology in the next section.

I end the present section with limiting cases of matter and of form, both controversial. In the broader picture, arguably, the system of matter and form extends to include prime matter at the very lowest level of analysis in the sublunary world, and the Unmoved Mover – on most accounts, "pure form" – which stands outside the sphere of natural objects altogether. In the Aristotelian "scale of being," the different elements all have as a constituent some portion of prime matter (if, as I suppose, this is a genuinely Aristotelian concept, see below); prime matter is the limiting case of the notion of matter, which applies throughout the sublunary sphere, and is absent only outside the sublunary world altogether, in the case of the Unmoved Mover, which (on the usual view) is itself the limiting case of the correlative notion of form. The Unmoved Mover is the limiting case of form, on the usual view, because all engagement with matter is absent from it. Just so, prime matter is the limiting case of matter, because all engagement with form is absent – of all the cases of matter, prime matter alone is not itself a compound of form and matter.

At the same time, because the Unmoved Mover has no constitutive matter, it has no shred of potentiality but, as Aristotle describes it, is pure actuality: the activity of thinking, engaged in thinking its own activity of thinking. And because prime matter has no constitutive form, in a certain sense it exhibits the maximum degree of potentiality: the potentiality for one or other of the four elements, each of which in turn has the potentiality for elemental transformation, and beyond that, as we have seen, for being mixed with the other elements into one or other uniform stuff; and so on all the way up to the living substances of nature.

Matter and Potentiality, Form and Actuality; the Teleological Conception of Matter

Matter and powers

One ingredient in Aristotle's conception of matter from the start is persistence: we will return to qualifications to this conception below. Persistence (or something similar) is presupposed in the idea that matter is a subject in turn for the privation and for the form that replaces it. More precisely, it is apparently a defining feature of matter that it have the *capacity* for receiving the form under the appropriate conditions of realization or, in unfavorable cases, for reverting to the privation:

> Matter in altogether the strictest sense is the underlying thing ("the subject") that is capable of receiving generation and destruction. (*GC* II.4 320a2–3)

This part of Aristotle's theory suggests the following view. His notion of matter has its basis in the brute fact about a given stuff or structure, *s*, that *s* has the *capacity for receiving or losing the relevant contraries* in a given case of coming to be or destruction. Here, the capacity in *s* for receiving or for losing contraries *plays a certain causal role*: the fact that *s* possesses the capacity in question contributes to *s*'s constituting (or ceasing to constitute) a thing of a given kind. And it is *because s* possesses properties that play this causal role that *s* qualifies as matter in the first place.

On this view, the property in *s* of being matter is (in today's terms) a *second-level functional property*: it is the (second-level) property of *s* that *s* have some (first-level) property – this or that capacity for receiving contraries, different in different cases – that plays a certain causal role in coming to be and destruction. Plausibly, the order of metaphysical priority runs from the first-level capacities to the second-level functional property: it is *because* a stuff or structure has the (first-level) capacities that play the causal role in question, that it has the (second-level) functional property of being matter.

Further complications concern the realization conditions for the capacities noted. The capacity in the matter for receiving contraries is the *passive* power for receiving the contrary relevant in a given case of generation or destruction – "matter qua matter is *capable of being acted on*" (*pathêtikon, GC* I.7 324b18) – and it is realized only in the presence of an agent with the appropriate *active* capacity. For the two powers to be actualized, what has the active power and what has the passive power must be "together" or otherwise in suitable proximity; and the two powers must be suited to each other and to the product in various ways.

Some examples may help. Marble (say), and bricks and timbers, both qualify as matter (for the record, not only a single item, but also a collection of parts, can count as matter) – better, as the matter *for* something. The marble, for example, counts as the matter for a statue, because it has the passive power for being acted on in such a way as to be made to receive or to lose the appropriate contrary or form, so that it is made to constitute a statue (or so that it ceases to constitute a statue, under the appropriately adverse circumstances). But the passive power in the marble is different from that lodged in the bricks and timbers: the passive powers of the marble leave it open to being made into a statue; those of the bricks and timbers to their being developed into a house.

In this account, marble counts as matter, *because it has the appropriate passive power* – the power for being made to receive the appropriate contrary or form, so that it can be made into a thing of the kind, statue, where statues are typified by the form in question. Meanwhile, the corresponding *active* power for the relevant form is lodged in the agent or sculptor, who has the form of a statue before his mind. Aristotle outlines the relevant active and passive powers at *Met* Θ.1 1046a22–8; and for a case study of the role of the relevant active and passive powers in the formation of the different bodily parts in the generation of an animal, see *GA* II.6 743a21–29.

Motion (kinêsis) and actuality (energeia)

In *Met* Δ.12 and Θ.1, Aristotle explains what he takes to be the core notion of potentiality: it is "a principle of movement or change in something else, or qua other." From this comes the notion of a passive power: "the principle in the very thing that is being acted on for passive change by the agency of something else, or qua other." Thus, the bricks and stones that are the matter for a house have the (passive) capacity for undergoing the change or *kinêsis* of being made into a house. And there is a corresponding active power in the agent – the builder – thanks to which he engages in the *kinêsis* of building the house.

But what of when the house is built? In *Met* Θ.6, Aristotle promises a new notion of potentiality, for which (he says) his discussion of the capacities correlated with motion (*kinêsis*) was merely preparation. Here, the capacity in the matter by virtue of which the matter constitutes the thing is the capacity for an actuality (*energeia*), in the special sense Aristotle explains (his terminology is not consistent in other works, perhaps not even in Θ.6). His first explanation is that a thing obtains actually when it does not obtain potentially (as the Hermes exists in the stone). Otherwise, he relies again on analogy (see above): its actuality (*energeia*) stands to the relevant capacity (*dunamis*) as (i) what is house-building stands to what can house-build; or (ii) what is awake stands to what sleeps; or (iii) what is seeing stands to what is sighted but has its eyes shut; or (iv) what has become distinct out of the matter stands to the matter; or finally (v) what has been wrought stands to the unwrought.

Of Aristotle's examples, it is not straightforward to place (i). The capacity for building my house is on its way to being realized in the *kinêsis* of placing the bricks and the rest, but is fully realized only when it is exhausted with the completion of the house. The capacity for building tout court, on the other hand, is realized as an *energeia* from moment to moment, as one builds. Later remarks in the chapter favor the first reading of this example; but they favor the second, *energeia*-style reading for (ii) and (iii). Aristotle explains that a *kinêsis* is incomplete: with slimming, or learning, or walk-taking, or building my house, the end is not present at every moment in the performance: we do not say that at every moment I am building my house, and that I have built it. Quite differently, however, with an *energeia*, one simultaneously is seeing and has seen, is living well and has lived well; in contrast to a *kinêsis*, an *energeia* does not finish once the end is achieved.

As for matter and *energeia* (or matter and substance, 1048b9) in cases (iv) and (v): barring disaster, presumably, or disuse – Aristotle himself offers no explanation – my house once finished is equally a house from each moment to the next, and the matter continues to exercise the *energeia* of successfully constituting a house.

Form as actuality

In *Met* Z and the opening chapters of *H*, Aristotle offers a three-fold view of substance, in which the *individual substance* is a compound of form and matter, the matter is a *potential* substance, and the form is the *primary* substance and "the substance of each thing and the cause of its being." Alternatively, form is "substance as actuality" – that is, the actuality of individual sensible substances (H.2 1042b10–11). Correcting Democritus, who saw three *differentiae* by which matter is ordered, Aristotle argues for *many* differentiae, so that *is* too is said in that many ways (b25–6). When we say of a threshold, for example, that it is – that it *is a threshold* – the being in question is to be explained in terms of the differentia or form thanks to which the matter constitutes a thing of the relevant kind. We are to look for the *kinds* under which the various differentiae fall, and to think of these as the *principles* of being (b32–3). In this way, the different notions of being distributed among the different kinds of individual substances are themselves subject to regimentation and, ultimately, explanation, where the explanation will run in terms of the new theory of form as the substance and actuality of sensible substances.

The notion of Form-As-Actuality is combined with the idea that the form is *actually* a so-and-so – in fact, the very so-and-so that the matter is *potentially*. The view of form as an actual so-and-so begins with the idea developed in Z.17 and H.2 that Socrates is an animal *thanks to his form*, so that his form is a cause or principle of being for Socrates. Add to this the so-called Transmission Principle of Causality (otherwise, the idea that "the cause is equal to or greater than its effect"), and we find that the substance-term, "animal," for example, *applies to the actuality or form* – to the substance of a given animal – as well as to the living animal (H.3 1043a29–37). Accordingly, Socrates and his soul are *homonyms* with respect to the term, "animal" – no single formula covers both uses. But, Aristotle adds (a37), this is *core-dependent* homonymy: Socrates is a core-dependent homonym of his soul with respect to the term, "animal." That is, the universal, animal, that applies to Socrates is definitionally dependent on the universal, animal, that applies to his soul.

The claim that Socrates and his soul each count as an animal is not an easy one, but it apparently recurs at Z.10 1036a16–17, 24, and Z.11 1037a5–10, cf. H.3 1043b3–4. The claim that the form of an animal is actually an animal can perhaps be understood in terms of the *content* of the form: it is thanks to its content that the form is the actuality of the compound material animal, and the form "brings" its content to the compound animal. The notion of Form-As-Actuality, and the idea that the form is actually a so-and-so (the very so-and-so that the matter is potentially) is an important component in Aristotle's solution to the problem of the "unity of substance" (below).

The teleological conception of matter

The role of matter as a *potential* substance – as matter *for* a thing of a given kind – underscores the *teleological* component in Aristotle's notion of matter. As before, we think of a stuff or structure as having the property of being matter *in virtue of* its having the relevant powers for being made into a thing of a given kind. The direction of metaphysical priority is important, because it allows the teleology inherent in Aristotle's view of the causal powers of a thing to be passed along to his notion of matter. Aristotle's view of the different passive powers in what counts as matter is the opposite of egalitarian. One of the powers of a given stuff or structure is the power to receive the form, ψ, that typifies a thing of kind k, where a thing of this kind is a desirable goal; but it is only "by way of a privation and a corruption" that, less desirably, it has the capacity to receive the privation of ψ. Wine and vinegar, which have a common matter, illustrate persuasively the different values attaching to the different products in which a given example of matter may find itself (H.5 1044b29–34).

Aristotle expressly tells us (*An* III.5 430a10–11) that matter is potentially a thing of a given kind; similarly, a given passive power is defined in terms of the actuality it is the power for (see, for example, *Cael* IV.3 311a4–6). For simplicity's sake, we may pretend that a given stuff or structure is the matter for a single desirable product; in many cases, however, in particular, where the product is an artifact, there may be more than one desirable product that the matter is for.

The teleological component in Aristotle's concept of matter is on display in his discussion in *Met* Θ.8 of the different ways in which actuality is prior in substance. What temporally comes to be last, he argues, is nonetheless *prior in form and in substance*. As always, "being is prior to becoming": as the matter moves from potentiality to actuality, the potentiality and the actuality alike are determined by the appropriate form – the matter "may go to" the form, and when the process is complete, it will be "in" the form (1050a7–10, 15–16). Otherwise put: from the first, a stuff or structure, *s*, counts as matter, because it has the passive power for being made into a thing of a given kind, *k*, where ψ is the form that typifies a *k*. And if, finally, the matter is "in the form," the passive power in *s* has been realized, and *s* is actually, or actually constitutes, a *k*, thanks to the form, ψ. Thus, the matter is all along "teleologically bound" to the form, and bound to it most fully when its potentiality is realized with the advent of the form.

Form, Matter, and the "Unity of Substance"

As we saw above, Aristotle moves directly from the account of the coming to be and destruction of individual substances to a conclusion about their metaphysical constitution: they are to be analyzed as *compounds* of form and matter. How should this claim be understood? One reading of Aristotle rejects the implications of "compounding" talk, in favor of the "projectivist" view that such language goes proxy for talk of the individual substance itself, under this or that causal description – form and matter are artifacts of our way of looking at individual substances, and not a feature they exhibit "in the real order." Suppose, however, as seems more reasonable, that for Aristotle these are the real parts of a thing and not merely our creations. Then he will owe us an explanation of how these different kinds of entity – the stuffs and structures (all of them concrete objects) that comprise the matter of the thing on the one side, the form (an abstract entity) thanks to which the matter constitutes the thing in question on the other – can together make up a unity.

In addition to Aristotle's positive answer to the unity question, there are two wrong answers he means to discredit. One mistake, discussed in *Met* Z.17, is to think that what is responsible for the unity among the obvious material parts, or elements (*stoicheia*), that make up a thing is yet another element, or is composed of elements; this suggestion invites an infinite regress of elements, so that there can be no single definite answer to questions about the true structure of the thing. Instead, if a thing is to be a unity, it must be not only its material parts, or elements, but "also something else" (1041b16–19). This new factor is both the cause of being for, and also the substance of, the thing (b26–31, cf. b7–9); as before, presumably (b8), it is a form. This role for form allows Aristotle to hold that there is a single definite answer to the question, What is the true structure of the thing, such that its *many* parts make up a *unified* whole? The correct answer involves the obvious material parts or "elements," together with a single unifying form or "principle" (*archê*), *internal* to the thing – a privileged one of its metaphysical constituents, of a different order from the stuffs and structures that are its matter.

The second mistake Aristotle argues against is to think that there is a single definite answer to the question about the true structure of the thing, but that it requires introducing a *special connecting relation* – a *logos henopoios* – the same in all cases, in addition to the obvious material parts and the form. Aristotle's positive view is that the unity of a thing is to be traced to its matter and, especially, its form, and to nothing more than these. So he must be able to say what it is about the matter and, especially, the form *by themselves*, such that the compound material substance that results from them is indeed a unity.

The argument against a special connecting relation appears in a difficult but important passage at H.6 1045b7–17. Assume that the principle of unity for a thing is also its substance and the cause of its being. If, then, a single notion, *sunthesis* (say), is the principle of unity for *two* things – for a bronze triangle and for a white surface – then, absurdly, the same content-less principle is vacuously the substance and cause of being for them both (cf. Z.11 1036b7–20; *Top* VI.14 151a20–6). Aristotle suggests that the mistaken talk of *sunthesis* and comparable notions results from the quest for "a unifying formula, and a difference, between potentiality and complete reality." Thus, *if* there is a "difference" between potentiality and actuality, or between form and matter, as people allege, then some unifying formula – *sunthesis*, *sundesmos*, or something similar – will be needed to connect them. In fact, however no "difference" of the kind alleged exists, and the "unifying formula," and the consequent talk of *sunthesis* and the rest, absurd as they are, are an unneeded solution to a nonexistent problem.

What "difference" have people wrongly seen between the matter and the form, and how are they mistaken? On some readings, Aristotle's solution to the unity of matter and form is that, in fact, these are one entity, not two; so the difference mistakenly found between them must be numerical difference. The proposed correction, that a thing's matter and form are identical, pitches us directly into the projectivist reading of Aristotle criticized above. Alternatively and, I think, preferably, Aristotle's solution in H.6 argues that a thing's matter and form are *alike* in a way that people had not expected, so that the difference they wrongly see must be *qualitative* difference. The view that a difference exists between the matter and the form takes these to be distinct items, with no relevant similarity between them. The view is corrected, not by supposing that the matter and the form are identical; rather, they are two, but they after all exhibit some relevant similarity. As we shall see, the matter and the form of a thing are alike in the way that in general the potential and the actual are alike. In particular, as Aristotle points out more than once in H.6, if I am about to make a bronze sphere, its matter is already potentially a sphere, and the form is actually the very same thing – it is a sphere.

But then, Aristotle asks, once the sphere is made, what is the cause thanks to which the potential sphere is actually (a) sphere? His first move is to set aside any efficient-causal story in telling how it is that a potential so-and-so actually constitutes a so-and-so. Once efficient causes are bracketed, however, what is left? He continues: "For nothing else is the cause of the potential sphere's actually being (a) sphere, but this was all along the essence of each of the two" (a31–3). One of the many uncertainties here is Aristotle's "nothing else." On one reading, he means there is no cause other than the agent, already dismissed in the previous sentence: on this showing, the count of causes stands at zero, and there is no cause: conspicuous among the sceptics are the projectivists, mentioned above. But the second part of his remark, "but this was all along the essence of each," suggests that there is a cause of unity after all. An intriguing possibility is that by "nothing else" Aristotle means that there is no cause *over and above the actual and the potential spheres themselves* – nothing over and above the form and the matter – that might explain why they are one. Once the efficient cause has been set to one side, only the actual and potential spheres – the form and the matter – remain as the cause of unity. In this way, no outside factor explains why the matter and the form make up a unity. It is consistent with this, of course, that there is a cause of their unity, but this must be something intrinsic to the matter and the form themselves.

What features are they of the form and the matter by themselves that allow the two together to make up a unity? Aristotle's account is at first sight conspicuously Fregean. On a Fregean account, a function is "unsaturated," as opposed to an object, which is "saturated," and the two together make up a "complete whole." Aristotle's distinction between element and principle in Z.17, for example, can seem a direct, if more prosaic, counterpart of Frege's contrast between saturated and unsaturated. The discussion in H.6 directly contradicts these expectations. Frege's distinction has to do with "formal" features of the items to be unified: it has no interest in the *content* of the items to be joined together. For Aristotle, by contrast, the question of how the matter and the form "fit together" in the thing has everything to do with their content. Does the compound of the two have a single, unified nature? How is it not subject to competing classifications – both bronze and equally (a) sphere (say) – thanks to the different natures of its constituent matter and form? Accordingly, his view of the problem of unity is distinctly unFregean. As Aristotle emphasizes, matter and form must be *suited* for each other – they must be similar in content – but in such a way that the matter is appropriately *subordinate* to the form. In this way, any story for how form and matter are united in a given compound material substance is not based on some purely formal feature of each, which holds across the board, for all choices of form and matter regardless of content. Aristotle's approach instead will be piecemeal, letting the content do the work in each case.

Thus, for Aristotle, the matter and the form each *has an essence* in a way that helps solve the unity problem ("this all along was the essence of the two," H.6 1045a33). It is essential to the matter and the form alike that it is (say) (a) sphere, each in its own distinctive way: "the one is matter, and the other form, and the one <is> potentially, and the other <is> actually" (a23–4) – that is, in terms of the sphere example, the matter is potentially (a) *sphere* and the form is actually (a) *sphere*. (This last is Aristotle's Form-as-Actuality assumption – see above.) Again, "the proximate matter and the form are the same and one, the one potentially, and the other actually . . . each thing is one thing of a certain kind, and the potential and the actual are in a way one" (b17–19, 20–1). Aristotle is not saying that the matter is the same and one as, much less identical with, the form. Rather, there is one and the same thing, in fact, one and the same kind, k, such that the matter is potentially (a) k, and the form is actually (a) k.

Aristotle is clear that for the compound sphere to exist, it must be the case that the matter is not only potentially but also *actually* a sphere: the form is actually (a) so-and-so (as before), *and the matter too is actually (a) so-and-so* (a30, 32–3, b22), where each is actually the same so-and-so, viz. (a) sphere. Once these stronger conditions are satisfied, a compound sphere exists.

But the terms on which the compound material sphere *exists* also guarantee that it is a *unity*. One component in securing unity is the similarity between matter and form, just noted; a second is his teleological conception of matter (above), which we can interpret in terms of degrees of *teleological dominance* and *dependence*. Accordingly,

1   The matter, m, is *potentially* (a) sphere, *because* (i) m is teleologically dependent on the form ψ and (ii) ψ is *actually* (a) sphere.

What, next, when – going beyond being a potential sphere – the matter actually is (constitutes) a sphere? The needed scheme involves a *deepening* of teleological dependence, but is otherwise the same as before:

2   The matter, m, "actually is" (a30, 32–3, b22) (a) sphere, *because* (i) m is fully teleologically dependent on the form ψ and (ii) ψ is actually (a) sphere.

The relation of full dependence here is just an intensification of (lesser) dependence in 1; the analysans in 2 and that in 1 diverge only in that dependence and dominance come in different degrees. As predicted, 2 brings to light a strong *similarity* between the matter and the form; they differ, however, in that the matter actually is (a) sphere thanks to some *other* entity, namely the form, while the form *in itself* is actually (a) sphere.

In summary: Aristotle interprets the question about the unity of matter and form as a question about their *content*. The matter and the form are distinct constituents in the finished substance; but the compound is not a "heap" of the two but a member of a single unitary kind, thanks to their similarity, and to the progressive domination of the matter by the form.

Prime Matter

The traditional view

Aristotle appears committed to the concept of prime matter traditionally ascribed to him above all in the early chapters of *GC* II (see especially II.1 329a24–b6, 7 334a16–18, 24–5). Foremost among the components of the traditional view of prime matter is persistence. If, in general, the coming to be and destruction of things is analysed in terms of a substratum that persists through the exchange of contraries (one of the first principles of natural philosophy established in *Phys* I, above), the same analysis should apply at the lowest level of the sublunary universe, in our account of the mutual transformation of the elements, in which one element is destroyed and a second comes to be. What persists through changes of this last kind, on the received view, is prime matter.

If prime matter persists, however, it does so without in any ordinary sense a qualitative nature of its own. According to Aristotle, prime matter is something that is "matter for the perceptible bodies," but is itself only "perceptible body in potentiality" (*GC* II.1 329a24–5, 33). More generally, it is not anything in itself, and a fortiori, it does not fall under any of the categories (*Met* Z.3 1029a20–3, 24–6). But like matter in general, it has the capacity for being and for not being (*GC* II.9 335a32–b6; *Met* Z.15 1039b27–31) – in particular, it is receptive of the elemental contraries, hot, cold, wet, dry, as the so-called elements, earth, air, fire, water (see above), come to be and are destroyed in the course of their mutual transformation. The various elemental contraries are occurrent properties of prime matter, and are all *accidental* to it. Meanwhile, its essential properties include the corresponding dispositional properties: it essentially has the capacity to receive this or that elemental contrary.

At the same time, prime matter by definition itself *has no matter* – as *prime* matter, it is not itself a compound of form and matter – so it cannot be subject to generation or destruction. Hence, the traditional account of prime matter, championed in Zeller (1897), as the eternal substratum for all change: prime matter is "that which is nothing, but can become everything – the Subject, namely, or substratum, to which no one of all the thinkable predicates belongs, but which precisely on that account is equally receptive of them all."

One correction to Zeller's formulation is by now standard: Aristotle's concept of prime matter does not commit him to a "featureless bearer of properties," but to something which is a bearer of properties but (with certain exceptions) has no *occurrent* features *of its own*. The idea that prime matter is the substratum of *all* change, is also open to question and, arguably, the controversial result of a polemical argument in *Met* Z.3 (below). I will ignore this broader claim about prime matter, in favor of the following more restrictive view about its role as the substratum of elemental change. For clarity, take a case of the transformation of a given amount, E, of earth into an amount, F, of fire. Suppose that E is a compound of matter, m_1, and a form, cd, composed of the two contraries, cold and dry: where "+" is the sign for the application of form to matter,

$$E = m_1 + (cd)$$

The resulting amount of fire, F, is a compound of matter, m_2, and the contraries, hot and dry, hd:

$$F = m_2 + (hd)$$

The transformation of E into F results from the "flipping" of the contrary, c, as it is replaced by its contrary, h. The remaining contrary, d, meanwhile, "jumps," and is present in both E and F. On the traditional view of the persistence of prime matter, finally, we are to suppose that $m_1 = m_2$. If all cases of transformation among the elements follow a similar pattern, we can generalize from this single example: in every case where one element (or pair of elements, *GC* II.4 331b12–26) transforms into some new element, the matter of the beginning element (or the matters of the beginning pair of elements) is (are) *identical* with the matter of the element that results.

Prime matter is not, then, the subject of *all* change, as Zeller claimed. It is properly subject only for the different elemental contraries (and only indirectly for the higher-level forms in the constitution of a thing, above the elemental contraries; and not at all for its accidents, see below). But if we can imagine a given portion of one element transforming into a portion of another, and from here on and then back through the cycle of transformations, in isolation from the various changes going on around it, *one and the same* amount of prime matter will underlie all the transformations in the history of the elemental portion we began with.

On the traditional view, some portion of prime matter persists through each elemental transformation. A minority view, by contrast, denies that the concept of a persisting prime matter is genuinely Aristotle's. Banishing prime matter from Aristotle's account replaces the traditional view, that $E = m_1 + (cd)$, with the claim that, instead, $E = (cd)$. On this view, Aristotle's theory is no longer a version of Bare Substrate Theory, but of Bundle Theory, where various properties are compresent without the benefit of an accompanying substrate. The merits of this rival view, and of the traditional account it means to replace, are a topic of ongoing debate (Bostock 2006: ch. 4; Charles 2004; Lewis 2008).

Entrapment and the Homonymy of the Body and Its Organs

The origins of the account of change and of the attendant analysis of individual substances in terms of a persisting subject and a form (above) lie largely, even exclusively, in dialectic. The various dialectical procedures at work in *Phys* I all take place well in advance of much if anything in the way of empirical inquiry. Do the results of *Phys* I (and their continuation in *Phys* II) hopelessly compromise the results of future empirical inquiry?

Consider, for example, Aristotle's technical notion of a mixture – the uniform stuff that is the result of mixing (see above). If a stuff is truly uniform, then the four elements that are its initial matter will not be evident in the stuff itself. Flesh, for example, is a uniform part, hence, flesh "all the way down" (and "all the way through") – however closely we look, in principle, there is only flesh there to be discerned. So must Aristotle give up the idea that the initial matter is also a constituent in the product? And is persistence on the part of the matter now a dead letter?

Comparable questions arise over the intersection of Aristotle's notion of matter and his notion of homonymy. A thing is *homonymously* a so-and-so, according to Aristotle, when it is not able to behave in the way typical of members of its purported kind. The hand of a statue (one of Aristotle's stock examples, *PA* I.1 640b34–64Ia5) is a hand "in name only," not because it has the wrong matter, but because it *cannot perform the function of a hand*. Likewise for the severed hand, or the hand of a corpse, which once had the ability to perform as hands should but have now lost that ability.

We have seen that matter essentially has the potentiality *for* some standard product, best of all, for a natural substance (see above). Homonymy, by contrast, typically has to do with a falling away from the standard product, resulting in the *lapsed* state of a substance or its parts. These two sides of the story – the passive power in the matter for the product, or the homonymous product which has fallen away from its proper state – both contribute to the strongly teleological cast of Aristotle's philosophy of nature.

If we apply the notion of homonymy just described to the stuff or structure that is a thing's concurrent matter, the tie between matter and thing will seem even closer than anything suggested so far. For example, imagine an animal whose constitutive form is the capacity for perception of a given particular sort – it is (a variety of) sensitive soul. The *de Anima* commits Aristotle to the view that the matter of sensitive soul is a body with the appropriately functioning sense-organs. On this view, the sense-organs that help constitute the matter of the animal must themselves, in their own right, have the capacities typical of sensitive soul, on pain of homonymy. If so, sensitive soul is *essential* to the sense-organs, and the matter of the animal cannot exist independently of the animal itself. And in general, perhaps, matter is not only essentially matter *for* a given product, but also it cannot exist independently of it.

The idea that in certain cases a form is essential to the matter on which it supervenes, lies behind a number of puzzling, if not outright sceptical, conclusions. Above all, the renewed challenge to persistence is obvious. If the matter of a thing cannot exist outside it, there seems no hope that the matter can exist before or after the thing does.

The Appeal to Homonymy also breathes new life into old worries about compounds and about the distinction between a thing and its matter. One difficulty asks how a compound or whole can be constructed out of parts that depend for their existence or nature on that very compound. A second difficulty threatens the very distinction between a form-matter compound and its matter. Aristotle's views on homonymy suggest that the living body that is Archimedes' matter requires the relevant form or soul to be truly living. At the same time, Archimedes himself requires that same form. But it appears that there is no material difference between Archimedes and Archimedes's matter. Accordingly, if Archimedes is a compound of form and matter – if there is nothing more to Archimedes than these two constituents – and if Archimedes and his matter have the same form and the same matter, then it seems to follow that Archimedes is identical with Archimedes's living body. What Aristotle thinks of as a compound of two items, a matter and a form, is identical with the matter that is only one of its two constituents. So are the projectivists above right after all?

Finally, if the proximate matter of an animal exists, only by virtue of actually constituting an animal of the appropriate kind, then the relation between matter and form here is not accidental. This again conflicts with the assumptions about persistence already noted. It is also in conflict with the "independence" assumption at work, for example, in *Met* Z.3, where the form that belongs to a given matter can be "stripped away" from it in thought, on the assumption (presumably) that the subject is *independent* of what is (metaphysically) predicated of it.

Persistence

It is an open question how deep these various difficulties cut. With respect to persistence, for example: in the case of a living thing, is there a lower level of matter where we find stuffs that are *not* essentially alive – that lie beyond the reach of the form or soul of the animal altogether – but which are still parts of the animal's concurrent (non-proximate) matter? Can there be a level at which one and the same matter can first be made to constitute the animal – is its "before" matter – and later be its concurrent matter?

On some accounts, blood has good credentials for being both the concurrent and the "before" matter of the animal: blood plays a part in the generation of an animal, and also in nourishing the animal once it is formed (*PA* III.5 668a27–8; *GA* II.4 740b34–7). Alternatively, it has been suggested that alongside the living bodies, functioning organs and all, which are essentially alive, there exist "non-organic" bodies that have the capacities of the living animal contingently, and hence can exist outside the living animal. Or, again, perhaps the difficulties of homonymy apply only to natural objects, while artifacts are immune. None of these suggestions, however, at best is more than a partial solution. Even if there are levels or varieties of matter beyond the reach of the form or soul of the whole living animal, this does nothing to solve our difficulties at the level of the uniform and nonuniform parts, which remain resolutely in the grip of the form of the whole animal.

If literal persistence by a thing's matter is not available, it may help to see the problem of persistence as that of *tracking* the stuffs and structures that comprise a living thing's matter, from before the creature comes into existence, through its lifetime, to after its death. A succession of stuffs and structures come into being at different stages in the formation of the animal, and each new stage comes with its own, new passive power for being made into a product at the next level – blood into flesh or sinew or bone (say); and flesh, sinew and bone together into a hand – under the influence of the form derived from the male parent. But once the creature is fully finished, with its own independent existence, the matter at every level is fully dominated by the form, which remains an external principle to the matter, but is now an internal principle to the living creature itself.

At death, finally, we subtract the form altogether – it is neither an internal nor an external principle to what remains. What remains is a body in name only – a degenerate version of what was formerly a living body (a body in the proper sense of the word). Not only is the active power in the form no longer in force; the passive power for being made to constitute a creature of the kind in question is also lost, as the different constituent stuffs and structures with their separate powers disintegrate or are dispersed.

Despite the transformations in the initial matter as the living animal is formed, there is a coherent route that can be traced through the progressive realization of powers in the matter and in the efficient cause. Perhaps there is here a notion, if not of the literal persistence by some single identifiable stuff or structure, at least of coherent development sufficient to preserve the outlines of the account in *Phys.* I (see above).

There remains the problem how matter persists in Aristotle's account of mixture above, where what counts as matter exists only potentially in the product but, Aristotle says, can (in some sense) be recovered from it. The account of persistence here is again difficult, but clearly it will have to give up the view of matter in this case as simply one or more of the spatially-determined parts in the finished mixture.

Compounds and their matter

In the case of the developing animal, its form is at first *external* to it, and becomes internalized only later in its development. But the various parts that make up the matter of the animal may never acquire an internal principle. In the case of blood, for example, heat is essential to the blood, and part of its definition; but the heat never becomes an internal principle (*PA* II.3 649b25–8). So heat is part of the form of blood, if anything is; but at the same time, it is not an internal principle or nature, even though the form of a thing and its nature strictly so-called are one and the same (*Met* Δ.4 1014b35–1015a11), and even though without an internal principle, blood is more like an artifact than a natural object (*Phys* II.1, above).

To be blood in the full sense, blood must have heat from the appropriate source. But heat is not part of the form of blood. Rather, it is the form-*analog* in blood (cf. *Met* H.2 1043a7): blood cannot lose its heat and still be properly blood; but since the heat is only a form-analog and not a form proper, it is not necessary that it be an internal principle.

Suppose, now, that similar results hold for the run of uniform and non-uniform parts of an animal. Life to the hand or eye, for example, is like heat to blood: in its natural, proper context, the hand or eye is alive, as blood is hot – but like the heat of the blood, the hand's life or the eye's is externally driven, in a way that is determined by the form of the whole animal. The form or soul of the animal is a principle internal to the living animal, governing its typical behavior; the same form or soul also governs the behavior of the animal's hand or eye, but it is an *external* principle relative to them. The living hand or eye of the animal, then, is not properly a substance, and has the form or soul of the animal as its constitutive form-*analog*.

We may now move up a level, and ask about the matter and form of the whole living animal. The animal itself exists, only because the form is present to the body. At the same time, we have supposed, the form of the animal is essential also to the body and its sense-organs. But if the body by itself has all the form the animal could ever need, doesn't this tend to show that the animal is identical with its living body, true to the "projectivist" conclusion, that thing and proximate matter are identical?

Although the animal's form is essential both to the animal and to its living body, it is essential to them in different ways. The relation of soul to Archimedes's body and its living organs (say) is the same as that of heat to blood: it is essential to them, but it is their constitutive form-*analog*, and an *external* principle of their behavior. But the form or soul can be external to his body, only because it is internal to Archimedes himself. Archimedes is a compound of form and matter, and the form is an *internal* principle of behavior relative to the compound, and it is his *constitutive form simpliciter*. And if Archimedes and his living body are related differently to the form in this way, the argument that they are identical collapses.

But if the distinction between a thing and its matter remains secure, what of the complaint that the very conception of a thing as a compound of form and matter is threatened by the dependence of the matter on the finished thing? Are Aristotle's critics right, that a whole cannot be constructed out of parts that are not independent of the whole, in the way that the matter of a thing apparently depends on the whole for its existence? Arguably, these complaints presuppose an unduly restrictive notion of whole and part – a notion (I suspect) according to which a whole is *nothing but* a construct out of its parts. Aristotle's account of the unity of substance is directly opposed to a reductive picture of wholes and parts of this kind. As we have seen (above), for Aristotle, the unity of substance requires that one part or parts of a thing – the stuffs and structures that count as its proximate matter – be dependent on another, privileged part – the form – even before the finished whole yet exists; and that those parts be more fully dependent on the privileged part, and not able to exist outside the whole, once the whole has come into existence. With this different conception of wholes and their parts, complaints that the parts, matter included, need to be there "in advance," ready to be pressed into service as ingredients of the future compound – and that they should exist unchanged as parts of the finished whole – evaporate.

(Metaphysical) predication

Finally, Aristotle speaks of a form's being (*metaphysically*) *predicated* of a given matter, apparently in much the way that its accidents are (metaphysically) predicated of the thing – but is the relation of (metaphysical) predication between a given form and a given matter *accidental?* Such a view does not sit well with Aristotle's teleologically driven conception of the stuffs and structures that are the matter for a living thing, or with the diagnosis of homonymy that threatens when the teleology fails. It also goes badly with his account of the unity of substance, where (on the more developed view of parts and wholes at work there) again the matter is not independent of the form and, hence, not independent of the finished whole. The contrary assumption, however, is alive and well in *Met* Z.3, for example, where Aristotle assumes that, in general, a subject is *independent* of what is (metaphysically) predicated of it, so that even the relation between a thing's form and its proximate matter is accidental. Such a view is also encouraged, perhaps, by Aristotle's frequent use of artifact examples, where the tie between matter and form may not seem so close. The artifact examples may be a case of oversimplification for the sake of exposition; the account in *Met* Z3, meanwhile, is likely driven by what I take to be the polemical needs of the moment. But the tension between the different views of the relation between form and matter, here and elsewhere, is a reality of Aristotle's text, and the subject of ongoing controversy.

Note

The angled brackets at quotations enclose additions by the translator to supply material needed in English but not expressly given in the Greek. Square brackets enclose the author's comments on the material being translated.

Bibliography

Ackrill, J. L. (1963). *Aristotle "Categories" and "De Interpretatione"* (Oxford: Clarendon Press).
Bogen, James (1992). "Change and Contrariety in Aristotle," *Phronesis*, 37, pp. 1–21.

Bolton, Robert (1991). "Aristotle's Method in Natural Science: *Physics I*," in Judson (1991).

Bostock, David (2006). *Space, Time, Matter, and Form* (Oxford: Clarendon Press).

Burnyeat, Myles (2001). *A Map of "Metaphysics" Zeta* (Pittsburgh, PA: Mathesis Publications).

Charles, David (2004). "Simple Genesis and Prime Matter," in de Haas and Mansfeld (eds.) (2004).

Charlton, W. (1970). *Aristotle "Physics" Books I and II* (Oxford: Clarendon Press).

Code, Alan (1976). "The Persistence of Aristotelian Matter," *Philosophical Studies*, 29, pp. 357–67.

Fine, Kit (1992). "Aristotle on Matter," *Mind*, new series, 101 (401), pp. 35–57.

Fine, Kit (1994). "A Puzzle Concerning Form and Matter," in Scaltsas et al. (eds.) (1994).

Fine, Kit [1995] (1996). "The Problem of Mixture," in Lewis and Bolton (eds.) (1996).

Fine, Kit (1998). "Mixing Matters," *Ratio*, 11 (3), pp. 278–88.

Furth, Montgomery (1988). *Substance, Form and Psyche: An Aristotelian Metaphysics* (Cambridge: Cambridge University Press).

de Haas, Francis and Jaap Mansfeld (eds.) (2004). *Aristotle: "On Generation and Corruption,"* Book II, *Symposium Aristotelicum* (Oxford: Clarendon Press), pp. 151–69.

Joachim, H. H. (1922). *Aristotle: "On Coming-To-Be and Passing-Away"* (Oxford: Clarendon Press).

Judson, Lindsay (ed.) (1991). *Aristotle's "Physics": A Collection of Essays* (Oxford: Clarendon Press).

Lewis, Frank A. (1982). "Accidental Sameness in Aristotle," *Philosophical Studies*, 42, pp. 1–36.

Lewis, Frank A. (1991). *Substance and Predication in Aristotle* (Cambridge: Cambridge University Press).

Lewis, Frank A. (2008). "What's the Matter with Prime Matter?" *Oxford Studies in Ancient Philosophy*, 31, pp. 123–46.

Lewis, Frank A. and Bolton, Robert (eds.) (1996), *Form, Matter, and Mixture in Aristotle* (Oxford: Blackwell).

Loux, Michael J. (1991). *Primary Ousia: An Essay on Aristotle's "Metaphysics" Zeta and Eta*, (Ithaca: Cornell University Press).

Loux, Michael J. (2005). "Aristotle on Matter, Form, and Ontological Strategy," *Ancient Philosophy*, 25 (1), pp. 81–123.

Makin, Stephen (2006). *Aristotle "Metaphysics" Book Θ* (Oxford: Clarendon Press).

Matthews, Gareth B. (1982). "Accidental Unities," in Martha Nussbaum and Malcolm Schofield, (eds.), *Language and Logos: Studies in Greek Philosophy Presented to G. E. L. Owen*, (Cambridge: Cambridge University Press), pp. 223–40.

Robinson, H. M. (1974). "Prime Matter in Aristotle," *Phronesis*, 19, pp. 168–98.

Ross, W. D. (1936). *Aristotle "Physics"* (Oxford: Clarendon Press).

Ryan, Eugene E. (1973). "Pure Form in Aristotle," *Phronesis*,18, pp. 209–24.

Scaltsas,T, Charles, D., and Gill, M. L. (1994). *Unity, Identity, and Explanation in Aristotle's "Metaphysics"* (Oxford: Clarendon Press).

Shields, Christopher (1999). *Order in Multiplicity: Homonymy in the Philosophy of Aristotle*, (Oxford: Clarendon Press).

Wedin, Michael (2000). *Aristotle's Theory of Substance: The "Categories" and "Metaphysics" Zeta*, (Oxford: Oxford University Press).

Williams, C. J. F. (1982). *Aristotle's "De Generatione et Corruptione"* (Oxford: Clarendon Press).

Zeller, E. (1897). *Aristotle and the Earlier Peripatetics*, 2 vols. (London: Longmans, Green, and Co.).

11

Aristotle on Universals

MICHAEL J. LOUX

I

In the *De Interpretatione* Aristotle defines the universal as "that which by its nature is predicated of a number of things" (17a38), and he goes on to contrast the concept of a universal with that of a particular; but in neither that work nor any other does he present us with a general statement of his views about this fundamental ontological dichotomy. Those views get presented piecemeal in a variety of texts. Much of what he has to say about universals is found in texts where he is attacking the Platonic Ideas, so his criticism of Plato makes for a natural starting point for any discussion of his views on universals. Perhaps his most sustained discussion of the Platonic Ideas is in an early treatise, *Peri Ideon* (*On Ideas*). Although little of the text survives in its original form, the first-century commentator, Alexander of Aphrodisias, provides a good sense of its contents in his commentary on the *Metaphysics*. In *Metaphysics* A.9, where he also discusses the Ideas, Aristotle mentions a number of arguments for the existence of Platonic Ideas and provides a cursory critique of those arguments ((990b11–17); virtually the same text is found in *Metaphysics* M.4 (1079a5–14)). The text in question makes up barely eight Bekker lines. Alexander, however, provides an extended discussion of the material presented there (for Alexander's commentary on this piece of text, see (Fine 1993)). He tells us that the points Aristotle summarily makes in A.9 are expanded and developed in Book I of *Peri Ideon*, and he goes on to lay out the main contours of that early discussion of Plato.

In the text from A.9, Aristotle mentions by name three lines of argument for the Ideas (the "arguments from the sciences," the "one over many" argument, and the "object of thought" argument) and contrasts them with what he calls the "more accurate" arguments. In Alexander's account, *Peri Ideon* construes Ideas as eternal, separately existing models or paradigms for the particulars making up the sensible world; and what the early text argues is that the three named arguments fail on two scores: first, none succeeds in identifying a theoretical role that only Ideas as so understood could play and, second, even if successful, none of those arguments would serve the purposes of the Platonist since they would establish the existence of Ideas even in cases where Platonists deny there are any. By contrast, *Peri Ideon* tells us that if sound, the "more accurate" arguments would succeed in giving us the existence of eternal, separately existing paradigms; but the early treatise contends that since they have necessarily false consequences, those arguments must likewise be rejected.

Alexander mentions three different arguments from the sciences. They all agree, first, in arguing that each of the various sciences has as its subject some entity distinct from the various particulars that come under its purview and, second, in identifying that entity with an Idea. According to Alexander, Aristotle argues that if any of these arguments succeeds in showing the need for entities over and above particulars, they do not succeed in establishing the existence of Ideas since we do not need separately existing paradigms to constitute the subject matter of the sciences. What Aristotle calls *ta koina* (the common things) would do as well. We are not told much about *ta koina*. Obviously, they are somehow common to all the particulars falling under a science; and, presumably, they do not exist separately or apart from those particulars. But according to Alexander, Aristotle goes on to say that even if there were an argument here that successfully established the existence of Ideas, the argument would not be acceptable to the Platonist; for that argument would apply to the case of the arts no less than to the sciences. Platonists, however, deny that there are Ideas corresponding to artificial objects. As they see it, there are Ideas only for natural objects.

The "one over many" argument tells us that (1) where, for some *F* (e.g., man), certain particulars agree in being *F*, there is some one entity, distinct from those particulars, that is predicated of each of them and (2) that object is an eternal and separately existing paradigm for those particulars. According to Alexander, Aristotle's reply to this argument parallels his response to the arguments from the sciences. He argues that if sound, this line of argument would not give us the Platonic Ideas. *Ta koina* would serve as well in the explanation of attribute agreement. But, Aristotle claims, the argument is not sound or, at least, no Platonist should think it is. The arguments works not only for notions like *man* and *animal*, but for negations like *nonman* and *nonanimal* as well, and no Platonist is willing to posit Ideas to correspond to negations.

The "object of thought" argument tells us that when we think of things like *horse*, we are thinking of some one determinate entity and not the various particular horses: the particulars can cease to exist while our thought and its content persist. What we are thinking about has to be the eternal and separately existing paradigm for the particulars. According to Alexander, Aristotle once again contends that if sound, this argument would yield Ideas where Platonists deny we have any. They restrict Ideas to the case of general contents; but we can go on thinking about a particular like Socrates even after he has ceased to exist. If we needed an Idea to accommodate our thought about *horse*, presumably we should need one to accommodate our thought about Socrates as well. But, Aristotle claims, even if the Platonist could find a way to limit the argument to the case of general contents, the fact would remain that we do not need Ideas to serve as the objects of abstract thinking. Aristotle's *koina* would do as well.

Alexander associates two distinct lines of argument with Aristotle's "more accurate" arguments. The first tells us that where a term (like "man") that signifies a determinate nature applies nonhomonymously or in a single sense to all the items in a group, then either (1) all those items have the signified nature fully and completely or (2) they are all likenesses of something that has the nature fully and completely or (3) they include both the model that has the nature fully and completely and things that are likenesses of the model. Alexander tells us that where "man" is predicated of things like Socrates and Plato, we have a case of (1), that where it applies to the figures in portraits of human beings, we have a case of (2), and that were we to lump together Socrates and his likenesses in portraits and call them all men, we would have a case of (3). The argument then focuses on the predication of terms that apply nonhomonymously, but, as we might put it, only defectively to sensible particulars. "Equal" is the example we are given. While it applies in a single sense to sensible particulars, no one of them has the nature of equality wholly and completely, so the predication is not a case falling under (1). But since no particular is perfectly equal to any other, the predication is not a case falling under (3) either. The only remaining possibility is that the application of the term "equal" to sensible particulars is a case falling under (2). Sensible particulars are called equal because they are likenesses of something that is wholly equal. So we have something that is a model or paradigm which sensible particulars copy or imitate, and it exists separately from all sensible particulars, so, for the case of "equal" at least, we have a Platonic Idea, and, presumably, the same line of argument works for any other predicate that applies nonhomonymously, but defectively to sensible particulars.

If we accept Alexander's explanation of the label "more accurate argument," we can see why this argument deserves that label. Unlike the first three lines of argument, this argument would, if sound, actually establish the existence of Ideas understood as separately existing paradigms; or at least it would do so for cases where we have what I have called nonhomonymously, but defectively applicable predicates. According to Alexander, Aristotle's difficulty with the argument is that among those cases we have predicates that apply only relatively. Indeed, "equal" is cited as just such a case. Nothing is equal simpliciter; a thing is equal only in relation to something else. Aristotle points out, however, that Ideas are supposed to be substances, things that subsist in their own right; but no relative has independent or subsistent being. Relatives are, as Alexander puts it, mere appendages to subsistent being. So what is wrong with the first of the "more accurate" arguments is that it entails the substantiality of things whose being is nothing more than relative.

The difficulty with the second "more accurate" argument is that it lands us in the infinite regress Aristotle regularly calls the "Third Man." As Alexander lays it out, it is difficult to distinguish this argument from the earlier "one over many" argument. One possibility (presented in (Fine 1993)) is that while the earlier argument is restricted to the case where we have a plurality made up exclusively of sensible particulars, this "more accurate" argument tells us that where, for some F, a plurality of objects, $a \ldots n$ (whether sensible particulars or *not*) all agree in being F, there is some entity, x, such that x is distinct from each of $a \ldots n$, x is itself fully and completely F, and each of $a \ldots n$ participates in x. If Alexander means to point us to an argument incorporating this premise, then we have an argument that would, if sound, establish the existence of separately existing paradigms and would as Aristotle claims, land us in the "Third Man." Consider the plurality made up of all the human beings in the sensible world. By our premise, there is some one entity they all share or participate in; that entity is distinct from each of them; and it is itself paradigmatically human. But, then, we have a new plurality of human beings – one made up of our original plurality plus the paradigmatic human being. That plurality will require a new paradigmatic human, which will, in turn, generate yet another plurality requiring a still further paradigm, and so on *ad infinitum*.

So one argument for the Ideas leads to the "Third Man." In texts later than the *Peri Ideon*, we meet with the more general claim that central theses of the theory of Ideas itself land their proponents in the sort of regress just outlined. According to Aristotle, the chief culprit here is the Platonist's treatment of Ideas as "thises." The claim is that the Platonist construes universals – things predicated of several individuals, things that are "suches" – as further individuals (*SE* 22 178b3–179a10; *Met* Z.13 1038b35–1039a3). Presumably, what makes this construction compulsory is the Platonist's contention that Ideas are paradigms or models for the particulars of which they are predicated. The paradigm for *F*-objects must itself be an *F*-object. Thus, the paradigm for human beings must have all the properties essential to human beings; it must be a further human being (*Met* B.2 997b5–12). But since no human being can be a paradigm for itself, we need a further paradigm to explain how our original paradigm manages to have its character; and we have our third man. (For a different reading, see Fine 1993: 60ff)

Ultimately, then, it is the paradigmatism at work in the theory of Ideas that leads to the regress. But Aristotle thinks there are other features of the theory of Ideas that have problematic consequences. He regularly rails against the separation of the Ideas, the Platonist's claim that Ideas inhabit not the changeable world of sense, but some immutable realm accessible only to intellect. What Aristotle argues is that in separating the Ideas, the Platonist leaves us without any plausible account of our knowledge of universals and makes it a mystery that universals should play a role in determining the character and structure of familiar sensible particulars (*Met* A.9 991a9–19 and M.5 1079b12–23). As Aristotle sees it, the Platonists are forced to resort to poetic metaphor and supernatural myth in their explanation of these facts (A.9 991a22–3 and M.6 1080a25–7), and the best we get are the sorts of pictures at work in the doctrine of the demiurge or the theory of recollection.

II

Of course, if metaphor is the best we can do here, then it remains unclear that the Ideas can play the roles assigned them by the various arguments in *Peri Ideon* – to provide the sciences with their subject matters, to explain the fact that familiar particulars have the attributes they do, and to provide intellectual or noetic acts with objects. But Aristotle is anxious to make good on the *Peri Ideon* claim that a theory of universals that replaces Ideas with what he there calls *ta koina* has the resources for accommodating the phenomena Platonists claim require the postulation of Ideas. As we have noted, *Peri Ideon* tells us little about *ta koina* other than that they are things predicated of several different objects and that they do not exist apart from the things of which they are predicated. *Ta koina*, of course, satisfy the *De Interpretatione* definition of the universal, and although some commentators have thought otherwise, there is good reason to believe that Aristotle construes his universals as nonlinguistic, extramental objects and that he understands predication in nonlinguistic terms as roughly our notion of instantiation (see, for example, *Cat* 2 1a20; *An. Post* I.24 85b16–22).

So *ta koina* are multiply instantiated entities, and they do not exist in separation from the things of which they are predicated; they are instead immanent in their subjects.

But just what does this come to? Aristotle never provides a single rigorous account of the separate/immanent contrast. Nonetheless, there can be little doubt that when he tells us that universals are immanent in the sensible objects of which they are predicated, Aristotle means to be rejecting the sort of two worlds account of Plato's middle dialogues where universals exist in an intelligible realm immune from all change. But the two worlds of the middle dialogues constitute a picture. The literal core of the picture is the idea that the existence of universals is independent of the mutable objects accessible to perception; and that idea entails that it is possible for at least some universals – those that can be instantiated exclusively by contingently existing sensible objects – to exist without any instances. Aristotle, by contrast rejects the possibility of uninstantiated universals. It is clear from the *Categories* and elsewhere that he takes it to be a necessary truth that every universal is predicated of some object or other (*Cat* 10 13b7–10; *Met* Λ.3 1070a23–4); and as Aristotle understands it, the upshot of this claim is that the existence of universals generally presupposes the existence of sensible particulars to serve as the ultimate subjects of predication. So we have a distinction between two accounts of the ontological status of universals. One is a theory where the existence of universals is independent of the existence of sensible particulars; in this theory, there are uninstantiated universals. The other rejects the idea of universals with no instances and insists that all universals are anchored in the world of sense. A natural way to express the contrast between the two theories is to say that in the one universals exist separately or apart from sensible particulars and that in the other they are immanent in sensibles.

For Aristotle, then, universals are common or shared entities: they are such as to be predicated of several different subjects, and they are immanent in their subjects in the sense that necessarily every universal has instances. What Aristotle wants to say is that a theory that construes universals in these terms has the resources for accommodating the phenomena discussed in *Peri Ideon*. Immanent universals can provide us with the subject matter for the various sciences; they can furnish us with objects for genuinely intellectual or noetic acts; and they provide the materials for explaining how familiar particulars have the properties and characteristics they do.

In the *Posterior Analytics* we find Aristotle repeatedly echoing the *Peri Ideon* line about science. A science is an interconnected network of demonstrations or explanatory syllogisms, and Aristotle denies that demonstration requires separated Ideas. What the sciences seek to elucidate and explain are facts involving immanent universals – the *koina* of *Peri Ideon* (*An. Post* I.5 77a5–9, I.22 83a33–35, and I.24 85a31ff). This view, however, is not without its theoretical costs. The propositions making up a demonstration are one and all necessary truths; and as Aristotle understands them, they are subject-predicate propositions. But if the subjects for necessary propositions are immanent universals, then there are immanent universals that are necessary beings; and Aristotle quite explicitly tells us this (*Met* Z.15 1039b20–1040a5). However, since he denies the possibility of uninstantiated universals, he is committed to the view known as the eternality of the species, roughly the view that, where for some kind, K, there is a body of scientific truths about Ks, it is a necessary truth that there are (in the occurrent, present-tensed sense) Ks. Accordingly, we get the result that it is impossible that there be a time at which there fail to be, say, oak trees, cats, or human beings: the relevant species are eternally and necessarily instantiated.

The *Peri Ideon* tells us that we need universals to serve as the objects of noetic acts, and in *De Anima* II.5, Aristotle tells us that universals are properly intelligible beings – things apt to be apprehended by intellect or *nous*, and contrasts them with the objects of perceptual experience – particulars (*An* II.5 417b19–23). But in Aristotle this contrast does not have the force it does in Plato. On the one hand, Aristotle wants to claim that everything is intelligible (*An* III.4 429a18), so, unlike Plato, he is committed to the idea that the same particulars that are grasped by perception can be the objects of noetic acts. On the other, he wants to defend an empiricist account of all our epistemic states (*An. Post* I.19 81a38–81b9; *An* III.8 432a4–9). Accordingly, he is committed to the idea that our apprehension of universals is anchored in perceptual experience. Now, some commentators have thought that a deep problem confronts Aristotle here. They have insisted that our ability to grasp universals on the basis of purely perceptual data requires some sort of very special noetic machinery, and they have claimed that Aristotle's brief and elusive comments about active *nous* in *De Anima* III.5 represent the attempt to identify that machinery. There is, however, little in that enigmatic chapter to substantiate this claim. Indeed, where Aristotle explicitly discusses the foundations of our thought about universals, he presents precisely the sort of account one would naturally associate with the view that universals are immanent in sensible particulars. He tells us that intelligible contents are literally contained in perceptual contents (*An* III.8 432a5), and the upshot is the sort of picture he presents in the last chapter of the *Posterior Analytics* (II.19), where we are told that beings whose perceptual experience is like ours in being intellectually informed are such that merely by perceiving the world they are put into epistemic contact with the universals that sensible particulars instantiate (see 100a4–100b5, especially 100a17).

It is in the *Categories* that Aristotle puts his theory of universals to work in explaining how familiar particulars have the attributes we associate with them. There we are told that there are two forms of predication: a universal can be *said of* a subject or *in* a subject (1a20 ff.). Where *U* is a universal and *s* its subject, then either *U* marks out *s* as what *s* is or *U* fails to do so. If the former, then *U* is said of *s*; if the latter, then *U* is in *s*. The kinds (species and genera) under which a thing falls as well as any universals that enter into their definition are related to the thing in the first way. Thus, *man* and *animal* are said of Socrates; *color* is said of *white*; and *virtue* is said of courage. But not all universals mark out their subjects as what they are. Some merely characterize or modify things that are antecedently marked out as what they are by other universals. If Socrates is pale, then the universal pallor is predicated of him; but being pale is not what Socrates is; what Socrates is a human being, so pallor is in Socrates.

Now, Aristotle's immanentist conception of universals structures the whole ontological theory of the *Categories*. That theory is thoroughly anti-Platonic. The underlying assumption is that universals are ontologically dependent on their instances (see, again, 13b7–10). Subjects, so to speak, provide metaphysical anchors for the universals predicated of them; they give them an ontological foothold in the world. Indeed, that idea is built into the Greek word for subject. The term is *hupokeimenon*, and it means "thing lying under." So subjects underlie the universals said of or in them; they provide them with a metaphysical foundation. But Aristotle did not think that just any subject provides the requisite grounding for a universal. He thought, for example, that the genus *animal* is said of the species *man*, that *virtue* is said of courage, and that *color* is in the genus *body*; but he did not think that these facts are sufficient to insure an onto-logical foothold for the universals *animal*, *virtue*, and *color*. In each of these cases, we have a universal predicated of another universal, and the latter is as much in need of an ontological anchor as the former. Ultimately, Aristotle thought, universals require as their subjects things that are not, in the same way, ontologically dependent on any-thing else; and he believed that only particulars present us with such things (2a35–2b7). His examples are an individual human being like Socrates and an individual horse like Secretariat. Such things together constitute the subjects of which all univer-sals are ultimately predicated; but since they are particulars, they are not predicated of anything else and so require no subjects to underwrite their existence.

Things like Socrates and Secretariat (things "neither said of a subject nor in a subject") Aristotle calls the primary substances (2a12–15), that is, the ontologically basic entities. The universals said of them (their species and genera) he call secondary substances (2a15–18). These substance kinds mark out the primary substances as what they are; they provide them with their essences. Universals from categories other than substance (quality, quantity, etc.) merely modify or characterize the primary substances in accidental ways, marking them out as qualified, quantified, or character-ized in one of the other ways associated with these categories. So in the *Categories* there is a two-way dependency relation between universals and the particular substances of which they are predicated. The particulars provide the universals with subjects or instances, thereby insuring an ontological foundation for them; but the universals, in turn, provide particulars with their character: the universals said of them furnish the primary substances with their essences; and the qualities, quantities, and other attri-butes that are in them furnish the primary substances with their various accidental determinations.

The *Categories*, then, takes particulars like Socrates and Secretariat to be the primary substances, and it construes both the kinds under which they fall and the accidents that modify them as universals predicated of them; or so, at least, one interpretation of that treatise would have it. The interpretation in question is widely held nowadays, so widely held that it has recently been called the standard interpretation (Wedin 2000). There is, however, an alternative reading, which is actually the older, more traditional reading. According to this alternative interpretation, the so-called accidental categories include not just universals, but individual or particular qualities, quantities, and the like – the sorts of things that nowadays are called tropes; and the claim is that it is these items that are ultimately responsible for the qualitative, quantitative, and other acci-dental determinations of primary substances. Thus, in addition to the universals *color* and *white*, the category of quality includes a whiteness that is unique or peculiar to Socrates, and it is this – the whiteness of Socrates – that is directly or immediately responsible for Socrates' characteristic complexion.

The debate between those who favor the so-called standard reading and those who defend the alternative reading has dominated almost all the recent literature on the *Categories*; see Ackrill (1963) and Owen (1965) for early and, by now, almost classic contributions to this debate; for more recent contributions, see Frede (1987) and Wedin (2000). Those who find tropes in the *Categories* argue that only individual accidents would satisfy the *Categories'* characterization of things that "are in a subject but not said of any subject" (1a23–4). Things not said of a subject are things that have no logical inferiors; they are the least general or most determinate items in their respective categorial lines. Obviously, nothing could be more determinate than a particular; and, we are told, Aristotle makes it clear that he has individuals in mind here because he associates an inseparability condition with the notion of inherence. He tells us that where x is in y, it is impossible for x to exist apart from y (1a25). However, a universal like *white* can obviously exist apart from any of the particulars of which it is predicated; it is only something like the whiteness of Socrates that satisfies the inseparability condition.

Those who defend the standard reading, by contrast, take the reference to things "in a subject but not said of any subject" to be a reference to fully determinate, yet repeatable qualities, quantities, and the like. On their reading, what Aristotle has in mind here is something like a fully determinate shade of white – say, winter white. Winter white is as specific a shade of color as there is, so it has no logical inferiors to be said of. It can, nonetheless, be found in numerically different substances at a single time. Defenders of this interpretation of the *Categories* argue that since Aristotle explicitly tells us that universals like *color* and knowledge can be in particulars (1b1 and 2a1–2), he cannot mean by the inseparability condition what defenders of the alternative interpretation claim he means. Finally, defenders of the standard reading point out that Aristotle tells us not only that all the items in the accidental categories are predicated of substances (3a1–5) but also that no particular can be predicated of anything else (*An. Pr* I.27 43a25–8 and 40).

III

As we have suggested, in the *Peri Ideon* and the *Organon* talk about the immanence of universals signals a repudiation of the Platonic two-worlds picture and the associated idea that there can be uninstantiated universals; but in later works like the *Physics* and, especially, the *Metaphysics*, talk of universals as things immanent in sensible particulars often has a different and more literal force. What Aristotle often means in these later works when he tells us that universals are in particulars is that the universals are components of or ingredients in sensible particulars. The idea is that particulars are composites or wholes and that universals are to be numbered among their constituents or ontological parts.

The source of this idea is Aristotle's attempt in *Physics* A.7 to provide an account of the coming to be of sensible particulars. It is a prephilosophical datum that the individuals of common sense come to be or are generated, but it is a datum that philosophers of a Parmenidean ilk wanted to challenge. They said that genuine coming to be would require a radical emergence *ex nihilo*, so that before the change we had nothing and after the change, something; and that, these philosophers said, is impossible. In defense of our prephilosophical belief in coming to be, Aristotle argues that if we take familiar particulars to be composites or complexes, then we can explain their coming to be without committing ourselves to any problematic emergence *ex nihilo*. His example is the musical man. He tells us that if we take the musical man to be a composite whose constituents are a certain substance – the man – and a certain quality – *musical*, then we have no difficulty explaining how the musical man comes to be. One constituent in the composite – the man – preexists the change. Prior to the change he is unmusical;

but, then, he comes to be musical; that is, he comes to have the other constituent – *musical* – predicated of him (190a13–21 and 190b17–23). There is nothing mysterious going on here; we do not have something just "popping" into existence *ex nihilo*. There is a substance; it exists before, during, and after the coming to be; what happens is merely that *it* gets changed. It comes to have predicated of it a quality not previously predicated, and the upshot is a composite – the musical man.

And Aristotle wants to claim that a parallel account works for the primary substances of the *Categories*, things like the individual man and the individual horse that were that treatise's examples of ontologically basic entities (*Phys* I.7 190b1–4). We are to construe a primary substance on the model of the musical man; we are to treat it as a predicative complex, a composite one constituent of which is predicated of the other. Then, we are to say that the subject constituent in the predicative complex preexists the coming to be of the composite and that what happens is merely that it comes to have the other constituent predicated of it. But, of course, we need confirmation that this is really what happens when something like a human being or a horse comes to be, and Aristotle tells us that observation provides the requisite confirmation (190b2). The paradigms of the *Categories'* primary substances are living beings – plants, animals, and human beings; and when we examine their coming to be, we find precisely the sort of pattern Aristotle describes. Living beings come to be from seeds, and there is always a continuity of stuff that takes us from seed to embryonic organism. The coming to be of the organism is simply the persisting stuff's taking on the structural and functional organization characteristic of a particular biological species, the species to which the resulting organism belongs. So like the musical man, living beings are predicative complexes, composites whose constituents include a subject entity and something predicated of it. But whereas in the case of the musical man, the subject was a full-fledged substance, in the case of a living being, the subject is the stuff of which a substance is made. Aristotle calls it matter; and whereas in the case of the musical man the predicated entity was something from an accidental category, the predicated entity in the case of a living being is one that makes the preexisting stuff constitute a particular falling under a determinate substance kind, and Aristotle calls it a form.

Plants, animals, and human beings, then, are hylomorphic composites; they are composites one of whose constituents is the appropriate sort of matter and the other, a substantial form predicated of that matter. The form is, of course, a universal, a substance determining universal. There is, Aristotle tells us, a single such form present in all the members of a substance species. So one constituent in a substantial composite is shared with all of the other members of the same species. What, then, distinguishes those members from each other? Aristotle tells us that matter is the principle of numerical differentiation within a substance species. In each individual belonging to the species there is a numerically different parcel of matter serving as the subject for the predication of the shared or common form (*Met* Z.8 1034a5–8).

Although this hylomorphic conception of substances is introduced in the *Physics*, it is refined and developed in the central Books of the *Metaphysics*. The resulting framework is very different from that outlined in the *Categories*. There, individuals like the man and the horse were ontologically basic; and although substance kinds (species and genera) were said of them marking them out as what they are, the individual substances were unanalyzable simples. Within the hylomorphic framework of the *Physics* and the *Metaphysics*, however, they turn out to be composite structures; and their being what they are turns out to rest on a prior type of predication; for the individual substance is a member of its proper substance species only because the substantial form associated with that species is predicated of the individual's matter. But, then, the predication of the species is grounded in the predication of the form. That, of course, implies that the matter and the form are metaphysically prior to the individual substance; and, Aristotle tells us, the form has a priority over the matter. Its predication takes a parcel of matter and makes it constitute a living being falling under a substance kind. Accordingly, Aristotle tells us that its form is the primary cause of the being of an individual living being. It is, as he puts it, the substance of the living being (see Z.17 and, especially, 1041b25–33).

So the middle Books of the *Metaphysics* hold that (1) forms are universals and that (2) they are the substances of the composites whose constituents they are. The difficulty is that in *Metaphysics* Z.13, Aristotle tells us that (3) no universal can be substance (1038b8–9). The result, it seems, is an inconsistent triad. That triad has been the focus of a major debate over the theory of the central Books of the *Metaphysics*. Just as the issue of particular versus universal accidents has dominated recent literature on the *Categories*, the triad just laid out has been the most discussed topic in recent scholarship on the middle Books.

The resulting literature is complex and highly technical. The best we can do in this sort of survey is to gesture at the main contours of the debate. In general, there are three different ways of dealing with the triad. One obvious strategy is to take the inconsistency at face value and to insist that it is an unfortunate consequence of the overall theory of the middle Books. There are scholars who endorse this strategy (see, e.g., Lesher 1971); but they constitute a distinct minority. Most scholars are unwilling to conclude that the ontological framework so painstakingly delineated in the central Books is at bottom contradictory. Accordingly, they deny that Aristotle actually holds all three of the propositions in the triad. Since it is beyond question that he takes forms to constitute the substance of familiar particulars, it is one of the other two members of the triad that Aristotle is typically taken to deny. Some commentators want to deny that, for Aristotle, substantial forms are universals (see, e.g., Frede 1987; Frede and Patzig 1988; Witt 1989). They take the upshot of Z.13 to be that the substance of each individual is a constituent idiosyncratic or peculiar to it. On this reading of the middle Books, the different members of a substance species have numerically different substantial forms; but while numerically distinct, those forms are all subject to a single definition. And defenders of particular forms insist that Z.13 is not the only place Aristotle commits himself to a doctrine of individual forms. That same doctrine they claim, is expressed in other texts as well (Δ.18 (1022a26–7), Z.6 (1032a6–8), and Δ.5 (1071a28–9) are examples).

Other commentators argue against the attribution of individual forms to the Aristotle of *Metaphysics* Z and H (see, e.g., Woods 1967; Loux 1979; Code 1983; Loux 1991; Lewis 1991). They point out that Aristotle repeatedly characterizes forms as things predicated of matter (*Met* Z.2 1029a23–4, Z.13 1038b6, and Θ.7 1049a34–6); they remind us of Aristotle's explicit denial that particulars can be predicated of things other than themselves (*An. Pr* I.27 43a25–8 and 40); and they point to Aristotle's claim in Z.8 that while the different individuals in a substance species have one and the same form, each has its own matter (1034a5–8) as something like a proof text for the attribution of general as opposed to individual substantial forms. They argue that none of the texts alleged to express a doctrine of individual forms actually does, and they claim that although Z.13 may appear to deny that universals can constitute the substance of familiar particulars, a careful reading of the chapter shows Z.13 to have a quite different point. As these commentators see it, what Aristotle is denying in that chapter is not that a universal can be the substance of the individual members of a kind. He is denying instead that where *K* is a genuine substance species, the thing that constitutes the substance of the *K*s can be a universal more general than *K*. On this reading, Z.13 has an antireductive force. Aristotle is claiming that where we have a genuine substance species, we have a group of individuals with an autonomous or *sui generis* form of being, and he is arguing that it is only if we posit an irreducibly fundamental or primitive principle as the substance of the members of that species that we secure that result. (For further discussion on this issue, see this volume, ch. 9, "Aristotelian Categories.")

Bibliography

Ackrill, J. L. (1963). *Aristotle's "Categories" and "De Interpretatione"* (Oxford: Oxford University Press).

Burnyeat, M. (2001). *A Map of "Metaphysics" Z* (Pittsburgh, PA: Mathesis).

Code, A. (1983). "Aristotle on Essence and Accident," in R. Grandy and R. Warner (eds.), *Philosophical Grounds of Rationality* (Oxford: Oxford University Press), pp. 411–44.

Fine, G. (1993). *On Ideas* (Oxford: Oxford University Press).

Frede, M. (1987). *Essays in Ancient Philosophy* (Minneapolis, MN: University of Minnesota Press).

Frede, M. and Patzig, G. (1988). *Aristoteles "Metaphysics" Z* (Munich: Verlag C. H. Beck).

Furth, M. (1988). *Substance, Form, and Psyche* (Cambridge: Cambridge University Press).

Lesher, J. (1971). "Aristotle on Form, Substance, and Universal: A Dilemma," *Phronesis*, 16, pp. 169–78.

Lewis, F. (1991). *Substance and Predication in Aristotle* (Cambridge: Cambridge University Press).

Loux, M. (1979). "Form, Species, and Predication in *Metaphysics* Z, H, and Θ," *Mind*, 88, pp. 1–23.

Loux, M. (1991). *Primary Ousia* (Ithaca, NY: Cornell University Press).

Owen, G. E. L. (1965). "Inherence," *Phronesis*, 10, pp. 97–105.

Scaltsas, T. (1994). *Substances and Universals in Aristotle's Metaphysics* (Ithaca, NY: Cornell University Press).

Wedin, M. (2000). *Aristotle's Theory of Substance* (Oxford: Oxford University Press).

Witt, C. (1989). *Substance and Essence in Aristotle* (Ithaca, NY: Cornell University Press).

Woods, M. (1967). "Problems in *Metaphysics* Z, Chapter 13," in J. Moravsick (ed.), *Aristotle* (New York: Doubleday).

12

Substances

S. MARC COHEN

Aristotle divides "the things that there are" or "beings" (*ta onta*) into a number of different categories. He is not always consistent about how many categories there are (ten in *Categories* 1b25 and *Topics* I.9 103b20, seven in *Physics* V.1 225b5 and *Metaphysics* K.12 1068a8), but the one he always lists first and regards as the most fundamental is the category of *substance* (*ousia*).

"Substance," the conventional English rendering of Aristotle's word *ousia*, is in fact misleading, suggesting as it does a kind of *stuff*. The English term "substance" entered the philosophical vernacular as a translation of the Latin *substantia*, which was itself an inadequate attempt to translate Aristotle. What "substance" and *substantia* both miss is the connection of the word *ousia* to the verb "to be" (*einai*). A better rendition might be "reality" or "fundamental being," but "substance" is deeply entrenched in the philosophical literature and will be used here. A good gloss would be to say that *ousiai* are the "ontologically basic entities" (Loux 1991: 2).

The Categories

In the *Categories*, Aristotle further distinguishes between *primary* and *secondary* substances, and quickly makes it clear that primary substances are ontologically basic: "if the primary substances did not exist it would be impossible for any of the other things to exist" (2b5). By "the other things" Aristotle means the secondary substances as well as the items in all the other categories – qualities, quantities, relatives, etc.

As examples of primary substances Aristotle gives "the individual man" (*ho tis anthrôpos*) and "the individual horse" (*ho tis hippos*) (2a13–14). Secondary substances include the species and genera under which the primary substances fall, such as *man*, *horse*, and *animal*. (2a15–18). Although he does not use the terms "universal" (*katholou*) and "particular" (*kath' hekaston*) in the *Categories*, it is clear that Aristotle would count primary substances as particulars and secondary substances as universals (see ch. 11, "Aristotle on Universals"). For he tells us that primary substances are "not said of a subject" (2a14), whereas a secondary substance such as *man* "is said of a subject, the individual man" (1a21), and this conforms to his definition of "particular" and "universal" in *De Interpretatione*: "I call universal that which is by its nature predicated of a number of things, and particular that which is not; man, for instance, is a universal, Callias a particular" (17a37–b1). So the difference between primary and secondary substances is that the former are particulars and the latter are universals.

What differentiates substances from everything else in the ontology of the *Categories* is that substances are "not in a subject" (1a20, 1b2, 2a14). Aristotle warns us that he is using this phrase in a somewhat technical sense: "By 'in a subject' I mean what is in something, not as a part, and cannot exist separately from what it is in." (1a24–5). This relation of *inherence* (as traditional jargon has it) is clearly one of ontological dependence – something *in a subject* is incapable of independent existence – but precisely what an inherent item is supposed to be dependent on has been a matter of significant scholarly dispute. (This dispute is thoroughly covered in ch. 9, "Aristotelian Categories," and will not be pursued here.)

Still, on any account of inherence, it is clear that, for Aristotle, shapes, sizes, and colors, for example, are inherent items. There are shapes (sizes, colors) only in so far as there are bodies shaped (sized, colored) in one way or another. Aristotle's claim is that all inherent items ultimately inhere in substances. One might well conclude from this that all of the properties of a substance inhere in it, and hence that to be *in a subject* is simply to be a property of that subject, but that would not be quite right. For the *Categories* also introduces the notion of the *differentiae* of a substance – roughly, the properties that are in the definition of the substance – and maintains that these are *not* inherent (3a21–5):

> the differentia is also not in a subject. For footed and two-footed are said of man as subject but are not in a subject; neither footed nor two-footed is *in* man.

Since the definition of a thing mentions its essential properties, it is clear that inherence corresponds to what Aristotle elsewhere calls *accidental* (*kata sumbebêkôs*) predication: for a non-substance F to inhere in a substance x is for F to belong accidentally to x. (For more detail on differentiae and inherence, see ch. 9, "Aristotelian Categories.")

So non-substances are accidents, and accidents are ontologically dependent on substances. But one might well wonder whether the dependence is not mutual. That is, one might suppose that substances depend on non-substances in just the same way. For a substance can no more exist without any accidents than an accident can exist without belonging to any substance. Aristotle never discusses this "reverse" dependence – he neither asserts nor denies it – but it is clear that he thinks that in some way the ontological dependence of non-substances on substances is asymmetrical. One possible account of the asymmetry is this. Since non-substances are accidental to the substances they inhere in, a particular substance can exist without the particular accidents that inhere in it. That is not to say that the substance might be lacking in accidents altogether, but only that it is capable of possessing different accidents from the ones it actually has. A particular accident, on the other hand, is ontologically dependent on the particular substance that it inheres in; it could not exist without that particular substance. (This account of asymmetry presupposes the interpretation of inherence recommended in ch. 9, "Aristotelian Categories.")

So much for the priority of substances over non-substances. But what gives primary substances the edge over secondary substances? One might suppose that Aristotle thinks that secondary substances are also inherent, but he denies this (3a9–11):

> as for secondary substances, it is obvious at once that they are not in a subject. For man is said of the individual man as subject but is not in a subject: man is not in the individual man.

There must, then, be another kind of ontological dependence than inherence, since secondary substances are ontologically dependent on primary substances, but do not inhere in them.

Aristotle addresses this issue by pointing out that a primary substance is *some this* (*tode ti*, 3b10), since it is "indivisible and numerically one" (*atomon kai hen arithmôi*, 3b12). A secondary substance, on the other hand, although its name may be singular, is not really *one*, for "*man* and *animal* are said of many things" (3b17). So a secondary substance is not a this but *a sort* (*poion ti*). Since he uses the same word, *poion*, for the category of quality, Aristotle realizes that he must quickly dispel the impression that secondary substances are qualities. The name of a secondary substance, he says (3b19–21):

> does not signify simply a certain qualification (*poion*), as white does. White signifies nothing but a qualification, whereas the species and the genus mark off the qualification of substance – they signify a certain sort of substance (*poion tina ousian*).

The idea here seems to be that what makes species and genera secondary is that they are just kinds or collections. A species is just a collection of individuals, and a genus is just a wider collection of the individual members of the species that fall under it. Without those individuals, there would be no species, and without the species there would be no genera. For the species *tiger* to exist, for example, is just for there to be individual tigers. It is the individual tigers and the other individual plants and animals that are the real things; their species and genera are simply the way the specimens are classified and organized. The species and genera of non-substance categories, such as *red* and *color* in the category of quality, are doubly dependent. For they are collections of individual qualities which are themselves ontologically dependent on substances.

Once again, one might wonder whether there is a mutual ontological dependence here, this time between primary and secondary substances. For although Aristotle never makes this claim in the *Categories*, it would seem that a given primary substance depends for its existence on its belonging to the particular species it belongs to. For Sheba to cease to be a tiger, one might say, is for her to cease to exist. In the *Topics*, Aristotle makes this dependence explicit (IV.5 125b37–40):

> it is impossible for a thing still to remain the same if it is entirely transferred out of its species, just as the same animal could not at one time be, and at another not be, a man.

And the fact that the *said-of* relation seems to amount to what Aristotle elsewhere calls *essential* (*kath' hauto*) predication makes this idea even more plausible. For when *x* is said of *y*, Aristotle tells us, both the name and the definition of *x* will be predicated of *y* (2a19–20). And the definition of *x* is the formula that signifies the essence of *x* (*Topics* I.5 101b38, VII.5 154a31). We will return to the topic of essence below. For now, it is enough to note that individuals would seem to depend on their species as much as the species do on individuals. But although this dependence of individuals on their species is implicit in the *Categories*, it is left undeveloped in that work (Furth 1988; Loux 1991). The message of the *Categories* is that the fundamental entities – the primary substances – are the individuals that do not in turn depend on other individuals.

In *Categories* 5, the chapter devoted to substances, Aristotle mentions some of their other salient features. Substances do not come in degrees: "of the species [of substance] themselves, one is no more a substance than another . . . the individual man is no more a substance than the individual ox" (2b23–7). Nor is one man more a man than another (3b36). In this respect substances contrast with qualities, "since one pale thing is more pale than another, and one beautiful thing more beautiful than another" (4a1–2). Substances also do not have contraries – "there is nothing contrary to an individual man, nor yet is there anything contrary to man or to animal" (3b25–6) – but this feature, he says, is not "distinctive" (*idion*) of substances, since quantities (e.g., "four-foot, or ten") also do not have contraries. What is "most distinctive" (*malista idion*) of substance, however, is that "what is numerically one and the same is able to receive contraries" (4a10). By this Aristotle means that substances alone are capable of undergoing change: "an individual man – one and the same – becomes pale at one time and dark at another . . . Nothing like this is to be seen in any other case" (4a19–21).

Substances, then, are not only the fundamental subjects of predication ("All the other things are either said of the primary substances as subjects or in them as subjects," 2a35), but also the fundamental subjects of change – substances alone *undergo* change, i.e., persist through change by remaining "numerically one" throughout. As we shall see, this hallmark of the substances of the *Categories* will be threatened by further developments in the *Physics* and *Metaphysics*.

Metaphysics Z

Aristotle begins *Metaphysics* Z, the treatise that contains his most extended discussion of *ousia*, with the words "being is said in many ways" (*to on legetai pollachôs*, 1 1028a10), but he quickly points out that this is not a case of mere ambiguity, or "homonymy," as he would call it, but of "focal meaning" (*pros hen* equivocity; see ch. 6, "Signification and Truth"). For one of the ways in which *being* is said is primary: "that which is primarily is the 'what', which indicates the substance" (1 1028a14–15). We may say that a thing "is white or hot or three cubits long" (1 1028a17), but that is to state its quality or quantity – to say *what it's like* or *how much it is* – not to say *what it is*, e.g., "a man or a god" (1 1028a17). And this is the primary sense of "is," for (1 1028a18–20):

> all other things are said to be because they are, some of them, quantities of that which *is* in this primary sense, others qualities of it, others affections of it, and others some other determination of it.

When we try to account for the being of these other things, then, we must make use of the sense of "is" in which only substances can be said to be. Although the primacy of substances proposed here is more elaborate than the doctrine of the *Categories*, it certainly recalls the earlier work's doctrine that the non-substances exist only because they "inhere in" substances. If one attempts to answer the central question of ontology – "What is there?" – with a list, one's catalog of entities might include qualities (colors, shapes, etc.) and quantities (meters, quarts, etc.) as well as substances (horses, tigers, etc.). But it is the substances that are fundamental, for the items in all of the other categories are dependent upon substances. Hence the central question in the study of being, Aristotle points out, can be reduced to a question about substance (1028b2–4):

> the question which, both now and of old, has always been raised, and always been the subject of doubt, viz. what being is, is just the question, what is substance?

At this point the reader might well expect Aristotle to give a brief answer, referring to the *Categories*: substances are, e.g., individual horses, tigers, and trees. (and, in a secondary way, the kinds – *horse, tiger, tree*, etc. – to which they belong). But it turns out that the answer is not so simple, for two reasons. First, a mere inventory might well be disputed. Should we include not just plants and animals but fire and water (1028b11)? What about stars, moon, and sun (1028b13), or "the limits of body, i.e., surface, line, point, and unit" (1028b16), or non-sensible eternal things (1028b19)? Different philosophers (Aristotle mentions Plato and Speusippus) give different answers. Second, providing such an inventory presupposes that we can answer the question of what entitles something to be included in it, and that is the question to which Aristotle now turns.

He begins Z.3 by proposing (1028b34–5) four candidates for the title of substance: essence (*to ti ên einai*), universal (*katholou*), genus (*genos*), and subject (*hupokeimenon*). We will examine the claims of these candidates momentarily, but it is worth noting at the start the way in which Aristotle introduces them. Each of them, he says, has a claim to be considered "the substance of each thing" (*ousia hekastou*, 1028b35). This locution, "the substance *of x*," is strikingly novel – nothing like it can be found in the *Categories* – and Aristotle's use of it further supports the idea that the question he is raising here is not "which things are substances?" but "what makes something a substance?" (Wedin 2000; Burnyeat 2001). The substance of *x* is presumably that feature of *x* in virtue of which *x* is a substance. Hence, Aristotle is asking whether the substance of *x* is (i) the essence of *x*, or (ii) a universal that *x* is an instance of, or (iii) a genus that *x* falls under, or (iv) a subject underlying *x*. (iv), the so-called *subject criterion*, recalls the doctrine of the *Categories* that a primary substance is what is neither in a subject nor said of a subject. Substances, that is to say, are subjects of predication that are not in turn predicated of anything else.

The remainder of Z.3 is devoted to the subject criterion, which leads Aristotle to propose a possibility never countenanced in the *Categories*: that the substance of *x* is the *matter* of which *x* is composed. The *Categories* was in no position to consider this possibility since the concepts of *matter* and *form* are not part of its conceptual framework. *Matter* makes its first appearance in the *Physics*, where Aristotle defines it as "the primary substratum (or subject, *hupokeimenon*) of each thing, from which it comes to be, and which persists in the result" (I.8 192a31). But if matter is the subject that persists through change, then it has the feature that Aristotle said at *Categories* 4a10 was "most distinctive" of substances. And since matter is also the primary subject of predication ("the predicates other than substance are predicated of substance, and substance is predicated of matter," 1029a23–4), it certainly has a prima facie claim, in the context of a hylomorphic analysis that was absent from the *Categories*, to be considered substance.

But Z.3 forcefully rejects the claim of matter to be substance. (Whether it also rejects the subject criterion is a matter of dispute.) It is "impossible" for matter to be substance, Aristotle says (1029a28), for a substance must be both "separable" (*chôriston*) and "some this" (*tode ti*). What is left unstated, but clearly intended, is that matter fails to satisfy these two conditions, although the conditions themselves are far from clear. It is generally agreed that the separability requirement concerns independent existence – for something to be separable is for it to be capable of existing on its own. The "thisness" requirement presents two main interpretative possibilities: (1) *individuality*, and (2) *determinateness*. According to (1) the objection to matter is that it is not a countable individual – it is just *stuff*. According to (2) the problem with matter is that it has no determinate nature – it is not of any specific kind. (The prevailing interpretation is (1), which recalls the characterization of *tode ti* we found in *Categories* 3b10; for (2), see Dancy 1978 and Gill 1989.) Note that the two requirements are independent of one another. A particular color or shape satisfies the "thisness" requirement (it is a countable individual) but not the separability requirement, for it is not capable of existing on its own – it is always the color or shape of some substance or other.

The problem with matter seems to be that it cannot simultaneously satisfy both requirements. The matter of which a substance is composed may in a way be *chôriston* in that it can exist independently of that substance (think of the wood of which a desk is composed, which existed before the desk was made and may survive the disassembly of the desk). But the matter is not, as such, any definite individual – it is just a quantity of a certain kind of matter – and so is not, as such, *tode ti*. On the other hand, the matter may be construed as *tode ti* in that it constitutes a definite individual substance (the wood just *is*, one might say, the particular desk it composes). But it is in that sense not separate from the form or shape that makes it a substance of that kind (the wood cannot be that particular desk unless it is *a* desk, i.e., unless it has the form and fulfills the function of a desk). So although matter is in a sense *chôriston* and in a sense *tode ti*, there is no sense in which it is both. It thus does not qualify as the substance of the thing whose matter it is.

The matter that is rejected in Z.3 may be something more abstract and recondite than wood or bronze, however. For Aristotle says that to arrive at matter we must systematically remove from a thing its "affections, products, and capacities" (1029a12), and eventually its "length, breadth, and depth" (1029a16). What we are left with, if anything, is matter. The matter we are left with is "of itself neither a particular thing nor of a particular quantity nor otherwise positively characterized; nor yet negatively" (1029a24). Matter so conceived, as stuff devoid of essential characteristics, has traditionally been given the label *prime matter*. Whether Aristotle himself is elsewhere committed to embracing such a conception of matter has been hotly debated (see ch. 10, "Form and Matter"). Here, at least, it seems that he thinks that the "ultimate subject" criterion would lead to the intolerable result that a single featureless stuff – prime matter – underlies all hylomorphic compounds and is therefore the substance of all of them.

The failure of matter's candidacy leaves Aristotle with two other contenders: "form and the compound of matter and form" (1029a29). He immediately dismisses the compound ("it is posterior, and its nature is obvious," 1029a31), and this may seem surprising, since a primary substance of the *Categories* counts as a compound of matter and form in the new hylomorphic framework. But if we recall that Aristotle's question is what the substance *of* something is, his move here makes sense. Perhaps the substance *of* a *Categories* substance is its form. Hence Aristotle proposes to "inquire into the third kind of substance [i.e., form]; for this is the most difficult" (1029a32).

When Aristotle immediately turns, in Z.4–6, to examine the candidacy of essence, it may seem as if the topic of form has been shelved. But this appearance is somewhat misleading. For *essence* is not really an alternative to *form*; it is a logical concept, linked (as we saw above) to the notion of definition, and does not by itself involve the hylomorphic concepts of form and matter. But neither does it exclude them. If the substance of *x* is its essence, and the essence of a hylomorphic compound is its form, then it will turn out that the substance of a hylomorphic compound is its form.

Aristotle's term for essence is the curious phrase *to ti ên einai* – literally, "the what it is to be." And he tells us that the essence of each thing (the *what it is to be* for that thing, as he puts it) "is what it is said to be in virtue of itself (*kath' hauto*)" (1029b14). *Kath' hauto* predication, as we saw above, is contrasted with accidental (*kata sumbebêkôs*) predication, and this connection between essence and *kath' hauto* predication conforms to his standard usage in the logical works (cf. *An. Post* I.4 73a34–5: "One thing belongs to another in itself (*kath' hauto*) . . . if it belongs to it in what it is (*en tôi ti estin*)"). Since the account (*logos*) of *x* that states its essence is the *definition* of *x*, Aristotle concludes that "there is an essence only of those things whose formula is a definition" (1030a6).

In making this last claim, Aristotle means to be ruling out a phrase like "pale man" from serving as the definiens in a definition (1031a5). Hence, even if we introduce a term (Aristotle's example is "cloak") into our language by stipulating that it means *pale man*, this does not make "a cloak is a pale man" count as a genuine definition, or *being a cloak* count as an essence. There will be essences corresponding to the species *man* and *tiger*, but *pale man* is not a species of animal and so has no corresponding essence. "Nothing," Aristotle concludes, "which is not a species of a genus will have an essence" (1030a11). This startling conclusion raises a number of questions.

First, what precisely is Aristotle ruling out here? Clearly he is contrasting genuine species, like *man*, with jury-rigged kinds, like *pale man*, and claiming that the latter do not have essences. But is he also contrasting species with their specimens? Does he mean that *man* has an essence but Callias does not? That is not likely. Aristotle's point would seem to be, rather, that the essence of an individual, such as Callias, must be something at the species level that does not distinguish one member of the species from another. Another possibility is that Aristotle is only considering universals at this point, and questions about individuals are not even in order.

Second, what about definitions of non-substances? Surely qualities (*white, musical,* etc.) are definable, and so they, too, should have essences. Aristotle concedes that they do, but points out that "'definition' (*horismos*), like 'what it is' (*ti esti*), is said in many ways" (1030a19). That is, items in all the categories are definable, so items in all the categories have essences – just as there is an essence of man, there is also an essence of white and an essence of musical. But, because of the *pros hen* equivocity of "is," such essences are secondary – "definition and essence are primarily (*protôs*) and without qualification (*haplôs*) of substances" (1030b4–6). Thus it is only these primary essences that are substances. (For a reconstruction of the "hierarchy of essences" hinted at here, see Loux 1991).

Third, has Aristotle radically altered his conception of the importance of the species, which in the *Categories* he called a *secondary* substance? Woods 1967 and Owen 1978 argued that he has, but that interpretation is now widely disputed. For Aristotle's claim at 1030a11 is not that a species *is* an essence, but that it *has* an essence. This essence will turn out to be the *form* of a hylomorphic compound. The distinction is easy to miss, since the word "*eidos*," which in the logical works meant "species" (in contrast to "genus"), has a new meaning in a hylomorphic context, where it can also mean "form" (in contrast to "matter"). (The distinction, established by Driscoll 1981, was missed by Woods and Owen). Indeed, Z.10 offers a new characterization of the species (secondary substances) of the *Categories* that is couched in terms of the notions of matter and form (1035b28–30):

> But man and horse and things that are thus predicated of particulars, but universally, are not [primary] substance but a kind of compound of a certain formula and a certain matter, taken universally.

Since a species is now conceived of as itself a kind of hylomorphic compound, it would be a mistake to think that Aristotle has promoted the species to the rank of primary substance. The *eidos* that is primary substance in Z is not the species that an individual substance belongs to; rather, it is the form associated with that species, a form that is predicated of the matter of which individual substances are composed.

The possibility that Aristotle has universals in mind in Z.4 comes into play again when we consider the central question of Z.6: "whether each thing and its essence are the same or different" (1031a15). (It must be pointed out that Z.6 is an unusually dense and difficult chapter that has attracted fierce scholarly debate, and there is nothing resembling general agreement about its message. What follows is just one possible interpretation.) If, as seems plausible, by "each thing" (*hekaston*) Aristotle means each *definable* thing, then it would seem that Aristotle's question pertains solely to universals. For "definition is of the universal" (Z.11 1036a27 and "there is no definition . . . of sensible individual substances" (Z.15 1039b27). Since Aristotle's answer (call it "the Z.6 Thesis") is that, properly qualified, each definable thing is the same as its essence ("each of the things that are primary (*protôn*) and self-subsistent (*kath' hauta legomenôn*) is one and the same as its essence," 1032a5), it seems clear that it is the substance *of* something that is here being claimed to be the same as its essence. For it is not Callias but the substance *of* Callias that is definable. Suppose that x is an individual substance and y is the substance of x. Then according to the Z.6 Thesis, on this interpretation, it is y (rather than x) that is identical to its own essence.

This interpretation is supported by Aristotle's claim (1031b29–30) that to deny the Z.6 Thesis would lead to an infinite regress (Code 1986). For to deny the identity of a definable thing and its essence is to say that that the thing and its essence have different definitions (since the identity of a definable object is given by its definition). But if the definition of y is different from the definition of the essence of y, then likewise the definition of the essence of y will be different from the definition of the essence of the essence of y, and so on, *ad infinitum*. And the regress must be rejected to avoid epistemological disaster, since "to know each thing is to know its essence" (1031b20), and an endless regress of essences would leave all of them unknowable, there being no highest-level essence to serve as the basis for the knowledge of all the others.

This reading of the Z.6 Thesis is also supported by several of Aristotle's subsequent claims. In Z.11 he says that "things which are of the nature of matter or of wholes which include matter are not the same as their essences" (1037b5–6), and this has the consequence, as he says, that Callias, in whom matter is present, is not a primary substance that is identical to its essence. Rather, "the [primary] substance is the indwelling form, from which along with the matter the so-called concrete substance is derived" (1037a29–30). The form of a living thing, Aristotle says, is its soul (see ch. 18, "The Aristotelian Psuchê"). Similarly, in H.3 he makes clear that it is the form (and not the composite of matter and form) that is the same as its essence (". . . soul and to be soul are the same, but to be man and man are not the same" 1043b2).

At this point in our journey through *Metaphysics* Z, we reach a fork in the road. For the next three chapters (Z.7–9) begin an investigation of "things that come to be" (*ta gignomena*) that seems to bear no obvious relation to the discussion of essence in Z.4–6, and it is generally agreed that these chapters were not originally written for this context. Since the discussion in Z.6 is smoothly resumed in Z.10, which concerns the relation between a definition and its definable parts, it is tempting to move directly from Z.6 to Z.10 (as does, e.g., Wedin 2000) and ignore the interpolated chapters. Still, it is not disputed that Aristotle wrote these chapters and probably placed them here himself, perhaps because they reintroduce the topic of form, which was left dangling at the end of Z.3 and at least nominally ignored throughout Z.4–6.

The individual substances we have been considering since Z.3 are hylomorphic compounds, and hence the role of matter and form in their generation must be accounted for. Both natural objects, such as plants and animals, and artifacts, such as houses, have the same requirements. Neither their matter nor their form is produced; rather, we put the form into the matter, and produce the compound (1033a30–b9). Both the matter and the form must pre-exist (1034b12). But the source of motion in both cases – what Aristotle calls the "moving cause" of the coming to be (see ch. 13, "Causes") – is the form. In the case of artistic production (e.g., housebuilding), the form is found in the soul of the artisan (1034a24, 1032b23). In natural generation, the form is found in the parent, where "the begetter is the same in kind as the begotten, not one in number but one in form – for man begets man" (1033b30–2). In both cases the form pre-exists and is not produced (1033b18).

The product of such a hylomorphic production is correctly described by the name of the form that produced it, not by that of the matter from which it was produced. What is produced is a house or a man, not bricks or flesh. Of course, what is made of gold may still be described in terms of its material components, but we should call it not "gold" but "golden" (1033a7). For it was not gold that came into being, but a statue (a golden one, to be sure), which cannot be identified with the gold of which it was made. For the statue came into existence just then, but the gold did not.

So the link between form and essence has been forged. The essence of a hylomorphic compound is its form. "By form I mean the essence of each thing, and its primary substance" (1032b1), Aristotle observes, and "when I speak of substance without matter I mean the essence" (1032b14). It is the form of a substance that makes it the kind of thing that it is, and hence it is form that satisfies the condition initially required for being the *substance of* something in the sense of its essence. The essence of a thing is its form. And this form is something that different individual substances share (1034a5–7):

> And when we have the whole, such and such a form in this flesh and in these bones, this is Callias or Socrates; and they are different in virtue of their matter (for that is different), but the same in form; for their form is indivisible.

In Z.10 and 11, Aristotle returns to the consideration of essence and definition left off in Z.6, but now within the hylomorphic context developed in Z.7–9. The main question these chapters consider is whether the definition of x ever includes a reference to the matter of x. If some definitions include a reference to matter, then the link between essence and form would seem to be weakened. The reason that this question arises is that Aristotle is committed to a kind of correspondence principle about definitions (1034b20–22):

> a definition is an account, and every account has parts, and part of the account stands to part of the thing in just the same way that the whole account stands to the whole thing.

Roughly, if y is part of x, then the definition of x must contain something that corresponds to y, namely, the definition of y. That is, the definition of a thing will include the definitions of its parts. For example, *animal* occurs in the definition of *man*, and since *animal* is itself definable, it should be replaced, in the definition of *man*, with its own definition. In this way a formula like *man is a rational animal* is only a shorthand for a proper, fully explicit, definition, one which will ultimately be composed of simple terms that are not further definable.

But there is a problem. Since a hylomorphic compound is partly matter, the definition of the compound would have to consist, in part, of the definitions of its material components. And this consequence is untenable. A circle, for example, is composed of two semicircles (for it obviously may be divided into two semicircles), but the definition of *circle* cannot be composed of the definitions of its two semicircular parts. For, as Aristotle points out (1035b9), *semicircle* is defined in terms of *circle*, and not the other way around. This priority of the whole over its material parts may seem arbitrary, but it is not. For if circles were defined in terms of semicircles, then presumably semicircles would be defined in terms of the quarter-circles of which they are composed, and so on, *ad infinitum*. The resulting infinite regress would make it impossible to define *circle* at all. For if, as Aristotle thinks, matter is not divisible into individual atoms, one would never reach the ultimate "simple" parts of which such a definition would be composed.

Aristotle's solution to this problem is that one must be clear about which whole it is that the matter is a part of. "The bronze is part of the compound statue, but not of the statue spoken of as form" (1035a6). Similarly (1035a17–20):

> the line when divided passes away into its halves, and the man into bones and muscle and flesh, but it does not follow that they are composed of these as parts of their essence.

Rather, "it is not the substance but the compound that is divided into the body and its parts as into matter" (1035b21–2). So the substance of a hylomorphic compound has been "purified" (Wedin 2000) – it contains form, but not matter.

As Aristotle seems to realize, however, this solution is only partially successful. We may grant that neither a particular batch of bronze nor even bronze in general enters into the essence of statue, since being made of bronze is no part of what it is to be a statue. But that is only because statues, although they must be made of some kind of matter, do not require any particular kind of matter. But what about kinds of substances that do require particular kinds of matter? Aristotle's distinction between form and compound cannot be used in such cases to isolate essence from matter. Thus there may after all be reasons for thinking that reference to matter will have to intrude into at least some definitions.

This is the problem that Aristotle tackles in Z.11, where he concedes that "some things surely are a certain form in a certain matter" (1036b23). For example, "the form of man is always found in flesh and bones and parts of this kind" (1036b4). It would thus appear that at least some definitions of (types of) hylomorphic compounds will mention matter. Nevertheless, Aristotle ends Z.11 as if he has defended the claim that definition is of the form alone. It is not surprising, therefore, that this chapter is considered difficult and controversial. What follows is just one possible account of his point here. Grant that there are cases in which it is essential to a substance that it be made of a certain kind of matter (e.g., that man be made of flesh and bones, or that "a saw cannot be made of wool or wood," H.4 1044a28). Still, this is in some sense a formal or structural requirement. A kind of matter, after all, can itself be analyzed hylomorphically. Bronze, for example, has a certain form – it is a mixture of copper and tin according to a certain ratio or formula (*logos*) – and this form is in turn predicated of some more generic underlying subject. The apparent reference to matter in a definition will thus always be to a certain kind or form of matter, and hence to a predicate, rather than a subject. At any rate, if one has in mind the prime matter alluded to in Z.3, there will be no reference to it in any definition, "for this is indefinite" (1037a27).

The Inconsistency

Let us now take stock of what we seem to have learned so far about substances in *Metaphysics* Z. The substance of a hylomorphic compound is a substantial form, which corresponds to a species. A substantial form is an essence, which is to say that it is what is denoted by the definiens of a definition. Since only universals are definable, substantial forms are universals that can be shared by different specimens of the same species.

Socrates and Callias are different substances, but they differ only in matter, and not in substance.

But now Z.13 seems to undercut this interpretation entirely by arguing that universals are not substances: "it seems impossible for anything predicated universally to be a substance" (1038b9); "it is plain that no universal attribute is a substance" (1038b35).

This leaves us with a fundamental tension in Aristotle's conception of substance, since he seems to be committed to each of the following three propositions:

(i)   Substance is form.
(ii)   Form is universal.
(iii)   No universal is a substance.

But these three propositions are mutually inconsistent, and dealing with the apparent inconsistency in Aristotle's theory of substance has fragmented his interpreters. Some believe that Aristotle is indeed committed to all of (i)–(iii) and that his theory of substance is therefore untenable. But most believe that on a proper understanding, the inconsistency can be avoided. There have been two main approaches to resolving the apparent inconsistency. The first is the "particular forms" approach, which denies (ii). According to this line of interpretation, a substantial form is not a universal but peculiar to a single particular. The substantial form of Socrates is thus distinct from the substantial form of Callias; each hylomorphic compound substance has its own substantial form. (Whether the substantial forms of conspecific particulars are only numerically distinct or differ qualitatively as well is a matter of dispute among proponents of this approach.) The second approach has many variants, so it is harder to characterize with a simple label, but it is unified by a rejection of particular forms. On one version of this approach, there is only one substantial form for all the particulars belonging to the same species, but it is not predicated of those particulars. Rather, it is predicated of the many different clumps of matter of which those particulars are composed. That makes a substantial form a universal in the sense that it can be predicated of many things, but not in the sense that it can be predicated of many different individual substances. Proponents of the particular forms approach include Sellars 1957, Hartman 1977, Irwin 1988, Frede and Patzig 1988, and Witt 1989. Opponents include Woods 1967, Owen 1978, Code 1986, Furth 1988, Lewis 1991, and Loux 1991. (For biological evidence bearing on this dispute, see ch. 23 in this volume.)

It would be difficult to imagine that Aristotle was unaware of this tension in his theory. For at the heart of the tension is a puzzle about whether the substance of something is universal or particular, and Aristotle himself lists a variant of it as one of the puzzles (*aporiai*) that lie at the heart of first philosophy. He presents it in the form of a dilemma (B.6 1003a6–13):

> We must ask whether [first principles, *archai*] are universals or what we call particulars. If they are universals, they will not be substances; for everything that is common indicates not a "this" but a "such," but a substance is a this . . . [I]f they are not universals but, as it were (*hôs*), particulars, they will not be knowable; for knowledge in all cases is of the universal.

In Z Aristotle works out the arguments in support of both of the horns of this dilemma (hence the tension), and presumably attempts to provide a resolution (see Code 1984).

But what resolution does he offer? This is where the two approaches differ, and I cannot hope to do justice to both in the present chapter. But it seems clear that any adequate interpretation must see Aristotle as recognizing something right in each horn of the dilemma. In what follows, I will sketch a line of interpretation that attempts to do that.

At the very beginning of Z.1 (1028a11–15), Aristotle presents two requirements for a substance: it must be both a "this" (*tode ti*) and a "what it is" (*ti estin*) (see Owen 1978; Code 1984). The first requirement argues against universals (since a universal is a "such," and not a "this"), and the second argues against particulars (since to know something is to know *what it is*, and knowledge is of the universal). So what is needed is something that is neither a universal nor a particular. But what could such a thing be? As we saw above, what is predicated of many things is a universal, and what is not predicated of many things is a particular. There does not seem to be room for something that is neither universal nor particular, and yet that is what a substantial form needs to be.

But recall that for Aristotle there are two ways of being predicated – essentially and accidentally. Let us call what is predicated essentially of many things a universal$_E$, and what is predicated accidentally of many things a universal$_A$. Many universals are both; red, for example, is a universal$_A$, since it is predicated accidentally of the many red things, but also a universal$_E$, since it is predicated essentially of the many shades and individual bits of red. Species and genera of substance, on the other hand, would seem to be universals$_E$ but not universals$_A$ (they are predicated essentially of their specimens, but not predicated accidentally of anything at all). Notice, however, that there is room for something that is a universal$_A$ but not a universal$_E$ – predicated accidentally of many things, but not predicated essentially of many things. We will return to this possibility shortly.

Since a particular (*kath' hekaston*) is just what is not universal, we can say that a particular is something that is neither universal$_E$ nor universal$_A$. To call something an individual (*tode ti*), however, is just to say that it is not a universal$_E$, that it is a bottom-level item in its category and not a fundamental classification under which other things fall. So every particular is an individual, but not every individual is a particular. This is what a substantial form is – a *tode ti* that is not a particular, and is therefore a universal$_A$.

Recall that in Aristotle's hylomorphic theory, form is predicated of matter, and so that is what substantial form is universally$_A$ predicated of. The form of *man*, for example, is not predicated (essentially) of the individuals Socrates and Callias (for it is not a universal$_E$); rather, it is predicated (accidentally) of the clumps of matter that constitute those individuals (for it is a universal$_A$). What is universally$_E$ predicated of both Socrates and Callias is the species *man*, so the species is not a *tode ti*. Note that this requires us to distinguish between the individual Callias and the clump of matter that constitutes him, but this seems right. For the former is member of the species *man* and the latter is not. The species predication *Callias is a man*, familiar to us from the *Categories*, is thus explained in this hylomorphic context by the form predication *These flesh and bones are a man* (Loux 1991; Wedin 2000). The term "man" in the first predication refers to the species (a universal$_E$) and in the second to the form (a *tode ti*, i.e., a non-universal$_E$).

The inconsistency is thus removed by taking (ii) and (iii) to be talking about different kinds of universals. (ii) asserts that form is universal$_A$, and (iii) denies that substance is universal$_E$. (See Modrak 1979 for a different way of distinguishing between kinds of universals.) We will conclude with a brief examination of some of the remaining passages in Z to see how well they accommodate this interpretation.

The first argument Aristotle gives in Z.13 purports to establish that it is "impossible for anything predicated universally to be a substance" (1038b9). Yet when we look at the details of the argument, we see that the problem it finds with the universal is that it is "common" (*koinon*) to many things, whereas "the substance of x is peculiar to x" (*ousia hekastou hê idios hekastôi*, 1038b10). A universal substance would then have to be, impossibly, both predicated of all its many instances and yet peculiar to (i.e., predicated uniquely of) each of them. So Aristotle concludes that such a universal is not the substance of any of its instances ("[W]hat will this be the substance of? Either of all or of none, but it cannot be of all," 1038b12–13). Notice that the implicit conclusion is not that no universal is a substance, but the weaker claim that no universal is the substance of any of the things of which it is universally predicated. The argument tells against both universals$_A$ and universals$_E$, although in different ways. A universal$_A$ is not the substance of any of its instances, since it is accidental to them, and the substance of a thing cannot be accidental to it. A universal$_E$, such as a species or a genus, on the other hand, is universally$_E$ predicated of all the specimens that fall under it, and so cannot be the substance of any of them. The universals that this argument is directed against are the species and genera of substances. But the argument does not tell against a substantial form that is universally$_A$ predicated of the various clumps of matter constituting the specimens of those species and genera. For although this form is predicated of many bits of matter, it is not the substance of the matter of which it is (accidentally) predicated. It is not part of the essence of the bricks and boards that compose a particular house (e.g., Frank Lloyd Wright's famous *Fallingwater*) that they should constitute a house.

What, then, is a substantial form the substance of? At this point it becomes tempting to say that the form is the substance of the individuals that are composed of these bits of matter. But that cannot be exactly right, since the form would then be the substance of many individuals and therefore not *idion* to (i.e., distinctive of) any one thing. Here it is useful to remember the Z.6 Thesis: each definable thing is identical to its essence. Since a substantial form is a definable thing *par excellence*, it must be identical to its essence. Since the essence of a substance is presumably the substance of that substance, a substantial form is the substance of itself. The form itself is the thing to which it is *idion*. It is the substance of those many individuals only in the following extended sense: it is by virtue of the form being universally$_A$ predicated of many bits of matter that those bits constitute the many individuals of which its associated species is universally$_E$ predicated.

In Z.17 Aristotle proposes to make a fresh start, beginning with the assumption that "a substance is a principle (*archê*) and a cause (*aitia*)" (1041a9–10). The job of such a principle or cause, he notes, is to explain why one thing belongs to another (1041a11); that is, it is to explain some predicational fact. What needs to be explained, for example, is why *Callias is a man*, or *Fallingwater is a house*. Notice that the explanandum in these cases involves a species predication, in which a species (*man*, *house*) is universally$_E$ predicated of an individual (Callias, Fallingwater). But the explanations that Aristotle provides for these species predications are couched in terms of a hylomorphic analysis: we must state "why these things, e.g., bricks and stones, are a house" (1041a26). In the explanation, the predicate is a substantial form (*house*) that is universally$_A$ predicated of the matter (bricks and stones) that constitute the house. "What we seek is the cause, i.e., the form, by reason of which the matter is some definite thing; and this is the substance of the thing" (1041b6–9) and "the primary cause of its being" (1041b27).

So Callias is a man (i.e., *man* is universally$_E$ predicated of Callias) because the form or essence of man is present in (i.e., universally$_A$ predicated of) the flesh and bones that constitute the body of Callias; Fallingwater is a house because the form of house is present in (i.e., universally$_A$ predicated of) the materials of which Fallingwater is made. In general, a species predication (involving a universal$_E$) is explained in terms of an underlying form predication (involving a universal$_A$). But these two predications have different subjects. The subject of the species predication is the specimen substance, a particular compound. The subject of the form predication is not the particular compound, but the matter of which that compound is composed. Form predications are thus more basic than, and explanatory of, their corresponding species predications. A substantial form, as a primary definable, is essentially predicated of itself alone, and is therefore, in a primary way, the substance only of itself. But the substantial form of a material compound, because it is predicated (accidentally) of the matter of the compound, is the cause of the compound's being (essentially) the kind of thing that it is. The form is therefore, in a derivative way, the substance of the compound as well. For when we ask the "what is it?" (*ti esti*) question about that compound, the form is the individual (*tode ti*) that our answer ultimately appeals to. The species-level substantial form is thus both a *tode ti* and a *ti estin*, as Aristotle has insisted that *ousia* must be.

Bibliography

Bostock, D. (1994). *Aristotle "Metaphysics" Books Z and H*, trans. with comm. (Oxford: Clarendon Press).

Burnyeat, M. (2001). *A Map of "Metaphysics" Zeta* (Pittsburgh, PA: Mathesis).

Code, A. (1984). "The Aporematic Approach to Primary Being in *Metaphysics Z*," *Canadian Journal of Philosophy*, suppl., 10, pp. 1–20.

Code, A. (1986). "Aristotle: Essence and Accident," in R. Grandy and R. Warner (eds.), *Philosophical Grounds of Rationality: Intentions, Categories, Ends* (Oxford: Clarendon Press), pp. 411–39.

Dancy, R. M. (1978). "On Some of Aristotle's Second Thoughts about Substances: Matter," *Philosophical Review*, 87, pp. 372–413.

Driscoll, J. (1981). "*Eidê* in Aristotle's Earlier and Later Theories of Substance," in D. J. O'Meara (ed.), *Studies in Aristotle* (Washington, DC: Catholic University of America Press), pp. 129–59.

Frede, M. (1987). *Essays in Ancient Philosophy* (Minneapolis, MN: University of Minnesota Press).

Frede, M. and Patzig, G. (1988). *Aristoteles "Metaphysik Z": Text, Übersetzung und Kommentar* (Munich: Verlag C. H. Beck).

Furth, M. (1988). *Substance, Form and Psyche: An Aristotelian Metaphysics* (New York: Cambridge University Press).

Gill, M. L. (1989). *Aristotle on Substance: The Paradox of Unity* (Princeton, NJ: Princeton University Press).

Gill, M. L. (2005). "Aristotle's *Metaphysics* Reconsidered," *Journal of the History of Philosophy*, 43, pp. 223–51.

Hartman, E. (1977). *Substance, Body, and Soul: Aristotelian Investigations* (Princeton, NJ: Princeton University Press).

Irwin, T. H. (1988). *Aristotle's First Principles* (Oxford: Clarendon Press).

Lesher, J. (1971). "Aristotle on Form, Substance, and Universals: A Dilemma," *Phronesis*, 16, pp. 169–78.

Lewis, F. A. (1991). *Substance and Predication in Aristotle* (Cambridge: Cambridge University Press).

Loux, M. J. (1991). *Primary "Ousia": An Essay on Aristotle's "Metaphysics" Z and H* (Ithaca, NY: Cornell University Press).

Modrak, D. K. (1979). "Forms, Types, and Tokens in Aristotle's *Metaphysics*," *Journal of the History of Philosophy*, 17, pp. 371–81.

Owen, G. E. L. (1978). "Particular and General," *Proceedings of the Aristotelian Society*, 79, pp. 1–21.

Sellars, W. (1957). "Substance and Form in Aristotle," *Journal of Philosophy*, 54, pp. 688–99.

Wedin, M. V. (2000). *Aristotle's Theory of Substance: The "Categories" and "Metaphysics" Z* (New York: Oxford University Press).

Whiting, J. E. (1991). "Metasubstance: Critical Notice of Frede-Patzig and Furth," *Philosophical Review*, 100, pp. 607–39.

Witt, C. (1989). *Substance and Essence in Aristotle: An Interpretation of "Metaphysics" VII–IX.* (Ithaca, NY: Cornell University Press).

Woods, M. J. (1967). "Problems in *Metaphysics* Z," in J. Moravcsik (ed.), *Aristotle: A Collection of Critical Essays* (New York: Anchor), ch. 13, pp. 215–38.

13

Causes

R. J. HANKINSON

This chapter is concerned with Aristotle's account of a key Greek concept, that of an *aitia* (sometimes *aition*), a cause or explanation, and of his analysis of the various types of entity that fall under it. I shall proceed by way of analyzing his best-known and most compendious treatment of the issue, in *Phys* II.3, and relating the findings of that analysis to other treatments, both theoretical and applied.

The term we are considering started life as an adjective (a fact which explains its alternative endings – scholars have searched, usually unsuccessfully, to find significant differences between them; certainly they seem interchangeable in Aristotle), *aitios*: to call something *aitios* for something else is to hold it responsible for it. The notion of responsibility thus signaled has, as in English, a broad semantic range, moral, causal, and eventually legal. But it is in the first instance primarily said of persons: if you are *aitios* for something, then it is down to you; and you are liable for praise (or blame) on its account. This usage goes back (at least) to Homer; and numerous examples of it can be found in the intervening period.

Aristotle and His Predecessors

Aristotle was acutely aware of the contributions of his predecessors, even while he was on occasion less than entirely fair to them. He was the first systematic historian of philosophy, and indeed thought that such a history was an indispensable part of the proper methodology of discovery. As he says in *Met* a.1 993a27–b8, knowledge is in a way difficult and in a way easy: difficult, since no one can know everything; easy, in that everyone knows something. Accordingly he submits the views of his predecessors on questions of nature, change and explanation to extensive, if at times vituperative, review; and in accordance with that methodological precept, he finds something of use in most of them.

From the sixth century onwards, Presocratic philosophers sought to account for natural phenomena (thunder, lightning, earthquakes, the structure and movement of the heavens) in naturalistic terms, as the result of the interplay between natural forces and the properties of materials. This process culminated in the complex physical systems of the fifth century, pre-eminently the atomism of Democritus, and the continuum-theories of Empedocles (based on four elements, earth, water, air and fire, compounded and dissolved by the two cosmic forces, Love and Strife) and Anaxagoras (for whom all macroscopic stuffs were mixtures of an indefinite number of elements, under the general control of Mind).

The early Presocratics at least attempted to understand the world; and for the most part their intuitions were reasonable, at least in that they were searching for basic principles of very general applicability. But they all fell short, he thinks, in their more or less exclusive concern for *material* explanations (*Met* A.3 983b6–984a19):

> While all generation and destruction may well be from one or more elements, still why does this occur, and because of what cause (*aition*)? For it can't be that the substrate itself moves itself. I mean for instance that neither wood nor bronze are responsible (*aitios*) for each of their changes: it's not the wood which makes the bed or the bronze the statue, but something else is the cause of the change in each case. To investigate this is to investigate the *other* cause, that from which comes the origination of change. (*Met* A.3 984a19–27)

Dynamism has to enter the picture somewhere, as thinkers such as Empedocles, with his contrasting cosmic forces, realized (A.4 985a2–10):

> People like this, then, seem to have grasped the two causes which we distinguished in the *Physics* [i.e. the material and the efficient: see further below], up to a certain point, but in a confused and unclear manner. (A.4 985a10–13)

Moreover some earlier thinkers went a little further:

> For neither fire nor earth nor anything else of that sort seem a likely cause of things either being or becoming good and beautiful, and nor did they seem so to them. Nor can it be right to entrust such a matter to chance and fortune. (A.3 984b11–15)

Aristotle commends Anaxagoras for introducing reason into the picture, as being part of the explanation for the goodness of things (984b15–22); although he shares Plato's dismissive attitude to his deployment of it (cf. *Phaedo* 96a–99d): he wheels it on like an *ad hoc* deus ex machina to get him out of difficulties, rather than employing it as a general principle (A.4 985a18–21). For Aristotle, as for Plato, no Presocratic was able seriously to account for the orderly arrangement of things. (Aristotle treats the Pythagoreans, as precursors to Plato (*Met* A.5); and the Pythagoreans (at any rate Philolaus) were certainly concerned with form, in the sense of that which imposes limitations, or structure, on matter's infinite variety. Plato also talks of form in terms of unity being imposed upon the quantitatively indefinite (*Met* A.6 987b18–988a1; cf. *Philebus* 16b–19b).)

For Plato, the appropriate questions to ask are not: What is everything made of? Or: How do the elements serve to explain the properties of things? But: Why are things arranged the way they are? The appropriate answer is: because it is better that way (*Phaedo* 99a–d; cf. *Timaeus* 28a–30c). The job of the theorist, then, is to show how things are indeed for the best, given various reasonable constraints imposed by the nature of the materials to hand, and to sketch an account of explanation consistent with these strictures. Grand, untestable physical hypotheses, such as the atomist notion that the worlds are held together by vortices, won't do the trick (*Phaedo* 99b); one must supply an intelligible answer to the question how have things come to be the way they are (it is for Plato a conceptual truth that nothing comes to be without an *aition*: *Timaeus* 28a); and a cause is, as he says in the *Cratylus* (413a), that because of which something comes to be. But this "because of" is artfully vague: what sorts of thing *are* appropriately said to be those because of which particular events occur or states of affairs are realized? In *Phaedo*, he identifies the materialists' error as that of confusing mere prerequisites (the material bases of things) with real causes (99a–b; cf. *Timaeus* 45b–46d). Properly causal questions are to be answered in terms of form and finality, structure and purpose.

Thus in Aristotle's assessment, Plato also really only distinguishes two types of cause, the material and the formal (A.6 988a7–17). He sums up: different thinkers have stumbled on different types of cause, the material, the efficient, and (albeit confusedly) the formal; but none, he thinks (in spite of Plato's insistence in *Phaedo* and *Timaeus* on the importance of teleological considerations), has done justice to the final cause, that for the sake of which things come into being (A.7 988a18–b21). Finally, in chapter 9, he subjects the Platonic theory of Forms to a series of sharp criticisms. The theory is both unnecessary and incoherent; Forms cannot explain why their particular sensible compliants come to be (991a19–32, 992a24–b9; cf. Λ.6 1071b14–17); and they cannot give a satisfactory account of our states of knowledge either (992b24–993a10); "to say that they are 'exemplars,' and that other things 'participate in' them, is to talk vacuously, and to indulge in poetic metaphors." Thus Plato's "naïve account of explanation," his insistence that he understands no way of explaining why particular things are beautiful "other than the presence within it of . . . Beauty itself" (*Phaedo* 100d), is just that: naïve. Of course for Plato there is much more to it than that: his is a metaphysical, and not merely a semantic theory. It is because it stands in the appropriate relation to a real object, the Form of Beauty, that a beautiful thing is beautiful. All the same, Aristotle surely has a point when he castigates the Platonists for the arbitrariness of their Formal postulates.

Three more features of Plato's account are worth brief consideration. First, the emphasis on the formal (indeed Formal) nature of causation allows Plato to adhere to what he takes to be a basic principle of explanation: if A is responsible for B, then it must be so invariably; it cannot also be responsible for not-B; equally, not-A cannot account for B either (*Phaedo* 100e–101b). Moreover, causal explanation typically involves the world of becoming; but ultimately the causes themselves must be in some sense eternal (*Timaeus* 28a–b). Finally, it would be "blasphemous" to hold that the universe as a whole "is ruled by the power of irrationality and randomness . . . to say that Mind orders everything is adequate to the visual evidence of the universe, the sun, moon, stars and all their revolutions" (*Philebus* 28d–e).

The Theory of the *Physics*

Aristotle, then, thinks that causation (and explanation) comes in a variety of forms, a variety which none of his illustrious predecessors has fully appreciated; and that is exactly what he says when he addresses the issue in his own voice in chapter 3 of Book

II of the *Physics*. There are four types of *aitia*: material, formal, efficient, and final, as later generations were to know them. They are all, he says (*Phys* II.3 194b16–17), different ways of answering the question "why," and are as such intimately associated with knowledge (an association we will pursue further later on): we do not really know a thing until we know why it is (194b17–23).

"In one way we say that the *aition* is that out of which, as existing, something comes to be, like the bronze for the statue, the silver for the phial, and their genera" (194b23–6). By "genera," Aristotle means more general ways of classifying the matter (e.g. "metal"; "material"); and that will become important. A little later on, he broadens the range of the material cause to include letters (of syllables), fire and the other elements (of physical bodies), parts (of wholes), and even premises (of conclusions: Aristotle re-iterates this claim, in slightly different terms, in *An. Post* II.11). Evidently, the material out of which something is made is relevant to its existence: but in what sense is it supposed to be explanatory? What "why" question does it answer? Here we need to look a little further afield, by way of considering the second type of cause, the formal (examples of which are given in the quotation above). Roughly speaking, form is a restriction of matter: a syllable is letters arranged in a certain way, the statue bronze thus elaborated. And this restriction-relation can apply at a variety of different levels. As Aristotle stresses in *Parts of Animals*, the elements (earth, air, fire and water) are matter for the primary, uniform stuffs (blood, bone, flesh) out of which as matter in their turn are created the non-uniform, organic parts of the body (heart, liver, hands), which in turn, as parts, are matter for the functioning body as a whole (*PA* II.1 646a13–24). Or, to return to one of Aristotle's favorite examples, the bronze is matter for the statue; but bronze is itself, as a metallic alloy, a particular formal development of its constituent metals, which are in their turn elaborations of the basic elements. At each level we can intelligibly ask: what are the structural features (form) in virtue of which the stuff or thing is what it is (at the level in question); and in what and out of what material substrate has that form been generated?

But granted that something's material basis is relevant to what it is, we still need to see how it matters to *why* it is what it is. Of course, we may refer to a statue as a bronze – and in that case the type of material it is made of clearly explains at least the appropriateness of the appellation. But such cases (where a formal type is picked out by its material basis) are relatively uncommon, both in English and in Greek. We need to consider a rather different question: what sorts of material can be endowed with sculptural form? The answer (at any rate for sculpture traditionally construed) will take the form of a relatively small disjunction: stone, wood, metal, terracotta, etc.; and that fact in turn is to be accounted for in terms of the necessary pre-requisites of statuary. The production of an enduring, stable, three-dimensional representational image mandates the selection of materials with a certain conjunction of properties (it's no good trying to make a bust out of cheese) and those properties themselves will directly account for certain features of the finished article, features which are appropriately explained, indeed, at the material level. Aristotle makes this point himself with the example of an axe. An axe is a device for cutting tough material, and so must itself be constructed from resilient material which in addition is capable of being sharpened to a lasting edge. Thus saws will, in general, be made of metal; at any rate, you can't make one of wool (*Met* H.4 1044a28–9; cf. *Phys* II.9 200a10–13).

The other side of this particular coin is, obviously enough, that set of formal features which are induced in the matter and make the thing what it is. As Aristotle emphasized in his historical survey in *Met* A, form is closely related to essence and definition: "another [cause] is the form and the exemplar; this is the formula (*logos*) of the essence (*to ti ên einai*), and its genera, for instance the ratio 2:1 of the octave" (*Phys* II.3 194b26–8). At first sight, the choice of example may seem surprising; but in fact it is pointed. Form is not just shape (of course, the form of a statue, particularly of a realistic portrait-bust, *involves* its shape). We are asking (and this is the connection with essence, particularly in its canonical Aristotelian formulation) what it is to be something. And it is a feature of musical harmonics (first noted and wondered at by the Pythagoreans) that intervals of this type do indeed exhibit this ratio in some form in the instruments used to create them (the length of pipes, of strings, etc.). In some sense, the ratio explains what all the intervals have in common, why they turn out the same.

Similar conditions hold in the natural world. The world divides naturally and realistically into kinds, members of each of which share a certain definitional structure, but one which can be expressed in such a way as to indicate the degree of affinity of the kind with its near neighbors in the scheme of things. These are Lockean, real definitions, accounts which spell out what it is to be a member of the kind in question. Thus (as it might be: Aristotle's actual texts are very sparing in their presentation of definitions other than *exempli gratia*) a human being is a rational, mortal animal: "rational" to distinguish it from other terrestrial creatures, "mortal" to distinguish it from the gods. Canonically, you define something by specifying its genus, and then saying what differentiates it specifically from its congeners; and this is a matter of isolating form (here notorious Aristotelian problems regarding the relations between form, matter, substance and essence may be sidestepped: cf. *Met* Z–H).

But additionally

> there is that which is the primary originator of the change and of its cessation, such as the deliberator who is responsible [sc. for the action] and the father of the child, and in general the producer of the thing produced and the changer of the thing changed. (194b29–32)

In other words the efficient cause. Aristotle's examples here are instructive: one case of mental and one of physical causation, followed by a perfectly general characterization. But they conceal (or at any rate fail to make patent) a crucial feature of Aristotle's concept of efficient causation, and one which serves to distinguish it from most modern homonyms. For Aristotle, any process requires a constantly operative efficient cause as long as it continues. This commitment appears most starkly to modern eyes in Aristotle's discussion of projectile motion: what keeps the projectile moving after it leaves the hand? "Impetus," "momentum," much less "inertia," are not possible answers. There must be a mover, distinct (at least in some sense) from the thing moved, which is exercising its motive capacity at every moment of the projectile's flight (see *Phys* VIII.10 266b29–267a11). Similarly, in every case of animal generation, there is always something responsible for the continuity of that generation, although it may do so by way of some intervening instrument (*Phys* II.3 194b35–195a3). We shall return to this later on.

In the case of the efficient cause too we may refer to the item in question in a variety of different ways. We may call the efficient cause of health the doctor, or more generally the professional, or more generally still a man (195a29–31); and we may refer to it "incidentally" (*kata sumbebêkos*), by its proper name ("Polycleitus"), or even as "a man" or "an animal," rather than in ways which makes its causal role patent ("the sculptor"): 195a32–7. These strictures apply to the other causal modalities; and they bring to the fore an important feature of Aristotle's theory. Properly so-called, his *aitia* are not extensional items. We cannot, in full propriety and with nothing disturbed, simply replace the proper *aition*-term in a cause-giving context with a co-referring expression. For when we refer to the cause of the sculpture as "a man," or even "Polycleitus" our referring-expressions conceal the explanatory facts, which we capture only by designating it in the appropriate way, as "the sculptor," or (even more precisely) as "the art of sculpture resident within him": for this is what really explains why this individual has managed to produce, non-accidentally (this will become important), the item in question. But while *aitia* proper are non-extensional, incidental *aitia* clearly are. If all we are concerned with is correctly identifying the factor responsible, rather than picking it out under the appropriate description, then extensionality reigns. Thus in this regard modern notions of cause closely approximate to Aristotle's incidental causes (or, more properly, causes incidentally identified).

Finally, let us consider final causes:

> Further, there is the cause in the sense of the end; this is that for the sake of which [something is undertaken]. As for instance health is the cause of walking. Why, then, is he walking? We say "in order to be healthy," and think that in so saying we have explicated the cause. (194b32–5)

Goals have an explanatory function; that is a commonplace, at least in the context of action-ascriptions. Less of a commonplace is the view espoused by Aristotle, that finality and purpose are to be found throughout nature, which is for him the realm of those things which contain within themselves principles of movement and rest (i.e. efficient causes); thus it makes sense to attribute purposes not only to natural things themselves, but also to their parts: the parts of a natural whole exist for the sake of the whole. As Aristotle himself notes, "for the sake of" locutions are ambiguous: "A is for the sake of B" may mean that A exists or is undertaken in order to bring B about; or it may mean that A is for B's benefit (*An* II.4 415b2–3, 20–1); but both types of finality have, he thinks, a crucial role to play in natural, as well as deliberative, contexts. Thus a man may exercise for the sake of his health; and so "health," and not just the hope of achieving it, is the cause of his action (this distinction is not trivial). But the eyelids are for the sake of the eye (to protect it: *PA* II.13) and the eye for the sake of the animal as a whole (to help it function properly: cf. *An* II.7).

The Model Applied: Causation in Nature

Aristotle's contention that final causes exist in nature is both crucial and controversial. He rejects the sort of providential teleology offered by the *Timaeus*: Aristotle's God is no designer, and has no concern for the running of the universe; "he" is an intellectual postulate designed to fill out metaphysical reality by allowing for something which is purely actual, a pure actuality which consists entirely in rational contemplation (the best activity) of the best thing (himself: *Met* Λ.7 1072b14–30; *NE* X.8 1178b20–3). For all that, God serves as a final cause for everything, since everything seeks to emulate his perfect activity, insofar as it is capable of so doing (*Cael* II.12). Thus even the elements, in their nisus to attain their natural places, are aspiring (albeit weakly) to divine perfection. It is significant in this context too that Aristotle says, of the elements, that they most fully realize their forms only while at rest in their natural places (*Cael* IV.3 310a21-b1; cf. 311a2–7), and that "the motion of something to its proper place must be supposed to be similar to other sorts of generation and change" (310a21–2). Equally, the elements, in any complex, are "for the sake of" that complex (*PA* II.1 646b5–10: in general, each level is "for the sake of" the next level up the ladder of complexity).

In a similar vein, animals reproduce because that is the closest they can get to immortality (*GA* II.1 731b31–5), which is obviously a good. Equally, sex-differentiation is explained in teleological and hierarchical terms: the male is superior to the female (the alleged reasons for this need not detain us), and it is better to concentrate the better functions in separate organisms, so far as that is possible (*GA* II.1 732a4–12). Male and female are required in the production of complex organisms (Aristotle is aware of plant-gender); and in the division of labor, the male supplies the form and is the initial efficient cause, while the female supplies, in the form of menstrual blood or its equivalents, the matter (*GA* I.2 716a4–7). This controversial story is worked out in the first two Books of *GA* (cf. esp. I.18–22); and it has excited much comment, some ill-informed, and provoked fierce controversy, in particular in regard to the question of how much the female contributes, and whether Aristotle ever calls it "seed" (*sperma*). Two things seem evident, however. First of all, the female doesn't just supply matter, in the sense of some basic raw material. Menses are concocted blood, blood worked up to a considerable formal extent (he says it is "seed, although not in its refined form: for it lacks only one thing, the source [*archê*] of soul": *GA* II.3 737a28–9). It is the final stage of information prior to that required for self-sustaining and regulating life. On the other hand, Aristotle is also clear that, controversial off-cases aside (Aristotle accepts the possibility of parthenogenetic reproduction; but he does not think its existence securely established: *GA* II.5 741a33–5), this material is not on its own capable of producing viable offspring. He instances the case of unfertilized eggs: they grow to a certain point as a result of the female's contribution alone, which of course shows that the latter is not inert; but equally, they cannot get beyond that stage without the imposition of external formal movements conveyed in the semen, which is blood concocted to a higher degree (it is in the male's capacity to engender this higher degree of concoctedness that his superiority largely resides): *GA* I.21 730a23–33, III.1 750b2–4. For all that, the menses have within themselves the potential for being ensouled (except for the highest, rational level, which in an obscure and controversial passage Aristotle says enters the conceptus "from without": *GA* II.3 736b8–29); and this is precisely what it is to be the matter in the appropriate sense.

What of the other causes? Here the picture is muddied by a certain obscurity in Aristotle's own attitude to the categorial status of the relata involved in causal and explanatory relations. Put another way, it is unclear precisely what items are supposed to enter into such relations. In one sense, this is to the good: the range of phenomena Aristotle's account is designed to cover is broad, and as we know from contemporary discussions of causation, there is no consensus as to what causation ranges over. Agents, events, processes, states of affairs, facts? All of the above? Aristotle's instincts here are catholic, but even so a little more precision, and explicit attention to the issue, would have helped. In the case of the efficient cause of generation, however, the answer initially seems to be clear enough:

> the female residue [i.e., the menses] is potentially what the animal is by nature, and it contains the parts potentially, although not actually, and because when something active and something passive come into contact . . . the one immediately acts and the other is acted upon in the manner in which they are active and passive. And the female provides the matter, the male the origin of the change. (*GA* II.4 740b19–25)

The doctrine of active and passive potentiality is spelled out in *Met* Θ.1 1046a4–18; and it obviously connects with the distinction between efficient and material causes. Equally obviously, our passage here makes the male the efficient cause, "the origin of the change." But how and in what sense? As noted above, Aristotle requires that there be a constantly operating cause effecting all stages of a process. It is easy enough to see how the male (in the sense of the father) may be thought of as the *originator* of the process that leads to the conceptus, and thence to foetus, child, and finally adult (although to put things that way perhaps involves a certain metaphysical bias against the female's role) – but in what sense (if any) can it be thought of as being active *through* that process? And how does its causal power get transmitted in the first place?

Aristotle is clear that the male semen serves solely as a vehicle for the transmission of form; once it has accomplished that, it simply evaporates, and no material part of it becomes part of the emerging conceptus (*GA* I.21; cf. II.3, 736a24–7; this view was later treated with scorn by Galen, but it turns out to be closer to the truth than Galen's own view). Offspring are formed "from" the male contribution only in the sense that bed is formed "from" the carpenter (GA I.21, 729b16–19). Aristotle refers to what is transmitted thereby as "motions" (*kinêseis*: 729b5, I.22 730b5–32, etc.), and while this is no doubt deliberately vague, the semen is conceptualized as the means by which the formal structures of the animal are initially induced in the receptive matter. The controversial details of this need not concern us; what matter are the consequences of this account for our understanding of Aristotle's concept of efficient causation (and, not incidentally, of formal and final causation as well). Another passage is worth quoting here at length:

> What is sought now is not the material out of which but the agency by which the parts come to be. For either something outside them makes them, or something which exists within the seed and the semen; and whatever it is must either be a part of soul, or soul, or something which possesses soul. But it seems unreasonable to suppose that anything outside could create anything to do with the viscera, or any of the other parts: for it cannot cause movement without being in contact, and nothing can be affected by it unless it causes movement. Therefore it must be something which exists within the fetation, either as a part of it or as distinct from it. (*GA* II.1 733b32–734a6)

Causation requires contact (as Aristotle spells out at *Phys* VII.2); the carpenter and sculptor work by touching the material they work on. The only difference in the case of nature is that nature operates by permeating its material, rather than simply working it from the outside (*GA* I.22).

The upshot of this is that we now have three distinct items as candidates for efficient cause of the developing embryo: the father, the father's semen (or perhaps rather the motions in it), and "something which exists within the fetation." Part of Aristotle's problem here is biological rather than conceptual: he realizes that he needs to account for its *continuing* development and growth, and in an organized way. Here, after all, is the nub of his disagreement with the atomists and other mechanists (who in this context include the Hippocratic author of *On Seed* and *The Nature of the Child*), who think that everything can be done at the level of elementary physical interactions. No such account is remotely satisfying to Aristotle: it leaves far too much to chance, and as he says (in a passage we will return to later) chance is the opposite of what happens regularly. That is to say, we cannot do without the notion of form, and of its transmission: what accounts for the regularity of natural production is just this, that creatures pass on their specific forms to their offspring. As Aristotle says on more than occasion, human begets human (*Phys* II.7 198a26–7; *PA* I.1 640a25–6). In this sense, it is the father who is the efficient cause in the sense of that which sets the process in train, but of course the father is not there throughout the whole process. This sort of efficient cause, in fact, seems to be on a par with the example given by Aristotle in *An. Post* II.11 94a36-b8, of the cause of the Persian Wars for the Athenians, namely some earlier act of aggression on their part.

But if the father sets things going, something still is needed (on Aristotle's non-inertial understanding of the dynamics of processes) to keep it going: and this comes in at at least two stages. First, the "motions" are transmitted, in the semen, to the menses and begin to inform it; but at a certain point, the structure of the foetus itself takes over and becomes self-directing (not of course self-supporting – it still needs external nourishment and protection from the mother – but the moulding process is controlled from within it). At this point, Aristotle's account becomes very sketchy in its details; but the general picture seems clear enough. Once it has achieved a certain level of internal complexity, the foetus has enough of its potentiality actualized to carry that process along. Of course most of its potentialities (at least *qua* animal as opposed to *qua* foetus) are not yet actual: but it is developed enough to carry on, as it were, under its own steam. At this point, the developing being contains its own efficient cause, that which pushes it towards the final realization of its form.

The Relations between the Causes

And this brings us back again to form and the final cause. In the case of animals themselves, their final causes just are to manifest to the best of their abilities the distinctive characteristics of the species they exemplify (this notion is of course central to the *Ethics*); and in order to do that, they must first realize their adult form. This latter is, in a perfectly obvious sense, that towards which they are tending, and which, unless they are impeded by external, unlucky circumstances, they will achieve. Aristotle just takes it is an obvious datum that the natural world is constructed and operates this way: it consists of a set of internal nisuses for perfection (cf. *Phys* II.8 199b14–33). Of course, in the contingent way of things, not every acorn will become an oak, not every human foetus a human adult. But these are the off-cases, the ones that need explaining (even if in absolute terms they may, as Aristotle is well aware, be far more common). Developmental biology is an error-theory: what needs explaining is why things fail fully to exemplify their form rather than why they manage to do so.

This brings into relief the strengths and weaknesses of Aristotle's theory. On the positive side, there is a certain obvious conceptual economy about the view that in natural processes naturally constituted things simply seek to realize in full actuality the potentials contained within them (indeed, this is what *is* for them to be natural); on the other hand, as the detractors of Aristotelianism from the seventeenth century on were not slow to point out, this economy is won at the expense of any serious empirical content. Mechanism, at least as practiced by Aristotle's contemporaries and predecessors, may have been explanatorily inadequate – but at least it was an *attempt* at a general account given in reductive terms of the lawlike connections between things. Simply introducing what later reductionists were to scoff at as "occult qualities" does not explain – it merely, in the manner of Molière's famous satirical joke, serves to re-describe the effect. Formal talk, or so it is said, is vacuous.

Things are not however quite as bleak as this. For one thing, there's no point in trying to engage in reductionist science if you don't have the wherewithal, empirical and conceptual, to do so successfully: science shouldn't be simply unsubstantiated speculative metaphysics. But more than that, there is a point to describing the world in such teleologically loaded terms: it makes sense of things in a way that atomist speculations do not. And further, Aristotle's talk of species-forms is not as empty as his opponents would insinuate. He doesn't simply say that things do what they do because that's the sort of thing they do: the whole point of his classificatory biology, most clearly exemplified in *PA*, is to show what *sorts* of function go with what, which presuppose which and which are subservient to which. And in this sense, formal or functional biology is susceptible of a type of reductionism. We start, he tells us, with the basic animal kinds which we all pre-theoretically (although not indefeasibly) recognize (cf. *PA* I.4): but we then go on to show how their parts relate to one another: why it is, for instance that only blooded creatures have lungs, and how certain structures in one species are analogous or homologous to those in another (such as scales in fish, feathers in birds, hair in mammals). And the answers, for Aristotle, are to be found in the economy of functions, and how they all contribute to the overall well-being (the final cause in this sense) of the animal.

In fact, Aristotle says, the final cause explanation is the most important of all (*PA* I.1 639b12–20), for it is this towards which the maturing specimen is tending, the fullest expression of the internal structure or *logos*, its form. Here formal and final causes come close to coinciding.; in fact, as Aristotle says in *Phys* II.7 198a24–7:

> Frequently three of these [sc. *aitiai*] coincide; for what something is and that for the sake of which it is are the same, while that from which motion first arises is the same as them in form: for man begets man.

So while evidently in the case of efficient causation considered in this way ("what is the primary origin of the thing in question?") the causal types do not coincide numerically, they do in form. And again, this should occasion no surprise; for the paradigm cases of Aristotelian production are to be explicated as involving the transmission of form from something which has it in actuality to something which is capable of taking it on; any other basic pattern of transmission would, Aristotle thinks, render the stability of natural processes inexplicable. Moreover, in cases of artificial generation, the same relations are maintained, even if the mode of production is different: when a sculptor produces a sculpture he does so because of the form of the art of sculpture which is internal to him; this is exactly why professional sculptors (and other technicians) are able regularly to achieve their goals, unlike the more haphazard results of the unskilled (cf. *Phys* II.8 199b14–26). And this is precisely why Nature, for Aristotle, is likened to a supremely skilful craftsman: it too does nothing by chance, and acts as an artisan that permeates its material, exhibiting formal, final and efficient aspects at the same time. It is important to realize, however, that this coincidence of causal categories is not, for Aristotle, a matter of reduction. It is not that the causal types are really at bottom one and the same thing, or that finality and efficiency are merely aspects of form (or the other way round). Rather all are explanatory features attributable to the same objects and processes: they exhibit equally formal, final, and efficient features (I shall have a little more to say about this later on in the context of discussing explanation and necessity). The final cause, then, exerts no mysterious pull from the future, dragging the currently incomplete development into full actuality; rather it merely serves to emphasize a crucial feature of regular efficient processes: they are goal-directed, and the fulfilment of those goals consists precisely in the full realization of form. As he puts it at *PA* I.1 640a3–7:

> The starting point for the former [sc. the theoretical sciences] is what is; but for the latter [natural science] it is what will be: since health, or a human, is of *this* nature, then such-and-such must be or have been generated; but it is not that, since this is or has been generated, then the other [i.e., the end] is or will be.

Chance and Explanation

We have seen how far Aristotle distances himself from any view which makes chance a crucial factor in the general explanation of things. And he does so on conceptual grounds: chance events are, he thinks, by definition unusual and lacking certain explanatory features: as such they form the complement class to those things which can be given full natural explanations. Aristotle deals with two related concepts, *tuchê* and *to automaton*, which I shall translate, tendentiously, as fortune and chance, at *Phys* II.4–6 (and in related passages).

For Aristotle, chance events (chance being the broader category which includes fortune as a proper subset of itself) are not uncaused, although definitionally they lack proper final causes. Fortunate events are ones which we are in some sense responsible for (although we have not foreseen their outcomes); chance includes cases where no deliberation of any kind could have taken place (even though the result may be to our advantage, as when a stampeding horse happens to avoid danger, or when a tripod falls in such a way that it can serve as a seat: *Phys* II.6 197b13–22). Some hold, Aristotle says, that "nothing comes to be because of fortune, but that there is a determinate cause for everything we ascribe to luck and chance" (*Phys* II.4 195b36–196a3). Aristotle rejects this; but it should not be inferred that he thereby rejects causal determinism. In fact Aristotle has no attitude to *causal* determinism as such (he doesn't clearly entertain the possibility); but for all that, what he says about *aitia* in these contexts is, I think, compatible with both determinism and its rejection, since his real concern is with explanation.

Aristotle offers an example. Consider the case of a man who goes to the agora for some unrelated purpose, but happens upon someone who owes him money and recovers the debt. He didn't go there for this purpose, but he might have done so (had he known), and the outcome is beneficial. This is a case of fortune (*Phys* II.5 196b29–197a8). And it is so because it does not exhibit the proper regularity we associate with purposeful events, whether deliberated or natural; things which happen either always, or for the most part, are outside the scope of chance (*Phys* II.5 196b10–14). In fact, Aristotle assimilates fortune and chance to the category of incidental causes (see above); what he means is that we might, "incidentally," pick out his going to the market as the occasion of the collection of the debt, in the same way as we might ascribe the sculpture to Polycleitus, or the man to my left. But this tells us nothing about the actual *reasons* for the action in this case. Thus this particular event (the recovery of the debt) has no genuine final cause, and the description "going to the market to collect the debt" does not properly apply to it (it wasn't *really* an action of that sort). Thus fortunate events lack genuine final cause explanations (again it should be stressed that this has nothing to do with whether the event itself was caused, only with whether it has a full explanation *under that description*).

At *Met* E.3, Aristotle considers another relevant case: a man becomes thirsty from eating spicy food, so goes to the well to relieve his thirst; there he comes upon brigands who kill him. The meeting is chance, a case of (mis-)fortune, which is to say that there is no determinate explanatory process that can take us from the man's predilection for hot foods to his death by violence. As Aristotle puts it, some causes are themselves generated. The point is that we can see the murdered man's going to the well as part of a coherent, explanatorily unified process (he eats, he gets thirsty, he seeks to assuage the thirst); equally (although Aristotle does not mention this), the presence at the well of the men who will kill him is no doubt also explicable, in terms of *their* desires, predilections, motivations. What has no genuine (i.e. structural) explanation is their happening to be there at the same time (again, obviously, this is perfectly compatible with their coincidence being *causally* determined). There is no general natural correlation between a taste for hot food and violent death.

Explanation and Generality

Here we may follow out another thread in the pattern. For Aristotle, explanations are properly speaking general, or at any rate generalizable. This is particularly obvious in the case of form and finality in nature, which can hardly be given a perspicuous characterization other than in general terms (form, in this sense, just *is* general). But it applies to the other categories too. Material explanations rely on the general potentialities of matter of that type; and efficient causes are, at least typically, ones which can be ranged under general explanatory categories. This feature of the Aristotelian position is given further formal substance from within the context of his general theory of scientific knowledge as outlined in *An. Post* I.1–6. According to Aristotle, properly to understand some proposition of a proper science (here = organized body of knowledge) consists in seeing either why it has axiomatic status (and hence relies on nothing else for its truth), or how it is logically dependent upon other axioms. All scientific truths are thus either basic axioms or derived theorems; and they are all, Aristotle holds, necessarily true (the details here, in particular epistemologically, are obscure; but we can afford to ignore them). Consider the proposition that all men are mortal. This is a theorem, and its theorematic status can be exhibited syllogistically, by finding that higher-order class of beings of which humans are a proper subset and which is such that membership of it is sufficient to explain mortality. One candidate for such a class is that of animals, all of whom are mortal. This yields the familiar argument: all men are animals; all animals are mortal; so all men are mortal. "Animal" functions as the middle term, mediating in the premises between the subject and the predicate of the conclusion. These formal constraints are necessary for a middle term to be explanatory; but they are not sufficient. It is obvious that any number of middle terms might yield sound syllogisms here (replace "animal" with "mammal," or "vertebrate" for example). But in Aristotle's view only one of them will be properly explanatory, for there will be at most one such term which is such that the predicate of the conclusion holds of its subject *in virtue of the fact that* it mediates in this way (intuitively, humans are not mortal because they are vertebrates, or mammals).

Moreover, there are cases where the crucial terms convert (i.e. all and only As are Bs); and yet only one form of the universal generalization will be such as to function properly in an explanation. Aristotle gives examples at *An. Post* I.13: all and only non-twinkling celestial objects are close to the earth; and planets both fail to twinkle and are close by; but only one syllogistic arrangement of such material yields a genuine explanation, and that is because it is their proximity which explains their non-twinkling, rather than the other way round. The argument "all planets don't twinkle; whatever doesn't twinkle is nearby; so all planets are nearby" does not explain *why* they're nearby. Explanation (at least of a single type) is asymmetric (elsewhere Aristotle does allow that two items may be mutually explanatory, as long as the explanation-type is different in each case: thus regular walking explains physical fitness (it's its efficient cause), while the fitness is the final cause of regular walking: *Phys* II.3 195a8–11).

This connection between explanation and logical derivation is important for several reasons, but most obviously it emphasizes the link between Aristotelian explanation and generality. We explain the stars' failure to twinkle by noting that they are part of a distinct class of objects none of which twinkle; anything, then, in the appropriate class will exhibit the same behavior. Equally, consider the example of the cause of the Persian war: this too, Aristotle thinks, can be exhibited syllogistically: the Athenians were aggressors (they raided Sardis), and aggressors are typically warred upon (*An. Post* II.11 94a36–b8). Of course, that's not the only reason for war – and some aggressors no doubt get away with their aggression. (This brings up the general question, which I cannot deal with here, of whether Aristotle thinks that the same cause can have different effects, or the same effect different causes; in brief, the answer is, for ordinary categories, yes: but a properly organized scientific language will match causes one-one with effects.) The generalities, then, need not be universal, which is why Aristotle repeatedly says that the appropriate connections must hold "either always or for the most part" (notoriously he does not spell out exactly how we are to interpret the latter condition; but it seems best to take it as meaning "in the majority of relevant cases," *vel sim.*). For Aristotle, in general the *failure* of some general process-type to result in its normal outcome is to be explained in terms of the interference of extraneous "material" factors, which will not themselves in general be susceptible of general characterization. The point is logical: if we can specify precisely when some general but non-universal correlation will fail to be instantiated, then by simply adding the specification we can replace the former with the latter: "for the most part, As are Bs" will become "All As, given conditions C, are Bs." But then we will have no genuine use (although we might of course have a provisional one) for the "for the most part" propositions in a completed science (cf. *Met* E.2 1027a5–26). Yet Aristotle suggests that such propositions will be an irreducible component even of mature natural science. That they will be so is due to metaphysical considerations: the off-cases just are too various to be susceptible of lucid explanatory grouping. They are, in Aristotle's own terminology, "indeterminate," *aoriston*: his own preferred characterization of the nature of the material (in his sense) itself.

The idea that all genuine explanations can be expressed canonically in syllogistic form is problematic, however; and Aristotle's own examples are confused and confusing. In particular, it is hard to make sense of his example of final cause explanation in terms of the middle term (in *An. Post* II.11 94b9–26), although we have no time to enter that interpretative minefield. Suffice it to say that any coherent attempt to do so will of necessity rely on what one might characterize as the formal characteristics of the items chosen to exemplify each explanation-type: thus we might give a "material" explanation of iron's suitability for saws in terms of the *formal* properties of iron itself, namely its ability to take on and preserve a sharp edge. And the same goes, *mutatis mutandis*, for efficient and final causes (an efficient cause is *one of the right type* to effect such an outcome). And this in turn goes a long way towards accounting for Aristotle's insistence that causal propositions must be necessary. Of course it may be a contingent fact, e.g., that the man met the ruffians at the well (since he had not set out to do any such thing, his action cannot be ranged under some suitable purposive generalization); but it is not contingent, at least in the explanatory sense, that, once he was there, that was the fate he suffered: that's just what happens when (other things being equal) you come upon ruffians. And if that may seem rather strained (as perhaps it should), the strain is caused more by Aristotle's insistence on the fundamental analogies between human action and production on the one hand and natural action and production on the other, rather than by the inapplicability to the latter domain of such considerations (which is what primarily interests him in any case).

226

Explanation, Necessity, and Finality

One more issue regarding necessity needs to be confronted. Both in the *Physics* and in the biological works, Aristotle distinguishes the roles of necessity and the final cause; but he does so in a way that makes them complementary. The appropriate sort of necessity to invoke (generally) in natural contexts is not the necessity of antecedent causal determination, as the materialists supposed, but what Aristotle labels "hypothetical necessity," the necessity of prerequisites: if you're going to produce a house, you need bricks, mortar, timber, etc.; but the materials themselves do not necessitate the generation of the house: they are necessary, not sufficient conditions for it (*Phys* II.9; *PA* I.1 639b20–640a9). This is, of course, another expression of Aristotle's opposition to material reductionism, and his insistence on the need for a more than merely metaphorical appeal to teleology. Of course the materials have something to do with the production of complex structural outcomes; they may even necessitate certain features of those outcomes (things made of heavy elements will be heavy; houses built of bricks will be brick-colored; eye-color, according to Aristotle, although functionally irrelevant, is determined by differential characteristics of the material, the eye-jelly: *GA* V.1 779a27–b7); but they don't necessitate the outcomes themselves. Here we need to invoke the moulding hand of nature, an irreducible organizational tendency inherent in complex structures which strives towards their reproduction and perfection.

But on many occasions, he will say that a particular outcome is the result both of necessity (here to be construed to mean that it is the inevitable outcome of prior states and processes) and teleologically determined, being for the good of the animal in question. Commentators have felt tension here, sometimes incoherence: for if the prior ("material-efficient") factors really do determine the outcome, what possible role is left for the final cause? The result may happen to be to the animal's advantage in some way: but what could be the content of saying that it has happened *because of* that advantage? Such considerations have led some commentators to suppose that Aristotle's account is hopelessly confused, or alternatively that he intended his teleology to be merely heuristic, "*als ob*," a set of Just-So stories. Neither alternative seems to me to be satisfactory. Nowhere, in all the passages where Aristotle talks in teleological terms about nature, does he so much as suggest that it's all supposed to be merely a *façon de parler*. But then how is it supposed to work? To take a much-discussed, entirely typical example:

> Deer are the only animals in which the horns are solid throughout, and are also the only ones to shed them, on the one hand for the sake of the advantage gained by the natural lightness, on the other from necessity because of their weight. (*PA* III.2 663b12–15)

Deer shed their antlers, both because it is good for them to do so (to remove an unnecessary burden), but also simply because they get too heavy for the bone-joints to support: and that is simply a consequence of the way in which the bony material is generated (and concentrated) in the first place. Where's the role for finality?

First of all, we should note that the production of horn, like everything else about an animal's metabolism, is for Aristotle the result of a complex set of trade-offs between what materials are available to the animal and how they can best be put to use. Aristotle regularly notes that, in cases where the use of material for one purpose would be superfluous or redundant, nature typically diverts it to some other use (at least if it can: otherwise it just gets rid of it; but as far as possible it puts such residues to work, thus, for example, endowing humans with abundant facial hair for protection, while at the same time evacuating "moist residues" produced by the brain: *PA* II.14 658b3–10). Thus only single-toed creatures have horns, since the many-toed have other means of defence (in the form of claws); moreover only large animals, with their natural predominance of heavy, earthy materials, produce horns; and when they don't the extra material is diverted to make tusks or more teeth (*PA* III.2 663b24–664a11). Even so, horns sometimes arise without conferring an advantage on their possessors; and they may even be a handicap (*PA* II.16 659a19). The basic point is that nature works within the constraints supplied by the material; but within those constraints it does indeed do some work. Indeed, this may be seen as the absolute heart of Aristotle's theory of natural explanation, and how he positions himself, by triangulation, in contrast with both the materialists and Plato. The mere materials on their own, considered reductively, with their limited set of internal properties, simply cannot contrive and maintain the abundant complexity of life. On the other hand, no non-metaphorical intelligent guiding hand is needed either: nature does not deliberate (*Phys* II.8 199b26–32); and it is not the case (a few hints apart) that in Aristotle's world there is any interspecies teleology: things are not providentially organized for us. Form just is a part, a repeating part, of nature. So in the case of the stag's antlers, it is true to say that they grow naturally, by material accretion; and that when they get to a certain size, they will simply fall off. But that growth and shedding is not to be explained simply in terms of the materials and their properties, nor even in terms of the actual collocations of the materials. They have to be seen as part of a self-regulating system, one in which material necessities play a role, but do not – cannot – account for all outcomes in terms of themselves alone.

Bibliography

Allan, D. J. (1965) "Causality Ancient and Modern," *Proceeding of the Aristotelian Society*, suppl. vol. 39, pp. 1–18.

Annas, J. (1982) "Inefficient Causes," *Philosophical Quarterly*, 32, pp. 311–26.

Balme, D. M. (1987) "Teleology and Necessity," in Gotthelf and Lennox (eds.) (1987), pp. 275–85.

Barnes, J. (1994) *Aristotle: "Posterior Analytics"* (Oxford: Oxford University Press).

Barnes, J. (ed.) (1995) *The Cambridge Companion to Aristotle* (Cambridge: Cambridge University Press).

Cooper, J.M. (1987) "Hypothetical Necessity and Natural Teleology," in Gotthelf and Lennox (eds.) (1987), pp. 243–74.

Frede, D. (1985) "Aristotle on the Limits of Determinism: Accidental Causes in *Metaphysics* E.3," in A. Gotthelf (ed.), *Aristotle on Nature and Living Things* (Bristol: Mathesis Publications).

Freeland, C. (1992) "Accidental Causes and Real Explanations," in L. Judson (ed.), *Aristotle's "Physics"* (Oxford: Oxford University Press), pp. 49–72.

Gotthelf, A. (1976) "Aristotle's Conception of Final Causality," *Review of Metaphysics* 30, pp. 226–54. (Revd. version with added postscript in Gotthelf and Lennox (eds.) (1987), pp. 204–42.)

Gotthelf, A. and Lennox, J. G. (eds.) (1987) *Philosophical Issues in Aristotle's Biology* (Cambridge: Cambridge University Press).

Hankinson, R. J. (1995a) "Science," in Barnes (ed.) (1995), pp. 140–67.

Hankinson, R. J. (1995b) "Philosophy of Science," in Barnes (ed.) (1995), pp. 109–39.

Hankinson, R. J. (1998) *Cause and Explanation in Ancient Greek Science* (Oxford: Oxford University Press).

Hocutt, M (1974) "Aristotle's Four Becauses," *Philosophy*, 49, pp. 385–99.

Matthen, M. (1989) "The Four Causes in Aristotle's Embryology," in T. Penner and R. Kraut (eds.), *Nature, Knowledge and Virtue* (*Apeiron*, 22.4, Edmonton, Alberta), pp. 159–79.

Moravscik, J. M. E. "Aitia as Generative Factor in Aristotle's Philosophy," *Dialogue*, 14, pp. 622–38.

Mure. G. R. G. (1975) "Cause and Because in Aristotle," *Philosophy*, 50, pp. 356–7.

Sorabji, R. R. K (1980) *Necessity, Cause and Blame* (London: Duckworth).

14

Heavenly Bodies and First Causes

SARAH BROADIE

At the opening of *Metaphysics* Λ, Aristotle characterizes the object of his inquiry as "the principles and causes of substances." He proceeds to a main division of substances into (*A*) those that are *changeable and perceptible*, and (*B*) those that are *changeless and non-perceptible*. He subdivides kind *A* into (*A₁*) changeable, perceptible, substances that are *eternal*, and (*A₂*) ones that are *perishable*. Examples of *A₂*, he says, are the plants and animals of our ordinary experience. Under *A₁* (as we know from a number of other passages) Aristotle places the heavens and what he calls "the parts" thereof: the sun, moon, planets, and stars. The question of what objects fall into section *B* is one that Aristotle regards as particularly difficult and contentious. However, it is clear from the context that the domain of the whole taxonomy is *the causal system of substances*. Hence if any substances are going to be recognized in division *B*, this will only be on the assumption of their standing in causal relations to substances in the other two divisions (*Met.* Λ.1 1069a18–b2).

We shall be returning to the question of identifying what falls into *B*. For the moment let us note an important implication of Aristotle's distinction between the *A*s and the *B*s: the *A*s, whether eternal or perishable, are corporeal, whereas the *B*s are incorporeal. This implication depends on two background assumptions: that everything corporeal is changeable, and that everything changeable is or is bound up with something corporeal. Straightaway, then, we are faced with one of the profoundest differences between Aristotle's metaphysics and the materialism which is orthodoxy for many philosophers today: Aristotle believes, or in *Metaphysics* Λ has arrived at believing, that there are incorporeal substances.

He also – and in this respect he is unbridgeably distant from all of us today – believes in two fundamentally different kinds of corporeal substance: perishable and eternal. For us, still rocking on the ripples from Cartesianism, it might seem no contrast could be more stark and basic than that between corporeal and incorporeal substance – Aristotle's *A*s in general and his *B*s. But Aristotle could with equal plausibility have reached his triple grouping by dividing substances first and most fundamentally into (*C*) *perishable* versus (*D*) *eternal*, and then subdividing *D* into (*D₁*): *eternal, changeable, and perceptible*, and (*D₂*): *eternal, immutable, and non-perceptible*.[1] Within the Aristotelian framework, the difference between the *C*s and the *D*s is as basic and rich in consequences as that between the *A*s and the *B*s. It is, *inter alia*, the difference between what is and is not divine.

230

To move forward we must take account of the main facts of Aristotelian cosmology. Aristotle's earth is a stationary sphere at the centre of the universe (*Cael* II.13–14). Round it revolves the multi-tiered heaven. Echelons of this system are marked out by the visible heavenly bodies situated at various distances: the moon is closest to the earth, next is the sun, then the five known planets (Mercury, Venus, Mars, Jupiter, Saturn), then the fixed stars (*Met* Λ.8). It is not the case that there is empty space between these luminaries, or between any of them and the earth; for Aristotle has elaborate arguments proving the non-existence of a vacuum anywhere in nature (*Phys* IV.6–9). Instead, the visible bodies are set in transparent rotating physical spheres centred on the earth. For the fixed stars there is one such sphere, furthest from the centre. In the case of the planets and the sun and the moon, one sphere each is inadequate to account for their complex movements. Rather, the immediate sphere of each is one of a nested set whose diverse rotations all contribute to the observable movements of the luminous object in question (*Cael* II.12 293b31–294a9; *Met* Λ.8).

Roundabout the earth, beneath the last sphere of the moon, are large regions corresponding to three of the four Aristotelian elements. Furthest from the centre is the region or "own place" of *fire*; next in is that of *air*; then that of *water* (which fortunately does not completely enswathe the earth). *Earth* is the fourth (*Cael* IV.3–5, on weight and lightness). The point of calling these "elements" is that they are the ultimate physical constituents of all physical compounds, including the materials of the bodies of living things (*Cael* III.3; *GC* II.8).

This system is unique: it comprises the entirety of the physical universe. The earth is at the absolute center of the world, not just at the center of its own particular system. The sphere of the fixed stars, together with everything it contains, is the sum total of physical reality; and within the circumference of that sphere is the entirety of space. The world is a severely finite sphere, but a sphere with no outside (*Cael* I.9; *Met* Λ.8 1074a31–8).

Everywhere in this universe there is orderly movement and change. The distinct heavenly spheres maintain an unalterable arrangement as they rotate incessantly about the centre, while closer in ("under the moon") there is constant interchange and displacement. Organisms die and give up the constituents of their bodies to the environment; minor portions of the four elements are constantly turning into each other by a cyclic transmutation. Hence in each of the regions occupied by the larger masses of the elements smaller portions of an alien kind are constantly forming. Portions which appear away from the natural place of their kind tend towards it by natural, unforced, locomotion. This behavior expresses their inherent tendency to be in that place. In equally unforced fashion, and expressing the same tendency, they come to rest there and stay unless disturbed. And the same tendency explains the dispositions of the larger masses. These tendencies are in a way purposeful, but they are not animistic. Aristotle is clear that the four elemental materials are mindless and inanimate.

He sees them as essentially characterized by their tendencies towards their natural places. It is the fundamental nature of earth to settle at and around the center of the universe, of fire to settle furthest out under the moon, of water and air to settle in their intermediate positions. Moreover, these four are themselves individually fundamental. Yes, they can transmute into each other, but the structures that enable this are wholly qualitative. The four are not modes or arrangements of some more fundamental

231

empirical matter M such that the particles of M which at a given moment constitute some fire can at a different moment constitute some air through rearrangement. There is no such M. The familiar four are physically ultimate corporeal kinds. Thus there are no universal laws of motion holding of all bodies, or of all fundamental bodies, as such. In the Aristotelian universe, not only are the natures of earth and fire, water, and air, each marked off by a distinctive set of chemical powers, but each has its own distinctive law of natural motion.[2]

It is therefore not surprising to discover that, for Aristotle, the existence of a sort of body whose natural motion is fundamentally different from those of the four sublunary elements, means nothing less than the existence, within the very same physical universe, of a type of physical substance that is fundamentally different from any of the kinds of matter we encounter on or near the earth, in our dealings with our immediate environment. Such an additional kind of substance has to be postulated, according to Aristotle, to account for the circular movement of the heavens. Under the influence of Aristotelian physics, this substance came to be known as the "fifth essence," but Aristotle calls it the *aithêr*. This was an already existing word meaning "sky." Its earlier use had been compatible with different theories as to the material of the sky: some philosophers had thought this was air, others a kind of fire. But in Aristotle's hands, "*aithêr*" comes to denote a *sui generis* kind of matter (*Cael* I.1–4).

This substance fills a theoretical role that is basic to Aristotle's cosmology: the role of *that which is necessarily eternally in movement*. Aristotle argues that time is infinite in both directions, that there is never time without physical change, and that these facts are necessary (*Phys* VIII.1–2). He argues that the necessary truth of the proposition "There is always physical change" can only be guaranteed if there is an eternal first cause of change, and that the immediate effect of such a cause must be a change that is individually absolutely unitary and unbroken. Such a change presupposes a single subject undergoing the change: a change produced by relay from one subject to another would lack the requisite unity. Consequently, there must be at least one eternal or everlasting substance eternally exhibiting a single change.[3] What could such a change be like? For various reasons it cannot be growth or shrinkage or qualitative alteration; it must be locomotion. And of the various types of locomotion only the circular kind can be without temporal beginning and end, hence everlasting and absolutely unbroken (*Phys* VIII.7–9). All this is established from the armchair. Then experience finally identifies for us some actual incumbents of this cosmic role. The overwhelmingly obvious candidates are the circling round the earth of the fixed stars, and the diurnal circling of the sun, which seem to be completely reliable and independent of anything that happens closer to home, and which have surely been going on since time immemorial. An interpretation is found that also covers the less plainly intelligible movements of the other luminaries, and the annual cycle of the sun. Thus the sun *circles* because, more fundamentally, it is set in, or is a part of, an otherwise invisible ethereal sphere that *rotates*, and likewise for the others. The objects in motion are first and foremost the spheres (*Cael* II.8 289b31–290a29). Our distant ancestors, Aristotle thinks, encapsulated a truth when they labeled the sky "*aithêr*," a compound (he believes) of "*aei*" ("always") and "*theei*" ("runs") (*Cael* I.3 270b16–25).

It is a key tenet of the theory that this "always-running" of the heaven is *natural* to it. Things can be subjected to enforced or counter-natural movement in Aristotle's universe. You can lift some earth up, and somehow fix it aloft, or whirl it about in a bucket on a string. Its weight – its natural rectilinear downward tendency – proves all this to be contrary to earth's nature. But since earth and the other elements can be forced against their nature, conceivably the celestial spheres consist of some of those materials kept forcibly in place and made forcibly to rotate. This is implied in the myth of Atlas, the Titan who stands on the earth and supports, while turning, the heavens; also in the theory of Empedocles, who held that the celestial system stays where it is because it has received a whirl that overpowers its downward tendency. Both pictures take the substance of the heavens to be of a downward, earth-like, nature overcome by alien force. To Aristotle any such view is anathema because of his commitment to the *eternality* of the celestial rotations. It is unthinkable to him that a substance should eternally and necessarily (thus, under all physically possible circumstances) have its natural tendency forcibly suppressed, especially if it is a *divinely living* substance (see below) (*Cael* II.1). For the same reason he could not have countenanced (so far as it applies to the heavenly spheres) the modern analysis of rotation as a product of continuous application of force to a body that would otherwise be moving, if at all, in a straight line.

So the places and movements of the celestial spheres are natural to them, which has the momentous consequence that they are physical substances quite different in kind from the sublunary elements or any compounds thereof. This difference is more absolute than the differences obtaining among those four elements themselves. For although the latter are irreducibly different, they share affinities in which the substance of the spheres can have no part. The cycle of inter-transformation is complete with the four; thus there is no room in it for any other sort of matter. The substance of the spheres is not, then, merely broadly ungenerable and imperishable, to the extent required for there to be an eternal subject of eternal motion, but is incapable of even the slightest decay since there is no kind of matter that it can turn into. Again, the four elements cohabit a space in that portions of each can move into and out of the regions of the others, displacing a corresponding amount of the matter that was there. But there is no possible agency whereby a portion of any of the four sublunary elements, or anything compounded of them, could be introduced into the region of the spheres, thereby displacing some *aithêr* into the sublunary realm. Every part of the *aithêr* is necessarily always in its natural region and engaged in natural rotation (*Cael* I.2–3). Finally, the sublunary four can combine into compounds, whereas *aithêr* cannot combine with anything. No amount of it can enter the sublunary realm to combine with any of the sublunary elements; no amount of them can enter the ethereal region to combine with anything there; and above the moon there is no other physical substance with which *aithêr* could combine.[4]

One can see the Aristotelian *aithêr* as occupying the theoretical role for which some of the ancient cosmologies postulated a spatially infinite corporeal first principle that, as it were, ensures the unity of the universe by spatially comprehending and containing everything else, and enduring through and beyond the lifetimes of all other things. Aristotle has a host of arguments against the possibility of an infinite body (*Phys* III.5; *Cael* I.5–7). But he does not, as later philosophers might, reject the notion by simply dismissing the need for a physical substance that somehow holds the world together throughout space and time and requires no holding together itself. Philosophers today

are likely to think that the physical world is unified by the fact that the same fundamental laws of nature apply to all matter anywhere anywhen. This vision is unavailable to Aristotle. Again in other post-Aristotelian philosophies what holds nature
together is a single pantheistic world-soul; and for yet others it is the will of a transcendent creator conferring existence immediately on all created beings. It should be noted
that a pantheistic theory has trouble, if not impossibility, in allowing the souls of
animate things within the world to be genuine though limited first causes of their
behavior, as distinct from channels or expressions of the universal soul. Aristotle's
theory of the *aithêr*, worked out in close harmony with his theory of the four sublunary
materials, offers a unifier that is physical and empirical (for the spheres are empirically
known through the sun, moon, and stars); that literally encompasses everything else
both in space and in time; that determines by its movements (in ways not yet mentioned) the ongoing framework in which the careers of all mortal beings take place;
that even so is self-contained in its own place, hence carries no threat of displacing
them or of overwhelming their powers with its own; and, finally, that allows genuine
metaphysical autonomy to the souls of mortal living substances and hence to those
substances themselves.

The eternal and necessary rotation of the spheres has loomed large in the account
so far, but now we must ask about the exact source of this motion. Aristotle's thoughts
on the question were not static, although the variation may sometimes be due to differences of conceptual emphasis. But there is one fundamental assumption to which
he seems to hold unwaveringly: that the heavenly rotations are expressions, in some
way, of soul and mind.

It is notable, however, that Aristotle accumulates major conclusions about the *aithêr*
by treating it simply as a kind of body whose natural movement is rotation, as if the
case is straightforwardly comparable to those of the four elements. Some of his most
telling arguments speak generically of simple (i.e. uncompounded) bodies and simple
natural movements, and depend on applying this generic perspective to all five kinds
(*Phys* III.5; *Cael* I.5–7). Apparently this had not always been Aristotle's approach. We
gather from Cicero that in a lost and relatively early work Aristotle distinguished
between "natural" and "voluntary" movement, and classed the movements of the sun,
moon, and stars as voluntary. Hence when eventually he designated the celestial rotation a "natural" movement, this must have been a very deliberate move. And indeed
he gains considerable theoretical advantages from putting the *aithêr* on broadly the
same generic footing as the sublunary four. To the modern reader, however, this
approach is bound to suggest the following train of thought: "Ethereal rotation is sufficiently explained by the corporeal nature of *aithêr*: no more needs to be said than that
aithêr rotates round the sublunary region as naturally as fire goes to the latter's periphery and earth towards its centre. But in that case, just as it would be superfluous, and
in any case absurd, to introduce soul, life, or mind to account for the movements of the
four elements, should one not adopt a similar view concerning the *aithêr*?" We may
think it strange that Aristotle, as far as we know, never confronts this objection to his
doctrine that the heavenly movements are due to life, soul, or mind.

We can, however, be sure that he would have rejected the objection outright. It
carries two barbs fashioned on analogy with the case of the four elements: one, the
suggestion that postulating life, soul, or mind for the celestial spheres is unnecessary

for explaining their motion; the other, that the postulate is absurd. The latter suggestion would itself have seemed absurd to Aristotle. To him, what makes it absurd to attribute soul to the elements is not that they have natural movements: after all, most animal species move about "from themselves" – this is paradigmatic of natural movement. But the animals and other living things of our ordinary experience are shapely and organized, and in them the source of continuing organization is the soul, which is also the source of their natural movements. What makes it absurd to attribute soul to the elements is, above all, that they are formless – mere tracts or masses lacking shape and inherent boundaries.[5] The ethereal bodies, however, instantiate the perfect shape of the sphere. Any feeling of ours that geometrical regularity belongs only to the lifeless and mechanical would not have been shared or even understood by Aristotle. Of course, if we think of the celestial spheres as Newtonian objects engaged in a curious kind of inertial motion unique to themselves, namely rotation, then it is gratuitous to explain this motion as stemming from soul. If, on the other hand, by analogy with the shapes of ordinary animals we see the sphericity of the sphere-body as the active expression of a soul that eternally holds this body at an invincible peak of physical wellness, form, and perfection, then in addition to not being absurd it is explanatorily most economical to see the body's unforced rotation as also expressing soul.

Beyond the moon, then, we have a system of divine beings. For the heavenly bodies are alive, and their life and activity is eternal. They are ageless, impassible, beyond reach of chance or brute force; their perfectly regular motion is effortless and therefore blissful. These, for the Greeks, are the attributes of gods. Men have always associated the heavens, or upper region, with gods, and Aristotle's systematic arguments for the eternity of the heavens now show the truth of this popular belief (*Cael* II.1 284a2–14; *Met* Λ.8 1074b1–14).

We may ask in what relation these beings stand to sublunary nature. In a somewhat obscure flight of thinking that is extraordinarily ambitious even for him (*Cael* II.3; cf. *GC* II.10), Aristotle brings the heavens and the sublunary world together by arguing, from the sheer assumption that god exists, (1) that there must be eternal rotation, (2) that there must be sublunary elements that come to be and pass away out of and into each other, and (3) that there must be more than one eternal rotation. The first proposition is proved from the premise that god is eternally active, from which Aristotle immediately deduces that the divine is in eternal motion. Evidently in this passage he simply identifies god's activity with that motion. The second is proved from the premises that the rotating body requires a central body, naturally at rest, round which to revolve: hence there must be earth; but there cannot be earth without its contrary, fire, and there cannot be contraries without intermediates, in this case air and water. The third is proved from the fact that these materials are constantly in flux, since not only do they transform into each other, but by constituting the bodies of the sublunary living species they underwrite the births and deaths of mortal individuals in a cycle without end. This flux implies that there must be more than one eternally rotating body. For if there were only one, it would be the one that is actually furthermost, i.e. the sphere of the fixed stars, whose movement spells eternal sameness, not variegation, hence cannot account for the eternally recurrent variation of coming-to-be. The latter is due to a rotation oblique to the first, involving a seasonally heat-causing luminary, the sun, that affects the areas of the earth differentially in different parts of its annual period.

The divine heaven may seem utterly aloof from the world of coming to be and passing away, but the above argument not only shows how its eternal activity entails the existence of transitory things, but (in the proof of the third proposition) actually treats coming-to-be as that which *explains* why the heaven is plural. The passage begins by asking for the explanation of this fact – presumably as if on the face of it a single rotating sphere would have been more rational – and concludes by stating that several are necessary because "there must be coming-to-be" – as if this were the end served by celestial plurality!

Along with the above argument, which straightforwardly identifies the activity of god with a physical movement, we should notice a similar passage where Aristotle speaks of the "first and highest" divine being, on which everything else in nature depends, as ceaselessly in motion (*Cael* I.9 279a22-b). Presumably, when he composed these passages Aristotle recognized just two kinds of substance relevant to the physical world[6]: both perceptible and subject to change or movement, one divine, ingenerable, imperishable, the other not. The reason for thinking this is that one consequence of introducing the third kind – non-perceptible and changeless – is that *it* straightaway comes to be identified with the "first and highest" divinity.

His recognition of the third kind probably results from a variety of conceptual leads or pressures. The order in which these are presented below is not meant to imply either an order of importance or a relative chronology of their occurring to Aristotle.

(1)   One of the most important differences between the heavens and sublunary substances is that the former are in perpetual motion, whereas the latter are sometimes changing and sometimes not, depending on the circumstances. We have already seen this in contrasting the fifth simple body with the four elements, but there is the same contrast between the fifth body and sublunary compounds. The contrast *substances that are essentially always changing/substances that essentially sometimes change and sometimes do not* suggests a possible third section: *substances that are essentially always changeless*. It is natural to wonder whether anything of this kind exists of causal relevance to the physical world. Of course, if one interacts with philosophers who believe that things do exist which fit that description on the ground that Platonistic Forms or Ideas exist, then, if one objects to the Ideas, and especially, as Aristotle does, to postulating them as causes of sublunary becoming, one might assume for a while that no substance belonging to the system of causes and effects is essentially changeless. On the other hand, if one then comes to think it even possible that the concept *causally relevant essentially changeless substance* could apply to something other than an Idea, one might be disposed to assume, even in advance of proof, that this concept will turn out not to be empty. The fact that elements of the concepts defining the other two sections can logically recombine in a way that unites *always* with *not-changing*, together with the fact that the concepts defining the other two sections evidently capture, in a scientifically commanding way, two great natural groups of known substances, might be enough to make it seem only rational to welcome the new concept as heralding a third natural grouping: which would be only a short step away from taking the third section not to be empty.

(2)   The religiosity towards Ideas which surfaced at times among "friends of the Forms," Plato himself having set the example in famous passages (*Cael* I.9 279a22–b), may have

struck Aristotle – since these were respectable philosophers – as intellectual intimations of the reality of some kind of genuine absolutely changeless and indeed awe-inspiring "separate" substance whose nature and role in the scheme of things the Idea-theorists had misunderstood. In short, there may be a parallel here with Aristotle's attitude to popular belief about the gods: some of it is childish and absurd, as for instance the anthropomorphism and theriomorphism, but some strands reflect a true intuition, for instance the part that connects divinity especially with the upper realms (cf. *Met* Λ.8 1074a38–b14). For another parallel, consider Aristotle's re-fashioning of the ancient notion of the physical infinite into his own theory of the shapely englobing heavens, so as to satisfy in a less problematic way (and thereby justify) the intellectual craving for an all-encompassing being. The suggestion is that he may have seen the theory of Ideas, too, not merely as a mistake and an obstacle to philosophical progress, but as foreshadowing the as yet undiscovered true theory of absolutely changeless causes.

In short, it is reasonable to assume on more than one ground that a certain hospitality towards admitting absolutely changeless causes (since in relation to changeable things they could only be causes, not also effects) helped to shape Aristotle's argumentation in this area.

(3) We come now to arguments. In the cosmology described above, the celestial spheres are alive and in movement. It is natural to say, without further analysis, that they *move themselves*. However, at some point Aristotle looked critically at the notion of self-movement, and concluded that, strictly, the phrase is incoherent. In fact, every so-called self-mover comprises one element that is *subject* of the movement and one that is its *source*, and these are necessarily distinct. From this Aristotle builds his famous general doctrine that every causal series of movements begins with an unmoved, motionless, first mover (*Phys* VIII.5 257a32ff; see also 256b13–257a31). This enables him to argue that a necessarily eternal movement must have a necessarily eternal first mover immutable in all respects. Since we know that there is necessarily eternal movement, we now know that there exists a kind of cause or principle that is absolutely changeless. Such a being is not perceptible, because only physical objects are perceptible, and nothing is a physical object that is completely immune to change. (Non-perceptibility also follows from the theorem that any mover responsible for eternal movement must be without magnitude. Aristotle bases this on the premises (i) that such a mover has infinite power, since its effect, the movement, is of infinite duration, and (ii) that if infinite power belonged to a physical magnitude, this magnitude would have to be infinite; but an infinite magnitude has already been proved impossible (*Phys* VIII.10; cf. *Met* Λ.7 1073a5–11). Baldly stated, these premises seem not particularly plausible. But the first makes sense if understood as assuming that the entire eternal movement, given its absolute continuity, is a single effect, not an infinite succession of finite stages. The second appears less arbitrary if one considers that an account of the sort of mover responsible for an eternal movement will be understood purely functionally: thus assigning a property P to such a mover embodies the claim that P is essential to its causal role or entailed by what is thus essential. It would be impossible to explain why one finite magnitude rather than another, even that of the relevant sphere itself, is essential or entailed by something essential to the role of mover responsible for eternal movement.[7])

How exactly does Aristotle get to the general doctrine that every causal series of movements begins with an unmoved, motionless, first mover? His assumptions are (A1) that everything in movement is moved by something, either itself or something else (*Phys* VIII.4–5 256b3), and (A2) that every causal series of movements begins from a first mover (*Phys* VIII.5 256a21–9). Hence every such series begins from a self-mover. The next block of argument shows that "self-mover" necessarily stands for something complex: nothing can move precisely itself. Therefore the mover-element in a self-mover cannot, as such, be moved at all: not by anything else, and not by itself. Aristotle takes this as meaning that the first mover of a series is motionless, without movement.

Why should we accept A1, that everything in movement is moved *by something*? Aristotle admits that it is hard to see the application to portions of the four elements in natural motion. They are not self-movers even in the loose sense because self-movers in this sense are animals – organic complexes (*Phys* VIII.5 256a21–9). Yet they seem not to be moved by anything outside them. Aristotle responds that even here the elements are moved *by something else*, because they owe their natural movements to agents which have removed impediments, and also (indirectly) to the agents of their coming-to-be in the first place. After shoring up A1 by this *ad hoc* stretching of the concept of *that by which something is moved* to cover enabling factors, Aristotle treats the premise as unassailable, and pushes on to apply it to the case of the eternal motion. But what he never considers is that something might just be in movement without being *moved by* anything, whether itself or something else. It would be unmoved in the sense of not being moved by anything, yet it would be not at all motionless. If this is a coherent description, and Aristotle says nothing to show otherwise, then why not apply it to the heavens in their eternal and unimpedible rotations? That would be to treat the motion of the heavens as metaphysically primitive. If the heavens are not moved *by* anything, they are not moved by motionless first movers. Nor are they self-movers in the loose sense. (Does this spell death to the idea that the heavens are animate? Not necessarily. The idea would be endangered if we insisted that the soul of an animate being is what moves the body, for if, as we are supposing, the celestial spheres *just move*, then they are not moved by any souls. However, it may be possible to think of the spheres' rotations as expressing their souls without thereby thinking of them as due to mover-souls. The case is not closed.)

(4)　Why does Aristotle find literal self-movement impossible? His reasons are crabbed in the extreme, but the spirit of them is important as it sheds light on his refusal, or inability, to consider that something might be in movement yet not *moved by* anything. Aristotle understands movement or change in general as "imperfect (or: incomplete) activity (or: fulfilment, or: realization)."[8] The subject of change S lacks a certain perfect or complete activity, say of that of being in the state F, and the change, i.e. S's becoming F, is the activity of the potential of S, when not-F, for being F; on the other hand, the agent or mover of this change is somehow already in possession of the complete activity of being F. The mover must differ from the subject or it would be both F and not-F. The crucial point is the connection between change of whatever kind and incompleteness. We may think we can frame the concept of a kind of physical substance that *just is* in movement, eternally and necessarily (and even animatedly), without any mover. But from Aristotle's standpoint, this would be incoherent. To fit the description, the substance must have complete autonomy over its activity, so that the activity, i.e. its movement, is completely unconditioned by any independent circumstance or origin. But how could a substance that essentially expresses its nature through movement, which is incomplete activity, be complete enough to enjoy such perfect autonomy over what it does? To give this its cosmological application: either the rotation of the heavens is not to be considered an incomplete activity, in which case we get the absurdity that it is not really a movement at all; or the rotation depends on a mover, and therefore on a first mover that will be non-physical.

(5)   It has been assumed all along that the first cause of heavenly rotation is sublime in the scale of value, even at the stage when it seemed reasonable to think of this first cause as the sphere itself in self-movement. Now if the excellence or goodness of something is rationally connected with its causality, so that it is by its goodness that it causes, not by anything else, then *final* causality, or some similar relation, must be the mode of causality in play (*Met* Λ.7 988b6 ff). Unaided goodness as such has effects or makes a difference only in so far as there is something that exists or acts for the sake of the good object, or out of love or appreciation of the good object as good. But the object's being a cause in this way does not require it to "do" anything "to" the beings which are affected. Conceiving of the first mover either as that for the sake of which the motion is engaged in, or as causing "as an object of love,"[9] reinforces the conclusion already reached that the first mover is necessarily motionless; for it gives a model of how something motionless can function as a cause. Of course, something whose nature is bound up with movement, such as celestial sphere$_n$, might function as an object of love for the sake of which sphere$_{n+1}$ is moving; so even if X is a necessarily *motionless cause* entails *X causes as that for the sake of which/object of love*, the converse does not hold. (The converse would hold, however, if it were the case that a sphere (1) subserves or loves X *as first cause of necessarily eternal movement*, and (2) is correct in taking X to be such a cause.[10])

These, then, are the ingredients of the theory of the third kind of substance presented in *Metaphysics* Λ.6–10. That theory has highlights omitted or not foregrounded above. It stresses the pure and complete *activity* of the third kind of substance. It identifies this activity with *intellection*, in that our own intellection at its best provides a model for our thinking about the activity of the supremely divine substances. It emphatically declares the supreme *pleasantness* of the life that is (rather than: is lived by) the supreme substance, "the principle on which depend the heavens and the world of nature." It displays its findings to the Platonists: "it is clear then from what has been said that there is a substance which is eternal and immovable and *separate from sensible things*." Finally, triumph of triumphs, it supplies what Platonism could not: an obvious, scientifically impeccable, procedure for deciding the number of these incorporeal substances and cosmic first causes. Since what they are is sources of eternal rotation, there must be as many of them as there are rotating spheres needed to account for the observed movements of sun, moon, and stars. For the precise number we look to the best astronomical theory (*Met* Λ.8).

The separate, incorporeal, unmoved mover of the furthest sphere is the supreme god, and the incorporeal unmoved movers of the other spheres are divinities too, being, like the former, eternal blissful sheer activities. We might expect this theology of incorporeals to demote the eternal corporeal and moving substances to non-divine status: but we would be wrong. Aristotle continues to assume that the heavens are divine. In fact, he sees this as giving us a special reason to affirm the eternity of the incorporeal, separate, causes of celestial motion: those causes have to be eternal precisely because they are causes of "so much of the divine as appears to us [sc. by sense perception]" (*Met* Λ.1; cf. *Phys* II.4 196a33; *NE* VI.7 1141a34–b2).

Its richness notwithstanding, the theory of incorporeal substance in *Metaphysics* Λ is incomplete. It primarily says what must be postulated to account for eternal celestial movement, and on this score some important issues remain unclear. For example, the supporting argumentation from *Physics* VIII often seems to treat first movers in general as efficient causes. How does this fit with the view that a first mover of the heavens moves as a final cause (or as an object of love)? Or are these alternative conceptions, marking different stages of Aristotle's thought? It is presumably as an ensouled being that each sphere loves its unmoved mover. Is the unmoved mover then the same as the sphere's soul (which is thus in love with the activity that it itself is, this activity being a divine intellection), or is the unmoved mover a being wholly distinct from the ensouled sphere? Is the latter implied by the assertion that it is "separate from sensible things"? If so, why is a substance as separate as *that* needed to account for necessarily eternal movement? Why does the sphere's love of its unmoved mover give rise to rotation? Are there two sphere-activities, rotation and loving the unmoved mover, or could these be different aspects of a single activity?

One might also ask: if the sphere-souls are fixated on their unmoved movers, while the latter, we are told in *Metaphysics* Λ.9 (although this may apply only to the ultimate mover of the all-containing sphere), engage only in "thinking on thinking," then how do any of these eternal causes, whether first and unmoved or in motion and intermediate, connect with the world of perishables? Aristotle answers this in *GC* II.10. Perishables are connected to the eternal through imitation. The imperishable eternal is imitated by the eternity of the perishable generations (cf. *An* II.4 415a26 ff.; *GA* II.1 7731b19–732a1). But what exactly is doing the imitation? Perhaps no perishable particulars as such; rather, their behavior exhibits an eternal pattern, and this is the imitation. But one might think of the particulars as themselves fixated on the imperishable and thereby contributing to the pattern. Their mindless willingness to exist in a miserably non-divine way, i.e. at the price of perishing and making room for others, is their mode of attention to the immortal. *What* do the perishables thus imitate? Not the ultimate causes, the incorporeal unmoved movers, but something that belongs on the level of imperishable *moved* movers, namely the annually circling sun.[11] Aristotle is clear that the sun, approaching and retreating from the terrestrial hemispheres, is efficient cause of the conditions of generation and perishing.[12] But the suggestion that the flux of the perishables in response to those conditions is a sort of imitative heliolatry[13] adds something: it gives them, too, an active and non-incidental part in ensuring the succession of the generations and thereby upholding the eternal completeness of the entire mortal-*cum*-immortal physical world.

Notes

[1] The kind C would have been the same as A_2, D_1 would have been the same as A_1, and D_2 would have been the same as B.

[2] Elemental inter-transformation: *GC* II.2–5; no single more basic physical stuff: *Cael* III.5.

[3] For the general point, see *Phys* VIII.6 259b32–260a11, 10, 267a21ff; for the eternity of the heavens specifically, see *Cael* I.3 and 9–12.

[4] Thus it is a mistake to call *aithêr* the fifth "element," although this label is often used.

[5] They are also without micro-structure.

[6] At *Cael* I.9 279a16–22, he speaks as if there are divine beings "outside the heaven"; but he does not suggest that anything physical is due to them.

[7] The argument is usually assumed to apply only to the mover as efficient cause, but the strictly functional reading abstracts from the mode of causality, hence could apply to a final cause. See below.

[8] *Phys* VIII.5 257b7–9 (for the translation of which see Graham (1999: 15, 97); the *Revised Oxford Translation*, vol. 2: 430, is incorrect); III.1–3; cf. VIII.1 251a8–9.

[9] Aristotle gives both formulations. Even if close in meaning, they are not equivalent. It is worth noting that Aristotle does not state that the spheres by their motion imitate the activity of the unmoved movers, although he is commonly interpreted as holding this. His explicit remarks about cosmic imitation ascribe it to perishables.

[10] But there may be an undesirable circularity in saying that X causes as object subserved, or as object of love, while at the same time saying that the subservience or love in question are for X as some sort of cause.

[11] Cf. *Met* Θ.8 1050b28–30; from the context, the objects imitated are the heavenly bodies.

[12] At *GA* IV.10 he also assigns a small role of this kind to the moon.

[13] This leaves it open whether the perishables imitate the sun's circle *simpliciter*, or as an effect (or representative) of the relevant unmoved movers.

Bibliography

Frede, M. and Charles, D. (eds.) (2000). *Aristotle's "Metaphysics" Lambda* (Oxford: Oxford University Press).

Gill, M. L. and Lennox, J. (eds.) (1994). *Self-motion* (Princeton, NJ: Princeton University Press).

Graham, D. (1999). *Aristotle, "Physics" Book VIII* (Oxford: Clarendon).

Guthrie, W. K. C. (1939). *Aristotle: "On the Heavens"* (Cambridge, MA).

Judson, L. (1994) "Heavenly Motion and the Unmoved Mover", in Gill and Lennox (1994), pp. 155–74.

Kahn, C. (1985). "The Place of the Prime Mover in Aristotle's Teleology", in A. Gotthelf (ed.), *Aristotle on Nature and Living Things* (Pittsburgh, PA: Mathesis), pp. 183–205.

Kosman, A. (1994). "Aristotle's Prime Mover," in Gill and Lennox (eds.) (1994), pp. 135–54.

Ross, W. D. (1966). *Aristotle's "Metaphysics,"* vol. I, intro. and ch. 4, "Aristotle's Theology" (Oxford: Clarendon).

Solmsen, F. (1960). *Aristotle's System of the Physical World* (Ithaca, NY: Cornell University Press).

Sorabji, R. (1988). *Matter, Space and Motion* (Ithaca, NY: Cornell University Press).

Waterlow [Broadie], S. (1982). *Nature, Change, and Agency in Aristotle's "Physics,"* ch. V (Oxford: Clarendon).

B. Physics

15

Mixing the Elements

THEODORE SCALTSAS

All bodies in the sublunary world are composed of mixtures of all the primary elements – fire, air, earth, and water. Aristotle argues for the primacy of these four elements in the constitution of objects in our world. He further develops an original theory of mixing of elements to explain the formation of uniform matter such as flesh, oil, or granite. His theory of the mixing of the elements has received much attention in the past couple of decades, resulting in an exciting array of interpretations that have also generated contributions to contemporary philosophy. In what follows I offer an account of Aristotle's theory of the elements and their mixtures that addresses the challenges encountered by earlier readings.

The Early Elements

The earliest conception of the elements out of which things in the world are made up, in Greek philosophy, is that of elemental *stuff* rather than particles. Thales of Miletus took water to be the fundamental element and everything else was derived from it. His student, Anaximander of Miletus, introduced the opposites into cosmological explanation and thought that things in the world are different combinations of the basic oppositions, the hot and cold stuff that came out of the subsisting omnipresent indefinite *apeiron*. A further disciple of Thales, Anaximenes of Miletus, took air to be the basic element of the cosmos, from which all other things derived by its thickening or rarefying. Still in domain of stuff-cosmology, Xenophanes of Colophon took earth to be the basic element, while Heracleitus of Ephesus held fire to be the elemental foundation of the world from which all other elements were derived.

The first departure from the qualitative explanation of the constitution, the generation, and the change of things is made by Empedocles of Acragas and Anaxagoras of Clazomenae, who could be described as stuff-pluralists, falling in between the first cosmologists and the atomists. Empedocles thought there were four kinds of stuff, earth, water, air, and fire, and the things in the world were combinations of parts of each kind of stuff. The elemental stuff remains unchanged in their combined state. Anaxagoras did not delimit the elements to the four kinds but allowed for numerous kinds, corresponding to the kinds of natural thing such as bone and flesh. Each kind was always combined with particles of the other kinds, and although the particles were divisible, they were unchanging.

Leucippus was the first cosmologist we would consider an atomist, along with his student Democritus of Abdera. For Leucippus matter consists of indivisible particles that are imperceptible and have particular geometrical shapes. For Democritus, who introduced the term "atomon" (indivisible, although it is a matter of controversy whether theoretically or only physically indivisible), atoms were unchanging, eternal solids of different shape, size, and weight. Atoms come together to form compounds giving rise to the different kinds of thing in the world. Both believed that the atoms moved in empty space.

Finally, Plato, in his late work the *Timaeus*, proposed that the world is built out of four types of ideal polyhedra, corresponding to earth, water, fire, and air. These are composed of plane triangles of particular shapes which are the indivisible geometrical atoms. Geometrical combinations of polyhedra of one or more kinds can produce polyhedra of another kind, thereby generating one kind of stuff from the others.

It is against this recent, for Aristotle's era, wave of atomism, that Aristotle reacts with a series of detailed criticisms and returns back to the qualitative cosmology of the elements, but embedded in a theory of powers. Although this invites comparisons to contemporary theories of matter, it is not what we shall study here. Rather, we shall focus on the interactivity of the elements in mixing, in order to uncover a further dimension of Aristotle's hylomorphism – his theory of the matter-form relation.

Aristotle's Elements

Aristotle sets out to explain the constitution of things in the world through the process of their generation and corruption. He begins with the elements: "an element . . . is a body into which other bodies may be analysed" (*De Caelo*, 302a15–16); if there is to be generation in the world, there needs to be more than one element; for otherwise, every thing would be that element in merely altered states (*Generation and Corruption*, 332a6–9). Change is to contraries (e.g. from being hot to being cold, GC 332a7–8); but contraries do not change into each other (e.g. it is not the hot which becomes cold, but the hot body, 329b1–2); nor do contraries underlie each other as matter (e.g. the hot does not constitute the cold, 329a32–3); rather, a third thing, the matter, underlies the contraries and remains through the change (332a7–18). The matter is inseparable from the contraries, and with them constitutes the elements (329a24–7).

Aristotle explores which contraries are the primary ones for the constitution of tangible bodies by considering several candidate pairs of contraries. He engages in a characterization of the various contraries such as viscosity, softness, hardness, liquidity, and solidity, in terms of their functional properties, on the basis of which he concludes that some are derivable from others: "all other differentiae are reducible to these four primary ones, whereas these cannot further be reduced to any smaller number" (330a24–6). The four primary contraries are the hot, the cold, the wet, and the dry (329b25–31).

On the basis of the four contrary qualities, Aristotle derives that their combinations result in there being four elements or primary bodies: "fire is hot and dry, air hot and wet (for air is something like steam), water cold and wet, and earth cold and dry" (330b3–5). The four elements have natural places in the sublunary world, and a natural movement by which they get there: "fire and air belong to that which moves towards the boundary, earth and water to that which moves towards the middle" (330b32–3). In *De Caelo* he explains that earth is absolutely heavy, and moves naturally downwards towards the centre of the universe, if not impeded, while fire is absolutely light, and moves naturally upwards. Air and water combine these properties and are intermediate, "since while they rise to the surface of some bodies they sink to the bottom of others" (311a23–4). Their natural movement is explained in terms of their lightness and heaviness: "that which produces upward and downward movement is that which produces weight and lightness" (310a31–2). Since, as we have seen in *Generation and Corruption*, all other differentiae of bodies are reducible to the four primary ones, "that which produces" the movement and the weight and the lightness is to be traced to the primary contraries.

The notion of being absolutely light and absolutely heavy in *De Caelo* is an indication of the way Aristotle understands the four primary contrary qualities. The hot, for example, in fire and air, is absolute heat, and the wet in water and air is absolute wetness. So understood, the four primary qualities in *Generation and Corruption* are in fact contradictories, as Williams also observes, rather than contraries.[1] But combinations of the primary elements produces material that possesses the contraries to various degrees.

Aristotle considers various alternative models for the generation of the primary elements, and concludes that their generation is reciprocal from one another. What makes this possible is their composition in terms of pairs of contraries which the matter of each element can lose or gain. Thus "from fire there will be air if one of its properties changes, the former having been hot and dry whilst the latter is hot and wet, so that if the dryness is conquered by wetness there will be air. Again from air there will be water if the heat is conquered by cold, the former having been hot and wet, the latter cold and wet, so that if the heat changes there will be water" and so on (331a26–32). No element has any type of priority over the others with respect to generation and corruption.[2]

Combining the Elements

Every object that is not uniform is composed of uniform stuff (321b18–19). Nonuniform objects are those whose parts are functionally and materially of different types, e.g. a tree, a house or an animal. The leaves of the tree are not roots, nor are they composed of wood, and the finger of an animal is not a tooth, nor composed of the same stuff as it. But the stuff that the nonuniform objects are composed of *is* uniform, e.g. flesh, bone, and blood for an animal, and wood and soft tissue for a tree. So uniform stuff is the material of the objects in the world around us. It is therefore significant for Aristotle's investigation of nature that an account be given of the generation of uniform matter. As we would expect, and as we shall see, there is an intimate connection between the primary elements and uniform matter. All uniform matter is composed of all four of the elements; it is generated by a process that Aristotle calls mixing. What is metaphysically significant is that mixing is different from, and does not involve, substantial composition, although a new entity is created through mixing. By that I mean that in a mixture, matter is not related to form in the way that matter and form make up a substance; the relation in a mixture is not that of constitution, which is why mixing enriches Aristotle's theory of hylomorphism. Understanding Aristotle's account of this alternative metaphysical phenomenon of generation is our task in what follows.[3]

We can hardly improve on Aristotle's introduction to the problem of mixing. He begins with a puzzle he inherited (327a33–b6): there are three possibilities, presumed exhaustive, of an account of mixing, none of which delivers the phenomenon. First, if the things that have been mixed still persist unaltered in the mixture, then they have not been mixed since they remain the same as they were before they entered the mixture. Secondly, if either of the original ingredients is destroyed in the process of mixing, then they are not mixed since there is only one remaining, while in a mixture the ingredients are in the same condition. Thirdly, it follows that there is no mixing if both ingredients are destroyed in the process, since they cannot be in the state of being mixed in the mixture if they are not at all (holôs ouk onta).

It may appear that the outlined possibilities suffer from a rather obvious lacuna, namely, that the first option can be subdivided into two: they both persist unaltered, or they persist altered. But this would not affect the puzzle. If both ingredients persist in the mixture, each of them in an altered state, since each could have been found in that same state independently of being mixed, there is no reason to suppose they are mixed; there is nothing that marks off their state as mixed rather than unmixed. This presupposes that for an ingredient to be mixed with another is not for them to come to some external relation that respects their claim to persistence. Such relations between items abound without the items thereby becoming mixed with each other. In general, we need to assume that for the puzzle to have a bite, no state in which the ingredients can be when unmixed will explain how they are in a mixture, since they can be in that state unmixed. That this is what Aristotle has in mind is confirmed by the fact that he takes this puzzle to invite us to differentiate between mixing on the one hand, and generation and corruption on the other (327b6–9); the qualification of the first horn that they persist unaltered plays no role in the dilemma; the relevant factors in the reasoning are only persistence and corruption, not alteration.

So we have learned that mixing cannot be explained in terms of the ingredients persisting or ceasing to be. But before offering his explanation of mixing, Aristotle introduces a further condition: "when two things are mixed each must exist as a separable thing" (327b21–2). A thing is not mixed with its affections, or its dispositions, since neither affections nor dispositions ever exist separately without belonging to some subject. What is initially surprising is that Aristotle invokes this separateness condition for mixing to exclude these cases, although he has just achieved the same effect on the basis of the conditions of the initial puzzle. He has just pointed out that affections and dispositions cannot be mixed with the things that have them because the affections and dispositions are preserved (327b15–17, b29–30). So these cases are already blocked by the first horn of the dilemma. If something persists, whether it enjoys an independent or a dependent existence, it cannot be in a state of being mixed while persisting. Affections and dispositions persist when they come to be possessed by a substance; when a body becomes white, "both remain in actuality . . . the body and its whiteness" (327b29–30). Why then introduce the separateness condition since persistence suffices? There may be more than one motivation, but what I take to be crucial in this clarification is that *ontological dependence* itself is different from mixing. This is of particular importance for the explanation Aristotle gives of mixing (in the very same passage, 327b22–6), which makes use of the notion of *potential* existence. It is not ontological dependence that is at the root of mixtures, because *ontological dependence does not undermine the actuality of the dependents*, as we just saw with the body and its whiteness; whereas *mixing must undermine the actuality of the ingredients*, if we are to escape the dilemma above.

Since the ingredients cannot cease to be, nor persist in a mixture, not only alteration but transformation, too (namely generation or corruption), is different from mixing. When wood burns, it is not being mixed with fire. Rather, it ceases to be and fire is generated (327b10–13). Growth is not mixing either, because one component persists, the growing one, and the other ceases to be, the nourishment (321a34–5, 322a11–13).[4]

Mixing by Division

Aristotle considers the mechanism of mixing by division as the main candidate for explaining the survival of the original ingredients in the mixture, and their recoverability; division generates small parcels of matter, preserving the kind and the parts of the original ingredients. The first account of mixing Aristotle considers is one where the parcels are so small that it is not possible to discern the parcels of one of the ingredients in the mixture from the parcels of the other ingredient (327b32–5) – I will assume, with Aristotle, that there are two ingredients only, for simplicity. I agree with Williams (1982: 146) that it is not necessary, in this first account, that the parcels of stuff are alternating between the two kinds. All that the present conception of mixture requires is that they be small enough for their difference in kind to be imperceptible, whether they are clustered together in small groups per kind or not. Aristotle immediately abandons this possibility, and the reasons why can be discerned from the conditions that characterize mixtures, which we gradually encounter in what follows.

There are three reasons that speak against mixtures *modulo* perception. The first and most important condition is that mixtures, according to Aristotle, are homoeomerous – uniform. At first glance, mixtures modulo perception appear uniform, which might suggest that they satisfy the uniformity requirement. But Aristotle tell us what he means by uniformity, which is a much more stringent requirement than uniformity in appearance: "just as a part of water is water so it is with what has been mingled" (328a11–12); so a part of a mixture must be the same kind of stuff as the whole mixture. Clearly, what looks uniform but consists of parcels of matter of two different kinds does not satisfy the criterion for being a homoeomer. Even if the whole is taken to be a ratio of the two different kinds of stuff, small enough parts of the whole will consist of one only kind of stuff.

The second reason against mixtures modulo perception is that the resulting whole is not a mixture but a composition of parts. This objection too is premised on the uniformity of mixtures. Since every part of a mixture is the same kind as every other part of it, mixtures are not compositions of parts that are different in kind in the way that salt and pepper, when intermingled, are. Finally, the third reason is the relativity of perception. Aristotle says that "'being mixed' would be relative to perception: one and the same thing will be mixed for one man whose sight is not sharp, whereas for Lynceus nothing is mixed" (328a13–15). Williams thinks that the relativity of perception is a defeasible objection to mixing modulo perception, since there comes a point of small-ness of parcels of matter which makes them indiscernible to human sight (1982: 146). So even Lynceus would not be able to tell that the mixture is not uniform. But there is no in-principle impossibility of (technologically enhanced) discernability, which suffices for the objection to stand.

Aristotle's second attempt at mixing by division is far more sophisticated and complex. We are again considering the division of the ingredients into small parcels (*eis mikra*) but now, they must be, not small enough to be indiscernible to perception, but small enough to be "arranged in such a way that every single part of either of the things mixed is alongside some part of the other" (328a1–2). As an example, consider salt and pepper so arranged. Aristotle examines whether such an explanation will satisfy two conditions regulating mixing. The one is that every body, including mixtures, is divis-ible, but not thoroughly divided, which is an Aristotelian metaphysical tenet. The second is that a mixture is uniform.

To show that the present account of mixture satisfies uniformity, he considers a second conception of uniformity (after the abandoned "uniformity in appearance"), which is that "every part of one [ingredient] would have to come to be alongside some part of the other" (328a5). At first glance, salt and pepper could satisfy this homoeo-merity requirement if properly arranged. But the impossibility of thorough division blocks this possibility. For a successful adjacency arrangement it would be necessary that each ingredient be divided into the smallest possible parts, which would then be arranged side by side, ensuring that no two parts of a single ingredient were adjacent. But since every body is divisible, but not thoroughly divided, every part of each of the ingredients will be divisible, and there will be no smallest parts (328a5–6). Hence, uniformity cannot be satisfied even on its second conception of adjacency of parts. The final blow is struck by Aristotle pointing out that even if it were satisfied, still this would not be a mixture because this conception of uniformity is not the appropriate one for mixtures. Adjacency is a type of composition, not mixing, whereas mixing requires a different kind of uniformity than composition.

Williams thinks that Aristotle fails to make his case against mixing being composi-tion (1982: 146–8). He argues that the reasoning we just rehearsed is valid only if Aristotle was attacking some form of atomism, as most commentators assume. But if the smallest parts are not assumed to be atoms, but infinitesimals, then further possi-bilities arise (pp. 146–7). Williams begins by challenging the logic of the following sentence:

> But if every body is divisible, given that a body mixed with another is homoeomerous, every part of one would have to come to be alongside some part of the other. (328a3–5)

Williams finds the sentence inconsistent on the atomist reading of this argument. If there is infinite divisibility, then there are no atoms, and hence uniformity *qua* adja-cency of atoms would be impossible; yet exactly the opposite seems to be suggested in

Aristotle's sentence above, which turns it into nonsense. In consequence, Williams suggests that possibly Aristotle is here entertaining an account of mixing based on a theory of infinitesimals (pp. 147–8), not atoms. According to it, "every (infinitesimal) part of B would have to get alongside some part of C and vice versa. Homoeomerous mixture = alternation of infinitesimal parts" (p. 147, where B and C are the ingredients of the mixture). According to Williams, this is the only way to make sense of Aristotle's quoted sentence above, and not through the traditional atomist reading of it. Furthermore, Williams wonders whether Aristotle's "rough rejection of it [is] a sign that he has not fully grasped its significance, that he has perhaps confused it with an atomist theory of indivisible *minima*" (p. 148). Aristotle's rejection of it is based on his claim that "there is no such thing as a thing's being divided into parts which are the smallest possible" (328a5–6).

Has Aristotle missed out on a possible explanation of mixing? Williams does not explain how this reading might help us make sense of Aristotle's sentence above, other than to say that we should think of infinite division resulting, not in atoms, but in limits or infinitesimals. Let us pursue this reading. Consider a mixture where the ingredients divide each other infinitely; there is total interpenetration. We could think of two lines, a red and a green one, merging into one line. Take the case of infinitesimals first, i.e. the points in the lines. The lines would be thoroughly mixed after their merger, in the sense that given any two points of one of the lines there would always be a point of the other line in between them. This would indeed satisfy the thorough divisibility and mixture requirements, as well as the conception of uniformity given in the sentence above as systematic juxtaposition (328a3–5).

The case of limits may be of even greater interest. Let us suppose the merger results in a line, every point of which is a limit for each of the two lines. I mean the following: every point in the merger is a point where each of the two lines meet – it is an end point, as it were, of each of the two lines, at which the two lines touch. Then we can think of each point as being the limit at which each of the two lines converges. In that sense, each of the two lines is present at each point (by converging on it)! Could it be that such an account of mixing would satisfy, not the systematic juxtaposition requirement of uniformity any more, but indeed the Aristotelian conception of uniformity, where every part of the mixture is of the same kind as the mixture (as in water)?

There are several reasons why Aristotle would not be satisfied either with the infinitesimals or with the limits conception of mixing. First, for Aristotle there is no thorough interpenetration, because no infinite process, such as the infinite division of bodies, can be actualized (328a5–6). Further, the solution in terms of the infinitesimals or the limits requires that the lines be composed of them, which introduces the problem of the dimensionless making up an entity with dimensions; points or limits cannot be *parts* of a line, whereas the division of a body for Aristotle is division into parts; when does this division cease to separate parts and isolates entities without dimension? Furthermore, at least on the account with infinitesimals, we still have mere composition, whereas Aristotle distinguishes mixing from composition (328a6–7); the components of such composition are either of the one or the other kind of stuff, hence it is not a proper Aristotelian homoeomer (like water). Finally, on either the infinitesimals or the limits account, we cannot explain how mixtures can have different proportions of ingredients (e.g. 2 : 3 parts respectively).

So Aristotle is neither confused, nor does he fail to fully grasp the significance of the suggestion made at 328a3–5. Even more importantly, this sentence is not inconsistent. Williams is wrong to accuse Aristotle of all these failings, because as we saw, infinitesimals do not provide an answer towards an account of mixing. How then are we to understand 328a3–5? It introduces mixing by division into parts. Even with every body being divisible, for Aristotle the end points of such division processes are not infinitesimals, since infinite processes are not actual. The end points of divisions would not even be atoms, since "there is no such thing as a thing's being divided into parts which are the smallest possible" (328a5–6). So division produces only small particles. Furthermore, it is clear that for the purposes of the hypothesis of mixing by division, Aristotle is introducing the term "homoeomer" in an everyday way of understanding it, namely as uniform juxtaposition, e.g. as it would apply to the sand on the beach which is homoeomerous: grains of different types of stone or shell are intermingled with one another uniformly. This is just the requirement of thorough juxtaposition in 328a3–5: given (*eiper*) that mixed bodies are uniform, every part of one would have (*deoi an*) to come to be alongside some part of the other. This explanation of a homoeomer is of course incompatible with Aristotle's understanding of it (as it applies to water), but he is setting up this alternative just to present his reasons against mixture by division, which he does in the lines that follow. It is that an intermingling of parts would be a composition, not a mixture; it would not be a proper homoeomer (like water), since it would have parts whose kind would be different from that of the whole (e.g. being just salt, or just pepper); and, finally, it would not be uniform even in the juxtaposition sense, because due to divisibility, some parts of each of the intermingled ingredients would always be adjacent to, or contained in, parts of the same ingredient (328a5–16). This completes Aristotle's criticism of mixing by division.

The Account of Mixing and Potential Persistence

Aristotle seeks the solution to the puzzle of mixing in the distinction between the ingredients surviving in potentiality, and their surviving in actuality. He is concerned to distinguish mixing of substances from the generation and destruction of substances on the one hand, and from the growth of substances on the other. In so doing, he generates a new metaphysical theory which accounts for the uniformity of the kind of stuff that substances are made of, e.g. blood or bark. I will first present in outline Aristotle's theory of mixing, and then examine how successfully his theory addresses the challenges it faces.

To be and not to be; that is the challenge. Aristotle says it is possible for the ingredients of the mixture to be and not to be in the mixture:

> Since some things that are, are potential, and some actual, it is possible for things after they have been mixed in some way *to be and not to be*. Some other thing which comes to be [*gegonos*] from them is actually [i.e. the mixture], while each of the things which were, before they were mixed, *still is*, but *potentially*, and has not been destroyed [*ouk apolôlota*]. This is the solution to the problem raised by the previous argument. (327b23–6, my emphasis.)

In this initial statement of the solution, we find the first of the two principles of the Aristotelian account of mixing regarding the fate of the ingredients in the process of mixing – they are not destroyed, but survive in potentiality. This is qualified by a further claim, which is related to the first, but regards the fate of the ingredients post-mixture:

> Things that are mixed manifestly come together from having formerly been separate, and are capable of *being separated again* [chôrizesthai palin]. (327b27–9, my emphasis)

The second principle is the requirement we encountered in the discussion of mixtures modulo perception about the nature of the new thing which comes to be, namely the mixture itself:

> a body mixed with another is homoeomerous . . . we say that if things have in fact been mixed the mixture has to be homoeomerous, and that just as a part of water is water so it is with what has been mingled. (328a4–12)

We can thus summarize the Principles of Mixing on which Aristotle's solution is based as follows:

PM1	*Survival*:	The ingredients that are mixed survive in the mixture in potentiality, not in actuality, and can be separated again.
PM2	*Uniformity*:	The parts of a mixture are of the same kind as the whole mixture.

There are issues to examine, question, and explain in relation to the two principles. We shall be aided by Aristotle's discussion of the ways in which mixing differs from other phenomena, and his examination of borderline cases of mixing.

Survival in the mixture is explained in terms of potentiality, but the latter notion is broad enough to allow for a variety of types of survival. To understand the type of potentiality at work in PM1, we need to determine the sense in which Aristotle claims the ingredients to still be in the mixture. We saw in 327b23–6 above that the ingredients that go into a mixture in some way are, even after they have been mixed; they are potentially the things *they were* before the mixture; and they *have not been destroyed*. But they also are not, because some other thing has come to be from them as ingredients. The sense in which they are not is given by an example Aristotle offers to contrast the survival of the ingredients with survival in accidental unities such as of the body and its whiteness. The first difference is that the ingredients that go into a mixture are not ontologically dependent entities in the way that an affection is, e.g. the whiteness of a body: "When two things are mixed each must exist as a separable thing, and no affection is separable" (327b22–3). The second difference is that "neither do they both remain in actuality like the body and its whiteness, nor do they perish – either of them or both – because their potentiality is preserved" (327b29–31). A body remains that very same body in actuality when it becomes white, and whiteness is in actuality when it qualifies the body.

The ontological dependence of whiteness on the body does not threaten its actuality, which consists in being the specific type of pale that white is. But if the ingredients of a mixture remained in actuality, their actuality would involve actuality of form, and of ontological separateness, not only separability. But we already know that Aristotle said in 327b22–3 that the things that are mixed remain only *separable*. Therefore, they are neither separate, ontologically independent, nor therefore could they retain their form in actuality, as when each is separate, in the way whiteness does, since being what they were would require their separateness. Another thing comes to be from them, and they become ontologically dependent on it while mixed, as its components. But they do not get composed into this new thing in the way that the parts of a substance are composed into the substance as a whole. Here the mixants do not become reidentified by being enformed by the substantial form of the new entity. The impact on their nature due to their demotion to ingredients in the mixture is of a different type than the assimilation of components into a new substance. We shall turn to the type of change suffered by their nature in what follows.

Separability, which Aristotle insists on for the ingredients in a mixture, is a fundamental requirement which characterizes mixing as a distinct type of process. It distinguishes mixing from the generation of a substance by specifying how the ingredients survive in the mixture; they are recoverable, while what is transformed in a generation is not recoverable. But more importantly, separability gives us a criterion for the potentiality of the ingredients in a mixture, which distinguishes this potentiality from other types of it. The criterion is that the ingredients in a mixture retain whatever their numerical recovery requires. They do not survive in the mixture, for then the mixture would be their mere alteration, which we found dismissed in the initial puzzle. But the recovery will be a recovery of things *numerically identical* to the initial ingredients, not of things like these ingredients.[5]

What is required to retain the potentiality for the recovery of the numerically identical entities? Aristotle does not offer the answer to this question, but a solution can be found to fit the framework of his account of mixing. In order to address this question we need to examine the second Principle of Mixing, Uniformity.

Uniformity, or homoeomerity, has figured in the preliminary discussion of mixing we examined in the above, in different senses, but finally as the requirement that a part of a mixture be the same type of stuff as the whole, as it is in water. What we have not encountered so far is the mechanism through which different ingredients together manage this feat, namely to produce a thing that is a single type of stuff, uniformly throughout. Aristotle describes this mechanism as follows:

> when the two are more or less equal in strength, then each changes from its own nature in the direction of the dominant one, though it does not become the other but something in between and common to both. (328a28–31)

Consider mixing two ingredients that can affect one another, e.g. honey and wine. The honey becomes less viscous and more watery or wet, due to the effect of the wine on it, and more sour, while the wine becomes thicker, less watery, and sweeter due to the effect of the honey on it. The causal interaction reaches equilibrium at some point, when neither the wine nor the honey, in their new tempered states, overtop the other in being watery, or acidic, or viscous or sweet. Both are equally viscous or acidic, etc. Thus the effect of each on the other stabilizes. But it does not stop, because then each

251

of the two would revert to its own nature of being more liquidy and sour, or more viscous and sweet.

It is fundamental to understanding Aristotle's explanation of mixing that we recognize that the *essential nature* of each of the ingredients of the mixture is changed, compromised. Their natures are not destroyed, because that would result in their corruption and the generation of new substances. Although their natures are not destroyed, they are altered, though not irrecoverably, since that would be destruction and the generation of a new type of substance. Their natures are altered under the causal influence of each on the other ingredient, while that influence lasts. We should think of the natures of each of the ingredients in a mixture as a compressed spring, which remains so while the force is exerted upon it, but is ready to recover its full length when released from the force exerted upon it. If we think of two springs pressing against each other until their powers equalize, we begin to see how the nature of each ingredient in a mixture imposes itself on the other, bringing about changes until their respective natures are compromised to the point of not being able to affect the other in any further way. They keep each other at this compromised state of tension and strength equilibrium by continuously affecting each other's nature, preventing any kind of superiority in causal efficacy. The result is a type of mutual normalizing of natures.

We are now in the position to address the question of the First Principle of how the ingredients retain the potentiality for numerical identity. The one factor is the inevitable fate of each ingredient in the mixture: it is altered by the other ingredient until the causal powers of their respective contrarieties are equalized; the other factor is that each ingredient must retain the potentiality to recover, or revert to, the object it was before entering the mixture. If these two factors cooperate when we mix, the result is a mixture; if not, the result is either compresence of different (unmixed) materials, or destruction of one or both of them. Therefore, however the potentiality of an ingredient to be the object it was is retained, this must not impede the causal equalizing of contrarieties in the ingredients. Aristotle requires that "each changes from its own nature [*phusis*] in the direction of the dominant one, though it does not become the other but something in between and common to both [*koinon*]" (328a30–1). By "dominant" Aristotle means any type of causal strength that each of the ingredients has on the nature of the other. What is common to both is the compromised state of each ingredient's nature when their causal efficacy is equalized. This means that neither is superior to the other in respect of any contrariety, such as hot or cold or wet or dry, or their derivatives, which are the characteristics that determine the nature of each ingredient. So the compromised natures are equal in wetness and heat, dryness and cold, etc.

That the ingredients should be "more or less equal in strength" (328a29) is also a tacit reference to the relative quantity of each ingredient. Aristotle has said in just the previous sentence that when there is gross inequality of quantity between two ingredients, then it is not possible for their opposite characteristics to keep each other balanced, but the one is overpowered by the other. Going back to our springs example, a small spring would be crushed by a very powerful one, not just compressed. Aristotle's example is the following:

> when many of them are juxtaposed to few or large ones to small, then indeed they do not give rise to mixing, but to growth[6] on the part of that which is dominant; for the other

changes into the dominant one: thus a drop of wine is not mixed with ten thousand pitchersful of water, for its form dissolves and it changes into the totality of the water. (328a24–8)

The nature of the drop of wine is destroyed by the causal effect of the large quantity of water around it. It is as if there were an inexhaustible source of opposite characteristics compromising those of the small quantity of wine, overwhelming the wine's characteristics until even their source is obliterated, leaving no trace of the wine's nature behind. Quantity plays a role in the outcome, as *causal strength* is measured in quantity as well as intensity of opposites. Thus extremely hot lava mixing with lukewarm mercury could result in equalising of temperatures, if there was plenty of lukewarm mercury around it. But high intensity, and comparatively large quantity are devastating; a drop of mercury in an erupting volcano would be destroyed.

So here is the metaphysical picture of mixtures so far: each ingredient in a mixture is changed in its essential nature, by having its characteristics compromised due to the causal interaction with the other ingredient. The nature of each ingredient is not obliterated by the causal interaction, but altered, so that it is not any more the type of material that it was before entering the mixture; what it is missing are the characteristics which are necessary for this type of thing, but which are now compromised. Although the ingredient does not possess these characteristics while in the mixture, it has not lost the power to restore them, if released from the causal interaction with the other ingredient.

But what does the restoration of the nature of each ingredient involve? On what is the *potentiality* for this restoration grounded? It is grounded on the only factor in which the *nature* of an ingredient could be anchored, namely, the *enformed matter* of that ingredient. The enformed matter is what constitutes the ingredient before entering the mixture. In the mixture, the matter of each ingredient is still enformed, but the form is altered, compromised by the causal effect of the other ingredient. The matter of each ingredient is divided up into small parcels in the mixture, as we shall see in what follows. But each part, say of honey, retains the potentiality to regain its original form when the causal influence is withdrawn.

To see how it is possible to retain the potentiality even for a complex form, we can consider an example, which is not a case of mixing. If we have a vase which we break up into small pieces, the form of the vase is retained in potentiality in the pieces, and can be restored if the pieces are glued together again. There is no vase once it is broken up into pieces, but it has not been destroyed in the sense that it can be restored. When restored, it is numerically the same vase as it was before it was broken up. Now consider two vases which crush onto each other. The tiny pieces from each vase become mixed up in the resulting rubble. But both the forms of the vases and the vases themselves can be restored. But achieving the latter requires more than restoration of shape; to restore numerically identical vases we need to select out the pieces of each vase. To see why, consider two identical vases which we cut up into tiny square pieces each, and then mix up the pieces. It is possible to restore two vases by putting the appropriately shaped pieces together, paying no attention to the origin of the pieces but only to their shape. Then we would have two new vases which would be identical in form to the original ones, but not numerically identical to either of the original ones. The numerical identity of the original and the restored vases requires restoring the same form and matter of each vase. The sameness of matter secures physical continuity and brings with it the historical features of the form of each vase.[7]

The same analysis applies to mixtures, too. The matter of each ingredient in a mixture is divided up into small pieces which interact with the pieces of the other ingredient, compromising the form of each other. But when each piece of each ingredient is not being affected by the other ingredient, then its form is restored; and when the pieces of the each ingredient are put together again, then each ingredient is restored. Each ingredient is restored because the original quantity of matter regains the same form, e.g. of honey or wine, as it had before entering the mixture. The same type of complexity that we encountered in the case of the vases can be encountered here too, e.g. by mixing two similar wines together. But their similarity does not change the metaphysics of the mixture. The same analysis of potentiality of forms and of ingredients remains, even if restoration is possible only in principle.

Aristotle's account of mixing applies to mixtures where the ingredients affect each other's nature. If the ingredients affect each other's *accidental properties*, then restoration of accidental features cannot be secured, although separation of ingredients is possible at least in principle. For example consider mixing hot and cold water. The quantities mixed will give rise to lukewarm water; they can even, in principle, be separated out again. But their original temperatures will not be restored to each of the ingredients by the separation. The reason is that the potentiality of form is not preserved, because there is no anchoring of the accidental features onto any particular matter; the original heat of each quantity of water is not tied to that quantity of water but to its previous environment. This contrasts with the case of the compromise of the nature of each ingredient; here the form of each ingredient is anchored onto the enformed matter of the ingredient; honey is sweet unless, and while, under the influence of, e.g., wine.

The formal and the historical continuity between the ingredient before entering, and after it enters the mixture is what distinguishes mixing from generation. In generation, although the same quantity of matter remains, it loses the form of the original object, and with it the historical continuity with that object, which is why that object cannot be restored. Even if the same form is repeated, as it could in a metal statue, the causal history of that form anchors it in the new, post destruction, environment, not in the matter/nature of the original statue. By contrast, the parcels of the enformed (but compromised) matter of an ingredient in a mixture are the seat of the physical, formal, and historical continuity with the original ingredient. They possess the potentialities for the restoration of the form and also the ingredient. In some cases, restoration may be physically possible, as in the case of salt and water. But in other cases it will be only in principle possible, as in the case of water and wine. Even in this case, the parcels of matter of the ingredients carry the potentialities for restoration, but separating them out from the mingled state they are in the mixture would be a physical feat.

This is what a mixture is for Aristotle. The ingredients that enter the mixture causally affect each other until their powers of contrarieties are equalized. This process deforms each of them, equalising their contrarieties, and keeps them in that common state while their causal effect on each other lasts. In that state, the matter of each ingredient is still informed by the nature of each ingredient, but the nature is compromised due to the causal effect of the other ingredient (328a28–31).

Uniformity is thereby achieved. Every part of the mixture is equipotent with every other part of the mixture. None is warmer or sweeter or drier than other parts of the mixture. Some of these parts are parts of the first ingredient, some of the second, and some of both; but their form in the mixture is the same, balancing excess or deficiency of causal power on each other. At the same time, each part of the mixture caries potentialities and continuities which are *not* shared by every other part of the mixture or by the whole. These are the ground for the possibility of the restoration of each ingredient after having been mixed.

Further Considerations on the Mechanism of Mixing

In the above, I have assumed that each ingredient is cut up into small pieces while in the mixture. This follows from Aristotle's account of causal interaction between ingredients, to which I will now turn. Causal interaction smoothes out differences in contrarieties: "what is active makes the patient like itself. For agent and patient are contraries, and coming to be is to the contrary. So it is necessary that the patient change into the agent" (324a10–13); "of agents, those are capable of being mixed which have a contrariety (for it is these which are capable of being acted upon by one another)" (328a31–3). Thus the ingredients of a mixture change each other into something that is common to both, since both act as agents and as patients until they equalize their contrarieties.

The way that causation is engendered is by the *contact* between the agent and the patient:

> for neither is acting and being affected possible in the strict sense for things which cannot be in contact with each other, nor can things be mixed unless they have first had some sort of contact . . . It is necessary for those things which are involved in mixing to be capable of contact with one another, and the same holds for anything which properly speaking acts on, or is affected by, another. (322b22–9)

Contact is a necessary condition for the agent to affect the patient. Thus the ingredients of a mixture need to be in contact with one another in order to affect each other. But contact by itself may not be sufficient for mixing to take place. Further conditions need to obtain to expedite mixing.

To understand the complexity of the mechanism of causation it would be helpful to consider how fire warms up the water in a pot. Fire warms up the pot by coming in contact with it. But fire does not come in contact with the water in the pot, although it manages to warm it up as well. This is achieved by fire warming up the pot, which is in contact with the water, and thereby warms up the water. The end result is that the heating effect of the fire extends to some distance from the point of contact between it and the pot. I will call this distance between the point of (agent-patient) contact and the furthest point in the patient which is affected by the agent the *causal range* of the agent on the patient.

Aristotle does not talk of the causal range of an agent on a patient, but it follows from his description of what expedites mixing. He says:

> amongst things which are divisible and capable of being affected those which are easily bounded are capable of being mixed, since they divide easily into small parts . . . For instance, liquids are the type of bodies most liable to mixing, for liquids are the most easily bounded of divisible things, unless they are viscous. (328a35–b4)

We can explain why those bodies which are divisible and easily bounded are most of all capable of being mixed. Being most easily bounded maximizes contact between agent and patient. Secondly, being divisible into small parts makes possible the causal effect of the agent to reach all the parts of the patient. Thus "small quantities put alongside small quantities mix better, because they change one another more easily and quickly" (328a33–4). The contact area increases and the distance which the effect has to reach decreases. Things which do not divide up easily resist mixing with whatever they are brought into contact: "liquids are . . . most liable to mixing . . . unless they are viscous (these have the effect only of multiplying and increasing bulk)" (328b3–5).

It therefore follows that for Aristotle, each of the ingredients of a mixture is divided into small parts and is in contact with the parts of the other ingredient. But the parts are not infinitesimal. We already saw that Aristotle does not believe that a division could be carried to completion (328a5–6). In fact, the division need be such as to allow each part of each ingredient, acting as agents, to causally affect through and through each part of the other ingredient acting as patient. The causal range of the efficacy of each ingredient will place an upper limit on how large the pieces can be in the mixture before mixing stops being possible. But if the parts into which each ingredient is divided are not too large for their causal range, the intermingling of parts of the ingredients will suffice to allow the causal equilibrium to be reached, reducing the ingredients to the common state that is the uniform nature of the mixture.

Thus, the common form of the mixture is *not* a *ratio* between ingredients. It is not that e.g. there are two parts of the one and three parts of the other ingredient in every part of the mixture we consider. On Aristotle's account, it may be that a part of the mixture derives fully from one only ingredient. But what makes the mixture uniform is that the form of that part of the mixture is the same as the form of a part that derives from the other ingredient; namely, the common form that results from the causal equilibrium between the ingredients.[8] So, there is in a sense mingling of parts of different origins, deriving from different ingredients, in a mixture, but unlike the composition of barley and wheat, there is no mingling of natures in a mixture, because of the uniformity of all parts irrespective of derivation.

The difference in origin of the parts in a mixture does not prevent the uniformity of the mixture. But does it have consequences for what can be derived from each part of the mixture? Aristotle in fact seems to make an even more stringent claim than that the initial ingredients of a mixture can be restored after they have been mixed. He seems to claim that any of the initial ingredients can be *derived*, not just from the mixture, but *from any part* of the mixture:

> It follows [from Empedocles' account] that fire and water cannot come to be from any particle of flesh whatsoever, in the way that with wax, whilst from this part a sphere might come to be and a pyramid from some other, it would always be possible for it to happen the other way round. This does in fact occur in this way, i.e. from flesh both elements can

come to be from any particle whatsoever. According to the account we have been discussing, however, it would not be possible: it would have to be the way that stone and brick come from a wall, one from one place and part, one from another. (334a31–b1)

This is *prima facie* a difficulty for the interpretation I am offering of Aristotle on mixing. On my explanation, the matter of the initial ingredients remains fragmented and deformed in the mixture. Isolating any such part of the mixture from the causal influence of the other parts of the mixture that are in contact with it would allow the compromised nature of the initial ingredient to be restored in that part, e.g. into water or earth. But Aristotle seems to claim here that from that part of the mixture either water or earth could be derived.

The claim is *not* that in every part of the mixture both ingredients are *present*. This could be somehow explained by a presence of a compromised part of one ingredient at a place in a mixture, or by the presence of the causal influence of the other ingredient on it. These are two senses in which both ingredients are present in every part of the mixture. But the claim here seems to be more stringent. Aristotle appears to want either of the initial ingredients to be *derivable* from any part of the mixture (*ex hotououn amfô ginesthai*, 334b35), not just present in every part of the mixture. Nor does he mean that any particle of the mixture can produce both ingredients at the same time. His example of the pyramid and the sphere shows that when the mixture is dissolved, from any part either the one or the other ingredient will be restored.

I believe that if Aristotle is claiming the omni-derivability of a mixture's ingredients from the mixture, the claim is unsustainable. The reason is the following: suppose that in one case of dissolution of a mixture, all the original matter of one ingredient comes to constitute the other ingredient, and vice versa; e.g. all the matter of the water that went into the mixture comes to have the properties of earth, and all the matter of the original earth comes to have the properties of water. Then we do not have the recovery of the initial ingredients, but only of some earth and some water, generated from the mixture. The resulting elements are not the original ingredients because their matter has totally changed. If we took them to be the same, then any pool of water would also turn out to be identical to any other pool of water, and similarly for parcels of earth. Hence, if Aristotle's claim is that either ingredient can be derived from any part of the mixture, the claim is simply false.

But maybe, on the other hand, Aristotle does not say that either of the original *ingredients* can be derived from any part of the mixture, but only that either of the *elements* that the mixture contains can be derived from any part of it: "from flesh both elements [i.e. fire and water] can come to be from any particle whatsoever" (334b35). If Aristotle is here indifferent as to whether we derive new parcels of earth from a part of the flesh, or the original ingredients, then my account has no difficulty accommodating this. In the case of the generation of the new element from the mixture, external causal factors would need to explain its generation according to any account.

Aristotle does not give us the mechanics of how the original ingredients can be restored from a mixture, let alone how either ingredient can be restored from any part of the mixture, if this is being claimed at all. The account I offered above in terms of the original ingredients remaining fragmented and compromised in the mixture supplies the mechanism for the first, to complement what Aristotle explains about mixtures. What his claim is about the second remains a speculation, which on either reading of it does not add content to his account, but if anything, misleads.

Notes

[1] C. J. F. Williams (1982).

[2] A further description of the Aristotelian account of the elements is offered by M. L. Gill (forthcoming).

[3] Aristotle's account of mixing has attracted much attention in recent literature, not only because it is challenging to unfold Aristotle's intuition towards its resolution, but also because this intuition is philosophically so promising. Its recalcitrance has given rise to very interesting and imaginative interpretations, such as Richard Sharvy's topological interpretation (1983: 439–57). But a very systematic and especially demanding philosophical analysis of the phenomenon has been given in Kit Fine's (1995/1997/1998) paper. Although I do not find myself in agreement with Fine's interpretation of Aristotle on mixture, I wish to register my enthusiasm for the excellence of the paper and my gratitude for the philosophical sophistication it takes its readers through, which is not often encountered in the exegetical literature. Fine concludes in what could be described as a two-tier analysis of Aristotelian matter, in terms of embedded levels of dispositions, which he also recommends as a promising conception of material powers in contemporary philosophy. Allan Code (1997) has outlined Aristotelian objections to Fine's interpretation. For a comprehensive review of the interpretations of mixing in the exegetical tradition, see Rega Wood and Michael Weisberg (2004). See also Bogen (1997), discussed in Fine (1998); Frede (2001).

[4] The phenomenon of growth is different from that of generation too. In growth, as in alteration, the object that grows persists in actuality and survives the change, but becomes altered; each part of it becomes larger due to another thing which accedes to it (321a19–22). The thing that accedes does not survive because its substance is destroyed (321a34) when it is assimilated in the growing object.

[5] Despite Aristotle's explicit assertion of the recoverability of the ingredients that go into a mixture, there are cases where the ingredients are recoverable in principle only. For example, consider mixing some hot and cold water. It will appear in what follows why I believe that even in such a case they are recoverable in principle.

[6] See note 4 above.

[7] Finally, if the two vases are pulverized and then mixed up, it may be only in principle possible to restore them again, but not in practice. The potentiality for the form and each vase to be restored would remain, but we may not be able to bring it about.

[8] When discussing the barley-wheat type of composition, Aristotle says that they are not mixed because the composition is not a homoeomer: "nor will the part have the same proportion [*logos*] as the whole" (328a9). It should not be thought that Aristotle is here defining uniformity in terms of the proportion of the ingredients being the same in every part of it as it is in the whole. This is clear from the fact that he immediately proceeds to give the example of water as a paradigmatic homoeomer. But it is also clear from the fact that he denies the possibility of division into infinitesimals (328a5–6) which would be a presupposition for such a definition of uniformity. What Aristotle is saying here is that in the barley-wheat composition we do not have even the same proportion of different ingredients in the part as in the whole (let alone the same stuff, as we do in the case of water).

Bibliography

Bogen, J. (1997). "Fire in the Belly: Aristotelian Elements, Organisms, and Chemical Compounds," in Lewis and Bolton (eds.), pp. 183–215.

Code, A. (1997). "Potentiality in Aristotle's Science and Metaphysics," in Lewis and Bolton (eds.), pp. 217–30.

Fine, K. [1995] (1997). "The Problem of Mixture," *Pacific Philosophical Quarterly*, 1995, pp. 266–369. (Repr. in Lewis and Bolton, (eds.), pp. 82–182; a shorter version of the paper is given in Fine's "Mixing Matters," *Ratio*, 1998, pp. 278–88.)

Frede, D. (2001). "On Mixture and Mixables," in Mansfield and de Haas (eds.), pp. 289–314.

Gill, M. L. (forthcoming). "The Theory of the Elements in *De Caelo* III and IV," in A. C. Bowen and C. Wildberg (eds.), *A Companion to Aristotle's Cosmology: Collected Papers on "De Caelo"* (Leiden: Brill).

Lewis, F. and Bolton R. (eds.) (1997). *Form, Matter and Mixture in Aristotle* (Oxford: Blackwell).

Mansfield, J. and de Haas, F. (eds.) (2001). *Aristotle: "On Generation and Corruption" I*, Proceedings of Symposium Aristotelicum 15 (Oxford: Oxford University Press).

Sharvy R. (1983). "Aristotle on Mixtures," *Journal of Philosophy*, pp. 439–57.

Williams, C. J. F. (1982). *Aristotle's "De Generatione et Corruptione,"* Clarendon Aristotle Series, ed. J. L. Ackrill (Oxford: Clarendon Press).

Wood, R. and Weisberg, M. (2004). "Interpreting Aristotle on Mixture: Problems about Elemental Composition from Philoponus to Cooper," *Studies in History and Philosophy of Science*, pp. 681–706.

16

Aristotle on the Infinite, Space, and Time

MICHAEL J. WHITE

In claiming novelty for their doctrines, those natural philosophers who developed the "new science" of the seventeenth century frequently contrasted "Aristotelian" physics with their own. Physics of the former sort, so they claimed, emphasized the qualitative at the expense of the quantitative, neglected mathematics and its proper role in physics (particularly in the analysis of local motion), and relied on such suspect explanatory principles as final causes and "occult" essences. Yet in his *Physics* Aristotle characterizes physics or the "science of nature" as pertaining to magnitudes (*megethê*), motion (or "process" or "gradual change" – *kinêsis*), and time (*chronon*) (*Phys* III.4 202b30–1). Indeed, the *Physics* is largely concerned with an analysis of motion, particularly local motion, and the other concepts that Aristotle believes are requisite to that analysis. These concepts, essential to the philosophy of nature, include those with which we are concerned in this chapter: the infinite, space, and time.

Aristotle on the Infinite (*to apeiron*): From Cosmological Principle to Mathematical Operation

Chapters 4 through 8 of the third Book of Aristotle's *Physics* are devoted to an analysis of *to apeiron*, variously rendered in English as "the unlimited," "the indefinite," and "the infinite." At the beginning of this discussion, Aristotle briefly states the relevance of the concept of the infinite to the science of nature (*physis*) or physics: since, as we saw, he holds that physics is concerned with "magnitudes (*megethê*), motion, and time," and since each of these is either unlimited or limited (*peperasmenon*), it is necessary for the investigator of nature to inquire into the unlimited, "whether it exists or not, and if it does, what it is" (202b30–6). He adds that virtually all those who have pursued the science of nature have made the infinite a "principle (*archê*) of things" (203a3–4).

Among those who accord substantial status to the infinite, he mentions the Pythagoreans and Plato. However, those whom Aristotle recognizes as being concerned more particularly with giving an account of sensible nature have, he claims, made the infinite a characteristic of (some of) the cosmological "elements" (*stoicheia*) – "such as water or air or what is intermediate between them" (203a18). After a bit more historical discussion, Aristotle concludes with five principal reasons that give rise to belief in the existence of the infinite: (1) From the consideration of time, which is unlimited. (2) From the unlimited "division of magnitudes" (Aristotle identifies this as a mathematical use of the infinite). (3) From the need of an unlimited "source" for generation and destruction if these processes are not to be exhausted. (4) From a regress argument to the effect that, if everything is limited by something distinct from itself, it is "necessary that there not be an [ultimate] limit." (5) From, especially, the following consideration: "not only number but also mathematical magnitudes and what is outside the heavens seem never to play out in thought" (203b23–5). These considerations are obviously of very different sorts, and it is not until chapter 8, the last of Book III, that Aristotle explicitly returns to them.

In general, Aristotle's strategy is to move away from the postulation of a cosmic role for the infinite to a much more restricted linguistic and mathematical account of it. He clearly dismisses the idea that the infinite is some sort of substance or substance-like entity or "stuff"; and in both the *Physics* and the *On the Heavens* (*Cael*), he argues against the thesis that there is to be found in the cosmos an unlimited or infinite physical magnitude. For example, in *Cael* I.5, the postulation of an infinite magnitude for the cosmos is claimed to be inconsistent with the observed circular movement of the heavens. If there were an infinite distance from earth, at the center of the cosmos, to the sphere of fixed stars, at its periphery, then any circular rotation would entail the impossibility of a point on the sphere's traversing an infinite linear distance in a finite time (271b26– 272a7). Aristotle's conception of the derivative ontological status of the infinite is adumbrated by a rhetorical question that he poses in *Physics* III.5: "Further, how is it possible for the infinite to be itself something (*einai ti auto*), unless number and magnitude, of which the infinite is an essential attribute (*kath' hauto pathos*) are themselves something? . . . It is clear, then, that it is not possible for the infinite to exist as something that exists in actuality or as a substance or a principle" (204a17–21).

In the development of his analysis of the infinite, Aristotle makes use of two separate classificatory schemas, a mathematical one and a metaphysical one. What I term the mathematical schema is his distinction between the unlimited or infinite with respect to addition (*prosthesis*) and the unlimited/infinite with respect to division (*diairesis*) (204a6–7). I use the term "mathematical" here because this distinction appeals to the two types of quantity distinguished by Aristotle in *Metaphysics* Δ.13. There is plurality or multitude (*plêthos*), which is *numerable* quantity, and there is magnitude (*megethos*), which is *measurable* quantity. The former, numerable quantity (plurality) is divisible into discrete units, which are not continuous with one another; but the latter, measurable quantity (magnitude) is divisible into parts that are continuous with one another (1020a7–12). The infinite by addition is manifest particularly in numerical, discrete quantity. Any number is some multiple of a unit, but another greater number can always be obtained by the addition of a unit. As Aristotle puts it in *Phys* III.7, "it is reasonable, too, to suppose that in number there is a limit in the direction of the fewer, but that in the direction of the more each multiple is always exceeded" (207b1–3). The infinite by division, however, pertains to measurable, continuous quantity. In Aristotle's words, "in the direction of the less, each magnitude is exceeded, but in the direction of the greater there is not an infinite magnitude" (207b3–5). Because of Aristotle's conviction of the finitude of the cosmos and his conception of magnitude (*megethos*) as ontologically dependent on the cosmos, he can maintain a sort of parallelism between the infinite with respect to addition and the infinite with respect to division: the infinite with respect to addition has a lower bound (a unit of numeration) but no upper bound, while the infinite with respect to division always has an upper bound (a definite magnitude to be divided, which can be no larger than the extension of the cosmos), but no lower bound.

It is clear that Aristotle sees a close connection between the infinite with respect to addition and the infinite with respect to division. In fact, he says that, in a sense (*pôs*), they are the same: "For in a determinate magnitude, addition occurs conversely [to division]; where division is seen to be *ad infinitum* (*eis apeiron*), there addition seems to tend to the determinate magnitude in question" (206b3–6). And, "it is always possible to think [of a bigger number] in the direction of more, since the bisections of a magnitude are unlimited (*apeiroi*)" (207b10–11). Aristotle's picture is that of idealized geometrical bisection – say, of a given line segment. He holds that the process or geometrical construction of bisecting the given linear *magnitude* can, in principle, be continued beyond any finite stage – in the direction of the "less." Consequently, the *number* of bisections that are made can, in principle, be increased beyond any finite stage – in the direction of the "more."

The degree to which Aristotle's analysis is influenced by the developing geometry of his day can be seen by his recognition of some fundamental geometrical principles. First, he notes that "if one takes a determinate part in a finite magnitude and adds in the same ratio [as that of the original part of the finite magnitude] – and does not add the same part of the original whole – then one does not traverse the original magnitude" (206b7–9). Aristotle seems to intend this to be a general claim about what would now be called a geometrical series: a series of terms added together each one of which is the member of a decreasing geometrical progression (that is, each term of which is the same proportional proper part of the preceding term). His commonsensical but important insight (which is relevant to his discussion of Zeno's Dichotomy and Achilles and the Tortoise paradoxes in *Phys* VI.2 and VIII.8) is that if one takes a "whole" and begins with a certain proper part of it (say, a half), and then adds to that part a half of it, etc. *ad infinitum*, one never surpasses the whole with which one began irrespective of how many terms in the series one adds. Although he does not explicitly say so, it seems overwhelmingly likely that Aristotle recognizes that one approaches the original magnitude ever more closely (without reaching it at any finite stage) as one continues to add parts standing in the given geometrical relation. These considerations, of course, form the basis of the so-called method of exhaustion in the later history of Greek geometry, although Aristotle neither here nor elsewhere ever indicates that he recognizes anything like the *actual* "sum" of an infinite geometrical series.

Immediately following his claim about geometrical progressions, Aristotle enunciates another claim that came to be of central theoretical importance to ancient geometry and, in particular, to the method of exhaustion: "if we increase the ratio so that the same magnitude [which is a proper part of the original magnitude] is always taken, one traverses [the original whole], because every finite magnitude is exhausted by any determinate magnitude whatsoever" (206b9–12). The principle in question, variously known as the postulate (or axiom) of Eudoxus or Archimedes, is fairly clearly stated here: for any positive magnitudes "of the same kind" $x > y$, there is some finite number $n > 1$ of additions of y to itself such that the result surpasses x.

The metaphysical aspect of Aristotle's analysis of the infinite in the third Book of the *Physics* is certainly as important as, and probably more familiar than, the strictly mathematical aspect of that analysis. Having refused to accord to the infinite any sort of substantial existence, Aristotle recognizes that refusal to acknowledge the existence of the infinite in *any* sense leads to "many impossibilities": "there will be some beginning and end of time, [some] magnitudes will not be divisible into magnitudes, and number will not be unlimited" (206a9–12). He proceeds to invoke his actuality–potentiality distinction. There must be *some* sense in which magnitude is infinitely divisible, he argues; otherwise, what he takes to be the absurdity of geometrical minima would be entailed. So, "it remains that the unlimited/infinite exists potentially (*dunamei einai*)" (206a18).

The import of Aristotle's claim that the infinite exists only potentially has been controversial, particularly among modern commentators. It does seem relatively clear that he ascribes a particular sort of potentiality to the infinite. The infinite does not possess the sort of potentiality that, he says, can become actual in the way that a statue that exists potentially in a block of marble can become actual. He further says that, although the infinite exists differently in time, in the generations of humans, and in the divisions of magnitude, it is generally true of it that "one thing is taken after another, but what is taken is always finite, and always different" (206a25–9). Later in this same chapter, *Phys* III.6, he contrasts his conception of the infinite with a more common conception – viz., that of many of his predecessors, who thought of the "infinite" as "that of which there is nothing outside." Rather, he says, the unlimited/infinite is "that of which there is always something outside" (207a1–2).

The upshot of Aristotle's metaphysical analysis of the infinite can, I think, be characterized as "processive." In other words, he holds that "the infinite" connotes processes that can always be taken a step beyond any finite step – such as enumeration, or the geometrical bisection of any finite magnitude, or the transit of the sun across the celestial equator. And he concludes that such processes, which are capable of indefinite continuation, are essentially incompleteable and that any "collection" produced by such a process is thus not a "whole" (*to holon*): "nothing which does not have an end is complete; and the end is a limit (*peras*)" (207a14–15). With respect to the particular case of the geometrically idealized bisection of a magnitude, "the bisections of the magnitude are infinite (*apeiroi*). Hence this infinite exists potentially but not actually. The number of bisections that can be taken always exceeds any particular multiplicity. But this number [of bisections] is not separable; nor does the infinity remain but, rather, is a coming-to-be, as is time and the number of time" (207b10–15).

In chapter 8, the last chapter of Book III of the *Physics*, Aristotle returns to his five arguments for the existence of the indefinite. But he here treats them as arguments that might be interpreted as establishing the existence of the indefinite "not only potentially, but as something separated (*aphôrismenon*)" (208a6). The two cosmological arguments for the existence of *to apeiron* are summarily dismissed. In order that coming-to-be should not fail, it is not necessary for there to be an actually infinite sensible body; rather, the destruction of one thing can be the coming-to-be of another, with the sum total of everything being limited. With respect to the infinite regress argument (each thing is limited by something else in such a way that there is no ultimate limit), Aristotle distinguishes touching and being limited. While the requirement that everything be touched by something else might lead to the regress, being limited does not: what is limited need not be limited by something distinct from that very thing.

With respect to what might be termed the mental "construction" of the indefinite/infinite, Aristotle takes a strongly anti-idealist position. It is absurd (*atopon*), he says, to suppose that one could make anything either larger or smaller than it is simply by *thinking* that it is or might be so. Perhaps somewhat more obscurely, he says that "time, motion (*kinêsis*), and thinking are infinite, but any part that is taken does not persist. Magnitude (*megethos*) is not infinite in thought either with respect to diminution or increase" (208a20–2). I believe that it is important to keep in mind that Aristotle is speaking of an *actual* infinity or "indefiniteness" in this chapter. Thus, his claim about magnitude comprehends several doctrines. Thought cannot, as it were, expand the extent of the finite cosmos to an unlimited/infinite extent. Nor can it decrease any given magnitude to some *actually infinitesimally small* size. Also, I believe that he holds that thought cannot increase the number of bisections of a given magnitude to some *actually infinite* collection of bisections. Number (*arithmos*) is always finite, and an actual collection always consists of a finite or definite number of elements. All these claims are consistent with the doctrines that Aristotle has asserted about the *potential* infinite. In particular, an idealized geometrical bisection of a definite, given magnitude can always be taken beyond any finite stage. Consequently, there is no limit to the smallness of continuous magnitude just as there is no limit to the numerousness of the collection of discrete elements yielded by the continuing bisection of such a magnitude.

With respect to time, motion, and thinking, Aristotle's attempt to avoid an actual infinite/indefinite is more problematic, although his strategy is clear enough. Time and cosmic motion Aristotle holds to be eternal, without beginning or end. But he claims that since the "parts" of these magnitudes do not exist contemporaneously, they do not constitute actually infinitely large magnitudes – or infinitely great collections if we think of time and motion as consisting of discrete, successive "measures" (e.g., the annual transit of the sun around the ecliptic). To think about the "parts" of time as contemporaneous (or not) seems to be conceptually problematic, however. Many commentators have questioned whether this maneuver can really save Aristotle from the need to postulate an eternity of time (and motion). It is also questionable whether the thought attributed to the unmoved mover(s) can be conceptualized in such a way that its eternity does not commit Aristotle to an actual infinity – particularly if such thought is non-discursive and non-developmental in the manner described by later Aristotelians.

It seems clear that Aristotle's conception of *to apeiron* in terms of processes or procedures that are capable of being extended beyond any definite stage constitutes a major innovation. As he himself points out in *Phys* III.6, his view is in opposition to another view of the infinite, according to which it is an all-inclusive, perfect whole that excludes nothing. The latter, un-Aristotelian conception continued to have a philosophical place, particularly in metaphysics and theology. A conception of the divine nature or attributes as "infinite" in something like the sense of "maximal," "greatest," or "fullest" would seem to require a notion of *actual* infinitude as opposed to the Aristotelian notion.

The relation between Aristotle's conception of potential infinity and ancient mathematical theory and practice is unclear. Views of contemporary scholars on this matter are quite diverse. At one extreme, there is the view of W. Knorr, according to whom "Aristotle's theory of the infinite shows remarkable insensitivity to the issues which must have occupied the geometers of his generation" (Knorr 1982: 122). In Knorr's estimation, it is plausible "to view Aristotle discussions in the *Physics* as an attempt to *save* the concept of the infinite, in the face of a movement among the geometers of his day to give up that concept" (Knorr 1982: 121). At the other end of the spectrum, T. Kouremenos speculates that, in the third Book of the *Physics*, Aristotle "rightly, and constructively as it turned out, objected to the pre-Eudoxean" proofs of certain geometrical theorems that supposedly appealed to mathematical conceptions of *actual* infinity (Kouremenos 1995: 93).

Whatever the relation between Aristotle's doctrine of the potential infinite and contemporary ancient mathematical practice, the Aristotelian conception became, in the long run, the orthodox view, particularly in physical and mathematical contexts. Despite the difficulty in working out the foundations of the calculus in terms of "Aristotelian" potential infinity (a problem that was finally solved by B. Bolzano, A. Cauchy, and K. Weierstrass in the nineteenth century), the basic Aristotelian view persisted in technical contexts until the work of Georg Cantor in the late nineteenth century. In contemporary mathematics, the Aristotelian influence is detectable in the so-called "intuitionist" and constructivist traditions. In words that could have been written by Aristotle himself, M. A. E. Dummett writes that "in intuitionistic mathematics, all infinity is potential infinity; there is no completed infinity. This means, simply, that to grasp an infinite structure is to grasp the process which generates it; to recognise it as infinite is to recognise that the process is such that it will not terminate" (Dummett 1974: 3).

Aristotle on Space: Magnitude (*megethos*) and Place (*topos*)

K. Algra has usefully distinguished three functions that "a concept of space may fulfil within a physical theory": "(a) a kind of prime stuff or 'reservoir of physical possibilities'"; "(b) a framework of (relative) locations"; and "(c) a container, the 'fixed stage where things play out their comedy,' a space *in* which things are and *through* which they can move, to paraphrase Epicurus" (Algra 1995: 15–16). To begin our discussion of Aristotle's conception of space, it is worth noting the Aristotle clearly rejects both one version of function (a) and one version of function (c). A conception of space that is a "kind of prime stuff" or "reservoir of possibilities" (such as that of Plato's receptacle [*hupodochê*] in the *Timaeus*) is rejected by Aristotle in favor of his conception of matter (*hulê*). And he also certainly does not accept a conception of space (like the Epicurean void [*to kenon*]) as having its own substantial ontological status, which could serve as a "container" for bodies and their local motions.

Algra notes that functions (a) and (c) "both identify space with extension" (Algra 1995: 18). Although Aristotle rejects the versions of (a) and (c) that I have mentioned, he does employ an important notion of extension, which has what might be termed spatial characteristics. This is his conception of *megethos*, which I translate as "magnitude." In *Categories* 6, Aristotle distinguishes discrete quantity (*poson*) from continuous (*suneches*) quantity. He includes lines, surfaces, bodies, time, and place in the latter

265

category. And in *Met* Δ.13, Aristotle also distinguishes quantity that is continuous from that which is non-continuous. A magnitude, he says, is quantity that is measurable (as opposed to numerable or countable), and a magnitude is divisible into parts that are continuous (1020a7–11). Among magnitudes, "that which is continuous in one [dimension] is length, that in two breadth, and that in three depth . . . Limited (or 'finite' – *peperasmenon*) length is a line, limited breadth a surface, and limited depth body" (1020a11–14). I think that is fair to say that Aristotle's conception of continuous quantity or magnitude is a geometrical conception. I shall postpone discussion of the continuous "quantities" of time and place, concentrating for the moment on magnitudes of the three spatial dimensions. There are both what might be called "structural" (geometrical or topological) and metaphysical features to be found in Aristotle's analysis of *megethos*.

Some of the former, structural features correspond to properties central to the developing geometry of the fourth century BCE. Aristotle's basic structural property, however, is continuity (*sunecheia*); and it does not have an explicit role in Euclidean geometry (where it appears principally in the notion of a "continuous proportion" of three or more terms). A principle of continuity of geometrical magnitude is assumed, however, in many Euclidean constructions: it guarantees the existence of points at the intersection of two lines, the existence of lines at the intersection of two surfaces or planes, etc. (See Heath 1956: vol. 1, 234ff) It is this conception that is adumbrated by Aristotle in his most formal definition, in *Phys* V.3, of continuity. Having stipulated that "something is contiguous (*echomenon*) [to something] that is successive to and touches it" (227a6), he proceed as follows:

> I say that something is continuous (*suneches*), which is a kind of being contiguous, when-ever the limit of both things at which they touch becomes one and the same and, as the word implies, they are "stuck together" (*sunechêtai*). But this is not possible if the extrem-ities are two. It is clear from this definition that continuity pertains to those things from which there naturally results a sort of unity in virtue of their contact. (227a10–15).

In *Phys* VI.1 Aristotle argues that his conception of continuity implies that "it is impossible that what is continuous be composed of indivisibles, e.g., a line from points" (231a24–5). I shall not here rehearse his argument. But he elsewhere explicitly recognizes other, closely connected corollaries of his conception of continuity. In *Phys* III.7, he comments that "what is continuous is in each case divisible to infinity (*eis apeira*)" (207b16–17) and in *Phys* VI.2, he gives what may seem to be an alternative definition of continuity: "I call continuous that which is, in each case, divisible to [parts] that are continuous" (232b24–5). The upshot of Aristotle's analysis is what I have elsewhere termed a principle of non-supervenience of continuity: "each partition of a continuous magnitude into proper parts yields parts each of which is pairwise continuous with at least one other part" (White 1992: 29). The partition of a continuous magnitude, however small (of one, two, or three dimensions) yields continuous magnitudes of the same dimension *ad infinitum* or "*eis apeiron*," in Aristotle's "potential" sense of *apeiron* (infinite): such a process of partitioning can be continued beyond any finite stage with the same result. A "finest," "foundational," or "atomic" partition – which would be a partition into indivisibles – is never reached. So, in addition to continuity, a second structural characteristic of magnitudes is this kind of infinite divisibility.

A closely related characteristic is a kind of density of one-dimensional or linear magnitudes. Since a line or line segment cannot be constituted of indivisibles (viz., points), Aristotle concludes in *Phys* VI.1 that there is always a line segment between any two points (231b9). I refer to this as the *distributive* density of points in a line: since there is a line segment between any two points that one might consider, one could always *construct* a particular point on that line-segment (by, for example, bisecting it with another line) and, thus, construct a distinct point between the two points with which one began. This distributive density is to be distinguished from the *collective* density of a collection of points. This is the conception of a line (or line segment) as constituted from or identified with a linearly ordered collection of points such that, for any two points in the collection, there is a distinct point in between. There is no indication that Aristotle ever conceived of a one-dimensional continuous magnitude as constituted from a collectively dense collection of points. For one thing, such a collection would evidently have to be *actually* infinite, a consequence that would be unacceptable to him.

We here arrive at the juncture between Aristotle's structural analysis of magnitude (*megethos*) and a more metaphysical dimension of his analysis. His conception of magnitude seems – and, I think, is – quite geometrical. One might wonder, then, whether he conceived of magnitudes in its several dimensions as having some sort of substantial "mathematical" existence – even though he clearly does *not* conceive of a magnitude in a given dimension as reducible to magnitudes in a lesser dimension (e.g., lines to points, surfaces/planes to lines, solids to planes). From his discussion in Books B and M of the *Metaphysics*, it is clear that he does not have a view of mathematical entities as having an independent, substantial status. Although its context is aporetic, the discussion of *Met* B.5 suggests a "constructive" view of lines, surfaces, and points: "they are all divisions (*diaireseis*) of body (*tou sômatos*), the first [lines] with respect to breadth, the second [surfaces/planes] with respect to depth, and the third [points] with respect to length" (1002a19–20). Moreover, points, lines, and surfaces "are not capable of being in the process or coming-to-be or perishing, although at one time they exist and at another they do not" (1002a32–5).

The general impression that magnitudes of null dimension (points), of one dimension (lines), and of two dimensions (surfaces) are ontologically dependent on physical (changeable and sensible) body is confirmed by Aristotle's discussion in *Met* M. Although this account of mathematical objects is difficult, Aristotle appears to hold that they are not, in reality, "separable" (*chôrista*) from sensible, physical reality. Rather, the geometer considers physical bodies *qua* geometrical, abstracting (*aphairein*) their spatial/geometrical characteristics and considering such properties separately from other kinds of property of such bodies. The first result is the idea of three-dimensional extension, abstracted from a consideration of the cosmos as a whole. The "limitations" of 3-D extension are three-dimensional solids (*sterea*), which Aristotle frequently refers to simply as "bodies" (*sômata*). Surfaces, lines, and points are then demarcated by further processes of geometrical demarcation or construction. In *Met* M.3, Aristotle notes that "arithmeticians and geometers" typically consider "what is not separable as separate." The arithmetician (the object of whose investigation is discrete quantity) considers a human being as a single, indivisible unit while the geometer considers him as a solid (1078a21–6). While Aristotle holds that such hypostatization does not produce *mathematical* errors, his view appears to be that, as an ontological matter, the continuous magnitudes investigated by the geometers exist only "materially" (*hulikôs*) in physical, sensible reality (1078a29–31).

This material dependence of spatial magnitude, in its several dimensions, on the physical cosmos creates a potential problem for Aristotle in view of his conception of the extension (*diastêma*) of the cosmos as bounded and finite (characteristics which amount to the same thing, for Aristotle). Shortly after the time of Aristotle, the codification of fifth- and fourth-century geometry by Euclid involved the assumption that the geometer has available magnitudes (say, lines, in one dimension) as large as he or she wants. In Euclid's *Elements*, this assumption appears in several places, including his statement of the famous parallel postulate, the fifth postulate of Euclid I: "if a straight line falling on two straight lines make [the sum of] the interior angles on the same side less than [the sum of] two right angles, the two straight lines, if produced indefinitely/ infinitely (*ep' apeiron*), meet on that side on which are angles less than the two right angles" (Heath 1956: vol. 1, 202). It should be noted that what is required is only the availability of linear magnitude that is *potentially* infinite, in Aristotle's sense: longer than any given finite magnitude. Indeed, there are several passages in the Aristotelian corpus where Aristotle himself assumes the availability of lines "as long as one wishes." (See White 1992: 156ff.)

The apparent problem is that, if there is only a finite cosmos from which we can "abstract" geometrical lines, it is unclear how we are going to come by lines of arbitrarily great finite length. As J. Hintikka expresses the issue, "the real problem here is that some of the lines that a geometer needs do not seem to be forthcoming at all, and of course *this* existential problem is not alleviated by the possibility of abstracting from certain attributes of lines. If the requisite ['physical'] lines do not exist, there is nothing to abstract from" (Hintikka 1973: 122). After claiming in *Phys* III.7 that "since there is no sensible magnitude that is infinite, it is not possible to exceed every definite magnitude – if it were there would be something greater than the heavens" (207b19–21), Aristotle proceeds to argue that his account does not destroy the science of the mathematicians. In a difficult passage, he seems to suggest the following three propositions: (i) the geometers do not need or use the (actually?) infinite; (ii) they require only that a finite (line?) can be produced as far as they wish; (iii) for purposes of demonstration, they need not be concerned whether the magnitude that they require is "among the magnitudes that exist" (207b27–34). Although these are plausible claims about fourth-century geometrical practice, what is problematic is the *reason* that Aristotle seems to give why geometers should not be concerned about the finitude of cosmic extension: "it is possible to have divided in the same ratio (*logon*) as the greatest magnitude another magnitude of any size one wants" (207b31–2).

What Aristotle apparently has in mind is the following strategy. Suppose that one is making a geometrical construction (or proving a theorem about a geometrical construction) that turns out to require more space (i.e., a greater extension) than is available in the physical cosmos. Not to worry: the construction can be made or theorem proved for an entirely similar figure that is small enough to fit into the cosmos, so to speak. Hintikka notes that, clever though Aristotle's maneuver may be, the result is not sufficient to save all theorems of Euclidean geometry, as the notion of "Euclidean geometry" came to be understood (Hintikka 1973, 118ff). T. Kouremenos has attempted another strategy to insure that Aristotle's spatial magnitude is Euclidean. If I understand him correctly, he argues that, despite the limit of physical magnitude in the cosmos, the geometer can "mentally extend" any magnitude – say, a line segment – as far as he or she wants without encountering any upper bound. Kouremenos wishes to interpret the sort of "abstraction" that the geometer performs on "available physical magnitudes" to include abstraction with respect to the *size* (length, breadth, depth) of such magnitude as well. So any physical restriction on the size of magnitudes is simply irrelevant to the "noetic" constructions of geometers (Kouremenos 1995: 53–62). Although I think that the balance of evidence weighs against Kouremenos' interpretation, it perhaps cannot be decisively eliminated.

While Aristotle's conception of magnitude (*megethos*) is strongly geometrical, his concept of place (*topos*) finds more direct employment in his physics. He begins Book IV of the *Physics* with the claim that the physicist or natural philosopher must acquire knowledge of place as well as the infinite. He gives two reasons for this requirement. The first is that "everyone assumes that the things that exist are somewhere (*pou*). But what does not exist is nowhere. Where is the goat-stag or the sphinx?" (208a29–31). The second reason is that "the most general and most proper kind of motion (or 'process' – *kinêsis*) is motion with respect to place, which we call locomotion (*phora*)" (208a31–2). An immediate problem is that, as we have seen, place is classified at *Cat* 6 5a13–14 as a kind of continuous *quantity* ("how much" – *poson*). Most, but not all, commentators have understood the *Categories* conception to be that of continuous three-dimensional extension (*diastêma*) "possessed by" or "corresponding to" a body. (See Algra 1995, 125.) However, one might think that there is at least as great a reason to assign place to the category of location ("where" – *pou*) in terms of the schema of categories specified by Aristotle at *Top* I.9 103b20–5. In fact, Aristotle proceeds in *Phys* IV.1 to distinguish, as the "kinds and parts" (*merê kai eidê*) of place, the six "directions" (*diastaseis*) of left, right, back, front, up, and down. He considers these to be cosmic regions – e.g., up is at the periphery of the cosmos, down at its center – and he identifies (at least some of) these places as the natural places of the four basic elements, each being a place where an element will go if not impeded and thus having a kind of "power" (*dunamis*) (208b8–22). There is, then, a positional function for Aristotle's conception of place – what K. Algra terms the notion of "place as localization" (Algra 1995: 136).

However, in the *locus classicus* of Aristotle's discussion of place, *Phys* IV.1–5, the emphasis is on the role of place in local motion, which is conceptualized as change of place. Aristotle claims that "it is necessary to recognize that place would not be investigated if there were not motion with respect to place" (*Phys* IV.4 211a12–13). In the same chapter, Aristotle lists his requirements for an adequate conception of place:

> we hypothesize first that place contains that of which it is the place and that it is not [a part] of that thing. Further, that a primary or first place is neither smaller nor larger [than the thing]. And further, that it can be left behind [by the thing] and is separable [from it]. In addition to these requirements, that every place admits of up and down and that each of the [elementary] bodies is carried to and remains in its proper place and that this is what makes [a place] either up or down. (210b34–211a6).

His list of potential candidates for a conception of place that satisfy these desiderata contains four items: "the form [of the body having a place], the matter, some sort of

269

extension (*diastêma*) between the extremities (*eschata*) [of the body], or the extremities if there does not exist an extension in addition to the magnitude (*megethos*) of the body that comes-to-be in [the place in question]" (*Phys* IV.4 211b7–9). The first three candidates Aristotle quickly dismisses. In the case of form and matter, these "belong" to a body in such a way that a body cannot leave behind one place and enter another, as is required for local motion. He comments that form, understood as shape (*morphê*), might seem to be place on account of its surrounding the body of which it is the shape since "the extremities of what surrounds and of what is surrounded are in the same [locus?]. Both [shape and place] are boundaries (or 'limits' – *perata*), but not of the same thing: form/shape (*eidos*) is the boundary of the thing, while place is the boundary of the surrounding body" (211b11–14).

Aristotle here hints at his final account of place. But before giving that account, he dismisses the third account of place as the extension (*diastêma*) coincident with the "bulk" of a body and confined by the "extremities" or shape of the body. What he seems to have in mind is a three-dimensional extension that is *distinct* from but "positionally coincident" with the three-dimensional *megethos* of the body itself; being distinct from the body, it can be left behind by the body when the body moves (changes place). Although the argument is obscure in detail, Aristotle dismisses this candidate (which resembles the account of *Cat* 6, as many commentators have noted) because it would yield "infinite places in the same thing" (211b20–1). According to what is perhaps the simplest account of Aristotle's infinite regress argument, place as a three-dimensional "entity" separate from the three-dimensional body that it contains, would require its own separate place, etc. *ad infinitum*. (For a more detailed and subtle interpretation of this argument, see Morison 2002: 122–32.)

Aristotle accepts a specification of the fourth candidate: "place is the primary ('first' or 'innermost' – *prôton*) unmoveable boundary (or 'limit' – *peras*) of that which surrounds [a body having place]" (212a20–1). In what appears to be a gloss on this definition, he adds that "a place seems to be a sort of surface and, as it were, a vessel and container" (212a28–9). According to what may be termed the standard interpretation of Aristotle's account, he is claiming that the place of a body is the innermost (two-dimensional) surface of the stationary surrounding body or "physical matrix or medium" containing the body; this innermost surface of the surrounding matrix would be topologically coincident with but formally distinct from the (two-dimensional) "shape" or surface of the body itself. This conception thus fits Aristotle's desiderata: place so defined contains the body whose place it is; it is neither larger nor smaller than that body, and it is left behind when the body moves and is "separable" from the body. The problematic aspects of this account of place are, however, well known. Things that are not three-dimensional physical bodies (e.g., points, lines, surfaces) would not seem to have their own proper places. It is not clear that things contained in *moving* or *moveable* vessels and matrices (e.g., olive oil in a jar or a boat in a flowing river) could have proper places. And, since the place of something is the innermost surface of the surrounding matrix, what happens when that matrix is changed – when, for example, the water in a pool containing an underwater sculpture is drained and the pool is filled with soil? Does the place of the sculpture change?

This last concern points up a more general problem with Aristotle's account. It seems that one function that an account of place should fulfill is to relate something to other things in its cosmic environment, so to speak. That is, places should be capable of being spatially integrated so as to fulfill the second of the functions of space distinguished by Algra: to serve as "a framework of (relative) locations" (Algra 1995: 15). It is not clear that Aristotle's account of place, as standardly interpreted, can satisfy the final desideratum in Aristotle's list: "that every place admits of up and down and that each of the [elementary] bodies is carried to and remains in its proper place and that this is what makes [a place] either up or down" (211a3–6).

I believe that this problem is a motivating factor in H. Lang's radical reinterpretation of Aristotle definition of place at *Phys* IV.4 212a20–1: "place is the *proton* unmovable *peras* of that which surrounds [a body having place]." Lang denies that "*proton . . . peras*" connotes the *innermost surface* of any surrounding body or medium. Rather, she interprets "*peras*" as a sort of *sui generis* limit and "*proton*" as "first," in the sense of outermost heavens or sphere of fixed stars in the Aristotelian cosmos: "place is first as the whole heaven is what first surrounds everything that is contained within the heavens" (Lang 1998: 99–100). According to Lang's view, this account of place as limit "renders the cosmos determinate in respect to the six directions, up, down, front, back, left and right, and so constitutes 'the where' of all things that are and are moved" (Lang 1998: 102).

While Lang's interpretation of Aristotle's account of place in *Phys* IV has not been widely accepted, it does point to a problem in Aristotle's account of place. According to the traditional interpretation, that account is quite "local": the place of something is defined exclusively in terms of the body/matrix that *immediately* surrounds it. But some uses of place-talk would seem to suggest a broader, more universal or "cosmic" framework of relative positions or what Algra calls "a kind of overall grid of locations" (Algra 1995: 227). I believe that Algra is correct, however, in suggesting that "the idea of a self-subsistent surface [*qua* place of something] as part of a kind of overall grid of (abstract) locations would be as alien to Aristotle's ontology as the idea of a self-subsistent three-dimensional extension" (Algra 1995: 230).

Aristotle on Time: The "Number of Motion" and "Ever-rolling Stream"

Of the three topics of this chapter – the infinite, space, and time in Aristotle's thought – the last has surely received the most attention. Since I cannot hope to do justice to the immense literature on the subject, I concentrate on two themes. One is his "physical" analysis of time, which issues in the formulaic definition found in *Phys* IV.11: "this, then, is [a] time: the number of motion with respect to the earlier [or 'prior' – *proteron*] and the later [or 'posterior' – *husteron*]" (219b1–2). The other theme, which borders on the ineffable, is the transitory, evanescent, or "flowing" character that attaches to our experience of time. In the words of the English hymn "St. Anne," "Time, like an ever-rolling stream, /Bears all its sons away." In Aristotle's less poetic but nonetheless poignant words, "a thing, then, is affected by time, as we are wont to say that time wastes things away and that all things grow old because of time and people forget on account of time – but not that one has learned or become young or beautiful [on account of the passage of time]. Rather, time is essentially the cause of corruption. For

271

it is the number of process (or 'motion' – *kinêsis*), and process does away with what exists" (*Phys* IV.12 221a30–b3).

Aristotle's principal "scientific" analysis of time occurs in the fourth Book of the *Physics*. It is useful, I believe, to begin our brief discussion of that analysis by drawing a distinction that is not explicitly made by Aristotle, the distinction between a geometrical or topological component and a metrical component of his account. By "geometrical/topological component," I refer to his conception of time as a continuous, linear dimension of *kinêsis* (process, motion, or change that is incremental and developmental). By "metrical component," I mean the idea of "*a* time" in the sense of a unit of temporal measure (defined in terms of some continuous and unitary but repeating or repeatable motion), or some definite multiple of such a unit.

To begin our discussion of the geometrical component, it is worth recalling that time (*chronos*) is one of the species of continuous quantity (along with lines, surfaces, bodies/solids, and place) distinguished by Aristotle in *Cat* 6. In view of Aristotle's general ontological proclivities, it is not surprising to find that he does not conceive of time as some substantive principle (*archê*) or entity *within* which occur processes and events that are metaphysically separable from that time. In *Phys* IV, he makes it clear that time, in this geometrical sense, is ontologically dependent on (but not identical with) *kinêsis* – motion, process, or continuous change, which includes not only local motion but also qualitative alteration (*alloiôsis*), increase (*auksêsis*), and decrease (*phthisis*) (see, e.g., *Phys* III.1 201a9–16). In *Phys* IV.14, Aristotle describes time as an "affect or state of motion (*kinêseôs ti pathos ê heksis*)" (223a18–19). It is also clear from the discussion of time in the *Physics* that Aristotle employs (in fact, is perhaps the first to employ) a sort of geometrical abstraction in his analysis of time. That is, he thinks of time as analogous to one-dimensional or linear magnitude ("a line"). Finite stretches or intervals of time are bounded, in both the prior (*proteron*) and the posterior (*husteron*) "temporal directions," by temporal "points" or instants (literally, "nows" – *ta nun*), which do not themselves have "positive measure" or duration but which serve as the limits of stretches of time.

Just as a line is not composed of points according to Aristotle, so time is not composed of nows or instants. "Insofar as the now (*to nun*) is a boundary/limit (*peras*), it is not time but belongs to it as a property" (*Phys* IV.11 220a21–2). And, "because time is a number of motion with respect to the prior/earlier and the posterior/later it is clear that it is continuous (for motion is continuous)" (220a24–6). Although the previous chapter, *Phys* IV.10, is aporetic in character, Aristotle there seems to claim that "the now/instant is not a part [of time], for the part measures [that of which it is a part], and it is necessary that a whole [time] is constituted of parts. So time seems not to be constituted of nows" (218a6–8). He also makes the following stipulation: "let it be [understood to be] impossible that nows are in immediate succession to one another, just as it is impossible for point immediately to succeed point" (218a18–19). The general geometrical picture that emerges is that of time modeled in the same way as linear magnitude (*megethos*). Any interval or stretch of time is continuous and "infinitely divisible" (in Aristotle's "potential infinity" sense) into smaller sub-intervals. Temporal "points" or instants can be demarcated or "constructed" (as, for example, the boundaries of processes and, perhaps, as instantaneous events). They are "distributively dense" within temporal duration; but no time, in the sense of interval of time, is constituted of such instants as parts. Both cosmic motion and the time that is an affect or property of that motion are without beginning and end, as Aristotle argues in *Phys* VIII.

Although Aristotle holds that time has neither beginning nor end, there is a fundamental cyclical character to his conception of time that is, I believe, introduced by the *metrical* component of his conception of time. In *On Generation and Corruption* II.11, he maintains that generation or coming-to-be which is "absolutely" (*haplôs*) necessary must be coming-to-be that is cyclical (338a3ff). Among motions that are eternally cyclical (and, hence, necessary in an absolute sense), the most obvious are the motions of the heavenly spheres, particularly the diurnal motion of the outermost sphere of fixed stars in Aristotle's finite, bounded cosmos. And these celestial motions provide the principal "numbers" that constitute time in the metrical sense.

In *Phys.* IV.12, Aristotle specifies some of the consequences of his metrical conception of "a time," in terms of a unit of time or definite multiple of such a unit. "A time" as the number of motion with respect to prior and posterior is not properly said to be fast or slow. Rather, it is "many or few and long or short: long or short *qua* continuous, and many or few *qua* a number" (220a32–b3). The idea is that time is a number insofar as its duration can be measured by a multiple of some unit, the unit being defined by a certain (repeatable) motion. Thus, there is a certain reciprocity of measurement between a time and a motion since "they are delimited by one another" (220b16). That is, a time measures a motion insofar as the motion's duration can be represented as a definite multiple of some temporal unit. But a motion measures a time insofar as a time *qua* temporal unit is defined in terms of some unitary, continuous motion. Aristotle here presents an analogy. We know the size of a herd of horses by determining their number (how many horses in the group). But the unit of measure (one horse) by which we enumerate the size of the herd of horses is determined by the nature of what is measured (220b18ff). Finally, Aristotle develops a metrical analogy between magnitude and time:

> Since a time is a measure of motion or being moved, it measures a motion by delimiting a given motion that measures out the whole [motion] – just as a *pêkus* [forearm and hand's length] measures length by delimiting a given magnitude [i.e., the linear magnitude of a forearm and hand] that measures out the whole length. (220b32–221a4)

In the "Corollary Concerning Time" to his commentary on Aristotle's *Physics*, the sixth-century CE commentator Simplicius reports that Strato of Lampsacus (the successor of Theoprastus as Peripatetic scholarch, who himself succeeded Aristotle) "does not agree that time is a number of motion, because number is discrete quantity, but motion and time are continuous, and what is continuous is not numerable" (Simplicius, *Phys*, CAG 9, 789). I believe that the most plausible Aristotelian response to Strato would be to point out the difference between the geometrical and metrical constituents of Aristotle's conception of time. From the geometrical/topological perspective, Strato is correct: as a continuous quantity, time does not possess an intrinsic metric. But from the metrical perspective, the assignment of a discrete but repeatable/repeating motion (e.g., a complete transit of sun around the ecliptic, or a complete diurnal rotation of the sphere of fixed stars – which accounts for the daily rising and setting of the sun in the astronomy of the fourth century BCE) introduces the notion of discrete "number" by which time may be measured. Time as a species of continuous quantity does not exhibit a single, intrinsic and obvious unit by which it can be measured – in the way that a discrete multiplicity, such as a herd of horses, exhibits the intrinsic and "natural" unit of one horse. But, once an extrinsic unit of measure has been selected for a continuous quantity such as time, one can speak of time in metrical terms as a "number of motion [viz., of motion-types *qua* units] with respect to earlier and later" (220a24–5).

There is an aspect of Aristotle's conception of time that does not fit well into either the metrical or geometrical categories. This is the picture of time as the "ever-rolling stream" or, alternatively, the picture of the *nunc fluens* ("flowing now"). In modern scholarship, this picture is sometimes presented in terms of J. M. E. McTaggart's A-series tense concepts (past, present, future) and his B-series concepts of temporal ordering (before, simultaneous with, after). As we have seen, Aristotle makes use of one notion of "nows" (*ta nun*) – that of temporal points, limits, or instants – in order to define stretches of time to which the B-series concepts can be applied. But the now (*to nun*) also appears as the notion of "the present," as in the A-series concepts: "the now is the link (*sunecheia*) of time, as has been said, for it links (*sunechei*) what has happened and what will happen" (*Phys* IV.13 222a10–11). It is not obvious, I think, whether Aristotle sees this latter, token-reflexive now as a *unique* temporal instant that, as it were, "moves through time," generating a unique past out of a partially indeterminate future or whether he conceives of *each* temporal instant as representing "the present" from its own perspective and possessing its own particular determinate past and partially indeterminate future.

What is more certain is that Aristotle holds that time is anisotropic: that is, the future is quite different from the past. In *Cael* I.12, for example, he notes that capacities or potentialities pertain not to the past but only to the present-or-future (283b13–14). And *de Interpretatione* 9, with its discussion of future sea-battles, has often been interpreted as attributing a sort of indeterminacy or "openness" to the future, while regarding the past as determinate or fixed. Indeed, the relation in Aristotle's thought between temporal concepts (past, present, and future), on one hand, and alethic concepts (truth, falsity, possibility, necessity), on the other, is a complex matter that cannot be explored in detail in this chapter. But it does seem that he accepts a commonsensical picture of the future as "containing" various possibilities in a way that the past does not. With the passage of time, some of these possibilities are actualized and some are not. The result is a past that is fixed in such a way that true propositions about it are *now* necessary and false propositions about it are *now* impossible. But it should be noted that these kinds of possibility and necessity are *relative* to a particular temporal perspective (now). Thus, the modal status of events and processes can change with the passage of time. Tomorrow's possible sea-battle, if it is actualized "come tomorrow," *then* becomes necessary (in something like the sense of unchangeable, unalterable, or irrevocable) ever thereafter. In contemporary tense and modal logic, this temporal and modal asymmetry of the past and future has been modeled by branching tree structures in which each temporal instant has a unique, linear past-branch but multiple linear future-branches, each representing a possible future from the perspective of the given temporal instant from which they branch. But whether such structures do adequate justice to Aristotle's conception of temporal passage, his conception of time as an "ever-rolling stream," is a controverted subject.

I have elsewhere (White 1992: 95) characterized an Aristotelian notion of "*Urzeit*" that is defined by the eternally cyclical (and, thus, in Aristotle's view necessary) cosmic motions. These motions define time as a linear continuum because their tokens or instances are temporally continuous with one another, without any intervening gaps. But they also supply the fundamental metrical character of time by providing the most basic units of temporal measurement. However, contingent, irregular, and idiosyncratic processes or *kinêseis* (which, in Aristotle's view, are sublunary) give rise to the asymmetry of the past and future and, consequently, constitute temporal anistropy.

In concluding this discussion of time, it is worth noting that in a brief passage in *Phys* IV.14, Aristotle raises the issue of the relation of time to soul (*psuchê*). In this passage, Aristotle may seem to introduce an idealistic element into his analysis of time. His basic argument appears in the following passage:

> if it is impossible for something which/who enumerates to exist then it is impossible for what is enumerated to exist. So it is clear that number would then not exist. Number is either what has been enumerated or what can be enumerated (*to arithmêton*). If nothing other than soul or the reason (*nous*) of soul is of such a nature as to enumerate, it would be impossible for time to exist without soul's existing, but only that of which time is the "when" (*pote*) – if, that is, it is possible for motion (*kinêsis*) to exist without soul. For the earlier and later exist in motion; and time is these [the earlier and later] *qua* enumerated. (223a22–9)

Whether this passage makes time as "ideal" or soul-dependent as it may seem to do is open to question (see Annas 1975). What Aristotle apparently claims is that the "earlier or later [that] exist in motion" – or what Waterlow terms the "temporal dimension of motion" (Waterlow 1983: 134) – would exist so long as motion exists even if soul did not exist. It would exist, that is, if *motion* itself could exist without soul. He seems further to imply that the existence of time in the metrical sense depends on the existence of soul or reason. But, in Aristotle's cosmology, reason *does* actually, eternally, and necessarily exist in the form of the celestial intelligences or unmoved movers responsible for the rotation of the celestial spheres. Since these are the very principles responsible for *Urzeit* or the fundamental metric of time, it seems plausible to suppose that these unmoved movers could supply the enumeration needed for time in the full, metrical sense.

Bibliography

Algra, Keimpe (1995). *Concepts of Space in Greek Thought* (Leiden: Brill).

Annas, Julia (1975). "Aristotle, Number and Time," *Philosophical Quarterly*, 25, pp. 97–113.

Cleary, John J. (1995). *Aristotle and Mathematics: Aporetic Method in Cosmology and Metaphysics* (Leiden: Brill).

Conen, Paul F. (1964). *Zeittheorie des Aristoteles* (Munich: Verlag C. H. Beck).

Coope, Ursula (2005). *Time for Aristotle* (Oxford: Oxford University Press).

Corish, Denis (1978). "Aristotle on Temporal Order: 'Now,' 'Before,' and 'After,'" *Isis*, 69, pp. 68–74.

Dummett, M. A. E. (1974). *Intuitionistic Logic and Mathematics*, part I (Oxford: Oxford Mathematical Institute Mimeograph).

Heath, Sir Thomas L. (1956). *The Thirteen Books of Euclid's Elements*, 3 vols., 2nd edn., revd. (New York: Dover Publications).

Hintikka, Jaakko (1973). "Aristotelian Infinity," repr. in *Time and Necessity: Studies in Aristotle's Theory of Modality* (Oxford: Clarendon Press), pp. 114–34.

Knorr, Wilbur R. (1982). "Infinity and Continuity: The Interaction of Mathematics and Philosophy in Antiquity," in Norman Kretzmann (ed.), *Infinity and Continuity in Ancient and Medieval Thought* (Ithaca, NY: Cornell University Press).

Kouremenos, Theokritos (1995). *Aristotle on Mathematical Infinity* (Stuttgart: Franz Steiner Verlag).

Lang, Helen S. (1998). *The Order of Nature in Aristotle's "Physics"* (New York: Cambridge University Press).

Lear, Jonathan (1979). "Aristotelian Infinity," *Proceedings of the Aristotelian Society*, 80, pp. 188–210.

Lear, Jonathan (1982). "Aristotle's Philosophy of Mathematics," *Philosophical Review*, 91, pp. 161–92.

Mendell, Henry (1987). "Topoi on Topos: The Development of Aristotle's Concept of Place," *Phronesis*, 32, pp. 206–31.

Morison, Benjamin (2002). *On Location: Aristotle's Concept of Place* (Oxford: Clarendon Press).

Waterlow, Sarah (1983). "Instants of Motion in Aristotle's *Physics VI*," *Archiv für Geschichte der Philosophie*, 65, pp. 128–46.

Waterlow, Sarah (1984). "Aristotle's Now," *Philosophical Quarterly*, 34, pp. 104–28.

White, Michael J. (1992). *The Continuous and the Discrete* (Oxford: Clarendon Press).

White, Michael J. (1993). "The Metaphysical Location of Aristotle's *Mathêmatika*," *Phronesis*, 38, pp. 166–82.

17

Change and Its Relation to Actuality and Potentiality

URSULA COOPE

What is change? Aristotle points out that there are many different types of change: change in respect of quality (for instance, change in color), change in respect of quantity (such as, growing and shrinking), change in respect of place (or "motion" as we would call it) and the kind of change that is the generation of a new substance (for example, the coming-to-be of an animal) (*Physics* III.1 200b33–4).[1] In *Physics* III.1–3, he provides a general account of change. Before looking in detail at this account, it is helpful to answer two questions. What is he attempting to achieve in giving it? And what are his criteria for success?

In part, his aim is simply to defend the possibility of change. Parmenides, he tells us, argued that change was impossible on the grounds that nothing can come from what is not. Aristotle replies to this argument in *Physics* I.7–9. He agrees with Parmenides that something cannot come into being from nothing, but claims that this does not rule out the possibility of change. What is F can come to be from what is not F, provided that there is some underlying thing that persists through the change. For instance, the change that is *becoming musical* is not simply the emergence of musicality from an absence of musicality. Rather, it is a change that occurs in some man, who is first unmusical and then musical.

Though he argues against Parmenides, Aristotle does concede that there is something puzzling about change. This is reflected, he thinks, in other thinkers' confused attempts to say what change is. In Plato's *Sophist* (256d), change is described as something that is not (since it is different from that which is) and yet also is (since it partakes in that which is). Aristotle tells us that change has been variously defined as "difference and inequality and that which is not" (201b20–1). There is, he thinks, something right about these earlier views. Change is closely connected to privation and what is not, and because of this it is, in a sense to be explained, "incomplete" (201b31–2). Nevertheless, none of these views provides a satisfactory definition. Things can, after all, be different and unequal without changing (201b21–2). A successful account of change must explain its connection with what is not, while showing how it can be among the things that are.

In his reply to Parmenides, Aristotle lays down a necessary condition for change: for there to be change there must be an underlying thing and two contraries. It might be thought that this suggests an obvious definition: change is simply the possession, by one persisting thing, of contrary states at different times. To define change in this way would be to advocate what is sometimes called an "at–at" theory of change. In modern times, Bertrand Russell has endorsed such a theory (for locomotion): "Motion," he says, "consists merely in the fact that bodies are sometimes in one place and sometimes in another, and that they are at intermediate places at intermediate times" (Russell 1981: 66). Aristotle would reject the at-at theory of change. Understanding why will help us to see what, on his view, a successful definition of change must be like.

There are at least two reasons why Aristotle would reject an at-at account of change. First, he is going to define time partly in terms of change (*Physics* IV.10–14). If this definition of time is not to be circular, he needs some account of change that makes no reference to time. Second, he assumes that changing cannot be reduced to being, successively, in a series of unchanging states. (This is implicit, I think, in his discussion of the continuity of motion at *Physics* VIII.8.) Though it is true that in the course of a change, the changing thing passes through intermediate states, *passing through a state* is different from *statically being in that state*. The mistake of the at-at theory is to assume that passing through a state is a way of statically being in that state (namely, being in it instantaneously), and hence that it can be understood independently of change. Aristotle rejects this assumption. For him, the notion of passing through a state is itself derivative from the notion of a change. Hence, change cannot be defined as being successively in different states at different times. (For a fuller discussion of this, see White 1992.)

We can now appreciate the difficulties Aristotle faces in providing an account of change. He wants an account that makes no reference to time. It must explain what change is, without reducing changing to being in a series of unchanging states. It must show that change is something real, and yet it must capture the insight (attributed by Aristotle to his predecessors) that change is closely connected with privation and what is not. He attempts to give such an account in *Physics* III.1–3, using the notions of actuality and potentiality. In this essay, I provide an interpretation of this difficult passage, and raise some problems for the account of change that emerges from it.

The Account of Change in *Physics* III.1–3

In *Physics* III.1, Aristotle defines change as the "actuality of that which potentially is, *qua* such" (201a10–11). This definition owes at least some of its obscurity to the notions of potentiality and actuality that it employs. I consider three different ways of understanding them. On the interpretation I defend, Aristotle uses the notions of actuality and potentiality to explain the relation between change and what is not. In defining change as a kind of actuality, he is making the point that change is something that is: it is a part of reality. In defining change as an actuality *of what potentially is qua such*, he is bringing out the relation between change and what is not.

According to Aristotle, to be potentially is to have a potential *for* some actuality. A potential is defined in relation to some actuality that is its fulfillment. For example, some bronze in the sculptor's workshop has the potential to be a statue; the actuality of this potential is *being a statue*. The doctor's patient has the potential to be healthy; the actuality of this potential is *being healthy*. Aristotle writes not only of the actuality of a potential but also of the actuality of what has the potential. The complete actuality (or fulfillment) of something that has the potential to be F *insofar as it is considered simply as having that potential* consists in its being F. Hence, the complete actuality of what is potentially a statue, considered simply as potentially a statue, is a statue. In our example, it is bronze that is potentially a statue. The complete actuality of this bronze *qua* potentially a statue is a statue. Similarly, the complete actuality of what is potentially healthy, considered simply as potentially healthy, is a healthy thing (or, in our example: the complete actuality of the patient, *qua* potentially healthy, is a healthy patient).

These examples immediately give rise to a puzzle for Aristotle's definition of change as a kind of actuality. For they suggest that the actuality is the product of a change, rather than the change itself. An account of change needs to capture what it is for some bronze to *become a statue*, but once the bronze is fully actual, *qua* potentially a statue, it already is a statue, and so is no longer becoming a statue. Similarly, the actuality of the patient's potential to be healthy would seem to be not the change that the patient undergoes (becoming healthy), but, rather, the result of this change: *being healthy*.

Each of the three interpretations I shall consider provides a different response to this puzzle. According to the first, the word I have translated "actuality" should, in this context, be translated "actualization." A change is, on this view, the actualization, or *process of becoming actual*, of a certain potentiality. According to the second interpretation, the puzzle I outlined above arises only because of a misidentification of the potentiality that Aristotle refers to in his definition. Change is the actuality of a potential for *changing*, not of a potential for being in a certain new state. For instance, the bronze's change into a statue is the actuality of its potential to *become* a statue (not of its potential to *be* a statue). On the third interpretation (which is the one I shall defend), the potential mentioned in the definition is a potential to be in some new state, but there are two different ways of being the actuality of such a potential. One kind of actuality is being in the new state, and the other is the process of changing into that new state. The point of Aristotle's definition and of his subsequent discussion is to pick out precisely the kind of actuality that is *change* as opposed to the actuality that is the *product* of the change.

Change as the actualization of a potential for being

Is Aristotle defining change as the *actualization* of that which potentially is, *qua* such? On this interpretation, he is defining change as the process by which a certain potential is actualized. For instance, the sculptor's bronze is potentially a statue; its change into a statue is the process by which its potential to be a statue is actualized. The doctor's patient is potentially healthy; *becoming healthy* is the actualization of this potential to be healthy (i.e. it is the process that results in being healthy). (For a defence of this interpretation, see Kostman 1987).

One objection to this interpretation is that it makes Aristotle's account of change circular. To define change as a process of actualization is singularly uninformative, for if one is puzzled about the notion of change, one is likely to be at least as puzzled by the notion of a process of actualization. By itself, this objection is not fatal, since it depends on certain assumptions about Aristotle's aims. If he meant to give a reductive account, then clearly this could not be achieved by defining change as a kind of actualization. If, on the other hand, he merely meant to exhibit the relation between change and other notions he already employs in his metaphysical writings (such as that of potentiality), then perhaps he would not regard the charge of circularity as troubling. The claim that any change must involve a process by which a potential for being in a certain new state is actualized is, after all, not simply a truism. (Indeed, far from being trivially true, this is an account of change with which one might well disagree. Consider, for instance, a dead leaf that is blown across the street by the wind. Is it really plausible to suppose that its movement is the actualization of some specific potential it has for being on the other side of the street?)

This interpretation does, however, face a more serious objection. As I have already explained, Aristotle is writing against a background in which the possibility of change, and the reality of changing things, has been called into question. Given this background, the challenge he faces is to explain how change can be part of reality. If he is to meet this challenge, he needs to show that change itself is a kind of actuality. To define change as the process by which a certain potential is made actual would be to restate the problem without saying anything to solve it. (See Waterlow 1982: 106–14.)

Neither of the objections outlined above is decisive. Both depend upon controversial views about what Aristotle hoped to achieve in giving his account of change. However, there are in addition two independent reasons for doubting this interpretation. The first is lingusitic. The Greek word that, on this interpretation, gets translated as "actualization" is *entelecheia*. This word is an Aristotelian coinage and means literally *having completion (or perfection)*. If Aristotle is using the word here to mean *the process of making actual*, then he is using it in a way that has no parallel elsewhere in his work. It is unlikely he would alter the meaning of a technical term in this way, especially in a passage that is designed to reveal the connections between change and the metaphysics of potentiality and actuality.

The other reason for doubting this interpretation lies in the details of the definition of change itself. As we have seen, Aristotle defines change as the *entelecheia* (actuality/actualization) of what potentially is, *qua* such. If the word *entelecheia* means *process of actualization*, then this definition seems unnecessarily complicated. *Any* process by which something that is potential is actualized is a change. Why, then, is it necessary to add the qualification "*qua* such"? What is more, Aristotle himself makes it clear that this qualification is an essential part of the definition. Bronze, he says, is something that is potentially a statue. The *entelecheia* of the bronze *qua* potentially a statue is a change (201b4–5), but the *entelecheia* of the bronze *qua* bronze is not a change (201a29–31). It is hard to make sense of this, if we understand *entelecheia* to mean *process of becoming actual*, for surely the process by which the bronze becomes actual, *qua* bronze, is a change: it is the change that is the coming-to-be of the bronze.

For all these reasons, it is preferable to understand *entelecheia* to mean actuality. If we adopt this translation, though, we are left with the question I raised earlier: how does the phrase "the actuality of what potentially is, *qua* such" manage to pick out change, as opposed to the state of completion which terminates a change?

Change as the actuality of a potential for changing

One answer is to understand the potential mentioned in the definition as a potential for changing. On this interpretation, the definition says that change is the actuality of what is potentially changing, *qua* potentially changing. The role of the *qua* clause is unproblematic. Change cannot simply be defined as the actuality of what is potentially changing, since there are some actualities of a thing that is potentially changing that are not changes. For example, what is potentially changing might be some bronze. There are some actualities of the bronze that are not changes: the actuality of the bronze *qua* bronze is *the bronze's being bronze*; the actuality of the bronze *qua* potentially a statue is (on this interpretation) *a statue*. The function of the *qua* clause is to pick out the actuality of the bronze (or, more generally, of what is potentially changing) that is a change. The actuality that is a change is the actuality of the bronze *qua* potentially changing. This interpretation of Aristotle's account is defended by Heinaman (1994).

There is some textual support for this interpretation. In spelling out his definition, Aristotle frequently mentions what appear to be potentialities for change. For instance, he says that alteration is the actuality of the "alterable *qua* alterable" (201a11–12). And later (201a27–9) he describes change as the actuality of what potentially is *"qua* changeable." The terms "alterable" and "changeable" are most naturally taken to mean (respectively) *having the potential to alter* and *having the potential to change*, rather than *having the potential to be in some new state*.

Moreover, one advantage of this interpretation is that it allows us to make sense of Aristotle's view that there are certain changes (such as the circular movements of the planets and the heavenly spheres) that go on forever. If Aristotle defines change as the actuality of a potential for changing, then there is nothing puzzling about the fact that he thinks that some changes are unending. If, on the other hand, he defines a change in terms of the changing thing's potential to be in some particular end state, then he faces a difficulty about accommodating these unending changes, for it is unclear how undergoing an unending change of this sort could be regarded as fulfilling a potential to be in some definite end state.

Nevertheless, there are good grounds for rejecting this interpretation. One drawback is that it (like the first interpretation I discussed) attributes to Aristotle an account of change that is circular: it defines change in terms of a potential to be changing. As I said above, the charge of circularity is not by itself a decisive reason for rejecting an interpretation, since its force depends very much on what Aristotle was aiming to do in giving an account of change.

A more important objection is that this interpretation makes it difficult to explain Aristotle's claim that change is an *incomplete* kind of activity or actuality (201b31–2).[2] He makes this claim when discussing his predecessors' views about change. The fact that change is an incomplete kind of actuality is, he thinks, what his predecessors were gesturing towards when they described change as inequality, difference and what is not (201b20–1). He boasts that it is a merit of his definition that it captures this fact about change (201b16–17).

The problem is that it is unclear in what sense change could be the *incomplete* actuality of a potential to change. How could a potential that is specifically for changing be more completely fulfilled than by something's changing? If I have a potential for walking, then surely I fully exercise this potential by walking (just as I fully exercise my potential for sitting still by sitting still). The main drawback of the proposed interpretation, then, is that it fails to explain what Aristotle himself thought was peculiar about change: the fact that change, though a kind of actuality, is an incomplete actuality.

Change as the incomplete actuality of a potential for being

Our discussion so far suggests certain requirements that a successful interpretation should meet. First, it should translate the word *entelecheia* as actuality, rather than actualization. Second, it should explain what is problematic about change: it should enable us to understand the sense in which change is incomplete and associated with what is not, while showing how change can nevertheless be something real. Third, it should give due weight to the *qua* clause in the definition. And finally, the definition should pick out processes of change rather than the products that result from them.

The interpretation I shall defend attempts to meet all these requirements. (Versions of this interpretation are defended by Kosman 1969 and by Waterlow 1982.) On this interpretation, change is the actuality of what is potentially in some particular different state, *qua* such. For example, the change that is *becoming a statue*, is the actuality of what is potentially a statue, *qua* potentially a statue. On this view, then, when Aristotle writes of what is potentially *changeable*, he is not invoking an irreducible potential for *change*: to have a potential for a certain change is to have a potential for being in some particular new state.

There are two questions that such an interpretation needs to answer. First, how does the definition (so understood) distinguish *changing* from *having the potential to be in some new state without changing towards it*? How, for instance, does it distinguish between *changing into a statue* and *statically being something that has the potential to be a statue* (e.g. statically being bronze)? Second, on this interpretation, how is the process of change distinguished from the state in which it results? How, for example, is the process of changing into a statue distinguished from the state of being a statue? Both of these questions can be answered by attending to the *qua* clause in Aristotle's definition. I shall examine each of them in turn.

Aristotle himself makes it clear that at least one function of the *qua* clause in his definition is to distinguish between the process of change and the state that a thing is in when it has the potential to be different but is not yet changing. He says, "by *qua* I mean this. The bronze is potentially a statue, but nevertheless it is not the actuality of bronze *qua* bronze that is change" (201a29–31). His point is that since what it is to be bronze is different from what it is to be potentially a statue, the actuality of the bronze *qua* bronze is different from the actuality of the bronze *qua* potentially a statue. The actuality of the bronze *qua* bronze is just *the bronze being bronze*. The actuality to which the definition refers is the actuality of the bronze *qua* potentially a statue.

But what is it for the bronze to be actual *qua* potentially a statue? There is a sense in which, before the bronze starts to undergo the process of changing into a statue, its potential to be a statue is dormant: the fact that the bronze has the potential to be a statue is not making any difference to how the world then is (although this fact about the bronze does, of course, make a difference to what might happen in the future). For the bronze to be actual insofar as it is potentially a statue is for the bronze's potential to be a statue to be making a difference in a certain way. Care is needed to spell out exactly what this amounts to. There are ways in which a potential can make a difference to the world, without that potential's being (in the sense we have in mind here) actual. A tyrant who wanted to prevent the manufacture of statues might order that all materials for making them should be confiscated and transferred to the royal vaults.

It could then be true of a certain lump of bronze that it was lying in the royal vaults precisely because it was potentially a statue. But the bronze's lying in the royal vaults would not count as an actuality of its potential to be a statue. Why not? The reason is that for a potential for being F to be actual at a certain time, it is not enough that that potential is making a difference to how the world then is: it must be making a difference in a way that is (in some sense) *directed at being F*.[3]

There are two ways in which the bronze's potential to be a statue might, in this sense, be actual. One is for the bronze to be a statue, the other is for the bronze to be in the process of becoming a statue. For all that has been said so far, either of these could count as the actuality of the bronze's potential to be a statue, *qua* potential. Our next question, then, must be: how can Aristotle distinguish between the process of change and the product of change?

The answer is once again found in the *qua* clause of the definition. When Aristotle says that change is the actuality of what is potentially F, *qua* potentially F, the point of the *qua* clause is partly to emphasize that the actuality in question is the actuality of something insofar as it is merely *potentially* F. A thing's potential to be F is most fully actual as a *potential*, when the thing is not yet F. Aristotle explains this, using as an example the process of housebuilding: "the actuality of the buildable, *qua* buildable, is the process of building. For the actuality is either the process of building or the house, but when the house is, the buildable no longer is" (201b9–11). "The buildable," here, is that which is potentially a house. By saying that when the house is, the buildable no longer is, Aristotle makes it clear that being *potentially* a house, in the sense he means here, is incompatible with actually being a house. The actuality of the buildable *qua* buildable is the actuality of what is potentially a house (bricks and mortar, for instance), when it is exhibiting its potential to be a house without yet being a house.

This explains Aristotle's claim that change is an incomplete kind of actuality or activity. The reason he gives for this is that "the potential, of which it is the actuality, is incomplete" (201b32–3). The potential is incomplete in that it is only retained for as long as it is not completely fulfilled. In the sense of "potential" Aristotle invokes here, a thing only has a potential to be F when it is not in fact F. We can now see why Aristotle thought there was something right about his predecessors' association of change with difference and what is not. A change is the fulfillment of a potential something has to be different from how it currently is (or, equivalently, to be in a state in which it currently is not). This brings out the puzzling nature of change. A change is, in a certain sense, aimed at its own destruction. When the potential mentioned in its definition is fully actual, the change is no longer occurring.

According to the view I have outlined here, a thing's potential to be F is actual *qua* potential just in case this potential is making a difference to the world that is (1) characteristic of its being a mere potential and (2) directed at being F. Both of these aspects of what it is for a potential to be actual *qua* potential are essential. One way in which a thing's potential for being F can make a difference is for that thing simply to be F, but this is not a way of making a difference that is characteristic of being merely a potential. Something that is merely potentially F is not in fact F. On the other hand, the actuality *qua* merely potential of a potential to be F is not simply a manifestation of the privative state of not-being-F. As Mary Louise Gill has pointed out (1989: 189–94), flaunting one's ignorance need not be part of a process of learning. Flaunting one's ignorance, though it is compatible with having the potential for knowledge, is not the actuality of a potential for knowledge, because it is not an actuality that is directed towards having knowledge.

An actuality that is a change must, then, be directed at some new state. What makes it possible for a change to exhibit this kind of directedness is an agent that is responsible for the change. The changes I have considered so far have all been changes that a thing undergoes as a result of the action of something else. The bronze becomes a statue because of the action of the sculptor; the bricks become a house because of the action of the housebuilder. Aristotle says that the thing that produces the change will always have the form that is responsible for the change: "what is actually a human being makes, out of what is potentially a human being, a human being" (202a11–12). When the production results from the application of some craft, the relevant form is in the soul of the craftsman. For instance, the housebuilder has the form of a house in his soul. It is the fact that the agent has the form responsible for the change that explains the directedness of the change. The direction of the change is, in a sense, set by the form in the agent. These bricks have the potential to be a house but they also have the potential to be a church. If they are becoming a house, then it is their potential to be a house that is (incompletely) actual. What makes it the case that it is *this* potential that is actual (rather than one of the others) is that the agent who is acting on the bricks is doing so in virtue of having the form of a house in his soul.

At the end of Aristotle's account of change, he turns to a discussion of what it is for one thing to act on another (*Physics* III.3). He concludes this with a revised version of his definition of change. Change, he now tells us, is "the actuality of what potentially acts and what potentially is acted upon *qua* such, both *simpliciter* and also in each particular case, e.g. building or healing" (202b26–8). I shall have more to say about this revised version of the definition below. Here I want simply to note the central role this definition accords to agency. On this definition, every change must have an agent: a change is, by definition, the actuality of that which is acted upon and of "that which potentially acts." This raises the question whether something can be the agent of one of its own changes. Aristotle holds that animals are self-movers (259b1–3). However, when he discusses self-motion in *Physics* VIII.5, he claims that for something to change itself is really for one part of it to change another part of it. Suppose, for instance, that an animal is causing itself to acquire the property, Fness. There must be some part of the animal that is already F. How otherwise (in the absence of an external agent) could its change be directed towards being F? But obviously the part of the animal that is becoming F cannot be the same as the part that is already F. An animal that is making itself F must, then, have one part that is becoming F and another part – a kind of internal agent – that is already F (*Physics* VIII.5 257a31-b13). His account of change in *Physics* III seems to imply that any change that is not guided by an external agent must have an internal agent of this sort.

Some Problems for This Account of Change

I turn now to some objections that might be made to Aristotle's account of change (as I have interpreted it). First, I shall consider an objection raised by Robert Heinaman, who has argued that this interpretation cannot make sense of Aristotle's claim that the action of changing something else is itself a kind of change. I shall then discuss the claim that Aristotle's account, on this interpretation, is incompatible with a view about the parts of a change that he adopts in *Physics* VI. I shall end by presenting three apparent counterexamples to Aristotle's account.

Changing something else

Aristotle's reformulation of the definition of change in terms of agency and patiency (III.3 202b26–8) brings out a striking feature of his account. For him, the class of changes includes not only changes that a thing undergoes (such as *becoming a house* and *becoming a sculpture*), but also what we might call "transitive changes": actions of producing change (such as *building a house* and *making a sculpture*). (In this respect the Greek word change, *kinêsis*, is rather like the English word "movement": "my movement" can refer either to a movement I undergo, such as falling over, or to my action of moving something else.) In presenting his revised definition, Aristotle makes it clear that his account of change is meant to explain not just what it is for something to be changed but also what it is for one thing to change another.

But can there be one account of change that applies equally to *being changed* and to *changing something*? What exactly does it mean to say that change is "the actuality of what potentially acts and what potentially is acted upon *qua* such" (202b26–8)? And what is the relation between this revised version of the definition and the earlier version, according to which change is "the actuality of what potentially is, *qua* such"?

Robert Heinaman has argued that the two versions of the definition are only consistent if the potential referred to in each case is a potential for *changing*, rather than a potential for being in some new state (1994: 35–6). On his view, the bronze's becoming a statue is the actuality of its potential for being made into a statue, *qua* such (this is "the actuality of what potentially is acted upon, *qua* such"), and the sculptor's making a statue is the actuality of his potential for making a statue, *qua* such (this is "the actuality of what potentially acts, *qua* such"). The one is the actuality of a potential for changing (in the sense of undergoing change); the other is the actuality of a potential for changing (in the sense of changing something else). On Heinaman's view, Aristotle's reformulation of the definition in terms of agency and patiency shows that the potential referred to in the phrase "the actuality of the potential, *qua* such" must all along have been a potential for changing. If this is right, then it is a reason for rejecting the interpretation I defended above, according to which change is the actuality of a potential for being in some new state, rather than of a potential for changing. There is, I think, a reply to this objection. I shall argue that the agent's potential that is actual during the change is, in fact, a potential for the being of a new state, but that it is a potential for the being of a new state in the patient rather than in the agent. Seeing how this can be so will be of central importance in understanding Aristotle's definition.

The problem to which Heinaman draws attention arises because there is no new state of the agent that the change that is the agent's action can plausibly be said to be directed towards. This suggests that when Aristotle describes the agent's action as the "actuality of what potentially acts, *qua* such," he cannot mean that the agent's action is the actuality of what has a potential for being in some new state, *qua* such. Consider,

285

for instance, the action of building a house. This, it would seem, is the actuality of what has the potential to build a house *qua* such; that is, it is the actuality of what has the potential to change something, *qua* such. If this potential to change something is also a potential for being in a new state, then there must be some new state that the house-builder's potential for building a house is directed towards. But what is this new state?

It cannot be a new state of the housebuilder. There are at least two reasons why not. First, the action of *building a house* is the kind of action it is in virtue of the fact that it is aimed at producing a house, not in virtue of the fact that the builder will end up in some particular new state. The structure of the action is determined by the goal of producing *a house*, not by the goal of producing some state in the agent. For example, the reason that in building a house one must lay the foundations before putting up the walls stems from facts about what it is to be a house, not from any facts about the condition of the builder after he has built the house. Second, Aristotle says that the action of producing a change in something else, though it is a change, is not a change that is in the agent. (At *Physics* III.3 202a28–31, he derives absurd consequences from the claim that the action is in the agent.) So, for example, the action of building a house is not a change in the housebuilder (*De Anima* II.5 417b8–9).[4] If the action of building a house is not a change in the housebuilder, it cannot be a change that is directed towards the housebuilder's being in some new state.

How, then, can the agent's potential for building a house also be a potential for the being of some new state? The answer, I think, is that the state that the agent's potential is directed towards is a state not of the agent, but of the thing the agent acts upon. The housebuilder's potential to build a house is a potential the housebuilder has for the being of a house; the sculptor's potential to make a statue is a potential the sculptor has for the being of a statue. Of course, it would be a mistake to say that the house-builder is potentially a house. The housebuilder, unlike the bricks and mortar, does not become a house. But nevertheless, the housebuilder, like the bricks and mortar, has a potential the complete fulfillment of which is *a house*. The incomplete actuality of this potential of the housebuilder (or, in other words, the actuality of this potential, *qua* potential) is the action of housebuilding.

Aristotle says that this action is a change that is *of* the agent but *in* the thing that is acted upon (*Physics* III.3 202b8). We can now see what he means by this. The action of housebuilding is a change (it is the actuality of a potential *qua* potential) and it is *of the housebuilder*, in the sense that it is the incomplete actuality of a potential of the housebuilder. But it is not a change that the housebuilder undergoes (since it is not a change that is directed at the housebuilder's being in a new state). It is, instead, directed at a new state of the bricks: being a house. It is the incomplete actuality of a potential for there to be a house. It is, thus, a change that is undergone by the material of the house: it is a change in the bricks and mortar that the housebuilder is acting upon.

The idea that something can have a potential that is fulfilled by something *else's* being in a new state might seem strange. Aristotle acknowledges this strangeness when he considers the possible objection that, if the agent's action is not in the agent, "the activity of each thing will not be in each thing" (*Physics* III.3 202a33–4). His response is that it is not absurd that the activity of each thing should be in another, provided the two things are related as agent and patient (202b5–8). In the *Metaphysics*, he points out that the teacher demonstrates his craft by exhibiting the pupil at work (Θ.8 1050a17–19): to see the fulfillment of the teacher as a teacher, one must look at what the pupil is doing.

We can now see that the change that is *making something F* and the change that is *becoming (or being made) F* can each be correctly described as an actuality of what has a potential for being F, insofar as it has a potential for being F. *Making something F* is the incomplete actuality of the agent's potential for something else to be F. The agent's potential for something else to be F is completely fulfilled when that other thing is F. For example, the housebuilder's potential for building a house finds its complete fulfillment in the existence of a house that he has built. *Becoming F* is the incomplete actuality of the potential to be F that is possessed by the thing that is acted upon. This potential is completely fulfilled when the thing acted upon is F. For example, the potential of the bricks for being a house is completely fulfilled when they constitute a house.[5]

I have explained how Aristotle's final formulation of the definition of change in terms of agency and patiency can be accommodated by the interpretation I have defended. Both the agent's action and the patient's change can be described as an incomplete actuality of a potential for being in some new state. The difference between them is that the agent's action is the incomplete actuality of a potential for something else's being in a new state, whereas the patient's change is the incomplete actuality of a potential for it itself to be in a new state.

Change-parts and divisibility

In *Physics* VI, Aristotle discusses the divisibility of time, change, and spatial magnitude. He presents, and replies to, Zeno's four arguments against the possibility of motion, and he defends the view that time, change and spatial magnitude are all alike infinitely divisible. A striking feature of this discussion is that it makes no mention of the *Physics* III account of change in terms of potentiality and actuality. This prompts the question: are these two different discussions complementary, each revealing different but compatible features of change, or are they in conflict?

There is reason to think that Aristotle's discussion in *Physics* VI is incompatible with his account of change as the incomplete actuality of a potential. (For a full discussion of the relation between the two accounts, see Waterlow 1982: 131–58.) More specifically, a claim he defends in *Physics* VI about the parts of change seems to be incompatible with his earlier account. In the course of arguing that every change is infinitely divisible, he claims that anything that is changing has already changed and that anything that has changed must previously have been changing (VI.6 237a17–19). By this he means not only that, for any moment during a change, there must have been a previous moment at which that change was already occurring, but also that any moment during a change must be a moment at which *another* change is completed. Thus, something that moves from a point A to a point B must, at any moment during this movement, have completed another movement (from A to some point between A and B): "In half the time it will have completed another change, and in half that another, and so on *ad infinitum*" (VI.6 237a26–8). To Zeno's argument that it is impossible to perform infinitely many changes in a finite amount of time, he replies that there are as many divisions in the time as in the change. Since time too is infinitely divisible, for each of the infinitely many changes, there will be a corresponding period of time.

The tension between this claim and the account of change in terms of actuality and potentiality becomes clear when we try to apply that account to the infinitely many sub-changes undergone by a changing thing. Is each of these sub-changes itself the incomplete actuality of a potential for being in some end state? If not, then for every change that exemplifies the *Physics* III account, there are infinitely many others that are counterexamples. On the other hand, if each of the sub-changes is itself the incomplete actuality of a potential for being, then the change as a whole seems to dissolve into its parts. According to the *Physics* III account, a change is unified by its directedness towards an end state: it is, throughout, the incomplete actuality of a potential to be in that end state. If the changing thing is, equally, manifesting potentials to be in infinitely many other states, then the special role of the end state is lost. On this view, the potential to be in a certain state can be completely fulfilled merely by passing through that state. It follows that the changing thing is directed no more towards the end state than it is towards any of the states it passes through on the way.

In *Physics* VIII, Aristotle recognizes this problem and revises the claim that anything that is changing must already have completed a change. He says there that it is impossible for a thing to complete a change without resting in the state to which it was changing. Thus, merely passing through an intermediate state in the course of a change does not constitute the completion of a change to that intermediate state. On this view, though a movement is infinitely divisible in the sense that there are infinitely many points at which it could be interrupted, a continuous movement does not contain parts that are themselves movements. In moving from A to B without stopping, I do not also complete movements to each of the points on my route.

Some possible counterexamples to Aristotle's account

Does the definition of change, as I have interpreted it, succeed in picking out all and only cases of change? There is some reason to think it does not. I shall discuss three apparent counterexamples. The first two are types of change that appear not to be classified as such by this definition. The third is a type of unchanging state that would, according to the definition, be a change.

The unending circular motion of the heavens Aristotle holds that the most primary kind of change is an unending rotary motion. He argues, in *Physics* VIII, that circular movement is the only kind of change that can go on forever and that, if there is to be change at all, there must be a change that goes on forever. All finite changes ultimately depend on the everlasting rotary motion of the outermost heavenly sphere. The agent of this everlasting motion is a first mover that is itself unmoved. Our question is: how can there be an unending motion of the sort he describes here, if motion (being a species of change) is the actuality of a potential to be in some definite end state?

The problem arises partly because the movement is unending and partly because it is rotary. Since the movement is unending, there is no end point at which it will naturally culminate. It cannot, then, be the incomplete actuality of a potential to be at such an end point (for the moving thing has no such potential). Moreover, since the movement is rotary, it is not even directed towards an unreachable end point (as something moving along a curve might be tending towards an asymptote). The path traced out by rotary movement is entirely occupied by the moving body. Any part of this path that is being approached by one section of the moving thing will already be occupied by another section. As Aristotle says, something moving with a rotary motion moves "around the mid-point rather than towards an extreme point" (VIII.9 265b6–7). In the course of *Physics* VIII, Aristotle twice reiterates his earlier definition of change as the incomplete actuality of a potential (at VIII.1 251a9–10 and again at 5 257b8–9), but he never explains how to avoid the conclusion that unending rotary motion is a counterexample to this definition.

Accidental change   On the account I have given, a changing thing is, by definition, heading towards some particular end state. This end state in terms of which the change is defined need not, of course, be the state of the changing thing when the change stops. External interference may bring it about that a change towards being a house (i.e. a change that is the incomplete actuality of a potential house) breaks off before any house has emerged. The important point is that, throughout the change, the changing thing is heading towards some state (in which it will end up provided there is no interference). As we have seen, Aristotle says that the agent of the change must in some sense already have the actuality towards which the change is directed.

This account works best for changes that are the productions of some craft (e.g. the art of housebuilding or of sculpture) and for natural changes (e.g. the growth of an acorn into an oak tree). There is an obvious sense in which such changes are all along directed towards some end. But there are certain changes that do not fit the account so easily. Consider, for instance, a stone that is inadvertently knocked out of the way by a walker. Its movement is not natural to it (since it is moving under the influence of an external force), but nor is this movement directed towards some end set by the agent: there is no potentiality of the walker that is fulfilled by the stone's being in one place rather than another. It is hard, then, to see what ground there is for thinking that this movement is the actuality of a potential to be in some particular place, rather than another. Aristotle could, of course, insist that there is some place at which this movement would stop (barring interference) and that the movement is the incomplete actuality of a potential to be in this place. But this seems arbitrary. There is no *independent* reason for supposing that a movement of this sort is (like the other changes we have considered) directed towards a particular end.

Opposed forces   On the account I have defended, could it ever turn out that an unchanging state was the actuality of what was potentially F, *qua* such? I have said that a potential to be F counts as being actual just in case it is making a difference to the world in a way that is directed towards the obtaining of F. Thus, the bronze's potential to be a statue is not actual when the bronze is lying unused in the royal vaults, but it is (incompletely) actual when the bronze is being made into a statue. Unfortunately, however, this does leave open the possibility of a potential's being incompletely actual without any change occurring.

Consider, for instance, a stone that is held stationary by the operation of two opposed forces, a force pulling it rightwards towards point A and a force pulling it leftwards towards point B. The stone's potential to be at A is actual, in the sense I have described. This potential is making a difference to the world (the reason the stone is stationary, rather than moving towards B, is because of the force pulling it to A), and the difference that it is making is, in an obvious sense, directed at the stone's being at A. For the same reason, the stone's potential to be at B is also actual. Both of these potentials are actual *qua* merely potential: the stone is not, in fact, either at A or at B. According to our definition, then, the stone is moving towards A and also moving towards B. Its potential to be at A is actual *qua* merely potential, and its potential to be at B is also actual *qua* merely potential. But in fact the stone is stationary. Aristotle takes it for granted that something cannot be moving in two opposite ways at the same time (see, for example, *Physics* VIII.8 264a16–20), so he cannot reply that in such a case the stone remains stationary in virtue of undergoing two opposite motions that cancel each other out.

To answer this objection Aristotle would have to spell out a sense of "incompletely actual" in which a potential for F was incompletely actual when (and only when) there was a change towards F. I cannot myself see any way to explain this without bringing in the notion of change (and hence incurring, after all, the charge of circularity).

Of the objections I have considered, these apparent counterexamples to Aristotle's account are, I think, the most troubling. I have shown that my interpretation can make sense of Aristotle's claim that the action of changing something else is itself a kind of change. And although Aristotle's account (as I have interpreted it) is inconsistent with a claim he makes about the parts of change in *Physics* VI, there is reason to think that he himself acknowledges this fact in *Physics* VIII (since in that Book, he rejects the relevant claim from *Physics* VI). The counterexamples I have presented are more difficult to explain away. Whether this is a problem for Aristotle's account or for the interpretation of it that I have defended, I leave the reader to decide.

Notes

[1] Though Aristotle lists change in respect of substance as a type of change (*kinêsis*) in *Physics* III.1, elsewhere he restricts change to quantitative, qualitative or locomotive change. See, for example, *Physics* V 225b10–11.

[2] The word for actuality here is *energeia* (often translated "activity"). Aristotle uses the words *energeia* (activity) and *entelecheia* (actuality) interchangeably in this passage. I shall translate both with the English "actuality."

[3] It might be objected that, when the bronze is simply lying in the sculptor's workshop, its potential to be a statue is already making a difference in a way that is directed at its being a statue. After all, the sculptor has only obtained the bronze because he intends to make it into a statue. Is the bronze, then, already actual *qua* potentially a statue when it is lying in the sculptor's workshop? If so, then according to Aristotle's definition, the bronze is at this stage already becoming a statue. This is not, I think, a serious problem for his account. There is often a certain amount of indeterminacy about when exactly any given change begins. On Aristotle's view, this is mirrored by the indeterminacy about when exactly a potential to be F counts as making a difference to the world in a way that is directed at being F.

[4] An exception is the builder's action of building when he is learning his craft. In that case, the action of building a house is part of the acquisition of the housebuilding craft, which is a change that the housebuilder undergoes: a change from not having the craft to having it.

[5] In fact, Aristotle says that the agent's action is one and the same change as the change undergone by the thing acted upon, though it is different "in being." For example, *building a house* and *becoming a house* are one and the same change (the change in the bricks and mortar that is directed towards being a house); building a house is that change considered from the perspective of the agent; becoming a house is that change considered from the perspective of the thing acted-upon. They must, he thinks, be one and the same change, since they are directed at the same end (in this case, being a house) and are in the same stuff (in this case, the bricks and mortar) (*Physics* III.3). For a fuller discussion of this see Coope (2004).

Bibliography

Bogen, J. (1992). "Change and Contrariety in Aristotle," *Phronesis*, 37 (1), pp. 1–21.

Coope, U. C. M. (2004). "Aristotle's Account of Agency in *Physics* III.3," *Proceedings of the Boston Area Colloquium in Ancient Philosophy*, 20, pp. 201–21.

Gill, M. L. (1989). *Aristotle on Substance: The Paradox of Unity* (Princeton, NJ: Princeton University Press).

Graham, D. W. (1988). "Aristotle's Definition of Motion," *Ancient Philosophy*, 8, pp. 209–15.

Heinaman, R. (1994). "Is Aristotle's Definition of Change Circular?' *Apeiron*, 27, pp. 25–37.

Hussey, E. (1983). *Aristotle's "Physics": Books III and IV* (Oxford: Oxford University Press).

Kosman, L. A. (1969). "Aristotle's Definition of Motion," *Phronesis*, 14 (1), pp. 40–62.

Kostman, J. (1987). "Aristotle's Definition of Change," *History of Philosophy Quarterly*, 4 (1), pp. 3–16.

Loux, M. J. (1995). "Understanding Process: Reflections on *Physics* III.1," in M. Sim (ed.), *The Crossroads of Norm and Nature* (Lanham, MD: Rowman and Littlefield), pp. 281–303.

Ross, W. D. (1955). *Aristotle's "Physics": A Revised Text with Introduction and Commentary* (Oxford: Oxford University Press).

Russell, B. (1981). "Mathematics and the Metaphysicians," repr. in *Mysticism and Logic* (Totowa, NJ: Barnes and Noble, 1981), pp. 59–74.

Waterlow, S. (1982). *Nature, Change and Agency in Aristotle's Physics* (Oxford: Oxford University Press).

White, M. (1992). *The Continuous and the Discrete: Ancient Physical Theories from a Contemporary Perspective* (Oxford: Oxford University Press).

C. Psychology

18

The Aristotelian *Psuchê*

CHRISTOPHER SHIELDS

Aristotle's Middle Way

"But how shall we bury you?" Faced with this question when on the verge of his state-mandated execution, the Platonic Socrates responds with a gentle chuckle, "In whatever way you wish – if you can catch hold of me and I do not elude you" (*Phaedo* 115c3–5). As he goes on to remind those among his intimates present at his end, Socrates understands death to be the mere separation of the body and soul. If they are apprehensive about the fate of his body, then they have misplaced their concerns. Since his soul lives on and he *is* his soul, Socrates will not be available for burial. "I have been making the point at some length now that after I have drunk the poison I shall no longer remain among you, but will have gone off to enter into the joys of the blessed" (*Phaedo* 115d2–4). As for the disposition of his corpse, Socrates is no more concerned than he might be for the fate of a threadbare overcoat discarded at the end of its useful life. Although he laments that some have remained unconvinced by his arguments for the immortality of the soul, Socrates finds himself at ease at the moment of his death.

Among those unconvinced by the arguments for the immortality of the soul given by Socrates in Plato's *Phaedo* is Aristotle. When investigating the nature of soul–body relations in his principal work on the soul, *De Anima* (*On the Soul*; soul = *anima* in Latin, or *psuchê* in Greek), Aristotle contends that it is clear "that the soul is not separable from the body" (*An* II.1 413a3–4). If it is not separable, then it perishes when the body perishes; so, although Socrates may be right that he will not be present at his own burial, this can only be due to the fact that he will be no more. It is not that he will be merely absent, hovering in the vaguely indicated realm of the blessed. Instead, he will have died, and his death will not have been the separation of the soul from the body but rather the cessation of the body's life functions.

It is easy to read in Aristotle's remarks a sort of recoiling from the excesses of Platonic dualism. If it is ancient, his dialectic is also modern. One philosopher notices that living beings are distinctive in various ways and posits as an explanatory factor a life force, a *soul*, and moves swiftly to the conclusion that since the soul is not identical with the body, it is separable and capable of a non-bodily, immortal existence. Others find this explanatory gambit extravagant, and scurry in the opposite direction to *reduce* the soul

292

to the body, or to some part or aspect of the body, by arguing that the soul is after all identical to some corporeal element or other. Finding the expected reductions more difficult to capture than might have been anticipated, other philosophers traipse further down this same path towards *eliminativism*. Because the soul is hardly an immaterial something, they reason, and since it cannot be shown to be identical with the body, as a whole or any of its parts or aspects, we must assign all talk of the soul to the idiom of an earlier, less enlightened day. Souls are as witches: while we can speak of witches and can see that our forbearers really did think that some women were possessed by the devil and so needed to be burnt at the stake for their good and ours, we do not suppose that the executioners simply failed to appreciate that witchery might be reduced to other, more familiar sorts of conditions. We have not discovered in the interim that witches are *really* women suffering from epilepsy or depression or are bipolar or manic depressive or are simply grotesquely oppressed – though they may well have suffered in some or all of these ways. Rather, we have come to understand that those who executed women on the grounds that they were witches did so wrongly and indefensibly not least because *there are no witches*.

Aristotle is no eliminativist. He maintains that Plato was in one important way right: there are souls. Further, and more strikingly, he argues vigorously against various attempts at reductionism. So, he accepts the existence of souls, as does Plato, but rejects their separability, in contrast to Plato. He evidently hopes, then, to forge some middle path between what he regards as the excesses of Platonic dualism at one end of the continuum and the unwarranted austerities of reductionism or eliminativism at the other. If he succeeds, then he will have identified a position well worth our serious consideration; otherwise, he will simply have failed in his attempt to effect a compromise between alternatives which, however polarized, have at least the virtue of uncompromising clarity. Our question then is this: does Aristotle's analysis of soul and body represent a subtle and exciting *tertium quid* or is it rather the dreary muddle of moderation?

The rudiments of Aristotle's account of soul are easily appreciated. As is the case with most of his mature philosophy, its central terms are cast in the language of *hylomorphism*: he says that the soul is the *form* of the body and the body is the *matter* of the soul (*An* II.1 412a19–21). Less clear is Aristotle's understanding of these terms. Less clear still, and also more contentious, is how we might best characterize and assess Aristotle's hylomorphic middle way. Any such characterization is reasonably pursued by considering hylomorphism in three stages: (1) its background assumptions; (2) its basic commitments; and finally, (3) its most arresting, and surprising, convictions. Thereafter we will be in a position to consider various complications which surround Aristotle's account of soul and, finally, to assess its viability.

The Background Assumptions of Hylomorphism

When Aristotle offers his positive account of the soul, he urges something which may seem a bit alien to an audience accustomed to thinking of the soul in broadly religious terms. In any event, it strikes many today as odd that Aristotle presumes that plants and animals no less than humans have souls. He contends, in fact, that *being ensouled*

293

and *being alive* are co-extensive, that is, that all and only living beings are ensouled. Aristotle maintains this co-extensivity thesis because he supposes that a sufficient condition for being alive is to be such that a being has "through itself nourishment, growth, and decay" (*An* II.1 412a14–15). He thinks that some bodies are natural and some artifactual: a computer is an artifact, whereas a tree is not. What differentiates a living being from an artifact is precisely that a living system contains within itself its own principles of change. Unlike an artifact, a living system moves without having been designed for this purpose by any intentional agent. Living beings simply show up equipped to seek out nutrition, to grow, if their environments permit it, and to perceive and think, if they are outfitted for this purpose. Further, there is an important distinction between two sorts of natural bodies: "Among natural bodies, some have life and some do not" (*An* II.1 412a13). Thus, he takes it as obvious that the various material elements, like earth and fire, are no more alive than artifacts. Accordingly, he supposes, we must observe a real division in nature, one which, like other natural divisions, requires an explanation. Aristotle's way of marking that division is by dividing the living from the non-living by the presence or absence of the soul: "what is ensouled is distinguished from what is not ensouled by living" (*An* II.2 413a22–3).

His way of explaining this division begins with the observation that *life* is not a simple or univocal notion:

> But living is spoken of in several ways. And should even one of these belong to something, we say that it is alive: reason, perception, motion and rest with respect to place, and further the motion attendant upon nourishment, decay and growth. (*An* II.2 413a22–4)

In speaking of life this way, Aristotle intends to indicate that once we have acknowledged a reasonably clear division between the living and the non-living, we should not rush forward to suppose that we have available to us some one single, univocal account of life. On the contrary, when confronted with the tremendous variety we observe in the community of living beings, we should acknowledge that "living is spoken of in many ways" – that what it is for an ox to live, for instance, is not the same as what it is for an amoeba to live. Though they both qualify as living beings, there will be appreciable differences in the conditions which so qualify them.

That said, if we introduce the soul as a principle of life, we will immediately cast the net of the ensouled relatively broadly. Someone whose primary interest in the soul stems from a religious conviction, or from a hopeful fascination in the prospects of *post mortem* existence, might not be at all disposed to regard rosebushes as ensouled. For Aristotle, who approaches the study of the soul informed by a biologist's interest in the character of living systems, it is natural and unremarkable that a jellyfish no less than Socrates should have a soul. Each is living and so each has a soul. This is, then, the first presupposition of Aristotle's hylomorphic approach to soul and body: all and only living beings are ensouled. Thus, the introduction of the soul is as uncontroversial as the claim that some beings are alive. Accordingly, supposes Aristotle, unless we are inclined to be eliminativists about life, unless, that is, we are prepared to contend that there are no living beings, we should admit the existence of souls.

If we will agree with Aristotle this far, we have perhaps not agreed to much of substance, since we have thus far introduced souls in a fairly deflationary sort of way. Souls have been introduced by Aristotle as a kind of explanatory posit: what they explain, in the first instance, if he is correct, is that some beings are alive and others are not. Beyond that, however, matters become more contentious and controversial. For in addition to being anti-eliminativist, Aristotle gives every indication that he is equally anti-*reductivist* about the soul. By contrast as Aristotle presents them in his historical survey in the first Book of his *De Anima*, many of his predecessors agreed with his anti-eliminativism only to adopt one form or another of reductivism, ranging from extremely crude hypotheses to the effect that the soul is to be identified with this or that material element – with fire or with water or with air – to some comparatively sophisticated suggestions to the effect that the soul is a harmony or attunement (*harmonia*) of the body (*An* I.4 407b30–408a28). According to this last theory, the soul is not identical with the body, but is rather something emerging out of the body, when it is in a certain condition, in something like the way that the property of *being well tuned* emerges out of the correct arrangement of the strings, sounding board and other parts of a violin. Although the attunement is not the same as any one part of the violin, or even with the whole of it, since the whole can exist in an untuned state, it supervenes on the violin as a whole, when it is appropriately configured.

Aristotle's reactions to all of these proposals, the subtle no less than the coarse, take a common theme. He holds that reductive accounts of all varieties fail to explain the fine-grained traits and capacities we attribute to the soul. In particular, to begin with the cruder forms of reductivism, no suggestion that the soul is really simply, for instance, *fire* can account for the fact that the soul moves the body but does not always tend upwards as fire does. At the more sophisticated end of the scale, he contends that the soul *initiates* change – that it is a datum to be explained that living beings, *insofar* as they are living, can propel themselves through space – and that living beings change by growing larger in a patterned and constrained way. Further, we find elements existing in inanimate bodies as well as living bodies. If the presence of the elements were sufficient to explain the soul, then all things would be living things. Thus, Aristotle contends in a manner characteristic of his anti-reductive tendencies:

> In general, why is it that not everything which exists has a soul, since everything is either an element, or made from one, several, or all of the elements? . . . And one might also raise a difficulty: what ever is it that unifies the elements? (*An* I.5 410b7–11).

Aristotle further expands his contention by asserting that the soul must explain not only local motion and growth, but the sort of motion we find in perception and thinking, and moreover, that the soul must be introduced to explain the unity of the body and not the other way around:

> So it is clear from what has been said that knowing does not belong to the soul because of its having been made from the elements; nor is the soul rightly or truly said to be moved. But since knowing belongs to the soul, as do both perceiving and believing, and further desiring and wishing and wants in general, while motion in respect of place comes to be in animals by means of the soul, as do growth and maturity and decay, we ask whether each of these belongs to the soul in its entirety. That is, is it by the whole soul that we think and perceive and move about and both do and experience each of the others? Or do we do

different things with different parts of the soul? Again, does living reside in some one of these parts, or in several, or in all? Or is it due to some other cause? To be sure, some say that the soul has parts and that thinking is by means of one part and desiring by means of another. What, then, holds the soul together, if it naturally has parts? It is surely not the body; on the contrary, the soul seems rather to hold the body together. At any rate, when the soul has departed, the body disintegrates and putrefies. (*An* I.5 411a24–b9)

Aristotle thus presumes that just as the bare fact of life justifies the rejection of eliminativism, the variety of living processes and activities justifies the rejection of reductivism.

It is instructive to appreciate the argumentative backbone of Aristotle's anti-reductivism. He argues:

1 Living systems display a range of phenomena, including limited, patterned growth, perception and thought.
2 Reductive accounts of the soul which attempt to identify the soul with individual elements, or blends of several elements, or with elemental epiphenomena, cannot explain these phenomena.
3 If (2), all such reductive accounts must be dismissed as explanatorily impoverished and so as inadequate.
4 Hence, reductive accounts of the soul must be dismissed as explanatorily impoverished and so as inadequate.

Of course, one will want to probe (2), especially in view of the fact that nearly all the versions of reductivism canvassed by Aristotle are bound to appear so empirically impoverished as to be of historical interest only. To the extent that this is so, however, the critic has at least come on board to the general Aristotelian program of investigating the distinctive character of living systems, if only by reflecting upon the general features material processes and events must exhibit in order to be identified with the phenomena of life.

Moreover, if we reflect on some features of perception and intentionality left relatively unassayed by Aristotle, including especially the phenomena of consciousness, then (2) does not appear to be so immediately or obviously objectionable. Minimally, it bears noting that there continue to be, to this day, lively and appropriate debates surrounding the prospects of providing reductive analyses of consciousness. Indeed, so lively are these debates that some participants, having despaired of any eventual success, have reverted to the forms of eliminativism disregarded by Aristotle as beneath serious consideration. From this remove, then, Aristotle's easy anti-eliminativism, however defensible it proves to be be, need not be accepted as unobjectionable on the basis of the considerations mooted.

Be that as it may, Aristotle's hylomorphic analysis of soul thus far proceeds against the backdrop of his paired rejections of reductivism and eliminativism. He supposes that there are living beings, and so that there are ensouled creatures, ranging from humble house plants to eminent sages; and he further maintains that the range of life activities manifested across this collection is so varied that it resists analysis in reductively materialist terms.

When turning to proffer his own preferred form of explanation, Aristotle relies on his general *hylomorphism*: he thinks that life activities are fundamentally understood, at root, on the model he has introduced to explain the existence of change in the universe. Appreciating why this might be so leads us to our second important background assumption of Aristotle's approach.

In the first Book of his *Physics*, Aristotle had sought to combat an eliminativism of a sort more severe and bewildering than any doubts about the existence of the soul could ever generate. Parmenides had argued with great ingenuity that contrary to all appearances *there is no change*. Aristotle in response introduced matter (*hulê*) and *form* (*morphê*), whence *hylomorphism*, as correlative notions: there is change, he reasoned, but all change requires a kind of persistence (*Phys* I.7 189b30–191a22). One thing persists through change, the matter, say some quantity of bronze, while another thing is gained or lost, a positive attribute, the form, perhaps a Hermes-shape. Simple though it is, this distinction permits Aristotle to defang an otherwise surprisingly compelling argument for the conclusion that there is no change. In its most general guise, then, Aristotle's hylomorphism is simply this: (i) there is change; (ii) a necessary condition of there being change is the existence of matter and form; hence, (iii) there are matter and form. (For an introduction to the details of this argument, see Shields (2003, ss. 4.3 and 4.4).)

For this reason, Aristotle assumes that his general hylomorphism provides the basic framework for the analysis of change. This same hylomorphic framework appears and re-appears throughout his psychological writings, first, in its most general guise, in his account of soul–body relations, and thereafter, in increasingly attenuated fashions, in his analyses of perception (*aisthêsis*) and thinking (*noêsis*). At root, in each case, his thought is the same: the birth of a living being, its perceptual encounters, and its episodes of thought are all, in suitably shaded ways, instances of change. Since it was invented precisely for the purpose of explaining change, hylomorphism provides the appropriate framework for investigating and analyzing these and other characteristic activities of living beings.

The Basic Theses of Aristotle's Psychological Hylomorphism

After reviewing the views of his predecessors in *De Anima* I, Aristotle opens the second Book of the same work by announcing the need to offer a view of his own. His view, in its most succinct expression, is this:

> It is necessary, then, that the soul is a substance as the form of a natural body which has life in potentiality. But substance is actuality; hence, the soul will be an actuality of a certain sort of body. (*An* I.1 412a19–21)

Noting an ambiguity in the notion of *actuality* (*energeia*), Aristotle expands:

> Actuality is spoken of in two ways, first as knowledge, and second as contemplating. Evidently, then, the soul is actuality as knowledge is. For both sleeping and waking depend upon the soul's being present; and as waking is analogous to contemplating, sleeping is analogous to the having of knowledge without exercising it. And in the same individual,

having knowledge occurs prior to contemplating. Hence, the soul is the first actuality of a natural body which has life in potentiality. (*An* I.1 412a22–9)

Finally, Aristotle finds the need to characterize the sort of body suitable for being ensouled. This seems only appropriate, since he has found cause to criticize his predecessors on just this account. Some of them thought that souls could come and go, the soul of a human transmigrating perhaps into a dog, as if, Aristotle scolds, the art of carpentry could find its expression through musical instruments such as flutes rather than wood-working gear (*An* I.3 407b24–6). As he sees things, by contrast, only certain sorts of bodies are suited to realize the life activities of souls:

> This sort of body would be one which is organic. And even the parts of plants are organs, although altogether simple ones. For example, the leaf is a shelter of the outer covering, and the outer covering of the fruit; even the roots are analogous to the mouth, since both draw in nutrition. Hence, if it is necessary to say something which is common to every soul, it would be that the soul is the first actuality of an organic natural body. (*An* II.1 412a29–b6)

Given the criticisms he offers of his predecessors, we can appreciate that hylomorphism represents Aristotle's attempt to offer an account of the soul which is neither Platonic nor eliminativist nor reductive. He situates himself between these alternatives by first agreeing with Plato, against the various eliminativists and reductionists, that all living beings have souls, none of which is identical to the elements or any configuration of the elements. He then proceeds to differentiate himself from Plato by arguing that a rejection of reductionism provides no reason for supposing that the soul is separable from the body. We can and must distinguish the soul from the body; but our doing so gives us no more reason to believe in the separability of souls than it does to believe in the separability of statue- or house-shapes from the matter in which they are realized. Statues and houses have forms without which they would not exist. Still, when a statue is smelted or a house razed, neither the shape of the statue nor the form of the house goes anywhere. There is no heaven for shapes. Thus, by parity of reasoning, as hylomorphism gives us no reason to believe in the separation of inanimate forms, so it gives us no reason to endorse the *post mortem* existence of souls. Put more abstractly, then, Aristotle's contention is that irreducibility does not warrant ontological independence.

That acknowledged, one might at this point enter a concern as to whether Aristotle is right to insist both that the activities of life are irreducible and that hylomorphism is sufficiently rich a framework to capture what is distinctive about them. One might well, after all, reasonably insist that the structure of a house *just is* its matter being suitably arranged or that the shape of a statue is no more than so much bronze organized in a certain way. Indeed, it seems to be just this sort of intuition which underwrites the easy contention that the forms of artifacts are inseparable. If that is so, however, then one may well wonder whether Aristotle's anti-reductivism extends to hylomorphic artifacts.

Taking these thoughts together, one may pose the following heuristic dilemma for Aristotle: either non-reductive materialism obtains for hylomorphic artifacts, in which case Aristotle's non-reductivism for living systems amounts to little, *or* hylomorphism is compatible with reductive materialism in the case of artifacts but not living systems, in which case the features of living systems rendering them unsuitable for reductive treatment equally threaten the extension of Aristotle's hylomorphic analysis to them. On the first horn, to say that a shape of some bronze is not the same as the quantity of that same bronze hardly implies that no suitably robust reductive materialism obtains. On the second horn, the worry is that Aristotle overtaxes his hylomorphic framework when he seeks to extend it beyond its home domain in the analysis of simple change. It is, it seems, the second horn with which Aristotle must contend, since it was precisely the features of living systems – e.g. constrained and patterned growth in two directions – which led him to reject the reductive approaches of his predecessors.

We can move towards an assessment of Aristotle's response to the second horn of this dilemma by focusing on some additional terms in his definition. Aristotle holds that as the form of the body, the soul is a *substance* (ousia) and the *actuality* (energeia) of the body. He says further that only a body of a suitable sort, one which is *organic* (*organikon*), may serve as the matter of the soul. In saying that the soul is the actuality of the body, Aristotle intends in the first instance that it is the soul which makes the body the body of a living being. That is, no body is actually a body unless ensouled. This in turn suggests that in thinking of the soul as a *form* of the body, Aristotle has a metaphysically robust conception in view: the soul is not a mere shape or configurational property of the body, but is, rather, the essence of the living human being. Two further claims help shore up his contention. The first is that a dead body, though inanimate, continues to have the general shape (*schēma*) of a human being (*PA* I.1 640b30–641a5). The soul is not this shape, but, rather, that which grounds the individual capacities of the living being. The souls of human beings are rational souls, and thus ground the activities characteristic of life at that level. This explains Aristotle's second contention, one which may sound initially opaque, that "for living beings being is life" (*An* II.4 415b13). He means not only that human beings are essentially alive, but that the kind of life available to the being is a function of the kind of soul present to the body. A rational soul actualizes a human body, and thus makes a suitable body a human being, whereas a perceptual soul makes a suitable body an animal.

As the actuality of the body, the soul is in this sense *prior* to the body. This is part of the reason why Aristotle had wanted to reject the relatively sophisticated *harmonia* theory, according to which the soul is a sort of epiphenomenal structure of the body. According to this account, the soul is manifested by the arrangement of the body in the way that the attunement of a guitar is created by the organization of the parts of the guitar. An attunement is fully determined and, so to speak, carried around by the instrument to which it belongs. Thus, by analogy to this approach, the soul is understood to be a mere feature of the body, something determined by the relations of the body's parts, and not something capable of acting upon the body. Aristotle has two complaints, the first of which is put most clearly in an early work. This is that the soul is a substance (*ousia*), and that as such it has kinds of independence and priority lacking in a mere attunement. (This criticism is made in an especially clear fashion in an early, mostly lost work of Aristotle, *Eudemus*. Fragments of this work have, however, been preserved. See Damascius, *Commentarious in Phaedonem* 383 = F45R[3].) The second criticism, more characteristic of the later *De Anima*, is related: the soul is not passively determined by the body. Rather, the soul *initiates* motion. The proper causes of our actions – our desires and decisions – are psychological events. If such events were mere epiphenomena, then they would be causally inert. Hence, since the *harmonia* theory treats them in just this way, it is to be rejected (*An* I.4 407b34–408a3).

What is to be put in its place is a theory which treats the soul as a substance in its own right. As we have seen, this need not commit us to Platonism, for the soul might be a substance without being able to exist independently of the body whose soul it is. Thus Aristotle's hylomorphism regards the body and soul as importantly *interdependent*. The soul will not exist without the body, and so is existentially dependent upon it. At the same time, the body would not be what it is without being ensouled, and so is dependent for its identity conditions on the soul. Although there is some tension inherent in this sort of thought, there need be no contradiction: *x* and *y* can be mutually interdependent so long as their forms of dependency are distinct. Thus, a chief operating officer of a corporation can depend upon his board of directors to have his decisions implemented, while the members of the board can depend upon their chief for leadership and direction.

That said, one form of dependence between soul and body is more readily understood than the other. If it is a form of the body, then, as we have seen, the soul may be supposed no more separable from the body than the structure of a house is from the bricks which constitute it. The dependency heading in the other direction is, by contrast, not immediately clear. How might Aristotle also maintain that the body depends upon the soul? Part of Aristotle's meaning is revealed in his contention that the body suitable for being ensouled in an *organic (organikon)* body (*An* II.1 412a28–b1). Although the term "organic" is likely these days to conjure up images of chemical-free farming, Aristotle's word is highly technical, meaning something more in the neighborhood of "organ-equipped" or, more likely, if more expansively, "well suited to be an organ of the soul." In general usage, an *organon* is a tool; thus, to say of the body that it is *"organikon"* is to say that it is a tool suitable for implementing the goals and activities of the soul (*An* II.1 412b15; cf. *PA* I.1 642a11; *Pol* I.5 1254a34).

This contention comprises two claims: first, that the body is a *tool*, and second, that the body is a *suitable* tool. Both claims are important. The body is a tool in the sense that it is subordinate to the ends of the soul, just as a plane is subordinate to the art of carpentry. Further, the body is a tool *of the right sort*. A plane levels and smooths wooden surfaces; a body is similarly suited to the psychic activities of the kind of soul it realizes. Thus, rosebushes do not perceive and so need not have perceptual organs. Cows, by contrast, do perceive and thus have organs suited to that task. This commitment, as we have seen, helps explain Aristotle's impatience with fanciful fables of soul-transmigration. Although we can easily imagine quaint stories in which candelabras speak, sing and dance, in fact we are misled by our imaginings if we think that a human soul could come to take up residence in a silver ornamental candlestick. In fact, metal thus configured cannot be made to serve the ends of life. Aristotle's claim that the sort of body suited to be ensouled must be organic thus reflects his judgment that the soul is the *final cause* of the body (*An* II.4 415b15–23): the body is as it is because it serves the ends of life.

If that is so, then Aristotle's hylomorphism carries with it a strong and central teleological commitment. We should not think of the soul as ephiphenomenal on the body, since living bodies by their nature implement the activities of life. Rather, the body in the first instance owes its configuration and character to its suitability as a general organ for implementing a determinate life directionality. As Aristotle sees things, it is appropriate to speak of the functioning of the parts of the body only relative to some role they play in securing the good of the organism as a whole. Thus, for example, we say that the kidneys *malfunction* when they cease to purify blood only because their normal activity bestows a continuing good on the well being of the organism whose kidneys they are. Some may scruple that kidneys do not *really* confer benefits, supposing that all such talk qualifies as an imposition of a normativity not found in nature. Aristotle has no such scruples: the proper activity of the soul is something good and it thus always makes ready sense to determine the functioning of the body's parts relative to this good. Thus, we are free to speak truly, objectively, and unapologetically about the functioning – and malfunctioning – of the organs of the body. From there, supposes Aristotle, it is a small step to infer that what holds for the parts of the body holds for the body as a whole: just as the organs are instruments for implementing their parts of maintenance of the life of the whole organism, so the whole body is itself, corporately, an organ of the soul. Thus is the body *organikon*: a soul is realized in a body as matter only when that body is suitably structured to implement the ends of the soul, namely living well.

Two Arresting Consequences of Hylomorphism

If we are happy to come along with Aristotle this far, then it is probably because we find the moderation in his approach congenial. Although he insists on the real existence of the soul, where this consists primarily in a commitment to the ineliminability and non-reducibility of life, Aristotle resists the stridency of a dualist's understanding of these commitments. He denies that the soul is separable from the body and thinks that it is wrong to view the soul and body as discrete and independently existing entities which come together in a single entity. It is towards this end that he thinks that it is appropriate to restrict the bodies suitable to realizing souls to those which are organic. Now, however, matters become more complex and difficult. We will briefly explore two such complexities, one in the form of a deep problem for Aristotle's view and the other in the form of an interesting result regarding the metaphysics of souls.

A problem for soul–body hylomorphism

A problem threatens. Although we have seen that it is in principle possible to maintain that the soul and body are inter-dependent, so long as their forms of dependence lie along distinct axes, it strains the very terms of hylomorphism to insist, as Aristotle does, that an organic body is one already living. (Ackrill (1972/3) originally formulated this problem most succinctly and forcefully. For different ways of approaching it, see Whiting 1992; Cohen 1992; Shields 1993.)

The problem is this: by insisting that an organic body exists when and only when it is alive, Aristotle threatens to vitiate the very hylomorphic framework whose trumpeted moderation permits him to forge a middle way between reductive materialism and dualism. Recall that in the background of Aristotle's approach to body and soul is a simple analysis of change: we say that so much bronze, some quantity of *matter*, becomes a statue of Hermes when it acquires the appropriate shape, some *form*. Now, of course, the process can be reversed. The statue might be smelted and recast over and over again, so that the same quantity of bronze comes to gain and lose again and again any number of distinct forms. The terms of hylomorphism are thus simple:

form : matter : : shape : bronze : : soul : body

Key to this analogy is the thought that the matter, the bronze in the case of the statue, can persist through the acquisition and loss of the form.

Partly because he restricts the suitable matter in the case of the living body to the one called *organic*, Aristotle simply denies that bodies have this ability:

> It has now been said in general what the soul is: the soul is a substance corresponding to the account; and this is the essence of such and such a body. It is as if some tool were a natural body, e.g. an axe; in that case being an axe would be its substance, and this would also be its soul. If this were separated, it would no longer be an axe, aside from homonymously. But as things are, it is an axe. For the soul is not the essence and structure of this sort of body, but rather of a certain sort of natural body, one having a source of motion and rest in itself.
>
> What has been said must also be considered when applied to parts. For if an eye were an animal, its soul would be sight, since this would be the substance of the eye corresponding to the account. The eye is the matter of sight; if sight is lost, it is no longer an eye, except homonymously, in the way that a stone eye or painted eye is.
>
> What has been said in the case of parts must of course be understood as applying to the whole living body. For there is an analogy: as one part is to one part, so the whole perceptive faculty is to the whole of the body which is capable of perception, insofar as it is capable of perception. The body which has lost its soul is not the one which is potentially alive; this is rather the one which has a soul. (*An* II.1 412b10–27)

The basic themes of Aristotle's final position are now all in view. What is added is a surprising claim: a dead body is a body *only homonymously*.

By this Aristotle means that when a body loses its soul, the corpse is no longer properly a body at all. Indeed, he compares that non-ensouled body to the sort of body we have in the case of a statue. Relying on the analogy between the functioning organs and the whole organ of the body which we have already seen, Aristotle now insists that just as an eye which cannot see is an eye in only the sense in which the eye of a statue is an eye – that is to say, not really an eye at all, although resembling one – so a body which has lost its soul is no more a body than a body painted in a picture. When asked to identify an eye in a statue, we would not in complying point to a real eye; but we would become chagrined if we were then asked to explain how the "eye" to which we were pointing is supposed to see anything, given that it is made out of marble. We would no doubt respond that the eye is *not a real eye*, but rather is called an eye because of its resembling or representing a real eye. Aristotle now makes the same claim about corpses: they are no more bodies than pictures of bodies. This is what is meant by saying that such bodies are only *homonymously* bodies: although they are called bodies, when pressed we will be forced to back away, and say that they are not really bodies.

This is, of course, linguistically odd, to say the least. The problem which concerns us however, extends much further. Our problem is that the hylomorphic framework in terms of which Aristotle has preferred to articulate his theory presupposes that the body, as matter, is only contingently enformed. The bronze of a statue is, after all, capable of gaining and losing forms with impunity. Now we are told that the living body, as matter, ceases to be a body altogether when it loses its soul, which is its form. Put most pointedly, the problem threatens incoherence: the body, as matter, is only contingently enformed; yet the body, since it is merely homonymously a body when unensouled, must be necessarily enformed. Hence, the body is and is not necessarily enformed, and is and is not only contingently enformed. Hylomorphism and homonymy do not make a happy marriage.

One might be tempted in view of this looming contradiction simply to encourage Aristotle, or his appointed defender, to rescind the homonymy principle. After all, it is precisely its application which threatened incoherence, after it had antecedently bequeathed extreme linguistic oddity. We do, and will, call corpses bodies; and we have no inclination to think that a corpse is no more a body than a representation of a body.

Aristotle's reaction to this encouragement will come in two phases. First, he will decline. It is not that he had capriciously made the point about homonymy. On the contrary, it follows from his claim that the suitable matter for living beings in the case of the soul is always *organic*. For it was this commitment which led him to suggest that the body is in various ways dependent upon the soul: the body is the single body it is because its sundry activities – seeing, eating, filtering, growing, touching – are all activities subordinated to a single end, a single life directionality (*An* II.4 415b15–20). Further, he will not be flummoxed by any linguistic oddity attending his contention. On the contrary, he expects his view to sound somewhat odd. This is the point of his attempting to illustrate it by means of uncontested instances of homonymy, such as the eyes and other body parts of statues.

The second phase of Aristotle's reaction itself comes in two sub-phases. The first will be to show how his view is at least not self-contradictory; for if it were, there would be no point in proceeding to the second sub-phase. This is that there is in fact good reason for thinking that a dead body is a body only homonymously.

In its most trenchant formulation, the problem about the homonymy of the body alleges that one and the same body is both necessarily and merely contingently enformed by the soul: the body, as matter, is contingently ensouled, whereas the body, as organic, is necessarily ensouled. Put thus sharply, it becomes clear that it is open to Aristotle to maintain that the organic body is not identical to the body which is only contingently enformed. He might, for example, suggest that the non-organic body is the body considered as a certain quantity without building in the diachronic identity conditions imposed by its being the body of a living organism, whereas the organic body is that body capable of sustaining material replenishment in the way that a normal body does through the course of its life. It is thus true, for instance, that in the organic sense, when we speak of Lenin's body, we speak of an ever changing diachronic continuant, that which began as a small infant in 1870 and ended as a stroke-riddled middle-aged man in 1924. Perhaps no part of the original quantity of the baby's body, considered as non-organic, was present in the body of the dying man, again considered as a non-organic. Still, there is some identifiable body, the organic body, which was wholly present at the beginning and at the end. If we think of the organic body as the one which is co-extensive with the life of Lenin, fully present at every moment of his existence, then we can begin to see how Aristotle could at least in principle draw a distinction between the organic and non-organic body.

If he may in principle distinguish one body from another, however odd his doing so may sound, then Aristotle will at least have answered the charge of internal inconsistency. For the organic body may be necessarily enformed while the non-organic body is only contingently enformed. There would then be no single body which was both necessarily and merely contingently enformed. Of course, bare consistency is not worth much, if the remaining commitments of the theory are uninformative. That allowed, if Aristotle is absolved of the charge of internal inconsistency, then his hylomorphism may provide the middle way he seeks. In that case, Aristotle's conception of soul and body will need to be judged on whatever explanatory merits its hylomorphic pedigree bestows upon it.

The unity of the soul

One explanatory benefit has already been mentioned, though as yet undeveloped: the soul, as the final cause of the body (*An* II.4 415b15–23), provides and grounds its unity. Recall that when criticizing some of his predecessors, Aristotle had complained that their reductivism left various facts about living systems unexplained. He put a rhetorical question to those who sought to identify the soul with some collection of elements: "And one might also raise a difficulty: what ever is it is unifies the elements?" (*An* I.5 410b10–11). He answered, implicitly, that it is the soul. He then raised a puzzle, not for his predecessors, but for himself. Suppose, he conjectured, that the soul itself has parts. "What, then, holds the soul together, if it naturally has parts? It is surely not the body; on the contrary, the soul seems rather to hold the body together" (*An* I.5 411b6–8). The conjecture is not an idle one. After all, Aristotle routinely treats the soul of human beings as having various distinct capacities, each of which receives its own extended analysis. (See the relevant chapters in this volume.) The most sophisticated souls, the souls of rational animals, comprise various faculties: (i) the nutritive faculty, the broadest of all faculties, which belongs to all (mortal) living beings (The qualifier "mortal" is required because Aristotle suggests that among divine beings, reason can exist without the lower capacities (*An* II.2 413a31–2; cf. *Met* Λ.8 1073a23–44.); (ii) perception (*aisthêsis*), which in fact commands the dominant portion of Aristotle's attention in *De Anima* (roughly one-third of the entire text; (iii) reason (*nous*) and (iv) locomotion, which receives only cursory treatment (II.2 413a20–4, b16–23, II.3 414a29–31). Aristotle eventually also introduces both imagination (*phantasia*) (*An* III.3 427a17–429a9) and desire (*orektikon*) (*An* III.10 433a21–30) though he is less clear whether these are to qualify as full-fledged capacities on par with the others. So, if the soul can be divided in these ways, then it seems to have parts; if it has parts, however, then something must account for its unity. If that cannot, on Aristotle's account, be the body, then what might it be? Moreover, if the soul comprises various parts, how will it be suited to ground and explain the unity of the body as Aristotle expects it to do?

It will not suffice simply to report, as many commentators seem disposed to do, that Aristotle treats the soul as a "set of capacities." To begin, the soul is not a set: it is, rather, a substance (*An* II.1 412a19–20, II.4 415b12–14). The more pressing problem in the present context is that a set is not an internal unity. A set is an extensional aggregate, a collection having no intrinsic principle of unity. Yet Aristotle wants to insist that not only is the soul an intrinsic unity, but the sort of unity whose presence as a final cause grounds and explains why the various activities of the body all qualify as activities of the same unified being, why, indeed, the body itself qualifies as a single unified being in the first instance. That said, if there is a worry about the unity of the soul, it resides not with Aristotle's interpreters, but with Aristotle himself. For it is he who insists both that the soul comprises various capacities and that it is an intrinsic unity.

One may approach this worry by contrasting two models of the Aristotelian soul. On the first, one may think of the soul as a sort of layer cake. The lowest layer will be the nutritive soul, as what is common to all and only living beings. This is "the first and most common capacity of soul, in virtue of which life belongs to all living things" (*An* II.4 415a24–5). Animals add another layer, perception (I.5 410b16–24, III.10 433b30). Finally, humans have the top layer, reason, "the part of the soul by which it knows and understands" (*An* III.3 429a9–10; cf. 3 428a5; 9 432b26, 12 434b3). On this approach, one can view the soul as a series of capacities stacked one on top of the other, each discrete and autonomous from the others. Although reasonably clear and accessible, this is not Aristotle's preferred model. For he denies, in an initially perplexing passage, that each lower soul of the soul is fully present alongside the higher:

> What holds in the case of the soul is similar to what holds concerning figures: for both figures and the ensouled, what is prior is present in potentiality in what follows in the series, for example, the triangle in the square, and the nutritive in the perceptive. We must investigate the reason why they are thus in a series. For the perceptive faculty is not without the nutritive, though the nutritive faculty is separated from the perceptive in plants. Again, without touch, none of the other senses is present, though touch is present without the others; for many animals have neither sight nor hearing nor a sense of smell. Also, among things capable of perceiving, some have motion in respect of place, while others do not. Lastly, and most rarely, some have reasoning and understanding. Among perishable things, those with reasoning also have all the remaining capacities, though it is not the case that those with each of the remaining capacities also have reasoning. (*An* II.3 414b28–415a10)

Significant in this passage is the suggestion that the lower souls are present *only in potentiality* in beings with higher-order souls. Rather than the picture presupposed in the layer cake model, according to which all souls would be present in a complex soul discretely and actually, Aristotle contends that lower souls are somehow contained in the higher souls without being actually present. In some sense, a triangle is potentially present in every square, though the converse does not hold; still, there is not, in every square, an actual triangle. So too in the case of the soul. In every rational animal there is a perceptual soul discernible, though there is no perceptual soul actually present.

Aristotle's manner of speaking may seem a bit odd. After all, as he says, if a being can reason, then it can also perceive; and it can perceive, then it can take on nutrition and grow. So, one might infer, it is, or ought to be on his account, obvious that the perceptual soul is *actually* present in the rational soul. After all, a human being could not perceive if perception were merely potentially and not actually available to him.

In fact, however, Aristotle's point is more nuanced. It is rather that the rational soul of a human being has perception in it in an integrated manner, as subordinate to reason, rather than as a discrete and self-contained module. To illustrate, extrapolating somewhat, consider two instances of perception, both of the same object, but involving significantly distinct kinds of perceivers. Arguably, their perceptual experiences would differ significantly. Thus, if a connoisseur of fine wines tastes a 1990 St. Emilion at the same moment as her dog slurps some from his bowl, their perceptual experiences will differ in any number of ways. Presumably, the connoisseur's conceptual repertoire will inform her experience, permitting her to make perceptual discriminations far beyond the ken of the dog. It is not that they will not both have experiences; for they are equally perceptual creatures. It is rather that the experiences of the intellectual soul will be such that its conceptual structure will infuse the experience in such a way that the subject will have a single, integrated experience of a sort differing in character from the differently integrated experience of the dog. To the extent that such a comparison is apt, it will be possible to make sense of Aristotle's suggestion as follows. A being with a rational soul has a perceptual capacity neither more nor less than a being with a perceptual soul. Still, the manner in which the perceptual faculty is present is distinct. A rational soul is not formed by the layering of a rational faculty upon the top of an actually existing perceptual faculty. Rather, a rational soul subordinates a perceptual faculty to its own ends, thereby integrating it into a unified, single soul.

Aristotle's concern with the unity of the soul is reasonable for anyone, but especially so for him, given his tendency to criticize his predecessors for failing to explain the unity of living beings. Since he believes that the soul as substantial form is the cause and ground of the unity of the whole living organism, he expects that it must itself be unified. For were it not, then we would need to ask anew about the ground of its unity, and the unity of what unifies that unifier, and so on into infinity (*Met* Z.17 1041b11–33). It will be preferable, then, to nip the regress in the bud and accept the soul as itself an intrinsic unity, as a being whose unity is contained in itself and not given by forces external to it. It will be possible to proceed this way on the assumption that the soul is not a set, or a layered aggregate of capacities, but rather as exhibiting the sort of ordering we find in the series of figures. There is a sense in which a square contains a triangle, and a pentagon a square, even though there is no actual square in the midst of the pentagon, nor any actual triangle in the midst of the square. Aristotle makes a similar point elsewhere about the asymmetric containment of the lower numbers in the higher. He thinks that five contains four, but not *vice versa* – though only in potentiality and not actually (*Met* B.3 999a6, M.6 1080b11). Similarly, the higher-order souls contain the lower order souls, though, again, only in potentiality.

One may wish to probe whether Aristotle is on defensible grounds in insisting upon the intrinsic unity of the soul. One cannot, however, fault him for wondering about the best way to model the integration of our various psychological capacities. We grow, perceive, and think; we desire, imagine and move; and we struggle with ourselves about how we ought to act. Sometimes our struggles find happy resolutions, and in other times they result in less pleasing outcomes, leading to remorse and regret. When we move through the world in these ways, we do so as unified psychological beings, not as loosely assembled components located in the same general bodily neighborhood. Aristotle rightly wonders how best we ought to explain and model these phenomena.

A Concluding Complication

These investigations into Aristotle's conception of the soul have been intended to highlight some of the richness of his approach to the study of the phenomena of life. Sensitive as he is to the various demands on explanatory adequacy, Aristotle has wanted to forge a middle way between what he regards as the impoverished frameworks of his reductivist predecessors and the extravagances of a Platonic dualism. It is often, and rightly, observed that he denies the separability of the soul: even while siding with Plato against the reductive tendencies of the Presocratics, Aristotle has not wanted to join with him in any easy inference to a thorough soul–body dualism. He would thus be doubtful about Socrates' confident conviction that death is the separation of the soul from the body, that the soul persists while the body perishes, that a life beyond awaits. As we have seen, he justifiably observes that a simple rejection of reductive materialism warrants no such inference. He offers as a moderate middle way his hylomorphism.

The moderation of Aristotle's hylomorphism may also prove unstable, by attempting to embrace more of the phenomena than any one position can comfortably accommodate. In this vein, it is well worth emphasizing something we have thus far neglected. Just after insisting that the soul is not separable from the body, Aristotle appends a rider often politely ignored by his current-day materialistically minded exegetes. Directly after concluding "that the soul is not separable from the body" (*An* II.1 413a3–4), Aristotle comments that this holds true at any rate of "some the soul's parts, if it naturally has parts" (*An* II.1 413a4–5). His reason for holding out: "The actuality of some parts belong to the parts of the body themselves. Even so, nothing hinders some parts from being separable, because of their not being the actualities of any body" (*An* II.1 413a5–7). We find Aristotle thus at once denying separability and making room for the possibility of some attenuated version of it; and we find him, again, puzzling not only over the existence and character of the parts of the soul but additionally over their sundry relations to their correlative bodily parts. Hylomorphism thus proves elastic and accommodating, perhaps to the point where its own precise commitments are difficult to determine, or where its resources begin to show the strain of overexertion.

In one way, of course, any instability or indeterminateness in Aristotle's conception of the soul is cause for criticism. All the same, his hylomorphism does provide a framework for thinking about soul–body relations which succeeds in acknowledging the full complement of phenomena we should wish to explain. We are one sort of living being among others, minded, embodied, and capable of change. We perceive and plan, imagine, desire and fear, and we engage in intentional, end-directed behavior. We are born, eat, grow, change, atrophy, and die; some of us, like Socrates, speculate along the way about how best we might understand our deaths. Should it be a criticism of Aristotle, or of us, that we struggle to explain the matter of mind in an idiom avoiding polarities with clarity purchased only at the cost of denying the phenomena? One might think it, on the contrary, a cause for commendation all around.[1]

Note

I thank Nathanael Stein for his comments on a draft of this chapter.

Bibliography

Texts, translations, and commentaries

Apostle, Hippocrates (1981). Aristotle's "On the Soul" (Grinell, IA: Peripatetic Press).

Hamlyn, D. W. [1968] (1993). *Aristotle "De Anima," Books II and III (with Passages from Book I)*, trans. with intro. and notes by D. W. Hamlyn, with a report on recent work and a revd. biblio. by Christopher Shields (Oxford: Clarendon Press).

Lawson-Tancred, H. (1986). *Aristotle: "De Anima"* (Harmondsworth: Penguin).

Monographs, articles, and book chapters

Ackrill, J. L. [1972/3] (1979). "Aristotle's Definitions of Psuchê," *Proceedings of the Aristotelian Society*, 73, pp. 1991–33.

Burnyeat, Myles [1992] (1995). "Is an Aristotelian Philosophy of Mind Still Credible? (A Draft)," in Nussbaum and Rorty (eds.) (1995), pp. 15–26.

Caston, Victor (1992). "Aristotle and Supervenience," in John Ellis (ed.) (1992), "Ancient Minds," *Southern Journal of Philosophy*, 31, suppl., pp. 107–35.

Caston, Victor (1997). "Epiphenomenalisms, Ancient and Modern," *Philosophical Review*, 106, pp. 309–63.

Caston, Victor (2000). "Aristotle's Argument for Why the Understanding is not Compounded with the Body," *Proceedings of the Boston Area Colloquium in Ancient Philosophy*, 16, pp. 135–75.

Charlton, William (1985). "Aristotle and the *Harmonia* Theory," in Allan Gotthelf (ed.), *Aristotle on Nature and Living Things* (Pittsburgh, PA: Mathesis), pp. 131–50.

Code, Alan (1991). "Aristotle, Searle, and the Mind–Body Problem," in Ernest Lepore and Robert van Gulick (eds.), *John Searle and His Critics* (Oxford: Basil Blackwell), pp. 105–13.

Code, Alan and Moravcsik, Julius [1992] (1995). "Explaining Various Forms of Living," in Nussbaum and Rorty (eds.) (1995), pp. 129–45.

Cohen, S. Marc. [1992] (1995). "Hylomorphism and Functionalism," in Nussbaum and Rorty (eds.) (1995), pp. 57–73.

Frede, Michael. [1992] (1995). "On Aristotle's Conception of Soul," in Nussbaum and Rorty (eds.) (1995), pp. 93–107.

Granger, Herbert (1993). "Aristotle and the Concept of Supervenience," *Southern Journal of Philosophy*, 31, pp. 161–77.

Granger, Herbert (1994). "Supervenient Dualism," *Ratio*, 7, pp. 1–13.

Heinaman, Robert (1990). "Aristotle and the Mind – Body Problem," *Phronesis*, 35, pp. 83–102.

Irwin, Terence (1991). "Aristotle's Philosophy of Mind," in Stephen Everson (ed.), *Psychology*, Companions to Ancient Thought, vol. 2 (Cambridge: Cambridge University Press), pp. 56–83.

Kosman, Aryeh (1987). "Animals and Other Beings in Aristotle," in Allan Gotthelf and James G. Lennox (eds.) (1987), *Philosophical Issues in Aristotle's Biology* (Cambridge: Cambridge University Press), pp. 360–91.

Matthews, Gareth (1977). "Consciousness and Life," *Philosophy*, 52, pp. 13–26.

Matthews, Gareth [1992] (1995). "*De Anima* 2.2–4 and the Meaning of Life," in Nussbaum and Rorty (eds.) (1995), pp. 185–93.

Nussbaum, Martha C. and Rorty, Amélie Oksenberg (eds.) [1992] (1995). *Essays on Aristotle's "De anima,"* first paperback edn., with an additional essay by M. F. Burnyeat (Oxford: Clarendon Press).

Robinson, H. M. (1978). "Mind and Body in Aristotle," *Classical Quarterly*, n.s., 28, pp. 105–24.

Robinson, H. M. (1983). "Aristotelian Dualism," *Oxford Studies in Ancient Philosophy*, 1, pp. 123–44.

Shields, Christopher (1988). "Soul and Body in Aristotle," *Oxford Studies in Ancient Philosophy*, 6, pp. 103–37.

Shields, Christopher (1988). "Soul as Subject in Aristotle's De Anima," *Classical Quarterly*, 38, pp. 140–9.

Shields, Christopher (1990). "The First Functionalist," in J-C. Smith (ed.), *The Historical Foundations of Cognitive Science* (Dordrecht: Kluwer), pp. 19–33.

Shields, Christopher (1993). "The Homonymy of the Body in Aristotle," *Archive für Geschiche der Philosophie*, 75, pp. 1–30.

Shields, Christopher (2003) *Classical Philosophy: A Contemporary Introduction* (London: Routledge).

Sisko, John (2000). "Aristotle's *Nous* and the Modern Mind," *Proceedings of the Boston Area Colloquium in Ancient Philosophy*, 16, pp. 177–98.

Sorabji, Richard [1974] (1979). "Body and Soul in Aristotle," *Philosophy*, 49, pp. 63–89; also in Barnes, Schofield, and Sorabji (eds.) (1979), *Articles on Aristotle* vol. 4 (London: Duckworth), pp. 42–64.

Wedin, Michael (1996). "Aristotle on How to Define a Psychological State," *Topoi*, 15, pp. 11–24.

Whiting, Jennifer [1992] (1995). "Living Bodies," in Nussbaum and Rorty (eds.) (1995), pp. 75–91.

Williams, Bernard (1986). "Hylomorphism," *Oxford Studies in Ancient Philosophy*, 4, pp. 189–99.

19

Sensation and Desire

DEBORAH KAREN WARD MODRAK

It would be difficult to exaggerate the importance Aristotle attaches to sensation (*aisthesis*). It plays a key role in how we come to have knowledge and how we hit upon the right thing to do. In Aristotle's treatise on the soul, the *De Anima*, the psychological capacity that is discussed at greatest length is the perceptual faculty of the soul and its various functions. These include the five senses, the common sense and imagination. Elsewhere in the corpus Aristotle extends the functions of the perceptual faculty to include memory, dreaming and consciousness.

Desire is another important concept in Aristotle's psychology. His account of it in the *De Anima* is quite compressed but without desire, there can be no action. Sentience and locomotion are the two characteristics that distinguish animals from plants. A concept of desire, broad enough to cover all types of motivation, is required, Aristotle recognizes, in order to explain self-movement.

In light of the multi-faceted nature of Aristotle's concepts of sensation (*aisthesis*) and desire (*orexis*), it would be wise to adopt a cautious attitude about identifying these notions too closely with the concepts we associate with the English terms "sensation" and "desire." This is especially true in the case of *aisthesis*. This Aristotelian term has been variously translated in different texts as "sensation," "perception," "awareness," and "consciousness." Aristotle's notion of *aisthesis* is much broader than our notion of sensation or even our notion of perception.

Sensation

Perception in general

In *De Anima* II.4, Aristotle lays the explanatory groundwork for the account of specific functions of the perceptual faculty of the soul in *De Anima* II.5–III.3. In the first Book of the *De Anima*, Aristotle argues that since psychic capacities are possessed, even when they are not being exercised, the soul should be identified with the capacities rather than their realization. Since a psychic capacity is a capacity for performing a certain kind of psychological activity, it will be defined with reference to the activity. Sight is the capacity for seeing; an analysis of sight must examine the nature of seeing. Cognitive activities such as seeing have the characteristics they have because their objects have the character they have. When a percipient looks at an orange, her eyes are affected by an orange, circular object, when the same percipent looks at an apple, her eyes are affected by a red, cylindrical object. In one case, an orange, round shape is actualized as the object of seeing; in the other, a red, cylindrical one. Aristotle says that the capacity for seeing is potentially what its object is actually. Hence he urges the psychologist to work back from the cognitive object (color) to the activity (seeing) to the faculty (sight).

Another feature of Aristotle's psychological theory is a commitment to psychophysicalism. Psychic activities are embodied. The soul does not see or feel anger; the person does (I.1 403a15–25). The soul as the form of the living being must be realized in appropriate matter in order for there to be a living creature with a variety of cognitive and other psychic capacities. Aristotle advises the psychologist to attend to structural features or form but also to recognize that psychic capacities are embedded in bodily organs (I.1 403b7–10). As he explains in *De Sensu* 1, "The most important characteristics of animals seem to be common to soul and body, for example, perception and memory and passion and desire and appetite generally as well as pleasure and pain" (1 436a7–10; cf. *An* I.1 403a16–18). Psychic capacities are first actualities of bodily organs. The relationship between sight and the eye is analogous to the relationship between the soul as a whole and the body (II.1 412b20–2). The eye must be made up of an appropriate material in order for seeing to take place. The transmission of color requires a transparent medium and hence, Aristotle argues, the eye must be made up of water or air. Since water is more easily confined, the eye is made up of water (*De Sensu* 2 438a14–23). The account that Aristotle gives of the individual senses is simultaneously about the formal features of perception and the physical basis for perception.

The general principles that Aristotle articulates for psychological analysis are brought to bear in his account of perception and the other capacities of the perceptual faculty of the soul. Having made psychic capacities a special kind of potentiality, that he calls first actuality, Aristotle labels the activities in which these capacities are realized second actualities. Perceiving is a second actuality, whereas the capacity for perception is a first actuality. Using perception as an illustration, Aristotle argues that the change from a first to second actuality is unique among changes in preserving and completing the capacity. When a cold object becomes hot, the cold is destroyed. However, when the capacity for hearing a particular sound is realized, the capacity for hearing is strengthened and the percipient will be more able to hear that sound in the future. If the sound is so loud that it causes deafness, this is not because the change from a first actuality (the capacity to hear) to a second actuality (hearing the loud sound) requires the destruction of the capacity, but because damage was done to the eardrum by the physical force of the sound.

> For that which perceives is a magnitude while neither what it is to be percipient nor the sense are magnitudes, but a certain form (*logos*) and power of the former. And it is clear from these considerations also why excess in the objects of sense destroys the sense organs; for if the movement is too strong for the organ, the form is destroyed – and this is the sense – just as the consonance and the pitch are destroyed when the strings are struck violently. (*An* II.11 424a26–32)

The five senses and their proper objects

To discover the nature of sight one must study seeing. Cognitive activities, however, are themselves the realization of particular kinds of objects, and so Aristotle suggests that our starting point should be the object of the activity, viz. color. There are five types of sense objects, each of which defines a sense. These are color, sound, flavor, odor, and the tactile qualities. There are five proper senses corresponding to the five types of sense object; the senses are sight, hearing, taste, smell, and touch. The senses are the foundation for all the other perceptual capacities and activities.

Aristotle investigates the nature of the five senses and their objects at length in the *De Anima* and the *De Sensu*. Each special sense perceives its proper object in itself (*kath' hauto*). In this context, "in itself" has both conceptual and causal significance. Conceptually, the special sense is defined in terms of its proper object. Sight is by definition the capacity to apprehend color. The color of the external object causes a change in the medium that is communicated to the eye.

> By in itself visible we mean not that the object is by its definition visible but that it has in itself the cause of its visibility. Every color can produce movement in that which is actually transparent, and it is its very nature to do so. (*An* II.7 418a30–b2)

The percipient is able to see whatever she sees in virtue of being affected by color and to hear whatever she hears in virtue of being affected by sound, and similarly in the case of the other senses.

The sense object is analyzed in terms of a pair of opposite qualities. Each sense is the capacity for realizing the ratio (*logos*) of a particular pair of opposite qualities; seeing is the realization of a ratio of light and dark. Every color falls along a continuum from light to dark. Sound is a ratio of sharp and flat; odor and flavor are ratios of sweet and bitter. Each pair of basic opposites defines a continuum along which other qualities perceptible by that sense fall.

> The types of flavors, just as in the case of colors, in their simplest form are contraries, sweet and bitter; next to them respectively are oily and saline; between these latter come pungent, rough, astringent and acidic. (*An* III.4 429b11–14)

When Aristotle tries to extend this model to touch, he concludes that there are several relevant pairs of opposite qualities, hot and cold, wet and dry, and hard and soft. Any tactile quality will fall somewhere on a continuum defined by one of these pairs of opposites. When the *logos* of perceptible qualities, the sensible form, is realized in the organ, perception takes place. A sensible quality such as blue is, from one perspective, a property of the blue object that exists independently of the perceiver; from another, it is a form that can be realized in an eye. The organ, Aristotle says, takes on the sensible form without its matter (II.12 424a17–19). Aristotle likens this process to the way soft wax takes on the shape of the signet stamp without absorbing any of its matter. The air becomes smelly but does not perceive the odor of the rotting cheese; the nose does not become smelly but smells the odor.

Each sense is associated with a specific bodily system. The sense organ is a composite of form and matter; the sense is the form of the organ. What Aristotle means by this description is that each sense organ has the function it has because it is structured in a particular way. The eye is a composite of sight and eye jelly (its watery matter). The eye (and other visual organs) can function in the way that it does because its matter is structured in a way that enables it to be the organ of sight. Color acts on transparent media, air and water, and is communicated through the medium to an organ that is made up of transparent material, the watery eye jelly. The eye is so constituted that the physical transmission of color to it results in the perception of color. Aristotle explains that the nose can smell odor while the air that transmits the odor cannot, because the nose has the structure that it has and its functional organization or form is the sense of smell.

In *De Anima* II and *De Sensu*, Aristotle explains how the physical characteristics of the external objects of perception cause changes in the peripheral sense organs. In every case, a change occurs in the organ as a direct result of a change communicated through a medium from the object to the organ directly or by contact. Color, which is a property of surfaces, causes a change in a transparent medium, air or water, in the presence of light. When this change is transmitted to the transparent eye jelly, the eye sees color. Sound is a motion in the mass of air between the sounding object and the perceiver that is communicated to the air of the inner ear. Temperature and solidity and other tactile characteristics are communicated by contact from the hot or solid object to the organ of touch within the skin.

Aristotle gives an account of the five senses that combines a causal theory of perception with a psychophysical account of each sense. The account begins with the external object and its ability to bring about a change in the medium and the organ. The visible form is transmitted by the medium to the eye. In the perception of a red object, the external object's redness becomes red as perceived and the percipient's capacity to see colors becomes the cognizing of red. This is a single event that can be analyzed from the side of the object or from that of the percipient. Each sense is a capacity of a bodily organ to be affected in a particular way by the objects in the environment and a capacity to experience a sensible quality as such.

The common sense

The five senses provide the foundation for all the other perceptual capacities and activities. Like the proper sensibles, the common objects are perceived in themselves. The common objects include motion, rest, number, figure, and size (II.5 418a17–20). These objects are perceived through the joint activity of several senses. Aristotle labels the special senses' capacity for joint activity the common sense. The common sense perceives certain objects, the common sensibles, in themselves. It is unlike a special sense, however, in being dependent upon the special senses, whereas each special sense, when apprehending its proper object, functions independently. One may, for instance, be blind but have exceptionally good hearing. The argument Aristotle gives to distinguish the common sense from a special sense turns on the difference between perceiving a common sensible in itself and perceiving it incidentally.

> Nor indeed can there be a special organ for the common objects that we perceive incidentally through each sense, for instance, motion, rest, figure, magnitude, number, and

unity . . . For each sense perceives one kind of object so it is clear that is impossible for there to be a special sense for any of these, for instance, for motion. For if so, it would be as we now perceive sweet by sight. This we do because we happen to have a perception of both and in this way we recognize them at the same time when they fall together. (*An* III.1 425a14–24)

In order to perceive the common objects jointly, the affected senses must be able to perceive the object individually. For instance, sight and touch perceive motion jointly, but sight may on occasion perceive motion without any other sense modalities being affected. When this happens, sight perceives motion incidentally but not in itself. Sight perceives color in itself; if the colored object is in motion, sight perceives motion incidentally; it perceives motion in virtue of perceiving color. However, when sight and touch act jointly, the percipient exercises a capacity that she possesses in virtue of having special senses that are capable of joint activity. This capacity cannot simply be reduced to the activity of the special senses because individually the senses are unable to perceive common objects in themselves. The common sense, Aristotle argues, is not a sixth sense. A special sense is by definition the ability to perceive a sensible characteristic that is not accessible through any other sense. Apart from metaphor, neither ears nor noses perceive color; sight is the capacity for sensing color. Were some bodily part, other than the eyes, to possess this capacity, it too would be an organ of sight, i.e., an eye. To reinforce this point, Aristotle argues that all the common objects are perceived through change (III.1 425a17). To perceive magnitude, for instance, the perceiver must note the changed perspective involved in perceiving different surfaces of the object.

Although the question whether the common sense is a special sense is a different question than whether it has an organ, the two are conflated in Aristotle's discussion of the common sense in *De Anima* (III.1 425a14–24). Elsewhere its having a specific organ that is distinct from all other sensory systems, as an eye is distinct from all non-visual sensory organs, is disentangled from the broader topic of its embodiment. The common sense does have a physiological basis as Aristotle makes clear in *De Somno* (2 455a28–b2) and *De Insomniis* (3 461a24–30). Its organ is not peculiar to it as are the organs of the five senses. It is the common terminus of all the individual sense organs in the heart. In *De Partibus Animalium*, Aristotle argues that the heart is better suited to be the central organ than the brain because it is centrally located; it is connected with all parts of the body through the vascular system; and it is irregular in shape (II.1 647a3–23). Blood transmits sensory impulses from the peripheral organs but it is not percipient because it is uniform. Perceptual activity can only take place in an irregularly shaped organ. The heart is percipient because it has an irregular structure. Perception takes places when impulses from the special organs reach the heart. Moreover, the central organ must be present in the developing embryo from the beginning, and the heart is the first organ to develop in the embryo (II.4 666a19–23, a35–6).

The common sense not only is the capacity to perceive the common objects in themselves; it is also the capacity for making various apperceptual judgments. Aristotle discusses two types of apperceptual awareness in *De Anima* III. In one instance, the percipient recognizes that the very same object is both white and sweet. This is a case of putting together the perceptual information received through two sense modalities and recognizing the unity of the object experienced through different senses (III.1 425b1–3). The activity of two senses is involved. Yet this is not a case of perceiving a common object, because each of the two qualities continues to be perceived in itself by its proper sense. What is involved is the ability to unify different types of perceptual experience. Sweetness and whiteness must be simultaneously apprehended. As Aristotle pictures such perceptions, they supervene upon the more basic perceptions of the special senses. They involve joint activity on the part of the special senses albeit of a different type than in the case of the perception of the common sensibles. Unlike Plato and many other later philosophers, Aristotle is not inclined to move judgments of this sort out of the sphere of perception and into that of reason. If the objects apprehended (in this case, sweet and white) are sensibles, then the apprehension is perceptual. If the cognitive grasp exceeds the scope of the individual senses, Aristotle assigns it to the common faculty of sense.

The second case of apperception mentioned in the *De Anima* is the recognition that color is different from flavor. This, too, requires the ability to perceive objects from several senses simultaneously. How exactly this happens is not fully explained by Aristotle, who cites the example of a point that is the end point of one line and the beginning of another (III.2 427a10–14). When a percipient recognizes that the whiteness and sweetness of a piece of candy are distinct and different sensibles, the objects of two senses are grasped in a single cognition. The white of the candy is a distinct form realized in the visual organs and the sweet, a distinct form realized in the organs of taste, but the perception of their difference occurs at their common terminus in the common sense. In *De Somno*, Aristotle elaborates further.

> Since each sense has a special function and a common function, the special function, for example, of sight is seeing, that of the auditory sense is hearing, and similarly with the other senses. But there is also a common faculty associated with them all, through which one is aware that one sees and hears (for it is not by sight that one is aware that one sees; and one judges and is capable of judging that sweet is different from white not by taste, nor by sight, nor by a combination of the two, but by some part which is common to all the sense organs). (2 455a13–21)

In *De Anima*, there is a type of apperception that takes place in the proper senses. Aristotle wonders whether it is "by sight that one perceives that one sees or by another sense" (III.2 425b13). He concludes that since the awareness of seeing would involve color, it too must belong to sight. However, he rejects this conclusion in *De Somno* where he quite firmly assigns all the types of apperceptual judgments discussed in *De Anima* to the common sense (1 455a13–21). These two positions can be reconciled. In *De Anima*, Aristotle considers the senses individually and bases his analysis on the objects that define the special senses and the common sense. Although he recognizes that the special senses possess a capacity for joint activity, he does not develop his account of this capacity in *De Anima*. In *De Somno* and *De Memoria*, where Aristotle's topics are sleep and memory respectively, his focus is on perceptual activity as a whole. In *De Somno*, he develops an account of a common capacity of the senses (2 455a16) and in *De Memoria* he makes use of this notion to locate remembering among the activities of the primary faculty of sense (1 450a11, 451a17). In short, when his attention is directed to perceptual experience in general, Aristotle recognizes the centrality of the common sense in order to give an adequate account of perception.

Perception of incidental sensibles

Proper and common sensibles are perceived in themselves (*kath' hauta*). They do not, however, exhaust the field of perceptible objects. Aristotle recognizes a third type of perceptible, the incidental object. Incidental objects are perceived in virtue of the perception of proper and common objects. A certain complex of colors, shapes, sounds, and movements acts on a percipient, who perceives a particular person, the son of Diares (II.6 418a20–4). The perception of the person occurs because the percipient's eyes are affected by the color and shape of the person, the perceiver's ears are affected by the sound of the person's voice, etc. Because such perceptions are dependent upon more fundamental perceptual activities, they are described by Aristotle as incidental (*kata sumbebekos*). The percipient who has never met the son of Diares nor been told by someone else that the person approaching is the son of Diares will perceive a man approaching rather than the son of Diares. In this case, too, the percipient perceives something, a man, incidentally. However, suppose the percipient were an infant, then the colored shape approaching might not occasion any incidental perceptions, although the infant would perceive the color, shape, sound and movement in themselves.

This aspect of the perception of incidental sensibles has led some scholars to conclude that this type of perception is not genuine perception but rather a kind of inferential perceptual judgment. Aristotle, however, repeatedly describes incidental object as sensibles and we should take him at his word. Aristotle distinguishes between perceptual and rational faculties of the soul in *De Anima*. Inference is taken to be a mark of rationality. The apprehension of incidental sensibles is discussed in the course of outlining the basic functions of the perceptual faculty. He nowhere suggests that reason is required for their apprehension. Aristotle has another motivation to keep incidental objects among perceptibles. Both as a psychologist and as an epistemologist, Aristotle takes our perceptions of the external world as basic. As a psychologist, he offers an account of the sensible features of physical objects. As an epistemologist, he focuses on the apprehension of the intelligible forms of objects as perceived. From this perspective, the apprehension of a natural kind such as human being is basic. The incidental sensibles, however, are perceived with less accuracy that the proper sensibles (III.3 428b19–25). Proper objects are perceived with the least amount of error (III.3 428b18–19) – at times Aristotle goes so far as to say with no error (II.6 418a12, a15, III.6 430b29; *De Sensu* 4 442b9). A proper sensible, unlike other sense objects, acts directly on a single sense, the addition of joint activity in the case of common objects or conceptualization in the case of incidental objects increases the potential for error.

Aristotle's describing ordinary objects such as people as incidental perceptibles is significant. His picture of perception is not one where the percipient judges that a colored shape is a person; it is rather one in which the percipient perceives a person. In order to perceive a person by sight, the percipient's eyes must be acted upon by a shaped color. In order to perceive the common sensible, shape, through sight, the percipient must be acted upon by a color. In short, perceptions are multi-layered from the standpoint of analysis and causality; at the most basic level, there are the proper sensibles, without which perception is impossible; at the next level, there are the common sensibles that act on more than one sense but do so along with each sense's proper object, and at the next level there are the incidental objects that do not directly act on any sense but are borne by concatenations of proper and common objects. However, at the level of perceptual experience, the world is presented as objects that have various characteristics and stand in various relations to each other.

Perceptual consciousness

Nor does Aristotle's account of perceptual activities end with immediate perceptual experience. He includes imagination, memory, and dreaming among the functions of the perceptual faculty of the soul. After considering various possible accounts of imagination in *De Anima* III.3, Aristotle ultimately concludes that imagination is a distinct cognitive function that is an activity, caused by and similar to perception, that occurs in percipients, and through which percipients do many things (III.3 428b10–17). Having assigned imagination to the perceptual faculty of the soul in *De Anima*, Aristotle extends the activity of the perceptual faculty to include dreaming, remembering, and sleeping in the *Parva Naturalia*. According to Aristotle, a dream is a kind of image and dreaming is an activity of the perceptual faculty qua faculty for imagination (*De Insomniis* 1 459a18–22). Sleep is a distinctive and routine shutting down of the central organ in which the common capacity of sense resides (*De Somno* 2 455a33–b3). Since the common organ is the terminus of the individual senses, its incapacitation extends to the other senses.

A similar explanatory strategy is employed by Aristotle in *De Memoria* to account for memory. Memory is a cognitive state in which an image is grasped in relation to what the image is an image of and it is a function of the primary faculty of sense (2 452a15–18). A feature that is implicit in his treatment of common and incidental sensibles in *De Anima* is made explicit here. Not only is the content of the perceptual state important to the definition of the state, but also how the content is apprehended. The perception of the river today may in all observable particulars be indistinguishable from yesterday's perception, and thus Aristotle's asks, what distinguishes today's memory of the river from a perception? What makes the content of a past perception, a content of a memory, is its apprehension in relation to a past perception or thought (1 450b26–451a8). It is striking that Aristotle assigns this degree of representational complexity to functions of the perceptual faculty. Because he has a broad and inclusive notion of the powers of perception, Aristotle is able to extend the functions of the perceptual faculty of the soul to include consciousness and sleeping.

Pulling together the picture of a central organ and a common capacity of perception from the *De Anima* and *Parva Naturalia*, one finds that Aristotle has given us an account of all aspects of consciousness under the rubric of an examination of the capacities of the perceptual faculty of the soul. Aristotle builds this account up from the functions of the special senses to the myriad forms of awareness he ultimately assigns to the common functions of the sense faculty as a whole. These are seated in an organ that is the common terminus of the senses. To the common capacity for sentience, Aristotle has assigned the perception of the common sensibles, the unification of the sensations received through different senses, the conceptualization of disparate sensible features

317

as manifestations of the same object, the introspective awareness of perceiving and the discrimination of differences among sensibles. Not only do all aspects of perceptual experience fall under the common capacity but also remembering and dreaming; sleep, too, is assigned to it by virtue of its being the opposite of waking consciousness. "Being awake," Aristotle says, "consists in nothing else but perceiving" (*De Somno* 1 454a5–6).

Desire

Aristotle's analysis of desire in *De Anima* III.9–11 follows along similar lines to that of his analysis of perception. Desire is a psychophysical disposition that is realized in an activity, desiring. There are three types of desire, each of which is defined in relation to its object. Desire is a distinct psychic faculty, albeit one that is dependent upon a faculty of presentation, perception or thought, for its objects.

Desire is of interest to Aristotle because he wants to explain the motive faculty of the soul. His question is: what gets us moving and why. Aristotle's theory of motion provides the context for his analysis of desire (433b10–21). The faculty of desire is that which moves us in virtue of being a psychic activity that prompts the movement of relevant bodily parts – muscles, sinews, and limbs and so forth – as is clear from the physiological account of desire and self-movement in *De Motu Animalium*. Desire is a moved mover and its object, the thing desired, is the unmoved mover of desire (*An* III.10 433b11, *De Motu Animalium* 10 703a5). Both are required to cause an agent to act. Aristotle considers and rejects the possibility that some other psychic capacity such as perception or thought occasions action. He concludes that only desire in one of its various forms is sufficient for movement that is initiated by an agent, human or non-rational animal. Aristotle defends his position by pointing out that we can entertain the thought of something pleasurable or frightening and not be motivated to act. Perceptions do not provoke actions unless desire is present. Desire, however, may influence our perceptions and thoughts. Aristotle's example is that of mistaking a stranger at a distance for one's lover (*De Insomniis* 2 460b3–8).

There are three types of desire that differ, Aristotle says, by definition and capacity (III.10 433b3–5). They are sensual desire (*epithumia*), emotion (*thumos*) and rational desire (*boulêsis*). Sensual desire aims at bodily pleasure and seeks to avoid bodily pain; rational desire aims at the good and emotion falls somewhere in-between. Rational desire belongs only to humans; non-rational animals and young children possess both sensual desire and emotion (*NE* III.2 1111b12–13). Because there are different types of desire, conflicts between desires may arise. Whenever we have conflicting motivations, Aristotle argues, we have conflicting desires. Cases where an agent appears to act against her desires are, for Aristotle, cases where the agent's rational desire has conflicted with and bested the agent's sensual desires or emotional ones. They are not cases where reason as such has become a motive capacity. On Aristotle's account, one can act on principle and against some of one's other desires and still be acting on desire. While different types of desire may conflict with one another, potentially conflicting objects of desire falling under a single type of desire will not produce actually conflicting desires of that type. Suppose I am thirsty and hungry and objects that would satisfy both are ready to hand. To act I must pick up one or the other. If the thought of a cool drink provokes more pleasure than the thought of food, I'll drink first. The sensual desire that was fully realized had a single focus. Sensual desire will always settle on what appears to be most pleasurable or least painful (*NE* III.2 1111b16).

Broadly speaking all forms of desire aim at a good that may be achieved through action. Aristotle calls this kind of good the practical good (*An* III.10 433a30). The practical good includes both what is actually good for the agent and what appears to be good to the agent. Every operative desire is aimed at achieving some very specific good; the desire for a piece of pizza causes the agent to eat a particular slice of pizza. Any number of different items may function as practical goods. The *Nicomachean Ethics* famously opens with these words: Every art and every inquiry, and similarly every action and every choice seems to aim at a good (I.1 1094a1–2). This is true on Aristotle's account of action and desire.

The objects upon which particular desires are focused are presented to the agent by some form of cognition. Broadly speaking, this may be some perceptual cognition (perception, imagination, memory) or a rational one (*An* III.10 433b12; *De Motu Animalium* 7 701a28–b1). The cognition is, on the one hand, a presentation of a particular object and, on the other, a presentation of it as pleasurable or otherwise desirable. In order to perceive the piece of pizza as desirable, one must not only recognize that it is a piece of pizza, but one must also perceive it under a description that makes it desirable. The description connects the pizza with one's desire for food; one's liking the flavor of pizza, and so forth. A person who has just eaten is unlikely to perceive a piece of pizza as desirable, even though he may quite like pizza and he recognizes that the object in front of him is pizza. In order for an object to prompt desire and hence an action, it must present itself to the agent as actually desirable at that moment. To perceive the pizza as desirable is to apprehend it as a good for oneself here and now. A prospective agent may believe, for instance, that one should eat when hungry and since he is currently hungry, he will eat the pizza. Desire, like perception, is realized through the actualization of its object as an object of awareness. It differs from perception and other cognitive functions in being the realization of affective characteristics. The object of desire is a cognitive object, an object of perception or thought, embedded in a presentation that not only has cognitive but also affective qualities. In the case of humans, the latter may be articulated as universal principles. In the case of other animals, there is no capacity for articulating general principles but the object of desire is, nonetheless, presented as desirable.

> Since one judgment and premise is universal and the other particular, for the one says that a person of this sort ought to do such and such, and the other says that this is such and such, and I am such a person, this opinion causes action, not the universal, or perhaps both; but the universal is more at rest; and the particular is not. (*An* III.11 434a16–21)

The particular judgment or presentation moves the agent because it occasions the presentation of an object, obtainable through action, as an object of desire. The psychic realization of an object of desire is a desiring. Actively desiring the object causes the agent to move to obtain it.

The theory of desire that is sketched by Aristotle in his psychological writings is filled out in more detail in his ethical ones. Desiring the right thing is central to Aristotle's

319

account of virtue. Virtue is a disposition to behave in various ways. A mark of virtue is taking pleasure in the right objects. Unless our desires are in line with our moral judgments, we will not be able to behave virtuously. Aristotle makes choice (*prohairesis*) a necessary condition for the possession of virtue, and he defines choice in terms of desire. Choice is deliberate desire (*NE* III.3 1113a11, VI.2 1139a23). Choice is desire for an end achievable through our own action that arises after deliberation. Sensual desire figures importantly in Aristotle's accounts of temperance and its opposite, profligacy, and weakness of will (*akrasia*) and its opposite, self-restraint. Aristotle draws a distinction between natural sensual desires and ones that are peculiar to individuals (*NE* III.11 1118b8–22, VII.4 1147b24–31). Natural sensual desires, such as those for food and drink and sex, are common to all humans. Peculiar desires are often permutations of natural ones, for instance, a desire for delicacies. People are much more likely to have excessive or inappropriate peculiar desires than natural ones. Appealing to this analysis of desire, Aristotle explicates the nature of temperance and self-restraint and the corresponding cases of morally problematic behavior. The temperate person has natural sensual desires that are appropriate to the occasion (VII.2 1146a12). The self-restrained person acts on rational desire that holds his inappropriate sensual desires in check (VII.1 1145a17, b8, VII.2 1146a10). In a broader sense, however, all virtuous action involves desiring the right objects at the right time and choosing the right means to achieve them.

The analysis of desire in terms of an implicit deliberation is briefly sketched in *De Anima* III.11. Aristotle fleshes this account out in the *Nicomachean Ethics* as part of his explanation of weakness of will. The weak-willed individual has in principle the same motivation to make the right choices as the temperate individual since they share the same moral principles. The problem as Aristotle sees it is to explain why the weak-willed agent's beliefs do not shape his desires. Aristotle's solution is ingenious. The weak-willed person's correct belief that sweet foods should be eaten in moderation, if brought together with the perception of a second dessert, would lead to the presentation of this particular bit of sweet food as undesirable. It does not, however, because the perception of the sweet dessert brings a different universal to the fore, "all sweets are pleasant" (VII.3 1147a27). The weak-willed person perceives the dessert as pleasurable, i.e. he desires it and acts accordingly. The self-restrained individual, by contrast, is well aware of the pleasurableness of the sweet food but successfully acts on rational desire against his sensual desire.

Aristotle's account of desire has sufficient flexibility to accommodate the movement of the simplest animals to the complexly textured motivations of human agents. The simplest creatures possess the senses of touch and taste, and this is sufficient to have some forms of sensual desire. Humans, on the other hand, often act on reason and principle. These types of motivation remain speculative until they are realized through rational desire. Because desire is realized through the apprehension of an object as desirable nothing further is needed to prompt action. Because different types of desire may conflict with one another, Aristotle has a ready explanation for the apparent failure of desire to issue in action. It is only apparent, because even the self-restrained individual who is fighting with his sensual desires is, nevertheless, acting on desire.

Together perception and desire distinguish animal life from plant life. These two faculties are also central to the life of rational animals. As rational animals, we are still dependent upon perception for all the materials upon which reason works and upon desire to motivate us to act. No matter how lofty the principles or how mundane the beliefs upon which we act, they must be applied to the particular situation in which the agent acts. For this to happen, both perception and desire must be realized in a cognitive presentation of the object of the act as desirable. Action follows seamlessly from this cognition. While a perception need not prompt any desire at all, every desire is dependent upon a cognitive presentation of its object. Since its object is always a particular, some form of perception is always involved–even in the case of rational desire.

Sensation (*aisthesis*) and desire (*orexis*) are fundamental notions in Aristotle's account of human psychology. As a consequence, they play a crucial role in other aspects of his philosophy from moral theory to epistemology. In a short sketch such as this, one can only hope to provide a broad overview.[1]

Note

[1] For a more detailed treatment of many of the topics discussed above, see Modrak (1987).

Bibliography

Broadie, S. (1993). "Aristotle's Perceptual Realism," in J. Ellis (ed.), *Southern Journal of Philosophy, Spindel Conference 1992: Ancient Minds*, 31, suppl. vol., pp. 137–60.

Everson, S. (1997). *Aristotle on Perception* (Oxford: Clarendon Press).

Freeland, C. (1992). "Aristotle on the Sense of Touch," in M. Nussbaum and A. Rorty (eds.), *Essays on Aristotle's "De Anima"* (Oxford: Oxford University Press).

Johansen, T. (1997). *Aristotle on the Sense-organs* (Cambridge: Cambridge University Press).

Kahn, C. (1966). "Sensation and Consciousness in Aristotle's Psychology," *Archiv für Geschichte der Philosophie*, 48, pp. 43–81.

Modrak, D. K. W. (1976). "*Aisthesis* in the Practical Syllogism," *Philosophical Studies*, 30, pp. 379–91.

Modrak, D. K. W. (1987). *Aristotle: The Power of Perception* (Chicago/London: University of Chicago Press).

Sisko, J. (1996). "Material Alteration and Cognitive Activity in Aristotle's *De Anima*," *Phronesis*, 41, pp. 138–57.

Sorabji, R. (1971). "Aristotle on Demarcating the Five Senses," *Philosophical Review*, 80, pp. 55–79.

Wedin, M. (1988). *Mind and Imagination in Aristotle* (New Haven/London: Yale University Press).

20

Phantasia and Thought

VICTOR CASTON

Aristotle's theory of cognition rests on two central pillars: his account of perception and his account of thought. Together, they make up a significant portion of his psychological writings, and his discussion of other mental states depends critically on them. These two activities, moreover, are conceived of in an analogous manner, at least with regard to their most basic forms. Each activity is triggered by its object – each, that is, is about the very thing that brings it about. This simple causal account explains the reliability of cognition: perception and thought are, in effect, transducers, bringing information about the world into our cognitive systems, because, at least in their most basic forms, they are infallibly about the causes that bring them about (An III.4 429a13–18). Other, more complex mental states are far from infallible. But they are still tethered to the world, in so far as they rest on the unambiguous and direct contact perception and thought enjoy with their objects.

Perception and thought are not exactly alike, of course. Aristotle notes that perception is concerned with external objects, which act on our bodies; whereas thought is triggered by something within. For this reason, we can think whenever we want, while perception depends on what is available in our immediate environment. In its most basic form, perception is about, and is caused by, individual perceptible objects. Thought, in contrast, is about universals; and these, Aristotle says, are "somehow in the soul" (An II.5 417b19–25). Thought, finally, is in some sense derived from, or dependent upon, perception (III.8 432a3–10). But not directly. Through the repeated perception of objects and our ability to form coherent memories, we acquire experience of the different types of things there are. As we further manipulate things and attain some knowledge of how they work, we begin to get a grip on the natures of things: to understand what it is to be a certain sort of thing and why something behaves the way it does (Met A.1; An Post II.19).

This processing of perceptual experience and the information gleaned from it requires that information is somehow preserved between experiences and so available for extraction. This belongs to another capacity, midway between perception and thought, which Aristotle calls "*phantasia*." The term is usually mistranslated as "imagination," but it designates something that has much broader functions, as one of the main forms of mental representation. By appealing to it, Aristotle believes, he can account for aspects of intentionality which his predecessors were completely unable to explain: our ability to have things present to mind which are absent from our environment and, importantly, our ability to get things wrong, to be in error. This basic form of mental representation, he maintains, arises naturally from perceptual activity and provides the material on which our understanding works to produce concepts.

Phantasia and thought are clearly both critical to Aristotle's overall account of content. But they also raise more metaphysical concerns about the relation of the soul to the body. On the one hand, Aristotle regards thought as requiring the bodily activity of phantasia and perception. On the other hand, he argues that the understanding is without a bodily organ of its own and that a second, very special type of understanding is actually "immortal and eternal." How these claims are to be reconciled is obviously of the greatest consequence to Aristotle's overall position and so not surprisingly the subject of some of the greatest controversy in the Aristotelian tradition.

Phantasia

After Aristotle completes his discussion of perceptual abilities in *De Anima* III.2, he turns to the topics of thought (III.4–6) and desire and action (III.9–11). But not immediately. In *De Anima* III.3, he introduces a new ability, distinct from all the rest, which he calls "*phantasia*." This ability will play a central role not only in his accounts of thought and desire, but also in his accounts of memory, dreams, passions, and aspects of perceptual experience that go beyond mere sensation. But as the first chapter of *De Anima* already makes clear, it has especially significant consequences for the understanding. This, among all mental capacities, is the most likely to be "separable." But, Aristotle warns, if it requires *phantasia*, even the understanding cannot exist apart from the body (*An.* I.1 403a8–10). And it does in fact require *phantasia*. In the last part of *De Anima* and in the *Parva Naturalia*, Aristotle repeatedly claims that we do not ever think without a *phantasma* (see n. 4), the state we have when we are using *phantasia* (III.3 428a1–2).

"*Phantasia*" and "*phantasma*" are most commonly rendered "imagination" and "image." But these translations are theoretically loaded and misleading. Like the cognates "fantasy" and "fancy," these terms have a long history in philosophy, psychology and poetics, especially in the last four centuries, which strongly colors our associations. But Aristotle stands at the beginning of this history, which evolves well beyond his original concerns. When we speak of imagination, we often have in mind a source of creativity and invention. But these are not a part of Aristotle's concerns when he introduces *phantasia*. And while there are connections with mental imagery and visualization, it might well be wrong to think of a *phantasma* as something which is *viewed* with the "mind's eye." Yet many intepretations make just this assumption, conditioned by the translation "image." But it is no part of the meaning of the Greek term. Such questions can only be resolved by looking at Aristotle's actual usage and the details of his theory.

Although Aristotle is not the first to use the term, "*phantasia*" is nevertheless a recently coined technical term. Derived from the passive verb "*phantazesthai*," it signifies the capacity through which things are made to *phainesthai*, to appear or seem to us to be the case. It thus has more to do with things' appearing a certain way in experience than with our inventing imaginary scenes. Plato actually defines *phantasia* as "a belief that comes about through perception" (*Sophist* 264A–B; cf. *Theaetetus* 152A–C). Aristotle rejects his claim that it is a kind of belief, but he too is thinking along similar lines. The sun *appears* to be a foot wide, he argues, even though we believe, and even know, that it is not, but larger than the whole earth (*An* III.3 428a24–b9), just as the two lines in a Müller-Lyer diagram (to use a modern example) continue to *look* unequal even after we have convinced ourselves that they are in fact equal. The way things appear to us thus has a certain independence from what we believe. Because of this, Aristotle regards *phantasia* as more rudimentary than belief and even more closely connected with perceptual experience than Plato had claimed.

"*Phantasia*," then, is just the term for experiences of this sort and whatever it is that enables us to have them. But what precisely is that? It is not perception in its most basic and strict sense, in Aristotle's view, since things can appear to us other than they are. Yet there is still a strong sense in which *phantasia* is *like* perception, and it clearly plays a part in perceptual experience more broadly conceived. In the last third of *De Anima* III.3 (428b10–429a9), Aristotle proposes that *phantasia* is a *trace* or *echo* of perceptual activity and so can bear a similar content to perception, even after the original perceptual encounter has ended. As a result, it can falsely represent how things are in the world. In the *Parva Naturalia*, Aristotle explicitly compares *phantasmata* to representations, suggesting that they are reproduced from perceptual activity like an impression from a signet ring (*Mem* 1 450a27–32). In these essays, he also discusses the underlying physiology more extensively, beginning with how the traces persist in the peripheral organs, where they can bring about after-images and other perceptual illusions (*Insomn* 2), and then how they proceed to the central perceptual organ (which, for Aristotle, is the heart). Along the way, they are subject to distortion, resulting in dreams that can deviate significantly from our waking experience (*Insomn* 3). Because these *phantasmata* can be stored for long periods in the walls of the heart (*Mem* 1 450a32–b11), we are able to remember experiences long past, as well as search for and retrieve particular items (*Mem* 2). There are even a few tantalizing details about the mechanisms of representation itself, at least as regards magnitudes and our ability to order them (*Mem* 2 452b7–453a4).

The richness of detail in the last third of *De Anima* III.3, corroborated by the *Parva Naturalia*, has rightly led many interpreters to emphasize this part of Aristotle's account. But it has also traditionally been construed in terms of mental images, especially before the rise of behaviorism, when introspection was still dominant in psychology. On this line of interpretation, *phantasmata* are not merely representations that bear the content of mental acts. The way they represent objects is by being *viewed internally*, by being themselves the *objects* of an internal mental act. Consequently, they are like the percepts from which they are copied by *subjectively resembling* them, though they are fainter and less vivid (cf. *Rhet* I.11 1370a28–9). The echoes of British empiricism here are not accidental. Such interpretations often allude explicitly to Hobbes' characterization of the imagination as a kind of "decaying sense" and Hume's description of it as a "faint and languid perception."

Growing concerns about mental images in the twentieth century have led to a re-examination of this reading. The most influential critiques were advanced by Malcolm Schofield (1978) and Martha Nussbaum (1978). Both allow that Aristotle in places treats *phantasmata* as mental images, but deny that this is essential to their function.

Schofield emphasizes Aristotle's sensitivity to ordinary language, especially skeptical or non-committal uses of the phrase "it appears that" in waking experience, which is more evident in the middle section of *De Anima* III.3 (427b6–428b9). He concludes that *phantasia* is a "loose-knit, family concept" (p. 106), best understood as a passive capacity for having "non-paradigmatic sensory experiences" (pp. 101–2). Nussbaum similarly regards Aristotle as lacking a "canonical theory" (p. 222). But she emphasizes the more positive role *phantasia* plays in Aristotle's account of action, both later in *De Anima* (III.9–11) and in *De Motu Animalium* (6–11). Here, she contends, Aristotle treats *phantasia* as a capacity to perceive objects *as* certain sorts of things, in particular *as* worth pursuing or avoiding. Both stress the interpretive character of *phantasia* and its pervasive role in ordinary perceptual experience, as opposed to dreams and visualization.

With the resurgence of interest in representational theories of mind in the last quarter of the twentieth century, the pendulum has swung back, at least in part. Deborah Modrak (1987), Michael Wedin (1988) and Dorothea Frede (1992) defend the overall coherence of Aristotle's theory against Schofield's and Nussbaum's critiques. But while both Modrak and Frede accept the traditional view that *phantasmata* are images, Wedin's account marks more of a new departure by construing Aristotle's account along "cognitivist" lines. *Phantasia* is not a full-fledged faculty in the Aristotelian sense, but a system of internal representation that subserves the other faculties, where representations or *phantasmata* are not themselves objects of *phantasia*, or indeed Humean images at all. Instead, they are to be understood as physical states of the body, which possess their content in virtue of their similarity to an object, together with their role in the cognitive system as a whole.

There is much to be said for this general approach, which can be developed even further. Aristotle explicitly treats *phantasmata* as representations that underwrite the content of mental states more broadly. Imagistic experiences and visualization are included among these. But active visualization is *not* necessary for these representations to bear content and perform their cognitive role. To use a scholastic distinction, they are that "by which" (*a quo*) mental states are about objects. But they are not in general something "towards which" (*ad quem*) mental states are directed – they are not in general themselves the objects of mental states. Criticisms of representational theories, from the early modern period on, often assume that a representation must be the object of some internal mental state in order to represent another object. But Aristotle does not appear to think that this is necessary. It may simply be that *by which* our mental states are directed at objects, without itself being an object of a mental state at all. The question of subjective resemblance, therefore, need not arise: *phantasmata* do not represent by being looked at and compared to the objects they represent.[1] To the extent that Aristotle does appeal to similarity, it is objective, *physical* similarities that matter, such as possessing magnitudes with the same proportions as those of the object or having similar causal powers with respect to the cognitive system (similar proportions: *Mem* 2 452b11–22; similar causal powers: *Insomn* 2 460b23–5; *MA* 7 701b17–22; 11 703b18–20). In fact, Aristotle explains similarity in artistic representation by reference to causal powers too, in distinguishing signs from likenesses (*Pol* VIII.5 1340a18–35; for more extensive discussion and defense of these claims, see Caston 1998a).

The suggestion that *phantasia* is a form of internal representation that underlies mental states quite generally also fits the contexts in which Aristotle invokes it. On

325

several occasions, he raises puzzles concerning intentionality and mental content, which he uses as a basis for rejecting other theories – any adequate theory, he believes, must have a solution to them. He rejects both pre-Socratic and Platonic accounts, for example, because they cannot solve *the problem of presence in absence* in its full generality – the problem, that is, of explaining how we can remember or more generally think of objects that are absent (whether they are simply absent from our immediate environment, or no longer existent, or have never existed at all). But a solution can be found, he believes, if we posit internal representations or *phantasmata*. (*Mem* 1 450a27–32, 2 452b11–16; *Peri Ideôn* 81.25–82.6, Harlfinger). Similarly a theory must have a solution to *the problem of error*, of explaining how it is possible for the content of our mental states to deviate not only from immediate stimuli in our environment, but from the way things are in the world more generally. This is the task Aristotle sets explicitly in the opening section of *De Anima* III.3 (427a17–b6). This passage, though overlooked by most discussions, makes clear the structure of the entire chapter. Aristotle taunts his predecessors for not being able to explain how error is possible given their simple causal model of cognition, according to which "like is known by like." On such a view a mental state is invariably about what brings it about and so always corresponds to actual conditions in the world – it cannot err or deviate from the way things are. What makes this critique especially interesting is that Aristotle's *own* account of the most basic forms of perception and thought does not differ in this regard and accordingly he takes both to be incapable of error. The difference is that Aristotle does not think that all cognition can be *reduced* to these two basic activities – the simple causal model of cognition that underlies them does *not* account for content in general. A different kind of activity is required: *phantasia*. In the second section of the chapter (427b6–428b9), he argues that *phantasia* is distinct from perception, thought, or any combination of the two. The way it is generated from perception, he argues in the third section (428b10–429a9), explains why its content is similar to perception, yet also capable of deviating from actual conditions in the world. *Phantasia* can represent the world falsely as well as truly (428b17) and thus is a key factor in explaining the complex behavior of animals (428b16–17, 429a4–8; a close reading of the chapter and its structure can be found in Caston 1996).

Thought

Aristotle's "noetic" – his account of *nous* or thought (*An* III.4–8) – is one of the most influential parts of his entire psychology. It is also one of the most controversial, as it is decisive for several issues of larger importance, including dualism and personal immortality. Given the predominance of these metaphysical issues in the literature, it is worthwhile to start with his views on content and intentionality instead, which have received comparatively less attention.

The content of thought

Aristotle's treatment of thought resembles, in certain large-scale features, his treatment of perception. Just as he distinguishes a basic form of perception, which we might call "sensation," from other forms of perception, he also singles out a basic form of thinking from more complex ones that include propositional thought and reasoning. This basic form of thinking is perhaps best thought of as "understanding."[2] Its object is always a nature or essence (*An* III.4 429b10–22, III.6 430b27–9), about which one *cannot be in error*: either one grasps it or one doesn't.[3] Its infallibility, like the infallibility of sensation, can be traced to the simple causal model that underlies both accounts. Understanding is *about* the object that *brings it about*, which causes the understanding to become like it in form, without becoming the object itself (*An* III.4 429a13–16; *Met.* XII.7 1072a30): "the understanding is related to what can be understood in just the way that what can perceive is related to what can be perceived" (*An* III.4 429a16–18). When people speak about the analogy between perception and understanding, these are the doctrines they principally have in mind.

But there are differences too, of course. As mentioned earlier, perception requires an external object, a sensible particular, while understanding is of a universal, which is "somehow in the soul"; hence, understanding is "up to us" in a way that perception is not (*An* II.5 417b19–25). Perception depends for its objects on what the environment furnishes, whereas the understanding depends on what is furnished by our own lower faculties. For humans, each act of understanding is grounded in *phantasia* and so ultimately perception: without any sensory experience, humans could not learn or grasp anything (III.8 432a3–8). But we can retain the contents of such experiences in memory, and this allows us to have the objects of understanding available to be thought whenever we want (II.5 417b19–26; III.4 429b5–9). For understanding grasps the forms it understands "in" these *phantasmata* and hence cannot occur without the presence of an appropriate *phantasma*.[4] The content of understanding thus depends in some sense on the quasi-perceptual content of individual *phantasmata* (see above) and is therefore constrained by it (e.g., *An* III.7 431b18–19; *Mem* 1 450a7–14). But even if concepts are "not without" *phantasmata*, they are not reducible to *phantasmata* either (III.8 432a12–13), since understanding is not of perceptible individuals, on Aristotle's view, but "of the universal" (II.5 417b22–3). This difference is presumably due to the nature of the interaction between *phantasmata* and the understanding. But on this key question Aristotle says very little. According to one common interpretation, the activity of the understanding consists in the literal "abstraction" of intelligible forms from material *phantasmata*, by actually stripping away or removing their matter to yield disembodied forms, freed from the particularity that is a consequence of material embodiment. But Aristotle nowhere says this. In fact, the only process he explicitly describes sounds more like selectively attending to parts of a *phantasma*'s content or, better, *ignoring* the rest, as we do for example when we use diagrams in geometry, ignoring those features of our drawings which are irrelevant to our purposes (*Mem* 1 450a1–10).

This basic form of thought is contrasted with a more discursive form he refers to as *dianoia*. This type of thinking involves the "combination and division" of basic concepts, to produce a new compound unity (*An* III.6 430a27–8, b5–6, 8, 432a10–12; cf. III.11 434a9–10), which is capable of falsehood as well as truth (*An* III.6 430a27–8, b1–4, III.8 432a10–12; *Int* 16a9–18). The analogy Aristotle draws with words and sentences suggests that he takes both combination and division to be forms of predication, where one concept is either applied to another or withheld from it. Understanding, in contrast, is like uttering a single word.[5] Aristotle offers few further details. Apart from the cryptic remarks at *An* III.6 430b20–3, for example, very little is said about how the mind "divides" concepts. Even combination is not entirely clear, given that "combining" and "dividing" ordinarily signify symmetric operations, whereas predication is nonsymmetric (for some speculations along these lines, see Caston 1998b). One would also like to know more about the basic "simple" concepts, which are uncombined and undivided, or perhaps even indivisible (on this question, see Berti 1978 and Aubenque 1979).

The metaphysics of understanding

Aristotle devotes considerably more attention to the metaphysics of understanding: the nature of the understanding as both a capacity and an activity, its relation to the body, and the existence of a second understanding, the so-called "agent intellect," which he says is alone immortal (*An* III.5 430a23). It will be possible here only to outline the major issues.

Aristotle begins *De Anima* III.4 by confronting a question that has dogged him throughout the treatise, namely, whether the understanding is "separable" (*chôristos*). Although he uses this term in a number of senses, even within this treatise, the question alive in every reader's mind is whether the understanding is separable *from the body*; and until this point, Aristotle has offered only hedged and qualified remarks (*An* I.1 403a3–b19, I.4 408b18–29, II.1 413a4–7, II.2 413b24–7, II.3 414b18–19, 415a11–12). Plainly, the understanding is separable "in account" – *conceptually distinct* from other capacities – because the account of what it is to understand something is clearly different from what it is to digest or to perceive. The question Aristotle now asks is whether the understanding is "separable in magnitude" as well (429a10–13) – that is, whether it is *spatially distinct*, by involving some discrete portion of the body, as for example sight involves the eyes. He then offers an argument to show that it does *not* have an organ of its own, but is "uncompounded" with the body (Anaxagoras' phrase), on the grounds that if it had any actual qualities of its own prior to its exercise – as it would, if it were compounded with the body – these would block it from understanding things that we can in fact grasp (429a18–27).[6] Prior to grasping something, there is nothing more to the understanding beyond the ability itself, like a slate on which nothing has yet been written (429a24–7, 429b31–430a2). This makes it even less vulnerable than our perceptual abilities. If anything, highly intelligible objects strengthen our ability rather than debilitate it (429a29–b5; for close examinations of this argument, see Shields 1997; Sisko 1999; Caston 2000).

On the face of it, this conclusion sounds like a strong affirmation of dualism. But its precise import is less clear in context. To begin with, it does not imply that the understanding can function independently of the body's involvement. As we have seen, all human understanding involves *phantasmata*, in so far as it grasps its objects "in" *phantasmata*; and given that *phantasia* is a function of the perceptual system (*Insomn* 1 459a15–18) and thus bodily, it follows that human understanding cannot take place without certain bodily activities. By Aristotle's own admission, this is enough to show a second consequence, namely, that the human understanding cannot exist separately from the body. For according to *De Anima* I.1, if the understanding "either is a kind of *phantasia* or not without *phantasia*, it will not be possible for it to exist without the body" (403a8–10). And in the chapter immediately following the present argument, Aristotle claims that this understanding is *perishable*, in contrast with another, very different type of understanding which "alone is immortal and eternal" (III.5 430a22–25; we will return to this second understanding, and the question of its identity, in the next section). So the argument of *De Anima* III.4 cannot entail anything as strong as is sometimes assumed.

Aristotle's stated conclusion is more modest and limited. It need mean no more than this: that there is no *organ* of understanding, that is, no *discrete part* of the body that is *dedicated* to its functioning, as there is for each of the other capacities that make up the soul. It is in this sense that Aristotle can claim that there is nothing more to the understanding, prior to actually grasping something, than its "nature," namely, the mere ability itself to understand. Beyond the equipment we already possess for other functions, there is no special apparatus for understanding that exists even when it is not being exercised. To go back to the question Aristotle raises at the beginning of the chapter, the ability to understand would be separate *only* in the sense of being conceptually distinct from our other abilities. It cannot further be located in some particular part of our bodies. It is, as was intimated earlier in the treatise (cf. II.1 413a4–7), part of the form of the body, but not the form of part of the body. And such a claim is compatible with various forms of materialism, even if it runs counter to our own view that there is an organ of cognitive activity, namely, the brain.

Some have felt that the understanding must be an "immaterial faculty" in a stronger sense, though, which no materialist could countenance (see Hamlyn 1978; Robinson 1983; Sisko 2000). But it is difficult to give these claims a precise meaning. There is a temptation to imagine an incorporeal *organ*, something analogous to a bodily sense organ, but dematerialized and, as it were, diaphanous. Such a view would conflict with Aristotle's stated argument, however. For an immaterial organ would have to be something *actual* beyond the mere ability of understanding, which would exist even when it is not being exercised – otherwise, it would be an "organ" only in name, and there would be nothing to distinguish this view from the minimalist reading given above. Yet if this organ is something actual prior to acts of understanding, it will have characteristics of its own that would obstruct the full range of understanding, against what Aristotle claims.

Any interpretation, in fact, other than the minimalist reading will confront the same objection. If the understanding, prior to its exercise, is nothing more than the mere ability to understand, there cannot be anything more to the understanding, whether material or immaterial, that exists between episodes of understanding. The capacity to understand is something that belongs to the human being as a whole, without any additional special apparatus.

Aristotle's argument has consequences for his views about cognition more generally. One of the most interesting features of the argument is the way it links the *constitution* of the understanding to the *contents* it is able to entertain. It rests on certain assumptions about how forms must be received for cognition to take place, and how the constitution of organs affects their performance in specific ways. Such assumptions are clearly important in trying to evaluate his views on mental content (for an attempt to spell out some of these assumptions more precisely, see Caston 2000).

The "agent intellect"

These difficulties pale, however, when we come to *De Anima* III 5, a chapter of a mere 16 lines. In it, Aristotle argues that there must be a *second* understanding, traditionally referred to as the "agent intellect" (*nous poiêtikos* or, in Latin, *intellectus agens*), which "alone is immortal and eternal" (430a22–3). There is not a phrase in the chapter whose interpretation has not been disputed. But plainly it is decisive for many issues. If each person has an agent intellect of their own, Aristotle is committed not only to personal immortality, but to a genuinely robust substance dualism, where the human soul – or part of it, at any rate – can exist independent of the body. It is not surprising that over the last 2,300 years it has occasioned more controversy than any other passage in the corpus.[7]

The chapter consists of two parts: an extended inference, arguing for the existence of the second understanding (430a10–17); and a compendious list of its attributes (a17–25). In every kind found in nature, Aristotle claims, there is (i) something that serves as matter and has the potential to become each of the things in that kind and (ii) something that is the productive cause that makes all the things in that kind, comparable to the way that art (*technê*) is related to matter and light makes potential colors into actual ones. This distinction, he argues, is also found in the soul: one understanding has the capacity to become all things, another to make all things. The latter understanding is not only separate, inviolable, and unmixed, it is also by its very essence in actuality – it is not the case that it sometimes thinks and sometimes does not. Thus, even though the capacity to understand precedes the activity of understanding in the individual, in the universe as a whole the activity of understanding is prior. This second understanding, taken separately just by itself, is alone "immortal and eternal." The other understanding is perishable.

The exact identity of the second understanding is very much in dispute. One tradition, championed by Thomas Aquinas and dominant throughout the twentieth century, holds that (*A*) each human being has an "agent intellect" of his own, which guarantees some form of continued existence after death.[8] But this isn't the only way to construe Aristotle's conclusion that the distinction between agent and patient can also be found "in the soul." It need not imply that both understandings can be found within *each* human soul, but only among souls generally.[9] The fact that this second understanding is supposed to be eternal and in activity by its very essence suggests that (*B*) it belongs to a different kind of soul, perhaps (1) one of the higher intelligences, as many of the medieval Arabic and Italian Renaissance commentators held (see Davidson 1992 and Kessler 1988), or even (2) God himself, as Alexander of Aphrodisias maintained (second to third century CE; see Moraux 1942). There is extensive overlap, in fact, between the attributes of the second understanding and those of the divine understanding listed in *Metaphysics* Λ.7–9, which is held to be unique (see Caston 1999: 211–12). On either (*B*1) or (*B*2), personal immortality is out of the question, as is substance dualism.

On *any* of these readings, though, Aristotle's naturalism would be in doubt. For they all take the second understanding to play a direct and essential role in the production of ordinary human thoughts, and this would seem to preclude a naturalistic account, whether the second understanding is supposed to be a higher intelligence, like God, or a human intellect capable of existing independently from the body. This result has been contested recently by Michael Wedin, who argues that Aristotle's account is "stubbornly naturalistic" (1988: 194). In fact, he claims that on the contrary it is thoroughly functionalist and cognitivist in spirit, especially the distinction between two kinds of understanding. Aristotle first explains the basic features of cognitive activity by positing a single, unified faculty of understanding in *De Anima* III 4. But he goes on to raise two puzzles at the end of the chapter (429b22–430a9), which prompt him to offer a deeper analysis, at a "lower, sub-personal level." *De Anima* III.5 offers us, in effect, a distinction between two "subsystems" within a single, unified mind that together allow us to think spontaneously, as self-movers. This strategy does not threaten naturalism, according to Wedin, because the "productive mind" is not *literally* divine, eternal, or independent of the body. It is active whenever it exists, but it does not exist at all times or function continuously (pp. 178–9, 189–90). It is eternal only in the sense that a mathematical object is, in so far as both are defined abstractly without reference to the body; yet neither can exist or function, according to Aristotle, without a body (pp. 190–3). Productive mind is separable only in so far as it is not the actuality or form of a discrete organ (pp. 182–3, 186).

Some may reject such an interpretation as overly deflationary: it is difficult not to take "eternal" as meaning existing at all times. But it would be wrong to blame Wedin's advocacy of "stubborn naturalism." The real culprit is the nearly universal assumption that the second understanding is instrumental in the production of episodes of ordinary thoughts. Absent this, it is easy to offer a naturalistic reading without being deflationary. The second understanding can be literally eternal, and even God, if the actual mechanisms of human thought involve nothing more than the first intellect together with the lower faculties. One of the greatest difficulties for the received tradition, in fact, has always been to specify what the second understanding is required to *do*. Suggestions run the gamut, including the abstraction of universals from images (which is itself explained in diverse ways), selective attention, the ability to think spontaneously, and even free choice. But these are entirely speculative. Aristotle says *nothing* determinate about how the second understanding would produce thoughts – in fact, this understanding is never expressly referred to outside *De Anima* III.5. And that chapter, beyond its initial distinction between an understanding that "becomes all things" and another that "makes all things," only offers analogies to art and to light, which have proven extremely malleable (to put it gently) throughout the tradition. So commentators have searched for gaps in Aristotle's account that need to be filled. But if the second understanding played such a critical role in the production of human thoughts, it would not have been to his credit to have introduced it in this way. It would be little more than a *deus ex machina*, a magical problem solver, mentioned only in an exceedingly telegraphic and cryptic manner. Worse, many proposals are difficult to reconcile with what Aristotle actually *does* say, in particular about the parallel between understanding and sensation. Whether one takes the "agent intellect" to act directly on our receptive understanding or indirectly by acting on an object of understanding (which in turn acts on the receptive understanding), *nothing comparable is found in the case of sensation.* Aristotle makes no similar call for an "agent sense," whose causal intervention is required if sensible objects are to have any effect on our senses. Instead, the sensible object acts directly to produce a sensation of itself. If the object of understanding cannot act similarly, as is traditionally assumed, then the parallel Aristotle draws at the beginning of *De Anima* III.4 between sensation and understanding cannot run deep at all: the simple causal model used to explain sensation will be inadequate for understanding. But what *precisely* is inadequate about this model in the case of understanding? What is it about the object of understanding that prevents it from acting in a parallel fashion? Before cognition, the objects of each faculty are only potentially cognized. Why should one have the ability to produce cognition unassisted and the other not? And what difference between the two activities demands the introduction of a new agent that is itself *a kind of understanding*, rather that some other kind of contributing cause (as, for example, heat is for digestion: *De Anima* II.4 416a14)? What remains of Aristotle's express claim that the understanding is related to its objects "*in just the way*" that sensation is to its objects (429a15–18)?

These difficulties are avoided if we deny that the second understanding is part of what *we* would call the causal mechanisms of thought.[10] The capacities Aristotle discusses at length in the *De Anima* are sufficient on their own to produce episodes of thought. Human understanding does in fact work on the same model as sensation: the object of understanding is able, on its own, to act on the receptive understanding, causing us to grasp it, just as sensible objects act on the senses. The second understanding is *not* a part of this account at all, but is introduced only against the backdrop of "the whole of nature" (430a10). At this point in his treatise, as at the climax of his other great works (*Met* Λ.7–9; *NE* X.7; *EE* VIII.2–3), Aristotle considers his subject in its larger, theological context. On this reading, the second understanding is simply God, who is said to be eternal and pure activity (*Met*. Λ.7 1072a25–26, b27–28; cf. 1075a10). His role as the Prime Mover, moreover, as something that is ultimately responsible for all movement in the universe, shows how Aristotle might have regarded him as "producing" all thoughts. According to Aristotle, God makes the heavenly spheres move "in the way a beloved does" (1072b3), by being the object of their striving, an endpoint towards which all their efforts tend. Aristotle explicitly regards this kind of final cause as an efficient cause (*poiêtikon kai kinêtikon*, Λ.10 1075b8–10, b30–5). But it is not a triggering cause, as moved movers are, which can only bring about change by direct contact (*GC* I.6–7). God is an unmoved mover, a standing condition that helps explain general patterns of change, rather than the occurrence and character of particular episodes. The intermittent and imperfect exercise of our capacity for understanding is something that can be fully appreciated only by reference to the most complete and perfect example of understanding, God. It is only then that we understand what understanding really is, in its essence. But episodes of understanding – why I succeed in understanding something on this occasion rather than fail to understand anything at all, or why I have an understanding of one thing rather than another – must be accounted for in entirely non-transcendent terms, by reference to the objects in my surrounding, my cognitive history, and my very human capacities. These are, one and all, the capacities of an embodied being, even if they are not all forms of a specific part of the body, and they all perish with the body at death. In this way, a naturalistic account of the causal mechanisms of human thought can be preserved. The idiosyncratic sense in which the second understanding is "productive" depends heavily on *Aristotle's* views about explanation, and in particular the central importance that teleology has for him. But it does not interfere with what *we* would call the causal account of thought.

Notes

[1] There are of course cases where we do reflect on our mental states – for example, when we wonder whether we are genuinely remembering or not (*Mem* 1 450b20–451a14), or whether we are dreaming (*Insomn* 3 462a5–7) – and in such cases, we do consider the similarity of their content to that of perceptual experiences. But this does not entail that *phantasmata* possess their content in the first place by subjective resemblance.

[2] Although Aristotle distinguishes these forms of perception and thought, he does not use a distinct terms; I am introducing "sensation" and "understanding" purely for convenience. On the nature of sensation, see Caston (2006: 327–8). Accordingly, I will speak of the capacity for understanding, or *nous*, as "the understanding," rather than using the traditional "intellect." The latter rendering masks connections in the Greek between the capacity and the activity, because there are no verbal forms in English cognate with "intellect" (unlike Latin, the origin of this rendering).

[3] *An* III.6 430a26–7, b27–8; *Met* Θ.10, 1051b15–32, 1052a1–4; cf. *Int* 1 16a9–13. The metaphor of touch is used at *Met* Θ.10, 1051b24–5; cf. Λ.7 1072b21.

[4] *An* III.7 431b2, III.8 432a4–6; also *An* III.7 431a14–15, III.8 432a8–10, a12–14; *Mem* 1 449b31–450a14.

[5] *Int* 16a9–18; *An* III.7 431a8–10, 14–16. On Aristotle's psychosemantics more generally, see Charles (2000) and Modrak (2001).

[6] Aristotle actually claims that the understanding grasps *everything*. But his argument only requires that being mixed with the body would prevent us from thinking *certain* things we actually can think. See Caston (2000).

[7] The most detailed account of ancient interpretations is still Kurfess (1911). In English, see Brentano (1977: 4–24); Kal (1988: 93–109); and Blumenthal (1996: ch. 11).

[8] Thomas Aquinas *ST* 1a q. 79 a. 4–5; *SCG* II 76–8; In III *De An.* lect. 10; *Quaest. De An.* a. 5; *De Spir. Creat.* a. 10. For representative examples from the twentieth century, see Ross (1949: 148–53) and Rist (1966).

[9] If anything, the logical structure of the argument requires that they belong to distinct kinds of soul: see Caston (1999: 205–11).

[10] See Caston (1999), as well as Frede (1996), which gives an allied reading, though different in both its motivations and details.

Bibliography

Aubenque, P. (1979). "La pensée du simple dans la Métaphysique (Z 17 et Υ 10)," in Pierre Aubenque (ed.), *Études sur la Metaphysique d'Aristote*, Actes du VIe Symposium Aristotelicum (Paris: J. Vrin), pp. 69–88.

Berti, E. (1978). "The Intellection of 'Indivisibles' according to Aristotle, *De Anima* III 6," in G. E. R. Lloyd and G. E. L. Owen (eds.), *Aristotle on Mind and the Senses*, Proceedings of the Seventh Symposium Aristotelicum (Cambridge: Cambridge University Press), pp. 141–63.

Blumenthal, H. J. (1996). *Aristotle and Neoplatonism in Late Antiquity: Interpretations of the "De Anima"* (Ithaca, NY: Cornell University Press).

Brentano, F. [1867] (1977). *The Psychology of Aristotle*, ed. and trans. Rolf George. (Berkeley, CA: University of California Press).

Caston, V. (1996). "Why Aristotle Needs Imagination," *Phronesis*, 41, pp. 20–55.

Caston, V. (1997). "Epiphenomenalisms, Ancient and Modern," *Philosophical Review*, 106, pp. 309–63.

Caston, V. (1998a). "Aristotle and the Problem of Intentionality," *Philosophy and Phenomenological Research*, 58, pp. 249–98.

Caston, V. (1998b). "Aristotle on the Conditions of Thought," *Proceedings of the Boston Area Colloquium in Ancient Philosophy*, 14, pp. 202–12.

Caston, V. (1999). "Aristotle's Two Intellects: A Modest Proposal," *Phronesis*, 44, pp. 199–227.

Caston, V. (2000). "Aristotle's Argument for Why the Understanding Is Not Compounded with the Body," *Proceedings of the Boston Area Colloquium in Ancient Philosophy*, 16, pp. 135–75.

Caston, V. (2006). "Aristotle's Psychology," in Mary Louise Gill and Pierre Pellegrin (eds.), *The Blackwell Companion to Ancient Philosophy* (Oxford: Blackwell Publishing), pp. 316–46

Charles, D. (2000). *Aristotle on Meaning and Essence* (Oxford: Clarendon Press).

Davidson, H. A. (1992). *Alfarabi, Avicenna, and Averroes on Intellect: Their Cosmologies, Theories of the Active Intellect, and Theories of Human Intellect* (New York: Oxford University Press).

Frede, D. (1992). "The Cognitive Role of *phantasia* in Aristotle," in Nussbaum and Rorty (eds.), pp. 279–95.

Frede, M. (1996). "La théorie aristotélicienne de l'intellect agent," in G. Romeyer-Dherbey (ed.), *Corps et âme: Sur le "De Anima" d'Aristote* (Paris: J. Vrin), pp. 377–90.

Hamlyn, D. W. (1978). "Aristotle's Cartesianism," *Paideia*, second special issue, pp. 8–15.

Kal, V. (1988). *On Intuition and Discursive Reasoning in Aristotle* (Leiden: E. J. Brill).

Kessler, E. (1988). "The Intellective Soul," in C. B. Schmitt, Q. Skinner, and E. Kessler (eds.), *The Cambridge History of Renaissance Philosophy* (Cambridge: Cambridge University Press), pp. 485–534

Kurfess, H. (1911). "Zur Geschichte der Erklärung der aristotelischen Lehre vom sog. *Nous Poihtikos* und *Payhtikos*," Ph. D. diss., Tübingen.

Lloyd, G. E. R. Lloyd and Owen, G. E. L. (eds.) (1978). *Aristotle on Mind and the Senses*, Proceedings of the Seventh Symposiuim Aristotelicum (Cambridge: Cambridge University Press).

Modrak, D. K. W. (1987). *Aristotle: The Power of Perception* (Chicago, IL: University of Chicago Press).

Modrak, D. K. W. (2001). *Aristotle's Theory of Language and Meaning* (Cambridge: Cambridge University Press).

Moraux, P. (1942). *Alexandre d'Aphrodise: Exégète de la Noétique d'Aristote* (Liège: Faculté de Philosophie et Lettres).

Nussbaum, M. (1978). *Aristotle's "De Motu Animalium,"* with trans., comm., and interpretive essays (Princeton, NJ: Princeton University Press).

Nussbaum, M. and Rorty, A. O. [1992] (1995). *Essays on Aristotle's "De Anima;"* first paperback edn., including and additional essay by M. F. Burnyeat (Oxford: Clarendon Press, 1995).

Rist, J. M. (1966). "Notes on Aristotle *De Anima* 3.5," *Classical Philology*, 61, pp. 8–20.

Robinson, H. (1983). "Aristotelian Dualism," *Oxford Studies in Ancient Philosophy*, 1, pp. 123–44.

Ross, W. D. [1923] (1949). *Aristotle*, 5th edn. (London: Methuen).

Schofield, M. (1978). "Aristotle on the Imagination" in Lloyd and Owen (eds.), pp. 99–141.

Shields, C. (1997). "Intentionality and Isomorphism in Aristotle," *Proceedings of the Boston Area Colloquium in Ancient Philosophy*, 11, pp. 307–30.

Sisko, J. (1999). "On Separating the Intellect from the Body: Aristotle's *De Anima* III.4, 429a10–b5," *Archiv für Geschichte der Philosophie*, 81, pp. 249–67.

Sisko, J. (2000). "Aristotle's *Nous* and the Modern Mind," *Proceedings of the Boston Area Colloquium in Ancient Philosophy*, 16, pp. 177–98.

Wedin, M. V. (1988). *Mind and Imagination in Aristotle* (New Haven, CT: Yale University Press).

334

D. Biology

21

Teleology in Living Things

MOHAN MATTHEN

Artifacts and the Four Causes

Aristotle's doctrine of four causes is central to his study of nature, but both in the order of his thought and in his exposition, it is modeled on the etiology of artifacts. In *Physics* II.3 and 7, which contain the clearest statement of his doctrine, the examples are, with one exception – "The father is a cause of the child" (194b30–1), "A man generates a man" (198a26–7) – drawn from action and craft. It is, in short, a central heuristic for Aristotle that the explanatory framework for understanding natural things, particularly living things, should be an image of the corresponding schema for artifacts. (He does sometimes say that art imitates nature, and this indicates that the ontological ordering does not necessarily recapitulate the methodological, but this point will not be pursued any further here.)

Let us say that a man wishes to make something, for instance, a house. The man, and at a finer level of detail his actions, originate the process, and are thus *efficient causes*. The house itself is the end (*telos*) of his actions or, in other words, their *final cause*; and it is also that for the sake of which (*hou heneka*) the man undertakes and plans his actions. *How* does the man decide what he must do? How, in other words, does he relate the house-as-end to the actions necessary for building it? He has a "model" (*paradeigma*) in mind, Aristotle says, and this is an "account (*logos*) of its essence" (194b26–7). The *paradeigma* or *logos* is the *formal cause* of the man's actions. It guides the man as he manipulates the building materials, the bricks, tiles, and so on. Together, these constitute the *material cause* of the house.

A builder's mental representation of the model of what he is building must be distinguished from the model itself: he thinks *about* a house; the house is one thing, his thought another. The thought plays a crucial role in the house-builder's deliberations. These deliberations too are efficient causes. (Aristotle says, *Phys* II.3 194b30, 195a22, that the deliberator is the cause, but he means that the trope (or predicative complex, *deliberating in the man* is so.) Similarly, the ability to represent the house he will build is an element of the house-builder's craft (195a5–6, 22), and this craft is an efficient cause. From all of this, we may conclude that the man's representation of the house is an efficient cause. (Cf. *MA* 6 700b17–19: "The things that move the animal are choice,

335

Table 21.1 The four causes of an artifact

Efficient cause (whence the action originates)	The man, the craft, the mental representation of the house
Material cause (what the builder's actions modify or shape)	Building materials
Formal cause (what the product is; this constrains the mental representation)	Essence of house (note difference from mental representation)
Final cause (product)	A particular house

deliberation, and appetite. All of these come to *mind and desire.*") The model itself is, as said before, the formal cause of his actions.

Aristotle assumes that the house-builder's representation of his end must correspond to what-a-house-is, i.e., that the "correct" account of a house constrains how he thinks of it. This does not seem right. A man may, after all, have a mistaken idea of what-a-house-is: he may entertain a faulty model. But Aristotle assumes that it is pretty much determinate what one is trying to create, so that men of even minimal competence will know what they are aiming at. This shows itself at *Physics* II.8 199a34–b5, where he recognizes only mistakes of execution – actions wrongly designed or executed for the sake of a correctly conceived end. He does not recognize mistakes of conception. This requirement has a rationale with regard to natural processes, as we shall see in section 6, but it is not clear that it is justified in the case of craft. But were Aristotle to allow that form need not constrain the craftsman's mental representation, it would not be clear what role form plays in craft. In all particular instances of production, the explanatory role of form would be trumped by the mental representation of form.

Aristotle claims that the efficient cause "often" coincides with the formal and the final cause. "These three things often come to the same thing: *what a thing is* and *what it is for* are one thing, and *that from which the change first originated* is the same in form as these" (*Phys* II.7 198a24–6). The identity of formal and final cause indicates that he defines artifacts functionally: a house is *for* shelter, and shelter is therefore a part (or perhaps the whole) of *what a house is*. Further, the form is represented in the builder's deliberations and is an efficient cause. In this (somewhat dubious) sense, the efficient cause is same in form as the end. As we shall see below, this statement has a very different and a very significant meaning in the realm of natural things. To summarize, then, we have table 21.1.

Goals vs. Functions

The artifact model outlined above is most straightforwardly applied to temporal sequences of actions, for it is these that have a *telos* or end: *telos* normally has a *temporal* meaning. That is, the *telos* (for instance, the house) is normally the last event or culmination of a series of events (the building process). Aristotle's framework is naturally suited to explaining what philosophers today call "goal-direction," the culmination towards which a series of actions is aimed. Accordingly, his examples in the *Physics* are all processes.

In other places, Aristotle extends the framework to the *functions* of artifacts, such as the house, i.e., to what such artifacts are *for*, and by analogy to natural functions. He uses what artifacts and natural things are for to explain why they have certain of their properties.

> A hatchet, in order to split [wood], must be hard; if it is hard, it must be made of bronze or iron. Similarly, since the body is an instrument – each of the parts is for something, and so also the whole – it is necessary that it be such and such and made out of such and such. (*PA* I.1 642a10–12; *Phys* II.9 200a10–13 makes the same point but with respect to a saw *coming to be*.)

The notion being introduced here is that of *hypothetical necessity*: it is necessary that the materials should be this way *if* the thing is to fulfill this function.

Shelter is what a house is for, its function, but it is a stretch to say that shelter is the *telos* of the house: the house is not a temporal sequence culminating in shelter. (Of course, the process of building the house *does* culminate in shelter, and here shelter is a *telos* in the temporal meaning of the term. My point is that the house itself is not a process, and so does not have shelter as a *goal*. Shelter is a goal of the building process, and a *function* of the house.) To ameliorate this oddity of usage, Aristotle talks about *energeia* or actuality. In *NE* I.1 1094a4–7, he writes: "A certain difference appears among ends (*telê*): some are actualities; others are achievements above and beyond (*para*) the actuality." The process of building falls into the second category: its *telos* is the house in which the building process culminates. The house itself falls into the first category: its actuality is at the same time its "end."

There is a degree of discomfort, then, that results from extending to the functions of substances a framework primarily constructed for the goal-direction of processes. The material cause of the process of building a house is the material that is shaped into a house: bricks, tiles, etc. This material exists independently of the house. And this is theoretically useful, since the intrinsic properties of the building material, i.e., the properties it has independently of its being incorporated into a house, can be used to explain certain features of the process in which that material participates.

Now, what is the material cause of the house itself (as distinct from that of the process of building it)? Aristotle sometimes suggests that the bricks, etc. play this role, but what about the *functional* parts of the house: the door, the roof, the kitchen, etc.? One might expect that as parts or constituents, these too would count as material causes. But there is a difference between such functional parts and bricks and mortar. Since the kitchen etc. are defined in terms of the role they play in the house, and since their playing this role depends on the house itself, they exist only when the house does. That is, they do not exist independently of the house. So their properties independently of the house cannot be used to explain the house. (This is true of *letters* which Aristotle claims as material causes of syllables (195a16). How alpha sounds depends on the syllable in which it occurs: it sounds different in αι than in αυ. There is no independent sound of α that explains the sound of these wholes.)

A similar situation obtains in the domain of living things. The material cause of the *generation* of an animal is the semen of the father and the menstrual blood (*katamênia*) of the mother. These, of course, exist independently of the generated animal, and they are crucial in explaining the process of generation. But what is the material cause of the animal itself? By analogy with bricks and mortar, Aristotle might be tempted to say: flesh, blood, and other such organic materials. These materials are defined functionally and do not exist independently of the whole animal: in this respect, they are more like the kitchen and roof than like bricks and materials. (Of course, flesh is homoeomerous, unlike the kitchen, but this is irrelevant to the present point.) In fact, flesh does not just lose its functional role but physically disintegrates outside the context of a living thing. Thus, the independent properties of flesh and the like cannot be used to explain the properties of the animal. They have no such independent properties.

The Argument from Non-Coincidence

Aristotle claims that the four causes are to be found in the realm of nature as well as that of craft. This raises some well-known philosophical perplexities. How can the goal, which comes temporally after a sequence of actions, *cause* or even *explain* the actions? What does it mean to say that a natural thing is "for the sake of something else"? And even if one could make sense of what this means, how can what-something-is-for explain its properties when there is no intervening mental representation?

Aristotle is well aware of these problems. However, he is convinced that nature *does* act for an end. Thus, he takes the perplexities of the preceding paragraph as difficulties to be solved, not as proofs of impossibility. In *Physics* II.8, the problem is stated in this way: "It is a puzzle what prevents one from saying that nature does *not* act for the sake of anything, nor because it is for the better." Certain students of nature – call them materialists – say that "Zeus does not rain so that the grain might grow; rather, it rains of necessity." ("Zeus rains" is apparently a hieratic formula [Sedley 1991]: Aristotle uses it here to allude to the materialists' assumption that goal-directed processes must be agent-driven.) Why, Aristotle asks, should we not say similarly that the front teeth come to be sharp and the back teeth flat "of necessity"? What compels us to take up the position that they come to be so arranged because it is better that they should be so?

In order to understand Aristotle's argument, it is important to appreciate his position on efficient causation. It is striking that in table 21.1, it is this category of causation that has the most diverse instances. Aristotle is full of detail about the origin of motion and about material constitution: these are, for example, the main concern of *On the Generation of Animals*, and also of the important short essay, *On the Movement of Animals*. His response to the materialists is certainly not to downplay or neglect these categories of causation – indeed, he appropriates materialist theories, or modifies them to suit his purposes. But he thinks that materialist (i.e., material plus efficient) causation is insufficient in the end.

Why? Is it because in addition to all available materialist causes, a formal or final cause is needed to achieve the result? Some commentators think so, for instance Allan Gotthelf (1976, section VI): "the development of a living organism is *not* the result of a sum of actualizations of element-potentials." According to Aristotle, the development of an embryo proceeds by a series of heatings and coolings, pushes and pulls, which effect the transformation of nutriment into the parts of the baby. Gotthelf seems to imply that even if all such "element-potentials" were to be actualized in the right sequence, the result would not come about without the final cause.

When Aristotle says that a process is "of necessity," he means that it is wholly driven by the nature of its constituents – "element-potentials" being a limiting case of constituency. Note the contrast with "hypothetical" necessity, the necessity that attaches to material constituents *if* a certain goal or function is to be achieved. For the sake of clarity, we will call the kind of necessity now being discussed *material necessity*. Suppose you flip a coin. The weight of the material causes the coin to come to rest on the ground. Since this is determined by the constitution of the coin, we say that it happens by material necessity.

On the traditional view of the text under consideration, Aristotle's intention is to argue that well-adapted parts of living bodies cannot come about by material necessity (Nussbaum 1978: 322). Gotthelf takes this to imply that materialist causes are insufficient to create these parts. On the traditional view, these parts are contrasted with inanimate rain: the materialist causes of rain are sufficient to make it fall. Further, a final cause is needed to explain the teeth: they come to be this way because it is better for taking in food. But no final cause is needed for rain: it does not fall in order to make the crops grow.

The traditional interpretation has rain contrasted with the arrangement of teeth; the former occurs by material necessity, the latter for the sake of something. However, David Furley (1985) has pointed out that this is *not* the contrast we actually find in *Physics* II.8. For Aristotle says: "It cannot be by luck or by coincidence when it often rains in winter, but only if it does so during the dog days; nor if it is extremely hot in the dog days, but only if so in winter" (198b36–199a2). The contrast drawn here is between rain *in summer* and the ontogenesis of teeth. The rain in winter is on the same side of the contrast as teeth; teeth come to be this way regularly, just as the rain falls regularly in winter (but not in summer).

Why does the rain in winter not fall by necessity? Aristotle's argument depends on a notion that we have neglected so far: that of coming to be "by coincidence." An outcome involving X is "coincidental" if it is not determined by causes that act on or involve X. Suppose that a flipped coin lands heads. This outcome is not compelled (let us say for the sake of argument) by the causes acting on the coin. These causes determine only that the coin will fall to the ground. Coming up heads simply *coincides with* this outcome, Aristotle would say, and has no further cause. It is by coincidence.

Appealing to coincidence in this way would be unsatisfying if the coin *always* landed heads. Things that happen regularly do not occur by mere coincidence. If a coin always landed heads, we would look for some cause of its landing heads. Supposing that this cause cannot be found in the material constituents of the coin, we would have to conclude that the coin does not land heads by material necessity. For instance, we might conclude that it does so because of its shape, not its material constitution. Similarly for the rain in winter and for the arrangement of teeth: they are *regular* occurrences – they happen "always or for the most part." They cannot be consigned to coincidence. (There is a lacuna in Aristotle's argument. Regular relative to what? Aristotle does not see the need to elaborate. It may be a regular occurrence that rain falls in summer *after a long spell of muggy days*. Thus, it is not clear that rain in summer is freakish *tout court*. As we shall see, a similar lacuna infects his treatment of spontaneous generation.)

Now, Aristotle believes that it rains when water is drawn up by the heat of the sun, cools in the upper atmosphere, and returns in liquid form (*Meteor* I.6). This cycle of material/efficient causes is in play whenever it rains, in winter just as much as in summer. Notice, though, that is no materialist cause that is capable of bringing it about that the sequence occurs in the right order. (Materialist causes include elements going to their proper places, heat being transferred, pushes and pulls, etc. None of these is sequence-compelling.) As far as the infrequent rain in the summer, this is no problem. The requisite sequence occurs infrequently and by coincidence. But this explanation will not suffice for regular winter rain, which implies a further cause.

Let us distinguish between two kinds of question.

- *Sufficiency* Does a particular series of materialist causes E suffice to bring about a particular result?
- *Regularity* Does a particular series of materialist causes E suffice to bring about a particular result *"always or for the most part"*?

Aristotle's theory concerning rain implies a positive answer to the question of *Sufficiency* (see Meyer 1992). In the dog days, E *does* bring about rain without any additional cause. If E is sufficient in the dog days, then it is so in winter. Here, at least, Gotthelf must be mistaken: this outcome *is* the result of a sum of actualizations of element-potentials. If the rain can occur in this way by the coincidental occurrence of material causes, why not the sprouting of teeth?

Aristotle's argument implies, however, a negative answer to the second question. When E occurs only infrequently, it need not be ascribed to *any* cause – it may have occurred just "by coincidence." But when E occurs regularly, we need to invoke a cause to explain *it* (cf. Matthen 1989: 178–9). This is especially so when E is a complex sequence. Perhaps very simple sequences can occur regularly by coincidence, but with complex occurrences this is very unlikely. There is in these cases an *overarching cause* of E.

Aristotle's claim is that when an event O, brought about by a complex sequence of constituent events occurs regularly, there must be an *overarching cause C* responsible for the material/efficient causes of O. C is responsible for O occurring regularly because it ensures that the materialist causes sufficient for O occur regularly. The materialist explanation that cites only E is deficient, then, *not* because it gives causally insufficient conditions, but because it does not specify all the causes of O. In *Physics* II.8, Aristotle is accusing his materialist opponents of incompletely specifying the causes of the rain in winter and of the ontogenesis of teeth. These opponents are missing the overarching cause of these events.

Craft, Form, and Spontaneity

How does Aristotle's argument from non-coincidence translate into a full-blown four-cause scheme for natural things? The case for materialist causation is straightforward: these are the causes acknowledged by his opponents. It has just been argued that Aristotle thinks that an overarching cause is needed regularly to bring these causes into play in the proper way. How does such an overarching translate into the formal and final causes that we have seen at work in artifacts?

There are two lines of thought to be considered here. First, according to Aristotle, a process (*kinêsis*) leading to an outcome *O* is the product of two potentialities (*dunameis*) matched to one another and in contact: a passive potentiality resident in the material in which the process takes place, and an active potentiality resident in the agent that works on that material (*Phys* III.1–2). For example, the process of building that culminates in a house is (standardly) brought about in bricks, etc. that possess the passive potentiality of becoming a house. Similarly, the house is brought about by the actualization of an active potentiality to build a house. This resides in the builder. In cases where the outcome is not merely by coincidence, i.e., where they are *properly* caused, these potentialities are matched not only to one another, but also to the outcome.

Now, the overarching causes spoken of earlier are potentialities matched to the outcome in this way. The overarching cause of the rain in winter (as we shall see later) is the obliquity of the Sun's orbit. This obliquity is non-accidentally the same as the Sun's potentiality to make it rain in winter. In living things too there is an overarching cause of well-adapted processes. Aristotle calls this the *nature* of a living thing. At the heart of the craft analogy is a comparison between the nature of a thing and a craftsman. Like a craftsman, the nature of a living thing brings about outcomes that are good for that living thing by acting upon the materials of that thing. Nature is an impersonal potentiality, to be sure, but it has the same relationship to matter as a craftsman. Just as a craftsman sequences his actions appropriately to his end, so too does nature; just as a craftsman sometimes makes errors of execution, so also does nature. In embryonic development there is an interplay between an active potentiality resident in the semen and a passive potential in the *katamênia* or menstrual blood. This interplay is sequenced and controlled by the form of the baby present in the semen. This form acts much as the skill of the builder does, fashioning the material present in the mother into a baby.

In addition to this rather technical argument, Aristotle also observes a number of other analogies between nature and craft. Processes under the control of nature are for the good. The winter rain is for the growth of plants (or perhaps specifically for the growth of crops planted by humans). (See below for more on how this could be so.) Teeth grow into an arrangement that enables animals first to tear and then to chew. Just as the builder builds for some good, so also does nature.

Where no such good generally comes to pass, Aristotle is not inclined to posit an overarching cause. When it rains in summer, the grain on the threshing floor might spoil. And it might be that this happens regularly: every summer, some farmer gets caught in a thunderstorm. But spoiling does not demand that water falls artfully on grain; no elaborate sequence of events is needed. Similarly death, destruction, and decay, though regular events, do not require any particular sequence. Natural organs and organisms decay with time under the influence of materialist causes. By contrast with the embryonic processes by which these are built, decay happens randomly. In development, the heart has to be fashioned first, to prepare for other developments; in decay, it makes no difference whether the heart goes first or last. Decay is not a *sequence* of events; it is merely an accumulation of events under materialist causation. As such, it does not need an overarching cause. The four causes responsible for the ontogenesis of a baby are given in table 21.2.

Table 21.2 The four causes of a living thing

Efficient cause	Potential matched to outcome: form instantiated in semen
Material cause	Material that is shaped by the efficient cause: *katamenia* in female, which waits for activation by semen
Formal cause	Essence of man, soul
Final cause	Baby

Though natural outcomes are standardly explained in this fashion, Aristotle recognizes a category of spontaneous events (*ta automata*) which are not caused by matched potentialities (*Phys* II.4–6). As we have seen, sometimes a potentiality for O will be at work, but bring about a distinct outcome O' because O' "coincides with" O. Aristotle's example is a man who goes to the market to buy groceries and there encounters somebody he wanted to meet, but did not expect to find (196a1–3). The potentiality at work here resided in the man's deliberation, which took him to the market. These deliberations did not foresee that the man was going to be there, and hence were not directed at meeting him. His trip to the market, however, coincides with finding the man: the two events are (accidentally) one on this occasion, though usually events of this type are not. Thus, meeting the man is on this occasion caused not by the potentiality to bring about *this* result, but by another potentiality. This is what makes it a spontaneous event.

In similar fashion, some lower animals come-to-be spontaneously. These organisms presumably come to be from relatively simple sequences of events; like the rain in summer, they can appear without the need for form as an overarching cause. Does this mean, contrary to observed fact, that these organisms do *not* regularly come to be? No: they come to be whenever the circumstances are right for their genesis – just as the rain in summer comes to be whenever rain-making factors come together. They do not, however, occur regularly in the life-cycle of other organisms of the same sort – they are not reproductively generated. There is a fundamental lack of clarity in Aristotle's notion of regularity, as we noted earlier.

Non-bodily Causes

In *Physics* II.9, Aristotle gives us an example of a wall with heavy stones forming the foundation and light things like wood on top. The fact that the stones are able to bear the weight of what is constructed on top of them is due to material necessity emanating from the nature of the stones. These stones are there by hypothetical necessity: that is, they are there because they are necessary for the function of the wall. Aristotle also makes a point about how the wall came to be. The stones did not get to the bottom by virtue of their weight. As far as the genesis of the wall is concerned, the natures of the constituents had nothing to do with it. The stones are at the bottom because they were put there by the builders.

In the discussion of generative processes in the biological works, Aristotle often seems to assign the building role to non-bodily entities. From one point of view, this is entirely explicable. Aristotle's materialist opponents think that natural organic processes are driven by element potentials. Aristotle thinks that form and final cause play a role as well. He cannot locate these non-materialist causes in body: to do so would be tantamount to accepting a completely materialist account.

Consider the following passage:

> As semen is a residue, and as it is endowed with the same movement as that in virtue of which the body grows through the distribution of the ultimate nourishment, when the semen has entered the uterus it "sets" the residue produced by the female and imparts to it the same movement with which it is itself endowed. The female's contribution, of course, is a residue too, just as the male's is, and contains all the parts of the body *potentially*, though none in actuality; and "all" includes those parts which distinguish the two sexes. Just as it sometimes happens that deformed offspring are produced by deformed parents, and sometimes not, so the offspring produced by a female are sometimes female, and sometimes not, but male. The reason is that the female is a deformed male. (*GA* II.3 737a18–29, trans. Peck)

Consider Aristotle's account of the sequence of events that takes place after the semen has entered the uterus. If the materialists are right, this sequence is driven by element potentials. In other words, the materialist line is that the mixture of semen and the "female residue" has properties that neither has on its own, properties that drive the mixture on its embryological path by material necessity. Aristotle denies this. He thinks that the semen imparts *its own* movement to the female residue. It cannot do this simply by materially acting on the *katamênia* – that is, it cannot do this without the operation of an overarching cause. For as noted in section 3 above, no material has the power to bring about sequences of events *regularly*. Significantly, Aristotle says above that sometimes the semen fails, and when it does, the female movement keeps going in its path of material necessity, thus *failing to produce a penis*. The deficiency here is ultimately a failure of form over matter. The deformed parent produces deformed offspring because the overarching cause fails to control.

The argument just given does not really demand that form be non-bodily. Form acts *through* element-potentials, but it is not clear what the nature of form itself is. The above argument implies that form would not be an element-potential itself. Does this mean that it is non-bodily? One might consider this an open question with regard to the interpretation of Aristotelian embryology, perhaps with regard to its content. There is, however, one reason why Aristotle might have been tempted to stray down an immaterialist path. He believes that *reason* or *noûs* is *not* a bodily activity. Accordingly, he argues that this activity requires something other than bodily causes: it enters from "outside" – from God, presumably – and it alone is divine (*GA* II.3 736b28–30). This non-bodily part is apparently carried with the semen and imparted to the fetus. The bodily part of the semen then disappears, leaving the ensouled fetus behind.

Global Teleology

The question must now be addressed: how is it that nature is organized in accordance with the craft analogy? The most obvious answer, and the one adopted by Plato, is that the world was constructed this way by a creator. Organisms are best constructed the way we find them, and in order to explain why the world and its creatures are so well-constructed, Plato appealed to the intentions of a superior being. This answer has the additional advantage of explaining why natural functions seem to be, as Aristotle says in *Physics* II.8, "for the better," since it could additionally be assumed that this creator created the world in accordance with its apprehension of the Good.

Aristotle disagrees with this whole approach. First, he does not believe that the world had a beginning in time (*GC* I.10–12), and for this reason he rejects the notion that the world is created. Secondly, he does not believe in a pre-existing and independent Good which things in the world measure up to. Rather, he believes in immanent goods. The good-for-humans is the ideal execution of human ways of acting in the world (*NE* I.7). The ways of acting come first as parts of human nature; the good-for-humans derives from them as their being performed well. So also for the Universe itself: its good is what it does. (The interpretation offered in the present section is taken largely from Cooper 1987.)

Now, one of the things that the Universe "does" is to be stable forever. It imitates the Prime Mover (Aristotle's God), who lives a perfectly homogeneous life, eternally contemplating itself. Many of the other activities of the Universe and many of its characteristics are teleologically subordinated to this one activity. Consider, for example, the sublunary sphere – the part of the Universe under the Moon – of which fire, air, water, and earth are the elements. Aristotle observes in *De Generatione et Corruptione* II.10 that these elements move in straight lines, either toward or away from the centre of the Universe. Left to themselves, they would separate out "in infinite time." Consequently, the Sun is placed on a displaced orbit which leads it on its annual path, first to the northern and then to the southern hemisphere. This movement causes the rain cycle, displacing the elements that would otherwise simply settle in their natural places. The rain in winter is caused by the obliquity of the Sun's orbit, which is in this way for the sake of the stability of the Universe. "That is why . . . the simple bodies, imitate circular motion," Aristotle says. "It is by imitating circular motion that rectilinear motion too is continuous" (336b31–37a7). In this way, the world is so structured as to imitate the homogenous eternal activity of the Prime Mover. This homogeneity is its good. (Incidentally, Aristotle attributes this structure to God in this text, but this is evidently not meant to imply that God *created* the Universe.)

Now, one might ask: why should the world be made *this* way? Could it not have been eternal by omitting the sublunary elements altogether and making do with the circularly moving starry element by itself? This is precisely the kind of question that Aristotle's immanent Good is supposed to circumvent. The question assumes that there is an external reason why the Universe should be the way it is, some independent good that it would instantiate by being so. Aristotle denies any such transcendentalist notion of the Good. The good of the Universe is the ideal performance of the parts and functions it happens actually to possess.

It is part of the way the world is that it contains certain species. The members of these species too aspire to the eternally homogeneous activity of the Universe and its Prime Mover. But it is impossible for *individual* things of this sort to be eternal. So they are eternal in the only way open to them: eternity as a kind. This they achieve by producing offspring (*GA* II.1 731b32–5). Obviously, their ontogenetic activities would not achieve this end if they did not produce creatures of the same kind as themselves. This is why animals reproduce: to preserve their kind. This is the best they can do by way of achieving eternity. (It follows that species themselves have no beginning or end.) This makes sense of Aristotle's claim that even "monsters" (*terata*) result from "erroneous" processes that are, nevertheless, for the sake of reproduction (*Phys* II.8 199b3–4). The process of creating offspring makes no sense to him if it is not for the sake of producing something of the same kind. This is the reason why in nature the formal cause and the efficient cause are one: man generates man.

This looks at reproductive activity from the point of view of the species themselves. But one could also look at things from the point of view of the Universe, as it were. As noted before, the Universe is itself stable. If its species were to perish, that stability would be undermined. Just as it would contradict the stability of the whole if the sublunary elements were to separate out in time, so also it would contradict the eternity of the whole if the species were to perish. Thus, animal reproduction does not only subserve the local good of each species; it also subserve the global activity of the Universe.

It is significant that the "starry element" plays a role in reproduction. Aristotle "proves" this by noting that various stages in ontogenesis are brought about by heat carried by the *pneuma* present in the semen (*GA* II.2 736a1–2). However, mere heat will not do, he says: fire will not produce a baby. He concludes that the *pneuma* that gives the semen its fertility carries a special sort of heat; it is "analogous to the starry element." This reaffirms the role of the starry element as an instrument for preserving the stability of the whole. Elsewhere, Aristotle insists that the heavens and the planets serve as divine instruments for maintaining "the cycle" in the sublunary world; they are described in *Physics* VIII.10 267a21–b9 and *Metaphysics* XII.7 1072a20–5 as intermediate between God (or the Prime Mover) and sublunary entities. Here too this element is given a similar role.

All of this suggests that the teleology of living things is part of a grander scheme by which the Universe itself maintains its stability. Such a suggestion undermines, as David Sedley (1991) has said, the school of thought that reads Aristotle as "refusing to extend the workings of . . . finality in nature beyond the internal structure and functioning of individual organisms." Sedley himself argues for a "broader interactive teleology," a "global teleology" which sees the Universe as a single large structure and the nature of living organisms as part of this larger structure (see also Matthen 2001).

Sedley argues that this structure is, as he puts it, "anthropocentric," in that much of the world does not merely subserve the imitation of eternity, but specifically serves the interests of human beings. In support of this interpretation, he adduces three important passages. The first is from *Politics* I.8 1256b10–22, where Aristotle claims that "plants exist for the sake of animals, and the other animals for the sake of men." The second piece of evidence is the rainfall passage from the *Physics*, which has been dealt with in detail above. Finally, there is a passage from *Metaphysics* XII.10 1075a11–25 where Aristotle suggests that the nature of the Universe aspires to the goodness of the Prime Mover and in so doing forms a joint-arrangement in which all creatures participate, each in their own way.

Sedley's hypothesis is controversial, to say the least (see Wardy 1993), but in the light of his work it now seems uncontroversial that Aristotle's teleology of the living world is not fragmented and species-bound in the way it was only recently thought to be. The final causes of each species connects in some way to the excellent activity of the whole Universe.

Note

Interpretive note: Aristotle often uses terms like "the sculptor" or "the doctor" to refer to a cause. Now, one might think that if "the sculptor" is the originator of a series of actions culminating in a statue of Hera, then Polycleitus (who happens to be the said sculptor) is the originator of those actions. But Aristotle does not quite accept this. He says: "Polycleitus is the cause of the statue *in a different way* than the sculptor; since the being of Polycleitus coincides with the sculptor" (195a33–5). G. E. L. Owen famously used to call statements like these "Aristotle's Principle of the Discernibility of Identicals" since they apparently differentiate Polycleitus from himself. In reality, it indicates that as far as Aristotle is concerned, "the sculptor" is *not* identical with "Polycleitus." In Aristotle's ontology, there are (1) individual substances (Polycleitus is one of them), (2) individual predicables or *tropes* (the instantiation of the sculptor's art in Polycleitus), and (3) "predicative complexes" (consisting of a trope together with the individual substance to which it belongs – see Matthen 1983). Thus he says: "A predicatively complex thing (*sumplekomenon*) may be given as cause – *not* Polycleitus, *nor* the sculptor, but Polycleitus-the-sculptor" (195b10–12). Note that these three things are assumed to be distinct. Aristotle does, however, think that they are "accidentally the same," by which he means that they are all either identical with Polycleitus or resident in him. Aristotle's causes are generally tropes or predicative complexes, not individual substances. Thus, he has a different view from the Stoics, who make bodies the terms of causal relations, and from the "agent-causation" theories recently entertained by some philosophers. Aristotle's view corresponds more closely to the event-causation paradigm that is standard today.

Bibliography

Charles, David (1991). "Teleological Causation in the Teleology," in Gotthelf and Lennox (1987).

Cooper, John M. (1987). "Hypothetical Necessity," in Allan Gotthelf (ed.), *Aristotle on Nature and Living Things* (Pittsburgh, PA: Mathesis Publications).

Furley, David (1985). "The Rainfall Example in *Physics* II.8," in Judson (1991a).

Gotthelf, Allan (1976). "Aristotle's Conception of Final Causality," *Review of Metaphysics*, 30, pp. 226–54.

Gotthelf, Allan and Lennox, James G. (1987). *Philosophical Issues in Aristotle's Biology* (Cambridge: Cambridge University Press).

Judson, Lindsay (1991a). *Essays on Aristotle's "Physics"* (Oxford: Clarendon Press).

Judson, Lindsay (1991b). "Chance and 'Always or for the Most Part' in Aristotle," in Judson (1991a).

Lennox, James (1991). "Teleology, Chance, and Aristotle's Theory of Spontaneous Generation," *Journal of the History of Philosophy*, 20, pp. 219–38.

Lewis, Frank A. (1988). "Teleology and Material/Efficient Causes in Aristotle," *Pacific Philosophical Quarterly*, 69, pp. 54–98.

Matthen, Mohan (1983). "Greek Ontology and the 'Is' of truth," *Phronesis*, 28, pp. 113–35.

Matthen, Mohan (1989). "The Four Causes in Aristotle's Embryology," in T. Penner and R. Kraut (eds.), *Nature, Knowledge, and Virtue*, Apeiron, 22, pp. 159–79.

Matthen, Mohan (2001). "The Holistic Presuppositions of Aristotle's Cosmology," *Oxford Studies in Ancient Philosophy*, 20, pp. 171–99.

Meyer, Susan Sauvé (1992). "Aristotle, Teleology, and Reduction," *Philosophical Review*, 101, pp. 791–825.

Nussbaum, Martha Craven (1978). *Aristotle's "De Motu Animalium"* (Princeton, NJ: Princeton University Press).

Sedley, David. (1991). "Is Aristotle's Teleology Anthropocentric?" *Phronesis*, 36, pp. 179–96.

Wardy, Robert (1993). "Aristotelian Rainfall and the Lore of Averages," *Phronesis*, 38, pp. 18–30.

Wardy, Robert (2005). "The Mysterious Aristotelian Olive," *Science in Context*, 18, pp. 69–91.

22

Form, Essence, and Explanation in Aristotle's Biology

JAMES G. LENNOX

Introduction

Aristotle's concept of form (*eidos*) is closely associated with two other key concepts in his metaphysics and natural philosophy, essence (*to ti ên einai*) and cause (*aition*). Yet in Aristotle's most sustained and detailed account of scientific explanation, the *Posterior Analytics*, a view of scientific definition and demonstration is developed which makes no reference to form or the distinction between form and matter. Moreover, the examples from the science of nature that Aristotle typically appeals to, such as thunder, eclipses, or leaf-shedding, leave the reader wondering how that theory would apply to natural substances. When we turn to Aristotle's most sustained scientific investigation of nature, his many integrated investigations of animals, we can see how his views about definition and demonstration are applied to his paradigm case of the natural unity of matter and form. In the domain of living things form is a functional concept, referring to the soul (*psuchê*), the integrated set of living activities of a body constituted to perform them. As such, form plays a key role in two very different explanatory contexts: that of explaining why each kind of organism is structured as it is; and that of explaining the amazingly complex and organized process of development. Development is the process by which biological forms, souls, are endlessly replicated. It permits a living thing to "participate in the eternal and divine." This "most natural" of an organism's formal capacities ensures "coming to be is for the sake of being."

Essence and Explanation in Theory and Practice

Aristotle's essentialism, as it is articulated in the *Posterior Analytics* (*An. Post*), is at once sophisticated and remarkably unlike what passes for "Aristotelian essentialism" in modern philosophy (Charles 2000). The goal of scientific inquiry, according to *An. Post* II, is knowledge of certain features of the objects of inquiry, features that both make the objects what they are and are the causes of most or all the other non-accidental features of those objects. The summary statement of the position in *An. Post* II.10 refers to a privileged kind of *definition*, one which is a rearrangement of the terms of a parallel *demonstration*. For example, in a scientific demonstration of why a certain noise

348

(thunder) occurs in certain clouds, the middle term identifies the cause of the noise (extinction of fire). This demonstration provides the materials for a definition of thunder as a noise that occurs in certain clouds due to the extinction of fire (*An. Post* II.10 93b38–94a9).

There are, however, two puzzling features of this discussion of scientific definition and demonstration. One puzzle is that the focus seems to be on determining the natures of the attributes in a domain of inquiry rather than on determining the nature of the substances in that domain. In other words, the *definitional* inquiry that is closely tied to the search for causal demonstration results in definitions of attributes. This discussion provides us with little insight regarding how one might pursue an inquiry into the essences of different kinds of animals.[1] A second puzzle is that on this view the content of a definition cannot be determined independently of causal inquiry. There is no access to essences that is independent of successful causal investigation.

These puzzles are exemplified by an example in *An. Post* that comes closest to the definitional and explanatory practices of Aristotle's biological works. The example is presented during Aristotle's discussion of converting problems (*problêmata*) at the level of ordinary experience into true scientific problems, where the predications to be explained are commensurately universal. Consider one of Aristotle's conversions, wherein a question about why this or that sort of tree suffers loss of leaves leads into a question about why all and only broad-leafed trees lose their leaves. Initially one might think that Aristotle has converted his initial question into an answer: All fig trees lose their leaves *because* they are broad leafed. But Aristotle argues that, though we may consider this a provisional explanation, the "because" here is not *immediate*; for one may now inquire into the (convertible) connection between being broad-leafed and losing leaves. For the sake of illustration, Aristotle suggests that leaf loss in all such trees is due to the solidification of the moisture where the leaves connect, and he claims that this cause will also enter into *the definition of leaf loss* for these sorts of trees (*An. Post* II.16 98a35–98b38; 17 99a21–9; for detailed discussion of these passages, see Charles 2000: 204–9; Lennox 2001b: 51–3, 88–9).

As in the meteorological and astronomical examples of earlier chapters (inquiries into "thunder" and "eclipse"), there is a definition corresponding to the demonstration, but it is a definition of the *attribute* (loss of leaves), not of the kind to which the attribute belongs *per se* (trees with broad leaves).

> If you take the primitive middle term, it is an account of the loss of leaves; for there will first be a middle in the one direction (that all are such); and then a middle term for this (that sap solidifies or something of that sort). What is it to lose leaves? It is for the sap to solidify in the connection of the seed. (99a25–9)

Also as in the earlier examples, it looks as if that subject – trees with broad leaves – is identified a posteriori, in the process of discovering an attribute that is commensurate with loss of leaves. In these cases, the subject kind is not identified prior to the demonstrative inquiry.[2]

Since the 1970s, a great deal of work has been done to narrow the distance between the understanding of Aristotle's essentialism derived from the *Analytics* and the explanatory and definitional practices of the biological works (Kullmann 1974; Bolton 1987;

Charles 2000: ch. 12; Gotthelf 1985, 1987b; Lennox 1987b, 1990).[3] This scholarship has shown us, for example, that when Aristotle finishes his account of the heart with the following words, he has in mind the idea of the relation of essence and explanation that is expressed in *An. Post* II.8–10:

> Regarding the heart, then, what sort of thing it is, what it is for the sake of, and the cause owing to which it is present in those animals that have it, let so much be said. (*PA* III.4 667b13–14)

And indeed, *PA* I.1, the philosophical groundwork of Aristotle's biology, defends the view that in the study of the products of natural generation, the cause identified as that-for-the-sake-of-which takes precedence over motive and material causes. This precedence ordering is given because in the case of things that come to be, the account of the essence (i.e. the definition) identifies the final cause (639b12–21). For example, Aristotle's general account of the heart concludes (i) that the heart is present for the sake of originating blood, (ii) that it is also the primary perceptive part, and (iii) that it is thus the primary organ of the perceptive capacity of soul, the capacity essential to being an animal (*PA* III.4 666a34–6).[4] The definition of a heart and the explanation of why animals with hearts have hearts are intertwined in precisely the way the *Posterior Analytics* would lead us to expect.[5]

Not surprisingly, then, the aforementioned puzzles about the account of essence in the *An. Post* also manifest themselves in the biological practice. It should be noted, for example, that the only "kind" that is mentioned in Aristotle's conclusion about the heart is "animal," and the only "subject" to which the part "heart" belongs is "those animals that have it." This is far more the rule than the exception in *PA*, and the reason again seems to follow from the principles of the *An. Post* II: in many cases the groupings of animals to which a part belongs commensurately are not easily identified and are typically picked out by reference to other differentiae. In considering, for example, animals with multiple stomachs (a group we now call "ruminants"), Aristotle explains why all of them have this feature. In so doing, he notes that they also share hoofs, horns, and a dearth of upper teeth, and this level of similarity is sufficient for Aristotle to give a single explanation that applies to all of them. Aristotle typically identifies them by a Greek nominal phrase that literally translates as "the ones that do not have both rows of teeth (*ta mê amphôdonta*)" (cf. *PA* III.2 663b29–664a3, III.14 674a32–b18; *An. Post* II.14 98a13–19). That group will be the subject of a demonstration that explains the possession of four stomachs, but it will be identified as subject only during the search for that demonstration.

Another grouping that Aristotle investigates that does not constitute an identified kind is the group of animals that possess lungs and also share a number of correlated features, all of which can be explained by reference to breathing. Aristotle concludes his discussion of the lung by claiming that, even though animals with a lung do not constitute an identified kind, the lung is nevertheless part of their being (*ousia*) – as much, he insists, as having feathered wings is part of the being of birds (*PA* III.6 669b8–12).

Until now I have been stressing the similarities (including the shared puzzles) between Aristotle's account of essence and explanation in the *Analytics* and the definitions and explanations one finds in the biological works. There are, however, important differences that derive from the abstractness of the account in the *Posterior Analytics*. Aristotle will often, and I suspect intentionally, exemplify the same philosophical point in *An. Post* II with an example drawn from mathematics and an example drawn from the investigation of nature. The account of definition and explanation provided must apply to both, since he is providing an account of knowledge as such. It has often been noted that neither in *An. Post* nor in the *Organon* in general is there any place for an analysis that divides being into material and formal aspects. Even when it is finally acknowledged that there are four distinct kinds of causes, there is no mention of matter and form, but rather of "necessitating ground" and "essence" (*to ti ên einai*) (*An. Post* II.11 94a20–4).

Aristotle considers the objects investigated by biology, on the other hand, to be *paradigmatic* of the unity of matter and form, and the closely related teleological unity of structure and function, characteristic of natural substances. How does this affect the understanding of essence, as presented in the *Posterior Analytics*? The example of the heart described above (and it is typical of the practice in *On the Parts of Animals*) suggests at least a significant amount of continuity. But that example also suggests that Aristotle's views about explanation and definition will involve essential reference to the functions of the soul and to the way matter is organized for the sake of performing the soul's functions.

Form, Function, and Biological Essentialism

After having outlined, in the opening pages of *De Partibus Animalium* I, the approach to the scientific investigation of living things that will give us true understanding of them, Aristotle tells us why it was left to him to identify this approach:

> One reason our predecessors did not arrive at this way is that there was no "what it is to be" and "defining substantial being" (*to ti ên einai kai to horisasthai tên ousian ouk ên*). Democritus touched on it first, not however as necessary for the study of nature, but because he was carried away by the subject itself; while in Socrates' time interest in this [sort of inquiry] grew, but research into the natural world ceased, and philosophers turned instead to practical virtue and politics. (642a24–31)

Coming as it does near the end of the *PA* I.1, the argument leading up to this claim of historical precedence provides us with several interpretive clues. The way of inquiry that was *not* employed prior to Aristotle will be the new path characterized in this chapter. When it comes to causal investigation, that sort of inquiry gives *priority* to natural ends over antecedent motive causes (639b11–21), and it introduces a special sort of necessity, the *conditional* necessity for antecedent materials and processes to be present *if* natural ends are to be achieved (639b21–640a8; 642a1–17). This causally prior end of natural development for which we are to search is not, however, an organism's body, at least not insofar as it is conceived as a mere anatomical structure. Instead, the end of organic development is *form*, conceived of in functional terms, the *soul* of the living thing (640b28–641a32, cf. 645b15–20).

351

There are, however, two quite distinct ways in which the form of a living thing enjoys causal/explanatory precedence in Aristotle's philosophy of biology. First, explanatory priority is given to *the function for the sake of which* the organisms being investigated have those parts. This is the central task of *De Partibus Animalium* II–IV, as exemplified in the example of the heart discussed earlier. In this domain, we find Aristotle moving in the direction of a kind of unified account of the essences of animal kinds. Second, explanatory priority is given to *the actual being* in accounting for the various stages of potentiality represented in animal development. This is the primary task of *De Generatione Animalium*. In this section we will look at the definitional and explanatory role of form in the discussion of animal being in *De Partibus*; in the next we will turn to its role in Aristotle's account of animal generation.

If Aristotle the biologist continues to hold that there is a tight connection between demonstration and definition, he must integrate that view with his views about the priority of "the cause for the sake of which" over motive causes and the priority of living form over living matter. Just such an integration is outlined in *PA* I.5. The causal priorities are especially clear in the following passage.

> Since every instrument is for the sake of something, and each of the parts of the body is for the sake of a certain action, it is apparent that the entire body too has been constituted for the sake of a certain complete action.[6] For sawing is not for the sake of the saw, but the saw for the sake of sawing; for sawing is a certain use. So the body too is in a way for the sake of the soul, and the parts are for the sake of the functions in relation to which each of them has naturally developed. (645b15–20)

The connection between essence and explanation here is as intimate as it was in the *Posterior Analytics*. The unity of matter and form in animals is to be understood as the unity of an instrumental structure and its functional capacity. The various features of a part are to be explained by reference to the function or action for-the-sake-of-which that part came to be and exists; the physical features of the animal as a whole are to be understood by reference to the animal's complex, yet integrated, way of life. The definition of a part that corresponds to such an explanation will necessarily make reference to the part's structure, but only in so far as that structure exists for the sake of performing its function or functions (645a33–6). To be the heart of a certain kind of animal is to be an instrument structured (and located) appropriately for the nutritive and perceptive functions of that (kind of) animal.

The resulting teleological unity of matter and form can be understood at any level of generality. In the previous chapter (i.e., *PA* I.4), Aristotle resolved an *aporia* raised at the very beginning of the Book (639a15–19). As he restates it in *PA* I.4:

> On the one hand, in so far as what is indivisible in form is a substantial being, it would be best, if one could, to study separately the things that are particular and undivided in form – just as one studies mankind, so too bird; for this kind has forms. But the study would be of any one of the indivisible birds, e.g. sparrow or crane or something of this sort. On the other hand, in so far as this will result in speaking many times about the same affection because it belongs in common to many things, in this respect speaking separately about each one is somewhat silly and tedious. (644a29–34)

This tack is not merely silly and tedious – according to the *Posterior Analytics* it is wholly mistaken, as it will fail to produce scientific knowledge. For, if the same feature belongs to a sparrow and a crane because they are birds, the first step toward understanding this feature must be to grasp that it belongs *per se* to bird, not to crane or sparrow (cf. *An. Post* I.4 73b25–74a3, 5 74a4–b4; cf. Lennox 2001b: 7–10).

Aristotle resolves the puzzle of animal groupings by identifying animals that share many differentiae at the same level of universality. The features of these animals vary in degree rather than in kind. As a consequence of these similarities, their forms will be more like one another than anything else. If a particular type of animal does not belong to such a grouping, we must speak of it separately (644b1–8).

Aristotle is implementing a view about "sameness in kind"; animals are to be brought together into kinds in virtue of differing only "by degree" or "by the more and less" (644a15–23). In chapter 4 he focuses on more and less variations in *parts* – variations in an animal's size, density, texture, color, and so on. These appear to be the features Aristotle thinks we will use in our *initial* identification of kinds – they are "better known to us." Prior to this discussion about the identification of kinds in chapter 4, however, chapter 1 had already insisted on the *definitional* and *explanatory* priority of the functional capacities of organisms and their parts. It is not surprising, then, that just prior to the passage we began this section with, arguing for the explanatory priority of actions to parts, Aristotle extends his resolution of the *aporia* regarding the particular and the general from parts to *actions*:

> Therefore one should first discuss the actions of animals – those common to all, those according to kind, and those according to form. I call "common" those [actions] that belong to all the animals, *and "according to kind" those [actions] whose differences from each other we see in degree; for example, I speak of bird "according to kind," but I speak of mankind, and everything without any difference according to its general account, "according to form."* (645b20–6)

Soul-based activities (*praxeis*) are both *common* and *formal* features. That is, at whatever level of generality or specificity one considers a function performed by a part, it is that for the sake of which that part exists – it is a soul function. Material features and formal features, structures and their functions, can be identified at various levels of universality. To refer to an action "according to form" is to refer to it at a certain level of universality; but actions and their capacities are *formal* features of the animal, aspects of its soul, regardless of the level of generality at which they are described.[7]

Earlier, I noted that Aristotle concludes his philosophical introduction to biology by arguing that the entire body has been constituted for the sake of a certain complete action" and that "the body is in a way for the sake of the soul, and the parts are for the sake of their functions." We can see this grand vision manifested in his actual explanatory practice in a chapter near the end of *PA* IV, where he discusses the external organs of birds. A study of the method employed in that chapter has an additional payoff. It will provide us with insight into the intimate connections between Aristotle's views about more-and-less variation of forms within kinds and his views about the explanation and definition of structure, both of which reference the essence of animal being, functional activity.

To comprehend fully that chapter, some background from the *Historia Animalium* is helpful. There, Aristotle commences his study with a discussion of the fundamental modes of similarity and difference among animals. This discussion meshes very tightly with those we have investigated in *PA* I.4–5. After focusing on the differences between parts within kinds – differences in degree or by more and less – he extends the analysis to three other fundamental features in terms of which animals are differentiated: actions (*praxeis*), character traits (*êthê*), and ways of life (*bioi*). Indeed *HA* in its entirety is organized around these categories of differentiae. And in the investigations of these latter three modes of difference in *HA* V–IX, a certain relationship among them emerges. Animals have the character traits and perform the actions they do in virtue of their way of life. In *HA*, way of life is absolutely fundamental (cf. *HA* I.1 487a11–488b10, VII.1–2 588a17, 588b4–590a18, VIII.1–7 609a19, 610a34, 612b18–22).

Our focus is, of course, on essence and explanation. Thus, as we examine the pattern of explanation in *PA* IV.12, in which *bios* is central, the dominant question will be: what is the relationship between *bios* and soul, understood as that "complete action" for the sake of which the body has the parts organized as it does?

In *PA* IV.12 Aristotle is moving on to discuss the external parts of birds, having already discussed the two-legged and four-legged land dwellers in chapters 10 and 11.[8] He first discusses the observable similarities and differences of their parts and notes correlations among them. He treats these as sufficient grounds for the groupings mentioned.

> Among birds, differentiation of one from another is *by means of excess and deficiency of their parts, i.e. according to the more and less.* That is, some of them are long-legged, some short-legged, some have a broad tongue, others a narrow one, and likewise too with the other parts. (*PA* IV.12 692b3–6)

He next notes that all birds have feathers and beaks, and that these parts differ *by more and less*, but are *analogous* to parts such as scales or trunks in other kinds of animals (692b15–18). When he moves on to discuss the neck, he begins to note correlations among the measurable variations in all of these parts, and then he offers a single, functional explanation for the correlated variations of parts. For example,

> those that are long-legged have a long neck, while those that are short-legged have a short one . . . for if the neck were short in those with long legs, the neck would not be of service to them for eating food off the ground; nor if it were long in those with short legs. *Again for those that eat flesh a long neck would be contrary to their way of life (bios).* (692b19–693a6; italics added).

The crook-taloned birds *also* have a type of beak that is correlated with talons, and both are explained by reference to their predatory way of life (693a10–13). By contrast, "all birds whose way of life (*bios*) includes swamp-dwelling and plant-eating have a flat beak; for such a beak is useful both for digging up and cropping off their nourishment" (693a14–17).

The modes of life (*bioi*) of the different birds account both for their differences and for the correlations among those differences. The focus of inquiry is the provision of functional explanations of the more and less variations within the kind "bird." The *explananda* of such explanations will be more and less differences between birds of one form and another.

This chapter shows us another side of essence, however. A number of features are identified as *idia* of birds – feathers (692b10), beaks (b15–16), and feathered wings (693a26). These are features properly identified as commensurate universals of the kind "bird." It is also claimed that it is of the being (*ousia*) of birds to be *blooded*, yet *winged* (693b5–7) and *able to fly* (693b12–13) – all features of wider extension than the kind "bird," though the combination is commensurate (cf. *An. Post* II.13 96a24–b14). Indeed, it is this *combination* of features in the being of bird *qua* bird that necessitates their peculiar form of bipedalism (693b5–14). Moreover, there appear to be fundamental presuppositions about the ratio of different elements in different kinds (694a22–27; Lennox 2001b: 194–5). These features are *not* explained in functional terms; nor are those that are direct consequences of them. Functional explanations enter only once one is attempting to account for the *differences* within a kind.[9]

The dominant theme of *PA* IV. 10–13 is the way in which each of Aristotle's "great kinds" (*megista genê*) has each of its parts differentiated in just the way needed so that all of the parts are able to function harmoniously together. Certain features and modes of activity are identified with the *ousia* or essence of birds generally; other universal features, such as bipedalism, are explained as a consequence of this combination of essential features. Each form of bird has each of these parts differentiated for its own way of life, or *bios*. This central explanatory concept requires the biologist to take a certain perspective on the animal's functional activities. Those activities must be looked at from an ecological perspective; and the parts, then, must be organized not only for a particular function, but also in terms of the functions they perform within the wider context of the animal's way of life. A hawk is essentially a carnivore that hunts by soaring at great heights; this means it must fly in a certain way, capture and kill prey of a certain kind, and eat in a certain way. All of these activities will differ in degree from those of other birds, and this dictates differences in the way its parts are constructed. Finally, it is not merely the *structure* of each part that will be explained by reference to a function; the *coordination* of various structures will be explained by reference to the various functions that are required for a particular way of life. The talons, hooked beak, strong, short neck, thick, streamlined wings, short tail feathers, and so on, must be organized in an integrated manner.

This discussion of the external parts of birds is the hard currency behind the promissory note of *PA* I.5. What was there referred to abstractly as a "certain complete action" for the sake of which the entire body of an animal is organized, we now see, the full complement of an animal's activities organized around the single goal of its specific way of life. *PA* I.5 makes it clear that this explanatory relationship takes precedence over the relationship between a single part and its activity, and we can now see why this is. A beak is hooked in order to perform a specific kind of nutritive function, that of overpowering and eating prey; but that attribute of the beak is a consequence of the hawk's way of life, as are a large number of other, coordinate, attributes.

Only in this chapter is the explanatory centrality of *bios* made explicit. To be precise: of 20 uses of the term *bios* in all of *PA*, 9 occur in the 3 Bekker pages of *PA* devoted to the external parts of birds. I have nothing but unsubstantiated speculation as to how this is to be explained. But the fundamental idea so beautifully illustrated here – that entire systems of organs are organized in a coordinated way and that this organization is related to some basic feature of the animal's way of life – can be found much more widely.

Does Aristotle consider the possibility that the way of life of a kind might change and lead to a significant change in the activities and structures that are organized for a particular way of life? As far as I can see, he does not consider the possibility. It is likely idle to speculate on the reasons for this. But if we now turn to the other way in which form has explanatory and definitional priority over matter in Aristotle's biology, we can at least see that there are reasons, rooted in his metaphysics, that would make any sort of "evolutionary" understanding of such changes difficult to accept.

The Priority of Being to Generation

Near the start of the chapter, we saw that a certain view of essence that is defended in the *Posterior Analytics* apparently undergirds the results of biological inquiry found in the *De Partibus Animalium*. One problematic aspect of this view is that the identification of biological kinds appears to be guided by the search for those groupings of animals whose features are commensurate with the feature to be explained. Among commensurately universal features there will be explanatory priority relations, and scientific explanation (demonstration) will display the feature or features that are explanatorily basic – the features that are in one sense or another the cause(s) of the others. Next, we tracked the way in which this explanation-driven view of essence is articulated and implemented in a biological context. The theory defended in *PA* I is that organisms, and in particular animals, are natural unities of matter and form. Form, however, is to be understood as the soul, the integrated functional capacities, of an organism; matter is to be understood as the body, organized so that it can perform the animal's living functions. The animal's body is the seat of its functional capacities; in the absence of those capacities its parts are what they are in name only. The many "more and less" anatomical differences that distinguish the parts of one form of a kind from another are defined and explained by identifying the functional contribution of those variations to the animal's way of life.

Of equal importance is that this natural, teleological unity that is the animal is prior in every respect *to the process of coming to be* that gives rise to it. Armed now with a concrete sense of how his explanation-based essentialism functions in a biological context, we are prepared to explore Aristotle's views about the *explanatory* priority of being to becoming in a biological context. The key is to be found in his understanding of the ability of organisms to replicate themselves.

Aristotle insists that the failure of earlier natural philosophers to inquire into definition and essence was in part due to their tendency to seek the efficient cause of organic development in the interactions of antecedent materials. In his view this is the opposite of the truth. The true efficient cause is an already actual organism that (in virtue of its nutritive/generative soul) produces a seed with a potency (*dunamis*) for becoming an organism of the same kind (641b25–32).[10] Against Empedocles, Aristotle holds, in what is surely an intentional echo of *Philebus* 54A7–9, that just as in the crafts, so in nature, "generation is for the sake of being; being is not for the sake of coming to be."

It is a principle he reminds us of in *De Generatione Animalium*, in order to highlight the methodological relationship between investigating animal being and animal development:

> For as was stated initially in the first accounts (*kat'archas en tois protois logois*), it is not because each thing's coming to be is of a certain sort that it *is* of a certain sort; rather it came to be such a thing on account of its *being* of this sort; for generation follows on and is for the sake of being; being is not for the sake of generation. (778b2–7)

Failure to appreciate the priority of being to becoming leads Empedocles to attempt to explain the beautifully adapted structures of mature organisms as mechanical consequences of antecedent events with no intrinsic connection to those organisms. Since Empedocles failed to recognize that each seed has a potency for the appropriate form, he didn't consider the source of that potency:

> its producer was prior – not only in account but also in time.[11] For one human being generates another; consequently, it is on account of *that* one being such as it is that *this* one's generation turns out a certain way. (640a22–6)

Empedocles, and others of his sort, consistently attempted to understand the features of mature organisms as coincidental outcomes of materially necessitated developmental processes. Actually, it is not clear that they would consider these interactions as having sufficient unity to be considered a single process. At least, this is how Aristotle understood their project (cf. Code 1997).

But what is the connection between these failures and the failure to search for an account of the essence? In one sense, once we attend to the Greek rather than our translations, the answer is obvious. It is *ousia* that Aristotle claims is causally prior to *genesis*, and it is the search for the definition of *ousia*, for *to ti ên einai* – the-being-what-it-is – that Aristotle is claiming his predecessors failed to appreciate. To put it plainly: they failed to give investigative priority to what is naturally prior!

In a deeper sense, however, the answer is not at all obvious. One could defend the causal/explanatory priority of the end state (i.e. the actual organism) relative to the process of development, and yet see this as unconnected to questions about the definition and essence of the natural substances that are those end states – as most modern defenders of teleology explanation do. We now need to ask how Aristotle understands the connection between essence and causal explanation when the *explanandum* is the animal's *generation* rather than its parts.

In words reminiscent of *Metaphysics* Z.7–9 and Θ.8, Aristotle begins his extended explanation of animal generation by stating a first principle:

> To understand how each thing comes to be it is necessary to grasp the following, making it our first principle: as many things as come to be by nature or by art come to be by means of a being in actuality from that which is potentially such as that being. (734b22–3)

He often reminds us of this first principle, as we saw in *PA* I.1, with the expression "For a human being generates a human being." This expression serves as a leitmotif for concretizing two different, though related, consequences of his teleology.[12]

1 *Natural, substantial generation* is *formal replication*. Formal replication is my short-hand for Aristotle's claim that in biological generation, organisms make another *like*, or *such as*, or *one-in-form* with, themselves. This is a point that can be made either with or without contrasting formal replication with chance production. (Passages without the contrast with chance include: *Phys* II.1 193b12, II.2 194b13, II.7 198a26; *PA* II.1 646a33; *GA* II.1 735a19–21 (with which compare *An* II.4 415a23–b8); *Met* Z.7 1032a25, Z.8 1033b32, Λ.3 1070a28, Λ.4 1070b31–4. Passages with the contrast include *GC* II.6 333b7; *Met* Z.8 1033b32, Λ.3 1070a8.)

2 *Act is prior to potency* (cf. *Phys* II.1 193b8, III.2 202all; *Met* Θ.8 1049b25, N.5 1092a16).[13] Earlier, we discussed Aristotle's criticism of Empedocles' attempt to explain the being of an animal by reference to its mode of coming to be. Aristotle ends that section of *PA* I.1 with the somewhat Delphic remark: "Again the seed is in potency (*dunamei*); and how potency (*dunamis*) is related to complete act (*entele-cheia*) we know." (642a1) The two items prior to the seed (one prior in *both* time and being, the other just in being) are the two beings non-accidentally related to the seed's potency: [i] the adult organism or organisms[14] responsible for producing a seed, and [ii] the fully formed organism toward which the seed is developing.

The priority of being to coming to be is one of those bedrock starting points that Aristotle shares with those working in the Parmenidean tradition, including Plato. Aristotle also shares with Plato the identification of *form* as the source and cause of being. The idea that the coming to be of natural substances is to be understood as the replication of form, on the other hand, allows Aristotle to do something his predecessors in that tradition could *not* do – it allows him to take unqualified, substantial generation seriously. Thus Aristotle's refrain, *anthropos anthropon genna*, is twice given in the *Metaphysics* as a sufficient reason for treating Plato's theory of Forms as unnecessary for an account of natural substances (*Met* Z.8 1033b–1034a1; Λ.3 1070a4–30; cf. Lennox 2001b: 147–54). But Aristotle also believes that only a proper understanding of the relationship of act to potency will permit one simultaneously to take substantial generation seriously while accepting the priority of being to coming to be.

Aristotle considers replication to be among a living thing's most natural activities (*phusikôtaton tôn ergôn, An* II.4 415a27, *phusei ergon*; *GA* II.1 735a19; cf. *Pol* I.1 1252a26–30) at least in the case of those living things that are not maimed or spontaneously generated. He tells us this in the *De anima*, in the process of arguing that the potency for nutrition and the capacity for generation are in fact one and the same. Living things perform this function, he claims, "in order that they may participate in the everlasting and divine as far as possible; for all desire this and do whatever they do in accordance with nature for the sake of this" (*An* II.4 415a27–b2; cf. *GA* II.1 735a16–23). This is a single potency because in both its nutritive and generative manifestations it has the same, single goal – self-maintenance.

Since, however, living things inevitably pass away, generation allows the maintenance, not of the animal itself but "what is like it, not one numerically, yet one in form" (*An* II. 4 415b7–8). The exercise of our nutritive potency, in its reproductive manifestation, is via a process of *formal replication*. It is not merely making another animal (or plant); it is making an animal *one-in-form* with the animal that is generating.[15] This is not a point about ontological level; it is a point about *the explanatory priority of soul*. "One-in-form" here is not in contrast to one-in-kind; it is in contrast to *numerical unity*. To exist eternally as a natural unity of matter and form would be to go on forever, as do planets and stars. In contrast, many living things have the ability to replicate themselves, so that something *numerically distinct from* but *formally like* them continues on. This fact, as we will see, allows the study of generation to be the object of a science.

The opening of the second Book of the *Generation of Animals* supplements this account with deeper metaphysical grounding for the idea that generation is formal replication. The goal of this discussion is to explain why it is *good* that there be male and female, and what such a distinction is *for* (731b22–4). Since, however, the male and the female capacities exist for the sake of generation, either generation must be taken as a given, or there must be a more basic cause for it. But as we have seen, coming to be is for the sake of being; Aristotle does not take it as a given.

While there are a number of interpretive problems associated with that passage[16], we can take from it at least two important messages for our purposes. Aristotle begins with the assumption that there are two fundamentally different kinds of natural beings – those that are eternal and those that come to be and perish. Those in the latter category can either be or not be, and being is the better state.[17] In the case of living things, this alternative is in fact the alternative between living and not living, and living just is being in possession of those functional capacities that constitute the soul. The soul, therefore, is the source of a living thing's continued living – the source and cause of its being in the better state.

However, by their very nature generated things cannot exist eternally in a numerical sense – unlike planets, for example. But being eternal *in a way* is better than simply going out of existence. Generation is a way that individual living things can share in the eternal. "On account of these causes there is a generation of animals." Generation is one more manifestation of the drive for self-preservation, our "most natural" function. Indeed, the discussion in *De Anima* concludes that "since it is just to designate everything according to its end, but the generation of a likeness of itself is its end, the primary soul would be a capacity to generate a likeness of itself" (416b23–6).

The understanding of generation as the replication of form, then, allows natural particulars a way of "participating" (*metechein*) or "partaking" (*koinônein*) in eternal being simply by activating one of their soul functions. Though by their very nature generated things cannot *be* eternal, the ability of certain living things to replicate their forms permits them *a share in* the eternal.[18] Formal replication is, concretely, what it means to say that coming to be is for the sake of being. At the most abstract level, this is the explanation for why every "complete" organism has a natural capacity to reproduce.

Of course, the product of generation is an animal, a unity of matter and form, not just a form. A human being generates in order to produce another human being; therefore the process of generation should be explained by reference to its end. In the study of natural coming to be, teleological explanation depends on a prior understanding of the essence of what is coming to be.

What is transmitted in sexual generation is a capacity of the soul to transform already prepared blood into tissues, by means of a heat that is specifically for carrying out nutritive/generative processes. Aristotle tells us that this heat acts according to a *logos*, a formula, that determines what it makes, where it makes it, and when it makes it. (For the details, see Henry, ch. 23, in this volume.) The heat, which is an instrument, must not be confused with the generative capacity (*GA* II.1 734b28–36).

That "motion from the generator" is, a few lines later, referred to as "the motion *of the nature*"; and, by contrast with the crafts, it is in the developing thing itself though "derived from another nature *having the form in actuality*" (735a3–5; and see "the productive potency" (740b36), and "the potency of nutritive soul" (740b30)).[19]

The male seed, and later the embryo, is a unity of matter and form; it possesses a productive and generative potency that, once present in the material prepared by the female, begins its work, starting with the construction of the heart. The activation of that potency is, like the potency itself, always referred to in the singular. There is one, single generation identified by reference to its end. Like the single process of building a house, biological development involves innumerable component movements; but these display a *logos*, an organized pattern, and it is this *logos* that constitutes the process of generation. From an Aristotelian perspective, that single potency and the coming to be that is its actuality[20] are primary, while the various instrumental movements subserve that single, goal-directed generation.[21] Yet prior even to it, to return to our starting point, is the end of generation, which is one-in-form with its efficient cause.

As in all such cases, the transmitted potency of the seed is that of a particular male parent. Thus, it is not just the capacity to make, for example, hawk in general; it must be the capacity to make a particular hawk. But if it makes a particular hawk, it makes a hawk; and if a hawk, a bird; and if a bird, a blooded animal. This, I take it, is the point of Aristotle's comment in *GA* IV.3, that when sufficient relapsing of the generative capacity of the male occurs, "only that which is common is left, i.e. to be a human being" (768b12–13). If none of the particular features of parents or their immediate ancestors (*mêtheni eoikenai tôn oikeiôn kai suggenôn*) emerge, what is left is a human being that lacks any of *that family's* particular features – Aristotle cannot mean that the result is human being in general. As he puts the point in *Metaphysics* Λ.5:

> These primary sources are not universal; for the particular is the source of particulars; for human being is the source of human being in general; but there is no such thing. Peleus is the source of Achilles, and your father of you. . . . and the causes of things in the same form are different, not in form, but because the causes of the particulars are other – your matter, form and mover are other than mine – though the same in the general formula. (1071a20–2, 27–9; cf. *Phys* II.3 195b6–10, b25–7)

Recall that in *PA* I. 5, in discussing the application of his grades of likeness to actions, Aristotle noted that to speak of actions *kat'eidos* – he uses human being as his example – is to discuss them at a level where "they have no difference according to the universal account" (*kata ton katholou logon mêdemian echei diaphoran*) (645b26–27). In the previous chapter, he refers to "last forms (*ta eschata eidê*)" as *ousiai* and exemplifies them by Socrates and Coriscus – but he immediately says that they are "undifferentiated with respect to form" (*kata to eidos adiaphora*) (644a24–6). In the context of explaining biological generation, we now see the same point being stressed. To say that every organism that is complete generates another one-in-form with it is not to make a point about essential membership in a kind. It is to make a point about *the manner in which form and end control coming-to-be*, at whatever level of generality one wishes to describe that process. It is in the way the account of the actual form takes precedence in the causal explanation of coming-to-be that we see how it is that, once again, there is an intimate relationship between essence and causal explanation in Aristotle's biological practice.

Biological replication is also the centerpiece of the argument for the priority in time and being of *energeia* to *dunamis* in *Metaphysics* Θ.8:

> But actuality is [not only prior in time but] also prior in being (*ousia*), e.g. father to child, human being to seed; because the former already has form, the latter not; and because everything which comes to be progresses to a principle (*archê*) and end (*telos*); for that for the sake of which is a principle, and generation is for the sake of the end. And the actuality is an end, and potency is attained for the sake of this. (1050a4–10)

The argument for the priority of being of the actual over the potential in account and even, in a certain sense, in time, rests on the possession of form. This argument serves as the metaphysical backdrop for Aristotle's opening move in his biological account of the teleological priority of an animal's non-uniform parts to its uniform parts. This priority is justified on grounds that "in generation, things are opposed to the way they are in being (*ousia*)" and that "the last stage in generation is primary in nature" (646a24–26). In his general summary of the point, he also reminds us that, even in time, another organism with the being that is primary in nature must already be present, as the generation's efficient cause:

> every generated thing develops from something to something, i.e. from a principle to a principle, from the primary mover that already has a certain nature to a certain shape or other such end. For a human being generates a human being, and a plant a plant, from the underlying matter of each. (646a30–5)

Once again it turns out the priority of the actual organism over the process of generation that temporally precedes it has two sides: it provides the basis for the proper identification of the developmental process *and* for its proper explanation. The actual parent is the productive source of that process; and the form of the actual organism provides our only means of determining why each stage of that process is occurring when, where, and how it is occurring. The kind of understanding of organic systems arranged for distinctive ways of life in the *De Partibus Animalium* forms the basis for accurate teleological explanations in the *De Generatione Animalium*. This is the import of the extremely difficult and extended discussion of why Aristotle's predecessors have failed in their attempts to explain the order in which the parts come to be in *GA* II.6 (742a17–743a1). As he puts it there:

> For, with parts, as with other things, one is by nature prior to another. But the prior exists in many ways. For that for the sake of which and what is for the sake of it are different, and while one of them is prior in generation, the other is prior in being. (742a18–22)

His point is at once highly abstract and of immense practical importance for the embryologist. Just watching things unfold will not tell you why they are unfolding as they are. You must know what the parts are for and which ones subserve which. Otherwise, the developmental process will make no sense. Again, a proper account of generation depends on knowing what the parts are. But, as Aristotle says in the opening paragraph of his study of animal generation, "the *logos* and that for the sake of which as end are the same" (715a8–9).

Conclusion

De Partibus Animalium elaborates the explanation-based essentialism of *Posterior Analytics* II, but in a context given scant attention in the *Analytics* – that of natural bodies that come to be and are for the sake of living. Given certain assumptions about Aristotle's essentialism, two aspects of the essentialism defended in *An. Post* are problematic: its focus on finding the essences of attributes rather than substantial kinds, and its method of identifying kinds that appeared to be dependent on explanatory context. Aristotle's theory of biological method in *PA* I and his practice in *PA* II–IV provide us with a deeper understanding of his commitments. There is a method for identifying large kinds (*megista genê*) such as bird, fish, or insect that is pre-explanatory; but this method has causal explanation as its goal, and the kinds are identified based on the possession of commensurate differentiae. (In the case of bird, for example, these include the possession of a beak, feathered wings, a form of bipedalism.) Moreover, the causal explanations are primarily *teleological*, specifically *functional* explanations of *differences along more/less continua* in the organs and tissues of organisms within these kinds. At the center of these explanations are certain basic activities (*praxeis*) that all play a role in the animal's way of life (*bios*). The organic activities that constitute the way of life of an animal are the explanation-based essences of the forms of a kind such as bird or fish. These kinds, however, also have essences – for example, birds are blooded, winged, feathered, beaked, flyers. Why birds have any of these features is not subject to teleological explanation. At this level, we reach explanatory bed-rock. That is what it is to be a bird. Period.

Aristotle's biology, however, includes a treatise that is self-consciously distinct from the *De Partibus Animalium*, namely *De Generatione Animalium*. "A human being generates a human being" echoes through Aristotle's metaphysics and natural philosophy. What does Aristotle find so significant in this apparent truism? It stresses, depending on which aspect of the phrase one emphasizes, three crucial points: being is prior to coming to be in two respects, as the motive source of generation and as its goal; coming to be is not a chance process but a goal-directed one; and generation is more precisely a formal replication, a sort of *formal* self-maintenance. Since every coming to be of an animal (save those that are spontaneously generated) is causally dependent in this way on a prior, actual organism of the same kind, and since the natural goal of that parent's capacity to reproduce is another organism, one-in-form with the parent, there does not appear to be a natural way for this theory to accommodate regular evolutionary change. In *Physics* II.8 Aristotle attributes to Empedocles a view whereby a "fitting arrangement" of teeth arises by chance and is perpetuated because it happens to be useful (198b24–31). But it is precisely the idea that the "fitting arrangement" arises by chance that Aristotle rejects. "Again whatever chanced along would need to come about in seeds [for this view to be true]; but those saying this do away both with nature and what happens by nature; those things are by nature which arrive at a certain end, having moved toward it continuously from a certain origin within them" (199b13–17). And that origin is provided by the form of the prior, actual parent.

In his ability to explain substantial coming to be without either appealing to separate forms or reducing coming to be to an incidental byproduct of chance, Aristotle makes one of his most fundamental advances over his predecessors. There are reasons rooted deep in his metaphysics for separating the account of animal being from the account of animal coming to be. But in the end it is the essence stated in the account of the substantial being that provides us with our only means of understanding and explaining the complex process of biological development.

Notes

[1] Aristotle is fully aware of this gap in the *An. Post* model, as two passages in the *Metaphysics* clearly demonstrate. In Z.17 he dismisses inquiries of the form "Why is an X an X?": "This much, then, is clear: one does not inquire why that which is a human being is a human being; therefore one inquires why one thing belongs to another (*that* it belongs must be clear; if it is not, one inquires about nothing); for example 'Why does it thunder?' [is an inquiry about] 'Why does a certain noise come about in the clouds?' For in this way the object of inquiry is one thing predicated of another" (1041a22–6). See Charles (2000: 283–309) and Wedin (2000: 405–52) for contrasting accounts of the relationship between the *An. Post* model and Z. 17.

The same point is made about the *An. Post* paradigm cases in H.4. In discussing the role of matter in a causal analysis of substance, he explicitly refers to eclipses as exemplary of cases where the *explanandum* exists by nature (*physei*) but is *not* a substance – rather, the subject is a substance. In this case, he notes, the moon is the subject (1044b8–11).

[2] This of course does not mean the general kind being investigated by the science in question – plant, animal, heavenly body, natural objects – cannot be familiar to us in advance. But, as the opening page of *PA* I.1 shows, the typical domain of investigation begins with only some such very general characterization and then a grab bag of categories that may or may not have value for a demonstrative science (see Lennox 1987a/2001b: ch. 1).

[3] The goal of eventually finding explanations of attributes at the level of commensurate universality is central to the methodology of the *Historia Animalium* as well, as a great deal of detailed research has made clear (Balme 1987b; Gotthelf 1988; Lennox 1987a, 2001b: ch. 1, 1991, 2001b: ch. 2). But the way in which this goal is pursued has serious implications for the kind of essentialism that can be reasonably defended on the basis of Aristotle's biological works.

[4] It needs to be noted that it is part of Aristotle's explicit theory that many animals that perceive lack hearts. *PA* III.4, however, is part of the discussion of the internal organic parts of blooded animals. Aristotle turns to the bloodless animals in Book IV, and when he does so he notes that they must have an analogue of the heart and blood (cf. *PA* IV.5 678b1–7)

[5] This claim of affinity between the *An. Post* Model and Aristotle's biological project has its critics of course. The most sustained and knowledgeable critic is Sir Geoffrey Lloyd; see for example Lloyd 1990 and Lloyd 1996: chs. 1–7.

[6] The majority of the manuscripts read *plêrous* (full, complete, whole) *praxis*, though Peck (1961: 102) and Düring (1943: 122–3) both follow ms. P, which reads *polumerous*. The vulgate makes good sense, given the substitution at b18 of "soul" for the disputed phrase. Nevertheless, since Aristotle will occasionally speak of "parts" of the soul when referring to its integrated functional

capacities, either reading could yield a picture of the body as a whole organized for a unified soul.

[7] Space limitations do not allow further development of this point, but it has important implications for the question of the ontological status of form.

[8] For a discussion of the overall plan of *PA* II–IV cf. Gotthelf (1987a: 172–8); and Lennox (2001a: 220–1, 254, 292–3, 315).

[9] Though due to space limitations the subject must be set aside, this leads to an intimate connection between division and explanation in Aristotle's biology (cf. *PA* I.5 645b1–3; Gotthelf 1997b: 215–30; Lennox 2001a: 175, 2001b: 7–38).

[10] This *dunamis* of the male parent conveyed by seed, analogous to the capacity of a shipbuilder, is nicely captured in Allan Gotthelf's phrase "irreducible potential for form" (Gotthelf 1987b).

[11] This passage is making, in a more specific context, exactly the same point as *Met* Θ.8 1049b18–27, where Aristotle is defending the claim that in one respect act is prior to potency *even in time*.

[12] This expression virtually always takes the form of an *explication*, introduced by the Greek particle *gar* (for, that is).

[13] See the papers of Kosman and Witt, in Scaltsas et al. (1994), for very different views of this priority. I have chosen the somewhat archaic renderings of "potency" and "act" for *dunamis* and *energeia* because, while I am in broad agreement with those concerned about the misleading character of "actuality" and "potentiality," I am less convinced that someone reading the English translations "activity" or "capacity" gains much insight into the Aristotelian concepts, especially in their extended, metaphysical applications.

[14] *Generation of Animals* occasionally restricts the term, in the case of sexual generation in animals, to the male semen. But more commonly it is a generic term by which he refers to both the male and female contributions when he is not differentiating them. Again, at least once he denies that the female contributes seed, but his typical and more common position is to stress that female animals contribute a different kind of seed.

[15] When the very potency (a power to heat informed with a *logos*) that transforms nutrients into blood and blood into the appropriate tissues in the appropriate places at the appropriate times is conveyed, via male seed, to a properly prepared portion of the female menstrual fluid, it has the same effect – that is, it transforms this prepared menstrual blood into the appropriate tissues at the appropriate places and times in order to constitute the appropriate organs.

[16] For two quite different interpretations see Balme (1992: 155–6); Lennox (2001 133–7).

[17] It may be that the belief that being is better than non-being is simply bedrock for Aristotle. But I can think of at least one way in which he could argue for it from principles he accepts. In setting up the teleological groundwork for his ethical theory, Aristotle makes the general claim that the good is properly said to be that at which all things aim (e.g. *NE* I.1 1094a2–3); and that if there is some end of everything pursued in action, this is the good of action (*NE* I.7 1097a18–23). Now, the existence of an eternal being is guaranteed; its existence is not dependent on any action on its part. But, for a thing that comes to be and passes away, and in particular for a living thing, continued existence is ever dependent on its performing the appropriate actions. And all living things, by nature as we might say (and as Aristotle certainly would say), are continually acting to maintain themselves, for the sake of continuing to live, i.e., to be. On the principles articulated in *NE* I, then, continued living or being qualifies as the good for such contingent beings. It is that toward which their activities are directed.

[18] Thus while I am in accord with Witt (1994) on seeing the dependence of coming to be on being in teleological terms, I think these passages argue decisively *against* the end being the "species" or "type" (cf. 224–8).

[19] And compare: "Just as the potency of the nutritive soul later, in the animals and plants, produces growth from nourishment using heat and cold as instruments (for the movement of the nutritive soul is in them, and each part comes to be according to a certain *logos*), so too that which comes to be by nature is constituted from the beginning" (740b30–4).

[20] This understanding of coming to be is thus very congenial to the account of Aristotle's understanding of motion given in Gill (1989: 183–206).

[21] The analogy with house building continues to be powerful. Even though many people work on building a house; even though they stop each day and go home and resume the next day; even though each of them acts independently and is involved in innumerably different activities on any given day – it is, nevertheless, natural to describe the on-going process of building a house as a *single* process. By comparison with this, biological development has far greater unity. And it is natural to describe the source of the unity in each case as a "blueprint," or as Aristotle would say, a *logos*, specifying the form the result is to take.

Bibliography

Texts and Translations

Balme, D. M. (1992). *Aristotle: "De Partibus Animalium" I and "De Generatione Animalium" I* (Oxford: Oxford University Press).

Balme, D. M. (2002). *Aristotle: Historia Animalium*, vol. 1: Books I–X: text (Cambridge: Cambridge University Press).

Barnes, J. (1993). *Aristotle: "Posterior Analytics,"* 2nd edn. (Oxford: Oxford University Press).

Bekker, I. (1831). *Aristotelis Opera*, vol. 1. (Berlin: De Gruyter).

Burnet, J. (1910). *Platonis Opera*, vol. 2. (Oxford: Oxford University Press).

Bywater, I. (1894). *Aristotelis: "Ethica Nicomachea"* (Oxford: Oxford University Press).

Drossaart Lulofs, H. J. (1965). *De Generatione Animalium* (Oxford: Oxford University Press).

Hicks, R. D. (1907). *Aristotle: "De Anima"* (Cambridge: Cambridge University Press).

Lennox, J. G. (2001a). *Aristotle: "On the Parts of Animals"* I–IV (Oxford: Oxford University Press).

Peck, A. L. [1937] (1961). *Aristotle: "Parts of Animals"* (Cambridge, MA: Harvard University Press).

Ross, W. D. (1922). *Aristotle "Metaphysics,"* 2 vols (Oxford: Oxford University Press).

Ross, W. D. (1936). *Aristotle "Physics"* (Oxford: Oxford University Press).

Ross, W. D. (1949). *Aristotle's "Prior" and "Posterior Analytics"* (Oxford: Oxford University Press).

Secondary literature

Balme, D. M. (1987a). "The Place of Biology in Aristotle's Philosophy," in Gotthelf and Lennox (eds.) (1987), pp. 9–20.

Balme, D. M. (1987b). "Aristotle's Use of Division and Differentiae," in Gotthelf and Lennox (eds.) (1987), pp. 69–89.

Balme, D. M. (1987c). "Aristotle's Biology Was Not Essentialist," in Gotthelf and Lennox (eds.) (1987), pp. 291–312.

Bolton, R. (1987). "Definition and Scientific Method in Aristotle's *Posterior Analytics* and *Generation of Animals*," in Gotthelf and Lennox (eds.) (1987), pp. 120–66.

Bowen, A. (ed.) (1991). *Science and Philosophy in Classical Greece* (New York: Garland Publishing).

Charles, D. (2000). *Aristotle on Meaning and Essence* (Oxford: Oxford University Press).

Code, A. (1987). "Soul as Efficient Cause in Aristotle's Embryology," *Philosophical Topics*, 15 (2), pp. 51–60.

Code, A. (1997). "The Priority of Final Causes Over Efficient Causes in Aristotle's PA," in W. Kullmann and Sabine Föllinger (eds.) (1997), pp. 127–43.

Detel, W. (1999). "Aristotle on Zoological Explanation," *Philosophical Topics*, 25 (1), pp. 43–68.

Devereux, D. and Pellegrin, P. (eds.) (1990). *Biologie, Logique et Métaphysique chez Aristote* (Paris: Éditions du CNRS).

During, I. (1943). *Aristotle's De Partibus Animalium: Critical and Literary Commentaries* (Göteborg: Elanders Boktryckeri Antiebolag).

Fortenbaugh, W. W. and Sharples, R. W. (eds.) (1988). *Theophrastean Studies* (New Brunswick, NJ: Rutgers University Press).

Gill, M. L. (1989). *Aristotle on Substance: The Paradox of Unity* (Princeton, NJ: Princeton University Press).

Gotthelf, A. (1985). "Notes towards a Study of Substance and Essence in Aristotle's *Parts of Animals* II–IV," in A. Gotthelf (ed.) (1985a), pp. 27–54.

Gotthelf, A. (1987a). "First Principles in Aristotle's *Parts of Animals*," in Gotthelf and Lennox (eds.) (1987), pp. 167–98.

Gotthelf, A. (1987b). "Aristotle's Conception of Final Causality," in Gotthelf and Lennox (eds.) (1987), pp. 204–42.

Gotthelf, A. (1988). "Historiae I: Plantarum et Animalium," in Fortenbaugh and Sharples (eds.) (1988), pp. 100–35.

Gotthelf, A. (1997a). "The Elephant's Nose: Further Reflections on the Axiomatic Structure of Biological Explanation in Aristotle," in Kullmann and Föllinger (eds.) (1997), pp. 85–96.

Gotthelf, A. (1997b). "Division and Explanation in Aristotle's *Parts of Animals*," in Günther and Rengakos (eds.) (1997), pp. 215–30.

Gotthelf, A. (ed.) (1985). *Aristotle on Nature and Living Things* (Pittsburgh, PA, and Bristol: Mathesis and Bristol Classical Press).

Gotthelf, A. and Lennox, J. G. (eds.) (1987). *Philosophical Issues in Aristotle's Biology* (Cambridge: Cambridge University Press).

Günther, Hans-Christian and Rengakos, Antonios (eds.) (1997). *Beiträge zur antiken Philosophie: Festschrift für Wolfgang Kullmann* (Stuttgart: Franz Steiner Verlag).

Kosman, Aryeh (1994). "The Activity of Being in Aristotle's *Metaphysics*," in Scaltsas, Charles and Gill (eds.) (1994), pp. 195–213.

Kullmann, K. and Föllinger, Sabine (eds.) (1997). *Aristotelishc Biologie* (Stuttgart: Franz Steiner Verlag).

Kullmann, W. (1974). *Wissenschaft und Methode* (Berlin: De Gruyter).

Lennox, J. G. (1987) "Divide and Explain: The *Posterior Analytics* in Practice," in Gotthelf and Lennox (eds.) (1987), pp. 90–119.

Lennox, J. G. (1990). "Notes on David Charles on *HA*," in Devereux and Pellegrin (eds.) (1990), pp. 169–83.

Lennox, J. G. (1991). "Between Data and Demonstration: The *Analytics* and the *Historia Animalium*," in Bowen (ed.) (1991), ch. 12, pp. 261–95.

Lennox, J. G. (2001b). *Aristotle's Philosophy of Biology: Studies in the Origins of Life Science* (Cambridge: Cambridge University Press).

Lloyd, G. E. R. (1990). "Aristotle's Zoology and His *Metaphysics*: The Status Questions: A Critical Review of Some Recent Theories," in Devereux and Pellegrin (eds.) (1990), pp. 7–36.

Lloyd, G. E. R. (1996). *Aristotelian Explorations* (Cambridge: Cambridge University Press).

Pellegrin, P. (1986). *Aristotle's Classification of Animals: Biology and the Conceptual Unity of the Aristotelian Corpus*, trans. Anthony Preus (Berkeley, CA: University of California Press).

Scaltsas, T., Charles, D., and Gill, M. L. (eds.) (1994). *Unity, Identity, and Explanation in Aristotle "Metaphysics"* (Oxford: Oxford University Press).

Wedin, M. (2000). *Aristotle's Theory of Substance: The "Categories" and "Metaphysics" Zeta* (Oxford: Oxford University Press).

Witt, C. (1985). "Form, Reproduction, and Inherited Characteristics in Aristotle's *Generation of Animals*," *Phronesis*, 30, pp. 46–57.

Witt, C. (1994). "The Priority of Actuality in Aristotle," in Scaltsas and Gill (eds.) (1994), pp. 215–28.

23

Generation of Animals

DEVIN M. HENRY

The Place of *GA* in Aristotle's Philosophy

The best way to understand the place of *Generation of Animals* in Aristotle's philosophy is to consider the way Aristotle himself envisions the proper organization of the study of living things. According to *Parts of Animals* I.1, biology starts by collecting the phenomena concerning each kind and then goes on to study its causes. The three main biological works – *HA*, *PA*, *GA* – seem to be organized in accordance with this. *HA* studies the differentiae of animals, while *PA* and *GA* provide their causal explanations. In this way *PA* and *GA* follow on the results of *HA* (though see Balme 1987a; cf. Lennox 1996). The relative order of *PA* and *GA* can also be understood in terms of the methodological recommendations of *PA* I.1. At 640a10–19, Aristotle tells us that the causal story must begin with the animal as it exists in actuality (the mature organism) and then go on to consider how it comes into being. In this way causal explanations proceed from the causes of *being* an animal (*PA*) to the causes of *becoming* one (*GA*); for coming-to-be is for the sake of being rather than vice versa (*PA* I.1 640a10–32; *GA* V.1 778b2–11; cf. Lennox 2001: xi).

The four causes of animal generation can be summarized as follows. The mother and father represent the material and efficient causes, respectively. The mother provides the matter out of which the embryo is formed, while the father provides the agency that informs that material and triggers its development. The formal cause is the definition of the animal's substantial being (*GA* I.1 715a4: *ho logos tês ousias*). The final cause is the adult form, which is the end for the sake of which development takes place. I shall return to this four-fold account at the end of the chapter once we have a better understanding of Aristotle's project in *GA*.

Male and Female as *archai*

Aristotle's investigation into animal generation begins from the observation that offspring come into being from the union of animals of the same kind and that male and female are the "starting-points" (*archai*) of this change:

Of the generation of animals, we must discuss various questions case by case in the order that they arise, and we must connect our discussion to what has been said. For, as we said above, the male and female may be put down first and foremost as starting-points of generation, the male as possessing the efficient cause of generation, the female as possessing the material cause. The most convincing proof of this [sc. that male and female are starting-points of generation] is drawn from considering how and whence sperma[1] comes into being. For although the things which are generated naturally come from this, we must not fail to notice how this comes to be from the female and the male. For it is because this sort of part is secreted from the two sexes (the secretion taking place in them and from them) that they are starting-points of generation. (*GA* I.2 716a4–13)

(That the male and female are starting-points of generation was already established in *GA* I.1 by observing that some animals come into being through sexual reproduction and that "these kinds possess sexes" (715a17–29). The idea that the male is the efficient cause while the female is the material cause is Aristotle's own theory, which he develops over the course of the first two Books (see below).)

This passage is relevant for understanding the general structure of Book I. For example, the statement that male and female are *archai* of generation is meant to lead to a discussion about the nature of sperma. According to common opinion (*endoxa*), sperma is the starting-point of generation since the development of the individual begins from it (compare *PA* II.7 653b18–19). Aristotle's statement is meant to correct this. Although sperma is in a sense the beginning of the change, natural generation must ultimately be traced back to the parents since sperma comes into being from them. Thus, by studying how sperma is produced and whence it comes (the project of the second half of Book I) we will be in a better position to see that male and female are the ultimate principles of generation. This in turn is necessary for showing that natural generation is a cyclical change and therefore eternal (*GC* II.11), and that it is through reproduction that individuals are able to achieve a kind of immortality and thereby partake in the divine (*GA* II.1; *An* II.4).[2]

The Nature of Sperma

Of the two main topics examined in Book I – the instrumental parts connected with reproduction and the nature of sperma – the account of sperma is more important for the argument of the *GA*.[3] The best way to understand Aristotle's project here is to see it as an attempt to formulate a series of definitions progressing towards a full scientific account of sperma which will be among the first principles of embryology (Bolton 1987). Beginning from a pre-scientific understanding of sperma as "the sort of thing from which naturally generated organisms originally come to be" (724a18–20), Aristotle goes on to provide a series of progressively refined scientific accounts:

1 Sperma is a certain kind of residue (725a3–4; cf. *An. Post.* II.8 93a21–8).
2 Sperma is a useful residue (725a11).
3 Sperma is a useful residue of ultimate nutriment (725a12–13, 726a26–9).

369

While (2) exhibits both the genus ("residue") and differentia ("useful"), (3) reveals a further feature of sperma that is said to be explanatory of certain others. For example, being a residue of ultimate nutriment (which in animals is blood or its analogue) is supposed to explain why offspring resemble their parents in species (725a26–7). For by "ultimate nutriment" Aristotle means "that which gets distributed to each part of the body and out of which they are directly formed" (725a11–13) and "that whose nature is to go to the whole body" (725a21–7).

When used in this generic sense, "sperma" thus refers to a useful residue of ultimate nutriment from which naturally generated organisms originally come into being.[4] In animals this account is further divisible into an account of male sperma and female sperma according to the different senses of "from which" specified in the definition (cf. 724b4–7). The offspring comes "from" male sperma *as mover*, in the way that the house comes "from" the carpenter, while it comes "from" female sperma *as matter*, in the way that the house comes into being "from" bricks.[5] Aristotle develops this theory in the closing chapters of Book I and into Book II. There we learn that just as none of the matter for the house comes from the carpenter's body, so too semen contributes nothing material to the construction of the offspring (*GA* I.21). Rather, it makes its contribution by means of a certain *dunamis* (*GA* II.1). This *dunamis* is the power to form the embryo, which Aristotle compares to rennet's power to curdle milk. In both substances vital heat is the active ingredient which is the seat of the *dunamis* (*GA* I.20 729a9–13, b26–9; cf. II.4 739b21–33, IV.4 771b21–4, 772a8–30). We also learn that female sperma lacks this *dunamis* because it lacks the same level of vital heat as semen. The female is colder than the male and so is unable to fully concoct her sperma. As such menstrual blood is colder, more fluid, and greater in bulk than semen (726b31–727a2, 738a12–15, a34–b2, 765b16–35; cf. *Meteorologica* IV.2 380a4–9).

The Transmission of Soul: *GA II.3*

Another question posed by the *GA* is how animal souls are transmitted in reproduction. According to the traditional interpretation, the father transmits all faculties of soul to the offspring using his semen as a vehicle. This was certainly Aristotle's initial position. Thus, early in Book II he says:

> As to the question of whether or not semen possesses soul, the same argument concerning the parts of the body also applies here. For no soul will be present anywhere except in that of which it is the soul and no part of the body will be such except homonymously unless it partakes of soul (just like the "eye" of a corpse). Hence it is clear that semen contains soul and is potentially [the parts of the body]. (*GA* II.1 735a5–12)

However, Aristotle was eventually forced to reconsider this view in light of a puzzle arising in *GA* II.3.

GA II.3 opens with the following question: What happens to the physical part of the semen once it has performed its function? On the one hand, Aristotle argues that the semen makes its contribution by means of a *dunamis* and not by supplying matter for the offspring's body (736a25–8). So the physical part of the semen does not remain in the finished product in the way that the bricks remain in the finished house. (Compare the analogy with the carpenter at *GA* I.21 729b14–20; I.22 730b8–23.) And yet, on the other hand, we do not find the semen inside the female after conception or being discharged from her at any point (737a13–15). So if the semen is not used up in the construction of the offspring's body, what happens to it?

Aristotle's worry is that his solution to this puzzle – the semen evaporates – is inconsistent with his earlier view that semen is the vehicle for transmitting soul to the offspring. The key here is the idea, stated in the passage quoted above, that no soul can be present anywhere except in that of which it is the soul (compare *GA* II.3 736b21–6). Something like this lies behind the requirement at *GA* II.3 736b13–16 that a thing must first possess soul potentially before it possesses it actually. To possess a soul *actually* is to possess organs with the capacity to perform certain functions (since "soul" is the first-actuality of the living body; cf. *An* II.1 412b11–15, 412b18–22, 413a1). Whatever possesses soul *potentially*, then, must be the sort of material that is capable of developing the right structures (cf. *An* II.5 417a26–7). So if semen possess soul potentially, it must be the sort of thing which is capable of developing functioning organs: it must be potentially "that of which it is the soul."

Now Aristotle has already concluded in Book I that animal sperma is potentially the parts of the body in virtue of being a residue of blood. Since semen is a form of sperma, it would appear to be a suitable candidate for conveying soul. As Aristotle says, "the semen of the hand or the face or the whole body is a hand or a face or the whole body, though in an undifferentiated way; in other words, it is potentially what each of those is actually" (*GA* I.19 726b17–20). The problem arises because Aristotle insists that male semen does not become any of those parts in actuality; the parts of the offspring are not formed from semen as matter but only as moving cause. Aristotle repeats this at the start of *GA* II.3: "The semen which is introduced into the female is not an ingredient in the thing which is formed but performs its function simply by means of the *dunamis* it contains." So why is this a problem for conveying soul?

For Aristotle, "soul" refers to a set of life-capacities possessed by the body (cf. *An* II.1 412b18–22: "if the eye were an organism, sight would be its soul"). This is why soul cannot exist apart from that of which it is the soul: capacities cannot exist apart from the things of which they are capacities.[6] Sight cannot exist in separation from the eye, nor the capacity to walk apart from legs (*GA* II.3 736b22–4). It follows from this that an Aristotelian soul cannot exist before its corresponding body has been formed *or after* that body has been destroyed.[7] Given the inseparability of soul and body (function and structure), there are only two ways that semen could serve as a vehicle for transmitting soul to the offspring.

One is for the semen to carry another body inside itself which acts as the material substratum for the soul transmitted. For example, semen could transmit sight by carrying eyes. However, Aristotle has already rejected this preformationist alternative in *GA* II.1 (733b31–734b4). The parts of the offspring do not come into the female already preformed inside the father's semen.[8] The other way would be if the semen itself were the material substratum of the soul it carried, that is, if the physical part of the semen stood to that soul as matter to form. This was Aristotle's initial position in *GA* II.1 when he said that semen contains soul and is potentially the parts of the body. If the semen then became those parts in actuality, it would come to possess soul in actuality as they developed from it. But that is not Aristotle's position. The parts of the offspring develop out of menstrual blood *not* semen. After the semen forms the embryo and triggers its development it evaporates and its bodily substance is destroyed (737a11–17).

Herein lies the problem. Since Aristotelian souls are inseparable from the bodies of which they are souls, when the semen perishes any soul it possesses must perish along with it. Hence semen cannot be a vehicle for transmitting soul from the father to the embryo:

> Clearly those capacities of soul whose activity is bodily cannot be present anywhere without a physical body; for example, the capacity to walk cannot be present anywhere without feet. And this also rules out the possibility of those capacities of soul entering [the embryo] from without (since it is impossible for them to enter on their own) as well as their entering by being transmitted in some body [namely semen]. For semen is a residue of nutriment that undergoes a change.[9] (*GA* II.3 736b21–5)

The complicated argument that runs through most of *GA* II.3 is an attempt to head-off this problem by providing a new account of how animal souls are reproduced. At 736b16–21 Aristotle considers several alternatives. The one he opts for is that some faculties of soul pre-exist in the embryo while others come into being as the embryo develops (without having been carried in by the semen). For example, the nutritive soul is already present in the embryo even before the semen makes its contribution (736a34–6 b8–13).[10] And it is "as they develop" that animals come to acquire sensory soul (736b1–2). Only intellectual soul is left with the possibility of "entering from without" (*thurathen*), since its activity is not associated with any bodily organ (736b26–30, 737a8–11). However, this idea is left obscure and undeveloped.

Reproductive Hylomorphism

Throughout the course of the *GA* Aristotle develops a thesis about the distinctive contributions of each sex to the process of generation, which I shall call "reproductive hylomorphism." In its most general formulation, the thesis states that the male contributes the form (*eidos*) while the female contributes the matter (*hulê*).[11] At first glance Aristotle's reproductive hylomorphism seems straightforward. The female provides a quantity of unformed matter which is given shape and form by the semen just as the sculptor forms the unsculpted bronze into a statue. But this characterization of the male and female contributions provides an inadequate picture of Aristotle's theory. While saying the mother provides the matter certainly does mean her contribution is used to make the parts of the offspring (and so in this sense is analogous to unsculpted bronze),[12] it is far from obvious what it means to say the father provides "the form."

A careful reading of the *GA* reveals two ways in which the father can be said to provide "form." According to the first formulation (the version that dominates Book I), providing form does not involve the formation of any complex structures with soul-functions. Rather, the semen is said to provide form to menstrual fluid in the way that rennet forms curds out of milk (*GA* I.20 729a10–14). The heat in the father's semen acts on the menstrual fluid, drawing in the bits of spermatic residue contained in it and fusing them together into one solid mass (cf. *GA* II.4 739b21ff, IV.4 771b22–4). The product of this event is not a fully formed organism but an amorphous seed which is the immediate product of fertilization. Once this seed has been formed, the heat in the semen triggers its development in the way that one triggers the movements of an automaton (*GA* II.5 741b7–9).

It is important to note that this first formulation of the matter-form thesis does not pick out the male's exclusive contribution to the process. At *GA* I.21 730a29–30 the male is said to contribute the principle that initiates change and determines the menstrual fluid (i.e. gives it form). Aristotle then suggests that in some species the female might be capable of supplying this principle herself, which he confirms in *GA* II.5 (cf. III.7 757b12ff). However, in this context Aristotle is only talking about the basic act of forming the embryo (which he likens to forming curds in milk) and triggering its development.

The second version of Aristotle's hylomorphic model is formulated in *GA* II.4. This is the more important formulation. Here the form that the father is said to provide is the offspring's *soul*, while the mother is said to provide its *body* (738b25–6). Yet, when we turn to *GA* II.5 we discover that this soul/body hylomorphism does not actually apply to the offspring's entire soul but only a part of it. In the final analysis, what the male *alone* is said to provide is the offspring's sensory soul. This is what Aristotle ultimately means when he says that the father's exclusive contribution to the generation of an animal is its "form." For the sensory soul is the form of an animal in the strict sense. It is the property that makes a living thing an *animal*.

Aristotle also reveals in *GA* II.5 that the mother's contribution is not confined to providing the offspring's body; she also provides part of its soul. In some species the female can generate embryos capable of (minimal) growth without being fertilized by the male, a phenomenon known as parthenogenesis. Parthenogenesis plays a significant role in the argument of the *GA*, since it allows Aristotle to isolate the unique contribution of the male parent. Aristotle observed that unfertilized "wind-eggs" never develop to the point where they begin to form sense organs, which (he thinks) shows that the father's contribution must be responsible for the development of the sensory system. The fact that wind-eggs develop at all, however, shows that the nutritive power of soul comes from the female. For those embryos grow (and decay) without any contribution from the male, but simply in virtue of the nutritive soul acquired from the female.[13]

There is one final issue to address concerning the semen's role in the process of generation. In general, the father's semen is directly responsible for three principal events: forming the embryo out of menstrual blood; constructing the embryonic heart (cf. 735a12–26); and triggering the development of the remaining parts. It is a common misconception that Aristotle thought the father's semen fashions the offspring in its entirety (e.g. Furth 1988, 119). This generally results from a failure to consider how the argument develops past Book I. Throughout Book II, for example, Aristotle repeatedly emphasizes that the proximate cause of generation is the offspring's own nature, which coordinates the sequence of changes (triggered by the semen) through its newly constructed heart. This is the main conclusion of the closing argument of *GA* II.1. There Aristotle argues that because the heart is the first part to be formed it must contain a generative principle. For at that point the embryo must be able to take over for the semen and build the rest of its body. This is also the point of the "rational argument" at *GA* II.4 740a5–24. Aristotle again argues that because the heart is formed before the other parts, it must contain "the principle from which the subsequent ordering (*diakosmêsis*) of the animal's body derives." For once this part has been formed the embryo must be able to "manage itself" (*hauto diokein*), just as the son who has been sent away from his father must be able to set up and manage his own household.[14] By locating the source of growth and development in the embryonic heart Aristotle was able to bring the theory of the *GA* in line with the *Physics*, which defines "natural" changes as those deriving from a principle in the thing itself *qua* itself (*Physics* II.1).

Aristotle eventually identifies the embryo's generative nature with its soul, which is said to be "the active power" that forms the parts of the body in the beginning:

> For, since the material out of which the organism grows and that out of which it is originally constructed are the same, the active power is also identical with the one which is operative in the beginning (but greater than it). If, then, this is the nutritive soul, it is also that which generates. And this is the nature of each organism, being present in all plants and animals alike. (*GA* II.4 740b35–741a2; cf. *An* II.4)

Here we encounter a problem. Aristotle says the offspring's nutritive soul is the agent that constructs the parts of the body, including the parts of the sensory system (see note 14). Yet he goes on to argue in *GA* II.5 that the nutritive soul comes from the mother *and* that the father alone provides the sensory soul. How are these two theses reconciled?

It is unlikely that Aristotle means to say that the mother's contribution is responsible for constructing the sense organs while the semen implants sensory soul in them. Aristotelian souls are not the sorts of things that are capable of being implanted in bodily organs from without (except perhaps intellectual soul). Soul is not an extra ingredient added to the organ over-and-above its structure. Once there is a properly constructed organ it straightaway possess the corresponding soul-function in virtue of its structure.[15] So if the nutritive soul is responsible for constructing the parts of the body, including the sensory parts, then *all* faculties of soul would be traced to the mother's contribution. And this contradicts the hylomorphism of the *GA*.

One solution to this puzzle is to distinguish the "nutritive soul" that *GA* II.4 identifies with the offspring's generative nature from the "nutritive soul" that *GA* II.5 says comes from the mother. The former is the power to construct the parts of the body in the beginning, which *DA* II.4 calls "the generative soul." The latter is the general capacity of a living thing to process nutriment and to increase and maintain its size. The mother supplies nutritive soul only in this minimal sense (basic metabolic functions). On this reading each parent will contribute part of the generative soul. The mother contributes the part that governs the development of the metabolic system, while the father contributes the part that governs the development of the sensory system (though see further below).[16] It is this latter part which is missing from the generative souls of those wind-eggs that are produced by females alone. And this is why their development stops at the point where fertilized embryos begin to develop sense organs.

Inheritance

One of the most interesting aspects of the *GA* is the theory of inheritance in *GA* IV.3 (Aristotle's central account of inheritance comes at *GA* IV.3 767a36–768b10). It has not been well understood by commentators and relatively little has actually been written about it. What I shall offer here is only a brief sketch of the theory (for a more detailed discussion of this see Henry 2006a).

In a key passage at *GA* 767b23–768a2 Aristotle sets out the basic mechanism underlying the phenomenon of inheritance:

(T1)   I speak of each *dunamis* in the following sense. The generator [*to gennôn*] is not only a male but also a particular sort of male, e.g. a Coriscus or a Socrates,[17] and it is not only a Coriscus but also a human being. And it is in this sense that, of the characteristics that belong to the generator insofar as it is capable of generating [*katho gennêtikon*] and not incidentally [*kata sumbebôs*] (e.g. if it is a scholar or someone's neighbor), some belong to it more closely while others more remotely . . . So, there are *kinêseis* present in the seeds of animals derived from the *dunameis* of all of these sorts of things [sc. male, Socrates, human], and in potentiality even those of its ancestors, although those of the individual are always closer.

This passage tells us two important things about Aristotle's theory of inheritance. First, it draws a distinction between the *heritable* properties of an individual (those that belong to the generator *katho gennêtikon*) and what we might call its *genetically incidental* properties (those that are *kata sumbebêkos*). The examples of genetically incidental properties are being a good scholar and being someone's neighbor. These properties are incidental to the generator *qua* generator precisely because they are not passed on in the act of reproduction; they are not heritable. Second, it sets out the mechanism that explains the transmission of an organism's heritable traits. The two central components of this mechanism are the "*kinêseis*," which are said to be present in the parent's reproductive material, and the "*dunameis*" from which those *kinêseis* are derived. The main interpretive difficulty that arises in connection with *GA* IV.3 is how to understand the mechanism in T1. Specifically, what are the *kinêseis* and *dunameis* supposed to be? Once we have come to understand how the mechanism works, we will not only be in a better position to understand Aristotle's theory of inheritance itself but more generally how he thinks biological form is passed on from one generation to another. For throughout the discussion Aristotle makes it clear that the same mechanism that explains resemblance in individual characteristics also explains resemblance in species-level properties (767b23–768a2, 768a13–14, 768b10–15).

Aristotle's hereditary concept of a *dunamis* here is not that different from his metaphysical concept of *dunamis* (see esp. *Metaphysics* Θ.1–6). According to *Metaphysics* Θ.1, a *dunamis* is a power or capacity for acting or being acted upon. Thus it is reasonable to suppose that the *dunameis* in our passage refer to specific developmental capacities (cf. Morsink 1982: 134–5). This hereditary concept of a *dunamis* is meant to provide the ontological basis for the distinction Aristotle draws in our passage between features that belong to an organism *katho gennêtikon* and those that are *kata sumbebêkos*. Unlike genetically incidental traits, each heritable feature of an organism can be traced to a corresponding *dunamis* in its generative nature, which is a capacity for the formation of just that trait. In this way T1 can be seen as an attempt to isolate the more precise (efficient) causes of reproduction. The *dunameis* are the causal entities behind the heritable features enumerated in that passage.[18]

The *kinêseis* (which are said to be present in the reproductive materials of organisms) function as the vehicles for transmitting these *dunameis* in the act of reproduction (see Witt 1985: 56, n. 26; Henry 2006a).[19] For lack of a better word I will simply translate *kinêsis* here as "movement." This need not imply that Aristotle thinks there are literal motions or changes occurring in the organism's sperma. He could be thinking of local motions (e.g. vibrations or waves) that somehow encode the characteristics of the parent's body. However, what *GA* IV.3 seems to provide is an explanatory framework for giving an account of inheritance at a more abstract level. As such, we should not expect the concepts being deployed there to be spelled out in concrete terms. If this is right, then Aristotle's spermatic "*kinêsis*" would be like Mendel's "factor" in that both concepts attempt to abstract away from the concrete physical basis of the vehicles of inheritance.[20]

The picture presented in T1 thus looks something like this. Socrates' semen carries a set of "movements" derived from various capacities of his generative nature, each of which is the productive source of a corresponding characteristic. For example, there will be one movement corresponding to his snub nose and another corresponding to his particular shade of eye-color. If each of these movements "dominates" (*kratein*), then Socrates' son will come to resemble him in both these respects.

According to the traditional interpretation, Aristotle failed to assign the mother a direct contribution to inheritance. Rather, maternal resemblance simply results from the semen failing to impose the father's likeness on the matter. On this reading the mother is at best an accidental cause of maternal inheritance insofar as the semen's failure is due to the recalcitrant nature of the material she supplies. However, when we turn to Aristotle's account of maternal inheritance we find something that does not sit well with this picture. As several commentators have noted, *GA* IV.3 introduces a set of maternal "movements" to account for resemblances to the mother's side of the family. Apparently Aristotle's idea is that, like the father, the mother contributes a set of spermatic movements associated with the features of her own body as well as those inherited from her ancestors. Maternal resemblance occurs whenever one of her movements dominates over the one from the father with respect to the same feature (e.g. nose shape, eye color).

This is most explicit in a passage where Aristotle introduces the causal mechanism behind the phenomenon of atavism (resemblance to ancestors).

(T2) [Atavism occurs when] the formative movements relapse into the ones which stand closest to them. For example, if the movement of the father relapses, it passes into that of his father (the least difference) and in the second instance into that of his grandfather. Indeed in this way too, on the female side just as on the male side: the movement of the mother passes into that of her mother, and if it not into that one, then into that of her grandmother. And in the same way for the more distant ancestors. (*GA* IV.3 768a14–21)

What T2 makes clear is that the inheritance of maternal traits is explained by movements coming from the mother *in the same way* that paternal movements explain resemblances to the father's side of the family. The most natural reading of this passage (and several like it) is to see these maternal movements as being functionally equivalent to those of her male counterpart: both serve as vehicles of inheritance. (For an alternative, though in my opinion implausible, interpretation of maternal inheritance, see Cooper 1988. For an assessment of the problem of maternal inheritance see Henry 2006b.)

Aristotle's theory of inheritance itself consists of three "general suppositions" (*katholou hupotheseis*):

> We must grasp the general suppositions: the one stated, that among the movements present in the parents' seeds some are present in potentiality while others are present in activity; and two others, that being dominated causes displacement into the opposite [movement], while relapsing causes a change into the movement which stands next on the blood-line. If it relapses a little, it passes into the movement which stands closer; if it relapses more, into the one farther away. (*GA* IV.3 768b5–10)

The first supposition concerns the existence of movements in the parent's sperma (cf. 768a12–14). The other two supply the principles that govern the interactions between the paternal and maternal movements. The outcome of these interactions will determine the pattern of inheritance for the particular offspring. By using these three general principles Aristotle was able to explain at least seven phenomena connected with inheritance (see *GA* IV.3 767a36–b7).

Individual Forms

Many scholars have suggested that Aristotle's account of inheritance has implications for how we understand his concept of form. Traditionally scholars have held that the form transmitted in the act of reproduction is the species form. According to this view, form is (a?) universal, includes only those features which are common to the species, and is shared by all members of the same kind. Those features that distinguish one member of the species from the next (e.g. eye color in humans) are accidental properties which result from the species-form being embodied in different quantities of matter. A corollary of this is that inherited resemblances are irrelevant to the science of biology, since there cannot be scientific knowledge of what is accidental (Sharples 2005: 105).[21] A second interpretation claims that the forms of particular organisms are themselves particulars (i.e. numerically distinct, non-repeatable instances) rather than universals shared by all members of the same kind (e.g. Frede and Patzig 1988; cf. Witt 1985). This is compatible with the view that form only includes features common to every member of the species, e.g. Socrates and Callias have numerically distinct human forms (for a discussion of these two positions in relation to the *Metaphysics* plus references, see ch. 12, on substance). Finally, others have argued that Aristotle was committed to a much more radical notion of *individual* forms which include features below the level of species. For one of the important lessons of the *GA* is that some individual differences are part of the form that is transmitted in the act of reproduction (Balme 1987b: 291–312; Cooper 1988: 32–8; Whiting 1990; Henry 2006a).

Aristotle's remarks on inheritance in *GA* IV.3 do seem to point towards individual forms in the last sense. Consider T1 again. Aristotle tells us that what the offspring receives from its parents is a series of *dunameis*, or developmental capacities, for different parts of its body. These *dunameis* are transmitted directly from parent to child through a series of *kinêseis*, or movements, carried in the animal's sperma. Contrary to the traditional view, Aristotle extends this mechanism to include not only the transmission of those *dunameis* that belong to Socrates as a human being but also those that are distinctive of him as a particular human being (e.g. a *dunamis* for snub-nose and blue eyes).[22] Thus it seems that the heritable properties of organisms include both species- *and* individual-level properties: all of these features are essential to Socrates "insofar as he is capable of reproduction" (*katho gennêtikon*). It is a short step from this to the notion of individual forms. For the *dunameis* enumerated in T1 are surely parts of Socrates' *formal* nature: they are capacities of his *generative soul*.[23] It follows from this that Socrates' form will be different from Callias' form insofar as his generative soul includes capacities for developing particularly Socratic (as opposed to Calliastic) features, such as a snub nose and bulging blue eyes. It is in this sense that Socrates' form is individual: Socrates' generative soul does not just include *dunameis* for parts of a human being but more specific *dunameis* for parts of a particular kind of human being, namely, a Socrates. These more specific *dunameis* (*dunameis* for resemblances that are peculiar to Socrates) are not found in Callias' generative soul.

Some have objected that this interpretation commits Aristotle to a division into subspecific types of soul (e.g. human souls divide into Socratic soul, Calliastic soul, etc.), for which there is no evidence (Witt 1985: 51). However, if the above analysis is right, then our passage gives us every reason to think that human souls do divide into Socratic souls and Calliastic souls. If the *dunameis* for those properties that Aristotle says belong to the generator *katho gennêtikon* are capacities of the generative soul (and there is every reason to think they are), then a Socratic soul *is* different than a Calliastic soul.

Whether or not *GA* IV.3 does imply individual forms, Aristotle clearly thinks the phenomenon of inheritance is scientifically explicable in terms of general principles (*katholou hupotheseis*). As such, the resemblances in question cannot be accidental, since what is accidental is intractable to scientific explanation.[24] At the outset of *GA* IV.3 Aristotle identifies seven phenomena that he thinks an adequate account of inheritance must explain. He then tries to explain those empirical regularities by relating them to the interactions between the various entities postulated there (the *kinêseis* and the *dunameis*), while the general suppositions supply the theoretical principles that govern the behavior of the mechanism. If this is right, then what we seem to find in *GA* IV.3 is the first real attempt to formulate a genuine science of inheritance (this insight was first noted by Morsink (1982), if perhaps for the wrong reasons). This conclusion does not sit well with the traditional view that inherited resemblances are accidental and thus irrelevant to the science of biology.

Four Causes of Generation

We are now in a position to set out the four causes of animal generation in more detail (this account does not apply to spontaneous generation, which is only subject to explanations in terms of material and efficient causation). According to the *GA* the mother and father represent the material and efficient causes, respectively. The mother provides the matter out of which the embryo is formed, and the father provides the agency that informs that material and triggers its development. This account is elaborated over the course of the *GA*. For example, although the embryo is originally constituted from menstrual blood, the emerging structures are built from nutritive blood supplied through the umbilical cord. This nutriment is processed into various types of "residue" by the embryonic heart, which serve as specialized matter for different parts (*GA* II.6, 744b13ff). A study of the material cause of animal generation would therefore include an account of these residues and how each contributes to the formation of the body.[25] Further, while the father is the primary efficient cause in that his semen provides the catalyst for the embryo's development ("that whence comes the beginning of motion"), as we have seen, the offspring's own nature is more directly responsible for the construction of its parts. This is the theory developed in the latter half of *GA* II.1 (734b20–735a26): the material supplied by the mother is formed by a series of processes which are initiated by the sire (who is in actuality what that material is potentially) and then controlled by the nature of the developing embryo itself.

The formal cause of generation is the definition of the animal's substantial being, while the final cause is the adult form, which is the goal of the process of development (*GA* V.1 778a33–5; cf. *Metaphysics* V.4 1015a12; *GC* II.9 335b6–7). At the outset of the *GA* I Aristotle tells us that these two causes refer to the same thing (715a4–5).[26] This is plain enough, since the form specified in the account of an animal's substantial being is also the *telos* of its natural development. Reference to this form therefore tells us what the embryo is coming to be (and therefore what it *is*) and properly identifies the series of changes as a single process of development. Since the sensory soul is the form of an animal *qua* animal, there is a strong sense in which the father can be said to contribute both the formal and final cause of animal generation (*GA* II.1 732a4–5). And yet, insofar as the mother also provides a part of the offspring's soul, she too can be seen as making her own formal contribution. This is especially true if the *GA* recognizes individual forms, since she is directly responsible for those features of the offspring that make it look like individuals on her side of the family (Balme 1987: 292–3).

Notes

I am grateful to Jim Lennox, Monte Johnson, Marguerite Deslaurier, Ursula Coope, S. Marc Cohen, Jim Hankinson, Robert Mayhew, Nick Fawcett, and Julie Ponesse for their helpful suggestions on earlier drafts of this chapter.

[1] There is no suitable English translation for *sperma* and so I shall transliterate it. Aristotle uses the term for many things: (1) generically for an organism's reproductive material (both male and female: e.g. 716a4–13); (2) specifically for male semen alone (technically *gonê*: e.g. 727b34); and (3) for the immediate product of fertilization (technically *kuêma*: e.g. 724b14–18

728b34–5, cf. 731a2–4). Unless otherwise indicated or qualified, I shall use "sperma" to mean (1), the reproductive material of animals in general.

[2] *GA* I also fulfills two promises from the *PA*. The first is to discuss both the instrumental and uniform parts connected with generation which had not been dealt with there (cf. *GA* I.16 721a27–30). (The "uniform parts" in question are sperma and milk, which are included among the useful fluids produced in the last stages of digestion (*PA* II.7).) The other is to discuss the hypothesis, introduced in *PA* IV.10, that the reproductive fluids are both "residues."

[3] Aristotle's own account of sperma does not begin until *GA* I.18 724b14. Prior to this he presents a dialectical argument against the view that sperma is composed of tiny bits of tissue drawn directly from the parts of the parent's body, which has come to be known as "pangenesis." This was the theory held by Democritus (e.g. IV.1 764a7–12).

[4] The last part of this definition, which specifies its function and end, is necessary to distinguish sperma from other types of useful residue of ultimate nutriment (e.g. fat: 727a33–7).

[5] See also *GA* IV.1 765b8–15, 766b8–15. Commentators are divided on whether or not Aristotle recognizes female sperma. There are some passages where Aristotle seems to deny that females produce sperma (e.g. 727a26–30); however, in those cases "*sperma*" appears to mean male semen (i.e. *gonê*). Female sperma is explicitly mentioned in several passages (e.g. 728a26–7, b23, 750b4–5, 767b16–17, 771b20, b22–3). Indeed, as we have seen, Aristotle thinks it is because the female produces sperma that she is a "starting-point" of generation (716a11–13). Nevertheless, Aristotle stresses that what she produces is not the *same kind* of sperma as the male "as some allege" (727b6–7, 728a27–31).

[6] Cf. *An* II.1 413a2–7: "The body is that which exists potentially; but just as the eye-jelly and the capacity to see make the eye, so too the body and the soul make the organism. Thus it is clear that no soul exists in separation from the body. Likewise for certain parts of the soul (if it naturally has parts); for in some cases the actuality of these [parts of the soul] is the actuality of the parts [of the body]."

[7] The exception here is intellectual soul, since it is not the capacity *of* any organ (compare the qualification on "some cases" in *DA* 413a2–7). Intellect presents a special puzzle when it comes to transmitting soul (736b5–8).

[8] One might point to a special pneuma inside the semen as the matter for the soul (cf. *GA* 736b30–737a7). I do not have space to discuss this alternative, except to say that this is not Aristotle's position.

[9] The change in question is the evaporation of the semen (cf. 737a15–6).

[10] This is confirmed in *GA* II.5 when we learn that this part of the soul comes from the mother (see below).

[11] *GA* I.20 729a9–12; I.21 729b18–19, II.1 732a4–5, II.4 738b26–8. In other places Aristotle simply says the male contributes the "starting-point of the change" (*arkhê tês kinêseôs*), e.g. I.2 716a4–7, I.21 730a24–30, II.4 740b25–6. Although this is not equivalent to his role as supplier of form, in certain contexts the two are bound up with each other.

[12] Aristotle even compares menstrual fluid to prime matter (*GA* I.20 729a32–3). As we shall see, this is not exhaustive of the mother's contribution to reproduction though.

[13] This is the traditional interpretation of *GA* II.5 (e.g. Peck 1990, xii). Allan Gotthelf has suggested to me that the father's contribution must include nutritive soul and that all *GA* II.5 commits Aristotle to is the idea that the mother *can* provide nutritive soul and *in some cases* (viz. wind-eggs) actually does so: but these cases should not be taken as a model for what normally happens.

[14] At *GA* II.6 744b16–27 the embryo's generative nature is compared to a household manager (*oikonomos*) that "constructs the flesh and the somatic parts of the other sense-organs out of the purest material, while it constructs bones and sinews and hair out of the residues."

[15] This is what Aristotle seems to mean by saying the organ and function come into being *together* and not one before the other (*GA* IV.1 766a5–7, cf. II.1 734b22–4: "Sperma . . . has a movement and a principle of such a kind that once the movement ceases each part comes into being ensouled."). Nevertheless, soul-capacities are explanatorily prior insofar as they explain why organs have the structure they do and thus why the nature of the embryo builds them in the way that it does (II.6 743a36–b18).

[16] This seems to be the force of Aristotle's statement at *GA* II.5, 741a13–14 that the father's contribution is "the capacity to make (*poiêtikon*) this sort of soul" rather than simply *being* that soul. On my reading, the way to "make" an Aristotelian soul is to construct the organs that discharge the corresponding capacity (since Aristotelian souls are capacities of organs). Thus, what the father directly supplies through his semen is the capacity to construct sensory parts (*see below*). Moreover, if we think of the generating capacities (*dunameis*) of the embryo's soul as capacities of the embryonic heart, then the way to cash this out is in terms of organising the region of the heart that governs the development of the sensory system. Likewise for the mother's contribution.

[17] By "a Coriscus or a Socrates" Aristotle means those properties that make the generator an individual, as opposed to a male or human being. For the significance of this see further below.

[18] For the idea that a science must attempt to identify the "more precise" causes of a phenomenon see *Physics* II.3 195b21–5.

[19] We also find *kinêsis* being used in this way in the account of sense-perception in *GA* V.1–2. For the idea of a *kinêsis* bearing informational content see Aristotle *On Memory* (e.g. 452b23–4: "the *kinêsis* of the fact" and "the *kinêsis* of the time"). For alternative accounts of T1 see Morsink (1982), Balme (1987a), Cooper (1988), and Furth (1988).

[20] Aristotle does attempt to give an account of the general principles of the theory (specifically, "displacement" and "relapse") in terms of physico-chemical processes (768b16–35). However, that account remains incomplete and quite tentative. Indeed, Aristotle tells us that the job of giving a complete description of these processes belongs to a different part of natural science. All we are given are some basic remarks about how the project of translating these principles into the language of Aristotle's chemistry might be accomplished.

[21] See *Metaphysics* K.8. This inference seems to depend on an equivocation of the term "accidental," namely "incidental" versus "by chance." Eye color may be accidental in the first sense even if not in the second, and K8 only applies to what is accidental in the second sense.

[22] Aristotle does not say exactly which individual differences he has in mind in T1; he only mentions properties that make the generator "a Coriscus or a Socrates" (as opposed to simply "a human being"). It does seem reasonable, however, that he has some kind of facial features in mind like eye color and nose shape, since these are the sorts of features where family resemblances are most conspicuous (the very phenomenon Aristotle sets out to explain in *GA* IV.3). But the specific examples are irrelevant. The point is that some sub-specific differences – whatever features make the generator "a Socrates" – belong to the individual *katho gennêtikon*.

[23] For the relation between "formal nature" and "soul" see *PA* I.1 641a22–33. In *De anima* II.4 Aristotle says that generative soul is essentially the capacity to reproduce the form and substantial being (*ousia*) of the individual in a different material body (415a26–8), while the nutritive soul is the capacity to maintain that form and substantial being in the same body (416b3–24). While both capacities essentially belong to the same part of the soul, the reproductive capacity is said to be teleologically primary (416b24–6).

[24] Lennox has convinced me that this would also be consistent with the view that inherited resemblances are due to the matter. For both *GA* V and *Meteorologica* IV show that we can have scientific knowledge of universal material-level causes.

[25] In *GA* I Aristotle tells us that "the parts" are matter for the animals: "the non-uniform parts are matter for the entire animal as a whole, the uniform parts for the non-uniform parts, and the so-called elements of bodies are matter for the uniform parts" (715a9–12, cf. *PA* II.1). However, these are material causes of *being* an animal; they are the matter out of which *the existing* animal is composed. Menstrual blood and the various "residues" of nutritive blood are material causes of *becoming* an animal; they are the matter out of which *the developing* animal is constructed. This reflects Aristotle's distinction at *PA* I.1 640a10–12 between studying animals as they actually exists and studying them in the context of generation.

[26] Compare *Physics* II.7 198a25–7. There Aristotle says that the efficient cause refers to something *specifically* the same as these (viz. the father), not *numerically* the same.

Bibliography

Balme, David (1987a). "The Place of Biology in Aristotle's Philosophy," in Gotthelf and Lennox (eds.) (1987), pp. 9–20.

Balme, David (1987b). "Aristotle's Biology Was Not Essentialist," in Gotthelf and Lennox (eds.) (1987), pp. 291–312.

Balme, David (1990). "Ανθρωπος ανθρωπον γεννα: Human Is Generated by Human," in G. R. Dunstan (ed.) (1990), *The Human Embryo: Aristotle and the Arabic and European Traditions* (Exeter: University of Exeter Press), pp. 20–31.

Bolton, Robert (1987). "Definition and Scientific Method in Aristotle's *Posterior Analytics* and *Generation of Animals*," in Gotthelf and Lennox (eds.) (1987), pp. 120–66.

Charles, David (2000). *Aristotle on Meaning and Essence* (Oxford: Oxford University Press).

Cooper, John (1988). "Metaphysics in Aristotle's Embryology," *Cambridge Philological Society Proceedings*, 214 (new series 34), pp.14–41. (Repr. in D. Devereux and P. Pellegrin (eds.) (1990), *Biologie, logique et metaphysique chez Aristotle* (Paris: Editions du CNRS), pp. 55–84.)

Furth, Montgomery (1988). *Substance, Form and Psyche: An Aristotelian Metaphysics* (Cambridge: Cambridge University Press).

Gotthelf, Allan and Lennox, James (eds.) (1987). *Philosophical Issues in Aristotle's Biology* (Cambridge: Cambridge University Press).

Henry, Devin (2006a). "Aristotle on the Mechanism of Inheritance," *Journal of the History of Biology*, 39 (3).

Henry, Devin (2006b). "Understanding Aristotle's Reproductive Hylomorphism," *Apeiron*, 39 (3).

Henry, Devin (2008). "Organismal Natures," *Apeiron*.

Lennox, James G. (1996). "Aristotle's Biological Development: The Balme Hypothesis," in W. Wians (ed.), *Aristotle's Philosophical Development* (Savage, MD), ch. 10.

Lennox, James G. (2001). *Aristotle's Philosophy of Biology: Studies in the Origins of Life Science* (Cambridge: Cambridge University Press).

Morsink, Johannes (1982). *Aristotle on the "Generation of Animals"* (Washington, DC: University Press of America).

Peck, A. L. (trans.) (1990). *Aristotle: Generation of Animals*, Loeb Classics, vol. 13 (Cambridge: Harvard University Press).

Sharples, Robert (1985). "Species, Form, and Inheritance: Aristotle and After," in Gotthelf (ed.) (1985), *Aristotle On Nature and Living Things* (Pittsburgh, PA: Mathesis), pp. 117–28.

Sharples, Robert (2005). "Some Thoughts on Aristotelian Form: With Special Reference to *Metaphysics* Z 8," *Science in Context*, 18 (1), pp. 93–109.

Whiting, Jennifer (1990). "Aristotle on Form and Generation," in J. Cleary and D. Shartin (eds.) (1990), *Proceedings of the Boston Area Colloquium in Ancient Philosophy*, 6 (Lanham, MD: University of America Press), pp. 35–63.

Witt, Charlotte (1985). "Form, Reproduction, and Inherited Characteristics in Aristotle's *Generation of Animals*," *Phronesis*, 30 (1), pp. 46–57.

Part IV

Practical Knowledge

A. Ethics

24

Happiness and the Structure of Ends

GABRIEL RICHARDSON LEAR

We want to know what the good is, Aristotle thinks, because "knowledge of it carries great weight for life and, just like archers with a target, we would be more likely to hit what we ought" (*NE* I.2 1094a22–4). I think most of us would agree that our interest in reading ethics is, at least in part, practical. We want to become good, to lead lives that are good, and to provide the good to our families and political communities (I.1 1094a7–10, II.2 1103b26–30, X.9 1179a35–b4). Given that this is the case, we may also agree with Aristotle that there is little point in studying philosophical accounts of happiness if we are too immature – too inexperienced in life to recognize when an account adequately captures what makes life worth living or too easily overwhelmed by passion to put our reflections into practice (*NE* I.3 1094b27–1095a11). If so, we may be disappointed to find that Aristotle's ethical treatises are not compilations of straightforward advice. On the contrary, one of their distinctive lessons is that very little practicable advice of a general nature can be given.

Even so, the *Nicomachean Ethics* and *Eudemian Ethics* have a practical focus in an interesting sense. Aristotle believes that we should guide our philosophical reflection about the good by keeping in mind the role it actually plays in life. In particular, he thinks we should conceive of it as the goal or end (*telos*) of practical deliberation and action. As he says in the very first sentence of the *Nicomachean Ethics*, "Every craft and every inquiry, and likewise every action and decision, seems to aim at some good. For which reason people have rightly concluded that the good is that at which all things aim" (I.1 1094a1–3).

This may not seem like an especially substantial starting point, but it is not an obvious one. Plato's Socrates, for instance, begins his investigation into another sort of value, the fine-and-beautiful (*kalon*), by asking what all fine things have in common (*Hippias Major* 289d). We might, then, begin an inquiry into the good by surveying all the things we recognize as good and looking to see whether there is some feature peculiar to them that they share. Aristotle's critique of the Platonic theory of the Good-Itself shows why he thinks an approach of this sort is unpromising: it is metaphysically incoherent (since good is said in as many ways as being) and, even if there *were* a form of the Good, it would be too abstract to provide any practical guidance (*NE* I.6). In theory, it might seem as if knowing the paradigm of goodness would help us identify good things as they come along. But according to Aristotle, this is not in fact the sort of good that guides the deliberations of doctors and sailors and other undisputed purveyors of good things. Notice that he does not deny that there is anything interesting to say about the way in which the goodness of all good things, human and non-human, is related. He wonders briefly whether they are all good by analogy, or by being related in various ways to some one good thing (I.6 1096b26–9). But he leaves this metaphysical issue aside as a distraction from the business of practical philosophy. What we are seeking, he says, is the best good achievable by human action (I.6 1096b30–5). In the *Eudemian Ethics* he is explicit that his teleological approach is to be preferred to Plato's precisely because his does and Plato's does not capture this practicable aspect of the human good (I.8 1218b4–10).

As we will see, Aristotle's approach is enormously powerful. It allows him to identify necessary features of the good – self-sufficiency and finality or completeness – since these are necessary features of an ultimate end. Using them as criteria, he can confirm the widespread belief that the highest good is happiness and evaluate common beliefs about what happiness is. (So, for instance, in *NE* I Aristotle argues that wealth is not the highest good because it is an instrumental and not a final end (I.5 1096a6–7).) Perhaps less obvious, the idea of the good as goal also provides the underlying rationale for thinking of happiness as excellent human functioning. The function of a thing just is the end to which it is naturally suited. It need not be the only typical activity this thing can perform. But where a thing has a function, this activity is the goal at which all its other activities are aimed. As Aristotle says in the *Eudemian Ethics*, "The function of each thing is its end" (II.1 1219a8).

Since Aristotle is so thorough-going in conceiving of the good as an end, understanding what this idea amounts to is an important first step for understanding his ethical theory as a whole. For there are good reasons to wonder whether this is in fact a fruitful place to begin. Consider: Aristotle is well aware that there is almost no limit to what we can desire. (In *NE* VII.5 he discusses rather lurid examples of people who like to eat babies.) He also knows that people disagree vehemently about whether things are desirable or not. Furthermore, anything we desire as an end will, once we possess it, have various effects and people will disagree about their desirability too. So not only does there seem to be no limit on what we can treat as an end, there also seems to be no limit on whether we treat an end as ultimate. We may wonder, therefore, how Aristotle hopes to build a realist account of the good from the mere observation that the good figures in deliberation and action as an end.

But those of us who approach the *Ethics* in a practical frame of mind will want to get clear about what is involved in conceiving of the good as an end for another reason, too. What in the final analysis does Aristotle think happiness is? Remarkably, this is not at all an easy question to answer, despite the fact that he discusses it at some length. The problem is that whereas in the first Book of our *Nicomachean Ethics* he implies that happiness is, or at least prominently includes, morally virtuous action, in the last Book he argues that morally virtuous action is happiness in only a secondary way and that the best good is theoretical contemplation. One of his principal reasons for drawing this conclusion is that contemplation is completely final as an end whereas morally virtuous action is not. Perhaps Aristotle here contradicts his earlier position. But we cannot determine whether or not he has nor can we consider how the two positions might be reconciled until we understand what Aristotle means by claiming that happiness is an absolutely final end. I will return to this problem at the end of the essay.

The Good Conceived as an End

Let us begin with the first lines of the *NE*: "Every craft and every inquiry, and likewise every action and decision, seems to aim at some good. For which reason people have rightly concluded that the good is that at which all things aim" (I.1 1094a1–3). Notice that craft (*technê*), inquiry (*methodos*), action (*praxis*), and decision (*prohairesis*) are all rational dispositions and activities. Thus Aristotle is not suggesting that *all* of our behavior, including a person's thoughtless munching of potato chips while he reads, is performed with the conscious intention of securing some good.[1] Still, there are puzzles.

The point at which actions and so forth aim is called its *telos* or end. In saying that ends are goods, Aristotle is not saying that ends are always *morally* good. The goodness in question here is quite general. Even so, we may doubt that this claim is true of the ends of a vicious or otherwise misguided person. Can we not pursue bad ends in the mistaken belief that they are good? Furthermore, not only does Aristotle assume that all ends are goods, he also believes that ends are better than the things leading to them. So he writes, "Some ends are activities, others are products beyond the activities. Of those whose ends are things beyond the activities, the products are naturally better than the activities" (I.1 1094a4–6). His claim that ends are *naturally* better than the things leading to them signals that their superiority is somehow objective. However, this claim is scarcely credible if every result of an activity, even every welcome result, counts as one of that activity's ends. Construction work, for example, strengthens your muscles. And this in turn may excite the envy of your peers. But having big muscles or being envied by one's peers are not obviously better than the activity itself of building a house.

These puzzles arise because we assume that an Aristotelian end is any result that the agent desires to achieve by his action. But the picture of ends that emerges in the first two chapters of the *NE* is importantly different. Genuine ends guide the activities leading to them and determine their distinctive character. For this reason, ends are the source of value for the things leading to them.

Consider again the results of construction. Even though it makes the workman strong and thus an object of envy, Aristotle says that the end of construction is a house (I.7 1097a20). What reason could he have for singling out this result as the proper end? For one thing, in the normal case at least, the objective of building muscle does not guide the activity of building houses. The carpenter pours the foundation, erects the frame, installs wiring and then plumbing in the precise order and way that he does because he aims to produce a house. In fact, even if he himself has no interest in the completed house, even if his principal desire is to build muscle, it will still be the case that his method of working gets its specific character from the fact that it is aimed at creating houses. Genuine ends, therefore, determine what the things leading to them are like.

Notice that the guiding function of ends is not completely exhausted by the fact that the craftsman happens to desire the end. It is of course true that desire is normally the route by which ends influence our behavior. Indeed, all behavior studied by philosophical ethics is like this. (Still, we should not forget that Aristotle explains *all* living behavior, including the spider's building of its web, the plant's setting down of roots, and our own processes of digestion and growth, in terms of its proper end. Since these activities are not all motivated by desire, it is clear that according to Aristotle ends, including human ends such as self-nourishment, do not always have their influence via desire.) Ordinarily, the craftsman sets about pouring the foundation because he wants to create a house. But imagine our builder is a new recruit to a construction team who does not really know what he is doing in pouring concrete. If he wants to do his job well, he had better figure out what the goal of his team's activity is.

The point is that ends determine the distinctive character of the things leading to them by setting the standards of their success. Pouring a concrete foundation may have many predictable results, but it is a good instance of the sort of activity it is only to the extent that it contributes to the making of the house. This is because foundation-pouring just is the activity of creating part of a house. A given individual may decide to pour a foundation in order to hide some incriminating evidence. But its success as foundation-pouring does not stand or fall with its effectiveness in that regard. From here we can see that pouring a foundation is worth choosing as the kind of thing it is because it helps bring a house into being. In other words, it is for the sake of a house that foundation-pouring as such is worth choosing. And that means that, in general, there is no value to this or any other construction activities as the kinds of thing they are unless houses are something good and worth choosing.

It is easier to see that ends play these normative roles in cases where the end is a product beyond the activity, but it is equally true in cases where the end is the activity itself. Think for example of dancing a waltz. The dancer moves his feet and holds his arms in one way rather than another in the particular order that he does because this is what it is to dance a waltz. Waltzing as an end guides his dancing activity. And moving his body in just this way is worth choosing because waltzing is (under the circumstances) a good thing to do.

We can see all these points at work in Aristotle's discussion of how ends themselves can in turn be worth choosing for the sake of other ends:

> Bridle-making and the other crafts of riding equipment fall under the craft of cavalry-riding, and this and every other military action fall under the craft of strategy, and in the same way other crafts fall under still others. In all these cases, the ends of the commanding crafts are more worth choosing than all the ends under their power. For the latter are pursued for the sake of the former. (I.1 1094a10–16)

Aristotle immediately reiterates that everything he has said about ends holds good regardless of whether the ends in question are the activities themselves or the products of activities. So, for example, even though riding is an activity whose end is in itself, this end is nevertheless worth choosing for the sake of the general's end. Notice that riding is instrumentally related to its higher ends even though it has its more proximate end in itself (*contra* Ackrill 1980: 18–19). The general's end is military victory which, Aristotle tells us later, is itself worth choosing for the sake of peaceful leisure

(X.7 1177b5–12). But riding is not a constituent either of victory or of peace, even though it is an activity which has, at least in the first instance, its end in itself.

Notice that the ends in this teleological hierarchy are not just any result of the activities leading to them. A proper end is the result which structures a body of craft-knowledge and guides its implementation. As we said before, this is not simply a psychological point. Although the general will want bridles because they help him achieve the victory he desires, there is no reason to think that this is so for the bridle maker. The bridle maker could conceivably be a slave or a citizen of the enemy state who cannot hope for any good from the general's success. He may be motivated by money. Nevertheless, victory is the ulterior end and good of bridle-making because it, rather than for example money, plays the normative role of an end in the bridle-maker's craft. Bridle-makers cut leather in a particular way because they aim to make a bridle, but bridles are in turn made the way they are because they are useful for horseback riding. And, presumably, the particular techniques of riding in battle take their character from the goal of military victory. (Aristotle makes this general point at *Physics* II.2 194a36–194b7.) Ultimately, then, bridles (of this sort) are the way they are because bridles (of this sort) are tools for riding in battle for the sake of military victory. That is the sort of thing these bridles are. In other words, genuine ends determine the standard of success for the things leading to them. This is why ultimate ends and the craftsmen who make them have authority (I.2 1094a26–7).

Finally – and this is Aristotle's principal point in this first chapter of the *NE* – things leading to the end are chosen and are worth choosing for the sake of the end and the end is more worth choosing than all the things leading to it. When he says that the end is *more* worth choosing, he does not mean that our desire for it is or ought to be more intense. He is instead drawing a conclusion from the logic of the "for the sake of" relation. Craft products are worth choosing for the sake of their end because they were made to be for its sake. This is what, essentially, they are for. (The same point holds for Aristotle's natural teleology as well. The *telos* of a plant's roots is to absorb food and this function determines the roots' nature or form.) Thus craft products are worth choosing as the particular kinds of thing they are only on the condition that their end is valuable too. (This seems to be what Aristotle means when he says later that the highest good is "the source (*archê*) and cause (*aition*) of goods" (I.12 1102a3–4).) From this point of view, the end is not more worth choosing merely in the sense of being preferable in a conflict, for if having the instrument did conflict with achieving the end, then on that occasion the instrument would not be valuable at all.

The Good as a Convergent End

In any chain of ends, the value of the end gives value to things leading to it. But a consequence of this is that the value of subordinate goods is only conditional. They are actually worth choosing only if the end to which they lead is actually good. Thus bridles really are worth choosing only if riding really is good; and its value depends on whether victory really is good, which in turn depends on the value of peace which depends on the value of . . . The upshot of it is that unless a chain of ends reaches an end that is not worth choosing for its contribution to some further goal but is, rather, sufficient of itself for its own value, none of the subordinate goods will actually be worth wanting. Aristotle puts this point in a rather poetic way: "we do not choose everything for the sake of something else, for if we did, it would go on to infinity, so that desire would be empty and frivolous" (I.2 1094a19–21). Thus, by the middle of *NE* I.2 Aristotle has described the teleological status of the highest good. It must be something worth choosing for itself alone and an end for the sake of which everything else we do is worth choosing (I.2 1094a18–19). He will go on in *NE* I.7 to derive two criteria for identifying the good conceived in this way – finality and self-sufficiency. But before we turn to that discussion we should reflect on how far we have, and how far we have not, come.

Just because all chains of desire must terminate somewhere does not imply that there is just one ultimate goal where all desire rests. (From the fact that everybody has a mother it does not follow that there is some one woman who is the mother of everyone. Likewise, it does not follow from the fact that every chain of ends terminates somewhere that there is some one good where all chains terminate.) Nevertheless, Aristotle writes from this point forward as if there is a single, convergent end. "Since every knowledge and decision aims at some good, what is the highest of all the goods achievable by action, the one at which we say the political art aims?" (I.4 1095a14–17). In fact the assumption that there is a single highest good seems already to have been in play in the first lines of the *Nicomachean Ethics*. If we assume Aristotle thinks he has demonstrated the existence of some one good that is the goal of all rational activity, then his argument is a failure. But he does not appear to be giving an argument for the existence of the good. He seems, rather, to be entering a discussion in which everyone already assumes that the good exists and arguing that we ought to agree with those who conceive of this good as an ultimate end.

One wonders who these people were. We can imagine people thinking that there must be some common account of the property of goodness that is the goal of all rational deliberation and action. However, as we have already seen, Aristotle believes that positing a univocal account of goodness involves a metaphysical mistake. (This was one of Plato's mistakes in positing the form of the Good.) But once one gives up the idea that there is a single property of goodness, it is not clear why one would assume that there is a single good at which all rational activity aims.

This is an important issue and it is one Aristotle does not address directly. In these first pages he seems to be influenced by his conception of politics as the art that governs other crafts in the *polis*. Since, he thinks, it is the master craft that directs all the rest, including the most esteemed, its end must be the best, the human good (I.2 1094a26–b7). Clearly, our confidence in this argument will depend on whether we agree with Aristotle that politics is a mastercraft of this all-encompassing sort. We can glimpse a different sort of rationale in the function argument. If the human function is our characteristic activity, if, that is to say, it is definitive of human being, then it is reasonable to suppose that the human function, and thus the human good, is in some way unified. (Otherwise human nature would not be unified.) In the *Eudemian Ethics* he suggests that it is simply foolish not to organize one's life with a view to a single end, as if there were pragmatic reasons for doing so (I.2 1214b10–11). Perhaps he thinks that the unity of our life depends on its having a single focus. But whether this is true or why it is important to keep one's life unified are not questions he answers.

Notice that Aristotle's assumption that all our chains of ends converge on a single good is considerably less surprising if this ultimate good turns out really to be just the set of all terminal ends. In that case, the appearance would be somewhat misleading that in his view all human activity aims at a single good. For this single good would not have any character over and above the individual constituent ends. In fact, this is an important interpretation of Aristotle's theory of happiness, as we will soon see.

The Meaning of *"Eudaimonia"*

Aristotle thinks we can all agree what to call the highest human good: it is *eudaimonia*, happiness (I.4 1095a14–20). But as for what happiness is, people disagree vehemently and sometimes even contradict themselves at different times of life.

> The many think it is something palpable and obvious, for example pleasure or wealth or honor. Some think it's one thing and others think its another – and often the same person thinks it's different things. When he is sick he thinks *eudaimonia* is health, but when he is poor he thinks it is wealth. (I.4 1095a22–5)

It is well-known that "happiness" can be a misleading translation of *eudaimonia* and this passage shows why. The goods mentioned here may cause us, as we say, to feel happy, but it is hard to see how they could be what happiness itself is.

In English the most common meaning of "happiness" is a certain feeling of either contentment or euphoria. *Eudaimonia* does not mean that. The point is not that it is nonsensical to say that *eudaimonia* is pleasure. A hedonist would make this very claim and Aristotle himself argues that one particular pleasant activity – excellent rational action – is the best. Rather, the point is that this is a claim for which one must argue. Just on its own, *eudaimonia* does not refer to a feeling.

For this reason, people sometimes prefer to translate *eudaimonia* as "flourishing." This leaves open the question of how important pleasure is in the human good (presumably flourishing for trees has nothing to do with pleasure at all). It also has the advantage of capturing (1) the objectivity of *eudaimonia* – both flourishing and *eudaimonia* are things people can easily believe they have when in fact they do not – and (2) the fact that judgments of *eudaimonia* refer to fairly significant periods of time – no one can be *eudaimôn* or flourish for just a short time or vacillate rapidly between these conditions and wretchedness (*NE* I.10). However "flourishing" is, I think, too organic or biological a notion to be a good translation. Aristotle thinks that animals can flourish, but they cannot be *eudaimôn* (I.9 1099b32–1100a3; X.8 1178b24–8). Indeed, the only living things other than adult human beings that can be *eudaimôn* are the gods; *eudaimonia* has connotations of blessedness. True, Aristotle ultimately claims that *eudaimonia* is excellent human functioning, but this is a position for which he must argue. It is not suggested to him by the very meaning of the word *eudaimonia*. In Aristotle's view, human beings are distinguished from the rest of the natural world by the fact that their flourishing is a matter of being *eudaimôn*.

Perhaps the most accurate and intuitive translation of *eudaimonia* would be "success." The *eudaimôn* person is like an Olympic victor (I.8 1099a3–7); his life is successful and, as we and Aristotle might say, well worth living. There is the further advantage that the popular theories of *eudaimonia* Aristotle canvases – pleasure, wealth, honor, excellent public service – are familiar answers to the question, what is success? But if we think of *eudaimonia* as success, we must be clear that it is success that applies to life as a whole. We must also be clear that what counts as success is an objective matter and does not depend on what our society happens to admire. Since this is an old-fashioned but not altogether alien sense of the word "happiness," and since "success" may strike some readers as being vulgar, we should stick with the traditional translation of *eudaimonia*, "happiness."

Happiness vs. the Happy Life

There is another confusion about the meaning of *eudaimonia* we should be careful to avoid. Aristotle says that living well and doing well are equivalent to happiness (I.4 1095a19–20). This may lead us to suppose that "happiness" and "the happy life" are interchangeable translations of *eudaimonia*. But it is important to be clear that *eudaimonia* is not equivalent to the happy life as we ordinarily use that term. By "happy life" we usually mean everything involved in the happy person's day to day activity, the sort of thing that might be plotted in a "life plan" or recounted in a biography. Suppose a person thought that happiness was a flourishing family-life. Then if he were to be happy, he would need to have a flourishing family. But since it is hard to imagine a family doing well without a house, the happy person would need to have a house, too. And so he would need cleaning supplies. On this view of happiness, the life story of the happy person makes reference not only to his family, but also to a house and cleaning supplies, so we might say that the happy life includes them all. But a happy life in this sense – that is, everything involved in the happy person's day to day activity – is clearly not the same thing as the flourishing family-life that is the focus and raison d'etre of all these other goods. This goal and organizing principle of the happy life is what Aristotle calls *eudaimonia*.

The distinction between happiness and the happy life seems not to be peculiar to Aristotle. As we saw, he reports popular opinion as admiring the life of pleasure and refined men of action as admiring the life of honor. Pleasure and honor are not the only constituents of these lives; they are their focus. But although the distinction between happiness and the happy life ought to be obvious, Aristotle thinks a failure to draw it is at the root of many disputes about the good (*EE* I.2 1214b24–6). In the *Eudemian Ethics* he warns us not to confuse the indispensable conditions of happiness with happiness itself:

> For the things without which we cannot be healthy [e.g., breathing, eating meat, and walking after dinner, I.2 1214b20–4] are not the same as being healthy and the same thing holds for many other things. The result is that living finely is not the same as the things without which it is impossible to live finely. (I.2 1214b14–17)

It is unlikely that anyone would include basic necessities, such as breathing and food, in their account of happiness. These after all are prerequisites for any life whatsoever, happy or miserable. We are liable to be confused, however, by those features of a happy life that are peculiar to it (life as such does not require them but the happy life does) but that are nevertheless not its focus. For example, if a person devotes himself to public service as the highest good and if he is successful in achieving it, he will receive honor. For (according to Aristotle) honor is the customary and appropriate response of a city to its benefactors. But although the happy political life includes honor, that does not imply that the happy person devotes himself to the pursuit of honor as the good which makes life worth choosing. Precisely because honor is typical of the happy political life, however, people can be confused into thinking that honor is the highest good. Aristotle is explicit that these subordinate parts of the happy life must not be conflated with happiness itself (I.2 1214b15–28). Happiness is the good which, once we have it, makes our lives successful, but it does not include everything we need to make that good our own, not even if it is characteristic of the happy person to have it.

The Finality Criterion

When we insist that *eudaimonia* is that good which is the focus or goal of the happy life, we are only spelling out Aristotle's starting point, that the good is that at which all rational activity aims. The question now is, what good thing is this? Aristotle's initial assumption that the good is an ultimate end bears fruit as soon as he begins to examine the common opinions. For instance, if the political life is happy then neither honor nor moral virtue can be the highest good, for neither of these goods is sufficiently ultimate. Public men who are worth their salt show by their behavior that they think virtue is better than honor; they want to be honored for virtue and by people with sense (I.5 1095b26–30). That is to say, they want honor for the sake of virtue, not virtue for the sake of honor. However, virtue, in turn, is brought to fulfillment in action under favorable circumstances. Thus simply on its own, virtue (the disposition) too is rather imperfect (*atelestera*, I.5 1095b32). Finally, he argues that wealth cannot be the good since it is worth having as a tool for doing other things (I.5 1096a6–7).

Notice that although some of the goods ruled out by Aristotle are purely instrumental (e.g. wealth), others are in fact desired for themselves (e.g., honor, virtue, and pleasure). The fact that a good can be an end worth choosing for itself and yet insufficiently ultimate to be the highest good leads him to elaborate his notion of finality more fully:

> We say that something pursued for itself is more final than something chosen because of something else; and something never chosen because of another thing is more final than things chosen for themselves and because of it; and something always chosen for itself and never because of another thing we call final in an absolute sense. (I.7 1097a30–4)

As it turns out, happiness meets the criterion of being most final. Honor, pleasure, virtue, and presumably all other goods worth choosing for themselves are also worth choosing on account of happiness while happiness, in turn, is worth choosing for itself alone (I.7 1097b1–6).

The passage quoted above has been the subject of substantial scholarly debate. The debate often manifests itself as a dispute about whether to translate *teleion* as "final," "perfect," or "complete," but the point at issue is how to understand the relationship between happiness and the other intrinsically good things Aristotle mentions. Are honor, virtue, and other middle-level ends worth choosing for the sake of happiness in the sense that they are constituents of happiness? If so, perhaps we should understand *teleion* to mean "having all its proper parts" – this is after all a sense of the word Aristotle recognizes (*Metaphysics* Δ.16 1021b12–13). In that case we should translate it as "complete." Happiness would be the most complete good because it includes all other intrinsically valuable goods as parts. (Hence, this has been called the *inclusivist* interpretation.) Or, on the other hand, does Aristotle believe that happiness is some monistic good distinct from all the middle-level ends chosen for its sake? (This is sometimes called the *dominant-end* view, on the grounds that it describes the highest good as dominating over all others.) In that case, we may prefer to translate *teleion* as "perfect," meaning "lacking nothing in respect of its proper excellence" (*Met* Δ.16 1021b14–17) or the more literal "final," meaning "possessing its end or *telos*" (*Met* Δ.16 1021b23–5). These, too, are senses of the word Aristotle recognizes.

The question we need to ask ourselves in reading this passage is what kind of perfection Aristotle has in mind in the particular case of the good. Since we see that he explicates the notion in terms of whether or not a good is worth choosing for the sake of something else, he evidently means that the highest good is perfect *in the sense of* being absolutely ultimate as an end. In itself it completely achieves its own end. Subordinate goods, on the other hand, are less *teleion* because, even though they are ends for the things leading to them, they also are worth choosing for an end beyond themselves. They are ends that, just in themselves, do not fully provide the good that makes them worth pursuing. So when Aristotle argues that happiness is most *teleion*, his point is merely that it is the good to which all other goods are teleologically subordinated. He leaves open whether some of them are worth choosing as constituents of happiness, as instrumental means to happiness, or indeed in any other way a thing may be chosen for the sake of something else.

The Self-sufficiency Criterion

It may seem that Aristotle closes the door on this question immediately when he argues, in the following passage, that the highest good, happiness, is self-sufficient (*autarkes*). In order to be self-sufficient a good must "on its own make life worth choosing and lacking nothing" (I.7 1097b14–15). How could a good make a life lack nothing unless it contained all intrinsically good things?

If we take this inclusivist interpretation literally, self-sufficiency becomes an unreasonable constraint on an account of happiness, since it implies that no one can be happy unless he has all, or at least an example of every kind of, the intrinsically good things there are. If a person fails to acquire some good thing he (reasonably) desires, he cannot be happy. Since such failure is inevitable for the finite beings we are and yet

Aristotle believes happiness is achievable by human action, it is charitable to look for another interpretation.

More important from the point of view of our current discussion, however, we should notice that Aristotle derives the self-sufficiency criterion from the fact that the good is an ultimate end: "The same result [viz., that happiness is the human good] seems to follow from self-sufficiency, too. For the final good seems to be self-sufficient" (I.7 1097b6–8). And his discussion concludes, "Happiness seems to be something final and self-sufficient because it is the end of practicable goods" (I.7 1097b20–1). The first step in understanding what the self-sufficiency criterion requires is understanding why in Aristotle's view it is so obviously a characteristic of an ultimate end.

Recall the argument in *NE* I.2 for why there must be some ultimate end at all. Unless there is an end that we wish for on account of itself, our activity of choosing one thing for the sake of another will continue infinitely "with the result that desire is empty and frivolous" (I.2 1094a21). Any end not only makes the things leading to it worth choosing, it also satisfies to some degree the rational desire that caused us to choose those subordinate ends in the first place. So for example, when we have finally completed building a house, the house satisfies the desires we had for laying a foundation, building saw horses, and so forth. Of course it does not satisfy these desires by including all those intermediate ends; it does so by being the object we wanted to achieve through them. Notice, though, the desire that led us to build a house is not really fully satisfied even once we have the house. For houses are worth choosing for the sake of the life we can live in them. When an end is ultimate, on the other hand, it fills rational desire completely. Since we want such a good for itself and not as a means to something else, there is no further objective left to want. This, then, is a (more modest) sense in which a most final end leaves us lacking nothing. It is also a conception of self-sufficiency that makes it derive from the finality of the highest good, as Aristotle says it should. It is interesting to notice, then, that this is precisely the sort of self-sufficiency he ascribes to the human good in *NE* X.6:

> If . . . among activities, some are necessary and worth choosing on account of other things while others are worth choosing for themselves, it's clear we must suppose that happiness is one of those worth choosing for themselves and not one of those worth choosing on account of another. For happiness lacks nothing but is self-sufficient. (X.6 1176a35–b6).

Inclusivism

The interpretations of finality and self-sufficiency for which I have argued do not preclude an inclusivist interpretation of *eudaimonia*. For all Aristotle has said, the good which is most final and self-sufficient as an end may turn out to be the sum of honor, pleasure, virtue, and other intrinsically valuable goods taken together. But the mere fact that the highest good is final and self-sufficient does not tell in favor of inclusivism, either. This point is important because the textual evidence of Book I strongly suggests that Aristotle has in mind a monistic conception of *eudaimonia*. So, for instance, he asks at I.4 1095a16–17, "what is the highest of all the goods achievable by action?" The common opinions he canvases – honor, pleasure, virtue, and wealth – are all monistic goods. As we have seen, Aristotle does not criticize these accounts for including too little but for being insufficiently final. When he offers his own substantive account of happiness, he says that "the human good is activity of the soul in accordance with virtue, and if there are many virtues, in accordance with the best and most *teleia*" (I.7 1098a16–18).[2] The close proximity of his discussion of the finality criterion suggests that the most *teleia* virtue is the most final virtue, i.e. the virtue whose exercise is most worth choosing for itself alone.

Scholars who advocate inclusivism reject this interpretation of "the most *teleia* virtue" on the grounds that in a similar passage in the *Eudemian Ethics* Aristotle is explicit that the most *teleia* virtue is the virtue that includes all its parts (II.1 1219a35–9). Now I am inclined to think that here, in the *Nicomachean Ethics*, by the most *teleia* virtue he means to refer to the one virtue whose activity is most final. A bit later he writes that "virtuous activities, or rather the best one (*mian*) of these" is happiness (*NE* I.8 1099a29–31). This interpretation also has the advantage of cohering with his argument in *NE* X.7 that activity of theoretical virtue is perfect happiness because it is more final than the activity of practical virtue. But even if we adopt the *Eudemian* reading for the *Nicomachean* claim that happiness is the activity of *teleia* virtue, it still will be the case that *eudaimonia* is not completely inclusive. For there will be intrinsic goods, such as honor, that are not among its parts. It is true that happiness "seems to need external goods in addition" (I.8 1099a31–2; cf. I.8 1099b4–5), but here we should recall Aristotle's warning not to confuse the goods necessary for happiness with happiness itself.

Textual evidence notwithstanding, inclusivist interpretations are attractive because they easily capture an important intuition about the place in the happy life of intrinsically valuable goods other than happiness. We tend to suppose that the happy life will include some measure of honor, pleasure, and virtue (the disposition of character rather than its realization in action) because these things are good in themselves. We do not value them only or even primarily for their consequences. Now if we assume that happiness includes all intrinsically valuable goods, then when the happy person seeks, say, pleasure for the sake of happiness, that "does not imply that pleasure is not intrinsically worthwhile but only a means to an end. It implies rather that pleasure *is* intrinsically worthwhile, being an element of *eudaimonia*. *Eudaimonia* is the most desirable sort of life, the life that contains all intrinsically worthwhile activities" (so writes John Ackrill (1980: 21), one of the most influential exponents of this interpretation). In other words, inclusivism gets intrinsically valuable goods into the happy life for the right reason, their intrinsic value. Monistic or dominant-end interpretations, on the other hand, seem to make the counter-intuitive suggestion that insofar as the happy person cares about being happy, he pursues these subordinate goods only for their instrumental value.

This philosophical motivation for inclusivism is powerful. However it is important to see that inclusivist interpretations have a significant philosophical cost. It is a cost we are well-placed to understand now that we have a clearer understanding of what Aristotle means by saying that the highest good is an ultimate end. Leave aside for the time being that happiness comes close to being conflated with the happy life in this view. (Inclusivist interpretations can and should keep these notions distinct, but I think they gain rhetorical power from the fact that often, in their formulation, they do not.) At least in some versions (and Ackrill's seems to be one of them), happiness is conceived simply as the sum total of all intrinsically valuable goods, whatever they may happen to be. There is no substantive character to *eudaimonia* knowable in advance of knowing its constituents. But a set like this cannot be an end in an Aristotelian sense.

There is nothing incorrect in itself in the inclusivist assumption that choosing something as a constituent part of a good thing is a way of acting for the sake of an end in Aristotle's sense. It is true that all the examples he gives in *NE* I.1 of choosing one thing for the sake of another are examples of choosing something as an instrument for the production of an independent good, but presumably he uses these examples because they show especially clearly the way that ends are "naturally better" than the things leading to them. We know from his biological works that bodily organs are for the sake of the living body they constitute and presumably he would want to say that flour is worth choosing for the sake of a cake. So in itself, this expansion of Aristotle's practical teleology seems acceptable. But notice that in these cases of constitution the end plays the normative functions of an end that we saw at work in Aristotle's instrumental examples. So for instance, it is because we aim to make a cake (rather than bread) that we choose cake flour. And the flour is good of its kind to the extent that it has the characteristics requisite for forming the batter of a good cake. Even though we choose flour as a constituent of the cake (or perhaps of the batter), the cake sets the standards of success for the flour and is its source of value. The sum of all things worth choosing for themselves cannot play this role, however, since its specific character depends on its constituents. It cannot determine what makes an honor, for example, a good honor nor can it explain why honor is in general something worth choosing. It cannot even tell us which constituents of happiness are more important than others. The most it can do is direct us not to choose one sort of intrinsic good at the expense of another. That is to say, it could function as a sort of side constraint on our pursuit of the constituents. But this role is far more limited than the one Aristotle describes. Happiness conceived in the standard inclusivist way is not "the source and cause of goods" (I.12 1102a2–4).

The Shape of the Happy Life

The picture of the happy life that has emerged is one in which all the agent's pursuit of various goods is aimed ultimately at some single kind of good activity. (What counts as a *single* kind is an important issue, but I will leave it aside here.) This highest good is conceptually independent of the things leading to it, including those subordinate goods that are also worth choosing for themselves. Middle-level ends, such as honor and pleasure, may be worth choosing for themselves, but their place in the happy life as such is to be explained by the fact that they are worth choosing for the sake of the highest good.

The happy life so described has an austere cast, but is it in addition a life of monomaniacal obsession? The charge of obsession depends, I suspect, on limiting our attention to the instrumental "for the sake of" relation. Since the value of instruments is in their ability to bring the end into being, they are no longer worth having once the end in question has been achieved. So if the only way subordinate goods were worth choosing for the sake of happiness was as instruments, then we would have no choice but to view the happy person as pursuing subordinate goods as necessary but dispensable steps towards the single best activity. On this interpretation lower goods might in fact have a permanent place in the happy life, but that would be only because our grip on the good is inconstant and imperfect.

However, there is good reason to believe that choosing something as an instrument is not the only way of acting for the good. In *NE* I.8 he marks out two reasons we need external goods. They are tools for virtuous action. But he also claims that being deprived of certain goods (he mentions good family, good children, and good looks) "disfigures blessedness" (I.8 1099b2). The implication is that we need these goods because they somehow ornament happiness. Later he says that many strokes of great good fortune "help to adorn" the virtuous life (I.10 1100b25–8). Now some of these goods, such as coming from a good family, are beyond our power to choose. But where it is in our power to pursue them, it seems reasonable to say that they are worth choosing for the sake of happiness in a non-instrumental way.

It is not at all clear why Aristotle thinks it so important to beautify the virtuous actions which constitute the human good. One possibility is that ornaments call to the agent's attention and celebrate his possession of the good. This does not increase the amount of the good that he has, but it helps him to delight in it and remain aware that he has achieved the good whose end is entirely in itself. Since rational creatures cannot possess the good unless they know that they do, the function of ornaments in the good life is potentially quite an important one. Perhaps this is the sort of rationale Aristotle has in mind. If so, notice that the highest good functions as a *telos* for our choice of ornaments to beautify it. It is a source of value for the ornament – because the best activity of virtue is good it is good to beautify it – and it determines what the ornament should be like – the ornament must fit the virtue in question or it will not be successful as an ornament.

In the *Nicomachean Ethics* Aristotle explicates his notion of an end by appeal to craft examples. But we should not infer from this that choosing something as an instrument is the only way of acting for an end. Not only is constitution a teleological relation, but so too, in appropriate circumstances, is ornamentation. Furthermore, in his scientific works he appears to claim that a certain variety of *mimesis* is a way of being oriented to a goal (Lear 2004: 72–84). What this shows is that a life clearly focused on a so-called dominant-end need not be devoted obsessively to *maximizing* that end. At least in principle it can involve a range of pursuits that make the highest good their focus in a non-instrumental way. Of course, the happy person will need to decide when to promote the good directly and when to act for its sake in other ways. But making that decision is the job of practical wisdom and will, presumably, depend on the circumstances. It cannot be decided in advance by an abstract account of happiness such as Aristotle gives us.

Concluding Remarks

Let us recall where we have come so far. Aristotle begins by proposing that the human good is an ultimate end. He infers from this conception that the end, happiness, must be final and self-sufficient. Since our rational human function is an ultimate end we have by nature whose excellent performance makes us good of our kind, Aristotle argues that the highest good is some sort of excellent or virtuous activity of reason. So, since the good turns out to be happiness and happiness is virtuous activity, it is reasonable to expect that this is the end we must keep in view as we deliberate.

Sometimes Aristotle's discussion seems to bear this expectation out. For instance, he says in Book VI that the practically wise person is expert at deliberating towards the end of living well, *eu zên* (VI.5 1140a28) and doing well, *eupraxia.* (VI.5 1140b7). These are synonyms for *eudaimonia* (I.4 1095a18–20). However, there are difficulties. In the first place, it is not clear how to square the idea that virtuous activity is the deliberative goal with his frequent description of the virtuous person as acting for the sake of the fine, *kalon* (III.6-IV.7 *passim*). Worse, it is hard to understand how virtuous activity itself *could* function as a deliberative goal, particularly if we assume that the virtuous activity in question is moral action (something the *NE* VI passage suggests). The aspiration to act virtuously in general seems too vague to determine, for example, whether in some particular situation it would be more generous to buy your friend a plane ticket or to give her the money directly. (The example and the worry come from Broadie 1991:227, 232–242 *passim*.) Finally, even if we can resolve this problem, there is the problem of Book X. For in the concluding chapters of the *Nicomachean Ethics* Aristotle argues that theoretical contemplation is perfectly final (*teleia*) happiness (X.7 1177b24). This, rather than morally virtuous action, seems to be the end for the sake of which we should "do everything" (X.7 1177b33–4). That seems to contradict the earlier implication that the wise person acts for the sake of fine actions.

It lies well beyond the task of this paper to suggest whether and how the final Book of the *Nicomachean Ethics* might be interpreted as consistent with the preceding Books. Still, there are two reasons I believe we should treat the unity of the *NE*, and in particular of Books I and X, as a working hypothesis. We should do so despite the fact that it, like all Aristotle's works, shows signs of having been cobbled together by someone, we know not who. First, *NE* X.6–8 argues for a substantive account of happiness in precisely the way we would expect given the discussion in Book I. So, for instance, Aristotle reminds us that happiness is an end (X.6 1176a30–2) that is ultimate and self-sufficient (X.6 1176b1–7); these are the criteria established before. He then uses these criteria to argue against pleasure and morally virtuous action and in favor of theoretical contemplation; these are the goods Aristotle mentions in Book I as the most plausible candidates for being the good. He also reminds us that happiness is the activity of our proper virtue (X.7 1177a16–17). He then goes on to argue that *nous*, whose activity is contemplation, is the most authoritative part of ourselves and so that contemplation is the most perfect expression of our human nature (X.7 1177b31–1178a7).

Second, the end of the *Eudemian Ethics* contains a similar surprise about the nature of happiness, but the surprise is not an inconsistency. Book I of the *EE* advises us to choose some good to be the target of all our choices (I.2 1214b10–11). It also treats happiness as the activity of the whole of virtue (II.1 1219a35–9). So we might expect, given the tenor of the *EE*, that the proper target of the happy life would be the combination of all virtuous activities, including especially morally virtuous ones. But in the last

Book of the *EE* Aristotle advises us to make all our choices by reference to their ability to promote the contemplation of god (VII.15 1249b16–19). This is not strictly speaking inconsistent with what he said before, but it is clear that commentators have felt it to be a surprise standing in need of explanation. The fact that in both the *NE* and the *EE* there appears to be a shift from the importance of moral action to the dominance of contemplation suggests that this represents a genuine feature of Aristotle's thought and is not simply the effect of poor editorial work by later generations.

Myles Burnyeat has argued that we should think of the Aristotelian corpus as being "an evolving system." "The surviving treatises, unlike the 'exoteric' works he sent to the booksellers, remained with him, always available for additions, subtractions, and other forms of revision" (2004: 179). (He finds evidence of this revision in the many "blank" cross-references found throughout the corpus.) If Burnyeat is right, then we should expect to find inconsistencies in the *Nicomachean Ethics* – either because Aristotle didn't notice the incompatibility of an addition to the text or, more interesting, because he had not yet decided which formulation was best. But we should also assume that, like any work in progress, the *NE* has as its goal a coherent and unified account of its subject matter, the human good. It is reasonable, then, to work to see whether some inconsistencies are only apparent. If a unifying interpretation makes good philosophical and textual sense, then our uncertainty about how the *NE* was composed should not stand in the way of our accepting, at least tentatively, that it is correct.

Readers are often disappointed that Aristotle ends up praising "his own" philosophical life, but we may also be disappointed that he gives serious consideration only to the voluptuary's life, the political life, and the philosophical life. Why so narrow a range of options? What about the life of artistic creativity or the life devoted to the worship of god? Might not the ends of these lives or of still others also meet the criteria of being a final and self-sufficient end?

In *NE* I.4 Aristotle warns that it is a waste of time to survey all the accounts of happiness that have ever been given. It is sufficient just to examine the most prevalent opinions and the ones that strike us as reasonable (I.4 1095a28–30). He does not explain why a more exhaustive investigation would be frivolous. Elsewhere, he suggests that reconciling philosophical theories to reputable opinions is warranted by the fact that all human beings, presumably by virtue of their rational nature, tend to hit on the truth to some degree or other (X.2 1172b36–1173a2; cf. *Rhetoric* I.1 1355a15–18). But that is not what he says here. On the contrary, he suggests that unless we have been brought up well, our sense of the reasonable will be so skewed as to make us unfit for practical philosophy (I.4 1095b4–6).

His method is sensible nevertheless. Remember that Aristotle thinks we do and ought to investigate the human good for practical reasons; we want to create happiness for ourselves and for others. From this point of view, understanding the flaws in every conceivable view of the good life is simply unnecessary. It is the most widespread views of happiness and the ones that seem attractive to us that we should examine since these are the ones most likely to affect the way we conduct our lives. Of course, if we discover that none of these opinions is correct then it will make sense to cast our net more widely. But that is not where we should begin. It is a consequence of this method, however, that the *Nicomachean Ethics* leaves unexplored conceptions of happiness that are widespread and plausible for us. A true measure of the power of his theory that the human good is an ultimate end, then, will be its ability to make sense of the sorts of life we ourselves are inclined to consider happy. As Aristotle himself reminds us,

> In practical matters truth is judged on the basis of facts (*ergôn*) and life, for in these matters they are authoritative. So it is necessary to examine what has been said [here] by bringing it to bear on facts and life, and if it harmonizes with the facts we should accept it; but if it is dissonant, we should suppose it to be mere words. (X.8 1179a18–22)

Notes

[1] This point should not be overstated, however. Aristotle is ready to accept that my munching potato chips may be caused by nothing more than an appetitive desire for pleasant food and an awareness that chips are pleasant, absent any judgment of good. Nevertheless, the fact that I am capable in general of being moved appetitively does have a teleological explanation culminating eventually in the way such behavior subserves specifically human, rational activity.

[2] *Teleia* is the feminine form of *teleion*, agreeing with *arête* meaning "virtue."

Bibliography

Ackrill, J. [1974] (1980). "Aristotle on *eudaimonia*," in A. O. Rorty (ed.), *Essays on Aristotle's Ethics* (Berkeley, CA: University of California Press), pp. 15–33; originally in *Proceedings of the British Academy*, 60 (1974).

Barney, R. (2007). "The Carpenter and the Good," in D. Cairns, F.-G. Hermann, and T. Penner (eds.), *Pursuing the Good: Ethics and Metaphysics in Plato's "Republic"* (Edinburgh: Edinburgh University Press), pp. 293–319.

Broadie, S. (1991). *Ethics with Aristotle* (Oxford: Oxford University Press).

Burnyeat, M. F. (2004). "Aristotelian Revisions: The Case of *De Sensu*," *Apeiron*, 37, pp. 177–80.

Cooper, J. M. (2004). "Plato and Aristotle on 'Finality' and '(Self-)sufficiency'," in *Knowledge, Nature, and the Good* (Princeton, NJ: Princeton University Press), pp. 270–308.

Heinaman, R. (1988). "Eudaimonia and Self-sufficiency in the *Nicomachean Ethics*," *Phronesis*, 33, pp. 31–53.

Irwin, T. (1985). "Permanent Happiness: Aristotle and Solon," *Oxford Studies in Ancient Philosophy*, 3, pp. 89–124.

Kullman, W. (1985). "Different Concepts of the Final Cause in Aristotle," in A. Gotthelf (ed.), *Aristotle on Nature and Living Things: Philosophical and Historical Studies* (Pittsburgh, PA: Mathesis), pp. 169–75.

Lawrence, G. (1993). "Aristotle and the Ideal Life," *Philosophical Review*, 102, pp. 1–34.

Lear, G. R. (2004). *Happy Lives and the Highest Good: An Essay on Aristotle's "Nicomachean Ethics"* (Princeton, NJ: Princeton University Press).

Richardson, H. (1992). "Degrees of Finality and the Highest Good in Aristotle," *Journal of the History of Philosophy*, 30, pp. 327–51.

25

Pleasure

GEORGE RUDEBUSCH

It doesn't work well to define pleasure as a perceived process; better to call it a *complete act* of the condition according to one's nature; and instead of "perceived," *unimpeded*.

NE VII.12 1153a13–15

Introduction

Conventional wisdom and many moral philosophers distinguish the *noblest* acts of human beings from the *pleasantest*, such that these acts can often be at odds with each other. In contrast, Aristotle's *Nicomachean Ethics* gives us a grand theory of human happiness that denies such a distinction (*NE* I.8 1099a21–32; likewise *EE* I.1 1214a1–8. All translations below are my own). The key to his grand unification is his theory of pleasure as the perfection of human nature in its acts.

Aristotle's writings on pleasures and acts, which often seem mere lecture notes, are scattered throughout his work. The interpreter is presented with a number of dots, as it were, which may be completed according to several possible patterns. Excellent interpretation is faithful and charitable. The task is to find the loveliest pattern that fits the dots.

The interpretation I give in this chapter tries to be faithful to Aristotle's texts and present a single consistent and defensible theory of pleasure that supports his grand moral theory unifying the noble and the pleasant as the identical best life for human beings. Though I do not discuss alternative interpretations in detail, I take any alternative interpretation to be inferior if it emends the text, finds multiple inconsistent theories, finds an indefensible theory of pleasure, or finds a theory that does not support the grand unifying project of Aristotle's ethics. I defend Aristotle's assumption that a single theory of pleasure is appropriate for the different kinds of pleasures human beings enjoy. Next, I defend his refutation of restorative accounts of pleasure, which are the only rivals to his theory. Finally, I give an interpretation of his positive account of pleasure in terms of the degrees of completion that human and divine acts can have.

Should We Look for a Unified Theory of Pleasure?

There seem to be two different kinds of pleasure. *Modal* pleasures are activities that are done or happen *in a certain way*, while *sensate* pleasures are feelings or *sensations.* Ryle's (1949: 108) famous golfing example illustrates the difference.

> Doubtless the absorbed golfer experiences numerous flutters and glows of rapture, excitement and self-approbation in the course of his game. But when asked whether or not he had enjoyed the periods of the game between the occurrences of such feelings, he would obviously reply that he had, for he had enjoyed the whole game.

Here the "whole game" is a modal pleasure; the "numerous flutters and glows" are sensate pleasures. In light of this difference in the *phenomena* of pleasure, some philosophers and psychologists since Ryle think it a mistake to look, as Aristotle does, for a single underlying *theory* of pleasure. But Aristotle is justified in his attempt at theoretical unity: modal and sensate pleasure share an organic structure. Both pleasures are reduced by depression (which appears related to neurochemical imbalances) and both are restored to the same extent by drug therapy (see Warburton 1996: 3).

The Phenomenon of Sensate Pleasure and the Restoration Theory

In fact most pleasure theorists treat sensate pleasure as a more basic phenomenon than modal pleasures.[1] There seems good reason to take sensate pleasure as the most basic pleasure to explain. It is common practice in psychology to use a scale rating experiences such as odors from 1 to 9, from "very, very unpleasant" to "neutral" to "very, very pleasant." People have no difficulty describing the intensity of sensate pleasures and pains in these terms. And this scale yields systematic and predictable results. For example, a neutral test odor (like plain water) will be rated unpleasant when presented in alternate trials with odors that the subject rates pleasant.[2]

When theorists take sensate pleasure as the basic phenomenon, they are likely to follow Plato's explanation of pleasure. According to that explanation, living organisms are a system of elements in balance. When the natural balance is destroyed, there is pain, such as overheating; as the natural balance is restored, there is the pleasure of restoring by cooling off. But restoring is pleasant only if it happens perceptibly. While there is variation in the terminology for restoration – "tension reduction," "successful striving," "achieving homeostasis" – these theories follow Plato's account that sensate pleasure is perceived restoration.[3]

Aristotle knew Plato's account of pleasure as perceived restoration and probably accepted this account in his early writings (Gosling and Taylor (1982: 194–6) and Bravo (2003: 62–4) discuss Aristotle's Platonic influences). But he came to reject the Platonic account.

405

How Aristotle Refutes the Restoration Theory

Aristotle refutes the Restoration Theory by pointing out a categorical difference between two kinds of act,[4] a difference in the unity of act and goal. *Incomplete* (the Greek word might as well be translated as *imperfect*) acts, like house construction, are not one with their goal. They move towards but have not yet reached it. *Complete* (or *perfect*) acts, like home living, *are* their goal (*NE* VII.12 1153a9–10). Aristotle gives criteria marking the difference between complete and incomplete acts. These criteria show that restoration, far from being pleasure, is not even in the same category as pleasure.

Criterion 1: present is perfect

Because it is one with its goal, a complete act is identical with its completion. For example, as soon as you see, you have seen; and as soon as you understand you have understood. Likewise pleasure is complete: as soon as you enjoy you have enjoyed; as soon as you feel it you have felt it. In contrast, restoration is incomplete: while restoring you have not yet restored (*Met* Θ.6 1048 b22–5; *Phys* VI.1 231b28–232a1).

Criterion 2: speed

Aristotle correctly defines speed in terms of some interval of change *in* some interval of time (*Phys* II.10 218b15–17). But only in incomplete acts is there a distance to cover between start and finish (for act and goal are not one). Thus quickness, slowness, and speed in general will be features of incomplete acts only. For example, you can restore your vision quickly or slowly, but when you finally *see*, you do not see quickly, slowly, or at any speed. By this criterion, pleasure is complete, for "while it is possible to *get* pleased quickly, as one can get angry quickly, it is not possible to *be* pleased quickly" (*NE* X.3 1173a34–b1).

These criteria show both that it is wrong to define pleasure as a perceived process of restoration and that it is a complete act (*NE* VII.12 1153a9–13).

Two Objections to Aristotle's Refutation

To many interpreters, Aristotle goes too far in rejecting any restoration as pleasure (prominently Urmson 1967: 329). The most important objections fall under two headings.

1   *Absurd conclusion.* Aristotle's conclusion that to feel bodily restoration is not pleasure conflicts with the observed facts about pleasure that we all have. Such an argument can be nothing more than an intellectual curiosity, like Zeno's proofs that motion is impossible.

2   *Word play.* Aristotle's argument depends upon his distinction between complete and incomplete activity. But the distinction is mere word play. Whether an act is complete or incomplete depends upon the words we use in describing it. Consider

the act of walking. If we describe it as *walking from A to B*, then it fits the criteria for an incomplete act: if you are walking from A to B you have not yet walked from A to B, and walking from A to B must happen either quickly or slowly or at some speed. On the other hand, if we describe it as simply *walking*, then it fits the criteria for a complete act: as soon as you are walking you have walked; and the speed of walking is undefined without an A and B between which to measure time. The same word play applies to pleasure. Described as *enjoying*, an act is complete: as soon as you enjoy you have enjoyed; and you cannot enjoy quickly or slowly. But described as *enjoying a movie*, an act is incomplete: if you are enjoying a movie you have not yet enjoyed the movie; and you can enjoy the movie quickly or slowly (for example with a remote control when watching a videotape: you can go fast forward through dull parts and savor good parts frame by frame). According to this objection, Aristotle's definitive distinction between complete and incomplete acts becomes trivial word play. (The classic statement of this objection is Ackrill 1965. I elaborate the classic reply of Penner 1970.)

Actualizing Potentials and Acts of Power

Aristotle's general theory of acts saves his account of pleasure from these objections. In that general theory, Aristotle distinguishes *potentials* from *powers*, using the following sorts of examples in *Metaphysics* Θ.6. (I follow Code 2003). Bricks and mortar have the potential to change into a house; a homeless person has the potential to change into a homeowner; and one unskilled in housebuilding has the potential to change into one skilled at housebuilding. Such potentials undergo a change as they go through the act: the bricks cease to be a pile and the tub of mortar is used up; the homeless person is no longer homeless; and the one who was unskilled no longer is. Indeed, although the bricks and mortar continue to exist after the house is built, the pile and tubful do not. The *formlessness*, however one might describe it, of the bricks and mortar does not survive the change when bricks and mortar become a house. Likewise one's *homeless-ness* does not survive the change when one acquires a house; and one's *ignorance* does not survive the change when one becomes wise.

Consider now, in contrast, the following *powers*. A house has the power actually to house occupants; a homeowner has the power actually to live in a home; and a house-builder has the power actually to build. Unlike potentials, powers do not change as they act: the house remains a house as it houses occupants; the homeowner remains so while living, using, and enjoying the home; and likewise the builder while building (*An* II.4 417b8–9; *NE* VII.14 1154b26–7).

As Aristotle points out, the word "housebuilding" is ambiguous. The *builder's act of housebuilding* leaves the builder unchanged, while the *housebuilding of the house-under-construction* changes the bricks and mortar by giving them form. Although these two acts coincide, they are different in form, just as a doctor's act of doctoring and a patient's act of recovery are different in form, though coinciding. The doctoring is a causal act of a power in the doctor, while the recovery is the actualizing of a potential of a different object, the patient. The difference in form between acts of power and actualizations of potential holds true even when doctors happen to heal themselves. In such cases there is an opportunity for word play: given their coincidence in place and time, one could play with words to try to prove that *to be a doctor* is *to be a patient*, or that *to doctor* is *to recover*. This word play should not keep us from recognizing the real difference between powers and potentials, although the serious theorist ought, as Aristotle often does, take the time to sort out the fallacies of such word play (*SE* 6 168b4–1. On Aristotle's identity conditions for actions, see Penner 1970: 413–14).

Levels of Completeness of Act

- *Level one: formed matter.* Aristotle correlates potentials and powers with different levels of completion (*An* II.1). He analyzes physical objects – axes, eyes, animals, and persons – as some condition, power, or form existing *in* some matter with potential. In an ax, the ax-form exists in the material of the handle and head; in an eye, the power of sight in an eyeball; and in an animal, soul in body. He calls the form in these cases a "level-one completion" (*entelecheia hê prôtê*, *An* II.1 412a27).
- *Level two: formed matter acting.* Aristotle's examples of "level-two completions" (so called by ancient commentators) are acts of power. For example, the acts of chopping, seeing, and consciousness *come to be upon* the ax, eye, and animal, as in general any performance comes to be upon one in condition to perform.

As the shape of a cookie cutter completes the cookie by existing in the dough, so does a condition of homeostasis (that is, the product of a restoration) complete an organism by existing in it. As a form completes some material, so at a second level does an act complete formed matter, uniting with it. Even the power of virtue is incomplete without its act (*NE* I.5 1095b31–1096a2).

Reply to First Objection: False Pleasure

Aristotle's general account of act saves his refutation of the Restoration Theory from the two objections. His refutation required a distinction between complete and incomplete act, so that he could categorize pleasures as complete and restorations as incomplete. The first objection was that his conclusion is impossible to take seriously because it conflicts with the observed fact that feelings of bodily restoration *are* sensate pleasures.

Aristotle disarms this objection. He diagnoses as mistakes the widespread, confident reports that quenching thirst and filling the belly are pleasures. In these cases the act of power and the actualizing of a distinct potential coincide in the same body (*NE* VII.12 1152b33–1153a7, VII.14 1154b17–20). Human cognitive inability to draw distinctions (*NE* X.1 1172b3) explains the widespread confusion in such cases. Aristotle does not deny that people feel pleasure when quenching their thirst. They are not mistaken about the fact that they feel pleasure; they are mistaken about the object of their pleasure. For example, they mistake the processes of being rehydrated or of acquiring knowledge for the pleasure of the act of the power to rehydrate or to learn. Bodily restoration and psychological fulfillments falsely appear to be pleasures. The process itself *appears* pleasant but *is* not, because the process of restoring or fulfilling coincides with the act of power (*NE* II.3 1104b30–4, VII.12 1152b30–3; Gottlieb (1993: 39, n. 10) recognizes this type of error).

Reply to Second Objection

The second objection to Aristotle was that the distinction between complete and incomplete acts is a matter of word play only and not a real difference. Aristotle's theory of distinct, coinciding acts again disarms the objection. It allows him to diagnose why these cases seem like word play: in walking and in enjoying a movie the act of power and the actualizing of a potential coincide in the same body or mind. The distinction is real, although the coincidence hides it from ordinary observation.

The words we use to describe an act – say, as *walking* or as *walking from A to B* – are irrelevant to its completeness or incompleteness. What matters is the real difference – however we choose to describe it – between on the one hand the causal power of an animal to control its location and on the other hand the potential of spatial bodies to undergo change in location. The causal power to walk survives the act of walking, while the potential of a body to move from A to B does not survive the move to B (in the sense that, once it is *at* B, it cannot *move to* B but only *away from* B).

The pleasures of movies are complex, involving both relief from dramatic tension and aesthetic appreciation. With respect to dramatic tension, the viewer's act of powers to view and comprehend coincides in the same mind with the actualizing of various cognitive potentials. One such potential is a thirst, as it were, *to find out what happens*. In such cases, the cognitive power to understand is unchanged by its act, while the thirst to find out ceases to exist at the moment of discovery. With respect to aesthetic appreciation, the cognitive act of power need not coincide with the actualization of a potential *in the agent*. Nonetheless, the screening of the film that is the object of the pleasure is the actualizing of a potential that the moving picture has, to move from first frame to last frame, a potential that does not survive the screening (in the sense that, once the movie is *at* the last frame, it cannot *move to* that frame but only *away from* it, by rewinding the film or resetting the digits).

The second objection used linguistic facts – such as whether the present tense of a verbal phrase implies a perfect tense, or whether an adverb like "quickly" or "slowly" has an established use with a verbal phrase – in order to prove the truth, for example, of the seemingly absurd sentence, "This incomplete act [watching a movie from beginning to end] is a complete act of enjoying." Whether the movie is a cliffhanger or an art film, Aristotle's theory has the power to admit the truth of the seemingly absurd sentence *as a matter of coincidence* yet to identify the real difference in form between the coinciding complete and incomplete acts.

Unforced Acts of Power Are Complete Human Acts

Aristotle's *Metaphysics* distinguishes power from potential as part of a general theory of act. This general distinction was enough to refute the Restoration Theory of pleasure.

409

But to develop his own positive theory of pleasure, Aristotle needs a further distinction between forced (or subordinate) and unforced (or free) power in the special case of human acts (*NE* I.5 1096a5–6).

In the case of a homeless person, building because forced by need, the point of the work is to acquire a home, a goal distinct from his act of making. Such building is a necessity and chosen for the sake of something else (*NE* X.5 1176b2–4). Though an act of power, it is subordinate to a higher power, namely, the person's prudence, which specifies the type of house to build, just as the military office of cavalry specifies to its bridlemakers the type of bridle to make (*NE* X.1 1094a5–12). While the homeless person builds, that act completes at level two that person's power to build. But that act is incomplete *in relation to that person's prudence*.

In contrast to such *subordinate* acts of power stand *free* acts of power, when the act is chosen for its own sake, that is, nothing is sought apart from the act (*NE* X.5 1176b4–6). In this case the man's act is not subordinate to the goal of prudence but is one with the goal (and indeed the act) of prudence. In relation to prudence the free or "leisure" act is more complete than the subordinate act.[5] An example of this contrast between subordinate and free acts occurs in friendship.

Aristotle defines the difference between complete and incomplete acts of friendship (*NE* VIII.3 1156a6). Complete friendship is for the sake of the beloved person; incomplete is for the sake of a utility or pleasure (*NE* VIII.3 1156b7) that merely *happens to coincide with* the beloved (*NE* VIII.4 1157b4–5).

Except for trivial amusements and inapplicable research, some utility typically coincides with the acts that human beings do – but when is a coinciding utility a motive for the act? In the case of friendship, Aristotle provides a criterion to determine whether an act is subordinate to some utility or freely chosen for its own sake: if the cessation of the utility causes the act to cease, then the act is subordinate to that utility (*NE* VIII.3 1156a22–4). This *shortcut test* generalizes from friendship to all other acts. For example, if I am engaged in the act of building, and you offer to finish building the house for me, and I accept, then my willingness to cut short my act of building shows my act's subordination to my need for a house. However, the fact that I refuse the shortcut you offer is not sufficient evidence that my act is free. I might build for an indefinite number of other goals, such as money, health, companionship, or prestige. In these cases, I might stop my act of building if you showed me relevant shortcuts to such goals.

Each shortcut that tempts me reveals a level-one incompletion in me recognized by my prudence: as cookie dough lacks shape, so I might lack property, wealth, health, etc. To whatever extent that I am subject to temptation by shortcuts, to just that extent my act is not free play – that is, pleasure – but subordinate, forced, and no fun. If in act I were to refuse all shortcuts, I would be free of lack, that is, complete at level one, and my act would be pure free play, that is, have complete unity with my goal in acting. This form of complete act is the general form of a complete or perfect human life (*NE* X.6 1176a30–1176b6). There is no forced activity, not even as a tiny component, in heaven.

Independent wisdom traditions share Aristotle's account of a perfect life. Confucius, for example, says the good man "never takes a shortcut in walking" and does not make his life a "utensil." Krishna advises Arjuna to make the "act" his aim, as opposed to its "fruits" (*Analects of Confucius*, 6.14, 2.12; *Bhagavad Gita*, 2.47–9).

410

Beauty in Act

When human beings act not out of need but freely, they see beauty in the act itself. This is most obvious in acts of perception. A builder might look at the house only in order to figure out what to do next: there is no special pleasure in that act of perception. But when the builder finds himself stopping for no other reason than to admire the project, it is because of beauty seen in it (I follow Annas 1980 and Brewer 2003: 151).

As Aristotle notices, this connection between seeing beauty in an act and taking pleasure in it explains why animals, though their sight and hearing in many cases are keener than human, never stop to admire visible or audible beauty. They cannot see or hear it, being incapable of feeling the pleasure of such perceptible objects, precisely because incapable of seeing beauty (*EE* III.2 1230b35–40; I follow Gonzalez 1991: 152–3).

Impeded and Unimpeded Complete Human Acts

In the case of acts of virtue, Aristotle distinguishes two ways in which a man might do an act for its own sake: either as a virtuous or as a self-controlled man (*NE* VII.9 1151b34–1152a4). Both these men might do the same act and do it freely for its own sake, because they see the beauty of the act – in other words, they understand its nobility or intrinsic value. This act is a pleasure, however, only for the virtuous man.[6] For, while the two men are alike in their power of understanding, in the virtuous man there is a harmony between his intellect and the rest of his character, while the self-controlled man must fight and win an inner conflict in his soul with the wrong desires. These impediments prevent the self-controlled man from enjoying the act. The disharmony in his soul does not keep his mind from recognizing the beauty in the act, but his wrong desires (to eat or sleep, say) make him conscious of himself and the passing of time, distracting his attention from the act. These impediments here coincide in a man who would accept no shortcut as he acts. This account of impediments generalizes to the pleasures of all human acts.

When cookie dough receives the shape of a cookie cutter it becomes complete at level one (see above). But there are varying degrees of that completion, because the cookie can take the shape of the cutter in ways ranging from poor to excellent. Just so an eyeball becomes complete when it gains the power of sight, but its power to see can vary from poor to excellent. In this way Aristotle speaks of the varying degrees of the health of the eye (and of the beauty of what is seen) as completing to varying degrees the eye's act of seeing: "The most complete act is the pleasantest, and the perception that is an act *from* an excellent power *upon* the very best of its objects is the most complete act" (*NE* X.4 1174b21–3).

At level one, an eye doctor completes or causes the perfection of my eye health by restoration of the condition existing in my eye at level one. The result is a change in my act of seeing. Instead of squinting and straining to see the beauty, working to make out its form, my vision clears as I experience eye health coming to be upon my act of seeing. This level-two completion – not the incomplete process of restoration as things come into focus but the act of effortlessly seeing the beauty – is pleasure.

> The pleasure does not complete the act in the same way as the power of perception and object of perception complete it [at level one] by being good, just as health and the doctor are not likewise causes of the act of health . . . The pleasure completes the act not as the [level-one] condition *existing in* it but as a [level-two] completion *coming to be upon* it, as for example peak performance comes to be upon those in optimal condition.[7]

In this way, Aristotle gives a lawlike account of the relation between pleasure and impediment.[8] For an act to be pleasure, the agent's relevant powers must be good, and the object must be the most beautiful of the objects in view (*NE* X.4 1174b15–16). Blurry vision, or an object that is a poorly formed image of beauty, impede the pleasure of vision, as could fatigue, hunger, worry, or brute incapacity to see beauty. Such defects in agent or object make them incomplete at level one, lacking health or beauty as cookie dough lacks shape. Insofar as the agent and object are both complete at level one in the relevant ways, the agent *by nature* will act from complete power, and the act will be a level-two completion:

> So long as the object of thought or perception and the power that is discerning or viewing are as they ought, pleasure *will* exist in the act. For while the active power and passive potential stay the same and stay in the same relation to each other, the same end [that is, the completion, namely, pleasure] as a fact of nature comes to be.[9]

Counterfeit Pleasure

One type of pleasure for the diseased is the genuine pleasure that coincides with recovery. But there is a counterfeit pleasure for the diseased that is not a pleasure of recovery. For example, different temperatures feel pleasantly warm to one with a dangerous fever than to one in health. These sorts of pleasures are not associated with recovery from disease but with the imbalanced state of disease, seeming, as they can when one is ill, to be a level-one completion with a corresponding pleasure. When a healthy person warms up after being chilled, the process is a real completion of a lack in the body, just as it feels; but the process of warming those who are fevered may well move them further away from the bodily temperature they lack. Their pleasure in the harmful warmth is illusion: there is no level-one completion of a state that is imbalanced and defective by definition (*NE* IX.9 1170a20–4). Hence their pleasure is not real, "even though it seems so to someone [in a bad condition]," and likewise for those with depraved character (*NE* X.5 1176a20–2).

Complete Acts Relative to the Agent's Nature

There is another part to Aristotle's definition of pleasure: it is an unimpeded complete act *according to nature* (*NE* VII.12 1153a13–15). As human beings we share a specific but differ in our particular natures and lives. For example, "the musician acts from the power of hearing upon musical notes; and the scholar acts from the power of intellect upon theoretical matters; and likewise for every one of us" (*NE* X.4 1175a11–17). But no one is simply a musician. "Our human nature is not simple, and something else is always there in us" (*NE* VII.14 1154b21–3). This complexity and variability explain why our pleasures never last long, changing from one thing to another.

Despite this *particular* variability, there is one *specifically* invariable act of human life: rational act. Human rational powers are of two types. *Intellect* has the power to reason, and *moral character* – such as anger, confidence, or fear – although unable to reason, can understand the commands of reason (*NE* I.7 1098a4–6). These are the two parts of soul that are at odds in the self-controlled (*NE* I.13 1102b12–18). The act of my life therefore will have a greater unity both insofar as my soul is united and insofar as the act is a unity with my particular and specific nature. This greater unity is at once greater completeness, excellence, and pleasure (*NE* X.5 1176a3–12).

Absolutely Complete Acts

In addition to the degrees of unity between an act and the agent's nature, there are also degrees of unity and completeness depending on the nature of the act itself. For example, acts of nutrition, growth, and reproduction by their nature do not involve perception. Plants, which lack perception, do these acts as well as perceptive animals. Such non-perceptive acts and their objects have only the weak unity of coinciding in time and place, as for example the coincidence of photosynthesis and light synthesized. In this case, the form of the act and the form of the object are distinct.

In contrast, the power to perceive is in its nature the power to receive the perceptible form of the object without receiving the matter (*An* II.12 424a18–24). In this unity of form, acts of perception are more complete than non-perceptive acts. As Aristotle hypothesizes, different kinds of perception are more or less muddied with matter in their acts, rendering the perceived form more or less obscure. The fact that we more easily abstract words for shapes and colors than for touches supports Aristotle's claim that there are degrees of purity in perception: that, for example, sight is *purer* than touch. Greater purity of form enables a more complete unity of the form in consciousness and the form of the object perceived (I follow Gonzalez 1991: 154–6).

By the same reasoning, the act of intellect is more unified with its object than acts of perception. For the objects of intellect, being immaterial, do not remain distinct from the intellectual act in their matter, as perceptible objects do. Since pleasure *is* completeness of act, Aristotle infers that the soul's acts of perception and thought are more pleasant than bodily acts of nutrition or reproduction, that sight is more pleasant than touch, and that intellect is more pleasant than sight (*NE* X.5 1175b36–1176a3).

Pleasure as Flow

Aristotle's account of pleasure explains the observations of Csikszentmihalyi, observations based on interviews with thousands of subjects across many cultures about

413

"optimal enjoyment." The reported key element is an act that is "an end in itself." Aristotle explains this key element as *complete act* (see above). Although the activities enjoyed vary enormously, descriptions of the characteristics and causes of enjoyment reportedly share many more similarities than differences – people mention at least one, and often all, of the following.[10]

1   *Effortless* involvement; attention absorbing, with by-products:
    (a)   consciousness focuses upon the activity and nothing else;
    (b)   merging of action and awareness;
    (c)   loss of self-consciousness;
    (d)   altered sense of time passing.

Aristotle's theory explains pleasure's effortlessness as *unimpeded* act, and explains attention's absorption in terms of the perceived *beauty* in the act. His theory of thought and perception, where at its best *the form of the object becomes identical to the form in consciousness*, explains why optimally (a) consciousness will be focused exclusively upon the object in such a way that (b) there is a merging of action and awareness to the exclusion of focus upon extraneous objects, such as (c) self and (d) time.

2   *Appropriate* to agent's ability, so that the activity produces neither frustration nor boredom.

Aristotle's theory of act *according to nature* explains why pleasure is appropriate to ability. Games are appropriate to natures that love games, easy games to beginners, and hard games to advanced players. (The same account explains pleasures of non-cognitive powers, as reported in McBride 1996.)

3   *Skillful* (nearly anything from reading to rock climbing), with by-products:
    (a)   unambiguous goals and feedback;
    (b)   sense of control and power over the world.

Aristotle's account of the greater pleasure of acts of intellect to bodily acts explains why optimal pleasure is skillful act (sect. 15).

Divine Act

It is a strength of Aristotle's theory that it explains an incompatibility in human lives. The more conventional life across cultures is social and domestic, producing material well-being and friendship. Such a life prefers pleasures of practical skills and moral character. Aristotle's theory explains the preference for such a life in terms of pleasures *relative to human nature*, unlike counterfeit pleasure, which is relative to human *defects*.

   Less conventional, though likewise found across cultures, is a life of intellect withdrawn from practical skills and moral character. This, too, Aristotle can explain. Since we possess intellect as part of our nature, and its act is more complete than acts of character and perception, the most complete and pleasant life *without qualification* would be to do everything as an act of the part of us that is at once best and pleasantest, by striving as far as possible to be like God (*NE* X.7 1177b25–1178a2).

According to Aristotle's theology, the ultimate unity of power, act, and object exists in God, in whom the three are one without qualification (*Met* Λ.9). Because of this absolute unity, God's pleasure is greater than any human intellectual pleasure. Moreover, because of God's unity, it is not accurate to say he experiences the greatest pleasure: he *is* ultimate pleasure. It is likely that some theoretical accounts of mystical experience, such as in Neoplatonism and possibly in Aristotle himself, are based in part on mystical experiences of a complete unity in act, of pleasure in power, and of beauty in object.[11]

Conclusion

Aristotle provides a unified theory of both sensate and modal pleasure. He explains away the common observation that sensate pleasure is a felt restoration, making modal pleasures basic, explained as acts of power. Pleasure is an act that is one with its goal, and cannot be a restoration, which lacks that unity. The common observation of restoration in sensate pleasures (such as quenching a thirst) fails to distinguish, because of their coincidence, an act of power from an actualization of potential.

In human beings, incomplete acts are of powers subordinate to distinct goals of prudence, while complete acts *are* the goals of prudence. Complete acts may yet need to be self-controlled, rather than effortless, to overcome impediments in the agent's soul, such as incomplete harmony of soul or another incompletion of the agent's or object's potential. But it is a fact of nature that a power in a complete agent, presented with the relevant complete object, will act. That act will complete the agent's *power*, if the agent is inactive, in the way that any peak performance completes an optimal condition. It will complete the agent's *act*, if the agent is acting incompletely, in the way that health completes acts of health as a patient recovers. This unimpeded, complete and completing act *is* pleasure.

Since pleasure is a complete act relative to an agent's nature, an act that seems complete and pleasant to a disordered body or soul is no more pleasant than complete. It is human nature to seek completion and pleasure in its specific rational, emotional, and perceptual acts. But acts of intellect, considered apart from the nature of their agent, are capable of greater unity than acts of perception, character, or body. It is the power of intellect, the divine part of us, that explains why sometimes we seek to become like God.[12]

Notes

[1] Plato, the first pleasure theorist, appears to recognize *only* sensate pleasures as pleasure. Jeremy Bentham, founding in 1789 the hedonism that shapes modern utilitarian thinking (*Principles of Morals and Legislation*), made sensate pleasures basic. In the past century Freudian, behavioral, evolutionary, and contextual accounts of pleasure make sensate pleasure basic, deriving

415

"higher" modal pleasures from them. Freud's (1949: 15–16) basic concept is "tension reduction," which is "felt" as "pleasure." The behaviorist Duncker (1941: 392) explains modal – "aesthetic and accomplishment" – pleasures as what "occurs" when a "striving" is "successful." A pioneer of evolutionary "opponent process theory" is Solomon (1980: 700): "the body achieves homeostasis, in part, by canceling out any departure from an optimal position by generating an opposite, countervailing departure." Rozin (1999) and Kubovy (1999) extend this model to music appreciation and other mental pleasures including acts.

[2] Parducci (1995: 22–5) reports the evidence for natural internal judgments of pleasure and the predictable results using the scale of sensate pleasure. On the basis of similar observations Plato makes a similar claim about the contextual nature of pleasure (*Republic* 583c–d).

[3] These quotations are cited in note 1. Plato's account is at *Philibus* 31b–32b, 43b–c; *Republic* 584c–585b, and *Timaeus* 64a–d. Some interpreters, beginning with the ancient commentator Damascius, are skeptical about attributing *only* the sensate-restoration view to Plato. Their strategy, in outline, is to treat the restoring pleasures as inferior or illusory, while treating Plato's pleasures of wisdom as comparable to Aristotle's modal pleasures. The most comprehensive defense of this reading is Bravo (2003), criticized in Rudebusch (2007).

[4] The word "act" translates the Greek *energeia*. As Code (2003: 253–5) shows, Aristotle uses the word *energeia* in at least four ways: to refer to (1) a process like the act of becoming a homeowner, (2) the goal of a process, like the act of homeownership, (3) a case where the process *is* the goal, like the act of home living, and (4) a generic sense of "act" containing the above three species. As Aristotle for technical reasons stretches the ordinary Greek usage of *energeia*, so do I with "act."

[5] A free act is more complete, *NE* I.5 1096a7–9, and leisured, *NE* X.7 1177b4–5. The subordinate acts are "makings," *poiêta*; the free acts are "doings," *prakta*, *NE* VI.4 1140a2.

[6] Gosling and Taylor (1982: 277) deny the plausibility of a lawlike connection between being virtuous and enjoying virtuous acts. Annas (1993: 369) distinguishes between being killed (unpleasant) and acting bravely (pleasant), solving the problem.

[7] *NE* X.4 1174b23–33. My interpretation permits me to translate this passage literally: *epiginomenon ti telos, hoion tois akmaiois hê hôra*. *Epiginomenon* means merely "coming to be upon," not – as often translated – "supervening" i.e. "coming to be upon *as additional or extraneous*." *Hôra* has a root meaning of time (like the English "hour"), but came to mean "peak time" and naturally "the event at peak time"; hence my translation "peak performance" is more accurate than the oft-used but too specific "prime of life" or "bloom of youth." *Akmaiois* is a substantive adjectival form cognate with the Greek and English noun "acme," meaning the "highest point" and more generally "optimal condition"; hence my "those in optimal condition." My interpretation of this passage solves the problems interpreters have had, since the ancient commentary of Michael of Ephesus (from whom we inherited the "supervenient *as swimming upon* [*epinêchetai*]" interpretation), in accurately fitting a good theory to the text without emendment or inconsistency.

[8] Owen 1977 and others deny that the "unimpeded act" account of *NE* VII can harmonize with the "pleasure completes the act" account of *NE* X. I follow Gosling and Taylor (1982: 250–3) and Bravo (2003: 71–2) in harmonizing the two Books.

One might raise an additional worry about *NE* X. Aristotle's discussion of hedonism there criticizes Eudoxus's argument for hedonism, concluding that "this argument seems to prove [only] that pleasure is among the goods, and no more a good than any other" (*NE* X.2 1172b26–7). If Aristotle himself holds that there are other goods besides pleasure, perhaps even unpleasant ones, then clearly he is inconsistent with his program to unify seemingly incompatible goods (as I argue above). But it is more faithful to the text, and also avoids the uncharitable accusation of inconsistency, to read chapters 2 and 3 of Book X as a critical review of the arguments of others, rather than Aristotle's own theoretical conclusions. In this reply again I follow Gosling and Taylor (1982: 250–3).

[9] *NE* X.4 1174b33–1175a3. Some alternative interpretations deny that Aristotle can speak of degrees of completion in the same way as he speaks of complete as opposed to incomplete act, most recently Bostock (2000: 155, n. 35), critical of Gonzalez's attempt (1991: 151). Alternative interpretations in general have problems finding a defensible and consistent theory fitting the words Aristotle actually uses. See Gauthier and Jolif (1970: 834–44) for a comprehensive review and van Riel 1999 for a recent alternative.

[10] Csikszentmihalyi (1990: 48–67) abstracted these features in apparent ignorance of Aristotle's theory. Their organization under three headings is my own.

[11] There is recognition of the pleasure in complete unity in Freud's account of Thanatos ("Death") as a primary human motivation. According to Freud, the Ego's attraction to Thanatos is the loss of objects in losing oneself. Mendosa (2003: 300–3) shows the parallel with Aristotle.

[12] For helpful comments I thank E. Kofi Ackah, Georgios Anagnostopoulos, Talbot Brewer, Mark Budolphson, David Ciavatta, Mehmet Erginel, Peter Kosso, Michael Malone, Terry Penner, Dennis Rusche, Daniel Russell, and especially Kym MacClaren.

Bibliography

Ackrill, J. L. (1965). "Aristotle's Distinction between *Energeia* and *Kinêsis*," in R. Bambrough (ed.), *New Essays in Plato and Aristotle* (New York: Humanities Press), pp. 121–41.

Annas, J. (1980). "Aristotle on Pleasure and Goodness," in A. O. Rorty (ed.), *Essays on Aristotle's Ethics* (Berkeley, CA: University of California Press), pp. 285–99.

Annas, J. (1993). *The Morality of Happiness* (Oxford: Oxford University Press).

Bostock, D. (2000). *Aristotle's "Ethics"* (Oxford: Oxford University Press).

Bravo, F. (2003). *Las Ambigüedades del Placer* [*The Ambiguities of Pleasure*] (Sankt Augustin: Academia Verlag).

Brewer, T. (2003). "Savoring Time: Desire, Pleasure and Wholehearted Activity," *Ethical Theory and Moral Practice*, 6, pp. 143–60.

Code, A. (2003). "Changes, Powers, and Potentialities in Aristotle," in N. Reshotko (ed.), *Desire, Identity, and Existence* (Kelowna: Academic Printing), pp. 251–71.

Csikszentmihalyi, M. (1990). *Flow: The Psychology of Optimal Experience* (New York: Harper and Row).

Duncker, K. (1941). "On Pleasure, Emotion, and Striving," *Philosophy and Phenomenological Research*, 1, pp. 391–430.

Frede, D. (1999). "Der Begriff der Eudaimonia in Platons Philebos," ["The Concept of Eudaimonia in Plato's Philebus"], *Zeitschrift für philosophische Forschung*, 53, pp. 1–26.

Freud, S. [1938] (1949). *An Outline of Psychoanalysis* (New York: Norton).

Gauthier, R. A., and Jolif, J. Y. (1970). *L'Éthique à Nicomaque* [*The Nicomachean Ethics*], 2nd edn., vol. 2 (Louvain: Publications Universitaires).

Gonzalez, F. J. (1991). "Aristotle on Pleasure and Perfection," *Phronesis*, 36, pp. 141–59.

Gosling, J. C. B. and Taylor, C. C. W. (1982). *The Greeks on Pleasure* (Oxford: Clarendon Press).

Gottlieb, P. (1993). "Aristotle's Measure Doctrine and Pleasure," *Archiv für Geschichte der Philosophie*, 75, pp. 31–46.

Kubovy, M. (1999). "On the Pleasures of the Mind," in D. Kahneman, et al. (eds.), *Well-being: The Foundations of Hedonic Psychology* (New York: Russell Sage Foundation), pp. 134–54.

McBride, R. L. (1996). "The Bliss Point and Pleasure," in D. M. Warburton and N. Sherwood (eds.), *Pleasure and the Quality of Life* (New York: John Wiley), pp. 147–54.

Mendosa, M. A. (2003). "La nozione di 'piacere' in Aristotele e in Freud," ["The Concept of 'Pleasure' in Aristotle and Freud"]. *Aquinas*, 46, pp. 275–305.

Owen, G. E. L. [1972] (1977). "Aristotelian Pleasures," in J. Barnes, M. Schofield, and R. Sorabji (eds.), *Articles on Aristotle:* vol. 2, *Ethics and Politics* (New York: St. Martin's), pp. 92–103.

Parducci, A. (1995). *Happiness, Pleasure, and Judgment: The Contextual Theory and Its Applications* (Mahwah, NJ: Lawrence Erlbaum Associates).

Penner, T. (1970). "Verbs and the Identity of Actions," in O. P. Wood and G. Pitcher (eds.), *Ryle: A Collection of Critical Essays* (New York: Anchor), pp. 393–460.

Rozin, P. (1999). "Preadaptation and the Puzzles and Properties of Pleasure," in D. Kahneman, et al. (eds.), *Well-being: The Foundations of Hedonic Psychology* (New York: Russell Sage Foundation), pp. 109–33.

Rudebusch, G. (2007). "Review of *Las Ambigüedades del Placer* [*The Ambiguities of Pleasure*], by F. Bravo. *Ancient Philosophy*, 26, pp. 192–6.

Ryle, G. (1949). *The Concept of Mind* (London: Hutchison).

Solomon, R. L. (1980). "The Opponent Process Theory of Acquired Motivation," *American Psychologist*, 35, pp. 691–712.

Urmson, J. O. (1967). "Aristotle on Pleasure," in J. M. E. Moravcsik (ed.), *Aristotle: A Collection of Critical Essays* (New York: Anchor Books), pp. 323–33.

van Riel, G. (1999). "Does Perfect Activity Necessarily Yield Pleasure?" *International Journal of Philosophical Studies*, 7, pp. 211–24.

Warburton, D. M. (1996). "The Functions of Pleasure," in D. M. Warburton and N. Sherwood (eds.), *Pleasure and the Quality of Life* (New York: John Wiley), pp. 1–10.

26

Human Excellence in Character and Intellect

GAVIN LAWRENCE

Initial Survey: The Role of the Human Excellences in Aristotle's Practical Philosophy

Practical philosophy

The *Nicomachean Ethics* is a work of "*practical* philosophy." Its concern is *Praxis*, action, but in a narrow sense of action that is not merely voluntary or intentional, but *rationally chosen*, i.e. it comes from or expresses the agent's *preferential choice* (*prohairesis*) (1111b6–8). Such action is *valued* by their agents: it is seen by them *as* being what is *best* to do or what they *should* do (*dei*), in the light of their views of human goods and bads; as what counts as human success (*eudaimonia*), and as acting or living successfully (*eupraxia; euzôia*). It is thus action that they stand four-square behind, seeing it as *them* – as realizing their selves, their values and character.[1] It is strictly *human* action – the *form of life* and *life-activity* that constitutes the function of the human in the adult perfection of its nature (*tetelesmenon*) (1098a3–5). Unsurprisingly then Aristotle denies that mere beasts, and children, choose or act in this sense (e.g.1111b8–9, 1139a19–20, 1100a1–3).

Corresponding to these two senses of action, we can distinguish *two* senses or forms of *character* (*eidê tou êthikou*: VI.13 1144b14–16). First there are patterns and dispositions that animals, children, and even adults, may all exhibit in their emotions and behavior. That is, even in living under the sway of the emotion of the moment (*kata pathos*), as against chosen, or valued, living (*kata prohairesin*), there may be certain natural, or acquired, dispositions and patterns, at the level both of species and of individual. Here we can talk of *natural* (*phusikê*) – or indeed of *habituated* (*ethistê*) – excellence and defect (*aretê, kakia*, virtue and vice). But in our talk of human character *strictly speaking* (*kuria*) a different sense is at issue (cf. I.13 1102a13ff, VI.13 1144b1–17). Here a character-trait, an excellence or defect, says something about the possessor's disposition as regards *Praxis* and emotion – it is a disposition of will, of values, of *preferential choice*, a *hexis prohairetikê*: II.5 1106a3–4, b36; *EE* II.5 1222a31, II.10 1227b2–3, 5–9, cf. III.7 1234a23–5; cf. *NE* V.5 1134a1–2, 1111b5–6), a disposition to behave in a way illuminated by the agent's reasoning about what is best, or wisest, to do or feel, and thus revealing of what they take to be good and bad, fine and base (cf. III.2 1111b5–6; *Poet* 1450b8–10).

Character in this sense is then primarily a settled disposition *to* choose, a disposition *of* the will; yet the relation to value and the will may also be less direct. Thus by "childishness" or "immaturity" – or "wildness" – in an adult we generally have in mind a character defect that has indeed to do with the will, or choice, but that is a disposition *in relation to* the will, not *of* it. For the point at issue is that such behavior *lacks* that prossession, or realization, of values and choice that is to be expected of a human by a certain age – it is a lack of character in the primary sense. Character in this primary sense is not something innate but something we develop as we live – as we grow from merely liking and disliking things to valuing them *as* good and bad, *as* fine and base, and shift from living by natural prompt to living by rational design, from merely reacting and behaving in certain ways to taking it that we *should* react and behave thus-and-so – and so taking control of our lives, and starting to see things in the context of a life to be achieved and constructed.

So these notions of human Praxis, of choice, and of strict, or human, character, all line up, and interweave, to define practical philosophy.

The project of practical philosophy

Aristotle begins the *NE* by introducing a *teleological* conception of the human good. It is *that for the sake of which* all fully rational human actions (i.e. *Praxeis*) are chosen – and indeed productions (*poiêseis*) as well. As their end, it is the principle of organization in human life (*NE* I.1–2). This good, the highest humanly attainable, is the object of *politikê* – practical wisdom in a political dimension – both to determine and attain; and the *Ethics*, as a political investigation (1094b10–11, cf. 1102a12–13), sets out to do this (1094a22–5, 1095a14–17, 1097a15–16, cf. 1096b31–5, 1102a14–15, etc.; *Pol* III.12 1282b14ff).

So what is this human good? Aristotle says that virtually everyone agrees that, *nominally*, it is *eudaimonia*, success (just as, presumably, they agree health is, *nominally*, the good of medicine or doctors). Like Plato, he understands *eudaimonia* as synonymous with living and acting successfully (*euzôia; eupraxia*: I.4 1095a17–20). So much is uncontroversial: controversy, he thinks, breaks out over what *more materially* constitutes it. Here are many different views – pleasure, wealth, health, honor, excellence, the Platonic Form of the Good, etc. (I.4–6). All give rise to various puzzles. Aristotle, with his "endoxastic" method, aims to provide an account of *eudaimonia* which does justice to these various views, and which, by clarifying them, reveals their true place and role in the account – preserving, refining, and integrating the truth in each. His resolution has two parts (cf. I.8 1098b9–12): an argument from the idea of human function (I.7 1097b22–98a20); a corroboration of its conclusion, by showing the sense it enables us to make of the other candidate views, and of various standard puzzles over *eudaimonia* (in I.8–12; cf. Lawrence 2001).

In the Function Argument, Aristotle invites us to look at the human as a functional item, something with an *ergon*. (A) Generally with functional items their good, and their success (*to eu*), is a matter of their functioning – of their doing *what it is for them as such to do* – successfully or well (*eu*): so, for instance, the good, and success, of a flute-player is flute-playing successfully, and, of an eye, seeing successfully. If the human is such an item, its good and success will similarly be constituted by its performing its own specific, or "proper," function – "humaning" – successfully. (B) To do something successfully is at least to do it *in accord with* (*kata*) the *excellences*, or virtues, (*aretai*) proper to it (and to do it unsuccessfully, or badly, is to do it in accord with its proper defects (*kakiai*)) (1098a8–12). (The connection is conceptual.) The excellences then at least provide the criteria, or modes, of success. (A*) The specific function of the human, "humaning," is, Aristotle argues, actual living, and living in a specifically human way: "the practical life of the part that has reason" (1098a3–4). I understand this life-activity to be reason-involving chosen action, *Praxis*, broadly understood to include the emotions, at least insofar as these are obedient to reason (*epipeithes logô*), as well as more strictly rational activities (I.7 1098a4–5 prefigure I.13 1103a1–3). (B*) If so, then *eudaimonia*, successful human living, consists in this Practical life-activity done *successfully*, i.e. in accord with its proper excellence(s).

So understood, the argument is rather formal, its points almost truistic. It doesn't aim to specify or justify any particular conception of the human excellences (cf. I.7 1098a20–22; *EE* II.1 1220a18–22). It aims instead to make clear *that* human excellence plays a *central role* in the account of the human good, and *what* that role is. There are two common mistakes here. (1) Some fail to appreciate that *eudaimonia* must centrally be a good of *soul*, of life – not a bodily good (physical beauty) nor an external one (wealth) – and so fail to accord excellence of human living a central place (cf. *NE* I.4, I.5; *Pol* VII.1; cf. *NE* I.8 1098b12–16). (2) But some who give human excellence a central role mistakenly suppose the human good actually consists in *being a good human*, in *possessing* these excellences (cf. I.5 1095b29–96a2, I.8 1098b30–99a7; *EE* I.4 1215a20–5). Aristotle is very clear about the grammatical ambiguity in "Gavin sees" between "Gavin has sight," so-called first actuality, and "Gavin is seeing," second actuality. Armed with this, it is evident that one's good, or success, as a human is *not* primarily a matter of *being* a good human, but of *living as a good human* – of "using" or realizing the human excellences in actually living well. If *being* a good human were the end of life, then putting a virtuous person into a dreamless sleep would not be to harm them, whereas it takes away *their life*, in its strictest sense, of *second actuality* (I.7 1098a5–7). In this way Aristotle clarifies the logic of the role of human excellence: the human good is not *having excellence*, but Practical living *in accord with* it (cf. I.8 1098b30–99a7; Lawrence 2001).

Yet this isn't all the argument tells us about the role of human excellence in the human good. In a further clause, 1098a17–18, Aristotle raises the formal possibility of there being more than one excellence of human activity. If so, then he claims human good is activity "in accord with the most final/perfect and best excellence." But are we to understand this *compendiously*, as referring to a perfect set of the excellences, or *selectively*, as referring to a single most final one? I believe the latter correct. Even so, the claim that the human good is activity in accord with the single best most final excellence can be understood as a claim that to constitute the human good without qualification (*haplôs*), the activity must *at least* – not at most – accord with the most final excellence. So understood, it leaves open that the activity, in realizing the single best excellence, *may* at the same time accord also with any other less final excellence, and even that it *must* do so (cf. Lawrence 1993, 2006).

To sum up. Aristotle's practical philosophy is *eudaimonistic* and *excellence-centered*. (1) The human good is *eudaimonia* – successful human living or doing. (2) Successful human living is Practical life activity, done successfully, i.e. *in accord with its proper excellence(s)*. If so, then (3) we need to specify these excellences (I.13 1102a5–7; *EE* II.1 1219b26ff; *MM* I.4 1185a37ff). Aristotle proceeds to do this (Books II–VI). (4) This puts him in a position to deliver a more substantial, if still outline, account of the *content* of successful human living (VI.13, X.6–8).

Human excellence

To examine *human* excellence, we must first consider the human soul, or living, at least in the broad outline suited to the political purpose of our investigation (I.13 1102a13–23, 23–6). Aristotle distinguishes within non-rational life-faculties (a) the nutritive soul, which is no part of specifically human excellence (1102a32–b12, 29–30, cf. VI.12 1144a9–11), and (b) a further non-rational, "appetitive and generally orectic" element that yet "in a way partakes in reason" (1102b30–03a1). This latter is non-rational in that it can oppose or strive against reason, as in the akratic and enkratic (1102b14–26); yet it can also hear or obey reason, as it does in the enkratic (b26–7); it may even be completely obedient and in tune with reason, as in the temperate and courageous (b27–8).[2] This element can thus be viewed rather as one that "has reason" *in a way*, i.e. with a qualification. If so, we can instead distinguish within the rational life-faculties two different elements, (E1) one that "has reason" *qualifiedly*, in the sense of "being able to listen to one's father," (E2) the other "*strictly and in itself*," i.e. *unqualifiedly*. This latter includes not only the "fatherly" voice of instruction and admonition, but also other strictly intellectual functions (1103a1–3; cf. *EE* II.1 1219b28–30). In line with this division of elements in human rational life-capacities, Aristotle distinguishes human excellences into the *characterological* (*êthikai*), such as liberality and temperance, and the *intellectual* (*dianoêtikai*), such as theoretical wisdom (*sophia*), good-judgment (*sunesis*: cf. VI.10) and practical wisdom (*phronesis*) (1103a3–10).

This distinction sets the agenda for Books II–VI. Books II–V focus on excellences of character, 6 on intellectual. The structure of II–V is elaborate. It divides into a *general* discussion of excellences of character (Books II.1–III.6) and a *detailed* one (Book III.6–V.11). The latter focuses on each particular character excellence, saying what it is (*tis*), its domain of concern (*peri poia*), and its manner of concern (*pôs*) – the whole discussion thereby making clear also how many (*posai*) they are (1115a4–5): Aristotle is thus aiming at completeness – not unreasonably since every area of human goodness is of concern to the politician (1129b14–27, 1130b22–4).

The *general* discussion covers various topics (III.5 1114b26–1115a3):

1 (II.1–4). The acquisition of character excellence by habituation (*ethismos*), and a reply to an obvious objection – a reply which allows Aristotle to provide three conditions on acting excellent-*ly*, i.e. from an excellence the agent possesses: he must act with knowledge of what is excellent (e.g. temperate, just), choosing what he does, and choosing it for its own sake, and his disposition must be firm and not easily changed (II.4).

2 (II.5–6). A definition of its nature. The Doctrine of the Mean (DOM): each excellence of character is flanked by defects of excess and of deficiency, and is a state that disposes us to find out and choose the mean, or correct, thing both to feel and to do, using the reasoning of a practically wise person.

3 (II.7). A detailed list (cf. "*diagraphê*," 1107a33) of the various excellences or means, and their respective excesses and defects.

4 (II.8–9). Further topics. II.8 explains why we are led to assume a duality of virtue and vice. II.9 draws the conclusion that excellence is *hard* – for it is a complex business to hit the mean: it then offers three strategic remarks by way of rough and ready help in hitting it.

5 (III.1). The voluntary, involuntary, and non-voluntary.

6 (III.2–3). Preferential choice – its non-reductive nature (III.2) and what it is (III.3).

7 (III.4). Wish, or rational desire, (*boulêsis*).

8 (III.5). An attack on the Socratic asymmetry thesis that the acquisition of excellence is voluntary, of badness involuntary; a defense of the symmetry, and an explanation of the sense in which we are responsible (*aitios*) for our states (excellences and defects) as well as our actions.

There are questions about the rationale for each topic, and for their order, in this general discussion, as also about the point of the extended detailed discussion of III.6–V: what is its contribution to the overall purpose of the *NE* (cf. II.7 1107a28–32)?

Book VI turns to the intellectual excellences. It begins by reminding us of the role of *phronêsis* in the doctrine of the mean (1138b18–34; cf. *EE* II.5 1222b7–8): to act correctly we must aim "for the mean and how the correct account [says]" – i.e. the account the *phronimos* would give (cf. II.6 1136b36–07a2). But so formal a formula is of no practical use: it is as if asked about the dosage, or application, of some medicament, one could say only "the amount that medicine instructs, and as the person with that knowledge [would instruct]." For something practical we need to determine "what the correct account (*orthos logos*) is and/i.e. what the determinant (*horos*) of this is" (1138b33–4). Fair enough. But the problem for the reader – raised e.g. by Ackrill (1974/1980: 15) – is whether these initial questions are ever answered in Book VI, or even in the *NE* at large.

Their answer at least requires that we delve into the excellences of rational thought (*dianoia*). As before, we perforce start with the soul. Aristotle now makes a further distinction *within* the *strictly* rational part (1139a1–15). With one of its subparts we intellectually view (*theorein*) things whose first principles *cannot* be otherwise, with its other, those whose first principles *can* be otherwise (be or not be). Correlative to these different objects are different parts of the soul. To these he gives the Platonizing names, *the scientific* (to *epistêmonikon*) and *the calculative* (to *logistikon*), or deliberative (*bouleutikon*). And, as in 1.13, we posit excellences to go with different proper functions (1138b35–1139a17). Aristotle's *first* task is to identify and describe the excellences of these two strictly rational parts: this occupies VI.2–11. His *second* is to answer the initial question(s) of Book VI. In VI.12–13 Aristotle raises and resolves two puzzles which bear on these – he makes clear the practical usefulness of *phronesis* and something of its determinant (*horos*), which he could not do without the distinction within the strictly

423

rational part, since the one will provide the needed *horos* for the other. (The structure of Book VI is very tight, while not sufficiently explicit.)

The complex chapter, VI.2, enlarges on the difference between the two forms of rational thought; and elucidates the roles of preferential choice and character in practical thought, and also its relation to skill (*technê*). Aristotle then, in VI.3–7, gives brief accounts of five states "by which the soul attains truth by assertion or denial" (1139b14–18). (1) Scientific, or demonstrative, understanding (*epistêmê*), (2) skill, and (3) practical wisdom are viewed as "states involving a true account/reasoning" – *hexeis meta logou alêthous* – and then differentiated by their end, demonstrative, productive and practical.[3] Added to these is (4) intuitive intellect (*nous*), which is of the immediate first principles (VI.6); and (5) theoretical wisdom (*sophia*) – a combination of *nous* and *epistêmê* (VI.7). This description of the five states is followed by further discussion of *phronesis* and its various forms (VI.7 1141b8– VI.9), of the conditions of good deliberation, *euboulia* (VI.9), and of related states like *sunesis* (VI.10–VI.11). VI.11 concludes:

> It has been said then (1) what practical wisdom and theoretical wisdom are, and (2) about what each are [i.e. their domain], and (3) that each is an excellence of a different part of the soul. (1143b14–17)

Many questions arise. Why does Aristotle, apparently unlike Plato, divide reason into theoretical and practical – and on what grounds? Are they any good? What lies behind the penchant for correlativity in VI.1 (1139a8–11)? It is one thing to think different objects demand different capacities (cf. *Rep* V 477c–d), quite another to suppose this requires the capacities to share certain properties of the objects, like being eternal, so that a part of the soul needs to be immortal (this connects with Aristotle's dualism). Again isn't he committed to other excellences of reason besides these two – for instance, *sunesis* (mentioned in I.13, and discussed in VI.10–11), and also technical excellence? Why do the notions of mean, excess, and deficiency not apply to the intellectual excellences (if, that is, II.7 1108b9–10, and *EE* II.3 1221a12 are interpolated)? And what of intellectual appetites, and emotions – or the intellectual dimensions of emotions – such as curiosity, wonder, excitement, adventure and daring, puzzlement and doubt (cf. *NE* 1111a30–1; *Met* A.1 980a1). These seem generally neglected.

In VI.12–13 Aristotle proceeds to two puzzles about these two rational excellences: (A) about why we should want either, given doubts about their bearing, or efficacy, on human happiness; and (B) about their relation – how can *politikê/phronêsis* be authoritative over all (cf. *NE* I.2), yet not so valuable as *sophia* (*NE* VI.7)?

(A)   He argues that, for *eudaimonia*, we need both. The contemplative activity of *sophia*, not itself concerned with human success as subject matter, yet is constitutive of it. And counter to the objector, excellence of character does *not* suffice by itself for fine and just actions – it needs practical wisdom, just as practical wisdom in turn needs it, a thesis of "unity" or mutual implication (*antakolouthia*), of the virtues (cf. II.2 1103b34). This is a reconfiguration of the I.13 distinction between excellences of character and of intellect, in light of the new distinction within the strictly intellectual part. There are now two excellences, one, practical wisdom with the excellences of character, the other, theoretical wisdom, and thus two basic kinds of human activity, each with its own excellence, and both are needed for successful human functioning (cf. Pakaluk 2005: 88–90).

(B)   Here Aristotle employs the formal possibility introduced in the function argument – that "if there were several excellences," then the human good would be living in accord with the best and most final excellence. This possibility is now seen to be realized. *Phronêsis* is in charge (*kuria*), but as regards *sophia* it issues instructions not *to* it, but *for its sake* – to create room for it in our lives, and to educate and equip us to engage in it, etc.

In *Met* E.1, Aristotle distinguishes three areas of human thought (*dianoia*), theoretical, practical, and productive. These have a certain proper structure, seen in the best life, the life of the best person, and the best society, in optimal conditions. It is the role of practical thought to use and command the productive skills and their products to help it organize human life at individual, domestic, and social levels – so as to live well (cf. VI.2 1139a35–b4, I.2 1094a26–b7), where this is a matter of providing as much free time as is ever humanly possible for doing the most valuable activity, pure theoretical reasoning, or contemplation (cf. Lawrence 2006). It is this tripartite structure that one looks to for the "*horos*" of the *orthos logos* (cf. VI.13 1145a8–11, VII.13 1153b21–5; *EE* VIII.3 1249a21–b25).

So much then by way of overview of practical philosophy in the *Nicomachean Ethics*, and of the general role of the excellences of character and of intellect in it. To fill it in would require full discussions at least of: (1) the acquisition of character excellence, and the conditions on such excellence; (2) its nature, and the doctrine of the mean; (3) the nature of practical wisdom; (4) the nature of theoretical wisdom and its activity, contemplation. All are difficult, and challenging to the interpreter. Here I focus on the second, and aim to convey some idea of what is relatively clear, and what still puzzling.

The Nature of Virtue and the Doctrine of the Middle/Mean (DOM)

The nature of virtue

In *NE* II.5–6 Aristotle turns to the nature of excellence of character, and gives an account, or definition, of it by genus (II.5) and differentia (II.6).

Its genus. There are, he says, three kinds of things in the soul – capacities, states, and passions (i.e. fits of emotions: *pathê*) (cf. *Cat* 8). "Gavin can be angry" ascribes a capacity for an emotion, anger. "Gavin is irritable" says how well or badly I am disposed in regard to anger – to feeling it, and displaying it (some complexity lurks here between feeling and displaying). "Gavin is angry" describes my present passion (1105b21–8). Aristotle offers largely grammatical arguments to show, by elimination, that excellences (and defects) are, in genus, *states* (1106a12, 14). They are not passions because (a) we are said to be good or bad people, and praised or censored, in regard to excellences, but not in respect of affections; (b) we are angry without choice, the excellences are choices or not without choice; (c) in respect of passions we are said to be "moved," in respect of excellences "disposed" in some way. They are not capacities either, for the first of these reasons; and also because we have capacities by nature, but not excellences (cf. II.1 1103a18–32).

Its differentia. Well, quite generally

425

the excellence of an X both perfects the X into a successful state, and renders its function successful: e.g. the excellence of the eye both makes the eye a good one and its function [good]. (1106a15–18)[4]

That is, the excellence of an X is that in virtue of which it is a *good* X, and that in virtue of which it x's excellently, i.e. successfully or well. If so, then human excellence will be that state

from [i.e. in virtue of which] which a human becomes a good one and from which he will discharge his own function well. (1106a22–3)

Such is the *formal* specification of the differentia in the case of the human. "But how <more concretely> is this achieved? We have already said, and it will be evident also as follows if we consider of what particular sort its nature is" (1106a24–6).[5] And the answer that follows is that excellence makes us good humans and perform our human function well, *in that* it is a state that disposes us to choose the correct, or mean, thing in passion and action as that is calculated by correct reasoning: it is

a state involving choice, being in a mean/middle, that is relative to us, which is determined by reason, i.e. by whatever reason the practically wise man would determine it." (1106b36–07a2)

Every part of the differentia generates considerable discussion (cf. Hardie 1968: 129). But the doctrine is, I believe, clear in the following respects. (cf. II.9 1109a20–4).

(M1)   An excellence of character is a state between two vices, one of excess and one of defect – of too much and too little – *vis-à-vis* emotions and actions in the particular sphere (*peri*) of human life to which this excellence and its defects belong. (E.g. gentleness is between irascibility and obtuseness, courage between rashness and cowardice: see the diagram of fourteen in *EE* II.3 1220b38–21a12, oddly including *phronêsis*, and the list of thirteen in *NE* II.7. For differences, see Woods 1982: 115.)

(M2)   Excellence can itself be called "a kind of mean," or middle (*mesotês tis*) *in that* or *because* it disposes its possessor to aim at (*stochastikê*) or choose (*prohairetikê*) – to search for and take (*zêtein kai haireisthai* 1106b6–7; *heuriskein kai haireisthai* 1107a5–6) – the mean (*to meson*) in action and passion, i.e. the humanly *correct* emotion or action (II.6 1106b27–8, II.9 1109a22–3; *EE* II.5 1226a6–12). Unsurprisingly, since it is actions and passions that are "continuous and divisible" – actions and passions of which strictly there is excess and deficiency and a mean/middle (1106b16–18; cf. *EE* II.3 1220b21–6).

(M3)   This mean, or correct, emotion and action is a mean or middle "relative to us" as against "in respect of the thing." It is not an arithmetic mean, a mid-point calculable from given extremes, and which is "one and the same for all" (i.e. for any creature). Instead, like health, it is not one and the same for all (1106a28–32). What it is depends on all the particulars of the situation (cf. *pros ton kairon* 2.2.1104a8–9). For actions occur among particulars (II.7 1107a31, III.1 1110b33–11a1, etc.). So, where relevant, it will include pertinent facts about the individuals involved [*pros hous*] as well as all other aspects: "to whom [*hoi*] one should, and how much [*hoson*] and when [*hote*] and for the sake of what [*hou heneka*] and the manner [*hos*]," as well as general facts about

426

human nature, its proclivities and susceptibilities. Aristotle illustrates this with the example of a trainer who looks to whom he is training and their particular conditions in determining their diet, rather than prescribing one and the same diet to all comers (1106a36–b5, cf. X.9 1180b7–11, versus *Statesman* 294d–e).

(M4)   This mean then is a product, or function, of all the relevant particular factors in the situation and is calculable only from a sensitivity to them and an experienced understanding of their import – that is, by whatever reasoning the practically wise would determine it (i.e. *orthos logos*). *Phronesis* involves this kind of *situational appreciation* (Urmson 1973: 162 ; Wiggins 1976/1980: 233, 237).

Practical wisdom is thus revealed as at the heart of the strict excellences of human character, indicating that the division of soul and excellences at I.13 is to be reconfigured (cf. VI.12–13) – or at least bringing home the fact that the subordinate, characterological, rational part was after all characterized by its power of listening to and obeying reason proper (I.13 1102b25–03a1), and that its dispositions are essentially dispositions to choose as reason dictates: so we were to expect an essential place in it *for the voice of reason to speak* (cf. p.421 and p.422 above).

So much then is, I think, clear. The claim that excellence is "in a mean relative to us" has generated confusion, and even prompted the curious idea that Aristotle is relativizing *excellences* to individuals (see the sensible discussion in Brown 1997). Firstly, *just as* excellence can be called a kind of mean *because* it aims at the mean in emotion and action (i.e. M2), *so* it can be called a mean relative to us *because* the mean it aims at in emotion and action is one relative to us. Secondly, the distinction between mean *in the thing* and mean *relative to us* draws on the contrast between two kinds of skill, arithmetical and those "relative to due measure," in Plato's *Statesman* (283c–285c, see p.18). This contrast surfaces again in VI.7 1141a22–33 where *sophia* is concerned with what is one and the same always (or, in every case, i.e. for all species), while *phronêsis* concerns specifically *human* goods and bads, just as medicine concerns *human* health; there would need to be a different *phronêsis*, and a different medicine, for fish, etc. This relativity to the human case is apparent again in II.8 1109a5–19, where specifically human susceptibilities are the first of two reasons why one opposing defect is the more opposed to the mean state than the other. *So* in "relative to us," the "us" is "us humans" (Brown 1997) – the correct action and emotion is not something common to all species, but, *like the healthy*, species-specific. Thirdly, this point about species-specificity, however, is compatible with claiming further that the mean or correct action and emotion is, like the healthy, relative to us not merely *qua* human, but also *qua individual* human agents in our particular circumstances, and with our particular proclivities etc.: it is after all not *man* that is cured, but *this* or *that* individual (cf. II.9 1109b1–4, I.6 1097a11–13, X.9 1180b7–13; *Met* A.1 981a15–20). This is no more than a situational relativism, which takes as relevant such facts about the individual agent as their being overweight, the father of the child, the recipient of the favor, etc. (cf. Hardie 1968: 135). For these are relevant to what is good and bad to feel and to do in the particular case (itself a completely objective "matter of fact").

The doctrine raises many other issues, among them how successfully and seriously Aristotle applies it: he himself is curiously content to note its different application in the case of justice (*NE* V.5 1133b29–34a1, cf. II.7 1108b7–9; any reference to justice is oddly absent from *EE* II.3). Ross (1949: 206, 207, 213–14) and Urmson (1973/1980:

427

164–70) raise a series of difficulties about courage, and further difficulties in certain other triads. We shall focus on some other issues.

The point of the doctrine: moderation and the substantiality/formality dilemma

It is *de rigueur*, at least since Urmson, to distinguish *a doctrine of the mean* from *a doctrine of moderation* (1973/1980: 160–3). But what is a doctrine of moderation? The injunctions "avoid extremes" and "nothing too much (*meden agan*), and nothing too little" may be called doctrines of moderation; yet there is nothing in such catchphrases obviously incompatible with Aristotle's DOM. It is only if we understand them as *methods of substantial determination* that we run into trouble. (View 1) If I take "avoid extremes" as an injunction to "live tepidly" – and understand this as an instruction to live constantly in a state of mild hunger, and irritation, and fear, etc., and to take life at a constant mild trot, and tango. . . this is evidently silly. The constancy and conjunction of such tepidities are practically, and perhaps logically, impossible. Moreover they undermine the notion of emotion and behavior as differential responses and sensitivities to the contours of situations – as things not completely insulated from external demand and input. (Suggesting that the excellences are dispositions to such tepidities is close to suggesting they are "impassivities" (*apatheiai*) *without qualification* (II.3 1104b24–6).) (View 2) Even if we emend this to: "where emotion E, and action A, are appropriate, feel E tepidly, and do A mildly," and understand these concretely, it is still evidently absurd: we need, on occasion, to be outraged by injustice, or to run like the wind. (For these two views cf. Urmson 1973: 160–1.) So the error is not in the catchphrases of moderation *per se*, but in their interpretation. But if not substantial, and silly, these injunctions then seem truistic, and of no help. So aren't we caught between a concrete stupidity and a vacuous formalism?

Now there is room for theses of moderation that are neither naively substantial nor safely formal, but rather *strategic practical advice* in the light of facts of human natural history and life – much as telling someone with a heart condition to take it easy, avoid strong emotions and violent exercise. Thus some human emotional and behavioral responses tend to go wrong in the direction of excess, others in deficiency – e.g. humans tend to go too much for pleasure rather than too little, and conversely with pain; to be too angry in various ways rather than not sufficiently angry, etc. (cf. II.8 1108b30–09a19, III.11 1118b15–16; Urmson 1973/1980: 161–2; cf. Kraut 1989: 339–41). We can refine this further within types of situation in the different spheres of the virtues, and even within a particular human's differential configuration of response and proclivity (cf. II.9 1109b1–7). These are important facts of our general human and individual behavioral and emotional topology. We appeal to such facts every day to understand others and to guide and critique our own behavior – e.g. decent people tend to go over the top emotionally and behaviorally in matters to do with their children.[6] If so, as a matter of general strategy, to hit the mean – to feel and act correctly – it is sensible to assume that e.g. certain emotions, like anger, fear, or the appetites, are likely exaggerated and so one should try to err in the other direction, and vice versa with others (and extend this to one's personal configuration) (II.9 1109b1–4).

428

The central point however is that DOM is evidently *not* itself a substantial decision procedure. This is obvious from (M4), where the mean in action and emotion in a situation is said to be determined by correct account (*orthos logos*), i.e. the reasoning the practically wise would use (II.6 1106b36–07a2). The point is made explicit in VI.1 1138b18–34:

> Since we said earlier that one should take the mean/middle, not the excess nor the deficiency, and the mean is as the correct account says, we now need to define this [i.e. discharge this debt] . . . But to say this is, while true, not at all clear: for in those other pursuits where there is knowledge [*episteme*], it is true to say that one should neither strain nor ease off too much or too little, but <do> the middle things [means] and as the correct account <says>. But if someone had only this, he would know nothing more – it is as if, concerning what sorts of things one should apply to the body, someone were to say "the amount that medical knowledge prescribes and in the manner the person with that knowledge [says]." (cf. *EE* VIII.3 1249b3–6)

This points to a way out of our dilemma. The doctrine is not *per se* substantial, but nonetheless incorporates essential reference to how the mean is to be determined. Of course this naturally leads us to ask in turn what "the correct account is" and "what is the determination/standard of that" (1138b33–4 cf. *EE* II.5 1222b7–8, VIII.3). And failing some answer *here*, the charge of vacuity will re-appear (cf. p.423). But the DOM is not now itself the focus of this charge.

Yet if the DOM is taken thus formally, what then is its *point*? In II.2 1103b31–4 Aristotle apparently set aside discussion of the *orthos logos*, and offered some thoughts about the mean as a rough help (1104a10ff). Nonetheless on returning to the mean, in II.6, and learning of its role in the *nature* of excellence of character, as its differentia (cf. 1106a24–6), we find ourselves back with an essential role accorded *orthos logos*. So where has this got us? Is the mean just a detour, something that Aristotle should abandon (cf. Barnes 1976: 23–6)?

What is abundantly clear from the definition is that, if it is a state that aims at the mean – the *correct* thing to do and feel – as that is determined by the correct reasoning of the *phronimos*, then its very nature is *essentially intertwined with* practical wisdom in a way that prepares us for the inter-dependency theses of VI.12–13 (cf. Ackrill 1973: 23; Müller 2004). It is not enough to suppose that the excellences dispose us to act and feel in ways that simply *match*, or accord with (*kata*), what reason says we should do or should feel – as it were two voices in harmony: they are dispositions to listen and follow reason, to choose or decisively desire what reason says. Yet *this* intertwining is evident even if the notion of the "mean" is equivalent simply to "correct" or "appropriate" or "best," and doesn't seem to hinge on anything to do with any distinct notion of "mean" (i.e. quantitative). It is time to look more closely at the DOM.

The doctrine: its nature, formality, and plausibility

(A) *The linear model*   In the initial idea – represented in the diagram of *EE* II.3 and in *NE* II.7 – each character excellence has its domain or field of concern in human life, often marked by a single typifying emotion (or in the case of courage, two), and certain

429

types of action; and to be affected, and to act, correctly is a matter of avoiding excess and deficiency, and hitting the mean or middle: the good "mean" states dispose one to *find and choose* the mean in their relevant action and passion. Each excellence is flanked by two extremes, one a defect of excess, the other of deficiency. For example:

	Excess	Mean	Deficiency
Anger			
States	*Orgilotês*	*Praotês*	*Anaisthêsia*
	Irascibility	Gentleness	Obtuseness/imperviousness

This linear model is Aristotle's basic, "mean," way of talking: getting it correct in action and emotion is getting the correct amount – not over-doing it, not under-doing it, but *just so*. Aristotle looks here to skills, especially such as medicine and fitness-training, to provide an illuminating parallel (II.2 1104a11–b3, II.6 1106a36–b16).

This way of ordering, or conceptualizing, the realm of character commits Aristotle to a frame whose nodules or joints may not be marked linguistically, and he feels free to invent names "for the sake of clarity and ease of following" (1108a16–19) – names often lacking because the type of error in one direction is not as common as error in the other in its domain (1107b6–8; cf *EE* 1222a36–b1), or else perhaps just linguistic accident (1107b29–31, 1108a5).

(B) *The category/aspect way of talking*   In "mean-speak," Aristotle says at 1106b18–21:

> e.g. it is possible to get frightened and sanguine and to appetitively-desire and to get angry and to pity, and *in general* to be pleased and pained, both *too much* and *too little* [*mallon kai hêtton*], and both [are] not [emoting] successfully.

He segues immediately into another kind of formulation – *category-* or *aspect-speak*

> The "when" and "on what grounds" and "towards who" and "for the sake of what" and "how/the manner" it should be, this is both mean and best, which belongs to excellence. (1106b21–3)[7]

There are many aspects to an action and to a passion, as generally to pleasure (cf. II.3 1104b21–4, 25–6), in any of which one can go wrong, and all of which one must get right if the action and passion are to be correct (cf.1106b28–31) – *no easy matter* to determine (1109a24–30, b14–16, 1126a32–5).

In this passage Aristotle clearly takes these two ways of talking as *of a piece*. To feel/do the *mean* thing is to feel/do what you should, towards whom should, when you should, etc. But how can Aristotle suppose them consistent? One claims we go wrong in only two ways – too much or too little; the other that we go wrong in many (cf.1106b28–31).

(C) *The star model*   The solution seems simple. Take each *aspect* in which one can go wrong, and claim that going wrong in each is going wrong in one of two directions, too much and too little. This is what Aristotle apparently does: so using anger as an example, he says:

excess occurs in all the *aspects* (both with whom one should not and on grounds one should not, and more than one should, and too quickly, and for too long). (IV.5 1126a8–11; cf. *EE* II.3 1221b10–18)

(Presumably the same holds of deficiency.) If so, then instead of the linear model's single line we have multiple lines, each representing an aspect of the emotion or action, all passing through the single mean point, at the centre of the star, and each extending either side in the direction of excess or deficiency. On this model, each error in an aspect is one of excess or deficiency in that aspect; this occurs with all aspects, although not necessarily with all in any one person at one time: one kind of fault can block another (1126a11–13) – you can't go wrong in every way, at least not at one time. (Aristotle does not pursue this more elaborate conceptual frame in detail with a finer grained, newly minted, vocabulary, marking excess and defect along each dimension, but focuses rather on faults that are already linguistically marked, presumably because humanly common – e.g. the irascible, the hypercholeric, the bitter, the difficult. These faults he analyses as particular configurations of excess/deficiency across several different aspects (1126a13–28). Nor again does he remark on the correlative possibility of different aspectual names for the mean.)

Is this resolution plausible? And what does mean-speak add to aspect-speak? Aspect-speak is clearly a sophisticated way of revealing the intricacy and difficulty of correct action and emotion – of registering and articulating just how much reasoning has to be sensitive to and to get correct. Mean-speak apparently commits us to a model of error in each aspect – of it being *quantitative*, or quantifiable, in the directions either of too much or of too little. But:

1 It doesn't seem that such a quantitative error of too much/too little makes sense in connection with every aspect: e.g. the object or the end in question (Ross 1949: 195; Hursthouse 1980–1; cf. Curzer 1996, for an attempted defense). If the talk of mean, excess, and deficiency is applicable to things that are "continuous and divisible" (II.6 1106a26–8; *EE* II.3 1220b21–7), are these various *aspects* of an emotion, or action, all ones which are, or are always, continuous and divisible?[8]

2 Even if each counterexample can be re-described as involving an error of excess or deficiency on the parameter of some other aspect, why suppose that this description will always capture the real nature of the fault?

3 And even if it does, why will it be illuminating, and not a somewhat opaque alternative? Is it supposed to have explanatory primacy, and gesture towards the possibility of some kind of "scientific" measurement?

Yet, as said, Aristotle offers the doctrine as some help (II.2 1104a10–19). But how?

1 Mean-speak provides a *conceptual frame* which imposes a certain order and completeness on a complex area of human life, a frame that illuminates a possible range of correctness and error beyond those caught by the accidents of language. Aristotle seems willing to admit the frame may be limited in its help (e.g. not fitting justice in the same way).

2 Aristotle offers mean-speak as having clear application in the case of skills, and is here drawing on a certain amount of background, Platonic (cf. *Statesman*), and

431

other (cf. Gauthier and Jolif 1970: 142–5). Aristotle himself also applies it else-where (e.g. in perception). Its quantificational nature links it perhaps to the art of measurement (cf. Plato's *Protagoras*), and the explanatory principles of the more and the less, and suggests a perspective of knowledge or science. But is this mere pastiche – mere scientism?

It may initially seem that the conceptual frame of mean and aspect chimes with philo-sophical commitments Aristotle feels he must make in the area. It is part of his func-tional approach to identify something that humans do, and can do well or badly, excellently or defectively, which segues into an investigation of the relevant excel-lences. This approach demands basic "neutral" specifications of our doings and emot-ings, with respect to which we can then be said to be well or badly disposed (cf. II.5 1105b25–8; Ackrill 1973: 22; Urmson 1973: 163, 166–9). We can grant that both functional approach and mean-speak require such neutral specification; but the functional approach doesn't thereby require mean-speak and its quantitative frame. Aspect-speak would seem sufficient, without the further thesis of the two directions of aspect error. Aspect-speak suffices to characterize the elements of situations that reason needs to consider in determining what is correct to do and to feel.

One question to press is clearly about the philosophical, or "scientific" background here, about notions of the mean, the more and the less, quantity and science, etc. Another is to ask about the explanatory relations of mean-speak and aspect-speak. (A) The Star Model in effect suggests that the two ways of talking are *joint* components of an explanation: aspect-speak brings out the complexity of *the scope* for possible error – *where* the agent can get it wrong; mean-speak characterizes *what it is* to get it right or wrong in each aspect, a matter of just right, too much, or too little. (B) In a way the Star Model can also be viewed as making mean-speak dominant, or rather a refinement. For one may agree that obviously and crudely one should do *what* one should, *to whom* one should, *when* one should, *for the end* one should, *in the manner* one should, etc.: what really needs explaining is how to determine this "should." Mean-speak then tells that this is a matter of getting all the aspects just right, neither too much nor too little. Naturally reason is needed to determine what the right amount is, but the question at issue has been made more specific – and *of the same general type* across the various dif-ferent aspects; moreover, being quantitative, it looks calculable, even if the calculation isn't one of a simple arithmetic mean. So theoretic progress seems to have been made. Yet the star model is, we claimed, at least *prima facie*, problematic. (C) This may lead us to wonder whether we can't view the explanatory dominance, or refinement, *in reverse*. We could view the quantitative mean-speak as an *initial* crude cut – a way of imposing rough order on a rationally messy and recalcitrant area of life. It has proved of help in bringing order to skills. So why not use it here? It systematizes and extends our vocab-ulary, and imposes order in rough, superficially quantitative, terms. But once we have this general crude structure, we are in a position to refine, or dissolve, it into the subtle-ties of aspect-speak. What one thought of crudely and initially as a matter of simple amounts, mores or less-es, is complexified through the lens of aspect. What starts as a model of quantity is reconfigured into a model that equally does justice to non-quanti-tative assessments. Alternatively, the following may be a better way to develop the suggestion. In *Statesman* 283c–284b2 Plato distinguishes between "two kinds and judgments" (*ousias kai kriseis*) of greatness and smallness – the relative greatness and smallness of objects to each other, and their greatness and smallness relative to *due measure (pros to metrion)*. Correlatively there are two kinds of skill at measurement, of excess and deficiency – those of arithmetical measurement and those which "are relative to due measure (*to metrion*) and the fitting (*prepon*) and the opportune (*kairon*) and the due (*deon*) and all the other characteristics that have abandoned the extremes for the middle (*meson*)" (284e2–8). Aristotle's "relative to us" can be assimilated to Plato's latter normative measure.[9] Taken that way, it is tempting to see aspect-speak as a *gloss* on what it is for the mean to be "relative to us": to get the right amount or measure of action and passion *consists* in acting to whom one should, when one should, etc., in short, what is fitting in every aspect (II.6 1106b21–3). The gloss distances us from literal quantity, while keeping the notion of its being a matter of rational calculation. This assimilation to Plato strikes me as the more plausible option. However I now want to turn to some other, somewhat neglected, puzzles.

Difficulty of virtue. Emotions vs. actions – two problems

Hitting the mean is, Aristotle says, a *difficult* business. It is complex in part because of the sheer number of aspects in which one could go wrong (II.9 1109a24–30); and in part because of our human nature, and our individual proclivities, which make us susceptible to error, especially over pleasure and pain (II.8 1109a12–19, II.9 1109b1–3; *EE* II.5 1222a36–9, etc.). So hard is it, Aristotle recommends a strategy not of going for the mean, but of avoiding the worse extreme (II.9 1109a30–b1). But how plausible is all this? We can grant that it is difficult to *become* virtuous. But once virtuous – once one has achieved a settled state, that is hard to corrupt, or even to tempt (cf. II.4 1105a32–3) – then why should the exercise of virtue be always hard? Admittedly issues arise that are difficult even for the virtuous to see their way through, and they too may seek advice (cf. III.3 1112b10–11). Yet it is, one would think, not difficult for the just to see that they should now pay their bus-fare, or return the book they borrowed: does this really call for deliberation? Indeed much of the landscape of proper human action and feeling seems transparent.[10] (1) Can we interpret 1109a24–6 as a claim about the hardness of attaining, rather than exercising virtue? It is not easy, and anyway Aristotle apparently claims deliberation is always involved. (2) Is it that even for ordinary actions to be done virtuously the agent must be cognizant of their simplicity, of the *absence* of complicating factors (the owner of the borrowed sword has not gone mad)? Yet this sensitivity, while again difficult to attain, does not seem hard to bring to bear in many cases. (3) Is it then that even in the simplest case the exercise of virtue is ever open to further development, to "precisification," to a deeper appreciation of what is before you and the possibilities of more delicate response: the moral beauty of the act is open to endless refinement as is the agent's sensibility and perception. Do you pay the fare with a smile, return the book with a gracious note . . . ? (cf. II.9 1109b18–23) (Is this the sense in which excellence is "more precise" than every skill (II.6 1106b14)? – a remark otherwise surprising in the light of III.3 112a34–b9: but see X.9 1180b11–13 and cf. V.9 1137a4–26.)

The DOM applies to *pathê kai praxeis* – emotions as well as actions (e.g. II.6 1106b16–24). This leads at least to the following two problems.

433

(A) *Urmson: problem 1*   Urmson distinguishes between various figures in the Aristotelian practical landscape by supposing that, with *the virtuous*, their emotion, action, and choice all "display the mean state," with *the enkratic or continent*, only their actions and choice, with *the akratic*, only their choice, and with *the bad*, none (1967/1980: 160, 163–4). So viewed the enkratic is one who hits the mean in action, but not in emotion. (cf. also Burnyeat 1980: 87; Curzer 1996: 130).

Urmson's schematic picture is neat. But is it so obvious that means of emotion and action can be separated as Urmson envisages? Can you hit a mean in action for yourself *without* in some sense also doing so in emotion? Can you *enjoy* doing the mean in action quite independently of such emotions, if any, as are relevant in the area? And in any case, won't having one's emotions correct, in some sense, feature, at least for many cases, *in* the mean of action (e.g. in the manner in which it is done)? And more generally how do emotion and action relate in Aristotle, and each to enjoyment? Isn't Aristotle tempted to think of emotions as area-specific determinations of like and dislike, enjoyment and disenjoyment? Let us pursue this further in connection with two questions.

First, does the enkratic *feel* as he should? Instead of Urmson's "no," why not answer "yes and no"? It is "yes," in that knowing the particulars of the situation – that these are éclairs and fattening, that health demands he lose weight – he knows he should in the situation get his appetites to focus on his health, and want not to eat them: and so he does, and he *enjoys* declining the éclairs "in the expectation that he reap the benefit later, or that he is even now being benefited in acting healthily" (*EE* II.8 1224b17–18); he is, in this small way, acting finely and he enjoys that. In this respect he feels as he should and is not emotionally frustrated. Nonetheless his emotions, here his appetites, are not *all* as they should be; for while some are rationally illuminated and focused on health, he has *other* appetites, wild and un-integrated – recalcitrant hankerings that will not as yet listen to reason. (Or again, he correctly feels generous and sees the fineness of giving *that* object as a present: he delights in the giving and the other's pleasure, and yet finds himself also with an un-subdued hankering to keep it for his own.) So we might say: *yes*, he is someone whose emotions do hit the mean, but not unqualifiedly so (*haplôs*): we must add some clause "although he still has some recalcitrant desires." The point is this: Urmson supposes the dividing line in the enkratic must be between emotion and action, but why not suppose it rather between two emotional thrusts (and their associated actions – thus preserving an emotion-action connection)? (b) Second, does the enkratic *act* as he should? Instead of Urmson's "yes," why not again "yes and no"? Yes, his action is chosen, correct, and enjoyed – he acts as he should, well and finely. Yet not so *without qualification* (*haplôs*). For, unlike the virtuous, he is also inappropriately pained by what he does, and so the action is not unqualifiedly enjoyed and is not wholly perfected (cf. *EE* II.8 1224b16–17); for it frustrates an appetite of his, and so is a source of friction, resentment, or regret to him, in a way it shouldn't be (feelings he presumably is also emotionally uncomfortable – annoyed and ashamed – to own since, correctly, he supposes he shouldn't have them). In this respect his action is marred – and marred in a way in which another, to his shame and chagrin, may pick up on or probe: "you can't be that good – I bet really you want one" "it's very generous, but wouldn't you rather keep it yourself? Are you really sure?" It is a perturbing element that on occasion we out, and even ruefully laugh at, relieved to acknowledge our imperfection ("ah my lower self"). The action in its full roundness as a Praxis doesn't ring clear as a bell.

"So the action is not enjoyed, taken as end, by his whole self." That is not quite right. It is not a question of *value ambivalence.* The rational valuing self in the enkratic *is wholly* – 100 percent – behind their action; they are tempted to do other than they think best, but not tempted, as yet, to suppose that other course best (cf. VII.10 1152a19–21). It is rather that they are not a whole, fully integrated, self; the work of reason in illuminating and integrating the material afforded by nature and social practice is not yet fully achieved – some material remains to be dominated or informed. Such imperfection, if acknowledged, can itself factor in as a determinant of the, suitably qualified, mean or correct thing for the agent to feel or do: the enkratic may correctly drink less than the wise at the party in order further to train his appetites. (He will need to explain the correctness of this in terms of his enkratic condition, in a way that the *phronimos* does not). And the reforming akratic, cognizant of his weakness or impetuosity, may correctly – indeed perhaps with the advice of the wise – choose to avoid parties altogether for the time being (although, to his dismay, he may find *this* decision too now assailed).[11]

(B) *Emotions as objects of choice*   The second problem concerns the idea not just of actions but of emotions too *as being objects of choice* and of practical deliberation: for the excellences allegedly dispose us to aim at and choose the mean in emotion as well as action. There is a double problem.

(P1) Most seriously, in contrast to actions, it can seem implausible to suppose we work out what to feel so as to choose, or decide, to feel it (cf. e.g. Adams 1985).

(P2) There is also a problem of consistency. *NE* II.5 1106a2–4 apparently says – and is so taken by Kosman 1980: 114 – that excellences involve choice while what we feel does not. But, *pace* Kosman, elsewhere Aristotle explicitly says we aim at the mean in *both* passion and action – and *stochastikê* surely goes proxy for *prohairetikê* (e.g. 1106b18–28, 1107a3–6, II.9 1109a23).

P2 is readily soluble. The II.5 remark that "we get angry and feel fear without choice (*aprohairetos*)" can easily be interpreted as: (i) at least *some* instances of feeling angry or afraid do not involve choice; or even as (ii) to say of someone "he is angry" doesn't imply anything about his choice – about whether he thought he should or shouldn't be angry, or didn't think at all. *Either way,* the point is enough to differentiate emotion and excellence, *compatibly* with allowing emotions to be objects of choice in fully developed or strict character. And that I take to be Aristotle's view. So we are back with P1.

P1 needs a paper to itself. For a start, what is it even to have, or be in, a *pathos*? "X is very angry with Y," or "in love with Z." We are talking of their current emotions, but at this precise moment X may have other things on his mind, as he times the boiling eggs. Then Y enters the room, and X explodes in a fit of anger: "it pours out." These seem two forms of occurrent emotion, with correlatively two points of correctness, two possible emotional "means": is X's basic current anger with Y correct? And is X's explosion correct? The two are complexly related. Or are these precisely means in emotion and action – if we are to regard expressions of emotion as actions, and actions as expressions of emotion (cf. Urmson 1980: 159)? But X's explosion could equally have been suppressed as to outward expression? Or would that still count as an action?

Again, what more precisely is the difficulty in P1? Is it that we have no use for such locutions as "he chose to be angry," or if we do that it describes something quite special and not what we feel Aristotle is after? We are tempted to think of emotions as natural reactions, indeed as authentic only if spontaneous (in the modern sense of undeliberated): in the shadow of Romanticism, we look for love as a *coup de foudre*, not as a nice judgment. And indeed one can think of emotions initially as natural reactions – involving immediate likes and dislikes – and our having natural patterns of such reactions (cf. natural virtues and vices). Yet such natural reactions quickly develop, in social and rational dimensions: our perceptions of what is before us are transmuted in the lens of social environment, of our experienced understanding and reflective sensibility, and our repertoire and vocabulary of response and engagement is open to immeasurable refinement (one has only to think of the possibility of linguistic response and its infinite, Jamesian, potential for nuance and tone). Most importantly, as our emotions and behavior become increasingly rationalized, they come to express our sense of how we *should* feel and behave, of emotion and behavior that we take to express our full selves, our values and views of how best to go on in human life. Investigation of our issue needs then to consider *the various ways we talk about the emotions* (their grammar). In particular we need to note the possibility of such talk as "*should* you have been so angry?" "did you *mean* to be so angry?" where the latter asks not about intention versus accident, but about a notion of meaning that has to do with the expression of a person's values (cf. Lawrence 2004: 300). So emotions, like actions, come, in a proper adult, to exist in this space – as expressions of full, or strict, character, imbued with value. In that sense a relationship of adult love is something worked at, and the work of much nice judgment. (Here I am somewhat aligned with Kosman's own view, 114, although finding more of it in Aristotle than he does).

Even granting this, it may still be queried whether we can talk sensibly of emotions as being deliberated *to*, or the objects of choice. Here many questions press on us, among them:

1　Does one *have* an emotion and deliberate about how best to *express* it? Does one choose, or *decide*, to express it – or to suppress its expression? And even if so, can it be that one also deliberated and chose to *have* that emotional response in the first place?
2　What does "deliberation" involve? Is noticing aspects of situations, and being then set on to look harder and uncover further aspects, a form of deliberation? And when one feels, say, sympathy or pity, or is righteously indignant, as a result of one's understanding of what is before one, and feels that response correct – how else *should* one feel *given these facts*! – may this be not a *considered* emotional response? The response incorporates a view of itself as precisely what is called for or merited. Can we not view such an emotional response to a situation as the drawing of the conclusion – just as much as an action can be the conclusion? We chose to feel that way, if that is what we mean by "choose": the bringing to bear of my character or evaluative being in response to what lies before me.

All this but a taste of our perplexity here, yet again suggesting that we need more understanding of Aristotle's view, and the topic itself, before it can be ruled out of court.

Emotions and actions vs. states, Urmson: problem 2

Urmson, somehow and mistakenly, thinks that if excellence were a disposition toward the mean in action and emotion, rather than a mean disposition, this would commit us to the silly doctrine of ("tepid") moderation (pp. 161–2). So he claims instead:

> It is perfectly plain, in fact, that for Aristotle what is *primarily* in a mean is a settled state of character. *In his definition* he says that excellence of character is a settled state in a mean; thus an emotion or action is in a mean if it exhibits a settled state that is in a mean. (1973/1980: 161, my emphasis)

This is confused and confusing.[12] *Confused* because (a) it is not clear what he means by an emotion or action "exhibiting" a settled state; (b) it would be surprising given Aristotle's general view of the priority of activity over state or capacity (cf. *An* II.4 415a16–20); and (c) it is not what Aristotle says. It is *primarily* action and emotion that are continuous and divisible; and it is clear that an excellence is a kind of mean *because* it disposes us to aim at – to seek and choose – the mean, or correct, thing in emotion and action (II.6 1106a27–8, cf. 1106b8–14, 15–18, II.9 1109a22–3, 30): this is a matter of the complex factors operative in the situation, and it is for *phronesis* to work out. Virtue disposes us to choose what reason delivers (presumably it counts as virtue only when the reasoning is correct, i.e. is such as the practically wise would use: cf. VI.9). So in fact *the reverse* is "perfectly plain": what is *primarily* in a mean is an action and emotion, and a state is a mean/in a mean in that disposes us to aim at that (i.e. M2).[13]

The claim that character is primary, over action and emotion, is potentially, although on Urmson's part unintentionally, *confusing* because this priority suggests theses to which some virtue theorists have unguardedly been drawn, and which their opponents have then taken as the core of "virtue theory" (e.g. Louden 1984; Tannsjo 2001). (i) First a criterial or constitutive thesis that an action or emotion is correct *because, or in that*, it is what the virtuous or wise person would choose (the direction of explanation runs that way); (ii) second, a related epistemic or methodological thesis that *the* way to discover the correct thing to do or feel is by asking a virtuous or wise person what they would do (or asking the same question of oneself). These are evidently misguided. The goodness or correctness of some action clearly consists in such facts as that e.g. it helps someone, relieves pain; nor does the wise person try and work out what best to do by asking themselves what the wise person would do (cf. Lawrence 2006: 50–1).

Aristotle's practical philosophy is completely alive to these particular points – as to many others. Yet if it suggests many solutions, it is even better in the problems it sets. I hope I have shown something of that.

Notes

[1] *Met* E.1 1025b23–4. Cf. *NE* VI.2 1139a18–20, 31–3; *EE* II.6 1222b18–20, II.8 1224a27–30, II.10 1226b21–3, and e.g. 1094a1–2, 1095a14–15 1097a21, III.1–3. See McDowell (1980: sect. 1–6); also Lawrence (2004). For complexities in the target of "how best to live," Lawrence (1993, 2005, 2006).

[2] (a) The enkratic described in I.13 seems one whose recalcitrant emotional part ultimately comes to order or is quieted ("obeys"), albeit *not as promptly* as the emotional part of the temperate, whose desires straightway fall into alignment with their perception of the situation confronting them. A different case would have the enkratic's tempting emotions *still* out of order – still *not* listening or obeying – even although defeated (*NE* VII.9 1151b34–52aa3; *EE* II.8 1224b16–17). The agent, though in no doubt about the correctness of their action, is still tempted and *tormented*. (b) Being, or becoming, in tune with reason, I take it, is consistent with the "actional displacement" of emotions – emotions that would naturally have issued in action need not disappear, but can be transmuted in various ways, into regretful, wistful, and wishful thoughts, into "oh-that-it-might-have-beens," and "if-onlys." The desired action may be satisfied in the imagination.

[3] Cf. VI.4 1140a3–5, 7–10, 20–3, VI.5 1140b5, 20–1; in VI.5 Bywater's OCT wrongly reads "*alêthê*" qualifying "*hexin*" rather than "*alêthous*" qualifying "*logou*."

[4] Cf. *Rep* 1.353b14–c7. The thesis is, as with Plato, *au fond* grammatical (though perhaps cast as metaphysical). Its excellence makes an eye a good one, and makes it perform its function successfully: i.e. is that in virtue of which it sees well. The "makes" here is formal (or final) – as at 1144a6 (and a8) – and not, *pace* Hutchinson (1986: 30), efficient causal.

[5] Is Aristotle referring back to the earlier mention of the mean at 1104a11–27, or, as Grant and Gauthier-Jolif (1958/1970: 136–7), argue, to the conditions on excellence at 1105a26–33?

[6] Perhaps this is particularly so with sudden emotions and actions – since they stem from natural programs that are relatively insensitive (cf. VI.13 1144b8–12); and it is the rare person who has rationally illuminated the very roots of such basic emotional and behavioral responses.

[7] For this way of talking see also e.g. II.9 1109a28–30, b14–16, III.7 1115b15–19, 33–4, III.11 1118b22–7, 1119a11–15, III.12 1119b16–17, IV.1 1120a24–6, b4, 20–1, IV.5 1126a4–6, 9–35, b5–6, etc. (cf. also III.1).

The list covers time – occasion (*hote*) as well as duration (*hoson chronon*); manner (*hôs*); quantity (*mallon*; *hoson*); speed (*thatton*); end (*hou heneka*); grounds/circumstances (*eph'hois*); to whom (*pros hous*); with whom (*hois*); by what/to whom (*hoi*: II.9); object (*HA* II.3 1104b22; *EE* II.3 1221a18); extent (*mechri tinos*: *EE* II.3 1221a15–19).

[8] (i) In the assessment of feelings and actions we appeal often to quantitative language of more and less – comparatives: "Don't be so cross"; "You could have been more sympathetic"; "You could have given them more"; "You are too often in the bar."

(ii) Yet there are also assessments not cast in quantitative terms: "that was cruel"; "I think you did it only for your own pleasure"; "you pitied the wrong person"; "you enjoyed hurting them"; "you tried to win – you should have tried to lose"; "you shouldn't take that – it's not yours"; "you should not have run away from the enemy, but towards them."

It is not obvious (i) and (ii) are equivalent, nor that one is always reducible to, or paraphrasable in terms of, the other. One idea would be that the non-quantitative assessments are in the vocabulary of points on the mean (of which there can be no further, no iterated, excess, deficiency, mean: II.6 1107a18–27), while the more basic quantitative vocabulary measures someone's place on the frame of the mean in terms of their excess/deficiency quantity of the neutral continuum – neutrally specified emotion or action. If something is wrong in an aspect, then the action/emotion will be too much/too little.

[9] For such "normative," circumstantially sensitive skills, there is much background here, in the medical tradition (cf. II.2 1104a13–18), and in rhetoric (e.g. in the model proffered by Plato's *Phaedrus*, and in effect given in Aristotle's *Rhetoric*). See also Hutchinson (1988).

[10] Cf. Anscombe (1962/1981: 45): "But people of the most horrible principles know quite well how to cry out against injustice and lying and treachery, say, when their enemies are guilty of them. So they in fact know quite a lot" (cf. 1135b34 and Burnet's note ad loc).

[11] There are complexities here, as can be seen by arguing conversely to Urmson that the enkratic may rather be quite similar to the *emotions* of the *phronimos*, and differ in his *action*. (i) Like the *phronimos*, he enjoys or likes the fineness of abstaining from the éclair, although he has an extra unintegrated and unsubdued appetite to eat it – a desire that is frustrated and perhaps clouds or qualifies his enjoyment of the fineness of his abstaining. (ii) If he acted as the *phronimos* – say, drinking two glasses of wine – the enkratic would not be acting as *he* should, given his condition, which calls for one glass. Perhaps we ought to say: "the enkratic does not act as he should *haplôs*, but acts as he should, *given his enkratic condition*" (which may on some occasion be identical with what he should *haplôs*). Drinking the one glass wasn't the correct thing to do, said without qualification (*haplôs*); but it was the correct thing, *for our enkratic* (so qualified).

[12] Urmson is, I think, misled by focusing on the definition at 1106b36–07a2, where Aristotle indeed apparently says that the *state* of excellence itself is in a mean that is determined by reason. This strangely suggests that reason primarily works out what the mean in *states* is. I expect it to say: "So excellence is a state involving choice – choice *of* the mean in action and emotion relative to us, as the correct account determines that," as indeed does the comparable passage in *EE*, 1227b5ff, and as do other passages in the *NE* (e.g. 1106b5–8, 27–8, 1109a2–04). So, I am suspicious of the current text. Broadie (1993: 95–103) offers a rather different treatment of these issues: see esp. 101.

[13] The source of the confusion, I suspect, is this: if every good action is supposed intermediate, then this seems a tepidity thesis, because obviously there are occasions where an extreme response is the mean or correct one (cf. Ackrill 1981: 136–7). This last is true; but it doesn't, I think, follow that there isn't always some possibility of over, or under, doing it – at least along some, and perhaps any, aspect: where one can act courageously, one can act rashly or with cowardice, etc. Something can be extreme without being the *extremum* (further discussion is needed e.g. about responses that are less than nothing). The problem dissolves somewhat if category speak resolves mean speak (cf. pp. 432–3).

Bibliography

Ackrill, J. L. (1973). *Aristotle's Ethics*, ed. with intro. (London: Faber & Faber).

Ackrill, J. L. [1974] (1980). "Aristotle on *Eudaimonia*," *Proceedings of the British Academy* 60, 339–59; repr. in A. Rorty (ed.) (1980), pp. 15–33.

Ackrill, J. L. (1981). *Aristotle the Philosopher* (Oxford: Oxford University Press).

Adams, R. M. (1985). "Involuntary Sins," *Philosophical Review*, 94, pp. 3–31.

Anscombe, G. E. M. [1962] (1981). "Authority in Morals"; repr. in *Collected Papers* (Oxford: Blackwell), vol. 3, pp. 43–50.

Barnes, J. (1976). *Aristotle's Ethics*, trans. J. A. K. Thomson, intro. J. Barnes (Harmondsworth: Penguin).

Broadie, S. (1991). *Ethics with Aristotle* (Oxford: Oxford University Press).

Brown, L. (1997). "What is 'the Mean Relative to Us' in Aristotle's *Ethics*?," *Phronesis*, 42, pp. 77–93.

Burnyeat, M. (1980). "Aristotle on Learning to be Good," in A. Rorty (ed.) (1980), pp. 69–92.

Curzer, H. J. (1996). "A Defense of Aristotle's Doctrine that Virtue is a Mean," *Ancient Philosophy*, 16, pp. 129–38.

Gauthier, R. A. and Jolif J.-Y. [1958] (1970). *L'Ethique A Nicomaque* (Louvain/Paris: Nauwelaerts).

Hardie, W. F. R (1968). *Aristotle's Ethical Theory* (Oxford: Oxford University Press).

Hursthouse, R. (1980–1). "A False Doctrine of the Mean," *Proceedings of the Aristotelian Society*, 81, pp. 57–72.

Hutchinson, D. S (1986). *The Virtues of Aristotle* (London: Routledge and Kegan Paul).

Hutchinson, D. S. (1988). "Doctrines of the Mean and the Debate concerning Skills in Fourth-century Medicine, Rhetoric and Ethics," in R. J. Hankinson (ed.), *Method, Medicine and Metaphysics* (Edmonton: Academic), pp. 17–52.

Kosman, A. (1980). "Being Properly Affected: Virtues and Feelings in Aristotle's *Ethics*," in A. Rorty (ed.) (1980), pp. 103–16.

Kraut, R. (1989). *Aristotle on the Human Good* (Princeton, NJ: Princeton University Press).

Lawrence, G. (1993). "Aristotle and the Ideal Life," *Philosophical Review*, 102, pp. 1–34.

Lawrence, G. (2001). "The Function of the Function Argument," *Ancient Philosophy*, 21, pp. 445–75.

Lawrence, G. (2004). "Reason, Intention and Choice: an Essay in Practical Philosophy," in A. O'Hear (ed.), *Modern Moral Philosophy* (Cambridge: Cambridge University Press), pp. 265–300.

Lawrence, G. (2005). "Snakes in Paradise: Problems in the Ideal Life," *Southern Journal of Philosophy*, 43, pp. 126–65.

Lawrence, G. (2006). "Human Good and Human Function," in R. Kraut (ed.), *The Blackwell Guide to Aristotle's "Nicomachean Ethics"* (Blackwell: Oxford), pp. 37–75.

Louden, R. (1984). "On Some Vices of Virtue Ethics," *American Philosophical Quarterly*, 21, pp. 227–36.

McDowell, J. (1980). "The Role of *Eudaimonia* in Aristotle's *Ethics*," *Proceedings of the African Association*, 15; repr. in A. Rorty (ed.) (1980), pp. 359–76.

Müller, A. W. (2004). "Aristotle's Conception of Ethical and Natural Virtue: How the Unity Thesis sheds light on the Doctrine of the Mean," in J. Szaif and M. Lutz-Bachmann (eds.), *Was ist das für den Menschen Gute? Menschliche Natur und Güterlehre* [*What Is Good for a Human Being? Human Nature and Values*] (New York: Walter de Gruyter), pp. 18–53.

Pakaluk, M. (2005). *Aristotle's "Nicomachean Ethics": An Introduction* (Cambridge: Cambridge University Press).

Rorty, A. (ed.) (1980). *Essays on Aristotle's "Ethics"* (Berkeley, CA: University of California Press).

Ross, W. D. [1923] (1949). *Aristotle*, 5th edn. (London: Methuen).

Tannsjo, T (2001). "Virtue Ethics," in D. Egonsson et al. (eds.), *Exploring Practical Philosophy* (Aldershot: Ashgate), pp. 167–85.

Urmson J. O. [1973] (1980). "Aristotle's Doctrine of the Mean," *American Philosophical Quarterly*, 10. (Repr. in A. Rorty (ed.) (1980), pp. 157–170.)

Wiggins, D. [1976] (1980). "Deliberation and Practical Reason," in A. Rorty (ed.) (1980), pp. 221–40.

Woods, M. (1982). *Aristotle's "Eudemian Ethics" I, II, and VIII* (Oxford: Clarendon Press).

Further Reading

Bosley, R., Shiner, R., and Sisson, J. (eds.) (1995). *Aristotle, Virtue and the Mean* (Edmonton: Academic).

Clark, S. (1975). *Aristotle's Man* (Oxford: Clarendon Press).

Cooper, J. (1999). *Reason and Emotion* (Princeton, NJ: Princeton University Press).

Dahl, N. (1984). *Practical Reason, Aristotle, and Weakness of the Will* (Minneapolis, MN: University of Minnesota Press).

McDowell, J. (1998). *Mind, Value, Reality*, essays 1–3. (Cambridge, MA: Harvard University Press).

Reeve, C. D. C. (1992). *The Practices of Reason* (Oxford: Oxford University Press).

Sherman, N. (1989). *The Fabric of Character* (Oxford: Clarendon Press).

Sorabji, R. (1973–4). "Aristotle on the Role of Intellect in Virtue," *Proceedings of the Aristotelian Society*, 74, pp. 107–29. (Repr. in A. Rorty (1980).)

Woods, M. (1986). "Intuition and Perception in Aristotle's Ethics," *Oxford Studies in Ancient Philosophy*, 4, pp. 145–66.

27

Courage

CHARLES M. YOUNG

I had got in a position where only a desperate maneuver could save me. Tarrasch had outplayed me in the opening, but he lacked the passion that whips the blood when great stakes can be gained by resolute and self-confident daring.

Em. Lasker on his great rival S. Tarrasch, in a newspaper interview after the second game of their 1908 World Chess Championship Match, as reported by the *American Chess Bulletin*, 1908

Introduction

Aristotle typically begins a discussion of an individual virtue of character by specifying its sphere of operation. He begins his treatment of temperance, for example, by telling us that it is concerned with pleasures (*Nicomachean Ethics* III.10 1117b25), his remarks on liberality by saying that it is concerned with wealth (IV.1 1119b22–3), and so on. Courage is not an exception to this general rule. What is unusual, though, is that Aristotle takes it that courage is concerned with two items, not the normal one. He says, as we should expect, that courage is concerned with things that occasion fear (III.6 1115a7). But he also says that it is concerned with things that occasion a second emotion (1115a7), *thrasos*, or cheer, as I shall call it. (I shall explain presently why I prefer the translation "cheer" to the more common "confidence.") And, while Aristotle discusses the nature of fear, and the fears specific to courage, at considerable length, both in the *NE* (III.6 1115a7–b6) and in the *Eudemian Ethics* (III.1 1228b4–1229a11 and 1229a33–b21), in neither treatise does he even attempt to explain the nature of cheer. There is, then, a major gap at the very heart of Aristotle's account of courage. Without some understanding of how Aristotle conceives of cheer, we cannot hope to understand his conception of courage.

Aristotle's inclusion of cheer within the scope of courage introduces other complications. One has to do with the doctrine of the mean. The doctrine of the mean characteristically associates each virtue with a pair of vices, one of excess and one of deficiency. Thus it links temperance with profligacy, a vice of excess, and with insensibility, a vice of deficiency (II.7 1107b4–8); magnificence with the deficient state of niggardliness and the excessive state of vulgarity (II.7 1107b16–20); and so on. The *EE* maintains this pattern, positioning courage between rashness and cowardice:

> Since courage is the best disposition concerned with fears and cheers, and the courageous person is neither like the rash (who fall short in certain respects and exceed in others) nor like the cowardly (who do the same thing, though in opposite ways – they fall short in fear and exceed in cheer), it is clear that the middle position between rashness and cowardice is courage. For it is the best state. (III.1 1128a36–b4)

In the *NE*, however, we find a more complicated picture. For the *NE* connects courage not with two vices but with three, each of which it characterizes, at least initially, as involving excess:

> Of those who exceed, he who exceeds in fearlessness has no name . . . but someone would be mad or insensitive to pain if he fears nothing . . . He who exceeds in cheer is rash . . . He who exceeds in fear is a coward, for he fears the wrong things, in the wrong way, and so on. And he is also deficient in cheer, though his excess in the face of pains is more apparent. (III.7 1115b24–1116a2; cf. II.7 1107a34–b4)

It will be straightforward and natural, I take it, to redescribe excess in fearlessness as deficiency in fear. Even when this is done, however, differences between the accounts in the two treatises remain. First, the *NE*, unlike the *EE*, seems to be committed to the view that both rashness and cowardice are vices of excess. Because the *EE* includes deficiency in fear as a part of rashness, it can count rashness as a vice of deficiency (as it seems to do, e.g., at III.3 1221a17–18). But, because the *NE* characterizes the rash person only in terms of excess, and because it says that, although the coward "is also deficient in cheer, it is his excessive [fear] in the face of pains that more clearly distinguishes him" (III.7 1116a1–2), it seems that it must regard both rashness and cowardice as vices of deficiency. Second, while the *EE* associates courage with only two vices, cowardice and rashness, the *NE* associates it with three. The *EE* has it that fear and cheer vary inversely, excessive fear and deficient cheer combining in cowardice and excessive cheer and deficient fear combining in rashness. The *NE* breaks the tie between excess in cheer and deficiency in fear, in this way allowing for more than two ways of failing to achieve the virtuous mean state and so for more than two vices.

In allowing that fear and cheer can vary independently of one another, the *NE* raises a question about the unity of courage as it conceives of that virtue. For it would seem that courage involves *two* mean states, one relative to fear – call it *fortitude* – and another relative to cheer – call it *discretion*. Why, then, does Aristotle not regard these apparently distinct mean states as two distinct virtues, as Ross (1923: 206) believes he should have? It is not enough to insist, with Hartmann (1932: 517–18) and Hardie (1968: 140), that the two states are "aspects" of a single virtue; this simply labels the problem without solving it. We need, rather, to specify the nature of discretion and describe the place of fortitude and discretion within the structure of Aristotelian courage.

The *NE* also has puzzling things to say about cowardice and rashness. Although the *NE* differs from the *EE* in treating excessive cheer and deficient fear as distinct vices, the two treatises agree in thinking that excessive fear and deficient cheer combine in cowardice (III.7 1115b33–1116a1; *EE* III.1 1128b1–2), and we need to understand why and how he sees these states to be connected. Regarding rashness, the *NE* seems to think that it is sometimes – even usually – a form of cowardice:

> Most rash people are rash-cowards (*thrasudeiloi*). For though they are full of cheer in these circumstances [viz., circumstances in which they can imitate courageous people], they do not stand firm against frightening things. (III.7 1115b32–3)

We need an account of rashness that makes plausible Aristotle's idea that rash people turn out to be cowards.

In addition to these problems, which are internal to Aristotle's account of courage, Aristotle's account of courage is arguably at odds with a number of theses that Aristotle holds about the virtues generally. One such thesis is the distinction drawn in *NE* VII (= *EE* VI) between virtue and self-control (*enkratia*), a distinction that Aristotle explains most fully in the case of temperance. (Although Aristotle restricts the sphere of self-control, properly speaking, to the sphere of temperance, it is clear that he envisages analogues of self-control for the other virtues. See e.g. VII.4 1148b9–14.) According to him, both temperate persons and self-controlled persons make correct choices and act in accordance with their choices (VII.9 1151a29–b4). But self-controlled persons succeed in acting as they choose only by mastering desires to do otherwise; temperate persons, in contrast, have no such contrary desires and so no need to overcome them (VII.9 1151b32–1152a3). Thus, as Aristotle sees it, self-control requires contrary desires for its manifestation, while temperance excludes such desires altogether. And in general, for Aristotle, the manifestation of a genuine virtue of character excludes the possession of contrary desires, while the manifestation of the corresponding form of self-control requires the mastery, and so presupposes the possession, of such desires. Against this background, Aristotelian courage emerges as a problematic Aristotelian virtue in that it can easily seem to resemble self-control more than temperance. Aristotle is clear on the point that courage is displayed only in the face of fearful things, notably loss of life (see e.g. III.6 1115a24–35). He seems equally clear on the point that courageous agents feel fear in the face of fearful things. Thus at III.7 1115b17–19 he characterizes courage in this way: "He then who endures and fears what he should and why he should, and as he should and when he should, and feels cheer similarly, is courageous." But any reasonable characterization of fear will surely mention a desire on the part of a fearful agent to avoid what he fears. If so, in allowing that courageous agents feel fear in relation to imminent loss of life, Aristotle seems to be committed to holding that courage is displayed only by agents who succeed in overcoming a desire to act in other than a courageous way. And in this critical respect, courage seems to be more like self-control than like temperance, more a form of self-control than a genuine Aristotelian virtue.

A final problem has to do with the notion of the fine (*to kalon*). Aristotle holds generally that an action counts as virtuous only if it is done because it is fine (see e.g. III.7 1115b12–13, III.8 1116b30–31, III.7 1116a11–12 for different ways in which he puts the point), and courage is no exception to this general rule: "The courageous man stands firm and does the deeds that manifest courage for the sake of the fine" (III.7

1115b23–24; see also III.7 1115b12; 1116a11–12 and 14–15; III.8 1116b2–3; 1116b30–31; 1117a8 17 b9 14–15). But the fine enters a second time into Aristotle's account of courage, specifying not only the motive required in an action if its agent is to count as courageous but also the very circumstances in which courageous action is possible. Courage, he insists, is not concerned with just any kind of fear but only with the fear of death (III.6 1115a10–24). It is not even concerned with death in all circumstances, but only with death in battle, for the reason that battle offers, in Aristotle's view, the finest circumstances in which to die:

> The courageous man is concerned with death in the finest circumstances; and such deaths are those that occur in battle, since such deaths occur in the greatest and finest dangers. (III.6 1115a29–31)

To understand Aristotelian virtue generally, we need to have some sense, at least, of what Aristotle means by the fine, and of what he is getting at in insisting that virtuous people act for the sake of the fine. And to understand Aristotelian courage, we need to understand, against this background, the special connection between courage and the fine.

Courage and Self-control

It will be useful to begin with the problem about courage and self-control. Does Aristotelian courage, like Aristotelian self-control, require contrary desires for its manifestation? According to Aristotle, courage is shown in the face of fearful things, notably loss of life. He also allows that courageous agents feel fear, even in the circumstances that call for courage (see e.g. III.7 1115b11–13). If, as seems reasonable, one desires to avoid what one sees as fearful, it would seem that in allowing that courageous agents feel fear in the circumstances that call for courage, Aristotle is committed to holding that courage is displayed only by agents who desire to act in other than a courageous way. If so, Aristotelian courage involves overcoming contrary desires and in this respect is a form of self-control, and not a genuine Aristotelian virtue.

One way in which Aristotle might avoid this result would be to say that fearful things are so-called because they are feared by most persons in all situations and even by courageous persons outside the circumstances that call for courage, but to insist that they are not feared by courageous persons in the circumstances of courage. If Aristotle said this, he could hold that courageous agents do regard imminent loss of life as fearful and that they do fear in ordinary circumstances, but at the same time he could deny that they desire to avoid loss of life in the circumstances of courage, on the grounds that they do not fear loss of life in those circumstances. On this line, then, courage would be like temperance in not involving contrary desires, and not like self-control.

There are passages that suggest that this is in fact Aristotle's view of a courageous agent's attitude towards loss of life in battle. The clearest such passage, perhaps, is *EE* III.1 1228b25–31:

> Things that are fearful to most people, and all that are fearful to human nature, we say are fearful absolutely. But the courageous person is fearless in relation to them, and he endures such fearful things, which are fearful to him in one way but not in another: they are fearful to him *qua* person, but *qua* courageous person they are not fearful to him, except slightly, or not at all. But these things really are fearful, because they are fearful to most persons.

Here Aristotle seems to drive a wedge between what is fearful and what a courageous agent fears of just the sort described above: fearful things are things that are fearful to most persons, but courageous agents are fearless in relation to them. Other passages also support understanding Aristotle in this way. At *NE* III.7 1115a32–3, for example, he says that "he who is fearless in the face of a fine death is properly called courageous" (see also *NE* III.7 1115a16 and III.8 1117a16–17).

In spite of such passages, though, this interpretation goes too far. For there are other passages in which Aristotle clearly allows that courageous agents experience fear, though in the proper degree, in relation to death in battle. He says, for example:

> Although [the courageous man] will fear even the sorts of things [that are not beyond human endurance], he will endure them as he should and as reason dictates, for the sake of the fine, since this is the end of virtue. (III.7 1115b11–13)

And a few lines later, he sums up thus:

> He is courageous, then, who endures and fears the right things, for the right reasons, in the right way, and at the right time, and shows cheer in similar fashion. (1115b17–19)

In the light of these and similar texts – note especially that it is excess in fearlessness, and not fearlessness *tout court*, that he characterizes as a vice at II.7 1107b1 and III.7 1115b24–28 – it is probably better to take Aristotle's considered view to be that courageous agents do feel (medial) fear, even in the circumstances that call for courage. When he describes courageous agents as fearless, Aristotle may have in mind a contrast between courageous agents and cowards, who experience excessive fear, or else – this is perhaps more likely – he may mean to be saying that courageous agents do not experience the possibly disabling symptoms of fear: nervousness, rapid heartbeat, and so on.

Even if we reject the idea that courageous agents are completely without fear in the circumstances that call for courage, we need not say that Aristotle is committed to holding that courage, like self-control, involves contrary desires. Consider again what he says about self-controlled people. Such people choose as they should and act as they choose, but they succeed in so acting only by overcoming desires to act otherwise. Contrary desires are thus presupposed in the manifestation of self-control. But the respect in which such desires are *contrary* is that their satisfaction is incompatible with action according to choice. One who, for example, desires to eat more than one should but who correctly chooses not to do so cannot both satisfy the desire and act in accordance with the choice; in such a case, desire and choice are strictly opposed. But there is no good reason to suppose that a courageous agent's desire to avoid loss of life is in a similar way contrary to his choice to act courageously. It is quite possible for an agent both to act courageously and to avoid loss of life. Indeed, from the agent's point of view this would seem to be the optimal outcome.

Probably the only way to think of a courageous agent's desire to avoid loss of life as parallel in the relevant way to a self-controlled agent's desire to do other than what she chooses is to construe the courageous agent's desire to avoid loss of life as a desire to take flight. An agent could not both flee and act courageously. But it is surely open to Aristotle not to construe a courageous agent's desire to avoid loss of life in this way but rather to construe it as a desire to preserve life and limb in the course of engaging in the acts that manifest courage. Fearing loss of life, a courageous agent can be expected to defend himself against his opponents as well as he is able, making every effort to preserve his life while fighting and taking only those risks he judged appropriate. But one thing he will not do – nor will he want to do – is run.

On the interpretation I am suggesting, then, Aristotle can have it both ways. He can admit – what he surely should admit – that courageous agents feel fear, in the proper degree, in the face of death in battle. He can also admit – what he also surely should admit – that courageous agents desire to preserve their lives, even in the circumstances that call for courage. But he need not admit – what he surely should not admit – that courageous agents, in the circumstances that call for courage, desire to take flight. If this is indeed Aristotle's view, he is not committed to holding that a courageous agent's desire to avoid loss of life is contrary to action in accordance with choice. On the suggested interpretation, then, courage is not a counter-example to Aristotle's doctrine that genuine virtues of character do not involve contrary desires.

The Object of Cheer

Courage is concerned with two distinct emotions, fear and cheer. While Aristotle is clear about the nature of fear, or at least about the fears relevant to courage, he says nothing – at least not in the ethical treatises – about the nature of cheer. Indeed, he says so little about cheer that any proposal about what he might have had in mind can only be speculative. Some speculations, though, are better than others in fitting what Aristotle does say and in attributing to him a plausible analysis of courage.

Aristotle discusses fear and cheer more fully in the *Rhetoric* than he does in the ethical treatises, and it will be convenient to work from what he says there. The *Rhet* gives us this definition of fear:

> Let fear (*phobos*) be defined as a kind of pain or disturbance arising from what strikes one as an imminent evil that produces death or pain. (II.5 1381a22–3)

Later in the same chapter, Aristotle uses this definition of fear to characterize cheer:

> Since it is clear what fear is, and what fearful things are, and what the states of mind are in which people feel fear, it is clear from this what cheer (*tharrein*) is, and what sorts of things are cheerful, and how the cheerful people are disposed. For cheer (*tharsos*) is the contrary of fear, and what's cheerful of what's fearful. (1381b13–16)

These characterizations of fear and cheer will be useful in coming to terms with the *NE*'s account of cheer, although we must not forget that the *Rhet* is interested in fear and cheer generally, and not just in the fears and cheers relevant to courage. For if fear is an instance of the schema:

(a) *pain* occasioned by what strikes one as an imminent *evil*;

and if cheer is the contrary of fear, it would seem that we have three possibilities for the schema that cheer instances. It might be an instance of any of these three schemata:

(b) *pleasure* occasioned by what strikes one as an imminent *evil*;
(c) *pleasure* occasioned by what strikes one as an imminent *good*;
(d) *pain* occasioned by what strikes one as an imminent *good*.

these being the different ways in which we might form a schema contrary to schema (a). I take it that instances of schema (d), if any is coherent, are not relevant to courage. So we may restrict our attention to schemata (b) and (c).

Danger as the Object of Cheer

J. L. Stocks was a philosopher who, prior to service in World War I, believed that Aristotle was wrong in thinking that an emotion like cheer is involved in the circumstances of courage. His own experiences during the war, especially his observations of a Lance Corporal in his command, convinced him otherwise. The soldier was "a very quiet boy." But:

> [a]s soon as the enemy put down a heavy barrage on our trench he was a different man. He bubbled with energy and impudence . . . I saw him in action many times after that before he was killed, and he was always the same. Whether in attack or defence, danger invigorated and transfigured him. It was not fear he had to conquer and control, but the exhilaration produced by the sight of such splendid opportunities for the use of his darling weapon. (Stocks 1919: 80)

Stocks's Lance Corporal was "invigorated" by "danger"; he felt "exhilaration"; and "[h]e bubbled with energy and impudence." If, as Stocks believes, this is Aristotelian cheer, then cheer instances our schema (b) – it is a pleasant feeling occasioned by what strikes one as an imminent evil, though also one that, for the Lance Corporal, provides an "opportunity."

The interpretation of Aristotelian courage that Stocks's view of cheer suggests is this: In the circumstances that call for courage, agents are faced with the prospect of loss of life. This naturally occasions in them the painful emotion of fear. However, human beings are also so constituted, happily, that the very same circumstances that occasion fear can also occasion a pleasant emotion, cheer. Agents who experienced only fear would face the prospect of death at best with reluctance or resignation. But agents blessed with cheer would find their fear matched or even overcome and so be able to face death with equanimity, if not enthusiasm. Plainly, both emotions need to be controlled. Too much fear would incline one not to fight at all, too little fear would incline one to expose oneself excessively to risk. Too much cheer would blind one to the risks that are there (as may have happened in the case of Stocks's paradigm: note "before he was killed" in the quotation above); too little cheer would make fighting unpleasant. Medial fear, met by medial cheer, would enable one to fight effectively.

Stocks may well be right in thinking that the emotion he describes exists and in supposing that it requires control in circumstances that call for courage. Whether Stocks's emotion is what Aristotle calls cheer, and whether the account of courage Stocks suggests is Aristotle's, are other matters. I think, in fact, that Stocks's view will not do as an interpretation of Aristotle.

In the first place, it would seem that cheer and courage as Stocks describes them could be found in a wide range of dangerous circumstances. Mountain-climbers and racing-car drivers, for example, report experiencing what Stocks calls cheer, and a need to control it. As we have seen, though, Aristotle believes that the display of courage is restricted to dangers occasioned by war (III.6 1115a29–31). It would seem, too, that cheer and courage as Stocks understands them could belong to the mercenaries of whom Aristotle denies true courage:

> But perhaps [courageous persons] are not the best professional soldiers, but rather persons who are less courageous, since they have no other good [than life to lose]: for these people face danger readily, and they trade their lives for small gains. (III.9 1117b17–20)

Secondly, Stocks's approach is hard to square with Aristotle's view of how rash people react to fearful things. In *EN* III.7, he describes them in this way:

> Most rash people are combinations of rashness and cowardice (*thrasudeiloi*); in circumstances [in which they can imitate courageous people] they are cheerful, but they don't endure frightening things . . . Moreover, rash people are impetuous, and they wish for dangers beforehand, but draw back when they are in them. (1115b32–1116a9)

These remarks suggest that Aristotle thinks that rash people are, or pretend to be, eager to fight before they actually have to face danger, but less than eager when the dangers are present. If cheer is, as Stocks suggests, an exhilaration felt in the presence of danger, one would expect cheer to increase, not to disappear, as danger approached. Certainly this is what happened with Stocks's Lance Corporal.

These objections are, I think, decisive against any interpretation of Aristotelian courage that, like Stocks's, sees Aristotelian cheer as a pleasant emotion occasioned by an imminent evil. Courage so understood could be found in circumstances in which Aristotle thinks it cannot be found, and cheer so understood could be expected to increase as the evil approaches, whereas Aristotle thinks it decreases. We may therefore abandon schema (b) and turn to schema (c), according to which cheer is a pleasant emotion occasioned by an imminent good.

Safety as the Object of Cheer

One future good that is certainly involved in the circumstances of courage is the agent's safety: his survival in as sound a condition as possible. Moreover, the *Rhet* gives us some reason to suppose that safety is what Aristotle takes to be the object of cheer. For immediately after he says that "cheer is the contrary of fear and what's cheerful the opposite of what's fearful" (II.5 1381b15–16), he gives us this characterization of cheer:

> [Cheer is] the hope for the means of preservation accompanied by its striking one that they are near, while fearful things are non-existent or far away. (II.5 1381b16–18)

This definition may overintellectualize cheer in calling it a "hope" (*elpis*): hope is not on the *Rhet*'s list of emotions, and it may be little more than a judgment about the future (see, e.g., Plato, *Laws* 644c). In view of the fact that *Rhet* II.5 1381a22–3 defines fear as a pain occasioned by what one takes to be an imminent and destructive evil and the fact that II.5 1381b15–16 says that cheer is the opposite of fear, the *Rhet* would have done better if it had defined cheer as a pleasure occasioned by its striking one that one will avoid an imminent and destructive evil. In what follows I shall assume that this is what is meant. If so, the *Rhet* defines cheer as an instance of schema (c): a pleasure occasioned by an imminent good.

The account of Aristotelian courage that this way of understanding Aristotelian cheer suggests is straightforward. In the circumstances that call for courage, agents are faced with threats to life and limb. There are two sides to this prospect, one negative, the other positive. On the negative side, there is the prospect of loss of life, and this occasions the emotion of fear. On the positive side, there is the prospect of surviving, and this occasions the emotion of cheer. Plainly both emotions will need control. But, because they have the same object – threats to life and limb – seen positively as the occasion of cheer and negatively as the occasion of fear, the two emotions can be expected to vary inversely from one another: whatever increases either would decrease the other. One who comes to believe, for example, that the enemy is not as numerous or as formidable as one had supposed will become both more cheerful and less fearful. And, if fear and cheer vary inversely with one another, we should expect that excessive fear will be found with deficient cheer in cowardice, and that deficient fear will be found with excessive cheer in rashness.

As we have seen, this is basically the account of courage, rashness, and cowardice that we find at *EE* III.1 1128a36–b4, and I take this as evidence that the *EE* understands cheer is the way under discussion. In the *NE*, matters are, as we have also seen, more complicated. Although the *NE*, like the *EE*, links excess in fear with deficiency in cheer under the heading of cowardice, it breaks the link between excess in cheer and defect in fear, treating those states as two distinct vices. It is true that there are only two places in which the *NE* is explicit on this point, and there are passages where we should expect to find the third vice mentioned and do not (so, for example, III.7 1116a4–9, which apparently summarizes the points made in 1115b24–1116a4, lacks the latter passage's mention of excess in fearlessness). But if we are to take the mention of the third vice seriously, we must try to find another interpretation of Aristotelian cheer as in figures in the *NE*'s account of courage. This conclusion is supported by our first objection to Stocks's account of Aristotelian cheer and Aristotelian courage (though not the second).

Success as the Object of Cheer

Safety is not the only future good that might serve as the object of cheer. There is also *success*. What will count as success will vary from case to case. Sometimes, as in the case of Horatius at the bridge, success will mean the preservation of one's city. (I discuss this case in the next section.) Sometimes, as with the Athenians at Marathon, success will be victory in an important battle. Sometimes, as in the case of the Spartans at Thermopylae prior to their betrayal by Ephialtes or the Texans at the Alamo, success is achieved if the enemy is sufficiently delayed. Sometimes, as in the case of the Spartans after their betrayal, success will be something more obscure: obedience to orders, and thereby making a statement, perhaps. In general, though, success will be whatever it is that the agent is fighting for in the circumstances that call for courage, whatever it is that inspires them – encourages them, as we say – to stand firm or go forward, at the risk of life and limb.

The suggestion I wish to develop is that Aristotle views success so understood as the object of cheer. The picture of Aristotelian courage that emerges from this way of understanding cheer is this. In the circumstances that call for courage, the *fears* that matter are certain unattained but avoidable evils, notably the loss of life and limb. The *cheers* that matter are unattained but attainable goods, notably success in battle. Faced with fears, persons feel fear and a desire to avoid them; similarly, faced with cheers, persons feel cheer and a desire to attain them. What is special about courage, Aristotle seems to think, is that the circumstances of courageous action require that fears be faced if cheers are to be attained. In such circumstances, it will be important for agents to avoid too much fear, lest they take flight, and to avoid too little fear, lest they welcome too much risk. It will likewise be important that they avoid too much cheer, lest they be blind to real risks that are there, and that they avoid too little cheer, lest they fail to press on. Courage is found in a middle position relative to each set of extremes. A courageous agent will experience medial fear or fortitude: he will not take flight, but he will attempt to preserve his life. He will experience medial cheer or discretion: he will press on, but not by exposing himself to too much risk. On this view of Aristotelean courage, then, both fortitude and confidence are essential to its display. Aristotelian courage has the complex structure it does, then, as a consequence of the complex nature of the circumstances in which, as Aristotle sees it, courage is called for.

This interpretation of Aristotelian cheer and Aristotelian courage finds some support from *NE* III.9 1117b17–20, a passage that caused difficulties for the other accounts of Aristotelian cheer that we have considered. There Aristotle says:

> Perhaps it is not courageous persons, but persons who are less courageous, who make the best professional soldiers. Less courageous persons have nothing good except life to lose; they face danger readily and trade their lives for small gains.

451

Here Aristotle clearly implies that the willingness to face death in battle does not, by itself, suffice for courage: both courageous persons and the "less courageous" persons mentioned here have this willingness. The less courageous risk their lives for trifles; what marks off genuinely courageous persons, apparently, is that they risk their lives only in the attempt to obtain something relatively worthwhile – whatever in their situation amounts to success.

Horatius at the Bridge

Let us see how this account works in a particular case: that of Horatius at the bridge. (I follow the version of the story in Livy, II.9.10. For other versions, see Polybius, *Histories* V.55.1, and Dionysius of Halicarnassus, *Roman Antiquities*, V.23–5; Virgil has a brief allusion at *Aeneid* VIII.646.651.) Late in the sixth century BCE, Lars Porsena, the king of Clusium, launched an attack on Rome in an attempt to restore the Tarquins to the Roman throne. To attack the city Porsena's army had to cross the Sublican bridge, which in those days provided the only access to the city from the west. In Macauley's melodramatic poem on this theme, the Romans realized that the city could be saved if the bridge were destroyed, but the attack came with such swiftness that it was – apparently – too late. As the Consul on the scene observed:

> Their van will be upon us
> Before the bridge goes down;
> And if they once may win the bridge,
> What hope to save the town?
> ("Horatius," XXVI)

But one Horatius Cocles saw a way to buy the needed time, and said:

> Hew down the bridge, Sir Consul,
> With all the speed ye may;
> I with two more to help me,
> Will hold the foe in play.
> In yon strait path a thousand
> May well be stopped by three.
> Now who will stand on either hand
> And keep the bridge with me?
> ("Horatius," XXIX)

The rest is history, or at least legend. Two men, Spurius Larcius and Titus Herminius, volunteered to stand with Horatius, and the three of them defended the far side of the bridge until its destruction was imminent. Horatius then sent his colleagues back to safety and faced the enemy alone until the bridge came down. After a prayer to the Tiber, he leapt into the river and swam across to safety, winning, in Livy's words, "more fame than credence from posterity."

Whatever the historical accuracy of this story, Horatius's action approximates a case of Aristotelian courage. He risks his life, but his doing so is prompted by the prospect of saving his city. As the Consul's remarks make clear, Rome falls if Prosena's army takes the bridge. Moreover, the prospect of saving Rome is, in Horatius's estimation, a realistic one. The delay of the opposing army is all that is necessary, and their delay can be secured by his fighting at the bridge. And interestingly, he is not willing to fight alone; he insists upon the assistance of two others. Horatius thus seems to exemplify all the features of Aristotelian courage. He feels medial fear – he is prepared to risk his life, but he takes appropriate precautions. And he feels medial cheer – his city can be saved only if he fights, and there is a real prospect of saving his city if he does.

Acting for the Sake of the Fine

Aristotle affirms the idea that only the fine can serve as a motive for virtuous action in two different kinds of context. Sometimes, his point is to contrast a virtuous action motivated by the fine with a superficially similar action motivated in some other way. Thus he marks off courageous agents from suicides as follows:

> To be willing to die in order to avoid poverty or erotic passion or something painful is characteristic not of a courageous man but rather of a coward. It is weakness to avoid troubles, and such a person endures (*hupomenei*) [death] not because it is fine [to do so] but to avoid an evil. (III.7 1116a12–15; see also IV.2 1123a19–25)

Here, I take it, Aristotle means to contrast both the actions and the motives of suicides and courageous agents. The contrast with respect to motives is explicit: Both suicides and courageous agents are willing to die, the former to avoid an evil, the latter because it is a fine thing to do. But there is an implicit contrast between their respective actions: Since a suicide's willingness to face death is not something that, properly motivated, would count as courageous, what the suicide does is a different kind of action than what the courageous person does.

More often, though, Aristotle's point in saying that virtuous people are motivated by the fine is to contrast the fine as a motive with some other motive or explanation for the *very same* (kind of) action. In III.8, for example, Aristotle takes up what he calls the "tropes" of courage: states of character that, though distinct from courage, are sometimes taken to be courage because they resemble it. Thus he marks of the courage of citizens from true courage on the grounds that "Citizens seem to endure dangers because of legal penalties and reproaches, and because of honors" (1116a18–19). Here, I take it, Aristotle's point concerns only the motives, and not the actions, of citizen-soldiers. His point is that, although both citizen-soldiers and the genuinely courageous will stand firm in the face of death, citizen-soldiers do so to avoid the legal penalties and reproaches attaching to cowardly conduct and to secure the honors that courageous conduct brings, while genuinely courageous people stand firm because it is fine to do so. Citizen-soldiers and courageous people do the same thing – stand firm in battle – for different reasons.

If these considerations are sound, then Aristotle's view of the circumstances of courageous action are more complicated than it might otherwise appear. The relevant distinctions between the suicide, the citizen-soldier, and the courageous person may usefully be phrased in terms of Aristotle's distinction in *NE* II.4 between performing a virtuous action and acting virtuously. According to this distinction, one performs e.g. a courageous action only if one does what a courageous person would do in one's circumstances, while one acts courageously only if one does a courageous act in the way a courageous person does. The suicide, the citizen-soldier, and the courageous person all face death willingly. In Aristotle's view, though, the suicide's act is not a courageous act; it is rather the act of a coward (III.7 1116a12–15). The citizen-soldier's act is a courageous act, but because it is done for the wrong reason, the citizen-soldier does not act courageously. Only the courageous person, who performs the courageous act for the right reason, counts as acting courageously. What marks off the suicide, on the one hand, and the citizen-soldier and the courageous person, on the other, is principally the kind of action each performs, while what marks off courageous people from citizen-soldiers is the motive for which they act.

What exactly is Aristotle's account of what motivates virtuous people? Aristotle never tells us what it is to perform an action for the sake of the fine or, for that matter, to perform it for its own sake, and a full discussion of the question is well beyond the scope of this essay. Appreciating the point that Aristotle contrasts performing an action for the sake of the fine with other motives for performing the very same action, however, may help us to get an idea of what he is getting at in insisting that virtuous people act for the sake of the fine. Suppose for the sake of the point that my lending a car to a friend who needs it counts as liberal: a proper use of my time and resources. Clearly, I might perform this action for any of a variety of motives. I might wish to place my friend in my debt; I might anticipate still greater favors from her in return; I might be trying to impress acquaintances; and so on. I suggest that at least part of what Aristotle is after in saying that virtuous people perform virtuous actions for their own sakes is that, if I am a liberal person, I am *not* motivated by any such factors, even if I know that my action will have the listed effects. But the point can be put in a positive way as well. I can lend my friend my car out of a recognition that doing so is an appropriate use of my property in the circumstances in which my friend and I find ourselves, and if I do so, the suggestion is, I act for the sake of the fine. So also Horatius at the bridge: If he chooses to face the enemy, with his comrades, on the far side of the bridge out of a recognition that doing so is an appropriate deployment of his physical and mental talents given the circumstances that face him and his city, he acts for the sake of the fine.

When is Death Fine?

That courageous people do courageous actions for the sake of the fine is a consequence of Aristotle's general claim that virtuous people do virtuous actions for the sake of the fine. But Aristotle appeals to the notion of the fine to characterize courageous actions themselves, and here his point is unique to courage. According to him, courage is shown in the face of the most frightening thing, and this is death (III.6 1115a25–6). But not every sort of death provides an occasion for courage, only a fine one (a28–30).

Fine deaths, he says are found only in battle, for the reason that battles provide "the greatest and finest risk" (a30–1). He concludes that "He is called courageous in the strict sense who is fearless in the face of a fine death and imminent dangers that threaten death, and these are above all the dangers of war" (III.6 1115a33–5).

Aristotle thinks, then, that courage is shown only in the face of a fine death. He also tells us what a fine death is: one that occurs in battle, the risks of battle being the greatest and finest of risks. He seems to think that the risks of battle are the greatest risks because in battle one risks death (see 1115a24–7). But what makes the risks of battle the finest risks? Aristotle does not answer this question for us.

No doubt the idea is that the risks of battle are the finest risks because in the typical case they are undertaken in the service of one's community. The very existence of a Greek city-state depended upon the willingness of its citizens to risk and, if need be, to sacrifice their lives in battle in order to secure its preservation. In consequence, those who risk and sacrifice their lives to save their cities received the highest of commendations and honors. Aristotle may be taking it simply as a datum that risking one's life in these circumstances counts as fine.

That this would indeed be Aristotle's view of the fine in courage finds some confirmation from a passage in III.9 quoted earlier. At 1117b17–20, he says this:

> But perhaps [courageous persons] are not the best professional soldiers, but rather persons who are less courageous, since they have no other good [than life to lose]: for these people face danger readily, and they trade their lives for small gains.

Here Aristotle makes it plain that, in his view, courage requires more than merely a willingness to face death in battle, for both a courageous person and a "less courageous" person are willing to face death. A "less courageous" person, having relatively little to lose, will risk his life for trifles. A courageous person – especially one who has many other virtues and so a happy life (see 1117b9–15) – has much to lose, and so, Aristotle seems to think, will risk his life only in the attempt to attain something worthwhile: I take it, in the star cases, the preservation of his city. There is nothing fine in risking one's life for "trifles." There is something fine in risking one's life for one's city.

Note

Many of the ideas expressed in this chapter began life in comments I made on a paper by D. Pears at a conference at the University of Minnesota in March 1976. My comments grew up into Young (1977) and Young (1980), Pears's paper into Pears (1978) and Pears (1980).

Bibliography

Hardie, W. F. (1968). *Aristotle's Ethical Theory* (Oxford: Clarendon Press).

Hartman, N. (1932). *Ethics*, vol. 2, trans. S. Coit (New York: Macmillan).

Macauley, T. (1910). "Horatius," in *The Lays of Ancient Rome and Miscellaneous Essays and Poems* (London: J.M. Dent and Sons), pp. 418–34.

Pears, D. F. (1978). "Aristotle's Analysis of Courage," *Midwest Studies in Philosophy*, 3, pp. 273–85.

Pears, D. F. (1980). "Courage as a Mean," in A. O. Rorty (ed.), *Essays on Aristotle's "Ethics"* (Berkeley, CA: University of California Press), pp. 171–87.

Ross, W. E. (1923). *Aristotle* (London: Methuen).

Stocks, J. L. (1919). "The Test of Experience," *Mind*, n.s., 28, pp. 79–81.

Young, C. M. (1977). "Aristotle on Courage," in Q. Howe (ed.), *Humanitas: Essays in Honor of Ralph Ross* (Claremont, CA: Scripps College Press), pp. 194–203.

Young, C. M. (1980). "Virtue and Flourishing in Aristotle's *Ethics*," in D. Depew (ed.), *The Greeks and the Good Life* (Fullerton, CA: California State University Press), pp. 138–78.

28

Justice

CHARLES M. YOUNG

Introduction

John Rawls (1999: 3) begins his *A Theory of Justice*, famously, by saying, "Justice is the first virtue of social institutions, as truth is of systems of thought." For Socrates, Plato, and Aristotle, each in his own way, justice is the first virtue of individual human beings. Thus Socrates in Plato's *Crito* maintains that for an unjust person life is not worth living. Plato's *Republic* argues that justice is the natural expression in the field of human relations of a properly oriented and healthy individual life. Aristotle argues in the *Nicomachean Ethics* that justice (in one use of the term) counts as the whole of virtue and that (in another use of the term) it is the virtue that expresses one's conception of oneself as a member of a community of free and equal human beings: as a citizen.

Preliminaries

Book V of the *Nicomachean Ethics* (*NE*) is our principal source for Aristotle's views on justice, although passages in other texts, especially *Politics* III, are relevant as well. The Book divides roughly into two main sections, chapters 1–5, which deals with justice as a state of character, and chapters 6–11, which takes up issues having to do with justice and responsibility. In what follows, I take up only some of many important topics that Aristotle's discussion of justice treats. There are many other topics that I am unable to take up, and those I do take up receive limited treatment. For other topics and more detailed treatments, see Keyt (1991), Kraut (2002: 98–177), and Young (forthcoming). The present chapter overlaps extensively with Young (2006).

Universal vs. Particular Justice

Justice as an individual virtue of character is unique in Aristotle's treatment of the virtues in that he feels a need to establish that it exists. His worry arises because the language of justice in Greek is sometimes used in a very general way – so generally, in fact, that it covers pretty much the same territory as the language of virtue itself. That the language of justice is so used in Greek Aristotle takes for granted; he feels that he must establish that the language of justice is also used in reference to an individual virtue of character.

To this end, Aristotle distinguishes in *NE* V.1–2 between two forms of justice. *Universal* justice (sometimes called *general* justice, sometimes *broad* justice), he tells us, amounts to the whole of virtue. *Particular* (*specific, narrow*) justice, in contrast, is an individual virtue of character coordinate with courage, temperance, liberality, etc., and is, like each of them, a part of universal justice. Aristotle warned us about this complexity in justice at the end of his brief accounts of the various virtues of character in *NE* II.7: "After this, we'll talk about justice, since it is not a simple notion, distinguishing its kinds and explaining how each is a mean state" (1108b7–9). Aristotle does explain in *NE* V.5 how particular justice is a mean state, but he does not explain how universal justice is. Presumably he takes it for granted that universal justice is a mean state in that it comprises a number of particular virtues, including particular justice, each of which is itself in some way a mean state.

Aristotle's argument for the existence of particular justice and, hence, for the distinction between universal and particular justice, appeals in the first instance to facts of linguistic usage. He tells us that the Greek adjective *unjust* sometimes describes one who disobeys the law and sometimes one who is greedy (*pleonektês*), i.e., *unequal* or *unfair* (*anisos*). Aristotle is right in claiming that the language of justice in Greek is ambiguous in this way. So, for example, people accused of breaking the law in Athens were accused in the indictments against them of "doing injustice" (*adikein*). Thus the charge against Socrates stated, "Socrates does injustice in corrupting the young and in believing not in the gods in which the city believes, but in other, new spiritual beings" (*Apology* 24b8–c1). And in *Republic* I, Thrasymachus, when he recommends injustice over justice, invites us to consider "the unjust man . . . who is able to be greedy on a large scale" (343e7–344a2). Thus *unjust* can be used to describe two different kinds of people, those who break the law and those who are motivated by greed. *Just* can similarly be used of those who conform to the law and of those who are not motivated by greed, and so, too, *mutatis mutandis*, with *justice* and *injustice*. Justice in the first sense – universal justice – will prove to be the same state as virtue generally. Justice in the second sense – particular justice – is a virtue coordinate with the other individual virtues of character that Aristotle takes up in *NE* III–IV.

There are problems with Aristotle's equation of universal justice with lawfulness. Aristotle thinks that the laws in any political community aim at the happiness of its citizens, whether all or some of them (V.1 1129b14–19). Laws might miss this mark in at least two ways. First, those who draw up the laws might be wrong about what the happiness of its citizens consists in but successful in creating laws that promote happiness so conceived. Aristotle himself thinks that happiness consists in the realization of rationality in thought and action and that the laws in a proper human community will promote this end. Oligarchs, in contrast, think that happiness consists in the attainment of wealth or property. Let us suppose for the sake of the point that Aristotle is right and the oligarchs are wrong. Let us also suppose that a group of oligarchs enact laws that do indeed promote the attainment of wealth. What are we to say about obedience to such laws? Is it just, because it conforms to the law? Or is it unjust, because it doesn't conform to what the law should be? Second, those who draw up the laws, whether or not they are right about what happiness consists in, might do a poor job of implementing the conception of happiness they hold. Thus a second group of oligarchs might think that a certain tax code promotes the attainment of wealth, when in fact it hinders it. Compliance with the code would conform with the law, but not with the law as it should be, nor even with the law as it should be by the oligarchs' own lights.

Aristotle does not articulate these problems, much less address them, although he does at least envisage the possibility of poorly crafted laws at V.1 1129b24–5. But a proposal that captures the spirit of his ideas would be to make ascriptions of justice and injustice relative. We might score political communities both on their views of the nature of happiness and on their success in implementing those views, and assess the justice and injustice of a community's policies accordingly. Thus policies can be just or unjust according as they promote the correct or an incorrect view of happiness, and just or unjust according as they promote the view of happiness they seek to promote. This proposal gives us a principled way of dealing with the cases raised earlier. Thus obedience to the law in the first oligarchy, which succeeds in implementing its incorrect view of happiness, will be unjust when seen from the perspective of a proper human community, but just when seen from the oligarchy's own perspective. Obedience to the law in the second oligarchy, which fails to implement its incorrect view of happiness, will be unjust both from the point of view of a proper human community and also unjust from its own perspective.

The identity of universal justice with lawfulness carries with it, for Aristotle, an identity of universal justice and virtue of character:

> But the law also prescribes certain conduct: the conduct of a brave man, for example, not to desert one's post . . . that of the temperate man, for example, not to commit adultery or outrage; . . . and so on with the actions exemplifying the rest of the virtues and vices, commanding these and forbidding those – rightly, if the law has been rightly enacted, not so well if it has been made at random. Justice in this sense is complete virtue. (V.1 1129b20–6)

For, again, the law aims to promote the happiness of citizens, and virtuous activity promotes happiness, so the law requires the same forms of conduct that the virtues of character require. The identity of universal justice, lawfulness, and virtue as whole thus brings together two major themes of Aristotle's moral and political philosophy: the moral idea that acting virtuously promotes happiness and the political idea that the political community exists to promote the happiness of its citizens.

The Scope of Particular Justice

Aristotle limits the scope of the goods with which particular justice and injustice are concerned to external goods or goods of fortune (V.1 1129b1–3). A list of external goods that Aristotle gives at *NE* I.8 1099a31–b8 includes friends, wealth, political power, good birth, satisfactory children, and personal beauty. Plainly justice and injustice won't have to do with all of these, and at *NE* V.2 1130b2 Aristotle accordingly narrows the list of external goods with which justice and injustice are concerned to honor, wealth, and safety. These all seem to be things that one might want more than one's fair share of, i.e., things that one might be greedy for.

It is easy to see how justice and injustice are possible with regard to honor and wealth, less easy to see with regard to safety. Aristotle may have in mind cases in which one person avoids risks that others are then forced to assume. At *Rhetoric* I.13 1373b20–24, he distinguishes between doing injustice to individuals and doing injustice to the community (*to koinon*), maintaining, e.g., that one who commits adultery or assault does injustice to some individual, whereas one who avoids military service does injustice to the community. It would be a mistake, however, to conclude from this example that an act of injustice to the community does not involve an act of injustice to some specific person. If I unjustly avoid military service, the victim of my injustice is not only my city but also the person, whoever he may be, who must serve in my place.

Note that particular justice, in being concerned with honor, wealth, and safety, overlaps with other virtues of character: with magnanimity (*NE* IV.3) and proper pride (IV.4), which deal with honor; with liberality (*NE* IV.1) and magnificence (IV.2), which deal with wealth; and with courage (III.6–9), which deals with safety. Presumably particular justice has a different concern with honor, wealth, and safety from that of the other virtues. Aristotle makes no effort to tell us what the difference might be, but perhaps his idea is that, e.g., my cheating on my taxes shows both something about my attitude toward wealth – a concern of liberality – and something about my attitude toward those other citizens who must shoulder the burden I have shirked – a concern of justice.

Justice and the Doctrine of the Mean: The Problem

Aristotle thinks that each virtue of character – courage, temperance, liberality, etc. – is associated, not with a single vice, the virtue's opposite (as Socrates and Plato thought), but rather with a plurality of vices. Thus he associates courage with rashness, cowardice, and arguably other vices as well; temperance with profligacy and insensibility; liberality with prodigality and a variety of strains of illiberality; and so on. Moreover, Aristotle holds – indeed he is famous for holding – a general thesis as to how the virtue in each sphere is related to its correlative vices: the "doctrine of the mean," as the thesis is called. In explaining the doctrine at *NE* II.6 1107a2–6, Aristotle distinguishes two sub-theses of it, which I shall call *Location* and *Intermediacy*. Location is the idea that each virtue is a mean state (*mesotês*) that is in some way "between" a pair of vicious states, one of excess and one of deficiency. Intermediacy is the idea that each virtue is a mean state expressed in actions and passions that are in some way "intermediate" (*meson*) relative to the actions and passions in which its correlative vices are expressed. Thus courage is in some sense located "between" rashness and cowardice, and courageous actions are in some sense intermediate relative to rash actions and cowardly actions. (For more, see Young, 1996, 89.)

Particular justice would seem to be a counterexample to both of these sub-theses. In the first place, Aristotle associates only one vice, injustice, with justice; he does not claim that it is a mean state between a pair of vices, one of excess and one of defect.

This problem about Location produces a problem about Intermediacy. If justice is indeed associated with only one vice, it is hard to see how the notion of intermediacy can have any purchase with regard to just actions. Aristotle's solution to these difficulties is, as we shall see, to find special senses in which Location and Intermediacy are true of particular justice. Even after he has done this, though, he will admit that Location breaks down, at least partially, in the case of particular justice: "Justice is a mean state, though not in the same way as the other virtues" (V.5 1133b32–1134a1).

Distributive and Corrective Justice

NE V.2 ends by dividing particular justice into two kinds, distributive justice and corrective justice; and these are the subjects, respectively, of V.3 and V.4. Aristotle's principal aim in these discussions is to find a way to represent what is just in distribution and correction as "intermediate" between two extremes. This will enable him in V.5 to give senses in which Intermediacy and Location hold for particular justice.

Distributive justice is concerned with the distribution of "honor, wealth, and other items that may be divided among those who share in a political arrangement" (V.2 1130b31–2). Earlier in V.2, Aristotle had listed safety along with honor and wealth (1130b2); presumably he means to include it among the "other things" here. On Aristotle's analysis, distributive justice involves the allocation to *persons* of *shares* of one of these goods (V.3 1131a19–20). Such a distribution will count as *just* if and only if equal persons receive equal shares (1131a20–4). Equality of shares – what counts as an equal share of wealth, honor, or safety – will typically be easy to measure. Equality of persons will often be more difficult. "Everyone agrees," Aristotle says, "that just action in distributions should accord with some sort of worth, but what they call worth is not the same thing" (1131a25–7). The distribution of political authority is a star example: democrats propose that free citizenship is the proper basis for its distribution, oligarchs propose wealth, and aristocrats virtue or excellence (a27–9). (Aristotle tries to resolve this dispute in *Politics* III.) For our purposes, though, we can set aside these problems. What matters for us is that just action in distribution distributes equal shares to equal persons. Here the kind of equality is what mathematicians call "geometric" equality or equality of ratio: A distribution involving two parties, Socrates and Plato say, will be just if and only if the worth of the share distributed to Socrates is to Socrates' worth as the worth of the share distributed to Plato is to Plato's worth, where *worth* is measured by whatever are the correct standards.

Why does Aristotle think that this counts in some way as intermediate? We can answer this question by looking at just and unjust distributions in a simple case. Suppose that Socrates and Plato invest money in some enterprise, and the time comes when the profits earned are distributed. Distributive justice requires that equal persons receive equal shares. Here the measure of equality of persons is the size of the investment each has made. Suppose that Socrates has invested 20 minae, that Plato has invested 10 minae, and that there are now 60 minae in profits to divide between them. Plainly it is just to give Socrates, who has invested twice as much as Plato has, twice as much of the profits as Plato: 40 minae for Socrates vs. 20 minae for Plato. An unjust distribution would be one that violates this proportion. Suppose a distribution goes wrong by 5 minae, either by giving Socrates 45 minae and Plato 15 or by giving Socrates 35 and Plato 25. Then the amount that Socrates receives in the just distribution – 40 minae – is intermediate between what he gets in the first unjust distribution – 45 minae – and what he gets in the second unjust distribution – 35 minae. Thus a just share is intermediate between a share that is too large by some amount and a share that is too small by that same amount.

Corrective justice, the subject of V.4, is concerned not with distributions but with restoring the equality between people when one has wronged the other. In such cases, the worth of the people involved does not matter: "It makes no difference whether a good man has defrauded a bad man or a bad man a good one . . . ; the law looks only to the distinctive character of the injuries, and treats the parties as equals where one is in the wrong and the other is being wronged" (1132a2–6). In a case in which one person has wronged another, an inequality between the two people has been created, and corrective justice seeks to restore equality by taking away the perpetrator's "gain" (or its fungible equivalent) and restoring it to the victim. Here the kind of equality is not geometric equality but what Aristotle calls (following the mathematical terminology of his day) "arithmetic" equality or equality of difference: The difference between the victim's position after the correction and his position before the correction is equal to the difference between the perpetrator's position before the correction and her position after the correction. An illustration: if Plato has taken 10 minae that belong to Socrates, corrective justice will take 10 minae from Plato and restore it to Socrates. Socrates will then be better off after the correction by the same amount that Plato will be worse off: 10 minae. And Aristotle claims that what is equal here is also intermediate, since the restored position of equality, in which each party has again what he had before, is intermediate between the improved position of the perpetrator and the impaired position of the victim. When Plato takes 10 minae from Socrates, Plato is up 10 minae and Socrates is down 10. When equality is restored, both are back at ground zero. Each is at a position intermediate between Plato's being up 10 minae and Socrates' being down 10. Thus both distributive justice and corrective justice aim at what is intermediate. (Note that corrective justice, as Aristotle understands it, is concerned only with the restoration of the original positions between the principals. Concerns over, e.g., punishment do not arise, and indeed would in most instances be posterior to the determination, in achieving corrective justice, of the nature of the wrong done. That more will be required of the offender than what he has inflicted is noted in *Magna Moralia* I 1194a37–b2.)

Political Justice

Having wrapped up his discussion of justice and injustice as states of character at the end of V.5, Aristotle takes up a new topic in V.6, only to drop it forthwith and return to the subject of justice and injustice:

> We must not forget that what we are seeking is also unqualifiedly just action and politically just action. This is found among people who share in a life aiming at self-sufficiency, people

who are free and either proportionately or arithmetically equal, so that for those who do not have these features there is no politically just action, but only something just in virtue of a similarity. For there is just action among those in relation to whom there is also law. (1134a24–30)

A problem in understanding this important remark is whether, in describing "what we are seeking" as "unqualifiedly just action and politically just action," Aristotle is referring to two separate actions (as in "I'll start my car and drive to town") or to one thing twice, the second time in a way that explains or explicates the first (as in "I'll obey the law and pay my taxes in full"). Are "unqualifiedly just action" and "politically just action" two names for two things, or two names for one thing?

The text of *NE* V.6, though not conclusive, leans toward the second option. In the first place, 1134a24–30 goes on to say that politically just action is found among people "who share in a life aimed at self-sufficiency," who are "free," and who are "either proportionately or numerically equal," but it nowhere tells us what unqualifiedly just action is. This makes sense if "politically just action" explicates "unqualifiedly just action," since the statement of what politically just action consists in will also be a statement of what unqualifiedly just action consists in. If unqualifiedly just action and politically just action are two different things, the lack of an explanation of what unqualifiedly just action is would be mysterious.

Secondly, 1134a24 goes on to say that there is no politically just action among people who are not free and equal, only "something just in virtue of a similarity" (*ti dikaion kai kath' homoiotêta*" (1134a29–30). Presently (1134b8–18), he will tell us that no unqualifiedly just action or politically just action obtains between master and slave, between father and child, or between husband and wife, only something "similar" (*homoion*). Thus the first passage contrasts politically just action with action that is just "in virtue of a similarity," while the second contrasts unqualifiedly just action and politically just action with something "similar." Presumably, we have the same contrast both times. If so, again unqualifiedly just action and politically just action are the same thing.

Politics III.6–7 confirms the point. There, Aristotle classifies political arrangements or constitutions into types according to whether (a) *one* person, a *few* people (typically the rich), or *many* people (typically the poor) rule, and (b) the arrangement is *correct* in promoting the common interest or *incorrect* in promoting the rulers' interest. Thus we have six possible political arrangements:

	Correct	Incorrect
One	Monarchy	Tyranny
Few (rich)	Aristocracy	Oligarchy
Many (poor)	Polity	Democracy

Near the end of *Politics* III.6, Aristotle makes it plain that unqualified justice is restricted to cities with good rulers: "It is clear that those political arrangements that aim at the common interest are correct in conforming to what is unqualifiedly just, while those that aim at the interest of their rulers alone are all mistaken and are perversions of the correct political arrangements" (1279a17–20). Thus Aristotle affirms that political

463

justice, as it is found in communities with correct constitutions, conforms to what is unqualifiedly just. It will be clear that unqualified justice and political justice coincide if he also holds that *only* such communities enjoy political justice. And indeed he does. *NE* V.6 1134a27 asserts that politically just action is possible only among persons who are free and equal. And according to *Politics* III.6 1279a21, communities with incorrect political arrangements do not meet the condition of freedom: "These political arrangements [viz., the incorrect ones] are despotic, and a city is an association of free men." Indeed, it is precisely because they are despotic that these arrangements are mistaken and perverted (a19–21). It is safe to conclude, therefore, that unqualifiedly just action and politically just action in *NE* V.6 are one and the same thing, differently described.

Aristotle's view that justice *tout court* does not exist between a master and a slave, between a father and a child, or between a husband and wife may have some bearing on the question why the discussion of justice as an individual virtue of character in *NE* V.1–5 and the discussion of justice and responsibility in V.6–11 belong together. Aristotle's reasons for thinking that justice *tout court* does not obtain in the first two cases is that one's slave or one's child is "as it were a part of one" (V.6 1134b11), and there no injustice towards "one's own" (b10). This may strike one as a poor way of making a couple of reasonable points, that a slave is one's property and that a child is one's responsibility until it comes of age, both of which Aristotle does make (b10–11). But Aristotle may have put his point as he did because he thinks that there is some sort of separateness-of-persons condition between parties that must be met before relations of justice are possible between them, and that this condition is violated in the case of master v. slave and father v. child. His acceptance of such a condition is confirmed by his view that justice *tout court* obtains "to a greater extent" between a husband and wife than between a master and a slave or a father and a child (b15–16): The separateness-of-persons condition is closer to satisfaction in that case, even though "domestic justice," as he calls it, still falls short of full "political justice" (b17–18).

If Aristotle does accept a separateness-of-persons condition as necessary for full relations of justice, this may help to explain why the discussion of justice as an individual virtue in V.1–5 belongs with the discussion of justice and responsibility in V.6–11. There is an obvious application of the doctrine of the mean to the case of justice: Justice disposes one to seek one's fair share of certain kinds of goods. Plainly one can also be disposed to seek more than one's fair share of these goods, and this is the vice of injustice towards others. Plainly, too, one can be disposed to seek less than one's share of the goods in question: Why isn't this injustice to oneself, the missing vice of deficiency? But much of the discussion of in *NE* V.6–11, is concerned to establish that one cannot be unjust to oneself. So the suggestion is that Aristotle realized that he is avoiding what many would take to be the obvious application of the doctrine of the mean to the case on the individual virtue of justice, and that part of the point of V.6–11 is to explain why, or at least to provide the beginnings of such an explanation.

Pleonexia

Aristotle begins his development of the distinction between universal and particular justice with the observation, "Both one who breaks the law and one who is greedy seem to be unjust" (V.1 1129a31–2), and his first argument for the existence of particular justice appeals crucially to the notion of greed (V.2 1130a16–24). Thus greed is central to Aristotle's conception of particular justice. Here "greed" translates *pleonexia*, literally, "having more." Other translations include "overreaching," "getting more than one's fair share," "aggrandizement," and "graspingness." So what, exactly, is *pleonexia*, that is, Aristotelian greed?

Nobody knows. Aristotle says at one point, though, that the motive for particular injustice is the pleasure that comes from gain (V.2 1130b19–22). This remark requires some qualification, since plainly it is common for people to act on the desire for gain without being unjust: consider, e.g., business owners or investors. But the notion of excess is built into the word *pleonexia*, so perhaps Aristotle's idea is that a desire for excessive gain is at the heart of greed: in particular, a desire for gain that goes beyond one's fair share (see Hardie 1968: 187). A case will help to illustrate the idea. Suppose that I owe you some money. I might want to keep the money I owe you so that I shall have more money rather than less. If I act on that desire, on the current suggestion I shall act unjustly.

One difficulty with this suggestion is that Aristotle associates the desire for excessive gain with the vice of illiberality (see, e.g., *NE* IV.1 1122a2–3 and *EE* III.3 1232a11–12). If he was right in saying that, then he is wrong in saying, at V.2 1130b19–20 that actions done from greed are not expressions of any of the vices discussed in *NE* III–IV. A second difficulty is that if there is such a thing as desire for excessive gain, and that desire were distinctive of injustice, then presumably there is also such a thing as a desire for deficient gain, i.e., for less that one is entitled to, and such a thing as a vice of deficiency, which is also associated with justice – injustice to oneself, say. But Aristotle makes no provision for any such vice (see V.5 1133b32–1134a1); indeed, he vigorously denies that one can be unjust to oneself (see V.11 1138a4–28). Furthermore, far from thinking that desiring less than one's fair share is vicious, Aristotle counts the willingness to accept less than one is entitled to as a mark of equity (V.10 1138a1–2): something better than justice.

A second difficulty with understanding Aristotelian greed as the desire for more than one's fair share is that greedy people desire not simply to have more rather than less, but also to have more than their fair share (on one form the suggestion might take, see Engberg-Pederson (1988: 59); or Curzer (1995: 215–17)) or to cause others to have less than their fair share (on another form of the suggestion, see Kraut (2002: 138–41)). Thus in the example in which I want to keep the money I owe you, I desire to have more rather than less. But I also desire to have more than my fair share (on the first version of the suggestion) or in causing you to have less than your fair share (on the second): the unfairness is part of what appeals to me.

There is no doubt, I think, that the states of mind under discussion are possible states and that they are bad states. The question is whether they are the states of mind that Aristotle thinks are constitutive of greed.

Consider the first case he gives in arguing for the existence of particular injustice at the beginning of V.2. One man commits adultery for pleasure, another for profit. The former action is profligate, the latter unjust. The most straightforward way to construe the profit example is to say, e.g., that the second man seduces the woman because someone paid him to do it, or because he wished to gain entry into her house in order to steal something. Perhaps we could construe profit broadly, so that getting more physical pleasure than he deserves, or disgracing the woman, or her husband, or her family, counts as profit (though it is unclear how this counts as securing excessive money, honor, or safety – the goods with which justice and injustice are concerned). But there is no good reason to read the example in this way, except to save the interpretation. So too with the other cases of unjust action in the *NE*.

Further, it is not clear that the states of mind under discussion are plausibly to be seen as unjust at all. As Rawls (1999: 385–6) notes, unjust people and evil people are both prepared to do wrong or unjust things. They differ in that unjust people want more than their fair share of goods the appropriate pursuit of which is legitimate, whereas evil people want this, and more. Evil people want, in addition, to display their superiority over others and to humiliate them. They love injustice itself, and not merely the external goods that injustice can bring. The states of mind under discussion are, I take it, much closer to that of Rawls's evil man than that of his unjust man.

Rawls says that unjust people want more than their fair share of goods the appropriate pursuit of which is legitimate. This remark suggests a way of understanding Aristotelian greed different from those we have considered so far. For if this is what unjust people are like, then the difference between just people and unjust people will be that just people desire external goods only when their appropriate pursuit is legitimate, while unjust people continue to desire such goods even when their pursuit is illegitimate. In our example, if I owe you money and I am just, I shall not want to keep your money. If I am unjust, I shall. So understood, Aristotelian greed is not to be identified simply with some form, simple or complex, of the desire for excessive gain. It consists, rather, in the absence of a certain restraint on the desire for gain. A just person does not want gain when it involves taking what belongs to another. An unjust person is not similarly restrained.

If this is indeed what Aristotle means by greed, he is right to say, as he does at V.2 1130b19–20, that actions performed from greed are not expressions of any of the vices discussed in *NE* III–IV, illiberality in particular. For the mark of illiberality is the desire for excessive gain, and the mark of injustice is the absence of a particular inhibition on the desire for gain. Evidently Aristotle is also right not to seek a second vice to associate with justice. For if justice consists in the appropriate curbing of the desire for gain and injustice in the failure to curb that desire appropriately, it is hard to see what is left for a second vice to consist in.

Justice and the Doctrine of the Mean: Aristotle's Solution

Aristotle attempts at the end of V.5 to square his account of justice with the doctrine of the mean. Recall that the doctrine has two parts: Location, according to which each virtue is in some sense "between" two vices, one of excess and one of deficiency, and Intermediacy, the idea that virtuous action is in some sense "intermediate" between the actions expressive of those vices. Here is what Aristotle says about justice and Intermediacy:

We have now defined the unjust and the just. These having been marked off from each other, it is plain that just action is intermediate between acting unjustly and being unjustly treated; for the one is to have too much and the other to have too little. (V.5 1133b29–1134a1)

This should come as a surprise. In the first place, Intermediacy should place just actions between two sets of actions that are not just. Here, though, Aristotle places just action between acting unjustly and being unjustly treated. Furthermore, as we saw earlier, Aristotle argued in V.3 that what is just in distribution is intermediate between a share that is too great and a share that is too small. He argued in V.4 that what is just in correction is intermediate between profit (viz., the profit that an unjust agent secures) and loss (viz., the loss that the agent's victim suffers). Here he tells us, with no preparation, that doing justice – doing what is just – is intermediate between acting unjustly and being unjustly treated. It is hard to see how the remarks on intermediacy here fits with the remarks on intermediacy in V.3–4.

One possibility is this: Aristotle means that (a) my treating you justly is intermediate between (b) my treating you unjustly, in which case I get more than my fair share, and (c) my treating myself unjustly, in which case I get less than my fair share. Some scholars (e.g., Curzer, 1995: 218–22) think this is what Aristotle should have said in any event, since it represents justice as "between" between a pair of vices, injustice to others and injustice to oneself.

One problem with this interpretation is that it takes no account of the explanations of intermediacy in V.3–4. A second problem is that, even if Aristotle would have a better view if he took this line – and this is not obvious – the fact remains that he does not. He never attempts to associate justice with a pair of vices. Moreover, he has what he regards as good and sufficient reason not to take this line – for he will argue at V.11 1138a4–28 that one cannot do injustice to oneself. Indeed, as we have seen, it is not far-fetched to suggest that part of the point of Aristotle's including the discussion of justice and responsibility that occupies most of *NE* V.6–11 is precisely to explain why he does *not* take the line under discussion.

A second possibility is this: Aristotle means that (a) my treating you justly is intermediate between (b) my treating you unjustly, in which case I get more than my fair share, and (c) your treating me unjustly, in which case I get less than my fair share. This interpretation has two disadvantages. First, it is awkward that in (a) and (b) I am the agent and you are the patient, while in (c) you are the agent and I am the patient. And second, apparently, the interpretation, like the preceding one, takes no account of the explanations of intermediacy in V.3–4.

We can, I suppose, swallow the first difficulty. And perhaps we can answer the second difficulty: Suppose I refuse to repay the money I owe you. Corrective justice will then require that my unjust gain – the money of yours that I have kept – be taken from me and restored to you. Thus corrective justice will bring about the very same outcome that would have been brought about if I had acted justly toward you in the first place. And since corrective justice aims at what is intermediate between gain and loss – between what I get if I act unjustly and what you lose if you are unjustly treated – we can say that just conduct aims at that intermediate situation as well. Similar remarks can be made about cases involving distribution.

An advantage of this interpretation is that it may go some way toward explaining why Aristotle thinks the discussion of distributive and corrective justice in V.3–4 is relevant to the analysis of justice seen as the contrary of Aristotelian greed, the subject of V.1–2. Unjust conduct as described in V.1–2 is conduct that corrective justice as described in V.3 exists to make good on: theft, adultery, murder, assault, robbery, breach of contract, etc. (See the end of V.2 for the complete list.) So why does Aristotle think the discussion of distributive and corrective justice is even relevant to the understanding of justice as the contrary of Aristotelian greed? Perhaps because he thinks the perspective of a distributor or corrector is a perspective my assumption of which will allow me to bracket my personal interest in the outcomes of the various choices I might make, and thus allow me to see, in a disinterested way, what justice requires of me.

In Young (1989: 246), I give an example that illustrates what Aristotle may have in mind. I back my car out of my driveway, destroying your bicycle, which you have left there. A predictable dispute arises. We agree that I owe you compensation to the degree that I was negligent in not looking before backing my car out and to the degree that you were not negligent in leaving your bicycle in my driveway. But we disagree about which of us was the more negligent. You stress my error in not looking before backing out my car. If you are rude, you note that it might have been a child, not just a bicycle, that I ran over. I stress your error in leaving your bicycle where you did. If I am rude, I express the hope that you take better care of your child than you do of your bicycle. (For what it is worth, I am told that California law holds me, as the party with the last chance to avoid the mishap, as fully responsible.)

To settle our dispute we might take it to a third party for adjudication. Each of us would expect the arbiter to decide the case from a disinterested perspective. The arbiter will treat each of us, and our respective claims, equally. She will look only at the fact that a bicycle left in a driveway by one person was destroyed by a second person who backed over it, and not care which of us owned the bicycle and which the car. And she will fix responsibility as the facts and the relevant principles demand.

The arbiter's decision helps us to see what justice requires of each of us in the original case. The arbiter assumes a disinterested perspective on the matter, seeing us only as two members of a community of free and equal persons, each with our own needs and interests. She is made aware of the facts of the case, and she is asked to fix responsibility as the facts and principles require. But this is a perspective that is open to each of us, independently of our actually submitting our case to a third party. Each of us can look at the situation from the arbiter's point of view without actually submitting the case to an arbiter. I can base my claims on a view of the appropriate degree of responsibility attaching to someone who, in such circumstances, ran over someone else's bicycle that brackets the fact that the responsibility is mine. You can do the same, *mutatis mutandis*. To the extent that we have achieved Aristotelian justice, I am suggesting, this is what we shall be disposed to do.

Aristotle's attempt to square his account of particular justice with Location, according to which each virtue is in some sense "between" two vices, one of excess and one of deficiency, is this:

Justice is a mean state of a sort, but not in the same way as the other excellences, but because it is related to an intermediate, while injustice is related to the extremes. (V.5 1132b32–1134a1)

Here Aristotle makes no effort to locate justice between a pair of vices. This is understandable, since there is no vice other than injustice with which it is associated. But he apparently thinks that justice nonetheless counts as a mean state since it is "related to an intermediate, and injustice is related to the extremes." Evidently, this is an attempt to exploit the analyses of distributive and corrective justice in V.3 and V.4, where what is just is identified with what is intermediate, and what is unjust is shown to involve both excess and deficiency. But it is far from clear that it gives us an interesting sense in which justice is a mean state. Aristotle does have a verbal point: As kindness aims at what is kind, so a mean state (*mesotês*) aims at what is intermediate (*meson*). But one could argue that the practical crafts (such as, e.g., medicine) aim at what is intermediate – indeed Aristotle argues exactly this himself in *NE* II.6 1106b8–14. But would one draw the conclusion that the practical crafts are mean states? Aristotle himself does not.

Conclusion

In coming to a final view of Aristotelian justice, we must appreciate how thoroughly *political* it is. Justice does have a political dimension for Socrates and Plato, but each sharply limits that dimension. Socrates, in Plato's *Crito*, believes that it is unjust to disobey the city's laws, except under very special circumstances. But the injustice of disobeying the law is secondary; it derives from the injustice of harming those responsible for our existence or those who have benefited us and the injustice of reneging on our promises (if we believe that the *Laws* speak for Socrates) or from injustice of harming others *simpliciter* (if we do not). Plato's *Republic* notoriously defends a strong analogy between justice in a city and justice in an individual. But justice in the city is principally a heuristic facilitating the discovery of justice in the individual, and what matters in individual justice is not its connection with the city but its role in helping us to achieve and sustain what really matters: an apprehension and appreciation of formal reality. Aristotle goes further than Socrates or Plato in making justice political. One way in which he does this is, of course, by equating universal justice with lawfulness. But with his analysis of particular justice he cuts more deeply even than this. For on the account offered earlier, Aristotelian particular justice invites us, in conducting our relations with others, to assume a perspective from which we view ourselves and those others as members of a community of free and equal human beings, and to decide what to do from that perspective. If we are able to achieve that perspective, and to embody it in our thoughts, feelings, desires, and choices, we shall have achieved Aristotelian particular justice. When we act from that perspective, we shall express a conception of ourselves as free and equal members of a political community: as citizens.

Bibliography

Curzer, H. J. (1995). "Aristotle's Account of the Virtue of Justice," *Apeiron*, 28, pp. 207–38.

Engberg-Pederson, T. (1988). *Aristotle's Theory of Moral Insight* (Oxford: Oxford University Press).

Hardie, W. F. R. (1968). *Aristotle's Ethical Theory* (Oxford: Clarendon Press).

Keyt, D. (1991). "Aristotle's Theory of Distributive Justice," in D. Keyt and F. D. Miller (eds.), *A Companion to Aristotle's "Politics"* (Oxford: Blackwell).

Kraut, R. (2002). *Aristotle: Political Philosophy* (Oxford: Oxford University Press).

Miller, F.D. (1995). *Nature, Justice, and Rights in Aristotle's "Politics"* (Oxford Clarendon Press).

Rawls, J. [1971] (1999). *A Theory of Justice*, revd. edn. (Cambridge, MA: Harvard University Press).

Young, C. M. (1989). "Aristotle on Justice," *Southern Journal of Philosophy*, 27, supple, pp. 233–49.

Young, C. M. (1996). "The Doctrine of the Mean," *Topoi*, 15, pp. 89–99.

Young, C. M. (2006). "Aristotle's Justice," in R. Kraut (ed.), *The Blackwell Guide to Aristotle's "Nicomachean Ethics"* (Oxford: Blackwell), pp. 179–97.

Young, C. M. (forthcoming). *Aristotle: "Nicomachean Ethics"* V, Project Archelogos.

29

Friendship

MICHAEL PAKALUK

Aristotle's discussion of friendship occupies fully one-fifth of the *Nicomachean Ethics* and a comparable fraction of the *Eudemian Ethics*. Commentators have pointed out that this alone shows the great importance he assigns to the subject. Indeed, Aristotle tells us explicitly why he thinks friendship is important: it is either a virtue or something closely associated with virtue, he says, and it is centrally necessary for human life (*NE* VIII.1 1155a3–5). Aristotle thinks that friendship is a kind of natural outgrowth of goodness of character and that friendships are the ordinary context in which the virtues are acquired and virtuous actions are expressed. Furthermore, friendship seems naturally adapted to assist us in our needs and aims throughout life. Aristotle remarks famously that "human beings are by nature social animals." It is in his account of friendship that Aristotle gives us his fullest explanation of distinctively human sociability. The criticism that one sometimes hears, that Aristotelian ethics is egoistic, can have weight only if one ignores the social philosophy developed in Aristotle's treatment of friendship.

Two Initial Difficulties

Aristotle begins his discussion of friendship by distinguishing three kinds of friendship: complete friendship; friendship for usefulness; and friendship for pleasure. It is important to grasp that he distinguishes these three forms, in the first instance, in order to resolve two difficulties. These difficulties, then, provide a constraint on interpretation: we must understand Aristotle's classification in a way that it is suitable to resolving these difficulties.

The first difficulty is this. Do similar people become friends ("birds of a feather flock together"), or rather people who are dissimilar? Someone might try to resolve this difficulty by appealing to physical nature generally. For instance, some natural philosophers who preceded Aristotle held that, in general, "like is attracted to like"; others held, instead, that "opposites attract." Aristotle regards such an approach as misguided: in ethics, he thinks, we should attend to human character and what is distinctive about human beings (VIII.1 1155b9–10). We should resolve this difficulty, then, by looking to the basis of friendship in human character, affection, and choice. This is what the distinction of friendship into three kinds is meant to accomplish.

471

The second difficulty is as follows. Friendships seem to vary in degree; that is, of any two friendships, or of any one friendship at two different times, it seems to make sense to say that they are friendships to the same degree, or that the one friendship is *more* or *less* a friendship than the other. But, it seems, anything that can be compared in this way, falls along a single scale; and things that fall along a single scale, do not differ in kind: thus friendships do not differ in kind. And yet it seems commonsensical to say that there are different kinds of friendship. How, then, is it possible to compare friendships in *degree*, if in fact they differ *in kind*? Wouldn't that be "comparing apples with oranges"? Aristotle's distinguishing three forms of friendship, then, is also meant to explain how different kinds of friendships may nonetheless be compared in degree.

From this brief description of Aristotle's approach to friendship, it should be clear that he takes a very different approach from what we might take today. He does not begin with psychological claims; nor, surprisingly, is he at first concerned with friendship as it relates to his general ethical theory. Rather, he is concerned to clarify the relationship between friendship and, on the one hand, theories of natural science (the first difficulty) and, on the other hand, the logical characteristics of schemes of classification (the second difficulty). His approach to friendship is, one might say, "metaphysical" rather than psychological or ethical.

Three Kinds of Friendship

In defining friendship, Aristotle does not start from the consideration of an individual acting on his or her own and then build up a conception of friendship as composed of such actions. (This is one reason why he is not beset with any problem about the "possibility of altruism.") Rather, he views a friendship structurally, as a relationship which essentially involves symmetry, reciprocity, and mirroring. A friendship is a relationship in which persons similarly love each other, and in which they reciprocally wish good things to each other "in that very respect in which they love" (VIII.3 1156a9–10). By "love" Aristotle means an affection which has as its cause something that one recognizes in another and esteems as valuable. By "wish" Aristotle means a resolve to bring about something which one regards as good. The element of wish in a friendship is related to the love present in the latter, somewhat as effect is related to cause: we recognize something in someone as valuable; this may result in love; and love then manifests itself in a resolve to bring about something good for that person. To say that friends wish goods to each other "in that very respect in which they love" is to say that the good wished for answers to the good loved. (Precisely how it does so, Aristotle thinks, varies among the different kinds of friendship.)

Aristotle's view that friendliness is inherently reciprocal is of a piece with his view that human beings are by nature social animals (I.7 1097b11, IX.9 1169b17). When a person smiles at someone, he expects a smile in return. When we (in our current convention) reach out a hand for a handshake in goodwill, we expect that the other person will extend his hand similarly. We presume that "one good turn deserves another." Aristotle similarly conceives of human action not, typically, as something that one person does to or for another, but as a step in a reciprocal action, or series of such actions, between two persons. This is why Aristotle begins his classification of friendship by presuming that, in a friendship, each friend will show toward his friend the same sort of love that his friend shows toward him. This is also why he presumes that the ordinary sense in which friends wish goods to each other "in that very respect in which they love," is that each aims to confer some good upon the friend which is equal and similar to the good recognized in that friend and which was the reason or cause of the love.

Since friendship for Aristotle is a social structure of reciprocated love and well-wishing, he thinks that there will be as many kinds of friendship as there are of love. But how many kinds of love are there? To answer this question, Aristotle once again does not proceed in a psychological but rather in a "metaphysical" way. We said that he regards love as an emotional response to something valuable that is recognized and esteemed in another, which results in a corresponding wish for that person's good. Love therefore involves a relation: love is always love *for* something (cf. Plato, *Symposium* 199e–210a). But, Aristotle thinks, when one thing is essentially a relation to something, then the former has as many kinds as the latter (cf. VI.1 1139a8–11). Thus, Aristotle thinks, there will be as many kinds of love as there are bases for loving someone (VIII.3 1156a6–8).

Aristotle holds that there are only three bases for love. We value or esteem anything whatsoever, and thus a person also, only because of goodness or pleasantness (VIII.2 1155b20). But there are two ways in which someone may be good or pleasant. A person may be good or pleasant either "in his own right" or "in relation to you." To say that someone is good in his own right is to say that he is a good human being: that is, that he has the virtues and acts accordingly. To say that someone is pleasant in his own right is to say that his life and actions are inherently pleasant. It was Aristotle's conclusion in his *NE* Book VII treatment of pleasure that only a virtuous person's life and actions are inherently pleasant (VII.13 1153b9–15). Thus, these two bases for love coincide, and they form the object of a single kind of love: to love someone because he is good in his own right just is to love him because he is pleasant in his own right. Aristotle calls a friendship in which this sort of love is reciprocated a "complete" friendship. (He calls it "complete" for a reason that will become clear shortly.)

But there is not a similar coincidence in someone's being good "in relation to you" and his being pleasant "in relation to you." To say that someone is "good in relation to you" is to say that he is useful to you. To say that someone is "pleasant in relation to you" is to say that he is entertaining. Clearly someone may be useful without being entertaining, or entertaining without being useful. Thus these two bases correspond to two other kinds of love and therefore friendship: friendship involving the reciprocation of love based on someone's being useful ("friendship for usefulness"), and friendship involving the reciprocation of love based on someone's being entertaining ("friendship for pleasure").

After Aristotle develops, in this "metaphysical" way, this distinction of three kinds of friendship, he confirms his scheme tentatively by a cursory appeal to experience. For instance, he points out that adolescents typically form friendships for pleasure; elderly people form friendships for usefulness (VIII.3 1156a24–b6). He also points out that a friendship of the one kind will display very different attributes from a friendship of the other kind – which confirms that he has indeed isolated distinct *kinds*. For instance, elderly people who merely need help from each other won't spend time with each other, because they are grumpy and bitter and do not find each other's company pleasant (VIII.3 1156a28, VIII.5 1157b13–24): this would be a friendship for usefulness which is clearly not a friendship for pleasure. Again, adolescents form and dissolve friendships sometimes on a daily basis (VIII.3 1156b1–6): these would be friendships for pleasure, but not for usefulness (because surely what is useful to them doesn't change so quickly).

Resolution of the Difficulties

The first difficulty was: Do similar or dissimilar persons become friends? Aristotle uses his theory of three kinds to give a mixed resolution. Because friendship involves reciprocity, in which the love and well-wishing of each friend must "answer to" that shown by the other, it is inherent in friendship that similar persons become friends: typically two persons who are friends will both be inherently good and pleasant, or both useful to the other; or both entertaining to the other. Aristotle regards this as something like the default condition of a friendship. He thinks that there can be friendships which combine different kinds (IX.1), but these are aberrant and relatively unstable. His favorite example of such a relationship is pederasty, where a distinguished and mature man befriends a pubescent boy. The man offers his prestige and knowledge, as a way of advancement to the boy, and therefore is "useful" to the boy. The boy offers his good looks and, typically, sexual favors to the man, and therefore is "pleasant" to him. This relationship, then, combines different kinds: the acts and affections on each side of the relationship do not "answer to" those on the other side in the standard way. But as the natural tendency of a friendship is to show itself in an exchange that is similar in kind, in this case the older man inevitably comes to expect that he be loved in return in the same way that he loves the boy. He wants to be loved romantically, as he loves the boy romantically; but because he is not physically attractive, his expectation, and the relationship, is ludicrous (VIII.8 1159b15–19, IX.4 1164a2–4, cf. VIII.4 1157a5–10).

But another sort of similarity or dissimilarity involves goodness or badness of character. Thus, one might also wonder whether a good person can become friends only with another good person, or whether bad persons can form friendships at all. And here Aristotle's resolution is that only a complete friendship is sensitive to the moral differences in persons. Only good persons can become friends in a complete friendship, precisely because the love in such friendships is based on good character. But in the other kinds of friendship, a good, bad, or morally intermediate person can form a friendship with a person of any of these types. Clearly, someone may be good in relation to you – that is, useful – without being a good human being, or he may be pleasant in relation to you – that is, entertaining – without being inherently pleasant (and therefore good) (VIII.4 1157a16–19).

Someone might object that it would be enough if people merely *took* themselves to be good: to love someone as a good human being, it is important not that he actually be good, but simply that the one who loves him believes him to be good. Aristotle has some sympathy with this view. He recognizes that people generally regard themselves as good, even if they are not, and he apparently thinks that a friendship of a limited and qualified sort can result (IX.4 1166a11–12, b2–6). Yet he is unwilling to give too much scope for this refractory sort of relationship. He holds, reasonably enough, that a friendship based on a recognition of the goodness of another's character will require spending time with another and becoming capable of trusting him in important matters (VIII.3 1156b24–29, VIII.4 1157a20–4). And if you take someone to be good, but he isn't, your trust in him will inevitably be disappointed; you will eventually be hurt or even betrayed.

We can now see how Aristotle resolves the second difficulty which motivated his discussion of the kinds of friendship. As we saw, Aristotle thinks that anyone who is loveable as being good in his own right will also be loveable as being pleasant in his own right. But he also holds that anyone who is good in his own right will also be "good in relation to you." The reason is the obvious one that people who are virtuous act in ways that benefit those around them. For instance, you'd do well to be fighting along-side a courageous person on the battlefield; you'd be fortunate if your associates were all enormously generous persons; and so on. Again, Aristotle thinks that anyone who is inherently good will be "pleasant in relation to you." This is perhaps less easy to see. But consider that Aristotle thinks that among human virtues are to be included "friend-liness" and "ready wit." Aristotle's virtuous person is not austere and moralistic, but competent and gracious.

We seen now why a friendship based on someone's being good and pleasant in his own right is a "complete" friendship: such a relationship, Aristotle says, contains within it every possible basis on which someone can be esteemed and valued (VIII.3 1156b17–24). (And this is an additional reason, Aristotle thinks, besides the enduringness of virtue, why such a friendship is remarkably stable.) In contrast, friendships based on usefulness or pleasure have a superficial resemblance to complete friendships. They capture just one aspect of a compete friendship. That is the reason, Aristotle says, that we regard them as friendships "to a lesser degree." It is not that we are placing all friendships on a single scale and evaluating them with respect to that; rather, we are recognizing, perhaps only implicitly, that one kind of friendship is the ideal, and we say that a relationship is more or less of a friendship insofar as it has or lacks characteristics that we look for in that central case (VIII.6 1158b5–11).

Egoism and Altruism in Friendship

Aristotle's distinction of three kinds of friendship, then, is developed in response to the two difficulties he raises. Yet once Aristotle presents this distinction, we may raise other difficulties with respect to it. This in effect is what John Cooper does in a widely studied article on Aristotelian friendship (Cooper 1977a). Cooper first raises a question about whether Aristotle's theory can account for our ordinary experience of friendship: Aristotle says that complete friendship is based on a recognition of the good character of another, and therefore only good persons can form such a friendship; yet if few of us are good, then few friendships are like that (VIII.3 1156b24–5), and Aristotle's theory could not serve to explain, then, those common relationships that we call friendships. Second, Cooper worries whether Aristotle's theory involves an untenably bleak view of human nature: if Aristotle holds that an altruistic regard for another person's good is found only within complete friendships, and that the other forms of friendship, in contrast, are merely expressions of self-interest; then, since he thinks that complete friendships are rare, he must hold the unappealing and untenable view that nearly all human relationships are expressions of selfishness.

In response to the first concern, Cooper points out that virtue, and the virtuous person, serve as *ideals* for Aristotle. In practice, most people will approximate these ideals only partially. If so, then someone who approximated, to some degree, the ideal of human virtue could presumably form friendships which correspondingly approximated the ideal of friendship. One might also add that Aristotle recognizes that even persons who are not virtuous often act as virtuous persons do in limited circumstances: for instance, even people who are not ideally virtuous will typically treat their own children in much the same way as a virtuous person would (VIII.8 1159a33–5).

In response to the second problem, Cooper proposes a particular interpretation of the three kinds of friendship. Cooper maintains that, for Aristotle, friends of all three sorts evince a genuine, disinterested goodwill toward one another. The three kinds differ merely in the *conditions* under which that goodwill is displayed. In a complete friendship, Cooper says, the goodwill of the friends is not conditioned in any way: the friends wish good to each other come what may. But in a friendship for usefulness or pleasure, the friends show goodwill toward each other only on the condition that the friendship remains generally useful or pleasant to them; moreover, neither friend will promote the good of another if this tends to destroy the ground of the friendship. For example, a friend for usefulness will do favors for his friend, even at cost to himself, so long as the friendship continues in a general way to be profitable to him over time; he wishes good to his friend in a disinterested way, but only on the condition that the friendship retains a useful character. Moreover, he won't wish any good to his friend that would imply that his friend would cease being useful to him. Suppose for instance that his friend is useful because the friend lives nearby and can help him with difficult jobs around the house: then he won't wish that his friend take a new and better job, if that means that his friend will move to a distant town and be unavailable for helping out.

So, according to Cooper's interpretation, friendships for usefulness or pleasure are subtle mixtures of altruism and egoism: altruism because they contain the same disinterested goodwill as does complete friendship; egoism because this goodwill is evinced only given certain (egoistic) conditions. But does this interpretation match Aristotle's thought? We saw that Aristotle is concerned with the nature of reciprocation in a friendship; he thinks that the actions of a friend should properly answer to those of his friend, and that friends wish goods to each other "in the very respect in which they love." At one point Aristotle illustrates this with the story of a musician who plays the flute for a dinner, believing that the dinner host has contractually agreed to pay him a good fee afterwards. That is, the musician conceives of his playing as part of an exchange of useful goods, a service for a fee. But after dinner the host declines to pay him, insisting that there has been a fair exchange of *pleasure*: "You pleased me with your playing; and I pleased you in return, because you were pleased insofar as you anticipated getting a handsome payment for your playing" (cf. IX.1 1164a13–22). What the story shows is that friends do not wish for, or accept, just any sort of good from the other: they regard only a certain *kind* of good as properly reciprocating what they render. For Aristotle, the *kind* of well-wishing is not a constant across different kinds of friendship.

476

The gloomy view that human beings are entirely selfish is not a real possibility for Aristotle on entirely different grounds. As we have said, he thinks that human beings are by nature social, and what is natural to us is unavoidable and spontaneous – we can hardly become used to acting otherwise (II.1 1103a19–23). As Aristotle points out, we can observe the innate sociability of human beings when we travel, since strangers spontaneously act in a friendly way toward us, simply because we are fellow human beings (VIII.1155a21–2). Human beings are naturally friendly to one another as herd animals are naturally gregarious. (Nor does Aristotle hold that mental acts or emotions must have one's own welfare as their object: he thinks that we frequently respond to one another with emotions that are not self-interested, such as pity or hatred.) Thus a natural friendliness will mark *any* sort of friendship, even if the friendship itself is constituted by a distinct and limited sort of reciprocity.

At the same time, Aristotle is sensitive to the distinction between friendliness and friendship. A person may be surrounded by a plethora of friendly associates and yet be unhappy, because he lacks a true friend (IX.9 1169b16–22). Surely it is this further thing that Aristotle wishes to isolate, in his identification of "complete" friendship. Just as Aristotle is interested in the reciprocal structure of friendships, rather than in the structure of particular actions, so he is interested in what a particular sort of friendship implies about the character and dedication, and life, of the person who enters into it. His mention of a willingness to spend time with another (IX.12 1172a1–3, VIII.5 1157b17–21), and, in another context, of being prepared to give up one's life for another (IX.8 1169a18–20), seems directed at this. Even if friendships for usefulness and pleasure did contain the disinterested goodwill that Cooper claims for them, there would be an important sense in which they were, nonetheless, not altruistic enough, because they would not represent the altruism of character and of a life which Aristotle seems more interested in as most characteristic of a genuine friendship.

Extended Friendships

It is commonly, and rightly, said that Aristotle regards friendship as a much broader phenomenon than those intimate personal relationships that we call friendships. This is evident from the role that Books VIII and IX play in his *Ethics*. These are not a treatise on friendship alone so much as Aristotle's discussion of human sociability generally: personal friendships; romantic bonds; the nuclear family; the extended family; "voluntary associations"; political society; business partnerships; and the market. In doing so, he is not simply following the ideas of his time (see Konstan 1997). Rather, his view about how friendships vary in degree, and his structural definition of friendship, allow for that wide extension of the notion. As we have seen, relationships count as more-or-less friendships insofar as they resemble the central case of friendship. But, more importantly, Aristotle defines a friendship as a reciprocation of love and the wishing of goods to another. That is, friendship includes both an affective component and some component of resolve and purposefulness. Thus he can count as a friendship not merely relationships that arise at first from emotions, so long as they have *some* purposeful aspect (such as love affairs between adolescents), but also associations constituted by deliberate resolve or even contract, so long as they admit the development of an aspect of emotion.

For Aristotle, every friendship involves a common good, which is the sort of reciprocity that the friends recognize. Understand a common good as a goal that two or more persons share and work together to achieve. Something as simple as a contractual agreement thus constitutes a common good: if I am a carpenter, and you are a farmer; and you and I agree that I-will-build-you-a-shed-in-exchange-for-one-hundred-bushels-of-apples; this agreed upon coordination of our action is a common good. We need to have a shared understanding of the exchange if the contractual arrangement is to work, which requires that each person see things from the other person's point of view: I have to understand how the shed I build has as much worth to you as the bushels that you convey have to me. Aristotle thinks that the terms of the exchange of a friendship for usefulness usually have to be stipulated fairly precisely, but that, in contrast, the exchanges of complete friendships are loose, because the manner of reciprocation is different – Aristotle says that these friends reciprocate with their "purpose" or "choice," and that the friends expect this to be equivalent, not the worth of the service provided (VIII.12 1162b16–21, VIII.13 1163a16–23).

If every friendship involves a common good that is aimed at purposefully and perhaps even contractually, then, Aristotle reasons, any association through which human beings aim at a common good purposefully is potentially a "friendship" of sorts. This is the correct way of understanding his extended comparison of the family and political society in VIII.9–12. In the comparison, Aristotle views political society as that association which shows most clearly the ways in which human beings may deliberately coordinate their actions for the sake of some shared goal. We can do this in three ways, corresponding to the three main kinds of constitutional government: kingship, aristocracy, and timocracy. ("Timocracy" is what we should call "republicanism.") Aristotle regards these structures as revealing the "justice" of an association. On the other hand, Aristotle views the family as that association which shows most clearly the different sorts of affection that we can cultivate toward one another; he seems to think that we first cultivate them within a family and then extend them outwards to others. Aristotle next maps family relationships onto political structures: the relationship between father and children is mapped onto kingship; that between husband and wife in governing the household in a complementary way is mapped onto aristocracy; and that among siblings is mapped onto timocracy. He then concludes that each association formed on a pattern of one of the kinds of political constitution (e.g. a club which is run "democratically") is capable of carrying along with it the affections typical of the family structure which is mapped onto that constitution (in this case, fraternal affection). Such affections will naturally arise so long as the due structure or "justice" of the association is preserved, that is, insofar as the ruling group serves the interests of the ruled rather than its own interests.

The argument is evidently meant to apply to every possible human association. It yields not only a theory of "civic friendship," but also a theory of what we should call "civil society." Aristotle pictures political society as a society of societies: he holds that the members of each subordinate society should naturally be motivated, not simply by a sense of justice or duty, but also by fellow-feeling and loyalty, which come from the recognition of a shared purpose.

A Friend as "Other Self"

We saw that Aristotle thinks he can rely on each person's having implicitly an ideal of complete friendship. We also saw that he is disposed to extend the notion of friendship very widely, to encompass cooperation and friendly affection as found in any human association. In both cases he relies on the notion of a friend as "another self," which he develops in the final chapters of his treatment of friendship (IX.4–9). Indeed, that a friend is "another self" explains why Aristotle defined friendship in the first place in terms of symmetry, reciprocity, and mirroring.

The Greek for "other self," *allos autos*, means literally "other same." The notion looks paradoxical and contradictory: either a thing is the same or different (we might think); it cannot be both different ("other") and the same. Aristotle of course recognizes the jarring character of the phrase. He does not, however, leave it simply as a paradox. He gives it a definite meaning: to say that each of two persons is an "other self" relative to the other, is to say that each is related to the other, in affection and well-wishing, as he is to himself (IX.4 1166a29–33). But how precisely can a person love and wish good to himself? For Aristotle, we can construe an action or intention as an expression of self-love, only if we somehow analyze a person into two, either synchronically or diachronically (IX.4 1166a33–1166b2). We analyze a person into two synchronically by regarding his "thinking part" as primarily what he is: a person then loves himself, at some time, if the rest of what he is contributes to the good of this part. Thus a person would fail to love himself, in this sense, if he showed weakness of will and failed to carry out what his thinking part enjoined. We analyze a person into two diachronically by considering the same person at different times. Thus a person loves himself in this way if what he does at one time benefits himself at another time – if, for instance, through delay of gratification when young he puts himself in a better position when old. Aristotle's argument that "a friend is another self" involves looking at self-love as shown in various synchronic and diachronic relations that a person has with himself, and arguing that friendship involves a kind of substitution, by which the friend comes to occupy one place in these various relations. So, for instance, for a friend to accept a sacrifice now so that his friend will be better off later is not unlike a good person's delayed gratification in his own case. Of course, there must be reciprocity: by definition, another person will not be another self, if you alone make such sacrifices for him, but he is not disposed to make a like sacrifice for you.

So Aristotle reduces the great diversity of phenomena of friendship, which we have noted, to a single core conception: a friend is another self. Insofar as any relationship counts as a friendship, to that extent it involves persons relating to one another as a good person relates to himself. But this conclusion leads rather naturally to two further discussions in IX.8–9, which are, surely, two of the most interesting chapters in the Aristotelian corpus.

The first is this: If a friend is another self, and a good person's self-love is a paradigm for friendship, then it seems that a person should love himself, and do so more than he loves anyone else; however, this goes against the common wisdom that we should avoid selfishness. Aristotle resolves the difficulty by drawing a distinction between good and bad self-love. Good self-love is when a person loves his thinking part. We saw that Aristotle in IX.4 analyses synchronic self-love as the relationship of a person to his thinking part; in IX.8, he apparently wishes to analyze all good self-love in this way. He draws on his general conception of a virtuous action as an achievement which gains for the agent an enduring rational good, which Aristotle elsewhere describes as something "noble" (*kalon*). To do a virtuous action, he thinks, is to render a noble good to the thinking part of one's soul. In bad self-love, in contrast, we aim to satisfy the non-rational, non-thinking part of the soul. It is only the good sort of self-love which is a model for friendship, and no one would object if someone loved himself to an extreme in that way (IX.8 1169a11–18).

As we said, Aristotle wants to claim not simply that a good person should love himself, but also, shockingly, that he should love himself more than he loves anyone else. We would expect that to be the case if self-love is a paradigm for love of others; but, still, the claim is shocking. For Aristotle, it is a necessary truth that a good person loves himself more than others in this way. The reason has to do with an asymmetry between loving and being loved. To love is to act; to be loved is to be acted upon. But Aristotle holds that the goods we can gain through acting, especially the "noble" goods that we attain through virtuous action, are incommensurably higher than any good that we might gain through being acted upon. Suppose, for instance, that one's friend has three million dollars, and he gives two million to his friend, keeping only one for himself. Someone might suppose that the giver has therefore shown greater love for his friend than for himself: after all, he gave him the greater sum. But Aristotle would say: assuming that the gift was genuinely virtuous (that is, that it was the expression of generosity, magnificence, or some other virtue, and defensible as such), then he achieved something "noble" in giving it; and this good is incommensurably greater than the merely useful sum of money which his friend received. Clearly, any good thing we do for another will have the same structure (IX.8 1169a19–b1).

Aristotle's distinction of two senses of self-love, good and bad, suggests that an important idea which underlies his entire theory of friendship is that of "identification." For Aristotle, each individual seems to be faced, in particular actions and in the development of his character, with a decision involving identification: which part of himself will he take himself to be? Will he identify with his thinking part, or with the non-thinking part of his soul? Aristotle seems to think that an individual acts well or not, and becomes a good or a bad person, depending upon which he chooses. It seems also to be Aristotle's idea that this choice of identification makes possible the identification with the other that one finds in friendship. That is, it is precisely because the thinking part is rational, that we can regard the thinking part of another to be the same as one's own, so that another person takes the place of oneself (as we have seen) in relations of self-love. In contrast, there is no sense in which one may intelligibly take another person's non-rational part as equivalent one's own. Thus someone who identifies with his non-thinking part condemns himself to isolation and to perpetual conflict with those who have made a similar act of identification (IX.8 1168b15–21).

We have seen that Aristotle aims to unify the various phenomena of friendliness in relation to the ideal of "other self": persons are friends precisely to the extent that each is an other self to the other. We have also seen that, on Aristotle's view of human sociability, we are constantly led by natural motives to become related to others in that way: within the family; with associates; in political society; and so on. The question then arises: *Why* do we act in this way? What is it about us that impels us to become related to others as we are to ourselves? Why should we care so much about this? – so much so that, as Aristotle says, we would not find life valuable if we had no friends (VIII.1 1155a5).

Given that Aristotle thinks that happiness (*eudaimonia*) is the inherent goal of our nature, it is not surprising that he gives his answer as to the purpose of friendship, when discussing the relation of friendship to happiness (IX.9). He adverts to the definition of happiness he had offered in I.7, as *activity in accordance with virtue over a complete life* (1098a16–18). As regards the first part of the definition, activity in accordance with virtue, it is clear what role friends are meant to play: they are invaluable for perseverance, constancy, and growth in virtuous action, since we do everything better with friends; moreover, we can more reliably grasp the deficiencies of our own character, and thus act effectively to remedy or improve it, with the help of our friends. Such at least seems to be the main lessons of a somewhat obscure and much-discussed preliminary argument which Aristotle gives (IX.9 1169b28–1170a13).

But Aristotle then turns to an even more perplexing argument, which he refers to as "better grounded in a consideration of the nature of things" (IX.9 1170a13). This argument, as it involves an analysis of what it means for a human being to be alive, seems to be related to the second part of the definition of happiness, that it involves "a complete life." Life is perception, Aristotle claims, and a distinctively human mode of life must consist of intellectual perception. To wonder, then, why we seek friends for happiness, is to wonder what role a friend plays as regards intellectual perception. Aristotle points out that whenever we think, we perceive that we think. Thus there is a distinction of two, and a kind of self-love, implicit in every act of perception. A friend who shares in thought with you, assumes the same relation to you, as you do to yourself in a single act of intellectual perception: just as *you* perceive that you think; so your friend perceives that you think; and just as you perceive that *you think*, so you perceive that your friend thinks. But, more than this, the friend takes on this role at exactly the same time, and to an almost identical extent, as you are taking on this role. Contrast with this a case of reciprocal giving: if you give a gift to your friend, the reciprocation is not complete until your friend gives something in response, and there never was any one time, in the exchange, in which your friend has to yourself the relationship, or nearly the same, that you have to yourself.

Aristotle seems to think that thus to share in thought with another is a kind of fulfillment of an incipient sociability that is present in the very reflexive character of a single act of human thought. A human life, then, can fail to be complete not simply in its length (as when someone dies young) but also, so to speak, in its breadth, if we fail to relate to the inner intellectual life of another as we are related to our own life. Aristotle's final word on the point of friendship for human beings, then, is that through it we understand and are understood.

Bibliography

Books

Blum, L. (1980). *Friendship: Altruism and Morality* (New York: Routledge, Chapman and Hall).
Konstan, D. (1997). *Friendship in the Classical World* (Cambridge: Cambridge University Press).

Pakaluk, M. (1998). *Aristotle: "Nicomachean Ethics" VIII and IX*, trans. with comm. (Oxford: Clarendon Press).

Pakaluk, M. (2005). *Aristotle's "Nicomachean Ethics": An Introduction* (Cambridge: Cambridge University Press).

Price, A. W. (1989). *Love and Friendship in Plato and Aristotle* (New York: Clarendon Press).

Smith-Pangle, L. (2003). *Aristotle and the Philosophy of Friendship* (Cambridge: Cambridge University Press).

Stern-Gillet, S. (1995). *Aristotle's Philosophy of Friendship* (New York: SUNY Press).

Articles in journals

Annas, J. (1977). "Plato and Aristotle on Friendship and Altruism," *Mind*, 86, pp. 532–54.

Annas, J. (1988). "Self-love in Aristotle," *Southern Journal of Philosophy*, suppl. 7, pp. 1–18.

Cooper, J. M. (1977a). "Aristotle on the Forms of Friendship," *Review of Metaphysics*, 30, pp. 619–48.

Cooper, J. M. (1977b). "Friendship and the Good in Aristotle," *Philosophical Review*, 86, pp. 290–315.

Kahn, C. (1981). "Aristotle and Altruism," *Mind*, 90, pp. 20–40.

Kosman, A. (2004). "Aristotle on the Desirability of Friends," *Ancient Philosophy*, 24, pp. 135–54.

Millgram, E. (1987). "Aristotle on Making Other Selves," *Canadian Journal of Philosophy*, 17, pp. 361–76.

Schwarzenbach, S. (1996). "On Civic Friendship," *Ethics*, 107, pp. 97–128.

Whiting, J. (1991). "Impersonal Friends," *Monist*, 75, pp. 3–29.

30

Voluntary, Involuntary, and Choice

ROBERT HEINAMAN

Aristotle examines voluntariness in *Eudemian Ethics* II.6–9, *Nicomachean Ethics* III.1 and 5, and *Nicomachean Ethics* V.8. It is not obvious how similar or different he considered the three accounts to be. While focusing on *NE* III.1 and 5, I will also refer to *NE* V.8, and to the *Eudemian Ethics* as well when I believe it throws light on the *Nicomachean Ethics'* position.

Aristotle is primarily interested in voluntary and involuntary *action*. He calls other things voluntary or involuntary too: emotions such as anger; states such as courage and health; being happy; undergoing something (*paschein*) – *being moved* by an agent. But the *Nicomachean Ethics* does not explain how the definition of voluntariness for action is related to these other cases. This is puzzling when we consider two aims of his discussion of voluntariness: to explain happiness and virtue or excellence of character. *Nicomachean Ethics* I defines happiness (*eudaimonia*) as the exercise of virtue. Human beings can think, therefore they have intellects, and theoretical and practical wisdom are the virtues of this kind of soul. There is also a desiring part of the soul (*orexis*) which in turn divides into an appetitive soul that explains why human beings have appetites such as lust and hunger; a kind of soul that Aristotle calls *thumos* which explains why human beings feel emotions such as anger and pride; and a third element – identical with the practical intellect (*An* III.9 432b5–6; *MA* 4 700b22–3) – is the subject of rational desires that Aristotle calls "wish" and "choice." The virtues of the desiring part of the soul are virtues of character such as courage.

When Aristotle defines *eudaimonia* as the exercise of virtue, this applies to virtues or excellences of both character and intellect. Obviously, then, to understand Aristotle's definition of *eudaimonia* we must understand what counts as the exercise of virtue. A virtue is exercised or actualized in actions and emotions but, for example, an action counts as an exercise of courage only if it is done voluntarily. If I stand and face the enemy involuntarily it hardly counts as a manifestation of courage. So to understand what the exercise of virtue is – and hence to understand *eudaimonia* – we must understand what counts as *voluntary* action.

In terms of metaphysics, a virtue of character is a potentiality actualized in virtuous acts and/or emotions. One form of the priority of actuality to potentiality in Aristotle's philosophy is priority in definition: a potentiality is defined in terms of the actuality that realizes that potentiality (*Met* Θ.8 1049b10–17; *An* II.4 415a18–20). His definition of the genus *virtue of character* as a mean between excess and deficiency follows this requirement: virtue, a potentiality, is a mean *because* it is productive of what is intermediate in a certain sphere of actuality – action and/or emotion (*NE* II.5 1105b25–8, 6 1106b14–16 and 27–8, 9 1109a20–4, V.5 1134a8–9). The same applies to definitions of specific virtues of character (*EE* II.7 1223a21–3).

This exposes the problem regarding the voluntariness of emotions: if both *eudaimonia* and virtuous conduct must be explained in terms of voluntary exercises of virtue, since emotions as well as actions are actualities of virtue, Aristotle needs to explain what it is for an emotion to be voluntary. This, he signally fails to do (cf. *An* I.3 406a26–7).

Aristotle's focus is action. *Nicomachean Ethics* III.1 points out two factors – compulsion and ignorance – either of which suffices for involuntariness; and then defines voluntary action in terms of their contraries (1111a21–3):

> Since the involuntary is that which is done under compulsion or because of ignorance, the voluntary would seem to be
>
> [a] that of which the origin (*archê*) is in the agent,
> [b] where he knows the particular circumstances of the action.

I will discuss the two conditions in turn.

Agent Causation

Straightforward compulsion occurs when (a) the "agent" contributes *nothing* to the "action" and (b) what happens is contrary to the person's desires.[1] For example, when the wind blows agent A to place p, A goes to p involuntarily, under compulsion, just in case A wanted to avoid p, and it was not up to A to go there or not (*NE* V.8 1135a26–8).

By contrast, the origin of voluntary action is "in" the agent, or, equivalently, the agent causes the action. Though obscure, this notion can be clarified to *some* extent. *Rhetoric* I.10[2] lists possible causes of what people do or undergo:

1. The person is the cause
    a. Due to habit
    b. Due to rational desire
    c. Due to irrational desire
        1. Due to spirit (*thumos*)
        2. Due to appetite
2. The person is not the cause
    a. Due to chance
    b. Due to necessity
        1. Due to compulsion
        2. Due to nature

Confusion sometimes results from failure to distinguish agent-causation from the idea of a nature causing something. Although the voluntary agent acts in accordance with nature (*EE* II.8 1224b35–6, 1225a17–27; cf. *Phys* VIII.4 254b15–17, 27–8), other natural phenomena are *determined by* nature independently of one's desires, thus excluding voluntariness: respiration, growth, hunger, growing old, one's hair turning grey, dying, etc. (*NE* III.5 1113b26–30, 1114a23–6, V.8 1135a33–b2, VI.12 1144a9–11; *EE* II.10 1226a22–6; *MA* 11). Though explained by reference to a person's internal nature (the soul) (cf. *GC* I.5 321b6–7, 322a10–13), in the relevant sense their origin is *not "in"* the agent (*Phys* VIII.6 259b8–11).

As the *Rhetoric*'s scheme indicates, A causes an action x only if it is caused by a desire of A.[3] Further, and importantly,

(1) A causes x if and only if it was up to A to x or not to x (and A xes).[4]

Someone who causes x could have caused the opposite (*Phys* VIII.4 255a5–10). Aristotle never explains under what conditions "it was up to A to x or not." We might seek help in *Metaphysics* Θ.2 and 5. There, Aristotle explains, non-rational potentialities such as fire's power to heat are powers to do *one* thing. When sufficiently near an appropriate patient, and other necessary conditions hold, fire necessarily heats the patient: it is not up to the fire to heat or not (*Phys* VIII.4 255a9–10). But rational powers are potentialities for opposites, as a doctor's power to heal is also a power to harm. Hence, when sufficiently close to an appropriate patient and, as things are *there and then*,[5] other necessary conditions exist, it is not settled what the doctor will do: that is determined by the doctor's "decisive" want (*Met* Θ.5 1047b35–1048a13; cf. *An* II.3 417a27–8, b23–4, III.9 433a4–8. "Decisive want" remains unexplained). As with the ability to walk, this feature of rational powers need not be based on knowledge as the power to heal is based on knowledge of health.

This requirement for something's being up to a person would explain why A's nature may cause what A does not: it is not up to A to grow old or not, for there are conditions sufficient to cause A's growing old, and conditions never exist such that if A decisively desires to grow old he will, and if he decisively desires not to grow old he will not.

We can also see why the involuntariness of compelled actions is due to their not being up to the agent: if A is *compelled* to hit B when someone grabs A's hand and uses it to hit B (*NE* V.7 1135a26–8, *EE* II.8 1224b13–14), there are circumstances sufficient to make A hit B, and it is not true that if A decisively desires to hit B he will, and if he decisively desires not to hit B he will not.

If (see n. 1) the *Nicomachean Ethics* accepts *EE* II.10 1225a19–33's cases of compelled actions on desires and thoughts out of the agent's control, such an action may be caused by the desire to perform it when *the agent* does *not* cause it: according to *EE* II. 7 1224b2–15, a compelling force is *external* to the agent. In such cases, perhaps, Aristotle would reject the claim that:

(i) if A decisively desires to x he will x, *and if he decisively desires not to x he will not x*.[6]

But even if, in such cases, Aristotle would reject (i), (i) does not provide a complete analysis of his idea of something's *being up to* an agent. As just noted, *EE* II.10 1225a19–33 refers to cases where it is not up to A to *desire* x or not (cf. *EE* II.6 1222b41–2). The notion of x *being up to* A ought to be the same whether x is an action or a desire, but

485

clearly nothing along the lines of (i) works when x is itself a desire. However the notion of *being up to* an agent should be explained, at least we can say that another requirement for agent causation is that the desire causing an action must be up to the agent to have or not.[7]

Agent causation also requires that nothing cause A to cause the action (*NE* III.4 1113b17–21; *EE* II.6 1222b39–42; *Phys* VIII.5 256a8). It is clear that an agent causing an action consists in the agent's soul being the efficient cause of the action; and that this involves some *desire* efficiently causing that movement (*An* III.9–11). Since Aristotle believes that, for example, a wish may cause a choice which causes an action (*NE* VI.2 1139a31–3), the requirement that nothing cause A to cause the action applies only to the initial cause of the action. It is doubtful that Aristotle has a clear explanation of when this is true. And despite the *Ethics*' (and the *Physics*'[8]) talk of nothing being the cause of A's causing the action, Aristotle speaks openly of the relevant part of the soul, in desiring some good, being *moved* to desire by the *un*moved mover of the action – the desired good, real or imagined, for the sake of which the agent acts (*An* III.10; *MA* 6 700b36–701a2, 7 701a33–b1, 33–34, 10 703a4–5; *Met* Λ.7 1072a26–b4). According to *MA* 8, voluntary (703b3–4) animal motion results from the following sequence of cause and effect: something regarded by the animal as good is perceived or thought of; this causes the animal to imagine possessing it; this causes the animal to desire it; this causes certain parts of the animal's body to change quality, and this change causes the change of place that is the action (Cf. *MA* 6 701a2–6, 7 701b10–32; *Phys* VIII.2 253a7–13, VIII.6 259b1–14). It is not credible to suppose that the *Nicomachean Ethics* abandons this view of how final causes which are also efficient causes (cf. *MA* 6 700b23–8; *Met* Z.7 1032b15–23) explain the agent's desire in cases of "self-movement" (see *An* III.10 433b27–30; *MA* 6 700b17–29). Certainly, *MA* regards its account of animal motion not as incompatible with but as *explaining* self-motion.

Then we might try to give some sense to the idea that the agent is the ultimate cause by noting that the final cause is determined to be such by the condition of the agent's soul. To explain this I must clarify what Aristotle says about choice (*prohairesis*).

Choice

Consider table 30.1.

Suppose A has the virtue of temperance. Then A's appetites are for a moderate amount of physical pleasure and the virtue consists, in part, in a disposition to so desire physical pleasure. But the virtue also consists in a dispositional desire of the practical intellect: a wish to enjoy a moderate amount of physical pleasure resulting from the belief that one should enjoy a moderate amount of physical pleasure.[9] Contrary to the impression made by *NE* II, all virtues are by definition states of the practical intellect – rational desires, wishes – which are caused by another state of the practical intellect: a belief that something is good. Some virtues such as temperance are also states of an irrational part of the soul but others such as justice are states solely of the practical intellect.

The just man has a *general*[10] belief that distributing goods in proportion to merit is good and consequently wishes to distribute goods in proportion to merit. The disposi-

Table 30.1 Aristotle's understanding of desire and virtue in the soul

Soul	Part	Condition	Activity
Rational soul	Theoretical intellect	Knowledge or error	Theoretical thinking
	Practical intellect	Practical wisdom wish	Practical thinking wish
Desiring part (ὄρεξις)	Thumos	Virtue or vice	Anger, etc.
Irrational soul	Appetitive soul	Virtue or vice	Hunger, lust, thirst, etc.

tional wish is what the virtue of character *is* (*NE* V.1 1129a6–10). Given appropriate particular circumstances, the general belief and wish result in an agent A's believing that he should distribute goods in proportion to merit and thus wish to do so here and now. When it is unclear how to achieve the wished-for end, A may deliberate about how to achieve it. If the deliberation succeeds, he may *choose* an action x which he believes himself capable of doing *for the sake of* realizing his wished-for goal of distributing goods in proportion to merit (*EE* II.10 1226a11–15, 11 1227b36–8). Choice is by definition the outcome of deliberation beginning from a wished-for goal believed by the agent to be good. The entire process of forming a choice beginning with a belief and ending in a decision occurs in the practical intellect. The goal of the just person is the distribution of goods in proportion to merit, the goal of the unjust person, perhaps, self-aggrandizement, but the end of the choice will always be a wished-for goal believed to be good.

Since actions may go wrong and fail to reveal the agent's goals, choice is a better indication of character than action because it reveals the agent's ends, the goods he wishes for and the bases of those ends: his beliefs about what is valuable (*NE* III.2 1111b6; cf. *EE* II.11 1228a2–4, 11–13). A truly just agent must choose just actions *for their own sake* (*NE* II.4 1105a28–32, VI.12 1144a13–20), that is, because they are just and not (e.g.) merely in order to avoid jail. Aristotle's claim is not obviously consistent with his repeated assertion (*NE* III.2–5) that, as an outcome of deliberation, choice is of the *means* to achieve an end that is not a result of deliberation (contrast *NE* VII.9 1151a35–b2). I understand him to mean (e.g.) that the just man who desires to achieve the end of distributing goods in proportion to merit will, after deliberation, choose to perform an action x in order to achieve that end, and, *as* "doing what is just," choose x for its own sake.

Not every choice fully reveals character. Continent and incontinent agents both choose to refrain from physical pleasure but in both cases the choice does not itself expose an important feature of the agents' characters: the presence of excessive desire for physical pleasure. The incontinent agent's decision to pursue physical pleasure is not a choice since it results from deliberation on how to satisfy an appetite rather than a wish (*NE* III.2 1111b13–15, VI.4 1148a4–10, VII.8 1151a6–7).

Not all voluntary actions are chosen since choice occurs only when the action is immediately preceded by deliberation aiming at realizing a wished-for goal. So actions done without deliberation, such as those done on the spur of the moment (*NE* III.2 1111b9–10), are not chosen though they can still express a mature adult's virtue or vice (III.8 1117a17–22).

Agent Causation (Cont.)

Recall that the final cause of an action causes the agent's desire to x, so A's desire to x will itself be caused. It might be suggested that this does not contradict the idea that A's resulting action is, when chosen, "self-caused" since the final cause – the wished for goal – is determined by the agent's beliefs and character. It is only because A is just and thus believes that he should distribute goods in proportion to merit and wishes to do so that the goal – the final cause – of distributing goods in proportion to merit exists in the first place, and causes him to wish to achieve it, deliberate, and then choose to x. When there is no deliberation or choice the final cause of the action still derives from the agent's character. Returning to the sequence of cause and effect from *MA* 11, the initial thought or perception of x will lead to action only if x is regarded by the agent as good. So, one might propose, the fact that there is a final cause of the agent's desire does not conflict with the idea of the agent being the ultimate cause of the action (cf. *NE* III.5 1114a31-b3, 22–24. *Phys* II.5 197a2 suggests that the end for the sake of which an agent acts is a cause that is *in* the agent).

NE III.1 suggests that there are only two possibilities: the agent does or does not cause the action, and in the latter case the agent contributes *nothing* to producing the action, and hence the action is compelled. A frequently noted problem is that Aristotle's examples of compulsion, both here and elsewhere (*NE* III.1 1110a3–4, V.8 1135a27–8; *EE* II.8 1224b11–15; *Met* Λ.7 1072b11–12; *Rhet* I.10 1369b5–6), appear to be cases not of compelled *action* but of things *happening to* someone involuntarily. The distinction between doing (*poiein, kinein*) and "suffering" (*paschein, kineisthai*) is central to Aristotle's metaphysics[11] so it is puzzling that he gives examples of the second as instances of the first.

After straightforward cases of compulsion, Aristotle discusses "mixed" actions that are both voluntary and involuntary (*NE* III.1 1110a4–b9; cf. *EE* II.9 1225a2–36). They are cases in which an agent has conflicting desires where one desire can be satisfied only at the cost of frustrating the other, and where the rational decision requires one to do something that is evil[12] in itself in order to avoid another evil or achieve some good. They include cases of acting under duress or threat. One example is of a man who, along with his family, is under the control of a tyrant who demands that he do something base (kill an innocent man, for example) in order to save his family. The threatened man desires *both* to save his family and not to kill the innocent man. Suppose he judges that the evil which would be the death of his family outweighs the evil of killing an innocent man, and decides, with reluctance, to kill the innocent man. Does he kill the man voluntarily or involuntarily?

Aristotle answers that *in itself* the action of killing was involuntary because, in general, killing is an intrinsic evil, something to be avoided for its own sake. But the particular action was voluntary. For in the unfortunate circumstances, the particular act of killing was worth choosing since it was rational to prevent the greater evil rather than the lesser evil; and that required killing the innocent man (cf. *NE* V.11 1152b26–31).

Aristotle's second argument for judging the action voluntary is that the origin of the action was in the agent. Consequently, it was up to the agent to kill the man or not, which establishes that the action was voluntary (III.1 1110a15–18).

Evidently, Aristotle thinks that if it were not up to the agent to kill or not, his action would be involuntary. The *Eudemian Ethics* holds that while some mixed actions are voluntary, others are involuntary because it is not up to the agent to perform them or not (*EE* II.8 1225a19–21, 25–33). Most believe, reasonably, that *NE* III differs in holding *all* mixed actions to be voluntary. I am inclined to disagree. Compare the following passages, the first two from the *EE*, the third from *NE* III.1:

> *EE* II.8 1225a19–21: Therefore many hold that love, some instances of anger, and natural impulses are involuntary, because their strength exceeds [our] nature (*huper tên phusin*) – and we pardon (*suggnômên*) them because they naturally compel [our] nature.

> *EE* II.8 1225a25–7: What is up to a man, which is what it all depends on, is what his nature is able to bear (*hê autou phusis hoia te pherein*).

> *NE* III.1 1110a23–6: In some cases there is no praise, but there is pardon (*suggnômên*), whenever one does what one ought not to do because of pressure *which overstrains human nature* (*ha tên anthrôpinên phusin huperteinei*) *and nobody could endure.*

The *Nicomachean Ethics* agrees with the *Eudemian Ethics* that only what is up to us to do or not is voluntary. And how, in *NE* 1110a23–6's language, can some threat or fear be *beyond* what a person's nature can bear, be what nobody *could* endure, if the resulting action is still up to the person to do or not? So I am inclined to think that, as in *EE*, Aristotle continues to believe that what exceeds our nature is involuntary. If so, given his commitment to

(1)　A is the cause of x if and only if it was up to A to x or not to x (and A xes),

it follows that in some cases of mixed action, the origin of the action is not in the agent, Aristotle's second reason (1110a15–18; cf. 1110b4) for describing the action as voluntary does not apply, his definition of voluntariness is not satisfied, and the action is involuntary.

Knowledge

For an agent to x voluntarily he must know that he is xing (*NE* III.1 1111a21–3, V.8 1135a23–8). Any action involves many factors, descriptions of it varying depending on which factors are referred to. While their range seems indefinitely large, *NE* III.1 1111a3 appears to limit their number to six: the agent, what he is doing, the object acted on, the instrument, the manner, and the actual result of the action. The agent may of course be aware of some of these factors but not others, so the action may be voluntary "under one description" and involuntary under another. Suppose A stabs and kills the man standing before him with a knife. A might realize that he is killing the man but not that he is using a knife. Then while A killed the man voluntarily, he killed the man with a knife involuntarily. As long as one factor is referred to in the act description "x" of which the agent was unaware, the agent xed involuntarily.

Further, one factor can be picked out with different descriptions. Suppose that, unknown to A, the man he killed was his father. Then although he voluntarily killed the man standing before him, he did not voluntarily kill his father.[13]

After distinguishing the non-voluntary from the involuntary (see n. 1), *NE* III.1 draws another distinction, that between acting *because of* ignorance and acting *in* ignorance. All actions done *because of* ignorance are also done *in* ignorance, but the converse does not hold (*NE* V.8 1136a5–7). A drunk may act in ignorance of what he does but will not do it because of ignorance but because of his drunkenness.

Ignorance of some factor x can refer to (i) total ignorance of x, (ii) failure to think of what one knows regarding x, or (iii) a false belief about x (implying (i)). But the force of "because of" ignorance is obscure. Ignorance is the absence of knowledge, and Aristotle says little on how the absence of something explains why something else is the case. According to *Physics* II.3 195a11–14 we will "sometimes" speak of the absence of x as explaining y when the presence of x would explain the presence of the contrary of y. Applied to involuntary action, this would mean that when A does x because of ignorance, the relevant knowledge would have brought about a different action. But this will not work for "non-voluntary" action (see n. 1) since in many such cases the agent would not wish to avoid the action, and hence knowledge would not have resulted in a different action.

The *Physics'* proposal also undermines the distinction between action because of ignorance and action in ignorance. The ignorant drunk acts not because of his ignorance but because of his drunkenness (*NE* III.1 1110b25–7). But often if a drunk had known what he was doing he would have acted otherwise. So on the proposed explanation of "because of ignorance" the drunk would act because of ignorance.

The distinction between (i) *because of* and (ii) *in* ignorance raises problems for both the understanding and the coherence of Aristotle's position. In *NE* III.1 (1110b24–7), the drunk's action falls under (ii), not (i). In III.5 (1113b14–1114a3) the drunk – one example of a negligent agent who is responsible for his ignorance – is someone of whom we can say that the origin of the action is *in him* since it was up to him to get drunk or not (III.5 1113b32–3), and his drunkenness caused his present ignorance. The drunk is mentioned after Aristotle says (III.5 1113b19–21) that those things of which the origins are in us are up to us and voluntary.

On one common and plausible interpretation – call it the *First Interpretation* – this passage in III.5 is arguing that the origin of the action of the negligent and/or drunken agent is in him, his action is up to him to do or not, *and is therefore voluntary*. If so, III.5, 1113b19–21 – "the acts whose moving principles are in us must themselves also be in our power and voluntary" – justifies the conclusion that the drunk's actions are voluntary, claiming that

(2) "Action x is up to A to do or not to do" (and "A xes") entails that "A xes voluntarily,"

even when A acts without knowledge.[14]

490

But the First Interpretation faces objections. (i) The drunk could not have acted voluntarily since he was unaware of what he was doing. It is absurd to suggest that a mother who, through negligence, failed to realize that she was poisoning her beloved child must have *voluntarily* killed her child.

(ii) *NE* V.8 asserts that the origin of the *involuntary* action performed by the negligently ignorant agent is *in* the agent (1135b16–19), implying (given (1)) that the involuntary action was up to the agent to do or not. This contradicts (2). In *NE* III.5, when discussing the voluntariness of virtue, Aristotle acknowledges that the fact that A is the cause of x, or that it was up to A to have x or not, establishes that A acquired x voluntarily only if A knew that he was causing himself to acquire x (1114a9–10, 12–13).

(iii) The First Interpretation contradicts Aristotle's definition of voluntary action in *NE* III.1 (1111a22–4):

(a) that of which the origin (*archê*) is in the agent,
(b) *where he knows the particular circumstances of the action.*[15]

Given that:

(1) A is the cause of x if and only if it was up to A to x or not to x (and A xes),

(a) entails that the action is up to the agent to do or not. Therefore, if Aristotle accepted

(2) "Action x is up to A to do or not to do" (and "A xes") entails that "A xes voluntarily,"

(a) would suffice for voluntariness when (b) was false. Hence, contrary to Aristotle's definition, (b) would not be necessary for voluntary action.

Furthermore, the drunk and the negligently ignorant agent, acting "in ignorance" (1110b27, 1113b30–3), do not know the particular circumstances of their actions, so on Aristotle's definition of voluntary action they cannot act voluntarily.[16] In *NE* V.8, 1136a5–9, the man who acts *not because of but in* ignorance acts *in*voluntarily. *NE* III.1 consistently takes it for granted that acting in ignorance suffices for involuntariness (1110b19–21, 1111a2, 7, 8, 16–17).

(iv) If Aristotle accepts (2) and thinks that, on its own, the fact that the origin of the drunk's action is in him suffices for the voluntariness of the action, he ought to deny that the origin of action which, unlike the drunk's, is involuntary *due to* ignorance, is in the agent. Otherwise he must say that the man acting *because of* ignorance acts voluntarily. But if the origin of the action of the man who acts because of ignorance is not in but external to him, Aristotle must also say – given his account of compulsion – that someone acting because of ignorance acts under compulsion. The same conclusion follows when we note that since Aristotle believes (1), if the man who acts because of ignorance does not cause his action, it is not up to him to act or not. Then the man who acts because of ignorance and not because of himself acts under compulsion. Hence, all involuntary actions due to ignorance are cases of compulsion – an absurd position.

In view of these problems the First Interpretation needs to be modified. *NE* 1113b19–21 – "the acts whose moving principles are in us must themselves also be in our power and voluntary" – should not be understood to affirm

(2)   Action x is up to A to do or not to do (and A xes) entails that A xes voluntarily.

Rather *NE* 1113b19–21 assumes that the agent under discussion knows what he is doing. *NE* 1113b19–21 responds to the suggestion that we are not voluntarily vicious and are not origins of our actions (1113b17–19) and is not concerned with the issue of knowledge. The same tacit assumption of knowledge in the agent is found in *NE* III.1's second argument for the claim that mixed actions are voluntary since the agent of such an action is its cause (1110a15–18; likewise at *EE* II.8 1225a9–11). Neither passage supports (2) and the *Nicomachean Ethics* rejects the *Eudemian Ethics*' erroneous view that ignorant, negligent, and drunken agents act voluntarily.

However, while *NE* III.1 and V.8 agree on this point, *NE* V.8 also *supports* the claim that the cause of involuntary actions due to *non*-negligent ignorance is *not* in the agent (1135b19). On this point, Aristotle is consistent (*Phys* II.5 197a1–2, b18–20; *EE* I.3 1215a12–14, II.6 1223a10–12, 1226b30–1; *Rhet* I.9 1368a4–7, 14–15, I.10 1368b33–1369a7; cf. *NE* III.5 1114b3–5). Since, like all chance events, lucky and unlucky actions are unusual (see *Phys.* II.5–6), it is reasonable to expect them not to occur (they are *para logon*: *NE* V.8 1135b16–17; *Rhet* I.5 1362a5–6, I.13 1374b5–6; *Phys.* II.5 197a18–20). So they are involuntary due to *non*-negligent ignorance. While, Aristotle holds, the agent causes involuntary action due to negligent ignorance, on the *Rhetoric*'s scheme of causes (see above) luck is a cause only if the agent is not the cause. So while my other objections stand, the fourth points to a difficulty not for the First Interpretation but for Aristotle. He is committed to the erroneous claim that all involuntary actions due to non-negligent ignorance, that is, *all* actions *due to* ignorance, are compelled: if, ignorance being the cause, the agent is not the cause of the action, (1) entails that the action is not up to the agent to perform or not. So it is done under compulsion.

Moral Responsibility

In the *Eudemian Ethics* one is morally responsible for all and only one's voluntary actions, and an agent causes all and only his voluntary actions (II.6 1223a9–20, II.11 1228a7–11). By contrast, the *Nicomachean Ethics* cannot allow that voluntariness or being the cause of an action suffices for moral responsibility. For it asserts that animals – obviously not morally responsible agents – act voluntarily (*NE* III.2 1111b8–9), and so cause their voluntary actions. Nor does involuntariness entail absence of moral responsibility: negligent involuntary action due to ignorance can be justifiably blamed (*NE* III.5 1113b23–5, 1113b30–1114a4). The *Nicomachean Ethics*' position is rather that an agent is morally responsible for an action if and only if he is capable of *praxis* and is the cause of what he does (or, equivalently, it was up to him – *NE* III.5 1114a21–

31). A *praxis* is *chosen*, and, as we saw, an agent capable of choice has a character involving beliefs about what is good and evil. Only such agents are capable of understanding what is of value and what is evil, so only such agents can know when they act virtuously or viciously, or understand that they should or should not perform such actions (cf. *Pol* I.2 1253a15–18). Hence, only such agents can be justifiably praised or blamed from a moral point of view for what they do (*NE* VI.2 1139a20; *EE* II.6 1222b19–20, 8 1224a27–30, 10 1226b21–2).

The distinction between (i) *ignorance* and (ii) *an agent* causing an action remains obscure. One might propose applying what *Phys* II.5–6 says about lucky and unlucky actions to all involuntary actions due to non-negligent ignorance. We could try: for an agent to cause an action the desire to do *precisely x* must cause the action x. In Aristotle's example of the man who goes to the market by luck and recovers money from a debtor, the cause of his getting his money back is not a desire to get his money back. Rather the man's *desire to go the market* was an accidental cause, not a proper (*kath' hauto*) cause, of his recovery of the money. And this accidental cause, as the *Physics* uses that word, was *external* to the agent.

But this proposal fails to capture Aristotle's position since he regards negligently ignorant agents as causes of their actions, but it is not true (for example) that the negligently ignorant mother who involuntarily poisons her daughter desired to poison her daughter.

I believe that Aristotle *cannot* determine when an agent as opposed to his ignorance is the cause of an action independently of the question of moral responsibility. Suppose that we have two cases in which A (a mature adult) opens the door and hits C, who, unknown to A, was lurking behind the door. *Case 1*: A could not have reasonably been expected to know or check whether C was there. Then, for Aristotle, not A but A's ignorance is the cause of his hitting C and A is not to blame. *Case 2*: A should have checked whether C was there before he opened the door, and then, according to Aristotle, not A's ignorance but A was the ultimate cause of the action. For it was up to A to check or not, and his failure to do so caused his ignorance which caused his action.[17]

Note first that this example shows that the question of whether or not Aristotle labels A the cause of the action may have nothing to do with the actual sequence of events: what happens, and what causes what, may be exactly the same in the two cases with the only difference lying in the absence or presence of knowledge in A, which he could have but failed to call to mind (perhaps the knowledge that someone might be behind the door). But, further, since (let's assume) in Case 1, A was not *compelled* not to check whether C was there, there too it was in A's power to check whether anyone was lurking outside the door even if he had no reason to do so and could not reasonably have been expected to do so. Checking or not checking was in A's control, was up to A. If in Case 2, as Aristotle claims, the fact that it was up to A to check or not makes him the cause of the action, that argument applies equally to Case 1 and shows that there too, where A is not morally responsible, A is the cause of the action. Aristotle has no basis for classifying the cases as he wants independently of an appeal to moral responsibility, and his attempt to base moral responsibility on agent causation does not work.

Moral Responsibility for Virtue and Vice

NE III.5 argues that people are morally responsible for their character. Aristotle begins with two arguments, one (1113b7–21) which assumes that virtuous action is voluntary, and a second (1113b21–1114a3) which assumes that our practices of punishment and reward are correct. But these are precisely the kinds of assumptions that doubters of the voluntariness of character could be expected to challenge, and two further arguments are given. The first (1114a3–10) relies on the notion of agent causation. Aristotle had argued in *NE* II that we acquire a virtue or a vice by habitually performing the kinds of actions that manifest it – for example, we become just by doing what is just. So, Aristotle now says, a man who spends his time in drinking and other self-indulgent behavior thereby becomes self-indulgent. Since the man caused the action that caused the self-indulgence, he acquired the vice voluntarily.

The argument is weak. Even if Aristotle is right that one acquires a character by performing the corresponding types of action, what if someone is unaware of this fact? Aristotle says that only a stupid person could fail know it (1114a9–10). But stupid people exist, and Aristotle provides no reason to think that a person ignorant of the consequences of his unjust behavior is voluntarily unjust. And how could only stupid people fail to realize that character is a consequence of actions? This is a *philosophical thesis* in competition with the views – noted by Aristotle himself (*NE* III.5 1114b6–16, X.9 1179b20–1) – that character is produced by nature or teaching.

Aristotle's second argument (1114a11–13) is that (i) a man who, for example, regularly does what is self-indulgent (ii) *knows* that he will thereby become self-indulgent, and therefore (iii) *wishes* to become self-indulgent, and therefore (iv) *voluntarily* becomes self-indulgent. But, as we see, there is no reason to accept the move from (i)–(ii). Nor is there any reason to accept the step from (ii)–(iii). A man may believe that by smoking he insures that he will acquire cancer, but it hardly follows that the man *wishes* to acquire cancer.

Determinism and Compatibilism

Aristotle takes it for granted that determinism is false. The *Nicomachean Ethics*, and in particular III.5, does not address the issue of the compatibility of voluntariness and moral responsibility with determinism. He believes that agents often cause their actions, and agent causation entails that an action *is up to the agent to do or not*; and the fact reported by the italicized phrase entails the falsity of determinism (cf. *EE* II.7 1222b41–1223a9). Since he believes that agent causation is a necessary condition for moral responsibility, he is committed to the proposition that if determinism were true we would not be responsible for our actions.

Criticisms

Apart from difficulties already mentioned, I can only briefly consider a few criticisms that might be made of Aristotle's account.

1   Some have criticized Aristotle for ignoring involuntary actions arising from convulsive movements or inability to control one's body. But, in fact, he could explain that they are involuntary because they are not up to the agent to do or not (cf. *MA* 11).

2   He has been criticized for failing to deal with cases of psychological compulsion. But he does mention them (*NE* III.1 1109b30–2; *EE* II.10 1225a19–21, 27–33) and, again, Aristotle can explain why they are involuntary by saying that having the mental state or performing the action is not up to the agent. It follows – given (1) – that the agent is not their cause (even if the action is caused by a desire)[18] and Aristotle's definition of voluntariness is not met. Nevertheless, as noted before, *NE* III does not explicitly address the question of the voluntariness of emotions, and it is unclear what it implies about them.

3   One sound criticism of Aristotle is that he requires *knowledge* of particular facts for voluntariness where belief would, at least frequently, suffice. If I want to kill Smith, and believe but do not know that he is behind the curtain, then if I voluntarily stab the man behind the curtain and thereby kill Smith, it could hardly be said that I did not kill Smith voluntarily because I merely believed and did not know that it was him.

4   Another objection is that Aristotle must explain knowledge as being either potential knowledge or actual knowledge (cf. *EE* II.9 1225b11–12). Roughly, I have actual knowledge of the individual x as F if I am actually perceiving it and/or thinking of it as F, and I have potential knowledge of x as F if I have a disposition that is the capacity to have such actual knowledge.

The difficulty is that neither sort of knowledge fits. I can voluntarily enter my house without *thinking* "I am entering my house." For the action to be voluntary I must be aware of the fact that it is my house, but such awareness cannot be identified with thinking of that fact. *NE* VII.10 1152a14–15 commits Aristotle to allowing that potential knowledge suffices for voluntariness, since it says that the akratic agent acts voluntarily because he acts with potential knowledge of the sort possessed by the drunk or man asleep. But Aristotle's claim that potential knowledge suffices for voluntariness is false, and indeed his comparison with the knowledge of the sleeping man exposes its utter implausibility. When a mother fails to recognize that the bottle she is holding in her hand contains poison, then when she voluntarily gives her baby the liquid in the bottle, her possession of potential knowledge that the bottle contains poison is obviously not enough to make it the case that she voluntarily poisoned her baby.

Notes

1 (b) is not explicit and may not represent Aristotle's view. But his remarks on compulsion elsewhere (*Phys* IV.8 215a1–4; *Cael* I.2 269a7–9, II.13 295a2–3; *GC* II.6 333b26–30; *Met* Δ.5 1015a36–b3, Λ.7 1072b11–12; *EE* II.6 1224a13–31, b2–15, 1225a2–5; *Rhet* I.10 1369b5–6) suggest that *NE* III.1 assumes it. That would explain why Aristotle calls compelled actions painful (*NE* III.1 1110b11–12, *Rhet* I.11 1370a9–10): the compelled act contrary to their desires. Further, when discussing involuntariness due to ignorance, *NE* III.1 distinguishes the

involuntary, what the agent regrets (wanting to avoid what is done) from the non-voluntary, what the agent does not regret (having no desire to avoid it) (1110b18–24). Aristotle draws no such distinction for compulsion although it applies equally to compulsion *if* one can be compelled to do what one has no desire to avoid.

But in *EE* II.8 1225a25–33 Aristotle allows, correctly, a *compelled* action to be caused by a desire for that action (neither the desire nor the action being up to the agent) where no contrary desire exists. This suggests that *NE* III.1 might not mention the presence of a contrary desire precisely to allow for such cases. If so, however, the resulting position contradicts the view presented elsewhere in *EE* itself according to which compulsion requires a contrary desire (1224a13–31, b2–15, 1225a2–5, cf. II.7 1223a29–35).

² Cf. *NE* III.3 1112a31–2, 5 1113b26–30, 1114a23–9, 6 1115a17–18, V.8 1135a33–b2, 16–19; *EE* II.6 1223a10–15, II.10 1226a22–6; *Phys* II.5 197a1–2, b18–20, VIII.6 259b7–11.

³ Cf. *EE* II.8 1224b7–15; *MA* 6 700b17–19, 7 701a33–b1. I do not mention habit since the *Rhetoric* connects it to the desire for pleasure (I.10 1369b16–18).

⁴ "A is the cause of x" entails "It was up to A to x or not to x": *NE* III.1 1110a15–18, 5 1113b20–1, 5 1114a18–19; *EE* II.6 1223a4–9; *Phys* VIII.4 255a5–10. "It was up to A to x or not to x (and A xes)" entails "A is the cause of x": *NE* III.5 1113b32–3, III.5 1114a19–21, 28–9; *EE* II.7 1223a2–4, 7–8; *Phys* VIII.4 255a5–10. Cf. *Phys* V.2 226a33–b1. Thus, the fact that "it was up to A to x or not" is not explicitly included in the definition of voluntariness in *NE* III.1 signals no important difference between the definitions of *NE* III, *NE* V.8 (1135a23–7) and the *Eudemian Ethics* (1225b8–10, 1226b30–2). Note too that, for Aristotle, (i) "It was up to A to x" and (ii) "It was up to A not to x" entail one another (*NE* III.5 1113b7–11; *Phys* VIII.4 255a9–10), and so either entails (iii) "It was up to A to x or not to x." The insignificance of the difference between these statements is seen in the *Eudemian Ethics*' first defining voluntary action in terms of (ii) (II.9 1225b8–10) and later in terms of (iii) (II.6 1226b30–2).

⁵ Having a general power to x in the sense that a parachutist falling to earth is able to walk is insufficient. A definition of a potentiality to x must refer to the presence of the conditions necessary for the potentiality to be exercised (*Met.* Θ 5 1047b35–1048a2, 1048a10–21), and the absence of any such conditions means that the agent lacks the potentiality to x (*Phys.* VIII.1 251b1–3).

⁶ I understand *EE* II.8 1225a26–36 to show that Aristotle would count the italicized clause as false.

⁷ I thank Norman Dahl for helping me to see that an earlier draft of the previous four paragraphs needed to be set out more clearly.

⁸ VII.5 256a8, 258a1–19, VIII.10 266b28–9, contradicted by VIII.2 253a11–21.

⁹ Appetite and wish conflict in continent and incontinent agents, agree in temperate and self-indulgent agents.

¹⁰ The virtuous man knows "general law (*nomos*), all those unwritten principles which are supposed to be acknowledged everywhere" (*Rhet.* I.9 1368b8–9), the ignorance of which is blameworthy (*NE* III.1 1110b31–3).

¹¹ III.1 (1110a2–3) even draws attention to this distinction by speaking of the subject of compulsion as "the agent or the patient" (*ho prattôn ê ho paschôn*). The discussions in *NE* V.9 and 11 are based on the distinction.

¹² The opposite of what is of intrinsic value, not necessarily the opposite of what is *morally* good.

¹³ *EE* II.7 1223b24–6, II.9 1225b3–5; *NE* V.8 1135a28–31; *Soph El* I.24 179a32–b33. *Rhet.* I.13 1373b37–1374a17 shows that Aristotle is well aware of the fact that a single action can be described in different ways, and, evidently, in *NE* 1135a28–31 the agent voluntarily kills the man and involuntarily kills his father though the man is his father.

[14] The *Eudemian Ethics* (II.6 1223a1–9, 16–18; cf. *Rhet.* I.10 1369b21–2) accepts (2), but on the understanding that "action x is up to A to do or not to do" entails that, if A acts, "A acts with knowledge."

[15] There is no relevant difference between this definition and *NE* V.8's definition (1135a23–7).

[16] A point not addressed by those who say that *NE* III claims that the drunk acts voluntarily.

[17] This last statement mirrors Aristotle's argument in *NE* III.5 1113b32–3. The argument in *NE* III.5 1113b30–33 presupposes that the action of the man acting in ignorance is caused by his ignorance.

[18] Note the *Eudemian Ethics'* obscure statement that psychologically compelled actions and mental states are "products" of (II.8 1225a28) but not "of" (1225a26–7) or "on account of" (1225a30) natural desire or thought.

Bibliography

Berryman, S. (2002). "Aristotle on *Pneuma* and Animal Self-motion," *Oxford Studies in Ancient Philosophy*, 23, pp. 85–97.

Bostock, D. (2000). *Aristotle's Ethics* (Oxford: Oxford University Press).

Broadie, S. (1991). *Ethics with Aristotle* (Oxford: Oxford University Press).

Charles, D. (1984). *Aristotle's Philosophy of Action* (London: Duckworth).

Cooper, J. (1975). *Reason and Human Good in Aristotle* (Cambridge: Harvard University Press).

Furley, D. (1978). "Self-movers," in G. E. R. Lloyd and G. E. L. Owen (eds.), *Aristotle on Mind and the Senses* (Cambridge: Cambridge University Press), pp. 165–79.

Hardie, W. F. R. (1968). *Aristotle's Ethical Theory* (Oxford: Clarendon).

Heinaman, R. (1986). "The *Eudemian Ethics* on Knowledge and Voluntary Action," *Phronesis*, 31, pp. 128–47.

Heinaman, R. (1988). "Compulsion and Voluntary Action in the *Eudemian Ethics*," *Nous*, 22, pp. 253–81.

Irwin, T. H. (1980). "Reason and Responsibility in Aristotle," in A. O. Rorty (ed.), *Essays on Aristotle's Ethics* (Berkeley, CA: University of California Press), pp. 117–55.

Irwin, T. H. (1980). "Review of A. Kenny, Aristotle's *Theory of the Will*," *Journal of Philosophy*, 77, pp. 338–54.

Kenny, A. (1979). *Aristotles Theory of the Will* (London: Duckworth).

Mele, A. R. (1981). "Choice and Value in the *Nicomachean Ethics*," *Journal of the History of Philosophy*, 19, pp. 405–24.

Mele, A. R. (1984). "Aristotle's Wish," *Journal of the History of Philosophy*, 22, pp. 139–56.

Meyer, S. S. (1993). *Aristotle on Moral Responsibility* (Oxford: Blackwell).

Rowe, C. J. (1982). "Review of A. Kenny, *Aristotle's Theory of the Will*," *Journal of Hellenic Studies*, 102, pp. 250–3.

Sorabji, R. (1980). *Necessity, Cause, and Blame* (London: Duckworth).

Woods, M. (1982). *Aristotle's "Eudemian Ethics"* (Oxford: Clarendon Press).

31

Aristotle on Action, Practical Reason, and Weakness of the Will

NORMAN O. DAHL

Aristotle on Action

Human action can be construed broadly to include reflex actions and involuntary actions, or more narrowly so that intentional actions constitute paradigmatic examples, if not the entire scope, of human action. What follows takes human action in the latter way.

According to Aristotle, there are two sources of action, mind (*nous*) and desire (*orexis*) (*De Anima* III.10 433a9–13). There are also three forms of desire: appetite (*epithumia*), spirited emotion (*thumos*), and rational desire (*boulêsis*). Aristotle does say at *De Anima* III.10 433a22 that what moves a person is a single faculty, the faculty of desire; and he says at *De Anima* III.9 432b26–7 and *NE* VI.1 1139a35–6 that mind or intellect moves nothing. However, there is no inconsistency here. Various forms of desire arise from the exercise of various aspects of mind. It is also clear from what follows the latter two passages that the mind that moves nothing is theoretical, not practical intellect. Practical intellect does aim at an end (*NE* VI.2 1139a36). Mind is a source of action because it contributes to the desires that move people to act.

An example of the most primitive form of action is a person who drinks water at hand because she is thirsty. She acts from appetite, and the aspects of mind that are involved are imagination and perception. To be thirsty is in part to be disposed to perceive drink as pleasant, and it is imagination that allows a person to perceive something as pleasant, and so to desire it. Perceiving the water at hand to be drink and thus to be pleasant, she desires to drink it, and drinks it. If asked why, she would respond, "I was thirsty. I wanted something to drink, and there it was." Appetite is something that humans share with animals, so its objects are such things as food, drink, sex, and shelter from the cold.

There is also a more complicated form of appetite. I see the leaves turning and calculate that winter is coming on, bringing with it cold weather. I recognize that given my current wardrobe I will be cold when winter comes, something I imagine to be painful and so desire to avoid. I recognize that I need a covering to keep me warm during winter, and that a coat is a covering. I see materials for making a coat lying about, so I set about making a coat to forestall being cold during winter. Mind's calculative ability allows me to calculate about the future by thoughts and images and then imagine a future object as painful, and so desire to avoid it (*De Anima* III.7 431b3–9). The same calculative ability allows me to deliberate about means to satisfy this desire. When I perceive that these means are at hand, I act.

Since Aristotle defines choice (*prohairesis*) as deliberate desire of things in our own power (*NE* III.3 1113a11–12), one might think that the foregoing is a case of acting from choice. However, Aristotle says that a weak-willed person acts from appetite contrary to choice (*NE* III.2 1111b14–15) and that a weak-willed person can act from deliberation (*NE* VI.9 1142b18–20). He also says that choice can't exist without moral character (*NE* VI.2 1139a33–5), something that doesn't come just with appetite. Acting from choice, thus, involves more than simply acting from appetite and deliberation. What more it involves will emerge shortly.

Humans are also capable of acting on spirited emotion (*thumos*), paradigmatic examples of which are fear and anger. These desires typically arouse people emotionally and physiologically. Anger arises when a person believes that he or someone he cares about has been insulted, something that leads him to view retaliation for the insult as pleasant, and so to desire it. Anger also involves a physiological change, for example, blood boiling about the heart (*De Anima* I.1 403a31–b1), something that explains why people who are angry are typically flushed. In a sense anger listens to reason (it arises from a belief that an insult warrants retaliation). But in itself it listens to reason hastily, and so can lead a person to retaliate to a perceived insult without further thought (*NE* VII.6 1149a25–b1).

It is also possible for those who experience spirited emotion or have appetites not to act on these desires. At *De Anima* III.9 432b30–433a9 Aristotle notes that a person can think of something fearful, be physiologically aroused by such a thought, and yet not flee. Mind commands him not to flee, and a person can desire to act, and act in accord with such a command. Such an exercise of mind can also allow a person to resist temptation from appetite. Still, a person may not always follow such a command. Weakness of the will is possible; and when it occurs the person acts in accord with desire contrary to mind's command.

What allows a person to act on such a command is rational desire (*boulêsis*). An exercise of mind can lead to the thought that certain ends are worth pursuing for their own sake, a thought in part influenced by a person's character. This can lead a person to view the pursuit of these ends as pleasant, and so to desire to pursue them. Such a desire is an instance of rational desire (*NE* III.4 1113a16–33). If deliberation determines that a certain course of action is the best way to pursue those ends, mind will command her to adopt that course of action. If she does adopt it, she will have acted from choice (*prohairesis*). If she doesn't, she will act from desire contrary to choice, exhibiting weakness of the will.

A person need not go through an immediately preceding process of deliberation in order to act from rational desire and choice. If in the past I have recognized that health is on the whole good, determined by deliberation that walking is the best way to maintain my health, and set aside a certain time on certain days to walk, I may recognize that now is one of those times, and without any further thought start walking. If asked why I am walking, I will answer on the basis of my prior deliberation that I am walking

499

because health is something that is good, the best way to preserve it is to walk, and now is one of the times I have set aside for that sort of walking.

There is also an important connection between any form of desire and the good.

At *Metaphysics* Λ.7 1072a27–8 Aristotle says that the apparent good is the object of appetite and the real good the primary object of rational desire. The point here is not that appetite can't have an object that is genuinely good. A temperate person will pursue certain bodily pleasures for their own sake (*NE* III.11 1119a15–18). These pleasures will be good to pursue. Nor is it just that imagination can be mistaken in perceiving an object as pleasant. It is that appetite is the primary source of error about what is good (*NE* II.3 1104b10–11, 21–3, III.4 1113a33–b1, VI.5 1140b13–19). Left unchecked, it will have as its objects things that are only apparently good.

Spirited emotion rests on the thought that its object is good in some way. (For example, anger arises from the thought that retaliation is warranted.) However, in so far as a person who acts from spirited emotion acts in haste, he may act for the sake of what is only apparently good.

Rational desire arises from the thought that its object is on the whole good. For many people this may still only be the apparent good, for they may be mistaken about what is on the whole good. But rational desire has a natural object – what is actually good. This is the conscious object of the rational desire of a good person, because she is able to recognize the truth about such matters (*NE* III.4 1113a16–33).

Thus, any form of desire can lead a person to take its object to be good. But it can also lead a person to desire what is only apparently good.

We can now understand something about the practical syllogism. Whatever else it is, the practical syllogism provides a model for explaining human action (Santas 1969). (For Aristotle's examples of practical syllogisms, see *De Motu Animalium* 7 701a12–33, *Metaphysics* Z.7 1032b6–21, and *NE* VII.3 1147a1–10, 25–36.) A practical syllogism has two sorts of premises and a conclusion. Its major premise is concerned with what is good, its minor premises with what is possible (*De Motu Animalium* 7 701a23o–25). Although some of the major premises in Aristotle's examples set out certain objects as wanted or needed rather than as good, there is no inconsistency here, for we have just seen that the object of a desire can either be the good or the apparent good. At *NE* III.3 1112b26–7 Aristotle defines "possible things" as things that can be brought about by our own efforts. This fits the minor premises in his examples, since they indicate means for bringing about the end set out in the major premise. The final minor premise is grasped by perception, and indicates that means for achieving this end are at hand (*De Anima* III.11 434a17–20; *NE* III.3 1112b33–1113a2, VI.8 1142a26–30). The conclusion of a practical syllogism appears to be an action (*De Motu Animalium* 7 701a13ff; *NE* VII.3 1147a22–9).[1]

If one compares this with what has been said about action from desire, one will see that the major and minor premises of a practical syllogism set out an agent's desire and the means he has determined will satisfy that desire, thus providing a basis for explaining his acting from that desire. Furthermore, whenever a person has so acted, there will be an action that can be regarded as the conclusion of the practical syllogism that explains his action. Indeed, the examples of action from appetite and rational desire I have given match (with some amplification) three of Aristotle's examples of practical syllogisms.

500

Aristotle on Practical Reason

Practical reason exists when desires and actions can be rational or irrational. A desire or action will be rational if a good exercise of reason would indicate that one should have that desire or perform that action. There are two ways in which an exercise of reason might provide such an indication. According to an *internalist* conception of practical reason, necessarily a good exercise of reason will (perhaps under certain ideal circumstances) motivate a person to act.[2] A rational desire will then be a desire that would be so motivated, and a rational action will be an action motivated by a rational desire. According to an *externalist* conception of practical reason, a good exercise of reason will (perhaps under certain ideal circumstances) yield the conclusion that one should have a certain desire or perform an action (for example, because it maximizes expected utility) without there being any necessary connection between this conclusion and motivation.

What follows operates with an *internalist* conception of practical reason. It provides a basis for actions and desires themselves to be rational or irrational, whereas arguably an externalist conception provides only a basis for rational beliefs about desires or actions.

Operating with such a conception, and taking practical reason to exist if and only if reason by itself can motivate a person to act, Hume denied that practical reason exists, arguing that reason by itself never moves a person to act (Hume 1964: 414–18, 458). However, one need not operate with such a narrow basis for practical reason. Practical reason can also exist if (perhaps under certain ideal conditions) a good exercise of reason together with something else (for example, a desire for an end) would move a person to act. Either way, though, there will be motivations that arise from a good exercise of reason that an agent wouldn't otherwise have. These will be rational desires, and actions motivated by them will be rational actions.

Besides its existence, the most interesting question about practical reason is its scope. Is it limited to instrumental rationality, or can certain ends also be rational to pursue? If they can, could this provide a basis for ethical behavior?

Aristotle does seem to grant the existence of instrumental rationality when he says at *NE* III.3 1112b16–17 that those who deliberate assume the end and determine which of its means would be the most efficient and best to pursue. Since such a deliberation can be engaged in well or badly, and since what results from it will be a desire to adopt the means settled on by deliberation (*NE* III.3 1113a11–12), it looks as if a good exercise of reason, perhaps together with the desire for an end, can produce a motivation to adopt means to that end.

Aristotle also seems committed to taking ethical behavior to be rational behavior, and so to taking the ends one should have to be the objects of rational desire.

In providing an initial content to *eudaimonia*, the good for human beings, Aristotle says at *NE* I.7 1098a16–18 that *eudaimonia* is rational activity in accord with virtue. Since the virtuous exercise of rational activity would seem to be rational as opposed to irrational activity, Aristotle seems committed to taking ethical behavior, behavior that achieves the human good, to be rational behavior. It is true that in filling out this conception of *eudaimonia* Aristotle first discusses ethical virtue, virtue of the part of the soul that listens to reason. But when Aristotle defines ethical virtue in *NE* II.6 he says that

501

it is a disposition to choose relative to a mean, a mean determined by reason, the kind of reason that a person of practical wisdom would employ (1106b36–1107a2). Practical wisdom is a virtue of the part of the soul that issues commands to the part that listens to reason, and so its exercise would seem to involve rational as opposed to irrational activity.

Also, in discussing specific ethical virtues Aristotle often takes pains to say that a specific virtue disposes a person to act as reason directs (for courage see *NE* III.7 1115b19–20; temperance, III.12 1119b12–18; good temper, IV.5 1125b33–1126a1).

Finally, Aristotle says that one can't have ethical virtue without practical wisdom (*NE* VI.13 1144b30–1) and that with practical wisdom comes all of the ethical virtues (*NE* VI.13 1145a1–2).

Aristotle, thus, seems committed to regarding ethical behavior to be rational as opposed to irrational behavior, and so to regarding the ends that one should aim at to be objects of rational desires. Still, one might question whether Aristotle's moral psychology provides room for this commitment.

Aristotle says at *NE* I.7 1098b3–4 that some first principles are arrived at by induction, some by perception, and some by habituation. At *NE* I.4 1095b4–6 he says that whoever has the right habits has or can easily get the starting points for ethical behavior. Taking the latter to include ends one should aim at, it looks as if it is habituation that provides a person with the right ends, not an exercise of reason.

Aristotle also says at *NE* VI.12 1144a7–9, 20–2 that ethical virtue makes a person's aim or choice right, practical wisdom providing the means for this aim or choice. At *NE* VI.5 1140a25–8 he says that the mark of practical wisdom is excellence in deliberation, and at *NE* III.3 1112b12–19 he says that deliberation is about means, not ends. This seems to limit practical wisdom to instrumental rationality. It is ethical virtue, something acquired through habituation (*NE* II.1 1103b21–5, II.4 1105b9–12, VII.8 1151a14–19) that provides one with the right ends (Smith 1996; Vasiliou 1996).

However, a closer look will show that Aristotle's moral psychology does provide room for taking ethical behavior to be rational behavior.

First, when Aristotle says that some first principles are arrived at by perception, some by induction, and some by habituation, this doesn't mean that some first principles can't be arrived at by more than one of these means. Indeed, we shall see how certain ends can be arrived at by both habituation and induction.

Also, the kind of habituation that allows a person to have or easily get first principles in ethics need not be "mindless" (Burnyeat 1980). Initially it will be guided by the reason of his parents, but then by his own, once he acquires the ability to exercise reason.

Furthermore, Aristotle can distinguish virtue from practical wisdom by saying that virtue provides one with the right ends and practical wisdom the right means and still allow practical wisdom to be concerned with the right ends. Virtue is a disposition (*hexis*) to choose what is in a mean. But possession of such a disposition is compatible with inaction (*NE* I.5 1095b32–3). A person needs something else before she will act on a given virtue. She will need to recognize that there are particular means at hand for acting on that virtue, means that are worth adopting in spite of any other ends she might take to be worth pursuing on that occasion. This falls within the province of practical wisdom. Practical wisdom, thus, involves means in a way that virtue does not. This allows Aristotle to distinguish virtue from practical wisdom by saying that virtue is (always) concerned with the right ends while practical wisdom (in part) provides one with the right means.

A similar thing can be said about Aristotle's remark at *NE* VI.5 1140a25–8 that deliberation is the mark of practical wisdom. The context of this remark is a distinction Aristotle draws between practical wisdom and knowledge (*epistêmê*). In this context deliberation is the mark of practical wisdom because *epistêmê* is entirely concerned with what is demonstrable and thus what can't be otherwise, whereas practical wisdom (in part) involves deliberation and deliberation is about what can be otherwise (*NE* VI.5 1140a35–b3).

There are also passages in which Aristotle says that true reasoning or practical wisdom grasps the right ends. He says at *NE* VI.2 1139a21–6 that since virtue is a state of character concerning choice, and choice is deliberate desire, both the reasoning must be true and the desire right if choice is to be good, and the latter must pursue what the former asserts. At *NE* VI.9 1142b31–4 he says that excellence in deliberation is correctness with regard to what conduces to the end of which practical wisdom is the true apprehension.

It is true that both these passages are ambiguous. But a closer look at their contexts shows that they do say that true reasoning and practical wisdom are concerned with the right ends. This is clearest in the case of 1142b31–4. Its context is a distinction Aristotle draws between excellence in deliberation and the kind of correctness in deliberation that a weak-willed or bad person can engage in. If the passage only said that excellence in deliberation occurs when practical wisdom provides one with a true apprehension of means conducive to one's end, there would be no such distinction. (For a comparable disambiguation of 1139a21–6, see Dahl 1984: 38–9.)

Taken together, two other passages confirm Aristotle's taking practical wisdom to provide one with the right ends. At *NE* VI.13 1144b1–14 he marks off natural virtue from virtue in the strict sense, saying that natural virtue is shared with children and animals and that although in some circumstances it leads a person to act rightly, in others it will lead a person astray. He goes on to say that natural virtue becomes virtue in the strict sense with the addition of thought (*nous*). At *NE* III.8 1116b23–1117a5 he calls attention to a phenomenon that has been taken to be courage, acting from passion, saying that animals exhibit this kind of behavior and that it is most natural. He says it will be genuine courage if choice and "that for the sake of which" (*hou heneka*) are added, "that for the sake of which" being an end. But if natural virtue becomes virtue in the strict sense when thought is added, and if natural courage becomes genuine courage when choice and "that for the sake of which" are added, then it is a correct exercise of reason that leads a virtuous person to the right ends.

But what sort of exercise of reason could this be? There are two candidates, neither of which excludes the other.

Since the time of Greenwood (1909) it has been commonplace to distinguish between constitutive means and instrumental means. If one wants to prepare a good meal, determining its menu would be a determination of constitutive means. Determining how to obtain and prepare the ingredients for this menu would be a determination of instrumental means. Taking deliberation to determine both constitutive and instrumental means, one can arrive at certain ends through deliberation – those ends sought for their own sake that constitute *eudaimonia* (*NE* I.7 1097a34–b5).

However, potential problems arise for this candidate. First, it presupposes that *eudaimonia* is an inclusive end constituted by a set of more specific intermediate ends. Although, such a conception of *eudaimonia* has often been attributed to Aristotle, it has also been argued that *eudaimonia* is a single end, contemplation (*theoria*), to which other ends contribute instrumentally (Kraut 1989) or approximate (Lear 2004). Second, it has been argued that it is demonstrable that certain intermediate ends are worth pursuing for their own sake (Winter 1997). Since what is demonstrable is necessary, but deliberation is about what can be otherwise (*NE* VI.5 1140a35–b3), if it is demonstrable that certain intermediate ends are worth pursuing for their own sake, then one won't recognize this latter by means of deliberation.

If these problems can be handled, then the foregoing provides one way in which a good exercise of reason can provide a person with the right ends. But even if these problems can't be handled, there is another way of understanding how an exercise of reason can lead a person to acquire certain ends.

One arrives at them in a way similar to the way in which one arrives at certain first principles of an Aristotelian science – by an exercise of perception, experience (and hence induction), and comprehension (*nous*).

Consider those first principles of an Aristotelian science that are definitions and so state the essences of certain kinds of thing that fall under the science – for example, the definition of thunder as extinction of fire in a cloud that Aristotle discusses in *Posterior Analytics* II.8 and 10. (What follows relies on Kosman 1973.) Experience based on sense perception provides one with a nominal definition of thunder, noise in a cloud. It also provides additional phenomena that an adequate definition of thunder should demonstrably explain – for example, that thunder is preceded by the kind of flash of light we call lightning, and that thunder is typically followed by rain. The extinction of fire in a cloud will be a definition stating the essence of thunder if it can provide the basis for demonstrations that explain all of these phenomena – for example, explaining noise in a cloud by the noise made by extinction of fire in a cloud, and lightning by the fire in the cloud that is extinguished when thunder occurs.

Such a first principle is arrived at by *nous* because *nous* grasps something undemonstrable through the recognition of certain things as instances of a universal. It is not until one sees the universals that experience discovers are associated with thunder (for example, noise in a cloud, noise in a cloud preceded by lightning, etc.) as instances of the universal, extinction of fire in a cloud, that one can see the latter as something that could demonstrably explain the phenomena associated with these universals.

Ends that function as first principles in ethics are arrived at in a similar way – except that the relevant kind of perception is not simply sense experience but a perception based on a certain kind of experience, and that the exercise of *nous* that is involved includes recognizing particular actions as instances of relatively specific universals and recognizing these relatively specific universals as instances, contributors, or approximations of the more universal end that is the good for human beings. That this is so emerges from *NE* VI.11 1143a35–b5. (See Dahl 1984: 42–5, 227–36, for a defense of the kind of interpretation of this passage that follows.)

Aristotle says there that *nous* is concerned with ultimates in both directions – in its grasp of first principles that serve as bases for demonstrations, and thus a grasp of something undemonstrable, and in its grasp of what is last and variable, an action that is to be done in a particular situation, something that is also undemonstrable because it is particular. The grasp of the latter provides the starting points for the apprehension of universal ethical ends. These starting points are apprehended by perception, and this perception involves *nous*. This perception arises from a capacity that has been arrived at inductively. That is why this exercise of *nous* only comes at a certain age (*NE* VI.11 1143b7–9). It is also why we ought to pay attention to the undemonstrated sayings of older and experienced people. Experience has given them the ability to see what to do in particular situations (*NE* VI.11 1143b14–16).

What is grasped through this inductively based perception is not just that a particular action is to be done. What is grasped is that the action is to be done because it is an instance of a certain kind (even if those whose undemonstrated sayings we should listen to can't articulate this kind). This sort of perception is a starting point for first principles in ethics because it is a recognition that certain particular actions are good to do because they instantiate certain ends, ends that can then be seen to constitute, contribute to, or approximate a certain conception of *eudaimonia*. This recognition involves *nous* because it involves the recognition of something undemonstrable, a particular action that is to be done, as an instance of an end worth pursuing for its own sake, the latter then being recognized as explicable by its instantiating, contributing to, or approximating a certain conception of *eudaimonia*.

What ends a person can arrive at in this way may be limited by her character and the ends she actually aims at for their own sake. But she can still arrive at ends that she hasn't previously aimed at for their own sake, and so at ends that would need to be integrated into her character. For example, a person who takes wealth to be the good for human beings and for whom wealth is her ultimate end may only be in a position to recognize that the honor that comes with wealth is more important than wealth itself, and so arrive at honor as a new end to be pursued for its own sake and the life of honor as what constitutes *eudaimonia*. Once this new end has been integrated into her character, she may then be able to see that it is what merits honor, virtuous activity, that is worth pursuing for its own sake rather than honor, and so come to take *eudaimonia* to be a life of virtuous activity. That is, by a series of such steps a person can come to acquire the ends one ought to aim at.

What lies behind the foregoing is the following general point. Human beings have a nature whose realization constitutes their good. It is also part of that nature to act in accord with one's conception of the good. Through experience with one's own actions and the actions of others one can inductively form a conception of the human good that involves the pursuit of certain ends for their own sake. This conception, together with one's nature, can then lead one to pursue those ends and their corresponding conception of human good, and through habitual action to integrate those ends and that conception of good into one's character.

A person's newly acquired belief that certain ends are worth pursuing for their own sake, whether through deliberation or an exercise of the above sort of inductive reasoning, will (perhaps together with a desire for the good, or a nature that disposes one to desire what one takes to be good) motivate her to pursue these ends and to integrate them into her character, something that will take a certain amount of habituation. The ends one ought to aim at, thus, do fall within the scope of practical reason.

As a result, according to Aristotle, ethical behavior does turn out to be rational behavior, and there is a sense in which his ethics is based on practical reason.

Aristotle on Weakness of the Will

Aristotle begins his discussion of weakness of the will (*akrasia*) in *NE* VII by setting out what has been said about it, phenomena that any adequate account of *akrasia* must be able to explain, and by calling attention to puzzles that any adequate account must be able to solve. The former includes that an *akratês* knows that what she does is bad but acts instead because of passion, and that an *akratês* is blameworthy (*NE* VII.1 1145b9–12). The latter includes the question of what sort of understanding a person can have if she acts against her better judgment (*NE* VII.2 1145b21–1146a9). It can't be practical wisdom, because a person who has practical wisdom will act on that knowledge (1146a7–9). It can't be belief, because when people act contrary to a belief about which they have some doubt, we pardon them; but we don't pardon an *akratês* (1145b36–1145a4). Socrates denied that it could be knowledge (*epistêmê*), saying that it would be astonishing if *epistêmê* were dragged about like a slave (1145b22–4). So what sort of understanding does an *akratês* have?

Since practical wisdom has been ruled out, and since practical wisdom constitutes full and complete practical knowledge, an *akratês* must lack full and complete knowledge of how she should act. As Aristotle has traditionally been interpreted, this means that an *akratês* suffers from a certain kind of ignorance (for example, Joachim 1951; Robinson 1969; Santas 1969).

That is just what one would expect given the view mentioned earlier that the conclusion of the practical syllogism is an action, and given Aristotle's admission that an *akratês* knows in general how he should act.

Aristotle seems to endorse the former view in *NE* VII when he says at VII.3 1147a26–32 that in practical matters, if a single opinion results from a universal opinion and an opinion concerned with particular facts, the person must immediately act. For example, if everything sweet ought to be tasted and this is sweet, then necessarily a person who is able to act and is not prevented (*kôluomenon*) must act accordingly. He grants that an *akratês* knows in general how she should act, and so possesses the major premise of the practical syllogism on which she should act (the syllogism of reason) when he says that an *akratês* who acts because of pleasure does not think that it best to pursue pleasure, but instead has the (correct) first principle (*NE* VII.8 1151a11–14, 20–6).

But if necessarily a person who has and combines the premises of a practical syllogism will act on it, and if an *akrates* has the major premise of the syllogism of reason but does not act on that syllogism, then he must fail to have or combine at least one of its minor premises. Armed with this expectation, *NE* VII.3 seems to bear it out.

At 1146b30–4 Aristotle distinguishes two senses of "know," one in which a person exercises knowledge she possesses, the other in which she does not. He says it would be strange for a person to act contrary to knowledge that she is exercising, but it would not be strange if the knowledge was not exercised.

At 1146b35–1147a10 he distinguishes two kinds of premise in a practical syllogism, a universal premise and more particular premises relating the universal premise to the situation at hand. He says that to fail to act on one's knowledge while failing to have or exercise the most particular of this latter sort of premise would not be strange, but that failure to act when one has and is exercising both sorts of premise would be extraordinary.

Aristotle then distinguishes a subclass of cases in which a person has but is not exercising knowledge, cases in which a person in a sense knows and in a sense does not know. These include people who are mad, asleep, drunk, beginners of science, and people who recite the verses of Empedocles. He says that this is the condition of people under the influence of passion, and that an *akratês* is in a similar condition (1147a10–24).

After affirming at 1147a26–32 that necessarily someone who combines the premises of a practical syllogism will act on it if able and not prevented, Aristotle offers an example of an *akratês*. A person has (perhaps for reasons of health) a universal opinion forbidding tasting a certain sort of food, an instance of which is in front of her. She also has the opinion that everything sweet is pleasant and that this (what is in front of her) is sweet. When appetite is present, one thing tells her to avoid this (*pheugein touto*), her universal opinion forbidding tasting foods of the relevant sort. But appetite moves her to taste it, contrary to that general belief (1147a32–5).

The last premise (*hê teleutaia protasis*), a premise about something perceptible and one that determines action, is the final minor premise of the syllogism of reason, the premise that tells her that the food in front of her is of the relevant sort. This is a premise that the *akratês* either doesn't have or has only in the way in which a drunken man uttering the verses of Empedocles knows what he is talking about (1147b9–12). The *akratês* thus falls within the subclass of those said in 1147a10–24 to have but not exercise knowledge.

As a result, Socrates' position seems to follow. Since the last term (*ton eschaton horon*) (the final minor premise of the syllogism of reason) is not universal and does not express knowledge in the way a universal premise does, it is not knowledge proper (knowledge of the universal premise of the syllogism of reason) that is overcome by passion, but perceptual knowledge (knowledge of its final minor premise) (1147b12–17).

We can now see what kind of understanding an *akratês* has. She knows in general how she should act in the kind of situation she is in. But she fails to apply this general knowledge to her particular situation, either because she fails to recognize she is in the relevant sort of situation, or because she fails to combine this recognition with her general knowledge. As a result, she is ignorant of what she should do in her situation.

But how then can an *akratês* be blameworthy? At *NE* III.1 1110b24–7 Aristotle distinguishes acting in ignorance from acting by reason of ignorance, saying that one can be blameworthy for the former, offering a drunken person as an example of someone who acts in ignorance. Since an *akratês* is in a condition like drunkenness (1147a17–18), he can be blameworthy even if he is ignorant of the particular action he should do.

Still, problems arise for this interpretation. Aristotle says at 1150b37 that *akrasia* is aware of itself. If an *akratês* is aware that she is acting akratically at the time she so

507

acts, then she must know what she should do in that situation. At 1150b19–22 Aristotle distinguishes weak from impetuous *akrasia*, saying that the former fails to abide by the conclusions of her deliberations, while the latter fails to deliberate. But if a weak *akratês* fails to abide by the conclusions of her deliberations, she must have drawn those conclusions and recognized how she should act in those situations. Finally, at *NE* I.13 1102b13–19 Aristotle says that there is a genuine conflict of motives in *akrasia*, something that couldn't happen if an *akratês* didn't combine the premises of the syllogism of reason, recognize how she should act, and be motivated to act accordingly.

An advocate of the traditional interpretation might try to accommodate the first two of these passages by saying that it is only after the fact that *akrasia* is aware of itself, and that when a weak *akratês* draws the conclusions of his deliberations he abides by them, but that when he fails to abide by them he no longer draws them. Still, it is difficult to see how this interpretation can acknowledge a genuine conflict of motives in *akrasia*. Such a conflict could only occur if an *akratês* recognizes what he should do in the situation he is in, thereby being motivated to act that way, at the same time that passion provides him with a contrary motivation.

There is, however, an alternative interpretation that fits all three of these passages (Dahl 1984). It too denies that an *akratês* has full and complete practical knowledge of what he should do in the situation he is in. But it allows him to recognize what he should do in that situation, taking his knowledge to fail to be full and complete practical knowledge because it fails to achieve the goal of practical knowledge, action. It takes seriously the second explanation set out above for why the ends one ought to pursue fall within the scope of practical reason. This explanation grants that a person can recognize certain ends as worth pursuing for their own sake without having fully integrated them into his character, and so without always being sufficiently motivated to act in accord with them.

This explanation, together with the above three passages, provides a different set of expectations from those that lie behind the traditional interpretation. Read in light of these expectations, what Aristotle says in *NE* VII.3 seems to bear them out.

The first thing to note is that this way of understanding *akrasia* is not incompatible with the conclusion of a practical syllogism being an action. When Aristotle says at *NE* VII.3 1147a26–32 that necessarily a person who combines the premises of a practical syllogism will act if able and not prevented (*kôluomenon*), what he says grants that a person can combine the premises of a practical syllogism and still not act on it because she is prevented from acting on it. If the conclusion of a practical syllogism is an action, what results from this combination won't be the conclusion of that syllogism. It will be what was earlier called a command of mind. But this combination still allows the person to recognize what according to that syllogism she should do. A closer look at Aristotle's use of the verb "*kôluô*" will also show that a conflicting motive can prevent a person from acting on a practical syllogism (Dahl 1984: 196–8). This then allows an *akratês* to recognize the particular action she should do, and to be beset by conflicting motives. Again, what Aristotle goes on to say in *NE* VII.3 seems to bear this out.

A person has a universal opinion forbidding tasting a certain sort of food, an instance of which is in front of him. He also has the opinion that everything sweet is pleasant and that this (what is in front of him) is sweet. One thing says to avoid this (*pheugein touto*) – his recognition of what he should do in his situation (a command of mind), something indicated by the demonstrative "this" ("*touto*"). But appetite for what is sweet is also present, and so he suffers from conflicting motives. Appetite then moves him to act contrary to his recognition of what he should do.

The last proposition (*hê teleutaia protasis*), a proposition about something perceptible and one that determines action is the proposition that results from combining the premises of the syllogism of reason, a command of mind. It is a proposition that an *akratês* either doesn't have (the impetuous *akratês,*) or has only in the way a drunken man uttering the verses of Empedocles knows what he is talking about (the weak *akratês*) (1147b9–12). The *akratês* thus falls within the subclass of those said in 1147b10–24 to have but not exercise knowledge.

A weak *akratês* is the practical analogue of beginners of science. Although they may believe the propositions they express when they offer a scientific demonstration, they fail to know that demonstration "for it has to become part of themselves, and that takes time" (1147a22). That is why one won't find a practically wise man or a natural scientist among the young. First principles of these subjects come from experience, and that takes time. The young also lack conviction about these things (*NE* VI.8 1142a 12–20). The practical analogue of a one who lacks conviction about scientific demonstrations is someone who recognizes that certain ends are worth pursuing for their own sake but are not yet "part of herself" because she hasn't fully integrated them into her character. As a result, she isn't always sufficiently motivated to act on those ends in the face of a conflicting motive. She fails to exercise her knowledge of what she should do in her situation because she fails to act on it.

As a result, Socrates' position seems to follow. Since the last term (*ton eschaton horon*), the proposition that results from combining the premises of the syllogism of reason, is not universal and doesn't express knowledge in the way a universal premise does, it is not knowledge proper that is dragged about like a slave. Rather it is perceptual knowledge (of what to do in that situation) that is dragged about by a conflicting motive (1147b12–17).

We now can see what kind of understanding an *akratês* can have. He can recognize what he should do in the situation that faces him. But he lacks full and complete practical knowledge of what he should do in that situation, because he has failed to fully integrate that knowledge and the general knowledge on which it is based into his character. As a result, he isn't sufficiently motivated to act on that knowledge in the face of a strong, conflicting motive.

An *akratês* is blameworthy, because a weak *akratês* knows that the particular action he performs is wrong, and because either the weak or impetuous *akratês'* failure to integrate his knowledge of what to do into his character falls under the responsibility for character that Aristotle argues for in *NE* III.5.

There is also another way in which such an *akratês* might lack full and complete knowledge of what she should do. If an *akratês'* appetite for pleasure leads her to believe falsely that the pleasure she ends up pursuing is worth pursuing for its own sake in that situation but still takes its value to be overridden by other considerations (Broadie 1991: 270–4), then there will be a sense in which she doesn't fully understand what she should do. She won't have a fully correct understanding of why she should act as she should. Here is something of which she is ignorant; but she needn't be ignorant of the particular action she should do.

Still, questions can be raised for this interpretation. Can *"hê teleutaia protasis"* be translated as "the last proposition" rather than "the last premise"? Is the practical analogue of a beginner of science someone who has failed to integrate his ends into his character? Aristotle says at 1147b6–9 that we need to go to natural scientists to see how the *akratês'* ignorance (*agnoia*) is resolved. But does the failure to integrate one's ends into one's character amount to a kind of practical ignorance? Could this be the kind of ignorance mentioned in the previous paragraph?

We may yet to have seen the last word on Aristotle on weakness of the will.

Notes

[1] Below are two examples of a practical syllogism. The first corresponds to an example of Aristotle's at *De Motu Animalium* 701a18–20 and the example I gave above of action from appetite and deliberation. The second is similar to my example of walking for the sake of health. It involves action from a rational desire based on previous deliberation, and it is drawn from Aristotle's discussion of weakness of the will. Although Aristotle does not explicitly mention a command of mind when he talks about the practical syllogism, we have seen that he does recognize its existence in cases of weakness of the will. That is why it is included in the second example. Its existence will be of some importance when we come to Aristotle's discussion of weakness of the will.

I.   Major premise: I want to avoid being cold in the coming winter. (Avoiding being cold in the coming winter is (apparently) good.)
Minor premises: I need a covering in order to avoid being cold in the coming winter.
   A coat is a covering.
   Making what I need is a good way of obtaining what I need
Final minor premise: Materials for making a coat are at hand.
Conclusion: I make a coat from the materials at hand.

II. Major premise: (For reasons of health) avoiding eating foods of a certain sort is good.
Final minor premise: This food in front of me is of that sort.
(Command of mind: Avoid eating this food!)
Conclusion: I avoid eating this food.

[2] *Internalism* with respect to practical reason is best understood as a family of views, each one affirming a necessary connection between reasons for acting and motivation. For example, necessarily, if under certain conditions a person recognizes, or sincerely believes, or affirms, etc. that he has a reason to act in a certain way, he will be motivated to act in that way. Since recognizing, or believing, or affirming that one has a reason to act in a certain way involves an exercise of reason that can be engaged in well or badly, a rational desire is a desire that would be motivated by a good exercise of reason, and a rational action is an action that would be motivated by a rational desire and hence motivated by a good exercise of reason. *Externalism* with respect to practical reason denies the existence of any such necessary connection between reasons for acting and motivation. Even under ideal conditions it is possible for a person to recognize, or believe, or affirm etc. that he has a reason to act in a certain way without being motivated to act in that way. Thus, a person can engage in a good exercise of reason concerning what he has reason to do without being motivated to do it. Nevertheless, desires and actions will be rational if they are in accord with the result of such a good exercise of reason.

Bibliography

Broadie, Sarah (1991). *Ethics with Aristotle* (Oxford: Oxford University Press).

Burnyeat, Myles (1980). "Aristotle on Learning to Be Good," in Amelie Oksenberg Rorty (ed.), *Essays on Aristotle's "Ethics"* (Berkeley, CA: University of California Press), pp. 69–92.

Charles, David (1984). *Aristotle's Philosophy of Action* (Ithaca, NY: Cornell University Press).

Cooper, John (1975). *Reason and the Human Good* (Cambridge, MA: Harvard University Press).

Dahl, Norman O. (1984). *Practical Reason, Aristotole, and Weakness of the Will* (Minneapolis, MN: University of Minnesota Press).

Greenwood, L. H. G (1909). *Aristotle, "Nicomachean Ethics," Bk. VI* (Cambridge: Cambridge University Press).

Hume, David (1964). *A Treatise on Human Nature* (Oxford: Clarendon Press).

Irwin, Terence (1978). "First Principles in Aristotle's *Ethics*," *Midwest Studies in Philosophy*, 3, pp. 252–78.

Joachim, H. H. (1951). *The "Nicomachean Ethics"* (Oxford: Clarendon Press).

Kenny, Anthony (1979). *Aristotle's Theory of the Will* (New Haven, CT: Yale University Press).

Kosman, L. A. (1973). "Understanding, Explanation, and Insight in the *Posterior Analytics*," in E. N. Lee, A. P. D. Mourelataos, and R. M. Rorty (eds.), *Exegesis and Argument* (New York: Humanities Press), pp. 374–92.

Kraut, Richard (1989). *Aristotle on the Human Good* (Princeton, NJ: Princeton University Press).

Lear, Gabriel Richardson (2004). *Happy Lives and the Highest Good* (Princeton, NJ: Princeton University Press).

McDowell, John (1979). "Virtue and Reason," *Monist*, 62, pp. 331–50.

Mele, Alfred (1981). "Aristotle on *akrasia* and Knowledge," *Modern Schoolman*, 58, pp. 137–57.

Robinson, Richard (1969). "Aristotle on *akrasia*," *Essays on Greek Philosophy*, (Oxford: Clarendon Press), pp. 139–60.

Santas, Gerasimos (1969). "Aristotle on Practical Inference, the Explanation of Action, and *akrasia*," *Phronesis*, 14, pp. 162–89.

Smith, A. D. (1996). "Character and Intellect in Aristotle's *Ethics*," *Phronesis*, 41, pp. 56–74.

Vasiliou, Iakovos (1996). "The Role of Good Upbringing in Aristotle's Ethics," *Philosophy and Phenomenological Research*, 56, pp. 771–96.

Wiggins, David (1975–6). "Deliberation and Practical Reason," *Proceedings of the Aristotelian Society*, 76, pp. 29–51.

Winter, Michael (1997). "Aristotle, *hôs epi to polu* Relations, and a Demonstrative Science of Ethics," *Phronesis*, 42, pp. 163–89.

B. Politics

32

The Naturalness of the Polis in Aristotle

C. D. C. REEVE

Natural Beings

Of the various things that exist, Aristotle says, "some exist by nature, some from other causes" (*Phys* 192b8–9). Those that exist (or come into existence) by nature have a nature of their own – an internal source of "change and staying unchanged, whether in respect of place, growth and decay, or alteration" (192b13–15). A feline embryo, for instance, has within it a source that explains why it grows into a cat, why that cat moves and alters in the ways it does, and why it eventually decays and dies. A house or any other artifact has no such source within it; instead "the source is in something else and external," namely, in the soul of the craftsman who manufactures it (192b30–1).

A thing's nature (*phusis*), function (*ergon*), and end (*telos*) – or that for the sake of which it exists (*hou heneka*) – are systematically related, since its end just is to actualize its nature by performing its function (*NE* 1168a6–9; *EE* 1219a13–17). If it cannot perform its function, it ceases to be what it is except in name (*Pol* 1253a23–5). Aristotle's view of natural beings is thus teleological: it sees them as defined by an end for which they are striving, and as needing to have their behavior explained by reference to it. It is this end, essence, or function that determines what the excellences or virtues (*aretai*; singular, *aretê*) of such a being are and what its good consists in. Most pertinently, it determines what the virtues of human character and thought are, and – since the human good is called "happiness" (*eudaimonia*) – what human happiness consists in. In the famous function argument of *Nicomachean Ethics* I.7, therefore, Aristotle first argues that "the human function is activity of the soul in accord with reason or requiring reason," and concludes that happiness must be rational "activity of the soul in accord with virtue, and indeed with the best and most complete virtue" (1098a7–18).

Many of the things characterized as existing by nature or as products of some craft are hylomorphic compounds – compounds of matter (*hulê*) and form (*morphê*). The matter of a statue is the stone or metal from which it is made, while its form is its shape. The matter of a human being is (roughly speaking) the body, the form, the soul. Even a polis is such a compound: its matter is its inhabitants; its form, its *politeia* or constitution. Though the natures of hylomorphic compounds owe something to their matter, "form has a better claim than matter to be called nature" (*Phys* 193b6–7): change in matter is consistent with their continued existence; change in form isn't (*Pol* 1276b1–13). A human being can survive through material change (he is constantly metabolizing), but if his form is changed, he ceases to exist.

The Polis as a Natural Phenomenon

Human beings, Aristotle claims, are by nature political animals (*Pol* 1253a7–18, 1278b15–30; *NE* 1162a16–19, 1169b16–22). Moreover, he also claims that the polis is itself a natural phenomenon – something that exists by nature (*Pol* 1252b30, 1253a1). The two claims are so closely related, however, that they are based on the very same argument (1252a24–1253a19).

Political animals are a subclass of herding or gregarious animals that "have as their function some single thing they all do together," so that bees, wasps, ants, and human beings are all political animals in this sense (*HA* 487b33–488a10). But human beings are more political than these others (*Pol* 1253a7–18), because they are naturally equipped for life in a type of community that is itself more quintessentially political than a beehive or an ant nest, namely, a household or polis. What equips human beings to live in such communities is the natural capacity for rational speech, which they alone possess. For rational speech "is for making clear what is advantageous or harmful, and hence also what is just or unjust . . . and it is community in these that makes a household and a polis" (1253a14–17).

It is, perhaps, as uncontroversial to say that human beings have a natural capacity to live in communities with others as it is to make parallel claims about bees and ants. But why should we think they will best actualize this capacity in a community of a particular sort, such as an Aristotelian household or polis? Why not think that, unlike bees and ants, human beings might realize their natures equally well either in isolation or in some other kind of political or non-political community? In *HA* 487b33–488a14, Aristotle himself allows that human beings "dualize" – that some live in groups, while others live solitary lives. Though he represents the latter as abnormal, we might instead take it simply to mark a difference in equally "natural" values or preferences.

We saw that Aristotle thinks that what exists by nature must have a nature that is an inner source of stability and change. When he says that the polis exists by nature, does he mean that it has a nature of this sort – a *standard* nature, as we may call it? The fact that he introduces his argument for the naturalness of the polis by saying, "as in other cases the best way to study these things is to observe their natural development from the beginning" (*Pol* 1252a24–6) is strong evidence that he does, since something that comes into existence by nature has a standard nature (*Phys* 192b8–9).

Not everything that has a standard nature, however, realizes or perfects its nature *by* nature: craft is sometimes needed "to perfect or complete the task that nature is unable to perfect or complete" (*Phys* 199a15–16). Thus to perfect their standard natures, human beings have to acquire the virtues of character and thought through habituation and the craft of education (*Pol* 1332a39–b11, 1336b40–1337a3; *NE* 1103a17–26). Nonetheless, things that have their standard natures perfected by craft are not products of craft, since their forms do not flow into them from the souls or minds of a craftsman (*Met* 1032a32–b10). Instead, potentialities that are parts of their natures are further actualized by craft. The mere fact that a thing needs to have its nature perfected by craft is no obstacle, therefore, to its nature being a standard one.

Like other animals, human beings have a natural desire to reproduce, because in this way they participate to some degree at least in the divine:

> The most natural act for any living thing that has developed normally . . . is to produce another like itself (an animal producing an animal, a plant, a plant), in order to partake as best it can in the eternal and divine. That is what all things strive for, and everything they do naturally is for the sake of that. (*An* 415a26–b2)

This desire leads human beings to form couples – a type of community or communal relation (*Pol* 1252a27–30). Since our desire to reproduce *is* something we share in common with the other animals, it is surely as natural for us to have it as it is for them. But it is easy to slide from what is un-contentious into what is controversial. Is Aristotle just claiming that sexual coupling for the purposes of reproduction is natural? Or is he saying more than this?

In the *Nicomachean Ethics*, the human desire for sexual union is further characterized as follows: "The friendship of man and woman also seems to be natural. For human beings naturally tend to form couples more than to be political, to the extent that the household is prior to the polis, and more necessary, and child-bearing is shared more widely among the animals" (1162a16–19). We might wonder, however, whether the empirical evidence actually favors the view that human beings form couples in the way suggested, or whether this is not rather a variable social norm than a norm of nature. More importantly, we might wonder whether human beings do naturally form *Aristotelian* households.

The domestic and political subordination of women to men is a natural thing for Aristotle. Women ought to be ruled by men, he claims, because they are "naturally inferior" to them, since the deliberative part of their souls "lacks authority" (*Pol* 1260a13). What he has in mind, apparently, is that women lack authority over others, because they lack the spirit (*thumos*) required for command (*HA* 608a33–b12; *PA* 661b33–4; *Pol* 1328a6–7). No doubt, the observation of oppressed Greek women, socialized into passivity, provided him with ample empirical justification for this view. A clear-eyed survey of un-oppressed or differently socialized women, however, would surely do much to undermine this as a general hypothesis. In any case, the fact that the subordination of women to men is built into the conception of the household shows how controversial that conception actually is.

Yet more controversial is Aristotle's claim that the household must contain natural slaves – "animate property" – people who supposedly benefit from being under the control of a master, because their souls altogether lack a deliberative element (*Pol* 1252b9–12, 1253b32, 1254a10, 1260a12). Even if there were such people, it is not clear why they would need masters, or why the latter would need them. Aristotle's own view is that masters and slaves form a union "for the sake of their own survival" (1252a30–1). But this is implausible. Animals also lack the capacity to deliberate, on Aristotle's view, yet they seem to survive quite nicely without human masters who can deliberate (cf. 1254b10–13). True, masters may benefit from having slaves to do the donkey work, while they spend their leisure on philosophy or politics (1255b36–7), but, since they have bodies of their own and are capable of working on their own behalf, it is unclear why they need slaves *in order to survive*. We don't have slaves and we survive. Not only is Aristotle's conception of the household politically and ethically controversial, then, it isn't clear that, even if we granted its controversial elements, we could succeed in showing that it is natural, because "naturally constituted to satisfy everyday needs" (*Pol* 1252b12–14).

Similar problems beset the next stage in the emergence of the polis: the village. The village, we are told, is "constituted from several households for the sake of satisfying needs other than everyday ones" (*Pol* 1252b15–16). To determine whether these needs are natural, we need to know what they are. Aristotle says that households have to engage in barter with one another when the need arises (1257a19–25). But this is not much help, because the things they exchange with one another seem to be just the sorts of things the household itself is supposed to be able to supply, such as wine and wheat (1257a25–8). To count as a village, moreover, a community of several households must be governed in a characteristic way, namely, by a king (1252b20–2). This is natural, Aristotle explains, because villages are offshoots of households, in which the eldest is king (1252b20–2). The problem is that households involve various kinds of rule, not just kingly rule. For example, a head of household rules his wife with political rule (*Politics* I.12). We might wonder, therefore, why a village has to be governed with kingly rule rather than with political rule, where all the heads of households would rule and be ruled in turn.

The final stage in the emergence of the polis, and the conclusion of Aristotle's argument that the polis exists by nature and that a human being is a political animal, is presented in the following terse and difficult passage:

> (a) A complete community, constituted out of several villages, once it reaches the limit of total self-sufficiency, practically speaking, is a polis. (b) It comes to be for the sake of living, but it remains in existence for the sake of living well. (c) That is why every polis exists by nature, since the first communities do. For the polis is their end, and nature is an end; for we say that each thing's nature – for example, that of a human being, a horse, or a household – is the character it has when its coming-into-being has been completed. (d) Moreover, that for the sake of which something is, that is to say, its end, is best, and self-sufficiency is both end and best. (e) It is evident from these considerations, then, that a polis is among the things that exist by nature, that a human being is by nature a political animal, and that anyone who is without a polis, not by luck but by nature, is either a poor specimen or else superhuman. (*Pol* 1252b27–1253a4)

The polis, (a) tells us, is unlike the village, because it is pretty much self-sufficient. What does this mean? It seems clear that basic human needs are sufficiently satisfied outside the polis for human life to be possible there: households and villages that are not parts of a polis do manage to persist for considerable periods of time (1252b22–4, 1261a27–9); individuals too can survive even in solitude (1253a31–3; *HA* 487b33–488a14). Nonetheless, more of these needs seem to be better satisfied in the polis than outside it (*Pol* 1278b17–30), and it is always need that holds any community together as a single unit (*NE* 1133b6–7).

In (b) what gives rise to the polis is distinguished from what sustains it once it exists. Fairly basic human needs do the former, but what sustains a polis in existence is that we are able to live well and achieve happiness only in it. Thus the polis is self-sufficient not simply because it satisfies essential needs, but because it is the community within which we perfect or fully realize our natures or functions (*Pol* 1253a31–7).

With (d) and (e) we come to the crucial clauses. The household, village, and polis are like embryo, child, and mature adult: a single nature is present at each stage but developed or completed to different degrees. Where is that nature to be located? According to (e), it lies within the individuals that constitute these communities – individuals that are political animals precisely because their natural needs lead them to form, first, a household, then a village, then a polis (*Pol* 1253a29–30).

Imagine a newborn baby. He is not born into a pre-social state of nature of the sort described by Thomas Hobbes in *Leviathan*; he is born into a family. Hence from the very beginning he is leading a sort of communal life. And because he is leading such a life he is acquiring virtue of a sort, namely, *household* virtue – household justice (*to oikonomikon dikaion*) is distinguished from the justice of the polis at *NE* 1134b15–18. That is why it is "in the household that we have the first sources and springs of friendship, constitution, and justice" (*EE* 1242a40–b1). Since the human function or nature is rational activity expressing virtue, each member of the household will have a nature of a sort that identifies him as a member of a household. This justifies us in speaking of a nature that is not simply constituted by the collective natures that individuals living anywhere would have, but of one that is the nature of household-dwellers as such. This common nature, located in the inhabitants of the household, is the nature of the household.

The same line of argument applies in the case of the village and the polis. Each community educates its inhabitants into a type of virtue that suits them to be members of it. As a result, each indexes their natures to itself. The clearest examples of this sort of indexing are provided by the various types of constitutions that a polis can have: a democracy should suit its citizens to it by stamping democratic virtues into their souls by means of public education; an oligarchy should do the same with oligarchic virtues; and so on (*Pol* 1310a12–36, 1337a10–18). Hence a citizen of a democracy has a nature that identifies him as such. When he performs his function or realizes his nature by engaging in rational activity expressing virtue, he shows himself to be, as it were, by nature democratic. But – to pick up the point made in (d) – this nature should not be thought of as wholly different from the one possessed by citizens of other constitutions or by members of a village or household. Rather it is the same nature realized, developed, or perfected to a different degree.

If someone has the virtues of character in their unqualified form, his conception of happiness will be correct and he will possess practical wisdom in its unqualified form (*NE* 1144b30–1145b2). It is only in the best constitution, however, that the virtues inculcated in a citizen through public education are the unqualified ones (*Pol* III 4, 1293b1–7). It follows that in any other constitution the virtues that suit citizens to it will not provide them with a correct conception of their happiness or with unqualified practical wisdom. Starting with the household, then, what we have is a series of types of virtue and types of practical wisdom suited to different constitutions, existing in a single nature that is realized or developed to different degrees in them.

It is for this reason that Aristotle thinks that human beings are by nature political animals, not just in the sense that, like bees, they are naturally found in communities, but also in the stronger sense that they perfect their natures specifically in a political community of a certain sort. The function argument has shown that human nature consists in rational activity, whether practical (political) or theoretical. Hence to perfect their natures human beings must acquire the unconditional virtues of character. But this they do, Aristotle has argued, only in a polis, more specifically, in a polis with a certain constitution – the best sort.

The move from household to village or from village to polis coincides with a development in human virtue and practical wisdom. If human beings were non-rational animals, this development would be one that occurred through the operation of non-rational natural causes. But because human beings have a rational nature, their natural development (which is always communal, as we have seen) essentially involves a development in their rational capacities; for example, an increase in the level of practical wisdom they possess. Suppose, then, that the household already exists. Adult males in it possess a level of practical wisdom which they bring to bear in solving practical problems. The household is not self-sufficient: it produces a surplus of some needed items, not enough of others. This presents a practical problem, which it is an exercise of practical wisdom to solve. And it might be solved, for example, by noticing that other nearby households are in the same boat, and that exchanging goods with them would improve life for everyone involved. But exchange eventually leads to the need for money and with it to the need for new communal roles (that of merchant, for example), new forms of communal control (laws governing commerce), new virtues of character (such as generosity and magnificence which pertain to wealth), and new opportunities for the exercise of (a further developed) practical wisdom. (This story is modeled on the one Aristotle tells at *Pol* 1257a14–b8.) It is by engaging in this boot-strapping process that practical wisdom both causes new forms of communal life to emerge and causes itself to develop from the vestigial forms of it found in the household to the unconditional form of it found in Aristotle's best constitution.

The appearance of the polis at a stage in this process can now be thought of as an exercise of practical wisdom or statesmanship, as the result, for example, of a legislator having crafted a constitution for a collection of suitably situated villages which, when appropriately realized by them and their members, will be a polis – a self-sufficient political community. Notice that Aristotle himself often characterizes the polis as something crafted by legislators, and likens statesmanship to a craft (*Pol* 1253a30–1, 1268b34–8, 1273b32–3, 1274b18–19, 1282b14–16, 1325b40–1326a5). If things possessing standard natures had to perfect their natures by nature, this sort of talk would be disturbing, since it would conflict with the characterization of the polis as existing by nature. But, as we have seen, many standard natures, including our own, need to be perfected by craft. That the polis's nature is among them is not only no threat to its being a standard nature, therefore. It is just what we would expect given the close ties between our natures and its nature.

The nature of a polis, understood in the way we have been discussing, is manifestly internal to it. So it has one of the defining marks of a standard nature. But does it have the others? Is it a source of stability and change? A polis is a hylomorphic compound, with its constitution as its formal component and its inhabitants as its material one (*Pol*

517

1276b1–13). Since, as we saw, a thing's form has a better claim to being its nature than its matter does, what we are really asking is whether a polis's constitution is a source of its stability and change in the way that a standard nature is. And surely it is. A polis can change its matter (population) over time, but cannot sustain change from one kind of constitution to another, or dissolution of its constitution altogether (1276a34–b1, 1272b14–15). Thus its identity over time is determined by its constitution. Since a population constitutes a single polis if it shares a single constitution, its synchronic unity, its identity at a time, is also determined by its constitution (1276a24–6). A polis can grow or shrink in size, but its constitution sets limits to how big or small it can be (*Politics* VII 4–5). What causes it to decay or to survive is also determined by the type of constitution it has (these constitution-specific causes are discussed in *Politics* V). Thus a polis's constitution does seem to be a standard nature, and the polis seems to meet all the conditions of natural existence. No wonder, then, that the various kinds of natures that a polis may possess are defined in the same way as the different natures possessed by animals belonging to different species (1290b25–39).

So far we have been discussing the individual human beings in a polis. But the very same process of nature-indexing that occurs in them as they become parts of a polis also occurs in the various sub-communities that make up that polis. When a village is not yet part of a polis, it is a kingship. But if it becomes part of a democratic polis, though it may have a village elder of some sort, it is no longer a kingship plain and simple. Though the village elder may exercise kingly rule over village affairs, he must do so in a way compatible with the democratic constitution of which his village is a part. And in that constitution he is under the authority of all the other male citizens as a real king is not. The same is true of the household. Various types of rule are present in it, as we saw, but these are transformed when the household becomes part of a polis (*Politics* I 12–13). Thus households and villages that are parts of a polis have natures that are transformed by being indexed to the constitution of that polis. This is what makes them genuine parts of it.

We have seen that Aristotle's characterization of the emergence of the polis is not very compelling: his conceptions of the household and the village are far too contentious to be credible. Nonetheless, he is surely right in thinking that we are (in some sense or other) social animals from the very beginning of our lives, and that more sophisticated forms of communal life emerge from more primitive ones through some sort of rational bootstrapping. We might agree with Aristotle in principle, therefore, while wanting to haggle over the details. But, details aside, has he really shown that we are indeed *political* animals, that we do perfect our natures in a *polis*?

In *Politics* I, Aristotle characterizes the polis in rather abstract ways: it is the community with the most authority, the most self-sufficient one, and one ruled in its own characteristic way. When he puts meat on these bare bones, however, we see that a polis is quite like a modern state: it establishes the constitution, designs and enacts the laws, sets foreign and domestic policy, controls the armed forces and police, declares war, enforces the law, and punishes criminals (*Pol* 1328b2–23). Our question can thus be put as follows: has Aristotle shown that human beings can only perfect their natures in a state? Or in another community just in case it is a part of a state?

Many believe that leading the good life involves practicing a religion and living according to its dictates as a member of a religious community or church. But there are many different religions with different such dictates. If the state enforced any one religion or exerted more than fairly minimal authority within the religions it allowed, it would have to prevent many of its citizens from leading the good life as they understand it. To ensure that this does not happen the state must apparently be neutral on matters of religion, church and state must be separate, and the good life must be lived in religious communities largely protected from state intrusion. People who conceive of the good life in this way, therefore, will not accept Aristotle's argument. They may see the need for a state, but they will reject the idea that we perfect our natures or achieve our good only or primarily as members of it.

Many believe, too, that leading the good life involves following the cultural traditions and speaking the language of their own culture or ethnic group. Aristotle would agree with them, but this is very largely because he assumes that a polis (or at least its citizen members) will be ethnically, nationally, and even religiously homogeneous (*Pol* 1127b22–36, 1328b11–13): he is no cosmopolitan. Modern states by contrast are increasingly multicultural and multiethnic. If they are to respect the rights of their citizens, and allow them (within limits) to pursue their own conceptions of the good, they need to be supportive of cultural and ethnic diversity. They should not use their coercive powers to promote one culture or one ethnicity at the expense of others. Again, this means that most people will achieve the good or perfect their natures as members of different ethnic communities, and not as members of a state as such.

Religion, nationality, and ethnicity aside, it is perhaps more natural for us to think of public political life as something we engage in order to "be ourselves," as we say, in our private lives and leisure time. We are most ourselves, we are inclined think, not in any public sphere, but in the private one. Politics, like work, is necessary, but it is valuable primarily for what it makes possible.

These styles of objection can of course be generalized. Many believe that, at least as things stand, there are many different, equally defensible conceptions of the human good and the good life. We want to make room in the state for these different conceptions. We want to be left free to undertake what John Stuart Mill calls "experiments in living," in order to discover new conceptions. Consequently, we do not want the state to enforce any one conception of the good life, but to be largely neutral. We want it to allow different individuals and different communities (religious, ethnic, national) to pursue their own conceptions of the good, provided that they do so in ways that allow others to do the same. If we hold views of this sort, we will not agree with Aristotle that we perfect our natures or achieve our good as members of the state. We will claim instead that we do so as members of communities that share our conception of the good, but that lack the various powers, most particularly the coercive powers, definitive of the state.

Needless to say, it might be responded on Aristotle's behalf that this criticism of his argument for the naturalness of the polis simply ignores the function argument, since it implicitly denies (or at least seriously doubts) that the human good just does consist to some extent in practical political activity. This is a reasonable response so far as it goes. But even Aristotle thinks that the function argument is compelling only to the degree that it is underwritten by the facts of ethical and political experience (*NE* 1098b9–11, 1145b2–7, 1179a17–22). And what is surely true is that those facts no longer underwrite it completely. What experience has taught *us* is that there are many different human goods, many different good lives, many different ways to perfect ourselves, and much need for further experimentation and discovery in these areas.

Correct and Deviant Constitutions

A constitution, on the traditional Greek conception, can be controlled by "the one, the few, or the many" (*Pol* 1279a26–8): it can be either a monarchy, an oligarchy, or a democracy. Aristotle accepts this view to some extent, but introduces some important innovations. First, he argues that differences in wealth are of greater theoretical importance than difference in numbers. Oligarchy is really control by the wealthy; democracy, control by the poor. It just so happens that the wealthy are always few in number, while the poor are always many (1279b20–1280a6, 1290b17–20). This allows him to see the importance of the middle classes, those who are neither very rich nor very poor but somewhere in-between (1295b1–3), and to recognize the theoretical significance of a constitution, a so-called *polity*, in which they play a decisive part (1293a40–b1). Second, Aristotle departs from tradition in thinking that each of these three traditional types of rule actually comes in two varieties, one correct, the other deviant (1289b5–11). Rule by "the one" is either a kingship (correct) or a tyranny (deviant); rule by "the few" is either an aristocracy (correct) or an oligarchy (deviant); rule by "the many" is either a polity (correct) or a democracy (deviant).

The crucial difference between correct and deviant constitutions is that the former aim at "the common advantage," the latter, at the advantage of the rulers (*Pol* 1279a26–31). The precise identity of the group in a polis whose advantage Aristotle thinks to be the common one is difficult to determine. Is it the citizens? the citizens and their families? the native inhabitants? – it is difficult to be sure. Let us refer to it simply as G, therefore, and ask: is the common advantage the advantage of the individual members of G, or that of G taken as some kind of whole? Is the common advantage to be understood individualistically or holistically?

Some passages in the *Politics* suggest that Aristotle had fairly significant holistic or organicist leanings. For example, his argument that individuals are parts of a polis in the way that hands are parts of individuals (1253a18–29) suggests that it might be as uncontroversial to sacrifice an individual for the good of the polis as it would be to sacrifice a hand for the good of the individual whose hand it is. His views on the use of ostracism, indeed, seem to show him endorsing precisely such a sacrifice. It clearly isn't advantageous to the person who is superior to everyone else in his polis to be ostracized from it, yet even correct constitutions may ostracize him, when doing so serves the common advantage (1284b4–20).

Aristotle also uses the doctrine that individuals are parts of the polis to justify significant intrusion of the polis into what we would consider the private sphere. "One should not consider that any citizen belongs to himself alone, but that each of them belongs to the polis, since he is a part of it. And it is natural for the supervision of each part to look to the supervision of the whole" (*Pol* 1337a27–30; cf. 1260b14–16). Hence the best constitution should have laws that regulate or constrain the freedom of association of many of its inhabitants (1327a37–40), their freedom to marry, reproduce, and rear their offspring (1335a4–b19, 1335b22–5), their freedom to have extra-marital affairs (1336a1–2), their religious freedom (1330a8–9), their freedom of expression and artistic freedom (1336b3–23), and even their freedom to dine as they choose (1330a3–8). These views sound a good deal worse than merely holistic.

Many other texts in the *Politics* suggest, however, that Aristotle means to be espousing some sort of individualism: "it is impossible for the whole to be happy unless some, most, or all of its parts are happy" (1264b17–19); "even when they do not need one another's help, they no less desire to live together. Although it is also true that the common advantage brings them together, to the extent that it contributes some share of noble living to each" (1278b20–3); aristocrats "rule with a view to what is best for the polis and those who share in it" (1279a35–7); "it is evident that the best constitution must be the organization in which anyone might to do best and live a blessedly happy life" (1324a23–5); "the best life, whether for a whole polis collectively or for an individual, would be a life of action" (1325b15–16); "a polis is excellent because the citizens who participate in the constitution are excellent. And in our polis all the citizens participate in the constitution" (1332a32–5). These texts show that Aristotle is an individualist in at least this important sense: he believes that the best constitution, and the very intrusive laws that are part of it, promote the virtue and so the happiness of the individuals in G.

The question is how is the apparent holism to be combined with the apparent individualism? In discussing ostracism, Aristotle makes it clear that in his view a just constitution may require members of G to do things that do not promote their individual advantage. At the same time, he thinks that such a constitution must promote the advantage of the individual members of G. These views are compatible provided that promoting the advantage of the individual members of G need be no more than *generally congruent* with their actually being advantaged. Thus, for example, a correct constitution that has no need of ostracism is better, Aristotle thinks, than one that does need it, presumably because the former constitution better promotes the advantage of each of the individuals in G than the latter. At the same time, if an individual in G actually threatens the stability of the correct constitution, and the justice it embodies, the constitution may have to sacrifice his advantage to that of the other members of G. What it does, in other words, is to sacrifice the advantage of an individual in G when failing to do so would risk destroying a constitution that promotes the advantage of each of the other members of G. In these circumstances, that is the closest the constitution can come to preserving the congruence I mentioned. In times of war or scarcity, this congruence is likely to be quite hard to preserve; in times of peace and plenty, much easier. But the general point remains: no constitution short of an omnipotent and omniscient one can absolutely guarantee that this congruence will always be absolute.

On this way of looking at him, then, Aristotle is neither an extreme individualist – who thinks that the happiness of the polis simply consists in the happiness of each of the individual members of G – nor an extreme holist – who thinks of the happiness of the whole of G as something distinct from the happiness of each of the individuals in it. He is a moderate individualist or moderate holist, someone who thinks that the happiness of a polis must be generally congruent with the happiness of the individual members of its G class.

The fact that there need be no more than this sort of general congruence between a polis's happiness and the happiness of the individuals in its G class explains why Aristotle's doctrine that individuals are parts of a polis is no threat to moderate individualism. A hand can perform its task only as part of a body, and there is general congruence between the health of a body and the health of all its parts. Yet in some circumstances, the closest we can come to preserving this congruence involves sacrificing a part. In this respect, Aristotle thinks, we are like hands. We will find this insufficiently reassuring only if we think that general congruence between the aim of a just polis and that of an individual in G is not enough, that more is required. Aristotle fails to provide that reassurance, but this may be a strength rather than a weakness of his view.

The Naturalness of the Best Constitution

One important difference between the various sorts of constitutions Aristotle distinguishes is that they have different aims or goals (*Pol* 1289a17–28), different conceptions of happiness: "it is by seeking happiness in different ways and by different means that individual groups of people create different ways of life and different constitutions" (1328a41–b2). Of these conceptions, as we saw, only one is unconditionally correct: the one that accords with nature, with the conclusion of the function argument. This is the conception embodied in a kingship or aristocracy (and to a lesser extent in a polity). Only in these constitutions are the social virtues both natural and unconditionally correct (1288a37–9, 1293b5–6).

In all the correct constitutions justice is thought to consist in distributing political goods (such as citizenship, participation in office, or constitutional authority) to citizens on the basis of their contribution to achieving the constitution's goal. They all agree that justice is based on merit. But because they disagree about what the goal of a constitution should be, they disagree about what this basis is. Oligarchs think it is wealth. So they think that the wealthiest should have constitutional authority, and that participation in office should be subject to a property assessment. Democrats think that the basis is freedom: all free citizens bring an equal share into the constitution, so all should participate equally in office and its prerogatives and get an equal share of social benefits. Aristocrats, in the best constitution, on the other hand, think that the goal is neither wealth nor freedom, but noble or virtuous living. Hence they think – correctly in Aristotle's view – that it is just for the distribution of political goods to be based on virtue (*Pol* 1283a24–6).

In the best constitution, therefore, the citizens (who are either men equal in their virtue and practical wisdom or their wives) and the non-citizens, who are either natural slaves or non-Greek serfs (*Pol* 1329a25–6), should be treated differently. But it does not follow, as Aristotle simply assumes, that it is just to treat the children of citizens and non-citizens in the same way as their respective parents. For example, it is not just, as Aristotle assumes, to distribute public education to the children of citizens and not to those of the non-citizens. Indeed, it is unjust even in Aristotle's own terms. For virtue is not something that young un-socialized children can possess, and so education cannot be distributed among them on its basis, as unconditional Aristotelian justice requires.

Aristotle's best constitution thus fails to meet its own standards of justice. That is a major problem, obviously, but it points the way to a yet more serious one and then to a possible solution. Aristotle believes that virtue is a social or political output, a consequence of receiving advantages, such as public education, that a constitution itself bestows. But no constitution can distribute *all* advantages on the basis of a property which is itself the result of the distribution of advantage. If justice is going to be based on some feature of individuals, it must be one that individuals do not acquire through a process which may itself be either just or unjust. Aristotle's theory of justice needs to be modified, so that the means of acquiring virtue (whether nutritional or educational) are distributed on the basis not of virtue itself, but of a feature, such as being human, that is un-problematically possessed to an equal degree by all the children born in the constitution, whether male or female, whether born to citizens or non-citizens. The best constitution would have to provide equal opportunities to *all* the children possessing this feature. Then, at the appropriate stage, it would have cull out as its future citizens those who had successfully acquired virtue in this way. If this process were fairly carried out, it would ensure that people acquired their virtue in a just way. Subsequent virtue-based distributions of advantage would then not be unjustly based.

That problem, perhaps now to some extent solved, has to do with the basis on which advantage is distributed in the best constitution. The next problem concerns what gets distributed. If someone is a natural slave or a non-Greek of one sort or another, Aristotle thinks that he has pretty much no natural potential for virtue. Provided that his lack of such potential is determined by a fair process, it will then be naturally and unconditionally just for the best constitution to assign him no share or a very small share in political advantage or in true happiness. It does not follow, however, that it will be just to assign him a share of what we might call political *disadvantage*. For example, there are some occupations that Aristotle thinks it would be disadvantageous for a citizen of the best constitution to have. Thus citizens can't be farmers because happiness cannot exist without virtue, leisure is needed to develop virtue (1329a1–2), and farmers do not have leisure (1318b11–12). For a similar reason they cannot be vulgar artisans or tradesmen, "since lives of these sorts are ignoble and inimical to virtue" (1328b40–1). But he thinks it is perfectly all right to require (I intentionally use a fairly weak verb) natural slaves to work as farmers. True, farming won't be disadvantageous to a natural slave in the way that it would be to a citizen, it won't have a negative effect on his capacity for virtue, but that doesn't mean that it won't be disadvantageous to him in other ways. Being required to be a farmer by a constitution, when one hates farming, might well be considered precisely such a disadvantage.

If Aristotle is right about farming, trading, and artisanship, the appropriate conclusion to draw is that they are ethically reprehensible occupations, because inimical to virtue, and that no one in the best constitution should have them in a way that threatens their virtue (*Pol* 1277b3–7, 1333a6–16). Perhaps, like political office itself, the citizens themselves should undertake them turn and turn about for short enough periods to leave their virtue and leisure sufficiently unscathed.

If the best constitution is to be unconditionally just, to repeat, distribution of political advantage must be proportional to virtue, it must be equal for the unconditional citizens, since Aristotle stipulates that they are equal in virtue. But how are we to tell whether or not the best constitution or any other constitution, for that matter, meets this requirement? Aristotle claims that when political advantage is justly distributed, people who are equal in virtue receive "reciprocally equal" amounts of it. This, he says, is what preserves the constitution (*Pol* 1261a30–1, *NE* 1132b33; *MM* 1194a16–18). But reciprocal equality is by no means easy to understand. In the *Nicomachean Ethics*, where it is called "proportional reciprocity," it is initially introduced in connection with the exchange of property of different sorts: if *n* shoes are equal exchange for 1 house, *n* shoes are reciprocally equal to 1 house. This is the sort of equality that applies to political advantage, Aristotle thinks, because, like exchangeable property, it isn't all of one sort (1261a32–b6, 1300b10–12). Political offices themselves, for example, are very different in nature, scope, and authority. If A holds political office *x*, and B holds a very different office *y*, how are we to ensure that A's share in ruling is equal to B's, that A's share of political advantage is the same size as B's? When we know the answer to this question, Aristotle thinks, we will have established a reciprocal equality between *x* and *y*, and be on our way to understanding what proportional equality applied to political advantage actually amounts to.

In the case of exchangeable goods, money provides the units of measurement (*NE* 1133a20–1). So 1 house equals *n* pairs of shoes, because 1 house equals *n* units of money (*n* dollars), while a pair of shoes equals 1 unit (1 dollar). But that does not tell us how to establish that 1 house equals *n* dollars or that 1 pair of shoes equals only 1 dollar. Indeed, this is just the original problem all over again, since it is no easier to establish equalities between shoes and money than it is to establish them between shoes and houses. There is some suggestion that Aristotle may have thought that need (*chreia*) offers us some assistance with this problem: "Everything, then, must be measured by a single standard. In reality, this standard is need . . . But need has come to be conventionally represented by money" (*NE* 1133a25–30). This suggestion is certainly interesting. But it is not easy to determine the conditions under which otherwise similar needs for different things are equal. What, for example, could explain the fact that a need for shoes is equal to a need for houses just in case the one is a need for *n* pairs of shoes, while the other is a need for 1 house? Aristotle himself may have been aware of this problem, since he says that things so different as shoes and houses "cannot become commensurate in reality," but that "they can become sufficiently (*hikanôs*) so in relation to our needs" (1133b19–20; also *Pol* 1283a4–10). But it is frankly difficult to see how we could establish commensurability between houses and shoes on the basis of need that would be adequate for Aristotle's purposes.

When we turn from exchangeable goods to virtue, political advantage, and the like, our problems multiply. Here we do not even have a credible unit of measurement like money to rely on, and it is even less clear how need might come into the picture. But if we are not able to tell some reasonable story, the claim that the best constitution is unconditionally just will be bound to seem like stipulation rather than fact. Indeed, the more fundamental claim that Aristotelian justice is true and unconditional justice, because it alone is based *on nature* will itself come to have that same appearance: it will seem less naturalistic metaphysics and more like wishful thinking.

Bibliography

Aubenque, P. (ed.) (1993). *Aristote "Politique": Etudes sur La Politique d'Aristote* (Paris: Presses Universitaires De France).

Dreizehnter, A. (1970). *Aristoteles "Politica"* (Munich: Wilhelm Fink).

Keyt, D. (1999). *Aristotle "Politics" Books V And VI*. Oxford: Clarendon Aristotle Series.

Keyt, D. and Miller, F. D., Jr. (eds.) (1991). *A Companion to Aristotle's "Politics"* (Oxford: Blackwell).

Kraut, R. (1997). *Aristotle "Politics" Books VII and VIII* (Oxford: Clarendon Aristotle Series).

Kraut, R. (2002). *Aristotle: Political Philosophy* (Oxford: Oxford University Press).

Lord, C. and O' Connor, D. K. (eds.) (1991). *Essays on the Foundations of Aristotelian Political Theory* (Berkeley, CA: University Of California Press).

Miller Jr., F. D. (1995). *Nature, Justice, and Rights in Aristotle's "Politics"* (Oxford: Clarendon Press).

Mulgan, R. G. (1977). *Aristotle's Political Theory: An Introduction for Students of Political Theory* (Oxford: Clarendon Press).

Newman, W. L. (1887–92). *The "Politics" of Aristotle*, 4 vols (Oxford: Clarendon Press).

Patzig, G. (ed.) (1990). *XI Symposium Aristotelicum: Aristoteles "Politik"* (Göttingen: Vanderhoeck & Ruprecht).

Pellegrin, P. (1993). *Aristote: "Les Politiques,"* 2nd edn. (Paris: Flammarion).

Reeve, C. D. C. (1998). *Aristotle: "Politics"* (Indianapolis, IN: Hackett).

Robinson, R. (1995). *Aristotle "Politics" Books III and IV*, 2nd edn, with a supple. essay by D. Keyt (Oxford: Clarendon Aristotle Series).

Salkever, S. G. (1990). *Finding The Mean: Theory and Practice in Aristotelian Political Philosophy* (Princeton, NJ: Princeton University Press).

Saunders, T. J. (1995). *Aristotle's "Politics" Books I and II* (Oxford: Clarendon Aristotle Series).

Simpson, P. L. P. (1997). *The "Politics" of Aristotle* (Chapel Hill, NC: University of North Carolina Press).

Simpson, P. L. P. (1998). *Aristotle's "Politics": A Philosophical Commentary* (Chapel Hill, NC: University of North Carolina Press).

Yack, B. (1993). *The Problems of a Political Animal: Community, Justice and Conflict in Aristotelian Political Thought* (Los Angeles, CA: University of California Press).

33

Rulers and Ruled

ROBERT MAYHEW

Aristotle's *Politics* opens with a brief chapter that makes three related points:

1. Every city (*polis*) is an association (*koinônia*), and every association is formed for some good; the city is the most sovereign of all associations, embraces all others, and aims at the highest of all goods. (1252a1–7; cf. *NE* I.1–2)
2. The next point (most of which I quote here) is central to the topic of rulers and ruled: "Those who think that being a statesman (*politikon*), king, household manager, and master are the same, do not speak well, for they believe each of these differ not in kind, but in whether [the ruled] are many or few: e.g., [the ruler] over a few is master; over more, a household manager; over a still larger number, a statesman or king – as if there were no difference between a large household and a small city." (1252a7–16)[1]
3. The method appropriate to the investigation of the above issue is the analysis of something (in this case, the city) into its parts (the other associations). This enables us to see the difference between the city and the other associations, and most important, to better understand the different kinds of rule that properly go with these different associations. (1252a17–23; as Schofield 1990: 8–9 argues, it is this method of analysis, and not dialectic, that Aristotle employs in *Pol* I.)

The best way to come to understand Aristotle on the different kinds of rulers and ruled is to follow the method he proposes. So I shall examine the different kinds of rule that correspond to the kinds of associations of which the city is composed, and discuss the implications of Aristotle regarding these as different in kind from political rule.

According to Aristotle, the city is composed of households, each of which has a head of household (an adult male citizen).[2] Household management consists of three parts: mastery (rule over one's slaves), paternal rule (rule over one's children), and marital rule (rule over one's wife) (*Pol* I.12 1259a37–9). Aristotle claims that political rule is different from every type of household rule. An examination of the kinds of rule that go to make up household management is crucial for grasping his own conception of statesmanship or political rule.

Mastery: Rule over Slaves

Aristotle believes that in nature – in a condition prior to the formation of a city – humans come together to form other associations, which in turn join together to form households, which in turn become villages, which finally come together to form a city. The pairs of humans that naturally seek each other out are (1) free men and slaves, and (2) males and females (*Pol* I.2 1252a30–4). The primary and smallest parts of a complete household are certain kinds of individual humans: master and slaves, husband and wife, parents and children (*Pol* I.3 1253b4–7).

To understand why Aristotle believes that free men and slaves would naturally join together, and why they naturally make up part of a proper household (and thus a proper city), we must understand the difference, as he sees it,[3] between a free man and a slave. This difference will also explain why the arrangement of master and slave is beneficial to both parties. (I must pass over many details of Aristotle's account of natural slavery, and the many controversies surrounding it. See Schofield 1990; Smith 1991; Simpson 1998: 28–46.)

That man is free who can exist for himself and not for another (*Met* A.2 982b25–6), while a natural slave is someone who exists for another. In fact, a slave is in a sense a part of another – a living part that is separate. (See *Pol* I.4 1253b32, I.4 1254a8–13, I.6 1255b9–12, I.13 1260a39–40; *Cat* 7 7a34–b1; *EE* VII.9 1241b17–24.)

A slave cannot exist for himself because master is to slave what soul is to body, and the body is by its nature ruled by the soul (at least in a virtuous human). (See *Pol* I.5 1254a34–6, 1254b4–6; *EE* VII.9 1241b17–24.) What Aristotle means by this becomes clearer as he tries in *Pol* I.5 to justify his account of natural slavery.

> Those who are as different [from others] as soul from body and human from animal – and this is the way it is for those whose function (*ergon*) is the use of the body, and who can do nothing better – are by nature slaves, for whom it is better to be ruled according to this rule. . . . For he is by nature a slave who is capable of being another's – and this is why he *is* another's – and who participates in reason enough to perceive it, but does not have it. (1254b16–23)

Aristotle makes two points in support of his claims: (1) a slave belongs to another, and (2) a slave is cognitively inferior or impaired: he can understand or follow reason, but does not possess it. The first point is dependent on the second, for one human properly is or becomes a part of another because of this cognitive lack.

What the slave lacks is the deliberative part of the soul.

> The freeman rules the slave in a manner different from which the male rules the female, or the man the child. And while the parts of the soul are present in all of them, they are present in different ways. For the slave does not have the deliberative part (*to bouleutikon*) at all, while the female has it but it lacks authority (*akuron*), and the child has it but it is incomplete [or "underdeveloped," *ateles*]. (*Pol* I.13 1260a9–14)

The slave can understand his master's instructions – dig the ditch, rake the leaves, fetch some water, buy these supplies – but he cannot run a household or in general plan a fully human life. This is why Aristotle elsewhere says that a slave can have pleasure, but not happiness (*NE* X.6 1177a6–9). For a slave shares in neither deliberation nor happiness, and so must rely on the deliberations of his master (*Pol* III.9 1280a31–4, IV.11 1295b21, VI.2 1317b13). This is the core of what is meant in saying that a slave shares his master's life (*Pol* I.13 1260a39–40).

Slaves can have a kind of virtue (*Pol* I.13 1259b21–8, 1260a33–6; *Poet* 15 1454a16–22), but this cannot be relied upon: they also require admonishment (*Pol* I.13 1260b5–7). Further, a justice of sorts can exist between master and slave, as can a low-grade kind of friendship, though not the sort of justice and friendship that can exist among equals (*NE* V.6 1134b8–12, V.11 1138b5–13, VIII.11 1161a32–b8; *Pol* I.6 1255b12–15).

Because of the natural differences between masters and slaves, this relationship is beneficial to both parties, and it would be harmful to the slave to try to live outside such a relationship. Nevertheless, the slaves' welfare is not the master's motive in possessing them. Unlike a head of household's rule over his wife and children – which is properly for their benefit (though obviously conducive to the man's as well) – his rule over slaves is for his own sake alone. (See *Pol* I.5 1254a21–2, 1254b6–9, I.6 1255b4–9, III.6 1278b33–7.)

Note that according to Aristotle, although natural slavery is justified, enslavement of normal humans (e.g., through conquest) is not (*Pol* I.6, VII.14 1333b38–1334a2).

Given their intellectual and moral limitations, a city of slaves is not possible (*Pol* III.13 1283a18–19, cf. IV.4 1291a8–10, IV.11 1295b13–23). But more important for our purposes, and as we saw in *Pol* I.1, mastery should not be a model for political rule. To make it so results in tyranny (*NE* VIII.10 1160b27–32). Beyond *Pol* I.1, Aristotle twice makes the point that mastery is not the same as other types of rule. For example:

> It is evident from these [previous remarks] that mastery is not the same as political rule, and that all the kinds of rule are not the same as one another, as some claim. For one is rule over people free by nature, while another is over slaves, and household management is monarchy (for every household is ruled by one), while political rule is over free and equal people. (*Pol* I.7 1255b16–20; see also I.3 1253b18–20)

One role of the discussion of slavery in *Pol* I is to make precisely this point.

Parental Rule and Marital Rule

Aristotle says that a free man rules over his wife and children as free people (i.e., not like slaves), but he does not rule each in the same way: "the rule over his wife is political, and over his children kingly" (I.12 1259b1).

A parent's rule over his children is quite natural, based as it is on the helplessness of children, and their initial lack of the cognitive tools necessary to plan and live a fully human life. Whereas adults are older and (in normal cases) fully developed, children are younger and underdeveloped (*Pol* I.12 1259b3–4). Further, and connected to this, children require moral training (see, e.g., *NE* II.1). Aristotle says that parental rule is like kingship, since a parent rules on the basis of age and affection (*Pol* I.12 1259b10–17; *NE* VIII.10 1160b24–7; more on kingship later). This comparison to kingship suggests that parental rule is: (1) absolute or complete rule (for rule is not shared), and (2) for the sake of the children. (On this second point, see *Pol* III.6 1278b37–1279a2.) Whereas the slave is part of the freeman for the slave's entire life, the child is a part of his parents temporarily – until he is old enough to think for himself and plan his own life.

> There is no injustice unconditionally in relation to what is one's own; one's possession, or one's child until he is old enough and separated, is as it were a part of oneself, and no one chooses to harm oneself. This is why there is no injustice in relation to oneself, and thus no political justice or injustice. For political justice is according to law, and found among those who are naturally suited for law – those to whom belongs equality in ruling and being ruled. This is why justice exists more in relation to a wife than in relation to children or possessions, for the former is household justice (though this too is different from political justice). (*NE* V.6 1134b9–12; see also V.11 1138b5–13)

It is no surprise that not only justice, but friendship, can exist between parents and children, though again it is not the same as that which exists among equals (see *NE* V.7 1158b11–28).

In rejecting the idea that all rule is the same – and specifically that paternal rule is the same as political rule – Aristotle would seem to agree with classical liberalism to this extent: government should not be paternalistic, and expect to supervise and control citizens to the degree that we recognize parents ought to in the case of their children. (This is not to say that nothing that comes under the scope of government in Aristotle's political philosophy would be considered paternalistic by modern Lockeans.)

Aristotle's views on marital rule are not as important as mastery and paternal rule in coming to understand, by contrast, his conception of political rule. But for the sake of completeness, and because Aristotle's views on women are notorious, I'll briefly discuss his account of it.

The relation of male to female is that of natural superior to inferior, and of ruler to ruled (*Pol* I.5 1254b13–14). But not all kinds of *ruled* are the same. Most important, a women is not the same as a slave. There is a natural distinction between the female and the slave – one that non-Greeks (e.g., Persians) fail to recognize (*Pol* I.2 1252a34–b7).

As in the other cases of human superiority and inferiority, this relationship too is based on a cognitive difference. A woman possesses deliberation, but it lacks authority (*Pol* I.13 1260a12–20). There is a scholarly debate about just what this means – does the woman's deliberation merely lack the *political* authority to overpower that of men, or the psychological power to control her own emotions? – but I cannot explore these issues here. (See Smith 1983.) Suffice it to say that according to Aristotle, a woman's cognitive abilities are superior to that of children and slaves, but not as good as a man's – which means, not sufficient to lead an independent life, nor to take part in the running of a city.

> Household management is different for a man and a woman, for the function of one is to acquire, and the other to preserve [or "to guard," *phulattein*]. Practical wisdom (*phronêsis*) is the only virtue peculiar to ruling. For the others, it would seem, must be common to both being ruled and ruling; practical wisdom, at any rate, is not a virtue of being ruled, but true opinion is. (*Pol* III.4 1277b24–30)

Women *can* possess the moral virtues, though these are different from the moral virtues appropriate to men. (See *Pol* I.13 1260a20–31, III.4 1277b20–3; *Poet* 15 1454a16–22; *Rhet* I.5 1361a4–11.)

Aristotle believes friendship is certainly possible between husbands and wives, but not the highest form of friendship (*NE* VIII.11 1161a22–25; *NE* VIII.12 1162a16–33; *EE* VIII.10 1242a19–32), and like parental rule, but unlike mastery, in marital rule the ruler is motivated by the desire to benefit his wife as well as himself (*Pol* III.6 1278b37–1279a2).

Finally, although the husband is said to rule the wife, marital rule is much closer to political rule than it is to mastery or even paternal rule, which resemble tyranny and kingship respectively.

> The community of man and woman appears to be aristocratic. For a man rules according to worth, and in those matters over which a man should rule; but what is fitting to a woman he renders unto her. But if the man rules everything, he changes this community into an oligarchy, for he acts contrary to worth, and not as one who is a better person. (*NE* VIII.10 1160b32–1161a1)

An aristocracy is a proper form of government, wherein the best people (i.e., best in virtue, and such people are usually the few) exercise political rule over the ruled (usually the majority of citizens), and they do so for the sake of the whole city. The ruled, however, still have some role to play in the running of the city, for example, serving on a jury and electing certain officials. Similarly, the husband, because of the male's cognitive superiority, is better equipped to participate in ruling the household and the city. But if the husband does not allow his wife to play any role in the running of the household, that is improper, resembling as it does oligarchy (a deviant form of government in which the few rule for their own sake) and not aristocracy. (We saw earlier that what is fitting for a woman is to be a guard who helps her husband preserve the household. Cf. Xenophon, *Oeconomica* 7.22–5, and see Mayhew 2004: 92–113.)

Contra Plato

When Aristotle claims in *Pol* I.1 (and again in *Pol* I.3 and I.7) that not all kinds of rule are the same, Plato is clearly one of his targets. In the *Statesman*, Plato has the Eleatic Stranger ask:

> Shall we posit statesman, king and master, and also household manager, as one thing, when we call them all by these names, or shall we claim that there are as many sorts of art (*technas*) as there are names used to refer to them? (258e)

Plato maintains that the former is correct (259a–261a).

Moreover, in the *Republic*, Plato in different contexts takes as his model for political rule kingship, paternal rule and mastery. First, the philosopher-kings are *kings* – they (and not law) are to rule completely over the city, for the good of the entire city. (On philosopher-kings, see *Republic* V 473c–e; on the rule of law being second-best, see *Statesman* 293c–e, 297d–e, 300b–301b). Second, the Platonic communism of women, children and property aims to eliminate privacy as much as possible (including private households), and encourages the use of such familial terms as "brother," "sister," "father," "mother," "son" and "daughter" to refer to all citizens of the appropriate age and gender. This suggests that Plato intends the city (or at least the Gold and Silver classes, but see Mayhew 1997a: 129–37) to be run as one big household (*Republic* V 457c–466d; cf. *Laws* 5.739c–e).[4] Finally, in *Republic* IX, Plato refers to the ruled as slaves:

> Why do you think vulgar and manual labor bring reproach? Or shall we say it is for any other reason than that when the best [i.e., rational] part is by nature so weak in someone, it cannot rule the beasts in him, but can only serve them, and can learn only the things that flatter them? . . . Therefore, in order that such a person be ruled by something similar to what rules the best person, we say that he ought to be the slave (*doulon*) of that best person who has the divine rule within himself. It is not to harm the slave that we think he ought to be ruled . . . but because it is better for all to be ruled by what is divine and wise (*phronimou*), especially when one has it as one's own within oneself, but if not, then imposed from outside, so that as far as possible all will be alike and friends, governed by the same thing. (9.590c–d)

Plato creates a sharp distinction between the rulers and the ruled. The rulers are philosophers, the ruled are not. The rulers possess knowledge, the ruled mere opinion. Because of these differences, the ruled are not capable of ruling themselves: they are "the ruled" by nature, much like slaves and children in Aristotle's political philosophy.

For Aristotle, however, this form of rule is not proper for normal adult humans, who in the best circumstances should retain a great deal of independence. If he is consistent, we should expect political rule to be the shared rule of equal and independent men – men who may lack philosophical wisdom, but who possess the cognitive abilities neces- sary for running their own individual lives and for taking part in the running of the city. Such citizens are separate entities, and not parts of another.[5] Political rule is not the rule of master over slave or even benevolent parent over child.

Political Rule

According to Aristotle's political philosophy, in one sense, humans do not rule – law does. The rule of law is best for free and equal humans who are citizens of the same city. But more precisely, law and men must rule together. Wanting law to rule alone is like asking god and intellect (*nous*) to rule (which is impossible); wanting humans to rule alone is like asking wild beasts to rule (which is undesirable), "for passion perverts rulers even when they are the best men," whereas "law is intellect (*nous*) without desire." So law rules, and humans are "guardians of and assistants to the laws." (See *Pol* III.16 1286a17–20, 1287a18–32; *NE* V.6 1134a35–b2.) In what follows, I focus not on law, but on citizens as rulers and ruled.

Aristotle defines "citizen" as one who shares in making decisions (in the political context) and in holding office (*Pol* III.1 1275a22–3, 1275b17–21). Holding office includes even serving on a jury and going to the assembly (*Pol* III.1 1275a26–32). What counts as a citizen will differ from one political system to another (*Pol* III.1 1275b3–5); and in the best city, at least, the laborer and the vulgar person should not be considered citizens (*Pol* III.5). Citizens are basically equal, and take it in turns to rule and be ruled; in fact, they learn to rule by first being ruled (*Pol* III.4 1277b7–10, III.6 1279a8–21).

To understand why citizens, who are basically equal, must share in rule, and why their shares in ruling and being ruled must be different – and, looking back, why it is right for superiors to rule over inferiors – we need briefly to examine Aristotle's account of justice, which is the topic of *NE* V.

There are basically two ways of understanding justice, one general and the other specific (*NE* V.1). Justice in the general sense is simply virtue in relation to others (*NE* V.1 1129b30–1130a13). Justice in the specific sense is equality or fairness (*to ison*, e.g., *NE* V.2 1130b9). There are two kinds of justice in the specific sense: distributive and rectificatory (*NE* V.2 1130b30–1131a1). The latter type, which covers economic exchanges as well as punishment and restitution in criminal cases, need not concern us. Relevant to our discussion is distributive justice, which deals with "distributions of honor, or money, or the other things to be divided up among those who are members of the political system (*politeias*)" (*NE* V.2 1130b31–2). Included in the things that can be distributed justly or unjustly are the offices and tasks by which citizens share in rule. (Aristotle's main discussion of distributive justice is *NE* V.3.)

I want to emphasize two points about distributive justice: (1) the distribution must be "according to worth" (*kat' axion*, *NE* V.3 1131a24), which depends on the context and a certain standard of what is worthy or good; and (2) this justice is based on "a kind of proportion" (*analogon ti*, *NE* V.3 1131a29). Justice is equal in that those who are of the same worth (in a certain relevant context) deserve the same goods and/or treatment, and unequal in that those who are not the same do not deserve the same goods and/or treatment. Where two parties are unequal, what each receives should be *proportionate* to the degree of inequality, i.e., to how different they are. For example, according to advocates of aristocracy, all citizens with a certain high degree of practical wisdom must have access to the highest political offices (and in this sense justice demands equality), but those citizens without the requisite practical wisdom will not be allowed to hold such offices (and in this sense, justice demands inequality). (See *NE* V.3 1131a25–9.)

Even among citizens who are similar and politically equal there will be differences (more on these shortly), though they are not as great as the differences between master and slave, parent and child, or even husband and wife. But as with the other cases of rulers and ruled, the fundamental difference between political rulers and ruled is a cognitive one.

Political rule is not the domain of a small group of philosophers. In all normal humans there is a functioning rational part of the soul; and the appetitive part of the soul, though non-rational and often in conflict with the rational, can obey reason. The intellectual virtue most important in the present context is practical wisdom (*phronêsis*). Practical wisdom "is a true state involving reason (*hexin alêthê meta logou*), concerned with action regarding what is good or bad for human beings" (*NE* VI.5 1140b4–6). Aristotle offers politicians (especially leaders like Pericles) and household managers as examples of those who use practical wisdom.

At the beginning of *NE* VI.8, Aristotle discusses the relationship between practical wisdom and political science (*politikê*).

> Political science and practical wisdom are the same state, but their being is not the same. Of practical wisdom concerning the city, the ruling part is legislative science (*nomothetikê*), while the part concerned with particulars has the name common to both, i.e., political science. This part deals with action and deliberation, for the decree is to be acted on as the last thing [reached in deliberation]. (1141b23–8)

There are two parts of political science: legislative science (the ruling part) and the part, also called "political science," which is concerned with particulars and involves action and deliberation. Aristotle continues:

> Practical wisdom seems most of all to be that type which is concerned with the individual himself, and this part has the name common to both, i.e., practical wisdom. Of the other parts, one is household management, another legislation, another political science, and of this last, one part is deliberative and another judicial. (1141b29–33)

There are four parts of practical wisdom:

1   Practical wisdom concerning oneself (also called "practical wisdom")
2   Household management
3   Legislation
4   Political science (in the narrow sense):
   (a)   deliberative
   (b)   judicial

Legislation and political science (in the narrow sense) correspond to the two parts of political science (in the broad sense) outlined at 1141b23–9. Aristotle suggests that everyone should have at least some concern for oneself, household management, and the city (*NE* VI.8.1142a7–10). This last would require at least some degree of practical wisdom concerning legislation and/or political science (in the narrow sense). This is important for Aristotle's conception of political rule.

In *Pol* III.4, Aristotle notes that the city is made up of dissimilar parts, "and therefore the virtue of all the citizens is necessarily not one." Most significant, being a virtuous ruler and being a virtuous citizen are not necessarily the same thing: "the excellent ruler is good and wise (*phronimon*), but the citizen need not be wise" (1277a10–16). The major difference between the ruler and the ruled is that the ruler will possess practical wisdom. I think Aristotle has the following in mind: The virtue of the ruler is practical wisdom in the full sense, including political science (broadly understood). Only men like Pericles will have the knowledge necessary to make laws and propose decrees, and the ability to act on that knowledge in all the particular situations in which a city finds itself. Such men will know best which laws should be passed and when they should be applied. But the non-ruler will still possess some kind of practical wisdom. He should have it concerning himself and his household, and perhaps some form of it concerning the city. Though he won't be able to participate in legislation, he will be able to take some part in deliberation (e.g., in the assembly) and in judgment (e.g., serving on a jury, electing certain officials). People with such cognitive abilities should not be left out of politics, for they will likely have something valuable to say.

In *Pol* III.11, Aristotle examines the ways in which it is best for the multitude to participate in running the city. He says that it is not safe for the multitude to share in the greatest offices, as their lack of practical wisdom (*aphrosunê*) may lead them to err.

> But not letting them take part and share in [ruling] is alarming, for when there are many who are without honor (*atimoi*) and poor, that city will necessarily be full of enemies. So it remains for them to share in deliberating and judging. This is why Solon and certain other legislators arrange for them to choose and audit officials, but do not let them rule [or "hold office," *archein*] alone. For all of them when brought together have an adequate perception (*hikanên aisthêsin*), and when mixed with those who are better, they benefit cities. (1281b28–36; see also III.15 1286a25–33)

The role offered the multitude fits well the two parts of "political science" (narrowly understood): the deliberative and the judicial.

There are two advantages to giving the multitude a part in ruling: (1) It avoids a situation that could give rise to factional conflict, namely, leaving many citizens entirely out of politics (cf. *Pol* II.5 1264b6–15). (2) The "adequate perception" of the multitude constitutes a genuine contribution to the running of the city (see also *Pol* III.4, III.11 1282a20–3).

In my discussion of political rulers and ruled, I had to skip over much of what Aristotle says about the precise functions of the rulers and the ruled according to the different kinds of political systems, and the precise means of determining how citizens will take turns ruling. It is important, however, to mention the following passage from *Pol* VII.14, wherein Aristotle discusses the basis in nature for the kind of ruling and being ruled he believes is appropriate for the very best city:

> Nature has provided the distinction [between rulers and ruled among equals] by making that which is the same in kind have a younger and an older part, of which it is proper for the former to be ruled and the latter to rule. No one takes offense at being ruled on the basis of age or thinks himself superior, especially if he will be repaid for the contribution when he reaches the appropriate age. (1332b35–41; see also VII.3 1325b7–10)

Even where this is not practiced, there would be some differences between political rulers and ruled, for the rulers "seek differences in outward appearance, in forms of address, and in honors received" (*Pol* I.12 1259b7–8; see also *NE* V.6 1134b2–8). But the important point is that (slaves, children, and women aside) the differences between humans are usually not that great; at least they are nothing like the differences

534

between philosopher-kings and the other citizens in Plato's *Republic*. Therefore, justice demands that political rule not be a rule of subordination, like mastery or paternal rule, and that unlike mastery or paternal rule, all citizens have some role in the running of the city.

The Kingship Problem

Aristotle discusses the kinds of political systems in *Pol* III.6. There are differences in the number of rulers (one, few, or many), and a further distinction based on whether rule is correct (i.e., for the benefit of the entire city) or deviant (i.e., for the sake of the rulers alone). Aristotle generates six different kinds of political system: kingship (correct rule by one), aristocracy (correct rule by the few), polity (correct rule by the many, taking the name for "political system" itself, *politeia*); tyranny (deviant rule by one), oligarchy (deviant rule by the few), and democracy (deviant rule by the many). (In *Pol* III.8, Aristotle says that rule by the few is actually an accidental feature of aristocracy and oligarchy, and that their defining features are in fact rule by the virtuous and rule by the wealthy, respectively.)

In aristocracies and polities, citizens will share in rule according to the conception of political rule described above (though which citizens have access to which offices, what is the selection process, etc. will differ depending on the type of political system). Kingship (*basileia*) is rule by one person, for the sake of the entire city (*Pol* III.7 1279a32–4). If this referred (exclusively) to some kind of limited monarchy, according to which the king rules by law and shares some aspects of rule with his fellow citizens, then kingship would not contradict the conception of rulers and ruled outlined above. But as we shall see, limited monarchy is not primarily what Aristotle has in mind in his account of kingship.

Aristotle discusses kingship at length at *Pol* III.14–17. (See Simpson 1998: 180–92.) In *Pol* III.14, he lists five types, including limited kingship (e.g. the Spartan type, which is like a permanent generalship under the law) and some forms that are mixed and tending toward tyranny. But the fifth type interests him most, and is most of all kingship:

> There is a fifth kind of kingship, when one has authority over all, just as each nation and each city has authority over common matters, being arranged according to household management. For just as household management is a certain kingship over a household, so kingship is household management of a city or one nation (or many). (1285b29–33)

He later calls this absolute kingship (*pambasileia*, III.15 1285b36, III.16 1287a8, IV.10 1295a18).

Aristotle writes that kingship does raise problems (*aporias*, III.15 1286a7). He devotes much of *Pol*. III.15 to whether law or men should rule, and the related issue of whether the multitude can contribute anything to rule, even where the rulers are superior. (I have already touched on both of these issues.) Eventually, Aristotle returns to an issue he raised at the opening of *Pol* III.14:

whether it is beneficial for a city or territory that is to be well governed to be ruled by a king, or not but rather have some other political system, or whether [kingship] is beneficial for some, but not beneficial for others. (1284b37–40)

Here is his initial response, in *Pol* III.15:

If the rule of many men who are all good is considered aristocracy, and the rule of one [good] man kingship, then aristocracy would be more choiceworthy for cities than kingship . . . , if many similar men can be found. Perhaps this is why people originally lived under kingships: because it was rare to find men who were very distinguished in virtue, especially when the cities they lived in were small. Further, they set up kings because of [the kings'] benefactions, which is the function of good men. But when it happened that many people similar in virtue arose, they no longer endured [being ruled by one person], sought something common and set up a polity. (1286b3–13)

Aristotle seems to be saying that kingship is not best normally, though it may be under primitive or otherwise less than ideal conditions. If he had stopped here, there would perhaps be no problem in mapping his account of kingship against his conception of rulers and ruled. But he does not stop here; moreover, the opening of *Pol* III.16 suggests that the passage just quoted does not (necessarily or exclusively) refer to absolute kingship (see 1287a3–6).

In *Pol* III.16, Aristotle returns to a discussion of absolute kingship, which is not according to law (1287a1–3). He immediately raises an unsurprising objection:

Concerning so-called absolute kingship (*pambasileias*) (this is where the king rules over all according to his own will): some think it is quite contrary to nature for one of all the citizens to have authority, in a city consisting of similar people. For in the case of those similar by nature, justice and worth must necessarily be the same according to nature; so if it is harmful to their bodies for unequals to have equal food and clothing, the same holds for honors, and similarly for equals to have what is unequal. That is why it is just [for equals] to rule no more than to be ruled, and therefore they should do this in turns. But this is already law, for the ordering [of ruling and being ruled in turn] is law. And it is more choiceworthy for the law to rule than any one of the citizens. (1287a8–20)

This is consistent with his conception of political rulers and ruled, and with the view of distributive justice on which it is based. Much of *Pol* III.16 is devoted to supporting this "anti-kingship" point of view.

Toward the beginning of *Pol* III.17, Aristotle reiterates the position we expect him to hold: "where men are alike and equal, it is neither expedient nor just that one man should have authority over all" (1288a1–2). But then he adds, surprisingly, that whether kingship is appropriate or not depends on the circumstances and especially on the kind of people in a particular city – and he says he has mentioned these circumstances earlier (1288a5–6). What is he talking about?

We might think of the primitive conditions that gave rise to kingship, which he mentioned in *Pol* III.15. But recall that he there did not have absolute kingship in mind (or at least not exclusively). Rather, he is clearly referring to this passage from *Pol* III.13:

If there is some one person who is so distinguished by his superior virtue – or more than one, though not enough to make up the full complement of a city – such that the virtue of all the others and their political capacity admit of no comparison with theirs (if there are many), or with his alone (if there is one), [he or] they can no longer be considered a part of a city. For they will be done an injustice if it is reckoned that they are worth equal things, when they are so unequal in virtue and in political capacity. For such a person would probably be just like a god among human beings. Hence it is clear that legislation is necessarily concerned with those who are equal in birth and in capacity, and that for the other sort there is no law – they are themselves law. (1284a3–14; see also VII.14 1332b16–27)

In *Pol* III.17, he applies this specifically to kingship:

When a whole family, or even some one person among the others, happens to be so distinguished in virtue as to be superior to that of all the others, then it is just for this family to be kingly and have authority over all, or for this one person to be king. For as was said before, this not only accords with that justice which the founders of all political systems, whether aristocratic or oligarchic or again democratic, are accustomed to put forward (for they all claim to be worthy of rule owing to superiority, although not the same superiority), it also accords with what was said earlier. For it is surely not right to kill or ostracize or exile such a person, or reckon that they are worthy of being ruled in turn. For it is not natural for the part to be superior to the whole, but this is what happens in the case of someone having such superiority. So the only alternative is that this sort of person be obeyed, and have authority not in turns but without qualification (*haplôs*). (1288a15–29; see also V.10 1310b9–14, 31–4)

This creates a problem for Aristotle's conception of political rule. For aren't the king's subjects – who may be virtuous citizens capable of the kind of independence described earlier and of running their own lives and sharing in rule – being treated like children or slaves? Isn't Aristotle's primary objection to modeling political rule after mastery or paternal rule precisely that it involves this sort of injustice?

This problem is easily resolved *if* Aristotle has in mind here rare circumstances in which most people, for whatever reason (e.g., a primitive stage of development, years of living under tyranny) are not capable of virtuous and independent sharing of rule. Aristotle would then be saying that the king is superior *relative to everyone else* in a particular city, who happen to be inferior with respect to virtue (and especially practical wisdom). But Aristotle stresses the potential king's superior virtue – he is like a god among humans – and not merely superiority relative to some debased populace, so this solution is speculative at best.

Like the closing chapters of *NE* X, which I believe have resisted the attempts of scholars to reconcile with the rest of the *Nicomachean Ethics*, so Aristotle's account of kingship creates problems for anyone attempting to present a completely coherent picture of his political philosophy. (On similar problems with kingship, see Miller 1995:234–39. Kahn 1990:373–74 offers a "biographical hypothesis," which attempts to explain the anomalies surrounding Aristotle's discussion of kingship by considering it in light of his relationship to the Macedonian royal family.)

In *Pol* V.10, Aristotle writes that "kingships no longer come into existence" (1313a3–4). Further, neither the ideal city of *Pol* VII–VIII, nor the best practicable city of *Pol*

IV.11, is a kingship. (They are arguably kinds of aristocracy and polity respectively.) So whatever problems Aristotle's account of kingship raises for his conception of rulers and ruled, they are not central. And they should not detract from the fact that with its connection to the rule of law, distributive justice based on worth, and the sharing of rule among citizens, Aristotle's conception of *political* rule is one of the more admirable features of his political philosophy.

Notes

[1] Translations from the Greek are my own. For the *Politics*, I have used the Greek text of Dreizehnter. For the rest, I have used the Oxford Classical Text editions.

[2] The city is in fact composed of villages (see *Pol* I.2 1252b15–18), which are composed of households; but since Aristotle's focus is on the kinds of people and rule that make up the household, we can skip discussion of the village.

[3] Owing to its subject matter (especially slavery and the status of women), the first draft of this essay was riddled with such expressions as "according to Aristotle," "as Aristotle sees it," etc. I have removed most of these as irritating intrusions. But please keep in mind that this essay describes *Aristotle's* views (as I see it) on rulers and ruled, and not my own.

[4] On Aristotle's criticism (in *Pol* II.1–5) of Platonic communism, which sheds further light on Plato's and Aristotle's different conceptions of rule, see Mayhew (1997a).

[5] Two passages in the *Politics* might suggest that for Aristotle the relationship between individual and city is that of part to whole: I.2 1253a3–29 and VIII.1 1337a27–30. According to some scholars, these support the conclusion that his conception of political rule is not as different from Plato's as I am arguing (e.g., Barnes 1990), or that his political philosophy is contradictory (e.g., Keyt 1991). I have argued (Mayhew 1997b) that these passages in fact support neither reading. See also Miller (1995: 194–234).

Bibliography

Barnes, J. (1990). "Aristotle and Political Liberty," in G. Patzig (ed.), *Aristotles' "Politik": Akten des XI. Symposium Aristotelicum Friedrichshafen/ Bodensee 25.8–3.9.1987* (Göttingen: Vandenhoeck and Ruprecht), pp. 249–63.

Kahn, C. (1990). "The Normative Structure of Aristotle's *Politics*," in G. Patzig (ed.), *Aristotles' "Politik": Akten des XI. Symposium Aristotelicum Friedrichshafen/ Bodensee 25.8–3.9.1987* (Göttingen: Vandenhoeck and Ruprecht), pp. 369–84.

Keyt, D. (1991). "Three Basic Theorems in Aristotle's *Politics*," in D. Keyt and F. D. Miller, Jr. (eds.), *A Companion to Aristotle's "Politics"* (Oxford: Blackwell), pp. 118–41.

Keyt, D. and Miller, F. D., Jr. (eds.) (1991). *A Companion to Aristotle's "Politics"* (Oxford: Blackwell).

Kraut, R. (2002). *Aristotle: Political Philosophy* (Oxford: Oxford University Press).

Mayhew, R. (1997a). *Aristotle's Criticism of Plato's "Republic"* (Lanham, MD: Rowman and Littlefield).

Mayhew, R. (1997b). "Part and Whole in Aristotle's Political Philosophy," *Journal of Ethics*, 1, pp. 325–40.

Mayhew, R. (2004). *The Female in Aristotle's Biology: Reason or Rationalization* (Chicago, IL: University of Chicago Press).

Miller, F. D., Jr. (1995). *Nature, Justice, and Rights in Aristotle's "Politics"* (Oxford: Oxford University Press).

Patzig, G. (ed). (1990). *Aristotles' "Politik": Akten des XI. Symposium Aristotelicum Friedrichshafen/ Bodensee 25.8–3.9.1987* (Göttingen: Vandenhoeck and Ruprecht).

Schofield, M. (1990). "Ideology and Philosophy in Aristotle's Theory of Slavery," in G. Patzig (ed.), *Aristotles' "Politik": Akten des XI. Symposium Aristotelicum Friedrichshafen/ Bodensee 25.8– 3.9.1987* (Göttingen: Vandenhoeck and Ruprecht), pp. 1–27.

Simpson, P. L. P. (1998). *A Philosophical Commentary on the "Politics" of Aristotle* (Chapel Hill, NC: University of North Carolina Press).

Smith, N. D. (1983). "Plato and Aristotle on the Nature of Women," *Journal of the History of Philosophy*, 21, pp. 467–78.

Smith, N. D. (1991). "Aristotle's Theory of Natural Slavery," in D. Keyt and F. D. Miller, Jr. (eds.), *A Companion to Aristotle's "Politics"* (Oxford: Blackwell), pp. 142–56.

34

Aristotle on the Ideal Constitution

FRED D. MILLER, JR.

The ideal constitution looms large in Aristotle's *Politics*, dominating three of the eight Books. Book II criticizes the ideals proposed by his predecessors, and Books VII and VIII set forth his own vision of the ideal city-state.

"Ideal" is a rough translation of Aristotle's Greek word *euchê*, literally "prayer." His ideal city-state exists "according to prayer" and is what we would "pray for." It would occur "if there were no external obstacles" (IV.1 1288b23–4). It would possess the most favorable resources, location, and a population with the appropriate size, natural aptitude, and class structure (IV.11 1295a29, VII.4 1325a36, 5 1327a4, 10 1329b25–, 11 1330a37). The mention of prayer indicates the role of luck: "We pray that our city-state will be ideally equipped with the goods that luck controls (for we assume that luck does control them)" (VII.13 1332a29). Hence, ideal theorizing is easier than actual legislating because it can assume conditions brought about by luck (VII.12 1331b21). Aristotle compares the ideal city-state to the mythical isles of the blessed (VII.15 1334a31). It is beyond the reach of ordinary city-states (IV.11 1295a29–31). However, "we should assume ideal conditions, but nothing that is impossible" (II.6 1265a18, cf. VII.4 1325b39). Hence, Aristotle's ideal state is not a utopia in the literal sense of "no place" (*ou-topia*).

Problems Concerning Aristotle's Ideal Constitution

Aristotle's ideal constitution presents several problems. One concerns *where* Aristotle intended to discuss his ideal constitution. It is in Books VII–VIII of the *Politics* as it has come down to us, following the treatment of actual constitutions in Books IV–VI. This ordering seems to be reflected in the synopsis of the *Politics* at the end of the *Nicomachean Ethics*:

> First, then, if there is anything that has been well said on any particular point by our predecessors, let us attempt to discuss that, and then, on the basis of our collected constitutions, try to observe what sorts of things preserve and destroy cities, and what sorts have these effects on each type of constitution, and what the causes are whereby some cities are finely governed and others the opposite. For when we have made these observations,

perhaps we shall have a better view, too, on what sort of constitution is best, and how each type is arranged, and what laws and customs it will have. (X.9 1181b15–23)

Scholars such as Newman, however, contend that the discussion of the best constitution originally followed directly after Book III, but the order of Books changed somehow during the transmission of Aristotle's writings. Indeed, Book III concludes with a transition to a discussion of the best constitution. There is however not much other evidence for (or against) this hypothesis. (Simpson's translation of the *Politics* follows Newman's reordering).

A second problem concerns *when* Aristotle wrote about the ideal state. Werner Jaeger argues that Books VII–VIII express a youthful utopianism, with Aristotle emulating Plato by erecting "an ideal state by logical construction." In contrast, Books IV–VI are based on "sober empirical study." The more mature Aristotle adopts a pragmatic, even Machiavellian approach to politics. Other scholars, however, favor a more "unitarian" approach to the *Politics* (as reflected in the above synopsis from the *Nicomachean Ethics*). Although much ink has been spilled since Jaeger attempted to distinguish chronological strata in Aristotle's political thought, it has not resulted in a clear consensus.

These philological issues point to a philosophical problem: are there major inconsistencies of doctrine in the *Politics*? Scholars such as Schütrumpf see Aristotle as basing his ideal constitution on moral standards which he eschews when he turns to practical politics in Books IV–VI. In the latter, for example, he justifies political decisions on the basis of stability rather than justice. This raises the question of whether the principles underlying the ideal constitution in Books VII–VIII are inconsistent with those that Aristotle applies when he deals with practical politics in IV–VI.

Ideal Theory and Political Practice

Aristotle takes up the relationship between ideal theory and the ordinary tasks of statecraft by comparing statecraft with gymnastics (*Politics* IV.1). A knowledgeable gymnastics coach should provide the sort of physical training that is beneficial for each sort of body. A skillful coach is able to train someone who is "naturally the best" to become a champion. But a good coach should also know what training is appropriate to prepare a less capable pupil for the contests. Further, some might come with modest aims; they might want to get in shape but not aspire to compete in athletic contests. A competent coach should be able to help them as well. Other craftsmen, including physicians, shipbuilders, and tailors, carry out a similar array of tasks. Analogously, "the good legislator and true statesman" must master tasks including the following:

1 "What the best constitution must be like if it is to be most ideal, and if there were no external obstacles" (1288b21–4).
2 "Which constitution is best for which city-states. For achieving the best constitution is perhaps impossible for many" (1288b24–7).

3 "Which constitution is best given certain assumptions. For a statesman must be able to study how any given constitution might initially come into existence, and how, once in existence, it might be preserved for the longest time. I mean, for example, when some city-state happens to be governed neither by the best constitution (not even having the necessary resources), nor by the best one possible in the existing circumstances, but by a worse one" (1288b28–33).

Task (1) involves *ideal theory*, prescribing the best constitution under the most favorable possible circumstances. Task (2) involves *second-best theory*, prescribing the constitution that is best for an actual community making allowances for the insurmountable limitations of its citizens and resources (compare Plato's *Laws* V.739a-b). Task (3) involves *ordinary political theory*, prescribing how to reform an actually existing constitution which may be far from good. Aristotle rebukes his predecessors for disdaining this job:

> One should not study only what is best, but also what is possible, and similarly what is easier and more attainable by all. As it is, however, some seek only the constitution that is highest and requires a lot of resources, while others, though they discuss a more attainable sort, do away with the constitutions actually in place, and praise the Spartan or some other. But what should be done is to introduce the sort of organization that people will be easily persuaded to accept and be able to participate in, given what they already have, as it is no less a task to reform a constitution than to establish one initially, just as it is no less a task to correct what we have learned than to learn it in the first place. That is why . . . a statesman should be able to help existing constitutions. (*Pol* IV.1 1288b37–1289a7)

Aristotle's idealistic precursors might retort that unbridled activism leads to unprincipled pragmatism. Minor changes that people will be easily persuaded to accept may only help to perpetuate an unjust regime. For example, if the statesman advises that the regime will be more stable if the laws are invariably enforced, what if the laws are thoroughly unjust? Won't task (3) lead to moral compromise?

This criticism overlooks the role of ideals in Aristotelian statecraft, which may be explained in terms of two principles. The first is *the principle of approximation*: "While it is clearly best for any being to attain the real end, yet, if that cannot be, the nearer it is to the best the better will be its state" (*De Caelo* II.12 292b17–19; cf. *Generation and Corruption* II.10 336b25–34). Aristotle uses health as an example. Some of us are already in a healthy condition, others can become healthy by reducing their weight or by exercising and thereby reducing their weight, and others can never become healthy due to an incurable disease. The person who is capable of becoming healthy by exercising and reducing should clearly do so, but even the person who can never become entirely fit (due for example to having suffered a stroke) should strive for a condition which resembles health by exercising as much as possible under the circumstances. The second is *the principle of causal convergence* (see *Topics* III.5 119a17–18). Given that C causes E, then the more a cause resembles C the more its effect resembles E. The hotter the water the closer it comes to boiling. The two principles combined imply that an ideal can serve as a standard even if it is not attainable. If an ideal condition I would bring about a completely good result *G*, the closer one comes to bringing about *I* then the more nearly the outcome would resemble *G*. For example, if an ideal diet would result in one's having an optimal level of cholesterol, then the closer one's food intake is to the ideal the closer one would come to the optimal level (other things being equal).

Granted that these two principles apply to politics, then the ideal constitution is relevant to every politics. Even if it is not practically attainable, we can use it as a guide in reforming existing systems in order to come as close as possible to our policy objective. Although the Aristotelian statesman recognizes ideals, he is not a utopian perfectionist who remains aloof from politics because the "heavenly city" is out of reach. For this statesman the best constitution serves as a *regulative ideal*. This approach may be described as *approximist*: Practical politics should aim at reforming existing systems so that they approximate this ideal as closely as is feasible. (Kraut offers a similar interpretation.)

Criticisms of Previous Ideal Constitutions

Politics II criticizes Plato's *Republic* at length, then more briefly considers Plato's *Laws* and the proposals of Phaleas of Calchedon and Hippodamus of Miletus, before discussing actual city-states "said to be well governed" (namely, those in Sparta, Crete, and Carthage). Aristotle undertakes this survey "in order to see what is correct or useful in them, but also to avoid giving the impression that our search for something different from them results from a desire to be clever. Let it be held, instead, that we have undertaken this inquiry because the currently available constitutions are not in a good condition" (II.1 1260b32–6). This suggests a criterion for evaluating alleged ideals: a proposed ideal should be an improvement on extant systems; it is not enough for it to be ingenious.

Aristotle's criticisms of Callipolis – Socrates' "beautiful city" (*Republic* VII.527c) – fall under four main headings: the aim of the constitution; communism; the happiness of the whole city-state; and philosopher-kings.

The aim of the constitution

Aristotle attacks Socrates' "hypothesis that it is best for the entire city-state to be one as far as possible," arguing that

> as it becomes more one it will no longer be a city-state; for the city-state is with respect to its nature a sort of multitude, and if it becomes more one it will be a household instead of a city-state, and a human being instead of a household; for we would say that a household is more one than a city-state, and one [human being is more one] than a household; so that even if one could do this, it ought not to be done; for it would destroy the city-state. (*Pol* II.2 1261a16–22; cf. *Republic* IV.422d1–423b6, V.462a9–b2)

According to Aristotle, Socrates wants Callipolis to have the same degree of unity as a human being. Instead, Aristotle objects, a city-state must be composed of persons who

543

are different in kind and able to perform different functions (1261a22–b10), and its aim should be not unity but self-sufficiency which requires division of labor (1261b10–15). Aristotle's charge that Plato views the ideal city-state as a kind of "super-individual" or "super-organism" has been often repeated (see Popper). However, Plato's defenders deny that he intends them in the extreme literal holistic sense assumed by Aristotle's critique.

Communism

Aristotle observes that a constitution is a way of sharing in the city-state. "But is it better for a city-state that is well-managed to share everything possible? Or is it better to share some things but not others? For the citizens could share children, women, and property with one another, as in Plato's *Republic* . . . So is what we have now better, or what accords with the law described in the *Republic*?" (*Pol* II.1 1261a2–9) This misrepresents Socrates, who only claims that the guardian class should have wives, children, and property in common (see *Republic* IV.423e–424a, V.449a–466d). Still, Aristotle's arguments remain timely in view of the rise of modern communism. It is worth noting he does not advocate unqualified privatization. He considers only three possible schemes: (1) common ownership, common use; (2) common ownership, private use; and (3) private ownership, common use. He omits option (4) private property, private use. He criticizes arrangement (1) which he ascribes to Plato along with option (2), and defends arrangement (3) – which he describes as "the present practice, provided it was enhanced by virtuous character and a system of correct laws" (II.5 1263a22–3). He argues that arrangement (3) is superior on five grounds: it is less apt to give rise to quarrels and complaints, it encourages greater care devoted to property, it facilitates friendship through common use, it fosters the natural pleasure of self-love through private ownership, and it makes it possible to exercise virtues such as generosity (1263a8–b38). He makes similar points about private families. Parents are more attached to and take better care of children whom they regard as their own (individually not collectively), and marriage enables men to exercise temperance towards their neighbors' wives.

Aristotle's objections are not fully developed. He takes it for granted that virtues such as friendship and generosity require private ownership. Plato clearly thought otherwise. Aristotle also assumes that the vicious tendencies associated with private ownership can be offset by moral education. Why cannot Plato make a similar argument regarding harmful tendencies associated with common ownership? Moreover, Plato might argue that "natural self-love" could be transmuted into altruism by means of education. Nonetheless Aristotle has clearly identified fundamental issues at the heart of the controversy between communism and individualism. His argument that individuals tend to take better care of their personal possessions than of common property seems to anticipate arguments by modern economists that privatization gives individuals a greater incentive to use property efficiently. The benefits and costs involved in using resources are more fully taken into account when they are "internalized" in private possessions. Property which is commonly owned tends to be overused, abused, or neglected, resulting in "the tragedy of the commons."

Happiness of the whole city-state

Aristotle also attacks Socrates' conception of happiness in the *Republic*:

> Further, destroying even the happiness of the guardians, he says that the lawgiver ought to make the city-state as a whole happy. But it is impossible for a whole to be happy unless most or all or some of its parts possess happiness. For being happy is not the same as [being] even; for the latter can belong to the whole, even if neither of its parts does, but being happy cannot. But if the guardians are not happy, which others are? For at any rate the artisans and the multitude of vulgar persons are surely not [happy]. (*Pol* II.5 1264b15–24)

Aristotle again offers an extreme holistic interpretation of Socrates' declaration that "our aim is to see that the city-state as a whole has the greatest happiness" (*Republic* IV.419a1–421c6, cf. V.465e4–466a6). This interpretation is supported by Socrates' comparison with painting a statue: "You mustn't expect us to paint the eyes so beautifully that they no longer appear to be eyes at all, and the same with other parts. Rather you must look to see whether by dealing with each part appropriately, we are making the whole statue beautiful" (IV.420d1–5). However, Plato's defenders (including Vlastos and Annas) reply that Socrates merely means that the laws should not promote the happiness of any particular group at the expense of all the others (see V.466a2–6, VII.519e1–520a1).

Philosopher-kings

Aristotle surprisingly omits the philosopher-king, which Plato describes as the key to the ideal constitution (V.473d3–5), but his objection can be gathered from what he says elsewhere. In the *Republic* rulers are craftsmen who require philosophical knowledge of the Forms – transcendent patterns or models which define what things are and provide an objective standard of perfection for them. Rulers ignorant of the Forms are like blind painters. They "have no clear model in their souls, and so they cannot – in the manner of painters – look to what is most true, make constant reference to it, and study it as exactly as possible. Hence they cannot establish here on earth conventions about what is fine or just or good, when they need to be established, or guard and preserve them, once they have been established" (VI.484c7–d3). Of paramount importance is the Form of the Good. "Because you've seen the truth about fine, just, and good things, you'll know each image for what it is and also that of which it is the image" (VII.520c). Socrates suggests the ideal city-state itself may exist in the realm of Forms: "Perhaps there is a model of it in heaven, for anyone who wants to look at it and make himself its citizen on the strength of what he sees" (IX.592b).

Aristotle would be unimpressed. On his view philosophical knowledge of the Form of the Good, even if there were such, would not yield expertise in any field:

> For all of them [i.e. craftsmen] seek some particular good, and though they look for whatever is lacking, they leave out knowledge of the Form of the Good. And yet it is hardly likely that all the experts should be unaware of so great a resource, and should fail even to go looking for it. But it is also difficult to see how a weaver or a carpenter

will be helped in relation to his craft by knowing this good "itself"; or how someone who has seem the Form itself will be a better doctor or a better general. (*NE* I.6 1096b31–1097a11)

Similarly, knowledge of the Form of the Good is too abstract to provide guidance in ethics or politics. Aristotle distinguishes between theoretical wisdom (*sophia*) which is expressed in the demonstrations about immutable realities offered by philosophers and practical wisdom (*phronêsis*) which is expressed in deliberation about actions concerning things that are good or bad for human beings. Philosophy belongs to the former not the latter; political science belongs to the latter not the former. Although the ideal state needs wise rulers, they do not need to be philosophers.

Aristotle's critique of the *Republic* provokes very different reactions. Some view it as insightful and devastating, while others find Aristotle uncharitable to Plato and at times downright misleading. His objections must be read critically and compared carefully with Plato's text. (Irwin and Saunders are more critical of Aristotle, while Mayhew and Stalley are more supportive.)

Critique of Plato's "Laws"

Aristotle's treatment of this dialogue is comparatively brief. He commits obvious errors: for example, misidentifying the main speaker as Socrates (unless he thought he was the Athenian Stranger in disguise) and attributing to the *Laws* the idea that the best constitution is a mixture of democracy with tyranny (II.6 1266a1–2). Aristotle is more indebted to the *Laws* than his discussion suggests, for example appropriating its proposal to assign two pieces of property to each citizen (cf. 1265b21–6 and VII.10 1330a14–15). He does recognize that the *Laws* offers a second-best alternative to the *Republic* (II.6 1265a1–10), but he regards it as a failure because it is too similar to Plato's ideal and it thus ultimately makes the same mistake as the *Republic*: for example, "it would need a territory the size of Babylon or some other unlimitedly large territory to keep five thousand people in idleness, and a crowd of women and servants along with them, many times as great. We should assume ideal conditions, to be sure, but nothing that is impossible" (1265a14–18). (See Saunders 1995: 126–35 on the strengths and weaknesses of Aristotle's critique.)

Critique of Phaleas of Chalcedon

Phaleas, a contemporary of Plato, proposed a constitution in which all citizens would have equal possessions. This would be mandated in new city-states; it would be brought about in established ones by requiring wealthy persons to give but not receive dowries and poor persons to receive but not give them. Aristotle complains that Phaleas overlooked predictable problems. If the wealthy have too many children, there will be a class of poor persons descended from wealthier persons, which may lead to revolution (II.7 1266b8–14). Aristotle also objects that merely equalizing property cannot ensure domestic tranquility, because people also fight over honors and political offices as well as property (1266b28–31). Aristotle accuses Phaleas of neglecting the role of culture and moral education in securing justice and peace. Education is of course fundamentally important in Aristotle's own ideal constitution.

Critique of Hippodamus of Miletus

Aristotle says that Hippodamus (born ca. 500 BC) was the first non-politician to propose an ideal constitution. He may have been influenced by the Pythagoreans in view of his fascination with the number three: he distinguished three classes of citizens (artisans, farmers, and soldiers), three types of property (sacred, public, and private), and three kinds of law (against assault, damage, and killing). Aristotle criticizes the division of citizens as impractical. Since the farmers would have no weapons and the artisans neither weapons nor land, they would become virtual slaves of the warrior class. "So it is impossible that every office be shared. For the generals, civic guards, and practically speaking all the officials with the most authority will inevitably be selected from those who possess weapons" (II.8 1268a20–3). Military power cannot be sundered from political power even in the ideal constitution. Hippodamus also wanted to institute honors for those who introduce useful political reforms. Aristotle regards this proposal as dangerous. Although he agrees that some laws need to be changed at some times, legal change should be kept to a minimum. People tend to have less respect for the laws when they frequently change. "For the law has no power to secure obedience except habit; but habits can only be developed over a long period of time. Hence, casual change from existing laws to new and different ones weakens the power of law itself" (1269a20–4). The best constitution must ensure continuity and stability. Ideal theory must not ignore ineluctable facts of human psychology.

Aristotle's Ideal State

Although *Nicomachean Ethics* X.9 1181b15–23 indicates that the study of actual constitutions will provide a basis for the study of the ideal constitution, it is hard to see exactly how the two inquiries are related. *Politics* III.7 offers a canonical classification of constitutions, in terms of whether they are correct (i.e. just and promote the common advantage) or deviant (i.e. unjust and promote only the rulers' advantage), and whether there is one, few, or many rulers.

Politics IV.2 ranks these constitutions from best to worst, working on the assumptions that correct constitutions have virtuous rulers, and deviant constitutions vicious rulers, and that virtue and vice both tend to become diluted and less effective when

Table 34.1   Aristotle's classification of constitutions

	Correct	*Deviant*
One ruler	Kingship	Tyranny
Few rulers	Aristocracy	Oligarchy
Many rulers	Polity	Democracy

they are spread over larger groups. Hence a kingship ruler would be the best and "most divine" and tyranny the "worst." This yields the following ranking from worse to best:

Tyranny → Oligarchy → Democracy → Polity → Aristocracy → Kingship

---

In Book IV this initial ranking is found to be too crude, because the most extreme form of democracy in which a mob takes the law into its own hands is worse than a moderate form of oligarchy in which a minority rules according to law. Aristotle ends up by equating polity with a *mixed constitution*, i.e. one that combines features of different constitutions. A polity recognizes the political rights of both rich and poor (see IV.8 1294a9–29). A mixed constitution which assigns citizenship and offices to different groups on the basis of free birth, wealth, and virtue is called an aristocratic polity; but it is a "so-called aristocracy," because the rulers are not all fully virtuous. This analysis yields a more complex ranking of constitutions:

Extreme Democracy → Moderate Democracy ↘
Extreme Oligarchy → Moderate Oligarchy ↗ Polity → Aristocracy → Kingship

---

It is unclear where the ideal constitution of Books VII–VIII would fit into either of the above rankings. Although Aristotle calls the ideal city the "best constitution" in Book VII.1, he ranks kingship as "first and most divine" at IV.2. He concedes that kingship would be better at VII.14 1332b16–23, but adds that "this is not easy to suppose" because the kings would have to be "like gods and heroes" (cf. III.13 1284a10–11). This suggests that kingship would be the best constitution if any godlike kings were on hand, but for normal human beings the ideal constitution is as described in Books VII–VIII. But if the ideal constitution falls short of kingship, is it an aristocracy or a polity? The former seems unlikely, because all the citizens are rulers. So it does not satisfy the definition of aristocracy: i.e., a few rulers aiming at the advantage of all the citizens. Because the citizens are comparatively numerous, some commentators argue that the ideal constitution must be a polity. But a polity would be too populous to be a feasible ideal state (as mentioned above in the critique of Plato's *Laws*.) Also, the citizens of polity possess only a lower grade of "military" virtue (III.7 1279b1–2). Hence polity, characterized as "the middle constitution," is contrasted with the ideal constitution in IV.11. Thus the ideal constitution of Books VII–VIII seems to combine features of aristocracy and polity, without falling neatly into either category. (See Kahn, Keyt, and Bates for discussions of this problem.)

Aristotle's presentation of the ideal regime divides into the following sections: the best way of life for the citizens (VII.1–3); the population, territory, and location (VII.4–7); social classes and political institutions (VII.8–10; physical layout (VII.11–12); and educational system (VII.13–VIII.4). Unfortunately the treatment breaks off abruptly and several promised discussions are missing. Aristotle's ideal constitution may be thrown into relief by considering three issues: In what sense does the ideal constitution aim at happiness? In what sense is the ideal constitution just? Do non-citizens receive just treatment?

Happiness in the ideal constitution

The aim of the best constitution is a happy and blessed life. "The best life, both for individuals separately and for city-states collectively, is a life of virtue sufficiently equipped with the resources needed to take part in virtuous actions" (VII.1 1323b40–1324a2, cf. 1323b21–6, VII.2 1324a24–5). The *Politics'* account of happiness as "a complete activation or use of virtue" echoes the *Eudemian Ethics* and agrees with the *Nicomachean Ethics* (*Pol* VII.13 1332a8; *EE* II.1 1219a38–b2; cf. *NE* I.7 1098a16–18, 10 1101a14–16). This suggests that the ideal constitution aims at happiness as understood in Aristotle's ethical works. The *Nicomachean Ethics* argues that the contemplative life, the life according to intellect, is the happiest, whereas the life devoted to moral virtue is only secondarily happy. Although commentators disagree over whether Aristotle's best life is a purely intellectual life, or a mixed life with contemplation as the best component, it is clear that a life devoid of philosophy would be an inferior life, even for one who consistently practiced the moral virtues in the political realm. Do the citizens of Aristotle's ideal constitution engage in philosophy?

Aristotle discusses whether the best life is the philosophical life or the political life in *Politics* VII.1–2. He merely refutes common objections to each: that the political life involves injustice, and that the philosophical life is inactive. He does not conclude here that the philosophical life is the better life, or that a purely political life is inferior. Later on in his discussion of education, however, he indicates that the ideal citizens will possess both moral virtue and philosophy: "For they will be most in need of philosophy, temperance, and justice the more they live at leisure amidst an abundance of such goods. It is evident, then, why a city-state that is to be happy and good should share in these virtues" (VII.15 1334a31–6). Commentators disagree however on what this reference to philosophy amounts to. Most hold that "philosophy" has here a broad, popular sense satisfied by leisurely activities such as music and poetry (see Solmsen, Lord, Kraut). Some contend that philosophy here includes contemplative activity; music is a preparation, rather than a substitute, for philosophy in the strict sense (see Depew). Aristotle's discussion of education concludes with music, however, and there is no indication that philosophy in the strict sense will be part of the curriculum. If Aristotle's ideal constitution offers only philosophy in a loose sense, its citizens will lead an inferior life from the standpoint of the *Nicomachean Ethics*. But perhaps Aristotle thinks that most people even in ideal conditions are capable of no more than this.

Justice in the ideal constitution

If Aristotle's ideal constitution is just, it aims at the common advantage (*Pol* III.7 1279a28–31, 12 1282b16–18; *NE* V.1 1129b14–19, VIII.9 1160a13–14). But what does Aristotle mean by the common advantage (*koinon sumpheron*)? There are two quite different ways of understanding the notion. One is *holistic*: the common advantage is the good of the whole city-state, which like an organism has an end distinct from, and superior to, the ends of its individual members. The other is *individualistic*: to promote the common advantage *is* to promote the ends of individuals. On the holistic view individuals would not have rights in any substantial sense. The claims of individuals

549

to political office or property would be contingent on whether their having it advanced the higher ends of the state. As noted earlier, Aristotle criticizes Plato's ideal state for being too holistic. But how does Aristotle himself think individual happiness should be taken into account: do the citizens have rights (i.e. just claims) under the constitution (e.g. political rights, property rights, and the right to education) or do they merely "share in the constitution" in some less definite sense? (See Miller and Schofield for opposing interpretations.)

To resolve this issue it is important to note that the common advantage can be understood in two different ways:

- *The overall advantage.* The city-state is happy only if some (for example, most) of the citizens are happy.
- *The mutual advantage.* The city-state is happy only if each and every citizen is happy.

Because the *overall* advantage permits trade-offs, that is, the sacrifice of some individuals' basic interests in order to promote the advantage of others, it is not deeply committed to the rights of individuals. The *mutual* advantage, on the other hand, requires that the happiness of *each* of the participants must be protected by political institutions. Hence, whether or not Aristotle's ideal constitution recognizes individual rights depends on whether it promotes the *mutual* advantage.

There is evidence that Aristotle's best constitution in fact aims at the mutual advantage. He says that "the best regime is that order under which anyone whatsoever might act in the best way and live blessedly" (VII.2 1324a23–5). The expression "anyone whatsoever" (*hostisoun*) implies that no citizens are excluded from a happy life. Further, the citizens of the best regime are genuine members of the city-state rather than mere adjuncts such as slaves and vulgar workers (VII.8 1328a21–5). If the citizens merely performed necessary functions, they would be indistinguishable from the adjuncts (cf. IV.4 1291a24–8). Genuine members must also partake of the end of the city-state (VII.8 1328a25–33, b4–5). The citizens are soldiers when they are younger and stronger, and officials when they are older and wiser. Aristotle thereby solves two problems with a single stroke. He avoids the alienation of military power from political authority in a manner consistent with distributive justice: "it is advantageous and just to distribute tasks to each group on the basis of age, since the division is based on merit" (VII.9 1329a16–17). When Aristotle describes the city-state as "a community of similar persons aiming at the best possible life" (VII.8 1328a35–6), he implies that *all* its genuine members, i.e. citizens, partake in this end. This is explicitly asserted in support of universal property rights: "a city-state must not be called happy by looking at just a part, but by looking at all of the citizens" (VII.9 1329a23–4). This supports the mutual-advantage interpretation.

Further, before discussing education, Aristotle lays down a principle to guide the founder of the best regime:

a city-state is excellent due to the fact that the citizens who partake in the constitution are excellent; but in our case all the citizens partake in the constitution. We must therefore inquire as to how a man becomes excellent; for even if all the citizens could be excellent without each of the citizens [being excellent], the latter would be more choiceworthy; for "all" follows from "each." (VII.13 1332a32–8)

Aristotle thus distinguishes between two principles which could guide the lawgiver:

- *All* the citizens (in a collective sense) should be excellent.
- *Each* citizen (as an individual) should be excellent.

"Each" is logically stronger than "all," because "each" entails, but is not entailed by, "all." For "all" is compatible with the overall advantage, that is, a state of affairs in which the interests of some citizens are sacrificed in order to advance the happiness of most of the citizens. "Each" requires the *mutual* advantage, that is, the promotion of the excellence of each and every citizen. The "each" principle, which is more choiceworthy, rules out the interpretation that the citizens share in the common good in a weaker sense, as for example when some citizens bask in the reflected excellence of others.

Accordingly, Aristotle maintains that all of the citizens should be educated in a common system education (*Politics* VIII.1 1337a20–32). His premise is not however that every citizen has a just claim to education. Instead it is that each citizen is a part of the city-state, so that he belongs not to himself but to the city-state. Hence, the care of each citizen naturally aims at the care of the city-state as a whole. This rationale might suggest that the citizens are like organs belonging to a political organism. But Aristotle is speaking of the citizen as a part of the city-state in a special sense: as a *member* partaking directly in the end of the whole, not as an *organ* merely performing a function subordinate to the higher end of the organism. Thus his argument is consistent with the mutual-advantage interpretation. Because humans are by nature political animals and interdependent, they require education in order to be fully developed (see *Politics* I.2). The citizens cannot be nurtured or educated in isolation from each other; they need a system in which they are all educated in common (compare I.13 1260b8–20). It is in this sense that the care of each aims at the care of the whole: all for one, and one for all. Hence, parents should not be free to raise their children however they wish. They must obey the laws and customs concerning the education of their children. Indeed, officials may intervene in many ways in the private conduct and household affairs of the citizens, including the regulation of marriage. Although the citizens have rights in Aristotle's best constitution, they are not the sorts of rights claimed by modern liberal theorists.

Do non-citizens receive just treatment?

Aristotle's ideal constitution is often criticized for its systematic injustice towards non-citizens. Taylor compares the ideal citizens to "an exploiting elite, a community of free-riders whose ability to pursue the good life is made possible by the willingness of others to forgo that pursuit." Some commentators (e.g. Nichols) find the injustice so egregious that they suggest that Aristotle's ostensibly "best" constitution must have been ironic. Perhaps this serious problem escapes Aristotle because in his view political justice applies only to the citizens not to adjuncts, who include slaves. He regards natural slaves as inferior beings incapable of political life because they share in neither happiness nor a life of deliberate choice (III.9 1280a31–4). This includes many non-Greeks who have a deficit of reason (Europeans) or of spirit (Asiatic) (VII.7 1327b23–38). The ideal city-state may even wage war to enslave barbarians, those who deserve to be slaves (14 1334a1–2). Aristotle also offers unconvincing arguments in *Politics* 1 that rule over natural slaves is just and advantageous for the slaves. "Ideally speaking," Aristotle says, the farmers should be slaves or, as a second best, barbarian serfs. "Later we shall discuss how slaves should be treated and why it is better to hold out freedom as a reward to all slaves" (VII.10 1330a25–33). Unfortunately this perplexing promise is not fulfilled in the *Politics* as we have it.

Another problem concerns the treatment of vulgar persons (*banausoi*). Aristotle's ideal citizens may not engage in vulgar professions because this way of life is low-born and opposed to virtue. Hence, vulgar workers should not possess political rights although workers are necessary for the city-state (VII.9 1328b37–40, 1329a19–21, cf. III.5 1278a8–11, 17–21 and IV.4 1291a1–2). The vulgar person suffers from "a kind of delimited slavery" and leads an ignoble life inimical to virtue (I.13 1260b1, VII.9 1328b40–1). This raises another problem, if the vulgar workers are free by nature but constrained to hold degrading jobs. For the exploitation of such persons would be unjust by Aristotle's own principles (see Annas 1996). It is not clear however whether Aristotle thinks the vulgar workers in the ideal city-state are free by nature. He describes "vulgar persons, menial workers, and others of this sort" as possessing "souls that are diverted from the natural condition" (VIII.7 1342a18–25). If they are born that way, they might be regarded as natural slaves. Otherwise they seem to be an unjustly oppressed underclass.

Finally, a female citizen has no political rights in Aristotle's ideal constitution. He scarcely mentions women outside the context of marriage and child bearing. He recommends a kind of moral education, but also, notoriously, claims that a woman's deliberative capacity "lacks authority" (I.13 1260a13–20). The *Republic*'s proposal that women have the same way of life as men based on comparisons with wild beasts meets with a scoff: "wild beasts do not go in for household management" (II.5 1264b4–6).

Many commentators not surprisingly regard the treatment of non-citizens as a regrettable blemish on Aristotle's ideal constitution.

Aristotle Legacy to Ideal Theory

Aristotle made two major contributions to subsequent ideal political theory. First is the principle that the ideal state should aim at human perfection: "What is most choice-worthy for each individual is always this: to attain what is highest" (VII.14 1333a29–30). Human perfection consists in the active development of human capacities and excellences. Self-development or self-realization as a social and political aim is common to a wide spectrum of modern political ideologies, from Marx to Mill and Humboldt. It is also acknowledged by John Rawls in his "Aristotelian principle." Second is Aristotle's articulation of an individualistic alternative to Plato's holistic ideal. This is well stated by Zeller: "In politics as in metaphysics the central point with Plato is the Universal, with Aristotle the Individual. The former demands that the whole should realize its ends without regard to the interests of individuals: the latter that it should be reared upon the satisfaction of all individual interests that have a true title to be regarded."

Note

Translations of Aristotle's *Politics* are by C. D. C. Reeve (1998); of Aristotle's *Nicomachean Ethics* by Christopher Rowe (2002); and of Plato's *Republic* by G. M. A. Grube and C. D. C. Reeve (1992).

Bibliography

Annas, J. (1981). *An Introduction to Plato's "Republic"* (Oxford: Oxford University Press).

Annas, J. (1996). "Aristotle on Human Nature and Political Virtue," *Review of Metaphysics*, 49, pp. 731–53.

Bates, C. A. (2003). *Aristotle's "Best Regime": Kingship, Democracy, and the Rule of Law.* (Baton Rouge, LA: Louisiana State University Press).

Depew, D. (1991). "Politics, Music, and Contemplation in Aristotle's Ideal State," in Keyt and Miller (pp. 346–80).

Irwin, T. H. (1991). "Aristotle's Defense of Private Property," in Keyt and Miller (pp. 200–25).

Jaeger, W. (1948) *Aristotle: Fundamentals of the History His Development* (Oxford: Oxford University Press).

Kahn, C. H. (1990) "The Normative Structure of Aristotle's *Politics*," in G. Patzig (ed.), *Aktendes XI: Symposium Aristotelicum 1987*, Gottingen, pp. 369–84.

Keyt, D. (1991). "Aristotle's Theory of Distributive Justice," in Keyt and Miller (pp. 238–78).

Keyt, D. and Miller, F. D. (eds.). (1991) *A Companion to Aristotle's "Politics"* (Oxford: Blackwell).

Kraut, R. (1997). *Aristotle "Politics" Books VII and VIII* (Oxford: Oxford University Press).

Kraut, R. (2002). *Aristotle: Political Philosophy* (Oxford: Oxford University Press).

Lord, Carnes. (1982). *Education and Culture in the Political Thought of Aristotle* (Ithaca NY: Cornell University Press).

Mayhew, R. (1997). *Aristotle's Criticism of Plato's "Republic"* (Lanhan MD: Rowman and Littlefield).

Miller, F. D. (1995). *Nature, Justice, and Rights in Aristotle's "Politics"* (Oxford: Oxford University Press).

Newman, W. L. (1897–1902). *The "Politics" of Aristotle*, 4 vols. (Oxford: Oxford University Press).

Nichols, M. (1992). *Citizens and Statesmen: A Study of Aristotle's "Politics"* (Lanham, MD: Rowman and Littlefield).

Popper, K. (1962). *The Open Society and Its Enemies*, 2 vols., 4th edn. (Princeton, NJ: Princeton University Press).

Saunders, T. (1995). *Aristotle "Politics" Books I and II* (Oxford: Oxford University Press).

Schofield, M. (1996). "Sharing in the Constitution," *Review of Metaphysics*, 49, pp. 831–58.

Schütrumpf, E. (1980). *Die Analyse der Polis durch Aristoteles* (Amsterdam: B. R. Grüner).

Simpson, P. (1997) The *"Politics" of Aristotle* (Chapel Hill, NC: University of North Carolina Press).

Solmsen, F. (1964). "Leisure and Play in Aristotle's Ideal State) *Rheinisches Museum*, 107, pp. 142–55.

Stalley, R. F. (1991). "Aristotle's Criticism of Plato's *Republic*," in Keyt and Miller (pp. 182–99).

Taylor, C. C. W. (1995). "Politics," in J. Barnes (ed.), *The Cambridge Companion to Aristotle* (Cambridge: Cambridge University Press), pp. 233–58.

Vlastos, G. (1977). "The Theory of Social Justice in the *polis* in Plato's *Republic*," in H. North (ed.), *Interpretations of Plato* (Leiden: Brill), *Mnemosyne* suppl. 50, pp. 1–40.

Zeller, E. (1897). *Aristotle and the Peripatetics*, 2 vols. (London: Longman's, Green, & Co.).

35

Excellences of the Citizen and of the Individual

JEAN ROBERTS

One might reasonably think that there could be no room in Aristotle's moral and political theory for any distinction between the virtue of an individual and the virtue of a citizen. Excellence or virtue is expressed in functioning well as the kind of creature one is; humans are, by nature, rational and political creatures. The human good lies in living excellently in accordance with that nature, in being a good rational and political being. The philosophical life, devoted primarily to the exercise of intellectual virtue, is distinguishable from the political life, devoted to the exercise of the virtues of character, the moral virtues. The political life and the life of moral virtue, however, are the same. The traits described as virtues of character in the ethical works are precisely those states that make the possessor a useful member of a political community of the size and complexity Aristotle takes as required for living a genuinely human life, his polis. Happiness and human virtue are constituted by excellent rational activity of a kind appropriate to those who are part of a self-sufficient human community and whose happiness is tied to that of their fellow citizens. Justice, the complete virtue, is by definition virtue with respect to others; practical wisdom, its intellectual side, is credited to those, like Pericles, who understand not merely their own good but that of man generally (*NE* 1129b25–7, 1140b7–11). The *Politics* fills out that picture when Aristotle says that "a city is excellent by its citizens being excellent" and "the best constitution is that which allows anyone to be at his best and live happily" (1332a32–4, 1324a23–5). Happiness and virtue for an individual human being can only be found by living as a member of a community, and the best communities are those in which the members achieve that happiness and excellence.

Given this conception of virtue it may then come as a surprise that Aristotle explicitly asks whether the good man and the good citizen are the same, and answers that they are not (*Pol* III.4). This question might now be understood as asking about the limits of political obligation, that is, as asking when or to what extent, on what grounds, the good man will be a good or obedient citizen. None of these, however, seem likely to be Aristotle's concern. Insofar as he thinks about the appropriate range or scope of law it is to complain of political structures that fail to aim full-bore at virtue; justice, as complete excellence in relation to others, is easily equated with law-abidingness (*NE* 1129b11–14). Aristotle's preference for willing subjects over forced subjects is not an indication that he takes either the legitimacy or the scope of governmental authority to be dependent on consent; unwilling subjects are for him a symptom of constitutional injustice, that is, of the rulers' ruling in their own interest rather than in that of the ruled. By the same token, there can be bad laws, but questions about correctness do not here collapse into questions of legitimacy or authority. Nor is there, at the other end, any general abstract question about the legitimacy of the state or about how citizenship might contribute to an individual's independently defined good, and hence no material there for adjudicating hypothetical conflicts between legal and moral obligation. It is not that Aristotle could not have conceived of the question about the grounds of legitimacy; he needed only to have noticed the sophistic conception of justice as a contractual compromise set up as Socrates' target in *Republic II*. (Even there though, tellingly, the issue is one of the grounding of morality in general rather than of political legitimacy specifically.) Aristotle, rather, simply begins with the claim that humans are political, understood in a way that cuts off any abstract discussion about the limits of governmental authority and leaves only questions about the relative success of different political structures in attaining happiness for citizens.

The distinctions Aristotle sees between the virtues of citizens, or civic virtues, and complete moral virtue are then neither introduced, nor used, to answer questions about the moral appropriateness of obedience to law. The question about the two kinds of virtue is asked not because he suspects or expects any conflict, nothing of that sort is ever hinted at, but simply because this is a work about political excellence and thus about the virtue of citizens. Just as it was natural to conclude the discussion of the household in *Politics* I with some general remarks about of the kind of virtue available to each of its various members, so here in embarking on a discussion of the relative value of various forms of political community it is natural to ask what the members of that community ought to be like if the community is to be good. One needs then to grapple with the fact that Aristotle had a conception of political philosophy that took the limits of citizen obligation to obey law as not only not a foundational question but apparently as a question of no interest at all. There are, however, more immediate, and also unaddressed, questions to be raised here. Given that Aristotle's conception of moral virtue is from the start a conception of political virtue, that the life of moral excellence is naturally characterized by him as the political life, what can civic virtue be that allows it to be taken as in any sense distinct from moral virtue? Complete moral virtue, which Aristotle sometimes calls simply justice, is practical wisdom, a fully reasoned understanding of the human good, combined with perfectly integrated and harmonious emotions and desires. The familiar virtues, like courage and generosity, are all parts of complete moral virtue. How then, moreover, can he assume, given that civic virtue does not seem to be, as the virtues of character apart from justice are, an aspect or part of complete moral virtue, that it is always compatible with moral virtue, as presumably it must be, given that both are virtues of the same creature under the same description?

Virtues of Citizens Distinguished from Complete Moral Virtue

Moral virtue, what makes a man (a male, that is) a good man, plain and simple, is of one kind. The arguments distinguishing it from the virtues of citizens rely primarily on the claim that the virtues of citizens are not of one kind. The explanation begins as follows:

> Just as a sailor is one member of a community, so too we say is the citizen. Insofar as sailors differ in capacity (for one is a rower, one a pilot, one a lookout, and another has yet another name of this kind), it is clear that the most accurate account of the virtue of each will be peculiar to each. (*Pol* 1276b20–5)

A line of thought apparently continued a bit later in the chapter with:

> just as an animal is composed of body and soul, the soul of reason and desire, the household of husband and wife, ownership of master and slave, so too the city is composed of all these and other dissimilar kinds, necessarily then the virtue of all the citizens is not one. (*Pol* 1277a6–11)

There are, in Aristotle's view, certain tasks that need to be performed in order for there to be a city: farming, making tools and instruments of various kinds, trading, fighting, ruling (legislating and judging), and praying and offering sacrifices (*Pol* 1328b5–23, 1290b38–1291b2). This is presumably what he has in mind here when he implies that different citizens, like different sailors, have different capacities. A city will be better to the extent that each and all of these things is done better. Aristotle is here clearly not using "citizen" in the quasi-technical sense marked out in his previous chapter, for someone who is eligible for judicial and legislative roles, but in the broader sense he often slips into, which seems to include any free adult. The remarks then suggest, in part, that being a good citizen is a matter of doing an excellent job in making some one of the many necessary contributions to the common life of the city.

The description of civic virtue is tied to the particular political circumstances in another way as well. The passage about sailors quoted above continues:

> Yet there is also a common account that fits all. For the safety of the voyage is the function of all of them; each of the sailors aims at this. The same holds for citizens. Although they are dissimilar, keeping the community safe is their function, and the constitution is the community. For this reason the virtue of a citizen is necessarily relative to the constitution. Since there are many forms of constitution, it is clear that there cannot be a single and complete virtue of the excellent citizen, but we do say that a man is good by having one virtue, which is complete. It is clear then that it is possible for someone to be an excellent citizen without possessing the virtue in accordance with which he would be an excellent man. (1276b25–35)

All the members of the community that constitutes the city, whatever their disparate functions and capacities, have in common the aim of safeguarding the community, but which traits are necessary or useful for that end apparently depends on the constitution, the basic governing structure of the city. Constitutions are distinguished based on the criteria in place for ruling or holding civic office, and more broadly into good or deviant depending on whether those in power aim at their own good narrowly or at the common good. The thought here seems to be that the virtue of a citizen in a democracy protects the democracy, of a citizen in an oligarchy protects the oligarchy, and so on, and that the activities involved in so doing are sufficiently different that they constitute the exercise of distinct virtues. Possibly, and following the point about the sailors, Aristotle is thinking that since different constitutions have (to some extent) different civic offices and roles there will therefore be different functions to perform in different cities; the talents and virtues of a monarch are useless in a democracy. In any case, he is conceiving of civic virtue in a quite specific way as doing those particular things that promote the good of the particular city a particular citizen happens to be a citizen of.

Thus there appear to be two different ways in which civic virtue can differ from complete moral virtue, one stemming from the necessary differentiation in civic role essential to the self-sufficiency of the polis, and one stemming from variations in basic governing structure. There is no further spelling out of the nature of the virtues of citizens; nor are there any questions explicitly put about the relation between those virtues and complete moral virtue once the case for their distinctness has been made.

Civic Virtue as Excellence in Civic Function

The claim that different citizens will require, as citizens, different virtues because of the different functions they perform within the political community seems entirely of a piece with the conclusions drawn in *Politics* I, 13 about virtue in various members of the household. Aristotle says there that "it is necessary that all partake of moral virtue, not in the same way but to the extent that is fitting to each with respect to function" (*Pol* 1260a18–20). Individuals need those abilities and characteristics required for the performance of their roles within the household or city. Only one of the necessary civic functions requires the exercise of complete virtue and that is ruling (1277b25–6). Thus Aristotle's answer to his question about the identity of the two kinds of virtue, although negative, is, characteristically, not unqualifiedly so; sometimes civic virtue is just moral virtue. A good man for Aristotle is not merely a decent person who doesn't abuse his fellows; that much is presumably required of all, since serious vice would impede the proper performance of any civic function. Complete moral virtue, however, requires practical wisdom, *phronêsis*, a reasoned understanding of the good for man that is fully integrated with desires and habits. This all suggests that the requirements for civic virtue may simply be weaker than those for moral virtue, except in the case of those actively ruling. If so, the distinctness of civic virtue from complete moral virtue will seem to lie primarily in its (varying kinds of) incompleteness. It is easy, for example, to imagine, as Plato did in the *Republic*, that excellent farming or shoemaking or fighting doesn't require a sophisticated understanding of the political good. Although none of those activities seems positively incompatible with that sort of knowledge, there is also the possibility that Aristotle was thinking of the relation between moral virtue and the virtue of non-ruling citizens as more exactly on the model of virtue in the household, where the virtues of different members are incompatible. A good woman would be a bad man and a good man a bad woman (1277b22–5). If that what he has in mind here then being a good citizen in any but a ruling role would not simply be, in effect, easier than being morally virtuous, but would require having characteristics that conflict with it. Both of these models may be in play.

> The virtue of these [rulers and subjects] are different, but it is necessary that the good citizen understand and be capable of both ruling and being ruled, indeed this is the virtue of a citizen, knowledge of the rule of the free from both sides. Both belong as well to the good man, even though the moderation and the justice of the ruler are different in kind. For it is clear that the virtue, for example, the justice, of the good man who is a free subject is not one, but takes different forms depending on whether he rules or is ruled, just as the moderation and courage of a man and of a woman are different. (1277b13–21)

Being a good ruler is different from being a good subject, but a good citizen will have both kinds of virtue. Moreover, Aristotle suggests, the good man will have both kinds. The difference between the two is not simply that only ruling requires practical wisdom, but that the virtues exercised in common are different depending on the role. Nevertheless, although the justice of a ruler and that of the ruled cannot be simultaneously exercised, a single person can be capable of both, and indeed being good, either as a citizen or as a man, requires precisely being so capable and able to play either civic role when appropriate. Aristotle is clearly in this context thinking of citizens as those eligible for public office, and hence of the primary civic duty as ruling, the one that requires *phronêsis* for excellent performance. The inclusion of the excellence of a subject in civic virtue so defined is no doubt due to its being seen as a necessary acquisition in the development of the virtue of a ruler. "It is rightly said that it is not possible to rule well without having been ruled" (1277b11–13). Moreover, since most citizens in most cities will hold office at some times and not at others, this dual virtue will be the one needed for proper performance of that dual civic role.

We see a clear example of all this in Aristotle's ideal or best city. In this city the law successfully promotes virtue in the citizens and everyone is good. In the case of citizens (again, taken narrowly, that is, those who are eligible for public office), civic virtue, as expected, coincides smoothly with moral virtue. Citizens in this city "one would pray for" will perform the military, ruling, and priestly functions in turn in the course of their lives. All citizens will then exercise complete moral virtue when ruling, but be both good men and good citizens before and after taking on that role. There is though a very different story about the rest of this community, all those who make the other necessary contributions to the city. These will not be citizens, precisely because they are not thought to be capable of virtue. The doing of manual labor and what Aristotle, in general, describes as banausic work (roughly, anything physical or aimed at earning money) prevents the development of virtue, for which he thinks leisure is needed (1328b37–1329a2). Not much explanation is given for this. The point may not be so much that *phronêsis* requires that a great deal of time be spent sitting about contemplating the good for man, which is apparently not the case even with those who rule virtuously in his best city, who spend much of their formative years in military service, but that a life spent working for wages leads inevitably to the valuing of money in a way that constitutes a distorted conception of the good. Or perhaps it is simply that if much of a life is spent in a kind of activity that requires little mental work that part of the person will lie fallow (1337b8–15). Also at work here may be Aristotle's assumption (cf. 1299a38–1299b1) that most kinds of work are best done by those who spend all their time on them. Thus, what might seem the obvious way of mitigating the bad effects of certain kinds of work, sharing it out among people, would only in Aristotle's mind result in everything being done badly. Aristotle's solution is to assign it to slaves and barbarians (1329a24–6, 1330a25–30), who he could then take to be natural slaves and the sorts of non-Greeks incapable by nature of complete moral virtue. This neatly allows the best city to live up to its billing as the one that allows everyone to be as good as he can be (1324a23–5).

Despite what one might be tempted to infer from the function argument in the *Nicomachean Ethics* (1097b–1098a18), complete moral virtue is not the excellent performance of characteristically human activity in which all human beings engage. Those who are natural slaves lack any deliberative capacity; women have it but it is not authoritative (1260a12–13). There is a kind of moral virtue available to, and needed in, women and slaves, but it is different and inferior to the virtue of free males. Moreover, there are apparently many others who lack the wherewithal for virtue without falling as far off the scale as natural slaves or women do: people who live in cold places and Asians and even some Greek peoples, who are said to lack either thought or spirit (1327b23–36). The picture, in general, is that it is all too easy to find members of the species not, by nature, capable of becoming fully virtuous and all too difficult to find a few who are. Given that great good fortune is believed to be required to come upon a population with enough potentially good men to have good men ruling, it follows naturally enough that there would be no shortage of those naturally fit only for banausic work to do the banausic work. All of this serves only to illustrate that Aristotelian moral virtue is available in the end to only a very tiny portion of the species. The virtuous life is not in the end an excellently lived human life, but the excellently lived life of the naturally best sort of human.

So there are clearly here cases in which the successful making of the appropriate contribution to the life of the city is incompatible with the exercise of complete moral virtue. This is not, of course, technically, an issue about the virtue of citizens and moral virtue since these are not citizens. In any case, the particular form that incompatibility takes is due to Aristotle's deeply inegalitarian assumptions about the human capacity for virtue in general, not to any particular picture of the relations between moral and civic virtue. There would not here be conflict in individual cases between being a good member of the polis and being a good man, since these are those members of the polis who are not good men.

Different Constitutions and Different Virtues

One might expect Aristotle to say that good citizens everywhere should be trying to change their cities into his best city, and that just this would constitute the virtue of citizens. There is, however, as we have just seen, a very serious impediment in his mind to this sort of improvement. "Since happiness is the chief good, and this is the actualization and a kind of complete use of virtue, and since it so happens that some are able to share in it while others are able to do so only to a small degree or not at all, it is clear that this is why there are several kinds and varieties of cities and a number of different constitutions" (1328a37–41). In a different context, Aristotle points out that although the virtuous would be most justified in complaining of lack of power, since their virtue makes them truly deserving of it and fit for it, they rarely do simply because their meager numbers make it pointless (1301a39–40, 1304b4–5). There are hardly ever so many as a hundred of them (1302a1–2). This sorry fact helps explain why it is part of the task of political science to describe not only the constitution of the best city, but also the constitution best for any given circumstances, the one best for most cities, and even what can be done for cities whose constitutions neither are nor are going to become the best they could be (1288b21–35).

Presumably the contents of the middle Books of the *Politics*, which describe what ought to be done with less than perfect cities, are a display of political science and to that extent of *phronêsis*. Presumably also then, ruling in accordance with the advice given there could be, although it need not be since advice can be followed by those who don't fully understand its rationale, likewise a display of *phronêsis* and hence complete moral virtue. To use Aristotle's own analogy, medicine can be practiced well even if the patient cannot be restored to perfect health. This seems plausible at least in the cases of the non-ideal but basically just constitutional forms, monarchy, aristocracy, and polity, grouped as such because those in power aim at the common good. As long as those in power are virtuous enough to aim at the common good rather than their own they may be doing all that can be done in the circumstances for their cities, and hence have the appropriate civic virtue, even if they and those they rule lack the completely integrated conception of the good required for complete moral goodness. The difference between the two seems not a matter of incompatibility. A good king doesn't have to be Socrates, but Socrates would be a good king.

It is not always so straightforward. The most common types of constitution, democracy and oligarchy, are severely defective; they are in fact simply unjust. What makes oligarchy and democracy bad constitutional forms is that those who rule, the wealthy in the former case and the poor in the latter, rule for their own good rather than for the common good. Different populations may be naturally fit for different political arrangements but no community is naturally fit for rule by rulers who aim at their own rather than the common good, as happens in tyrannies, oligarchies, and democracies, as Aristotle defines them (1287b37–41). Aristotle says many times that civic virtue is relative to the particular constitutions of cities. Does being a good citizen in a city with an unjust political arrangement require the promotion of that injustice, which is to say, moral vice? If so, wouldn't being a good citizen in an unjust city be disturbingly like being a good thief or murderer? This is a variation of the familiar question about why Aristotle thinks it part of political science to advise the far less than perfect, and, in particular, why he is willing to give advice to unjust rulers aimed apparently at their retaining power.

Again, if being a good citizen is preserving the constitution and the constitution is an unjust one, doesn't the good citizen have thereby to be unjust? Won't, for example, the good ruling citizen of an oligarchy have to do whatever he can to keep power, unfairly, in the hands of the wealthy few? This would seem obviously to be the case if preserving constitutions were simply preserving the status quo. Even a cursory look at Aristotle's advice on preserving deviant forms of constitution makes it clear, however, that this is not what he means by preserving constitutions. Since injustice tends to destroy cities, they are all preserved by bringing them closer to just ones. Safeguarding the city or constitution is, in general, a matter of preventing revolution or collapse rather than preventing any sort of change. Aristotle does say that it may not always be worth changing a bad law if the benefit is small, since there is a cost to disrupting the habit of obedience that needs to be considered in such cases (1269a1318). In general though he seems not only to allow but to encourage significant changes. As a general matter he recommends diffusing the consolidation of power in the hands of self-interested parties that characterizes unjust arrangements. Doing so is claimed to be in the interest of those unjust or deviant regimes, but it does also make them less deviant. Oligarchies are more stable when those out of power are treated justly (1308a3–11). All cities are helped by making it impossible for those who hold office to profit from it (1308b32–3). Education appropriate to the constitution, taken as the most important factor in the preservation of cities, is described as precisely not impressing on the citizens the mistaken views of the good embedded in the constitutional structure. Citizens of oligarchies are not, that is, to be encouraged in the pursuit of wealth, nor citizens of democracies in unreflective pursuit of freedom (1310a11–28). Even the tyrant is pushed toward justice.

Aristotle does not, however, go quite so far as to say that deviant regimes are to be preserved by turning them into correct ones. His advice seems, rather, to be that they are to be brought as close to that as is possible, consistent with their remaining the kind of constitutions they are. It is sometimes supposed that Aristotle writes about the preservation of deviant regimes in the belief that nothing is worse for a city than constitutional change, and so once a deviant structure is in place, although it can be monkeyed with, it should not be changed even for the better. This is an inference from the fact that Aristotle gives the advice he does. The thought is that he would not give advice to the unjust unless he thought that even injustice is better than nothing, and that constitutional change somehow amounts to complete destruction of the community without which no one can even live, much less live well. It is not a view explicitly espoused by Aristotle. As Aristotle himself comes to note, the lines marking off one constitutional form from another get very blurry in practice (a polity can not implausibly be described as either a democracy or an oligarchy, for example); it would not be easy to say at what point exactly an oligarchy that had been gradually made more democratic turned into a polity. For Aristotle to believe that introducing a new constitutional structure inevitably did some kind of damage that it could never be in the interest of any city to suffer, while also believing that all the steps on the way to that change were beneficial to the city, he would have to be believing that there is something about that last step into the new form that makes it completely unpalatable in a way that none of the earlier steps were. The question can be put most easily in connection with the tyrant. Why would anyone think that it could be in the tyrant's and the city's interest for the tyrant to treat his subjects fairly and generally act almost like a monarch instead of a tyrant, but not in the city's interest for him to go all the way and become a monarch instead of a tyrant?

So, the assumption that Aristotle really believed that it was better for deviant constitutions to stay that way is not only morally implausible but also politically and practically implausible. At this point it is important to remember that the discussion of the preservation of deviant constitutions is introduced at the beginning of Book IV as analogous to giving advice about physical training to those who don't want to be athletes. Recall that the political scientist is supposed to think about, not only the best constitution possible, but also the best under particular circumstances, the best for most cities, and finally even those that are not the best possible, but are simply "based on a presupposition." The last are those that are not even the best that could be achieved under the circumstances. The analogy with those not interested in athletic training suggests that Aristotle, in giving advice about the preservation of deviant constitutions, takes himself to be speaking to a very particular audience, those who want to retain power in an unjust arrangement and whose self-interest has to be straightforwardly appealed to in order to get them to improve their cities. This is surely why the discussion of deviant constitutions is based "on the assumption" that the constitutions in question are to stay in place, and why justice is not recommended as something intrinsically good but as an instrument for the retention of power.

The upshot of all this is that good ruling will always be a near approach to, or approximation of, justice, and only the basic moral deficiencies of the ruler will prevent it from being complete moral virtue. The tyrant is the clearest example of this. Insofar as the tyrant who follows Aristotle's advice is a good citizen it is by pretending to be a better man than he is. Whether he thereby becomes a genuinely good citizen is a question that gave even Aristotle himself a moment's pause. His detailed advice to the tyrant ends by claiming that following such advice will not only lengthen his time in power, but will also make him, as a matter of character, "either well-disposed with respect to virtue or half-virtuous and not wicked, but half-wicked" (1315b8–10). Here, again, civic virtue is whatever of moral virtue the particular nature in question allows.

Good Men in Bad Cities

I have so far been asking the question about the relation between civic virtue and moral virtue in the case of those who rule in cities of various kinds, and have now argued that the virtue of citizens is always compatible with moral virtue, the significant difference in the end being that in various ways good citizens need not always be possessed of or exercising complete moral virtue. The difference between the two kinds of virtue has to do with the one being tied to specific roles and political circumstances which can often be served well without full moral virtue. In the case of those few who are possessed of complete moral virtue there is no difference between the two. The good ruler who is also a good man will not have different obligations or aims as a ruler or citizen than those he has as a man. Whatever moral virtue the good citizen who is not quite a fully good man has will be constituted precisely by his civic virtue. These are not then in the end competing kinds of virtue at all, as one would have expected given Aristotle's silence on the question.

The case might, however, seem different for citizens who are not ruling but ruled. Generally, what about that rare citizen who is a virtuous man in a less than best city? The laws will not be those of the best city, whose laws simply direct one to act virtuously. Won't this citizen sometimes be told to act in ways that he can see are bad, and won't he then have to choose between being a good citizen and being a good man? Aristotle, as I mentioned earlier, appears to have absolutely no interest in this question.

The entire *Politics* is written for, and from the point of view of, those who rule; the task of political science as he conceives of it is the genuinely practical one of advising the ruling elite. Political theory is concerned about how rulers should rule rather than about why the ruled ought to obey. Anything said about the ruled is said about them as subjects rather than as moral agents. Moreover, even had Aristotle looked at things from the point of view of the ruled, questions about how those better in character than their cities ought to act would probably not have seemed pressing. Although it is possible for virtue to arise outside the best city, it is not very common since people tend to be the sort of people their cities make them, and virtue is in any case rare.

That aside, and more importantly, the question as posed, which assumes the potential of conflict between moral and civic virtue, is not one that can be recognized within Aristotle's framework. Questions about whether particular laws ought to be obeyed on particular occasions, which certainly Aristotle can recognize, need not be interpreted as questions about whether the moral good should trump the civic good or whether moral virtue supersedes civic virtue. To interpret them that way is to assume not only that the two kinds of virtue have different aims that can therefore conflict, but also that the good citizen always obeys the law. Neither of these holds here. Although Aristotle thinks it is generally the case that obedience to law preserves the constitution, he says nothing that suggests that being a good citizen means mindless obedience to any and every law. Being a good or just man is essentially a matter of doing what promotes the good of others, particularly one's fellow citizens. Being a good citizen is aiming at the preservation of the constitution, which is presumably worth doing because it serves the common good. The common good being served may well not be the ideal good; being a good citizen may not amount to making a successful contribution to the complete virtue and happiness of all the citizens of a city. It will though be a contribution to whatever happiness is available in the circumstances. This is exactly what the good man aims at as well.

Aristotle certainly does not deny that there can be bad laws. Deviant constitutions will have laws that constitute unjust treatment of many of the citizens. Any constitution can have laws that do not properly reflect the constitution, and prescribe behavior that actually tends to destroy the constitution. Not all cities will have good rulers and legislators and so there is always a chance of there being laws that are not those a man of virtue would have made. One might think that a virtuous man (in either sense) ought not to obey any laws he would not himself have enacted, but Aristotle's view is unlikely to be so simple. Aristotle shows no sign of thinking of disobedience to law as a way of reforming bad law; it is always destructive of the constitution. This will make him inclined to think that good citizenship requires obedience. It will also make him inclined to think that moral virtue requires obedience even when the law is bad simply because the orderliness that comes of widespread obedience to law is better than its absence.

There can thus be a question about whether or not a particular law should be obeyed; the question will be whether obedience or disobedience best serves the common good. It will be a question at once about what good citizenship requires and about what moral virtue requires. It will not be a question about whether being a good man allows one to be a good citizen. It will involve regular Aristotelian deliberation involving proper recognition of the ways in which the circumstances of the proposed action affects its goodness. That an action is an act of disobedience to established law is a morally relevant feature that will need to be brought into the deliberation. It is morally relevant because disobedience tends to be harmful to the constitution, and the preservation of the constitution is tied to the common good. What counts as the right action in any case, what the good man and the good citizen will do, depends on the details of the particular situation in which action is to be taken. Some of those details will be details about the particular political community in which the good man finds himself. Being a good citizen requires doing what safeguards the political community, and it is possible, although unlikely, that disobedience rather than obedience will do this better. Questions about obedience to law are not, in any case, for Aristotle instances of a conflict between qualitatively different sorts of consideration as they seem to be when the issue is framed as one of conflict between moral rightness and duty to the state. A question about whether a particular law ought to be obeyed is not a question about whether one owes more to the city or to oneself, or about whether one should be a good man or a good citizen; it is simply a question about how to be good.

Note

Much of the material in this chapter began life as an invited talk at the Pacific Division Meetings of the American Philosophical Association in 1998. I am grateful to Roderick T. Long for his comments on that occasion, and to Angela Smith and Cass Weller for more recent discussion.

Bibliography

Annas, J. (1996). "Aristotle on Human Nature and Political Virtue," *Review of Metaphysics*, 49, pp. 731–53.

Barnes, J. (1990). "Aristotle and Political Liberty," in G. Patzig (ed.), *Aristotles' "Politik"* (Gottingen: Vandenhoeck and Ruprecht), pp. 249–63.

Curren, R. R. (2000). *Aristotle on the Necessity of Public Education* (Lanham, MD: Rowman and Littlefield).

Keyt, D. (1999). *Aristotle, "Politics" Books V and VI* (Oxford: Clarendon Press).

Mulgan, R. G. (1977). *Aristotle's Political Theory* (Oxford: Oxford University Press).

Newman, W. L. (1902). *The "Politics" of Aristotle*, 4 vols (Oxford: Clarendon Press).

Roberts, J. (1989). "Political Animals in the *Nicomachean Ethics*," *Phronesis*, 34, pp. 185–204.

Roberts, J. (2000). "Justice and the Polis," in C. Rowe and M. Schofield (eds.), *The Cambridge History of Greek and Roman Political Thought* (Cambridge: Cambridge University Press), pp. 344–65.

Robinson, R. (1995). *Aristotle, "Politics" Books III and IV* (Oxford: Clarendon Press).

Rowe, C. (2000). "Aristotelian Constitutions," in C. Rowe and M. Schofield (eds.), The *Cambridge History of Greek and Roman Political Thought* (Cambridge: Cambridge University Press), pp. 366–89.

Taylor, C. C. W. (1995). "Politics," in J. Barnes (ed.), *The Cambridge Companion to Aristotle* (Cambridge: Cambridge University Press), pp. 233–58.

36

Education and the State

RICHARD STALLEY

In the last two Books of the *Politics* Aristotle investigates the best *politeia* or constitution, that is, the best way of organizing a city (*polis*). These Books have puzzled some readers, mainly because an inquiry of this kind seems to presuppose an idealistic or utopian approach to political theory, whereas Aristotle is generally seen as a practical, empirically minded philosopher, deeply interested in the problems of existing cities and concerned to ameliorate their condition rather than to describe ideals that are unlikely to be achieved in practice. At one time it was fashionable to suppose that these Books represent an early Platonic phase in Aristotle's thought. This solution is less popular now, partly because of scepticism about the general idea that Aristotle began as a Platonist and then developed more distinctive philosophical positions and partly because it is clear that the investigation of the best city was always part of Aristotle's programme for political philosophy. However there are still difficulties in relating these Books to the more practically oriented discussions elsewhere in the *Politics* (Rowe 1991).

It is sometimes assumed that Aristotle saw his best constitution as a model which might actually be used in founding a city. He does indeed stipulate that it should not assume anything "impossible" (VII.4 1325b37–9). But he also describes it as the constitution that one would "pray for" (VII.4 1325b36, VII.5 1327a4, VII.10 1330a25–6, cf. II.1 1260b29). Moreover he shows no interest in questions about how or where it might be brought into being or how it might be preserved. So he seems to be concerned that the constitution should be consistent with the general facts of human nature and the human condition but not to be particularly worried about how it might be implemented. There is a contrast here with Plato. The ideal city of the *Republic* is very remote from ordinary experience but is not simply the one we would pray for. Plato specifies circumstances (albeit unlikely ones) in which it could come about and is much concerned with its preservation (450c, 456b–c, 473c–474b, 499c, 540d). In the *Laws* he discusses in detail the circumstances in which the city might be established (702a–e, 704a–712a, 739a–e, 745e–746d). There is therefore a sense in which Aristotle's account of the best city is more idealistic than Plato's. In this chapter I shall show that this "idealism" is closely connected with other elements in Aristotle's ethical and political thought. However it does not mean that these Books have no practical implications. I shall argue that, particularly because of their concern with education, they have a direct relevance to real life.

Aristotle defines the city as an association, or partnership, for the sake of the good life (I.1 1252a1–7, I.2 1252b27–30. III.6 1278b17–30, III.9 1280a25–b23). Not surprisingly, therefore he begins his investigation of the best *politeia* by considering what way of life is most to be preferred, since "those who live under the best *politeia* that can be achieved in their circumstance should do best provided nothing unexpected happens" (VII.1 1323a17–19).[1] For his account of the best life he draws, as one would expect, on his ethical works.[2] He begins with a familiar distinction between external goods, goods of the body, and goods of the soul. External goods include such things as wealth, power, and reputations. The good of the body is health. The goods of the soul are the virtues, that is, forms of human excellence such as courage, temperance, justice, and wisdom (VII.1 1323a21–6 cf. *NE* II.1 1098b12–16; cf. *EE* II.1 1218b31–4, VIII.3 1249a14–16; cf. Plato *Laws* 743e). According to Aristotle most people and most cities make the fundamental mistake of preferring external goods. In reality we need only a modicum of these since they have value only insofar as they serve the goods of the soul. The latter are fine or noble or, as we might say, "genuinely valuable for their own sake." Our happiness is thus "proportionate to our virtue and wisdom and to the virtuous and wise acts that we do" (VII.1 1323a26–b23). The same goes for the city. It can be happy only if it does fine deeds, for which it needs the virtues. This idea that the individual and the city should seek things good in themselves, rather than those that are good merely as a means, underlies much of the argument of Books VII and VIII. Positively it is the central principle on which Aristotle constructs his own best *politeia*; negatively it underpins his criticism of existing cities as dominated by commercial or military considerations.

As we know from the *Ethics*, the claim that human good consists in virtuous activity is open to different interpretations. The moral virtues are most fully displayed in active citizenship while the intellectual virtues are best exercised in the theoretical contemplations of the philosopher. It is disputed whether Aristotle thinks the truly happy life would somehow combine both kinds of activity or whether he would give priority to the life of the philosopher (see also this volume, ch. 24, "Happiness and the Structure of Ends"). In *Politics* VII he raises a similar issue by asking whether we should prefer the active political life or a life that does not depend on externals, such as "the theoretical life which some see as the only one worthy of a philosopher" (VII.2 1324a25–35). A similar issue arises for cities: must the good life involve active engagement with other cities or could it be solitary?

Aristotle responds to these questions by first correcting a mistaken view of the active life. Some hold that happiness, for cities and for individuals, consists in ruling over others despotically (i.e. as a master rules over slaves). But, Aristotle claims, despotic rule has nothing valuable about it, and is indeed positively evil (VII.3 1325a24–9). It is, on the other hand, a fine thing to participate in a government of equals where offices are shared in rotation (VII.3 1325b7–8). So he rejects the ideal of the Spartans, who see military success as the main object of legislation, and replaces it with an alternative conception of the active political life as one of "ruling and being ruled."

Those who advocate a life of inactivity are also mistaken. Their underlying thought seems to be that, since activity depends on externals, only an inactive life can be genuinely free and self-sufficient. But, in Aristotle's view, this cannot be right because happiness necessarily involves activity (VII.3 1325a31–3). He solves the problem by arguing that the active life need not be one that involves relations with others. We are most genuinely active when we engage in thinking for its own sake. Similarly a city which avoids relations with others can still be active by virtue of what goes on within it (VII.3 1325b16–29). These moves soften the contrast between the political and the philosophical lives without, in themselves, solving the problem. But they do perhaps point the way to a solution. Aristotle may be suggesting that if we understand the two kinds of life correctly we will see that a city could be constructed in such a way as to give scope for both.

Aristotle's proposals for the construction of his best city sometimes seem unoriginal – many of them closely follow Plato's *Laws*. But they are structured by his concern that the citizens individually and collectively should follow a life of virtuous activity without being diverted to the pursuit of external goods. The population must be large enough for self-sufficiency but also small enough for the citizens to know one another and share in ruling and being ruled (VII.4 1326a5–b25). The territory must not be so large as to encourage luxury (VI.5 1326b26–38). The harbor, which is needed for the import of essential goods, must not become a general centre of trade (VII.6 1327a17–25). The physical space of the city should be planned so as to minimize the corrupting effects of commerce (VII.12 1331a30–5). The citizens should have the right kind of natural temperament, combining a vigorous spirit with intelligence (VII.7 1327b36–1328a7). In making the last point Aristotle pays most attention to spirit. He argues that this makes people capable of friendship. It also enables them to be free and exercise rule because it is "a ruling and unconquerable element" (VII.7 1328a7). Here he explicitly gives spirit a more important role than Plato would allow it, but does nothing to suggest that spirit is more important than intelligence. Presumably both are necessary if one is to rule well.

More striking to most readers is the distinction between citizens and non-citizens. Aristotle claims that in a city, as in a natural organism, those elements that form part of the whole should be distinguished from those that may be necessary to the existence of the whole but are not parts of it. Because the city is an association of equals for the sake of the best possible life, its members (i.e. those who are regarded as parts of the whole) must be able to share in that life (VII.8 1328a21–b2). The functions necessary to the existence of the city include farming, the crafts, bearing arms, the provision of property, the service of the gods and, most importantly, the political function of determining what is in the public interest or what is required by justice (VII.8 1328b4–14, cf. IV.4 1290b37–1291b2). Aristotle argues that the military, political, and religious functions should belong to citizens. When young they will bear arms, in middle age they will exercise the political functions, and when they are older they will serve as priests (VII.9 1329a2–16, 27–34). Citizens should also own property – they all will, in fact, have their own farms (VII.9 1329a17–26). The central point here is that to be a citizen is to share in the activities of ruling and being ruled. In youth, when they are subject to military discipline, citizens will learn to rule by being themselves ruled. That fits them to fulfil the main political functions when they reach what Aristotle would consider the prime of life. The religious functions offer them an honorable role in retirement.

This conception of citizenship is attractive but what disturbs most modern readers is the inference drawn by Aristotle that those who work at farming, craftsmanship, and trade cannot be citizens. The reason for excluding farmers is that they lack the leisure needed for the development of virtue and for participation in politics. The same may go for craftsmen, wage-earners, and traders but in their case Aristotle has more specific anxieties. "Banausic" occupations, such as practicing a craft, may distort the natural development of mind or body, while working for a wage is seen as a form of slavery. Because he is controlled by the demands of his employer the wage-earner is not free. The trouble with traders is that they aim to acquire wealth in the form of money. This is intrinsically valueless but can be accumulated without limit. To engage in trade is thus to disqualify oneself from genuinely virtuous activity (VI.4 1319a25–30, VII.9 1328b33–1329a2, 1329a19–24, VIII.2 1337b5–15). Crafts and trades must therefore be assigned to resident foreigners while land must be farmed by slaves or, failing that, by barbarian serfs (VII.10 1330a25–32).

Aristotle's position here has been the focus of a good deal of criticism (Nussbaum 1990; Mulgan 2000), but it reflects the view adopted elsewhere in the *Politics* that those he calls "banausics" (those involved in crafts and manufacturing) cannot be citizens in a well-ordered city (III.5 1277b33–1278a12). No doubt this depends in part on sheer prejudice, but it follows naturally from Aristotle's view of the city as an association or partnership for the sake of the good life. He can plausibly claim that only those who participate in the good at which an association aims can be members in the full sense. So, if the city is such an association, membership must be open only to those who share in the good life. The conception of the good life, set out in the opening chapters of *Politics* VII implies that it requires leisure and is inconsistent with "banausic" occupations. Thus, if we are unhappy with the restrictions Aristotle places on citizenship, we have two alternatives. One is to reject his view of the city as existing for the sake of the good life rather than for the sake of survival or material needs. That would be to abandon most of what he has to say about politics. The alternative is to reinterpret the conception of a good life in such a way as to make it available to those whom Aristotle would exclude. I shall consider later whether this is a genuine possibility.

From Book VII, chapter 13, Aristotle's primary focus is on education, but, intriguingly, he opens this section by making what appears to be a fresh start: "We have now to speak of the *politeia* (constitution) itself and to explain the nature and character of the elements required if a city is to enjoy a happy life and be well-governed" (VII.13 1331b24–6). He goes on to make explicit the importance of distinguishing between ends and means. In constitution-making, as in anything else, we must direct our activities to the right end and be aware of the distinction between the end and the equipment that is necessary for its achievement (VII.13 1331b26–1332b7). The end of constitution-making is happiness understood as "the complete actualization and practice of virtue" (VII.13 1332a9; cf. *EE* II.1 1219a38–9; *NE* I.7 1098a16–17). This implies that education in virtue is the primary role of the legislator. As Aristotle puts it, the legislator has to consider "How a man can become good" (VII.13 1332a35–6).

The idea that education is the central task of the legislator should not surprise those familiar with Aristotle's ethical writings or with other Books of the *Politics*. Because the city exists for the sake of a good life it must provide training in virtue. As is clear in the *Ethics*, to be virtuous one must have appropriate feelings of pleasure and pain. We come to have these feelings by being habituated to behave in the right kinds of ways. It is thus a central task of the city to habituate the young to correct behavior. Existing cities make the mistake of leaving education largely to the family. But, even so, law also plays an important role. It lays down guidelines for conduct and takes over from the parents as children grow older (*NE* II.1 1103a31–b6; II.3 1104b3–28, V.5 1130b22–9). So at the end of the *Nicomachean Ethics* Aristotle marks the transition to politics by arguing that training in virtue requires good laws (*NE* X.9 1179b34–1180a5).

The interweaving of education and politics is also clear from the way in which Aristotle defines the *politeia* (constitution) of a city. It is not just a body of law or system of government but embraces the city's whole way of life (IV.11 1295a40–b1). This implies that education is central to the constitution, for only through education can a way of life be transmitted to succeeding generations. In fact Aristotle sees little point in legislation without education. He criticizes Plato's proposals for the abolition of private property by arguing that the aims to which they are directed should be achieved primarily through education (II.5 1263b37–40). Similarly he claims, as a general principle, that citizens must receive an appropriate education if a constitution is to survive (V.9 1310a14–19, VII.1 1337a11–21). As we might put it, different constitutions presuppose different kinds of values. A constitution will survive only if citizens have been educated to absorb those values.

Given these points it is not surprising that Aristotle sees education as a public responsibility (Curren 2000). It is too important to be left to the initiative of individuals. Moreover, because children are being trained for partnership in a single community, their education should also be common to them all (VII.1 1337a21–7). So, while they will be educated within the family up to the age of seven, education thereafter will be provided by the city – provided that is for boys of citizen families: Aristotle says nothing about the education of women or non-citizens, even though he recognizes elsewhere that, since women constitute half the free population, a study of constitutions should consider their education (I.13 1260b18–20).

According to Aristotle, there are three factors which contribute to human excellence: nature, habit, and reason (VII.13 1332a40–b10; cf. *NE* II.1 1103a14–26). Insofar as the legislator can control the natural characteristics of the citizens he does so in their initial selection. Human beings resemble animals in being capable of habituation but, unlike animals, they also have reason and may be led by it to act against nature and habit "if they have been persuaded that some other course is better" (VII.13 1332b6–7). So, although the nature of human beings is fixed, "the rest is entirely a matter of education; they will learn some things by habituation and others by listening" (VII.13 1332b10–11).

The scheme of education Aristotle proposes interweaves two lines of thought familiar from the *Ethics*: the theory of the human soul and the doctrine of leisure. The human soul, in Aristotle's view, contains two parts. One of these has reason in itself, while the other, although not intrinsically rational, is capable of listening to reason. To be a good human being requires the virtues of both parts (VII.14 1333a16–29, VII.15 1334b12–28). These are, of course, the moral and intellectual virtues distinguished in the *Ethics* (*NE* I.13 1102a26–1103b10). The reasoning part is further subdivided into practical and theoretical elements. Just as the body exists for the sake of the soul so the lower elements of the soul exist for the sake of the higher. Those with the requisite capacities should therefore prefer the activities of the highest element. Since the lower elements develop before the higher, educators should attend first to the body, then to the appetitive part of the soul and finally to reason (VII.15 1334b17–28).

Aristotle's doctrine of leisure combines this psychological theory with the distinction between activities that are genuinely valuable and those that are only conditionally so. Just as work must be undertaken for the sake of leisure and war for the sake of peace, so necessary and useful actions in general must be undertaken for the sake of those that are fine and noble (VII.14 1333a30–b5). Correspondingly we need three kinds of virtue. Courage and endurance are needed for work, justice and temperance for both work and leisure, and the love of wisdom (philosophy) simply for leisure (VII.15 1334a11–40). It is clear here that the best use of leisure involves theoretical reason. A similar point is made in the *Nicomachean Ethics* where it is suggested that genuine leisure is incompatible not only with war but also with political activities and that the best activity is therefore philosophical contemplation (*NE* X.7 1177b4–26).

The idea that leisure is ultimately what gives life its value would have appealed to many of Aristotle's contemporaries. But Aristotle has a very distinctive conception of what leisure is. In particular he distinguishes it from play or amusement. Although both afford pleasure they are, in Aristotle's view, quite different. Play or amusement is valued primarily as a means of relaxation from work. Leisure, on the other hand, involves not only pleasure but happiness and well-being. Different people conceive of this pleasure in different ways but the best pleasure is that which is valued by the best individual and comes from the finest activities (VII.3 1337b28–1338a9). We can understand this in the light of Aristotle's account of pleasure which treats pleasures as inseparable from the activities out of which they arise. We take pleasure in activities when we engage in them freely and without constraint. Indeed, Aristotle defines pleasure as "unimpeded activity" (*NE* VII.13 1153b7–25, X.5 1175a20–b35; *EE* VII.15 1249a17–21). It follows that the value of the pleasure depends on that of the activity. The most valuable pleasures are those that arise from the finest activities, ones that involve the intellectual virtues. Games and other kinds of amusement are not valuable in themselves but can have secondary value if they help us to relax and renew our energies for more important tasks.

All this implies that education should not be concerned purely with what is useful, nor, for that matter, with amusement. It should also prepare children for what Aristotle calls *diagôgê* (a life of leisure) (VIII.3 1338a9–13). In discussing the curriculum Aristotle starts from the four subjects commonly taught in his day: reading and writing, drawing, physical education, and music. The first two are useful for many purposes and physical education has been seen as useful for inculcating courage (VIII.3 1337b23–7). Aristotle criticizes the intensive training which is intended to turn out athletes but in fact prevents the proper development of the body. He also attacks, once again, the Spartan system. The characters it produces are not so much courageous as savage and unfitted for the things that really matter. It thus has a "banausic" character. It gave the Spartans military success only so long as no other states provided their young men with proper training (VIII.4 1338b9–38).

Aristotle treats musical education much more fully. He considers three possible purposes it might serve: amusement, character-formation, and leisure (VIII.5 1339a11–25). It obviously can be a pleasant form of amusement but more is needed to justify its place in education. Like Plato, Aristotle pays a good deal of attention to its role in the development of character, discussing which musical styles and instruments are appropriate for this purpose (VIII.5 1340a14–19, VIII.7 1341b19–1342b34). Here he appeals, in part, to accepted views which see some kinds of music as "inspirational" and recognize that the representational element in music is often itself enough to arouse sympathetic feelings. He gives these ideas a more precise form by relating them to his own account of moral development. Music, it seems, helps one "to form right judgments on and feel delight in good characters and noble actions." It thus plays a part in encouraging the young to take pleasure in the right things (VIII.5 1340a14–18). It also has a particular capacity to represent directly feelings and states of character. It is superior in this respect to the visual arts which represent these only indirectly by depicting external appearances (VIII.5 1340a18–35). Training in the right kinds of music is thus a means of acquiring the unity of right judgment and feeling that is constitutive of moral virtue.

However Aristotle sees a further purpose for musical education. Because leisure is more important than work, the city must include in the curriculum subjects which prepare children for the right use of leisure, that is, subjects which are not merely useful but valuable in themselves. Music is the pre-eminent subject of this kind. It is a traditional part of education but is not useful for purposes such as money-making, household management, the acquisition of knowledge, or politics. Its value must therefore lie in the part it plays in a life of leisure (VIII.3 1338a13–17). Aristotle finds support for this view in the poets (VIII.3 1338a 21–30). But, although Aristotle has deep respect for accepted opinion he cannot rely exclusively upon it. To make good his claims about music's part in the life of leisure he must demonstrate that it is a truly valuable activity which involves the rational element in the soul. Although he does little to justify this claim explicitly, he makes it clear that musical education enables us, not only to feel the right kinds of emotion, but also to discern goodness and nobility of character (VIII.5 1340a15–18). Children should learn to play an instrument, as opposed to merely listening, because that helps them to judge correctly which things are noble and to enjoy them rightly (VIII.5 1340b35–40). Aristotle allows that other studies may also have this kind of value. For example, drawing can teach children to contemplate beauty with respect to bodies (VIII.3 1338b2). The reason for his concentration on music may be that this subject is least likely to be seen as useful. It is, therefore particularly fitted to make the point that education should aim at the right use of leisure. However Aristotle holds that music could be studied in the wrong way. Children should not, for example, aspire to a professional level of skill. That would be banausic – it would impede other activities and hinder the child's physical and mental development. To take part in competitions would be banausic because it involves playing for the pleasure of others rather than for one's own improvement (VIII.6 1341a5–17, b8–19).

Music and physical education are the only subjects Aristotle discusses at any length. He includes drawing in the curriculum with some hesitation. Children will also learn subjects such as reading and writing, which are important, not just for their everyday practical utility, but because they make other kinds of study possible (VIII.3 1338a37–40). There is no indication what these other kinds of study are. Perhaps they include mathematics, in which citizens must surely have some instruction. There does not appear to be room for subjects such as astronomy and biology. It is striking that, in the text as we have it, there is nothing about poetry as such. Perhaps Aristotle means to include it in "reading and writing" or under the broad heading of "music." Plato had, of course, emphasized the need to teach poetry with an improving moral content. Emphasizing music may help Aristotle to distance himself from the Platonic view which emphasized moral education rather than the correct use of leisure.

There is also some uncertainty about when the various subjects could be taught. For the first seven years children will be educated at home. Until the age of five they should not be required to engage in study or do "necessary" work since that would impair their development. They will have games and other activities to prevent their bodies being idle but these should not be of a kind that is laborious or unsuitable for a free person. Public officials should supervise the stories that they hear and their general way of life, taking particular care that they spend as little time as possible in the company of slaves and are not exposed to bad language. Between five and seven they will observe the lessons of older children. From then on education will be provided by the city. Between the ages of seven and fourteen children will receive light physical training. From the age of seventeen there will be a period of strenuous exercise which Aristotle sees as incompatible with other studies. The three years between fourteen and seventeen are set aside for "other subjects," but this period seems hardly long enough for all the studies, apart from physical education, that Aristotle is committed to including. Perhaps he envisages that other subjects will be studied alongside the light physical training between the ages of seven and fourteen.

A more contentious question is whether Aristotle envisages any kind of education after the age of twenty-one. Since the best kind of life is that of theoretical reason, some scholars have supposed that Aristotle intended his citizens to have a period of philosophical training after that age. But there is no hint of this in the text. Moreover there is a clear indication that Aristotle does not think that everyone is capable of the theoretical life (VII.14 1333a27–9). This makes it unlikely that he would prescribe a course of philosophical training for all citizens.

A very different interpretation has been suggested by some scholars who believe that Aristotle cannot have expected his citizens to engage in philosophy as that term is now understood. They argue that, when he suggests that philosophy is needed for leisure, he is using the term "philosophy" in a broad sense to embrace what we might call "culture" including literature and music. The claim is then that Aristotle's best regime will be ruled, not by philosophers but by "gentlemen." The lives of these people are devoted to the practice of virtue but what distinguishes them from virtuous characters as commonly understood is that they do noble deeds because they see them as valuable in themselves rather than as contributing to some other good. They resemble philosophers in that they prefer leisure to occupation but they spend their leisure "in the enjoyment of what is noble and beautiful" rather than in "the pursuit of scientific truth" (Lord 1984: 200–2). It is, however, difficult to reconcile this view with the facts (1) that Aristotle clearly intends his citizens to live the best kind of life – the life we would pray for; (2) that within his account of the best state and of its education system he explicitly designates the life of theoretical reason as best for those who can achieve it (VII.14 1333a16–30); and (3) that in the same contexts he also associates genuine leisure with theoretical reason (VII.14 1333a30–b5). It is clear therefore that the lives of the citizens collectively must include in substantial measure activities which involve the exercise of this form of reason. This may not imply that all citizens must engage in philosophical activity in the narrow sense but it must mean more than that they simply live a generally cultured life.

Aristotle's conception of education and its relation to the good life would, no doubt, be clearer if we had the completed account of his best city. But his treatment of music gives some indication of what he has in mind. Music serves as means of developing the character and as a source of amusement and relaxation. It can do this because it involves the lower elements in the soul which develop in childhood. But these are not the only reasons why Aristotle thinks music should play a part in education. He also holds that, studied in the correct way, music involves the intellect. It can therefore serve as a prime example of the genuine use of leisure. It is an activity that is worthwhile in itself because it involves the unconstrained activity of the highest elements in the human mind. As the poets suggest when they make the gods enjoy music, it is a godlike way in which to spend one's time. But the same could be said of other subjects if they are studied in the right way. There are grounds for supposing that Aristotle would give philosophical contemplation a pre-eminent role among such activities. It gives scope for the exercise of theoretical reason in its purest form. One might also argue that only where philosophy is practiced will it be possible for the city to retain a clear understanding of the distinction between activities that are valuable in themselves and those that are merely useful or enjoyable (Depew 1991). But this goes well beyond anything said in the text as we have it.

Aristotle's account of the best constitution and its system of education is an integral part of his ethical and political theory. In his view anything that exists by nature is to be understood teleologically. An organism, for example, has an end, the achievement of which constitutes its well-being. Of course, a particular specimen may not achieve that end. Indeed the majority may fail to do so. But they do, nevertheless, all tend towards it (see also, this volume, ch. 21, "Teleology in Living Things"). This is why, in the *Ethics* Aristotle seeks to discover what constitutes the good life for a human being by investigating the natural function of man (*NE* I.7 1097b22–1098b8). Human beings cannot flourish without a city. A city is not an organism but, because it exists in order that human beings may fulfill their proper function, it resembles an organism in having an end towards which it is naturally directed and which constitutes its well-being (*Pol* I.2 1252b27–1253a39). So we cannot fully understand human good without knowing what it is for the city to flourish. A truly excellent city may be even rarer than a truly excellent human being but it is essential to Aristotle's scheme that he should be able to describe both.

Aristotle certainly did not expect to remodel any existing city on the lines of his ideal. This was partly because the best city requires unusually favorable circumstances but also because most people mistakenly identify the good with power and wealth rather than with virtuous activity. In these cities a wise statesman may be able to do no more than make modest improvements. But he will be better equipped to do this if he has a clear conception of the truly just city. This is one way in which the account of the best city could be relevant to the real world. But Aristotle's view of education gives them a more immediate relevance. Although he believes that education should be a central concern of the city he recognizes that, in practice, it is usually treated as a private responsibility of the family. As he points out in the last chapter of the *Nicomachean Ethics*, this means that, with regard to education, ordinary citizens are in the position of legislators. They have the opportunity to help children and friends towards the virtuous life. They will be better able to do this if they learn to legislate (*NE* X.9 1180a29–b7). For that they need to study politics. If there is any part of the *Politics* that serves this purpose it is the Books that discuss the best city. They describe not only the best way of life but also the ways in which children might be educated for that life.

Although Aristotle is concerned with life in a Greek city-state, his account of education may be of wider interest. Many modern educationists would sympathize with his criticisms of educational practices that concentrate purely on what is useful. They might also be attracted by his account of the proper aims of education. He believes that it should prepare children for a life which includes participation both in public affairs and in activities that are valuable in themselves because they involve the exercise of rational powers. It must therefore encourage the development and integration of all of one's capacities under the direction of reason. But, for all its attractions, Aristotle's view has obvious problems. He assumes that those who work for a wage, are employed as manual workers, or engage in trade cannot share in the good life. Since virtually everyone now falls into one of these categories, this suggests that the Aristotelian good life is simply a dream and that an education based on it must certainly be irrelevant and perhaps positively disabling.

If we are to retrieve anything from Aristotle's philosophy of education we need to challenge his pessimistic view of the occupations he calls "banausic." We might argue that these occupations need not engross their practitioners' lives to the extent that they cannot engage in worthwhile activities. At least in developed modern societies, the jobs by which we earn our livings do not normally occupy all our time. We can, therefore, have leisure to participate in the political community and engage in other worthwhile activities. Moreover the occupations in question need not be so corrupting as Aristotle supposes. Working as a craftsman, for example, involves choice and rational judgment. Employment can be organized so that working for a wage is not a form of servility. It is possible to engage in trade without coming to see the accumulation of wealth as the sole purpose of life. In other words, we do not need to draw a sharp distinction between those who can and those who cannot live a life of worthwhile activity.

Aristotle himself recognizes some of these points. In discussing the lives of the young citizens who learn to rule by obeying the rule of others, he notes that activities which are servile in one context may not be in another. What makes an act valuable is not the task itself but the end to which it is directed (VII.14 1333a6–11). Conversely, acts which are appropriate for a free citizen "if they are done for one's own sake or for that of one's friends, or to attain virtue" are "menial and or servile" when done "frequently for other people's purposes" (VIII.2 1337b17–21). Evidently what matters is not so much the particular activity but the attitude of mind with which one undertakes it.

This suggests a different way of understanding the exclusion of banausics from citizenship. Aristotle believes that, because certain occupations distort the character in ways which prevent people from living a truly good life, those who follow these occupations cannot be citizens. We might reply that the cause of corruption is not the occupations themselves so much as their social context and the attitudes with which they are undertaken. We may not be able to live exactly the kind of life Aristotle would regard as worthy of a free citizen, but we can organize our affairs so that we can come closer to it. If we think of education in an Aristotelian way we can see how it might play a central role in this. As his account of music makes clear, education can initiate children into the kinds of activity that are worthwhile in themselves and it can give them a grasp of the difference between things that are valuable for their own sake and those that are valuable only as a means. So, although Aristotle's best city may be an unattainable ideal, it does have a relevance to the real world.

Notes

[1] Translations from the Greek are my own.

[2] Verbally it is often closer to the *Eudemian Ethics* than to the *Nicomachean Ethics* but the doctrine of the two is, in relevant respects, fundamentally the same. There are also parallels with the surviving passages of Aristotle's lost work, the *Protrepticus*.

Bibliography

Curren, Randall (2000). *Aristotle on the Necessity of Public Education* (Lanham, MD: Rowman and Littlefield).

Depew, David J. (1991). "Politics, Music, and Contemplation in Aristotle's Ideal State," in Keyt and Miller (1991), pp. 346–80.

Keyt, D. and Miller, F. (1991). *A Companion to Aristotle's "Politics"* (Oxford and Cambridge, MA: Blackwell).

Kraut, Richard (1997). *Aristotle: "Politics" Books VII and VIII* (Oxford: Clarendon Press).

Kraut, Richard (2002). *Aristotle: Political Philosophy* (Oxford: Oxford University Press), pp. 192–239.

Lord, Carnes (1984). *Education and Culture in the Political Thought of Aristotle* (Ithaca, NY: Cornell University Press).

Lord, Carnes (1990). "Politics and Education in Aristotle's *Politics*," comm. by D. A. Rees, in Patzig (1990), pp. 202–19.

Miller, Fred D., Jr. (1995). *Nature, Justice, and Rights in Aristotle's "Politics"* (Oxford: Clarendon Press), pp. 191–251.

Mulgan, R. G. (2000). "Was Aristotle an Aristotelian Social Democrat?" *Ethics*, 111, pp. 79–101.

Nussbaum, Martha C. (1990). "Nature, Function and Capability: Aristotle on Political Distribution," comm. by David Charles, in Patzig (1990), pp. 153–201.

Patzig, Gunther (ed.) (1990). *Aristoteles' "Politik": Akten des XI. Symposium Aristotelicum* (Göttingen: Vandenhoeck and Ruprecht).

Rowe, Christopher (1991). "Aims and Methods in Aristotle's *Politics*," in Keyt and Miller (1991), pp. 57–74.

Solmsen, Friedrich (1964). "Leisure and Play in Aristotle's Ideal State," *Rheinisches Museum für Philologie*, 107, pp. 193–220.

Part V

Productive Knowledge

A. Rhetoric

37

The Nature and Goals of Rhetoric

CHRISTOF RAPP

In general, rhetoric is concerned with the persuasive in all fields of discourse. Aristotle himself defines the art of rhetoric as the capacity of discerning what is persuasive and what is not. The goal of Aristotle's work *Rhetoric*, however, is much more restricted, insofar as it does not discuss the persuasive in general, but rather focuses on the persuasiveness of public speeches. Such speeches are typically given at well-defined occasions: in the people's assembly, at judicial trials, and at certain ceremonial gatherings; this is why Aristotle is mainly interested in the three respective genres of public speech, namely the deliberative-political speech (*genos sumbouleutikon*), the judicial – either accusing or defending – speech (*dikanikon*), and the ceremonial or epideictic speech (*epideiktikon*). This, of course, is not to say that the *Rhetoric* has nothing to tell us about the principles of persuasiveness in general: it is plain that a theory of the persuasive public speech somehow presupposes a general theory of persuasiveness. Nevertheless, Aristotle's approach to rhetoric is essentially informed by the idea that an art of rhetoric is particularly useful for those addressing an amateurish and sometimes even depraved mass audience, while we need no additional technique of persuasion, or almost none, when teaching, say, geometry to our students.

When observing speakers who deliver their speeches at these public events we will find that some of them are more successful than others and that some of them proceed arbitrarily, while others do these things through an acquired ability or method. Hence it is possible to investigate the reasons as to why some of them are successful and some are not, and once we have grasped the causes of persuasiveness in public speech, we are in a position to construct a theory or, in Aristotle's terminology, an art (*technê*) of persuasiveness in public speeches, i.e. an art of rhetoric.

What would such an art of rhetoric look like? Surprisingly enough, it turns out that the art of rhetoric that Aristotle develops in his work *Rhetoric* can borrow concepts and theorems from various disciplines and especially from such disciplines as the philosopher happens to be interested in. Above all, Aristotle makes it clear that he sees rhetoric as closely related to dialectic, which he understands as the art of arguing on the basis of other people's opinions. But the rhetorician in the Aristotelian sense needs not only the logical proficiency of the dialectician but also the competence of the "political" philosopher who, in Aristotle's terminology, is concerned with character, virtue, and the laws and institutions of the *polis*. But that does not yet exhaust the art of rhetoric:

Aristotle also admits that style (*lexis*) – a topic that originally belongs to literature and has been discussed in the theory of tragedy – may have a certain impact on persuasion. Finally, the last chapters of his *Rhetoric* tackle a topic that was prominent in the manuals of his time but has not even been announced in the previous parts of Aristotle's own book, namely the division and ordering of several parts of a speech.

Hence, even a quick glance at Aristotle's *Rhetoric* reveals that, for him, the art of rhetoric is a blend of several approaches and heterogeneous disciplines. The following survey will try to distinguish and characterize the various approaches. At the end of the chapter we will return to the general purpose and goals of Aristotle's art of rhetoric.

The Dialectical Approach

In the opening line of the book *Rhetoric* Aristotle calls the discipline of rhetoric a "counterpart" (*antistrophos*) to dialectic (*Rhet* I.1 1354a1). This is clearly an allusion to Plato's *Gorgias* (464bff), where Socrates characterizes rhetoric as the counterpart to cookery in the soul. Though this is a much debated slogan, there is no doubt that Aristotle wants to understand rhetoric either as analogous or similar to, or as a special application or proper part of, dialectic (actually, Aristotle makes both kinds of statement in one and the same line, when he says that rhetoric is a part of and similar to dialectic: *Rhet* I.2 1356a30ff). How can this similarity be substantiated? In *Topics* I.2 Aristotle cited what he called *enteuxis* (encounter with the people) as one of the situations in which dialectic is useful (*Topics* I.2 101a30–4), because it allows us to debate with people on the basis of their own convictions. Aristotle is clearly referring back to this passage in *Rhetoric* (I.1 1355a29), when he speaks of *enteuxis* and says that rhetoric builds its arguments from generally accepted (*koina*) views (*Rhet* I.1 1355a27). Hence rhetoric here seems to be a form of dialectic practiced when facing the people. The basic idea behind this dialectical approach seems to be the following: rhetoric concerns the *pithanon*, the persuasive, and the *pistis*, the process of persuasion; persuasion is a kind of proof (*apodeixis*), since we tend to be most convinced of something when we think that it has been proven (*Rhetoric* I.1 1355a5–6). A proof is a kind of *sullogismos*, and it is the task of the dialectician to investigate all types of *sullogismoi* (*Rhet* I.1 1355a8–10). We can understand what Aristotle meant in describing the process of persuasion as a proof, or a rhetorical proof, based on his remark that the orator takes his arguments from generally accepted views, that is, views accepted by the audience. Hence the underlying analysis of the process of persuasion will probably look like this: in order to convince the audience of a sentence B, the dialectically instructed speaker will take up a sentence A already approved by the audience from which the target sentence B deductively follows, or at least seems to follow. Given certain subsidiary conditions, whoever is convinced of proposition A will also be convinced of proposition B once he learns that there is an inferential connection between both propositions. This analysis of persuasion assigns rhetoric to the purview of dialectic, since according to Aristotle's definition, dialectic concerns inference from accepted (*endoxa*) premises and since the opinions that are generally or for the most part accepted, which can be used as rhetorical premises, make up a subset of all accepted premises.

This dialectical analysis of the rhetorical process of persuasion has a number of far-reaching consequences. Above all, this analysis makes it inevitable that inferences or apparent inferences, proofs or proof-like means will play a central role in his method of persuasion. And indeed, Aristotle states that the rhetorical proof, the enthymeme, is the "body of persuasion" (*Rhet* I.1 1354a15), which is most probably the metaphorical way for saying that it is the core of persuasion. The concept of the enthymeme has been subject to many scholarly controversies, but on closer examination it turns out that Aristotle essentially regards it as an argument or proof that has been adjusted to the conditions of public speech. And since every proof is a syllogism, the enthymeme is a kind of syllogism, or syllogism of a kind. Hence Aristotle says that in order to formulate good enthymemes we must have the same competence that is required for all other kinds of syllogisms and additionally we must have a further competence concerning the differences between regular and rhetorical *sullogismoi* (*Rhet* I.1 1355a11–14). He adds that there are exactly two factors that the dialectician has to keep in mind if he wants to become a rhetorician as well. Firstly, the typical subjects of public speech do not – as do the subjects of dialectic and theoretical philosophy – belong to the things that are necessarily the case, but are among those things which are the goal of practical deliberation and can also be otherwise (*Rhet* I.2 1357a22–4). Secondly, as opposed to well-trained dialecticians, the audience of public speech is characterized by an intellectual insufficiency; above all, the members of a jury or assembly are not accustomed to following a long chain of inferences (*Rhet* I.2 1357a3–4). Therefore enthymemes need not be as precise as a scientific proof and should be shorter than ordinary dialectical arguments. This, however, is not to say that the enthymeme is defined by incompleteness and brevity. Rather, it is a sign of a well-executed enthymeme that the content and the number of its premises are adjusted to the intellectual capacities of the public audience.

By emphasizing the dialectical nature of rhetoric in chapter I.1 of the *Rhetoric* Aristotle also defuses a series of objections that could be levelled at any study of rhetoric that a philosopher would compose. The implicit background of the Book's first chapter is the charge that rhetoric could not be a *technê*, since it does not have any particular range of objects that it conveys knowledge of. Aristotle dispenses with this objection in emphasizing that dialectic, whose fundamental methodical character no one would doubt, also lacks a delimited range of objects, and that rhetoric plays the same role in the acts of accusing and defending that dialectic does for those of criticizing and supporting a thesis. Against the prejudice that rhetoric only aims at slander, distracting the judge, and agitating emotions that obscure judgment, Aristotle could respond that this may hold true of conventional rhetoric, but not of a dialectically conceived rhetoric with the rhetorical proof, the enthymeme, at its center.

The Moral-psychological Approach

So far one could have the impression that Aristotle's theory of rhetoric is exclusively based on dialectic. That rhetoric can be understood as a specific way of applying dialectic is certainly the basic idea for Aristotle's project, which he deliberately states at the beginning of the book in order to formulate what marks his project off from all the other manuals of rhetoric. But the situation changes when it comes to the introduction of the three technical means of persuasion (*pisteis*) at the beginning of the second chapter of the first Book. The doctrine that there are three such means of persuasion constitutes the core thesis of the first two Books of Aristotle's *Rhetoric*, and it structures the agenda of these two Books. "Technical" means of persuasion must rest on a method and they must be provided by the speaker himself, whereas pre-existing facts, such as oaths, witnesses, testimonies, etc. count as non-technical. Technical means of persuasion are situated either in the character of the speaker, in the emotional state of the hearer, or in the argument (*logos*) itself. Persuasion is accomplished by character whenever the speech is held in such a way as to render the speaker worthy of credence. The emotional dispositions of the audience are important for rhetorical persuasion, since we do not judge in the same way when we grieve or rejoice or when we are friendly or hostile. Finally, we persuade by the argument itself when we prove or seem to prove that something is the case. For Aristotle, there are two species of arguments: inductions and deductions (*Posterior Analytics* I.1 71a5ff). The inductive argument in the domain of rhetoric is the example (*paradeigma*), and the deductive argument in rhetoric is the enthymeme (*Rhet* I.2 1356a1–13).

These are the famous three technical means of persuasion: *êthos*, *pathos*, and *logos*. This three-fold division has always been met with marked sympathy among the recipients of the *Rhetoric*, and practically all subsequent modernizations of Aristotle have preserved exactly this tri-partition of the persuasive process, although variously weighted. Obviously, this indicates a kind of appreciation for the fact that a philosopher made famous for his achievements in logic, philosophy of science, and metaphysics remains sensible enough not to reduce everything to inferential validity and conclusiveness. Despite the not unwarranted success of this approach, the Aristotelian tri-partition of persuasion is still encumbered by a couple of obscurities; for example, Aristotle never tells us explicitly why there are just these three means of persuasion. The best we can do for the theoretical justification of this theory is to take recourse to the triangle of object, speaker, and addressee and associate each of the three persuasive means with one of these three factors. Nonetheless, this model is introduced not in chapter I.2, where we would expect a justification of the tripartite analysis of persuasion, but rather in chapter I.3, in order to distinguish between the three genres of speech (*Rhet* I 3 1358a37–b2), which could have been justified just as easily without this triangle.

However, once the doctrine of the three means of persuasion has been introduced, Aristotle reveals for the first time in the *Rhetoric* that he regards the discipline of rhetoric not just as an application of dialectic, but also as derived from moral psychology. Immediately after the introduction of this doctrine he continues: "Since persuasion comes about through these three means, it is clear that to grasp an understanding of them is the function of one who can form *syllogismoi* and be observant about characters and virtues and, third, about emotions (what each of the emotions is and what are its qualities and from what it comes to be and how). The result is that rhetoric is a certain kind or offshoot of dialectic and the study of character (which can be called '*hê politikê*')" (*Rhet* I.2 1356a20–7).

582

In this passage, rhetoric or, rather, the specific competence that is needed for either the elaboration of a rhetorical theory or the practice of rhetoric, is clearly characterized as a blend or combination of dialectical expertise and ethical theory. In this context the dialectical competence is clearly responsible for the logical and argumentative aspect of persuasion. The use of the word *hê politikê* (literally: the political art), with which he describes the second required competence, is not surprising here, since Aristotle often uses it to embrace the practical disciplines of ethics and political philosophy. But it is remarkable that he introduces moral philosophy as the "study of character," which is probably due to the fact that he wants to highlight the particular function of moral philosophy within rhetoric or the field where moral philosophy and rhetoric overlap, namely a certain expertise in questions concerning character. Since a person's character is manifested in her emotional responses, it seems clear that the study of character is apt to include *êthos* and *pathos*, character and emotion, as well; and this specific focus justifies the parlance of "moral psychology."

We understand, then, that rhetoric is an offshoot of dialectic and moral psychology precisely because we need dialectic in order to construe arguments, i.e. deductions, inductions, and deduction-like inferences (this is the *pistis* called "logos"), and we need moral psychology in order to persuade by character and emotions, i.e. the *pisteis* of *êthos* and *pathos*. It is important to note here that the expertise that is achieved in moral psychology is applied to purposes which are not connected with the internal goals of moral philosophy – we do not apply this expertise in order to understand what it means for the character to be good or bad or to distinguish between appropriate and inappropriate emotional responses. On the contrary, Aristotle uses expertise in moral psychology for a completely different purpose, namely for the questions of how the speaker can influence the listeners' emotions by speech, and not by education, and how the speaker can present himself as having a certain type of character. And "presenting oneself as having a virtuous character" is by no means the same as "acquiring and shaping a virtuous character." Even if a speaker happens to have a good or virtuous character, this would not be enough to make the audience think of him as credible and trustworthy.

Having the appropriate emotional responses is crucial for Aristotle's concept of moral virtue, and being morally virtuous is more or less the same as having a good character. Now, since in Aristotle's *Rhetoric* emotions and character play a crucial role, many authors jumped to the conclusion that an Aristotelian rhetorician must be concerned with the formation of good and virtuous characters.[1] I think that this approach is in principle mistaken, for the simple reason that the aim of rhetorical persuasion is a certain judgment (*krisis*), not an action or practical decision (*prohairesis*). Of course, it is true that, in the long run, the improvement of decisions and judgments in the assembly could improve the general state of the *polis*, and the state of the *polis* again can have an important impact on the education of its citizens; hence a successful virtuous speaker who aims at the continuous improvement of his *polis* will not remain without effect on his fellow citizens' character. But still, this indirect, long-term effect must be distinguished from the direct pedagogical influence of speeches, since for Aristotle the process that we would call "moral education" should ideally start in youth and has to be connected with praise and blame, with individual punishment and reward; and, most of all, it is a process that normally takes years of constant encouragement and exhortation, so that there is little hope that a speech, anonymously directed at hundreds of adult listeners, could directly help to improve the character of the audience. At the end of the *Nicomachean Ethics* Aristotle writes: "Now if speeches were in themselves enough to make men good, they would justly, as Theognis says, have won very great rewards, and such rewards should have been provided; but as things are. . . . they are not able to encourage the many to nobility and goodness" (X.9 1179b4–10).

At the beginning of the second Book of the *Rhetoric*, where Aristotle switches from the discussion of argumentative means of persuasion to the non-argumentative ones, he says: "But since rhetoric is concerned with making a judgment (*krisis*) . . . it is necessary not only to look to the argument, that it may be demonstrative and persuasive but also to construct a view of himself as a certain kind of person and to prepare the audience" (II.1 1377b20–4). It is fairly clear from this passage that *êthos* and *pathos* are introduced into rhetoric precisely because they have an influence on our judgments, and not because the speaker tries to improve the character of his audience. The mechanisms by which *êthos* and *pathos* influence the judgment are relatively simple: we do not judge in the same way, Aristotle says, when we grieve or rejoice or when we are friendly or hostile. Thus, the orator has to "prepare the audience," i.e. arouse its emotions precisely because emotions have the power to modify our judgments in a predictable way: to a judge in a friendly mood, the person about whom he is going to judge seems not to do any wrong or only in a minor way; but to the judge in an angry mood, the same person will seem to do just the opposite (see *Rhet* II.1 1378a1–5).

As for *êthos*, if the speaker appears to be credible, the audience will form the second-order judgment that propositions put forward by the credible speaker are true or acceptable. This is especially important in cases where there is no exact knowledge but rather room for doubt. But how does the speaker manage to appear as a credible person? He must display practical intelligence (*phronêsis*), a virtuous character, and good will (*Rhetoric* II.1 1378a6ff); for, if he displayed none of these, the audience would doubt that he is able to give good advice at all. Again, if he displayed *phronêsis* without virtue and good will, the audience could doubt whether the aims of the speaker are good. Finally, if he displayed *phronêsis* and virtue without good will, the audience could still doubt whether the speaker puts forward the best suggestion, though he might know what it is. But if he displays all of them, Aristotle concludes, it cannot (rationally) be doubted that his suggestions are credible. This is Aristotle's official description of *êthos* as one of the technical means of persuasion. It takes no more than 13 Bekker-lines to explain the underlying theory. The chapters on various types of character (*Rhet* II.11–17) are not intended as a contribution to *êthos* in the technical sense. Here and there in the *Rhetoric* the speaker finds suggestions for how to present himself as virtuous, but the other two factors of *êthos* are mostly neglected.

As we have seen, the art of rhetoric needs the specific competence of the moral philosopher or psychologist precisely because two of the three technical means of persuasion rely on concepts that fall under the competence of moral psychology, namely *pathos* and *êthos*. The dialectical approach to rhetoric must be supplemented by the moral-psychological one, since conclusiveness of argument is not the only factor that influences the judgment of the public audience.

Rhetoric as Dealing with Accepted Beliefs (*endoxa*)

The three genres of speech have different targets: In the judicial speech we try to persuade the jury of what is just or unjust, in the deliberative speech we try to persuade the people of what is good and useful or bad and harmful to the *polis*, and in the ceremonial speech we try to praise someone or something as noble or to blame him for being shameful. Hence the orator in the public speech must know what it is to be just/unjust, good/bad, noble/shameful, or, at least, he must know what people regard as just, good, noble, etc. And indeed, major parts of the *Rhetoric* are dedicated to the definition of such concepts and to listing those things that are said to be just, good, noble, etc. And these are not the only concepts that are relevant in the public speech: Since happiness, for example, is regularly regarded as the highest good, the orator is also expected to know what happiness consists in and which are the things that contribute to happiness, and, to take another example, since virtue is regarded as noble and praiseworthy, the orator should know what virtue consists in and which are the most appreciated virtues, etc. Therefore the prospective rhetorician can learn from the *Rhetoric* that happiness, for example, is to be defined as "*eupraxia* combined with virtue or as self-sufficiency (*autarkeia*) in life or as the most pleasant life accompanied with security or as abundance of possessions and bodily goods with the ability to defend and use these things" (*Rhet* I.5 1360b14–18), or that "good" is "whatever is chosen for itself and that for the sake of which we choose something else and what everything having perception or intelligence aims at or what everything would (aim at) if it could acquire intelligence" (*Rhet* I.6 1362a21–5), or that virtue is "an ability (*dunamis*) . . . that is productive and preservative of goods, and an ability for doing good in many and great ways, actually in all ways in all things" (*Rhet* I.9 1366a36–b1).

That the rhetorician must be equipped with at least provisional definitions of those ethical concepts is an additional requirement, because it is neither explicitly included in the dialectical competence for deductions and conclusiveness nor in the moral-psychological competence for *pathos* and *êthos*. On the one hand it seems plausible to assume that those concepts can be imported from the ethical-political theory (which we have called "moral-psychology" so far), because all of them derive from an ethical context. Beside its relevance to the two non-argumentative means of persuasion, *pathos* and *êthos*, this could be a second major respect in which moral psychology could contribute to the theory of rhetoric. On the other hand Aristotle indicates that the respective definitions of those ethical concepts do not represent his own well-considered philosophical views, by introducing them with a "*estô* – let it be," by which he distances himself in a way from the content of the sentence that follows. And indeed, since these concepts and their definitions occur as parts of propositions which are to be used in arguments from plausible and accepted premises, the definitions of these concepts should be subsumed under the broader heading of "*endoxa*." The selection of accepted propositions or *endoxa*, however, seems to fall in the competence of the dialectician. Therefore it is not entirely clear whether Aristotle wanted to entrust the dialectician or the ethical-political philosopher with the selection of the relevant concepts and propositions. In any case, in order to assess the status of these "endoxic" definitions, which, after all, occupy a considerable part of the *Rhetoric*, it would be useful to know whether these definitions just represent common-sense or whether they also inform us about

Aristotle's own ethical views. There are, however, some indications that we should not expect a clear-cut distinction.

Accidental selection of principles

Since for Aristotle dialectic is a procedure for finding arguments for and against any and all theses, any commitment to certain particular premises and positions is foreign to dialectic as such. Yet it still makes pragmatic sense for the dialectician to be informed about more or less successful premises. Aristotle's concrete recommendation in the *Topics* is to amass collections of accepted opinions in the various areas of knowledge – in part by studying the pertinent texts (*Topics* I.14 105b12–15) – in order to deploy them as premises in dialectical disputes. Now, if the dialectician is especially skilled in sorting through these accepted opinions according to their prospective success, then something remarkable occurs, for among the most successful dialectical premises will be found some that are also useful for scientific demonstration. But in reaching scientific principles the dialectician is no longer practicing dialectic in the strict sense, but rather has overstepped these bounds and entered into the individual disciplines of the principles thus grasped (*Rhet* I.4 1359b12–16). Interestingly enough, it is in the *Rhetoric* that Aristotle is particularly sensitive to this kind of problem, and it seems as if Aristotle even regards this tendency as a threat to his dialectical conception of rhetoric, for he says: "to the degree that someone makes better choice of the premises, he will have created knowledge different from dialectic and rhetoric without its being recognized; for if he succeeds in hitting on first principles, the knowledge will no longer be dialectic or rhetoric but the science of which one grasps the first principles" (*Rhet* I.2 1358a23–6). It should be added that "accidentally hitting on first principles" is perhaps not the same as the identification of a true general proposition *as* principle, since in the latter case we also have to assess the explanatory power of the respective proposition, which is only possible if we apply them to possible demonstrations. But in any case, principles must be true propositions, so that Aristotle seems to expect that some of the selected *endoxa* will happen to be true sentences or even principles that are by no means opposed to his own philosophical convictions.

Ambiguity of provisional definition and general conviction

The rhetorician has to be equipped with opinions that are accepted by the majority of people in order to mention these opinions or to build rhetorical proofs around them. For his purpose, generally accepted (*koina*) opinions are more effective than first principles, since the latter cannot do the same job if they are not generally known or generally accepted. This seems to be the reason why the first Book of the *Rhetoric* gives us lists of accepted opinions of what is good, just, pleasant, etc. The second Book of the *Rhetoric* starts with a different program: from chapter 2 to chapter 11 it lists definitions of various emotions. When Aristotle switches from the first Book with its endoxic definitions to the definition of emotions he emphasizes that he is about to provide definitions in the same way as he did before: "Just as we have drawn up a list of sentences (*protaseis*) on the subjects discussed earlier [i.e., in the first Book], let us do so about these [i.e., the emotions] and let us analyse them in the way mentioned" (*Rhet* II.1 1378a26–9). He seems to assert that the definitions of the various emotions will have the same status as the sentences or definitions about what is good, just, pleasant, etc. in the first Book. And indeed, he introduces the definition of most of the emotions with the same formulation "*estô* – let it be," thus indicating that he does not want to be committed to the details of the definition that follows. This is an interesting development, since the role of the emotions is not really compatible with what is going on in the first Book: as we said, Aristotle gives us generally accepted sentences in the first Book of the *Rhetoric* because it is important for the speaker to know what people think about the good, the just, the pleasant, etc. in order to hit upon their very convictions when formulating proofs with those accepted sentences as premises. But the situation is different with the use of the emotions: in order to arouse the emotions of the audience the speaker has to know what the emotions are like and *not* what people think they are like: even a broadly accepted sentence can be false, but with a false understanding of the nature of a certain emotion we will not succeed in arousing this particular emotion. Conversely we can succeed in arousing a certain emotion on the basis of an appropriate definition, even if the audience addressed is completely ignorant of this definition. It seems then that we have at least two different uses of *endoxa* within the *Rhetoric*: In the first use the speaker needs them as premises of his arguments, since a certain subset of *endoxa*, the opinions that are commonly accepted (the *koina*), represent the convictions of the audience; in the other use we are obviously faced with definitions that are *endoxa* in the sense that they do not represent the full and definite scientific definition. In this context the respective definitions are provisionally adopted and contain, most probably, something that Aristotle would regard as an appropriate description of the emotion in question; but since the context of rhetoric is not the right place to argue for those definitions, they are introduced without any background theory. Furthermore, it is not possible to assign some *endoxa* to the first, and some others to the second kind of use, because Aristotle sometimes ascribes different applications to one and the same list of *endoxa*, e.g. when he declares that the definitions of the various emotions in the second Book can also be applied for certain purposes from the first Book.

Confusion of accepted definitions and accounts of accepted views

As we have seen, the *Rhetoric* is interested in *endoxa* partly because the rhetorician has to engage the convictions of the audience. Therefore, what we expect to find in the corresponding chapters of the *Rhetoric* are catalogues of commonly held opinions. But even a quick glance at the *Rhetoric*'s first Book is sufficient to tell that Aristotle is far from collecting empirically held views: in chapters I.4–14 quotations, for example, are relatively rare. Also, the chapters that present the lists of *endoxa* are not just collections or catalogues; on the contrary, some of them are deductively structured insofar as they articulate consequences that can be derived from an initial definition of the respective concept. Furthermore, there are some examples which were most probably never meant as commonly accepted convictions: when it comes to the definition of pleasure in chapter I.11, for example, Aristotle applies the Platonic definition that pleasure is a certain *kinesis* of the soul and a sudden and perceptible settling down (*katastasis*) in its natural state (*Rhet* I.11 1369 33–5). It would be unpardonably naïve to think that such a definition gets introduced because it was, at a certain time, particularly popular among the Athenian judges and councilmen; it is even likely that ordinary people who participated in the democratic institutions had never heard of the Academic controversies about the nature of pleasure, from which the quoted definition was taken. Therefore it is much more plausible to assume that here we are dealing with a definition borrowed from a context of philosophical discussion and found suitable as the background to certain kinds of pleasure that seem to have been especially popular, i.e. the pleasures we enjoy when satisfying our bodily needs. The relevant difference would be that between a commonly accepted definition of pleasure and a definition of commonly appreciated pleasures; although the latter definition itself is not commonly known and accepted, the concepts of restoration and nature, which are used in this definition, can be used for some unproblematic and widespread assumptions about the nature of pleasures, for example, that habit is pleasant, because what becomes habitual is almost like nature, that necessities are unpleasant, etc.

In light of these indications we will have to draw a more differentiated picture of *endoxa* in the *Rhetoric*: First, the fact that the definitions in the first Book of the *Rhetoric* are presented as *endoxa* and not as true and primary principles does not imply that they are always mistaken; very often the difference between *endoxa* and scientific or philosophical sentences just lies in the degree of precision; also, the well-considered, philosophical definitions have to cover the entire phenomenon, while non-refined *endoxa* are typically restricted to certain parts of the phenomenon; for example, when defining *eudaimonia* in the *Rhetoric* Aristotle gives us four unconnected definitions, each representing different aspects of *eudaimonia* (virtue, self-sufficiency, pleasure, external goods). Second, even if a certain definition given in the *Rhetoric* coincides with the corresponding teaching in the philosophical writings, this does not mean that the same definition in the *Rhetoric* must be taken as the result of a philosophical discussion; sometimes *endoxa* just happen to have the same content as scientific or philosophical principles, which can be due to the phenomenon of "accidental selection of principles": the rhetorician wants to formulate a plausible and broadly accepted conviction, but accidentally hits on a principle whose correctness can be affirmed by philosophical investigation. Third, most of the definitions of ethical concepts given in the *Rhetoric* are not meant as quotations of actually stated opinions. As the diagnosed "confusion of accepted definitions and accounts of accepted views" teaches us, the attempt to ascribe the given definitions to certain schools or individuals seems to be futile (even if some of the definitions, e.g. in the case of *eudaimonia*, may have historical paradigms), and it is also instructive to regard those definitions as Aristotle's own formulations for what he himself conceived as the popular views about things such as happiness, virtue, etc. This again is the reason why we often find his own vocabulary in the endoxic definitions. Fourth, we have to keep in mind that in some cases the endoxic definitions oscillate between the roles of provisional definition and generally accepted conviction. In these cases the content of the definitions given may come close to Aristotle's own well-considered views, but then the difference lies in the fact that the *Rhetoric* wants to *apply* the respective concepts without being interested in the theoretical background, while the philosophical inquiry into the same concepts would be interested precisely in those theoretical presuppositions that are absent from the *Rhetoric*.

The Stylistic Approach

So far we have seen that the nature of rhetoric is to be characterized as a hybrid of at least two types of competence, the competence of the dialectician and the competence of the moral-political philosopher. In addition, the use of the three technical means of persuasion depends in various ways on the knowledge of certain *endoxa*. Everything that the rhetorician has to know about those "means of persuasion" is developed at length in the first two Books of the *Rhetoric*. But once we proceed to the third Book of the same work we find two further approaches which are entirely independent from the previous ones and are affiliated with quite different disciplines: In chapters 1–12 of the third Book Aristotle discusses *lexis*, i.e. diction or linguistic form, and in chapters 13–19 he discusses the parts of the speech and their ordering (*taxis*). Where do these additional approaches come from and how do they fit into the dialectical and political approaches to rhetoric?

As far as diction, *lexis*, is concerned, Aristotle seems to think that it is a topic that originally derives from literature (*Rhet* III.1 1404a20–1). And indeed, the topic of *lexis* also plays a role in Aristotle's book *Poetics*, where diction is discussed as one aspect of tragedy besides plot, melody, thought, etc. Ultimately, the discussion of diction or style in the *Poetics* consists in the distinctions between various kinds of words, such as ordinary word, strange word, ornamental word (*epitheton*), and metaphor, together with some considerations as to how these various kinds of words are to be deployed in the language of tragedy. The *Rhetoric*'s discussion of *lexis* actually seems to presuppose the treatment of diction from *Poetics* 20–22 (*Rhet* III.2 1404b7–9) and adjusts its distinctions to prose style, for which the poetic kinds of words, those that are mentioned in the *Poetics*, turn out to be inappropriate. The *Poetics* itself at one point refers to a treatise about rhetoric (*Poetics* 1456a35), which apparently had not yet included any treatment of *lexis*; hence it is tempting to think that a discussion of *lexis* was not intended at the time that the basic core of the *Rhetoric* I and II was composed and that chapters III.1–12 were added to Books I and II afterwards.

It is also remarkable that the topic of *lexis* had not earned a single word of mention before the transition from the second to the third Book of the *Rhetoric*; here, at the beginning of the third Book, Aristotle justifies the inclusion of the stylistic approach that has to deal with *lexis* as follows: "Our next subject will be *lexis*. For it is not enough to know *what* we ought to say; but one must also know *how* to formulate it" (*Rhet* III.1 1403b15–16). Later on, he adds: "The subject of *lexis*, however, has a certain small, but necessary impact on every teaching; for to speak in one way rather than another does make some difference with respect to clarity" (*Rhet* III.1 1404a8–10). In the same context he retrospectively subsumes the content of the first two Books, the three technical means of persuasion and everything that he has said about the "What" of speech, under the heading of "*dianoia*," thought, and opposes it to *lexis*. At first glance, this seems to be a clear-cut distinction, which allows us to regard the discussion of *lexis* as complementary to the topic of the first two Books. One could, however, raise doubts as to whether the discussion of the first two Books was really confined to the "What" of speech and refrained from commenting on the "How": For example, much of the advice that Aristotle gives for the formulation of the enthymeme in the first two Books seems to rest on the assumption that it is more or less the same argument that can be

589

formulated in different ways. The "elenctic" enthymeme, e.g., is characterized in terms of *lexis* when Aristotle says that it brings the opposites together in concise form, thus making the argument clearer (*Rhet* II.24 1400b26–9). And in the discussion of metaphor, which belongs, without any doubt, to the question of diction, to *lexis*, Aristotle recommends that the rhetorician not formulate the metaphor "from far away (*pôrrothen*)," and he gives the same advice for the formulation of the enthymeme, which is the central persuasive tool within the domain of thought or *dianoia* (*Rhet* II.22 1395b22 – 5 and I.2 1357a3 – 4).

All in all, one can get the impression that the stylistic or linguistic approach to rhetoric was not included in Aristotle's original concept of an art of rhetoric. Even so he eventually became aware of the fact that the selection of words by which we express one and the same argument could have an impact on persuasiveness, because it directly affects the clarity of what we say. Alternatively, we could refer to Aristotle's own statement that by nature the question of how persuasiveness can be produced from the things themselves is prior to the question of how to formulate these things in words (*Rhet* III.1 1403b18–20); on the basis of this statement one could argue that at first Aristotle elaborated what he himself regarded as primary, namely the subject of thought, *dianoia*, whereas the discussion of style was added as a sort of supplement.

The Conventional Approach

In chapters III.13–19 Aristotle discusses the various parts of a speech; this again seems to be an entirely different approach. Given Aristotle's general attitude to the rhetorical techniques of his predecessors and given the fact that their *technê* was centered around the division of parts of speeches (*Rhet* I.1 1354 b17–20) it is surprising, to say the least, that Aristotle also participates in this kind of discussion. This is particularly true in view of the fact that Pre-Aristotelian rhetoric used to organize the art of rhetoric in accordance with the several parts of a speech and their ordering, while Aristotle had explicitly replaced this traditional structure of the rhetorical art by his system of the three technical means of persuasion. Nevertheless, the end of the second and the beginning of the third Book of his *Rhetoric* tries to accommodate the respective chapters with the idea that the discussion of parts and their order (*taxis*) is what naturally follows the treatment of *dianoia* and the treatment of *lexis*. That this is more of an ad-hoc-systematization than the execution of a logically structured plan becomes clear when we consider that the chapters on *taxis* not only distinguish various parts but also repeat methods that have already been treated in the previous Books. Further, the terminology of the chapters on *taxis* is not always in line with the rest of the *Rhetoric*. And finally, it is remarkable that Aristotle adopts a four-part-model of speech (prologue – statement of the case – proof of the case – epilogue) though he had stressed that there are only two necessary parts (statement and proof of the case), neither of which corresponds to any of the traditional speech parts. In this context it might be of some significance that this four-part-model is more or less the same as Theodectes' division of speech, with whom Aristotle was said to be acquainted. We can speculate, then, not without plausibility, that the last chapters III.13–19 of the *Rhetoric* build upon a model of speech and rhetoric that Aristotle had adopted from someone else, perhaps from Theodectes, and that it was written quite independently from the rest of the work. Anyhow, it is clear that the approach to rhetoric that Aristotle himself or a later editor labelled as "*taxis*" is much closer to the style of traditional rhetoric than what we can learn from, say, the dialectical approach.

Thus, the final approach to rhetoric that we can identify in Aristotle's work *Rhetoric* is extraordinary, insofar as it is – as opposed to the previous approaches – more or less the conventional way of treating rhetoric. But why should we assume that Aristotle could have contributed to a project whose shortcomings he clearly saw? One part of the explanation could be this: according to ancient testimonies Aristotle collected previous rhetorical theories in a book called *Technôn Sunagôgê*; further Aristotle himself mentions a work by the name of *Theodecteia*, and some think that this was Aristotle's report on Theodectes' art of rhetoric. If Aristotle had composed collections of previous arts of rhetoric, including those which were focused on the parts of the speech, it is not difficult to imagine that he took one of these schemes, perhaps the one he regarded as the least bad, in order to illustrate how he himself would make use of the various parts of a speech. Another part of the explanation is probably this: Although he did not think that the division of speeches into parts and subparts is a preferable approach to the topic of persuasion, he came to acknowledge that a certain structure of the speech can even support an argumentatively ordered art of persuasion, as for example when the preamble is used to clarify the subject-matter of the speech (*Rhet* III.14 1415 a21–3) and the epilogue to lay out the conclusions that have been reached (*Rhet* III.19 1419 b28–32).

The Purpose Of Rhetoric

The previous sections have tried to characterize the nature of rhetoric by the several approaches to the topic of persuasion that we can find in Aristotle's book *Rhetoric*. It remains to comment on the possible goals and uses of Aristotle's technique of persuasion. In this context the question arises as to whether Aristotle's rhetoric was designed for certain moral purposes or whether it is a morally neutral technique of persuasion. Since this discussion sometimes suffers from a significant ambiguity we should distinguish from the very beginning between two senses of what it means to be a goal or end. We can call the goal or end "internal" if it is meant to define the nature and the specific standards of a thing, and we can call it "external" if it just indicates what an independently definable thing or art can be used for. A similar distinction can be found in Aristotle's own terminology: he regularly uses the concept of *ergon* to refer to the proper function of a thing. To define the good and flourishing state of something in accordance with its own inherent measures we have to refer to this *ergon*. In the case of productive arts or crafts the *ergon* is a product which, once it has been generated, exists alongside the exercise of the respective crafts. In these cases it is the quality of the product which defines the good or excellent exercise of the respective craft. Here the use or usefulness of the craft in question is defined by its *ergon*. In other cases there are *erga* which define the inherent standard of the respective thing or capacity, but do not determine or restrict the possible uses. Dialectic and rhetoric are in this latter class: here, Aristotle carefully distinguishes between the *ergon*, which defines the nature of these disciplines, from its various uses, i.e. what it is useful for (*chrêsimon*). For example, the internal end of dialectic is to provide a method which enables us to argue for or against any given proposition (*Topics* I.1 100a18–21). But this does not yet determine what we use the dialectical skill for; the list of possible uses includes argumentative gymnastics, encounters with the people, and the selection of principles (*Topics* I.2); and still more applications are conceivable.

The same distinction between internal and external ends can be found in rhetoric. In several passages (*Rhet*. I 1 1355b10ff, I 2 1355b26–8, et al.) Aristotle explicitly refers to the *ergon* of rhetoric, and these passages coincide in saying that the internal end of rhetoric is to see or to discern what is persuasive and what is not. We are experts in rhetoric if we succeed in detecting what is potentially persuasive in any given case. Obviously, such an expertise does not by itself restrict the range of possible uses. Whatever uses we may contrive for rhetoric, it is clear, then, that they are not imposed by the nature of the rhetorical art, which is neutral with respect to possible uses. Given that Aristotelian rhetoric is based on dialectic (see above), this is a natural consequence, since it is even one of the benefits of dialectic that it helps us argue for both sides of an opposition. For the dialectician it makes no difference whether he argues for or against a given thesis. Once we regard rhetoric as part of dialectic the same must be true of rhetoric and, indeed, Aristotle makes it clear that dialectic and rhetoric are equally concerned with both sides of an opposition (*Rhet* I.1 1355a29–30). Ultimately, he says, rhetoric aims at the judgment (*krisis*) that the audience is going to make, i.e. at influence on that judgment (*Rhet* II.1 1377b20–2). And he also stresses that the rhetorical *technê* makes it possible for the speaker, for example, to demonstrate that people are both enemies and friends and to make them so when they are not . . . and to bring the audience "to whatever side he chooses" (*Rhet* II.4 1382a16–19).

Three kinds of objection could still be raised against this neutrality-thesis:

First possible objection   In an oft-quoted passage from the first chapter of the *Rhetoric* Aristotle says that one should not use rhetoric for bad purposes (*Rhet* I.1 1355a31). One could be inclined to think that this remark expresses something like a moral commitment on the part of the Aristotelian rhetorician. However, this is not exactly what the respective passage expresses: Listing the benefits of rhetoric, Aristotle says that rhetoric allows us, just as dialectic does, to argue for both sides of an opposition. Since one could think that this feature is beneficial only for those who argue for the opposite of what is true, good and just, Aristotle hastens to explain what the respective feature consists in, exactly: Even if we do not actually attempt to argue for opposite states of affairs, the capacity to detect the persuasive aspects of both sides is important, since it represents an essential aspect of the full competence of discerning what is persuasive and what is not. And this epistemic advantage, again, can be of strategic use, for example, when one has to react to fallacious or deceptive arguments of the opponents.

Hence, the remark that we should not use rhetoric for bad purposes can be seen as a comment on the external ends that Aristotle himself finds to be preferable. But by no means does it attempt to deny the possibility of misuse. On the contrary, the passage reaffirms that rhetoric, as all goods (except virtue), can be used for good as well as bad purposes, i.e. that it is morally neutral in terms of its internal ends.

Second possible objection   For Aristotle, rhetoric is not only characterized by its affinity to dialectic, but is partly also derived from moral philosophy; hence, it could be argued, we can expect a strong inclination within rhetoric towards the goals of moral philosophy. However, it turned out in section 2 (see above) that moral philosophy is introduced precisely because of its competence regarding *êthos* and *pathos* and that this competence is needed for the two corresponding means of persuasion (*pisteis*). These means of persuasion in turn aim at the audience's judgment. They are methodical ways of influencing other people's judgments and are not as such committed to any pedagogical or moral goal.

Third possible objection   The *Rhetoric* makes very much of accepted opinions (*endoxa*). Concerning these *endoxa* it is a well-known fact that Aristotle's ethical writings often mention them and sometimes develop their own theories on the basis of certain accepted opinions. Moreover, some of the *endoxa* that are referred to in the *Rhetoric* bear a striking similarity to certain views developed in the ethical writings. On the basis of this observation one could argue that because of the prominent role of *endoxa* Aristotelian rhetoric is always and necessarily interwoven with ethical theory. However, as we saw above, the presence of *endoxa* in the *Rhetoric* does not prove any ethical commitment: As opposed to the ethical writings, where commonsense convictions are introduced, among other reasons, in order to confirm, to correct, or to adjust the philosophically developed hypotheses about *eudaimonia*, the art of rhetoric deploys accepted opinions precisely because the process of persuasion has to take the already existing convictions of the audience as starting points or premises, no matter whether these convictions seem to be reasonable or not. Nevertheless, it would be inappropriate to expect that those *endoxa* are flatly opposed to Aristotle's own ethical views, firstly, because *endoxa* can happen to be true principles, secondly because the formulation of these *endoxa* reflects Aristotle's reconstruction of popular opinion, thirdly because some *endoxa* in the *Rhetoric* are not only used as general convictions, but also as arbitrarily adopted definitions (see above). Hence, it would also be mistaken to conclude from certain similarities between the *Rhetoric*'s *endoxa* and the ethical writings that the *Rhetoric* is based on the results of moral psychology or that it is meant to communicate or even to make use of the insights from the ethical writings.

External ends

We have not spoken so far about the possible uses that Aristotle himself envisages for rhetoric in general and for his own art of rhetoric in particular. An initial approach to this question would be this: if the art of rhetoric as such is neutral, its benefits or harms depend on the type of person who uses this instrument. And given the value that Aristotle's political philosophy puts on the participation of the virtuous person in public affairs, it is safe to conclude that for Aristotle rhetoric is beneficial when used by the reasonable and decent powers within this *polis*, while dangerous or even harmful when used by the depraved ones. In this context, it is tempting to speculate about whom his lectures on rhetoric were meant to address: Insofar as at least parts of his *Rhetoric* make extensive use of dialectical vocabulary, it is likely that the target group he had in mind was not entirely inexperienced in dialectics, and this again indicates that the group he addressed stood in a certain relation either to Plato's Academy (where he lectured as a younger man) or to his own Lyceum. And that these are not the kind of people that

Aristotle regarded as being extraordinarily susceptible to the temptation of misusing rhetoric for egoistic goals, is at least likely.

However, even if we concede that rhetoric is more beneficial when used by a virtuous speaker than by, say, a demagogue or potential tyrant, one could still ask why the virtuous speaker should use rhetoric at all: For, given that the virtuous speaker, if anyone does, knows what is good for the *polis*, given that he would never misuse a public speech for egoistic or shameful goals and given that he would never try to deceive his audience, what, then, does he need rhetoric for, if he just has to spell out what is good, just and true? Actually, there is one passage where Aristotle seems to respond precisely to this objection: there (*Rhet*, I.1 1355a24–9) he says that in dealing with some sorts of people it is not easy to persuade them on the basis of one's knowledge; for if it is knowledge that we want to mediate to the others, we have to teach them, but teaching in the proper sense is impossible under certain circumstances. But why, one could object, should it be impossible to teach a public audience about what is good and true? Aristotle does not explicitly address *this* question, but gives many hints that contribute to an appropriate answer:

(1) In general, Aristotle seems to be thoroughly aware of the fact that the responses of a mass audience follow different rules than the reactions of individual interlocutors (see, e.g., *Rhet* III.12 1414a8–9). (2) Furthermore, in Aristotle's view, the process of teaching and learning in the proper sense is structurally similar to the scientific proof (*apodeixis*); this means roughly that the teacher offers certain premises and conclusions and that the student has acquired the piece of knowledge in question if he understands that and how the conclusion follows from the given premises. Within that process of learning proper, it is important that the student assumes the transmitted premises to be true, even if he is not yet able to understand why they are true and what they explain (see *Topics* VIII.5 159a28–30 with *Sophistical Refutaions* 2 165b1–3). This again requires that the student trusts his teacher, whereas, in the situation of controversial public speeches, there are no reasons of principle why the addressee should trust the premises of the one speaker rather than the premises of the other or why he should trust any of the premises. (3) Similarly, learning and knowing in the paradigmatic sense are of things that are necessarily the case, while there is often no exact knowledge of the subjects of public speech (I.2 1357a22–33), because rhetoric deals with particular things that do not happen by necessity, but allow of two possibilities and even leave room for doubt. (4) Furthermore, the public speech is characterized by certain constraints and impediments, which make it difficult, if not impossible, to communicate what one regards as the truth: above all, there are time limits for speaking; additionally, the judicial speech, to take one example, has to address certain mandatory points, which consume time and distract from the central point the speaker wants to drive home; furthermore, the audience is often preoccupied by contrary opinions or hostile attitudes that may have been stirred up by the opposing speaker; finally, the public audience is not always as attentive as it should be and does not base its decisions on the relevant facts alone. All these are factors that make the public speech so different from the didactic situation of teaching and learning. (5) Last but not least, Aristotle frequently refers to the corrupt and depraved character of the mass audience (see, e.g., *Rhet* II.21 1395a32–b3, III.1 1403b35–1404a8, III.14 1415b4–6) and sometimes also to the shortcomings of the constitutions (*Rhet* III.1 1403b27–35). Concerning the

latter factor, constitutions are to be blamed if, for example they allow the orator in the public speech to address things that are outside the subject (*exô tou pragmatos legein*) and distract the audience from the case at hand. Concerning the former factor, the weakness of the average listeners, Aristotle distinguishes between their intellectual and moral insufficiencies. Due to their moral deficiencies the listeners let themselves be distracted, e.g. by emotional appeals and flattery, or decide in accordance with their own particular interest. Due to their limited intellectual capacities they are not able to follow long and complex arguments, so that the rhetorical argument will either suppress logically required steps or will avoid premises that are too general and too far removed from the conclusion; in the process of learning proper, in contrast, one would have to introduce all premises in the required order.

Maybe, then, it is necessary to use rhetorical means of persuasion if we want to effect anything in public gatherings. But why should we use the Aristotelian art of rhetoric rather than the conventional manuals of his time? This brings us, at last, back to where we started, namely to the question of what the general nature of Aristotle's rhetoric consists in. In the criticism of his predecessors Aristotle makes it clear that, as opposed to the tricks of the traditional rhetoric, the technique of his dialectic-centered rhetoric (see above) does not attempt to obscure the facts, but rather aims at identifying the persuasive aspects in every given case. And that such an argumentative type of rhetoric which allows a treatment of the respective subjects in a pertinent and transparent way is preferable goes without saying – at least from a philosophical point of view. Additionally, Aristotle seems to think that his art of rhetoric is even more effective than the so-called "arts" that are based on flattery and deception, since the famous doctrine of the three technical means of persuasion (see above) rests on an analysis of which factors influence the formation of a judgment. And with such a theoretical foundation at his disposal, the Aristotelian rhetorician should be superior to adherents of any other rhetorical style.

Note

[1] The assumption that Aristotle's art of rhetoric ultimately pursues the change or even improvement of the listeners' character can be found in various versions: cf. Garver (1994: 108); Johnstone (1980: 8ff); Rorty (1992: 73); Woerner (1990: 282).

Bibliography

Cope, E. M. [1867] (1970). *An Introduction to Aristotle's "Rhetoric"* (Cambridge: Cambridge University Press); repr. (Hildesheim: Olms, 1970).

Cope, E. M. [1877] (1970). *The "Rhetoric" of Aristotle, with a Commentary*, revd. and ed. J. E. Sandys, 3 vols. (Cambridge: Cambridge University Press, 1877). (Repr. Hildesheim: Olms, 1970).

Dufour, M. and Wartelle, A. (1960–73). *Aristote, "Rhétorique,"* ed. and trans., 3 vols. (Paris: Les Belles Lettres).

Furley, D. J. and Nehamas, A. (eds.) (1994). *Aristotle's "Rhetoric"* (Princeton, NJ: Princeton University Press).

Garver, E. (1994). *Aristotle's "Rhetoric": An Art of Character* (Chicago, IL, and London: University of Chicago Press).

Grimaldi, W. M. A. (1972). *Studies in the Philosophy of Aristotle's "Rhetoric"* (Wiesbaden: Franz Steiner Verlag).

Grimaldi, W. M. A. [1980] (1988). *Aristotle, "Rhetoric" I–II: A Commentary* (New York: Fordham University Press).

Johnstone, C. L. (1980). "An Aristotelian Trilogy: *Ethics, Rhetoric,* and the Search for Moral Truth,"*Philosophy and Rhetoric,* 13, pp. 1–24.

Kassel, R. (1976). *Aristotelis Ars Rhetorica* (Berlin and New York: De Gruyter).

Rapp, C. (2002). *Aristoteles, "Rhetorik,"* trans., intro., and comm., 2 vols. (Berlin: Akademie Verlag).

Rorty, A. O. (1992). "The Directions of Aristotle's *Rhetoric,*" *Review of Metaphysics,* 46, pp. 63–95.

Rorty, A. O. (ed.) (1996). *Essays on Aristotle's "Rhetoric"* (Berkeley/Los Angeles/London: University of California Press).

Woerner, M. (1990). *Das Ethische in der "Rhetorik" des Aristoteles* (Freiburg and Munich: Alber Verlag).

38

Passions and Persuasion

STEPHEN LEIGHTON

Appealing to the passions with aims of persuading listeners was a familiar ploy in ancient Athens. Gorgias celebrated speech's power to arouse various passions and in doing so persuade (*Helen*, 8–10). Greek literature displayed and evoked the passions, often with aims of persuading. Athenian democratic practices and its courts permitted and fostered appeals to them. Even so, the nature of the passions, their means of persuasion, and the appropriateness of their persuasions were neither well understood nor agreed upon. Plato noted the power of particular passions to affect and beguile audiences and even speakers themselves, but questioned whether one was in one's right mind at such times (*Ion* 535b–e; cf. *Phaedrus* 267d). Moreover, he contested the appropriateness of passions to particular virtues (*Phaedo* 68c–69b), their role in a proper search for knowledge (*Phaedo* 66b–e), their place in the development of character (*Republic* III 386a–b, 387c, 390a, 396d), as well as their place in the fine arts generally (*Republic* X). At his trial, Socrates repudiated an appeal to pity (*Apology* 34b–35b).

Aware of such diverging views, but methodologically disposed to pursue the coherence in and sense behind beliefs and practices, Aristotle attempted to grasp the nature of the passions and their significant roles in a variety of practical disciplines, including ethics, poetics, and rhetoric.[1] It is in the latter context that one finds his seminal thoughts on the connections between passions and persuasion. Thus it is in his *Rhetoric* that one is best able to comprehend Aristotle on the matter – though what can be gleaned for rhetoric will have application elsewhere.

The *Rhetoric* seems to express differing positions on the passions' contribution to persuasion. While granting their power, the *Rhetoric*'s opening chapter suggests that the passions are external to rhetoric, merely personal appeals that warp a jury and cast shadows upon judgment (*Rhet* I.1 1354a16–18, 25, b8–12; cf. *Pol* III.15 1286a31–5, III.16 1287a20–32).[2] At times Aristotle seems to idealize persuasions that appeal simply to an argument's logical structure (*Rhet* I.1 1354a11–18, III.14 1415a34–b9). More characteristically, however, the *Rhetoric* makes room for and endorses appeals to the passions. Indeed, appealing to the passions, along with the character of the speaker and the argument itself, form the three modes of rhetorical persuasion provided by speech (III.1 1403b10–13, I.2 1356a2–4, 13–19).

For Aristotle, then, an art of rhetoric will have an interest in understanding the nature of the passions. This involves grasping "what each of the passions is and what

597

are its qualities and from what it comes to be and how" (I.2 1356a23–5). The *Rhetoric*'s main discussion of the passions identifies the passions as a significant grouping, characterizes its salient features, offers representative examples, sets forth the terms of their analysis for rhetoric, and uses those terms to discuss several passions (II.1 1378a20–II.11 1388b31). Simply to have envisaged and set forth this program is itself an impressive feat within philosophical psychology and rhetorical theorizing.

The *Rhetoric* tends to deal with passions in opposing pairs (anger and calmness, love and enmity, fear and confidence, etc.), though related passions are introduced (e.g. hatred is contrasted with anger), and the interdependencies and interconnections amongst several passions are explored. The analyses of particular passions are interesting and often quite penetrating. Strikingly, the *Rhetoric* is not deeply concerned to illustrate their rhetorical deployments (but see II.4 1382a16–19, II.5 1383a8–12, and II.8 1386a33–b7). It may be that Book II's sustained discussion of the passions has a different origin, and been adapted to its present setting (Kennedy 1963: 122).

The *Rhetoric's* Conception of the Passions

The *Rhetoric* characterizes the passions as:

> those things through which, by undergoing change, people come to differ in their judgments and which are accompanied by pain and pleasure, for example, anger, pity, fear, and other such things and their opposites. (*Rhet* II.1 1378a21–2)

Aristotle takes the passions to be a significant grouping in several works, each time characterizing it in light of ongoing concerns. The *Rhetoric*'s understanding has debts to the other investigations, particularly to his ethical studies. However, whereas his ethical studies likewise note a connection between passions, pleasures, and pains (a debt that goes back to Plato's *Philebus*), the connection between the passions and differences in judgment is found only in the *Rhetoric*. Again, whereas the examples listed in the ethical works include bodily desire (*epithumia*), the *Rhetoric* here does not. These differences seem significant. Bodily desires (e.g. desires for food, drink, and sex, *NE* III.11 1118b9–15; *Rhet* 1.11 1370a16–27), whilst accompanied by pleasure and pain (*Top* VI.3 140b26–32; *NE* VII.7 1150a25–6; *Rhet* II.7 1385a21–4), are not available to rational persuasion (*EE* II.8 1224b1–2). The exclusion of these desires here, combined with the *Rhetoric*'s claim of differences in judgments, serves to characterize the passions in a way tailored to ongoing concerns.

The *Rhetoric*'s characterization and understanding of the passions, then, is offered with concerns for persuasion in mind, rather than to provide a general theory of the passions. Indeed, the latter would require an analysis in terms of all four causes, whereas more circumscribed studies need not (*An* I.1 403a25–b19). The *Rhetoric*'s near silence on the material nature of the passions and particular passions should be understood in light of this. If so, the *Rhetoric*'s failure to discuss the material nature of particular passions or the passions as a whole does not reflect commitments at odds with what Aristotle writes elsewhere, but only local concerns. That is, rhetoric's concern is for the available means of persuasion in each case (*Rhet* I.1 1355b9–12, b25–6). That anger has to do with the boiling of the blood (*An* I.1 403a25–403b1) or that fear involves bodily chilling (*PA* II.4 650b27–30; *Prob* X.60 898a5–6; *Rhet* II.13 1389b32) seems unrelated to the concern for persuasion. Accordingly, the *Rhetoric* says little on the passions' material nature.

When the *Rhetoric* depicts the passions as accompanied by pleasure and pain, and speaks of some as disturbances, Aristotle seems to be thinking of the passions as occurrent, psychically disrupting phenomena (Cooper 1996: 245–6). Some passions are accompanied by both pleasure and pain. Anger's definition, for example, speaks of a pain brought on by insult, but Aristotle quickly notes that anger is also attended by pleasures that arise from expectations of and dwelling upon revenge (*Rhet* II.2 1378a30–1378b10). We also learn that exacting revenge will be pleasant (*Rhet* I.10 1369b11–15; *NE* III.8 1117a5–7). Other passions seem more centered on their painful nature. Fear, for example, concerns a pain or disturbance from imagining some destructive or painful future evil (*Rhet* II.5 1382a21–2). Strikingly, Aristotle takes no steps to include pleasure in fear's analysis, as he has for anger. So too regarding his account of pity. This need not mean that pleasantness cannot be associated with fear or pity, but only that there is no joy in the arousal of either. Any pleasantness that comes to be associated with them, then, is not integral to these passions, as it is for anger.[3]

While none of the passions as characterized by the *Rhetoric* are simply or fundamentally pleasant, passions such as joy seem likely to be so understood (*Top* II.6 112b21–5; *NE* II.5 1105b22). Some passions appear to be neither pleasant nor painful in themselves. The analysis of the passion kindness, for example, makes no mention of pleasure or pain as components. Another passion, shamelessness, is cast as lacking passion for or belittling (which Aristotle understands to be painless, *Rhet* II.3 1380a36) matters that would otherwise beget shame (II.6 1383b14–16). When contrasting hatred with anger, Aristotle suggests that while anger is painful, hatred is not. We are left with the impression of coldness and hardening rather than any pain or distress in this passion (*Rhet* II.4 1382a11–13; see Cooper 1996: 248). It seems that the passions' accompaniment by pleasure and pain holds in general, "for the most part" (*EE* II.2 1220b12–14; see Woods 1982; Leighton 1984; Fortenbaugh 2002: 106–14).

The *Rhetoric* makes no effort to differentiate the passions, their pleasures, pains, or disturbance in terms of a distinctive or characteristic "felt" nature. While differences of this sort may exist, Aristotle's interest is in differentiating the passions logically and causally. Anger, its pain is begotten by an insult given and taken, with the pain and the begetting cause serving as constituents of anger; fear, its pain is begotten by a danger taken to be threatening to oneself or one close, with the pain and the begetting cause serving as constituents of fear; pity, its pain is begotten by the recognition of undeserved disaster threatening another, with the pain and the begetting cause serving as constituents of pity; and so forth (see Fortenbaugh 11–12, 110–11).[4]

The above glosses oversimplify. Aristotle's accounts of particular passions involve quite subtle and complex perceptual-cognitive structures, a sometimes complex sentient nature, and in some cases desires and behavior too.[5] To give a somewhat fuller elucidation of one passion, anger arises when one is pained upon becoming aware of the belittlement (or intended belittlement) of oneself or someone close, by another in a position to belittle one. This requires complex social and personal relations and understandings between the person belittling and the person belittled, including matters of power, motivation, and self-worth. Belittled persons take themselves to have been treated as without worth for good or ill by particular persons. This treatment they take to be unprovoked and unjustified, but given voluntarily, unrepentantly, without fear, and for no benefit (*Rhet* II.2 1378a30ff, 1379a33–4, II.3 1380a9–16). Persons roused to anger expect better treatment, particularly at the hands of those they judge to be their inferiors or persons dear to them (II.2 1378b35–1379a9, 1379b2–3). They are more readily roused if already distressed, if expecting the opposite treatment, or if the belittlement concerns matters they take seriously (II.2 1379a19–29, 34–8). Further, belittled and now angry persons want, entertain, and actively seek revenge for their belittlement, one that they deem possible and conspicuous – something that brings pleasure to them (II.2 1378b1–10, II.3 1380b20–4). The full subtlety and complexity of Aristotle's depictions of various passions can be tremendously rewarding to explore, to relate to matters of value, to juxtapose with our own understanding of apparently similar passions.

The sentience and perceptual-cognitive features of passions seem to set out the passions as a group, the normal conditions necessary for a passion to be. For some passions this is all that is required for them to be.[6] Other passions can involve and even require further features. As we have seen, anger's definition speaks of a desire to retaliate, and is further connected to pleasures centered on revenge. These too help to determine something as anger. Interestingly, Aristotle queries but upholds a necessary link between anger and revenge (*Top* VIII.1 156a31–b3). Seemingly, then, a paradigmatic case of anger involves not only particular perceptual-cognitive networks and the pain of belittlement, but also requires a desire for revenge, pleasure in its contemplation, revenge itself (unless somehow offset), and the pleasure in its achievement.[7] By contrast, the structures of fear and pity prove less elaborate (above). Determining whether there are required features integral to particular passions beyond the basic perceptual-cognitive and affective will be discerned on a passion-by-passion basis.

Passions that do not require additional features for them to be (e.g. fear, pity, shame, indignation) can still be related to additional features. The situation parallels the earlier point about sentient complexity. While fear requires and is explicated in terms of its particular perceptual-cognitive complexity and relevant pain (whereas anger requires additional elements), it does not follow that fear cannot also be linked to additional elements, e.g., particular ends, desires, behavior, or pleasures. Rather, what follows is that fear (unlike anger) does not to require these further elements. If so, then when and where further connections are made requires an explanation beyond the basic structural requirements of the passion. That explanation is liable to involve situational concerns, including the particular context in which the passion presently arises. For example, whether a particular arousal of fear (pain or disturbance begotten by imagining some destructive or painful future evil threatening oneself or one close) begets desire, associated behavior, etc., can depend on whether one is on the field of battle, at the theatre, at sea, impoverished, sick, or before a jury. Presumably, fear on the field of battle is liable to beget desire, perhaps to flee, whereas the same desire or any other desire or ensuing activity is unlikely in the theatre, even though one is mightily afraid (Leighton 2003).

600

Persuasion and the Passions

One way the passions are involved in persuasion is by being present in the premises and conclusions of rhetorical arguments. A rhetorician can argue, using knowledge of a given passion, to derive particular conclusions. For example, an understanding of love enables one to argue in terms of it, drawing out implications about its goodness, its bad forms, the role of deficiencies, benefiting, suffering, hate, and so forth (*Rhet* II.4 1382a16–19, II.25 1402a37–b8). As important as persuasion concerning the passions is, the *Rhetoric*'s most innovative contribution to the passions' persuasive prospects is not in terms of the material of arguments, but as a persuasive mode, one in which jurors are moved to feel various passions and are persuaded thereby (see II.9 1387b18–21, II.10 1388a27–30, III.1 1403b10–13). It is because Aristotle also makes room for persuasion by the passions themselves that his thought comes to grips with the issues and concerns raised by Gorgias and Plato.

According to Aristotle, things do not seem the same when moved by various passions, where this concerns how one comprehends matters, the importance one attaches to them, and even one's hopes for dealing with them (II.1 1377b31–1378a5). Aristotle understands the passions' influence to be more extensive than the verdicts rendered, policies adopted, and so forth. Not only are those angered liable to render unfavorable verdicts upon those with whom they are angry, but also their anger affects supporting judgments and the importance attached to matters more generally. For example, angered persons will be liable to construe ongoing matters in terms of insults given, to find these to be particularly egregious, etc. By contrast, those moved by other passions, e.g. those feeling friendly toward or pity for someone, are liable to quite different assessments of an alleged wrongdoing, its importance, supporting evidence, and ensuing prospects.

The perceptual-cognitive complexity of the passions can help explain how particular passions change how things seem, and so persuade. Take fear aroused in the deliberations of public policy, imagining an advocate having moved a previously unemotional audience to fear an opponent, and what he or she proposes. In being brought to fear an opponent (and his or her proposals), an audience comes to take itself to be endangered, and is pained by this (II.5 1382a21–2). Thus, the audience has come to see the advocate's opponent (and his or her proposals) in particular terms, with fear's pain serving to disturb and thereby help to ensure that the matter is attended to. Further, since the *Rhetoric*'s account of fear connects it to thinking about what can be done (II.5 1383a5–8), the arousal of fear can also move audiences to deliberate about how to deal with relevant matters, for example, how to avoid or endure a feared policy, the particular planks of that policy, and the influence of those they fear. An audience's fear of an opponent, her or his proposals, affects how things seem, and can do so in ways that effectively defeat an opponent's proposals, the basis for those proposals, and her or his persuasive prospects. In contrast, the advocate's own proposals gain credence. Related analyses can be offered regarding the influence of anger, pity, shame, etc.[8]

The foregoing can also help to explain the absence of impressions, beliefs, passions, sympathies, etc., that might otherwise be extended. For example, an audience's indignation over something is opposed to their pity for the same matter. This is so, in part at least, because indignation views another as realizing unmerited good fortune (II.9

1386b10–15). Perceiving matters so precludes viewing the same matters as unmerited misfortune – an impression integral to pity (II.8 1385b13–16). Here the perceptual-cognitive structure relevant to one passion is at odds with the structure relevant to another. To the extent that one is in the grips of the one passion concerning a particular matter, one is thereby excluded from the grips of the other with respect to the same matter, and many ensuing judgments and appearances. Accordingly, an audience's indignation toward an accused can forestall pity for them or thoughts that the accused has suffered undeservedly or sympathy for their plight.

A number of passions conflict with one another. Fear excludes anger, and vice versa (II.3 1380a31–4, II.12 1389a25–8); envy bars pity (II.10 1388a25–8); fear, when great, tends to drive out pity (II.8 1385b32–4). Hatred and anger seem to be competing reactions, but whereas hatred excludes pity, anger does not (II.4 1382a1–15), and so forth. Moreover, passions can be coordinate with one another. For example, those who envy another's prosperity are liable to spiteful pleasure in the other's misfortune (II.9 1386b33–1387a2, II.10 1388a23–5). This too can be useful when persuading an audience.

So seen, rhetoricians by moving audiences to particular passions, by focusing on already existing or arising passions, by diminishing, heightening, or eliminating other passions can get their audiences to comprehend particular persons and matters in specific ways, give these a particular importance, see ensuing prospects accordingly, and motivate deliberation and specific courses of action.[9] We are unlikely to adopt policies of those we are angry with or indignant towards; we are liable to forgive or find faultless those we pity or love.

Other means of persuasion by the passions besides ones that rely on the cognitive-perceptual complexity of passions deserve notice. Several passions have an explicit or implicit *telos*. This too can influence persuasion. On Aristotle's view, those who love another wish for the benefit of the beloved for the beloved's own sake, and are inclined, as they can, to bring this about (II.4 1380b36–1381a1). One form of benefiting can be judging in particular ways. This might come about in several ways.

Insincerity is one possibility. Here through feelings of love, one behaves like those of bad character who do not say what they truly think (II.1 1378a11–12). One stands by one's beloved, judging the beloved well and an opponent basely, howsoever one comprehends the merits of the matter. While this can be relevant to rhetoric, it seems unlikely to be the sort of case that primarily interests Aristotle: insincere pronouncements due to one's passions are not a matter of things not seeming the same through passion.

Love's benefiting can also occur in sincere ways. Love's goal of benefiting will incline lovers to be generous to their beloved. Accordingly, where matters are underdetermined or where complex issues need to be put together to be comprehended, lovers will incline to understand in ways that benefit not hinder a beloved, and hinder not benefit a beloved's foe. We are little surprised when lovers find their beloved wondrous, and do so on what seems (to an outsider) very meager achievement. Those angry, and wanting revenge, will be liable to put things together quite differently. Even the sentience of particular passions can influence how things seem insofar as pleasant things we are inclined to focus on, whereas painful things we tend to avoid (*An* III.7 431a8–11; cf. *MA* 8 701b35–6; *Rhet* III.14 1415b3–4). Accordingly, we will strive to get over the pain of passion, but are liable to indulge any pleasure it brings. A clever rhetorician can play upon this in drawing us toward some things and away from others, thereby influencing our understanding of matters.

Other means of persuasion by the passions have less to do with the logical-teleological structure of particular passions. Aristotle appreciates Gorgias' recommendation that one spoil one's opponents' earnestness with laughter, and their jesting with earnestness (III.18 1419b3–6, III.14 1415a34–8, cf. Plato, *Gorgias* 473E). The point seems to be to set a contrary mood to that set by one's opponent, thereby changing and diverting the direction of thought and passion from what it presently is. In so doing, one might change an audience's focus, the importance it attaches to matters, perhaps even to instill or remove a particular passion and ensuing judgments. So too, Aristotle speaks of an orator seeking to evoke pity, and wishing to heighten the effect by putting matters before our eyes with "gestures and cries and display of feelings and generally in their acting," including dressing like those who have already suffered (*Rhet* II.8 1386a32–3). Here again the attempt to evoke passion and, in turn, influence judgment is not based on reasoning or the logical-teleological structure of the passion, but does so by exhibiting certain appearances relevant to particular passions, with others picking up and being moved by these (see below).

A further aspect of passions' persuasiveness deserves notice. For the most part, the foregoing allows rhetoricians to remain distant, manipulators of the passions, unmoved by the same. Aristotle, however, makes room for speaking with passion (III.7 1408a10–19, III.16 1417a36–7). Moreover, the influence of a speaker's own passions had not gone unnoticed (Plato, *Ion* 535b–e). It seems that rhetoricians themselves can be moved by the very means they employ to move others. This itself is interesting, and can help to explain how rhetoricians (and persons displaying emotion generally) can come to understand matters. It becomes important to persuasion because Aristotle supposes (as do we) that people tend to take up passions expressed by a speaker (cf. III.7 1408a16–25, 1408b10–20, III.16 1417a36–b7). If so, this provides a further, less direct means in which persuasion can occur, an emotional contagion of sorts. A speaker moved to and displaying passion regarding something (or even feigning the same) persuades by infecting an audience with his or her passion. Presumably, the infection of listeners by a speaker's passion may spread further amongst an audience, with members noticing, feeding on, and feeding the passions of each other.

Aristotle also identifies numerous stylistic devices that can affect persuasion. The language chosen, loudness of voice, pitch, rhythm, acting, even the use of certain tenses is thought to have emotional weight (III.1 1403b26–31, III.7 1408b10–19, III.12 1413b8–12, III.16 1417a12–16). Generally, an appropriate style expresses the passion and character suited to the subject matter (III.7 1408a10–11).

Any persuasiveness the passions might bring can be limited or offset in diverse ways. According to Aristotle, the deliberations of public policy allow few opportunities to arouse passion (III.17 1418a27–9). Again, the character of the speaker and the argument presented can affect matters. So too, can the character of the audience – something affected by their stage of life (II.12 1388b31ff), but also by the particular form of government, customs, and so forth (I.8 1365b21–30). Even whether there is one judge only can prove significant (III.12 1414a10–12).

Rousing the Passions

For the most part, the foregoing depicts various ways in which rhetoricians can be persuasive by playing upon the passions of an audience. To be truly successful in persuading, not only must roused passion further persuasion, but also rhetoricians must be able to instill particular passions in an audience. Emotional contagion and the stylistic devices just discussed are means for achieving this, but hardly suffice to account for the matter. How and on what bases can Aristotle account for rousing the passions themselves?

The *Rhetoric* approaches the passions from the vantages of (1) the state of mind of those roused, (2) against whom they are usually directed, and (3) the basis/grounds (*epi poiois*) for their being so directed (*Rhet* II.1 1378a22–9). Not only does understanding these enable one to appreciate the complexity of diverse passions, but also Aristotle takes knowledge of all three to be necessary to arouse particular passions (and, presumably, to play upon existing passions). The third of these is particularly significant to present concerns.

On Aristotle's depiction of the passions and his articulation of particular passions, passion aroused affects how things seem and the way we understand matters (discussed above). Aristotle's identification and subsequent use of basis or grounds (3) commits him to the view that begetting and change in passion can itself be based on reason and reasoning. Thus not only does being in one emotional state versus another move one to see things in particular ways, but also the emotional state one is in is itself responsive to reason and persuasion (e.g. II.5 1383a8–12). Rhetoricians can take advantage of whatever passions happen to be present, but also, through argument and other forms of persuasion can beget, foster, increase, diminish, redirect, and squelch particular passions, associated changes of judgments, appearances, and so forth. Not only does roused passion affect how one sees things, matters of salience, motivation, etc., but also passion itself can be roused, shaped, augmented, and diminished by distinctly rational means. For example, fear can be begotten by being persuaded of the danger to oneself that someone or something embodies; pity, by being persuaded that there are others suffering undeservedly matters that one also is liable to. In similar ways, various passions can be begotten, augmented, shaped, and eliminated.

Holding that passions are available to reason does not entail that they are readily or wholly at its behest. Nor does Aristotle suggest this (but see Nussbaum 1996). Rather, Aristotle holds that though available to reason, the passions remain unruly in important respects – a view that manifests itself in various ways throughout Aristotle's writings. For example, in the *NE*'s discussion of how the parts of the soul interact, Aristotle is at pains to make clear that while the appetitive part of the soul (which houses the passions) is open to persuasion, it is so only to a degree (*NE* I.13 1102b14–1103a4). This is reflected in the operations of rage (*thumos*) which attends to reason, but often mishears it, and reacts accordingly (VII.6 1149a25–35). When reflecting on the bodily nature of the passions and its influence, Aristotle observes that not all upon being made aware of a danger are moved to fear, and that some are moved to fear (or perhaps to something like fear) on little or no basis (*An* I.1 403a19–24). Again, time is seen to put an end to anger; and exhausting anger on one matter hinders its arising elsewhere (*Rhet* II.3 1380b6–15). Further, passions have a kind of inertial force, with the result that having been set in motion they are not simply available to reconsideration, recall, or other counter measures (*Mem* 2 453a26–9).

The passions' unruliness, in turn, can influence persuasion. For example, Aristotle credits Philocrates with planning to take advantage of the unlikelihood that anger would be directed toward him once it had been spent elsewhere – even though the conditions for anger with him remained (*Rhet* II.3 1380b7–13).

Still, the passions remain available to reason. Because they are, explanations paralleling how passions bring about changes of judgments (above) can be redeployed, but now to explain the arousal of the passions themselves. For instance, the earlier example of an advocate using fear to warn of the dangers of an opponent and her or his policies can be redeployed, but now to explain the arousal of fear itself in those previously unafraid. In addition, the basis or grounds (3) also allow one to explain the arousal of passions where that has little to do with the logical-teleological structures relevant to particular passions. Moving others to laughter, for example, fosters a joyful mood, and takes a step towards calming them (*Rhet* II.3 1380b2–3). Displaying rage at or contempt for another can serve to move an audience (via emotional contagion) to feel antagonistic towards that person. The arousal of these passions, in turn, affects how things seem, and judgment.

Rhetoricians can move audiences to the passions through reasoning; the presence of the passions, in turn, influences how things seem and judgment. Throughout, rhetoricians need to be cognizant of the unruliness of the passions and how that can affect persuasion, and the variety of ways of moving others that do not depend on an appeal to reason.

Tactics

There is no single answer to the question of what approach should be taken when trying to persuade. All three modes of rhetorical persuasion can be deployed. In some situations and before some audiences, the simple logic of the matter can suffice. So too can confidence in the character of the speaker, and, of course, appeals to the passions. A skilled rhetorician needs to be prepared to deploy all the appropriate uses of these individually, and in consort (Cope 1877: 119–20; Fortenbaugh 2002: 18). When the passions are deployed, the ways in which the passions' influence can be offset needs to be taken into consideration (discussed above). As well, consideration needs to be given to the fact that some parts of a presentation prove particularly fertile ground for arousing passions, e.g. the epilogue (*Rhet* III.19 1419b10–13, 24–7). Even so, by making the appeal to passions a mode of persuasion, and by the nature of his discussion of the passions, Aristotle renders the whole presentation ripe for an appeal to them, giving the passions an importance not seen in previous ways of thinking about rhetoric, nor followed up in ensuing theorizing (Solmsen 1938: 394).

The Legitimacy of the Passions

The way(s) in which the passions' persuasiveness can find a proper place in rhetoric deserves thought. We should keep in mind that Aristotle grants that appeals to the passions can be problematic, yet appealing to them is one of the modes of persuasion. As well, appreciating Aristotle's position in light of reservations articulated by Plato proves valuable.

While Aristotle mounts no specific defense of the passions' appropriateness to persuasion, his thoughts on the role of rhetoric, his placement of the passions in other domains, and his philosophical procedures shed light on the matter. One part of the explanation can be seen in terms of the nature of Aristotle's inquiries. Appeals to the passions in rhetorical argumentation were widespread, and often effective. Since one feature of Aristotle's philosophical style is to seek the coherence and sense in ongoing practices, he is bound to recognize the passions' place within rhetoric, and to make the best sense of appeals to them that he can. Moreover, since rhetoric itself is to discern the available means of persuasion (above), an art of rhetoric must understand the passions' persuasive power – howsoever particular persuasive means are judged. In this regard the rhetorician's situation is akin to the physician's: even if the practitioner may not properly employ every means of achieving his or her end, an understanding of the art is not had until all are understood (*Top* I.3 101b5–10).

The strategic advantages of appealing to the passions seem relevant. Even where Aristotle expresses reservations about the passions, he does not question their effectiveness. That effectiveness, therefore, needs to be understood. The interest is not simply theoretical, but affects the practice of rhetoric. Aristotle holds that one should be able to reason persuasively on both sides of an issue. In saying this, he is not recommending that we do so: we are not to make people believe what is debased. Rather, by being able to persuade on both sides, one better understands matters, and is better poised to fend off unjust arguments of others (*Rhet* I.1 1355a26–33; see also *Top* I.2 101a31–7). This should be so whether the persuasiveness of a speech comes by means of argument, character, or passion. Thus, rhetoricians need to be adept in the deployment of the passions, and in responding to their deployments.

Aristotle also observes that it would be strange if one ought to be ashamed at being unable to defend oneself with one's body, but not so with words (*Rhet* I.1 1355a38–1355b2). Since persuasion by the passions is one mode of persuasion by speech, our ability to defend ourselves by means of the passions appears appropriate on this basis also. It may be tempting to suppose that Aristotle is here making room for persuasions that can be fundamentally self-serving, simple expediency, noble or not. If so, this would cohere with those parts of the *Rhetoric* where Aristotle seems to be offering straightforward advice on how best to win an argument (e.g. I.9 1367a33–b7, I.15 1375a25–b25, but see Grimaldi ad loc). The passage, however, deserves a less cynical reading. A failure to be able to defend oneself with one's body, one's words, or one's passions may be shameful, but this need not mean that any use of them is valuable or without shame. As Aristotle proceeds, he makes it clear that he is not interested in defending an unjust use of speech (I.1 1355b4–7). So seen, his point coheres with his more characteristic views on rhetoric, and advice that we should not persuade persons to believe what is debased. The extent to which Aristotle's discussions do endorse less than noble ways of proceeding (and one can suppose the same regarding the passions) remain noteworthy but minor currents in his thoughts on rhetoric.

The foregoing helps to justify a place for the passions in rhetorical persuasion (including passions such as fear, anger, pity, etc). Still, particular passions require further consideration. For example, while shame is an appropriate passion to feel, it is only appropriate at certain times of life or in those of failed character (*NE* V.9 1128b10–34). If so, then arousing shame in an audience will be problematic, lest one arouses it in those who should not feel it, or fails to arouse it in those who should. Again, envy is a passion that Aristotle finds useful to rhetoric (*Rhet* II.10 1387b22–3, 1388a25–8, III.19 1419b25–8), but one that it is inappropriate to feel (*NE* II.6 1107a8–17). Arousing a passion that it is inappropriate for audience members to feel is hard to justify without invoking strategic justifications of a cynical sort.[10]

Finding a place for the passions within rhetoric and justifying rhetoric's need to understand that place leaves open the question of how laudable that place is. That the passions' place in rhetoric can be laudable is, in part, justified by the foregoing, but can be seen more clearly in light of Plato's concerns for rhetoric, particularly the *Gorgias'* doubts about an art of rhetoric (462b), and the *Phaedrus'* endorsement of one with the proviso that it becomes more philosophical and concerned with truth (271a–c, cf. 261a–b, 263b–c, 269d–270a, 259e–260d).

Aristotle adheres to the *Phaedrus* insofar as he endorses an art of rhetoric (*Rhet* I.2 1355b27–34, I.4 1359b6, II.24 1402a25–7). Moreover, his *Rhetoric* pursues various means for enhancing rhetoric's practice, some of which suit the *Phaedrus'* proposals. For example, the *Rhetoric*'s analyses of particular passions and persons at different ages, in part, help to meet the *Phaedrus'* insistence that one understand the psychology of one's audience (*Phaedrus* 271a, d; *Rhet* II.1 1378a20–II.3 1390b10). Aristotle does not, however, seem interested in elevating rhetoric into something akin to philosophy: rather, rhetoric, as he makes sense of and endorses it, is the normal practice of rhetoric, something that includes persuasion by the passions. As Aristotle worked to integrate the passions in ethics and poetics, so too he does for rhetorical practice and theory – doing so against the background of Plato's suspicions. We have seen that the integration of the passions within rhetoric can be justified in terms of the nature of rhetoric itself, the characteristic presence of passions within rhetoric, and certain strategic uses. In addition, Aristotle seems to have a further justification for the presence of the passions.

Aristotle is keenly aware that human practices and disciplines vary from one another in diverse ways. What is appropriate within a discipline such as rhetoric need not be appropriate within other disciplines, and *vice versa* (*NE* I.3 1094b11–27, I.7 1098a26–b8, II.2 1104a1–11). Given this, the fact that Aristotle fails to deploy, approve, or justify the use of the passions in, say, first philosophy or mathematics does not require or intimate the same for his understanding of the theatre, ethics, politics, or rhetoric. On the contrary, Aristotle takes it that appeals to the passions can be appropriate in these latter domains.

Part of the justification for thinking so can be seen in the striking epistemological differences between disciplines. Consider the differences between rhetoric and, say, first philosophy. The latter requires all the care and detail for which Aristotle as a philosopher is justly famous. One moves slowly, tentatively and carefully, demanding the utmost in intellectual rigor and precision, with arguments pursued as fully as possible. Similarly, regarding mathematics, physics, etc. Rhetoric is different:

the educated person seeks exactness in each area to the extent that the nature of the subject allows; for apparently it is just as mistaken to demand demonstrations from a rhetorician as to accept [merely] persuasive arguments from a mathematician. (*NE* I.3 1094b24–6)

Rhetoric often appeals to commonplaces, things worthy of belief, reputable yet conflicting opinions (*Rhet* I.1 1355a21–29, I.2 1356a4–10, 1358a10–35, I.4 1359b2–17, II.24 1402a31–4; cf. *Top* I.2 101a30–4). So seen, rhetoric does not always concern things that *qua* philosopher one can claim to know, and uncertainty can exist. Moreover, the audiences to be persuaded were often a diverse crowd. They could not be relied upon to be able to bring things together from distant starting points, or to follow complex reasoning (*Rhet* I.2 1357a3–12, III.18 1419a17–19).[11] Still, crowds can prove to be better and less corruptible judges than single persons (*Pol* II.15 1286a30–1). Humans have a natural disposition for what is true, and largely find the truth (*Rhet* I.1 1355a14–17) or the best understanding (*Rhet* II.25 1402b31–3). True and just things tend to prevail (*Rhet* I.1 1355a21–3).

The truths discerned, however, do not allow for the kind of precision available in areas such as mathematics, but instead indicate matters roughly and in outline, speaking to what is so for the most part (*NE* I.3 1094b11–27, II.2 1104a1–12). As well, the arguments deployed often concern matters that are so for the most part, with their conclusions derived from probabilities, examples, evidences, and signs (*Rhet* I.2 1357a30–6, I.3 1359a6–10, II.25 1402b12–23). Moreover, as Plato's recording of Socrates' trial reveals, the circumstances of rhetoric could be highly charged, with important matters quickly taken in and determined.

It is unsurprising, then, that the procedures appropriate to philosophical investigation or mathematics have little role here. If Plato was skeptical about the nature of public debate and sought to elevate rhetoric into something akin to philosophical investigation, Aristotle was more optimistic about such debates and our understanding of them (*SE* 34 183b22–34, 184a6–b8). His *Rhetoric* seeks to provide a more realistic understanding of rhetoric's workings and nature. As Aristotle's ethical and poetical thought makes evident, feeling the passions and being the object of another's passions can be appropriate, can immediately and insightfully comprehend and assist in dealing with matters at hand. This, when taken together with the evident persuasiveness of the passions, enables their deployment in rhetoric to be effective, and appropriate in a way that is laudable. They can assist in coming to the right determination of matters in their circumstance – where this is not a matter of luck or chance, and where deliberations in the style of first philosophy, mathematics, physics, etc., can have no serious application or hope of success. In context, not only are appeals to passions intelligible, but they can be intelligent as well.[12] Had Socrates sought the pity of his jurors, that appeal might have succeeded even where his more careful arguments failed. Appealing to the passions can be persuasive and justified; rhetoricians are right to appeal to them; audiences can be appropriately persuaded by them.

Still, as noted at the outset, particular appeals can be inappropriate, misused, warping, and prove overwhelming (see also *Rhet* III.7 1408a23–5). However, the fact that the passions and their deployments can be used inappropriately no more counts against their proper use than does the fact that goods such as strength, health, or wealth can be misused (1.1 1355b2–7). Disciplines like rhetoric, politics, ethics, and aesthetics are best served when they make use of the passions and their persuasions, and are most ennobled when they do so in appropriate ways.[13]

Notes

[1] In the passages from Aristotle that we will be concerned with "*ta pathê*" (here rendered "the passions") can also be translated as "the emotions." One does not go very far wrong with either translation, but "the passions" more neutrally indicates the continuity amongst several of Aristotle's discussions. Translations of the *Rhetoric* are based on those of George A. Kennedy (1991); translations from the *Nicomachean Ethics* are those of Terrence Irwin (1999).

[2] That these passages do repudiate an appeal to the passions is disputed. See, for example, Cope (1867: 140), Grimaldi's commentary on the relevant passages (1980: vol. 1), and Wisse (1989: 17–19).

[3] Most, perhaps all, passions should find pleasure in remembrance and hope (*Rhet* I.11 1370a26–b10). It is tempting, therefore, to think that something must be amiss, either in the above interpretation or (failing that) in Aristotle's thinking. If, for example, fear or pity also can be related to pleasure, should not these passions be understood to have a structure like that of anger, one that includes both pleasure and pain? More generally, should not every passion be rendered in parallel structural terms? Certainly, there is nothing to prevent one from creating a logic of passions along these lines. Moreover, Aristotle has as a precedent the *Philebus'* understanding of pleasure and pain, notably those of the soul (*Philebus* 31b–32b, 47dff). Yet, in his discussion of particular passions, Aristotle seems not to make a similar attempt (but see Frede). Rather than prescribing a single logical grid upon which each of the passions is to be fitted in fundamentally parallel ways, Aristotle appears to provide analyses more attuned to how particular passions are experienced and understood. In so doing, he can be more sensitive to the place passions have in our moral, ethical, and political lives, and their uses in rhetoric.

[4] This is not meant to endorse (nor foreclose) the possibility that the pains of these emotions are themselves intentional states with cognitive content (Nussbaum 2001: 64).

[5] Discerning the ontological status of the "cognitive" component of the passions and particular passions is problematic. The *Rhetoric's* characterization of the passions indicates that they affect our judgments, where the immediate concern seems to be for formal verdicts rendered. As well, (we shall see) the passions affect how things appear. Again, a number of passions are depicted in terms of their sentient nature, and others in terms of desire. All have discernible and specifiable logical structures. Unfortunately, Aristotle does not specify whether the passions or particular passions require and are constituted by judgments in a wider sense (or beliefs or evaluations, etc.) or whether the passions simply affect these, or can involve them, in the context of rhetoric. Again, because Aristotle elsewhere allows for many passions in non-human animals (creatures without a rational soul), a role for judgment or belief or evaluation as a necessary constituent for the passions or particular passions becomes problematic (but see Nussbaum 1996, Fortenbaugh 2002: 94–103, et al.). Thus, I speak of "perceptual and/or cognitive structures" or "networks" in a way that is uncommitted to whether (or just where) the passions, passion types, or particular arousals of a passion are constituted by appearances, beliefs, judgments, evaluations, etc. Even the "perceptual" needs qualification. Many passions are specified in terms of appearances. Characteristically, these will be perceptual, but not necessarily (e.g. in dreams, *An* III.3 428a5–7).

[6] However, as noted above, some passions appear not to be accompanied by pleasure or pain. Moreover, we are following Aristotle here in simply sidelining the question of the bodily nature of the passions for present purposes.

[7] The "unless offset" qualification can be important. For while those angered seek revenge, their anger can be quelled in various ways. Where so, the need for revenge can also be quelled (*Rhet* II.3 1380a9–20).

[8] Whether any changes in judgment that ensue are changes "all things considered" or are more restricted in scope is not determined here. From what Aristotle writes elsewhere, it seems likely that he means it in the latter way, though, presumably, sometimes it can achieve the former. So seen, a rhetorician by moving one to a particular passion will strive to achieve a change of judgments "all things considered," but can be satisfied if the changes prevail in their ongoing circumstances.

[9] Konstan elegantly uses Thucydides' recording of the generals' speeches in illustration of this (2006: 141ff).

[10] In the *Philebus* Socrates takes envy to have a role in comedy (48bff). Aristotle might allow for this, justifying its depiction on stage and its arousal in an audience in terms of our delight in imitation and learning (*Poet* 4 1448b5–23). In a different way, learning is relevant to rhetoric also (above), and this could be used to explain why rhetoricians must be prepared to deal with envy when aroused. Even so, this seems insufficient to justify arousing envy in jurors or those present at deliberations of public policy – given the *NE*'s concerns.

[11] Cope takes Aristotle to be offering "the rigorous observance of the rules of his art" and humouring the audiences' "perverted inclinations" (Cope 1867: 5–6). There may be a place for the latter, but as we shall see, Aristotle's concerns for the epistemological situation and the receptivity of the audience are more optimistic and noble.

[12] The view argued for is meant to show the appropriateness of emotional appeals to persuasion in the context of rhetoric. This contrasts with views such as those of E. Garver, where an appeal to passions within rhetoric seems applicable only where reason does not point in a single direction (1994: 109). It is also meant to suggest that Wisse's thought that passions within rhetoric are intelligible but not intelligent, is too mild (p. 73).

[13] I would like to thank R. Bosley, L. Judson, D. Mirhady, and C. Rapp for their assistance in helping me think through these matters, and Georgios Anagnostopoulos for his support and the wonderful opportunity to reflect on this topic.

Bibliography

Aristotle (1991). *On Rhetoric*, trans. George A. Kennedy (Oxford: Oxford University Press).

Aristotle (1999). *Nicomachean Ethics*, trans. T. Irwin (Indianapolis, IN: Hackett).

Cooper, J. M. (1996). "An Aristotelian Theory of the Emotions," in Rorty, pp. 238–57.

Cope, E. M. (1867). *An Introduction to Aristotle's "Rhetoric"* (London: Macmillan).

Cope, E. M. (1877). *The "Rhetoric" of Aristotle, with a Commentary* (Cambridge: Cambridge University).

Fortenbaugh, W. W. (2002). *Aristotle on Emotion*, 2nd edn. (London: Duckworth).

Frede, D. (1996). "Mixed Feelings in Aristotle's *Rhetoric*," in Rorty, pp. 258–285

Garver, E. (1994). *Aristotle's "Rhetoric": An Art of Character* (Chicago, IL: University of Chicago Press).

Grimaldi, W. (1980). *Aristotle, "Rhetoric" 1: A Commentary* (New York: Fordham University Press).

Grimaldi, W. (1988). *Aristotle, "Rhetoric" 2: A Commentary* (New York: Fordham University Press).

Kennedy, G. (1963). *The Art of Persuasion in Greece* (Princeton, NJ: Princeton University Press).

Konstan, D. (2006). *The Emotions of the Ancient Greeks: Studies in Aristotle and Classical Literature* (Toronto: University of Toronto Press).

Leighton, S. (1984). "*Eudemian Ethics*, 1220b11–13," *Classical Quarterly*, 23: pp. 135–8.

Leighton, S. (1996). "Aristotle and the Emotions," in Rorty, pp. 206–237.

Leighton, S. (2003). "Aristotle's Exclusion of Anger from the Experience of Tragedy," *Ancient Philosophy*, 2, pp. 361–81.

Nussbaum, M. (1996). "Aristotle on Emotions and Rational Persuasion," in Rorty, pp. 303–23.

Nussbaum, M. (2001). *Upheavals of Thought: The Intelligence of the Emotions.* (Cambridge: Cambridge University Press).

Rorty, A. O. (ed.) (1996). *Essays on Aristotle's "Rhetoric"* (Berkeley, CA: University of California Press).

Solmsen, F. (1938). "Aristotle and Cicero on the Orator's Playing upon the Feelings," *Classical Philology*, 33 (4), pp. 390–404.

Wisse, J. (1989). *Ethos and Pathos from Aristotle to Cicero* (Amsterdam: Adolf M. Hakkert).

Woods, M. (1982). *Aristotle: "Eudemian Ethics," Books I, II, and VII* (Oxford: Clarendon Press).

B. Art

39

Aristotle's *Poetics*: The Aim of Tragedy

PAUL WOODRUFF

"Every art . . . aims at some good," says Aristotle (*Nicomachean Ethics* I.1), and so we may reasonably ask what is the good at which he thinks tragedy aims. If we could identify that good, we would expect it to provide the standard by which he judges the practice of the art of tragedy; he would commend those plays or plot devices that serve to bring about the good that is peculiar to tragedy, and he would disparage those that block the achievement of that good.

Indeed, Aristotle does speak of the function of tragedy (*ergon*) and also of its aim (*telos*), to which he appeals in his judgments, as we would expect from what I have said.[1] But although he assumes that tragedy has its own specific aim, he does not explain in the *Poetics* what he takes this to be. In technical terms, Aristotle's argument presupposes that tragedy has a final cause, but does not specify the nature of that cause.

Aristotle gives us many hints, however, supplying a number of candidates for the answer to our question. Here are the main ones:

(1)   All poetry aims at being *kalon* (*beautiful* or excellent, 47a9); the proper size and order of tragedy is given by standards of beauty that may be applied to animals as well as to plays (50b36, cf. 512a31). Neither beauty nor excellence can stand alone as aims of tragedy, however. Aristotle would want to specify the beauty or excellence that is specific to tragedy; tragedy aims at excellence and beauty in a specific sort of mimesis.

(2)   The art of tragedy is a kind of *mimesis* and therefore ought to share in the general aim of mimesis. But the *Poetics* is not explicit about what that aim is, although the text does introduce two products of mimesis (at which mimesis may be supposed to aim), pleasure and understanding. At most, the *Poetics* suggests a complex account of the aim of mimesis (see Halliwell 2002: 177–206, "The Rewards of mimesis"). In itself, however, mimesis seems to take on the aims of whatever it is mimetic of; for example, when medicine is mimetic of nature, then, like nature, it aims at health. So mimesis as such may not have its own proper aim.

(3)   One of the products of mimesis is *understanding* (*Poetics* 4), and we may infer that this is at least part of the aim of mimesis and therefore of tragedy. Aristotle nowhere

612

says directly that tragedy leads to, or aims at, understanding, but this (or something like it) has been a popular candidate in recent years for the aim Aristotle would propose for tragedy (this line of interpretation begins with Golden's influential article of 1962).

(4)   Aristotle thinks that tragedy should aim to produce a distinctive *pleasure*, and the pleasure of learning, we know from chapter 4, is one of the products of mimesis. The pleasure specific to tragedy, however, is the kind that derives "from pity and fear by way of mimesis" (53b9–13, cf. 51b23, 53a35, 62a16, a19). Pleasure in Aristotle is never a free-standing goal, so this hint calls us to ask what kind of pleasure he means; more precisely, since pleasure belongs to the activity that it completes, we should ask in what activity the tragic audience is to take pleasure (*Nicomachean Ethics* X.4; on the point, see Halliwell 2002: 205).

(5)   Aristotle prefers tragedy that arouses *pity and fear* in an audience and holds that at least part of the aim of tragedy is to arouse these emotions (*Poetics* 13 and 14, cf. 52a2–3, 52a36–b1). This sits oddly with the idea that tragedy aims at pleasure, however, for pity and fear are, on his theory, painful.[2]

(6)   "The aim is a certain kind of *action*, not a quality" (50a17); "the actions and the story are the aim (*telos*) of tragedy, and the aim is the most important of all [of the elements of tragedy]" (50a21–2). By "actions" Aristotle apparently means whatever is presented on stage through mimesis, not the behavior by which the performers represent those actions (50a16); similarly, the agents ("those acting," *hoi prattontes*) are what we would call the characters who are represented by the performers. To say that action is the aim of tragedy, in context, means that the other elements of tragedy (such as character) serve the larger aim of achieving mimesis of action. But it cannot mean that the mimesis of action is the final aim of tragedy. If the mimesis of action had no further aim, any action would do. But we have seen that tragedy must select those actions that have the power to arouse pity and fear.[3] So action serves the arousal of emotion, and therefore it is not at the top of the hierarchy of aims in tragedy.

(7)   Aristotle uses the word *katharsis* in his definition of tragedy, in the place where he leads us to expect he is identifying the aim of tragedy (*Poetics* 6.49b27). But *katharsis* is even harder to understand than mimesis, for Aristotle has nothing further to say about *katharsis* as the aim of tragedy in the *Poetics* (the word appears at 55b15, referring to the ritual purification of Orestes in Euripides' play, *Iphigenia in Tauris*, 1029ff). Surprisingly, he does not appeal to *katharsis* in his account of the features that are desirable in tragic poetry. When evidence fails us, as in this case, the wisest course is to remain silent. I shall, however, consider a number of interpretations of *katharsis* below.

(8)   "What a thing is and what it is for are [often] the same," says Aristotle elsewhere (*Physics* II.7); perhaps the most Aristotelian answer to our question is that the aim of tragedy is to actualize its own *nature*–to be what tragedy most truly is. What tragedy most truly is–that is the *essence* identified in its definition (49b23). Tragedy reached the

end of its development when it realized its nature, and its nature determined such features as its proper meter (49a15, a23). This answer refers us to the definition of tragedy, which is the main subject of the surviving chapters of the *Poetics*. If we take the whole definition seriously, as I will argue we should, then the task of understanding the aim of tragedy is no different from what we used to think was the larger job of interpreting Aristotle's treatment of tragedy in the *Poetics* as a whole.

What then is the aim of tragedy as Aristotle understands it? The text does not warrant a simple answer; the most plausible answers will make use of all the features mentioned above. Few of these candidates could be omitted from an adequate account of the subject in our text. Aristotle clearly implies in the arguments of the *Poetics* that a good tragedy must be a beautiful instance of mimesis, that it must give pleasure to its audience, that it must present actions which arouse pity and fear, and that it must satisfy his definition of tragedy. One condition we could safely omit, with no cost to our understanding of the argument of the *Poetics*, is the requirement that a good tragedy must achieve *katharsis*. That is because this condition does no work in the argument; it does not support any of Aristotle's judgments about how tragedy should be made. I will review interpretations of *katharsis* in this paper, because they loom large in discussions of our subject, but with no commitment to the relevance of katharsis to Aristotle's discussion of tragedy as we have it. We can say the same about understanding; nowhere does Aristotle prefer this plot to that one on the grounds that it leads to a deeper understanding.

What Is Tragedy?

The question "What is the aim of tragedy?" makes sense only if tragedy is a distinct something that can have a distinct purpose. To have a specific aim (Aristotle holds) it must be something that can be defined. And indeed he takes it to be definable, opening his discussion of tragedy with a definition at the start of chapter 6.

Certainly, Aristotle is writing about the species of play developed for the Athenian tragic festivals during the fifth (and perhaps the later sixth) century BCE, and of which a small percentage has survived (readers wishing to educate themselves about ancient Greek tragedy should start with the excellent companion edited by Gregory 2005). We might begin by asking after the aim of ancient Greek tragedy as we know it, and to work back from this to an understanding of Aristotle's account. But Aristotle is writing two or three generations after the great age of Athenian tragedy, and we cannot assume that he knew how tragedy functioned in Athenian life in the mid-fifth century.[4] However well informed I may be about fifth century tragedy, my opinion of its historical aim remains an uncertain guide to interpreting Aristotle's.[5]

Aristotle appears to be mainly interested in poetic texts. These are what he has available, and he says that tragedy can have its special effect even on those who merely read it (62a11). It is tempting for modern readers to infer that the *Poetics* is a work of literary criticism divorced from concerns about performance. But poetry had up to then been composed or written primarily for performance, so the distinction is probably not one Aristotle would have made. Moreover, Aristotle's account of tragedy refers to features that tragic plays can have only in performance (see Scott 1999). So we should resist the temptation to think of the *Poetics* as concerned with literature narrowly conceived.

Mimesis[6]

The concept of mimesis is too obscure to admit of translation, so I will adopt it directly as an English word. In any case, knowing the purpose of mimesis avails us little unless we also know what differentiates the purpose of tragedy within the more general purpose of mimesis. Aristotle is puzzlingly silent about why he thinks it important to classify tragedy as mimetic, and he does not appeal to generic features of mimesis in discussing the workings of tragedy.

Mimesis can produce two products at the same time, according to *Poetics* 4: mimesis brings about instruction and at the same time it gives pleasure. Human beings are naturally curious, and so they enjoy learning by means of mimesis. That is why mimesis is naturally planted in human beings and is a distinctively human practice. Does this theory help us to understand the purpose of tragedy? True, Aristotle takes tragedy to be pleasure-giving, as we have seen, but he nowhere says that it is also instructive. In fact, chapter 4 does not claim to expound the general purpose of mimesis, but merely to explain why it is that mimesis is natural for human beings: We naturally take pleasure in learning, and we learn through mimesis, so we naturally take pleasure in mimesis.

Chapter 4 thus leaves open the question of what mimesis is for,[7] as well as the question how it is that we learn or gain in understanding through mimesis (on mimesis and learning, Halliwell's 2002 brilliant discussion should be required reading). This at least seems clear: the pleasure to be had from mimetic learning, according to chapter 4, requires that we be aware that mimesis is going on. We can't be totally deceived about it. If we are learning by imitating our elders, we enjoy this because we know we are acting as they act; if we learn by recognizing that an image is an image of a certain thing, we are aware that imaging is in play. But mimesis may also have effects on people who are not aware that mimesis is going on (as in the case of an unconscious patient receiving medical treatment that is mimetic of natural healing). But such a person is denied the special pleasure of learning through mimesis. The patient is, simply, healed. It follows that not all of the good that comes from mimesis comes by way of a recognition that mimesis is going on. mimesis can aim at goods that are independent of understanding.

On mimesis in general, we have much to learn from Aristotle in other texts. The reason that I do not translate the word as "imitation" or "representation" or "expression" is simply that none of these words can serve in all the contexts in which Aristotle uses mimesis or its verbal cognate. Two kinds of context are especially challenging and instructive:

1   *Technê* brings about through mimesis what nature would normally achieve directly; *technê* thus completes nature (*Physics* 199a15, cf. 194a21). *Technê* (professional expert knowledge) covers arts such as medicine: nature heals us naturally, but, when this fails, a skilled doctor can achieve nature's goal by means of his art.

Aristotle does not say this explicitly, but he seems to mean that medicine fools the body into accelerating or completing a natural process which, other things being equal, nature would accomplish without the assistance of medicine.

2   Music and dance achieve a mimesis of character and emotion: "In the tunes themselves are *mimêmata* of types of character" (*Politics* 1340a38–39, with 18–22). An explanation for this is found in *Problemata*: Melody and rhythm are motions, and so are actions of a certain character (919b26ff and 920a3ff. For the role of motion in emotion, see *De Anima* 403a16. I am indebted to Victor Caston for this account of the matter). Both music and action, when perceived, set up corresponding motions in the minds of spectators. Courageous music will have the same emotional effect on your soul as courageous action. You can habituate yourself to courageous emotion by doing courageous things, but you can achieve the same result by listening to courageous music.

The analogy between music and medicine is clear: That music does for the soul what medicine does for the body is an old Pythagorean idea (Aristoxenus, fr 26 [Wehrli], discussed by Halliwell in his 1986, p. 187 with note 23), but here is an Aristotelian theory to explain it: music achieves mimesis of courageous behavior by getting the soul to do what the soul would naturally do in a truly courageous person; medicine achieves mimesis of nature by getting the body to do what it would do naturally if it could. mimesis is an intervention in natural processes. The underlying theory is that mimesis is the art of arranging for something to have an effect or part of an effect that by nature belongs to a different kind of thing.

Although Aristotle does not apply this theory explicitly to tragedy, we can imagine how this could be done.[8] Consider pity and fear in the *Bacchae*. In the natural course of events, while watching the *Bacchae*, I would feel pity for Agave only if I believed she had just torn her son apart, and I would fear for her if I believed she was about to tear her son apart. But, as I well know, Agave will not tear her son apart offstage while I am watching the chorus raging at him. I have nothing to fear, and nothing to pity. The point holds whether I am watching history or fiction being staged: it is only being staged. The effect of mimesis is to make me react to this staged action almost as if I believed that Agave was about to tear her son apart.

I do not need to know that mimesis is taking place in order to be affected by it. If I did not know that the action was being staged, the mimetic effect would be more like the natural one. In the usual case, however, I am complicit in the mimesis, and this complicity allows me to take pleasure in what would be a painful experience in nature. mimesis carries most of the emotional power that actions in the world would naturally have, by art, into the theater. But not all. Because, in the world, those emotions would be painful, but here, in the theater, they will be pleasant. And this crucial difference must be due to mimesis: the spectator has the motions in his soul that belong to pity and fear, but not the set of beliefs that would make those motions painful – not the beliefs that these fearful actions are actually taking place.

Like other cases of mimesis, tragic mimesis is an intervention in a natural process, producing the effect that naturally would arise from witnessing an actual event. If I know that the action is staged, then the effects that would naturally depend on belief occur in the absence of belief, owing to mimesis. It is as if mimesis deceives my emotions without deceiving me; it provides me with an emotional impression to which I do not assent, but which moves me as if I did. And now we can see why mimesis can have a role in the presentation of history as well as fiction: If the actions of history are presented in a web of likelihood or necessity, then they will arouse my emotions. Tragedy is a mimesis of emotion-arousing actions because it arouses the audience partly in the way that such actions would. It makes no difference whether the actions in question are invented or actual. Either way, mimesis in tragedy makes things lifelike enough to arouse emotions.

Understanding

My account of mimesis leaves out learning altogether, and in this I am deliberately setting myself against the trend of modern scholarship. Even those who reject the strong view that the aim of tragedy is education find some place in tragic mimesis for the increase of understanding (see Halliwell 2002b, "The Rewards of mimesis," for a subtle and elegant discussion of pleasure, understanding, and emotion in tragedy). But passages in the *Poetics* that deal with the aim of tragedy offer us nothing to support the understanding view. Moreover, we have good reason to doubt that tragic mimesis could serve the primitive educational function suggested in Chapter 4, where we are to imagine the pleasure a child takes in recognizing the object of an image. Tragic mimesis is essentially capable of deception (for an example, see 61b9–12, cf. 60a13, ff, and a26, with my note 27 below). That is because tragic mimesis aims at *eikos* (what is likely or plausible), hoping by means of this to be persuasive. But what is plausible is not always true, as Aristotle knows. Like Plato, Aristotle rejects the claim of rhetoric to improve our understanding of the truth by generating what is merely *eikos*.[9]

Aristotle says that poetry is more philosophical than history (chapter 9), and some scholars have ridden this very hard to bring it into the stable of the theory that tragedy's aim is educational:

> Here's the difference [between history and poetry]: the one tells what has happened, the other what is such that it could happen. That's why poetry is more philosophical and more serious [about ethics] than is history; for poetry tells more of the universal, history of the particulars. (51b3–8)

By "such that it might happen" we learn from a later context that Aristotle means "what is likely" [*eikos*]. From this you might infer that poetry is meant to be didactic in presenting universal truths, while history deals narrowly with particulars. You might also infer that "poetry" is a near synonym for "fiction," and that Aristotle is proposing a philosophical purpose for fiction in general. But all these inferences are wrong.

First, the two categories–what happened and what is likely to happen–are not exclusive; in fact, much of the first is contained in the second, because, if our expectations are well-adjusted to reality, we will find that much of what happens does indeed seem to us to be likely to happen, and of course everything that happens is possible. Aristotle shows that he understands the point a few lines later, when he allows that poetry may represent actions that have taken place–if it represents them as necessary or likely

(51b29–32). So poets are not forbidden to represent actions that are particulars, nor are poets required to invent the actions that they put on stage.[10] Moreover, the historian is not forbidden to treat patterns of events that are likely or, as Aristotle also says, that occur as they do often or for the most part.[11]

Second, we must not place much emphasis on "more philosophical"; judging from the context of the *Poetics* as a whole, Aristotle does not expect tragic plays to do philosophical work in the usual sense.[12] Nor does he mean that tragic plots are composed of universals or that their agents are what we would call types. The temptation to think otherwise is strong, and excellent scholars have succumbed to it.[13] mimesis aims at *eikos*, however, not because it hopes to teach its audience what is plausible. That would be backwards. The audience already has a sense of what is plausible and a set of expectations about how each type of character will behave. They already subscribe to the generalizations, for example, that young men are bold and old men cautious. Playwrights appeal to these in using mimesis to give the story the power to arouse emotions, but this does not mean that their material is universal. Such generalizations are not always true, and playwrights are not strictly bound by them. *Eikos* is not constituted by generalizations; in the final test, what is eikos is plausible in a particular case, and what may be so in one case may not be (or may not be in the same way) in another. In short, as both Plato and Aristotle recognize, *eikos* is not the stuff of philosophy.[14]

What Aristotle means by consistency of character is not strict correspondence to a type, but rather the lifelikeness that comes with likelihood. The agents of Aristotelian tragedy must have two features: the power to arouse pity and fear, and the capacity to effect action (to be agents). Types or universals do not have these features. Aristotelian agents arouse pity and fear in virtue of their harmony with what is likely or necessary; moreover we accept them as the agents behind events for the same reason. When people act out of character we expect to find that a *deus ex machina* or some other power is at work, and this diminishes their agency. In Sophocles' *Ajax*, we accept him as the agent for acting out rage at the generals, but not for being deluded into taking cattle in their place. This delusion, which is not likely for him, is due to Athena, and is kept off-plot by being placed before the play opens.[15] But to observe this is not to classify Ajax as a universal or to show that the play is about universals. Familiar empirical generalizations lie behind judgments of what is likely; they are not the stuff of philosophy, and, since they are fairly obvious, we don't need to go to the theater to learn them: it is likely that a strong, blunt soldier should care deeply about his honor, as Ajax does. The playwright draws on common wisdom, not on philosophy, and what he does is a drawing on, not a teaching.[16]

Katharsis[17]

Aristotle's definition of tragedy in the opening of Chapter 6 seems to offer this as the aim of tragedy: "through pity and fear achieving the *katharsis* of such experiences" (1449b27), where the "experiences" are usually taken to be the emotions themselves. Aristotle does not say what he means by this, and the more plausible readings of the Greek in the phrase I have just quoted do not seem consistent with other comments he makes on tragedy. Hence the problem of this essay.

Wise commentators leave this word un-translated and undefined, like mimesis. "Katharsis" too has become an English word, although not one with an agreed-upon meaning. Interpretations of *katharsis* are a cemetery of the living dead; not one of the proposed accounts remains unburied by scholars, and yet not one of them stays in its grave. Views long since pronounced dead are dug up, only to bedevil the discussion of the *Poetics* until scholarly undertakers put them under once again. Many scholars interested in the question focus on the text of the *Poetics* itself, working back from Aristotle's judgments about plot and character to hypotheses as to what Aristotle took the aim of tragedy to be. Others work out a theory of *katharsis* from Aristotle's writings on politics, ethics, and psychology.[18] The difficulty, of course, is to bring these two approaches together.

We are faced with a dilemma. If we try to make out the meaning of the word *katharsis*, and then to read that into the later chapters of the *Poetics*, we will wrench them out of shape; if we look to the purpose of tragedy as applied in the later chapters, and then try to read that into the word *katharsis*, we will stretch that word farther than the Greek will bear.

Before Aristotle, and generally in ancient Greek, the word *katharsis* means "cleansing" (on the word's usage, see Halliwell (1986: 185–8), on which this paragraph is based) and had one use in medicine (for purgation–the effect of a laxative) and another in religious ritual (for purification, which participants in ritual must undergo). In addition, Greek writers use the word by way of metaphor for experiences outside the realms of medicine and ritual, e.g., for intellectual clarification (Plato, *Phaedo* 114c). Apparently a further technical use, derived from Pythagorean theory, was available to Aristotle (Halliwell 1986: 187, n. 23).

Now, as we shall see, a good tragedy arouses the emotions of pity and fear for appropriate objects, and there is nothing false or corrupting or dirty about pity and fear in themselves or as they are experienced by a tragic audience. It follows that there is nothing foul in our emotions to clean or to purify or to purge, and we are left with a serious problem of interpretation.

The central chapters of the *Poetics* evaluate different types of plot according to how well they serve the purpose of tragedy, but these make no use of the concept of *katharsis*. Analysis of these chapters and related texts offers our best hope of seeing what Aristotle took to be the aim of tragedy, but I would not recommend connecting the result with any meaning that could reasonably be given the word *katharsis*. The phrase I have quoted is the only one that uses the word in this way in the *Poetics* (see note 7). The word *katharsis* stands alone, orphaned, with no author or explanatory text to support it. If Aristotle meant to put it here, he failed to integrate it into the larger text that it is our duty to elucidate.

Five Questions for Interpreters

These questions are too technical for thorough discussion in these pages, but readers need to know that any account of *katharsis* will either answer these questions directly or assume an answer. All of them remain subjects of controversy:

619

(1)   *Is the katharsis in question a katharsis of emotions or of emotion-producing incidents?* The text does not determine an answer to this fundamental question; the Greek word, *pathêmata*, can mean either. Most scholars, drawing on *Politics* VIII, conclude that Aristotle refers here to a katharsis of emotions. But others point to the parallel use of the word at 59b11–12, where *pathêmata* plainly means "scenes of suffering" (this is Halliwell's translation, 2002), and this rendering is chosen by those who adopt either the intellectual or the dramatic interpretation (recently and notably by Nehamas 1992: 307, who adopts a version of the dramatic account of *katharsis*).

(2)   *Must we take into account the use of the word in Politics* VIII.5–7? The texts that seem most relevant are:

> We say that music should be used not only for one benefit, but for more: these include education and *katharsis* (what we mean by "*katharsis*" we will leave plain for now, but we will make it clearer later in our work on the poetic), and a third, which is recreational[19] and releases tension. (1341b38–41)

> Some are liable to be possessed by spiritual enthusiasm, as we see happening from sacred music: when this fills their souls with extreme excitement, it settles them down, as if by a medical treatment that is a *katharsis*. The same thing happens to people who are prone to pity or fear and are in general highly emotional, and to others as well, insofar as they are subject to such things: all receive a *katharsis* and relief, along with pleasure. (1342a7–15)

Most scholars make extensive use of this text, because the first passage looks like a reference to our text, the *Poetics*. But Aristotle may here be referring to another work on poets. It is possible, and some would say likely, that the *Poetics* itself never contained a passage explaining *katharsis*. The text we have is only a substantial fragment, and opinions differ on this point. Aside from the *Politics*, which is not clear on this point, we have no evidence that the *Poetics* ever contained a passage on *katharsis*, and, indeed, from the text we do have, it seems unlikely that it did. We seem to have everything he wrote about tragedy, and what we have ought to contain the explanation of *katharsis*, if it was ever part of the book (Belfiore 1992: 338–9).

Note that the intellectual account of *katharsis* is inconsistent with the *Politics* passage, so that adherents of that view must set this evidence aside, as must backers of the didactic theory.[20] Indeed, the contexts are different enough that they have reasonable arguments for doing so.

We should, however, draw as much as we can on Aristotle's works in interpreting this one. Other things being equal, an account of the *Poetics* that comports well with other texts is more attractive than one that would make the *Poetics* an anomaly. We may well appeal to the *Rhetoric* and the *Ethics*, as well as to the *Politics*, where these are helpful. But we cannot require that an account of the *Poetics* be perfectly consistent with other writings of Aristotle. We know that, in some other areas, his thinking changed over time, and he may well have changed his view of poetry.[21]

(3)   *Is katharsis supposed to be like an allopathic or a homeopathic remedy?* Applying fear to rid yourself of fear would be homeopathic, while applying fear to rid yourself of anger would be allopathic.

Most scholars, working from the evidence of *Politics* VIII, take it that *katharsis* is homeopathic (for example, Halliwell 1986: 194). But Pythagorean *katharsis* is evidently allopathic, and so is much of Greek medicine. In any case, as we have seen, not all scholars agree that the interpretation of our *katharsis* phrase should be limited by *Politics* VIII. And one scholar has ably defended an allopathic interpretation of both texts (Belfiore 1992: chs. 8 and 9).

(4) *Must we take the katharsis phrase as part of an answer to Plato's criticism of tragedy?* Many scholars take for granted that Aristotle designed the *Poetics* to answer Plato's challenge for a defense of poetry, hoping, through the theory of *katharsis*, to endow tragedy with a purpose high enough to confound Plato's attack on tragic poets.[22] We have no way of knowing that this is true. Aristotle may have Plato's attack in mind, and certainly he shows considerable awareness, through indirect allusions, to Plato's various writings on poetry and mimesis (see Halliwell 1986, pp 331–36, for a list of parallels between the *Poetics* and various Platonic texts). But when Aristotle's main purpose in a text is to refute a Platonic doctrine, as in *Ethics* I.6 or *Politics* II.2, he makes it clear that this is his target. In the *Poetics* he does no such thing. We cannot support the assumption, therefore, that Aristotle's purpose in identifying the aim of tragedy is to defend poetry against Plato's criticism.

In any case, the parallels between Plato and Aristotle on poetry are a bit ragged. A crucial case concerns mimesis. Plato offers a division of poetry into three kinds–mimesis, which is the impersonation of characters through direct speech; pure narrative, which permits only indirect reports of speeches; and a mixture of the two (*Republic* 3.394bc). The passage in the *Poetics* that is supposed to correspond with this divides the modes of mimesis (not the modes of poetry) into only two–narration and impersonation. There is a double clash here: Plato has three categories, and Aristotle seems to have only two,[23] while Aristotle takes narration to be a mode of mimesis, as Plato does not. If Aristotle really intended to tackle Plato's account of mimesis in the passage, why would he confuse the issue in this way? More likely he had a faint recollection of Plato's teaching on the matter and unconsciously echoed that, without perfect accuracy, in his own work. Aristotle starts with a broader concept of mimesis, one that allows for pure narrative to be mimetic, but he gives no argument for this, as he would if he wished to undermine Plato's case against mimesis as such. Indeed, Aristotle is so far from answering Plato's attack on mimesis that he does not even mention Plato's complaint that mimesis involves deception, although Aristotelian mimesis plainly can be deceptive.[24]

Assuming that Aristotle means to answer Plato has led fine scholars to bad conclusions. An admirable writer of the eighteenth century, Thomas Twining, has given an elegant, but illegitimate, argument against the proposal of the Abbé Batteaux that the effect of katharsis is to render painful emotions pleasurable (Twining 1789: 239). That, says Twining, would be no use against Plato, who is well aware of the seductive pleasure that dramatic performance affords an audience. Indeed, the seductiveness of theater is one of Plato's counts against it. So far so good. But we cannot infer, as Twining does, that this interpretation of katharsis is therefore false, because we do not know that Aristotle introduced *katharsis* in his definition of tragedy in order to refute Plato. Truly, an interpretation of Aristotle would be more attractive to us (and perhaps to him as well) if it showed that he had the basis for a sound reply to Plato. But this cannot be a requirement on interpretation. Batteaux is not far off: Part of the effect of mimesis must be to render otherwise painful emotions into pleasurable ones; it is *through* mimesis that these emotions give pleasure (53b9–13). If that undermines an Aristotelian answer to Plato, so much the worse for the assumption that the *Poetics* **is** meant as an answer to Plato.

(5) *Does the katharsis phrase belong in our text at all?* In a recent article, Gregory Scott argues that the phrase about *katharsis* may not belong in the text at all, and urges that it should be purged from the text (Scott 2003). Indeed, Aristotle may have interpolated the phrase himself, planning to bring the *Poetics* into line with other things he had written about poets. We'll never know for sure, but the phrase is doubly awkward. The definition is supposed to flow from what has been said before, but this part does not. And the whole definition is supposed to have work to do in the more developed account of tragic mimesis later in the book. But this part does not. Whether or not the *katharsis* phrase is an interpolation, it is not woven into the fabric of the book, and we had best set it to one side as we work to understand the text of the *Poetics* (Halliwell 2002 does just that, p. 206, with n. 7). Indeed, we will see that the most attractive accounts of *katharsis* are not derived from readings of the *Poetics*, but from a broader understanding of Aristotle's moral and psychological works.

A Short History of *Katharsis* Interpretation

Readers of this chapter will nevertheless want to know what has been concluded about *katharsis*. The following list of five types of interpretations is based on Halliwell, who discusses the history of each in some detail, often providing useful objections.[25] I have modified the list slightly, and I present it here plainly, without arguments pro and con.

1 *Didactic*. The aim of tragedy is to teach a moral lesson by placing bad examples before our eyes, thus warning us away from actions governed by excessive emotion.
2 *Ethical*. Any of a variety of views according to which the experience of tragedy on stage helps us to develop habits of emotion that constitute good ethical character. Within this we can distinguish three subtypes, of which only the third remains a serious contender: (a) Stoic-type theories: tragedy accustoms us to bear hardship; (b) moderation theories: tragedy helps us bring our emotions closer to the mean, as is required by Aristotelian ethics; (c) complex ethical theories: the experience of tragedy purifies ethical character and clears the mind at the same time.[26]
3 *Therapeutic*. Tragedy aims at the pleasurable release of emotion. Defenders of this theory understand *katharsis* on the medical model; its goal is simply pleasure, with no ethical side effects.
4 *Intellectual*. Tragedy aims at clearing up the audience's understanding of the events portrayed. Theories in this family draw on the claim in *Poetics* 4 that mimesis produces understanding; they take the word "*katharsis*" in its well attested use for intellectual clarification. Intellectual accounts have been aired by a number of scholars in recent years. A new recognition of the role of cognition in Aristotle's

account of emotions, however, has blurred the line between intellectual accounts and ethical ones, generating what I have called the "complex ethical" subtype.

5 *Dramatic.* Tragedy achieves *katharsis* by organizing its incidents in a way that washes away the audience's impression that the actions portrayed are cursed or morally repellent. A recent exponent paraphrases the *katharsis* phrase as follows: "carrying such incidents to their appropriate resolution through a course of events that provoke pity and fear" (Nehamas 1992: 308. A fine exposition of this view, not mentioned in Halliwell, is Srivastava 1982.)

The Nature of Our Question

None of these theories answers the question of this essay, which concerns the aim of tragedy as laid out in the *Poetics*, for the simple reason that none of these theories is laid out in the *Poetics*. We have a great deal of textual evidence that does bear on the question, however, and I reviewed that at the start.

The one firm constraint on interpretation of any text is the text itself; we must be as true as we can to as much of the *Poetics* as we can. At the same time, we should be agnostic about those issues that the text does not settle. One of those is *katharsis*. We may frame and evaluate hypotheses on the subject, but we would be irresponsible as scholars if we claimed that the text determines an answer to the riddle of *katharsis*. It does not.

The *Poetics* is a ruin of a book; much has been lost, and the smaller surviving fragments do not help with reconstructing his theory of tragedy (see Janko 1987 for a sober reconstruction on the basis of fragments of the last book on comedy). In reading the *Poetics*, and seeking for the Aristotelian purpose of tragedy, we may be like visitors to an archeological site. Here are most of the remains of an arch; some stones are missing, and the remaining ones are damaged by time. How are we to reconstruct the arch? One hypothesis would be that the arch stood (when it stood) only because it was locked by a keystone, which has now been lost. What can we learn about the keystone from the stones that have survived? That is the mode of search for those who think there is a keystone and it is *katharsis*.

Perhaps, however, the original arch had nothing but more stones of the kind we have seen, so that it depended equally on all of its stones, including the ones that we now see on the ground. Then we would do our best to study the stones we have, as being equally important as those that are lost. Then we would have less speculation ahead of us and, to break the analogy, more hard work with the text. This is the model I prefer. It steers us back to the entire text, and it calls attention to the eighth candidate I listed above–the proposal that the purpose of tragedy is to realize as fully as possible the essence of tragedy. This, after all, is the subject of most of the surviving chapters of the *Poetics*.[27]

Notes

[1] The *ergon* of tragedy is mentioned in the first sentence of chapter 13 (1452b29–30; cf. 50a31, 62b12); the *telos* is invoked in the argument that plot is primary (1450a18, a22–3, cf. 60b24–

6, 62a18–b1, 62b12–15). On these usages, see Halliwell (2002: 204). The *Poetics* covers Bekker pages 1447a–1462b of the Aristotelian corpus; in subsequent citations of passages from this work the first two digits of the Bekker pages will be omitted.

[2] "Fear is a pain or disturbance arising from the impression of an impending evil that is painful or destructive" (*Rhet* II.5.1); "let pity then be [defined as] a certain pain at an evil that is destructive or painful, occurring to someone who does not deserve it, such that you might expect it to happen to yourself or someone who belongs to you, and when it appears to be near" (*Rhet* II.8.1).

[3] "The mimesis is not only of complete action, but of [actions] that arouse pity and fear" (52a2–3). That it is the actions that must arouse emotion is clear from the following: "The most [appropriate] kind of plot, and most [appropriate] kind of action is the kind described above; such a recognition and reversal [occurring together] will yield pity or fear – the kind of action of which tragedy is supposed to be a mimesis" (52a36–b1).

[4] Many scholars hold that Aristotle wrote the *Poetics* during the Lyceum period, 335–323. Halliwell's hypothesis is that at least the thought behind the book dates from the time Aristotle spent at Plato's Academy (367–347). Sophocles died in 406, Euripides probably in the same year, and their like was never seen again. For dating the *Poetics*, see Halliwell (1986: 324ff).

[5] A case in point: A study of the surviving tragedies would not suggest to us Aristotle's claim that tragedy is a mimesis primarily of action, unless "action" is construed to cover such things as expressing grief. Grieving takes up nearly a third of the *Oedipus Tyrannus*, for example, and looms large in most tragedies.

[6] For useful summaries of treatments of mimesis see Somville (1975: 45–54), and, more recently, Halliwell (1986: 110ff). Halliwell offers a major contribution to the subject in his 2002a *passim*.

[7] "It is important to note that Aristotle is here concerned with the *origin of a process* which culminates in the development of tragedy. Children begin learning by their early imitations of the adults around them, and in learning they derive a rudimentary form of cognitive pleasure: but this is only an explanation of how elementary forms of imitation naturally arise among humans. It is not an explanation of the peculiar pleasure of tragedy" (Lear 1992: 322). Richer accounts of *Poetics* 4 are given by those who defend either the complex ethical account of *katharsis*, or the intellectual one.

[8] What follows is a speculative proposal for how to apply the art/mimesis/nature theory to tragedy, developed at greater length in Woodruff (1992). For a different (but attractive) proposal, see Belfiore (1992: 53ff).

[9] Plato, *Phaedrus* 272e–274a. For Aristotle, the matter is more complicated. He holds that probabilities (generalizations that are *eikos*) are what occur only for the most part (*Rhetoric* II.25.8), and contrasts them with necessities, which are always true. He also distinguishes between what is probable absolutely and what is probable in a particular case–that is, under specified circumstances. The former is really probable, and the latter only apparently so (II.24.11). The *Poetics* does not recognize the distinction, but it gives us no reason to think Aristotle would demand any more than apparent probability for tragic incidents, as this would be enough to arouse pity and fear.

[10] This implies that actual events can be the objects of mimesis, although Aristotle does not make the point explicit. mimesis is required for presenting actual events as lifelike enough that they have the power to arouse pity and fear; on Aristotle's theory, mimesis does this by bringing out the way in which likeliness and necessity connect actions with each other and with the character of their agents; only the mimesis of probable chains of incidents arouses emotion effectively (*Poetics*, ch. 16, 1454a16–20, cf. ch. 15).

[11] G. de Ste. Croix has shown that Aristotle elsewhere must take historical characters also to be likely in the relevant sense ("Aristotle on History and Poetry," *The Ancient Historian and His*

Materials, in A. Rorty (1992: 23–32): "if we are to derive episteme from it [a particular action] we have to take the further step of recognizing the general (the universal or the necessary) in the particular" (Rorty 1992: 28).

[12] See Halliwell's excellent discussion (2002: 197ff, esp. 199): "The implication of Aristotle's theory in its entirety is that poetry needs the convincingness of vivid particulars precisely in order to open up for its audience the quasi-philosophical scope of comprehension and discernment that it is capable of providing."

[13] Alexander Nehamas, for example, "Mythology; The Theory of Plot" (1983: 180–97). I quote from pp. 190–1. See also his "Pity and Fear in the *Rhetoric* and the *Poetics*," in Rorty (1992).

[14] See note 9 above. As for consistency of character, Aristotle allows that an agent may behave in ways that are consistently inconsistent (54a27), and, indeed, the great playwrights often have their agents deviate from type. Cadmus is bold in the *Bacchae*, and Haemon is (at least initially) respectful in the *Antigone*, and shows his boldness only when provoked (as seems plausible in his particular case).

[15] The example is mine, but it illustrates Aristotle's evident meaning. Keep in mind that Aristotle's word "character" refers not to an agent, but to qualities that an agent, or a speech, or even a piece of music may have. What we mean by a "character in a play" is captured by Aristotle's word "agent" [*ho prattôn*]. An expanded version of this argument is given in my "What is Creon? Character in Aristotle's *Poetics*," unpublished.

[16] Lear (1988: 324–6), makes a good case for not reading much into "more philosophical" here: "Something does not have to be very philosophical to be more philosophical than history [as Aristotle understands it]" (p. 326); but see de Ste. Croix (1975).

[17] See Halliwell (1986: 350ff), for a summary discussion of scholarly views about *katharsis* with good critical comments; see also Scott (2003), for arguments against more recent accounts.

[18] Halliwell's recent comment on the issue (2005: 404): "Our best hope is to combine *Politics* VIII.5, 1341a21–42a15, which applies the term to certain musico-poetic experiences, with the general tenets of Aristotle's moral psychology of the emotions as expounded in the *Ethics* and *Rhetoric*."

[19] Janko (1992: 344), takes this word, *diagôgê*, to mean "educative entertainment," as it does in some other philosophical texts.

[20] *Politics* 1341a23 contrasts *katharsis* with understanding: *aulos* music produces the first but not the second; we may infer that for Aristotle the means for producing *katharsis* in general do not produce *mathêsis* (understanding). Therefore, the *Politics* passage would, if relevant, rule out any account of katharsis as a kind of *mathêsis*.

[21] His lost dialogue, *On Poets*, for example, may have been closer to *Politics* VIII.5–7 than is the part of the *Poetics* that we have.

[22] This line of interpretation, which is notably present in Halliwell (1986: 184, 355) and Janko (1992: 352), goes back to Proclus, "On the *Republic*," 1.49. Writing over eight hundred years after Plato's death, Proclus may have been drawing inferences from the same evidence that is available to us, or he may have been responding to a tradition based on a work of Aristotle's other than the *Poetics*, such as the lost dialogue *On Poets*.

[23] On the interpretation of the passage, see Woodruff (1992: 78–9). Lucas (1968: 67) and Janko (1987: 72) adopt the two-category reading; Halliwell the three-category reading of Aristotle (1987: 77).

[24] "In composition, one should prefer the convincing but impossible over the possible but unconvincing" (61b9–12, cf. 60a13ff and a26). This implies that good tragedy can be deceptive.

[25] His excellent appendix on the matter is in Halliwell (1986: 350–6). More recent attempts at explaining *katharsis* are mentioned in Halliwell (2002: 206, n. 70) and in the following footnotes.

[26] Belfiore (1992: esp. 345). This is the one type of interpretation I cover that is not listed by Halliwell, but it comes close to capturing most recent work on the topic, including his own proposal: "that tragic katharsis in some way conduces to an ethical alignment between the emotions and the reason" (1986: 201). In this type I would class Lear: tragic *katharsis* allows us to "experience tragic possibility," to alert us to the possibility of emotions that even well-educated people do not have in ordinary life (1992: 333–4). Lear, however, argues against any educational interpretation, on the grounds that tragedy must be pleasant and useful for fully educated persons. Janko takes a position of this kind, but opposed to Lear on this point: *katharsis* involves both emotional and intellectual clarification, with the result that its audience comes to feel appropriate emotions in the right way (1992: 347). Nussbaum's account derives from an Aristotelian theory that takes emotions to be "genuine sources of understanding," and this leads her to a philosophically sophisticated version of the complex ethical view (1992: 281).

[27] I am grateful to E. Belfiore for her advice on this piece. Also, I must express a deep debt to Stephen Halliwell, whose scholarship on the *Poetics* has taught me more than I could acknowledge piecemeal. All translations are my own, unless otherwise indicated.

Bibliography

Belfiore, E. (1992). *Tragic Pleasures: Aristotle on Plot and Emotion* (Princeton, NJ: Princeton University Press).

de Ste. Croix, G. E. M. (1975). *The Ancient Historian and his Materials*, ed. B. Levack (Gregg Publishing); cited here in Rorty (1992), pp. 23–32.

Golden, Leon (1962). "Catharsis," *Transactions of the American Philological Association*, 93, pp. 51–60.

Gregory, Justina (ed.) (2005). *A Companion to Greek Tragedy* (Oxford: Blackwell).

Halliwell, Stephen (1986). *Aristotle's "Poetics"* (London: Duckworth).

Halliwell, Stephen (1987). *The "Politics" of Aristotle: Translation and Commentary* (London: Duckworth).

Halliwell, Stephen (1995). *Aristotle "Poetics,"* ed. and trans. Stephen Halliwell, in *Aristotle, Longinus, Demetrius* (Cambridge, MA: Harvard University Press).

Halliwell, Stephen (2002a). *The Aesthetics of mimesis: Ancient Texts and Modern Problems* (Princeton, NJ: Princeton University Press).

Halliwell, Stephen (2002b) "The Rewards of mimesis: Pleasure, Understanding and Emotion in Aristotle's Aesthetics," in Halliwell, pp. 177–206.

Halliwell, Stephen (2005). "Learning from Suffering: Ancient Responses to Tragedy," in Gregory, pp. 394–412.

Janko, Richard (1987). *Aristotle: "Poetics"* (Indianapolis, IN: Hackett).

Janko, Richard (1992). "From Catharsis to the Aristotelian Mean," in Rorty, pp. 341–58.

Lear, Jonathan (1988). "Katharsis," *Phronesis*, 33, pp. 297–326; cited here in Rorty (1992), pp. 315–340.

Lucas, D. W. (1968). *Aristotle "Politics"* (Oxford: Clarendon Press).

Nehamas, A. (1983). "Mythology: The Theory of Plot," in J. Fisher (ed.), *Essays on Aesthetics: Perspectives on the Work of Monroe Beardsley* (Philadelphia: Temple University Press, 1983), pp. 180–97.

Nehamas, Alexander (1992). "Pity and Fear in the *Rhetoric* and the *Poetics*," in Rorty, pp. 291–314.

Nussbaum, Martha (1992). "Tragedy and Self-Sufficiency: Plato and Aristotle on Fear and Pity," in Rorty, pp. 261–90.

Rorty, Amelie (1992). *Essays on Aristotle's "Poetics"* (Princeton, NJ: Princeton University Press).

Scott, Gregory (1999). "The Poetics of Performance: The Necessity of Spectacle, Music, and Dance in Aristotelian Tragedy," in Salim Kemal and Ivan Gaskell (eds.), *Performance and Authenticity in the Arts* (Cambridge: Cambridge University Press).

Scott, Gregory (2003). "Purging the *Poetics*," *Oxford Studies in Ancient Philosophy*, 25, pp. 233–62.

Somville, Pierre (1975). *Essai sur la poetique d'Aristote* (Paris: J. Vrin).

Srivastasa, Krishna Gopal (1982). *Aristotle's Doctrine of Tragic Katharsis: A Critical Study* (Allahabad: Kitab Mahal).

Twining, Thomas (1789). *Aristotle's "Treatise on Poetry," Translated with Notes* on the *Translation, and on the Original, and two Dissertations on Practical, and Musical, Imitation* (London).

Woodruff, Paul (1992). "Aristotle on mimesis," in Rorty, pp. 73–96.

40

The Elements of Tragedy

ELIZABETH BELFIORE

Introduction

The first sentence of the *Poetics* gives a clear statement of the goals of Aristotle's treatise: "Concerning the poetic art itself and its forms, what sort of power each one has, and how one should organize plots if the poetic composition is going to be good, and again, of how many and what kinds of parts [it consists], and similarly concerning the other things belonging to the same method of inquiry, let us speak beginning according to nature, first from first things" (*Poet* 1 1447a8–13). The work ends with a similar statement of goals: "Concerning tragedy and epic, themselves and their forms and parts, how many they are and how they differ, and what are the causes of their being well or not well [made], and concerning criticisms and solutions, let so much have been said" (26 1462b16–19). Following the agenda laid out in its opening sentence the *Poetics*: (1) considers the poetic art (one kind of mimesis)[1] as a whole, and its "forms" (that is, genres); (2) distinguishes the different "powers," that is, emotional effects produced by different genres of poetry; (3) examines how plots are best constructed, and, (4) discusses the parts of tragedy and of the tragic plot. However, at least in the text that has been transmitted to us, Aristotle's focus is narrower than his opening sentence suggests. While chapters 23 and 24 are devoted to epic, and comedy, which may have been the subject of a lost second book (Janko 1984, 1987), is given a brief treatment in chapter 5, the heart of the treatise (chapters 6 through 22) is concerned with a single genre: tragedy. Within this discussion of tragedy, moreover, Aristotle concentrates, as his opening statement indicates, on one part of tragedy: the plot. Thus, while Aristotle's ideas cannot be generalized into a universal literary theory, the *Poetics* is an invaluable source of information about a specific poetic genre, Greek tragedy, as performed in Athens in the fifth and fourth centuries BCE, according to specific rules and conventions.

Mimesis and the emotional effects of tragedy (the first two items on the list above) are the subject of Paul Woodruff's essay in this volume. My own contribution is concerned with items (3) and (4) in this list, and follows the order in which these topics are discussed in the *Poetics*. Below, I consider the relationship between the elements of tragedy and Aristotle's definition of tragedy. I next focus on the two most important parts of tragedy: plot and character. The following section studies the parts that make up simple and complex plots, and I go on to analyze the criteria for good and bad plots set out in chapters 13 and 14.

The Elements of Tragedy and Its Definition

Aristotle defines tragedy as "mimesis of a serious and complete action, having magnitude, in sweetened speech, with each of the kinds [of speech] separate in the parts, enacted and not narrated, by means of pity and fear accomplishing the katharsis of these kinds of emotions" (6 1449b24–8). As will be seen shortly, this definition explains why tragedy has those particular elements that belong to it: complication and solution, and what I will call its qualitative and quantitative parts.[2] First, however, it is essential to examine briefly Aristotle's concept of an action that is serious, complete, and has magnitude.

Tragedy is mimesis of a serious action because, in the first place, it is mimesis of the actions of serious people, those who are better than us in a social and ethical sense (2 1448a1–5, 16–19, with 13 1453a10–12). Tragedy is also mimesis of a serious action because events in the plot occur in a particular way. According to Aristotle, poetry is "more philosophical and more serious than history" because it states "the universal," that is, "what kinds of things a certain kind of person says or does according to probability or necessity" (9 1451b5–9). Events that follow one another by probability or necessity are those that occur "because of" and not merely "after" other events (9 1452a4–6, 10 1452a18–21); that is, they are efficiently caused by other events, and do not merely happen by chance. Modern examples might be drawn from murder mysteries, in which the detective discovers the chain of events leading up to a crime. Even events that in fact happen by chance, Aristotle writes, are more effective if they seem to occur for a reason. Consider a statue of a certain man that happens by chance to fall and kill the murderer of this man. In a good plot, the poet might make it appear as though the statue, animated by a desire for revenge, fell of its own accord (9 1452a6–10). The idea of probability or necessity also helps to illuminate the concepts of "complete" and "magnitude" in the definition of tragedy. A tragedy has magnitude, and is one, whole, and complete, if it is a mimesis of a series of events moving from beginning, to middle, to end, according to probability or necessity, either from bad to good fortune, or from good to bad fortune (7 1450b23–31, 7 1451a12–15).

A plot that is not one, whole, and complete is defective in one or more ways. It may be "double," having a happy ending for good people, and an unhappy ending for bad people (13 1453a31–3), or it may be a mimesis of more than one action, recounting, for example, all the things that happened to Odysseus (chapter 8). A defective plot may also be "episodic," having "episodes that occur after one another but not according to probability or necessity" (9 1451b33–5).

Aristotle's use of Greek terms cognate with "episode" is controversial and inconsistent. In chapter 12, an "episode" is an "act" between choral odes. In chapter 17, however, an "episode" is opposed in some way to the events that make up the plot. I have argued that Aristotle distinguishes between the probable or necessary events that make up the plot ("the universal": 17 1455b1), and the merely plausible "episodes." His meaning is clearest from the examples he gives in chapter 17, two of which are from Euripides' *Iphigenia in Tauris*: Orestes' madness "by means of which he was captured," and "the rescue by means of the purification" of Orestes. The madness and purification are "episodes" that are "appropriate" to the story (17 1455b12–15). Orestes' capture and rescue, on the other hand, are not merely "episodes," but are included in Aristotle's outline (below) as events of the plot itself because they follow by probability or necessity from previous events. There are a number of different plausible ways, besides madness and purification, in which a poet writing about the Orestes story might bring about his capture and rescue. For example, Orestes might be captured as he attempts to break into the temple, and Iphigenia might give his guards a drug to effect escape (Belfiore 1992a: 111–31, 1992b: 365–6).

A tragedy that is serious, complete, and has magnitude has two sections, a complication and a solution: "By 'complication' I mean the [tragedy] from the beginning until the last part from which it changes to good or bad fortune. By 'solution' I mean the [tragedy] from the beginning of the change until the end" (18 1455b26–9). The beginning of the change from good to bad, or from bad to good fortune, marks the structural and emotional focal point of the tragedy. Such a change begins, for example, when Iphigenia recognizes her brother in Euripides' *Iphigenia in Tauris*, and, instead of sacrificing him, helps him to escape.

The definition of tragedy alludes to the *quantitative* parts of tragedy, the distinct portions of speech and song into which a tragedy is divided, when it states that "each of the kinds [of speech are] separate in the parts" (6 1449b25–6, 29–31). These parts are (1) the prologue, that part of the tragedy before the entrance of the chorus, (2) the "episodes," the "acts" between choral songs, (3) the *exodos*, that part of the tragedy after the last choral song, and (4) the choral parts, which include (a) the *parodos*, the first song of the chorus, and (b) *stasima*, choral songs with certain metrical characteristics (12 1452b15–27). Tragedy has these quantitative parts because it is a performative genre in which entrances and exits, and different ways of performing–spoken dialogue or song–played a major role. "Song," moreover, is "the greatest of the sweeteners" (6 1450b16) of speech, and "sweetened speech" is part of the definition of tragedy.

Aristotle derives the six *qualitative* parts of tragedy from its definition. These are: (1) *plot*, (2) *character*, (3) *thought*, (4) *style*, (5) *song*, and (6) *spectacle*. *Plot*, "the composition of the events" (6 1450a4–5), is a necessary part of tragedy because tragedy is defined as mimesis of action (6 1449b24, 36), and it is plot that accomplishes this kind of mimesis (6 1450a3–4). *Character* and *thought* are parts because the action is done by people acting, who necessarily are of a certain kind with respect to their character and thought (6 1449b36–8). Aristotle's term "*character*" (*êthos*) refers to that which gives the agents of the dramatic action (our "characters") certain ethical qualities (6 1450a5–6, 19), and "shows what kind of choice someone makes" (6 1450b8–9, 15 1454a17–19). Aristotle defines *thought* as speeches "in which people make demonstrations or reveal their opinions" (6 1450a6–7, 1450b11–12), and he includes under "thought" proof and refutation and the arousal of emotion (chapter 19). *Style*, "the composition of the verses" (6 1449b34–5), or "verbal expression" (6 1450b13–14), and *song*, which Aristotle does not define, constitute the medium of tragedy, a genre in which verses are sung as well as spoken. Finally, because tragedy is performed and not narrated, *spectacle*, the "visual arrangement," is a necessary part of it (6 1449b31–3).

The *Poetics* has a somewhat ambivalent attitude toward spectacle and performance (Halliwell 1986: 337–43). Although spectacle creates a powerful emotional effect, it requires the least poetic skill, and does not produce the "proper pleasure" of tragedy. In fact, just hearing the story of Oedipus, without seeing it enacted, would arouse pity and fear. Moreover, the poet who arouses emotion by means of spectacle is lacking in skill and produces what is not appropriately fearful, but merely "monstrous" (6 1450b16–20, 14 1453b3–11). The "monstrous" is fear produced by visual effects, such as the masks and costumes of the Furies in Aeschylus' *Eumenides*, figures described as "terrible to see" (line 34), resembling Gorgons or Harpies, black, abominable, and with dripping eyes (48–54). The appearance of the Furies causes extreme fear in the old priestess (36–38), but properly tragic pity and fear in this play are aroused by the plot: the story of Orestes' sufferings after he has killed his mother.

It is apparent from Aristotle's account of the qualitative parts of tragedy that his concerns differ in some important respects from those of modern literary critics (Belfiore 2000b). His concept of "character" is narrower than our "characterization," for it refers specifically to ethical choice. Moreover, nothing in the *Poetics* corresponds to the modern categories of point of view (or focalization), or to what modern critics call "themes." That is, the *Poetics* does not discuss the philosophical, political, social, or religious ideas that may be expressed in tragedies. In fact, Aristotle barely mentions the gods, who play such an important role in the extant tragedies.

Plot and Character

According to Aristotle, plot is the most important part of tragedy, while character (*êthos*: that which gives ethical qualities to the agents of the dramatic action) is secondary. Plot, "the organization . . . of the events . . . is the first and most important part of tragedy" (7 1450b22–3); "the first principle and as it were the soul of tragedy is the plot; second is character" (6 1450a38–9); "without [mimesis of] action there could be no tragedy; without character there could be" (6 1450a23–5). Although Aristotle's insistence that plot is much more important than character goes counter to many modern ideas about drama, it makes a great deal of sense within the context of his theory of tragedy. Tragedy is mimesis of action (6 1449b24, 36), as opposed to other objects, such as characters and emotions (1 1447a28), and it is plot, and not character, that is mimesis of action (6 1450a3–4).

Because tragedy is imitation of action and not of character, it is the structure of the plot, rather than character, that accomplishes the function of tragedy, the arousal of pity and fear and the production of *katharsis*. "Ethical speeches," writes Aristotle, will not accomplish "that which is the function of tragedy" as well as the plot and "the organization of events" will (1450a29–33). This idea is expressed graphically in Aristotle's comparison of plot to a white outline drawing and of character without plot to coloring smeared on at random (1450a39–b3).

Aristotle provides examples of events without character when he gives outline sketches of the plots of Euripides' *Iphigenia in Tauris*, and of Homer's *Odyssey*:

> A certain girl, after being sacrificed and disappearing from the view of those sacrificing her, was settled in another land where the custom was to sacrifice strangers to the goddess. She came to hold that priesthood. A while later, it happened that the brother of the priestess arrived . . . He arrived, was seized, and when about to be sacrificed [by his sister], he made himself known, either as Euripides or as Polyidus wrote it, saying, as was plausible, that not only was it his sister's fate to be sacrificed, but his own also. From this [revelation] comes rescue. (17 1455b3–12)

> A certain man is away from home for many years, carefully watched by Poseidon and alone. Moreover, things at home are in such a state that his possessions are wasted by suitors and his son is plotted against. He himself arrives, storm-tossed, and making himself known by some, attacks and is himself saved while he destroys his enemies. This is what is proper [to the story]: the rest is episode. (17 1455b17–23)

In these plot outlines, Aristotle focuses on what he considers to be the bare events of the story and omits much of what modern readers find most interesting. He does not mention, for example, Iphigenia's hatred of the father who sacrificed her, the noble friendship between Orestes and Pylades, or the theological problems raised by a goddess who demands human sacrifice. Nor does he discuss Homer's characterization of Odysseus as "the man of many turns," who overcomes the obstacles to his homecoming, or Penelope's prudence and resourcefulness in fending off the suitors.

In giving priority to plot, Aristotle is not saying that character is unimportant, or that there can be good tragedies without it. In fact, two tragedies with the same plot might well be distinguished from each other in part by their use of character, as happens in the case of the two Iphigenia tragedies summarized by Aristotle, that of Euripides and that of Polyidus (about whom nothing is known apart from this passage), in the example given above. Aristotle's point is that tragedy arouses pity and fear because it is mimesis of specific terrible and pitiable events, such as fratricide, parricide, and incest, and not because it portrays an individual with particular ethical and psychological qualities, who makes choices that are noble or blameworthy. It is significant that Aristotle's analysis of plot types does not identify the agents of the dramatic action in ethical terms, for example, as "the villain," or "the hero," but as being related to each other, as brother, son, father, and mother (14 1453b20–21: see below).

Simple and Complex Plots

After discussing the qualitative parts of tragedy in chapter 6, Aristotle focuses on the most important of these parts, the plot. He identifies two kinds of plots: simple and complex (chapter 10). Simple plots, like that of Homer's *Iliad* (24 1459b14), proceed from good to bad fortune (or vice versa) without recognition or reversal (a change in direction within the movement of the plot). Simple plots have only a *pathos*, a destructive or painful event. Complex plots, like that of Sophocles' *Oedipus the King*, are superior (13 1452b30–2) because, in addition to *pathos*, they also have reversal, recognition, or both. Each of these three parts of the tragic plot – *pathos*, recognition, and reversal (11 1452b9–10) – contributes in its own way to the arousal of pity and fear (see, e.g., 11 1452a38–b1, 14 1453b14–22).

Pathos

Aristotle defines *pathos* in *Poetics* 11 1452b11–13: "The *pathos* is a destructive or painful action, for example, deaths in full view, and great pain, and wounds, and things of this kind." That the *pathos* is the most important of the three parts of the plot is apparent not only from the fact that it is the only part that belongs to every plot, whether simple or complex, but also from Aristotle's account of comedy. Comedy's subject matter, "the laughable," is directly opposed to the tragic *pathos*, for it is "an error and ugliness that is painless and not destructive" (5 1449a34–5). Aristotle does not explicitly say whether or not a tragedy can have more than one *pathos*. His examples in chapter 14, however, suggest that tragic plots usually have one major *pathos* with important consequences for the good or bad fortune of the agents of the dramatic action.

Aristotle's inclusion of "deaths in full view" in his definition of the *pathos* is puzzling, because deaths seldom or never occur on the stage in Greek tragedy. It is possible, then, that *pathos* includes events that are narrated in vivid language (Janko 1987: 97). A *pathos* need not actually take place in order to arouse pity and fear in the best way; it need only be "about to occur" (14 1453b18, 21). For example, when Iphigenia is about to sacrifice her brother, the audience reacts with pity and fear to this imminent act of kin killing. Indeed, according to Aristotle's *Rhetoric*, fear is aroused by the expectation of an imminent destructive or painful evil (II.5 1382a21–2) and pity is aroused when an evil "appears near" (II.8 1385b13–16).

Aristotle makes it clear that the best tragic *pathos* is a destructive and painful event that takes place within family relationships. In discussing events that arouse pity and fear, Aristotle states that they must necessarily occur (1) between kin, (2) between enemies, or (3) between neutrals. Events that take place between enemies or neutrals, he says, are not pitiable, "except in respect to the *pathos* itself" (14 1453b14–19). The best *pathos* is one that occurs between close kin: "When the events take place within family relationships, for example, when brother kills brother, or son father, or mother son, or son mother, or is about to kill them, or does something else of this kind, this is to be sought [by the poet]" (14 1453b19–22). In excluding harm of enemy by enemy from the best plays, Aristotle indicates that deaths in battle, like those celebrated in Homer's *Iliad*, do not arouse pity and fear most effectively, even though they are painful and destructive. Thus, when the sons of Oedipus kill each other in battle, in Euripides' *Phoenician Women*, it is the fact of their relationship, and not simply their deaths, that best arouses pity and fear. Although Aristotle's examples are exclusively of murder, the words "or does something else of this kind" suggest that these instances are exemplary rather than restrictive. Indeed, Aristotle discusses tragedies in which the *pathos* is betrayal (14 1454a8), rape (16 1454b36–37), and incest (16 1452a25–6). In these tragedies, kin does not kill, but instead does serious harm to kin.

The Greek term I have translated as "family relationship" is *philia*, a word that can refer to relationships between either kin or unrelated friends. Aristotle's statement at 14 1453b19–22, quoted above, and his examples in chapter 14 indicate that at least the primary reference here is to blood kinship: Orestes kills his mother Clytemnestra (1453b23–4); Medea kills her children (1453b28–9); Oedipus kills his father and marries his mother (1453b30–1); and Iphigenia is about to kill her brother (1454a4–

633

7). Blood kinship is also the central focus in many other Greek tragedies (Belfiore 2000a). Of the thirty-two extant tragedies, three represent sibling harming sibling, or being about to harm sibling (Aeschylus: *Seven against Thebes*; Euripides: *Iphigenia in Tauris*, *Phoenician Women*). In twelve of the extant tragedies parent harms child, or child parent (Aeschylus: *Eumenides*, *Libation Bearers*; Sophocles: *Electra*, *Oedipus the King*; Euripides: *Bacchae*, *Electra*, *Herakles*, *Hippolytus*, *Ion*, *Iphigenia in Aulis*, *Medea*, *Orestes*). These are the same relationships cited in *Poetics* 14 1453b19–22. In a number of other tragedies, however, husband is murdered by wife (for example, Aeschylus' *Agamemnon* and Sophocles' *Women of Trachis*). Accordingly, some scholars oppose the view that the *Poetics* is exclusively concerned with blood kinship, and instead expand the category of *philia* relationships to include spouses, or other kinship-like relationships, such as that between host and guest.[3]

The idea that tragedy is centrally concerned with family relationships is deeply rooted in Aristotle's views on the importance of these relationships in human nature and society. According to his *Politics*, "the human being is by nature a political animal," that is, one whose nature it is to live, in the first place, in families (I.2 1253a2–3, 1252a26–31). This concept of human nature is the basis for Aristotle's belief that "lack of *philoi* [kin or friends] and isolation [is] most terrible" (*EE* 1234b32–3). According to this view, Oedipus is pitiable not so much because he suffers blindness, pain, and the loss of wealth and power, as because he is irrevocably cut off from the family relationships that make him part of the human community.

Reversal

In addition to *pathos*, complex plots also have recognition, reversal, or both. Aristotle defines reversal (*peripeteia*) as "the change to the opposite of the things done, as was said" (11 1452a22–3). It is important not to confuse the reversal of complex plots with the tragic change (*metabasis*: 11 1452a16) that belongs to simple as well as complex plots. The tragic change is the whole movement of the plot between the two end points of good and bad fortune (7 1451a12–14), whereas reversal is a change in direction within the movement between these two end points. Most scholars believe that Aristotle's remark, "as was said," after the definition of reversal, is a reference back to his statement that pity and fear are aroused when events occur "contrary to expectation, because of one another" (9 1452a4; Dupont-Roc and Lallot 1980: 231–2; Halliwell 1987: 116–18; Lucas 1968: 129). In reversal, the expectations of the agents of the dramatic action, and of the audience are overturned (Halliwell 1987: 116). More specifically, in reversal, the action of an agent of a dramatic action is prevented from achieving its intended result and instead arrives at an opposite actual result (Belfiore 1992a: 141–53). Aristotle's example of Sophocles' *Oedipus the King* confirms this interpretation. A messenger arrives with the intention of bringing Oedipus good fortune. As it happens, however, he produces the opposite result, for his revelations lead to Oedipus' discovery that he has had the supreme bad fortune to commit parricide and incest (11 1452a23–6). Within this scene, then, the action doubles back upon itself, moving first toward good fortune, and then back again in the direction of bad fortune.

Recognition

Aristotle defines recognition in chapter 11: "Recognition, just as the word also indicates, is a change from ignorance to knowledge, either to friendship or to enmity, of those defined with respect to good or bad fortune" (1452a29–32). There can be recognitions of inanimate objects, and recognition that one has done something, but recognition of persons is the best kind, because it leads to good or bad fortune (11 1452a33–b3). In Sophocles' *Oedipus the King*, Oedipus commits parricide and incest in ignorance, and afterwards recognizes that Laius and Jocasta are his parents. This recognition leads to Oedipus' bad fortune. Recognition can also lead to good fortune. For example, in Euripides' *Iphigenia in Tauris*, when sister is about to kill brother, in ignorance of his identity, she recognizes him in time, and, as a result, is able to escape with him to Greece. Thus, Aristotelian recognition is not simply a mental state in which someone comes to acquire knowledge. Instead, because it is one of the three parts of the plot, recognition must be an actual event arousing pity and fear and affecting the movement of the dramatic action between good or bad fortune.

Recognition involves more than mere knowledge of identity, however. The definition of recognition as "a change . . . either to friendship or to enmity" indicates that it also involves the realization that one is in a state of friendship or enmity with the person recognized. Some specific examples from tragedy illustrate what Aristotle means when he defines recognition as a change "to friendship" or " to enmity." Orestes merely recognizes the identity of a person when he recognizes that the woman he sees is Electra (Aeschylus's *Libation Bearers*, line 16). The recognition that fits Aristotle's definition, on the other hand, begins at line 212, when Orestes reveals his identity to Electra, and the siblings pledge loyalty to each other and enmity to their mother. This recognition is a change "to friendship;" it is a recognition that a state of friendship exists between the siblings, that they are prepared to act as friends. The same play has a good example of a recognition that is a change "to enmity." When Clytemnestra understands that Orestes is her son she also understands that he has acted as an enemy to her by killing her lover, Aegisthus. As a result, she in turn acts as an enemy to Orestes, and calls for an ax to kill him (887–9).

Aristotle devotes chapter 16 to a discussion of six ways of bringing about recognition. The least skillful way is by means of signs. For example, Odysseus is recognized by his scar (1454b20–30). Other inferior kinds of recognitions include: recognitions made up by the poet, recognitions from memory, recognitions from reasoning, and recognitions from false inference. The best kind of recognition, however, is that which arises "from the events themselves." For example, in Euripides' *Iphigenia in Tauris*, Iphigenia is recognized by her brother because she wishes, as it is likely that she should, to send letters to her friends (1455a16–19).[4]

In the best complex plays, reversal occurs together with recognition (11 1452a32–3). This point in the play is also the beginning of the change from good to bad, or from bad to good fortune; that is, it marks the end of the complication and the beginning of the solution. A tragedy can, however, have more than one recognition (11 1452b7–8).

General Principles

A good plot, whether simple or complex, is a mimesis of pitiable and terrible events that take place between close family members (14 1453b19–22), and that occur not by chance, but according to probability or necessity (9 1451a38, b5–10). Each of the three parts of the plot makes an important contribution to this kind of mimesis.

Aristotle explicitly states that recognition and reversal should come about according to probability or necessity (10 1452a18–21, 11 1452a23–4). Although the *pathos* is not explicitly said to do so, that it should occur according to probability or necessity is implied by the fact that it is one of the three parts of a plot (11 1452b10) that is itself constructed according to this principle. Moreover, in a good plot, one family member would not kill another for no reason.

Philia, the relationship among family members, is also important in all three parts of the plot, each of which is defined in terms of, or depends for its emotional effects upon, the existence of family relationships among the agents of the dramatic action. The *pathos* that best arouses pity and fear is said to be murder or other serious harm, actual or imminent, of people within family relationships (14 1453b15–22). Recognition is a change from ignorance to knowledge of *philia* (14 1453b31). Although reversal need not involve family relationships, in the best plays, reversal and recognition occur at the same time (11 1452a32–3). In the *Oedipus*, for example, Oedipus' recognition that he has committed parricide and incest is coincident with a reversal, because it leads directly to his downfall. Family relationships are also important in reversal because reversal is a change of the action from good to bad or from bad to good fortune (11 1452a22–3), and family relationships are important to good fortune.

Good and Bad Tragic Plots

In chapters 13 and 14, Aristotle considers "how one should organize plots if the poetic composition is going to be good" (1 1447a2–3) by evaluating and ranking a number of specific kinds of plots. His analysis in these chapters creates difficulties, however, because the criteria used in chapter 13 seem to many scholars to be inconsistent with those used in chapter 14. After discussing each chapter in turn, this section briefly considers the question of consistency.

Unhappy endings

In chapter 13, Aristotle argues that the best tragedies are those with unhappy endings. Euripides, he writes, is the most tragic of the poets, because most of his tragedies end in bad fortune (13 1453a22–30). Unhappy endings, however, are not the only consideration. The best plots, according to Aristotle, portray "the person between these [two extremes of virtue and vice]." That is, they portray "someone not outstanding in virtue or justice, who changes [from good] to bad fortune, not because of vice and depravity, but because of some *hamartia* [mistake]. He is one of those with great good reputation and good fortune, for example, Oedipus and Thyestes and eminent men from families like these" (13 1453a7–12). The best plot, then, according to chapter 13, is a mimesis of (1) a change from good to bad fortune, (2) of someone between the two extremes of virtue and vice, (3) who falls because of a *hamartia*, and (4) who has great good reputation and good fortune.

Aristotle's requirement that the bad fortune in the best plot be due to *hamartia*, and his example of Oedipus, have been the subject of much controversy. *Hamartia* is a noun cognate with the verb *hamartano*, whose primary meaning is "to miss the mark," especially in throwing a spear. Now Aristotle excludes vice as a cause of the change to bad fortune because vicious people deserve bad fortune, and so do not arouse pity and fear. It is clear, then, that *hamartia* causes a change to bad fortune without marking a person as vicious. There is little agreement, however, about what *hamartia* is, or about the specific *hamartia* Oedipus commits in Sophocles' play. Some scholars argue that *hamartia* is a nonculpable factual mistake (Else 1957: 378–85; Lucas 1968: 299–307). Others hold that the concept can also include some mistakes for which a person is to blame (Halliwell 1986: 220–2; Heath 1996: xxxi–xxxiii; Sherman 1992; Stinton 1975). Each of these interpretations involves difficulties. An innocent mistake might seem to be lacking in dramatic interest, and to exclude the probability or necessity that a good plot requires. Innocent mistakes can lead to car accidents, for example, but car accidents caused by mere mistakes are not usually good subjects for drama. On the other hand, if *hamartia* includes blameworthy mistakes, it is not clear how these mistakes differ from the mistakes Aristotle wants to exclude: those that result from vice. I argue that the kind of *hamartia* in question in *Poetics* 13 is indeed a nonculpable factual mistake, but one that also has certain other characteristics. For example, like Oedipus's parricide, it is a "big mistake" (1453a16), with significant consequences, done in ignorance of important facts (Belfiore 1992a: 166–70).

This best kind of plot can be better understood by comparison with three inferior plots also discussed in this chapter. Aristotle first states that the best plot is complex and is a mimesis of fearful and pitiable events (13 1452b30–33). Next, he states that the agents of the dramatic action may be outstandingly virtuous, vicious, or between these two extremes, and that they may move from good to bad fortune, or from bad to good fortune. Aristotle lists and briefly comments on four ways in which a plot may combine these three possible ethical qualities of the agents of the dramatic action with the two ways in which the plot can move between good and bad fortune (1452b34–1453a12). I list these possibilities below, in order from best to worst:

1 A person between the two extremes moves from good to bad fortune because of *hamartia*.
2 A vicious person moves from good to bad fortune.
3 An outstandingly virtuous person moves from good to bad fortune.
4 A vicious person moves from bad to good fortune.

The first plot is the best (1453a22–3), because it best arouses pity and fear. According to chapter 13, the best tragedies end in bad fortune (1453a23–6). Moreover, someone between the two extremes of virtue and vice arouses pity by being undeserving of the bad fortune he or she suffers, and arouses fear by being like us (1453a4–6). That is, the observation of the sufferings of others who, like ourselves, are neither vicious nor exceptionally virtuous, arouses in us the fear that we might also suffer bad fortune

(Belfiore 1992a: 231; Dupont-Roc and Lallot 1980: 239; Halliwell 1986: 176). This plot is also superior because it has *hamartia* and portrays someone like Oedipus or Thyestes, who is powerful and wealthy (1453a10–12).

The other three plots are inferior because, even though all of them could portray people in great good fortune, they fail to arouse pity and fear in other respects. In addition to lacking pity and fear, plot (4) is "most untragic," because it lacks "the *philanthropon*" (1452b36–1453a1), an aspect of tragedy that has been variously explained as "poetic justice," "sympathy," or a pleasing quality of the plot (Carey 1988). Plot (2) is superior to plot (4) because it has the *philanthropon*, although it lacks pity and fear (1453a1–4). This plot is also superior to plot (3), which is said to be *miaron*, "repulsive," in addition to lacking pity and fear (1452b34–6).

It is not difficult to see why Aristotle calls plots (2) and (4) inferior. These plots do not arouse pity because vicious people deserve to suffer, and they do not arouse fear because vicious people are not like us; at least, we do not usually think of ourselves as vicious. Moreover, the bad fortune of a vicious person often results from vice rather than *hamartia*. Aristotle's reasons for considering plot (3) defective are harder to understand. This plot does not arouse fear because it portrays someone superior to ourselves, but it might well contain *hamartia*. And why does Aristotle think that it is "repulsive" (*miaron*) instead of arousing pity (1452b35–6)? One possible answer is to argue that Aristotle must have held that the suffering of an outstandingly virtuous person seems so cruel and unfair that the indignation it arouses overpowers any other kind of response (Stinton 1975: 238–9; Halliwell 1987: 125).

Aristotle does not mention two other kinds of plots that end in good fortune: (5) someone who is outstandingly virtuous moves from bad to good fortune, and (6) a person between the extremes of virtue and vice moves from bad to good fortune. It is easy to see why (5) would be inferior. This plot does not arouse pity because it is not a mimesis of undeserved suffering, and it does not arouse fear because it does not portray someone like us. More difficult to understand is why Aristotle omits (6), especially since this is the very plot pattern that is said to be the best in chapter 14: that of Euripides' *Iphigenia in Tauris*. This is one of the reasons why the two chapters appear to be inconsistent.

Happy endings

In chapter 14, Aristotle does not explicitly state that the best plots have happy endings. He does, however, write that the best plot is one like that of Euripides' *Iphigenia in Tauris*, that in fact has a happy ending, and he ranks the *Oedipus* second. Aristotle still holds that the best plots are those that arouse pity and fear most effectively, but he now uses different criteria in ranking plots.

The agents of the dramatic action, he states, may be family members, enemies, or neutrals (1453b15–17), and, Aristotle writes, "it is necessary for them to act or not to act, and to do so with or without knowledge" (1453b36–7). There are, then, three kinds of criteria for good plots in chapter 14: (1) what kinds of human relationships exist, (2) whether an agent acts or does not act, and (3) whether an agent acts with or without knowledge. The first criterion was discussed above: in the best tragedies, the agents are close kin. In the second criterion, "not to act" means, as Aristotle's discussion shows, to be about to act (1453b20–1, 1453b38, 1454a6, 8) without actually doing so. Third, acting with or without knowledge means, as Aristotle's examples make clear, acting with or without knowledge of a family relationship. Aristotle ranks plots according to these three criteria. He immediately excludes those in which enemies or neutrals harm one another, saying that these lack pity and fear (1453b17–19). In the rest of the chapter he is concerned only with plots in which kin harm or are about to harm kin. Aristotle uses the second and third criteria – (2) someone acts or does not act, and (3) does so with or without knowledge – to create a hierarchy of plots different from that in chapter 13. I list them below, in order from best to worst, along with Aristotle's examples (1453b27–1454a8):

1 Someone is about to act, without knowledge; recognition takes place and the act does not occur. Example: Euripides' *Iphigenia in Tauris*.
2 Someone acts, without knowledge, and then recognition occurs. Example: Sophocles' *Oedipus the King*.
3 Someone acts, with knowledge. Example: Euripides' *Medea*.
4 Someone is about to act, with knowledge, but does not act. Example: Haimon's attack on Creon in Sophocles' *Antigone*.[5]

In all of these plots, pity or fear is aroused by the occurrence, or prospect, of kin killing. As we have seen above, however, the best plots also arouse pity and fear because they make good use of the three parts of the tragic plot: *pathos*, recognition, and reversal.

Aristotle states that (4) is the worst plot because it is "without a *pathos*" (*apathes*) (1453b39). This statement is puzzling because a destructive or painful event also fails to occur in (1), which is not said to lack this part of tragedy. As an example of (4), Aristotle cites a minor scene in Sophocles' *Antigone*: Haimon lunges at his father with a sword and misses (1231–4). This example makes it clear that the event is not "about to happen" in the same way in which Iphigenia is about to sacrifice her brother in *Iphigenia*. Haimon does not plan in advance to kill his father, and his miss is due simply to chance, rather than resulting from other events according to probability or necessity. In (1), on the other hand, we may infer that the imminence of the sacrifice arouses pity and fear, and allows it to count as a *pathos*, even though it does not actually take place.

Plot (3), in which someone acts with knowledge, is said to be "second [worst]" (1454a2). Aristotle does not explain why acting with knowledge is inferior to acting without knowledge, but two reasons can be inferred. First, plot (4), in which someone is about to harm kin with knowledge, but does not do so, is *miaron* ("repulsive": 1453b39), and plot (2), in which someone actually harms kin, without knowledge, lacks the *miaron* (1454a2–4). It appears, then, that a plot is "repulsive" if it portrays someone harming kin, with knowledge of the relationship. Sometimes, of course, there might be mitigating circumstances, like the oracle that commands Orestes to kill his mother in Aeschylus' *Libation Bearers*. In most cases, however, someone who, like Medea, kills a relative, with full knowledge of the relationship, would be a vicious person, and thus a bad subject for tragedy, according to the criteria of chapter 13. The second reason why acting with knowledge would be inferior to acting without knowledge is that such a plot would lack recognition.

Aristotle writes that plot (1) is "best" (1454a4) without stating why it is superior to (2). One plausible account of his reasoning is as follows. In both plots, ignorance is followed by recognition, but only in (1) does recognition necessarily occur at the same time as reversal. For example, in Euripides' *Iphigenia in Tauris*, when sister is about to sacrifice brother, bad fortune would necessarily follow if she discovered who he was after doing the deed. When she learns that it is her brother she is about to kill, however, Iphigenia immediately stops her preparations for the sacrifice, and instead plans with him how they can both escape. The recognition thus makes a happy ending probable or necessary. In plot (2), on the other hand, recognition after the *pathos* takes place makes an unhappy ending necessary, for to harm kin in ignorance and then learn that one has done so is necessarily to suffer bad fortune. In this plot, recognition need not occur together with a reversal, and, in fact, reversal need not occur at all. For example, a man might, as happens in Euripides' *Heracles*, kill his family in a fit of madness and then learn what he has done. Far from bringing about a change back toward good fortune within the movement of the plot toward bad fortune, this knowledge increases Heracles' bad fortune. In some plots of type (2), of course, recognition and reversal occur at the same time. In *Oedipus the King*, the messenger, arriving with the intention of giving Oedipus good news about his parents, actually brings him bad news that leads to recognition and reversal (1452a24–6). As will be shown below, this combination of recognition and reversal is due to the skill of the poet and is not an essential element in plot (2).

In *Poetics* 14, then, Aristotle ranks plot types according to how well they arouse pity and fear by making the best use of the three parts of the tragic plot, *pathos*, recognition, and reversal. Plot (1) necessarily has all three parts of the plot, and reversal coincides with recognition. Plot (2) has recognition but may lack either reversal, or reversal coincident with recognition; plot (3) lacks recognition, and plot (4) lacks *pathos*, as well as recognition.

Did Aristotle change his mind?

The rankings of plots in chapters 13 and 14 make sense according to the criteria given in each chapter. Problems arise, however, because the two chapters rank the same plot differently. In chapter 14, the *Iphigenia* plot type, that ends happily, is said to be best, while the *Oedipus* type is only second-best (1454a2, 4–7). In *Poetics* 13, on the other hand, the *Oedipus* plot type, with its unhappy ending, is called the best (1453a22–3). Many attempts have been made to explain this apparent inconsistency. Some scholars argue that Aristotle changed his mind after writing chapter 13 (Bywater 1909: 224–5); others that the *Oedipus* is the best play, while the *Iphigenia* contains the best scene (Else 1957: 450–2; Lucas 1968: 155). Another interpretation is that Aristotle thought that there are different kinds of excellent plots (Dupont-Roc and Lallot 1980: 258–9; Heath 1996: xxxv). I argue, instead, that Aristotle preferred the *Oedipus* plot type, provided it is skillfully constructed so as to contain a reversal coincident with a recognition (Belfiore 1992a: 174–5).

As noted above, Sophocles' *Oedipus the King* is an example of plot type (2) in chapter 14, that makes good use of all three parts of the tragic plot so as to arouse pity and fear, just as does the *Iphigenia in Tauris* plot. It has a *pathos*, and, according to 11 1452a32–

3, it contains a reversal that is coincident with a recognition. The arrival of the messenger appears at first to contribute to Oedipus' good fortune. However, his subsequent revelation of Oedipus' identity produces the opposite effect (11 1452a24–6), thus reversing the movement back to bad fortune. This plot, then, has all of the advantages of the *Iphigenia* plot, according to the criteria of chapter 14. In addition, it has the advantage, according to the criteria of chapter 13, of having an unhappy ending. A skillful poet can succeed in combining all of these advantages in a single play. Aristotle's remarks about the poet's craft support his interpretation: "The best tragedy according to the principles of craft is created from this plot" (13 1453a22–3), that is, from the plot with an unhappy ending. Moreover, these tragedies "appear most tragic on stage, if they succeed" (13 1453a27–8). On the other hand, the *Iphigenia* plot pattern provides a kind of formula or recipe that is easy for poets to follow even if they have no extraordinary skill. These poets will not write the very best plays, but they will succeed in creating a plot that arouses pity and fear if they just follow the recipe: *pathos* about to occur, in ignorance, followed by recognition, which leads, necessarily, to reversal. This recipe has been discovered by chance rather than skill (14 1454a9–12).

Although it is not easy to determine which single tragedy Aristotle preferred, it is clear that his two favorites were Sophocles' *Oedipus the King* and Euripides' *Iphigenia in Tauris*. His reasons for liking both tragedies are evident, but he did not clearly and explicitly award first prize to either one.

Conclusion

Aristotle's *Poetics* provides a careful analysis of the elements of tragedy as a whole, and of the tragic plot, showing how each of them, singly and in combination, contributes to the arousal of pity and fear within this poetic genre. His treatise devotes most attention to the plot, the most important of the six parts of tragedy. The tragic plot is a formal structure, a "universal," governed by the principle of probability or necessity, concerned with significant human actions. Simple plots have only one part, the *pathos*, a painful or destructive event, while the best plots, the complex, also have recognition (a change from ignorance to knowledge, and to friendship or enmity), reversal (a change in direction within the movement of the plot from good to bad, or from bad to good, fortune), or both. In the best tragedies, the *pathos* is a destructive or painful event in which kin harms, or is about to harm, kin. The focal point of the best tragic plots, their emotional and dramatic climax, is the beginning of the solution, when reversal and recognition occur together, and a change of fortune begins. Aristotle admires plays with both unhappy and happy endings. What makes them "tragic," in his view, is not the direction of the change, but the fact that it takes place.[6]

Notes

[1] Mimesis: 1 1447a13–16. Because the translations "imitation" and "representation" can be misleading, I follow Halliwell (2002: 13–14) in retaining the Greek term "mimesis." All translations are my own, from the text of Kassel (1965).

[2] On the terminology "qualitative" and "quantitative" see Janko (1987: 219).

[3] Blood kinship: Else (1957: 349–50, 391–8, 415); other relationships: Belfiore (1992a: 72–3, 2000a: 5–9); Gudeman (1934: to judge by his list at 257–8); Janko (1987: 95–6), on 1452a31.

[4] In the play, Iphigenia is about to sacrifice two men she does not recognize as Orestes and his friend Pylades. She agrees to allow Pylades to escape to Greece on condition that he take a letter to her friends. When she reads the letter to the two men, she reveals that she is Orestes' sister (*Iphigenia in Tauris* 725–71).

[5] In our text of the *Poetics*, Aristotle lists only three of these four possibilities at 1453b27–36: (1) through (3) on my list. Moreover, he says that the last possibility he lists in this passage is "the third" (1453b34), immediately before stating that these are the only possibilities (1453b36–7). It is clear, however, that a mention of (4) has dropped out of our text, for Aristotle goes on to say, at 1453b37–8: "Of these, the worst is to be about to act with knowledge but not to act."

[6] I am indebted to Eugene Garver and Paul Woodruff for helpful comments on an earlier draft of this chapter, and to Peter Belfiore for editorial assistance.

Bibliography

Belfiore, E. (1992a). *Tragic Pleasures: Aristotle on Plot and Emotion* (Princeton, NJ: Princeton University Press).

Belfiore, E. (1992b). "Aristotle and Iphigenia," in Rorty, pp. 359–77.

Belfiore, E. (2000a). *Murder among Friends: Violation of Philia in Greek Tragedy* (Oxford: Oxford University Press).

Belfiore, E. (2000b). "Narratological Plots and Aristotle's Mythos," *Arethusa*, 33, pp. 37–70.

Bywater, I. (1909). *Aristotle on the "Art of Poetry"* (Oxford: Oxford University Press).

Carey, C. (1988). " 'Philanthropy' in Aristotle's *Poetics*," *Eranos*, 86, pp. 131–9.

Dupont-Roc, R. and Lallot, J. (1980). *Aristote: "La Poétique"* (Paris: Éditions du Seuil).

Else, G. F. (1957). *Aristotle's "Poetics": The Argument* (Cambridge, MA: Harvard University Press).

Gudeman, A. (1934). *Aristoteles: Peri "Poêtikês"* (Berlin and Leipzig: Walter de Gruyter).

Halliwell, S. (1986). *Aristotle's "Poetics"* (London: Duckworth).

Halliwell, S. (1987). *The "Poetics" of Aristotle: Translation and Commentary* (London: Duckworth).

Halliwell, S. (2002). *The Aesthetics of Mimesis: Ancient Texts and Modern Problems* (Princeton, NJ: Princeton University Press).

Heath. M. (1996). *Aristotle: "Poetics,"* trans. with an intro. and notes (London: Penguin).

Janko, R. (1984). *Aristotle on Comedy* (London: Duckworth).

Janko, R. (1987). *Aristotle, "Poetics" I*, trans. with notes (Indianapolis, IN, and Cambridge: Hackett).

Kassel, R. (ed.) (1965). *Aristotelis De arte poetica liber* (Oxford: Oxford University Press).

Lucas, D. W. (1968). *Aristotle: "Poetics"* (Oxford: Clarendon).

Rorty, A. O. (ed.) (1992). *Essays on Aristotle's "Poetics"* (Princeton, NJ: Princeton University Press).

Sherman, N. (1992). "*Hamartia* and Virtue," in Rorty, pp. 177–96.

Stinton, T. C. W. (1975). "*Hamartia* in Aristotle and Greek Tragedy," *Classical Quarterly*, 25, pp. 221–54.

Index